Battle of the Little Big Horn Series
Volume One

Custer's Last Fight

The Story of the Battle of The Little Big Horn

by

David C. Evans

Upton & Sons
El Segundo, California
1999

UPTON & SONS
917 Hillcrest Street
El Segundo, California 90245

LIBRARY OF CONGRESS CATALOG CARD NUMBER 98-60136
ISBN-0-912783-30-3

To Dan & Brian:

Learn well the lessons of history . . .

Lest you repeat them to your sorrow!

Contents

Foreword

From June 25 to 26, 1876, warriors of the Lakota and Cheyenne Nations defeated the 7th United States Cavalry in three separate engagements along the banks of the Little Big Horn River in southeastern Montana Territory. In the one hundred and twenty-two years since its prosecution, the Battle of the Little Big Horn has become one of the most widely discussed and hotly debated conflicts in our history, rivaled only by Gettysburg in sheer volume of written material.

Little Big Horn. Its very name, at one and the same time a contradiction and source of controversy with proponents about equally divided between the traditional Little Big Horn and the now cartographically correct Little Bighorn, contributes to the allure and mystique of the battle. What are the reasons for our fascination with this battle that has become not only a part of our folklore but symbolic of the conflict between the white and red races? The casualties suffered by either the forces commanded by George Armstrong Custer, who preferred his middle name of Armstrong to George, or by Marcus Reno were the most suffered by the United States Army in a single engagement with Indians on the great plains; eclipsing the dubious record set by William Judd Fetterman against many of these same Lakota and Cheyenne a decade earlier. The magnitude of the disaster, while undoubtedly adding fuel to the heated debate that continues to this day, cannot be the sole answer. American history records several "popular" disasters of equal, or greater, proportion: Alamo, Bataan, the Arizona at Pearl Harbor, and Titanic; none of which capture our collective imagination like Little Big Horn. In fact, considering only the total number of military casualties, Little Big Horn ranks no higher than third on the list of great defeats suffered at the hands of Indians on the North American Continent. First position on the list belongs to British General Edward Braddock who lost his own life while suffering 914 casualties in 1755. Fortunately his colonial aide, George Washington, came through unscathed. The United States Army suffered its worst defeat at the hands of Chief Little Turtle's Miamis who destroyed the army of General Arthur St. Clair in western Ohio in 1791, killing 35 officers and 622 soldiers in the process.[1]

The nation, totally unprepared for a defeat, was stunned by the magnitude of the disaster. One recalls the image of Braddock, lying mortally wounded in the path of retreat, endlessly murmuring *"Who would have thought it?"* The defeat at the Little Big Horn, considered a national disaster by the general public, cast a pall over the young nation's centennial celebrations. In the wake of this catastrophe, which riveted the national attention like no event since the Lincoln assassination, little notice was taken of the general mismanagement of the campaign and poor performance of the troops. The nation's crack cavalry regiment had been defeated; not only had a field-grade officer been killed (a rare occurrence in itself, see Appendix 17), but he had been a hero of the republic, playing no small part in preserving the Union. How could the nation who had developed the telephone and stood on the verge of inventing the incandescent lamp and the phonograph, have been soundly defeated by a rabble of stone-age savages? One begins to comprehend the confusion, embarrassment, and outrage expressed by the general public when it is recalled that much smaller forces held upwards of 1,500 of these same warriors at bay in the Hayfield, Wagon Box, and Beecher's Island Fights. A chagrined army, trying vainly to stem the public outcry, found itself embroiled in a controversy of ever widening proportions.[2] This war, brought on by an administration eager to secure the Black Hills for its greedy populace, was to have been a simple exercise ending with the complete subjugation of the bands in the unceded territory. Instead, the administration had an unparalleled disaster on its hands. A scapegoat was needed to divert attention from the command structure and the administration, and, as General Nelson A. Miles noted, it is easy to kick a dead lion.

The controversies started almost immediately and touched on every facet of the conflict imaginable. Had Custer disobeyed his orders, rushing headlong to disaster? Did Reno show the white feather in the valley fight? Did Benteen dawdle while his comrades, awaiting the precious ammunition he was ordered to bring, were being annihilated? Did Custer attempt to cross at Medicine Tail Coulee? Was Custer killed early at the river, or was he the last to fall? Could Custer and his regiment have won? Could they have been saved? Rather than subsiding with the passage of time, the controversies increased both in number and vehemence in the succeeding years. Aggravating the situation, and continuing to the present day, are self proclaimed authorities who, to paraphrase English biologist Thomas Henry Huxley, have done everything in their power to prevent *"the slaying of a beautiful hypothesis by an ugly fact."* While most of these were motivated by either an intense admiration for, or aversion to, Armstrong Custer, some were driven by their desire to preserve the good name of the United States Army and the honor of the regiment. A case in point is Edward Settle Godfrey. Godfrey, never an admirer of Reno, stopped short of labeling Reno's conduct at Little Big Horn as cowardice when he testified at the 1879 court of inquiry; branding him instead as guilty of *"nervous timidity."* What might Godfrey's testimony have been had he known of Reno's suggestion to abandon the wounded the night of June 25th? Godfrey, unaware of this incident while testifying at the court of inquiry, had full knowledge of the event prior to publishing his 1892 *Century Magazine* article; however his concern for the honor of the regiment forced him to refer to the incident in veiled terms decipherable by only the most astute students of the battle.

Admire him or despise him; Armstrong Custer stands as the dominant figure of Little Big Horn and the principal architect of its appeal, dominating every work on the campaign. Perhaps, this is fitting; for, with his death, he achieved immortality not only for himself but his regiment.[3] He and his regiment have become more than fallen heroes of the republic; they have become symbolic of the Indian fighting army with Custer the archetypical Indian hating frontier soldier. The irony that Custer was often in outspoken opposition to the very policies he has come to symbolize has been lost in much of the present literature.[4] As Steve Arnold and Tim French have noted, at the time of the battle Custer was seen as a symbol of sacrifice – a price to be paid for the nation's progress. Today, however, Custer is viewed either as *"the eternal villain or the great fool."*[5]

The reasons behind this shift in perspective was obvious to John B. Lundstrom: *"The historical criticism of Custer can be divided into three distinct phases. The first comprised the writings of those military men and their allies who knew Custer and had some personal motive for their hostility. They had something to gain in attacking Custer, either revenge or a personal defense of their own actions or of someone else they championed. The second echelon of Custer critics emerged in the early 1900's, forty or more years after his death. These writers were revisionists, who wrote largely in reaction to the attacks of the Custerphiles on the military critics. Intent in their response to what they considered injustice, they endeavored to uncover every fact and slant every interpretation which might be injurious to Custer's reputation. In their zeal to right the supposed wrongs, they made heroes out of those military men who criticized Custer the loudest. The final group of critics was a relatively new phenomenon, rising out of the new trend of Western history. These new revisionists hoped to correct what they felt was a totally erroneous treatment of the Indians by biased, largely uninformed white historians. In order to dramatize their cause against the whites, they selected Custer as a primary figure to attack largely because he was so well known (if not understood) by the general public."*[6] The evidence will be presented and the reader will form his own conclusions. This, however, is not a Custer Book. It is a book about an event in our history that continues to tantalize and enthrall, and the men, both red and white, whose struggle has enriched our national heritage.

After so long, how can one hope to unsnarl the tangle of myth, legend and falsehood surrounding this best known of all Indian Wars battles? In his Civil War Memoirs, Custer himself remarked upon the difficulties facing the military historian:

> *"It often becomes a matter of surprise to the reader of general history, or to the seeker after historical truths, particularly if the latter relate to the incidents of battles or to the conduct of military campaigns, that marked and sometimes apparently irreconcilable discrepancies occur in the recorded testimony of those who were prominent actors in the same event."*[7]

Fortunately, we have the pioneering research of Douglas Scott, Richard Fox Jr., and others into the archaeological aspects of the battle. A wealth of personal accounts has also survived, including the eye witness accounts of Indian participants. Indian accounts, considered unreliable and ignored or denigrated during the past century,[8] are being confirmed by archaeological discoveries and becoming more popular with current researchers. These data serve as the cornerstone in the attempt to reconstruct what happened to Armstrong Custer and five companies of cavalry on June 25, 1876.

While we will never know with absolute certainty what happened that hot June day, a careful sifting of the data allows us to draw some informed conclusions. In this work I have relied heavily upon the archaeological evidence. Remaining cognizant of the biases of some previous authors, not to mention the current infatuation with revisionist history, I have attempted to have multiple sources for critical conclusions. Some of the data will probably forever tantalize and elude us – such as how were the place names in the Indian accounts established? Since we can no longer interrogate either the participants or their interpreters, we must accept their place names as recorded unless we have strong evidence to infer otherwise. There is some danger in this approach in that the Indian testimony is typically nonspecific and great care must be exercised to refrain from sifting the evidence to fit previously established conclusions. To that end, I have accepted ALL of the Indian accounts in my research, not just carefully selected ones. In the case of the action at the "South Skirmish Line," this approach has led to a rather surprising and unconventional conclusion. Key primary source material is provided in appendices to aid the reader in forming his own conclusions. I have also been over the ground several times to gain insight into possible scenarios and to better comprehend Indian accounts (it is instructive to note that various prominent features of the topography look markedly different based upon one's direction of approach). Where conflicts in a given individual's accounts occur, I have typically given more weight to the account written most closely following the event. This methodology results in some disturbing commentary on the questioning and testimony of various officers at the 1879 Reno Court of Inquiry. In all cases I have attempted to meticulously identify any suppositions and conclusions that are strictly my own. To this end, my personal theories as to the movements of Custer's immediate command are presented in a separate chapter. Being cognizant that the terms "troop" and "squadron" were not in vogue at the time of the battle, coming into general usage in 1883 and 1901 respectively, I have taken the license to use them interchangeably with "company" and "battalion" where I thought it improved the narrative.

I have attempted to include enough material and sources to provide grist for the serious student of the battle while hopefully providing an entertaining narrative for the novitiate. Any discussion of the Little Big Horn itself would be incomplete without an explanation of preceding events and how they may, or may not, have contributed to the outcome. An examination of the 1868 Washita campaign, and the annihilation of Major Joel Elliott and his detachment, aids in understanding the possible forces working on Major Marcus Reno during the valley fight. Similarly, we will explore the Belknap affair to ascertain its role, if any, in the disaster.

Mere description of the events as we know them, or pure speculation no matter how imaginative, would result in a sterile and incomplete narrative. I have therefore included many personal anecdotes to remind us that these were flesh and blood individuals, with much the same fears and desires as ourselves. It is frustrating that the historical data on the Indian participants is so meager; making, of necessity, the personal accounts somewhat one sided.

To complete the narrative, I have included a brief epilogue summarizing the end of the campaign and subsequent fate of its major participants. An appendix containing selected biographies has also been included. Sufficient footnotes are provided to enable the serious student to further his research and identify alternate points of view. After much soul searching, I have included a section on the rationale for the disaster. This is not an attempt to place the blame on any individual or individuals, nor a catalog of 20/20 hindsight pointing the way to the victory expected by the nation and the military high command. I have simply tried to present the actions of key individuals in the context of their knowledge, or what one may reasonably presume they should have known, at the time the events described transpired.

In the following pages I will attempt, as best I can after carefully weighing and presenting the evidence, to reconstruct the events surrounding this last great struggle between two competing cultures. During our journey we will witness acts of great heroism, both red and white, pathos, willful disobedience, self sacrifice, implacable remorse, and the epitome of wifely devotion. Irony will be a frequent companion. Perhaps the greatest irony of all being that the detractors of Armstrong Custer, by the very frequency and ferocity of their attacks, have ensured his immortality. Some will disagree with my conclusions, and they may very well be right! It would be rash indeed for anyone to claim they know with absolute certainty all that transpired that fateful June day, especially when speculating on the motivation of key individuals. Perhaps on this one point we may all agree: legends are part of great events and insofar as they preserve the memories of gallantry and self–sacrifice they serve their purpose. May the legends of the Little Big Horn never die!

I wish to express my gratitude to Dick Upton and Art and Chris Sowin for their tireless efforts in obtaining the out of print sources that were so necessary to this narrative. To Richard Buchen, reference librarian, Southwest Museum for providing here–to–fore unpublished Cheyenne accounts from the George Bird Grinnell folder (copies of these were furnished to Richard Fox whose manuscript may have an earlier publication date). My thanks to Dan Old Elk, great grandson of the Crow scout Curly, for sharing the views of the family on the battle. An especial debt of gratitude is due Loren Brooks, Marvin Knutson, Christina Old Elk, and Pat Secrest for their willingness to share the historic sites on their land. Jim Court, former superintendent of the battlefield, devoted many hours to showing me the various locations and arranging interviews and access to the sites. The battlefield staff, especially Chief Historian Doug McChristian, Leann Simpson and Mike Moore have furnished valuable support and information. A very special thanks is due to Museum Curator Kitty Belle Deernose for tirelessly acceding to my near constant requests for more data. I also wish to thank Dave Wagner and Mike Charnota for not only accompanying me on journeys to some of the more inaccessible locations, but for serving as willing sounding boards and devil's advocates for my evolving theories. My gratitude for the assistance furnished by proof readers Mary Evans (thanks mom for continuing a practice begun in Junior High School), Dave Wagner, and Lieutenant Colonel Ronald C. Hale, USA ret., can never be properly expressed. Heartfelt thanks to Frank and Kathy Varacalli for the use of their basement and for special understanding at a time when it was sorely needed. Finally, to Jim Mundie, tireless seeker of source material and a constant source of inspiration and fresh ideas, my warmest thanks. Any errors or inaccuracies in the text are, of course, my sole responsibility.

Centreville Virginia, 1998

[1] See Geoffrey Regan "Snafu: Great American Military Disasters" page 56.

[2] It seems incredible that the only adversary to ever force the United States to sign an unfavorable peace treaty, wiped out the commands of Lieutenant Grattan and Captain Fetterman, sacked the city of Julesburg on two separate occassions, derailed a train, and sent General George Crook and his 1,300 man army hastening to the rear cannot be acknowledged by history for its demonstrated military prowess. It is interesting to note that the recent trend in ascribing the disaster to a general loss of command and control due to mass hysteria and "combat fatigue" merely puts on new coat of paint on the old Cheyenne argument that Custer's troops committed mass suicide. Rather than elevating the role of the Indian, which apparently is the goal in these "political correct" times, these arguments only serve to re–enforce the old ethnic bias that the Indians were incapable of defeating the troops. Ergo, the soldiers must have made some disastrous mistakes, such as allowing themselves to be killed without defense due to "combat fatigue" or mass suicide. Those who continue in vain the frustrating search for the ultimate mistake made by the army on June 25, 1876, ignore the obvious: the soldiers didn't lose, the Indians won!

[3] As Voorheis Richeson noted: *"The Seventh Cavalry's claim to renown is certainly unusual, if not wholly unique; generally a command is remembered because of some brilliant victory. This one is remembered because of an overwhelming defeat."* See Elizabeth Atwood Lawrence "His Very Silence Speaks" page 309.

[4] In fact Custer had offered to share his supplies with the Indians at Standing Rock Agency during the winter of 1874 – 75. See Lt Col Melbourne C. Chandler "Of Garryowen In Glory" page 46 and Colonel Charles F. Bates "Custer's Indian Battles" page 26.

[5] See "Custer's Forgotten Friend: The Life of W. W. Cooke" page 40.

[6] See Tom O'Neil "George Armstrong Custer" A Historical Overview" pages 14 - 15.

[7] See John M. Carroll "Custer In The Civil War: His Unfinished Memoirs" page 70.

[8] Great caution must be exercised when using an Indian account. First, it is usually impossible to know at this juncture whether the interviewer asked leading questions allowing his subject to discern a "proper" answer. Secondly, interpreters, as a class, have proven to be highly variable in both their accuracy and fidelity to their task. Lastly, but far from least importance, is the cultural gap that separated the white and red races in the 19th century. To fully comprehend Indian accounts, the researcher must view them in the context of Indian culture where feats of war were viewed in individualistic terms with the sole "objective' (to use the whiteman's term) being to win honors and recognition.

Artist's rendition of the Washita Fight. In reality, the surprised Cheyenne, many only partially clothed in the bitter cold, almost immediately abandoned the village; fighting a rear guard action to screen the escape of the women and children. *Photo Courtesy Little Bighorn Battlefield National Monument.*

Chapter 1

The Battle of the Washita

The sun was setting that Monday, June 26, 1876. The largest concentration of Indians ever assembled on the North American Continent climbed southwest out of the valley of the Little Big Horn River in Montana Territory heading for the Big Horn Mountains on the horizon. The shattered and demoralized remnants of the fabled 7th U. S. Cavalry, entrenched on the heights overlooking the river, watched the indistinct shapes fade, then disappear in the haze produced by dust from the hooves of innumerable ponies mixed with the smoke of the prairie fires set to conceal their movement. The ethereal quality of the scene seemed to hypnotize, lulling the exhausted observers into a dream–like state obscuring the reality of the past two days.

It had been no dream; rather a nightmare. Four and one–half miles to the North, Lieutenant Colonel George Armstrong Custer along with 208 members of his famed regiment, including four family members, lay dead; their bodies strewn along the ridges and ravines like the white marble boulders they resembled.

How could it have happened? While there had been previous disasters in our history of conflict with the native Americans: Braddock , St. Clair, Dade and Fetterman [1], none carried the impact of the Custer disaster. The national ego received a staggering blow when the terrible news reached Philadelphia at the height of the centennial celebration. A nation celebrating an unparalleled century of progress could not accept the death of a cultural hero and the loss of its finest regiment of cavalry at the hands of stone age savages. Clearly, the troops could not have been defeated in fair combat with the foe. Someone must have erred, thus precipitating the disaster. The public demand for an explanation focused attention squarely on George Armstrong Custer and away from other commanders and the campaign as a whole.

The summer campaign of 1876 was the largest military operation undertaken by the U. S. Army during the Indian wars. [2] Using the same tactics that had proven successful on the southern plains at the Washita and in the Red River War, Sheridan ordered three large columns to converge on the Powder River country. [3] Each column was of sufficient strength, it was believed, to deal the enemy a fatal blow. The only concern was that the Indians might be able to elude the troops and thereby avoid a decisive conflict. General George Crook, with 10 companies of the 3rd Cavalry, 5 companies of the 2nd Cavalry, 3 companies of the 9th Infantry, and 2 companies of the 4th Infantry, would march north from Fort Fetterman, Wyoming Territory, to intercept any Indians attempting to escape to the south (see Chapter 7 for the table of organization of Crook's 1325 man force). Colonel John Gibbon, with 4 companies of the 2nd Cavalry and 6 companies of the 7th Infantry, would march eastward down the Yellowstone River from Fort Ellis, Montana Territory, to either keep the Indians south of the Yellowstone or drive them toward General Alfred H. Terry's Dakota Column (see Chapter 6 for the table of organization of Gibbon's 478 man Montana Column). The final column, the Dakota Column, commanded by General Alfred H. Terry would march west, from Fort Abraham Lincoln in Dakota Territory, up the Yellowstone, forming the third element of the pinchers. The Dakota Column, totaling 1114 men (see Chapter 8 for the table of organization), was comprised of the entire 12 companies of the 7th Cavalry under the command of Lieutenant Colonel George Armstrong Custer, 5 companies of the 6th Infantry, and 2 companies of the 17th Infantry.

Fittingly, Custer had struck the village on the Little Big Horn at the zenith of its fighting strength. The campaign had gotten off to a poor start and the situation, rather than improving, had deteriorated. In March, Colonel Joseph J. Reynolds attacked a Cheyenne village on the

Powder River capturing a vast amount of stores and the pony herd. The attack and securing of the village was poorly managed resulting in Reynolds burning the badly needed stores. While the destruction of the village could technically be termed a tactical victory, the Indians reaped the moral victory by recapturing their pony herd. Indian spirits and disdain for the U. S. Army soared as the warriors rode away with their recaptured ponies in plain sight of the troops who offered no pursuit.

The confidence of the Indians was further bolstered in May as they observed Colonel John Gibbon march up and down the Yellowstone assiduously avoiding an armed confrontation. Another confidence builder was supplied in early June when Sitting Bull dreamed of *"many soldiers falling into camp."* The final boost to Indian morale and determination was received only eight days before the fight on the Little Big Horn when a large force of Lakota and Cheyenne stalemated General George Crook's advance on the Rosebud. Although Crook and the military high command would claim this day long battle as a victory, the largest column of troops in the field had been forced to return to its base of supply, where it would remain immobile for two months, its objective unfulfilled. Although the Lakota and Cheyenne had not sent a large force of warriors into the field against U. S. Troops since the disastrous Wagon Box and Hayfield fights of August 1867, Crook did not attempt to inform either General Terry or Colonel Gibbon that large numbers of warriors were in the field fighting with uncharacteristic determination and cohesion.

In the following pages we will explore the factors influencing the course of events that culminated in the Battle of the Little Big Horn. Along the way we will both prove and debunk some of the myths associated with this most famous of clashes between the red and white cultures on the northern plains. We will come to understand the symbols from this conflict that invest our folklore: Little Big Horn as the archetypical desperate struggle against overwhelming odds, and George Armstrong Custer as stereotype of the arrogant, rash, Indian hating frontier officer.

Commencing with the Battle of the Washita River in Oklahoma Territory, the 7th Cavalry has enjoyed the reputation of being the finest and most experienced regiment in the Indian–fighting army. While the 7th Cavalry could boast of 29 engagements[4] with Indians prior to the Little Big Horn, only three engagements were of any consequence, two occurring a week apart during the Yellowstone Expedition of 1873. Of these three, only the Washita Fight could properly be termed a battle.

Given the relative inexperience of the 7th Cavalry in major engagements with plains Indians, it is not surprising that there are many similarities between the battles of the Washita and Little Big Horn. Therefore, a rather detailed examination of the tactics and events of the Washita Fight is required to aid our understanding of the events to occur at the Little Big Horn eight years later.

Frustrated with the inability of both current cavalry tactics and his field commanders to deal effectively with the Indians,[5] Major General Philip H. Sheridan wired Custer who was serving out a one year suspension from rank and pay as the result of his court–martial:

Fort Hays, Kansas, September 24, 1868.

General G. A. Custer, Monroe, Michigan:

Generals Sherman, Sully (Lieutenant Colonel Alfred Sully. Sheridan used his, as well as Custer's, brevet rank of General, DCE), and myself, and nearly all the officers of your regiment, have asked for you, and I hope the applications will be successful. Can you come at once? Eleven companies[6] of your regiment will move about the first of October against the hostile Indians, from Medicine Lodge Creek toward the Wichita Mountains.

P. H. Sheridan, Major General Commanding[7]

The application was successful, as documented in a War Department telegram of September 25:

"The remainder of your sentence has been remitted by the Secretary of War. Report in person without delay [to] General Sheridan for Duty."[8]

Custer was on the next train west. Arriving at Fort Hays on September 30, Custer immediately set to work to hone his regiment into an efficient fighting machine.[9] The horses were shod, and, as an aid in communication,[10] the companies were "colored." All of the horses were arranged according to color and each troop commander, according to rank and seniority, was given the choice of color for his company.[11] Although the concept of "coloring" the companies was not new, the companies of the 2nd Cavalry having their horses matched in color when the regiment was organized in 1855,[12] this decision by Custer was not universally popular with his officers. Captain Albert Barnitz recorded in his journal under the date of November 10:

"General Custer is requiring all the company commanders to exchange horses, so as to secure a uniformity of colors in each company. I have bitterly opposed the scheme, but must comply I suppose. All my old horses were well trained, and very carefully trained, and the men were much attached to them, and now, just as we are to march on the campaign, every thing is to be turned topsy turvy! – There is much dissatisfaction among the men, in consequence which will result in numerous desertions hereafter.[13] Had the change not been insisted upon until after the campaign, and just as we were going into garrison, it would have been far better."[14]

The training of the men was not neglected. Godfrey wrote in his 1928 article for the *Cavalry Journal*:

"Drills and target practice were pushed to the limit.[15] Forty of the best shots were selected for a separate organization under the command of Lieutenant Cooke. We youngsters named it the 'Corps d'elite' and the name stuck throughout the campaign."[16]

Recognizing the inadvisability of the army's cost cutting practice of sending troops into the field without adequate training on their weapons, Custer ordered extensive target practice prior to all of his major campaigns with the single exception of the Little Big Horn. Given this track record, it is probable that, without the interference of the Belknap affair which detained Custer in Washington for many weeks, extensive target practice would have been conducted prior to the Little Big Horn Campaign as well. As a final measure in preparing his command, Custer led his men on a two week "shakedown" march.[17]

General Sheridan and his staff arrived at Camp Supply[18] on November 21st. As Sheridan had brought some remounts with him, Custer availed himself of the opportunity to select a personal mount, a fine animal he named "Dandy."[19] Like Custer, Sheridan was convinced that it was futile to pursue the Indians over vast reaches of prairie where their fleet ponies could easily outdistance the overburdened cavalry mounts.[20] He concluded that the only tactic that promised success was to catch the Indians in their villages while immobile, and lay waste their base of supply. Sheridan's plan for the winter campaign was relatively simple: have three columns converge on the valleys of the Canadian and Washita Rivers in Western Indian Territory.[21] Hopefully one of the columns would encounter the Indians in one of their favorite winter haunts.

On November 18,[22] Major Andrew W. "Beans" Evans led a column composed of six companies of the Third Cavalry and two companies of the Thirty-seventh Infantry, a total of 563 men, and four mountain howitzers out of Fort Bascom, New Mexico. Their objective was to march eastward down the South Canadian. On December 2, Major Eugene A. Carr led seven companies of the Fifth Cavalry out from Fort Lyon Colorado. Directed by a young scout named "Buffalo Bill" Cody, they united with Captain William H. Penrose's 4 companies of the Tenth Cavalry and the remaining company, Troop L, of the Seventh Cavalry on the north fork of the Canadian. This column of 650 men was to operate southward toward the Antelope Hills and the head of the Red River. The third column, commanded by Lieutenant Colonel Alfred Sully, assembled at Fort Dodge and consisted of eleven troops of the Seventh Cavalry, more than 800 strong,[23] and five companies of the Third Infantry. After establishing Camp Supply near the junction of the North Canadian River and Wolf Creek, the column was to be joined by the 19th Kansas Volunteer Cavalry under former Governor Samuel J. Crawford.[24]

Before the expedition could depart, however, Sheridan had to settle a question of rank and command. Godfrey relates:

> *"At that time the Rules and Articles of War provided that when troops of the regular army and volunteers came together, brevet rank took effect. Both Sully and Custer were lieutenant colonels. Colonel Crawford of the 19th Kansas was the senior in rank. General Sully issued an order assuming command of the troops by virtue of his brevet rank of brigadier general, U. S. A. When this order reached General Custer, he issued an order assuming command by virtue of his brevet rank of major general U. S. A. Sully contended that as between officers of the regular army this should not obtain. General Sheridan decided in favor of General Custer. General Sully was relieved from duty with the expedition and ordered to Fort Harker to command the District of the Upper Arkansas."*[25]

With the infantry detailed to garrison duty at Camp Supply, and Sheridan's unwillingness to wait any longer for the arrival of the 19th Kansas, the Washita Campaign became an exclusive Seventh Cavalry affair under the command of Lieutenant Colonel George Armstrong Custer.

The thermometer read 7 below zero[26] when the 7th marched out of Camp Supply on the morning of November 23rd with the band playing *"The Girl I Left Behind Me."*[27] . Shortly before departure, Sheridan asked Custer if he wanted to delay until it stopped snowing. Custer declined adding that the snow would keep the Indians in their villages and conceal his movements. The orders from General Sheridan couldn't have been more favorable:

> *"You will proceed south in the direction of the Antelope Hills, then toward the Washita River, the supposed winter seat of the hostile tribes. You will destroy their villages and ponies, kill or hang all warriors, and bring back all women and children alive."*[28]

Thanksgiving morning, November 26th, Major Joel Elliott, with troops G, H, and M, was ordered up the north side of the Canadian to search for sign.[29] Under the guidance of scout

Moses E. Milner, popularly known as "California Joe", the remainder of the command, including the large wagon train, crossed to the south side of the Canadian. Just as the rear guard was crossing, a galloper from Major Elliott was observed. Scout Jack Corbin reported that Major Elliott had cut the fresh trail of a war party of approximately 150 warriors. Custer ordered Corbin to take a fresh mount and return to Elliott with orders to follow the trail until nightfall at which time he was to halt and await the arrival of the balance of the regiment.[30]

"Officer's Call" summoned Custer's officers for a conference.[31] Custer related the information obtained from Corbin and stated his intention to pursue the enemy until they were brought to battle. Recognizing the need to travel light, Custer ordered that each trooper carry 100 rounds of ammunition and small amounts of coffee, hard bread, and forage on his saddle.[32] The wagon train (less 7 wagons and an ambulance commanded by Lieutenant James M. Bell), which must be left in the rear so as not to encumber his march, was to be guarded by a detail of about 80 men obtained from the different troops,[33] mounted on the command's poorest horses. Under the command of one officer, the train would proceed as rapidly as possible on the cavalry's trail.[34]

According to Francis M. Gibson, assigned to Company A but serving as the Second Lieutenant of Company F at the Washita, the command of the wagon train was not one to be relished. He related:

> "... *General Custer well knew there was not an officer of the regiment who would be left behind if he could avoid it, so realizing the futility of calling for a volunteer for this duty, he very naturally decided that the officer of the day and his guard, with an additional detail, should remain with the wagons. When the Adjutant, Lieutenant Moylan, communicated this order to Captain Hamilton,[35] who happened to be officer of the day, it simply crushed him. He was in command of the squadron composed of "A" and "D" Troops, and the thought of it going into action without him, was a blow to his soldierly pride and sensitiveness that almost stunned him, so he hastened to General Custer, and made such a strong and manly appeal to be permitted to lead his squadron, that the General acquiesced, provided he could find another officer willing to take his place. As these were the best terms he could make, he hurried off to Lieutenant Mathey, who he remembered was suffering from snow–blindness, and pleaded and reasoned with him until Mathey very unwillingly, and entirely our of consideration and respect for Hamilton, consented to relieve him as officer of the day, and take charge of the wagon train.* "[36]

The command then set out on a course to intercept Major Elliott. The going was difficult requiring the lead troop to be rotated at frequent intervals to spare the horses the arduous task of breaking the trail through the snow. They joined with Elliott's command at 9 PM and, after an hour's rest, pressed ahead. As the trail freshened, the Osage scouts were dismounted to preclude the possibility of blundering into the village in the dark. Soon Little Beaver, chief of the Osage, smelled smoke and, within a mile, discovered the remains of a small fire made by herd boys from the village. About 12:30 AM, Little Beaver reported the village in sight.[37] Custer went ahead with the two Osage scouts and observed the pony herd which, according to Custer, might have been a buffalo herd. Informed by the scouts they had heard a dog barking, Custer was not convinced.

> "I waited quietly to be convinced; I was assured, but wanted to be doubly so. I was rewarded in a moment by hearing the barking of a dog in the heavy timber off to the right of the herd, and soon after I heard the tinkling of a small bell; this convinced me that it was really the Indian herd I then saw, the bell being one worn

around the neck of some pony who was probably the leader of the herd. I turned to retrace my steps when another sound was borne to my ear through the cold, clear atmosphere of the valley – it was the distant cry of an infant; and savages though they were and justly outlawed by the number and atrocity of their recent murders and depredations on the helpless settlers of the frontier, I could not but regret that in a war such as we were forced to engage in the mode and circumstances of battle would possibly prevent discrimination."[38]

Lieutenant Gibson related:

". . . all officers were ordered forward to report to General Custer. He informed them briefly of what he had seen and heard, and suggested that they should all proceed as noiselessly as possible to the crest with him, and he would point out the location of the village and the features of the country surrounding it. This was done, and the general plan of attack was explained. The design was to surround the village as completely as was possible for eight hundred men to do so, and at daylight at a given signal to make a simultaneous attack from all sides. There were still several hours before daylight, and ample time for the attacking columns to get into position."[39]

Captain Benteen's squadron, Troops H and M, was initially detailed to guard Lieutenant Bell's wagons 2 or 3 miles back on the trail. Godfrey related:

"Just after dismissing the officers and as we were separating, General Custer called my name. On reporting, he directed me to take a detail, go back on the trail to where Captain Benteen and the wagons were, give his compliments to Captain Benteen and instruct him to rejoin the command, and Lieutenant Bell to hold the wagons where they were till he heard the attack which would be about daybreak."[40]

Custer divided the regiment into 4 battalions: Major Elliott, with troops G, H, and M was sent to attack the rear of the village; Captain Thompson with troops B and F was sent to the right; Captain Edward Myers with troops E and I was sent in on the left of Thompson. Custer kept the two squadrons under Captain Hamilton, troops A and C, and Captain West, troops D and K, along with Lieutenant Cooke and his 40 sharpshooters under his personal command.[41]

All being in readiness, the troops settled down for the long cold wait until dawn. Shortly before dawn the heavy overcoats and haversacks that would encumber the troops during the impending action were discarded and left under the protection of a trooper from each company to await the arrival of Lieutenant Bell's wagons.[42]

As the first faint streaks of dawn appeared on November 27, 1868, Custer, who would become known to the Crow as the "Son of the Morning Star," witnessed a spectacular atmospheric display:

"We were standing in a group near the head of the column when suddenly our attention was attracted by a remarkable sight and for a time we felt that the Indians had discovered our presence. Directly beyond the crest of the hill which separated us from the village and in a line with the supposed location of the latter we saw rising slowly but perceptibly, as we thought, up from the village and appearing in bold relief against the dark sky as a background something which we could only compare to a signal rocket, except that its motion was slow and regular. All eyes were turned to it in blank astonishment and but one idea seemed to be

All eyes were turned to it in blank astonishment and but one idea seemed to be entertained, and that was that one or both of the two attacking column under Elliott or Thompson had encountered a portion of the village and this that we saw was the signal to other portions of the band near at hand. Slowly and majestically it continued to rise above the crest of the hill, first appearing as a small brilliant flaming globe of bright golden hue. As it ascended still higher it seemed to increase in size, to move more slowly, while its colors rapidly changed from one to the other, exhibiting in turn the most beautiful combinations of prismatic tints. There seemed to be not the shadow of doubt that we were discovered.

"The strange apparition in the heavens maintained its steady course upward. One anxious spectator, observing it apparently at a standstill, exclaimed: 'How long it hangs fire: why don't it explode?' still keeping the idea of a signal rocket in mind. It had risen perhaps to the height of half a degree above the horizon as observed from our position when, lo! the mystery was dispelled. Rising above the mystifying influences of the atmosphere, that which had appeared so suddenly before us and excited our greatest apprehensions developed into the brightest and most beautiful of morning stars."[43]

As the troops moved closer to the village with the lightening sky, a warrior, roused by a barking camp dog, discovered the approach of Major Elliott's battalion and fired a single shot at the troops. Hearing the shot, Custer immediately ordered the band to play *"Garry Owen,"* the prearranged signal for the attack, marking the first time the 7th's band would play the regiment into battle:[44]

"Our hearts so stout have got us fame

For soon t'is known from whence we came;

Where'er we go they dread the name,

of Garryowen in glory."[45]

It was of little consequence the fighting air was cut short due to the freezing of the instruments; another legend had been born. With an answering cheer reverberating down the tree lined valley, the 7th surged forward into its first major action. The 51 lodge village of Southern Cheyenne was taken completely by surprise, falling into the hands of the troopers within minutes.[46]

It is ironic that this attack on Black Kettle's village occurred two days short of the fourth anniversary of the Chivington massacre of these same Cheyenne at Sand Creek. In the case of the Washita, Black Kettle had ample warning of the coming attack. Only the day before, he had returned from a conference with Colonel William B. Hazen at Fort Cobb where he was told General Sheridan had troops in the field and was the only officer authorized to make peace.[47] Moving Behind, a girl of 14, recalled:

"Someone in the camp said that a warning had been issued for us to move at once. They planned to have the camp move. But somehow they refused to move away at once. If they only could have listened and done what they were told to do! They did not feel sure about the warning. Not a soul knew about the secret plans that were being laid.

"I felt rather strange late that evening.

> *"Black Kettle's wife (Medicine Woman, DCE) became very angry, and stood outside for a long time because they were unable to move that evening. She was disappointed. Sometimes your own feelings tell you things ahead; perhaps this was what that woman felt. She talked excitedly, and said, 'I don't like this delay, we could have moved long ago. The Agent sent word for us to leave at once. It seems we are crazy and deaf, and cannot hear.'"[48]*

The day before the battle, Crow Neck had seen Custer's column while returning for a worn out horse he had left behind the previous day. When he reached the village, he told his host, Bad Man, what he had seen and recommended that Bad Man bring in his horses in preparation for a move. Bad Man did bring in his horses, but, apparently, a general warning was not raised in the camp.[49] Chief Black Eagle of the Kiowa told of another warning received by the Cheyenne:

> *"On the night of the 26th November, a party of Kiowa Indians returning from an expedition against the Utes, saw on nearing the Antelope Hills on the Canadian River, a large trail going south towards the Washita. On the arrival of the Kiowas at the Cheyenne camp, they told the Cheyennes about the trail they had seen, but the Cheyennes laughed at them. One of the Kiowas concluded to stay at the Cheyenne camp that night, and the rest of them went on to their own camp, which was but a short distance off."[50]*

While there was no general agreement regarding the validity of the threat posed by the soldiers, it was decided to move the village downstream the next day to be closer to the other bands. It was further decided to send emissaries to communicate to Sheridan the Cheyenne desire for peace.[51] As a final precaution, it was decided, that in the event of an attack by the soldiers, a white flag should be raised over Black Kettle's tepee. Double Wolf was charged with this responsibility, but, instead of standing guard as ordered, he sought the warmth of the sleeping robes within his lodge. He awoke at the first sounds of the attack and rushed from his teepee only to become one of the first casualties of the battle.[52] In fairness to the memory of Double Wolf, it is extremely doubtful that a white flag would have had any more effect on the troopers than the American Flag flying over Black Kettle's lodge had at Sand Creek.

Chief of Scouts Ben Clark described the charge:

> *"I rode right beside Custer just ahead of the command. He would allow no one to get ahead of him. His horse cleared the stream at one jump and up the bank we went and into the village."[53]*

After shooting one warrior, and bowling over another with his horse, Custer, accompanied by Clark, went to a low hill from which he could observe and direct the fight. A short time later, Clark noticed a large group of women and children attempting to escape to the south. They were pursued and fired upon by Captain Myers' troopers. Clark asked the general if he wanted those people killed. Custer replied:

> *"No. Ride out there and give the officer commanding my compliments and ask him to stop it. Take them to the village and put them in a big tipi and station a guard over them.'[54]*

The Cheyenne, Moving Behind, told of another instance of soldier clemency:

> *"The soldiers would pass back and forth near the spot where I lay. As I turned sideways and looked, one soldier saw us, and rode toward where we lay. He stopped his horse, and stared at us (Moving Behind's aunt, Corn Stalk, was hiding with her, DCE). He did not say a word, and we wondered what would happen. But he left, and no one showed up after that. I suppose he pitied us, and left us alone.*[55]

Captain Benteen likewise was not in a killing frenzy. He confronted a Cheyenne youth of about 14 and signed to him to surrender. He received three shots in return, one through the sleeve of his overcoat and one wounding his horse in the neck. When the boy continued his charge, Benteen rolled free of his fallen mount and fatally shot the youth.[56] While several accounts claim this youth to have been the son, or nephew, of Black Kettle, no name is given for this youth which casts grave doubt on the accuracy of this claim of royal lineage.

Attempting to show clemency did not always end well for the soldiers. Lieutenant Algernon Smith, while charging the village, ordered his trumpeter, Private Daniel Morrison, not to fire at a Indian wrapped in blanket, believing the figure to be a woman. Just then the Indian, an old man, loosed a arrow that struck Morrison in the right temple. Morrison shot and killed the old man, and may have taken his scalp.[57]

While the charge was brief in duration, it was costly for both sides. Black Kettle and his wife, Medicine Woman, as well as many of the Cheyenne warriors, were killed during the initial charge. Seventeen warriors took shelter in a shallow depression and exacted a toll on the soldiers until they were picked off by Cooke's sharpshooters. There was a further report of 38 dead warriors discovered in a ravine after the fight, but this appears to be an exaggeration as the total warrior population of the village probably did not exceed 75. The 7th also suffered heavily in the initial assault. Captain Hamilton, who had pleaded so forcefully to be allowed to command his squadron in the attack, was shot through the heart and killed instantly. Private Charles Cuddy, Company B, was shot through the head and died a short time later. Private Augustus Delaney, also of Company B, was shot in the chest and died some ten hours later. Finally, Private Benjamin McCasey, Company H, was shot in the ribs, the arrow penetrating his lungs. He died on November 30th.[58]

Captain Albert Barnitz was nearly fatally wounded during the initial charge. Rather than charging through the village, he had diverted about three quarters of a mile up the hills to the south where he engaged in a duel with the Cheyenne warrior Magpie. Barnitz had been shot about three inches above and four inches to the left of his naval. The bullet, ranging upwards, had exited about three and a half inches from his spinal column, rupturing the case of the stomach and breaking a rib, but otherwise not harming any vital organs.[59]

Major Joel Elliott, the regiment's second in command, noticed some dismounted Indians escaping downstream through a gap in the lines.[60] Seventeen men, including Regimental Sergeant Major Kennedy, responded to his call for volunteers. As he spurred in pursuit, he waved to Lieutenant Owen Hale and called:

> *"Here goes for a brevet or a coffin."*[61]

Godfrey, ordered to round up the ponies, passed through the village without encountering a single warrior. His 1928 narrative describes his actions:

> "*After passing through the village, I went in pursuit of pony herds and found them scattered in groups about a mile below the village. I deployed my platoon to make the roundup and took a position for observation. While the roundup was progressing, I observed a group of dismounted Indians escaping down the opposite side of the valley. Completing the roundup, and starting them toward the village, I turned the herd over to Lieutenant Law who had come with the second platoon of the troop and told him to take them to the village, saying that I would take my platoon and go in pursuit of the group I had seen escaping down the valley.*

> "*Crossing the stream and striking the trail, I followed it till it came to a wooded draw where there was a large pony herd. Here I found the group had mounted. Taking the trail which was well up on the hillside of the valley, and following it about a couple of miles, I discovered a lone tepee, and soon after two Indians circling their ponies. A high promontory and ridge projected into the valley and shut off the view of the valley below the lone tepee. I knew the circling of the warriors meant an alarm and rally, but I wanted to see what was in the valley beyond them. Just then Sergeant Conrad, who had been a captain of Ohio volunteers, and Sergeant Hughes, who had served in the 4th U. S. Cavalry in that country before the Civil War, came to me and warned me of the danger of going ahead. I ordered them to halt the platoon and wait till I could go to the ridge to see what was beyond. Arriving at and peering over the ridge, I was amazed to find that as far as I could see down the well wooded, tortuous valley there were tepees— tepees.*[62] *Not only could I see tepees, but mounted warriors scurrying in our direction. I hurried back to the platoon and returned at the trot till attacked by the hostiles, when I halted, opened fire, drove the hostiles to cover, and then deployed the platoon as skirmishers.*

> "*The hillsides were cut by rather deep ravines and I planned to retreat from ridge to ridge. Under the cavalry tactics of 1841, the retreat of skirmishers was by the odd and even numbers, alternating in lines to the rear. I instructed the line in retreat to halt on the next ridge and cover the retreat of the advance line. This was successful for the first and second ridges, but at the third I found men had apparently forgotten their numbers and there was some confusion, so I divided the skirmishers into two groups, each under a sergeant, and thereafter had no trouble.*"

> "*During this retreat we heard heavy firing on the opposite side of the valley, but being well up on the side hills we could not see through the trees what was going on. There was a short lull when the firing again became heavy and continued till long after we reached the village, in fact, nearly all day.*

> "*. . . On reaching the village I turned over the pony herd and at once reported to General Custer what I had done and seen. When I mentioned the 'big village,' he exclaimed, 'What's that?' and put me through a lot of rapid fire questions.*

> "*. . . the General sent for me and again questioned me about the big village. At that time many warriors were assembling on the high hills north of the valley overlooking the village and the General kept looking in that direction.*[63]

In between conversations with Lieutenant Godfrey, Custer, accompanied by the interpreter Romeo, had gone to one of the lodges containing the captured women and children. Interrogating one of the women,

> *"She informed me, to a surprise on my part almost equal to that of the Indians at our sudden appearance at daylight, that just below the village we then occupied, and which was a part of the Cheyenne tribe, were located in succession the winter villages of all the hostile tribes of the southern Plains with which we were at war, including the Arapahoes, Kiowas, the remaining band of Cheyennes, the Comanches, and a portion of the Apaches; that the nearest village was about two miles distant, and the others stretched along through the timbered valley to the one farthest off, which was not over ten miles."*[64]

The arrival of the warriors from the downstream villages put the 7th in a precarious position. Instead of being the aggressors, the 7th now found itself in the unenviable position of being nearly encircled by a warrior force that was continually increasing in strength. While the escort for the supply train was inadequate to handle such a sizable force should the Indians discover their presence, of more immediate concern was the safety of Lieutenant Bell and the reserve ammunition. Lieutenant Bell had started for the village at the first sounds of firing, but the steep icy banks of the river made for slow going. When he arrived on the ridge where the haversacks and overcoats were cached, the surrounding terrain was swarming with warriors. Noticing Bell's arrival, the Indians immediately attacked. Abandoning all hope of recovering the warm clothing and rations, Bell loaded the guard on the wagons and headed for the village at the best speed he could make under the difficult conditions. He sped along the snow encrusted ridge amid a hail of fire that killed several of his mules. He reached the village without the loss of a man; his tar soaked wagon wheels afire from the friction of applying the brakes during his mad dash to safety.[65]

The reserve ammunition safely in hand, Custer sent skirmishers forward to keep the warriors at bay, then set about complying with Sheridan's orders to destroy the village and pony herd. Lieutenant Godfrey was ordered to burn the village and allow no looting. Godfrey graciously allowed the Cheyenne captives to rescue some personnel items before destroying all the Indian stores save some *"small curios"* that undoubtedly went into the pockets of the troopers of Company K.[66]

> *"As the last of the tepees and property was on fire, the General ordered me (Godfrey, DCE) to kill all the ponies except those authorized to be used by prisoners and given to the scouts.[67] We tried to rope them and cut their throats, but the ponies were frantic at the approach of a white man and fought viciously. My men were getting very tired so I called for reinforcements and details from other organizations were sent to complete the destruction of about eight hundred ponies. As the last of the ponies were being shot nearly all the hostiles left. This was probably because they could see our prisoners and realized that any shooting they did might endanger them."*[68]

The destruction of the village completed, and the immediate threat from the warriors checked, Custer was finally free to focus his attention on the whereabouts of Major Elliott and his detachment. Earlier in the day, Godfrey had suggested to Custer that he may have heard Elliott firing:

> *". . . I told him that I had heard that Major Elliott had not returned and suggested that possibly the heavy firing I had heard on the opposite side of the valley might*

have been an attack on Elliott's party. He pondered this a bit and said slowly. 'I hardly think so, as Captain Myers has been fighting down there all morning and probably would have reported it."[69]

With their objective secured, Custer dispatched Captain Myers to search for Major Elliott and his detachment. Captain Myers took his troop approximately two miles down the valley in search of Elliott and his party but was unable to discover anything.[70] The fate of Elliott would not be known with certainty until the next month when Custer, accompanied by Sheridan, revisited the battlefield and discovered the horribly mutilated remains.

The village and Indian property destroyed, Custer's thoughts again focused to the supply train following in his wake. To remain on the battlefield was to invite disaster not only for the train but for his troopers without rations and the necessary warm clothing. He also knew a retreat would only encourage the warriors observing the command from just out of rifle range to fall upon his rear. He settled on a bold tactical stroke – a feint toward the remaining villages. Mounting the regiment, the column moved boldly toward the downstream villages with the band playing *"Ain't I Glad to Get Out of the Wilderness."* When the warriors on the hilltops discerned the cavalry's intentions, they broke off surveillance and rode to warn their villages. Their warnings were heeded and the villages were struck and the people began moving forthwith. Custer marched down river until darkness concealed his movements. He then counter marched until a halt was ordered at 2 AM; rejoining his supply train about 10 the next morning. The Battle of the Washita was over.[71] When Custer followed up this victory with his masterful stroke in securing the release of Sarah Catherine White and Anna Belle Morgan,[72] his reputation as an Indian fighter was secured.[73]

A great victory, the first since the Civil War, had been won. An entire village of 51 lodges had been destroyed. Fifty three prisoners had been taken. Many warriors, including Chiefs Black Kettle and Little Rock, had been killed.[74] Yes, it had been a great victory, the first for Custer and the Seventh Cavalry; but at what price had the victory been won? Two officers, one the grandson of Alexander Hamilton, and twenty enlisted men had been killed, or would eventually die from wounds. Clara Blinn and her young son Willie, captives in Satanta's Kiowa camp, had been slain as soon as the presence of troops was discovered. Beyond, and far surpassing, the human toll was an intangible, the 7th Cavalry, a unit not two and one half years old, had been rent asunder. In leaving the field without ascertaining the fate of Major Elliott and his detachment and recovering their bodies, regardless of the sound military reasons for so doing, Custer sowed the seeds for a schism in his officer corps that would ultimately contribute to his ruin a scant eight years later.

> *"A day or two after the fight, Benteen went to Ben Clark, one of Custer's scouts who had heard Elliott's call for volunteers and seen him ride off the field, and asked him if he would 'be willing to make the statement that Custer knowingly let Elliott go to his doom without trying to save him.' Clark knew the circumstances of Elliott's going off, and that Custer had known nothing of it till some time later, so, in his own words, he 'refused to have anything to do with the matter.'*
>
> *". . . Clark says that Benteen made the charge of the abandonment of Elliott because he was 'anxious to weaken Custer's prestige.'"*[75]

The schism was visible to all when Benteen's highly critical letter was published in the February 9, 1869 edition of the *St. Louis Daily Democrat*. Benteen seems to revel in his description of officers and men lounging, eating, and sleeping in the captured village while the ring of death slowly tightened around Elliott and his little band. Were this true, all the officers, Benteen included, would be equally guilty of callously abandoning Elliott to his fate. In light of this it must be noted that no participant, not even the vitriolic Benteen, mentions any protest associated with leaving the village prior to ascertaining the fate of Elliott.

Custer had erred in leaving the field without recovering the bodies of Elliott and his detachment; he now compounded his error. Assembling his officers, he took them to task over the letter in the *Daily Democrat;* stating he would horsewhip the guilty party. Custer, apparently believing the letter to have been written by a junior officer, was dumbfounded when Benteen confessed to the deed. While Benteen's account of the incident leads one to believe that the implied threat to "shoot it out" with Custer caused his commander to back down, not even Custer's most ardent detractors have ever accused him of any timidity what so ever. It is most probable that Custer was so taken aback by Benteen's confession that he simply ended the interview and, to our knowledge, never broached the subject again. Utterly fearless on the battlefield, Custer shied away from personal confrontations. Custer's unwillingness to meet the issue of disloyalty and insubordination by one of his senior officers head on, rather than the often charged abandonment of Major Elliott, was the major impact of the Washita on the Little Big Horn. Without the required reprimand, Benteen grew more vocal in his criticisms of his commander and the schism in the officer corps festered until the officers were divided into two cliques, one pro, and one anti–Custer. Rather than take positive action to resolve the situation, Custer resorted to the expedient of "banishing" those officers of the anti–Custer faction to remote posts while retaining those loyal to him at Fort Lincoln. The regiment would become schizophrenic, functioning as two distinct groups, with parallel yet distinct chains of command, one loyal and located with Custer while the other was located with and loyal to Benteen, Custer's chief antagonist.

We cannot close our discussion of the Washita fight without remarking on the controversy surrounding the status of Black Kettle's village. Custer's detractors have argued long about Black Kettle's tireless efforts to reach a lasting peace with the white men. Custer's supporters have argued equally persuasively about the depredations committed along the Solomon and Saline Rivers in the spring of 1868. When all the rhetoric is swept aside, two facts stand out. First, no chief, and no band of plains Indians, pursued peace more diligently than Black Kettle and his Southern Cheyenne. The second indisputable fact is that the trail of a war party, including many of Black Kettle's young warriors, their hands stained with the blood of Kansas settlers, led the 7th Cavalry to the Cheyenne winter camp. Speaking of this war party, scout "California Joe" remarked:

> *"It was learned afterwards that this band had killed the mail carriers between Forts Dodge and Larned, an old hunter near Fort Dodge, and two couriers sent back by General Sheridan with letters."*[76]

The fact that the army was never able to develop a means of distinguishing the guilty from the innocent and the Indians could not comprehend the white man's concept of justice and ownership of land and property only magnifies the tragedy.

---

[1] On July 8, 1755, British General Edward Braddock led his force of British regulars into a trap laid by French Captain Hyacinth de Beaujeu. Three hours later, Braddock, having suffered in excess of 975 casualties from his 1459 man force, lay mortally wounded , carried from the field by his colonial aide, George Washington. See Wilcomb E. Washburn and Robert M. Utley, "The American Heritage History of the Indian Wars," pg 88. There is some reason to believe that Braddock's defeat by a vastly inferior force (de Beaujeu commanded a combined force of approximately 400 French

troops and Indian allies) was due, in part, to his failure to heed his scouts. See John S. Grray, "Custer's Last Campaign," pg 134. This same charge would, of course, be applied to Custer as a result of the Little Big Horn.

In 1791, a large force of Miamis under chief Little Turtle defeated the army of General Arthur St. Clair in western Ohio near the Indiana border. St. Clair was repulsed with losses of 632 killed and 264 wounded from his 1400 man force. See Francis B. Taunton, "No Pride in the Little Big Horn," pg 72, and Paul Andrew Hutton, "Soldiers West," pg 7.

On December 28, 1835, Major Francis L. Dade led his 111 man force into a Seminole ambush. Only two men escaped with their lives. See Fairfax Downey "Indian Wars of the U. S. Army: 1776 - 1865" pages 119 - 121.

Captain, brevet lieutenant colonel, William Judd Fetterman and his force of 80 officers and men were decoyed and annihilated by a combined force of Lakota and Cheyenne near Fort Phil Kearny on December 21, 1866. Fifteen days earlier, Fetterman, accompanied by the two officers who would die with him, had been decoyed and ambushed by these same warriors, being saved only by the timely arrival of a relief force under Colonel Carrington. See Paul I. Wellman, "Death on Horseback," pp 51 – 54 and Cyrus Townsend Brady, "Indian Fights and Fighters," pp 20 – 22 and 24 – 32. Fetterman, his boast of being able to ride through the Lakota nation with 80 men ringing hollowly through the corridors of time, justifiably serves as the archetypical frontier officer, arrogant and rash with a total disregard for the capabilities of his enemy. Custer's character, as well as his behaviour at the Little Big Horn, has often been compared with that of Fetterman.

[2] See Brian C. Pohanka "Their Shots Quit Coming," pg 20.

[3] The original plan had called for a winter campaign, but the unusually severe weather prevented all but General George Crook's force from taking the field.

[4] See Appendix 17 for a complete listing of 7th Cavalry actions against Indians.

[5] Sheridan had once told a major in the 6th Michigan Cavalry that whenever his troops ran into trouble, he wanted to see Custer and the Michigan Brigade. It was obvious to Sheridan that Custer was the man to solve his problem on the southern plains. See Paul Andrew Hutton "The Custer Reader" page 30.

[6] Company L was serving in Colorado Territory. See Lt Col Melbourne C. Chandler "Of Garryowen In Glory" pages 13 and 28.

[7] See Lawrence Frost "Battle of the Washita" in "Great Western Indian Fights" pages 175 – 176. Sheridan had good reason for wanting his Civil War subaltern with him. The typical caliber of frontier commander with which Sheridan had to contend was aptly demonstrated on the march to establish Camp Supply. On the last day out, Custer's Osage scouts discovered the trail of a large war party heading north. Custer petitioned General Sully to be allowed to follow the back trail of this party and strike their village. General Sully refused on the grounds that the Indians were aware of the presence of troops in the area and therefore surprise was impossible! See Paul Andrew Hutton "The Custer Reader" pages 162 – 163.

[8] See Jeffry D. Wert "Custer" page 268.

[9] Custer's return was favorably received by the regiment, an enlisted man remarking: *". . . we were all very glad to see him again, as he was the only man capable of taking charge of the regiment."* His

impact was immediately felt as noted by an officer: *". . . we had unconsciously fallen into a state of inertia, and appeared to be leading an aimless sort of existence, but with his coming, action, purpose, energy and general strengthening of the loose joints was the order of the day."* See Jeffry D. Wert "Custer" page 269.

[10] See Richard A. Thompson "Crossing the Border with the 4th Cavalry" page 51.

[11] See General E. S. Godfrey "Some Reminiscences, Including the Washita Battle, November 27, 1868" page 483.

[12] See John K. Herr and Edward S. Wallace "The Story of the U. S. Cavalry" page 76.

[13] Barnitz was a fine officer, but not much of a prophet as there were no desertions recorded during the Washita Campaign.

[14] See Robert M. Utley "Life in Custer's Cavalry" page 204.

[15] Some of the troopers complained in vain that the drill was "damned doughboy work and they hadn't 'listed in the cavalry for such." See Fairfax Downey "Indian–Fighting Army" page 80.

[16] See General E. S. Godfrey "Some Reminiscences, Including the Washita Battle, November 27, 1868" page 483.

[17] See Stephen E. Ambrose "Crazy Horse and Custer" page 312 and Jay Monaghan "Custer" pages 307 – 308.

[18] Located 3 miles above the junction of Wolf Creek and the North Canadian River (sometimes called the Beaver) in Oklahoma Territory, the post was established by the Washita Expedition, then commanded by Lieutenant Colonel Sully, on November 18, 1868. Today, the post is known as Fort Sill. See Stan Hoig "The Battle of the Washita" page 80.

[19] See Lawrence A. Frost "General Custer's Libbie" page 179. Frost puts Sheridan's arrival on November 22 but this seems in error as both Godfrey and Sheridan list the date as the 21st. See Robert M. Utley "Frontier Regulars" page 150.

[20] Speaking of the 1867 campaign, Custer had remarked: *"I am of the opinion, . . . justified by experience, that no cavalry in the world, marching, even in the lightest manner possible, unencumbered with baggage or supply trains, can overtake or outmarch the Western Indian, when the latter is disposed to prevent it."* See Paul Andrew Hutton "The Custer Reader" page 105.

[21] This strategy, which was so successful in 1868, would result in defeat for two of the three columns in the 1876 campaign. See Robert M. Utley and Wilcomb E. Washburn "Indian Wars" page 222.

[22] The three columns were to have departed on November 1st, but, due to delays with supplies, the date was changed to November 12. Evans' column, the first to depart on active campaigning, missed the rescheduled departure date by almost a full week. See Brigadier General E. S. Godfrey "Some Reminiscences, Including the Washita Battle, November 27, 1868" page 483.

[23] See Robert M. Utley "Frontier Regulars" page 150. Unlike the Little Big Horn, on this occasion the strike force of the 7th contained many raw recruits. See Brigadier General E. S. Godfrey "Some Reminiscences, Including the Washita Battle, November 27, 1868" page 483.

24 See Robert M. Utley "Frontier Regulars" pages 149 – 150 and Brigadier General E. S. Godfrey "Some Reminiscences, Including the Washita Battle, November 27, 1868" page 483.

25 See Brigadier General E. S. Godfrey "Some Reminiscences, Including the Washita Battle, November 27, 1868" page 487. Captain Miles Keogh, who was to have a prominent role in the 1876 campaign, was detailed as part of General Sully's escort and missed the 7th's only true battle with plains Indians prior to the Little Big Horn. See Stan Hoig "The Battle of the Washita" page 82.

26 See John K. Herr and Edward S. Wallace "The Story of the U. S. Cavalry" page 163.

27 Godfrey noted that there *". . . was no woman there to interpret its significance."* See Brigadier General E. S. Godfrey "Some Reminiscences, Including the Washita Battle, November 27, 1868" page 488.

28 See D. A. Kinsley "Favor the Bold: Custer the Indian Fighter" page 82.

29 See Robert M. Utley "Life in Custer's Cavalry" page 215.

30 See Brigadier General E. S. Godfrey "Some Reminiscences, Including the Washita Battle, November 27, 1868" pages 488 – 489.

31 Custer would also inform his officers of his evolving strategy at the Crow's Nest the morning of June 25, 1876. See George A. Custer "My Life on the Plains" pages 302 – 303, and Brigadier General E. S. Godfrey "Some Reminiscences, Including the Washita Battle, November 27, 1868" page 489.

32 This same sentiment of relentless pursuit was expressed by Custer at his June 22, 1876 officer's conference. At that conference, he also ordered that 100 rounds of carbine ammunition be carried by each trooper.

33 At Little Big Horn, Custer would detail a sergeant and six men from each troop to guard the pack train. If he developed this criteria at the Washita, he would have detailed 77 men to guard the wagon train.

34 See George A. Custer "My Life on the Plains" page 303.

35 Captain Louis McLane Hamilton, a grandson of both Alexander Hamilton and President Jackson's Secretary of State, Louis McLane, commanded Troop A at the Battle of the Washita. See Stan Hoig "The Battle of the Washita" page 119.

36 See Captain Frank M. Gibson "Our Washita Battle" page 22. Note that Mathey would also command the pack train at Little Big Horn, while Captain McDougall would command its escort.

37 See Brigadier General E. S. Godfrey "Some Reminiscences, Including the Washita Battle, November 27, 1868" page 491.

38 See George A. Custer "My Life on the Plains" pages 319 – 320.

39 See Captain Frank M. Gibson "Our Washita Battle" page 18. Note that Custer did not have a similar opportunity at Little Big Horn to advise his officers in detail of the impending action as his battle plan was evolving as he conducted his reconnaissance in force. Note also that Custer

battle plan was evolving as he conducted his reconnaissance in force. Note also that Custer deployed to attack Black Kettle's village without knowledge of the large concentration of Indian bands within the immediate vicinity.

[40] See Brigadier General E. S. Godfrey "Some Reminiscences, Including the Washita Battle, November 27, 1868" pages 491 – 492.

[41] See Cyrus Townsend Brady "Indian Fights and Fighters" page 157. Note that Custer would also operate with 4 tactical units at the Little Big Horn (commanded by Benteen, Reno, Keogh, and Yates), rather than the five used at the Washita. This change may have been due to a change in tactics that designated a squadron being comprised of 3 troops rather than the two which had been in effect at the time of the Washita Fight.

[42] See Brigadier General E. S. Godfrey "Some Reminiscences, Including the Washita Battle, November 27, 1868" page 492.

[43] See George A. Custer "My Life on the Plains" pages 330 – 331.

[44] While the 7th Cavalry band was largely a creation of Major Alfred Gibbs (See Robert M. Utley "Life in Custer's Cavalry" page 146), Custer knew well the effect of music on the troops during a fight. He had his regimental band habitually play *"Yankee Doodle"* during Civil War engagements perhaps learning from Sheridan who had his own band play during the battle of Dinwiddie Court House. See Frederic F. Van de Water "Glory Hunter" page 94.

[45] See Edward Smith Luce "Keogh, Comanche and Custer" pages 120 - 121.

[46] See George A. Custer "My Life on the Plains" page 335.

[47] At this meeting Black Kettle had confessed his inability to prevent his young men from raiding into Kansas. See Robert M. Utley "Frontier Regulars" page 151. Hazen, branded by history as callous because of his refusal to accept the surrender of Black Kettle's Cheyenne and Big Mouth's Arapahos, merely recognized the reality of the situation. He had assumed his post as military commander of the Southern Indian Military District in September, after the winter campaign had been planned. He was also undoubtedly aware of General of the Army William T. Sherman's order to Sheridan that Fort Cobb not serve as a haven for the raiding bands. See Robert M. Utley "Frontier Regulars" page 145 and Paul Andrew Hutton "Soldiers West" page 198.

[48] See Theodore A. Ediger and Vinnie Hoffman "Some Reminiscences of The Battle of the Washita" page 2.

[49] See George Bird Grinnel "The Fighting Cheyennes" pages 301 – 302.

[50] See Stan Hoig "The Battle of the Washita" page 93.

[51] See Robert M. Utley "Cavalier in Buckskin" page 65.

[52] See Elmo Scott Watson and Don Russell "The Battle of the Washita, or Custer's Massacre?" page 4.

[53] See Robert M. Utley "Cavalier in Buckskin" page 67.

54 See Robert M. Utley "Cavalier in Buckskin" page 68.

55 See Theodore A. Ediger and Vinnie Hoffman "Some Reminiscences of The Battle of the Washita" page 4. Much has been made by some authors of the killing of women and children during this engagement. While the forgoing should dispel the distortion that a wanton slaughter of helpless women and children was ordered by Custer and executed by the 7th, it is true that a significant number, perhaps as many as 40, of the Cheyenne casualties were women and children. When denouncing the conduct of U. S. troops during the Washita fight, as is so popular among today's revisionist historians, it is well to remember that the Indian did not recognize the concept of non–combatant status for any adversary. It is to the credit of Custer and the 7th Cavalry that they attempted to discriminate targets during this action. It is one of the unfortunate consequences of war that they were only partially successful.

56 See Charles K. Mills "Harvest of Barren Regrets" page 168.

57 Lieutenant Smith describes the wound as minor while Custer described the arrow as sticking in the trooper's skull until removed. Custer's account mentions Morrison scalping the old man while Smith does not. It is difficult to accept Custer's account on this matter. While it was certainly a rather common practice for soldiers to scalp Indian dead, it is highly unlikely a trooper with an arrow protruding from his skull would have the inclination to go "trophy" hunting. It is therefore probable that Custer's account was influenced by journalistic considerations while Smith's presents the sterile facts of the incident. See Stan Hoig "The Battle of the Washita" pages 133 and 209.

58 See Stan Hoig "The Battle of the Washita" pages 140 – 141.

59 See Stan Hoig "The Battle of the Washita" pages 132 – 133. The severity of the wound would force Barnitz's retirement from military service. Although he lived to the age of 77, an autopsy revealed that the cause of death was a growth around his old wound. Also found in his body was a fragment of his army overcoat, driven into his body forty–four years earlier by a ball fired by the Cheyenne warrior Magpie. See Robert M. Utley, "Life in Custer's Cavalry" page 247.

60 Thompson squadron was prevented from forming a proper junction with Elliott's command due to the open nature of the terrain in his front requiring him to hold his command further from the village in order to escape detection. Because his squadron was furthest to the rear, they were the last to enter the village forming the corridor through which some Cheyenne escaped. See Stan Hoig "The Battle of the Washita" page 129.

61 See Brigadier General E. S. Godfrey "Some Reminiscences, Including the Washita Battle, November 27, 1868" page 493. There has been great debate over the exact strength of Elliott's detachment. Subtracting the four men who died either in the village, or later from wounds received in the village, from the twenty two 7th Cavalry fatalities, we are left with eighteen, Major Elliott and seventeen enlisted men. As a total of seventeen bodies were found where Elliott was killed (fourteen of which were recognizable), it appears that the eighteenth man may have been carried away for torture, or else killed some distance from where Elliott made his stand. See Stan Hoig "The Battle of the Washita" pages 202 – 210.

62 Just as Little Big Horn would witness the largest concentration of Indians on the Northern Plains, the winter camps along the Washita probably comprised the largest assemblage of Indians on the Southern Plains. In this instance, however, the various villages were beyond effective supporting distance of each other.

[63] See Brigadier General E. S. Godfrey "Some Reminiscences, Including the Washita Battle, November 27, 1868" pages 493 – 495. Note that Godfrey would again display coolness under fire in reorganizing his retreat from Weir Point at Little Big Horn when his skirmishers failed to maintain their proper intervals.

[64] See General George A Custer "My Life on the Plains" page 344. At Little Big Horn, Custer obviously remembered the shock he had suffered on the Washita with the arrival of the warriors from the down stream villages. Not wanting to repeat the same mistake of improper reconnaissance probably accounts for his irritability when informed at the Crow's Nest that his command had been discovered.

[65] See Colonel Charles F. Bates "Custer's Indian Battles" page 13. As Lieutenant Bell was on leave of absence from Company D, the responsibility to bring up the reserve ammunition fell to Captain McDougall and Lieutenant Mathey at Little Big Horn. Unfortunately for the regiment, neither displayed Bell's tenacity nor his devotion to duty.

[66] See Brigadier General E. S. Godfrey "Some Reminiscences, Including the Washita Battle, November 27, 1868" page 496.

[67] Custer has been severely criticized in some quarters for this slaughter of animals. It is to be noted that, regardless of how distasteful it may have been for a cavalryman to kill a horse, a plains Indian on foot was one less warrior with which to contend. Others would adopt this tactic including Colonel Ranald Mackenzie who, rather than experience a repetition of Indians recapturing their mounts, killed 2000 ponies captured at Palo Duro Canyon in 1874.

[68] See Brigadier General E. S. Godfrey "Some Reminiscences, Including the Washita Battle, November 27, 1868" page 496. This subtle reference to using the Indian noncombatants as a "human shield" is an important one. When Custer feinted down the valley, he kept the prisoners behind the advance companies, rather that at the rear of the column. demonstrating their use as a shield. Later we will explore the possibility that Custer attempted to implement this same stratagem in a final attempt to secure victory at Little Big Horn.

[69] See Brigadier General E. S. Godfrey "Some Reminiscences, Including the Washita Battle, November 27, 1868" pages 495 – 496. It is ironic, or perhaps poetic justice as some would suggest, that just as Custer failed to ride to the sound of Elliott's firing at the Washita, six of the seven companies commanded by Reno and Benteen would similarly ignore the sounds of Custer's firing at the Little Big Horn.

[70] See Brigadier General E. S. Godfrey "Some Reminiscences, Including the Washita Battle, November 27, 1868" page 497, and General George A. Custer "My Life on the Plains" page 370.

[71] Charles J. Brill credits scout Ben Clark with devising the feint strategy and goes on to state that Custer fed his command, at Clark's insistence, prior to the downstream movement (See "conquest of the Southern Plains" pages 177 – 178). Given the circumstances surrounding the movement, and the fact that neither Godfrey, Gibson, or Custer mentions a meal break, I find it highly unlikely that a meal break was taken. As far as the author of the feint, it truly doesn't matter. What matters is that Custer implemented this bold strategy and that it was successful in extricating the command and its prisoners from the field with the fruits of victory intact.

[72] Sarah White had been captured by the Cheyenne at her family's homestead near Concordia, Kansas in mid-August while the recently married Anna Morgan was abducted from her home on

the Solomon River near Delphos, Kansas. Knowing that an attack on the village where the women were held would result in their death, Custer resisted the temptation to fight and took several hostages which he used to obtain the women's release.

[73] To quote historian Milo Quaife: *"Custer's last campaign on the Southern Plains . . . was a remarkable performance which deserves far greater renown than has ever been accorded it. In its conduct he displayed a complete mastery of Indian psychology and of the art of frontier warfare."* See Lawrence A. Frost "General Custer's Libbie" page 181.

[74] No actual body count was made on the field. Instead Custer received estimates of Indian casualties from his officers some twenty four hours after the fight. Estimates ranged from a low of about 20 warriors killed to as many as 140. Custer claimed 103 Indians killed. It must be noted that a large number of the fatalities must have been women and children despite the efforts of the military to spare them. Perhaps Ben Clark's 1899 estimate of the dead being about equally divided between warriors and noncombatants is the closest we can come to the truth at this late date. It is certain that the Cheyenne suffered a significant number of fatalities given the nature of the action and a count of 51 warriors and 52 women and children killed in a village of 51 lodges is not unreasonable given the circumstances. See Stan Hoig "The Battle of the Washita" pages 200 – 201.

[75] See Colonel Charles F. Bates "Custer's Indian Battles" page 16.

[76] See Joe E. Milner "California Joe" page 167.

Chapter 2

The Treaty of 1868

Searching for a new Indian policy in the wake of the Fetterman disaster, an Indian Peace Commission was established by act of congress on July 20, 1867. The charge to the commission was to call together the warring chiefs, determine the cause of their hostility, attempt to negotiate treaties that would remove the causes of the war, provide for the safety of the frontier settlements and Pacific railroads, and institute some plan for the ultimate civilization of the Indians. If the peace commissioners were unsuccessful, the act authorized the President to call out four regiments of cavalry *"for the purpose of conquering the desired peace."*[1] The seven member commission was to be composed of four members named in the act, each of whom was opposed to the use of military force to subdue the Indians, as well as three general officers appointed by the President. The congressional appointees were Commissioner of Indian Affairs Nathaniel G. Taylor, Missouri Senator J. B. Henderson, chairman of the Senate Committee on Indian Affairs, Samuel F. Tappan, and General John B. Sanborn. President Grant's appointees, Lieutenant General William T. Sherman, General William S. Harney, and General Alfred H. Terry were all advocates of military force being the only practical solution to the problem. In October, due to pressing duties as General of the Army, Sherman was replaced by General Christopher C. Augur, Commander of the Department of the Platte.[2]

The composition of the peace commission, as well as the congressional act that established the commission, demonstrates the schizophrenic nature of dealings with the Indians by the United States Government. The commission, comprised almost equally of "hawks" and "doves" was doomed to ultimate failure from the beginning as an examination of the congressional charge reveals. First, the cause of Indian hostility should have been obvious to even as obtuse a body as the United States Congress; white men were continually invading prime Indian hunting grounds. This problem had an obvious solution – deny white access to Indian hunting grounds. Because this solution was patently unacceptable to a race attempting to fulfill its "manifest destiny," a different root cause of the hostilities must be found, one which could be resolved in a manner beneficial to the interests of the United States. While a difficult undertaking from a logical or ethical point of view, this was certainly no insurmountable task for individuals trained in the art of rhetoric, especially when the other party involved did not understand the language.

The problem of securing the safety of the frontier settlements and railroads and establishing a process for the civilization of the Indian was another matter however. The essential fact, that very few of either the white or red races recognized, was that culturally the two races could never hope to coexist. The concept of land ownership by individuals was totally alien to the Indian. Consequently, he could neither understand nor appreciate the white man's seeming obsession with the concept. Similarly, the white man could not comprehend that war was the only way to gain prestige among the Plains Indians; defining the entire sense of being and self worth for the Indian male. While whites would agree that there was an heroic and glorious aspect to war, they could not accept deeds of valor as war's ultimate objective. The ultimate aim, from a white perspective, was to inflict the maximum amount of damage on the enemy so that he would change his behavior in the desired manner. This concept of war was, of course, incomprehensible to the Indian who abhorred high casualty rates, because it took a minimum of fifteen to sixteen years to generate replacements. The essential point here is that, in order to achieve a lasting peace, the male dominated red culture would have to be redefined. The men would have to abandon the war path and learn to achieve prestige and self esteem in other areas, preferably the same as recognized by the white race. In short the Indian male's entire psyche and being would have to undergo a complete change. It is little wonder that the Indian has yet to be totally assimilated into the American culture.[3]

On the morning of October 9, 1867, the commission departed Fort Harker for the prearranged treaty site on Medicine Lodge Creek, Kansas. A portion of the escort was comprised of 150 troopers of the 7th Cavalry under the command of Major Joel Elliott who had been excused from Custer's court martial at Fort Leavenworth expressly for this duty. The 7th cavalry's Edward Settle Godfrey, then a second lieutenant fresh from West Point, found himself in charge of two of the new gatling guns. When he requested target practice for the inexperienced gun crews, Godfrey was informed that he would have to pay for any ammunition so expended. The gun crews marched as part of the escort without ever having fired a shot.[4]

The first general council was held on October 19th. The Comanches and Kiowas signed the treaty the next day although correspondent Henry M. Stanley and Major Elliott, who wrote an official report of the conference, charged that instead of reading the treaty in its entirety to the chiefs, only a few pleasing extracts were provided through the interpreter.[5] The Plains Apaches followed suit, signing on October 25th leaving the commissioners free to concentrate on the Cheyenne, who were viewed as the government's principal antagonists.[6] The Cheyenne, who had been making excuses for their nonattendance since the 14th, arrived in strength on the 27th and agreed to a council that would include the Arapaho on the following morning.

Senator Henderson opened the meeting by apologizing for General Winfield Scott Hancock's burning of the Cheyenne village the previous year.[7] He then got to the crux of the matter by explaining that the Cheyenne must stop raiding the settlements and railroads and confine their hunting to south of the Arkansas River. If they complied, they would be given livestock and farming equipment, and have a grist mill and warehouse for annuity goods built for them on their reservation. Buffalo Chief, who had been chosen to speak for the Cheyenne Nation, claimed the territory north of the Arkansas *"where the bones of our fathers lie buried."* He went on to state:

> *"You think you are doing a great deal for us by giving these presents to us, but we prefer to live as formerly. If you gave us all the goods you could give, yet we would prefer our own life, to live as we have done. You give us presents and then take our land – that provokes war."*[8]

The commissioners were square on the horns of a dilemma. The treaty was already drawn up awaiting signature and the key issue for both sides was ownership of the country north of the Arkansas. How could this impasse be resolved? The solution was really quite simple, Senator Henderson, with John Smith and George Bent acting as interpreters, pulled the Cheyenne Chiefs to one side and promised them they did not need to immediately go to their reservation and they could continue to hunt north of the Arkansas as long as the buffalo remained and they stayed away from white settlements. Later, when the buffalo were gone, they could move to their reservation where the Great White Father would take care of them. Of course, the language of the treaty instrument actually signed remained unchanged, requiring the Cheyenne to forever renounce all claim to the country north of the Arkansas.[9] To their credit, correspondent Stanley, Major Elliott, and General Augur protested vehemently against this deception. Their protests were ignored. Stanley would later recount:

> *"The Chiefs have signed it merely as a matter of form. Not one word of the treaty was read to them. How, therefore, can the treaty have been a success? Bull Bear and Buffalo Chief, even while they signed said: 'We will hold that country between the Arkansas and the Platte together. We will not give it up yet, as long as the*

buffalo and elk are roaming through the country.' Do the above words seem anything like giving up all claims to that country? And yet, if a white man, acting under the knowledge that all that country belongs to the whites, will go and make a home for himself, it will soon be a burning brand – a signal for war. If war is once thus commenced who are to blame? The commissioners."[10]

The 7th Cavalry's Captain Albert Barnitz, who was present as part of the escort, was also not deceived:

*"After the council the Cheyennes were with great difficulty persuaded to sign the treaty. They were superstitious in regard to touching the pen, or perhaps they supposed that by doing so they would be 'signing away their rights' – which is doubtless the true state of affairs, **as they have no idea that they are giving up, or that they have ever given up the country which they claim as their own** (emphasis the author's), the country north of the Arkansas. The treaty all amounts to nothing, and we will certainly have another war sooner or later with the Cheyennes, at least, and probably with the other Indians, in consequence of misunderstanding of the terms of present and previous treaties."*[11]

The sentiments of the majority of the commissioners were of long standing. John Quincy Adams, 6th President of the United States, having asked in 1802:

"What is the right of a huntsman to the forest of a thousand miles over which he has accidentally ranged in quest of prey? . . . Shall the fields and vallies (sic), which a beneficient (sic)God has formed to teem with the life of innumerable multitudes, be condemned to ever lasting barrenness?"[12]

Perhaps the prevailing white attitude was best summarized by a Governor of Georgia:

"Treaties were expedients by which ignorant, intractable, and savage people were induced without bloodshed to yield up what civilized people had the right to possess by virtue of that command of the Creator delivered to man upon his formation – be fruitful, multiply, and replenish the earth, and subdue it."[13]

Amazingly, this fraud and deception on the part of the peace commissioners would not precipitate the 1868 war on the Southern Plains which would culminate in the Battle of the Washita. Instead, a seemingly insignificant raid on the pony herds of the Cheyenne and Arapaho by the Kaws would ignite the conflagration when a retaliatory Cheyenne war party began raiding the settlements along the Solomon and Saline Rivers.

Having dealt with the tribes of the southern plains, the commissioners journeyed to Fort Laramie to treat with Red Cloud and the Lakota. This would be a difficult undertaking, for, despite the failure of their two major summer offensives, [14] the Lakota and their Northern Cheyenne allies controlled the Powder River Country and had, for all practical purposes, closed the Bozeman Trail. When they arrived on November 10th, the commissioners found a message from Red Cloud: Withdraw all troops from the Bozeman Trail. Only then would peace be discussed. Without Red Cloud's presence, nothing could be accomplished. Frustrated, the commissioners departed for Washington, but returned to Fort Laramie in April of 1868 with the text of a full treaty. [15] Spotted Tail, Red Leaf and other Brule chiefs signed the treaty on April 29th. Man Afraid of the Oglala and One Horn of the Minneconjou signed on May 25th and 26th respectively. With the closure of the forts along the Bozeman Trail in August, the last obstacle to the treaty was removed. Little Wolf of the Cheyenne accentuated the Indian position when his warriors burned the "hated post on the piney", Fort Phil Kearny, while the rear elements of the evacuating column were still visible on the trail. Although the terms of the treaty proclaimed a military defeat for the United States, the commissioners considered their mission successfully completed when Red Cloud "touched the pen" on November 6, 1868.

There has been so much controversy over the terms of the treaty that I have reproduced the entire text in Appendix 16. The articles of most interest are Article II, which establishes the boundaries of the reservation, Article XI, which establishes the right to hunt outside reservation boundaries, and Article XVI, which establishes the Powder River Country as unceded Indian territory. Article XVI clearly states the Powder River Country belongs exclusively to the Indians and *"no white person or persons shall be permitted to settle upon or occupy any portion of the same; or without the consent of the Indians, first had and obtained, to pass through the same. . ."* There was a similar prohibition against white trespass on the reservation in Article II, exempting only *"officers, agents, and employees of the government as may be authorized to enter upon Indian reservations in discharge of duties enjoined by law. . ."* Article XI, however, states *". . . the tribes who are parties to this agreement hereby stipulate that **they will relinquish all right to occupy permanently the territory outside their reservation as herein defined** (emphasis the author's), but yet reserve the right to hunt on any lands north of North Platte, and on the Republican Fork of the Smoky Hill river, so long as the buffalo may range thereon in such numbers as to justify the chase."* Clearly, this ambiguity would lead to trouble.

The ink barely dry on the document, both parties set about reinterpreting the terms of the agreement. Red Cloud's immediate concern was his refusal to use Fort Randall on the Missouri River as the site for his agency as stipulated in the treaty. He intended to continue to trade at Fort Laramie. The fact that the post was outside the boundaries of the reservation was of no interest to Red Cloud. This type of performance, signing a treaty to obtain some wanted short term concessions, food, and ammunition, while resolved to ignore any provisions determined to be unfavorable, was typical of both sides. While Red Cloud remained off the reservation, refusing to relocate to Fort Randall, Army Chief of Staff Sherman was forming his own interpretation of the treaty. On June 9, 1870 he wrote to General Augur *"I suppose we must concede to the Sioux the right to hunt from the Black Hills . . . to the Big Horn Mountains, **but the ultimate title to the land is regarded as surrendered** (emphasis the author's)."*[16]

Buried within Article XI were statements giving virtual *carte blanche* to the United States for the construction of railroads, wagon roads, mail stations and *"other works of utility or necessity"* in both the unceded territory and upon the reservation itself. The United States did stipulate that any such construction on the actual reservation would require some form of compensation to the Indians for damages. This article provides the legal basis both for the Stanley Expedition of 1873 and, along with the portion of Article VI reading *"The President may, at any time, order a survey of the reservation. . .,"* the Black Hills Expeditions of 1874 and 1875. While a careful reading of Appendix 16 will show that none of the three expeditions named were a technical violation of the treaty, they clearly represented neither good faith nor ethical behavior on the part of the United States.[17] The Stanley and two Black Hills expeditions will now be examined in more detail to determine their contribution to the Battle of the Little Big Horn.

On June 20, 1873 the escort for the Northern Pacific Railroad survey departed Fort Rice under the command of Lieutenant Colonel David S. Stanley. The column was comprised of 4 companies of the 8th infantry, 6 of the 9th, 3 of the 17th, 1 of the 6th, 5 of the 22nd, 2 Rodman guns manned by Company E of the 22nd infantry, and 10 troops of the 7th cavalry,[18] under Lieutenant Colonel Custer; in all numbering some 1540 soldiers, 275 wagons and ambulances, 353 civilian employees, including Chief of Scouts Charley Reynolds and the President's son, Fred Grant, and 75 Arikara scouts, including Bloody Knife, who was to become Custer's favorite Indian scout.[19] Also along, in charge of the engineers, was Custer's old West Point comrade and Civil War nemesis, Thomas L. Rosser. The steamer *Far West* was one of three used to supply the expedition.

The Stanley Expedition of 1873 is noteworthy for two engagements, August 4th and 11th, between the 7th Cavalry, under the direct command of Armstrong Custer, and the Lakota along the Yellowstone River. While these skirmishes can hardly be termed battles, they represent the only significant actions involving Indians and the 7th Cavalry in the interval between the Battles of the Washita and Little Big Horn. Of interest from a biographical perspective, were the confrontations between Stanley and Custer. While the clashes were over seemingly trivial matters, they were rooted in Stanley's excessive drinking and Custer's desire to be free from direct supervision. The feud culminated when Stanley ordered Custer's arrest and placed him at the rear of the column, only to deliver an abject apology two days later when sobriety returned. This ended the rift between the two as well as Stanley's command of the expedition which, for all intents and purposes, passed to Custer.

On August 4th Custer, true to his custom, was scouting ahead of the cavalry column to pick its route. His escort consisted of Companies A (Captain Myles Moylan, First Lieutenant Algernon E. Smith, and Second Lieutenant Charles A. Varnum)[20] and B (First Lieutenant Edward G. Mathey, and Second Lieutenant Benjamin H. Hodgson) a total of approximately 85 men and 5 officers. During the noon rest stop a decoy party of 6 Lakota were fired upon and driven off from the cavalry's picket line. The decoys withdrew to a safe distance and waited for the cavalry to saddle and start the pursuit. Custer, accompanied by his brother Tom,[21] brother-in-law and adjutant James Calhoun and twenty troopers, took the advance.

Fearing an ambush, Custer halted the advance and proceeded with two orderlies in order to discern the Lakota's intent. Their ambush thwarted, a large party of 300 – 400 warriors burst from the concealment of a heavy growth of timber. Custer, returning to the squadron, dismounted a skirmish line and checked the Lakota's charge, Bloody Knife scoring the first hit. Due to the vast numerical superiority of the Lakota, Custer took to the defensive placing every trooper except the horse holders on the firing line. Due to the extent of his front, Custer abandoned the usual custom of allocating one trooper for every four horses, requiring each trooper to control 8 horses. The fire fight continued for over three hours during which time the Lakota tried unsuccessfully to both flank and force back the dismounted skirmish line. Even firing the prairie grass was of no effect in dislodging the troops. Finally, running short of ammunition, Custer ordered a charge which apparently was delivered at the same time the Lakota discovered the advance of Troop L down the valley. With reinforcements in view, and not desiring to sustain further casualties, the Lakota broke off the attack.[22]

The loss sustained by the troops in this action was one man and two horses wounded while it was estimated that 2 to 4 Lakota were killed and 5 ponies were killed or severely wounded. Early in the day some warriors had broken off from the war party and gone in search of stragglers. The small party discovered veterinary surgeon Dr. John Honsinger and sutler Augustus Baliran about a mile from the column and quickly killed them and took their horses. Private John Ball strayed too far from the column while hunting and met a similar fate.

On August 8th, the expedition came across a large camp site that had been recently abandoned. Custer was ordered in pursuit with 4 squadrons[23] of the 7th. The trail was littered with abandoned camp equipment indicating to Custer that the flight was a precipitous one which he ascribed to the defeat on August 4th. Custer was 24 hours behind the Lakota when he reached their crossing point on the Yellowstone, which was within 2 miles of the Big Horn, the evening of the 9th. Custer tried, unsuccessfully, as Gibbon would three years later, to cross the Yellowstone all the next day, much to the disgust of Bloody Knife and the other Arikara.

At dawn on August 11th, the Lakota appeared in great numbers[24] across the river and poured a heavy fire into the cavalry camp. Custer mounted his command and withdrew the majority to the shelter of the bluffs in his rear, sending only a few skirmishers, including his orderly, Private John H. Tuttle, E Troop, to exchange shots with the Lakota marksmen across the river. Private Tuttle, who Custer characterized as *". . . one of the most useful and daring soldiers who ever served under my command"* was killed after dispatching at least 3 warriors.[25]

The Lakota then crossed strong parties above and below the cavalry camp in an attempt to gain the bluffs in the troops' rear. A platoon[26] of L Troop, under Second Lieutenant Charles Braden, was detailed to the left to hold a commanding knoll. When this unit checked the advance of some 200 Lakota, Custer ordered the band to play *"Garry Owen"* and launched a counter attack that drove the warriors for over 8 miles.[27] Custer, in addition to having a horse shot from under him, lost one trooper killed and one officer and 20 men wounded. Custer estimated that as many as 40 Lakota had been killed in the engagement.

Several items are worthy of note regarding these actions with the Lakota. First Captain Benteen was absent from both actions being detailed to command the garrison left at Stanley's Stockade on the Yellowstone near the mouth of Glendive Creek.[28] Perhaps Benteen, when detailed on his scout to the left at the Little Big Horn, reflected on the possibility of being left out of that fight as well. Coupled with the erroneous intelligence received from Custer's two messengers, his reflection may have induced his tardy arrival at the river which would then be attributable to pouting and sulking rather than mere dawdling. Custer's attempt at crossing a swollen Yellowstone could only have reinforced the lesson learned in 1867 that it was fruitless to pursue Indians across the plains as they would routinely go where troops could not follow.

Custer had also learned a great deal about tactics employed by the Lakota. He knew that they could be extremely aggressive when an enemy was outnumbered and held at bay, as his two companies had been on August 4th. He also knew that the Lakota were unwilling to stand in the face of a determined cavalry charge. While it is true that the Lakota did not, as a rule, meet cavalry charges head on, a striking exception being the Battle of the Rosebud, Custer misinterpreted their retreats as "cowardly" acts rather than the tactical withdrawals to buy time and reassess the situation that they really were. In sum, the army had probably overestimated the prowess of the Lakota prior to the 1873 Yellowstone Expedition as evidenced by a certain amount of overcautious and tentative behavior.

Unfortunately, the experience gained in 1873 led the army to grossly underestimate the prowess and determination of the Lakota warrior when embarking on the 1876 expedition. This failure to appreciate the true character of the Lakota can perhaps be best understood by viewing the results of the August 4th fight from both the Lakota and cavalry perspectives. Custer was obviously pleased to have driven the Indians from the field with the loss of only one man wounded. Custer rightly, by white standards, claimed victory when he was left in possession of the field. It would have astonished Custer to learn that the Lakota viewed the outcome as equally favorable. The Lakota had also realized their objective, the winning of war honors. The Indians had killed three men in the raid and disengaged when they desired with minimal casualties. Custer's report details the numerous "bravery runs" conducted by the Lakota in front of his skirmish line. Knowledgeable as he was for his day, the fact that Custer did not recognize these feats of bravery as an objective of plains Indian warfare demonstrates the white man's general lack of understanding of the Indian's motivations in war.

"But the foemen fled in the night,

And Rain–in–the–Face, in his flight,

Uplifted high in air

As a ghastly trophy, bore

The brave heart, that beat no more,

Of the White Chief with yellow hair."

The above is the operative verse of Longfellow's *"The Revenge of Rain–in–the–Face."* Although the poem clearly refers to Armstrong Custer, there is no more enduring legend of the Little Big Horn than that of Rain In The Face revenging himself upon the corpse of Captain Tom Custer by cutting out and eating the heart. Libbie Custer[29] believed this event had occurred and so stated in *"Boots and Saddles."* This belief was undoubtedly supported by the horribly mutilated condition of Tom Custer's corpse, being identifiable only by the "T.W.C." inscribed on his arm in India ink.

The roots of the legend lie in the August 4, 1873 action against the Lakota previously discussed. Recall that coincident with that action, two civilians, veterinary surgeon Honsinger and sutler Baliran, had been killed when separated from the column. During the winter of 1874 – 75, word reached Charley Reynolds that Rain In The Face was not only responsible for the killings, but was "wintering" at Standing Rock Reservation. Upon receiving this information, Armstrong Custer dispatched a detachment of cavalry under Captain George Yates to arrest the culprit. Tom Custer accompanied the column and was personally involved in subduing and arresting Rain In The Face. It seems incredible that any arrest resulting from military action could have been contemplated, let alone ordered. Apparently the driving force behind this action was the belief that, since Honsinger and Baliran were both unarmed civilians, the killings constituted murder rather than self defense against an armed invading enemy.

Rain In The Face was taken to Fort Lincoln for incarceration. He was personally interrogated by Armstrong Custer on several occasions. After one particularly lengthy interrogation, Custer announced that Rain In The Face had confessed to the killings. Interestingly, the military then lost all interest in the case, neither pursuing the fugitive nor disciplining the soldier on guard at the time Rain In The Face escaped from the guard house after 3 months of confinement.[30]

There are several possible explanations for this seemingly bizarre behavior on the part of the military. First there was a significant outcry for due process on the part of sympathetic whites. They rightly pointed out that even if a murder had been committed, the army had no jurisdiction and were illegally holding their prisoner. They further argued that the military expedition of 1873 constituted an armed invasion of Lakota hunting grounds and the Lakota would naturally assume any white men found in the region to be a part of the column and consider them to be armed belligerents. Indeed, this same argument resulted in a dismissal of charges against Rain In The Face when he was brought to trial for the murders several years later.[31] What is most probable however, is that Custer, somehow convinced of his innocence, simply allowed Rain In The Face to escape.

In any event the legend goes that Rain In The Face not only swore vengeance, but that, although painfully wounded, he actually recognized one or both of the unshaven and unkempt Custers amid the smoke, dust and turmoil of battle and then exacted his terrible revenge. Stories of "unbiased" death bed confessions not withstanding, it defies all logic that there could be any substantive truth to this legend.

In his annual report for 1873, General Sheridan had recommended that a military base be established in the Black Hills.[32] While it can be argued, I suppose, that a military installation could be considered *"other works of utility or necessity"* under Article XI of the treaty of 1868, the intent of the government was clearly to project a powerful military presence in the heart of the Lakota Reservation regardless of the precise interpretation of the treaty or the understanding of the parties involved at the time. Sheridan acknowledged as much in his annual report for 1874 which reads in part:

> *"In order to better control the Indians making these raids toward the south,[33] I had contemplated, for two or three years past, to establish a military post in the country known as the Black Hills, and in my last annual report, recommended the establishment of a large post there, so that by holding an interior point in the heart of the Indian country we could threaten the villages and stock of the Indians, if they made raids on our settlements. With this view I mentioned the subject in the presence of the President, the honorable Secretary of the Interior, the honorable Secretary of War, and the General of the army, last fall, and meeting with a favorable response from the Secretary of the Interior, who has exclusive charge of Indian affairs, I set to work to make a reconnaissance of the country about which dreamy stories have been told, especially by Father De Smet.*

> *"I first thought that Fort Laramie, which is not much more than one hundred miles from the Black Hills, would be the best place to start the reconnaissance from, but on visiting Fort Laramie last fall, and again in the winter, I found the condition and the temper of the Indians such as would probably provoke hostilities. I then turned my attention to Fort A. Lincoln, on the Missouri River, at the end of the Northern Pacific Railroad, where most of the Seventh Cavalry, under command of Lieut. Col. George A. Custer was stationed, as the most suitable place to start from, although the distance was three times as great as from Fort Laramie. On visiting Fort Lincoln in the spring, I found everything favorable. . . I then returned and secured the necessary authority for the reconnaissance, and directed General Terry to organize the expedition and put Colonel Custer in command, whom I thought especially fitted for such an undertaking."[34]*

General Terry, a member of the peace commission, summed up the opinion of the army and the administration in a letter to General Sheridan:

> *"I am unable to see that any just offense is given to the Indians by the expedition to the Black Hills. . . From the earliest times the government has exercised the right of sending exploring parties of a military character into unceded territory, and this expedition is nothing more."[35]*

Terry cites Article II of the treaty which permitted authorized officers and agents of the government to enter the reservation. Conveniently, he could not believe that this provision was intended to exclude military forces, and he doubted if the Indians had so understood it even though he knew full well that such an occurrence had never been explained to them. He piously continued:

> *"Can it be supposed that it was the intent of the treaty to set apart, in the heart of the national territory, a district nearly as great as the largest State east of the Mississippi River - two-thirds as large as the combined area of the six New England States - within which the government should be forbidden to exercise the power,*

which it everywhere else possesses, of sending its military forces where they may be required?"[36]

Nothing was going to stand in the way of the expedition. Custer and the 7th cavalry had been selected to survey *paha sapa*, the sacred Black Hills, to determine the best location for the proposed fort. Sheridan wired Custer on May 15, 1874:

"Prepare at once to outfit an expedition to the Black Hills to investigate rumors of large gold deposits & survey area for possible establishment of Military Posts."[37]

Before the expedition could depart, Custer insisted on making his usual preparations. Extensive training was provided for the many new recruits,[38] and Custer ordered a heavy regimen of target practice for the troops. One other item was required prior to departure, receipt of the new Springfield Model 1873 carbine which would remain standard issue during the 1876 campaign. The carbines and new ammunition were issued to the troops on July 1st.[39]

These preparations did not go unnoticed by the Lakota. During the time Custer was training his command, Running Antelope, along with delegations numbering up to 200 persons from the Grand River Agency, repeatedly petitioned Custer to abandon the expedition. Custer would patiently explain the peaceful nature of the enterprise and proceed with his preparations.[40] What did the protests of a few reservation Indians matter? The *Bismarck Tribune* summed it all up in an editorial that ran on June 17th:

"This is God's country. He peopled it with red men, and planted it with wild grasses, and permitted the white man to gain a foothold; and as the wild grasses disappear when the white clover gains a footing, so the Indian disappears before the advances of the white man.

"Humanitarians may weep for poor Lo, and tell the wrongs he has suffered, but he is passing away. Their prayers, their entreaties, can not change the law of nature; can not arrest the causes which are carrying them on to their ultimate destiny – extinction.

"The American people need the country the Indians now occupy; many of our people are out of employment; the masses need some new excitement. The war is over, and the era of railroad building has been brought to a termination by the greed of capitalists and the folly of the grangers; and depression prevails on every hand. An Indian war would do no harm, for it must come, sooner or later . . ."(emphasis the author's)[41]

When assembled, the expedition was a considerable force: 10 companies of the 7th Cavalry (companies D and I under Major Reno were again escorting the Northern Boundary Survey Commission), Company G of the 17th and I of the 20th Infantry to protect the wagons, and artillery consisting of 3 gatling guns and a three–inch Rodman gun. The expedition had a large civilian contingent as well including reporters Nathan H. Knappen, of the *Bismarck Tribune*, Samuel Barrows, ,of the *New York Tribune*, and William Eleroy Curtis, of the *Chicago Inter-Ocean*, miners Horatio Nelson Ross, and William McKay, a member of the Dakota Territorial legislature, and photographer William H. Illingworth. Numbered among the 51 "bug hunters", as the scientists were referred to by the troopers, were zoologist/paleontologist George Bird Grinnel and his assistant Luther North, geologist Newton H. Winchell, and botanist A. B. Donaldson. There were 3 civilian guides, Charley Reynolds, Louis Agard, and Boston Custer accompanying his brothers in the field for the first time. Filling out the scouts were 3 Lakota, 2 Blackfeet, 25 Santees and 23 Arikaras [42]. Of the Arikara, Goose, Little Sioux, Strikes Two, Young Hawk, and Custer's personal favorite Bloody Knife, would accompany the 7th to the Little Big Horn two years later.

Bloody Knife, half Uncpapa himself, had not wanted to accompany the expedition at first as he considered it a sacrilege to enter the dwelling place of the Lakota Gods. He had also lost a son to a Lakota raiding party that the 7th Cavalry had failed to intercept just a few days prior to the departure.[43] Custer finally won his promise to accompany the expedition with a promotion. When some well meaning officers toasted his newly won sergeant's chevrons, it was more than he could master with his usual equanimity and he wound up drunk and disorderly in the guard house.[44]

On July 2, 1874 the expedition departed Fort Lincoln. They would return on August 30 after traveling a distance of 883 miles (1,205 miles if all the side trips are counted). This being Boston Custer's first experience in the wilderness with his brothers, he was subjected to the usual ration of Custer family pranks. Bos, as he was affectionately known, would put rocks in a wash basin to soak each night because brother Tom assured him that those "sponge stones" would soften up. History does not record how many nights it took Boston to "wise up." Armstrong had confided in a letter to Libbie that Boston, astride his mule, had demonstrated endurance but no aptitude for speed. Accordingly, when the proper undulating terrain presented itself, Armstrong told Boston he needed to ride ahead. He would ride slowly until just over the divide, then spur his mount to a gallop only to slow when he again came into view ascending the next divide. It took Boston quite a while, according to Armstrong, to discover why the distance between the two kept increasing when they were both traveling at the same gait.[45]

On August 2, miner Horatio Nelson Ross discovered gold.[46] Custer's initial dispatch, written August 2 – 3 was restrained in the extreme:

> *"As there are scientific parties accompanying the Expedition who are examining into the mineral resources of the region, the result of whose research will accompany my detailed report, I omit all present reference to that portion of our exploration until the return of the Expedition, except to state what will appear in any event in the public prints, that gold has been found at several places, and it is the belief of those who are giving their attention to the subject that it will be found in paying quantities.*

> *"I have upon my table forty or fifty small particles of pure gold, in size averaging that of a small pinhead, and most of it obtained today from one panful of earth.*

> *"As we have never remained longer at our camp than one day, it will be readily understood that there is no opportunity to make a satisfactory examination in regard to deposits of valuable minerals.*

> *"Veins of lead and strong indications of the existence of silver have been found.* ***Until further examination is made regarding the richness of the deposits of gold, no opinion should be formed*** *."(emphasis the author's)*[47]

Correspondent Samuel Barrows, *New York Tribune,* was equally restrained in his report of August 10, it appeared in the August 28 edition, when he noted there was no way to determine the value or extent of the gold field. He reminded his readers the region belonged to the Lakota, concluding:

> *"Those who seek the Hills only for gold must be prepared to take their chances. Let the overconfident study the history of Pike's Peak. The Black Hills, too, are not without ready made monuments for the martyrs who may perish in their parks."*[48]

Nathan H. Knappen, correspondent of the *Bismarck Tribune*, must have quickened the collective pulse of a nation attempting a recovery from the panic of 1873 with his August 2 report that ran on August 12:

> *"Here in Custer's Valley, rich gold and silver mines have been discovered, both placer and quartz diggings; and this immense section, bids fair to become the El Dorado of America."*[49]

William Eleroy Curtis, *Chicago Inter–Ocean*, showed no restraint what–so–ever in his August 7 dispatch that ran on August 27:

> *"They call it a ten dollar diggin's, and all the camp is aglow with the gold fever. . . From the grass roots down it was 'pay dirt', and after a dozen pans or more had been washed out, the two persevering men who will be the pioneers of a new golden State came into camp with a little yellow dust wrapped carefully up in the leaf of an old account book."*[50]

Apparently everyone had been caught up in the fever, including Armstrong Custer. In his next report, dated August 15, he continued his vivid description of the geography of the country explored and offered his opinion that the land was unsurpassed for either ranching or farming. Never once specifically mentioning the suitability of any location for establishing a military post, although that was the primary purpose of the reconnaissance, he concluded:

> *"I referred in a former dispatch of the discovery of gold. Subsequent examinations at numerous points confirm and strengthen the fact of the existence of gold in the Black Hills.*
>
> *"On some of the water courses almost every panful of earth produced gold in small, yet paying quantities. Our brief halts and rapid marches prevented anything but a very hasty examination of the country in this respect, but in one place, and the only one within my knowledge where as great a depth was reached, a hole was dug eight feet in depth. The miners report that they found gold among the roots of grass,[51] and from that point to the lowest point reached, gold was found in paying quantities.*
>
> *"It has not required an expert to find gold in the Black Hills, as men without former experience in mining have discovered it at an expense of little time or labor."*[52]

All that remained was for the dependable Charley Reynolds to take the message to the outside world which, out of deference to the prowess of the Lakota assumed to be lurking in the vicinity, was accomplished by the expedient of having his horse shoed backwards.[53]

The Thieves' Road had been opened, and the tide of invading white men, lusting for quick riches, would successfully resist all attempts to close it. In the process Custer, *Pahuska*, the Long Hair, had earned a new sobriquet among the Lakota, Chief of the Thieves and the United States had inexorably entered upon the path of armed confrontation with the Lakota Nation.

As previously stated, agreement on gold being found in the Black Hills in paying quantities was not unanimous. It was therefore decided to send in a second expedition the following year to settle the matter once and for all. although miners had already descended on the Black Hills in droves.[54] Disregarding the fate of Ezra Kind,[55] Moses "California Joe" Milner and three companions, John Hickey, Nelse DeLude and George Barnes, entered the hills in March of 1875. Having scouted for Custer the previous summer, "California Joe" was familiar both with the territory and the danger posed by the Lakota. He had little difficulty in convincing the party to leave the hills when he discovered fresh signs of war parties in the vicinity. Before they could leave however, they were attacked by a Lakota war party. DeLude was killed and the remainder of the party was chased all the way to Fort Laramie.[56]

Lieutenant Colonel Richard Irving Dodge commanded the escort for the Jenny Geological and topographical Survey. The 16 civilians included Professor Walter P. Jenny (Chief Geologist), Mr. Newton (assistant geologist), Mr. Tuttle (astronomer), Dr. V. T. McGillicuddy (engineer and topographical officer), and Mr. Patrick (botanist). The escort consisted of 363 men (6 companies) of the 2nd and 3rd cavalry and parts of two companies (91 additional men) from the 9th infantry and one twelve pound howitzer. The train included 4 ambulances, 61 wagons, 397 mules; a herd of 134 beef cattle, one butcher and 3 herders to supply fresh meat.[57] The expedition left Fort Laramie on May 25, 1875 returning on October 13, 1875. For the only time in her life, Martha Jane Canary, more popularly known as "Calamity Jane," would accompany a military expedition from beginning to end.[58]

The Jenny expedition confirmed the presence of gold in the Black Hills. While Jenny, from the New York School of Mines, saw little hope that individual miners working with pan and rocker could succeed, he believed teams of miners with more sophisticated equipment could bring out gold in profitable amounts. Stemming the resultant white tide would prove an impossible task.

---

[1] See James C. Olson "Red Cloud and the Sioux Problem" page 58.

[2] See James C. Olson "Red Cloud and the Sioux Problem" page 59.

[3] The answer ultimately settled upon, of course, was to partition the races. This was accomplished by assigning the Indian to reservations. The attempt to assign the Indian to tracts of land deemed valueless by white men was not always successful. The history of U. S. treaties with the Indians is replete with broken promises and renegotiations necessitated by the tardy discovery that reservation land assigned to the Indians, always in perpetuity, was really of value to the white race after all.

[4] See Don Rickey, Jr. "Forty Miles A Day on Beans and Hay" pages 99 – 100.

[5] See Stan Hoig, "The Battle of the Washita" pages 29 – 30.

[6] See Stan Hoig, "The Battle of the Washita" page 32.

[7] Frustrated by his inability to force the Cheyenne to a peace council, Hancock had razed their deserted village on Pawnee Fork and then, relying primarily on Custer's 7th Cavalry, spent the rest of the summer in futile pursuit across the plains.

[8] See Stan Hoig, "The Battle of the Washita" pages 35.

[9] See Stan Hoig, "The Battle of the Washita" pages 36.

[10] See Stan Hoig, "The Battle of the Washita" pages 37.

[11] See Robert M. Utley, "Life in Custer's Cavalry" page 115.

[12] See Robert M. Utley, "The Indian Frontier of the American West 1846 – 1890" page 36.

[13] See Robert M. Utley, "The Indian Frontier of the American West 1846 – 1890" page 36.

[14] Large bodies of Lakota and Cheyenne had been defeated by small parties of soldiers armed with new breech loading rifles in the Hayfield Fight near Forts C. F. Smith, and the Wagon Box Fight near Fort Phil Kearny in early August.

[15] See Remi Nadeau, "Fort Laramie and the Sioux" page 242.

[16] See Paul L. Hedren, "The Great Sioux War 1876 – 77" page 260.

[17] Although the Stanley and Black Hills Expeditions have received the majority of historian's attention, there were two prior incursions; the Northern Pacific Railroad Survey of 1871 and a similar expedition in 1872. See Judson Elliott Walker "Campaigns of General Custer" pages 29 - 30.

[18] See E. Lisle Reedstrom "Custer's 7th Cavalry" page 78. Troops D and I, under the command of Major Marcus A. Reno, were escorting the Northern Boundary Survey.

[19] Custer had counseled long with Bloody Knife the night of June 19th trying to determine the probable disposition of the Lakota and where they were likely to be encountered. Bloody Knife's prediction that the Lakota would be found in the vicinity of the Tongue River would prove accurate and cement their relationship as *sihuan* (friends). See Ben Innis "Bloody Knife!" page 86. Libbie Custer commented on her husband's regard for Bloody Knife: *". . . sometimes petulant, often moody, and it required the utmost patience on my husband's part to submit to his humors; but his fidelity and cleverness made it worthwhile to yield to his tempers."* See Ernest Lisle Reedstrom "Bloody Knife: Custer's Favorite Scout" page 24.

[20] Varnum, the only officer to remain mounted throughout the engagement, was cited by Custer for gallantry in this and the subsequent engagement on August 11. See Colonel T. M. Coughlan "Varnum – The Last of Custer's Lieutenants" page 4.

[21] This is taken from Custer's official report on the action. While the report makes no mention of how, or in what capacity, Tom Custer was detailed from his troop (M), it is possible that Tom was serving as Aide–de–Camp to his brother, as he would 3 years later at the Little Big Horn.

[22] See Elizabeth B. Custer "Boots and Saddles" page 281 – 283 and John M. Carroll "The Yellowstone Expedition of 1873" pages 54 – 55.

[23] A squadron being 2 companies at that time.

[24] Custer estimated he had engaged 800 to 1000 warriors in this fight.

[25] See Elizabeth B. Custer "Boots and Saddles" pages 286 – 287. *"When the firing commenced in the morning, he (Tuttle, DCE) took a Springfield sporting rifle and with two other men, took station behind a tree and began picking off the Indians as they exposed themselves on the opposite bank. He had killed three Indians in the following manner: Observing one in full view on the bank, he remarked to the men with him, 'watch me drop that buck,' fired and down the Indian went, two others rushed to the assistance of the one killed, and Tuttle by rapid use of his breech loader, succeeded in killing them both. The Indians naturally became enraged at this kind of slaughter and directed their fire at Tuttle who incautiously looking out to get another shot, received a ball over his left eye which killed him instantly."* See Bruce Liddic and Paul Harbaugh "Camp on Custer" page 46.

[26] This deployment not only served as a turning point in the August 11th action, but demonstrates that Custer embraced the use of small tactical units which until recently had been overlooked in army regulations. As we shall see later, I believe that Custer again used platoons as tactical units at the Little Big Horn.

[27] See Elizabeth B. Custer "Boots and Saddles" pages 287 – 289.

[28] See Robert M. Utley "Cavalier in Buckskin" page 119.

[29] Elizabeth Bacon Custer, wife of Armstrong Custer, was known to her intimates as "Libbie."

[30] See Edgar I. Stewart "Custer's Luck" page 60. Rain In The Face maintained that his fellow prisoners, two grain thieves, were aided in their escape and that although the sentry saw them escaping, he made no attempt to stop them. See Usher L. Burdick "David F. Barry's Indian Notes On The Custer Battle" page 39.

[31] See Thomas B. Marquis "Rain–in–the–Face and Curly, The Crow" page 3. Dr. Marquis, in an excellent argument based upon traditional hunting grounds, presents his rationale for doubting that Rain–in–the–Face was even present at the August 4th action.

[32] See Lawrence A. Frost "General Custer's Libbie" page 211.

[33] Indians from the Department of Dakota habitually raided into Nebraska, the Department of the Platte, due to the scarcity of settlers in Dakota.

[34] See Donald Jackson "Custer's Gold" pages 14 – 15.

[35] See Donald Jackson "Custer's Gold" pages 23 – 24.

[36] See Donald Jackson "Custer's Gold" pages 23 – 24.

[37] See D. A. Kinsley 'Favor the Bold: Custer the Indian Fighter" page 156.

[38] See Katherine Gibson Fougera "With Custer's Cavalry" page 95.

[39] See Lawrence A. Frost "With Custer in '74: James Calhoun's Diary of the Black Hills Expedition." page 19.

[40] See Donald Jackson "Custer's Gold" pages 17 – 18.

[41] See Evan S. Connell "Son of the Morning Star" page 241.

[42] See O. G. Libby "The Arikara Narrative of the Campaign Against the Hostile Dakotas June, 1876" page 163.

[43] See Lawrence A Frost "With Custer in '74: James Calhoun's Diary of the Black Hills Expedition" page 54 and Donald Jackson "Custer's Gold" pages 18 – 19.

[44] See Big Horn Yellowstone Journal, Winter 1993, pages 19 – 20.

[45] See Lawrence A Frost "With Custer in '74: James Calhoun's Diary of the Black Hills Expedition" page 37, Note 57.

[46] See Lawrence A Frost "With Custer in '74: James Calhoun's Diary of the Black Hills Expedition" pages 60 – 61.

[47] See Lawrence A Frost "With Custer in '74: James Calhoun's Diary of the Black Hills Expedition" page 68.

[48] See Donald Jackson "Custer's Gold" page 90.

[49] See Donald Jackson "Custer's Gold" page 89.

[50] See Donald Jackson "Custer's Gold" page 90.

[51] Note that while Custer is generally credited, or discredited, with making the "grass roots" statement, it had actually been coined by correspondent William Curtis eight days earlier.

[52] See Lawrence A Frost "With Custer in '74: James Calhoun's Diary of the Black Hills Expedition" pages 79 – 80.

[53] See Lawrence A Frost "With Custer in '74: James Calhoun's Diary of the Black Hills Expedition" page 62. John Henley, First Sergeant of B Troop, told Walter Camp that rather than shoe Reynolds' horse backward, Saddler John E. Bailey, also of Company B, made boots for the horse that gave the appearance of the horse being unshod: *". . . he (Reynolds, DCE) devised special leather sandals cinched with drawstrings for the horse. Pulled over the animal's iron shod hoofs, the sandals would leave tracks like those of a shoeless Indian pony."* See Bruce Liddic and Paul Harbaugh "Camp on Custer" page 61. Private Daniel Newell of Company M, however, claimed that he shoed the horse backwards. See John M. Carroll "The Sunshine Magazine Articles" page 4.

[54] Jenny estimated there were 800 miners already in the Black Hills. See Donald Jackson "Custer's Gold" page 114.

[55] Ezra Kind and 6 others had entered the hills to seek gold in 1833. Kind, the last surviving member of the party, had scraped the following poignant lines on a slab of sandstone:

"Got all of the gold we could carry our ponys all got by the Indians I have lost my gun and nothing to eat and Indians hunting me."

See Donald Jackson "Custer's Gold" page 3.

[56] See Joe E. Milner "California Joe" page 222.

[57] See Joe E. Milner "California Joe" page 224.

[58] See Joe E. Milner "California Joe" page 230.

Custer's wagon train for the 1874 Black Hills expedition. Any column encumbered by such methods of transporting subsistence was doomed to failure in the attempt to pursue the highly mobile plains tribes.
Photo Courtesy Little Bighorn Battlefield National Monument.

Chapter 3

The War Department Assumes Control

Special Indian Commissioner Chris Cox had summed up the results of Custer's Black Hills Expedition in the Annual Report of the Commissioner of Indian Affairs for 1874:

> *"The glowing reports of General Custer (whether true or false) have aroused the frontier, and scores of organizations, more or less extended, are preparing to visit the Black Hills in the coming spring. Already small parties have ventured into the forbidden region and bloodshed has been the result. The tide of emigration cannot be restrained. The exodus will be effected. It may cost blood, but the ultimate occupation of this unceded territory by the white settlers is inevitable."[1]*

The 7th Cavalry had barely returned to Fort Lincoln before the nation's press raised the cry to annex the Black Hills. The September 3, 1874 editorial of the *Yankton Press and Dakotian* is typical of the attitude of the times:

> *"The abominable compact (the treaty of 1868, DCE) with the marauding bands that regularly make war on the whites in the summer and live on government bounty all winter, is now pleaded as a barrier to the improvement and development of one of the richest and most fertile sections in America. What shall be done with these Indian dogs in our manger? They will not dig the gold or let others do it. . . They are too lazy and too much like mere animals to cultivate the fertile soil, mine the coal, develop the salt mines, bore the petroleum wells, or wash the gold. Having all these things in their hands, they prefer to live as paupers, thieves and beggars; fighting, torturing, hunting, gorging, yelling and dancing all night to the beating of old tin kettles. . . Anyone who knows how utterly they depend on the government for subsistence will see that if they have to be supported at all, they might far better occupy small reservations and be within military reach, than to have the exclusive control of a tract of country as large as the whole State of Pennsylvania or New York, which they can neither improve or utilize."[2]*

The fall of 1874 was not the first time white men had cast covetous eyes on the Black Hills. Charles Collins, editor of the *Sioux City Times* and a leader in the move to invade the hills, received a letter from General Terry in April of 1872 warning against a contemplated trespass into the region:

> *". . . the consummation of which it will be my duty, under the law, and my instructions, to prevent, by the use, if necessary, of the troops at my disposal."[3]*

While the stern warning had the desired effect of keeping the would be trespassers in check in 1872, the panic of 1873 had so swelled the ranks of prospective emigrants that the *Bismarck Tribune* was led to rhapsodize:

> *". . . the time has come when the entire army could not much longer keep the country from being over run by the invincible white man – by the hardy pioneer."[4]*

This same sentiment had been expressed in the congress by Senator John Sherman, brother of the general. As early as the summer of 1867 he had recognized the futility of attempting to curb the lust for gold:

> *"If the whole Army of the United States stood in the way, the wave of emigration would pass over it to seek the valley where gold was to be found."*[5]

The army was quick to react. On the same day that the inflammatory editorial was published in the *Yankton Press and Dakotian*, General Sheridan wired General Terry:

> *"Should the companies now organizing at Sioux City and Yankton trespass on the Sioux Indian Reservation, you are hereby directed to use the force at your command to burn the wagon trains, destroy the outfits and arrest the leaders, confining them at the nearest military post in the Indian country. Should they succeed in reaching the interior you are directed to send such force of cavalry in pursuit as will accomplish the purpose above named."*[6]

Apparently recognizing the realities of the situation, Sheridan added:

> *"Should congress open up the country for settlement by extinguishing the treaty rights of the Indians, the undersigned will give a cordial support to the settlement of the Black Hills."*

Sheridan expected action from his subordinates, and that's exactly what he received. During 1875, Custer, Crook and Dodge all had troops in the field clearing the Black Hills of miners. In the period from July 15 to August 26, 1875 the 7th Cavalry arrested 44 miners for attempting to illegally enter the hills.[7] An even more dramatic event occurred on May 21, 1875 when Captain Anson Mills burned a wagon train of mining equipment destined for the Black Hills.[8]

As zealous as the troops were, Senator Sherman's observation had been prophetic; the tide could not be stemmed. Groups of miners eluded the troops and arrived in such numbers that it was estimated that 11,000 miners were in the hills by the fall of 1875. The Grant administration sat squarely on the horns of a dilemma. The destruction of civilian property could not continue. Besides, it had proven to be ineffective. There appeared to be only one avenue of escape. On June 18, 1875 the Secretary of the Interior appointed a committee, headed by Senator William B. Allison of Iowa, to purchase the Black Hills. Also serving on the committee was Brigadier General Alfred H. Terry.

The committee met with Red Cloud on the banks of the White River, about 8 miles east of Red Cloud Agency, on September 20. Almost immediately, the Lakota requested a private council of the tribes in order to determine a price for leasing the Black Hills. On the 24th the commissioners gathered to hear the Lakota reply. As many as 7,000 armed, belligerent warriors ringed the commissioners and their small military escort. Disaster almost ensued when Little Big Man rode into the assemblage and announced he had come to kill the white men who were plotting to steal the Lakota's land. Acting upon the sound advice of Spotted Tail, General Terry bundled the commissioners into army ambulances and hurried then to Camp Robinson.[9] On the 27th, meeting with a much smaller delegation of Lakota, the commissioners were stunned when Red Cloud demanded:

> *"There have been six nations raised, and I am the seventh, and I want seven generations ahead to be fed. . . These hills out here to the northwest we look upon as*

the head chief of the land. My intention was that my children should depend on these hills for the future. I hoped that we should live that way always hereafter. That was my intention. I sit here under the treaty which was to extend for thirty years. I want to put the money that we get for the Black Hills at interest among the whites, to buy with the interest wagons and cattle. We have much small game yet that we can depend on for the future, only I want the Great Father to buy guns and ammunition with the interest so we can shoot the game. For seven generations to come I want our Great Father to give us Texan steers for our meat. I want the Government to issue for me hereafter, flour and coffee, and sugar and tea, and bacon, the very best kind, and cracked corn and beans, and rice and dried apples, and saleratus and tobacco, and soap and salt, and pepper, for the old people. I want a wagon, a light wagon with a span of horses, and six yoke of working cattle for my people. I want a sow and an boar, and a cow and bull, and a sheep and a ram, and a hen and a cock, for each family. I am an Indian, but you try to make a white man out of me. I want some white men's houses at this agency to be built for the Indians. I have been into white people's houses, and I have seen nice black bedsteads and chairs, and I want that kind of furniture given to my people. . . . I want the Great Father to furnish me a saw–mill which I may call my own. I want a mower and a scythe for my people. Maybe you white people think that I ask too much from the Government, but I think those hills extend clear to the sky – maybe they go above the sky, and that is the reason I ask for so much. . . ."[10]

On September 29th, the commission offered the sum of $400,000 per year to lease the Black Hills. If the Lakota preferred to sell, the government would pay 6 million dollars payable in 15 annual installments. The offer was far too little to be accepted. Spotted Tail suggested they let the matter rest for the time being.

Trying to salvage something from their failure, in October the Allison Committee made a shocking recommendation. Congress should fix a "fair" price for the hills which would then be presented to the Lakota as a "finality." If the Lakota rejected the offer, all rations and annuities would be cut off.[11]

The administration had to act. President Grant, who had met with the commissioners in Cheyenne and expressed his disappointment over their failure to reach an agreement with the Lakota,[12] summoned Generals Sheridan and Crook, Commissioner of Indian Affairs Edward P. Smith, Secretary of the Interior Zachariah Chandler, and Secretary of War William Belknap to the White House on November 3, 1875.[13] While no transcripts of that meeting have come to light, some conclusions regarding that meeting are obvious. First, while the order prohibiting white entry into the Black Hills would remain in effect, the army would "look the other way" as the miners swarmed into the region.[14] Second, the Treaty of 1868 would be abrogated and the Indians living in the unceded territory would be ordered to their permanent reservations. All this was to be accomplished in the name of political expediency which, once again, would triumph over moral obligations. The scenario was complete on November 9 when Indian Inspector Erwin C. Watkins, recently returned from an inspection tour of the Missouri Agencies, concluded his report on the *"wild and hostile bands"* in the unceded territory:

"The true policy, in my judgment, is to send troops against them in the winter, the sooner the better, and whip them into subjection."[15]

All that remained was Commissioner Smith's December 6 wire to the Lakota and Cheyenne agents ordering them to notify the bands in the unceded territory to return to their agencies by January 31, 1876 or be considered hostile.[16] Apparently no one seriously considered the possibility of a new Indian war with determined resistance on the part of the non agency bands. Commissioner of Indian Affairs Smith summed up the possibilities in his annual report for 1875 and set the tone for the gross underestimate of Indian strength to be encountered during the 1876 campaign:

> ". . . except under extraordinary provocation, or in circumstances not at all to be apprehended, it is not probable that as many as five hundred Indian warriors will ever again be mustered at one point for a fight; and with the conflicting interests of the different tribes, and the occupation of the intervening country by advancing settlements, such an event as a general Indian war can never again occur in the United States."[17]

As with many facets of the Little Big Horn, the order to come in has been surrounded in a meaningless controversy that only serves to obscure the events. While there is no concrete evidence that the major Lakota bands under Crazy Horse, Sitting Bull and Gall ever received the order, some Lakota did comply. Captain John G. Bourke wrote of the period January through February 1876:

> "Telegraphic advices were received from Fort Laramie to the effect that three hundred lodges of northern Sioux had just come in to Red Cloud Agency."[18]

Further corroboration is provided by Red Cloud Agent James S. Hastings in his February 24, 1876 telegram:

> "Over one thousand Indians from the north have arrived in obedience to your request communicated to them by couriers sent from here. More are expected daily."[19]

The controversy over whether the Indians received the order, understood it, had a sufficiency of time and clement weather to comply with the order, or, whether the bands in the unceded territory would have remained out regardless of the circumstances merely obscures the real issue. The national government had abrogated the treaty without justification and a full scale war would be the result. General Hugh L. Scott, who would be posted to the Seventh Cavalry as a second lieutenant fresh from West Point following the Little Big Horn disaster, said it very succinctly in an account published in the November 1, 1939 edition of the *Rapid City Journal*. After branding Commissioner Smith's ultimatum *"a crime against humanity,"* Scott added: *"But I never saw one (Indian participant in the Little Big Horn Fight, DCE) who admitted that he had gone out there (the unceded territory, DCE) to fight. Our ideas about that are altogether wrong. The Indians were attacked at the insistence of the Interior Department while they were peaceably attending to their own business, with no desire to fight. To be sure, it was dangerous for white men to be in that country, but white men had no business being there and were trespassers."*[20]

The time limit having expired, the office of the Commissioner of Indian Affairs somewhat belatedly telegraphed the various agents on January 18 to halt the sale of arms and ammunition to the Indians and to seize any such articles that were likely to reach the bands in the unceded territory.[21]

This halting of the sale of arms and ammunition did not achieve the desired result. The winter of 1875 – 76 came early and was unusually severe. Agents had requested additional rations but authorizing legislation was not passed until spring.[22] This needless bureaucratic delay contributed to another winter of near starvation on the reservations and undoubtedly convinced many young men to head for the unceded territory with the coming of the spring thaw. In addition, sympathetic agency Indians had at least 6 weeks from the initial order to obtain the armaments needed by the bands in the unceded territory. Clearly a case of barring the barn door after the horse has gone. [23]

True to the time table established at the November 3rd meeting, Secretary of the Interior Chandler dutifully wrote to Secretary of War Belknap on February 1, 1876:

"Sir: On the 3rd December last I had the honor to address a communication to you relative to the hostile Sioux roaming in the Powder River country, under the leadership of Sitting Bull, informing you that I have directed couriers to be sent from each of the Sioux agencies, informing that chief that he must come in with his followers to one of the Sioux agencies, before the 31st ultimo, prepared to remain in peace near the agency, or he would be turned over to the War Department, and the Army be directed to compel him to comply with the orders of this Department.

"The time given him in which to return to an agency having expired, and the advices received at the Indian Office being to the effect that Sitting Bull still refuses to comply with the directions of the Commissioner, the said Indians are hereby turned over to the War Department for such action on the part of the Army as you may deem proper under the circumstances.

"I enclose copy of communication from the Commissioner of Indian Affairs, dated the 21st ultimo, recommending that hostilities be commenced."[24]

On February 7 Sheridan received his authority to proceed and Terry received his orders from Sheridan on the 10th. [25] Sheridan planned to stick with his proven strategy. While General Patrick Edward Connor had pioneered the tactic of using three converging columns in his 1865 Powder River Campaign, Sheridan had further refined the tactic during his 1868 and 1874–75 campaigns on the southern plains to add the dimension of winter campaigning. Sheridan had demonstrated that it was unnecessary to kill a multitude of Indians in order to be successful. Starvation, exposure, loss of property, and the loss of morale attendant with constant pursuit and harassment, would exact the necessary toll on the enemy. Finally, Sheridan's columns would be commanded by three subordinates, Armstrong Custer, George Crook, and John Gibbon, who had cooperated effectively during the Appomattox Campaign that brought a successful close to the Civil War.

Early in 1876 the 7th Cavalry was widely scattered; see Table 3 – 1 for the location of the various elements of the regiment and their arrival time at Fort Lincoln. General Terry, commanding the Department of the Missouri, recognized the necessity of uniting the 7th for the first time in its history [26] and wired General Sheridan on February 16:

"I earnestly request that the three companies of the 7th Cavalry now serving in the Department of the Gulf may be ordered to rejoin their regiment in this Department. The orders which have been given recently render indispensably necessary a larger mounted force than the nine companies of the 7th now in this Department. These nine companies comprise about 620 men all told, and of these 550 could be put in the field for active operations. This number is not sufficient for the end in view. For if the Indians who pass the winter in the Yellowstone and Powder River country should be found in one camp (and they usually are so gathered) they could not be attacked by that number without great risk of defeat. [27]

Element	Location	Arrival At Fort Lincoln
Headquarters, A, C, D, F, and I	Fort Lincoln	N/A
E and L	Fort Totten	17 April 1876
H and M	Fort Rice	6 May 1876
B, G and K	Detached service with the Department of the Gulf	1 May 1876

Table 3 – 1 Location of 7th Cavalry Units – February 1876[28]

While the 7th cavalry was concentrating at Fort Lincoln, an ever widening stream of Indians was exiting the agencies. While it is impossible to determine with any degree of certitude how many Indians left the agencies in 1876,[29] and how many of those were actually in the huge village during the Rosebud and Little Big Horn fights, two facts are clear. First the Indian agents consciously misstated the numbers of Indians leaving the reservations for the unceded territory,[30] and the army, while at times fairly accurately surmising the strength of the opposing force in message traffic to higher authority, consistently acted as if they would be meeting a greatly inferior force. A case in point is General Terry who wrote Sheridan two days before the 7th's departure from Fort Lincoln:

"It is represented that they have fifteen hundred lodges, are confident and intend to make a stand."[31]

When one considers that the usual estimate of the number of warriors in a village was two or three per lodge, Terry must have expected to encounter 3,000 to 4,500 warriors.[32] Yet, a month later, after receiving intelligence of a massive Indian trail, he detached only a portion of his command to deal with the Indian force. The point here is that the military leadership was so preoccupied with the perceived problem of forcing the Indians to stand and fight that all other considerations, such as enemy strength and armament, were virtually ignored.

We are indebted to John Gray for his extensive research into the concentration of the village attacked by the 7th Cavalry on June 25, and the interested reader is referred to his excellent *"Centennial Campaign."* The first major increase in Sitting Bull's village occurred in mid March with the arrival of Crazy Horse's Oglalas and the surviving Cheyenne from the Reynolds Fight. By mid May the arrival of Lame White Man and Dirty Moccasins (also referred to as Black Moccasins) had swelled the Cheyenne circle to over 100 lodges. With the arrival of Gall and Crow King after the Rosebud Fight, the village reached its zenith of 1,500 to 2,000 lodges containing 2,500 to 3,500 warriors. While any attempt to provide a "roster" of warriors participating in the Battle of the Little Big Horn must, of necessity, be incomplete, Appendix 9 contains a listing, by band, of Indians known to have been present in the village. Appendix 10 contains a listing of Indians who were probably present, although their participation remains undocumented.

---

[1] See Lawrence A. Frost "General Custer's Libbie" page 214.

[2] See Donald Jackson "Custer's Gold" pages 8 – 9.

3 See Donald Jackson "Custer's Gold" page 10.

4 See Robert M. Utley "Cavalier in Buckskin" page 134.

5 See Robert M. Utley "Cavalier in Buckskin" page 134.

6 See Donald Jackson "Custer's Gold" page 107.

7 See Katherine Gibson Fougera "With Custer's Cavalry" page 221. In a typically schizophrenic government performance, the miners were released by sympathetic civilian courts almost as fast as they could be arrested by the military.

8 See John M. Carroll "Papers of The Order of Indian Wars" page 5.

9 See George E. Hyde "Spotted Tail's Folk" pages 236 - 239.

10 See James C. Olson "Red Cloud and the Sioux Problem" pages 208 – 209.

11 See Robert M. Utley "Cavalier in Buckskin" page 145.

12 See J. W. Vaughn "The Reynolds Campaign On Powder River" page 7.

13 See Evan S. Connell "Son of the Morning Star: page 249, Paul Andrew Hutton "Soldiers West" page 89, and Robert M. Utley "Cavalier in Buckskin" page 146. General Sherman was not present being in St. Louis where he had moved his headquarters in an ongoing dispute with Secretary Belknap. See Robert M. Utley "Cavalier in Buckskin" page 146.

14 A confidential letter from General Sheridan to General Terry written in November of 1875 stated that Grant had decided that while the orders forbidding miners to go into the Black Hills should not be revoked, the troops should make no effort to keep them out. The letter closed: *"Will you therefore quietly cause the troops of your Department to assume such attitude as will meet the views of the President in this respect?"* See Colonel Charles Francis Bates "Custer's Indian Battles" page 27.

15 See Robert M. Utley "Cavalier in Buckskin" page 146.

16 See James C. Olson "Red Cloud and the Sioux Problem" page 216.

17 See James C. Olson "Red Cloud and the Sioux Problem" page 214.

18 See Paul L. Hedren "The Great Sioux War 1876 – 77" page 49.

19 See Paul L. Hedren "The Great Sioux War 1876 – 77" page 50.

20 See Thomas E. O'Neil "Custer Chronicles II" pages 25 - 26.

21 See Edgar I. Stewart "Custer's Luck" page 79.

22 In January, agent Hastings had reported his supply of flour and beef would be exhausted prior to March 1st. See J. W. Vaughn "The Reynolds Campaign On Powder River" page 8.

[23] The army had received a report from Standing Rock Reservation on Christmas eve, 1875 that Indians friendly to Sitting Bull had been trading hides for ammunition. See Edgar I. Stewart "Custer's Luck" page 78.

[24] See Evan S. Connell "Son of the Morning Star" page 250.

[25] See Edgar I. Stewart "Custer's Luck" pages 81 and 83.

[26] After the Civil War it was highly unusual for an entire regiment to serve together. Uniting the 7th Cavalry for the 1876 campaign was therefore somewhat unusual. See Edgar I. Stewart "Custer's Luck" page 162.

[27] See John S. Gray "Centennial Campaign" page 38.

[28] See Edgar I. Stewart "Custer's Luck" page 83.

[29] Captain James Egan, Second Cavalry had reported in May that *"nearly all the young men have left"* Red Cloud Agency. See Remi Nadeau "Fort Laramie and the Sioux" page 271. On May 7 Egan had encountered a war party of 100 lodges and 700 - 800 warriors on the Powder River trail headed north. See Edgar I. Stewart "Custer's Luck" page 190.

[30] Typically Indian agents didn't report the exodus of young men to join the non–reservation bands because the profit they made was based upon the number of Indians present on the reservation. See Richard Upton "The Custer Adventure" page 59. Sheridan's annual report to Sherman of November 25, 1876 states that the army's count of Indians at the agencies which was completed September 1st indicated less than 1/2 the numbers present as previously reported by the agents. See John M. Carroll "General Custer and the Battle of the Little Big Horn: The Federalist View" page 77.

[31] See Francis B. Taunton "Sufficient Reason?" page 12.

[32] "Portugee" Philips told *Rocky Mountain News* correspondent Robert E. Strahorn there were 18,000 to 20,000 Indians in the Powder River Country, of which 4,000 were warriors. Strahorn reported this information in his dispatch of February 27, 1876. See J. W. Vaughn "The Reynolds Campaign On Powder River" page 10.

Chapter 4

The Belknap Affair

The Belknap Affair is yet another of the controversies surrounding the Little Big Horn that has been so blown out of proportion that its true significance has almost been lost to history. This incident serves as the foundation for the theory Custer, smarting under presidential rebuke and covetous of the White House himself, recklessly sacrificed himself and his regiment in a vain dash to restore lost prestige. We will see that the Belknap Affair, while exerting a negative influence on the outcome of the battle, was neither a major contributing factor to the defeat, nor exerted the influence over Custer so popularly held.

The roots of the scandal lie in the handling of post traders. The position of sutler had been abolished in 1866 although the term remained in general use. Prior to 1866 sutlers had generally been unofficially franchised by the commander of the regiment and served at his pleasure. This system was rife for abuse and consequently was replaced in 1866 by a system of trading establishments. Prior to 1870 the post trader was appointed by the commander of the regiment subject to approval of the Commanding General of the Army. In 1870 the law was amended so that the Secretary of War was responsible for such appointments making them political plums.[1] While the post commander was to supervise the post trader, the system offered great opportunity for graft and corruption.

While stationed at Fort Sill in 1869, Colonel William B. Hazen had discovered evidence of kickbacks paid by post traders to obtain their monopolies. In February 1872, Hazen provided his friend James A. Garfield, a member of the House Committee on Military Affairs, an excerpt from a contract between John S. Evans, post trader at Fort Sill, and Caleb P. Marsh, a close personal friend of Secretary of War William Worth Belknap. The contract called for Evans to pay the sum of $12,000 annually for the exclusive privilege of trading at Fort Sill *"so long as William W. Belknap is Secretary of War."*[2] Although Garfield and chairman John Coburn were initially outraged by this documentation, their ardor had cooled considerably by the time Hazen was called to testify before the committee in March. The end result of the congressional "investigation" was for Belknap to sign a departmental order prohibiting traders from leasing their operations to a second party. This tactic, while diffusing the political situation, had no effect on graft in post traderships in general and the Evans – Marsh contract in particular. As for Hazen, Belknap vowed to *"send him to hell"* but settled on Fort Buford, Dakota Territory, instead.[3]

Heister Clymer, Chairman of the House Committee on Military Expenditures began an investigation of Secretary Belknap, his former Princeton College roommate,[4] on February 1, 1876. On February 10 the scandal broke wide open when the *New York Herald* demanded an investigation into corruption in the War Department, charging Secretary Belknap with farming out traderships and implicating President Grant's brother Orvil.[5] Within a month Clymer had such a body of evidence that he was able to convince Belknap to resign during a March 1st meeting.[6] The resignation did not satisfy Belknap's accusers and they proceeded to collect evidence for an impeachment trial in the United States Senate; that body having determined by a simple majority vote they had jurisdiction.[7]

On March 15, 1876 Custer received a subpoena to testify before Clymer's committee. Being anxious to prepare for the coming campaign, he wired General Terry for advice. Terry, a lawyer in civilian life, responded that the subpoena authorized Custer to proceed without official orders but suggested Custer request to provide his testimony via telegram. Custer wired this request early on March 16:

> *"I am engaged upon an important expedition, intend to operate against the hostile Indians and I expect to take the field early in April. My presence here is deemed very necessary. In view of this, would it not be satisfactory for you to forward me such questions as may be necessary, allowing me to return my replies by mail?"*[8]

Later in the day, fearing that his request would be construed as an attempt to avoid testifying, he withdrew the request and began preparations for his March 21 departure.[9]

The political bombshells were not over however. On March 16 the New York newspaper *The Nation* ran the following editorial:

> *"Orvil Grant . . . appeared. . . before the Committee on the War Department and told his own story of his jobs as an Indian trader in a simple artless way that could be diverting if it were not for the picture it presents of the views entertained by the Presidential family on 'the science of politics.' Mr. Grant appears to have been an unsuccessful man, who, when all else failed, tried to get a living in some easy way out of the Government and accordingly applied to his brother to license him as an Indian trader. . . Of course the traders in paying him profits paid him simply for his influence with his brother, the President, and Orvil confessed to the committee in the plainest manner that what was regrettable in his eyes in the whole affair was not his use of his 'influence' but the smallness of the amount he made out of the traderships. . . We are not surprised to hear that General Grant is very much annoyed by their investigations and says they are carried on for 'partisan purposes.' Orvil appeared. . . to be a man entirely devoid of what is called a sense of honor in matters pertaining to public funds and is well worth study. . . as an illustration of the moral tone of 'administration circles.'"*[10]

Custer was sworn before the committee on March 29. He testified that the effect of the 1870 law putting the appointment of post traders in the hands of the Secretary of War had added greatly to the discomforts and inconveniences of life on the frontier. He then went on to provide some hearsay testimony accusing Belknap of using the post traderships as articles of traffic. Custer then recounted how when officers and enlisted men had begun purchasing articles elsewhere, because of exorbitant prices, the post trader had complained to "higher authority" and was upheld in his position that military personnel must purchase from him exclusively.

Regarding the visit of the Secretary of War to Fort Lincoln, Custer testified that the post trader had sent a basket containing several bottles of wine to the Custer residence for entertaining the distinguished visitor, but, as Custer did not drink, they were returned unopened. Due to his personal feelings regarding Belknap's poor moral character, Custer did not meet him at the edge of the post as was customary, waiting for him in his office instead, and refused to entertain the secretary in his home. Custer did, however, have the customary salute fired.

Regarding Orvil Grant, the President's younger brother, Custer testified that Grant had secured the appointment of J. W. Raymond as post trader at Fort Berthold. Custer also vaguely implicated Grant in other unspecified frauds.[11] He went on to express the opinion that the extension of the Great Sioux Reservation to include the east bank of the Missouri River was made to further the profits of the traders by securing them a monopoly on trade in the region. He concluded his testimony by stating his opinion that had the Secretary of War been a man of integrity and honesty, these frauds could not have been perpetrated.

Perhaps the most damaging testimony given by Custer concerned some 8,000 bushels of corn that had been delivered to Fort Lincoln as part of an attempted fraud in which Custer implicated Orvil Grant. Custer had refused to accept the shipment when he noted the sacks were marked "Indian Department" and that they had been duly inspected by Indian Inspectors. The inspection certificate demonstrated to Custer that the corn had indeed been destined for an agency and that the supplier, no doubt operating in conjunction with someone at the agency, intended to double bill the government for the grain. Custer had dutifully registered his reason for refusing the shipment through the proper channels, Department Commander Terry to Sheridan to Sherman and thence to the Secretary of War. A response came back through official channels ordering Custer to accept the shipment.[12]

Recalled on April 4, Custer testified about Secretary Belknap's March 15, 1873 "gag order" which provided that *"no officer, either active or retired,"* should *"directly or indirectly, without being called upon by proper authority, solicit, suggest or recommend action by members of Congress for or against military affairs."*[13] He concluded his testimony with his belief that Colonel Hazen had been "exiled" to Fort Buford for discussing the Fort Sill business.

An interesting side bar to the Clymer Committee was provided by Major Reno. Left in command of the 7th Cavalry during Custer's absence, by early April he had become concerned over preparations for the expedition and wired General Terry:

> *"From Custer's telegrams and the papers it seems he will not soon be back. In the meantime the expedition here is making large expenses and Sitting Bull waiting on the Little Missouri. Why not give me a chance, as I feel I will do credit to the army?"*[14]

Unwilling to accept Terry's mild refusal to his entreaty, Reno went over Terry's head straight to General Sheridan on April 16:

> *"Expedition ready when transportation from Abercrombie and cavalry companies from Rice arrive. Why not give me a chance, sending instructions what to do with Sitting Bull if I catch him. He is waiting for us on the Little Missouri."*[15]

Sheridan responded with uncharacteristic diplomacy to this gross violation of the chain of command, replying on April 17:

> *"General Terry has entire charge of the expedition. I do not feel like interfering with him in his plans."*[16]

These too gentle rebukes from higher command authority may have helped induce Reno to disobey his orders on his subsequent scout to the Rosebud.

Since the Board of Managers preparing to conduct impeachment proceedings against Belknap, had no charges in their indictment pertaining to Custer's testimony, he easily won his release and, with the approval of the required military authorities, departed Washington on April 20th. Since the impeachment proceedings had commenced on April 17,[17] Custer must have been amazed when a summons overtook him at his New York publishers on April 24. Since Custer's testimony could contribute nothing but hearsay, some have speculated that this was a device of

President Grant to keep Custer out of the campaign. [18] Custer consulted General of the Army Sherman, who had relocated his headquarters to Washington on April 5 under the promise of noninterference from the new Secretary of War. Sherman, in turn, induced the Secretary, Alphonso Taft, to intercede in the matter. Custer suddenly fell from Sherman's and Taft's good graces when Grant exploded on the afternoon of April 28. Custer telegraphed the details to General Terry on April 29:

"I telegraphed you yesterday that Secretary Taft would address a communication to impeachment managers looking to my early return to my command. The suggestion was made to Secretary through General Sherman. The Secretary stated to Sherman he would write the letter after cabinet meeting, but at the latter he mentioned his intention to the President, who directed him not to write the impeachment managers requesting my discharge, but to substitute some other officer to command expedition. I saw Sherman's dispatch and the reply to Sheridan. I at once sought an interview with the managers and obtained authority from them to leave. Would have started this evening, but General Sherman suggested that I delay until Monday in order to see the President." [19]

Within twenty four hours the decision on command of the Dakota column had been made. Terry had recommended either Colonel Sykes, Twentieth Infantry, or Colonel Thomas L. Crittenden, [20] Seventeenth Infantry, as possible replacements for Custer and rejected Major Marcus Reno for lack of rank. Sheridan dismissed the colonels and suggested Terry himself command the column.

Promptly at 10 a.m. on Monday, May 1, Custer presented himself at the President's ante-room. For hours he waited until General Rufus Ingalls, Acting Quartermaster-General interceded on his behalf. Grant responded that he would not admit Custer. Convinced further waiting was useless, Custer sent the following note to the President:

"Today for the third time I have sought an interview with the President – not to solicit a favor, except to be granted a brief hearing – but to remove from his mind certain unjust impressions concerning myself, which I have reason to believe are entertained against me. I desire this opportunity simply as a matter of justice, and I regret that the President has declined to give me an opportunity to submit to him a brief statement, which justice to him, as well as to me, demanded." [21]

General Sherman being in New York, Custer secured written permission from the Adjutant-General and Inspector-General to leave Washington. Even so he delayed, hoping to see Sherman personally, until nearly train time. The next day Sherman wired Sheridan:

"I am this moment advised that General Custer started last night for St. Paul and Fort A. Lincoln. He was not justified in leaving without seeing the President or myself. Please intercept him at Chicago or St. Paul, and order him to halt and await further orders. Meanwhile, let the expedition from Fort Lincoln proceed without him." [22]

On the morning of May 4 Custer was greeted in Chicago with the above order and detained, a euphemism for being placed in arrest. Stunned, hurt and baffled, Custer sent Sherman three telegrams. The first reminded Sherman that Custer had his verbal permission to leave Washington as well as the written permission of both the Inspector-General and Adjutant-General. The second reminded Sherman of his promise Custer would go on the expedition in command of his own regiment and that Sherman had been equally anxious for Custer to return to his regiment at the earliest possible instant to complete preparations for the summer campaign. The final telegram requested his detention be served at Fort Lincoln to allow him to be near his family. After consultation with Grant, Sherman granted this last request.

On May 4, the *New York World* attacked this treatment of Custer in a scathing editorial. Grant's action in removing Custer from command of the Dakota Column was labeled *"the most high–handed abuse of his official power which he has perpetrated yet."* After recounting the circumstances of Custer's attempts to see Grant and the intercessions of Sherman and Secretary Taft on Custer's behalf, the editorial fired a last broadside: *"There has never been a President of the United States before who was capable of braving the decent opinion of the country so openly and shamefully as this, for the sake of wreaking such a miserable vengeance."[23]*

Grant was furious. He demanded an explanation from General of the Army Sherman for some of the statements supporting Custer in the editorial. Sherman sent the President a written response that withdrew all military support for Custer regardless of the right of the case. Judging from Sherman's disclaimer, Grant apparently was also concerned that Custer's arrest, after receiving the proper written endorsements, might add more fodder to the political fire:

> *"I say most emphatically that General Custer, though relieved as a witness by the Committee, was not justified in leaving Washington under the circumstances of the case and that the enclosed newspaper paragraph gives a wrong statement of the whole case.*

> *"I surely never protested to the President or to anybody, nor did I ever intimate that General Custer 'was not only the best man but the only man fit to lead the expedition, etc.' I believe the Army possesses hundreds who are competent for such an expedition and I knew that General Terry, who is perfectly qualified for the highest military duty, had already been chosen to conduct the same expedition.*

> *"I will show this letter and its enclosures to the Secretary of War, and most respectfully report that General Custer is now subject to any measure of discipline which the President may require. Whether he is responsible or not for the enclosed newspaper paragraph I have not the means of knowing and I surely cannot believe that he could so report the case."[24]*

Having secured his release from detention in Chicago, Custer proceeded to St. Paul where he convinced General Terry to intercede on his behalf. That he easily won Terry to his cause is not surprising. Terry, basically an honest man and cognizant of his own inexperience [25] as an Indian fighter, merely echoed Custer's past superiors. When a crisis arose, they sent for the man who would obtain results – Custer. On May 6 Custer sent the following telegram, through military channels to President Grant:

> *"I have seen your order transmitted through the General of the Army directing that I be not permitted to accompany the expedition to move against the hostile Indians. As my entire regiment forms a part of the expedition and I am the senior officer of the regiment on duty in this department I respectfully but most earnestly request that while not allowed to go in command of the expedition I may be permitted to serve with my regiment in the field. I appeal to you as a soldier to spare me the humiliation of seeing my regiment march to meet the enemy and I not share its dangers."[26]*

General Terry added the following endorsement:

"In forwarding the above I wish to say, expressly, that I have no desire whatever to question the orders of the President or my military superiors. Whether Lieutenant Colonel Custer shall be permitted to accompany the column or not, I shall go in command of it. I do not know the reasons upon which the orders given rest; but if these reasons do not forbid it, Lieutenant Colonel Custer's services would be very valuable with his regiment."[27]

General Sheridan, on May 7, added his own endorsement and "politically correct" castigation of Custer's actions:

"The following dispatch from General Terry is respectfully forwarded. I am sorry Lieutenant Colonel Custer did not manifest as much interest in staying at his post to organize and get ready his regiment and the expedition as he now does to accompany it. On a previous occasion in eighteen sixty–eight I asked executive clemency for Colonel Custer to enable him to accompany his regiment against the Indians, and I sincerely hope if granted this time it may have sufficient effect to prevent him from again attempting to throw discredit on his profession and his brother officers."[28]

The final act of contrition, which seems also to bear Terry's mark, was for Custer to wire Clymer and rescind the only truly damaging portion of his testimony. The following telegram from Custer to Clymer was also sent on May 6:[29]

"General Terry, commanding the Department of Dakota, informs me that the report I forwarded from Fort Lincoln, regarding certain corn delivered at that post for the use of the Army, in Indian sacks, was received at his headquarters in this city, and after due investigation was acted upon finally by his authority; and that it was he and not the late Secretary of War who sent the order to Fort Lincoln directing that, under certain restrictions, intended to protect the Government, the corn in question should be received. The receipt of the order was reported to me and I at the same time derived the impression that the order emanated from the War Department. As I would not knowingly do injustice to any individual, I ask that this telegram may be appended to and made part of my testimony before your committee."[30]

Grant finally relented as General Sherman's telegram of May 8 to General Terry related:

*"The dispatch of General Sheridan enclosing yours of yesterday touching General Custer's urgent request to go under your command with his regiment has been submitted to the President who sends me word that if you want General Custer along he withdraws his objections. Advise Custer to be prudent, not to take along any newspaper men who always work mischief and to abstain from any personalities in the future. Tell him I want him to confine his whole mind to his legitimate office, and trust to time. **That newspaper paragraph in the New York World of May 2nd compromised his best friends here and almost deprived us of the ability to help him** . (emphasis the author's, DCE)"[31]*

In addition to hinting at Sherman's complicity in the affair, the forgoing very aptly characterizes Custer. His competence was obviously highly regarded by his superior officers,[32] but, politically, Custer was a "bull in a china shop." Having no grasp of politics himself, Custer, much like World War II's George S. Patton, must have been a near constant source of embarrassment to his "politically correct" superiors whenever he chanced upon a political situation.

Custer had regained command of his regiment and been taught a valuable lesson about the dangers of mixing in political circles. Custer's detractors relate the story that, on the very morning he was restored to command of the 7th, he chanced to meet Captain William Ludlow,[33] a member of Terry's staff and of Custer's 1874 Black Hills Expedition. According to the story, Custer exulted in his restoration to command and boasted that he would be able to *"swing clear of Terry"* and run the campaign to his own satisfaction.[34] It is difficult to know how to credit this story. Since the story originated with Colonel Hughes,[35] no copy of the alleged letter from Ludlow has been found, and it is so out of character for Custer who was typically fiercely loyal to his superiors in public, there is strong reason to believe that it was a fabrication as part of the general cover up that occurred after the disaster.[36]

What effect did the Belknap Affair have on the campaign and what role, if any, did it play in the annihilation of 5 companies of the Seventh Cavalry? In chapter 10 we will see that, rather than recklessly rushing to defeat in order to expunge this blot on his honor, Custer moved methodically, even slowly, on the Indian trail. Did the Belknap Affair then have no effect on the campaign? I believe that it was an influencing, rather than a contributing, factor; the degree of which can never be known with certainty. One fact is crystal clear, however, Custer's detention in Washington caused him to take the field in a major campaign for the only time in his career without subjecting his command to rigorous training, including some much needed target practice.[37]

---

[1] See Daniel O. Magnussen "Peter Thompson's Narrative of the Little Bighorn Campaign 1876" pages 32 – 33. The change in the law was triggered when Secretary of War Belknap, exceeding his authority, dismissed the post trader at Fort Laramie. When General Sherman protested, the law was changed giving the Secretary the power to appoint post traders. See Edgar I. Stewart "Custer's Luck" pg 120.

[2] See Paul Andrew Hutton "Soldiers West" page 202 and Fred Dustin "The Custer Tragedy" pages 30 – 31.

[3] See Paul Andrew Hutton "Soldiers West" page 203.

[4] See Lawrence A. Frost "Custer Legends" page 180.

[5] See Edgar I. Stewart "Custer's Luck" page 121.

[6] See John S. Gray "Centennial Campaign" page 61. Belknap personally delivered his resignation to President Grant the next day. See Edgar I. Stewart "Custer's Luck" page 122.

[7] See Colonel Charles F. Bates "Custer's Indian Battles" page 24.

[8] See John Upton Terrell and Colonel George Walton "Faint The Trumpet Sounds" page 130.

[9] See John S. Gray "Centennial Campaign" page 62. Custer has been falsely accused by many authors of forcing himself upon the committee. The historical record clearly shows that Custer's actions were a direct response to a congressional subpoena.

[10] See Edgar I. Stewart "Custer's Luck" pages 124 – 125.

[11] While seemingly damning to the President's brother, and politically naive in the extreme, Custer's testimony wasn't nearly as injurious to Orvil Grant as Grant's own testimony had been.. Under oath, Orvil Grant admitted receiving four post traderships in 1874 and installing subagents to run them although War Department circulars of 1872 and 1875 specifically stated traders were to run the business themselves and not *"to farm out, sublet, transfer, sell or assign the business to others."* See Edgar I. Stewart "Custer's Luck" page 122. General George A. Forsyth, of Beecher's Island fame, cast Custer's testimony in the proper legal perspective when he stated *"It was apparent that he did not know anything. His evidence was all hearsay, and not worth a tinker's damn."* See John Upton Terrell and Colonel George Walton "Faint the Trumpet Sounds" page 130 and Frederic Van de Water "Glory Hunter" page 275.

[12] See W. Kent King "Massacre: The Custer Cover–Up" page 102.

[13] See Edgar I. Stewart "Custer's Luck" page 130.

[14] See John S. Gray "Centennial Campaign" page 87.

[15] See John S. Gray "Centennial Campaign" page 87.

[16] See John S. Gray "Centennial Campaign" page 87.

[17] In his testimony, Belknap would protest his innocence while condemning both his deceased and current wife who were sisters. Whether the Senate believed him to be corrupt, or merely a poor judge of women, he was acquitted on August 1 by the politically popular "Scotch verdict" of not proven. A majority of the Senate had voted for conviction, but, fortunately for Belknap, this was 5 votes short of the 2/3 majority required by law for conviction. See Colonel Charles F. Bates "Custer's Indian Battles" page 24.

[18] Custer had made two rejected efforts to pay a duty call on President Grant during his first week in Washington which seems to indicate Grant was nurturing a grudge over Custer's testimony regarding his brother. See John S. Gray "Centennial Campaign" page 63.

[19] See John S. Gray "Centennial Campaign" page 67.

[20] Terry felt that a Department Commander had no place in the field and that is probably why he recommended Sykes and Crittenden instead of himself. Ironically, Colonel Crittenden's son, on detached duty from the Twentieth Infantry, would be killed serving with Company L at the Little Big Horn.

[21] See John S. Gray "Centennial Campaign" pages 68 – 69.

[22] See John S. Gray "Centennial Campaign" page 69.

[23] See Frederic Van de Water "Glory Hunter" pages 283 – 285.

[24] See Frederic Van de Water "Glory Hunter" page 285. We shall see later that, apparently, Sherman knew a great deal more about the affair than he was willing to confess to Grant.

[25] Ironically, Terry's inexperience would be aptly demonstrated on the very day Custer met his fate.

[26] See Edgar I. Stewart "Custer's Luck" page 135.

[27] See Edgar I. Stewart "Custer's Luck" page 136.

[28] See Edgar I. Stewart "Custer's Luck" pages 136 – 137.

[29] While it cannot be proven, or disproved, that this telegram caused Grant to relent and rescind his punishment of Custer, it is instructive to note that this telegram removed the only charge of substance that Custer had brought against either Grant's personal friend Belknap or his brother Orvil.

[30] See Frazier and Robert Hunt "I Fought With Custer" pages 130 – 131.

[31] See Tom O'Neil "Politics and 1876" page 24.

[32] Sherman himself, while ordering Custer's detention in Chicago, believed *"Custer was not only the best man but the only man fit to lead the expedition now fitting out against the Indians."* See Lawrence A. Frost "General Custer's Libbie" page 222.

[33] William Ludlow was one of the cadets (the other being Peter W. Ryerson) involved in the fight that cadet Custer did not stop resulting in his court-martial just prior to his West Point graduation. See Minnie Dubbs Millbrook "Cadet Custer's Court-Martial" page 62.

[34] See Frederic Van de Water "Glory Hunter" page 293.

[35] During the 1876 campaign, Captain Robert Patterson Hughes served as Aid–de–Camp to his brother–in–law, General Terry. In 1896 he wrote an article, "Campaign Against the Sioux," that attempted to disprove much of Godfrey's 1892 *Century Magazine* article. He, along with Major Brisbin, is the source of the controversy accusing Custer of disobeying Terry's orders and implying that there was a plan for close cooperation between the commands of Custer and Gibbon.

[36] This evidence will be presented incrementally within the general context of the narrative. The reader is encouraged to withhold judgment on this matter until he has completed the entire narrative.

[37]Custer's training regimen, which he had religiously followed prior to previous campaigns, was unusual for frontier units. See Bill O'Neal "Fighting Men of the Indian Wars" page 103.

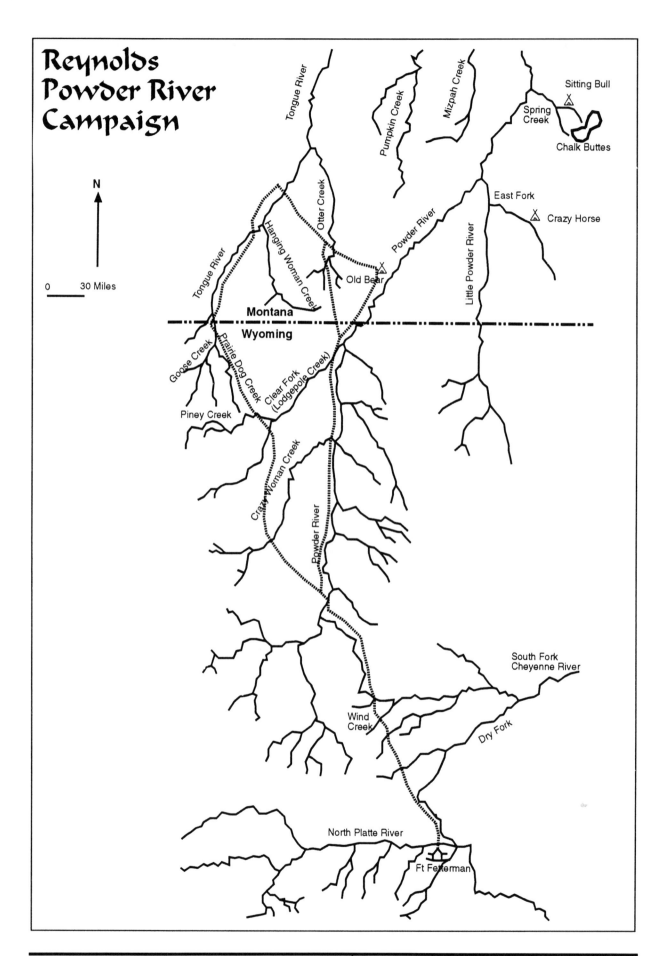

Reynolds Powder River Campaign

N

0   30 Miles

Tongue River

Pumpkin Creek

Mizpah Creek

Sitting Bull

Spring Creek

Chalk Buttes

Otter Creek

Powder River

East Fork

Crazy Horse

Tongue River

Hanging Woman Creek

Little Powder River

Old Bear

Montana

Wyoming

Goose Creek

Prairie Dog Creek

Clear Fork
(Lodgepole Creek)

Piney Creek

Crazy Woman Creek

Powder River

South Fork
Cheyenne River

Wind Creek

Dry Fork

North Platte River

Ft Fetterman

Chapter 5

Crook's Winter Campaign

Sheridan had originally planned to conduct a winter campaign. The severity of the winter in Dakota Territory and the absence of Custer were factors, but not the only factors, that combined to force a delay in launching the campaign. By the time authority was received to move against Sitting Bull, Terry's intelligence indicated the village had moved from its reported site near the mouth of the Little Missouri to the Powder River. Feeling the necessity to consolidate more of a mounted strike force than presented by the seven troops of the 7th cavalry on duty at Forts Lincoln and Rice, Terry decided to wait for spring.[1]

On February 22, Major James Sanks Brisbin left Fort Ellis, Montana with Companies F, G, H, and I of the 2nd Cavalry, and 12 men from Company C, 7th Infantry to serve a 12–pound Napoleon gun, to relieve a party of trappers and wolfers besieged at Fort Pease.[2] In all, Brisbin's force consisted of 14 officers and 192 enlisted men. Encountering no resistance, and much to the disgust of several of the "rescued," the civilians were successfully relieved, the column returning to Fort Ellis on March 17, the same day that Reynolds struck the Cheyenne village on Powder River.[3] Regardless of the fact that not one Indian had been sighted and no shots had been fired in the vicinity of the supposedly besieged civilians, the army considered the campaign to be off to a promising start.

In the meantime, Brigadier General George Crook, Commander of the Department of the Platte, was assembling his Big Horn Expedition at Fort Fetterman, Wyoming Territory. Heavy clothing was issued to the troops to protect feet, knees, wrists and ears from the numbing cold. Lieutenant John G. Bourke describes the clothing worn by a typical cavalryman:

"Commencing with the feet, first a pair of close–fitting lamb's–wool socks was put on, then one of the same size as those worn by women, so as to come over the knees. Indian moccasins of buckskin, reaching well up the leg, were generally preferred to boots, being warmer and lighter; cork soles were used with them, and an overboot of buffalo hide, made with hairy side inward and extending up nearly the whole length of the leg, and opening down the side and fastened by buckles. . .

"For underwear, individual preferences were consulted, the general idea being to have at least two kinds of material used, principally merino and perforated buckskin; over these was place a heavy blue flannel shirt, made double–breasted, and then a blouse, made also double–breasted, of Mission or Minnesota blanket, with large buttons, or a coat of Norway kid lined with heavy flannel. . . nothing in the world would keep out the cold but an overcoat of buffalo or bearskin or beaver, although for many the overcoats made in Saint Paul of canvas, lined with the heaviest blanket, and strapped and belted tight about the waist, were pronounced sufficient. The head was protected by a cap of cloth, with fur border to pull down over the ears; a fur collar enclosed the neck and screened the mouth and nose from the keen blasts; and the hands were covered by woolen gloves and over–gauntlets of beaver or musk–rat fur."[4]

Bedding consisted of one canvas wrapper, one plaid heavy blanket, one comforter, one pair of buffalo robes, one large wolf or beaver robe, one rollable mattress, one pillow and case, and one large rubber poncho.[5]

The column was composed of ten troops of cavalry (companies A, D, E, F, and M of the 3rd and A, B, E, I, and K of the 2nd) and two companies (C and I) of the 4th infantry. There were eighty–six mule-drawn wagons, three or four ambulances, and 400 pack mules, divided into five divisions of 80 mules each, one for each of the two troop cavalry squadrons. The train was commanded by Thomas Moore[6] who was Crook's personal "mule packer" throughout most of the general's career. The half–breed scouts recruited at Red Cloud and Spotted Tail Agencies were commanded by Major Thaddeus H. Stanton[7] and included such famous personalities as Frank Grouard, Louis Richaud, Baptiste "Big Bat" Pourrier, Baptiste "Little Bat" Garnier, Louis Changrau, Speed Stagner, and Ben Clarke. Mr. Robert Edmund Strahorn of the *Rocky Mountain News* was the sole correspondent accompanying the column.[8] While Crook accompanied the column as an observer, over–all command was vested in Colonel, Brevet Major General, Joseph J. Reynolds of the 3rd Cavalry.

Following a heavy snow fall the previous night, and in the teeth of a cold north wind, the Big Horn Expedition, 883 men strong, departed Fort Fetterman on March 1. The troopers carried both the Springfield carbine and the Colt revolver. Sabers, considered of little use in the post Civil War army, were left behind.[9]

In his annual report to the Secretary of War, Crook would write of the winter campaign:

"The object of the expedition was to move, during the inclement season, by forced marches, carrying by pack animals the most meager supplies, secretly and expeditiously, surprise the hostile bands and, if possible chastise them before spring fairly opened and they could receive re-inforcements from the Agencies. . ."[10]

Crook was certainly correct in calling it the "inclement season" as the temperature hovered between – 23 and – 26 degrees Fahrenheit from March 11 through the 17th. The first night out, the expedition lost its entire supply of fresh meat when Indians stampeded the beef herd. It was no consolation to the troops, or to John Wright the wounded herder[11] shot through the lungs, that all 45 beeves dutifully wandered back into Fort Fetterman the next day.[12] The evening of March 5th the column camped on the Powder River just opposite the ruins of Fort Reno. Just at sunset the Indians, presumed to be Lakota, struck again. In a brief exchange of gun fire, Corporal Slavey, Company C 4th Infantry, was slightly wounded in the jaw and the warriors withdrew.[13]

On March 7 Crook halted briefing on the Crazy Woman Fork of the Powder. Here he ordered the wagon train and the infantry to return to Fort Reno while the cavalry was to press on in pursuit. Each trooper was allowed to take the clothing on his back along with either a buffalo robe or two blankets. Fifteen days at half rations of bacon, hard tack, coffee and sugar were carried in addition to 200 rounds of ammunition per trooper.[14] The command made a night march of 35 miles, departing their campsite at 7 PM. The weather continued bitterly cold. The fact the mercury congealed in the thermometer the nights of the 10th and 11th indicated lows of at least – 39 degrees Fahrenheit.[15] Lieutenant Bourke describes the difficulties attendant with preparing breakfast in such temperatures:

"Our cook had first to chop with an axe the bacon, which over night had frozen hard as marble; frequently the hatchet or axe was broken in the contest. Then if he had made any 'soft bread,' that is, bread made of flour and baked in a frying pan, he had to place that before a strong fire for several minutes to thaw it so it could be eaten, and all the forks, spoons, and knives had to be run through hot water or hot ashes to prevent them from taking the skin off the tongue. The same rule had to be observed with the bits when our horses were bridled."[16]

These temperatures cooled the ardor of even the most dauntless of Crook's troopers one of whom *"got out of his tent, and in the frosty air of midnight shouted loudly enough for all the command to hear him, 'I want to go ho–o–o–ome!'"*[17] An additional casualty was sustained on March 10th when Corporal Moore's, Company D 3rd Cavalry, led horse slipped on the icy ground and fell on him. For the remainder of the campaign Moore was transported on a travois.[18]

Early in the afternoon of March 16, the advance, accompanied by General Crook, discovered two Indians on Otter Creek and gave chase; but could not overtake them. Crook decided to camp to give the appearance to any watching Indian scouts that the column was merely heading for the Yellowstone and had no interest in pursuing the two hunters. Crook then divided the command into two detachments, a strike force of six companies under Colonel Reynolds comprised of companies E, F, and M, 3rd Cavalry, and E, I, and K of the 2nd Cavalry; in aggregate 15 officers and 359 enlisted men,[19] retaining the remaining four companies and pack train under his personal command. The principal guide for the expedition, Frank Grouard, General Crook's aide, Lieutenant John G. Bourke, and correspondent Strahorn also accompanied the strike force. The pack train and escort under General Crook was to proceed to the mouth of Lodgepole Creek on Powder River to await the return of Reynolds' force. All being in readiness, Reynolds led his column out about 5 PM.[20]

About 4 AM on the 17th, Reynolds halted his column in a ravine and sent his scouts ahead. Frank Grouard returned about dawn with the intelligence that the two Indians previously sighted had been members of a party of 40 whose trail was being followed by the other scouts. The command started forward and, after traveling a short distance, observed a dense smoke which was taken to be a large village. As they were deploying to attack, Frank Grouard again returned to inform the column *"the smoke came from one of the burning coal–measures of which Montana and Wyoming were full."*[21] Their disappointment was short lived as Grouard soon returned with the welcome news that a large village had been sighted on the left (west) bank of the Powder under a high bluff. Despite their best attempts at stealth, the troops had been sighted in their camp on Otter Creek by hunters who reported to the village the night of March 16. The council of old men appointed 10 "wolves" to watch the movements of the soldiers, but they missed Reynolds' command in the dark.[22]

There has been much confusion about both the location and composition of this village. While many authorities place the village site on the Little Powder River, it seems fairly certain that the village was in fact located on the Powder River about 10 miles north of the Little Powder and consisted of approximately 100 lodges sheltering between 350 and 700 people of whom 150 to 200 were warriors.[23] Generally conceded to have been a combined Cheyenne and Lakota village, there is much confusion as to the principal chiefs involved. The Cheyenne are generally conceded to be the band of Old Bear although some authors believe the band to have been Low Dog's. Authors who have attributed the Cheyenne contingent to Two Moon fail to note that, while present at the battle, he did not attain the status of chief until elevated to that stature by the government subsequent to his surrender. There has been great acceptance that the Lakota were led by Crazy Horse but this is clearly in error as all Indian accounts of the fight note that the survivors traveled to the village of Crazy Horse in search of succor. It is possible that this misconception is due to the scout Frank Grouard, known to the Lakota as "The Grabber," who had been captured and adopted by Sitting Bull in 1869 and was well acquainted with Crazy Horse. As it happened, He Dog, brother friend of Crazy Horse, was in the village with his small band and it is possible that Grouard, recognizing some of the horses, mistakenly assumed the village to be that of Crazy Horse.[24]

Although the command had marched 54 miles in the last 24 hours, there was no time for rest. Reynolds quickly made his dispositions for the attack. He ordered a mounted pistol charge by Company K, 2nd Cavalry,[25] Captain James Egan commanding. The other company of the battalion, Company I, 2nd Cavalry under battalion commander, Captain Henry E. Noyes was to drive off the pony herd assisted by Major Stanton's scouts. Captain Alexander Moore was to take his battalion (Company E 2nd Cavalry and Company F 3rd Cavalry) to the left and position himself to be able to block the Indians in their flight from Egan. [26] Captain Anson Mills with his battalion (Companies E and M 3rd Cavalry) was to remain in reserve. Later Colonel Reynolds would dispatch Captain Mills and his company to support Captain Moore.

Crook's aide, Lieutenant Bourke, along with correspondent Strahorn went in with the advance. Just on the outskirts of the village the troops had to descend a deep ravine at the bottom of which a 15 year old youth, who had been driving the ponies to their morning watering, stoically awaited his fate. Just as Bourke leveled his pistol, Egan admonished him *"Don't shoot, we must make no noise!"*[27] Thus spared, the youth's war cry aroused the sleeping village.

The startled Indians tumbled from the warmth of their sleeping robes and commenced an immediate withdrawal to the high bluffs keeping up an effective fire against the troops and their horses as they went. Many acts of bravery were performed while the warriors attempted to delay the troops long enough for the women and children to escape. Chief Little Wolf and Wooden Leg personally took several children to safety under a hail of bullets before turning their full attention to the troopers. Although blind, holy man Box Elder secured his *Onohtsemo*, Sacred Wheel lance, before he would agree to leave the village. [28]

Once the initial shock of the attack subsided, the warriors counter attacked and forced Egan to take shelter among a plum copse along the bank of the river. The warriors continued to pour in an effective fire from the very positions they were expected to occupy, but the anticipated covering fire from Captain Moore's battalion did not materialize as he had taken up an entirely different position than the one ordered. [29] To this point Egan had sustained a loss of one man killed and three wounded. Of equal importance, he had lost 6 horses killed and another 3 wounded. At this critical juncture, Mills swept the rest of the village to the left of Egan's line. Within a half hour the village was in the hands of the troops and the major portion of the pony herd had been captured and secured.

At this point Colonel Reynolds entered the village with Lieutenant John Burgess Johnson's reserve company. Colonel Reynolds had at least three options open to him. First, he could hold the village and send word to Crook to meet him on the village site thereby making use of the meat and robes captured in the village. He could burn the village in its entirety, or he could pack the meat and robes on the captured ponies, burn the lodges and other camp equipment, and march to his rendezvous with Crook at the mouth of Lodgepole Creek. While Captain Mills would subsequently testify that Colonel Reynolds had agreed to hold the captured village, the village and all equipment, including the badly needed meat and robes, were ordered destroyed. To their credit, the troopers spared an Indian woman discovered in one of the lodges. [30] The destruction of the village was completed in about an hour's time. Captain Egan's and Captain Moore's commands then commenced to withdraw without orders leaving both of Mills' flanks exposed. Thus left hanging, and his appeals for support to Colonel Reynolds and Captain Moore unheeded, Mills had no choice other than to withdraw. [31] Mills had only gone a few yards when Captain Noyes' company arrived. They were tardy in relieving Mills as, after capturing and securing a portion of the pony herd, [32] they had unsaddled and made coffee.

Assistant Surgeon Curtis E. Munn had secured the 5 wounded to travois in preparation for the move. When he requested that the bodies of Privates Peter Dowdy and George Schneider be similarly secured from the field hospital area, known as Hospital Rock, Colonel Reynolds refused, stating that the retreating column could not carry them off. [33] At about this time, Captain Mills was informed that Private Lorenzo E. Ayers, of Mills' own company, had been left wounded upon the field. When Mills informed Colonel Reynolds of the situation he was told it was too late to do anything about it and Mills was ordered to proceed with his withdrawal. Mills sent a message to Captain Noyes, who was covering the withdrawal, requesting him to bring in the wounded man. Noyes had already evacuated the village and felt himself spread too thin to attempt to dislodge the Indians and rescue the wounded man. He sent back word that it was up to Mills to take his own wounded off the field.[34] Private Jeremiah J. Murphy, Company M, 3rd Cavalry, tried to evacuate Ayers on his own but was unsuccessful.[35] He later described the last harrowing sight he had of his stricken comrade with 10 to 15 warriors dancing around the prostrate figure.[36] To the lasting shame of the army, Private Ayers would not be the only enlisted man during the 1876 campaign to be left to the clemency of an enemy that did not recognize noncombatant status. Equally disturbing to frontier veterans was the abandonment of three dead troopers[37] to be brutally mutilated by the enraged Indians.[38]

Reynolds had lost 4 killed and 6 wounded; while Indian losses were 1 Lakota and 1 Cheyenne, Chief Eagle, a little chief of the Elkhorn Scrapers, killed, and 2 or 3 warriors wounded.[39] The soldiers had achieved their primary objective of destroying much valuable property, including a large store of ammunition, and leaving the inhabitants shelterless in the extreme cold. However the successful counter attack and the fact that a wounded man and the 3 dead troopers had been left in their hands served to bolster Indian morale.

Immediately, scouts were sent to follow the troops. When Reynolds camped for the night, he placed no guard upon the ponies as his troops *"were exhausted"* and he didn't order the ponies shot due to a *"shortage of ammunition."*[40] When the Cheyenne were sighted driving off the pony herd next morning, Reynolds failed to order a pursuit due to the *"poor condition of his mounts."*[41] When Crook arrived at the rendezvous at about noon, he had about 100 Indian ponies he had recaptured when the triumphant raiders had stumbled into his column. These he immediately ordered shot to prevent their recapture and feed his hungry troopers.[42]

The damage had been done however. Indian morale had received a tremendous boost with the recapture of the pony herd and the lack of pursuit by the soldiers.[43] Soldier morale, despite the technical victory achieved, was correspondingly low. Lieutenant Bourke described the situation *". . . large number of desertions at Fort Russell in early 1876, the men saying they were unwilling to serve under officers who would abandon the dead and wounded."*[44] General Sheridan noted in his annual report of November 25, 1876 that the recapture of the pony herd *"greatly modified"* the success of Crook's winter campaign.[45]

While the Cheyenne and Oglala survivors struggled toward the village of Crazy Horse and thence to the camp of Sitting Bull, Crook pondered what course the campaign should take. In his report on the fight Crook indicates that he intended to use the captured village and equipment as a base of supply to pursue action against any other villages that might be in the vicinity. While it is not clear that Crook either had sufficient ammunition to continue his campaign, despite the abundance of supplies captured, or had ever conveyed his "plan" to Colonel Reynolds, he was left with but a single option, retreat.[46] John Bourke summed up:

> *"We had no beef, as our herd had been run off on account of the failure to guard it; we were out of supplies, although we had destroyed enough to last a regiment for a couple of months; we were encumbered with sick, wounded, and cripples with frozen limbs, because we had not had sense enough to save the furs and robes in the village; and the enemy was thoroughly aroused, and would be on the qui vive for all that we did."*[47]

Crook, sustained by the slaughtered pony meat, and nursing 66 cases of frostbite, then embarked on the first "starvation march" of the 1876 campaign reaching Fort Fetterman on March 26.[48]

The conduct of Colonel Reynolds immediately came under question. The criticism was so severe as to cause him, on three separate occassions, to request a court of inquiry.[49] The criticisims were finally put in the form of formal charges by General Crook. Crook felt that Reynolds had failed in four specific instances:

1.　　A failure on the part of portions of the command to properly support the first attack (Captain Alexander Moore, DCE).

2.　　A failure to make a vigorous and persistent attack with the whole command.

3.　　A failure to secure the provisions that were captured for the use of the troops, instead of destroying them.

4.　　And most disastrous of all, a failure to properly secure and take care of the horses and ponies captured, nearly all of which again fell into the hands of the Indians the following morning.[50]

Colonel Reynolds responded by filing charges against Captains Moore and Noyes.[51] All three officers were ultimately convicted. Colonel Reynolds was convicted of *"conduct to the prejudice of good order and military discipline."* He had unsuccessfully argued that he'd had no orders and *"had been left to his own discretion."* The judge advocate general ruled that Reynolds' instructions *"were not in the form of positive formal orders, but they clearly and intelligently expressed the wishes of the commander of the expedition. . ."[52]* Reynolds, ordered suspended from rank and command for one year, retired while serving his suspension. While the true purpose of a court martial was to enforce discipline, rather than dispense justice, the Reynolds case introduced into military law the important concept that a commander's *"wishes and desires"* carried the full force of orders.[53] Captain Moore, convicted of neglect of duty, was suspended from command and confined to the limits of the post for 6 months. Captain Noyes was convicted of conduct prejudicial to good order and military discipline and sentenced to be reprimanded by his Department Commander , General Crook.[54]

The winter campaign was over. The April 1, 1876 issue of the *Army and Navy Journal*, quoting from the *New York Tribune*, proudly proclaimed:

> *"This engagement severely crippled if it does not entirely break up the only hostile band now infesting this portion of the frontier."[55]*

Crook knew better. In his report of May 7, 1876 he noted the four failures mentioned above and them summed up the successes as follows:

1.　　A complete surprise of the Indians.

2.　　The entire destruction of their village, with their camp equipage, and large quantities of ammunition.[56]

Crook did not confine his criticism to the failure of his own troops. In a report to General Sheridan, Crook had reopened the old conflict between the Army and the Indian Bureau. He characterized the village as *"a perfect magazine of ammunition, war material and general supplies,"* he went on to charge that *"Every evidence was found to prove these Indians to be in co–partnership with those at the Red Cloud and Spotted Tail agencies, and that the proceeds of their raids upon the settlements have been taken into those agencies and supplies brought out in return."*[57] This attack, of course, only served to insure there would be no cooperation between the Army and the Indian Bureau in the coming summer campaign; giving the agents one more reason to understate the numbers of Indians leaving the reservations for the unceded territory.

---

[1] See Francis B. Taunton "Sufficient Reason?" page 10. Colonel Robert Patterson Hughes, Terry's brother–in–law and a Captain at the time of the '76 campaign, in his January 1896 article "The Campaign Against the Sioux in 1876," referring to Terry's intelligence that Sitting Bull had moved to the Yellowstone, perhaps as far as the Powder, quoted Sheridan *"If Sitting Bull is not on the Little Missouri, as heretofore supposed to be, I am afraid but little can be done by you at this time."* (See Colonel W. A. Graham "The Story of the Little Big Horn" page 5 of the appendix). What Sheridan actually wired was *"I am not well enough acquainted with the character of the winters and early springs in your latitude to give any directions, and you will have to use your own judgment as to what you may be able to accomplish at the present time or early spring."* (See Francis B. Taunton "Sufficient Reason?" page 32). This article, written after the deaths of Terry and Sheridan, along with its corroboration, and misinformation as to Custer's written orders supplied by Major James S. Brisbin forms the foundation for the charge that Custer rashly rushed to defeat in direct disobedience of his orders. A careful reading of Hughes' article reveals not only a concerted effort to place the blame for the disaster squarely on Custer's shoulders, but also an attempt to remove any possibility of criticism being attached to General Terry for any aspect of the campaign. While it was proper for Terry to await the consolidation of the 7th, Hughes apparently felt the need to protect Terry from any criticism associated with Crook taking the field alone.

[2] Fort Pease, founded by Fellows D. Pease on June 25, 1875, was located on the Yellowstone opposite, and about three miles below, the mouth of the Big Horn River.

[3] See John S. Gray "Custer's Last Campaign" pages 129 – 130. For a commentary on the lack of necessity for the relief operation see W. Boyes "Surgeon's Diary With the Custer Relief Column" page 2.

[4] See John G. Bourke "On the Border With Crook" pages 252 – 253.

[5] See Fred H. Werner "The Soldiers Are Coming!" page 10.

[6] Moore's sister was the famed prohibitionist Carrie Nation. See J. W. Vaughn "The Reynolds Campaign On Powder River" page 30.

[7] Stanton served in the dual capacity of commander of the scouts and correspondent for the *New York Tribune*. Crook was reprimanded at Reynolds' subsequent court-martial for allowing this situation to exist. See J. W. Vaughn "The Reynolds Campaign On Powder River" page 29.

[8] See John G. Bourke "On the Border With Crook" page 254.

[9] See Fred H. Werner "The Soldiers Are Coming!" page 10.

[10] See Edgar I. Stewart "Custer's Luck" page 87.

[11] See J. W. Vaughn "The Reynolds Campaign On Powder River" page 45.

[12] See Edgar I. Stewart "Custer's Luck" page 88 and John G. Bourke "On the Border With Crook" page 256.

13 See J. W. Vaughn "The Reynolds Campaign on Powder River" page 205.

14 See John G. Bourke "On the Border With Crook" page 259 and Fred H. Werner "The Soldiers Are Coming" page 15.

15 See John G. Bourke "On the Border With Crook" page 263.

16 See John G. Bourke "On the Border With Crook" pages 264 – 265.

17 See Don Rickey, Jr. "Forty Miles A Day On Beans and Hay" page 266.

18 See J. W. Vaughn "The Reynolds Campaign on Powder River" page 205 and John G. Bourke "On the Border With Crook" page 262. Interestingly enough this humane method of transporting the wounded would not occur to members of the Dakota column when transporting the 7th Cavalry's wounded to the steamer *Far West*.

19 See Neil Mangum "Battle of the Rosebud: Prelude to the Little Bighorn" page 4.

20 See the official report of Colonel J. J. Reynolds contained in J. W. Vaughn "The Reynolds Campaign on Powder River" page 207 and John G. Bourke "On the Border With Crook" pages 269 – 270. Note that Borke gives the departure time for Reynolds' column as 5:30 PM.

21 See John G. Bourke "On the Border With Crook" page 272.

22 See Thomas B. Marquis "Wooden Leg: A Warrior Who Fought Custer" page 164 and Peter John Powell "People of the Sacred Mountain" page 941. The name of only one of these scouts, Wooden Leg's cousin Star, has come down to us. See Peter John Powell "People of the Sacred Mountain" page 941.

23 See Edgar I Stewart "Custer's Luck" page 90, Fred H. Werner "The Soldiers Are Coming" page 28, and Neil Mangum "Battle of the Rosebud: Prelude to the Little Bighorn" page 5.

24 See George bird Grinnell "The Fighting Cheyennes" page 347.

25 Incredible as it sounds, Company K was Colonel Reynolds' only option for a charge upon the village. In the camp on Otter Creek it had been decided that the assault would be made with carbines and all of the other companies had left their pistols with the pack train. See J. W. Vaughn "The Reynolds Campaign on Powder River" page 70.

26 See J. W. Vaughn "The Reynolds Campaign on Powder River" page 208, Fred H. Werner "The Soldiers Are Coming" page pages 57 – 58 and John G. Bourke "On the Border With Crook" page 272.

27 See John G. Bourke "On the Border With Crook" page 273.

28 See Peter John Powell "People of the Sacred Mountain" page 941 and Thomas B. Marquis "Wooden Leg: A Warrior Who Fought Custer" page 166 – 167.

29 Although he had been ordered to take a position north of the village to support Egan's attack, Moore actually took position on a ridge about 1000 yards south of village. Moore, although

remonstrated with by Captain Mills and Major Stanton, refused to move further forward as he feared his troops would be discovered and alarm the village. See J. W. Vaughn "The Reynolds Campaign on Powder River" pages 74 – 75. This performance would not have surprised General Crook for, during the Apache campaign of 1871, Captain Moore had failed to take the position ordered resulting in the escape of a band of 60 Apache. See Martin F. Schmitt "General George Crook His Autobiography" page 164.

[30] Bourke claims the woman had been wounded in the thigh at the beginning of the fight, (see John G. Bourke "On the Border With Crook" page 276) while the Indian accounts state the woman was blind (see Thomas B. Marquis "Wooden Leg: A Warrior Who Fought Custer" page 168, Mari Sandoz "Crazy Horse" page 307, and Peter John Powell "People of the Sacred Mountain" page 944). Wooden Leg goes on to state that all the woman's possessions, including the tepee were spared.

[31] During the retreat, Blacksmith A. Glavinsky, Company M, 3rd Cavalry, displayed conspicuous gallantry, having to be repeatedly recalled by his officers from exposed positions. For this action, Glavinsky was awarded the Medal of Honor. See W. F. Beyer and O. F. Keydel "Acts of Bravery" page 207.

[32] In fact only about half of the pony herd had been captured. See J. W. Vaughn "The Reynolds Campaign on Powder River" page 111. During this action the mount of John Wright, the herder wounded in the stampeding of the beef herd the night of March 1 – 2, was recaptured. See Fred H. Warner "The Soldiers Are Coming" page 54.

[33] See J. W. Vaughn "The Reynolds Campaign on Powder River" page 116.

[34] See J. W. Vaughn "The Reynolds Campaign on Powder River" apges 116 – 117.

[35] For his attempt, Private Murphy was awarded the Congressional Medal of Honor. See J. W. Vaughn "The Reynolds Campaign on Powder River" page 118.

[36] See J. W. Vaughn "The Reynolds Campaign on Powder River" page 118.

[37] In addition to privates Dowdy and Schneider, whose bodies were abandoned in the field hospital, the body of Private Michael McCannon was left on the field.

[38] The Indians were indeed savage in their treatment of enemy corpses. They believed that a man entered the spirit world in the same condition in which he departed this one. They therefore did their utmost to render the dead incapable of inflicting any harm upon them in the next life. Hence the gouging out of eyes and amputation of limbs, etc. There is a persistent rumor, propagated by some modern writers, that Private Ayers was literally cut to pieces by the Cheyenne and perhaps even eaten. We are indebted to Stanley Vestal for laying this rumor to rest with the following account of a trick played upon a Lakota who was too hungry to ask for hospitality:

" . . . *When Little Shield arrived, he found three Cheyennes roasting fresh meat over a hot fire.*

"Little Shield stood by the fire for a while, warming himself. Close by on a big platter were several pieces of raw meat awaiting their turn at the blaze. Little Shield was hungry; he thought the meat looked very appetizing that cold morning (day after the fight, DCE) He could not speak Cheyenne, so after a while he just went over and helped himself to a piece of meat and began to cook it for his breakfast. The Cheyennes watched him take it, but made no objection. They began to talk among themselves.

"When Little Shield's meat was done to a turn, he began to eat it. He had swallowed half a dozen juicy morsels when one of the Cheyennes came over and talked to him in the sign language. Said he, 'We found a dead fat soldier lying over yonder. We cut him up. That meat you are eating is part of him. That is soldier meat.'"

Little Shield did not know that the Cheyenne, like the Lakota, never ate human flesh and was unable to discern the joke being played on him. The result was that many Lakota believed the Cheyenne ate the dead soldier. See Stanley Vestal "Warpath" pages 180 – 181.

[39] See Thomas B. Marquis "Keep the Last Bullet For Yourself" page 75 and Peter John Powell "People of the Sacred Mountain" page 944.

[40] See Fred H. Werner "The Soldiers Are Coming" page 33.

[41] See Thomas B. Marquis "Wooden Leg: A Warrior Who Fought Custer" page 169 and John G. Bourke "On the Border With Crook" page 279. In his official report, Reynolds indicates that the Indian ponies simply *"strayed away."* No mention is made of seeing the retreating Indians who were clearly visible to the command. See Fred H. Werner "The Soldiers Are Coming" page 61.

[42] See John G. Bourke "On the Border With Crook" page 280 – 281 and Edgar I. Stewart "Custer's Luck" page 94.

[43] During the preparations for the summer campaign, Spotted Tail told one of Crook's staff officers: *"If you don't do better than you did the last time, you had better put on squaw's cloths and stay at home."* See Mark H. Brown "The Plainsmen of the Yellowstone" page 249.

[44] See John G. Bourke "On the Border With Crook" page 285.

[45] See John M. Carroll "General Custer and the Battle of the Little Big Horn: The Federalist View" page 73.

[46] Correspondent Strahorn, in an account of the fight dated prior to the rendezvous with Crook, confirmed the general intended to use the captured supplies for his command's subsistence. See Jerome A. Green "Battles and Skirmishes Of the Great Sioux War: 1876-1877" page 14.

[47] See Evan S. Connell "Son of the Morning Star" page 85.

[48] During the march, Crook was forced to destroy or abandon 58 cavalry horses and 32 mules. See J. W. Vaughn "The Reynolds Campaign On Powder River" page 158.

[49] See Fred H. Werner "The Soldiers Are Coming" page 63.

[50] See John M. Carroll "General Custer and the Battle of the Little Big Horn: The Federal View" page 119.

[51] See Neil Mangum "The Battle of the Rosebud: Prelude to the Little Big Horn" page 9. Reynolds would maintain he only filed charges against Noyes and Moore because of Crook's assurance that to do so would result in no charges being filed against himself. See J. W. Vaughn "The Reynolds Campaign On Powder River" pages 169 - 170.

[52] See Samuel W. Calhoun "Did Custer Disobey?" Volume 6 of Greasy Grass, May 1990, page 14.

[53] See Francis B. Taunton "Sufficient Reason?" pages 73 – 74.

[54] See Edgar I. Stewart "Custer's Luck" page 94.

[55] See Edgar I. Stewart "Custer's Luck" page 96.

[56] See John M. Carroll "General Custer and the Battle of the Little Big Horn: The Federal View" page 119.

[57] See James C. Olson "Red Cloud and the Sioux Problem" page 217.

March Of The Montana Column

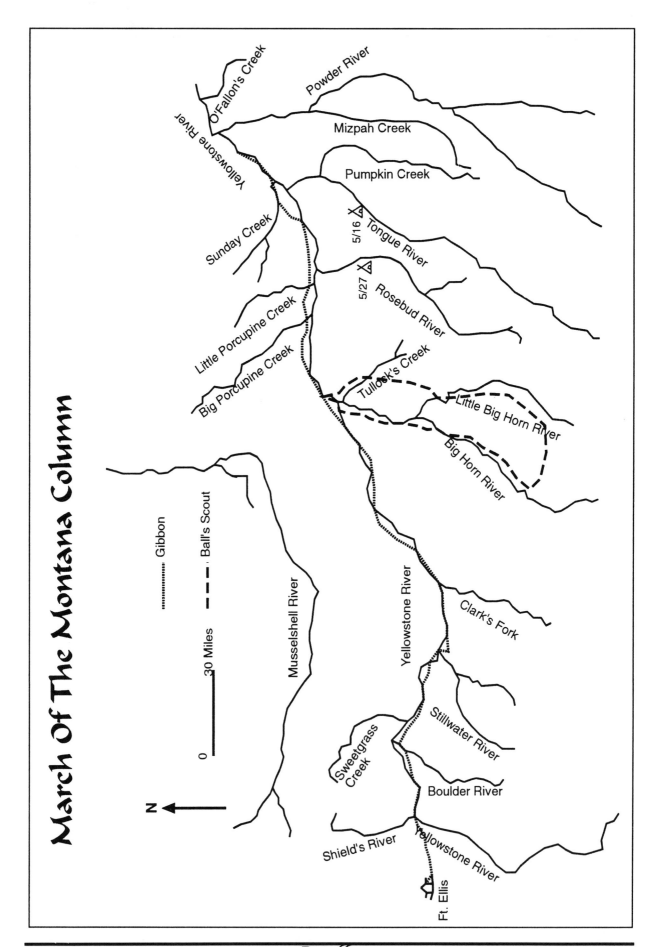

O'Fallon's Creek

Powder River

Mizpah Creek

Pumpkin Creek

Yellowstone River

Sunday Creek

5/16 △ Tongue River

5/27 △ Rosebud River

Little Porcupine Creek

Big Porcupine Creek

Tullock's Creek

Little Big Horn River

Big Horn River

·········· Gibbon

- - - - Ball's Scout

30 Miles

0

Musselshell River

Yellowstone River

Clark's Fork

Stillwater River

Sweetgrass Creek

Boulder River

Shield's River

Yellowstone River

Ft. Ellis

N

Chapter 6

The March of the Montana Column

On Friday, March 17, 1876, while Colonel Reynolds attacked Old Bear's Cheyenne village on the Powder and Major Brisbin led his Battalion of the Second Cavalry into Fort Ellis after the successful "relief" of Fort Pease, the Montana Column began concentrating for the summer campaign. Five companies of the Seventh Infantry (A, B, H, I, and K totaling 11 officers and 195 men),[1] under the command of Captain Charles Cotesworth Rawn, Company I, marched out of Fort Shaw about 10 AM bound for Fort Ellis.[2] Concurrently, Captain Walter Clifford, commanding Company E, Seventh Infantry, 2 officers and 25 men,[3] departed Camp Baker for Fort Ellis. The march was conducted under terrible climatic conditions, the command suffering much from snow blindness and frostbite.[4] The snow on the direct road to Fort Ellis being too deep, Captain Clifford abandoned that trail and dug his way to the Missouri River reaching Fort Ellis on March 22nd. The Fort Shaw battalion, now commanded by Captain Henry Blanchard Freeman, arrived at Fort Ellis on March 28.[5]

At 7:30 am on Thursday, March 30, the infantry battalion,[6] under the command of Captain Freeman, marched for the Yellowstone. Interestingly, First Lieutenant James Howard Bradley, Company B, Seventh Infantry, noted in his journal of that date:

"We learned today that General Crook, of the 17th Infantry, attacked a large Sioux village on Little Powder River (actually Powder River, DCE), drove away the Indians with considerable loss, captured and destroyed the camp, and also captured the greater part of the ponies but lost them afterwards through the fault of some of his subordinates. He then returned to Fort Fetterman, withdrawing his forces for the present from the field."[7]

On April 1, John W. Power's 12 contract wagons, carrying 60 days supplies, joined the infantry battalion in their camp on Shield's River[8] and the Yellowstone. That same day Colonel Gibbon and his staff, accompanied by Companies F, G, H, and L of the Second Cavalry commanded by Captain Lewis Thompson[9] of Troop L, departed Fort Ellis. Gibbon had wired General Terry for final instructions on March 30th:

"In view of the information from General Crook, am I not operating in a wrong line by going south of the Yellowstone, instead of north of it? Brisbin reports a large fresh lodgepole trail leading north from the mouth of the Rosebud. He thinks Sitting Bull is on the Big Dry Fork, toward which this trail leads. Must I limit my offensive operations to Indian reservation lines, or may I strike Sitting Bull wherever I can find him?"[10]

Terry's response was received the following day and would necessitate a change in plans.

"Until I learn what General Crook's further movements may be and until Custer starts, I think you ought not to go south of the Yellowstone, but should direct your efforts to preventing the Indians from getting away to the north. I doubt that Sitting Bull is on the Dry Fork. All information here points to the Powder River as his present location, and General Crook is positive that such is the fact. I think that if you move to the mouth of the Big Horn, by the time that you reach it I shall be able

to send you information of the movements of Crook and Custer, upon which you will be able to determine your course. If, however, you find that you can strike a hostile band anywhere, do it without regard to reservations; but in doing it, be careful not to neglect the great object of keeping between the Indians and the Missouri. Custer has been delayed by the blockade of the Northern Pacific road (due to heavy snow drifts, DCE). We have not yet been able to send up his train or his supplies. I hope that the road will be open next week. Make ample arrangements to communicate with Ellis."[11]

The change in plans reached the Fort Shaw Battalion in their camp on Big Deer Creek, on April 4th. Now fearing that the Indians would attempt to escape toward the north, the command was ordered to keep on down the Yellowstone toward the fords near the Rosebud instead of turning off toward abandoned Fort C. F. Smith as originally planned.[12] Colonel Gibbon and the cavalry rendezvoused with the Fort Shaw Battalion near Crow Agency on April 7.

Gibbon recognized he was badly in need of scouts who knew the territory where the campaign was to be prosecuted. Accordingly, on April 9, the task of enlisting Crow scouts was begun. Lieutenant Bradley was placed in command of the scouts assisted by white interpreters Thomas H. LeForge and Barney Bravo. Both interpreters had lived among the Crow for many years and were referred to by Bradley as "squaw–men." It is interesting to note that Bradley mistakenly calls LeForge "LeForgey" despite the fact that they spent much time together on the march; Bradley paying LeForge one dollar per day out of his own pocket to tutor him in the geography of the country and Indian customs.[13] The "swearing in" of the scouts was accomplished with great formality as described by Colonel Gibbon:

"We wished to bind them to their contract in some way, and in casting round for a method were informed that the Crow's way to take an oath was to touch with his finger the point of a knife. After this solemn proceeding if he failed to stand up to his pledges he was a disgraced man; but what was far more likely to keep him faithful was the belief that a violation of the oath laid him open to direful calamities in the way of disease and misfortune, not only to himself, but to all the members of his family! All the volunteers were paraded, and an officer (Lieutenant Bradley, DCE) presented to each in succession a hunting knife, on the point of which each one gravely placed the tip of his forefinger and the deed was done."[14]

Wanting some assurance that the military would keep their part of the bargain in terms of the Crow receiving the same pay, rations and allowances as the white soldiers, the scouts consented to having Lieutenant Bradley "touch the knife" to seal his pledge. After being issued a six inch wide strip of red cloth to be worn above the left elbow as an identifying mark, the conscription of the Indian scouts was complete.

The Montana Column was now fully constituted as shown in Tables 6 – 1 and 6 – 2. In addition to the 24 government and 12 contract wagons, all under the supervision of wagon master Matt Carroll, there were three pieces of artillery: two .50 caliber gatling guns and a twelve pound Napoleon, served by a detachment of the infantry commanded by Second Lieutenant Charles A. Woodruff of Company K.[15]

Wednesday, April 12, was spent in camp preparing for the advance. As the amount of stores on hand exceeded the capacity of his supply train, Gibbon detailed Company A, Commanded by Captain William Logan, and one of the gatling guns to guard the temporary depot.[16] Bradley describes the preparation of the Crow and his means of getting "off on the right foot" with his charges:

"Bravo came up toward evening with most of the Crow scouts, accompanied by a number of their friends whose presence we had not bargained for. In the evening they entertained the boys with songs accompanied with a thumping of a buffalo robe spread before them – a mystic ceremony termed 'making medicine'; that is to say, conjuring for good luck. They were in danger of pushing their incantations into the 'wee small (sic) hours' of the night, but, thinking it best to begin with them at once as I mean to continue, I explained to them the mystery of 'taps' and got them quieted down so as not to interfere much with the general repose of the camp."[17]

I.	Expedition Commander –	Colonel John Oliver Gibbon, 7th Infantry
II.	Cavalry Commander –	Major James Sanks Brisbin, 2nd Cavalry
III.	Infantry Commander –	Captain Henry Blanchard Freeman,[18] 7th Infantry
IV.	Expedition Staff –	1st Lieutenant Levi Frank Burnett, 7th Infantry, Adjutant
		1st Lieutenant Joshua West Jacobs, 7th Infantry, Quartermaster
		1st Lieutenant James Howard Bradley, 7th Infantry, Chief of Scouts and Mounted Infantry
		1st Lieutenant Holmes Offley Paulding, Assistant Surgeon
Company A, 7th Infantry		Captain William Logan, 1st Lieutenant Charles Austin Coolidge
Company B, 7th Infantry		Captain Thaddeus Sanford Kirtland, 2nd Lieutenant Charles Austin Booth
Company E, 7th Infantry		Captain Walter Clifford, 2nd Lieutenant George Shaeffer Young
Company H, 7th Infantry		Captain Henry Blanchard Freeman, 2nd Lieutenant Frederick Monroe Hill Kendrick
Company I, 7th Infantry		1st Lieutenant William Lewis English, 2nd Lieutenant Alfred Bainbridge Johnson
Company K, 7th Infantry		Captain James Madison Johnson Sanno, 2nd Lieutenant Charles Albert Woodruff
Company F, 2nd Cavalry		2nd Lieutenant Charles Francis Roe
Company G, 2nd Cavalry		Captain James Nichols Wheelan, 1st Lieutenant Gustavus Cheeny Doane, 2nd Lieutenant Edward John McClernand
Company H, 2nd Cavalry		Captain Edward Ball, 1st Lieutenant James George MacAdams
Company L, 2nd Cavalry		Captain Lewis Thompson, 1st Lieutenant Samuel Todd Hamilton, 2nd Lieutenant Charles Brewster Schofield

Table 6 – 1 Table of Organization of the Montana Column[19]

Element	Officers	Men
Gibbon and Staff	3	0
Infantry Battalion	13	220
Cavalry	10	186
Non–Combatant (Surgeon, teamsters, etc.)	1[20]	20[21]
Crow Scouts	0	23
White Interpreters	0	2
Total	**27**	**451**

Table 6 – 2 Strength and Composition of the Montana Column[22]

Getting off on the right foot with his Crow scouts was not as easy as Bradley records in his journal. Lacking understanding of the Crow mentality (a deficiency that, to his credit, he would remedy with LeForge's assistance), he had ordered a roll call of his scouts the day after their enlistment. It had proven a miserable failure as the Crow had no intention of submitting to any form of rigorous discipline. After receiving the complaints of his newly enlisted scouts, Gibbon counciled Bradley on the treatment of his charges and the roll calls ceased.[23] As planned, the Montana Column took the field at 7:15 A. M. on April 13 for the continuation of the march down the Yellowstone.

On April 15, while marching through the lower extremity of Clark's Fork Bottom, Bradley recorded some curious behavior on the part of the Crow:

> *"Today we passed a pile of small stones situated on the ground overlooking the Yellowstone, just below the Place of Skulls.[24] I noticed that some of my Indian scouts paused there, picked up a stone, spit upon it, and cast it upon the pile. Upon inquiry I found that this was done as an act of devotion which they believed would insure them good fortune in their enterprise."[25]*

While encamped near Fort Pease on the morning of April 21, a disturbing dispatch was received from General Terry, as Gibbon recalled in his *American Catholic Quarterly Review* article:

> *"The dispatch was dated at St. Paul on the 15th (six days before), and informed me that General Crook would not be prepared to take the field before the middle of May, that the third column (Custer, DCE) had not yet started, and directed that I proceed no farther than the mouth of the Big Horn unless sure of striking a successful blow."[26]*

Bradley summed up the command's feeling in his journal entry of that date:

> *". . .We were to have acted in conjunction with these forces (Crook and Custer, DCE), but we are now, when well advanced in the Sioux country, left unsupported. General Crook's victory (March 17 attack on Old Bear's village, DCE) was not so decisive as we have regarded it, while the fighting seems to have demonstrated that there are heavier forces of warriors to encounter than had been counted upon. General Terry fears that the Indians may combine and get the better of us; and we are therefore to cease our advance for the present and remain in this vicinity until further orders, in a state of inactivity unless sure of striking a successful blow. Now for tedious camp life and a long campaign."[27]*

Terry's concern for the safety of the Montana Column was echoed in a May 1 letter from Montana Territorial Governor Benjamin Franklin Potts to Secretary of War Alphonso Taft:

> *"It is now evident that the Yellowstone Valley will soon be the scene of bloodshed. The Sioux Indians are numerous and determined and great apprehension is felt for the safety of our eastern settlements. . . . I fear his (Gibbon's, DCE) force is not sufficient to meet the Sioux if they concentrate their entire strength . . . and attack his little band."[28]*

The caution contained in Terry's message is the first indication that more Indians may be in the anticipated area of operations than initially believed and there was some indication that the various scattered bands may concentrate at some point. Gibbon, had been in the process of composing a status message to Terry, dealing primarily with supply problems, when the latter's dispatch arrived. He continued his message:

"10:40 a.m. I had just got this far when a courier arrived with your dispatches of the 15th. I have in accordance with the directions moved my camp alongside Fort Pease, where I am strong enough to defy the whole Sioux nation, should they feel inclined to come this way, but I think they will be felt in the direction of the Black Hills mines first, whatever they do afterwards. The position here is so strong that one company can easily hold it and let all the rest loose in case we see a chance to strike. In the meantime I will send back for Logan's company and the supplies left with him, and make requisition on McClay & Co. (the Diamond R firm hired to transport supplies for the Montana Column, DCE) for freighting another month's supplies down and make this my depot.

"I have today sent scouts to the north of us where some sign was seen yesterday.[29] Will keep my scouts busy every day in various directions and think also I will send a company of cavalry with good scouts in the direction of C. F. Smith to communicate with that citizen party on the road.[30] If there are any Sioux in that direction, I imagine I shall soon hear of it. Hoping we shall be able to definitely settle this Sitting Bull matter, I am . . ."[31]

The tone of this message is very positive indicating Gibbon's complete confidence in, not only being able to defend himself even if attacked in large numbers, but in being able to project a sufficient force to be successful if only Sitting Bull can be located. To that end, Gibbon intends to keep up constant patrols. Unfortunately for the success of the campaign, and as a contributing factor in the subsequent defeat of Custer and the Seventh Cavalry, this attitude would soon change in a most remarkable manner.

True to his word, On April 23rd Gibbon dispatched Captain Freeman and Second Lieutenant Frederick Monroe Hill Kendrick along with Company H of the Seventh Infantry as escort for 27 wagons; 22 of which would be used in bringing up the supplies left at Logan's camp; the remaining 5 contract wagons to proceed to Fort Ellis, their services no longer being required. This action was followed up the next day by dispatching Captain Edward Ball, in command of Companies H and F (Second Lieutenant Charles Francis Roe[32]) of the Second Cavalry, up the Big Horn River on a scout to abandoned Fort C. F. Smith. Accompanying the column were scouts LeForge and Jack Rabbit Bull.

Ball's route took him up the west bank of the Big Horn River to the adobe ruins of Fort C. F. Smith at the mouth of Big Horn Canyon. They then followed the old Bozeman Trail southeast to the head of the Little Big Horn River; continuing down that stream, passing the remains of the 1875 sundance camp. After following the river for a few more miles, they crossed the divide and followed down the rugged valley of Tullock's Fork, reaching the base camp on the afternoon of May 1st without finding any fresh sign of their quarry. An interesting sidelight, heavy with irony, occurred during the noon halt on April 29. The site of their "nooning" was 3 to 4 miles upstream from the future site of the Custer fight. Second Lieutenant Edward John McClernand, Company G, Second Cavalry, recalled the actions of scout Jack Rabbit Bull during that noon halt in his journal entry for June 27, the day the Custer dead were discovered:

"Taking an abandoned hard–bread box and a piece of charcoal he covered it with a lot of drawings, which he said would tell the Sioux that we meant to clear them out, and then sticking a handful of green grass in the cracks, he added, 'and this will tell them we are going to do it this summer.' It is a little strange, considering the hundreds of miles we have marched over, that this taunt should have been left almost on the very spot where the one desperate fight of the campaign took place."[33]

During Ball's absence, two events occurred that served to shake the command's confidence in their Crow scouts. Bradley notes in his journal for April 24, the day Ball departed:

> *"Captain Clifford and Lieutenant Johnson with two men went down the valley hunting this morning, which afforded the camp an excitement and me an opportunity for a scamper. They were sighted by the Crow scouts at some distance below and mistaken for Sioux, whereupon the latter made a tragical rush for our camp to give the alarm. As they appeared in view across the valley running in single file at a lively speed, occasionally deviating from a direct line to describe a small circle indicating that they had seen an enemy, quite an excitement was aroused in the camp. The soldiers gathered in throngs, while the Crows formed in line, shoulder to shoulder, behind a pile of buffalo–chips, placed for the purpose and stood there swaying their bodies and singing while the scouts approached. As the leader of the scouts came up, he paused to kick over the pile of buffalo–chips, which was equivalent to a solemn pledge to tell the truth, then sat down surrounded by his fellow Crows and, after resting a minute or two, told what he had seen.*

> *"The Crows, full of enthusiasm, rushed after their horses and stripped for a fight; while I got my detachment in the saddle as quickly as possible, and away we went down the valley looking for a brush and hoping to bag a few Sioux. About eight miles down we found the trail of the party seen by the scouts, and behold it was the trail of Captain Clifford and his little hunting party, who, ignorant of the commotion they had innocently aroused, had ridden on to other fields. We returned to camp considerably crest–fallen, and with impaired confidence in the judgment of the Crows."[34]*

This first instance of "crying wolf" was clearly on the mind of the troops when it was repeated on May 1st. Bradley relates:

> *"About noon four of the Crows, who had crossed the river and gone up to the mouth of the Big Horn, were seen running rapidly along the summit of the rocky ridge on the opposite shore, occasionally describing the circle that indicates an enemy seen. When they got near enough to be heard, they shouted that the Sioux were close at hand and begged that a boat be sent over for them instantly. The boat was sent, and they were soon safe on this side telling their story, which was to the effect that dense swarms of mounted men in three bodies were pouring down Tullock's Fork, that they were undoubtedly Sioux, and that we might expect them soon to attack the camp. This information caused no excitement, as Capt. Ball was expected to return today, and by way of Tullock's Fork, so that the mounted men were pretty certain to prove to be his two companies of cavalry. And so it turned out, for about 3 P.M. he arrived in camp."[35]*

Bradley's disappointment in the performance of his Crow scouts, compounded by his frustration over Gibbon's failure to strike the village, resulted in the following bitter journal entry for May 30:

> *"It turns out that we have not wanted any Sioux villages, but had it been otherwise, it seems likely that we would have continued to want them for all that the Crows would have found for us. They are mortally afraid of the Sioux, and, even when they pluck up courage and start, the slightest misadventure suffices to convince them that their 'medicine' is bad, and then back they come."[36]*

On May 3rd, the Montana Column found the signs of the enemy they had been seeking so desperately. Bradley's journal relates:

"We have found the Sioux, or rather, they have found us. Reveille passed off as usual this morning, everyone turning out of bed and falling into ranks to answer to his name, and then turning into bed and falling asleep for another doze. But presently it was discovered that Bostwick's (Henry Bostwick, DCE) horse (Shavy) and mule, which had been picketed out the evening before to graze just outside the line of sentinels and about three hundred yards from camp, were gone. Investigation proved them to have been taken by Sioux, and as soon as the Crows heard of the circumstance, they rushed to the island just above camp where they had left their horses over night to graze, but every head was gone – thirty-two in all, gobbled by the Sioux. A search around the camp disclosed the fact that they had been in close vicinity to our sentinels, a broken saddle, three blankets, several wiping-sticks and other articles being found. The rascals managed the thing very adroitly, indeed."[37]

Bradley's supposition that the raiders were Lakota proved to be incorrect as interpreter Thomas LeForge explained:

"That record (Bradley's journal entry, DCE) sets forth quite well the essential features of this raid upon us. To be specific, though, it seems fitting to correct the record by attributing the daring deed to Cheyennes. Information as a basis for this correction came to me many years afterward, in a prolonged conversation with Two Moons, a Cheyenne chief. He was the leader of the band who stole our horses that night. He told me various corroborative details that convinced me he actually was there. He described exactly the arrangement of our camp. He knew right where the tents of the officers were located. With a blanket wrapped about his whole body so that only one peering eye could be seen, – a mode of dress favored by Indians, and which makes them all look alike, – he idled a few minutes about these tents and stood looking into the opening of one of them wherein a group of officers were engaged in a game of cards."[38]

Bradley availed himself of the opportunity to relieve some of his frustrations over the way he was forced to handle his Crow allies as he continued his May 3 narrative:

"The Crows had a good cry over their loss, standing together in a row and shedding copious tears, after which they set out to follow the trail of the robbers. It was found to lead down the valley to a point about eight miles below, where it crossed the stream. The Crows heard shots upon the opposite bank, which seemed to indicate that the Sioux were not very anxious to get out of the way and had little dread of pursuit. Fearing to cross, the Crows turned back. The trail indicates that about fifty Sioux were engaged in the affair, about twenty of whom reconnoitered our camp and secured the horses while the remainder held themselves in reserve a little way off. Of the seventeen Crows now with us, not one has a horse. It is an unfortunate state of affairs, as it will greatly impair their usefulness as scouts. The General (Gibbon, DCE) has been disposed to allow them every possible latitude to prevent the restraints of service from becoming too irksome to them, and so has permitted them to look after their horses in their own way, believing that their instinct and training would enable them to judge rightly what precautions were necessary. As commander of the scouts, and therefore personally concerned, I will add this has

not been my theory. I have desired to practice a more rigorous discipline with the Crows, and would have done so had I been unrestrained."[39]

As it turned out, the dismounting of the Crow scouts did not have an adverse effect on the operations of the Montana Column. What did effect operations was a growing mutual lack of trust and respect between the soldiers and their Crow allies and a significant change in attitude on the part of Colonel Gibbon.

By this juncture, Bradley had apparently lost all respect for the judgment of his Crow charges feeling them to be timid when confronted by the enemy. It is unfortunate that Bradley, like most 19th century white officers, did not understand the manner in which the Indians made war – a quest for personal honor and reward rather than achieving strategic and tactical objectives by inflicting maximum damage upon the enemy force. When the Indian saw little potential for winning honor or obtaining spoils, his 'objective" in going to war, he simply avoided combat. To his way of thinking, the loss of 2 or 3 warriors was a disaster of epic proportions; one to be avoided if at all possible. This resulted in a style of fighting that required either complete surprise, or significant numerical superiority, on the part of the aggressor force. If these conditions could not be met, combat was avoided and no social stigma accrued. The whites, with their Anglo–European concept of wars of attrition, interpreted this attitude as cowardly. Hence white officers had little interest in an Indian scout's assessment of the size or cohesiveness of the enemy force. White officers were perfectly content to restrict the function of their Indian "wolves" solely to locating the enemy force.

The scouts, on the other hand, had little respect for the abilities of white soldiers and sought to keep then out of harms way to the extent possible. Thomas LeForge confided that sometimes valuable intelligence was withheld from the troops:

> *"In fact, many signs of Sioux that we scouts discovered were not reported. To do so might have caused merely a fruitless sally of troops – or, worse, a disastrous encounter. Our observations convinced us that there were many more Sioux in the country than our present forces could handle."[40]*

This mutual lack of respect couldn't have come at a more inopportune time. The Lakota and Cheyenne, having finally been encountered, began to exhibit uncharacteristically aggressive behavior. The military response to this was to do nothing. Recall Gibbon's April 21 message to Terry was full of optimism – the only pessimistic note being a concern that the Indians might not be found. Suddenly, and uncharacteristically for the Civil War commander of the "Iron Brigade," Gibbon became indecisive and cautious, refusing even to follow the trail of the stolen Crow ponies.[41]

On May the 4th, two mail couriers were fired upon when about 10 miles from camp. Gibbon tried to induce the Crow scouts to go in search of the village on foot, but they refused.[42] On May 6 First Lieutenant Holmes Offley Paulding, Assistant Surgeon, First Lieutenant Samuel Todd Hamilton, Company L, Second Cavalry, Muggins Taylor, and a trooper were followed closely while out hunting.[43] Crow Scouts Half Yellow Face, mounted on Bradley's horse, Mink, and Jack Rabbit Bull surprised a party of three Lakota capturing three of their ponies. Bradley requestd permission to take his detachment of mounted infantry and some Crow scouts down river to *"see what I could find."* Gibbon initially refused but later consented on the condition that the departure be postponed until the evening of May 7.[44] Captain Clifford, in his journal entry of May 7, may have summed up the current feelings of the command. Bradley quotes him:

"The entire force of scouts went down the river and are very liable to be scooped up by an overwhelming force of Sioux."[45]

While this attitude may have been peculiar to Clifford, and not shared by Gibbon, the timid response of the military, especially after May 17, to the frequent and aggressive behavior of the enemy patrols suggests that Gibbon, finding himself alone in a very hostile environment, had determined against making any offensive movements until the other columns arrived in the theater of operations.

Clifford's fears were unfounded as Bradley's detachment returned without sighting the enemy. They had found plenty of sign, including 3 abandoned war lodges and tracks recognized as being made by Bostwick's mule. Gibbon's official report, contained in its entirety in Appendix 14, makes no mention of any signs reported during the period between the loss of the Crow horses and May 17. Being advised by General Terry that Custer would soon take the field, the march down river toward the Rosebud was resumed on May 10. On the 11th, Crow scouts found *"a place in the willows close to camp where four of them (Lakota scouts, DCE) had lain last night."[46]*

On May, 15 Bradley was informed by his Crow scouts they had discovered the trail of a party of approximately 30 Lakota. Bradley continues:

> *"After gathering the story of the Crows, I reported with it to the General, and then requested permission to do a little village-hunting myself, stating my belief that the thirty Sioux whose trail had been found by the Crows had come from a village on Tongue River, and promising to find it if there was one there. After some hesitation, fearing the destruction of my detachment, he finally consented, leaving the details to me. I made up a party consisting of twelve men of my detachment, eight volunteers from the infantry companies, and Bravo with five Crows – twenty-seven including myself. I had hoped for some volunteers from the cavalry, having been promised some by Major Brisbin, but none came forward. During the day three days' rations were got ready and other preparations made, and toward evening the men left camp one by one so as not to excite suspicion of a watchful enemy, and gathered upon the bank of the river covered by the timber. The river (Yellowstone, DCE) was very high and running like a mill-race, but aided by Captain Clifford with his boats we crossed in about twenty minutes without accident, swimming the horses, and just at dark all were assembled upon the opposite bank. The most of the command had gathered to see us off, and a good deal of apprehension was felt on our behalf, not a few feeling assured that we would never return."[47]*

Despite some initial reluctance on the part of the Crow, Bradley's detachment sighted the village about 4 P.M. on the 16th. The village, as anticipated, was on the Tongue, about 35 miles distant from Gibbon's camp near the mouth of the Little Porcupine. Bradley returned to camp reporting to Gibbon just after daylight on the 17th. According to Bradley, after about an hour's deliberation, Gibbon ordered a movement on the village[48]. Bradley describes the preparations and the outcome:

> *"Captain Sanno's (James Madison Johnson Sanno, Seventh Infantry, DCE) company (K) of the infantry was to remain in charge of the camp, the rest of the force constituting the column to advance against the Sioux. This column comprised five companies of infantry and four of cavalry, the mounted detachment, and Crow scouts, numbering in the aggregate 34 officers and 350 men, including the Crow scouts, to which are to be added about eight of our civilian camp followers, making*

our total effective force 392 men. We were to carry one blanket and 150 rounds of ammunition per man, and seven days' rations, thirty pack mules being provided as transportation. Taking as a basis the time occupied by my detachment in crossing, it was estimated that the entire command would be over by dark, when we would have made a forced march and got as near the village as possible before daylight, being governed by circumstances as to the time and method of attack.

"To render the camp as compact and defensible as possible, the most of the tents were taken down, and Captain Sanno bestirred himself vigorously in the construction of rifle–pits and other preparations for defense. The cavalry were ordered to cross first, the infantry holding themselves in readiness to follow as soon as the cavalry were done with the boats. The crossing began about noon, perhaps a little earlier, at a point about a mile above the camp, and for four mortal hours it went on at a most tedious, discouraging rate, about ten animals being got over per hour, though the officers and men engaged in it seemed to have done their best. What the trouble was I did not then understand, and I don't now, and I have never seen anybody that did. Everything worked at cross purposes, accident succeeded accident, and at last, after many narrow escapes on the part of both men and horses, four of the latter were drowned. The General had evidently chafed under the delay, but, where to all appearances everything was being done that men could do, saw no chance to accelerate matters. It had become evident that not even the cavalry would be over by dark, and when there came the catastrophe of the drowning of the four horses, it proved to be the last straw that broke the back of our warlike enterprise. Orders were given to recross the cavalry horses already over the river and my detachment, which had remained on the other side, and the expedition was abandoned. Before dark we were all together again in camp, tents were repitched, and everything had settled into its accustomed state.

"And so we failed to march against the foe. There ever will be a difference of opinion as to the propriety of the course pursued, but as I am not writing a critical history I will not take this advantage of my fellow officers to record mine. . .[49]

"The Crows who, when the order to advance on the village was given, were the most jubilant, were now, on the other hand, the most crestfallen and depressed. The crossing of a stream is such a simple matter for them that they do not understand how it should have proved an insuperable obstacle to our advance, and they are inclined to look upon it as a device to conceal our cowardice.[50] *I often talk with them and explain the mysteries and advantages of our prolonged movements and combined operations of different columns, which appear very perplexing compared to their simple methods of a dash in and out with a single force, but I fear it all avails little when they recall to mind a little passage that occurred in the course of our council with them in April. Said one of their speakers, Old Crow: 'If the Crows go with you, and they find a camp, they will bark like a dog. Will you then jump on the camp and fight right there?'*

"General Gibbon – 'That is what we want.'

"Old Crow – 'That is good.'

"One circumstance remains to be mentioned that had undoubtedly much to do with the General's decision not to march on the camp. Within an hour after my arrival from the village, the Sioux appeared in view on the prairie on the opposite side of the stream. My first impression was that it was the party of thirty returning from their bootless up-river trip; but those who saw the Indians estimated their number at not less than seventy-five, so that it must have been a party from the village on Tongue River. They had undoubtedly become in some way aware of our visit and followed us in; and had not the darkness favored us, we should probably have had to fight before we got back. They remained in the vicinity all day, killed several buffalo in plain view of my men, and two or three times tried to creep upon them. In the afternoon, when I went over to recross my detachment, and sent the most of them over, they came down within two hundred yards of us. My guard gave the alarm, and seizing our guns, we charged up the hill, but by the time we gained the summit, they were far out of range. I counted seventeen still in sight, but there were undoubtedly men who were concealed from view by a swell of the prairie. Whether or not they knew we were trying to cross is uncertain, but it is fair to presume that they did. If so, it would of course have been impossible for us to surprise their camp."[51]

Surgeon Paulding was not so sympathetic toward his commander when he noted:

"The Indians had evidently followed Bradley's trail which must have been very large through the mud— So that any chance of surprising a village was busted before the start & Gibbon was glad to throw the responsibility on the cavalry of causing the expedition to be abandoned."[52]

The remarks Private Eugene Geant confided to his journal were even more caustic:

"It looks to me that whoever was in charge did not understand his work or did not care to cross the river."[53]

Gibbon, in his annual report for 1876, cites only the drowning of the horses in the Yellowstone which *"had become a rapid torrent"* as rationale for abandoning the movement; omitting all mention of the warriors sighted on the opposite bank. Interestingly, he placed the location of the village at 35 miles away on the Rosebud rather than the Tongue. Later we shall see that this "mistake" was undoubtedly calculated to preclude any criticism of his actions. In any event, Gibbon had made the right choice given the circumstances. Whether or not Gibbon was aware of their presence, the Lakota and Cheyenne watching from across the river would have easily warned the village before a successful movement by the infantry, which would have required the better portion of two days to reach the village, could have been accomplished. To continue with the attempt might have resulted in the village scattering, the single event most feared by the military. Regarding this difficulty in crossing the horses, Gibbon would cryptically remark in his annual report:

*"The inadequate means at the disposal of the troops became painfully apparent at an early day. Operating on one bank of a deep and rapid stream for a distance of several hundred miles, my column was **entirely without the means of crossing to the other bank** (emphasis the author's) to strike exposed camps of the hostile bands."[54]*

Gibbon was not the first frontier officer to have difficulty fording the Yellowstone, nor was he alone in ignoring the help available from Indian allies.[55] Custer and the Seventh Cavalry had been unable to ford the Yellowstone while the Lakota they pursued on August 11, 1873 accomplished the feat with ease. Similarly, Custer did not seek the aid of his Arikara scouts in accomplishing a crossing.

In any event, armed with the intelligence that the hostile force was indeed south of the Yellowstone, it would seem that Gibbon should have ferried his force to the south bank before proceeding toward the Rosebud. This movement would have his force in position not only to deny the use of the fords to the enemy as currently planned, but to strike a rapid blow should another opportunity present itself. Failing this, he should have crossed once he reached the good fords in the vicinity of the Rosebud. As we shall see later, he not only remained on the north bank, but assumed an exaggerated defensive posture, akin to being under siege. Additionally, he did not inform General Terry of the sighting of the village or the aborted attempt to attack it although couriers were regularly sent between them.

The evening of the 17th a rather humorous event took place. About 10:30 P. M. the pickets opened fire on what they thought was an Indian swimming in the river. LeForge, who thought Bradley *"was a clean and fine young man, held in respect by all who had anything to do with him, but it appeared to me he often interjected too much red–tape formality into situations where the contingencies of Indian warfare rendered the tedious procedure an actual hindrance to efficiency,"*[56] described the incident:

> *"But a joke at the expense of this earnest Lieutenant (sic) came up while we were in camp across from the mouth of the Rosebud. Soon after dark one night a picket– guard mistook a floating log for a swimming Sioux, and he fired at it as it drifted past him. Of course, the camp was aroused. Bradley called out the scouts and hurried us all over to the river's bank. He had us all lie down and creep here and there through a brushy and reedy area where we knew there was an abundance of mosquitoes, frogs, and snakes. He himself was scurrying back and forth while giving orders to us about the proper mode of locating the enemy. He peered into brush–piles and out over the waters of the Yellowstone. The joke was that all of this time he was carrying in his hands a lighted lantern. In due time it became settled that an inanimate log had caused the alarm. I think our Crows enjoyed as much as did the soldiers the ensuing talk about the humor of the situation – a well–educated army officer using a lighted lantern at night in a hunt for hostile Sioux."*[57]

On the 18th, Captain Thompson was ordered on a three day scout to the Tongue. In addition to his own Company L, he was supported by Captain James Nichols Wheelan and his Company G of the Second Cavalry. The next day brought some welcome news. General Terry had taken the field with the Seventh Cavalry and a rendezvous was expected within a month. In addition, at least two steamboats, the *Josephine* and *Far West* had been secured to support the movement. In the meantime, Gibbon's command was ordered to remain in the vicinity and keep the enemy south of the Yellowstone.

On May 20th, Crow scouts reported that the day before they had encountered a large war party moving from the direction of the Tongue River into the valley of the Rosebud. Fearing for the safety of Captain Thompson and his command, Gibbon ordered the remaining cavalry and five companies of infantry to proceed down river to their relief. To expedite the march, 10 wagons were supplied to convey the infantry in turn. The relief force and Thompson's command passed each other and joined at the base camp on the 21st. They had lain in ambush for a war party of 40 or 50 that was attempting to cross the Yellowstone about three miles above the Tongue. After testing the depth of the river with poles, the Indians apparently decided the water was too deep and withdrew. Captain Freeman's journal contains an interesting entry for May 21st. While it is unclear exactly whom Freeman is referring to, it may have been regimental quartermaster Lieutenant Joshua W. Jacobs, the entry indicates an officer found an Indian grave at the mouth of the Rosebud. Among other articles recovered, or robbed, from the burial was a letter written by Fanny Wiggins Kelly who had been taken captive on July 12, 1864 and rescued on December 9, 1864.[58]

On the 22nd, a three man hunting party was fired upon in the hills back of the camp. Wheelan's Company G was ordered down stream while Bradley's detachment was sent up stream in an attempt to intercept the raiders. Bradley found the fresh trail of 8 to 10 Indians but, after a ride of about 24 miles, returned to camp without sighting the enemy. While out hunting on the morning of May 23, George Herendeen heard rapid firing in the hills. Companies G, H and L responded to the alarm, but arrived too late to save Privates Henry Rahmeir and Augustus Stoker, both of Company H, Second Cavalry, and Citizen teamster Matt Quinn. who had been absent from camp without permission. Although all of the bodies had been mutilated, only Stoker had been scalped.[59]

After a post mortem examination by Dr. Paulding, the bodies were buried at 7 P. M. that evening. Crow scouts Little Face and Shows His Face shed tears and donated their best blankets for the funeral. Dr. Paulding described the funeral:

". . . wrapped in a blanket & covered also with a green blanket put on the body by Show His Face, the Crow Chief to testify his grief – (It was a better blanket than the one he wore on his person). . . . At the time of the funeral a large band of Sioux were looking on from the bluffs across the Yellowstone. They had been seen fooling around in small bands all day on both sides of the river. Gibbon said at first they were 'nothing but game' – 'Elk' – Wonder if there are really any Indians in the country, perhaps we are all mistaken."[60]

Just at dusk several Lakota appeared on the opposite bank, about a mile away. One warrior, sporting a magnificent war bonnet, shook it defiantly at the troops before retiring. Believing they might be fired upon during the night, Gibbon ordered the 12 pounder moved to a more advantageous position near the river bank. Commencing that evening, the command either slept on their arms on a skirmish line, or rose at 2 A. M. to assume defensive positions in anticipation of a dawn attack; the order being rescinded on June 4th. Gibbon was now clearly on the defensive and, apparently, considered himself besieged.

On the 27th, Bradley and his detachment were ordered across the river to determine what had become of the Indians who had not been sighted since the 24th. Within four hours they had discovered the village in its new location on the Rosebud, only about 18 miles distant from Gibbon's camp. As Bradley noted *". . . the fact that they had moved down within easy striking distance ssemed to prove that they held us in no awe."*[61] Bradley reported to Gibbon before noon, recording in his journal for May 27th:

"Everybody wondered why we were not ordered over to attack the village; but the General probably had good reasons. The village was only eighteen miles distant, we had half a day to cross in, and by leaving the horses behind, could have been over the river ready to begin the march at dark, when we would easily have reached the village before day. The absence of Lieutenant English's company (First Lieutenant William Lewis English, Company I, Seventh Infantry, had left May 23 as escort to John W. Power's contract train, their service having been terminated. DCE) left us with an available force of only about 350 men, and whether that was enough to have attacked successfully is uncertain. It was subsequently ascertained that the

village contained about 400 lodges, representing a fighting force of between 800 and 1,000 warriors. It was pretty big odds, but I imagine the majority of our officers would not have hesitated to give them a trial, and there are some who assert confidently that we would have gained a rousing victory, dispersed the village, and prevented that tremendous aggregation of force a month later that made the massacre of Custer's command possible. On the other hand, we might ourselves have been massacred."[62]

Surprisingly, this is a very dispassionate assessment by a subordinate. Even the disrespectful Dr. Paulding was restrained when, upon learning of the discovery of the village, he remarked: *"Don't know whether Gibbon's instructions or disposition will allow us to go for them."[63]* The instructions from Terry, who really had no idea where the Indians were, required Gibbon to move to Glendive Creek, where the Indians were thought to be concentrating, to cooperate with the Dakota Column. Only a few hours after Bradley's report Gibbon composed the following to General Terry:

"I have reached this point (opposite the mouth of Rosebud) and have scouted the country on both sides of the Yellowstone. **No camps have been seen**, *(emphasis the author's) but war parties of from twenty to fifty have been seen to the south of the river and a few on the north side. One of these latter murdered three of our men whilst out hunting on the 23rd inst.*

"As soon as my train arrives from Fort Ellis, which is expected about the first of June, I will resume the march down the Yellowstone with supplies which will last till about July 10th, and I can draw no more from there, the supply being nearly exhausted. In the meantime I will keep scouting parties out, up and down the river, and watch closely for any movement of the Indians to the northward.

"A steamboat, if you have one at your disposal, will be of great assistance in passing troops across the river for effective cooperation if necessary. I have a few small boats which can be used, but they require, of course, a good deal of time. I send this by men in one of them. The three are Pvts. Evans (William Evans, DCE) and Stewart (Benjamin F. Stewart, DCE), Co. E., 7th Infantry (volunteers), and Williamson[64], a citizen scout (John Williamson, DCE), and if they get through successfully will deserve commendation. The danger by river is less than by land. . .

"P.S. **A camp some distance up the Rosebud was reported this morning by our scouts. If this proves true,** *(emphasis the author's) I may not start down the Yellowstone so soon."[65]*

This letter has to be one of the most incredible in the entire history of Indian warfare. *"No camps have been seen."* The utter gall of this statement, given his entire command was mobilized for an attack on the 17th defies belief! Again, Gibbon's official report provides the clues necessary to our understanding. Neither Gibbon's annual report, nor his later *American Catholic Quarterly Review* article, mentions the discovery of the village on the Rosebud on May 27th. Both, however, discuss the sighting of the village on May 17, and the abortive attempt to attack it, but misstate its location as being on the Rosebud rather than the Tongue. This, to my mind, represents a carefully orchestrated deception designed to deflect any criticism attendant to Gibbon's conduct. Why, at the time he wrote his report, did Gibbon choose the Rosebud rather than the Tongue as the site of his single village sighting? Quite simply he had no other choice as Reno's scout and Custer's movement up the Rosebud confirmed the Indians had been on that stream in force. As for definitely establishing if Sitting Bull's village was indeed on the Rosebud, Gibbon would continue to allow the Crow scouts, who wanted no part of an active reconnaissance of the village, to "scour" the countryside in all the wrong locations. Bradley and his mounted detachment, who had satisfied the army's primary campaign objective on two separate occasions, would be withheld from further searches for the village.

Gibbon's annual report for 1876 states: *"Had we been called upon to operate against only the Indians known to be hostile, any one of the three columns sent against them would have been amply sufficient to cope with any force likely to be brought against it. . ."* This, of course, is just what the army wanted to have on the official record. Had the Indian Agents not withheld valuable information, any of the three columns was more than able to take care of itself. Therefore, the blame for the disastrous campaign did not lay with the army. At the time of the two sightings, however, Sitting Bull's village was exactly the size anticipated by the army. Why then did Gibbon not act on the 27th? Clearly, his white–washing annual report statement notwithstanding, he did not feel strong enough to attack at that juncture, and had already decided, as Crook would later, that he was not going to make any movement toward the Indians without re–inforcement. Further, Gibbon must have been convinced that others would not have agreed with his rationale for remaining inactive; else he would have used his orders, requiring inaction unless sure of success, as justification for not moving on the village.

Gibbon had been the only commander in the field for a month. Moreover, his scouts had brought him just the information desired; the location of Sitting Bull's village. Gibbon's conduct undermined the morale of his own troops [66] and greatly increased the morale of the enemy who obviously felt Gibbon's force was afraid to engage them. The worst aspect of his subterfuge, was the deliberate withholding of vital information about the enemy force. This resulted in Custer leading his strike force unaware of the precise location of his objective, although Gibbon could have readily obtained that intelligence by continued surveillance of the village, and being totally ignorant of the belligerent temperament and high morale of the enemy force. While the Indians concentrated in their massive village, rather than gathering the intelligence necessary for victory, Gibbon spent his time sending patrols marching up and down the Yellowstone; seeking the enemy in locations where he knew them not to be. Gibbon's actions would be a contributing factor in Custer's ultimate defeat.

---

[1] Bradley lists 12 officers but this is found to be incorrect as the addition of Company E's 2 officers would then bring the total number of officers, when the concentration was completed, to 14. All authorities, including Bradley, agree that the infantry battalion, excluding Gibbon and the 2 lieutenants on his staff, contained exactly 13 officers.

[2] Colonel John Gibbon, Regimental Adjutant First Lieutenant Levi Frank Burnett, and Regimental Quartermaster First Lieutenant Joshua West Jacobs, remained behind, overtaking the command enroute on the 22nd. See Lieutenant James H. Bradley "The March of the Montana Column" pages 7 – 8, and 15.

[3] The number of enlisted men is derrived from Bradley's totals of 220 enlisted men for the 6 infantry companies and 195 for the 5 companies departing from Fort Shaw. Loyd Overfield contends that Company E contained 35 enlisted men (See Loyd J. Overfield II "The Little Big Horn, 1876" page 119), but his estimate of only 139 enlisted men for the remaining 5 companies is too much at variance with Bradley's report. When coupled with the omission of Captain Rawn from Overfield's company rosters, I am forced to conclude this analysis is in error and have therefore accepted Bradley's numbers.

[4] First Lieutenant James Howard Bradley, Company B, 7th Infantry, commanded the Montana Column's Crow Scouts and mounted infantry, known as the "shoo-flies." He was stricken with

snow blindness on the 19th, but had fully recovered and rejoined the command on the 24th. His journal contains an excellent account of the malady. See Lieutenant James H. Bradley "The March of the Montana Column" pages 13 and 16. We are indebted to his skill as a historian. His journal, incomplete at the time he was killed in action at the Battle of the Big Hole in 1877, is a primary source of information about the campaign. Captain Rawn was not so lucky. Also stricken on the 19th, he relinquished command to Captain Freeman, and returned to Fort Shaw for treatment on the 20th. It was several weeks before he was able to rejoin the command in the field. See Lieutenant James H. Bradley "The March of the Montana Column" pages 13 – 14.

[5] See John M. Carroll "General Custer and the Battle of the Little Big Horn: The Federal View" page 97.

[6] Captain Clifford's company, detailed as escort for the 24 wagon government train, had departed earlier for the Crow Agency, arriving there on April 1. See John M. Carroll "General Custer and the Battle of the Little Big Horn: The Federal View" page 97.

[7] See Lieutenant James H. Bradley "The March of the Montana Column" page 28.

[8] Early trappers had named this stream Twenty–five Yard Creek, but Captain William Clark had named it Shield's River in 1806 to honor one of his men. See Lieutenant James H. Bradley "The March of the Montana Column" page 29.

[9] Major Brisbin, suffering from an attack of rheumatism, was on crutches and unable to mount a horse. He insisted so vigorously on accompanying the expedition that Gibbon consented to his going although he was initially confined to travel in an ambulance. See John M. Carroll "General Custer and the Battle of the Little Big Horn: The Federal View" page 97.

[10] See John S. Gray "Centennial Campaign" pages 72 – 73.

[11] See John S. Gray "Centennial Campaign" page 73.

[12] The original plan was for Gibbon to move due east from the site of abandoned Fort C. F. Smith on the Big Horn River, to strike any villages in the valleys of the Little Big Horn, Rosebud, or the Tongue. Crook's withdrawal forced a change in plans requiring Gibbon to guard the Yellowstone to prevent the Indians from escaping northward. Gibbon immediately set out for the mouth of the Rosebud as the two principal fords used by the Indians were immediately above and below that point. See Edgar I. Stewart "Custer's Luck" page 104.

[13] See Thomas B. Marquis "Memoirs of a White Crow Indian" pg 207.

[14] See Colonel John Gibbon "Last Summer's Expedition Against The Sioux and Its Great Catastrophe" page 277.

[15] Bradley states that one of the gatling guns had been taken from Fort Shaw. While the source of the other field pieces is not specifically stated, it is generally assumed they were obtained at Fort Ellis.

[16] See Lieutenant James H. Bradley "The March of the Montana Column" pages 50 – 51.

[17] See Lieutenant James H. Bradley "The March of the Montana Column" page 51.

[18] Replaced Captain Charles Cotesworth Rawn effective March 19 when Rawn was returned to Fort Shaw due to snow blindness.

[19] See Lieutenant James H. Bradley "The March of the Montana Column" page 50.

[20] First Lieutenant Holmes Offley Paulding who had transferred to the Seventh Infantry from the Seventh Cavalry in October of 1875. See Roger Darling "A Sad and Terrible Blunder" page 117.

[21] Most prominent among these were the following: Henry S. Bostwick had been post interpreter at Fort Shaw since July 12, 1870. He accompanied the expedition as First Guide and Interpreter. See John S. Gray "Custer's Last Campaign" page 138. George Herendeen, who was to figure prominently in the controversy surrounding Custer's alleged disobedience of orders, had spurned Gibbon's $16 per month offer of employment as teamster tendered at Fort Ellis. He subsequently was hired as a guide for $150 per month, the highest rate of pay in the Montana Column. See John S. Gray "Custer's Last Campaign" page 139. Clearly the most famous of this assemblage was the half–breed scout Mitch Boyer. Hired as a guide, Boyer enjoyed a reputation as scout second only to the legendary Jim Bridger. See Edgar I. Stewart "Custer's Luck" page 105.

[22] See Lieutenant James H. Bradley "The March of the Montana Column" page 50.

[23] See Roger Darling "A Sad and Terrible Blunder" page 111.

[24] The Place of Skulls was the site of a great disaster for the Crow. Almost 4,000 souls had succumbed to small pox on this site; the skulls of the victims subsequently being placed on a natural shelf some two–thirds of the way up the rock wall of the bluffs.

[25] See Lieutenant James H. Bradley "The March of the Montana Column" pages 54 – 55.

[26] See "Gibbon on the Sioux Campaign of 1876" page 12. Terry's annual report for 1876 provides some illumination on this order: *"It was not intended that this column should seek for and attack the hostile Sioux independently, unless, indeed, some favorable opportunity should present itself. Its duty was to guard the left bank of the Yellowstone, and, if possible, prevent the Indians from crossing it in case they should attempt to do so. . ."* See Michael J. Koury "The Terry Diary" page 2.

[27] See Lieutenant James H. Bradley "The March of the Montana Column" page 68.

[28] See Paul L. Hedren "The Great Sioux War 1876 - 77" page 180.

[29] One of the sentinels thought he saw a signal light on the bluffs the night of April 19 – 20, but an investigation by the Crow scouts turned up no sign of human presence. Also the fresh tracks of two horses discovered by the scouts turned out to have been made by wild horses. Despite these "false alarms," Gibbon obviously felt compelled to do some further scouting.

[30] This was a party of nearly 200 prospectors led by William Langston that had left the Crow Agency on April 10 intent on prospecting along the Bozeman Trail from Fort C. F. Smith to the Big Horn. Gibbon had met with Langston prior to the party's departure from Crow Agency and obviously hoped the prospectors would flush any Lakota in the vicinity toward his command.

[31] See John S. Gray "Centennial Campaign" pages 75 – 76.

[32] Lieutenant Roe would supervise the detachment erecting the monument on Custer Hill in 1881. See Robert M. Utley "Custer and the Great Controversy" page 107.

[33] See Edward J. McClernand "On Time for Disaster: The Rescue of Custer's Command" page 148.

[34] See Lieutenant James H. Bradley "The March of the Montana Column" pages 71 – 72.

[35] See Lieutenant James H. Bradley "The March of the Montana Column" page 85.

[36] See Lieutenant James H. Bradley "The March of the Montana Column" pages 128 – 129.

[37] See Lieutenant James H. Bradley "The March of the Montana Column" page 87.

[38] See Thomas B. Marquis "Memoirs of a White Crow Indian" pages 212 – 213. Unlike a later story dealing with the escape of the Crow scout Curly from the Custer Battlefield by disguising himself in a Lakota blanket, the story of Two Moon is believable in that the temperature was very cold; snow falling the afternoon of May 3rd.

[39] See Lieutenant James H. Bradley "The March of the Montana Column" pages 87 – 88.

[40] See Thomas B. Marquis "Memoirs of a White Crow Indian" pages 221 – 222.

[41] See W. Boyer "Surgeon's Diary With the Custer Relief Column" page 5.

[42] See Lieutenant James H. Bradley "The March of the Montana Column" pages 88 – 89.

[43] See W. Boyes "Surgeon's Diary With The Custer Relief Column" page 5.

[44] See Lieutenant James H. Bradley "The March of the Montana Column" pages 89 – 90.

[45] See Lieutenant James H. Bradley "The March of the Montana Column" page 90.

[46] See Lieutenant James H. Bradley "The March of the Montana Column" page 94.

[47] See Lieutenant James H. Bradley "The March of the Montana Column" pages 96 – 97.

[48] Recalling that Bradley had not actually seen so much as a single tepee, due to an intervening ridge, it is interesting to note that Gibbon ordered this movement with only a vague idea of the location of the village and no real intelligence as to its size or surrounding terrain. This, of course, is exactly the situation Custer would find himself in on the morning of June 25. His subsequent decision to attack was, as Gibbon's action shows, in consonance with the military procedures of the times and should not be judged by current military standards.

[49] Ellipsis are indicated in the original publication of the journal.

[50] Noted Custer historian John Gray states that offers by the Crow to swim the horses across the Yellowstone were ignored. See John S. Gray "Custer's Last Campaign" page 153. While Gray doesn't cite his source for this statement, and I have been unable to locate a source on my own, it seems plausible the offer was made. Even if the offer was not made, it would appear that the

obvious solution would be to have Bradley repeat his feat of two days previously when he swam his horses across, or to enlist the Crow to help in this endeavor.

[51] See Lieutenant James H. Bradley "The March of the Montana Column" pages 103 – 106.

[52] See W. Boyes "Surgeon's Diary With The Custer Relief Column" page 7.

[53] See Charles M. Robinson III "A Good Year to Die" page 101.

[54] See John M. Carroll "General Custer and The Battle of the Little Big Horn: The Federalist View" page 101.

[55] This refusal of the offer by the Crow scouts to swim the cavalry horses across the Yellowstone would not be the last time a commander of the Montana Column would ignore the special talents of his Indian auxiliaries. See John S. Gray "Custer's Last Campaign" page 153.

[56] See Thomas B. Marquis "Memoirs of a White Crow Indian" pages 228.

[57] See Thomas B. Marquis "Memoirs of a White Crow Indian" pages 229.

[58] See George A. Schneider "The Freeman Journal" page 46.

[59] Without mentioning his name, Gibbon indicates that Stoker's knife was subsequently recognized and recovered from Custer's battlefield.

[60] See W. Boyes "Surgeon's Diary With The Custer Relief Column" page 12.

[61] See Lieutenant James H. Bradley "The March of the Montana Column" pages 124.

[62] See Lieutenant James H. Bradley "The March of the Montana Column" pages 126.

[63] See W. Boyes "Surgeon's Diary With The Custer Relief Column" page 13.

[64] John Williamson undertook the mission in the line of duty while privates Benjamin F. Stewart and William Evans were paid an additional $100 for volunteering. See John S. Gray "Centennial Campaign" page 85. Along with Private James Bell, also of Company E, Seventh Infantry, Evans and Stewart would volunteer to carry dispatches from General Terry to General Crook on July 9th.

[65] See John S. Gray "Centennial Campaign" pages 84 – 85.

[66] Bradley confronted nine of his fellow officers on May 29th when it came to his attention that at least one of them doubted he had sighted a village on the 27th. See Roger Darling "A Sad and Terrible Blunder" page 118.

Chapter 7

The Battle of the Rosebud

In terms of total combatants engaged, the Battles of the Rosebud and the Little Big Horn were the largest battles contested on the great plains. Size alone, however, does not qualify the Battle of the Rosebud for study in relation to the 1876 campaign. The significance of this battle, in relation to the Little Big Horn, lies in three areas: understanding how, and why, the tactics, determination, and cohesiveness of the Lakota and Cheyenne warriors deviated from what the military expected; the performance of the officers and troops; and the subsequent attempts at cover–up to maintain personal reputations. To that end, a detailed discussion of the ebb and flow of the battle will not be presented and the interested reader is referred to J. W. Vaughn "With Crook at the Rosebud" and Neil C. Mangum "Battle of the Rosebud: Prelude to the Little Bighorn."

General Crook experienced considerable difficulty in organizing his summer campaign. As noted in chapter 5, soldier morale was low, a primary cause of which was the abandoning of the dead and a wounded man during the disastrous Powder River Campaign of the previous March. Some fence mending was required and Crook traveled to Fort Russell on May 9th to meet with the officers of the Third Cavalry, where Colonel Reynolds and Captain Moore were still awaiting court–martial. Concluding his business in Cheyenne, Crook set out for Red Cloud Agency to enlist scouts for the coming campaign. Crook had proven during his Tonto Basin Campaign in Arizona just how effective Indian scouts could be in hunting their brethren. When the soldier's scouts were of the same tribe as the hunted, the effect on the "hostiles" was demoralizing in the extreme. Arriving while agent James S. Hastings was absent, Crook was quickly able to secure the promise of chiefs Sitting Bull of the South,[1] Rocky Bear, and Three Bears to furnish some thirty–five to forty young men. This satisfactory state of affairs was quickly reversed upon agent Hastings' return. Bourke relates:

> *"When Agent Hastings returned there seemed to be a great change in the feelings of the Indians, and it was evident that he had done his best to set them against the idea of helping in the campaign."*[2]

Crook had incurred the wrath of both E. A. Howard, agent at Spotted Tail, and Hastings for his verbal attack on the agencies after the March 17 fight on Powder River. Crook claimed Old Bear's camp was *"a perfect magazine of ammunition, war material and general supplies."* In documents sent to the Congress, he charged:

> *"Every evidence was found to prove these Indians to be in co–partnership with those at the Red Cloud and Spotted Tail agencies, and that the proceeds of their raids upon the settlements have been taken into those agencies and supplies brought out in return."*[3]

While these charges could not be substantiated, they obviously caused the agents considerable discomfort and they defended themselves vigorously. It is little wonder that Crook met with such a chilly response to his request for Indian scouts. Trying to salvage what he could from the situation, Crook attempted to validate the peaceful attitude of the agency Indians. He was shocked when Red Cloud informed him:

> *"The Gray Fox must understand that the Dakotas and especially the Oglalas (sic) have many warriors, many guns and ponies. They are brave and ready to fight for*

their country. They are not afraid of the soldiers nor of their chief. Many braves are
ready to meet them. Every lodge will send its young men, and they will say of the
Great Father's dogs, 'let them come!'"[4]

The *New York Herald* correspondent who recorded Red Cloud's speech showed remarkable insight into the Lakota psyche when he credited their attitude, in part, to the March 17 debacle on Powder River:

". . . The miscarriage of the winter campaign has been to confirm them in their
vain glory. They ascribe the hasty withdrawal of General Crook from their country
to fear instead of its real cause. . ."[5]

Crook was forced to leave the agency without any Lakota allies, undoubtedly fuming anew over the botched winter campaign, but without fully comprehending the import of this new found Lakota confidence to which his command had contributed so greatly. While things had not gone well, in terms of enlisting Lakota scouts, they almost turned into disaster on the trip up White Earth Creek where a band of Lakota lay in ambush. Fortunately for Crook, the target of the ambush, his normal escort had been augmented by those of the paymaster and Inspector General, as well as by a party of about a dozen civilians. Surprised by the size of this force, the Lakota let it pass unmolested, contenting themselves with venting their wrath on an unlucky mail–rider named Clark.[6] The remainder of Crook's trip to Fort Fetterman was uneventful.

Although Crook's column was the last of the three columns to take the field, it would be the first to become engaged. The command consisted of 10 companies of the Third Cavalry, 5 companies of the Second Cavalry, 2 companies of the Fourth Infantry, and 3 companies of the Ninth Infantry; a total force of 47 officers and 1002 men.[7] The expedition was organized as shown in Table 7 – 1.[8]

In addition to hundreds of pack–mules, the column had a train of 103 six–mule wagons. Also accompanying the column, disguised as one of the male teamsters, was the notorious "Calamity Jane." As the command neared old Fort Reno, she was discovered, clad in female attire, and finally sent back to Fort Fetterman with the wagon train several days after the battle.[9]

All finally being in readiness, the Big Horn and Yellowstone Expedition departed Fort Fetterman at noon on May 29, 1876.[10] Captain Meinhold, with two companies, *"was sent on in advance to reconnoiter (sic) the country, and report the state of the road as well as any signs of the proximity of large bands of the enemy."*[11] Captain Van Vliet's company was pushed ahead to keep a look–out for the Crow and Shoshone scouts who had promised to join the command in the vicinity of old Fort Reno.

Arriving at Fort Reno on June 2nd, Crook found only the detachment of Captain Van Vliet, who had seen no sign of the proffered Crow or Shoshone scouts. In desperate need of Indian scouts, Crook dispatched his three white scouts, Frank Grouard, Louis Richaud, and Baptiste Pourrier on the perilous 300 mile journey to the Crow Agency, then located on the Stillwater near Livingston, Montana. It was agreed that the main command would push on to Goose Creek, near present–day Sheridan, Wyoming, because of its ample water supply and fresh grazing.[12]

The command pushed on from Fort Reno on June 3rd, camping on Crazy Woman Creek. The next days' march brought them to Clear Creek. In exploring the surrounding area, Ninth Infantrymen discovered, and vandalized, an Indian burial scaffold; using the wooden support poles for kindling. Correspondent Finerty remarked on the soldier's conduct:

"Thus the relationship of all men to each other in point of savagery was established. The Sioux defaced the white graves at Reno (Fort Reno, DCE). The whites converted the Sioux pedestal into kindling–wood. It was all the same to the dead on both sides."[13]

I.	Expedition Commander –	Brigadier–General George Crook
II.	Cavalry Commander –	Lieutenant Colonel William Bedford Royall, 3rd Cavalry
III.	Infantry Commander –	Major Alexander Chambers, 4th Infantry
IV.	3rd Cavalry Battalion Commander – Major Andrew Wallace Evans, 3rd Cavalry	
V.	2nd Cavlary Battalion Commander – Captain Henry Erastus Noyes, 2nd Cavalry[14]	
VI.	Expedition Staff –	Captain Azor H. Nickerson, 23rd Infantry, Aide–de–Camp
		2nd Lieutenant John Gregory Bourke, 3rd Cavalry, Aide–de–Camp
		Captain George Morton Randall, 23rd Infantry, Chief of Scouts
		Captain William Sanford Stanton, Engineer Corps., Chief Engineer Officer
		Captain John V. Furey, Chief Quartermaster
		1st Lieutenant John Wilson Bubb, 4th Infantry, Acting Commissary of Subsistence
		Captain Albert Hartsuff, Assistant Surgeon, Medical Director
Company A 3rd Cavalry		1st Lieutenant Joseph Lawson, 2nd Lieutenant Charles Morton
Company B 3rd Cavalry		Captain Charles Meinhold, 2nd Lieutenant James Ferdinand Simpson
Company C 3rd Cavalry		Captain Frederick Van Vliet
Company D 3rd Cavalry		Captain Guy Vernor Henry
Company E 3rd Cavalry		Captain Alexander Sutorius, 1st Lieutenant Adolphus H. Von Leuttwitz, 2nd Lieutenant Henry Rowan Lemly
Company F 3rd Cavalry		2nd Lieutenant Bainbridge Reynolds[15]
Company G 3rd Cavalry		1st Lieutenant Emmet Crawford
Company I 3rd Cavalry		Captain William Howard Andrews, 1st Lieutenant Albert D. King, 2nd Lieuenant James Evans Heron Foster
Company L 3rd Cavalry		Captain Peter Dumont Vroom, 2nd Lieutenant George Francis Chase
Company M 3rd Cavalry		Captain Anson Mills, 1st Lieutenant Augustus Choteau Paul, 2nd Lieutenant Frederick Schwatka
Company A 2nd Cavalry		Captain Thomas Bull Dewees, 2nd Lieutenant Daniel Crosby Pearson
Company B 2nd Cavalry		1st Lieutenant William Charles Rawolle
Company D 2nd Cavalry		1st Lieutenant Samuel Miller Swigert, 2nd Lieutenant Henry Dustan Huntington
Company E 2nd Cavalry		Captain Elijah Revillo Wells, 2nd Lieutenant Frederick William Sibley
Company I 2nd Cavalry		Captain Henry Erastus Noyes, 2nd Lieutenant Frederick William Kingsbury
Company C 9th Infantry		Captain Samuel Munson, 1st Lieutenant Thaddeus H. Capron
Company G 9th Infantry		Captain Thomas Bredin Burrowes, 1st Lieutenant William Lewis Carpenter
Company H 9th Infantry		Captain Andrew Sheridan Burt, 2nd Lieutenant Edgar Brooks Robertson
Company D 4th Infantry		Captain Avery Billings Cain, Fi1strst Lieutenant Henry Seton
Company F 4th Infantry		Captain Gerhard L. Luhn
Surgeons		Julius Herman Patzki, Stevens, McGillicuddy, and Powell
Masters of Transportation		Charles Russell and Thomas Moore
Guides		Frank Grouard, Louis Richaud, and Baptiste "Big Bat" Pourrier

Reporters Joseph Wasson (*Philadelphia Press, New York Tribune*, and *San Francisco Alta California*), Robert A. Strahorn (Chicago *Tribune, Denver Rocky Mountain News, Cheyenne Sun*, and *Omaha Republican*), John F. Finerty (*Chicago Times*), Thomas B. MacMillian (*Chicago Inter–Ocean*), and Reuben H. Davenport (*New York Herald*)

Table 7 – 1 Table of Organization of the Big Horn and Yellowstone Expedition

The troops were visited by two miners in their Clear Creek camp. Lieutenant Bourke described the meeting:

> *"Here we were visited by messengers from a party of Montana miners who were traveling across country from the Black Hills back to the Yellowstone; the party numbered sixty–five, and had to use every precaution to prevent stampede and surprise; every night they dug rifle–pits, and surrounded themselves with rocks, palisades, or anything else that could be made to resist a charge from the Sioux, whose trails were becoming very thick and plenty. There were many pony, but few lodge–pole, tracks, a sure indication that the men were slipping out from Red Cloud and Spotted Tail agencies and uniting with the hostiles, but leaving their families at home, under the protection of the reservations."[16]*

Crook was resolved not to experience a repeat of the loss of his herd as occurred the first night out on the winter campaign. Bourke describes the elaborate precautions taken by the troops:

> *"To prevent any stampede of our stock which might be attempted, our method of establishing pickets became especially rigid: in addition to the mounted vedettes encircling bivouac, and occupying commanding buttes and bluffs, solid companies were thrown out a mile or two in advance and kept mounted, with the purpose of holding in check all parties of the enemy which might attempt to rush down upon the herds and frighten them off by waving blankets, yelling, firing guns, or other tricks in which the savages were adepts. One platoon kept saddled ready for instant work; the others were allowed to loosen the cinches, but not to unsaddle."[17]*

On the 5th, the column camped on the site of Fort Phil Kearny. Like Reno, old Fort Phil Kearny stirred the emotions of the men. The next day, June 6th, they crossed over Lodge Trail Ridge, near the site of the Fetterman Fight. Goose Creek, and the promise of good fishing that had several of the officers carrying their fishing poles, was only a dozen miles away when Captain Noyes, accompanied by ten men, went in advance to stake out a good camping site and to lay claim to the choicest fishing holes. Inexplicably, however, the command turned north, away from the forks of Goose Creek, and followed Prairie Dog Creek for 18 miles, most of the distance covered in a pelting rain. When the command failed to arrive, Noyes back tracked along their trail. Reaching the main body's camp after dark, Noyes wisely decided to wait until morning to make his appearance lest some nervous picket fire on the small party. It is extremely difficult to understand what happened when Noyes reported to Crook the morning of the 7th. It being obvious to all of Crook's officers that they had taken a wrong turn, the habitually taciturn Crook, ordered the advance continued along Prairie Dog Creek; camping for the night at its confluence with the Tongue, a distance of 17 additional miles in the wrong direction. Crook, as was his habit, never explained his rationale, and Bourke omits mention of the affair entirely stating only that Noyes had *"wandered off"* in search of fishing holes and remained out all night.

Unbeknownst to the soldiers, Lame Sioux, who along with Wooden Leg was a member of an eleven man Cheyenne hunting party, had discovered their camp. The Cheyenne trailed the column to the camping place on the Tongue; lingering to observe the departure of the Crow scouts on the morning of the 8th before returning to the village on the Rosebud to make their report.[18] The Crow had stumbled upon the camp about midnight of the 7th and had attempted to converse with the pickets. Courier Ben Arnold, frustrated by his inability to distinguish either voices, or the dialect, finally responded in Lakota. Hearing a reply in the tongue of their mortal enemies, the Crow withdrew. Crook, who had correctly guessed the identity of the midnight visitors, was justifiably upset by Arnold's slip of the tongue.

Crook was joined in this camp by the sixty–five miners[19] and received dispatches from General Sheridan via two couriers. The dispatches notified Crook *". . . that all able–bodied male Indians had left the Red Cloud Agency, and that the Fifth Cavalry had been ordered up from Kansas to take post in our rear; also that the Shoshones had sent one hundred and twenty of their warriors to help him, and that we should look for their arrival almost any day."*[20]

About 6:30 P.M. on the 9th, a small Cheyenne scouting party under Little Hawk sent to observe the soldiers, opened fire from the bluffs across the Tongue. After an hour's skirmishing, the Cheyenne withdrew leaving Crook with Sergeant John Warfield, Company F, Third Cavalry slightly wounded in the right arm; Private Emil Renner, Company D, Second Cavalry, with a flesh wound in the left thigh; three horses, including Captain Andrew Burt's beautiful white, and one mule killed. An additional "casualty" was the stove–pipe of Captain Mills' Sibley stove. It was perforated to the point of resembling Swiss cheese.[21] Notable in the action was Captain Mills detailing every eighth trooper as a horse–holder instead of the one in four prescribed by the tactics of the period.[22]

On the 11th, Crook finally marched to where he was supposed to go in the first place, Goose Creek. On the 13th, still anxious about his Indian allies, Crook sent a detail under Lieutenant Samuel Swigert to old Fort Phil Kearny to attempt to locate the Shoshone. They returned in the evening without having sighted their prospective allies. All questions were answered when scouts Frank Grouard and Louis Richaud, accompanied by Chief Old Crow, returned the afternoon of the 14th. Crook was informed it had indeed been the Crow who had hailed his camp the night of the 7th. They had withdrawn fearing they had stumbled upon a Lakota village. Returning later, they discovered the camp, obviously made by soldiers, abandoned. Fearing the troops had retreated, the Crow were unsure they wanted to support the soldiers and the main force, about 175 strong, remained a few miles away with "Big Bat" Pourrier.

Old Crow provided some interesting, but dated, information on the Montana Column. Crook was informed of the theft of the Crow's horses on May 3rd, Gibbon's abortive attempt to cross the Yellowstone on the 17th, and that Gibbon was encamped opposite the mouth of the Rosebud and the Lakota were crossing the Yellowstone at will. The Crow believed the village to be on the Tongue, but Frank Grouard told Crook: *"from all signs I had seen I supposed they were on the Rosebud."*[23]

Crook then dispatched Captain Burt, Louis Richaud, and Old Crow to bring in the main body. Before dusk the entire group of Crow scouts, numbering 176, under their chiefs Old Crow, Medicine Crow, and Good Heart had entered the camp.[24] After a welcoming ceremony, Crook had his officers assemble shortly after retreat. Bourke records the meeting:

> *"We were to cut loose from our wagons, each officer and soldier carrying four days' rations of hard bread, coffee, and bacon in saddle–pockets, and one hundred rounds of ammunition in belts or pouches; one blanket to each person. The wagons were to be parked and left behind in a defensible position on the Tongue or Goose, and under the protection of the men unable for any reason to join in the forward movement; all the infantrymen who could ride and who so desired were to be mounted on mules from the pack–trains with saddles from the wagons or from the cavalry companies which could spare them.[25] If successful in attacking a village, the supplies of dried meat and other food were to be saved, and we should then, in place of returning immediately to our train, push on to make a combination with either Terry or Gibbon, as the case might be."[26]*

Some authorities have formed the opinion that Crook was not serious about prosecuting the campaign; citing as evidence his order to carry only 4 days' rations. I believe this criticism to be unjust. The reticent and uncommunicative Crook was a logistical genius; his organization of pack trains serving as a model for the army until well into the twentieth century. I believe he had devised a strategy to further increase his mobility. Crook had determined to emulate his adversaries and "live off the land." Rather than depend on the hunt to replenish his supplies, he would use the food stuffs and clothing from captured villages. Crook had claimed this same stratagem for his earlier campaign on the Powder River, but there is reason to believe the concept was not formulated until after that campaign's conclusion. [27]

Brilliant in concept, the plan contained a fatal flaw; being grounded on a false premise. For success, Crook must capture village after village, much as the Pacific island hopping campaign of World War II; each captured citadel, in turn, serving as the base and staging area for the next assault. Unfortunately for Crook, the Indians were not in their usual small scattered villages. They had concentrated in a single, massive, mobile city.

Just as the conference ended, the long awaited Shoshone scouts, 86 in number, galloped up to headquarters. Included in this number were *". . . three white men – Cosgrove, Yarnell, and Eckles – all Texans; and one French–Canadian half–breed, named Luisant. Cosgrove, the leading spirit, was, during the Rebellion, a captain in the 32d Texas Cavalry, C. S. A., and showed he had not forgotten the lessons of the war by the appearance of discipline and good order evinced by his command. . ."* [28]

The composition of Crook's strike force, which departed at 5 A.M. on June 16 is given in Table 7 – 2. The 1325 effectives represented the largest force sent against Indians on the Northern Plains since the 1865 campaign of General Patrick E. Connor. [29] Morale was high, for as Bourke stated:

"No one now doubts we shall be victorious; the only discrepancy of opinion is in regard to the numbers we may find." [30]

The Crow were equally expectant of a great victory as Captain Nickerson related:

"It must have been soon after daybreak, that I was startled by a series of groans and cries as though the author was enduring excruciating torture. I jumped up, ran to the front of my tent, turned back the flap and peered out. Riding down through the camp, came an old Crow warrior, nearly as naked as when he was born, but painted and tattooed in approved form, and carrying his rifle which, from time to time, he swung in the air, as a drum major would handle his baton or staff. His wild eyes appeared to be fixed on objects, invisible to the outer world, and which he seemed to think were hovering about him, great tears rolled down his cheeks, as he pleaded, prayed and exhorted – the empty air. He was going through that species of savage incantation known as 'crying for scalps'." [31]

A noon halt was ordered on the divide of Spring Creek. While scouts went in search of the Lakota, the soldiers settled down for a long rest, some boiling coffee. The scouts made for a herd of buffalo seen grazing in the distance. As luck would have it, the herd was, at that moment being stalked by two hunting parties of Cheyenne. One band, under Little Hawk, was from the main village, now located on the South Fork of Reno Creek, some thirty miles to the north; the second group being from Magpie Eagle's camp on Trail Creek. After trading visual insults with Frank Grouard and the Crow Plenty Coups, the Cheyenne retired to their respective villages while the scouts made their report to General Crook. [32] Crook went into camp at the head of the south fork of Rosebud Creek at 7:20 P.M. secure in the knowledge he was marching in the right direction. A tragedy was narrowly averted when correspondent Finerty's accidentally discharged revolver merely burned and broke his saddle.[33] Bourke proved himself a prophet when he wrote in his diary:

"We are now right in among the hostiles and may strike or be struck at any hour."[34]

Element	Strength
Second Cavalry Battalion, Captain Noyes	269
Third Cavalry Battalion, Captain Mills	207
Third Cavalry Battalion, Lieutenant Colonel Royall	327
Mounted Infantry Battalion, Major Chambers	175
Crow Scouts	176
Shoshone Scouts	86
Packers	20
Montana Miners	65
Total Force	**1325**

Table 7 – 2 Crook's Strike Force June 16, 1876[35]

While Crook and his troopers rested peacefully, the Indian village was in an uproar . Little Hawk and his Elk Society brothers[36] howled like wolves as they approached the camp to indicate that the enemy had been sighted. A council of all the chiefs, Lakota and Cheyenne, was held to determine what to do. Although the Cheyenne women began preparations to move the village, the chiefs decided to wait until it was determined what the military's intention was. This did not sit well with the young men who decided to attack the soldiers anyway. Crazy Horse, recognizing the inevitability of a fight, realized some control must be exercised if the undertaking was to be successful. He said a large warrior force, under older chiefs, should be left to guard the village, while the remainder of the warriors rode out to attack and drive the soldiers away. Crazy Horse advised the young men that victory would require a different type of fighting on their part:

". . . let every man think carefully before shouting the Hoye! (Lakota acclamation of ascent, DCE) This was a new kind of war that had come to the country of the Lakotas, not the old one of driving off a few raiding Snakes (Shoshone, DCE) or Crows who made a little fighting between the time of the hunts and the other things of their lives. With the white warriors it was killing every day, killing all the time.

"These soldiers of the Great Father do not seem to be men like you. They have no homes anywhere, no wives but the pay–women, no sons that they can know. Now, my friends, they are here in our country looking for us to kill. In this war we must fight them in a different way from any the Lakotas have ever seen, not with the counting of many coups or doing great deeds to be told in the victory dance. We must make this a war of killing, a war of finishing, so we can live in peace in our own country."[37]

Shortly after the council broke up the warriors started for the Rosebud. They set out on their all night journey in many different bands; some traveling eastward over the divide, then angling south toward the big bend of the Rosebud; while others traveled down the South Fork of Reno Creek arriving on the field via Sioux Pass.[38] Other warriors, including the Uncpapas, left later; arriving after the start of the fight, but serving as re–inforcements for the warriors already engaged. While estimates of the size of the warrior force range from 750 to 1,500, a figure of 1,000 is probably not unreasonable. While Crook would not enjoy a significant numerical superiority over his adversaries, he would at least achieve parity. Notable among the Cheyenne participants were Spotted Wolf, principal Cheyenne chief in the fight, along with chiefs American Horse, Two Moon, and Lame White Man.[39] Also accompanying the war party, although too weak from the ordeal of his sun dance to actively participate, was Sitting Bull.[40] The bands of Crow King and Gall has not yet joined the great encampment. Their fighting would be restricted to the Little Big Horn, now only eight days away.

Crook resumed his march at 6 A.M. on the 17th, but traveled only 5 or 6 miles before halting between the two bends in the stream. Immediately many of the soldiers unsaddled and started fires to make morning coffee.[41] Crook's Crow scouts reported that they had seen sign of Lakota in the area and suggested the command remain in bivouac until they investigated. Crook agreed, immediately sending out pickets along the base of the bluffs to the north.[42] When a half hour had elapsed without further word from the Crow scouts, the command relaxed; Crook becoming engaged in a game of Whist with Bourke and several others.[43]

While Crook and his command rested, four Crow scouts topped a rise eleven miles north of the bivouac and commenced firing at two Lakota and two Cheyenne scouts from Young Two Moon's band. Upon hearing the firing, the remainder of Young Two Moon's band surged forward dislodging the Crow from the hill.[44] Some members of Crook's command heard the firing but misinterpreted it as was the case with Captain Sutorius. Only the evening before, the captain had remarked: *"We will have a fight tomorrow, mark my words – I feel it in the air!"*[45] Upon hearing the firing, however, he thought: *"They are shooting buffaloes over there."*[46]

The Crow, one of their number seriously wounded, dashed wildly back to camp shouting *"Ota Sioux"* as they approached; the Lakota and Cheyenne warriors at their heels engaging Crook's pickets. The Battle of the Rosebud had begun!

Crook had been caught napping,[47] however, luck was on his side. He scampered to a small hill to obtain a personal view of the enemy's dispositions, leaving the disposition of troops to subordinates. Fortunately, they were equal to the task at hand. Captain George Randall, chief of scouts, led his scouts to a plateau about 500 yards north of the disorganized troops. Here, the Crow and Shoshone scouts were able to check the advance elements of the Lakota and Cheyenne force. While this holding action consumed only about twenty minutes, it was all the time Major Andrew Evans needed to make his initial dispositions.[48] The loyal scouts had saved Crook's command from disaster. It would not be the last time their direct intervention saved soldiers that day.

What Crook saw from his hilltop position must have amazed him:

"In all of Crook's experience with the Apaches, there had been nothing like this - massed Indians, more of them than were Crook's own numbers, (Crook's force may have been slightly outnumbered, more probably the weight of numbers was equal or slightly in favor of the troops, DCE) drawn up for open battle, rampant to engage the army on its own terms. Nothing of that sort had happened before in the Plains wars, and after this campaign, it would never happen again."[49]

Crook returned from his observation post and immediately resumed command, but Crazy Horse had the initiative and would retain it throughout the day. Not realizing that Crazy Horse had convinced the young men to try new tactics, Crook scattered his forces by responding to enemy pressure at widely dispersed areas of the field.[50] This was exactly what Crazy Horse wanted as his charges and counter–charges were designed to string out the troops into small detachments that could be beaten in detail. When directly confronted, the Lakota and Cheyenne warriors would initially fall back; only to re–concentrate and strike savagely at the strung out soldier flanks or rear.

Captain Mills couldn't help but admire the skill and horsemanship of his adversaries:

"These Indians were most hideous, everyone being painted in most hideous colors and designs, stark naked, except their moccasins, breech clouts and head gear, the latter consisting of feathers and horns; some of the horses also being painted, and the Indians proved then and there that they were the best cavalry soldiers on earth. In charging up towards us they exposed little of their person, hanging on with one arm around the neck and one leg over the horse, firing and lancing from underneath the horse's necks, so that there was no part of the Indian at which we could aim.

"Their shouting and personal appearance was so hideous that it terrified the horses more than our men and rendered them almost uncontrollable before we dismounted and placed them behind the rocks.

"The Indians came not in a line but in flocks or herds like the buffalo, and they piled in upon us until I think there must have been one thousand or fifteen hundred in our immediate front, but they refused to fight when they found us secured behind the rocks, and bore off to our left. I then charged the second ridge, . . ."[51]

Not everyone concerned fought well; especially Oglala Jack Red Cloud, 18 year old son of the famous chief. Upon leaving the reservation he joined the Cheyenne circle of Magpie Eagle and American Horse.[52] Young Red Cloud went into the fight wearing his father's magnificent long trail war bonnet and sporting the engraved winchester presented to his father by the U. S. Government. David Humphreys Miller described the humiliation of Jack Red Cloud by the Crow scouts Buffalo Hard To Hit and Along The Hills[53]:

"The first thing a warrior must do if his horse is killed, as any fighting man knows, is to remove the bridle calmly and coolly before running for safety. Red Cloud's failure to do so showed the enemy Indians how untried he was in battle. Running away on foot with the bonnet streaming out behind him made him a prime target.

"The crowning disgrace, of course, was the refusal of the Crows to kill him after they had grabbed away his war bonnet and rifle as trophies. Instead of shooting him or riding him down with their ponies, they had simply struck him with their quirts – then rode away laughing, while he begged them to come back and finish him off."[54]

Some of Crook's troopers, as would later be reported about the Custer soldiers at the Little Big Horn, attempted to surrender. Baptiste Pourrier recounted:

> *"After Col. Henry was wounded there were two of his men who were killed by Cheyennes. They were dismounted and their horses had got away from them. Two Cheyenne warriors charged on them. The Crow Indians started to charge on these Cheyennes and save the soldiers' lives, which they could easily have done, but General Crook told Bat to call them back. Bat did so. The Cheyennes rode on to the soldiers, who gave up their guns from their hands to the two Indians who instantly shot the two men with their own guns."*[55]

These two acts were far outweighed by many acts of heroism. After rescuing Captain Vroom's surrounded troop, Captain Henry began a withdrawal to a less advanced position. He was shot full in the face, the bullet tearing the whole visage out under both eyes. Weak from shock and loss of blood, he fell from his saddle. As the troops continued their withdrawal, the Lakota launched a charge to finish the soldier chief. Help came from an unexpected quarter:

> *"With their war cries echoing from the farthest bluffs, they plunged headlong into the thick of the hostile array. Old Washakie of the Shoshones was there. So was Luishaw. Of the Crows, Alligator Stands Up and Plenty Coups were foremost.*
>
> *"Rearing, snorting horses, kicking up a dust cloud so dense the riders could hardly see – knife thrust and tomahawk blow – the Sioux ranks opened. Washakie, Alligator Stands Up and their warriors stood over Henry's limp body.*
>
> *"The hostiles fought desperately with the scouts. It created a diversion which stopped the Indian advance at its height. Royall and Vroom had time to catch their breath. Now they came back up the hill, driving Crazy Horse's warriors, reoccupying the ground held so heroically by a handful of savage scouts, and getting possession of the captain's unconscious body."*[56]

Captain Henry was not the only soldier rescued by the scouts that day:

> *"Sergeant Van Moll (First Sergeant John W. Van Moll, Company A, Third Cavalry, DCE) was left alone on foot. A dozen Sioux dashed at him. Major Randall and Lieutenant Bourke, who had probably not noticed him in the general melee, but who, in the crisis, recognized his stature and his danger, turned their horses to rush to his rescue. They called on the Indians (the scouts, DCE) to follow them. One small, misshapen Crow warrior mounted on a fleet pony outstripped all others. He dashed boldly in among the Sioux against whom Van Moll was dauntlessly defending himself, seized the big Sergeant by the shoulder and motioned him to jump up behind. The Sioux were too astonished to realize what had been done until they saw the long–legged Sergeant, mounted behind the little Crow, known as Humpy, dash toward our lines like the wind. Then they opened fire, but we opened also and compelled them to seek higher ground. The whole line of our battalion cheered Humpy and Van Moll as they passed us on the home stretch."*[57]

As their crowning achievement, the scouts, along with two infantry companies, covered Royall's perilous withdrawal to the main command. To his credit, Lieutenant Colonel Royall, unlike Major Reno eight days later, was the last man off the field.[58] While First Sergeants John Henry Shingle, Company I, and Michael A. McGann, Company F, Sergeant Joseph Robinson,

Company D, and Trumpeter Elmer A. Snow, Company M, all of the 3rd Cavalry, were awarded Medals of Honor for their conduct at the Rosebud,[59] the considerable contributions of the Crow and Shoshone scouts went both unrecognized and unrewarded. Adding insult to injury, an ill-informed Captain Mills proclaimed: *"These Indians (Lakota and Cheyenne, DCE) lived with their horses, were unsurfieted with food, shelter, rainment or equipment, then the best cavalry in the world; there like will never be seen again. Our friendlies were worthless against them; we would have been better off without them."*[60] The reader may judge for himself, had the Crow and Shoshone not been present, whether or not Mills would have survived to make any statement about the Battle of the Rosebud.

Narrow escapes were the order of the day. Private Phineas Towne, Company F, Third Cavalry, recounted:

"I had not gone more than one third of the distance from our position to where the horses were when I overtook three other soldiers of my own troop carrying a sergeant by the name of Marshall (David Marshall, Company F, Third Cavalry, DCE), who had been shot through the face. I knew that time was precious and none to lose. I could not give them the cold shoulder by passing them without giving a helping hand. Glancing back, I saw the hostiles coming over the hill. I said to the others, 'Quick, here they come!'

"At that instant my comrades, to save themselves, dropped the wounded sergeant and hastened to their horses. The sergeant, seeing that I was the only one left, said:

"'Save yourself if you can, because I am dying. Don't stay with me.' I replied:

"'Dave, old boy, I am going to stay right here with you and will not desert you.'

"Grasping him with all my strength, I carried my comrade until it was useless to carry him any farther, for he was dead. I then laid him down and left him and hurried to get away.

"I don't think that I had gone more than ten yards when I was surrounded by about twenty or more of the most murderous looking Indians I ever saw. You can talk of seeing devils; here they were in full form, painted in the most terrifying manner, some with their war bonnets adorned with horns of steers and buffalo. It was enough to strike terror to anyone's heart.

"I knew that my time had come, I knew that I would be taken prisoner. I fought, but it was fighting against terrible odds. There I was down in that ravine, alone and in the midst of a lot of murderous savages.

"Taking my carbine from me and throwing a lariat over my head and tightening it about my feet, I was helpless. This was all done in an instant, while I struggled and fought in vain, until I was struck on the head with something which rendered me unconscious and caused me to fall. As I went down a bullet struck me in the body.

"I think that when the bullet struck me I regained my consciousness, because I realized I was being dragged at a lively pace over the ground by a pony at the other

end of the lariat. It was, I think, the intention of the Indians either to drag me to death at the heels of the pony or after getting me away to torture me in some other manner.

"They captured one other comrade of mine by the name of Bennett (Richard Bennett, DCE), of L Troop, Third Cavalry, and completely cut him to pieces. His remains were buried in a grain sack.

"After I was dragged in this manner for some distance, my captors were charged by one of the troops of cavalry, and to save themselves from capture abandoned me and made their escape. Thus I was enabled to regain my liberty."[61]

Acts of heroism were by no means limited to the soldiers and their Indian allies. Although the Lakota and Cheyenne had adopted Crazy Horse's tactics, usually ignoring coups and scalps until the fighting was over in that part of the field, many brave deeds were performed. Early in the fighting, Young Two Moon, nephew of chief Two Moon, and five others were cornered in some rocks. They decided to try to escape one at a time:

"This crippled man Limpy was last, and he waited until all the rest had gone. Then just as he was ready to start, his horse was shot. It stampeded, kicking, and bucked him off and fell.

"The soldier scouts on the ridge saw him all by himself behind the rocks there, with his horse lying out in the open, and they started down to count coup and kill him. Two Moons (Young Two Moon, DCE) had gotten across to safety, but when he looked back he could see what was happening to Limpy, so he turned back after him. He ran his horse over beside him to pick him up, but Limpy could not get on. The bullets were hitting close to them and the horse was jumping around, so Limpy let go, and Two Moons galloped out and made another turn and hollered, 'Get ready!' When he came in this time, Limpy managed to get up a sand rock and to jump on behind Two Moons when he came by. They reached safety, riding double like that, and found a Sioux who had an extra horse for Limpy to ride, so he was all right."[62]

Although it was his first fight, Limpy knew the importance of retrieving his horse's bridle. Shortly after his horse was shot:

". . . he ran around behind some sand rocks to take cover, but right away he started worrying about his bridle. If he left it behind he would not have any, so he decided to go after it. He ran over to the horse as they started shooting. He got the strap under the chin untied, and while he was pulling it the rocks were hit two or three times. Pieces flew out and just missed him. But he managed to get back behind the sand rocks and Two Moons carried him to safety."[63]

During the fighting, the Cheyenne Young Black Bird, a nephew of the slain Chief Black Kettle, noticed a dismounted warrior trying to escape the troops. Lashing his winded pony to greater effort, Young Black Bird caught up to the warrior and discovered it was Young Two Moon. He called out *"My friend, come and get on behind me."* They had gone only a short distance before the pony became winded again and had to stop. Fortunately, Contrary Belly came along leading a horse he had taken from a Crow or Shoshone scout. Mounting Young Two Moon on the captured pony, they made their way to safety.[64] After the battle, Young Black Bird was known as White Shield.

Undoubtedly the most famous feat of individual bravery connected with the battle was the rescue of the Cheyenne Chief Comes In Sight.

> *"At the beginning of the fight he had charged the soldiers many times, and when they were fighting the upper group of soldiers, as he was riding up and down in front of the line, his horse was killed under him. White Elk was also riding up and down the line, but was going in the opposite direction from Chief Comes In Sight, and it was just after they had passed each other that Chief Comes In Sight was dismounted. Suddenly White Elk saw a person riding down from where the Indians were toward the soldiers, pass by Chief Comes In Sight, turn the horse and ride up by him, when Comes In Sight jumped on behind and they rode off. This was the sister of Chief Comes In Sight, Buffalo Calf Road Woman.'*[65]

For this reason the Cheyenne have always called the fight *Ksee sewoistaniwe itatane*, "Where the girl saved her brother."[66]

As the battle neared its climax, Crook made a crucial mistake. Not appreciating the seriousness of the situation, he ordered Captain Mills, with his 3 companies of the Third Cavalry, to march down the valley and strike the village that Crook was sure was near by. After he had traveled about 2 miles, Mills was re–inforced by Captain Noyes and his 5 companies of the 2nd Cavalry. While hotly pressed by the enemy, Crook had ordered almost half of his force to disengage and go village hunting![67] Believing Mills movement to signal a retreat, the Lakota and Cheyenne pressed their attack on Lieutenant Colonel Royall's isolated battalion with renewed vigor. When Crook had to choose between leaving his wounded undefended and covering Royall's withdrawal to the main command, he ordered Mills recalled.[68] Mills, rather than returning via his original line of march, exited the canyon to find himself in the rear of the Indians who were forming to charge Crook's position once again. Believing these to be fresh army units, the warriors withdrew. After 6 hours of fierce fighting, the Battle of the Rosebud was over.

Crook still believing the village to be near at hand, reformed the command and started down stream. He got to the point where Mills had been recalled when his Crow scouts refused to proceed further, fearing an ambush.[69] Unwilling to continue without his scouts, Crook returned to the battlefield. When Crook went back over the field in August, he found the remains of an Indian camp just below the battlefield leading him to believe he had been correct in his judgment. The campsite Crook discovered in August had, in reality, been occupied on June 30 as the Indians left the Little Big Horn valley.

Much has been made of the theory that Crazy Horse, master of the ambush, had set a trap for Crook in the "narrow" canyon of the Rosebud. It is extremely unlikely that such a plan existed. First, the valley of the Rosebud, at the point in question, is at least a half mile wide tending more to gentle slopes than craggy precipices. Second, had Crazy Horse planned an ambush in the canyon, he would clearly have used his old decoy tricks and withdrawn up the canyon to lure the soldiers into the jaws of the trap rather than retiring toward the village on Reno Creek. Last, regardless of my esteem for the leadership abilities of Crazy Horse, I cannot accept that a horde of warriors could be held in ambush for six hours while a battle raged within their hearing.

Since he had camped upon the field after the fight, Crook, of course, claimed victory. In his annual report for 1876, reproduced in full in Appendix 15 as is the complete sub report of the Rosebud fight, Crook made much of his "success" stating that, with less than one thousand men, he had defeated the entire warrior force thrown against Custer driving them from the field *"in utter rout."* Only the proper care of his wounded prevented him from following up his "victory."[70] In later years, the general would sometimes speak of the battle as a defeat, blaming Royall, whom Crook commended for his conduct in his official report of the battle.[71] While refusing to label the battle a defeat, Sheridan wasn't fooled. In his annual report, reproduced in full in Appendix 13, he noted:

> *"The victory was barren of results, however, as, on account of his wounded and a lack of rations for his troops, General Crook was unable to pursue the enemy."*[72]

Barren of results indeed! Claiming 13 dead warriors abandoned on the field, and only the most modest army casualties of 10 killed, including one Shoshone scout, and one officer and twenty enlisted men wounded,[73] which represented 2.3% of his effective force, the "victorious" Crook found himself unable to either follow the "routed" enemy, establish surveillance over them, or make any offensive movements for seven weeks! Crook could rationalize, and the army could attempt to white–wash, all they wanted. The fact remains, with less than 3% of his force out of action, Crook's offensive was stopped dead in its tracks; a tactical defeat by the definition of any "civilized" army in world history. The nation's press, whose favor was assiduously courted by Crook, likewise was not fooled. An unknown correspondent for the *Helena Daily Independent* provided some scathing commentary in the June 30 edition of that publication:

> *". . . sent to Fetterman and this post (Laramie, DCE) for infantry, which makes it pretty plain that the Indians are too many for him. It is reported here that General Sheridan, to whom a report of the battle has been made, has refused the reinforcements and ordered Gen. Crook to advance.*

> *"The officers of the post speak in terms of unmeasured condemnation of Gen. Crook's behavior, and denounce his retreat in the face of the savage enemy as* **cowardly** . *(emphasis from the original)*

> *"It is also reported that the Crows refused to stay with Crook any longer, and have gone off in a body to Gibbon on the Yellowstone. They call Crook the 'Squaw Chief' and say he's afraid to fight.*

> *"The news of the battle brought consternation to the military here, and as the details of the affair become known, it is looked upon as humiliating and disgraceful to the last degree.*

> *"The idea of two regiments of American cavalry being stampeded by savages and having to* **rally behind** *friendly Indians is regarded as incredibly revolting to the pride and honor of the army." (emphasis from the original)*[74]

In the same edition, the *Independent* editorialized:

> *"It is now clearly evident that General Crook was not the man to be intrusted with the conduct of the military expeditions in the Powder River country. His disastrous defeat at the hands of Crazy Horse last winter (Reynolds Fight on Powder River, DCE), although variously reported at the time and toned down as much as possible left the general impression upon the country that want of proper management was at the bottom of the result.*

"The Independent claimed at the time and has repeatedly urged since that the expedition should have been instituted from the banks of the Yellowstone, and not from the frontiers of Wyoming. It should have been intrusted to General Gibbon, and not General Crook. Events now transpiring clearly demonstrate that we were right. His recent battle with the Sioux on the Rosebud, even if he obtained the victory he claims, is nothing more than a practical defeat, since his retreat leaves the country in the possession of the Indians and all of his work will have to be done over again. But this is not the worst. The driving the Indians into the Bad Lands gives them possession of fastnesses in which they are the most secure and in which the most protracted resistance can be made. The War, if possible, should have been prosecuted on the plains instead on in the hills.

"If Gibbon and Custer had been permitted to acquire possession of the Powder river country early in the spring, and advancing in the direction in which General Crook has come have taken the savages in front and rear at the same time, the war would long since have been over. But instead of this the plan of the campaign has been botched from the beginning. Crook has delayed for months after the others were ready, and in his eager desire to monopolize the honors of the campaign has suffered two defeats, both of which have been more or less disastrous.

"The result of these engagements is to embolden the Indians to more depredations and to render the whole stretch of country between the Yellowstone and the Platte river untenantable by white men. It is not two to one that Crook, despairing of success when he has encountered two defeats, will withdraw from the Rosebud with the same precipitation that he did last winter from the mountains, and surrender the country he was sent to render peaceful and safe to the murderous discipline of the scalping knife of the Sioux. The retreat ordered after the battle on the Rosebud justifies this impression. With three days rations in the knapsacks and supply trains within fifth miles he falls back for provisions. Attacked by the Indians, he maintains his ground just long enough to demonstrate his readiness to retreat. He may out–General the indolent Apache, but he is no match for the daring and aggressive Sioux." [75]

While Crook's troopers spent the night of June 17th burying their dead on the banks of the Rosebud, the Cheyenne hurried to their village to commence 4 days of victory celebrations including a renewal of the Sacred Hat Lodge. [76] Captain Mills echoed the true feelings of the command upon their return to their Goose Creek base: *"General Crook and all of us made very brief reports of the fight, having little pride in our accomplishment."* [77]

Unfortunately, Crook wasn't able to disguise the graves as well as he planned, for when Standing Bear, accompanied by other victorious Lakota returned two days after the battle, they disinterred, robbed and mutilated the soldier dead. [78]

Crook set out for Goose Creek on the 18th transporting some of the wounded on travois. Just prior to departure, the command observed three or four Lakota mourning their dead on the battlefield. [79] Crook arrived at Goose Creek on June 19, at which point the Shoshones departed, the Crow having left the night before.

Although he habitually complained to his staff about not receiving word from General Terry, Crook made no attempt to inform Terry of the vital information he posessed: [80] that the enemy was in much stronger force than previously believed and that they were fighting with unsuspected cohesion and tenacity. One of Crook's troopers noted of the battle: *"They were in front, rear, flanks, and on every hilltop, far and near. I had been in several Indian battles, but never saw so many Indians at one time before, . . . or so brave.*[81]

On June 21, while General Terry and his staff planned their offensive, Crook sent his wounded back to Fort Fetterman. Rather than rushing to re–enter the campaign after seeing to the care of his wounded, Crook, and most of the command spent the time between June 21 and August 3, when they did re–enter the campaign, hunting and fishing. In fact Crook was on a hunting expedition when Terry's couriers arrived to inform him of the Custer disaster.[82] Indeed Crook had not even bothered to request the re–inforcements he obviously felt were critical to resuming operations. His annual report lamely explained: *"Knowing as I do, from personal knowledge, the large numbers of Indians in other localities who require the restraining influence of troops, I have carefully refrained from embarrassing the division commander (Sheridan, DCE) by calls for re–inforcements. I have rather left that matter entirely to him, satisfied that he understood the necessities of the case, and would send me troops as fast and as early as he could get them.* ***I mention this simply from the fact that there has been much of an unpleasant nature said in regard to the matter****. (emphasis the author's)"* I suspect much of an unpleasant nature had indeed been said, especially by those who had no desire to turn the summer campaign into a gigantic picnic and who had knowledge of Sheridan's dispatches of June 19th urging Crook to strike.[83] When Sheridan renewed his order to *"Hit them again, and hit them harder!"* on July 10, Crook could only reply: *"I wish Sheridan would come out here himself and show us how to do it. It is rather difficult to surround three Indians with one soldier!"*[84]

Crook's world had been turned upside down. He fully appreciated the magnitude of his defeat; his offensive having ground to a halt. Obviously, his initial strategy of gobbling up isolated villages in turn disintegrated as he realized the enemy was concentrated in heretofore unimaginable force. The swiftness and savagery of the enemy assault had left him stunned, as at Cedar Creek. How could he best cope with this dilemma? He hadn't a clue! That, in my opinion, is the reason he hadn't wired for re–inforcements. He had no concept of how many he needed, or how, or where to apply them. Crook would reach the nadir of his apprehension and indecision when he reported to Sheridan on July 23rd:

"I find myself immeasurably embarrassed by the delay of Merritt's column . . . On Powder, Tongue, and Rosebud Rivers the whole country is on fire and filled with smoke. I am in constant dread of attack; in their last (of July 10) they set fire to the grass, but as much of it was still green, we extinguished it without difficulty; but should it be fired now, I don;t see how we could stay in the country. I am at a loss what to do . . . All indications are that the Sioux are in the Big Horn mountains, from which they can see clear to the Yellowstone and discern the approach of Terry's column . . . I don't think they will fight us combined, but will scatter . . . Should the Indians scatter unhurt, they would have greatly the advantage over us, as we would be obliged to divide accordingly, while their thorough knowledge of the country and rapidity of movement would enable them to concentrate on and destroy our small parties . . ."[85]

The forgoing illustrates how confused, disoriented, and uncertain Crook had become. He didn't feel he could surprise the enemy if they remained concentrated in a single massive village, and he certainly wanted no further part of a pitched battle with them on even terms. Further, if they scattered, he must divide his command in order to catch them. Once caught, he felt he'd have a "wildcat by the tail," with little chance for a successful conclusion. What should he do? Keep the troops concentrated, or divide into small independent units? Due to his indecision, Crook's was no longer an effective fighting force. Except for stumbling upon, and defeating, a small village at Slim Buttes in September, he was effectively out of the campaign for good.

The legacy of the Rosebud was the defeat of the Seventh Cavalry at the Little Big Horn. Already buoyed by Gibbon's obvious timidity, Lakota and Cheyenne morale soared with Crook's defeat. And still Sitting Bull's promise of "soldiers falling into camp" was unfulfilled! Clearly the warriors considered themselves invincible! Crook would also not even attempt to get critical information to Terry regarding the enemy force. While Crook knew there were more Indians in the village than the army had planned for, the warrior's rank would swell even further with the arrival of Gall's and Crow King's Uncpapa bands. In addition, Crook now knew the Indians would not be running from the army, they would be attacking with a new found cohesiveness and determination. Crook knew well the value of intelligence; at Antietam, he *"had to get a good many men killed"* when ordered to take a bridge of unknown location although Sturgis had assaulted it earlier in the day.[86] Even so, he left Terry and Custer to gather the vital intelligence he possessed without assistance. Perhaps Libbie Custer sensed the tragedy about to occur when she penned the letter her husband would never receive; it being returned unopened after his death:

"I cannot but feel the greatest apprehensions for you on this dangerous scout. Oh Autie, if you return without bad news the worst of the summer will be over.

*"The papers told last night of a small skirmish between General Crook's cavalry and the Indians. They called it a fight. The Indians were very bold. **They don't seem afraid of anything.** (emphasis the author's)"*[87]

---

[1] Sometimes referred to simply as Sitting Bull, this Oglala chief, signer of the Treaty of 1868, is not to be confused with the more famous Uncpapa of the same name.

[2] See John G. Bourke "On the Border With Crook" pages 286 – 287.

[3] See James C. Olson "Red Cloud and the Sioux Problem" page 217.

[4] See James C. Olson "Red Cloud and the Sioux Problem" page 218.

[5] See James C. Olson "Red Cloud and the Sioux Problem" page 219.

[6] See John G. Bourke "On the Border With Crook" pages 288 – 289.

[7] See J. W. Vaughn "With Crook at the Rosebud" page 8.

[8] See J. W. Vaughn "With Crook at the Rosebud" pages 10 – 11 and 199 – 212, Neil C. Mangum "Battle of the Rosebud: Prelude to the Little Bighorn" pages 26 – 27, John G. Bourke "On the Border With Crook" pages 289 – 290, and John M. Carroll "Roll Call on the Little Big Horn, 28 June 1876."

[9] See John M. Carroll "The Papers of the Order of Indian Wars" page 6 and J. W. Vaughn "With Crook at the Rosebud" page 13.

[10] See Neil C. Mangum "Battle of the Rosebud: Prelude to the Little Bighorn" page 28.

[11] See John G. Bourke "On the Border With Crook" pages 291.

[12] See Neil C. Mangum "Battle of the Rosebud: Prelude to the Little Bighorn" pages 32 – 33.

[13] See Neil C. Mangum "Battle of the Rosebud: Prelude to the Little Bighorn" page 34. In this barbaric act, Crook's troops were not alone. Gibbon's men had, and Custer's would, commit the same sacrilege during their marches.

[14] Note that although charges were preferred against Noyes for his conduct during Reynolds' attack on Old Bear's Cheyenne village, he, unlike Captain Moore, was allowed to accompany the expedition. This may indicate that the charges against Noyes were not considered serious by Crook.

[15] Note that Captain Alexander Moore was under arrest at Fort D. A. Russell for his actions in the Reynolds attack on Old Bear's Cheyenne village.

[16] See John G. Bourke "On The Border With Crook" page 293.

[17] See John G. Bourke "On The Border With Crook" page 293.

[18] See Neil C. Mangum "Battle of the Rosebud: Prelude to the Little Bighorn" page 36 and Thomas B. Marquis "Wooden Leg: A Warrior Who Fought Custer" pages 193 – 195.

[19] This was the party of Captain St. John. See John F. Finerty "War Path and Bivouac" pages 71 – 72. They had left a message inscribed on a board that was discovered by the detachment of Captain Van Vliet on the 29th of May and had sent the two messengers that arrived on June 4th.

[20] See John G. Bourke "On The Border With Crook" page 296.

[21] See Neil C. Mangum "Battle of the Rosebud: Prelude to the Little Bighorn" page 40.

[22] See Neil C. Mangum "Battle of the Rosebud: Prelude to the Little Bighorn" page 39.

[23] See Neil C. Mangum "Battle of the Rosebud: Prelude to the Little Bighorn" page 43.

[24] See John G. Bourke "On The Border With Crook" page 301.

[25] Major Chambers set about training 176 of his infantrymen to ride the mules. Frank Grouard recalled: *"I never saw so much fun in all my life. The valley for a mile in every direction was filled with bucking mules, frightened infantrymen, broken saddles and applauding spectators."* See Mark H. Brown "The Plainsmen of the Yellowstone" page 263.

[26] See John G. Bourke "On The Border With Crook" pages 302 – 303..

[27] Prior to commencing operations for the Tonto Basin Campaign, Crook had personally led his command on a "shakedown" march. It is possible he intended to repeat this procedure prior to commencing active operations in the summer campaign of '76. If this was the case, it would provide an explanation for Crook's lackadaisical approach to the march.

[28] See John G. Bourke "On The Border With Crook" page 306.

[29] See Neil C. Mangum "Battle of the Rosebud: Prelude to the Little Bighorn" page 47.

[30] See J. W. Vaughn "With Crook at the Rosebud" page 30.

[31] See J. W. Vaughn "With Crook at the Rosebud" pages 30 – 31.

[32] See Neil C. Mangum "Battle of the Rosebud: Prelude to the Little Bighorn" pages 47 – 48.

[33] See John G. Bourke "On The Border With Crook" pages 310 – 311.

[34] See Neil C. Mangum "Battle of the Rosebud: Prelude to the Little Bighorn" page 50.

[35] See J. W. Vaughn "With Crook at the Rosebud" page 31.

[36] The other members of Little Hawk's party were Yellow Eagle, Crooked Nose, Little Shield and White Bird. See Jerome A. Greene "Lakota and Cheyenne" page 24.

[37] See Mari Sandoz "Crazy Horse: The Strange Man of the Oglalas" page 315.

[38] See J. W. Vaughn "With Crook at the Rosebud" page 45.

[39] See J. W. Vaughn "With Crook at the Rosebud" pages 45 – 46 and Thomas B. Marquis "Wooden Leg: A Warrior Who Fought Custer: page 201. Vaughn lists Little Wolf as being in the battle, but this is obviously in error as his band did not reach the encampment until the afternoon of the Custer fight.

[40] See the account of Kills Eagle in Tom O'Neil "Indians At Greasy Grass" page 19.

[41] See Neil C. Mangum "Battle of the Rosebud: Prelude to the Little Bighorn" page 52. Finerty states that, due to the horses being tired from the previous day's 35 mile march, the troops were ordered to unsaddle and graze their horses. Captain Noyes, in his official report also states the troops were ordered to unsaddle. See John F. Finerty "War Path and Bivouac" page 126 and See Neil C. Mangum "Battle of the Rosebud: Prelude to the Little Bighorn" page 132.

[42] See J. W. Vaughn "With Crook at the Rosebud" page 48 and Martin F. Schmitt "General George Crook: His Autobiography" page 194.

[43] See J. W. Vaughn "With Crook at the Rosebud" pages 48 – 49.

[44] See George Bird Grinnell "The Fighting Cheyennes" page 333.

[45] See Wayne Michael Sarf "The Little Bighorn Campaign" page 92.

[46] See John F. Finerty "War Path and Bivouac" page 126.

[47] In his address on the Battle of the Rosebud to the 1917 annual meeting of the Order of Indian Wars, retired General Anson Mills was less than complementary of his former commander when he stated:

> *"General Crook had previously to do only with the semi-nomadic tribes, and from conversations with him I felt he did not realize the prowess of the Sioux, though it*

was hard to think that he was not well informed by his numerous guides, scouts and especially the 250 friendly Indians."

See John M. Carroll "The Papers of the Order of Indian Wars" pages 7 – 8.

[48] See John M. Carroll "The Papers of the Order of Indian Wars" page 14 and J. W. Vaughn "With Crook at the Rosebud" page 50.

[49] See S. L. A. Marshall "Crimsoned Prairie: The Indian Wars" page 128. Marshall ignores the experience of the Platte Bridge, Fetterman, Hayfield, and Wagon Box Fights.

[50] See John F. Finerty "War Path and Bivouac" pages 128 – 129.

[51] See Stanley Vestal "Warpath and Council Fire" pages 223 - 224.

[52] See Peter John Powell "People of the Sacred Mountain" page 954.

[53] See Peter John Powell "People of the Sacred Mountain" page 1366.

[54] See David Humphreys Miller "Custer's Fall: The Indian Side of the Story" page 63.

[55] See J. W. Vaughn "With Crook at the Rosebud" pages 99.

[56] See Paul Wellman "Indian Wars of the West" pages 135 – 136. Although he would lose the sight of one eye, Henry survived to retire as a Brigadier General in 1898.

[57] Se John F. Finerty "War Path and Bivouac" page 133.

[58] See Neil C. Mangum "Battle of the Rosebud: Prelude to the Little Bighorn" page 82.

[59] See W. F. Beyer and O. F. Keydel "Acts of Bravery" pages 207 and 210.

[60] See Stanley Vestal "Warpath and Council Fire" pages 229 - 230.

[61] See Cyrus Townshend Brady "The Sioux Indian Wars" pages 206 – 208.

[62] See John Stands In Timber and Margot Liberty "Cheyenne Memories" page 188.

[63] See John Stands In Timber and Margot Liberty "Cheyenne Memories" pages 189 – 190.

[64] See Peter John Powell "People of the Sacred Mountain" page 998.

[65] See George Bird Grinnell "The Fighting Cheyennes" page 336.

[66] See George Bird Grinnell "The Fighting Cheyennes" page 336.

[67] See Neil C. Mangum "Battle of the Rosebud: Prelude to the Little Bighorn" page 83.

[68] See John M. Carroll "The Papers of the Order of Indian Wars" page 10.

[69] See Fred H. Werner "Before the Little Big Horn" page 29.

[70] Had Crook been as zealous of pursuing the Indians as his report indicated, he could have returned to his base camp on Goose Creek, replenished his supplies, rested for 24 hours, and still have had time to unite with Custer prior to June 25.

[71] See Martin F. Schmitt "General George Crook: His Autobiography" page 196. Crook maintained his defeat at the Rosebud was due to the failure of Nickerson and Royall to follow his orders to concentrate the cavalry and charge the Indians in his front. Again, this appears to be solely a self serving argument. Crook showed no compunction about court–martialing Colonel Reynolds after the Powder River debacle. He would certainly have court–martialed Nickerson and Royall if they had repeatedly failed to follow his orders. It should also be noted that Captain Henry's recollection of the Royall – Crook controversy supported Royall.

[72] See John M. Carroll "General Custer and the Battle of the Little Big Horn: The Federal View" page 74.

[73] This omits 4 Crow and 2 Shoshone scouts wounded in the action. See John M. Carroll "The Papers of the Order of Indian Wars" page 16. Bourke, Cook's Aide–de–Camp believed that the soldiers suffered 57 casualties. See John G. Bourke "On The Border With Crook" page 315.

[74] See J. W. Vaughn "With Crook At The Rosebud" page 160.

[75] See J. W. Vaughn "With Crook At The Rosebud" pages 161 - 162.

[76] Powell believes this was partially done to reconcile two warrior societies, the Elkhorn Scrapers and the Kit Foxes, who had become bitter rivals. See Peter John Powell "People of the Sacred Mountain" page 999.

[77] See "Great Western Indian Fights" page 233.

[78] See John G. Neihardt "Black Elk Speaks" page 104 and Raymond J. DeMallie "The Sixth Grandfather" page 177.

[79] See John G. Bourke "On The Border With Crook" page 317. John Stands In Timber notes that one Lakota was so grief stricken over the loss of his brother that he took a suicide vow and was killed in the Custer fight eight days later. Although the names of the two Lakota brothers are not recalled by the Cheyenne, the warrior taking the suicide vow may have been the Sans Arc Long Road who was killed almost within Reno's lines on June 26. See "Cheyenne Memories" page 186.

[80] See John S. Gray "Centennial Campaign" page 201.

[81] See Stephen E. Ambrose "Crazy Horse and Custer" page 421.

[82] See John G. Bourke "On the Border With Crook" page 319.

[83] See Martin F. Schmitt "General George Crook: His Autobiography" page 197.

[84] See John F. Finerty "War Path and Bivouac" pages 197 – 198.

85 See John S. Gray "Centennial Campaign" page 205.

86 See Martin F. Schmitt "General George Crook: His Autobiography" pages 97 – 98.

87 See Marguerite Merington "The Custer Story: The Life and Intimate Letters of General George A. Custer and His Wife Elizabeth" page 303.

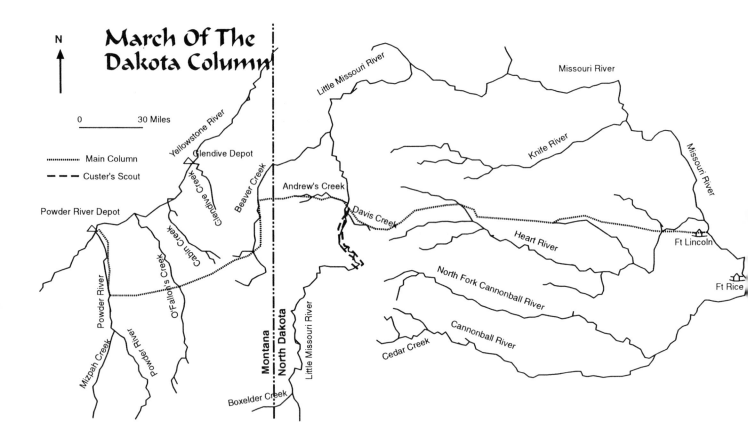

Chapter 8

The March of the Dakota Column

With the severe Dakota winter and Belknap hearings finally behind them, Terry and Custer made final preparations for the departure of the Dakota Column. Arriving at Fort Abraham Lincoln[1] on the evening of May 10, Terry assumed command of the expedition on the 14th. He advised Sheridan of his current planning and prospects for the campaign in a May 15th letter:

> *"Information from several independent sources seems to establish the fact that the Sioux are collected in camps on the Little Missouri and between that and the Powder River. I have already ordered Colonel Gibbon to move eastward and suggest that it would be very desirable for General Crook's column to move up as soon as possible. It is represented that they have 1500 lodges, are confident, and intend to make a stand. Should they do so, and should the three columns be able to act simultaneously, I should expect great success. We start tomorrow morning."[2]*

A great deal remained to be accomplished, and everyone pitched in with renewed vigor to expedite the departure. Correspondent Mark Kellogg noted the flurry of activity in his last dispatch prior to departure:

> *"General George A. Custer, dressed in a dashing suit of buckskin, is prominent everywhere. Here, there, flitting to and fro in his quick, eager way, taking in everything connected with his command as well as generally, with the keen, incisive manner for which he is so well known. The General is full of perfect readiness for the fray with the hostile red devils and woe to the body of scalp hunters that comes within reach of himself and brave companions in arms."[3]*

The command being in readiness, Custer attended to some personal details. Both Custer, whose hairline was beginning to recede rather severely, and Varnum had cropped their hair close on the eve of departure.[4] Custer's final act was one of contrition. Libbie Custer describes the scene:

> *"A day before the expedition started, General Terry was in our house alone with Autie (the General's pet name). A's thoughts were calm, deliberate, and solemn. He had been terribly hurt in Washington. General Terry had applied for him to command the expedition. He was returned to his regiment because General Terry had applied for him. I know that he (Custer) felt tenderly and affectionately toward him. On that day he hunted me out in the house and brought me into the living-room, not telling me why. He shut the door, and very seriously and impressively said: 'General Terry, a man usually means what he says when he brings his wife to listen to his statements. I want to say that reports are circulating that I do not want to go out to the campaign under you.' (I supposed that he meant, having been given the command before, he was unwilling to be a subordinate.) 'But I want you to know that I do want to go and serve under you, not only that I value you as a soldier, but as a friend and a man.' The exact words were the strongest kind of a declaration that he wished him to know he wanted to serve under him."[5]*

It is difficult to know what to make of this little scene. The staging and theatrics are pure Custer, but the need to quash rumors is not in character. Perhaps, given his recent rebuke in Washington, we should take it on face value; Custer had had enough of rumor and innuendo and wanted to make sure he was getting off on the right foot with his new commander. If this is the case, Custer's strategy may have backfired as some authorities, Roger Darling for one, believe the incident served to make Terry more wary and critical of Custer. In any event, Terry, like most commanders who had Custer as a subordinate, would have some difficulties with Custer during the march to the junction with Gibbon's column. Terry's diary complains of Custer's penchant for playing *"wagonmaster"* and his once leaving the column in an attempt to find a better trail *"without any authority whatever."*[6] This last may indicate a hint of jealousy on Terry's part as his own path finding abilities, which he would exercise on the Montana Column's march to the confluence of the Big Horn and Little Big Horn Rivers, would prove woefully inadequate.

There was to be one final delay, due to weather. Explaining this latest delay to Sheridan via telegram on May 16, Terry took the opportunity to amplify his request to have Crook started early:

> *"The storm was very severe yesterday, making the plain below the post on which we are encamped almost impossible for wagons loaded as ours are. It has not rained now since sunrise and I am very confident that we shall be able to pull out and make a short march tomorrow. I have no doubt of the ability of my column to whip all the Sioux whom we can find. I suggest Crook's immediate movement with the idea that if he moved up he would force them toward us and enable us to get at them more easily."*[7]

Sheridan, perhaps recalling this would be Terry's first Indian campaign, and realizing the difficulty in coordinating operations, wired his response the same day:

> *"I will hurry up Crook, but you must rely on the ability of your own column for your best success. I believe it to be fully equal to all the Sioux which can be brought against it, and only hope they will hold fast to meet it. Keep me as well posted as you can, and depend upon my full assistance in every respect. You know the impossibility of any large number of Indians keeping together as a hostile body for even one week."*[8]

The first part of the message contains a restatement of Sheridan's campaign strategy, proven successful in the Washita and Red River War Campaigns: operate three independent columns, each sufficiently strong to defeat the enemy force anticipated, in a relatively compact area. As long as the enemy "held fast," there could be no question of the ultimate victory. The only concern given consideration by the military was the possibility of the enemy escaping. The last line indicates it was Sheridan's opinion that the largest force with which the troops would have to contend would be the contemplated 300 – 400 lodges containing a maximum of 800 warriors. Any larger force that was discovered would undoubtedly disintegrate, for logistical reasons, before their might could be brought to bear against the troops. This view, representing the conventional wisdom of the times, proved to be disastrously incorrect.

The expedition was certainly a formidable one. It consisted of twelve companies of the Seventh Cavalry,[9] commanded by Lieutenant Colonel George Armstrong Custer, two companies of the Seventeenth Infantry, one company of the Sixth Infantry, a platoon of gatling guns,[10] guides, interpreters, and a contingent of Arikara scouts.[11] The wagon train was composed of 114 six–mule wagons, 37 two–horse wagons, 70 other vehicles including ambulances, and 85 pack mules.[12] The Organization of the expedition is presented in Table 8 – 1.[13]

Much has been made of the fact that correspondent Mark Kellogg accompanied the expedition, dying with Custer at the Little Big Horn, despite General of the Army William T. Sherman's May 8 order that Custer not take any newspapermen *"who always make trouble"* along. This fact is typically cited as verification that Custer was prone to disobey orders. Clement A. Lounsberry, editor of the *Bismarck Tribune,* who was to have accompanied the expedition but sent Kellogg as a last minute replacement, maintained that General Terry, not Custer, authorized Kellogg's participation. [14] Since General Crook took five reporters into the field for the summer campaign, it is obvious that Sherman's order was targeted solely at Custer, probably for the statements published in the *Herald* regarding the Belknap affair. In any event, Sherman's May 8 order was to Terry, not Custer, so if there is any question about violation of orders it rests with Terry, and not with Custer.

While the 7th Cavalry was an impressive force, comprised of 32 officers and 720 men, when it left Fort Lincoln, there were problems within the regiment. Although cavalry companies were allowed 70 enlisted men in 1876,[15] they were seldom fully staffed. Table 8 – 1 shows that the 7th's companies ranged in size from 47 (Benteen's H) to 66 (McDougall's B). Perhaps more damaging than the 135 "missing" troopers authorized by regulation, was the absence of some of the more experienced officers. Thirteen officers,[16] 2 of the 3 majors, 4 captains, and 7 lieutenants were not with the regiment when it marched to the Yellowstone.[17] Custer had requested Major Lewis Merrill, an experienced Indian fighter on duty with the centennial commission in Philadelphia, accompany the expedition. The request, initially granted, was subsequently revoked by President Grant. [18]

This loss of senior officers was compounded by the movement of officers within the regiment to fill the company vacancies. Lieutenant Charles DeRudio, who should have commanded E Troop, [19] was ordered to "switch places" with Lieutenant Smith of A; Second Lieutenant Jack Sturgis, son of the commanding officer, was reassigned from Troop M to E; First Lieutenant James Calhoun, of C Troop, and an officer from the Twentieth Infantry, Second Lieutenant John J. Crittenden, were assigned to Troop L. With Tom Custer detailed to his brother's staff, 5 of the 12 companies, including three of the five that would die with Custer, were not led by their regular commander. While a case can be made that Company L's commander, Captain Michael V. Sheridan, being habitually assigned to his brother's staff, constituted no true loss, it must be remembered that none of the officers regularly assigned to L were present at the Little Big Horn. [20] While there was some time on the march from Fort Lincoln for the officers and men to get acquainted, they had never trained nor fought together. I believe this resulted in reduced performance on the part of some companies at the Little Big Horn.

There has been some question about the regiment's reputation as an Indian fighting unit.[21] The 7th was a fine outfit, as even notorious custerphobe Frederick Van de Water had to admit: *"He (Custer, DCE) never ceased his remedial pounding and at last he made the 7th Cavalry, in drill at least, the best horse soldiers on the plains."*[22] This sentiment is echoed by Captain Charles King, 5th Cavalry, who recalled:

> *"Each company as it comes forward opens out like the fan of a practiced coquette and a sheaf of skirmishers is launched to the front. Something in the snap and style of the whole movement stamps them at once. There is no need of fluttering guidons and stirring trumpet calls to identify them. I know the 7th Cavalry at a glance."*[23]

Element	Officers	Enlisted
Department Headquarters – General Alfred H. Terry	10	0
Adjutant – Captain Edward Worthington Smith, 18th Inf		
Quartermaster – 1st Lieutenant Henry James Nowlan, 7th Cav		
Acting Commissary of Subsistence – 2nd Lieutenant Richard Edward Thompson, 6th Inf		
Engineer Officer – 1st Lieutenant Edward Maguire		
Ordnance Officer – Captain Otho Ernest Michaelis		
Chief Medical Officer – Captain John Winfield Williams, 7th Cav		
Aid-de-Camp – Captain Robert Patterson Hughes, 3rd Inf 1st Lieutenant Eugene Beauharnais Gibbs, 6th Inf		
Veterinary Surgeon – C. A. Stein		
Battalion 6th Infantry – Major Orlando Hurley Moore	1	0
Company C, 6th Infantry – Captain James William Powell, Jr., 2nd Lieutenant Bernard Albert Byrne	2	46
Company D, 6th Infantry – Captain Daniel Hamilton Murdock, 1st Lieutenant Frederick William Thibaut	2	39
Company I, 6th Infantry – 2nd Lt. George Branton Walker	1	39
Gatling gun battery – 2nd Lt. William Hale Low, Jr. 2nd Lt. Frank Xavier Kinzie	2	32
Company B, 6th Infantry – Captain Stephen Baker, 1st Lieutenant John Carland	2	40
Company C, 17th Infantry – Captain Malcolm McArthur, 1st Lieutenant Frank Dillon Garretty, 2nd Lieutenant James Dallas Nickerson	3	50
Company G, 17th Infantry – Captain Louis H. Sanger, 1st Lieutenant Josiah Chance, 2nd Lieutenant Henry Perrine Walker	3	45
7th Cavalry Staff – Lieutenant Colonel George Armstrong Custer Major Marcus Albert Reno Adjutant – 1st Lieutenant William Winer Cooke	3	4
Company A, 7th Cavalry – Captain Myles Moylan, 1st Lieutenant Charles Camilus DeRudio	2	53
Company B, 7th Cavalry – Captain Thomas M. McDougall, 2nd Lieutenant Benjamin Hubert Hodgson	2	66
Company C, 7th Cavalry – Captain Thomas W. Custer,[24] 2nd Lieutenant Henry Moore Harrington	2	61
Company D, 7th Cavalry – Captain Thomas B. Weir, 2nd Lieutenant Winfield Scott Edgerly	2	61
Company E, 7th Cavalry – 1st Lt. Algernon E. Smith, 2nd Lieutenant James Garland Sturgis	2	53
Company F, 7th Cavalry – Captain George W. Yates, 2nd Lieutenant William Van Wyck Reily	2	60
Company G, 7th Cavalry – 1st Lt. Donald McIntosh, 2nd Lieutenant George Daniel Wallace	2	60
Company H, 7th Cavalry – Captain Frederick W. Benteen, 1st Lieutenant Francis Marion Gibson	2	47
Company I, 7th Cavalry – Captain Myles W. Keogh, 1st Lieutenant James Ezekiel Porter	2	54
Company K, 7th Cavalry – 1st Lt. Edward S. Godfrey, 2nd Lieutenant Luther Rector Hare	2	63
Company L, 7th Cavalry – 1st Lt. James Calhoun, 2nd Lieutenant John Jordan Crittenden	2	64
Company M, 7th Cavalry – Captain Thomas H. French, 1st Lieutenant Edward Gustave Mathey	2	60
Indian Scouts – 2nd Lt. Charles Albert Varnum[25]	1	37
Band	0	14
Civilians, Guides, Interpreters	0	6[26]
Medical Corp – Elbert J. Clark, James Madison DeWolf	2[27]	0
Totals	**56**	**1058**

Table 8 – 1 Composition of the Dakota Column

Appendix 17 provides a complete list of all 7th Cavalry actions against Indians, a list of engagements between the U. S. Army and Indians resulting in more than 20 casualties, total casualties in engagements with Indians on the plains, total engagements with Indians for each cavalry regiment for the entire Indian war period as well as the period from July 1866 through June 1876, and a list of field grade, major and up, officers killed during the Indian Wars. The data show, at the time of the Little Big Horn, 7 of the nation's 10 cavalry regiments had participated in more engagements with Indians than the 7th Cavalry. While most of these actions were minor in scope, typically involving no more than a single company, the 7th itself had been involved in only three major actions, one offensive, the Washita, and two defensive, August 4 and 11 during the Stanley Expedition of 1873; clearly not an extensive record of victory over Indians. While the data indicate that there is some room for argument as to which was the frontier army's "best" regiment, Indian fighting experience, or lack thereof, was not a factor at the Little Big Horn. [28] As a final note, although Custer's personal experience with Indians was not extensive, he had "done it all": a successful offensive action, successful defensive actions, and a too little recognized diplomatic action in securing the release of white captives Mrs. Anna Belle Morgan and Miss Sara C. White. In terms of breadth of experience with Indians, Custer had no peer.

Appendix 11 lists the participation of 7th Cavalry officers, present at the Little Big Horn, in the regiment's major campaigns. The data show that while Myles Keogh was a thoroughly experienced officer, neither he, nor First Lieutenant James Porter, had participated in any of the regiment's major conflicts. While I have seen no evidence to indicate this posed a problem for Company I at the Little Big Horn, the same cannot be said for C Troop. With the reassignment of the company's captain, Tom Custer, and First Lieutenant, James Calhoun, C was left with only one officer, the relatively inexperienced Second Lieutenant Henry Moore Harrington. As will be shown in Chapter 9, Harrington harbored some very morbid thoughts about the campaign. When his mental state is considered within the context of his inexperience, we have a possible explanation for the poor performance of Company C; a major factor in turning a check into disaster.

A corollary to the question of inexperience is that of the number of recruits contained in the various companies. While Lieutenant Godfrey apparently believed in his later years that inexperience of the troopers was *"...an important factor in the defeat"*,[29] it is apparent that the 7th had no higher percentage of recruits than was the norm for the period.[30] In any event, as most of the recruits were left behind at the Powder River depot, the number of recruits was not a contributing factor in the defeat of the 7th.

Perhaps the major problem within the regiment was the schism among the officers. As the 7th marched out of Fort Lincoln, many of the officers harbored a grudge against their commander. Many authorities believe the 7th was split into pro and anti– Custer factions with *"McDougall and Godfrey, and possibly Gibson"* regarded as neutral.[31] I have been unable to come up with concrete evidence of a major split among the officers. I will present only the instances of factionalism I have been able to gather, and not the opinion of others.

As has already been noted, Lieutenant DeRudio was smarting under his reassignment. Rather than command Company E, by his right of seniority, he would be compelled to serve under Captain Moylan, an officer he disliked.[32] While there is no evidence of deep seated dislike between Reno and Custer, Reno had cause to question his relationship with his commander, and was probably beginning to mistrust Custer. During Custer's spring absence, Reno had discharged interpreter Frederick F. Girard[33] and drafted a complaint against Captain Weir for insubordination.[34] Upon his return, Custer rehired Girard and dismissed the complaint against Weir.

Godfrey shared Weir's dislike for Reno. The August 14, 1876, entry in Godfrey's field diary is instructive:

> *"Maj. Reno has been playing 'ass' right along and is so taken up with his own importance that he thinks he can 'snip' everybody and comment on the orders he receives from Genl Terry's Hdqurs. and insult his staff, so there is not any one the personal staff on speaking terms."* [35]

> *" I under stand that he (Terry, DCE) has said if he had not so much respect for the officers of the Regt. he would put some other field officer on duty with the Regt. It seems that Reno's self important rudeness makes him unbearable."* [36]

Clearly the most grievous schism involved the senior captain of the regiment, Frederick Benteen. Benteen, who typically resented his commanding officers (including Major Joel Elliott at the Washita and Colonel Samuel D. Sturgis during the Nez Perce campaign), had an especial dislike for Custer that, rather than subsiding with the passage of time, ripened into an obsessive hatred after Custer's death. While the reasons for this hatred remained hidden from his family,[37] they will be explored in detail within the context of Benteen's testimony at the Reno Court of Inquiry. Whenever the opportunity presented itself, Benteen never failed to impugn Custer's character. A case in point is Benteen's testimony at Custer's court–martial relating to the shooting of deserters, an event that Benteen did not witness:

> *"It was like a Buffalo Hunt. The dismounted deserters were shot down, while begging for their lives, by General Custer's executioners: Major Elliott (sic), Lieutenant Tom Custer, and the executioner-in-chief, Lieutenant Cooke. . ."* [38]

Another case in point is Benteen's commentary on the suicide of Major Wyckliff Cooper:

> *"Major Cooper was out of whiskey when he shot himself because that damned fool Dr. Coates, acting under orders from Custer, wouldn't even give him a drink to straighten out on."* [39]

Benteen's notorious Washita article has been discussed in Chapter 1, and his exchange with Custer along the Yellowstone will be discussed in Chapter 10.

What of Custer's role in this schism? Custer's meteoric rise in rank during the Civil War had robbed him of some important seasoning. He had advanced directly from staff officer to General. It was one thing to plan and execute the grand strategy of a campaign, but quite another to forge the alliances required for successful command of small tactical units. During the Civil War, victory piled upon victory was sufficient to win the loyalty and admiration of his officers and troops; for the lonely monotony of frontier service, it was not. On the frontier, Custer's lack of command experience at the platoon and company levels caused him grief on more than one occasion. He was unable to see this shortcoming himself, believing himself admired by all his subordinates. His letter to Libbie concerning garrisoning Fort Lincoln demonstrates:

> *"Our location for next winter is settled. We shall be at Fort Lincoln, and the decision is satisfactory to me. I presume you wish you were here to give the lieutenant–colonel of the battalion (a reference to himself, DCE) a little advice as to what companies shall be designated for each station. So far as this reason alone is concerned, I am glad that you are not here, as I not only would not wish you to attempt to influence such a decision, but that no person or persons might have just*

ground for imagining that you had done so. The officers are hinting strongly in the endeavor to ascertain 'Who goes where?' but thus far none are any the wiser, for the simple reason that I have not decided the matter yet in the case of a single troop.

*"It is a delicate, and in some respects an undesirable task, as **all, so far as I know, desire to go to Fort Lincoln.** (emphasis the author's)"[40]*

Ignoring the factionalism did not cause it to go away. This element would have an effect on the decisions made by Custer as well as the performance of Reno, Benteen, and Weir.

Godfrey describes the departure from Fort Lincoln:

"On the 17th day of May, at 5 A.M., the 'general' (bugle call to take down tents and break camp, DCE) was sounded, the wagons were packed and sent to the Quartermaster, and by six o'clock, the wagon-train was on the road escorted by the infantry. By seven o'clock the 7th Cavalry was marching in column of platoon around the parade-ground of Fort Lincoln, headed by the band playing 'Garry Owen,' the Seventh's battle tune, first used when the regiment charged at the battle of Washita. The column was halted and dismounted just outside the garrison. The officers and married men were permitted to leave the ranks to say 'good-by' to their families. General Terry, knowing the anxiety of the ladies, had assented to, or ordered, this demonstration, in order to allay their fears and satisfy them, by the formidable appearance we made, that we were able to cope with any enemy that we might expect to meet. Not many came out to witness the pageant, but many tear-filled eyes looked from the windows.

"During this halt the wagon-train was assembled on the plateau west of the post and formed in column of fours. When it started off the 'assembly' was sounded and absentees joined their commands. The signals 'Mount' and 'Forward' were sounded, and the regiment marched away, the band playing 'The girl I left behind me.'"[41]

Private Theodore W. Goldin provided additional detail on this leave taking:

". . . A few hundred yards further along and we approached the 'Barracks' as we called the quarters of the laundresses and married enlisted men, and it was here the first real partings took place. Close beside the roadway were clustered the wives and little ones of many a trooper, some of the women holding up little babes for a last farewell to 'daddy.' Once or twice I saw bronzed troopers reach out, catch the little ones in their arms and clasp them close, then pass them back to the wife and mother who had kept pace with the moving column. Now and again some trooper would rein out of line, bend low in his saddle for a farewell hand clasp and kiss. To all these somewhat unmilitary actions the officers were kindly oblivious. . .

". . . All at once the music changed. What possessed that band master I never knew, but at his signal the band broke into the wailing notes of 'The Girl I Left Behind Me.' That was too much for the bravest women, and one and all with tear-bedewed cheeks, they hurried inside, closed the doors behind them, and many a gallant officer had looked his last on the face of her he loved better than life itself. It was all over now."[42]

It is small wonder there were few dry eyes in the garrison at the conclusion of the first verse:

"The hour was sad I left the maid,
    A ling'ring farewell taking;
Her sighs and tears my steps delay'd –
    I thought her heart was breaking.
In hurried words her name I bless'd,
    I breathed the vows that bind me,
And to my heart in anguish press'd
    The girl I left behind me."[43]

The last verse, however, probably expressed the credo of the regiment and its commander:

"The hope of final victory
    Within my bosom burning,
Is mingling with sweet thoughts of thee
    And of my fond returning.
But should I ne'er return again,
    Still worth thy love thou'lt find me;
Dishonor's breath shall never stain
    The name I'll leave behind me."[44]

Although the last verse sent the troops off with bouyed spirits, the feeling was not universally held, as the Arikara scouts took the occasion to sing their death songs rather than their war songs.[45] As the morning fog lifted, a mirage was produced so that the line of troops and wagons seemed to march both on the earth and in the sky. Surprised and delighted, Libbie Custer remarked *"How beautiful and how strange!"* to sister–in–law Maggie Calhoun waiting beside her.[46] Later, Libbie and most of the women, would consider the sight an omen of impending doom. Miles Keogh may have had a premonition of disaster prior to embarking on this, his first major campaign with the Seventh Cavalry. He wrote long time friend Nelly Martin:

"We leave Monday on an Indian expedition and if I ever return I will go on and see you all. I have requested to be packed up and shipped to Auburn (Auburn New York, the Martin family home, DCE) in case I am killed, and I desire to be buried there. God bless you all, remember if I should die – you may believe that I love you and every member of your family – it was a second home to me."[47]

For the march, the regiment was divided into two wings; the wings being subdivided into two battalions of three companies each.[48] The right wing, commanded by Major Reno, was comprised of the battalions of Captains Keogh (companies B, C, and I) and Yates (companies E, F, and L); the left wing, commanded by Captain Benteen, was comprised of the battalions of Captains Weir (companies A, D, and H) and French (companies G, K, and M).[49]

The first day's march covered about twelve miles,[50] the troops going into camp on the Heart River at 1:30 P.M. The camp afforded good grass with an abundant supply of wood, water, and rattlesnakes. Richard A. Roberts, Captain Yates' brother–in–law, claimed that he and Autie Reed, nephew of the Custers, killed 9 of the reptiles at this camp.[51] The men were paid their three months back wages in this camp by the paymaster, Major William Smith.[52] Smith had been instructed by Terry[53] to accompany the column, rather than pay the troops at Fort Lincoln, as he feared the temptations of the saloons and bawdy houses of Bismarck would be too great for the men to resist, resulting in desertions and unnecessary delays.

On the morning of the 18th, Libbie Custer and Margaret Custer Calhoun, who had been allowed to accompany the column on the first day's march, prepared to return to Fort Lincoln with the paymaster's party. Custer's striker, John Burkman, described the farewell:

""Next mornin' the General sent Miss Libby back to Fort Lincoln with scouts and the paymaster from the boat to protect her. I was standin' holdin' her horse ready to help her mount. Even now, arter all these years, it brings a lump into my throat, rememberin' how she clung to Custer at the last, her arms tight 'round his neck, and how she cried. She want one to take on usually but seemed like she jist couldn't go back and leave him that day. Thar was tears in his eyes too and he kept tellin' her she was a soldier's wife, she must be a brave little woman, soon he'd be back and then we'd all have good times at Fort Lincoln agin.

". . .Then we stood watchin' her ride away across the prairie, the General and me. She looked so little and so young and she was leanin' way over with her head bent and we knowed she was cryin'. We watched till she was jist a speck way off on the plains.

"Custer's face went white and he was awful sober. 'A good soldier,' he said, low and quiet, 'has to serve two mistresses. Whilst he's loyal to one the other must suffer.'"[54]

Libbie, not daring to look back, repeated a line of poetry to herself:

> There's something in the parting hour
>   Will chill the warmest heart;
> Yet kindred, comrades, lovers, friends
>   Are fated all to part.
> But this I've seen, and many a pang
>   Has pressed it on my mind –
> The one who goes is happier
>   Than he who stays behind.[55]

After her return to Fort Lincoln, Libbie would write:

"With my husband's departure, my last happy days in garrison were ended; as a premonition of disaster that I had never known before weighed me down. I could not shake off the baleful influence of depressing thoughts. This presentiment and suspense, such as I had never known, made me selfish; and I shut into my heart the most uncontrollable anxiety, and could lighten no one else's burden. The occupations of other summers could not even give temporary interest."[56]

The second day's march proved extremely difficult due to the amount of corduroying required on the slippery banks of the Heart. The command went into camp at 2 P.M. having covered a distance of only eleven miles. Godfrey described the order of march after the first day as follows:

". . . one battalion was advance-guard, one was rear-guard, and one marched on each flank of the train. General Custer, with one troop of the advance-guard, went

ahead and selected the route for the train and the camping–places at the end of the day's march. The other two troops of the advance–guard reported at headquarters for pioneer or fatigue duty, to build bridges and creek crossings."[57]

In line of march, after the advance–guard came General Terry and the headquarters staff with a company of infantry, next the battalion of gatling guns followed by the wagon train, four wagons abreast with an infantry company at each end. One wagon was assigned to each troop for the transport of five day's' rations and forage. The beef herd and remuda were driven alongside the wagons. Last in line came the cavalry battalion assigned as rear–guard.[58]

Camps were typically arranged in the form of a parallelogram. The cavalry wings camped on the "long" sides facing each other, with the headquarters and guard located on the end nearest water and the wagon train and infantry battalion on the far side.

In order to break the monotony of the regular military routine, and to improve marksmanship, hunting was allowed. This served not only to provide fresh meat, prolonging the longevity of the beef herd, but to enrich the hunters who were allowed to sell their bounty. Ree scouts Strikes Two and Goose claimed to have earned $200 and $128 respectively from their prowess, charging $2 for the hind quarters of a deer and $1 for the front quarter, back or saddle.[59]

During a particularly difficult portion of the march, Custer determined that a little music might cheer the troopers engaged in the pioneer duty of clearing a road. Sending the sergeant major of the regiment, William H. Sharrow, to deliver his order, Custer was amused when informed that many of the instruments were "out of order" and the band couldn't play. Custer had the band marched to the pioneer wagons and received the explanation of Chief Musician Felix Villiet Vinatieri in person: *"General, many of ze instrument she is out of ordair, and ze museek she cannot make."* Custer then turned to the officer in charge of the pioneer wagons and stated: *"Lieutenant, if you have any picks, shovels and axes that are not out of 'ordair,' see that everyone of these men are properly equipped and find a place where they can work."* As private Goldin noted: *". . . all the rest of that damp, hot, muggy afternoon those lily-fingered bandsmen, band master and all, under the direction of an Irish sergeant, worked as some of them had never worked before, and came into camp with lame backs, blistered hands and mosquito bitten faces. The cure was, however, effective, and from that afternoon on, whenever they saw the head of the column diverge from the trail for the customary hourly breathing spell, those bandsmen would tune up and nearly blow their lungs out."[60]*

Nothing was ever truly dull with the Custer Clan in attendance, and the march from Fort Lincoln was no exception. Consummate practical jokers, the Custers gave as good as they got. Two incidents of the march are recounted by Roberts:

"All the Custers were fond of a good practical joke, and often attempted them on each other. One day the General, Tom Custer and his bosom friend, Col. Cooke (Cook's brevet rank. At the Little Big Horn Cooke was a First Lieutenant, DCE), thought they would play a joke on 'Boss' Custer, their youngest brother who was with the expedition.

"Boss often used to stray away from the column and hunt on his own hook, so they resolved to give him a surprise and at last reaching favorable ground they put their joke into execution, which was this, to follow Boston at a distance (disguised as Indians) and then when they had gotten him away to suddenly jump up from behind a 'divide' or low hill in the prairie and act like Indians and see if Boss

would turn tail and make a break for the column or see what he would do. Well, they found out. Just as soon as Boss heard them he dismounted, picketed his horse, stamping the lariat pin into the ground, and lay down flat on the ground and opened fire and kept it up so rapidly that the conspirators had to turn tail themselves and finally make signals to Boss who they were.

"It was evident that Boss was made out of the same grit and nerve as his brothers, and no more practical jokes were played on him.

"Another joke played by one of the Custers (Col. Tom) (again this is a brevet rank, Tom Custer was a captain at the Little Big Horn, DCE) was this: A large piece of spongy looking rock was found by one of them, and handing it to one of the young lieutenants (Second Lieutenant John Crittenden, DCE), told him that if he would soak it in water twice a day for two weeks he would have at the end of that time an elegant sponge, and it would be doubly valuable as a souvenir.

"The susceptible young man carried this rock strapped to his saddle bags and faithfully carried out the programme for at least a week, when he came to the practical joker and said that he could not notice that the sponge was getting any softer, and that he guessed he had not gotten a good piece. 'Not at all', said Tom Custer. 'You just mix some salt in a bucket each night and it will be all right.'

"Well the boy even tried that before he found out he was being played upon. I will drop the subject the same as the Lieutenant did the sponge stone."[61]

While the march was difficult due to bad weather,[62] nothing of import occurred until May 23rd. Early that morning, while chasing an elk in advance of the column, Custer came upon a fresh–burning campfire, and at dusk, Indians were observed watching the troops from a bluff about three miles away. The command was halted, after a march of only eight miles, while the country ahead was thoroughly scouted. While no further signs were detected, it was clear that the column was under observation.[63]

A curious incident, that fueled one of the seemingly infinite controversies associated with the Little Big Horn, occurred during the march and will be related at this juncture. During one of Custer's nocturnal visits to the Arikara camp he told them through the interpreter Girard:

"When we return, I will go back to Washington, and on my trip to Washington I shall take my brother here, Bloody Knife, with me. I shall remain at Washington and be the Great Father. But my brother, Bloody Knife, will return, and when he arrives home he shall have a fine house built for him, and those of you present will be the ones appointed to look after the work that will be placed in charge of Bloody Knife. You will have positions under him to help in what he is to do and you can, when you wish to speak with me or send me word, gather at Bloody Knife's house and decide what the message will be. Then he will send it to me. He will be given the whole tribe of the Arikara to be the head of. I will have papers made out for each of you here, then you will have plenty to eat for all time to come, and you and your children.

"When these papers are in your hands, you will have food to eat always. In case your child is hungry and wants something to eat, take your papers to any citizen

and he will divide with you. Take them to any store, and when they are read, they will speak and tell what you wish and you will get it. You will be the ones after we return who will have charge of the Arikara tribe."[64]

Most authors quote only the portion of the first paragraph that deals with Custer being named president and Bloody Knife being made chief of the Arikara. That Custer would have presidential ambitions, especially after his "political skinning" in the Belknap affair, is ludicrous. Proponents of the "Custer for President" theory seem somehow to believe that news of a victory would have reached the democratic convention in St. Louis in time for Custer's nomination thus necessitating his "rush to disaster." They conveniently forget that news of the defeat did not reach the convention until well after the candidate had been selected,[65] and Custer's name was never mentioned on the convention floor. [66] It is instructive to note an August 27, 1866 letter from Libbie Custer to her cousin Rebecca Richmond: *"It is my wish to have Autie avoid politics but I can say nothing to prevent him because I know he is so conscientious in what he is doing. He believes all I have feared and thought for a long time that there will, before long, be another war if such a congress is allowed to dictate laws to our country as did last winter. He believes men; soldiers and all should work to prevent it and so I do not oppose his present movements. He has positively declined running for Congress and will do so on no consideration – much to my delight . . ."* [67] When the entire account of Custer's visit to the Arikara camp in viewed in context, what we have is a basic "pep talk" to the scouts with rewards for all being promised. Promises that Custer had no ability to keep, it might be noted. The reason Custer felt compelled to deliver this talk has been lost to history.

On the 27th, they reached the *Mauvaises Terres*, the Badlands of the Little Missouri. Lieutenant Edward Maguire described the desolate landscape:

"These bad lands as seen from a distance present a very striking and picturesque appearance, forcibly reminding one of the ruins of a great city destroyed by fire.

"The effect is heightened by occasional patches of brilliant red clay, which glistens in the sunlight like beacon fires."[68]

General Sully had used almost the same language in 1856, labeling the badlands *"hell with the fires burned out."*[69] An Irish recruit, noting the sulphurous smell, agreed: *"Soy, Buddy, hell hain't more ner half a mile from here, that's wan dam sure thing."*[70]

Herder Roberts, although impressed by the desolation of the area, noted the bucolic beauty of the scene:

". . . scattered all through this beautiful desolation were patches of dark green grass, which added beauty to the scene.

"I remember that when the sun was setting behind the conical domes, that his blood red surface seemed to dance and made even the green grass a blood color, so remarkable was the scene that I called General Custer's attention to it."[71]

The Lakota would have been amused by the soldier's descriptions. Every Lakota knew the strange formations had been formed in part by the bones of *Uncigila,* the great water monster.[72]

During the march up Davis Creek on May 28, several troopers carved their names in a sandstone formation. Still visible are:

F. Neely
Co M 7th Cav
May 1876

and

W. C. Williams
Co H 7 Cav
1876

On the morning of the 30th, the expedition reached the first objective of the march, the Little Missouri River. Believing themselves to be in close proximity to the enemy, Custer forbade any discharge of firearms.[73] Terry had expressed the belief that he might find the Indians on that stream as it was one of their favorite wintering places. Custer, along with troops C, D, F, and M, guided by Lieutenant Varnum and a dozen of the scouts, patrolled up the stream for 20 miles without finding any evidence of habitation by the Indians within the last six months.[74] Reluctantly, Terry concluded his quarry would be found farther west; the hopes for a speedy campaign had vanished.[75]

Tom Custer recalled a humorous incident on the march in a letter to his niece Emma Reed: *"Aut (Armstrong Reed, DCE) and Bos (Boston Custer, DCE) went along also. Dick, Aut's pony got into the quick sand and he had to jump off in the river, and we of course laughed, and asked him if he was looking for specimens etc."*[76]

On the 29th, Sheridan had sent Sherman a lengthy report expressing his belief that the Indians couldn't remain concentrated for more than a week to ten days. While confident any of the three columns in the field was strong enough to prevail, he feared they were so strong that the Indians might simply return to their reservations without a fight, thereby forcing the campaign to be repeated. He therefore repeated his request to build two forts on the Yellowstone and to give control of the agencies to the army. While Custer was scouting the Little Missouri on the 30th, Sheridan forwarded to Sherman Crook's disturbing news that all agency Indians capable of taking the warpath were then, or very shortly would be, in the field.

On June 3rd, after a two day delay due to a freak spring snow storm, the march was resumed. That day they received a report from Gibbon, via Major Moore at Stanley's Stockade,[77] that the Indians were south of the Yellowstone in force and noting the killing of Rahmeir, Stoker, and Quinn on May 23rd. In his own dispatch, Moore reported that the steamers *Josephine* and *Far West* had both reached the stockade, and that, while the *Josephine* had already unloaded her cargo and left the river, the *Far West* would remain until Terry's arrival. Now that the Indians had been located, at least in a general sense, Terry issued new orders. Gibbon was to remain where he was until further orders. Major Moore was to take a boatload of supplies and establish a new depot at the junction of the Yellowstone and the Powder.

On the 7th of June, while moving from O'Fallon's Creek to the Powder, guide Charley Reynolds became lost and Custer, who was a natural born pathfinder, found the only practicable route through the valley of the Powder. The column camped that night on the Powder,[78] which has been variously described as the *"filthiest stream in America or elsewhere,"* and being *"too thick to drink and too thin to plow"* and finally as *"four hundred miles long, a mile wide, and an inch deep."*[79] Scouts sent to the mouth of the river returned the next day with mail and news that Gibbon's couriers had not been able to get through the Lakota and had turned back. That afternoon, June 8, Terry, escorted by Moylan's Company A and Keogh's Company I, marched to the mouth of the Powder to a rendezvous with the steamer *Far West*.

The *Far West*, one of the best known boats in western history,[80] had been built in Pittsburgh in 1870. Drawing 4 1/2 feet when loaded to capacity (397.81 tons), she was 190 feet long with a beam of 33 feet. She was powered by two 15 inch engines of 5–foot piston stroke, built by the Herbertson Engine Works of Brownsville, Pennsylvania, and carried three boilers. There were also two capstans, one on each side of the bow, which proved very useful in navigating the rapids and shallow portions of the river.[81] Having very little superstructure, she was eminently suited for duty on the Yellowstone, deserving her reputation:

> *As speedy a craft as the river'd float,*
> *She could buck the bends like a big horn goat.*

The *Far West* was skippered by the celebrated Captain Grant Marsh. [82] Although he was, at that time, the only captain to have navigated the upper Yellowstone, he would earn lasting fame for bringing the 7th's wounded to Fort Lincoln in record time.[83] Interestingly, after 1876, Captain Marsh would never again command the *Far West*.[84]

On board the steamer, Terry found Major Brisbin, who, accompanied by Captain Clifford and Company E of the 7th Infantry, had arrived in skiffs the previous day. Anxious to ensure that no blame accrued to either himself, or the Second Cavalry, for Gibbon's failure to engage the Indians, Brisbin apparently informed Terry of at least one sighting of Sitting Bull's village as well as the abortive attempt to cross the Yellowstone. Dr. Paulding noted in his diary for June 9th:

> *"It seems Brisbin took the boats clear down to Powder River & found the steamer*
> *'Far West.' Terry was then coming down with Custer, down the Powder River valley*
> *& got in at night. The boat will come up to us this morning & we will then turn back*
> *& go up the river again with the boat. Brisbin of course accomplished his object in*
> *getting in the first word with Terry & Gibbon is very hot about it apparently."*[85]

Terry then issued orders to Major Moore to transfer all supplies from Stanley's Stockade to the Powder River Depot, and to Colonel Gibbon to move downstream for an officer's conference. On the 9th, Terry steamed up river, meeting Gibbon at a point about 10 or 15 miles below the mouth of the Tongue. Despite Gibbon's assurances that the Indians were either on the Tongue or the Rosebud, Terry decided to scout the upper reaches of both the Tongue and Powder rivers before moving further west.[86] Gibbon furnished the famous Mitch Boyer[87] to serve as guide for the proposed scout. Terry, after ordering Gibbon to march his command to the mouth of the Rosebud, steamed down to rejoin the 7th on the morning of the 10th.

Upon his arrival, General Terry issued Special Field Order No. 11, which is contained in its entirety in Appendix 3, assigning Major Reno to conduct a reconnaissance of the Powder River. Noting that the normal forage allowance for cavalry horses in garrison was fourteen pounds of hay and twelve pounds of grain per day, it can be readily seen how difficult the march would be since only two pounds of grain per day was allocated.[88]

Terry verbally cautioned Reno to stay away from the Rosebud to preclude warning the Indians believed to be there. This indicates that Terry believed the intelligence about the location of the Indians he had received from Gibbon on the 9th. The scout by the 7th Cavalry was to ensure there were no Indians east of the presumed location of the village. On the 12th Terry reported to Sheridan how he intended to proceed if Reno's scout developed no new information:

"I intend then if nothing new is developed, to send Custer with nine companies of his regiment up the Tongue and then across to and down the Rosebud while the rest of the Seventh will join Gibbon and move up the Rosebud. Have met Gibbon and concerted movements with him."[89]

It is key to note that, although unstated, the village was presumed to be on the lower reaches of the Rosebud. Should the village be further up the Rosebud, this plan for cooperation between Gibbon and Custer could not work as Custer must arrive well in advance of Gibbon. It is also instructive to note Terry felt the need to balance the strength of Custer's and Gibbon's columns by detailing three companies of the 7th Cavalry to augment Gibbon's force. This report to Sheridan may also shed some light on Reno's selection to lead the scout. There had apparently been some speculation among the officers as to why Custer had not been selected. Godfrey commented in his journal; *"It has been a subject of conversation among officers why General Custer was not in command but no solution yet has been arrived at."*[90] Roger Darling feels that Terry was demonstrating he was in complete command while testing Custer's willingness to serve in a subordinate role,[91] while John W. Bailey believes that Custer was being punished for his conduct on the march from Fort Lincoln.[92] Perhaps the solution is as simple as this: the scout was to be minor in nature, no contact with the enemy was anticipated,[93] and, if the 7th was to conduct future operations in two detachments, Reno needed some practical experience in Indian campaigning. In any event, Reno was selected for the assignment. Just prior to departure, Custer and Reno were checking on the health of the scouts' horses.[94] It is instructive to note how Custer and Reno, called "Man With The Dark Face" by the Arikara,[95] handled the cases of scouts wanting to accompany the expedition, although their horses had galls:[96]

"At the Powder River when Custer was inspecting the horses and forbidding those with disabled horses from going on with him, Howling Wolf (this may have been Red Wolf, DCE) hid his horse, thinking to evade the inspection. Custer asked Howling Wolf by signs where his horse was. Howling Wolf replied: 'I put him on the island in the river, so he will be strong for the journey. He is as smooth and without galls as he was when he was a colt.' Custer said impatiently: 'Bring him here very quick or I will shoot him.' Howling Wolf brought the horse and Custer said (here the narrator made a face which would resemble Custer's in such a case): 'See that gall on his back, as large as my hand? What do you mean by your story?' Howling Wolf said to Custer: 'You see the gall is behind the saddle. It is natural to him and was there when he was born. See, he is sound under the saddle. He can out–travel any horse but yours and should he fall I will keep up with you on foot.' Custer laughed, and said: 'Since you are a wolf you may go.' Howling Wolf had been riding for several days with the saddle far back so as to have his horse in good trim when they should meet the Dakotas."[97]

"Reno told High Bear (may have been Bear Comes Out, DCE) that he could not go with the rest because his horse was badly galled. High Bear said to him: 'You see the sun there, if you say it does not move I will not dispute you.' This is the polite way the Indians have of telling any one that his opinion is totally wrong. Reno (not understanding the figure of speech) said to Girard: 'Tell him any man who is not a fool would agree with me, and that he will show himself a soldier by agreeing with me without question.' High Bear grew very angry at this and said to Reno: 'If only one of us is to go on we will decide by a fight which one is to go. The one killed in the fight will not go.' Reno thereupon threatened to shoot High Bear and High Bear started for him with his knife. Bloody Knife sprang between them and said: 'General Custer is my brother and I forbid this fight.' Then Bloody Knife turned to

Reno and said: 'I wish for my sake you would let him go.' So Reno consented to let him go. [98]

In addition to preparing for Reno's scout, the regiment was stripped for action; all unnecessary equipment, including the regiment's sabers, being left behind. Over Custer's protest, the band was dismounted, their white horses distributed to the dismounted cavalry.[99] The 7th would go into a major action without the band for the first time. In addition to the band, Custer's 4 dogs[100] and herder Richard Roberts were also left behind. Roberts' horse had given out and he had been unable to secure another. Yates was finally able to secure a horse for Roberts, but the 7th marched up the Rosebud before Roberts arrived to claim his mount.[101] According to Jacob Horner, then a private in Company K, there was one mount available for either himself or Private Charles Schmidt of Company L. Schmidt was successful in the quest for the horse and rode to his death with Custer's command.[102] There being a shortage of pack mules, some animals were taken from the wagon traces.[103] Private Goldin recounts the training of these "shave tails:"

"A few experienced packers had come up with this outfit, and they were mainly used as pack masters and instructors to whip into shape the soldier packers detailed in each troop, few if any of whom had ever seen, let alone knowing anything, about a pack sling or the much used 'diamond hitch,' and for a couple of days, from early morning until after sunset, intensive training of men and mules was the order of exercises, and those of us who were immune from this work spent every leisure moment on the sidelines of the training field.

"The mules, accustomed to nothing but the old chain trace harness, rebelled at the strange looking apparatus they were called upon to wear, and the men, green and inexperienced, had the time of their lives in getting the clumsy saddles in place. This accomplished, the work of instructing them in the fine points of putting on a pack that would stay, was next in order, and it was there the laughing, yelling spectators sure received the full worth of their admission fee. It was not at all uncommon to see some stubborn mule on whose back had been cinched a side pack of anywhere from two to four boxes of hardtack, a center pack of a sack of bacon or sugar or coffee, with an axe or two, pick and a shovel stuck here and there for good measure, turned loose to get accustomed to his burden. some of them were quite tractable, and took their new work quietly, but most of them rebelled. For a moment or two they would stand still, looking back to discover what sort of a thing this was that had been fastened to them, and then with a bray or a squeal they would proceed to give an exhibition of plain and fancy bucking that soon left the training field littered with a scattered mass of broken boxes, battered camp kettles and other impedimenta.

"Once relieved of their packs the mules would fall to grazing until rounded up and the process repeated again and again, until at last, broken in spirit, and sore on back and sides, the poor brutes would surrender and meekly amble off with their poorly cinched loads until they saw an opportunity to get in a jam and make a wholesale loosening and dumping of leads a possibility."[104]

One final note on preparations is in order for the sake of completeness. When the *Far West* arrived at the Powder River, on–board was a trader by the name of James Coleman, who was apparently in the employ of a John Smith. He set up a tent and did a land office business selling whiskey at $1.00 a pint. This sale of liquor to the troops, along with Wooden Leg's

The steamer *Far West.* Captained by Grant Marsh, the steamer supplied the troops during the 1876 campaign and carried the wounded to Fort Lincoln. *Photo Courtesy Little Bighorn Battlefield National Monument.*

Burial scaffold in a tree similar to the interments desecrated by Custer's troopers on the march to the Little Big Horn. While this was the preferred method of Lakota burial, after the battle the Lakota buried at least some of their dead in tepees left standing on the abandoned village site. *Photo Courtesy Little Bighorn Battlefield National Monument.*

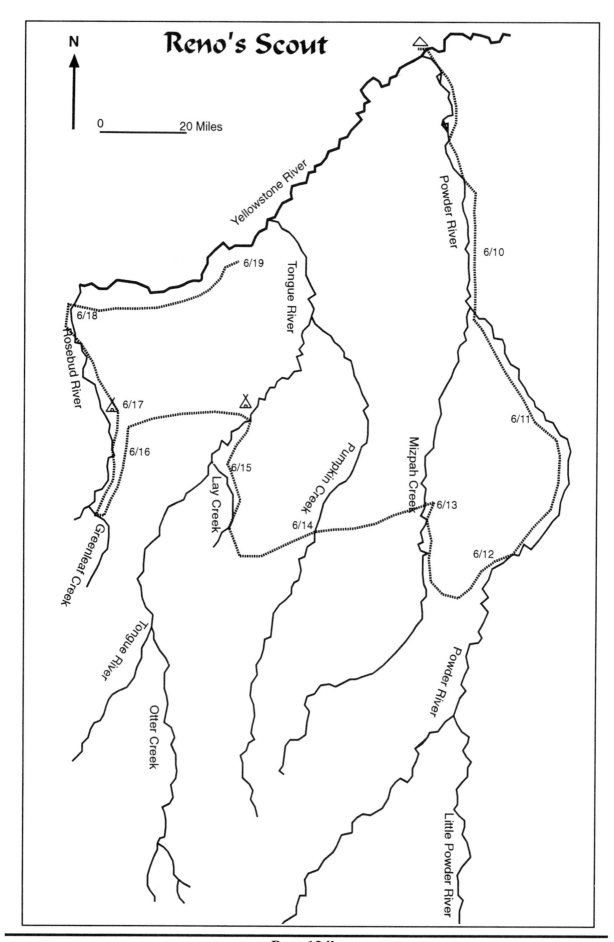

Reno's Scout

N

0   20 Miles

Yellowstone River

Powder River

6/10

6/19

Tongue River

6/18

Rosebud River

6/17

Mizpah Creek

6/11

6/16

6/13

Lay Creek

Pumpkin Creek

6/15

6/14

6/12

Greenleaf Creek

Tongue River

Powder River

Otter Creek

Little Powder River

account of finding whiskey filled canteens among the dead, is the source of the ridiculous rumors that intoxication was the reason for the 7th defeat at Little Big Horn.[105]

As ordered, Reno departed on his scout at 3 P.M. on the 10th.[106] In concert with his assignment as Aide–de–Camp to his brother, Tom Custer did not accompany Reno; C Troop continuing to be commanded by Second Lieutenant Harrington.[107] The right wing of the regiment, less Company B, which would be detailed to guard the pack train, would perish with Custer on the 25th and Second Lieutenant Jack Sturgis' official itinerary of the scout would be lost to history.[108] Fortunately, Sergeant James Hill, of Company B, also kept an itinerary which, along with the diary of Dr. DeWolf, is the source of most of our knowledge about the scout.[109]

Reno averaged almost 27 miles per day[110] on his march through some very rough country. There is no doubt that this scout was tiring to the men and animals and was probably the reason some of the trooper's horses would give out at the Little Big Horn.[111] The gatling gun, pulled as it was by condemned cavalry horses, gave much trouble. To cross some ravines, the gun had to be unlimbered and hauled over by hand.[112] When the gun upset on June 15 in the vicinity of Liscom Buttes,[113] three men were injured.[114] Finally, when Reno reached the Yellowstone on the 18th, he had left the gun some distance in the rear on a high hill as it would require ropes to bring the gun down. On the 19th, the gun was brought into camp.[115] It seems obvious that this performance helped to convince Custer not to take the guns when they were offered to him on the 21st.

On the morning of the 13th, Reno abruptly deviated from his orders. Instead of following the Powder River to the mouth of the Little Powder, he struck out for Mizpah Creek, camping on that stream at 2 p.m. after marching 22 miles. Companies B and C were then ordered to scout down the Mizpah, which they followed for 13 miles returning to camp at 10 p.m. after marching a total distance of 48 miles.[116] As the scout had not uncovered any recent signs of Indians, Reno again departed from his orders and marched due west on the 14th to arrive on Pumpkin Creek, about 40 miles south of the location Terry had contemplated, at 1 p.m. Proceeding due west again on the 15th, Reno arrived at Tongue River at 2 p.m. after a march of 28 miles.

The march down the Tongue commenced at 5 a.m. on the 16th. About 2:30 p.m. they went into camp about three miles east of the Rosebud Valley while the scouts went ahead to reconnoiter. The scout's mission bore fruit when they discovered the village site Bradley had seen on May 17th. The scouts carefully studied the abandoned campsite, determining the village contained about 360 lodges which would indicate a warrior force of approximately 800, just the size force the military had anticipated. The scouts uncovered additional evidence that the pony herd had been driven inside the camp circles at night.; a sure indication an attack on the camp was expected and that the warriors were prepared to meet it.[117] Encouraged by this intelligence, Reno marched the command from 8 p.m. until midnight, covering 40 miles during the entire day's march. It is interesting to note that the route of Reno's night march was southwesterly, while the trail from the abandoned village indicated the Lakota to be moving first northwesterly then southward up the Rosebud Valley. Although he never attempted to explain why he violated his orders and marched to the Rosebud, Reno appears to have set a course designed to intercept a slow moving village.[118]

The command, moved carefully now as Reno ordered no bugle calls sounded or *"loud notes be made,"*[119] followed the trail upstream on the 17th until they discovered an entrenchment showing evidence of a fight. This was one of the campsites of the Yellowstone Wagon Road Expedition of 1874.[120] Reno halted the command after only a 2 hour march and again sent scouts ahead. While we can not be certain how far they progressed, time and distance considerations indicate they could have gone no further than Lame Deer Creek. Upon the return of the scouting party, Reno questioned Forked Horn about the trail:

> "'What do you think of this trail, Forked Horn?' Forked Horn replied: 'If the Dakotas see us, the sun will not move very far before we are all killed. But you are leader and we will go on if you say so.' The commanding officer (Reno, DCE) said: 'Custer told us to turn back if we found the trail, and we will return, these are our orders.'"[121]

Reno had a dilemma. His scouts informed him that they believed the village could be overtaken in two day's fast march.[122] While his Arikara scouts argued the enemy was too strong for Reno's force, he had additional problems to ponder. He only had four days' rations remaining, an amount insufficient to see him to the mouth of the Tongue. Also he would undoubtedly arrive late for his junction with the remainder of the regiment. At 4 P.M. on June 17, Reno, reluctantly according to private Kennedy[123], decided to turn back, unaware that Crook had just been defeated about 40 miles away. Reno marched directly to the Yellowstone arriving opposite Gibbon's camp at noon on the 18th. Gibbon, believing the force to be Terry's, attempted to send a message across the swollen river. Henry Bostwick attempted to swim across, but was forced back by an attack of cramps.[124] Next to try were Jack Rabbit Bull[125] and another Crow scout. Gibbon describes the scouts' preparations:

> "The Indians stripped and commenced their preparations for their cold swim by rubbing themselves all over with red paint. I had the curiosity to inquire the object of this, and was surprised to learn that it was to protect them against the attack of **alligators**. As the alligator is an animal unknown to the waters of this region, the fact referred to is a curious evidence of the southern origin of the Crows, at the same time that it shows how traditions are transmitted for long ages in a barbarous tribe. Having completed their preparations against the attack of an animal of which perhaps their progenitors long ago had a wholesome dread in more southern waters, the note to General Terry was tied in the scalplock of one of them, and the two men started on the run for a point higher up the river. There providing themselves with a log of dead wood, they plunged into the water, and singing to keep up their courage, they were swept past us down the swift current, and after a swim of nearly a mile landed safely on the other side, and were seen through our glasses to approach the party opposite. All this took time, and being curious to know who was in the party, one of our officers tied a handkerchief to a stick, and commenced waving it from side to side as a signal. It was soon answered in the same way, and before our Crows had reached the opposite bank, the army code of signals was spelling out for us the information we wanted."[126]

Having ascertained the identity of the party, Gibbon sent Reno a note for delivery to General Terry:

> "Col. Reno made his appearance at the mouth of the Rosebud today and I have communicated with him by signal and by scouts swimming the river. He had seen no Indians, but I gather from the conversations which the scouts had with Mitch Boyer (sic) that they found signs of camps on Tongue River and Rosebud, and trails leading up Rosebud. I presume the only remaining chance of finding Indians now is in the direction of the headwaters of Rosebud or Little Big Horn.[127] I have been anxiously looking for the boat and shall be glad to meet you or to hear of your future plans."[128]

Reno marched his command down river toward the Tongue on June 19th. Camping about 8 miles short of his objective, after a march of thirty–three miles, he sent the following report, along with Gibbon's note, to General Terry:

> *"I am in camp about eight miles above you. I started this a.m. to reach your camp, but the country from the Rosebud here is simply **awful** and I had given orders to cache the gun, but Kinzie is coming in all right. I am sure you cannot take wagons to Rosebud without going some distance up Tongue River.*

> *"I enclose you a note from Gibbon, whom I saw yesterday. I can tell you where the Indians are **not**, and much more information when I see you in the morning. I take it the Tongue River is not fordable at the mouth and I will necessarily have to camp on this side. I have had no accident, except breaking the tongue of Kinzie's gun carriage. My command is well. I will be on Tongue River opposite your camp about 8 a.m. My animals are leg weary and need shoeing. We have marched near to 250 miles."*

This is truly a remarkable report. Reno not only admits his disobedience of orders by stating that he has been to the Rosebud, but he doesn't attempt to neutralize his commander's reaction by imparting the intelligence he has gathered relative to the size of the enemy force and its direction of travel. When his report unleashed the inevitable maelstrom, Reno compounded his problem by becoming silent and sullen.

Terry's reaction was swift. He dispatched his aid, Captain Robert Hughes, with orders for Reno to remain where he was and to obtain additional information. Custer was ordered to march the remainder of the regiment down the south bank of the Yellowstone to Reno's position. As Terry noted in his diary entry for June 19th, *"Reno gave him (Hughes, DCE) no reason for his disobedience of orders."*[129] Terry was less reserved in his June 21st letter to his sisters:

> *"Here we lay in idleness until Monday (June 19, DCE) evening when to my great surprise I received a note from Colonel Reno which informed me that he had flagrantly disobeyed my orders, and he had been on the Rosebud, in the belief that there were Indians on that stream and that he could make a successful attack on them which would cover up his disobedience. . . . He had not the supplies to go far and he returned without justification for his conduct unless wearied horses and broken down mules would be that justification. Of course, this performance made a change in my plans necessary. . . ."*[130]

Reno was chastised quite severely by Custer over his performance on the scout. Private Thompson related:

> *"General Terry and Custer joined us on the banks of the Yellowstone and, confirmed by those in position to know, that when Reno made his report concerning the discovery of the Indians trail and the supposed direction in which they were moving, General Custer upbraided him very bitterly for not finding out the exact number and the direction the Indians were taking instead of supposing and guessing. There were some sharp questions and short answers; but General Terry interposed and smoothed the matter over."*[131]

A change in plans was necessary. While Reno's scout had verified Bradley's unreported sightings, it was clear that the Indians were either high up the Rosebud, perhaps near its headwaters, or were over on the Little Big Horn; probably on its upper reaches. Therefore the previously planned movements of Gibbon and Custer could not be successful as Custer would undoubtedly encounter the Indians long before Gibbon could get into position. At this juncture, one point is crucial to our understanding the campaign and later cover up; on June 19, 1876, the military had absolutely no reason to believe that the Indians were to be found on the **lower** reaches of the Little Big Horn.

On June 15, as the band played *"Garry Owen"* from a nearby bluff, Custer led the left wing of the regiment toward its appointed rendezvous at the mouth of the Tongue. A tragedy had struck prior to the departure when Sergeant Henry Fox, Company D, 6th Infantry, had drowned when his mail-laden skiff capsized. The mail was saved due to the efforts of Captain Grant Marsh and Mark Kellogg who stayed up all night drying the letters.

The Arikara scout Red Star describes the end of the march:

> *"We marched up on a hill overlooking the Elk River (Yellowstone, DCE) and then down to the mouth of the Tongue River. Right at this point was an abandoned Dakota camp.[132] Here lay the body of a soldier, and all about him were clubs and sticks as though he had been beaten to death, only the bones were left. Custer stood still for some time and looked down at the remains of the soldier."[133]*

An anonymous article, probably authored by Custer, in the July 23 edition of the *New York Herald* gave a slightly different account of the discovery of the trooper's body:

> *"Upon the march from Powder to Tongue River, Custer, who was riding at the head of the column as it marched through a deserted Indian village of last winter, came upon the skull and bones of a white man. Near these remains was found the uniform of a cavalry soldier, as shown by the letter 'C' on the button of the overcoat and the yellow cord binding on the dress coat. Near by were the dead embers of a large fire, shown with attendant circumstances, that the cavalryman had undoubtedly been a prisoner in the hands of the savages, and had been put to the torture usually inflicted by Indians upon all white men falling into their hands as captives. Who the unfortunate man was and the sad details of his tragic death will never be known."[134]*

Godfrey noted some savage behavior on the part of the troops at this location:

> *"A number of their dead, placed upon scaffolds, or tied to the branches of trees, were disturbed and robbed of their trinkets. Several persons rode about exhibiting trinkets with as much gusto as if they were trophies of their valor, and showed no more concern for their desecration than if they had won them at a raffle. Ten days later I saw the bodies of these same persons dead, naked, and mutilated."[135]*

Isaiah Dorman, the black interpreter who was married to a Lakota woman, unwrapped a body and threw it into the river. This caused great concern on the part of Red Star who reported: *"Isaiah threw the body into the river, and as he was fishing there later, they suppose he used this for bait."[136]*

The *Far West*, with General Terry on–board, reached the mouth of the Rosebud the morning of June 21. The Montana Column, with the gatling gun battery, was started for the mouth of the Big Horn within the hour. Colonel Gibbon and Major Brisbin remained behind for an officer's conference. Terry's new strategy was contained in message to Sheridan written early on the morning of the 21st:

> "No Indians have been met with as yet, but traces of a large and recent village have been discovered 20 or 30 miles up the Rosebud. Gibbon's column will move this morning on the north side of the Yellowstone for the mouth of the Big Horn, where it will be ferried across by the supply steamer, and whence it will proceed to the mouth of the Little Horn, and so on. Custer will go up the Rosebud tomorrow with his whole regiment and thence to the headwaters of the Little Horn, thence down the Little Horn.
>
> "I only hope that **one** of the two columns will find the Indians. I go personally with Gibbon.(emphasis the author's)"[137]

The plan outlined above was not just a movement of the previous plan one river to the west, but a re–evaluation of the situation. Custer would now march with his entire regiment rather than the 9 companies previously planned. The 7th must be sent to the headwaters of the Little Big Horn because the current intelligence indicated the Indians would most likely be found on the **upper** reaches of either that stream or the Rosebud. No mention of cooperation between the commands was made, in fact, Terry's *"only hope"* is that *"one of the two columns will find the Indians."* Terry's plan had become a reconnaissance in force, rather than a cooperative attack.

The purpose of the officer's conference the afternoon of June 21 was not to determine how to defeat the enemy, but, as Gibbon recalled: *"to prevent the escape of the Indians, which was the idea pervading the minds of all of us."*[138] Apparently the conference concluded without controversy, although Custer was the only officer present who thought as many as 1500 warriors might be encountered.[139] However, after Custer's tragedy, there would be a great difference of opinion as to the details of the conference pertaining to cooperation between the two columns.

The *New York Herald* for July 8, 1876, quoted an unnamed officer in Gibbon's command: *"It was announced by General Terry that General Custer's column would strike the blow, and General Gibbon and his men received the decision without a murmur."*[140] Major Brisbin also wrote that *"The Montana Column felt disappointed, but General Terry's reasons for affording the honor of the attack to general Custer were good ones."*[141] Bradley echoed those sentiments in his journal entry for June 21:

> "Prior to his departure (Custer's, DCE) a conference took place on the boat between Generals Terry, Gibbon, and himself with reference to a combined movement between the two columns in the neighborhood of the Sioux village about the same time and assist each other in the attack, it is understood that if Custer arrives first, he is at liberty to attack at once if he deems prudent. We have little hope of being in at the death, as Custer will undoubtedly exert himself to the utmost to get there first and win all the laurels for himself and his regiment."[142]

There was one chronicler who thought a plan of mutual cooperation, including a junction of the commands, had been decided upon. Dr. Paulding's diary entry for June 25 includes: *"Started to move up Tullock's Fork to strike the mouth of the Tongue River (Paulding obviously means Little Big Horn, DCE) where we are to meet Custer on the 27th."*[143]

Custer had stated he planned to average 30 miles per day, at first. This indicates he would probably increase his rate of march if he closed upon the enemy. In fact, Custer would average about 31 miles per day from his departure until his arrival on Last Stand Hill. As the Arikara were not familiar with the terrain to be traversed, Terry gave Custer six of Gibbon's Crow scouts to serve as guides. Also detailed to Custer was George Herendeen, who was to bring Terry the results of Custer's inspection of the upper reaches of Tullock's Fork. For this hazardous service, Herendeen was to be paid an additional $200. [144]

The intelligence that the Indians were probably on the upper reaches of either the Rosebud or the Little Big Horn was bolstered by the fact that the upper Little Big Horn was a favorite hunting ground of the Lakota. In fact, had large herds of antelope not been sighted near the mouth of the Little Big Horn, the village would have gone up stream rather than down after the Rosebud fight. [145] It is therefore reasonable to assume that the portion of Custer's orders requiring him to pass by the Indian trail and continue to the headwaters of the Tongue[146], to prevent the Indians passing around his left flank, were discussed at length during the conference.

After the conference, which ran from about 3 pm to nearly sunset, [147] Custer was offered the battery of gatling guns as well as Gibbon's entire force of cavalry. [148] At this juncture, most authors launch into a discussion of Custer's rationale for refusing these additional elements. Custer's refusal is not the point and an analysis of his refusal will be deferred until Chapter 10. The real point is what does this offer to augment Custer's force say relative to Terry's plan for the campaign. First, it denotes significant indecision on Terry's part. Recall that early that morning he had started the battery and Gibbon's cavalry, along with the rest of the Montana Column, toward the mouth of the Big Horn. Now, just a few hours later, and with no new intelligence, he offers to recall and counter march a significant portion of the command. The second point is that this offer of the Second Cavalry demonstrates that Custer's column was to operate totally independently. Terry stated in his annual report dated November 21, 1876:

> *"This plan was founded on the belief that at some point on the Little Big Horn a body of hostile Sioux would be found; and that although it was impossible to make movements in perfect concert, as might have been done had there been a known fixed objective point to be reached, yet, by the judicious use of the excellent guides and scouts which we possessed, the two columns might be brought within co-operating distance of each other, so that either of them which should be first engaged might be a 'waiting fight' – give time for the other to come up. At the same time it was thought that a double attack would very much diminish the chances of a successful retreat by the Sioux, should they be disinclined to fight. It was believed to be impracticable to join Colonel Gibbon's column to Lieutenant–Colonel Custer's force; for more than one–half of Colonel Gibbon's troops were infantry, who would be unable to keep up with cavalry in a rapid movement; while **to detach Gibbon's mounted men and add them to the Seventh Cavalry would leave his force too small to act as an independent body.** (emphasis the author's)"[149]*

This report, while disjointed and self contradictory, makes several things crystal clear. First rapid movements for Gibbon's column were not contemplated. If the infantry couldn't keep up with the 7th Cavalry, how could it keep up with a rapid movement of the 2nd Cavalry? Secondly, Terry recognized that his offer of the gatling guns and 2nd Cavalry to Custer would render Gibbon's remaining force impotent. Since Terry admitted, in other documents, to making those offers, one can only conclude that Gibbon's force was not planned to play any major role as it would have been *"too small to act as an independent body"* had Custer accepted the offer.

The final subterfuge is contained in Terry's confidential report of July 2, see Appendix 5: *"We calculated it would take Gibbon's column until the twenty–sixth to reach the mouth of the Little Big Horn and that the wide sweep which I had proposed Custer should make would require so much time that Gibbon would be able to cooperate with him in attacking any Indians that might be found on that stream."* Gibbon, apparently providing back up to this subterfuge, wrote Terry on November 5, 1876:

> *"We both impressed upon him (Custer) that he should keep constantly feeling to his left, and even should the trail turn toward the Little Big Horn that he should continue his march southward along the headwaters of the Tongue, and strike west toward the Little Big Horn. So strong was the impression upon my mind and great my fear that Custer's zeal would carry him forward too rapidly, that the last thing I said to him when bidding him good-by, after his regiment had filed past you when starting on the march, was, 'Now, Custer, don't be greedy, but wait for us.' Poor fellow! Knowing what we do now, and what an effect a fresh Indian trail seemed to have on him, perhaps we were expecting too much to anticipate a forbearance on his part which would have rendered cooperation between the two columns practicable."[150]*

With everything being keyed upon a date of June 26, it is instructive to note that Terry's written orders to Custer, see Appendix 4, make no mention what–so–ever of any junction with Gibbon on the 26th, or any other date.[151] Proponents of the plan for mutual cooperation between Custer's and Gibbon's columns do not explain why the single most important element of the plan for cooperative action, the date of the combined attack, is not mentioned in Custer's **written** orders. Instead, the orders state of Gibbon's march: *". . . is now in motion for the mouth of the Big Horn. As soon as it reaches that point it will cross the Yellowstone and move up at least as far as the forks of the Big and Little Horns. Of course **its further movements must be controlled by circumstances as they arise** . . .(emphasis the author's)"* Apparently only the strike force was required to be in position at the "appointed" time. The all–important blocking force was free to go where circumstances dictated. The forgoing clearly demonstrates that the so called cooperative plan of action was fabricated after the disaster as a means of focusing blame on one who could no longer defend himself.

One of the greatest controversies surrounding the Little Big Horn is the question "Did Custer disobey his orders?" Over the years scholars have minutely analyzed each word and bit of punctuation contained in Terry's order to Custer. The amount of written debate on this order is rivaled only by that afforded to Lord Raglan's four orders to Lord Lucan resulting in the ill-fated charge of the Light Brigade. No document, much less this one, can stand such scrutiny and remain intact. The situation is very clear, however; that while Custer did not violate the intent of his orders, he definitely violated the letter of his orders in two instances. First, he was ordered to continue south rather than follow the Indian trail discovered by Reno. It is evident that this portion of the orders was included to preclude the Indians escaping around Custer's left flank. Since the Indians did not escape around Custer's left flank, I suppose "Custer's Luck" held in–so–far as to make this only a technical violation of his orders. Similarly, Custer did not scout Tullock's Fork as ordered. While this element will be pursued in greater depth in Chapter 10, suffice it to say, this disobedience, like the previous one, did not violate the intent of Terry's order and had no bearing on the subsequent tragedy. General Sherman, reviewing the findings of a Civil War court of inquiry, noted:

> *"It would be an unsafe and dangerous rule to hold the commander of an army in battle to a technical adherence to any rule of conduct for managing his command. He is responsible for results, and holds the lives and reputations of every officer and soldier under his orders as subordinate to the great end – victory. The most important events are usually compressed into an hour, a minute, and he [the commander] cannot stop to analyze his reasons. He must act on the impulse, the conviction, of the instant, and should be sustained in his conclusions, if not manifestly unjust. The power to command men, and give vehement impulse to their*

joint action, is something which cannot be defined by words, but it is plain and manifest in battles, and whoever commands an army in chief must choose his subordinates by reason of qualities which can alone be tested in actual conflict."[152]

Finally, there is the subject of Mary Adams, Custer's black cook. The claim is that after the conference, Terry accompanied Custer to his tent at which time Terry gave Custer *carte blanche* as to his movements. This conversation was reputedly overheard by Mary Adams who swore out an affidavit which, in an unexplained manner, subsequently came into the possession of General Nelson A. Miles. While there is no doubt in my mind that Mary Adams accompanied the expedition,[153] and was present in the camp at the mouth of the Rosebud on June 21, I am unable to credit this story. There remain three basic questions that must be satisfactorily answered for the story to be believed: If Miles had such an affidavit, how did it come to be in his possession, and why has it never been produced? Similarly, if Terry indeed gave Custer *carte blanche*, why didn't his written orders, delivered the next morning, reflect that conversation?

---

[1] Fort Lincoln was located across the Missouri River from Bismarck, North Dakota, not far from the present site of Mandan. Originally named Fort McKeen, within a year it was renamed Fort Lincoln with the infantry post occupying the original site on the bluffs while the new cavalry post was built on the flats below. The fort did not have a stockade, although the infantry post had a blockhouse, and the construction was primarily frame. On the cavalry post were three barracks, to house six companies, seven detached officer's quarters, a granary, office and dispensary, guardhouse, commissary storehouse, quartermaster storehouse, laundresses' quarters, quartermaster stables, six cavalry stables, accommodating 600 horses, and an ordnance depot. See Edgar I. Stewart "Custer's Luck" page 56 and Ernest L. Reedstrom "Bugles, Banners and War Bonnets" page 82.

[2] See John S. Gray "Centennial Campaign" page 89.

[3] See Frederic F. Van de Water "Glory–Hunter" page 300.

[4] See Frederic F. Van de Water "Glory–Hunter" page 301.

[5] See Roger Darling "A Sad and Terrible Blunder" page 18.

[6] The latter event occurred on May 31. See Michael J. Koury "The Terry Diary" page 19.

[7] See John S. Gray "Centennial Campaign" page 90.

[8] See John S. Gray "Centennial Campaign" page 90.

[9] A Seventh Cavalry roster, as of June 14, 1876, is provided in Appendix 1.

[10] There has been a continuing, and meaningless, controversy over the number, and caliber, of gatling guns on the expedition. While most authorities cite 3 guns, Custer's Special Order No. 48, dated March 18, specifically calls out *"four pieces."* Regarding the caliber of the weapons, the eight 45–70 caliber gatlings at the Rock Island Arsenal designated for the Department of Dakota had not been delivered. Official War Department correspondence indicates 3 half inch (50 caliber) guns accompanied the expedition while First Sergeant Hugh A. Hynds, Twentieth Infantry, gatling gun detachment, recalled two 50 caliber and two one inch guns. See Ernest L. Reedstrom "Bugles, Banners and War Bonnets" pages 268 – 274.

[11] The name Arikara means "Horns" and refers to the ancient manner in which the Arikara, popularly known as Rees, wore their hair with two pieces of bone standing up, one on each side

of the crest. See Bruce Grant "Concise Encyclopedia of the American Indian" page 25. It is difficult to know exactly how many Arikara accompanied the expedition. Many had several names which were used at various times in the several narratives. While most authorities quote a number between 41 and 45, my analysis, after adding in the 8 Arikara left at the Powder River Depot, indicates 31 Arikara, 5 Lakota, and a half–breed Pikuni Blackfoot accompanied the expedition. See Appendix 1.

[12] See Ernest L. Reedstrom "Bugles, Banners and War Bonnets" page 111.

[13] Note that Major Orlando Hurley Moore's Companies C, D, and I of the Sixth Infantry did not march from Fort Lincoln; being transported by the steamer *Josephine* from Fort Buford to Stanley's crossing of the Yellowstone. See Loyd J. Overfield II "The Little Big Horn, 1876" page 109.

[14] See Sandy Barnard "Mark Kellogg's Role During the 1876 Campaign" page 7. Photographer Stanley J. Morrow was also to have accompanied the column but his shipment of chemicals from Chicago was delayed and the regiment marched without him. See Gregory Michno "The Mystery of E Troop" page 207.

[15] See John S. Gray "Centennial Campaign" page 285.

[16] Some authors list the number of absent officers as fourteen, but, as the regiment's commander, Colonel Samuel D. Sturgis, was habitually kept on detached duty by Sheridan so that Custer could command the regiment, I have not included him in my count.

[17] See Edgar I. Stewart "Custer's Luck" page 137.

[18] See Edgar I. Stewart "Custer's Luck" page 177.

[19] See Walter Camp "Custer in '76" page 83.

[20] In addition to Captain Sheridan serving as Aide–de–Camp to his brother, First Lieutenant Charles Braden was on sick leave and Edwin Philip Eckerson, the company's newly appointed Second Lieutenant, wasn't scheduled to report until June 19th.

[21] The 7th had, and retains, the reputation of being the finest Indian fighting frontier regiment. This opinion is not universally held as Robert Utley, for example, feels that Mackenzie's 4th, with its record of 5 major victories: McClellan's Creek, Remnolina Mexico, Tule Canyon, Palo Duro Canyon, and the Dull Knife fight at Willow Creek, may have been the nation's finest Indian fighting regiment. See Robert M. Utley "Frontier Regulars" page 209.

[22] See Frederic F. Van de Water "Glory–Hunter" page 187.

[23] See Frederic F. Van de Water "Glory–Hunter" page 187.

[24] There is strong evidence that Captain Custer served as Aide–de–Camp to his brother during the campaign. Since it is uncertain just when this assignment was made, I have listed him with his troop.

[25] Bob Tailed Bull was the Indian leader of the Ree scouts. As such he wore a sergeant's chevrons. The Ree scouts were each paid $16 per month (a private was compensated at $13 per month) and

paid an additional $12 per month for each pony they furnished. See Edgar I. Stewart "Custer's Luck" page 180.

[26] Civilians Mark Kellogg, correspondent, Harry Armstrong "Autie" Reed, herder and nephew of the Custers; Guides Boston Custer, Charles "Lonesome Charley" Alexander Reynolds; Interpreters Isaiah Dorman, and Frederick F. Girard. Custer had been impressed with Dorman's work as interpreter at Fort Rice. On May 14th Custer issued an order to the commander at Fort Rice to assign Dorman to the expedition. As an added incentive, Custer increased Dorman's pay from $50 to $75 per month. Unfortunately, Dorman was never able to collect any of his increase as the army owed him $102.50 at the time of his death. See W. Boyes "Custer's Black White Man" page 6.

[27] Drs. Elbert J. Clark and James Madison DeWolf were the only doctors with the column when it departed from Fort Lincoln. Dr. Clark was replaced by Dr. Henry Rinaldo Porter as a 7th Cavalry surgeon on June 14th. Dr. George Edwin Lord was attached to the 7th at the same time. See John S. Gray "Centennial Campaign" page 274.

[28] While approximately only 172 7th Cavalry troopers at the Little Big Horn had taken part in the August 1873 engagements, other factors, such as disobedience of orders and poor intelligence, were much more important in determining the battle's outcome.

[29] See Thomas B. Marquis "Keep the Last Bullet for Yourself" pages 52 – 53.

[30] See Joe Sills "The Recruits Controversy: Another Look" page 8.

[31] See Barry C. Johnson "A Captain of Chivalric Courage" page 9.

[32] Myles Moylan had risen from the ranks to command Company A. When the class conscious bachelor officers refused Moylan admittance to their mess, Custer took him into his own home as a boarder. See Edward Settle Godfrey "The Field Diary of Edward Settle Godfrey" page 61. Although not one of the bachelor officers referred to by Godfrey, the class conscious and aristocratic DeRudio probably held Moylan in contempt due to his "humble" beginnings.

[33] See John S. Gray "Centennial Campaign" page 87.

[34] For details of the incident, and DeRudio's reassignment, see Robert M. Utley "Gossip and Scandal" page 18, "Research Review: The Journal of the Little Big Horn Associates" Vol. 3 No 1, June 1989. Weir was clearly insubordinate in the incident cited and would continue to be so, with good reason, at the Little Big Horn.

[35] See "The Field Diary of Edward Settle Godfrey" page 36.

[36] See "The Field Diary of Edward Settle Godfrey" page 37.

[37] See Charles G. du Bois "Kick the Dead Lion" page 98.

[38] See Evan S. Connell "Son of The Morning Star" page 173.

[39] See D. A. Kinsley "Favor the Bold: Custer the Indian Fighter" page 74. It should be noted that the outspoken, tee totaling Custer was less than gracious when speaking at the internment: *"Gentlemen, this is not the death of a soldier. It is unnecessary, standing as we do in the presence of such an example, that I should say more."* It should also be noted that Custer noted in his field

book Cooper's family later accused him of indirect homicide. See D. A. Kinsley "Custer: Favor The Bold: A Soldier's Story" page 354.

[40] See Elizabeth B. Custer "Boots and Saddles" page 291.

[41] See E. S. Godfrey "Custer's Last Battle 1876" page 5.

[42] See Theodore W. Goldin "With The Seventh Cavalry In 1876" pages 8 - 9.

[43] See Elizabeth B. Custer "Following the Guidon" page 316.

[44] See Elizabeth B. Custer "Following the Guidon" page 316.

[45] See Thomas B. Marquis "Keep the Last Bullet for Yourself" page 62.

[46] See Margaret Leighton "Bride of Glory" page 198.

[47] See Lenora A. Snedeker "Attention! An Article of Historical Opinion" Newsletter of the Little Big Horn Associates, May 1995, page 5.

[48] See E. S. Godfrey "Custer's Last Battle 1876" pages 5 – 7.

[49] See Joe Sills Jr. "Were There Two Last Stands?" page 13.

[50] Lieutenant Maguire, charged with keeping the itinerary, recorded the distance marched as 13.40 miles. As the column started from their camp some little distance south of Fort Lincoln, Maguire's figure, in terms of the distance of the Heart River Camp from Fort Lincoln, is somewhat over stated.

[51] See Richard A. Roberts "Custer's Last Battle" page 15. Both Roberts and Reed had been hired as herders for the column's 114 head beef herd. See Earle R. Forrest "Witnesses at the Battle of the Little Big Horn" pages 40 – 41.

[52] See O. G. Libby "Arikara Narrative" page 60.

[53] See Fred Dustin "The Custer Tragedy" page 49. Note that Charles Windolph, the last surviving enlisted man of the regiment, believed that Custer was responsible for the order. See Frazier and Robert Hunt "I Fought With Custer" page 53.

[54] See Glendolin Damon Wagner "Old Neutriment" pages 123 – 124.

[55] See D. A. Kinsley "Favor the Bold: Custer the Indian Fighter" page 30.

[56] See D. A. Kinsley "Favor the Bold: Custer the Indian Fighter" page 200.

[57] See E. S. Godfrey "Custer's Last Battle 1876" page 7.

[58] See Edgar I. Stewart "Custer's Luck" pages 212 – 213.

[59] See O. G. Libby "Arikara Narrative" page 72.

[60] See Theodore W. Goldin "With The Seventh Cavalry In 1876" pages 10 – 11.

[61] See Richard A. Roberts "Custer's Last Battle" pages 19 – 21.

[62] Not to demean the hardships attendant to the march, Burkman noted: *"It don't sound much in the tellin' to say a wheel come off'n a wagon, or a wagon got stuck in the mud but for us that had to tug and sweat and cuss in the blazin' sun for maybe half a day, it meant a lot."* See Edgar I. Stewart "Custer's Luck" pages 214.

[63] The identity of this band has never been established; however, they were probably one of the many small parties leaving the reservation for the unceded territory. Correspondent Kellogg said that, on two other occasions, hunting parties had found warm embers. See Edgar I. Stewart "Custer's Luck" pages 216.

[64] See O. G. Libby "The Arikara Narrative" pages 62 – 63. For a slightly different version see Ben Innis "Bloody Knife!" page 119.

[65] Placed in nomination were Senator Thomas F. Bayard of Delaware, Governor Thomas A. Hendricks of Indiana, William Allen of Ohio, Winfield Scott Hancock of Pennsylvania, and Governor Samuel J. Tilden of New York.

[66] See Thomas Marquis "Custer On The Little Big Horn" page 10. To state that Custer was improperly motivated on the campaign is to say he went against his military training and judgment. There is no evidence what-so-ever that this was the case. Quite to the contrary, Custer's major failing on the campaign was an unusually conservative attitude. Custer was undeniably ambitious. But it was a brigadier's commission he coveted, not the white house. The truth behind this aspect of the Custer Myth was discerned by Tony Forsyth in an early April letter to Secretary of War Belknap: *"The fact of the matter is that both Hazen, and Custer, are now working to make capital with the Democratic party – **they want stars** ."* (emphasis from the original). See Robert M. Utley "Cavalier in Buckskin" page 164.

[67] See Alice O'Neil "Custer and Politics" Newsletter of the Little Big Horn Associates May 1994, page 5.

[68] See Richard A. Roberts "Custer's Last Battle" page 17.

[69] See Paul L. Hedren "The Great Sioux War" page 256.

[70] See Theodore W. Goldin "With The Seventh Cavalry In 1876" page 11.

[71] See Richard A. Roberts "Custer's Last Battle" page 18.

[72] See Richard Erdoes and Alfonso Ortiz "American Indian Myths and Legends" pages 237 - 242.

[73] See Edgar I. Stewart "Custer's Luck" pages 217 – 218.

[74] See Edgar I. Stewart "Custer's Luck" page 218.

[75] At this point Terry began to become concerned for his reputation, confiding to his sisters: *"I did hope & I had reason to hope that we should find the Indians here in force prepared to fight but now I*

fear that they have scattered and that I shall not be able to find them at all. This would be a most mortifying & perhaps injurious result to me. **But what will be will be.** *(emphasis from the original)"* See James Willert "The Terry Letters" page 9.

76 See Tom O'Neil "Garry Owne Tid Bits VII" page 29.

77 Privates Evans, Stewart, and Bell had set off in a skiff on May 27, traveling by moonlight. Fortunately they used muffled oars as Evans recalled their passing by an Indian village: *". . . nearly given away by their dogs, who howled and barked while we pulled like good fellows until morning."* See Paul L. Hedren "Three Cool, Determined Men" page 18.

78 The Powder River received its name from the fine black sand along its banks that resembles gunpowder. See Edgar I. Stewart "Custer's Luck" page 14.

79 See Edgar I. Stewart "Custer's Luck" page 222.

80 The other steamers chartered for the 1876 campaign were the *Carroll, Yellowstone, Benton, Silver Lake, E. F. Durfee*, and the *Josephine*. See David H. Grover "Custer's Navy" page 74.

81 See Joseph Mills Hanson "Conquest of the Missouri" page 238.

82 Grant Marsh had explored the Yellowstone River on the *Far West* in 1873 and had taken the *Josephine* about a dozen miles up the Big Horn River in 1875. See David H. Grover "Custer's Navy" page 73.

83 See Edgar I. Stewart "Custer's Luck" pages 223 – 224.

84 See Fred Dustin "The Custer Tragedy" page 58. The *Far West*, bound for St. Louis from Rocheport, Missouri, would strike a snag at Mullanphy Bend and sink on October 20, 1883.

85 See W. Boyes "Surgeon's Diary With the Custer Relief Column" page 17.

86 Godfrey claimed this decision was reached before Terry departed for his rendezvous with the *Far West* "*. . . it was given out that the 7th Cavalry would be sent to scout up the Powder River . . ."* See E. S. Godfrey "Custer's Last Battle 1876" page 10.

87 Born in 1837, the son of a French trader and Lakota mother, Boyer was the protégé and pupil of Jim Bridger.

88 See Daniel O. Magnussen "Thompson's Narrative" page 76.

89 See Edgar I. Stewart "Custer's Luck" pages 227 – 228. In a dispatch three days later Terry informed Sheridan of his intention to accompany Gibbon's column. See Francis B. Taunton "Sufficient Reason?" page 19.

90 See Michael J. Koury "Diaries of the Little Big Horn" page 9.

91 See Roger Darling "A Sad and Terrible Blunder" page 48.

92 See John W. Bailey "Pacifying the Plains" pages 137 – 138. While it is tantalizing to speculate as to the outcome had Custer commanded the scout; reaching the Indian trail while the warriors were

busy fighting Crook, it is difficult enough to determine many of the events that actually transpired without indulging in idle speculation as to what might have been.

93 Kellogg's dispatch for June 12 stated: *"Gen. Custer declined to take command of the detachment, which Maj. Reno now heads, not believing that any Indians would be met with in that direction."* See John S. Gray "Custer's Last Campaign" page 182. Custer, who obviously had given Kellogg his information also sent a news dispatch on the 12th: *"Feeling that he ought to send a scout up Powder River to clear it of any small detached band of Indians lurking away from the larger village, Terry decided to send six companies of 7th Cavalry and one gatling gun . . . all under Maj. Reno, to scout the Powder River as far as the Little Powder. . . . It is not believed that the . . . [party] will find the Indians, as their present abiding place is . . . on the Rosebud."* See John S. Gray "Custer's Last Campaign" page 183.

94 Eight scouts would be left behind at the depot, 6 to carry mail, 1 sick, and 1 had only a colt to ride. See O. G. Libby "The Arikara Narrative of the Campaign Against the Hostile Dakotas June 1876" page 74.

95 See O. G. Libby "The Arikara Narrative of the Campaign Against the Hostile Dakotas June 1876" page 74.

96 Chafing of the skin caused by the rubbing of the saddle.

97 See O. G. Libby "The Arikara Narrative of the Campaign Against the Hostile Dakotas June 1876" page 73.

98 See O. G. Libby "The Arikara Narrative of the Campaign Against the Hostile Dakotas June 1876" pages 73 – 74.

99 Due to the shortage of mounts, some 78 troopers had marched all the way from Fort Lincoln. Those who could not obtain a mount were left behind with the recruits at the Powder River depot. See John M. Carroll "The Jackass Dragoons" in A Seventh Cavalry Scrapbook #2 page 3. See also Walter Camp "Custer in '76" pages 123, 138 and 149. Despite the fact Reno had wired Department Headquarters in St. Paul on February 9, requesting an additional 70 horses for the 5 companies stationed at Fort Rice, the required additional mounts were not forthcoming.

100 See Fred Dustin 'The Custer Tragedy" page 93. John Burkman, Custer's striker, maintained two of the dogs accompanied the regiment to the Little Big Horn.

101 See Richard A. Roberts "Custer's Last Battle" page 24 and See Earle R. Forrest "Witnesses at the Battle of the Little Big Horn" page 47.

102 See John M. Carroll "I Fought With Custer" in A Seventh Cavalry Scrapbook #7 page 20.

103 See Walter Camp "Custer in '76" page 145.

104 See Theodore W. Goldin "With The Seventh Cavalry In 1876" pages 13 - 14.

105 See Edgar I. Stewart "Custers' Luck" pages 228 – 229.

106 See Daniel O. Magnussen "Thompson's Narrative" page 64.

[107] See Daniel O. Magnussen "Thompson's Narrative" pages 52 and 68.

[108] See Edgar I. Stewart "Custer's Luck" pages 235.

[109] The itinerary, found among the field notes of Walter Camp in the Harold B. Lee Library at Brigham Young University, was written from Hill's notes by Sergeant James E. Wilson of the Engineer Corps on June 21, 1876. See R. "Dutch" Hardorff "The Reno Scout: The Itinerary of Sergeant James Hill" page 3.

[110] See Daniel O. Magnussen "Thompson's Narrative" page 76.

[111] Note that Terry's diary entry for June 21 indicates 13 mules were injured, or worn out, during Reno's scout. See Michael J. Koury "The Terry Diary" page 23.

[112] See John S. Gray "Custer's Last Campaign" page 188.

[113] See Roger Darling "A Sad and Terrible Blunder" page 55.

[114] See John S. Gray "Custer's Last Campaign" page 194.

[115] See Daniel O. Magnussen "Thompson's Narrative" page 75.

[116] See R. "Dutch" Hardorff "The Reno Scout: The Itinerary of Sergeant James Hill" page 6.

[117] See Edgar I. Stewart "Custer's Luck" pages 235 – 236.

[118] See R. "Dutch" Hardorff "The Reno Scout: The Itinerary of Sergeant James Hill" page 9.

[119] See John S. Gray "Custer's Last Campaign" page 191.

[120] George Herendeen, a member of that expedition, would have been able to explain how well two pieces of artillery had served the small party in their almost constant fighting with the Lakota, but there is no indication his opinion was ever solicited.

[121] See O. G. Libby "The Arikara Narrative of the Campaign Against the Hostile Dakotas June 1876" pages 70 – 71.

[122] See R. "Dutch" Hardorff "The Reno Scout: The Itinerary of Sergeant James Hill" page 9.

[123] See John S. Gray "Custer's Last Campaign" pages 192 – 193. Private Francis Johnson Kennedy of Company I. Kennedy, being under age, had enlisted under the name of Francis Johnson. Bitten by a rattlesnake in the badlands prior to crossing the Little Missouri River, Kennedy was with the pack train at the Little Big Horn. See John M. Carroll "A Seventh Cavalry Scrapbook" page 25.

[124] See Edgar I. Stewart "Custer's Luck" page 233.

[125] See Thomas B. Marquis "Memoirs of a White Crow Indian" page 238.

[126] See John Gibbon "Gibbon on the Sioux Campaign of 1876" pages 20 – 21.

[127] On June 16th, Gibbon's scouts had noticed a large smoke in the vicinity of Tullock's Fork. This, apparently, is the reason Terry would insist Custer scout the region on his subsequent march up the Rosebud. It should be noted that in both his official report and article for the *American Catholic Quarterly*, Gibbon states that this smoke was seen on the Little Big Horn. It should be remembered that at the time of Gibbon's official report and popular account, the surviving campaign leadership was trying to establish a myth of cooperation between Custer's and Gibbon's detachments predicated on the certain knowledge that the Indians were on the Little Big Horn. Noting that no further intelligence relative to the location of the village was obtained before Custer struck it, this communication demonstrates that, while the military may have inferred the trail led to the Little Big Horn, they did not know for a certainty where the Indians would be found. Given the route the village actually followed, the trail would have to be followed past the big bend of the Rosebud to verify it turned toward the Little Big Horn. As John Gray so aptly demonstrates in Centennial Campaign, Reno's scouts did not have time to follow the trail that far. In addition, had they reached the big bend of the Rosebud, they would have witnessed Crook's fight, an event they couldn't have failed to report.

[128] See John S. Gray "Centennial Campaign" pages 135 – 136. Gibbon knows that this information will necessitate a change in plan. It is ironic that Gibbon, and not Reno, should be the one to inform Terry of Reno's visit to the camp sites discovered by Bradley a month earlier.

[129] See Michael J. Koury "The Terry Diary" pages 22 – 23.

[130] No such letter is contained in the Terry collection at Yale University. The quote is from Terry's aid, and brother–in–law, Robert Patterson Hughes. Given their relationship by marriage, and that during the march from Fort Lincoln they had pitched their tents together so they shared a sitting room as well as a bedroom, Edgar I. Stewart and John Gray accept the validity of the letter, but Fred Dustin does not. It is almost certain that Terry wrote his sisters on that day as the last mail had been on June 12 and a mail was to sent on the 22nd. The content of the letter would also probably be known to Hughes. Although the exact wording is subject to question, due to Hughes later defense of Terry's actions, it is reasonable to assume that the letter read about as Hughes quoted. See James Willert "The Terry Letters" page 47.

[131] See Daniel O. Magnussen "Thompson's Narrative of the Little Bighorn Campaign 1876" page 78. This exchange was of little consequence as Custer was frustrated over Reno's lack of initiative and fearful that Reno may have alerted the enemy to the presence of the troops. Since he had disobeyed orders, Custer believed Reno should either have attacked, or , at least obtained positive information about the size and location of the village. For his part, Reno was justified in being short with his regimental commander as he had been operating directly under Terry's orders and was not responsible to Custer in the matter. It should also be recalled at this juncture that there are indications Reno had indeed contemplated offensive operations. Why Reno did not attempt to either defend, or at least explain, his actions to his superiors remains a mystery. As the subsequent controversy had no effect on the campaign I omit reference to Custer's and Kellogg's articles highly critical of Reno's performance. Roger Darling in "A Sad and Terrible Blunder" page 56, notes Terry *"frequently mentioning the indiscretion to newsmen at the end of the 1876 summer campaign."* The suggestion is this course was adopted to divert attention from Terry's own poor performance in the campaign.

[132] The Lakota had occupied this site the previous winter. Later Miles City, Montana would be built on the site of this Indian camp. See E. S. Godfrey "Custer's Last Battle 1876" page 11.

[133] See O. G. Libby "The Arikara Narrative" page 75. Libbie Custer wrote in "Boots and Saddles" that the body was found in the remains of a fire. Although this unfortunate trooper has never been

identified, many authorities speculate the remains to have been one of Custer's troopers from the 1873 Stanley Expedition. To my mind, this is highly unlikely as it would either have required the Lakota to have kept their prisoner, with his uniform intact, for over two years before torturing him to death, or to have camped, without disturbing any of the signs, on a site occupied 2 years previously. What is most likely is the unfortunate was a deserter, or trooper whose enlistment had recently expired, who happened to be in the wrong place at the wrong time.

134 See Robert J. Ege "Curse Not His Curls" page 72.

135 See E. S. Godfrey "Custer's Last Battle 1876" page 11.

136 See O. G. Libby "The Arikara Narrative" pages 75 – 76.

137 See John S. Gray "Centennial Campaign" page 140.

138 See John Gibbon "Gibbon on the Sioux Campaign of 1876" page 22.

139 See Edgar I. Stewart "Custer's Luck" page 243.

140 See Francis B. Taunton "Sufficient Reason?" page 25.

141 See Robert M. Utley "Cavalier in Buckskin" page 175.

142 See James H. Bradley "The March of the Montana Column" page 143.

143 See W. Boyes "Surgeon's Diary With the Custer Relief Column" page 19.

144 See Edgar I. Stewart "Custer's Luck" page 245.

145 See Charles Kuhlman "Legend Into History" page 37 and Thomas B. Marquis "Wooden Leg: A Warrior Who Fought Custer" page 204.

146 Note that the use of the Tongue River here is not an error. As the headwaters of the Rosebud lie north of the headwaters of the Little Big Horn, ordering Custer to only proceed that far before turning to the Little Big Horn would leave the 7th short of the headwaters. The Tongue, however, rises south of the Little Big Horn and therefore represents a proper objective for the southern most point of Custer's march.

147 See E. Lisle Reedstrom "Custer's 7th Cavalry" page 120.

148 Brisbin maintained Custer was only to get the 2nd Cavalry if Terry went in overall command and that the offer was made after the conference. Terry's confidential report of July 2, reproduced in its entirety in Appendix 5, indicates Terry offered Custer the cavalry and Gatling guns during the conference.

149 See John M. Carroll "General Custer and the Battle of the Little Big Horn: The Federal View" pages 87 – 88.

150 See Cyrus Townshend Brady "Indian Fights and Fighters" page 367.

[151] Custer was ordered to report to Terry *"not later than the expiration of the time for which your troops are rationed"* which would have been July 7 as he carried 15 days' rations. See Walter Camp 'Custer in '76" page 261 and W. A. Graham "The Custer Myth: A Source Book of Custeriana" page 130.

[152] See Louise Barnett "Touched By Fire" page 303.

[153] Among other evidence, there are letters from Autie Reed written June 21st and Tom Custer on June 5 indicating Mary Adams was with the command (see Charles K. Hofling "Custer and the Little Big Horn: A Psychobiographical Inquiry" page 103 and Tom O'Neil "Garry Owen Tid Bits VII" page 30); the statement of saddler John G. Tritten to Walter Camp (see Dale T. Schoenberger "The End of Custer" page 273); and canceled checks proving Mary and Maria Adams were two different people (see Charles M. Cook "Little Big Horn Survivors"). See also Robert M. Utley "Cavalier in Buckskin" page 171. An interesting corollary, which, in my opinion, also cannot be credited, is the account of Private John F. Donahue of Company K who claimed to overhear Terry tell Custer to strike in cooperation with Gibbon on June 26 unless he feared the escape of the Indians in which case he was to use his own judgment. See W. Kent King "Massacre: The Custer Cover-up" pages 147 - 148.

Chapter 9

Premonitions of Disaster

Coming events cast their shadows before them. Nowhere is this more true than in the case of the Little Big Horn disaster. Before embarking on the Seventh Cavalry's march up the Rosebud, let us pause and reflect on the various dreams and visions that seemed to foretell the calamity to occur on the Little Big Horn. Charles Deland wrote in his history of the Sioux:

> *"Everywhere among the narratives of various writers and informants concerning this expedition and who were members thereof, this remarkable and prophetic fact of premonition of impending doom of the participants, is woven as if some spirit of evil were lingeringly but persistently hovering over camp and march as a kind of presiding genius."*[1]

We will see in the next chapter that Lieutenant Edward S. Godfrey was apparently one of those filled with a sense of impending doom; at least his 1892 *Century Magazine* article is replete with references to an all pervading sense of melancholia enveloping the command like a shroud. We will see in the following accounts that these premonitions were not restricted to the soldiers. Was it mere coincidence that the Sacred Hat bundle of the Cheyenne was unwrapped for one of the few times in its history the week before the Custer fight?[2] While the mood expressed by Godfrey was by no means universally held, the accounts that follow are a collection of the experiences of those for whom the veil parted for an instant, revealing the disaster that lay just ahead.

Perhaps the most celebrated psychic event associated with the Battle of the Little Big Horn is Sitting Bull's sundance vision. This vision, however, was but one in a series of psychic experiences for Sitting Bull that had begun at the annual sundance conducted a year prior to the battle. The *wiwanyag wachipi*, or sundance, which may have originated with the Cheyenne, was the most sacred of all Lakota religious ceremonies. Black Elk, Oglala Holy Man, described the preparations:

> *"First a holy man was sent out all alone to find the waga chun, the holy tree that should stand in the middle of the dancing circle. Nobody dared follow to see what he did or hear the sacred words he would say there. And when he had found the right tree, he would tell the people, and they would come singing, with flowers all over them. Then when they had gathered about the holy tree, some women who were bearing children would dance around it, because the Spirit of the Sun loves all fruitfulness. After that a warrior, who had done some very brave deed that summer, struck the tree, counting coup upon it; and when he had done this, he had to give gifts to those who had least of everything, and the braver he was, the more he gave away.*

> *"After this, a band of young maidens came singing, with sharp axes in their hands; and they had to be so good that nobody there could say anything against them, or that any man had ever known them; and it was the duty of any one who knew anything bad about any of them to tell it right before all the people there and prove it. But if anybody lied, it was very bad for him.*

"The maidens chopped the tree down and trimmed its branches off. Then chiefs, who were the sons of chiefs, carried the sacred tree home, stopping four times on the way, once for each season, giving thanks for each.

"Now when the holy tree had been brought home but was not yet set up in the center of the dancing place, mounted warriors gathered around the circle of the village, and at a signal they all charged inward upon the center where the tree would stand, each trying to be the first to touch the sacred place; and whoever was the first could not be killed in war that year. When they all came together in the middle, it was like a battle, with the ponies rearing and screaming in a big dust and the men shouting and wrestling and trying to throw each other off the horses.

"After that there was a big feast and plenty for everybody to eat, and a big dance just as though we had won a victory."[3]

During this ritual, which served as a rite of passage to manhood, the individual suffered self–inflicted torture to prove his bravery and placate his gods. According to Stanley Vestal, the four great virtues taught by the dance were bravery, generosity, fortitude, and fecundity. Typically the dancer had his breasts gashed, although often it was the muscles of the lower back which were used, by the medicine men who then inserted skewer sticks just beneath the muscles which underlie the skin. Over the ends of these sticks was placed a buckskin thong which was fastened to the lariats attached to the central pole. The lines were then drawn tight so that the young man had to stand upon his toes to prevent being suspended by his breast and shoulders, the integument sometimes stretching three or four inches out of the body. Facing the sun, he would blow his eagle bone whistle while dancing about. Neither food, drink, nor sleep was allowed until the dance ended with the young man collapsing as the sticks finally tore through the muscles. It is easy to imagine that visions did indeed come to those who had undergone this ordeal. White Bull's account of the 1875 sundance is published here, I believe, for the first time:

"In the summer of 1875 the Sioux and Cheyennes had a meeting at the mouth of Lame Deer Creek to hold a sun dance. Sitting Bull's Sioux, Hunkpapa (sic), Crazy Horse, with Spotted Eagle and Spotted Elk, a few Minneconjous and one village of Cheyennes under Little Wolf.

"After the medicine lodge had been built, Sitting Bull rode into it on his war–horse, a black horse with a white stripe in the face, given to him by White Bull. This horse was well known to all as a good running horse. Sitting Bull dismounted and leading his horse, danced all around the circle of the medicine lodge. He carried no arms but wore a war bonnet. Sitting Bull was painted all over with yellow clay. He wore only a breech clout and moccasins. His face was painted black from the corner of one eye over the temple and across the forehead down to the other eye, but on each side this black line had two forks; the lower part of his face was painted black. About each wrist were two black lines and two black lines about each ankle. On his chest was a round black disc which represented the sun and on his right shoulder–blade a crescent which stood for the moon. Painted over the horse's hips came a crooked trail in white clay, down to the top of the hip, and from there down it ran straight down the right side of the hip and leg. From the corners of the horse's mouth were zigzag lines in white clay running to the root of each ear. From his shoulders back to where the rider's legs would come were dots of white clay, put on by the tips of a person's out–stretched fingers. These dots represented hail. He danced to the back of the lodge, and stopping there danced forward to the pole and

then back to his place. He called out, 'I wish my friends to fill one pipe and I wish my people to fill one pipe,' that is to say, he wanted the Cheyennes and the Sioux to fill pipes and smoke together, showing that they would act together. Black Crane, a Cheyenne afterwards killed on the way up from the south (a reference to the flight of the Cheyenne from Oklahoma Territory in 1878, DCE), filled one pipe and a Sioux filled another. Sitting Bull took the Cheyenne's pipe in his right hand and had Black Crane stand on his right. He took the Sioux pipe in his left hand and had the Sioux stand on his left.

"Now those in the medicine lodge began to sing. While Sitting Bull held the two pipes in front of him, the bowls directed toward the pole and danced toward it, he made motions as if he were approaching an enemy. All this time he led his horse, which followed him back and forth. As he danced forward and back he spoke now and then. Once he said, 'I have nearly got them,' meaning that the Great Power had nearly given his enemies to him. He made the motions of approaching and retreating and of drawing toward him three times, but the fourth time he did these things he spread his arms and swept them through the air and closed them over his chest, meaning that he had surrounded his enemies and had them in his power. Then after this he lifted his hands up to the sky and offered the pipes to the Great Spirit and said, 'We have them. The Great Spirit has given our enemy into our power.'

"No one then knew who the enemy were – of what tribe. Sitting Bull finished his dance by a song of triumph and thanksgiving saying, 'The Great Spirit has given our enemies to us; we are to destroy them; we do not know who they are; **they may be soldiers** *.' (emphasis the author's)*

"He sang his song first, and all the others joined in, perhaps six or seven hundred warriors in the whole camp. In those days there were only two men in the Sioux tribe who had plenty of courage and good sense. These two were Crazy Horse and Sitting Bull. Sitting Bull was a little the older of the two."[4]

In late May of 1876, Sitting Bull had a second vision associated with the coming fight. He had gone up on a butte to meditate and fell into a trace. In his dream he saw a great dust storm approaching from the east. The dust screened rank upon rank of soldiers who followed in its wake, closing upon the Indian village which was represented by a fleecy white cloud. The dust storm collided with the cloud with a terrible fury, accompanied by a tremendous thunderstorm and torrential rain. After the storm abated, the dust had dissipated, but the white cloud remained intact.[5] The dream could have but one meaning, the village would be attacked by an undetected column of soldiers from the east, but the warriors would prevail.

The final corroboration came during the June sundance. The 1876 sundance probably ran from the 11th to the 14th of June[6], although some authors place it as early as June 4th. Under the watchful eye of Black Moon, Uncpapa conductor of the sundance,[7] Jumping Bull carefully cut 50 pieces of skin from each arm of his adopted father, Sitting Bull.[8] In the vision that followed, Sitting Bull heard the voice of his *sicun* saying *"I give you these because they have no ears"*.[9] At the same time he saw mounted soldiers and Indians falling upside down into the Lakota camp. Now the meaning of the three visions was crystal clear– the village would be attacked by soldiers; but the Indians would be victorious. One can only imagine the effect this vision, coupled with the recent victory over Reynolds on the Powder, had on the young warriors. They must have felt that no power on earth could withstand them, and, after they had punished Crook on the Rosebud, even the staunchest of doubters must have been convinced of their invincibility.

Visions and prophecies were not new to Sitting Bull. He had once foretold his own wounding during a raid on the Flatheads.[10] Given this predilection and the magnitude of the coming victory, it is not surprising that the 1876 sundance vision was not Sitting Bull's only psychic experience related to the Little Big Horn.

Perhaps Sitting Bull sensed the coming fight again on the eve of the battle. Henry Oscar One Bull, a nephew of Sitting Bull, related the following episode that occurred the evening of June 24, 1876:

> *"The night before the fight with Long Hair, Sitting Bull went out to the ridge where the monument now stands. He sang a thunder song, then prayed for knowledge of things to come. As he repeated for me later, he wailed aloud, offering a filled pipe as he prayed:*

> *"'Wakantanka, hear me and pity me! I offer you this pipe in the name of my people. Save them. We want to live! Guard my people against all danger and misfortune. Take pity on us!'*

> *"Then he stuck slender wands in the ground to which he tied tiny buckskin bags of tobacco and willow bark. Next day Long Hair's horse soldiers would knock them all down, but that night my uncle knew that Wakantanka had heard his prayer."*[11]

Perhaps there is corroboration for this story. Lieutenant Varnum, while following Custer's trail to the battlefield on the 27th, came upon some Indian medicine bags on a hillside that had been trampled under the hooves of Custer's horses.[12]

Premonitions and psychic experiences were not unknown to Libbie Custer. The first experience connected with her husband's last campaign occurred the day the regiment departed. An early morning fog was beginning to burn off and, Captain George Yates' brother–in–law noted a beautiful rainbow under which nearly the entire expedition passed.[13] Some saw more than a idyllic scene in the morning mist. Libbie Custer related:

> *"From the hour of breaking camp, before the sun was up, a mist had enveloped everything. Soon the bright sun began to penetrate this veil and dispel the haze, and a scene of wonder and beauty appeared.[14] The cavalry and infantry in the order named, the scouts, pack mules, and artillery, all behind the long line of white–covered wagons, made a column altogether some two miles in length. As the sun broke through the mist a mirage appeared, which took up about half of the line of cavalry, and thenceforth for a little distance it marched, equally plain to the sight on the earth and in the sky.*

> *"The future of the heroic band, whose days were even then numbered, seemed to be revealed, and already there seemed a premonition in the supernatural translation as their forms were reflected from the opaque mist of the early dawn."*[15]

Sunday, June 25, 1876 was a day filled with foreboding for Libbie Custer. Once again her thoughts had strayed to her recurring nightmare of the naked Indian warrior brandishing a fresh scalp.[16] There was a difference this time; however, as she knew the blond scalp the warrior brandished had been her husband's. Her melancholy only increased as she recalled the news that the largest column in the field that summer, commanded by General Crook, had been soundly thrashed by the same Indians sought by her husband. The officer's wives habitually gathered at the Custer residence on Sundays, and the 25th was no exception. Libbie related:

"A picture of one day of our life in those disconsolate times is fixed indelibly in my memory.

"On Sunday afternoon, June 25, our little group of saddened women, borne down with one common weight of anxiety, sought solace in gathering together in our house. We tried to find some slight surcease from trouble in the old hymns; some of them dated back to our childhood days, when our mothers rocked us to sleep to their soothing strains. I remember the grief with which one fair young wife threw herself on the carpet and pillowed her head in the lap of a tender friend. Another sat dejected at the piano and struck soft chords that melted into the notes of the voices. All were absorbed in the same thoughts, and their eyes were filled with faraway visions and longings. Indescribable yearning for the absent, and untold terror for their safety, engrossed each heart. The words of the hymn,

'E'en though a cross it be,

'Nearer, my God, to Thee,'

came forth with almost a sob from every throat.

"At that very hour the fears that our tortured minds had portrayed in imagination were realities, and the souls of those we thought upon were ascending to meet their Maker."[17]

A vacancy occurred on Custer's staff with the detailing of Major Lewis Merrill to the centennial exhibition in Philadelphia in March of 1876. Custer wanted the first lieutenant of Company H, Francis M. Gibson, for the position. Gibson and his wife were overjoyed at the prospect of being posted to Fort Lincoln and they waited impatiently for the transfer papers to come through. Katherine had almost completed packing when the papers, requiring only Frank's signature, arrived. As she touched the papers, an unshakable feeling of dread came over her. So strong was this feeling of impending disaster, she argued for a day and a night against accepting the transfer. Finally, Frank gave in to the demands of his wife and declined the transfer, remaining with Company H and surviving the Little Big Horn.[18]

The vacancy on Custer's staff still remained and Katherine related:

"Upon my husband's declining the Lincoln transfer, he (Second Lieutenant Jack Sturgis, DCE) had come springing over to our quarters, and with eyes shining had asked eagerly, 'If you really don't want that transfer, Gib, do you mind if I take it?'

"'Not at all, Jack,' replied Frank promptly. 'It will mean so much to you being at Lincoln with your parents.'

"'Yes, indeed,' agreed the boy, his whole face lighting.

> *"For one wild moment I wanted to put my hand on his arm and plead, 'Oh, don't do it, Jack; don't do it,' but a warning glance from my husband checked the impulse. Besides, it wouldn't have done any good. The boy was too set upon it. Well, he had no difficulty in achieving the transfer, with General Sturgis' influence, and the day that he came to say good–by he was simply radiant with happiness. Poor, poor Jack!"[19]*

At the conclusion of the night march of June 24th, Peter Thompson lay down with his comrades in C Troop to grab what sleep they could. He relates:

> *"I will state here that I am too hard–headed to believe in dreams, but will here relate one which, in spite of my unbelief, disturbed me. I had laid down under a tree and had fallen into a doze when I dreamed that the Indians attacked a small detachment of us soldiers. We were all dismounted and the Indians put us to flight. At this point I awoke expecting to find it real, but seeing the outstretched forms of my comrades, I composed myself and laid down to sleep again., But my dream instead of being cut off by my awaking began to run in the same channel, only this time I alone was the victim. An Indian with an uplifted axe came after me, there was no lagging but a fair and square race, and for the life of me I could not tell why I ran from the Indian. Just as the savage got close enough to me to strike I awoke only to find all vanish into thin air. But as profoundly had the dream impressed itself upon me that I could get no more sleep.[20]*

On March 5, 1876, Corporal Thomas Eagen, Company E, wrote his sister for the last time (spelling and grammer have not been corrected in order to preserve the flavor of the original, DCE):

> *"Dear Sister,*
>
> *i take the preasent oppertunity of letting you no that i will soon be on the move again. We ar to start the 10th of this month for the Big horn country. The Indians are gettin bad again. i think that we will have some hard times this summer. The old Chief Sitting Bull says that he will not make peace with the whites as long as he has a man to fight. The weather very cold hear at preasent and very likely to stay so for two months yet. Ella, you need not rite to me again until your hear frome me again. Give my love to sister Mary and Brother Jonny. Remember me to your husband. As soon as i get back of the campaign i will rite you. **That is if i do not get my hair lifted by some Indian** (emphasis the author's, DCE). Well i will close, so no more at preasent."[21]*

Before sunup on June 25, 1876, an old woman died in the Uncpapa camp. Her name has been lost to history, but she was the wife of Four Horns, an uncle of Sitting Bull. Sitting Bull was deeply moved by the death of his aunt and later told his nephew, Henry Oscar One Bull, that the death of such an important woman made him wonder if the promised victory of many soldiers falling into camp might not come that very day.[22]

The night of June 23, 1876, an blind old Cheyenne Medicine Man named Box Elder dreamed that the soldiers would shortly attack the camp. His warnings to tie the war ponies near at hand conveyed to the village on the mornings of the 24th and 25th caused great consternation among the Cheyenne as he was known to have the gift of prophecy. Box Elder, and his father Horn before him, were reputed to have received their psychic powers directly from the wolves. In spite of his reputation, the warning went largely unheeded.[23]

Other warnings the morning of June 24th were ignored. A crier had gone around the Sans Arc circle crying that the soldiers would arrive the next morning. Very early that morning in the Cheyenne circle, Old Brave Wolf, although blind, had howled like a wolf. His call had been answered by a real wolf, howling twice. The meaning was clear – there would soon be meat for the wolves.[24]

While performing a healing ceremony for a wounded Cheyenne a few days prior to the Custer Fight, the shaman White Bull heard spirits calling from Bear Butte, the sacred mountain of the Cheyenne. These spirits foretold the coming victory.[25]

Interestingly, Lieutenant George Wallace, Company G, had a premonition of disaster, not for himself, but for Armstrong Custer. While walking back to their bivouac from the Officer's conference of June 22nd, Wallace discussed his thoughts with Lieutenant Edward S. Godfrey:

> *"I walked back with Wallace who said he believed Genl Custer would be killed as he had never heard him talk as he did, or his manner so subdued.[26]*

Perhaps Second Lieutenant Jack Sturgis, son of the regiment's full colonel, and the man who had accepted the transfer refused by Lieutenant Gibson, had a premonition of his death. He wrote a young lady about two weeks before the battle:

> *"Good-by. Perhaps I am bidding you my last farewell, as I am ordered out a couple of days hence to be scalped by the red-men."[27]*

One of the more bizarre and gruesome psychic incidents involved Second Lieutenant Henry M. Harrington. His was a pervasive premonition that he would be captured and burned alive.[28] Lieutenant Hare recalled that early in the campaign, Lieutenant Harrington had made sketches of himself tied to a tree with naked savages dancing around him as he burned. Fortunately, the sketches were sent to a friend, not to his wife.[29]

In the next chapter, I will relate how Charley Reynolds, certain of his approaching death, divided his belongings among the scouts the night of June 24th. Early in the expedition, however, he had a premonition that this was to be his last campaign. Fred Girard testified at the Reno Court of Inquiry in 1879:

> *". . . Mr. Reynolds and I were bosom friends and camped together, and twice on the expedition out he came and told me that he had a presentiment of his death – that he would never return from that expedition and I advised him to go to see Gen. Terry and get from him leave to stay out. If I was in the same position I would do it; and he went to Gen. Terry, and Gen. Terry shamed him out of it."[30]*

Second Lieutenant Benjamin H. Hodgson, Company B, was wounded in the leg as his horse jumped into the Little Big Horn during the retreat from the valley. His horse having been killed, probably by the same bullet, he called for assistance. According to First Sergeant John Ryan, and Private William Slaper, both of Company M, Trumpeter Charles "Bounce" Fischer, also of Company M, had Hodgson hold onto his stirrup and in that manner conveyed him across the river.[31] Cognizant Custer had ordered all stirrup hoods removed (except for guidon bearers),

Hodgson had mentioned some days before the battle that if he became dismounted or wounded in battle he intended to take hold of a stirrup to assist him from the field.[32] Unfortunately his planning went for naught as he was fatally shot upon reaching the presumed safety of the Little Big Horn's east bank.

While cooking dinner at the evening halt on June 24th, Custer's scouts discussed the outlook. According to William Jackson, Bloody Knife was very pessimistic:

> *"It is as I have told Long Hair: this gathering of the enemy tribes is too many for us. But he will not believe me. He is bound to lead us against them. They are not far away; just over this ridge, they are all encamped and waiting for us. Crazy Horse and Sitting Bull are not men–without–sense; they have their scouts out, and some of them surely have their eyes upon us. Well, to–morrow we are going to have a big fight, a losing fight. Myself, I know what is to happen to me; my sacred helper has given me warning that I am not to see the set of to–morrow's sun."*[33]

---

[1] See Evan S. Connell "Son of the Morning Star" page 262.

[2] See Margot Liberty and John Stands in Timber "Cheyenne Memories" page 77.

[3] See John G. Neihardt "Black Elk Speaks," pages 96 – 98 and James R. Walker "Lakota Belief and Ritual," pages 176 – 191.

[4] See Grinnell Interviews, Southwest Museum, Highland Park, California.

[5] See Robert M. Utley "The Lance And The Shield" apge 136.

[6] Henry Oscar One Bull, a nephew of Sitting Bull, said the vision was given to Sitting Bull three days before the fight with Crook on the Rosebud, making the vision the 14th of June. See Leslie Tillett "Wind on the Buffalo Grass" page 60.

[7] Vestal, Stanley "Sitting Bull," page 149 and Peter John Powell "People of the Sacred Mountain," page 952.

[8] Vestal, Stanley "Sitting Bull," page 149.

[9] See David Humphreys Miller "Custer's Fall: The Indian Side of the Story," page 43, Edgar I. Stewart "Custer's Luck," page 195 and Stanley Vestal "Sitting Bull," pages 150 – 151.

[10] See Stanley Vestal "Sitting Bull: Champion of the Sioux" page 119.

[11] See Leslie Tillett "Wind on the Buffalo Grass" page 60 and Stanley Vestal "Sitting Bull: Champion of the Sioux" page 158.

[12] See Evan S. Connell "Son of the Morning Star" pages 319 – 320.

[13] See Richard A. Roberts "Custer's Last Battle" page 14.

[14] Initially Libbie had remarked, *"How beautiful and how strange!"* to sister–in–law Maggie Calhoun (see Margaret Leighton "Bride of Glory" page 198). Apparently, she later considered the sight of the troops marching in the sky to be a harbinger of death.

[15]See Elizabeth B. Custer "Boots and Saddles" page 218.

[16]Libbie Custer had a fear of Indians since studying the Raisin River Massacre that had occurred at Monroe during the War of 1812. The victorious British had left the wounded Kentuckians unguarded and they were butchered by the British's Indian allies. (See Lawrence A. Frost "General Custer's Libbie" page 14). Libbie had her first childhood nightmare about this event. See Margaret Leighton "Bride of Glory" page 4.

[17]See Elizabeth B. Custer "Boots and Saddles" pages 221 – 222.

[18]See Katherine Gibson Fougera "With Custer's Cavalry" pages 250 – 254.

[19]See Katherine Gibson Fougera "With Custer's Cavalry" pages 258 – 259. Jack Sturgis was assigned to E Troop at the Little Big Horn and, although his body was never identified, he was presumed killed with his troop on June 25th.

[20]See Daniel O. Magnussen "Peter Thompson's Narrative of the Little Bighorn Campaign 1876" page 96. Peter Thompson was one of the stragglers from Company C that joined Reno's command on the bluffs. Despite having been in the army only 9 months, and contrary to his dream, he served with distinction, being wounded while a member of the water party on June 26th.

[21]See John M. Carroll "They Rode With Custer." Corporal Eagen was killed in action with the Custer column on June 25th.

[22]See Leslie Tillett "Wind on the Buffalo Grass" page 60.

[23]See Peter John Powell "People of the Sacred Mountain" page 1008 and David Humphreys Miller "Custer's Fall: The Indian Side of the Story" page 52. Box Elder's warning the night before the attack on Dull Knife's village in November of 1876 would also be ignored. See Richard G. Hardorff "Lakota Recollections" page 135.

[24]See Peter John Powell "People of the Sacred Mountain" page 1008 and Richard G. Hardorff "Cheyenne Memories of the Custer Fight" page 11.

[25] See Richard G. Hardorff "Cheyenne Memories of the Custer Fight" page 37.

[26]See "The Field Diary of Lt. Edward Settle Godfrey" page 9.

[27]See Elizabeth Atwood Lawrence "His Very Silence Speaks" page 106.

[28]A *New York World* article of November 20, 1887 quotes Reno as stating that he and several officers saw three men burned at the stake the night of June 25th and that one of them appeared to be Harrington. Given the distance involved, over three miles, and the quality of the field glasses in use at that time, it is highly improbable that anyone could have identified a person at such a distance at night. I have been unable to locate any of the "other officers" statements to corroborate the alleged statement. See "Was Lieut. Harrington Burned?", Big Horn Yellowstone Journal, Vol I., No. 4, Autumn 1992, page 10.

[29]See Mari Sandoz "The Battle of the Little Big Horn" pages 145 and 168.

[30]See Robert M. Utley "The Reno Court of Inquiry" page 136 and Ronald H. Nichols "Reno Court of Inquiry" page 127.

[31]See John M. Carroll "They Rode With Custer."

[32]See Colonel W. A. Graham "The Custer Myth: A Source Book of Custeriana" page 140.

[33]See James Willard Schultz "William Jackson Indian Scout" pages 129 – 130. Ben Innis "Bloody Knife!" pages 133 – 134 believes that Bloody Knife's statement was made to Custer shortly after the regiment crossed the divide on June 25th. It is possible Bloody Knife may have made the statement on more than one occasion.

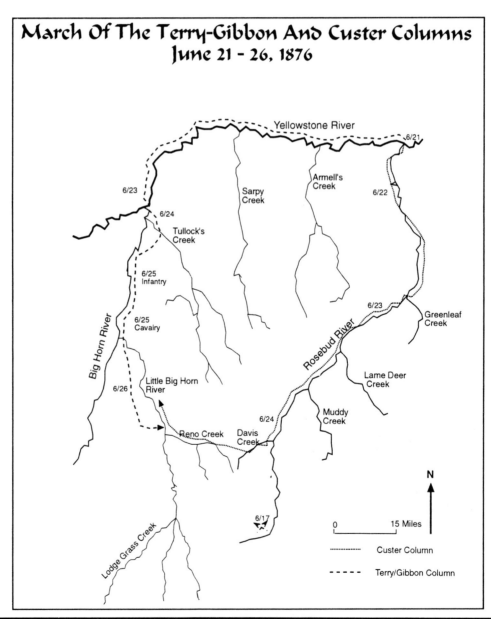

March Of The Terry-Gibbon And Custer Columns June 21 - 26, 1876

Chapter 10

The March Up the Rosebud

When Custer returned from the officers' conference held on board the *Far West* the afternoon of June 21st, he was moody and morose.[1] The reason behind this uncharacteristic behavior continues to perplex historians who feel this had some bearing on the subsequent disaster. Some authors argue that Custer was still smarting from his treatment by Grant, and that expunging this affront to his dignity, and blight upon his record, had become an all consuming passion that dominated his every waking moment. It cannot be denied that Custer possessed a rather advanced ego, which is not at all unusual in an individual who has attained great success and adulation at an early age, and he was undoubtedly concerned with "clearing his good name." This explanation, however, ignores the fact Custer had been his "old self" during the march from Fort Lincoln, especially so while scouting the Little Missouri. Similarly, while Custer was apparently disheartened when Reno was given the assignment to scout up the Powder River in preference to himself, he was now in exactly the position desired: an independent command with plenty of rations and the authority to attack and subdue the enemy force. What then is the explanation? As is true of most events and attitudes associated with the Little Big Horn, the question defies simple interpretation. Perhaps the forces that Godfrey felt hung like a cloud of impending doom, with which so many of the command seemed in tune, were in communion with Custer that night, or, perhaps Custer was unsettled by the indecision exhibited by Terry at the officer's conference and feared a repetition of Hancock's disastrous 1867 expedition. Given the gulf that separates us in time from these events, and the personal biases that unfortunately color so much of our primary source material, we will probably never have a completely adequate understanding of the feelings and prejudices that were driving Armstrong Custer on the eve of his departure from the Yellowstone. Ultimately, the reasons behind Custer's moodiness are unimportant. What is of interest is the question: Did Custer perform his duties adequately at the Little Big Horn, or did he let his emotions and personal motivations conspire to lead himself and his command to disaster? The answer will be discovered in an analysis of Custer's actions from the time he left the Yellowstone until he dispatched his second messenger, John Martin, with Adjutant Cooke's order to hurry the ammunition packs.

Upon taking his leave of Terry and Gibbon, who had accompanied him to his tent, Custer ordered *"Officer's Call"* sounded, and, when the officers were assembled, he gave them their orders.[2] Fifteen days rations of hard bread, coffee, and sugar as well as twelve days rations of bacon [3]and fifty rounds of carbine ammunition per man were to be transported on the pack mules.[4] Additionally, each man was to carry on his person, or in his saddle bags, 100 rounds of carbine and 24 rounds of pistol ammunition and twelve pounds of oats. Custer's suggestion that additional forage be carried on the pack mules, was met with resistance by some of his officers; primarily those assigned to the right wing, who felt that their mules had been pretty well used up on Reno's scout. He replied in what Godfrey described as an excited manner, which was considered unusual for him:

> *"Well, gentlemen, you may carry what supplies you please; you will be held responsible for your companies. The extra forage was only a suggestion, but this fact bear in mind, we will follow the trail for fifteen days unless we catch them before that time expires, no matter how far it may take us from our base of supplies; we may not see the supply steamer again."* As he turned to enter his tent, he added: *"You had better carry along an extra supply of salt; we may have to live on horse meat before we get through."* [5]

Page 153

According to Godfrey, the suggestion to carry extra salt was complied with while the one to take extra forage was not. It was at this conference that the battalion and wing assignments that had been in effect since the departure from Fort Lincoln were abolished and all company commanders were ordered to report directly to Custer.[6] While Reno would later assert that Custer told him command assignments would be made on the march, this directive was probably the result of Custer having lost confidence in Reno's abilities because of the just concluded scout to the Rosebud.

Most of the officers dispersed after the conference to attend to necessary details, although some, including Benteen, remained behind to discuss the possibilities of the campaign. According to a 1911 interview conducted by Walter Camp with Richard E. Thompson, who at the time of the battle was a second lieutenant in Company K of the 6th Infantry serving as Acting Commissary of Subsistence for the Dakota Column, Benteen and Custer engaged in a somewhat heated debate over the events of the Battle of the Washita. Benteen was said to have stated that, if the regiment got into a fight, he hoped he would be better supported than he was at the Washita; an obvious reference to the abandoning of Major Elliott in whose battalion Benteen had served that day. Custer then chided Benteen for having killed an Indian boy during the fight although that action was taken in self defense after repeated attempts to induce the youth to surrender had been ignored. Thompson went on to state that the discussion *"... waxed rather warm at this time, and it was plain to see that Benteen hated Custer."* [7] While I have been unable to uncover further corroboration of this story, the events depicted, and statements credited, are quite in character for both Benteen and Custer. Since this was to be the first major engagement sought by the 7th subsequent to the Washita, the two skirmishes during the Stanley Expedition being initiated by the Lakota, it is reasonable to assume that prior combat with the Indians would be a topic of conversation. Given the circumstances surrounding the deaths of Major Elliott and his men, it is probable that the specter of the Washita weighed heavily upon the minds of several of the officers. As the outspoken and antagonistic Benteen would have had no reservations in expressing his views, the exchange, as reported, probably occurred.

According to Godfrey: *"... nearly everyone took time to write letters home, but I doubt very much if there were many of a cheerful nature. Some officers made their wills; others gave verbal instructions as to the disposition of personal property and distribution of mementos; they seemed to have a presentiment of their fate."* [8]

While it is true that some officers, including Myles Keogh,[9] did make their wills that evening, it does not seem extraordinary that men whose profession is war, on the eve of departure for a march that is almost certain to end in combat, would be somewhat apprehensive and concerned with leaving their affairs in order. Several 7th Cavalry officers joined a poker game on the *Far West* that didn't break up until well after dawn. It is known that Keogh participated in this game that probably included several of the regular players (Captains Custer, Yates, and French as well as Lieutenants Cooke, Edgerly, and Godfrey). Keogh was assisted in the preparation of his will by former lawyer John Carland of the boat guard (First Lieutenant, Company B, 6th Infantry) only after the game broke up.[10] This observation of Godfrey's regarding a general impression of impending doom, was probably more the result of reflection on the subsequent disaster than being a true barometer of the feelings expressed at the time.

Perhaps the most celebrated member of the group who was sure disaster awaited the command was scout "Lonesome"[11] Charley Reynolds whose premonition of disaster was so strong that, on two separate occasions, he asked General Terry to relieve him of his responsibilities.[12] Shamed by Terry into rescinding his request, he accompanied the 7th, although he had been laid up on the *Far West* for several days with a seriously infected thumb, the result of a tumor that rendered his left hand practically useless.

Boston Custer, for one, seems to have looked forward to the march with anticipation, as his letter to his mother of June 21st indicates. Boston states he will try to get *"one or two Indian ponies with a buffalo (sic) robe"* for younger brother Nevin. He also passes along the consoling fact that nephew Armstrong Reed, called Autie after his famous uncle, who had accompanied the expedition in expectation of improving his health, *". . . has not been sick a day."* He also mentions that Reed intends to bring home a bow, six arrows, and *". . . a nice pair of moccasins (sic)"* which were obtained from an Indian grave pulled down *". . . the other day"* by Reed with the assistance of Boston and Tom Custer.[13] He does not mention that the general had told himself and Autie Reed they were to remain behind on the *Far West*.[14] Later, perhaps before Boston penned his letter, Armstrong relented and allowed Boston and Autie to accompany the column, ensuring a common fate for every member of his immediate family.

Among those who spent their time that evening in correspondence with loved ones was Acting Assistant Surgeon James DeWolf, who has been characterized as having been unlucky in the extreme. On the eve of departure he wrote to his young wife, Fannie:

> *"Darling wife – . . . [We] are fitting up for a scout under [Brevet] General Custer with 12 companies of cavalry up the Rosebud, across to the Big Horn River & down that to the Yellowstone. . . We marched about 25 miles a day, in all about 285 miles. (This refers to Reno's scout which DeWolf accompanied. The actual distance traveled, according to DeWolf's journal was 241 miles., DCE). I and Dr. [Henry R.] Porter messed together and had a nice time. We had just been getting a supply for the next scout. The commissary is a very good supply on the boat. We found no Indians, not one. All old trails. They seem to be moving west and are driving the buffalo. I think it is very Clear that we shall not see an Indian this summer. (emphasis the author's, DCE) The post–trader or John Smith has opened his whiskey &, of course, you all know what will follow for the time we remain here. (This statement, as well as Indian accounts of finding canteens filled with whiskey after the Custer fight, probably gave rise to the stories of Custer's troopers being drunk, DCE). [Brevet] General Gibbon's command is encamped opposite us. The boat will take our battery (the gatling guns, DCE) over to him this evening. It has hurt three men already (the battery) by upsetting. Dr. [George E.] Lord (George Edwin Lord, DCE) has joined us and will take Dr. [John Winfield] Williams' place as Chief Medical Officer on this scout...*

> *"We usually start at 5 A.M. and march until 1 or 2 P.M. which is not hard and is fun when there is any trail but I fear we shall not find even a sign that is new this time . (emphasis the author's, DCE) It is believed that the Indians have scattered and gone back to their reservations. Yesterday I went out with Dr. Porter, Lt. [Henry M.] Harrington and Lt. [Benjamin H.] Hodgson pistol shooting and came out second best. Porter was best, so you see some of the cavalry cannot shoot very well. Hodgson & I are harassing (joking, etc.) each other & have some nice times. He is Adjutant of the Right Wing '6' Companies of Cavalry. Reno's command. I hope when we return from this scout we shall be nearly ready to return, then darling only think, we will have 300 or 400 miles to march home again. We had two cases of slight sunstrokes (it was before the whiskey was opened) . . . Rosebud Creek takes its name by being profusely bordered by the wild roses like those of Warner. I send you one in this letter.*

> *. . . Well darling, I must close this as the boat moves down the river some little distance & the mail closes tonight & I want to be sure this goes in this mail for it has been 11 days since I wrote or had a chance to write. You must remember*

darling that one feels pretty tired after getting into camp and then we have so much to do to fit up again for this. Everything goes on pack mules & dirt is plentiful. Love & kisses darling. My regards to all. from your loving Hub"[15]

Before his wife would receive this letter, DeWolf would be killed and scalped within view of the remnants of Reno's battalion as they climbed the bluffs in their panic retreat from the valley of the Little Big Horn. In an attempt to spare the feelings of the young widow, Dr. Porter was something less than entirely candid when, on July 28th, he wrote of her husband's death:

". . . I was just behind him as we crossed the river. I saw him safe across and then he turned up a ravine a little to my left which was the last I saw of my friend and companion – alive. As soon as we reached the bluff, I found he was missing and soon found his body which I had buried the next day. **I know it will be a great relief to you when I say that his body was not mutilated in the least – that he was not scalped** *(emphasis the author's, DCE) or his clothes even taken. The Indians had stolen his revolver but not troubled him otherwise. . ."* [16]

While this gallant gesture of denying the mutilation of DeWolf's body was in keeping with the sensitivities of the times, it, and similar gestures, have served to obscure some of the relevant facts surrounding the battle.

Correspondent Mark Kellogg, was busily engaged in writing dispatches for his newspaper and packing for the march, his activities not concluding until well after midnight. His dispatch reads in part:

". . .tomorrow, June 22nd, General Custer with twelve cavalry companies will scout from its mouth up the valley of the Rosebud **until he reaches the fresh trail discovered by Major Reno, and move on that trail with all the rapidity possible in order to overhaul the Indians whom it has been ascertained are hunting buffalo and making daily and leisurely short marches** [17]. *(emphasis the author's, DCE) Gibbon's part of the command will march up the Big Horn valley in order to intercept the Indians if they should attempt to escape from General Custer down that avenue."*[18]

Other last minute preparations were being made. Scout George Herendeen, who accompanied Custer to bring General Terry the result of the examination of the upper end of Tullock's Creek [19], was busy securing a mount. From a selection of more than twenty 7th Cavalry horses, he finally decided upon the mount of Private Dennis Lynch. Being without a mount, the dejected Private Lynch was detailed to look after Custer's baggage on board the *Far West*. Had his mount not been selected, Private Lynch felt he would have ridden to his death alongside his comrades of Company F.[20]

Ever the pragmatist, Bloody Knife held council with the other Arikara scouts. He explained the general plan of the soldiers to catch and defeat the Lakota and emphasized that there were many of the enemy ahead of them. If the soldiers should be beaten, the retreat was to be made in small groups with the rallying point to be the camp on the Yellowstone at the mouth of the Powder River. [21] This duty being accomplished, Bloody Knife went off alone and, with some of post trader Smith's finest, probably obtained with the assistance of Girard, proceeded to get drunk.

Thursday, June 22, 1876

Armstrong Custer had spent a busy night in correspondence. Next morning his striker, John Burkman, found *"He must o' jist dropped off. He was hunched over on the cot, jist his coat and boots off, and the pen still in his hand."* [22] One of the letters was, of course, addressed to his wife. In it we see the residual anger for the perceived failure of Reno's scout, the lack of proper intelligence on the size of the opposing force, and his boyish delight in the respect shown by his newly obtained Crow scouts:

> *". . .Look on my map and you will find our present location on the Yellowstone, about midway between Tongue River and the Big Horn.*

> *The scouting party has returned (Reno's, DCE). They saw the trail and deserted camp of a village of three hundred and eighty (380) lodges. The trail was about one week old. The scouts report that they could have overtaken the village in one and a half days. I am now going to take up the trail where the scouting party turned back. I fear their failure to follow up the Indians has imperilled our plans by giving the village an intimation of our presence. Think of the valuable time lost! But I feel hopeful of accomplishing great results. I will move directly up the valley of the Rosebud. General Gibbon's command and General Terry, with steamer, will proceed up the Big Horn as far as the boat can go. . . I like campaigning with pack–mules much better than with wagons, leaving out the question of luxuries. We take no tents, and desire none.*

> *I now have some Crow scouts with me, as they are familiar with the country. They are magnificent–looking men, so much handsomer and more Indian–like than any we have ever seen, and so jolly and sportive; nothing of the gloomy, silent red–man about them. They have formally given themselves to me, after the usual talk. In their speech they said they had heard that I never abandoned a trail; that when my food gave out I ate mule. That was the kind of a man they wanted to fight under; they were willing to eat mule too. . ."* [23]

At 11 AM on the morning of June 22nd, Custer wrote to Libbie for the last time:

> *"My Darling – I have but a few moments to write as we start at twelve, and I have my hands full of preparations for the scout. Do not be anxious about me. You would be surprised how closely I obey your instructions about keeping with the column. I hope to have a good report to send you by the next mail. A success will start us all toward Lincoln.*

> *I send you an extract from Genl. Terry's official order, knowing how keenly you appreciate words of commendation and confidence in your dear Bo: 'It is of course impossible to give you any definite instructions in regard to this movement, and, were it not impossible to do so, the Department Commander places too much confidence in your zeal, energy and ability to impose on you precise orders which might hamper your action when nearly in contact with the enemy.'*

> *Your devoted boy Autie."* [24]

While Private Burkman was taking down the General's tent, Charley Reynolds came up complaining: *"This damned hand kept me awake all night. Dr. Porter says it's a felon (tumor, DCE). He says I ain't fit to march but I'm goin' along. Do you know anything for it?"* Burkman knew of a bread–and–milk poultice, but, having neither, he improvised with hardtack and water. Reynolds' thumb remained wrapped until he went into battle on the 25th when he apparently removed the bandage as it was not found on his body afterward.[25]

At precisely noon on June 22nd [26] the Seventh Regiment of United States Cavalry began its journey into immortality by passing in review before General Terry, Colonel Gibbon, and Major Brisbin. As the companies passed, General Terry received the salute and had a pleasant word for each officer. The somber mood of the previous day had departed, and Terry, Gibbon and Custer were in fine spirits. Gibbon described the scene:

> *"The bugles sounded the 'boots and saddles,' and Custer, after starting the advance, rode up and joined us. Together we sat on our horses and witnessed the approach of the command as it threaded its way through the rank sage brush which covered the valley. First came a band of buglers sounding a march, and as they came opposite to General Terry they wheeled out of the column as at review, continuing to play as the command passed along. The regiment presented a fine appearance, and as the various companies passed us we had a good opportunity to note the number of fine horses in the ranks, many of them being part–blooded horses from Kentucky, and I was told there was not a sorebacked horse amongst them. General Custer appeared to be in good spirits, chatted freely with us, and was evidently proud of the appearance of his command. The pack–mules, in a compact body, followed the regiment, and behind them came a rear–guard, and as that approached Custer shook hands with us and bade us good–by. As he turned to leave us I made some pleasant remark, warning him against being greedy, and with a gay wave of his hand he called back, 'No, I will not,' and rode off after his command. Little did we think we had seen him for the last time, or imagine under what circumstances we should next see that command, now mounting the bluffs in the distance with its little guidons gayly fluttering in the breeze."* [27]

Mark Kellogg, mounted on his mule, had been to Gibbon's right during the review. He started after Custer, General Terry calling him back to say good–bye.[28]

Girard, who claimed to have been momentarily detained by his "official duties" said he overheard Terry remark

> *"Custer is happy now, off with a roving command of fifteen days. I told him if he found the Indians not to do as Reno did, but if he thought he could whip them to do so."* [29]

One task that did delay Girard's joining the departing column was informing the Arikara scouts that they should sing their death songs.[30] They obliged by mounting their ponies and riding around the camp singing their dirge. This act completed, they assumed their place in line of march.

While it is difficult to ascertain the exact strength of the 7th Cavalry on that date, the regimental adjutant, Lieutenant Cooke, being killed with Custer and all records lost; an educated guess would be the command consisted of 28 line officers, 3 doctors, 92 non–commissioned officers, 489 enlisted men, 36 Indian scouts, including the six Crows detached from Gibbon's command, 2 interpreters, 2 guides, 1 courier, 12 civilian packers/teamsters and 2 citizens, for a total effective force of 667 men. Refer to Appendix 1 for a detailed 7th Cavalry Roster.

As the column moved out up the Rosebud the regimental band struck up *"Garry Owen."* The six Crow scouts were in the lead, followed by two groups of Arikara scouts, under the leadership of Soldier and Bob Tailed Bull, one on either side of the river. The cavalry, in column of fours, marched up the east bank of the river and went into camp about 4 PM after covering a distance of twelve miles, [31] averaging a rate of march of 3 miles per hour.

About sunset, Custer had *"Officer's Call"* sounded and the officers dutifully assembled at his tent. Godfrey related:

> *"It was not a cheerful assemblage; everybody seemed to be in a serious mood, and the little conversation carried on, before all had arrived, was in undertones."* [32]

When all the officers had assembled, Custer told them that, being deep in hostile territory, and, surprise being of the essence, no bugle calls would be sounded except in an emergency. He said that the troop commanders would be responsible for their companies, but that he would personally decide when the marches would begin and where and when camp would be established. All other details such as reveille, stables, grazing, etc., would be left to the discretion and judgment of the company commanders who were all experienced officers and should know what was necessary. The stable guards would awaken the troopers at 3 AM and the command was to be ready to march by 5 AM. During the march care was to be exercised to keep the column well closed up with the companies always within supporting distance of each other. The marches were to be in easy stages averaging 25 to 30 miles per day.[33] The officers were cautioned to husband their rations and the strength of the horses and mules wisely as they might be out a great deal longer than the period for which they were rationed, as he *"intended to follow the trail until we could get the Indians, even if it took us to the Indian agencies on the Missouri River or in Nebraska."* [34]

During the day, the packs, for which each company had been separately responsible, had caused great trouble; some breaking down just as the regiment was leaving camp, and the train had straggled badly. The principal reason, of course, was this first army mule train to be organized in the Department of Dakota, was, to a large extent, composed of mules taken out of the wagon traces, thus forming, according to Lieutenant John Bourke, *"the saddest burlesque"* one would ever expect to see in a pack train. [35] Accordingly, Custer now ordered that the pack train be combined. The command of the train, consisting of approximately 175 mules (see Table 10 – 1), 70 troopers, and 6 civilian packers, fell to First Lieutenant Edward Mathey, just as command of the wagon train at the Washita had eight years earlier. Lieutenant Mathey was ordered to report to Custer at the end of each day's march the relative efficiency of the company packers. [36] This improved the situation somewhat, although the pack train continued to give problems. Additionally, the three companies whose mules had proven most unmanageable during the previous day's march were to be detailed as escort, their position in march to be amidst the dust cloud at the rear of the column. Since Benteen was the senior officer in the affected companies on June 22nd, he was given overall command of the escort for June 23rd.[37]

Custer then explained that General Terry had offered Second Lieutenant William Low Jr. and his battery of gatling guns as well as Major Brisbin's battalion of the Second Cavalry, and he had refused both. Custer explained they would be traveling over uncharted territory, and it could be assumed that the country might be so rough that the guns would seriously impede his march.[38] As for the battalion of the Second Cavalry, Custer stated that, judging from the number of lodge fires observed by Reno, he anticipated the village to contain no more than 1000 warriors. He had also consulted the reports of the Commissioner of Indian Affairs and determined, if any reliance could be placed in those reports, that even though re–inforced with young men from the agencies, the hostiles could not put a force exceeding 1500 warriors in the field.[39] He appealed to his officer's *esprit de corps* by declaring that the 7th could whip a force that size with no assistance. Indeed, if the 7th was unable to subdue the hostile force, the support of an additional battalion would not alter the outcome. He ended by stating that the additional cavalry might actually weaken his command by creating jealousy among its component parts. [40] As usual, Benteen was quick to find fault with his commander's judgment, and stated *"I, for one, am very sorry you didn't take them. I think we will regret not having them."* [41]

Custer appealed to his officers for loyalty and cooperation while complaining that some of his official actions had been criticized. He was willing to accept recommendations, but those recommendations must come in the proper form. According to Lieutenant Edgerly, he went on:

"But I want it understood that I shall allow no grumbling, and shall exact the strictest compliance with orders from everybody. . ."

Number of Mules	Assignment
12	Ammunition
144	12 Per Company
4	Headquarters Staff
2	Medical Officers
2	Tools, Camp Outfits, etc.
11	Scouts, Packers, Civilians
175	**Total**

Table 10 – 1 Composition of Custer's Pack Train

At this point Benteen interrupted:

"It seems to me you are lashing the shoulders of all, to get at some; now, as we are all present, would it not do to specify the officers whom you accuse?"

Custer, stammering with the effort to control his anger, replied:

"Colonel Benteen, I am not here to be catechized (sic) by you, but for your own information, will state that none of my remarks have been directed towards you." [42]

What incident was preying upon Custer's mind we will probably never know, [43] but his remark about strict compliance with orders hit dead center. The failure of key officers to follow orders would be a major factor in the magnitude of the disaster that was now less than 72 hours away.

The final action taken at the conference was for the officers to synchronize watches with Lieutenant Wallace, who kept the official itinerary. [44] This conference, which was so out of character for Custer, left his officers dumbfounded. Godfrey wrote:

"This 'talk' of his, as we called it, was considered at the time as something extraordinary for General Custer, for it was not his habit to unbosom himself to his

officers. In it he showed a lack of self-confidence, a reliance on somebody else; there was an indefinable something that was not Custer. His manner and tone, usually brusque and aggressive, or somewhat rasping, was on this occasion conciliating and subdued. There was something akin to an appeal, as if depressed, that made a deep impression on all present." [45]

Lieutenants Godfrey, Gibson, McIntosh and Wallace [46] were walking back to their bivouac together when Wallace remarked:

"Godfrey, I believe General Custer is going to be killed. I never heard him talk that way before." [47]

Again, Godfrey dwells on the aura of doom he seemed to believe had settled upon the march. In this case, however, Wallace's declaration is contained in Godfrey's field diary and we have ample substantiation for the incident. Lieutenant Edgerly's letter to his wife of July 4th, however, describes an entirely different atmosphere:

"After Custer got through, Reno, Porter, Dr. Lord, Calhoun, Moylan, Smith, Weir, Gibson, and Crittenden came to my little shelter tent and sang for about an hour. Calhoun told us there that his wife had sent him a large cake and that the day after the fight he intended sending a piece around to each officer of the command." [48]

It is probably safe to say that, while the Indian scouts were becoming more apprehensive with each step taken nearer the enemy, and some of the officers and men were definitely caught up in a web of melancholia, a feeling of impending disaster by no means permeated the command.

While going through the herd to satisfy himself about the security of the animals, Godfrey chanced upon a council of the Indian scouts which included Mitch Boyer and Half Yellow Face. Godfrey had been silently observing for a few minutes when Boyer asked him, at the urging of Half Yellow Face:

"Have you ever fought against these Sioux?"

When Godfrey, who had been engaged against the Lakota during August of 1873 with the Stanley Expedition, answered affirmatively, Boyer continued:

"Well, how many do you expect to find?"

When Godfrey passed along Custer's estimate of a maximum of 1500, Boyer asked:

"Well, do you think we can whip that many?"

Again Godfrey answered affirmatively, to which Boyer replied with great emphasis:

"Well, I can tell you we are going to have a damned big fight." [49]

Friday, June 23, 1876

The command moved out precisely at 5 AM on June 23rd as Custer had ordered. Bloody Knife, having regained a portion of the composure characteristic of his race, had rejoined the command at breakfast, although he led rather than rode his horse into camp.[50] Custer was in the lead followed by Sergeant Major William H. Sharrow carrying the regimental standard and Sergeant Robert M. Hughes carrying Custer's personal battle flag, a red over blue swallowtail guidon with white crossed sabers. His wife had made the original of this battle flag when Custer commanded the Third Cavalry Division during the Civil War. The course of the Rosebud meanders a great deal in the narrow valley, requiring the river to be forded five times in the first three miles.

About five miles out they came upon the large lodge pole trail Major Reno had discovered on his recent scout.[51] Custer, his scouts gathered around him, studied the trail for a time, and then, addressed Lieutenant Varnum, in command of the scouts:

> *"This is where Reno made the mistake of his life. He had six troops of cavalry and rations enough for a number of days. He'd have made a name for himself if he'd pushed on after them."* [52]

About three miles further on, they came to the camp–site that Lieutenant Bradley had discovered on May 27th. Here another halt was made and the officers busily engaged in attempting to determine the exact size and age of the camp–site. When Charley Reynolds noted in his diary that this camp–site was about 20 days old,[53] he was in error by just about a week. It was noted that a good many wickiups, constructed of bushes with the tops drawn together and covered with skins to provide temporary shelter, had been present at this camping place.[54] It seems incredible that the veteran officers of the 7th, upon whom so much would depend in another two days, should have so little knowledge of their foe that they surmised these wickiups were erected to house the village canine corps.[55]

Six more miles found the column near Teat Butte and another abandoned campsite. The column again halted to examine the remains and to allow the pack train to close up. Nine miles further on, at the mouth of Greenleaf Creek, they came across the third, and final, camp–site they would discover that day. Charley Reynolds was again in error by about a week when he estimated the age of the camp to be about 12 days.[56] Wallace recorded in his journal what was probably the prevailing opinion of the officers:

> *"All the signs were old, but everything indicated large numbers, and in each bend of the stream were traces of some former camp. The ground was strewn with bones and cuttings from buffalo hides; and the Indian ponies had nipped off almost every spear of grass."*[57]

In retrospect, we note that Custer and the 7th Cavalry had received ample warning of the number of Indians they were shortly to encounter. In places the trail was 300 yards wide and deeply rutted. The camp circles were from 1/3 to 1/2 mile in diameter.[58] Perhaps it was the conviction that the enemy force numbered no more than 800 warriors, only Custer placing the number of warriors as high as 1500, that lulled the officers into a false sense of relative security resulting in misinterpretation of the trail signs that were all too easily read by the Crow and Arikara scouts. That this opinion had been widely held since Reno's scout can best be shown by recalling correspondent Kellogg's dispatch of June 21st, which refers to *"daily and leisurely short marches"* the Indians were known to be making. What Wallace, and the others, believed to be short leisurely movements of a single camp were, instead, the camp circles of several large bands traveling together. A hostile bastion that, rather than taking flight at the first hint of danger, must be reduced by force of arms.

The regiment marched another 10 miles, totaling 33 for the day, and went into camp at 4:30 PM having averaged a rate of march somewhat less than 3 miles per hour, the walk rate for cavalry. The straggling pack train did not arrive until near sunset. According to Private Peter Thompson of C Company, two amusing events served to break the monotony of the day's march:

> *"One of our men named Bennett (Private James C. Bennett, of Company C, DCE) was mounted on a bob–tailed horse, which had proven to be very tricky. While crossing a shelvingrock, overhanging a deep and rocky gorge the horse stood stock still and lifting up the right hind foot began to scratch his ear. Bennett looked around helplessly, first down the rocky gorge and then at his laughing comrades. As soon as he could he induced his horse to stop combing his ear and edged away from that locality.*[59]

> *Then one of our mules named Barnum, stumbled and fell. He went rolling down the hill with two boxes of ammunition on his back. As we watched his rolling we made calculations as to how much mule would be left in case the ammunition exploded. But contrary to all expectations, when he reached the bottom of the hill, he scrambled to his feet again with both boxes undisturbed and made his way up the hill again and took his place in the line as soberly and quietly as if nothing had happened."* [60]

More will be heard of Barnum and his adventures with the ammunition packs when we discuss the siege of Reno Hill.

During the day's march, Benteen had changed the disposition of his pack train guard. Instead of marching all three companies in rear of the packs as ordered, he placed one company in advance of the train, one on the right flank, about mid–train, and the last in rear. Upon his arrival in camp, Benteen informed Adjutant Cooke of this "alteration" he had made in Custer's orders. According to Benteen's account of the incident, he asked Cooke to pass his disposition of the guard along to Custer before some less experienced officer made the mistake of blindly following Custer's orders resulting in the loss of the train to the enemy. The tone of this conversation was such as to elicit no surprise when Cooke told Benteen if he wanted Custer to know about it, he would have to notify him himself. Benteen admitted he was close to insubordination, but, apparently, he could let no opportunity to correct his commander pass without comment.[61] Benteen concluded the event, with obvious relish:

> *"So, the next morning as General Custer was passing, I chose to do so; telling him, that I could not, without endangering the safety of the packs, carry out the orders he had given me concerning the marching of the battalion composing the 'Packs' guard. I then told the arrangement I had made of the battalion; and this from the fact that from the time he left me at the bivouac of the night before, not one sight of his command had been gotten. The General said, 'I am much obliged to you Colonel, and I will turn over the same order of march for the rear guard to the officer who relieves you.'"*[62]

After his baiting conversation with Cooke, Benteen spent some time fishing, without success, as the *"attempt resulting mostly in 'water–hauls'."* [63] Returning from his fishing expedition, Benteen noted the arrival of Doctor Lord, several hours behind the column. The doctor was afflicted with dysentery, known as the "Dakota Quickstep," and had stopped some distance from the camping place to rest.[64] Being exhausted, he refused both food and drink, wanting only to sleep.[65]

Saturday, June 24, 1876

The regiment marched at 5 AM,[66] the morning of June 24th. Almost immediately, Custer was informed that smoke signals had been seen in the valley of Tullock's Creek. When Godfrey called Custer's attention to them, Custer replied that his scouts were well out on the divide separating the Rosebud from Tullock's Creek, and that if there was any substance to the rumors, the scouts would have reported it. Godfrey subsequently became convinced that the "smoke puffs" were, in reality, *"cloudlets of mist formed during the night in the valleys and wafted over the hill–tops by the morning breeze."* [67]Within an hour the Crow scouts returned reporting fresh tracks made by 3 or 4 ponies and one man on foot. Acting on the presumption that these tracks were made by a nearby scouting party, Custer hurried ahead with two companies, the remainder of the column following a half mile in the rear. While Custer's investigation turned up nothing,[68] this incident, along with the earlier reports of smoke signals, may have convinced Custer that his command was under surveillance. In an attempt to lessen the dust, thereby aiding concealment, Custer ordered the regiment to advance in parallel columns.[69] We know, as Custer could not, that these tracks probably were made by members of Little Wolf's band of Cheyennes who had been following Custer's command, and would continue to dog their foot steps until the battle was joined.

At 1 PM, when just beyond Muddy Creek (this creek should not be confused with Lame Deer Creek which had previously been known as Muddy Creek), Custer ordered the lunch halt.[70] Up to this point the command had covered only 16 miles in 8 hours, definitely a methodical, cautious pace. While the men rested and made coffee, Custer ordered the Crow scouts to follow the trail ahead and to return by sundown. They were to search diligently for any trails diverging from the main one, especially any that might divert to the left, the only open avenue of escape. They were also to keep a special look–out in the direction of Tullock's Creek. Custer had been informed by both Godfrey and Herendeen of a small lodge pole trail that had diverged from the main trail near Lame Deer Creek. At this halt, Custer ordered Varnum and a detachment of the Arikara scouts back to investigate.[71] Varnum maintained that Custer ordered this reconnaissance because he feared the party of Indians had left the valley. Herendeen confirms this in his account stating:

> *"Custer said he did not want to lose any of the lodges, and if any of them left the main trail he wanted to know about it." [72]*

Varnum, after changing horses, made the twenty mile circuit "for nothing" as:

> *"A small branch stream had steep banks and the Indians' travois had gone up the stream to get a crossing & then returned to the Rosebud valley." [73]*

In a letter written to Walter Camp in 1909, Varnum described the incident a trifle differently. There he stated that Custer was quite perturbed with him for missing the Indian side trail. Varnum then went on to detail how he had his scouts deployed in a screen and that he doubted Godfrey's report. Varnum further stated that it was immediately prior to his starting back for Lame Deer Creek that Second Lieutenant Luther Hare was detailed from Company K to the scouts as Varnum's second in command. This is in conflict with other accounts stating Lieutenant Hare was not detailed to the scouts until Varnum was ordered to the Crows Nest later that night. Given that Varnum was in a position to know exactly when Hare was assigned to the scouts, and since the 1909 version is not too complimentary of his own performance, it appears probable that this is the correct account. When Varnum returned about 3 PM with his intelligence, Custer could breath a little easier; none of the enemy had managed to escape; he could be assured of finding them all on the stream known as *piji sla wakpa* – the Greasy Grass.

While awaiting the return of the Crow scouts, Custer pondered the fresh evidence the day had uncovered. Prior to crossing Lame Deer Creek, the trail had been well–defined and heavily rutted, resembling a poorly plowed field, interrupted at intervals by a large camp–site. After crossing that stream, the valley was virtually covered with lodge pole trails and camp–sites. In addition, the trail was noticeably fresher. Was the village breaking up and scattering as the soldiers feared? Perhaps Custer's scouts were unable to tell him that this fresh trail was actually superimposed on the older trail previously discovered by Reno,[74] indicating vast numbers of the foe; or did he ignore their council? According to Scout "Billy" Jackson:[75]

> "On the third day, we struck the trail of the hostiles, the one that Reno had found several days before. And what a trail it was; a trail all of three hundred yards wide, and deeply worn by travois, and lodge–pole ends. We went into camp close to the trail, and, cooking our supper, we scouts counciled together about the outlook. All agreed that at least fifteen hundred lodges of the enemy had made that broad trail. Said Bloody Knife: 'My friends, this big trail proves what we heard, that the Ogalalla, Minneconjou, Sans Arc, and Teton Sioux have left their agencies to join Sitting Bull and Crazy Horse; but I am sure that even this trail does not account for all that have left their agencies. There surely are other trails of them; and trails, too, of Cheyennes and Arapahoes.'
>
> 'Many Yanktonnais and Assiniboin have answered Sitting Bull's call for help, and joined him,' said Frank Girard (Fred Girard, DCE).
>
> 'Yes. They too,; Bloody Knife continued. 'It is as I have told Long Hair: this gathering of the enemy tribes is too many for us. But he will not believe me.'" [76]

Of the soldiers, apparently only Private Henry M. Brinkerhoff of Company G,[77] was able to discern the truth when he wrote:

> "About 2 p.m. we crossed a large Indian trail going directly north and coming from the south, and we then knew that the agency Indians were on their way to join the hostile Sioux camp. All signs pointed to the fact that there were a great many warriors in the bunch, as the trail in some places on the crossing of the Rosebud was a mile wide."

Custer, along with his officers, still believed they were on the trail of a single band of approximately 350 to 400 lodges supporting a fighting force of 800 warriors. During this halt, Custer, with Girard acting as interpreter, went to consult with the Arikara scouts. Stabbed put on quite an athletic demonstration, dodging imaginary bullets after which he said to Girard:

> "I want you to tell Custer that I showed him how we fight, for when his soldiers go into the fight they stand still like targets while the Sioux are dodging about, so it is hard to hit them. But they shoot the soldiers down very easily." [78]

Custer complimented the Arikaras on their fighting ability and went on to explain that when he had brought the Lakota to battle, he did not expect them to fight alongside the soldiers; it was Custer's desire that they drive off the Lakota pony herd.[79]

Couriers from the Crow scouting party arrived at 4 PM very much excited as they had, according to Wallace, found *"a fresh camp at the forks of the Rosebud. It was now generally believed that the Indians were not more than thirty miles away."* [80] This estimate of the proximity of the enemy force proved to be chillingly accurate. The scouts also brought several Lakota trophies to Custer, scalps and beards of white men. In response to these grisly relics, Custer signed to the Crows that he had been sent by the Great Father in Washington to stop these Lakota from killing white people, and that although he might be killed, the Lakota would surely feel his wrath.

> *"I do not know whether I will pass through this battle, but if I live, I will recommend you boys and you will be leaders of the Crows."* [81]

At 5 PM the command moved out, crossing to the left bank of the Rosebud. [82] Almost immediately they passed through several large campsites. At the largest of these, the frame of a great sundance lodge was still standing. In this lodge was found the scalp of a white man. As the scalp, according to Godfrey's field diary, *"was not quite dry"* it was assumed to belong to Private Augustus Stoker, Company H, Second Cavalry, [83] who was killed, along with Private Henry Rahmeir, also of Company H, Second Cavalry, and civilian teamster Quinn, while hunting outside Gibbon's camp on May 23rd. [84] Sergeant Jeremiah Finley of Company C retrieved the grisly trophy and it was undoubtedly still in his saddlebag when he went into action on June 25th. [85]

The soldiers were insensitive to the signs left in the camp, but the Arikara scouts were not. Red Star cataloged the discoveries:

> *"Here there was evidence of the Dakotas[86] having made medicine, the sand had been arranged and smoothed, and pictures had been drawn. The Dakota scouts with Custer said this meant the enemy knew the army was coming. In one of the sweat lodges was a long heap or ridge of sand, on which Red Bear, Red Star, and Soldier saw figures drawn, indicating by hoof prints Custer's men on one side and the Dakotas on the other. Between them dead men were drawn lying with their heads toward the Dakotas. The Arikara scouts understood this to mean that the Dakota medicine was too strong for them and that they would be defeated by the Dakotas. Young Hawk saw in one of the sweat lodges where they had camped, opposite the entrance three stones near the middle, all in a row and painted red. This meant in Dakota sign language that the Great Spirit had given them victory, and that if the whites did not come, they would seek them. Soldier saw offerings, four sticks standing upright with a buffalo calf–skin tied on with cloth and other articles of value, which was evidence of a great religious service. This was also seen by Strikes Two, Little Sioux, and Boy Chief. All the Arikara knew what this meant, namely, that the Dakotas were sure of winning."* [87]

It is no wonder then, that, when scouting the trail ahead, the Arikaras mistook the prehistoric rock carvings at Deer Medicine Rocks [88] for further signs of impending Lakota victory. [89] It is to their credit that, in the face of this powerful medicine, they performed all required tasks; indeed exceeding them by fighting shoulder to shoulder with the soldiers.

After about a half hour's investigation, Custer had *"Officer's Call"* sounded, the first bugle call since his injunction of the 22nd. [90] The only item on the agenda Godfrey mentions is the discovery of the pony and dismounted Indian signs by the Crow that had actually been reported at 6 AM. [91] It seems improbable that Custer would countermand his order regarding bugle calls for so trivial a matter given the age of the information imparted and the absence of a true emergency. If this account is to be credited, we must assume that the earlier events of the day convinced Custer that he was under continuing observation by Lakota scouting parties and any further attempt at concealment was futile.[92] There is further evidence that Custer believed he had been discovered; after leaving the "sundance camp" Custer ordered the companies to march on separate trails to keep down the dust.[93] If Custer indeed felt he was under continuing observation it makes the night march of June 24th, for which he has been severely criticized, not only understandable, but imperative to regaining the initiative.[94]

Godfrey goes on to mention that as the conference broke up, a stiff southerly breeze blew down Custer's personal battle flag, the standard falling toward the rear. Godfrey, being near, picked it up and replaced it, only to see it again fall toward the rear. He then *"bored the staff into the ground where it would have the support of a sagebrush."* Godfrey says the incident made no impression upon him at the time, but after the battle, the superstitious Wallace told Godfrey he had observed the incident and considered the fact of its falling to the rear a bad omen, feeling sure they would suffer a defeat.[95] The timing of this revelation explains Godfrey's diary which does not mention the incident along with his account of other events of the 24th. Instead, the diary contains the following entry dated June 24, but placed in an open space between entries for June 21 and June 22:

> *"While the officers were separating at the 'Sundance' camp Genl Custer's guidon fell down to the rear. I picked it up & stuck in the ground. Soon it fell again to the rear; this time I stuck it in some sage brush & ground so that it stuck. I never thought of it again till after the fight when my attention was called to it by Lt. Wallace who seems to have regarded it as a bad omen."* [96]

The regiment moved again, slowly, so as not to get ahead of the scouts who were performing their tasks with methodical diligence, and camped at 7:45 PM after a march of 28 miles,[97] averaging a rate of march of less than two miles per hour. Godfrey indicates that it was general knowledge that a night march was to be ordered, as attested to by the fact that, except for those items necessary for the preparation of dinner, the mules were not unpacked; but he doesn't elaborate as to the source of this information.[98] At this camp Lieutenant Cooke asked Lieutenant Gibson to witness his will stating he felt the impending fight would be his last.[99]

The remainder of the Crow scouts returned shortly before 9 PM with the intelligence that the trail led over the divide into the valley of the Little Big Horn.[100] Custer must have been greatly relieved at this news. The village had not broken up and scattered as he had feared throughout the day, indeed, after Lame Deer Creek, no diverging side trails had been noted.[101] The Indians almost surely were where the soldiers thought they would be found. The Montana Column under Terry and Gibbon would block the northern avenue of escape. If the Indians attempted to retreat in that direction, the Montana Column would serve as the anvil against which the hammer of the 7th Cavalry would drive the Lakota, crushing them forever. If the Lakota stood their ground, Custer was confident the 7th would have little trouble sweeping over them. Custer then sent for Varnum, known to the Arikara as "Peaked Face" due to his long thin features, who related the following:

> *"He said that the Crows believed we would find the Indians in the Little Big Horn valley. That in the divide between the Rosebud and that stream was a 'Crow Nest,' a big hollow, where the Crows used to go and hide when on horse–stealing expeditions against the Sioux. That from there they could see in the early morning when the camp fires started, and tell whether they were there or not, and estimate their strength. Custer said he wanted an intelligent white man to go with them and get what information he could from them & send him a message with that information. I said, 'That means me.' He said he did not like to order me on such a trip and that I had already had a hard day of it. I said he made me Chief of Scouts, and I objected to his sending anyone else unless he had lost faith in me. He said he thought that was about what I would say, and for me to go. He said I was to leave*

about 9 o'clock and get there before daylight. I would take the Crows & interpreters and I said I wanted one white man to talk to and asked for Charlie Reynolds, which he approved."

"He said he would start at 11 o'clock and be at the base of the divide before morning & he thought I could locate him from the bluffs where I would be. Having ridden over 50 miles, I started at 9 P. M. for a ride of 20 more with only Indians & one white man. I took about a dozen Ree scouts for messengers.[102] I arrived at the 'Crow Nest' about 2 A. M. It was a disagreeable ride, in single file, keeping near the brush and a small tributary to the Rosebud, and the feeling that the one white man with me was the only person I could depend upon in case of trouble, as the Indians would all scatter on their own account in case we were attacked, made me feel I was not in the safest kind of an expedition."[103]

Varnum suffered a minor mishap on the journey as he related in personal correspondence in 1929:

"I left the Rosebud at nine o'clock at night, June 24th. We went up a timbered stream on its right bank, the stream, of course, on our right. We went into the timber on two occasions and dismounted, and the Crows went into the brush and made some kind of cigarettes and smoked. Later we crossed the stream, and in crossing in the timber, I lost my hat when I was in the stream.

". . . When the command came along, my hat was found hanging in a tree and brought to me, so Custer must have followed our trail."[104]

About 9:30 PM, Custer assembled his officers. The general told them that the trail led over the divide into the valley of the Little Big Horn. He said that the regiment would march at 11 PM in order to get as near the divide as possible before daylight. The command would remain hidden during the day while the scouts located the village and surveyed the surrounding country. The reconnaissance completed, final preparations would be made for a dawn attack on Monday, June 26th. [105] Before breaking up, according to Private William Taylor of A Company, some of the officers, including Sturgis, Moylan, and Edgerly, engaged in an impromptu concert, singing *"Annie Laurie," "Little Footsteps Slow and Gentle," "The Good Bye at the Door,"* and *"Doxology."* They closed, somewhat irreverently Taylor thought, with *"For He's a Jolly Good Fellow."*[106] History does not record the opinions of Big Crow and Black White Man, members of Little Wolf's band of Cheyenne, who observed the command in this camp. [107]

Before discussing the night march, it is necessary to divert ever so slightly to discuss the controversy associated with Tullock's Creek. You will recall that Terry's orders of June 22nd specifically required Custer to scout the upper reaches of Tullock's Creek, and that George Herendeen had been attached to the 7th for the sole purpose of carrying the results of that examination through to Terry. Much has been made of Custer's failure to comply with this part of his orders, and that he did indeed disobey this particular aspect of his orders cannot be denied. Brisbin maintained Custer failed to send Herendeen through to Terry because *"He did not wish us to know where he was or what he was doing, for fear we would get some of the credit of the campaign."*[108] George Herendeen, who had a bonus of $200 at stake in the venture, had this to say in a January 1878 article for the *New York Herald*:

"On the morning of the 24th we broke camp at 5 o'clock and continued following the trail up the stream. Soon after starting Custer, who was in advance

with Boyer, called me to him and told me to get ready, he thought he would send me and Charley Reynolds to the head of Tullock's Fork to take a look (it would be necessary to send Reynolds so that Custer could obtain a report of the findings as the distance from the column to the forks and back and then on to Terry would exceed a horse's endurance, DCE). I told the General it was not time yet, as we were traveling in the direction of the head of Tullock, and I could only follow his trail. I called Boyer, who was a little ahead back and asked him if I was not correct in my statement to the General, and he said, 'Yes; further up on Rosebud we would come opposite a gap, and then we could cut across and strike the Tullock in about fifteen miles ride.' Custer said, 'All right; I could wait.'" [109]

Next day, however, when the column was opposite the jumping off point for Tullock's Creek, Herendeen, eager to earn his bonus, reported to Custer saying *"General, this is Tullock's, and here is where I leave you to go to the other command."* Custer merely looked at Herendeen without answering. The scout kept near him for some time, expecting to be called and dispatched to Terry, but, finally seeing that he was not wanted, fell back and followed along. [110]

What caused Custer to change his mind? It appears that, by the time it was necessary for Herendeen to leave the column, Custer was convinced, or feared, that his command was under continuing surveillance by enemy scouting parties and that he needed to make a night march concealing his location in an attempt to somewhat regain the element of surprise. He also knew that the village had not broken up and scattered and that he was on a hot trail; although he had been following it rather cautiously judging from his rate of march. He did not know precisely where the Indians were, however, he did know they had turned down Davis Creek and crossed the divide, away from the Tullock; he probably saw no reason to look where he knew them not to be [111] as he had done during the Hancock Campaign. [112] Additionally, he appears to have kept Mitch Boyer, who was thoroughly familiar with the country, near him, and Boyer may have told him that the water of the upper Tullock was alkaline and would not support a large village. Some authors feel that Custer did indeed "scout" the Tullock, either by giving it a cursory examination *"the valley of which was in general view from the divide,"* [113] or by ordering the Crow scouts to pay close attention to this area, although Varnum maintained no such request was made of his scouts. [114] Others conjecture that Custer was going to send Herendeen to Terry with the results of the reconnaissance of June 25. While all this makes for interesting conjecture, two facts remain abundantly clear; Custer's failure to "adequately" scout the Tullock had absolutely no bearing on the campaign whatsoever, and his failure to do so was in direct violation of the orders of his superior officer. [115] It is probable that had events concluded differently, Custer could easily have been exonerated of any malfeasance because the Indians indeed were not on the Tullock. My own interpretation of the facts is that nothing associated with the failure to scout the Tullock indicates willful disobedience on Custer's part; however, Custer should have sent Herendeen through to Terry on the morning of June 25th to inform the Department Commander that the village had been sighted and the 7th was moving to the attack before the Indians had the opportunity to scatter. Custer's subordinates would exercise similar judgment regarding strict obedience of orders, the appropriateness of which, given the unsatisfactory outcome of the action, is hotly debated to this day.

Prior to the night march, the company commanders made final preparations. Perhaps lieutenants Smith and Gibson revived their long standing joke concerning Smith's gold watch fob. According to Mrs. Gibson;

"Frank had always admired the bauble, and about the mess table or campfire nights, Algy used to say, 'Gib, if I'm killed first, I will the fob to you, and if you go first I get your Bloodstone ring.' Whereupon someone would shout, 'And if you're both killed together, then who gets the loot?' and this would evoke loud claims

and counterclaims, midst hearty laughter. However, when the jest became a grim reality,[116] *Mrs. Smith insisted upon presenting the fob to my husband, which he wore to the day of his death, and often as his hand strayed toward it, a detached, faraway look would creep into his eyes, followed by a sort of brooding silence as the past unfurled."* [117]

"Lonesome" Charley Reynolds, who probably would have survived the campaign had Custer decided to scout the Tullock, sunk ever deeper into his melancholia. Somehow he knew, as men who are attuned with the forces of nature are given the vision to know, that tomorrow's sunrise would be his last. Accordingly, he distributed the contents of his haversack: shirts, tobacco, a sewing kit. Scout Billy Jackson said that some of the men refused to accept anything from Charley, while others took what he offered but only with reluctance *"We had little appetite for our coffee and hardtack, and the meat that we were broiling."* [118] For both Custer, renowned for "Custer's Luck," and Charley Reynolds, whom the Indians called "Lucky Man," the allotted amount of luck, as well as time, was about to run out. [119]

In the Lakota end of the Great Encampment a Dying Dance was being held in honor of almost two score young Cheyenne and Lakota warriors who had taken suicide vows. [120] Among the Cheyenne taking the vow were Whirlwind and Noisy Walking who would give the full measure of their manhood on the morrow. In the Cheyenne circle, however a great social dance was held which kept many young warriors in their sleeping robes until Reno's troopers attacked.

After midnight, the Cheyenne warriors Big Foot and Wolf Tooth, went out from their camp, in defiance of the chief's order not to molest the soldiers, to where their horses were hobbled. They cautiously forded the Little Big Horn; for the elite Kit Foxes guarded the camp that night and the young men would be severely punished if discovered. They spent the rest of the night hidden in the brush on the east bank of the river. [121]

Despite the celebrating, an aura of impending trouble hung over the village like a pall. At mid day a crier in the Sans Arc circle had gone around warning that:

"The soldiers are coming; they will be here tomorrow. Be ready!" [122]

The 7th marched at either 11 PM, as scheduled, or 1 AM based upon whose timepiece you credit. [123] This apparent discrepancy, while of no particular importance in recounting the details of the night march, becomes troublesome when attempting to put the events of June 25th in sequence. Wallace, in the official itinerary, states the command was *"Unable to start until near 1 A. M., and owing to delays, with the pack train, had gone only about eight miles by early daylight, when the column was halted and the men prepared coffee."* [124] Godfrey records the starting time as 11:30 PM, [125] while Reno, Benteen, Edgerly, Hare, Moylan, and Herendeen indicate the command got off, as scheduled, at 11 PM, [126] with Benteen reporting the following on the pack train:

"If it took a minute to cross that pack train over the 'Muddy,' it took two hours; other side of creek Colonel Keogh hunted me up, he being the officer in charge of rear guard; – he was making the very air sulfurous (sic) with blue oaths, telling me of the situation; however, from having been there very many times myself, I knew it better than he did; so I consoled him with, 'Never mind old man, do the best you can, and it will all come out right.'"

"I don't begin to believe that Job ever had much to do with shaved tailed[127] *pack mules."* [128]

Whatever the difficulties associated with starting the pack train, the march was conducted in pitch blackness which made keeping the column closed up a trying affair. Benteen records that the movement was carried out at a trot, [129] but this seems incredible given the circumstances. Groping their way forward in the darkness, Benteen was able to maintain the trail by the expedient of listening for the clanking and banging of loose equipment from the company immediately in his front. [130] Godfrey, being partially deaf, had to resort to marching his company in the column's dust cloud. The column halted about 2 AM after having marched 8 miles and waited for daylight. [131] Benteen did not unsaddle or unbridle as, receiving no orders, he thought the halt unauthorized. Godfrey, on the other hand, eased his mounts and lay down to sleep. [132] Benteen mentions joining Reno and Hodgson for a breakfast of coffee, hardtack and *"trimmings."* Godfrey mentions coffee also, but says the water was so alkaline that the horses refused to drink it. [133]

During the march, Girard, Half Yellow Face, and Bloody Knife rode with Custer at the head of the column. When Custer kept insisting that he didn't want any of the Lakota to escape, Bloody Knife told him not to be too particular about the small camps as they would find all the Indians they wanted once they struck the main village. [134] Girard estimated that they would find not less than 2500 hundred warriors, and possibly as many as 3000, although later he corrected himself and settled on an estimate of 1500 to 2000. [135]

While this march was conducted under trying circumstances, at least one officer had not lost his sense of humor. Lieutenant DeRudio had been ordered by Captain Moylan to ride to Company A's pack mules to make sure all was in order. Setting out with a single orderly, Trumpeter William G. Hardy, DeRudio had no trouble in reaching the train. Upon his return however, he blundered into the midst of a group of *". . .whooping Indians. He drew the pistol Benteen had loaned him and cocked it. From the group of Indians surrounding him came the high–pitched laugh that DeRudio recognized as Captain Thomas W. Custer's. The Indians were friendly scouts – Rees, not Sioux."* [136]

It is now appropriate to take stock of the situation. The regiment is halted approximately 10 miles from the divide separating the valleys of the Rosebud and Little Big Horn. The Indian village is suspected to be in the valley of the Little Big Horn, and scouts have been ordered forward to a high point from which this supposition can be confirmed. The plan is to conduct a thorough scout of the region on the 25th followed by a dawn attack on the 26th.

It is difficult to find serious fault with Custer's actions to this point. The night march, for which he has been severely criticized, was tactically sound as it poised the regiment within striking distance of the enemy, which, of course, was the purpose of the campaign: force the Indians to battle and deal them a crushing blow. [137] The final march had not been conducted at a rapid pace, exhausting both men and animals as some have contended, having covered 36 miles in about 21 hours. [138] We have seen that the marches followed the plan laid out by Custer on board the *Far West*; to average 30 miles per day, as, from the time of the regiment's departure from the Yellowstone to its arrival at Last Stand Hill, the column averaged 31 miles per day. The march of June 24th averaged less than 3 miles per hour, a walk pace for cavalry, with frequent stops including one of four hours duration. The night marches also averaged less than 3 miles per hour and included prolonged stops for dinner as well as the rest stop when within 10 miles of the divide. While it cannot be denied that horses, as well as men, were tired and somewhat worn, this was primarily due to the rigors of the campaign and not the rate of Custer's march from the Yellowstone. The source of the "worn out men and horses" controversy is Custer's old nemesis, Benteen, who told Terry that the command, as of the morning of June 25th, had marched 92 miles in two and one half days, an average of almost 37 miles per day, when they had, in reality, only marched 73, an average of about 29 miles per day. [139] Custer's rate of march was not over what was experienced by other columns anticipating combat during the 1876 campaign. General Crook, after marching 40 miles on June 16th had planned to march an additional 50 miles on the 17th, [140] his plans being upset when he encountered Crazy Horse and his warriors on the Rosebud. In July, Colonel Wesley Merritt drove his 5th Cavalry 85 miles in 31 hours to cut off the Cheyenne at War Bonnet Creek.[141] Other Indian Wars examples were Mackenzie marching his command 140 miles in 38 hours with no stops for sleep during the Remolino Campaign in Mexico, and Wesley Merritt marching the 5th Cavalry 170 miles in less than 3 days to relieve the siege at Milk River in October of 1879.[142] While it is undeniable that the defeat at Little Big Horn provided ample grist for second guessing, the controversy surrounding Custer's rate of march has probably been due more to his continuing ability to elicit strong emotional responses from his chroniclers than to any valid tactical considerations.

We have seen that Custer moved rather slowly and methodically on a hot trail being obviously concerned with ensuring that none of the Lakota escaped the net now closing upon them. He had, in fact, halted his pursuit and sent his scouts along his back trail when the possibility arose that a small party might have broken off from the main trail. The impression one forms, to this point, is of a thoroughly professional soldier stalking his foe, his attention riveted on contingencies to prevent the escape of that enemy. I am unable, from the evidence available, to conclude, as some others have, that Custer was obsessed with the rebuke of his Commander–in–Chief, driving his men unmercifully until they collapsed, virtually defenseless, before the enemy. Indian Agent James McLaughlin probably summed it up best:

"I knew Custer personally but not well.

". . .General Custer was not the dashing, devil–may–care, hard–riding and fast–fighting mounted soldier that the romancers have made him out. He was a careful, painstaking man and officer, devoted to his profession of arms and properly appreciating the tools he had to work with. The dash that was supposed to be his principal characteristic was merely part of the plan of a man who knows the essentials to success. He was not careless of consequences in any of the matters of life. He was a reserved and reticent man. He held the admiration of his officers and soldiers, not because he was their idol, one whom they might follow unthinkingly, but because they knew him to be a thorough soldier. He might go into an undertaking when he knew the chances were against him, but he would not do it in a spirit of bravado."[143]

The fault that may be found with Custer, as well as his white subordinates, at this stage, is rather one of omission: the glaring failure to discern the truth as revealed by the Indian trail and campsites. When this error was compounded by the division of the regiment, the fate of the 7th Cavalry was sealed.

---

[1]Edgar I. Stewart believes that Gibbon and Terry, as well as Custer, were *"oppressed"* by their thoughts the evening of June 21st. See Custer's Luck, page 248.

[2]The following account is taken largely from Godfrey's 1892 *Century Magazine* article, as his field diary only notes that an officer's conference was held and omits further detail. Although this account had the advantage of sixteen year's reflection, it did not incite any controversy among the survivors of the campaign and can therefore be accepted without reservation.

[3]The disparity between the amount of bacon and hard bread carried is probably the reason some authors have stated that only twelve days rations were carried.

[4]Godfrey, E. S. "Custer's Last Battle 1876," page 14

[5]See E. S. Godfrey "Custer's Last Battle 1876," page 14. The admonition to carry salt indicates that Custer anticipated a chase of more than the fifteen days for which his command was rationed.

[6]See Colonel W. A. Graham "The Custer Myth," page 130, E. S. Godfrey "Custer's Last Battle," page 14, and Edgar I. Stewart, "Custer's Luck," page 247.

[7]See Charles K. Mills "Harvest of Barren Regrets," page 235.

[8]See E. S. Godfrey "Custer's Last Battle 1876," page 15. Godfrey's narrative paints a picture of a cloud of impending doom hovering over the melancholy 7th as it plods along, powerless to meet its fate. Other accounts will show that this mood was anything but pervasive.

[9] Six officers destined to die on Custer's battlefield were insured by New York Life: George A. Custer ($5,000), George W. Yates ($5,000), Miles W. Keogh ($10,000), James Calhoun ($5,000), John J. Crittenden ($10,000), and James E. Porter ($5,000). It should be noted that New York Life records have transposed the amounts for Yates and Keogh. See R. "Dutch" Hardorff "Captain Keogh's Insurance Policy" page 17.

[10]See Ernest L. Reedstrom "Bugles, Banners and War Bonnets," page 99. Keogh gave his will to Lieutenant Henry Nowlan in a sealed envelope with instructions to send it to his sister Margaret in Ireland if anything should happen to him. He was insured by New York Life for $10,000 (policy number 98–830), $1,000 of which was to go to Nowlan. The balance, after Keogh's debts were paid, was to go to his sister along with his personal effects excepting a small Russian leather valise. Keogh had left this valise with Mrs. Eliza Porter, wife of his second in command. His will instructed it be turned over to Dr. Octerlay of Louisville *"to be given to the party he knows of."* (Keogh's will is reproduced in full in R. "Dutch" Hardorff "Captain Keogh's Insurance Policy" page 18.) His personal papers were to be burned unless Nowlan thought they were of some value, in which case they were to be sent to his sister in Ireland. See "Myles Keogh: The Life and Legend of an 'Irish Dragoon' in the Seventh Cavalry," pages 132 – 133.

[11]According to *Chicago Inter–Ocean* reporter William E. Curtis, Reynolds earned his sobriquet *"because of his seclusiveness – an absent, silent way he had, that made him a wonder and a mystery among the loud–tounged, open–mouthed, bolsterous men of his class – and they called his silence and reserve 'lonesomeness,' It was lonesomeness."* See "Custer's Scouts", Big Horn Yellowstone Journal, Vol. 2, No. 1, Winter 1993, page 17.

[12] See Edgar I. Stewart "Custer's Luck," page 248. While we only have Girard's Reno Court of Inquiry testimony on this incident, it is well documented that Reynolds distributed his personal belongings among the scouts the evening of the 24th, his premonition of disaster being so strong.

[13]See Marguerite Merington "The Custer Story," pages 306 – 307.

[14]Glendolin Damon Wagner, on page 134 of "Old Neutriment," tells of Armstrong Custer's plan to leave young Reed behind while Frederick Van de Water, in "Glory Hunter," page 320, states both Boston Custer and Autie Reed were to remain behind. According to Van de Water, they induced the general to relent on the morning of June 22nd.

[15] See Richard. Upton "The Custer Adventure," pages 16 – 17.

[16]See Richard. Upton "The Custer Adventure," pages 17 – 18.

[17]From this dispatch we may infer that the decision to turn onto the Indian trail discovered by Reno, rather than continuing south as Terry had ordered, had already been made and communicated; or, at the very least, Kellogg had surmised that Custer would not depart from a fresh trail. Here also we have early evidence that the camp circles of the various bands had been misinterpreted as representing ***"leisurely short marches"***. This latter error in observation was a major contributing factor in the subsequent defeat of the 7th. It also indicates that if there truly was a plan of cooperation for Custer's and Gibbon's commands,it was not known by the sole reporter with the Dakota Column.

[18]See Edgar I. Stewart "Custer's Luck," page 240.

[19]George Herendeen had been engaged as a scout by General Terry on June 21 for $100 per month. See John S. Gray, "Custer's Last Campaign," page 200.

[20] This account is taken from Walter Camp's 1909 interview with Herendeen. See "Custer in 76," page 221. Apparently Private Lynch was able to secure another mount as he was with the pack train on June 25. See Walter Camp "Custer in 76" page 139.

[21]See Edgar I. Stewart "Custer's Luck," page 252.

[22]Wagner, Glendolin Damon "Old Neutriment," page 137.

[23]See Elizabeth B. Custer "Boots and Saddles," pages 274 – 275.

[24]See Marguerite Merington "The Custer Story," pages 307 – 308.

[25]See Glendolin Damon Wagner "Old Neutriment," pages 138 – 139.

[26]See Edgar I. Stewart "Custer's Luck," page 252.

[27]See Colonel John Gibbon "Last Summer's Expedition Against the Sioux and Its Great Catastrophe," page 23

[28]See Sandy Barnard "Mark Kellogg's Role During the 1876 Campaign," page 3.

[29]See Edgar I. Stewart "Custer's Luck," page 253. It is difficult to determine whether or not to credit this statement as there was bad blood between Reno and Girard and neither Terry, Gibbon, nor Brisbin make mention of the remark. It is probable, however, that Terry felt these sentiments even if he did not verbalize them.

[30]See O. G. Libby "The Arikara Narrative," page 77.

[31]Times and distances marched, unless otherwise noted, are from the official itinerary of Lieutenant George D. Wallace. See Michael J. Koury "Diaries of the Little Big Horn," page 15.

[32]The major source for the June 22nd officers conference is E. S. Godfrey, "Custer's Last Battle," see pages 15 – 16.

[33]See Edward Settle Godfrey "The Field Diary of Edward Settle Godfrey," page 9. Since Godfrey mentions this rate of march with no comment, it may be inferred that, none of the officers took

exception to the rate of march contemplated. The same had not been the case with Custer's proposal to carry the extra forage and salt.

[34]See E. S. Godfrey "Custer's Last Battle 1876," pages 16 – 17.

[35]General George Crook was the only officer of rank in the army at that time who understood that pack mules must be specially trained and dedicated to that type of service. The difficulties Reno and Custer experienced would have been no surprise to Crook given that the mules were taken from wagon teams.

[36]See Colonel W. A. Graham "The Custer Myth," page 134.

[37]See John M. Carroll "The Benteen – Goldin Letters," page 177.

[38]Custer has been unjustly criticized for not taking at least the proffered artillery. His, however, was an astute judgment as the guns had been, and would continue to be, a hindrance to the column they accompanied. Dr. DeWolf's letter of June 21st reports three men were injured when a gun overturned. See Edward S. Luce, "The Diary and Letters of Dr. James M. DeWolf" page 81. Also recall that on his scout to the Rosebud, Reno had temporarily abandoned his gun, later recovered, because of the rough country. See Walter Camp "Custer in '76" page 53. To compound the unwieldiness of the weapons, they were pulled by horses that had been condemned as they were no longer serviceable. See W. A. Graham, "The Custer Myth," page 134.

While the firepower of this weapon was impressive, it could not have been used to advantage, due to the broken terrain, at any location other than Reno's valley fight. Since Reno was ordered in hot pursuit of a presumably fleeing village, it is unlikely he would have been ordered to take the guns had they been present. Even if he had been so ordered, the Little Big Horn was approximately 5 feet deep where Reno crossed, and the guns were mounted on 48 inch wheels, making it unlikely that the guns could have crossed at that point. See Robert Ege "Curse Not His Curls" page 105. Nor was Custer the only frontier officer who disdained the weapon, General Nelson A. Miles thought gatling guns useless for fighting Indians because they were cumbersome, jammed easily with overheating and black powder residue, and did not out range a rifle. See Wayne Michael Sarf "The Little Bighorn Campaign" page 118. General Crook had so little use for the weapon that in April of 1876 he declined to accept the nine 45–70 Gatling guns reserved for the Department of the Platte. See Ernest L. Reedstrom "Bugles, Banners, and War Bonnets" page 274.

Fred Girard probably summed it up best in his 1909 interview with Walter Camp when he related a conversation he had with Custer prior to reaching the Yellowstone:

"Custer said he would have some Gatlings along, and if he got within range of a village he would make short work of it. I told him 'General, don't you be deceived in believing you can get Indians to stand while you grind out shots with a Gatling. I would advise you to leave Gatlings behind and take a twelve–pounder that will throw shells. Then if you get within a mile or two of an Indian camp, you can make then scatter pretty lively."

Fred Dustin in "The Custer Tragedy," page 72, notes that a twelve pound Napoleon accompanied the Montana Column, but there is no indication that it was offered to Custer. Girard was right of course, the gatling guns would have made no difference at Little Big Horn for the reasons stated above; but a twelve–pounder, firing grenades and canister from Battle Ridge might have greatly influenced the outcome. See Walter Camp "Custer in '76" page 229.

[39]See E. S. Godfrey "Custer's Last Battle 1876," page 16. Note that this estimate of Custer's was larger than that of any other commander in the campaign.

[40]See Colonel W. A. Graham "The Custer Myth," page 134.

[41]See Evan S. Connell "Son of the Morning Star," page 261. It seems obvious from his somewhat rambling explanation that Custer was rationalizing. Indeed, it seems clear that Custer intended this to be solely a 7th Cavalry action and no other unit was to share in the glorious success to come.

[42]The "standard" rendition of this incident as contained in Colonel W. A. Graham "The Custer Myth," page 177 and Edgar I. Stewart "Custer's Luck," pages 256 – 257 has been given here. Lieutenant Edgerly gives a slightly different flavor to the conversation. He recalls Custer replying to Benteen's question with a firm *"I want the saddle to go where it fits."* Only after much further discussion does Custer wearily reply with the statement quoted above. This latter account seems more in keeping with the two personalities involved and may, in fact, be correct. (See Charles K. Mills "Harvest of Barren Regrets," page 239.

[43]It is interesting, but purely speculative, to consider, in light of Custer's abolishing the battalion assignments that had been extant since the departure from Fort Lincoln, that Custer may have begun to doubt Reno's willingness to carry out orders.

[44]Godfrey makes no mention of any discrepancies in the various timepieces, which is not surprising given the circumstances. The reason this item is worthy of note is that approximately 48 hours later, several of the officer's watches disagreed by as much as two hours. This has caused considerable controversy regarding the timing of the events of June 25th as well as contributing to premature hair loss on the part of historians attempting to reconstruct the action.

[45]See E. S. Godfrey "Custer's Last Battle 1876," page 17.

[46]Edgerly excludes McIntosh from the party while Godfrey's account similarly omits Gibson.

[47]See Katherine Gibson Fougera "With Custer's Cavalry," page 267, Edgar I. Stewart "Custer's Luck," pages 256 – 257, Mari Sandoz, "The Battle of the Little Bighorn," page 22, and Colonel W. A. Graham "The Custer Myth," page 135.

[48]See John S. Gray "Centennial Campaign," page 154.

[49]See Edgar I. Stewart "Custer's Luck," page 257. The "damned" was omitted from the 1892 *Century Magazine* article in concert with the delicacies of the times.

[50]See O. G. Libby "The Arikara Narrative," page 77 – 78.

[51]The official itinerary of Captain George D. Wallace. See Michael J. Koury "Diaries of the Little Big Horn," page 16.

[52]See Edgar I. Stewart "Custer's Luck," page 258.

[53]From the Diary of Charlie Reynolds. See Michael J. Koury "Diaries of the Little Big Horn," page 32.

[54]There has been much subsequent conjecture relating to the presence of wickiups in the village on the Little Big Horn. Many authors argue that wickiups were erected only after the fight on the 25th in compliance with the Lakota belief of moving camp whenever a death occurred. The presence of wickiups in the village as early as May 27 would lead one to the inescapable conclusion that a large body of transient warriors had joined the village after wintering at the agencies. The irksome part of this account is that the presence of wickiups is not mentioned in any of the diaries or journals kept during the march. We have only Godfrey's 1892 *Century Magazine* article and a questionable translation from an interview with Crazy Horse to support this statement. What is the truth? Like so many things associated with the Little Big Horn, it is difficult to say, and whatever conclusion is reached is subject to conjecture. It appears probable, in this case however, that Godfrey is mistaken, a late May date being in conflict with numerous Indian accounts placing the arrivals of the various bands that comprised the final encampment in early to mid June.

[55] See E. S. Godfrey, "Custer's Last Battle 1876," page 17 and Edgar I. Stewart, "Custer's Luck," page 258.

[56]?From the diary of Charlie Reynolds. See Michael J. Koury "Diaries of the Little Big Horn," page 32.

[57]The official itinerary of Captain George D. Wallace. See Michael J. Koury "Diaries of the Little Big Horn," page 16.

[58]See Edgar I. Stewart "Custer's Luck," page 259.

[59]See Daniel O. Magnussen "Peter Thompson's Narrative of the Little Bighorn Campaign 1876," pages 91 – 92.

[60]See Daniel O. Magnussen "Thompson's Narrative," page 92.

[61]See John M. Carroll "The Benteen – Goldin Letters," pages 163 – 164.

[62]See John M. Carroll "The Benteen – Goldin Letters," page 164 and Edgar I Stewart "Custer's Luck," page 260.

[63]See John M. Carroll "The Benteen – Goldin Letters," page 164.

[64]See Ben Innis "Bloody Knife" page 129.

[65] See Colonel W. A. Graham "The Custer Myth," page 178, Edgar I. Stewart, "Custer's Luck," page 259, and John M. Carroll "The Benteen – Goldin Letters," pages 164 – 165.

[66]The official itinerary of Captain George D. Wallace. See Michael J. Koury "Diaries of the Little Big Horn," page 16.

[67]See Edgar I. Stewart "Custer's Luck," page 260.

[68]See Edgar I. Stewart "Custer's Luck," page 261.

[69]See E. S. Godfrey "Custer's Last Battle 1876," page 18.

[70]The official itinerary of Captain George D. Wallace. See Michael J. Koury "Diaries of the Little Big Horn," page 16.

[71]See John M. Carroll "Custer's Chief of Scouts," pages 60 – 61.

[72]See John S. Gray "Centennial Campaign," page 159. If Custer appears to have been overly cautious in watching for divergent trails, one must remember that in his only prior action against an Indian village he had encountered many camps strung out along the Washita River. Therefore, he would be extremely interested in intelligence relevant to any potential decomposition of the village he was trailing. Additionally, the military was fixated upon the fear the Indians would scatter before they could be brought to battle.

[73]See John M. Carroll "Custer's Chief of Scouts," page 61.

[74]See Robert M. Utley "Custer and the Great Controversy," page 24.

[75]See James Willard Schultz "William Jackson: Indian Scout," pages 128 – 129.

[76]This remark by long time associate Bloody Knife seems to indicate a disregard for valuable intelligence on Custer's part. Let's examine the situation a little further. Custer has been ordered to pursue, and bring to battle, the enemy force. At least one of his Indian scouts has counciled abandoning the pursuit as there are too many of the foe. Since plains Indians historically shied away from pitched battles, preferring small hit and run raids, how is Bloody Knife's council to be credited? Should Custer throw away the objective of the mission and return to the Yellowstone? Should he halt his pursuit until he can communicate with Terry? What can he tell Terry about the size and location of the hostile force? It seems clear Custer had no alternative on June 24th, regardless of the council of his scouts and the evidence of trail signs, but to continue his pursuit at least until he had definite knowledge of the location and strength of the enemy force. An additional fact to consider is that Indian scouts habitually overestimated the strength of the enemy and almost invariably advised that the attacking force was too weak to be successful.

[77]Private Brinkerhoff was promoted corporal effective June 25th to fill one of the vacancies caused by the deaths of Corporals Martin and Hageman.

[78]See O. G. Libby "The Arikara Narrative," pages 80 – 82.

[79]See O. G. Libby "The Arikara Narrative," pages 80 – 82.

[80]The distance was calculated from the age of the pony droppings which were less than 2 days old. See the official itinerary of Captain George D. Wallace, Michael J. Koury "Diaries of the Little Big Horn," page 16 and Robert M. Utley "Cavalier in Buckskin," pages 177 – 178.

[81]See Evan S. Connell "Son of the Morning Star," page 268.

[82]The official itinerary of Captain George D. Wallace. See Michael J. Koury "Diaries of the Little Big Horn," page 16.

[83]See E. S. Godfrey "The Field Diary of Edward Settle Godfrey," page 10. John Gray, noted Custer historian, asserts that Herendeen positively identified the scalp as belonging to Stoker.

[84]See John S. Gray "Centennial Campaign," page 156.

[85]See J. E. Kanipe "Tarheel Survivor of Custer's Last Stand" Research Review, June 1993, page 26.

[86] There are many names for this plains Indian nation – Sioux, Nakota, Dakota, or Lakota, the latter three being based upon how the language is pronounced. In any event, the nation was comprised of four main divisions: Eastern Dakota, Santee, Teton, and Yankton. The Teton was further divided into 7 tribes: Blackfeet, Brule, Uncpapa, Minneconjou, Oglala, Sans Arc, and Two Kettle. See Bruce Grant "Concise Encyclopedia Of The American Indian" page 105. Since the Teton prefer to refer to themselves as Lakota, I have adopted that nomenclature throughout this volume except for direct quotes.

[87]See John S. Gray "Centennial Campaign," pages 157 – 158 and O. G. Libby, "The Arikara Narrative," pages 78 – 79. Edgar I. Stewart "Custer's Luck," page 262 is positive that most of the signs left by the Lakota in the "Sundance Camp" were interpreted by the Dakota scouts with Custer's column.

[88]See Roger Darling "A Sad and Terrible Blunder," page 133.

[89]See O. G. Libby "The Arikara Narrative," pages 78 – 79.

[90]See Fred Dustin "The Custer Tragedy," page 97.

[91]See E. S. Godfrey "Custer's Last Battle 1876," page 18.

[92]There is ample Indian testimony that Custer's command was, in fact, under continuing surveillance. The Cheyenne Warriors Low Dog and Red Tomahawk observed Custer's camp on June 23, and on June 24th Custer was seen by Cheyenne scouts and a band of 4 or 5 Lakota lodges headed for the White River Agency (See Grinnell Interviews). The morning of June 24, Lame White Man told Twin Woman, his wife, that soldiers had been seen on the Rosebud (Custer) and that the *Far West* had been seen on the Yellowstone. These sightings apparently came from Roan Bear and his people who were on their way to the Black Hills. While this band continued on their way, they sent word to the village via a returning party of scouts they had encountered (See Margot Liberty and John Stands in Timber "Cheyenne Memories," pages 191 – 192). In response to this intelligence the Cheyenne Chiefs decided to wait and see what the soldiers would do rather than moving to attack them. *"If they want peace, we will talk with them. If not, we will fill them up with fighting."* (See Peter John Powell "People of the Sacred Mountain," page 1006.

[93]See E. S. Godfrey "Custer's Last Battle 1876," page 18 and John S. Gray "Custer's Last Campaign," page 213. In places the dust was 4 to 6 inches deep. See John Upton Terrell and Colonel George Walton "Faint The Trumpet Sounds," page 262.

[94]Wallace states in his official itinerary of the march that *"Gen. Custer then decided to continue on that night (June 24, DCE)* **to conceal the movement**, *(emphasis the author's, DCE) locate the Indian village the next day, and attack at daylight the following morning."* See Michael J. Koury "Diaries of the Little Big Horn," page 17.

[95]See E. S. Godfrey "Custer's Last Battle 1876," page 18.

[96]See "The Field Diary of Edward Settle Godfrey," page 8 – 9, Fred Dustin ":The Custer Tragedy," page 97, Edger I. Stewart "Custer's Luck," page 263, Colonel W. A. Graham "The Custer Myth," pages 135 – 136, and Mari Sandoz "The Battle of the Little Bighorn," page s 40 – 41.

[97]Official itinerary of Captain George D. Wallace. See Michael J. Koury "Diaries of the Little Big Horn," page 16.

[98]See Edgar I. Stewart "Custer's Luck," page 266.

[99]See Katherine Gibson Fougera "With Custer's Cavalry," pages 276 – 277.

[100] The official itinerary of Captain George D. Wallace. See Michael J. Koury "Diaries of the Little Big Horn," page 16 and Edgar I. Stewart, "Custer's Luck," page 266.

[101] According to Herendeen, Custer was so concerned with the village breaking up that *"Towards evening the trails became so fresh that Custer ordered flankers to the right and left and a sharp lookout had for lodges leaving to the right or left. He said he wanted to get the whole village and nothing must leave the main trail without his knowing it."* See John S. Gray "Centennial Campaign," page 161.

[102] Mitch Boyer, all of the Crow scouts, except Half Yellow Face, who remained with Girard and Custer, as well as the Rees Forked Horn, Black Fox, Red Foolish Bear, Strikes the Lodge, Red Star and Bull accompanied Varnum and Reynolds to the Crow's Nest. See John S. Gray "Custer's Last Campaign," page 225.

[103] See John M. Carroll "Custer's Chief of Scouts," pages 61 – 62.

[104] See Thomas E. O'Neil "Custer Chronicles II" pages 14 - 15.

[105] See E. S. Godfrey "Custer's Last Battle 1876," page 19 and Graham, Colonel W. A. Graham "The Custer Myth," page 136. It should be noted that Godfrey goes on to explain that it was not unusual in Indian warfare to engage the enemy without first establishing the exact size of the opposing force.

[106] See Edgar I. Stewart "Custer's Luck," page 268. Later in life, Taylor recalled this incident in his poem "On The Rosebud:"

> "Years have passed, and the bones of the singers
> Are mingled in the dust of the plain,
> Yet often at twilight I fancy
> I hear once more that refrain,
> 'I'd lay me down to die.'

> "And green, ever green in my memory
> Are the songs I heard that night
> By our Officers sung on the Rosebud
> In the twilight before the fight."

See William O. Taylor "With Custer On The Little Bighorn" page 123.

[107] See Edgar I. Stewart "Custer's Luck," page 268.

[108] See Charles G. du Bois "Kick the Dead Lion," page 67. Regardless of Brisbin's personal feelings about Custer and his attempt to divert adverse publicity from Terry, it is undeniable that even had Custer sent Herendeen to Terry on the morning of June 25th as he was ordered, Custer would not have changed his subsequent actions one iota – the result of the Battle of the Little Big Horn was totally independent of the Tullock and the messenger to Alfred H. Terry.

[109] See Charles G. du Bois "Kick the Dead Lion," pages 67 – 68, Robert J. Ege "Settling the Dust," page 8, and Colonel W. A. Graham,"The Custer Myth," page 262.

[110] See Fred Dustin "The Custer Tragedy," page 97.

[111] Both Herendeen (1911) and Girard (1909) told Walter Camp that the question of going to Terry came up when the command was halted near the Crow's Nest on June 25th. Herendeen's account:

" Early on June 25, I told Custer that Tullock's Fork was just over the divide, but he replied rather impatiently that there was no occasion to send me through, as the Indians were known to be in his front and that his command had been discovered by them. He said the only thing he could do was to charge their village as soon as possible. . . It appeared to me at the time that Custer was right and there really was no use in scouting Tullock's Fork."

See John S. Gray "Custer's Last Campaign," page 242.

[112] In the 1867 Hancock campaign, Custer had followed his orders literally and marched away from where all signs indicated the Indians to be, to the headwaters of the Republican. He was not about to repeat that mistake and spend the rest of the summer chasing after wil 'o the wisps. See Robert M. Utley "Cavalier in Buckskin," pages 52 – 54.

[113] See E. S. Godfrey "Custer's Last Battle 1876," page 18.

[114] See Graham, Colonel W. A. "The Custer Myth," page 153, John S. Gray "Centennial Campaign," page 165, and Colonel T. M. Coughlan "Varnum – The Last of Custer's Lieutenants" page 9. Godfrey, while decrying the whole idea of cooperation between Gibbon's and Custer's commands, theorized that perhaps Herendeen would have been sent to Terry the night of the 25th with the result of the day's reconnaissance. See Colonel W. A. Graham "The Custer Myth," page 148.

[115] Colonel Nelson A. Miles and Captain Robert G. Carter, argued that Terry's order to Custer was merely a letter of instructions. If this were so, Custer would not be obligated, by military law, to obey as *". . . mere instructions would not in general fulfill the definition of an order or 'command' . . nor would a mere statement of his wishes and views by a superior, however pointedly impressed upon the inferior in his entering upon the duty."* (See William Winthrop "Military Law and Precedents" page 574). While Carter noted that the document did not carry the customary "by order of," declaration, the fact a written document was prepared seems to indicate Terry meant the document to carry the full weight of an order.

[116] Captain Moylan retrieved the gold watch fob from a back pocket of Smith's trousers where the Indians had overlooked it. See Katherine Gibson Fougera "With Custer's Cavalry," page 275.

[117] See Katherine Gibson Fougera "With Custer's Cavalry," page 276.

[118] See James Willard Schultz "William Jackson Indian Scout," page 130.

[119] The coincidence of the 7th Cavalry nearing the village during the few days of its peak strength was only the start of a run of extremely bad luck for Custer.

[120] See Peter John Powell "People of the Sacred Mountain," page 1007.

[121] See Peter John Powell "People of the Sacred Mountain," page 1007.

[122] See Peter John Powell "People of the Sacred Mountain," page 1007.

[123] John Gray credits the disagreement of the time pieces to faulty memories on the part of the participants rather than to a mechanical malfunction of watches. See "Centennial Campaign," page 224.

[124] Since it took between 1 1/2 and 2 hours to cross Mud Creek, Wallace's starting time of 1 am may, in fact, refer to when the pack train finally moved out putting the entire column in motion while the 11 P. M. starting times may refer only to the column's advance elements. See Edgar I. Stewart "Custer's Luck," page 269. The quote is from the official itinerary of Captain George D. Wallace. See Michael J. Koury "Diaries of the Little Big Horn," page 17.

[125] See E. S. Godfrey "The Field Diary of Edward Settle Godfrey," page 10.

[126] See William Hedley "'We've Caught Them Napping!' – The Little Big Horn Time Warp," page 60.

[127] According to Fairfax Downey, these "shave tailed" mules were *perverse, untrained, bumptious, their manes had been roached and their tails shaved to distinguish them from the more tractable old-timers. Their name 'shavetails,' was transferred by the Army to all newly joined, spick-and-span know-it-all second lieutenants, who still bear it, most of them without knowing why.* See "Indian Fighting Army" pages 164 - 165.

[128] See John M. Carroll "The Benteen – Goldin Letters," page 166.

[129] See John M. Carroll "The Benteen – Goldin Letters," page 166 and Edgar I. Stewart "Custer's Luck," page 270.

[130] See John M. Carroll "The Benteen – Goldin Letters," page 166.

[131] See E. S. Godfrey "Custer's Last Battle 1876," page 19. Godfrey thought the command had marched about 10 miles, but I have used the official itinerary compiled by Captain Wallace which gives the distance traveled as 8 miles.

[132] It is appropriate here to note that Benteen's accounts of the march, and subsequent battle paint a portrait of Custer as being completely derelict in his duty; totally consumed by thoughts of imminent glory. This is the same Benteen who could not see the reason for the *"frequent and sometimes quite lengthy halts"* of June 24th, although the fact that they were on a fresh trail, whose signs needed to be interpreted, was obvious even to the greenest recruit (See John M. Carroll "The Benteen – Goldin Letters," page 179.). It should also be recalled that Custer had made each troop commander responsible for his own company on June 22nd. Godfrey, not burdened by Benteen's vindictiveness, had no problem in ascertaining the reality of the situation, hence he unsaddled.

[133] See E. S. Godfrey "Custer's Last Battle 1876," page 19.

[134] See John S. Gray "Custer's Last Campaign," pages 226 – 227 and Edgar I. Stewart, "Custer's Luck," page 271.

[135] The courier from Fort Lincoln carrying General Sheridan's warning about 1800 lodges departing a single reservation arrived about 1 week after the battle. See Colonel W. A. Graham "The Custer Myth," page 149 and E. S. Godfrey "Custer's Last Battle 1876," page 14.

[136] See Charles K. Mills "Charles C. DeRudio," pages 24 – 25.

[137] Reno, in his official report on the battle, notes Custer informed his officers that approaching the divide in daylight was certain to result in the discovery of the troops. See E. Lisle Reedstrom "Custer's 7th Cavalry" page 135.

[138] Mileage and travel times are taken from the official itinerary kept by Captain George D. Wallace.

[139] John S. Gray has done the definitive research in this area. The reader is referred to "Custer's Last Campaign," page 205 for times and distances marched from noon of June 22 until the halt at Busby on June 24th. The excellent description of the terrain of the Rosebud Valley found in "Custer Country" (Ralph E. Scudder, pages 18 – 20) demonstrates that the topography would not have been a factor in any fatigue experienced by the troops.

[140] See Edgar I. Stewart Custer's Luck," pages 197 – 199 and 201.

[141] See Paul L. Hedren "The Great Sioux War," page 202.

[142] See Bill O'Neal "Fighting Men of the Indian Wars" pages 161 and 167.

[143] See James McLaughlin "My Friend The Indian:" pages 119 – 120.

Chapter 11

The Crow's Nest

Varnum roused himself from his sleep of an hour's duration as the first gray streaks of dawn appeared in the eastern sky.[1] It was Sunday morning, June 25, 1876. Varnum, his eyes still red and sore from his exhausting 70 mile ride of the previous day, climbed the steep slope to the vantage point that would show whether there were Indians on the Little Big Horn. Upon reaching the lookout, Varnum was informed by the Crow scouts that a large village was in the valley of the Little Big Horn behind a line of bluffs, and they pointed out the pony herd. When Varnum could not spot the herd, he was told: *"Look for worms on the grass."*[2] Varnum tried in vain to locate the ponies. All he could see was *"two tepees ,(sic) one partly wrecked or fallen over."*[3]

Varnum quickly scribbled a note informing Custer of the Crow's report. Arikara scouts Red Star and Bull[4] were selected to carry this message to Custer, the smoke from the command's breakfast fires being easily visible from the Crow's Nest.[5] A curious incident occurred when Custer received this message, as Red Star relates:

> *"Custer said to Bloody Knife by signs, referring to Tom (Tom Custer, DCE), 'Your brother, there, is frightened, his heart flutters with fear, his eyes are rolling from fright at this news of the Sioux. When we have beaten the Sioux he will then be a man."*[6]

It is difficult to know what to make of this statement. Armstrong Custer could have no question of his brother Tom's courage, being a double Medal of Honor winner during the Civil War. Given Custer's earlier conversation promising rewards for the Arikara after the successful conclusion of the campaign, I believe this was an attempt on Custer's part to instill confidence in his Arikara scouts. Custer knew that Indians were easily impressed by numbers and the 7th would clearly be outnumbered in the coming fight. Since he would need his Indian allies to support his attack by capturing the pony herd, freeing all of the troops except the pack train detachment for active combat, he probably felt their confidence needed to be bolstered.

The village the scouts had sighted some 15 miles away, just below the mouth of Reno Creek,[7] was, in reality an immense city; stretching for almost three miles along the west bank of the river, and comprising anywhere from 7,500 to 12,000 people, of whom 2,500 to 4,000 were warriors.[8] In addition to the six major circles in the village (Cheyenne, Oglala, Minneconjou, Uncpapa, Blackfeet and Sans Arc), there were a considerable number of Brules, Assiniboines, and Santees (called Waist and Skirt People because of two piece women's dresses which were unique among plains Indians).[9] According to Wooden Leg, the circles were laid out from north to south along the west bank as follows: Cheyenne, Sans Arc, Minneconjou, and Uncpapas. Away from the river, and southwest of the Cheyenne and Sans Arc, were the Oglalas. Between the Oglalas and Uncpapas, but nearer the Uncpapas were the Blackfeet.[10] Most of the Cheyenne were in the encampment including Old Bear and Dirty Moccasins, two of the tribe's four "old man" chiefs. Little Wolf, an "old man" chief as well as the leading chief of the Elk Warriors, was the only one of the 30 warrior society chiefs not in the encampment.[11]

Custer, clad in blue-gray flannel shirt,[12] buckskin trousers, long boots and a wide brimmed white hat, started for the Crow's Nest.[13] Riding bareback on Dandy,[14] Armstrong was accompanied by Tom Custer, Girard, Bloody Knife, Red Star, Bob Tailed Bull, and Little Brave. Varnum observed the approach of this party and rode out to meet them. Armstrong Custer ordered his brother back to the main column to ascertain why it was moving up without orders before accompanying Varnum to the observation point.[15] Custer strained, trying to see the village through the morning haze, but was unable to see anything indicating the presence of a village. In an attempt to secure a better view, Custer, accompanied by Charlie Reynolds, had moved to a higher peak immediately south of the Crow's Nest. Unable to see anything even with field glasses, Custer expressed doubt that a village had been sighted.[16] When informed of this situation, Mitch Boyer told Custer: *"If you can't find more Indians in that valley than you ever saw together before, you may hang me."* To which Custer replied, *"It would do a damn sight of good to hang you, wouldn't it?"*[17] Custer's testiness may have been triggered by Varnum's report of sighting scouts who were presumed to come from the village. Varnum recalled:

> *"Soon after this (sending the Arikara messengers to Custer, DCE) I saw an Indian, mounted, leading a pony on a long lariat, & a boy, also mounted, riding behind. (This was probably the boy Deeds and his father Brown Ass, DCE) They were riding parallel to the divide and evidently heading for a gap to cross the ridge. The Crows wanted them headed off & killed. Reynolds, Boyer, two Crows & myself started off to do it. We got into a tangle of ravines. We heard a sound of Crow calls from the hill. Our Crows answered & then we turned back. I asked Boyer what it meant and he did not know.*

> *"On returning we found the Indian had changed his course, but soon afterwards he did cross the divide & went down the slope towards Custer's advancing column. We could see the dust of the column, but not the troops at that time. This Indian continued on a long distance & then stopped for a while & suddenly disappeared. He had evidently discovered the advance of the troops.*

> *"Later I saw seven Indians[18] in single file riding on the crest of a ridge running north from the divide & parallel to Custer's advance. Outlined against the sky their ponies looked as large as elephants. Suddenly they disappeared, but two black spots reappeared. Evidently they also had seen the troops & the two black spots were Indians watching them."[19]*

Custer did not initially believe that the command had been discovered. Upon leaving the observation point, he was confronted by Half Yellow Face, known to the Arikara as "Big Belly":

> *". . . Big Belly got up and asked Custer through the Crow interpreter (Mitch Boyer, DCE) what he thought of the Dakota camp he had seen. Custer said: 'This camp has not seen our army, none of their scouts have seen us.' Big Belly replied: 'You say we have not been seen. these Sioux we have seen at the foot of the hill, two going one way, and four the other, are good scouts, they have seen the smoke of our camp.' Custer said, speaking angrily: 'I say again we have not been seen. That camp has not seen us, I am going ahead to carry out what I think. I want to wait until it is dark and then we will march, we will place our army around the Sioux camp.' Big Belly replied: 'That plan is bad, it should not be carried out.' Custer said: 'I have said what I propose to do, I want to wait until it is dark and then go ahead with my plan.*

> *"Red Star as he sat listening first thought that Custer's plan was good. The Crow scouts insisted that the Dakota scouts had already seen the army and would report its coming and that they would attack Custer's army. They wanted him to attack at once, that day, and capture the horses of the Dakotas and leave them unable to*

move rapidly. Custer replied: 'Yes, it shall be done as you say.' The army now came up to the foot of the hill and Custer's party rode down and joined the troop."[20]

The arguments of the Crow scouts had not convinced Custer to abandon his original plan of using the 25th for reconnaissance and attacking at dawn of the 26th. Custer recalled his near disaster on the Washita and was determined to conduct a thorough reconnaissance before committing the troops. As the column approached the Crow's Nest, Tom Custer and Calhoun rode out front to inform the general of another encounter with the Lakota. Sergeant William A. Curtiss, of Yates' Company F, accompanied by a squad,[21] had gone over the back trail to retrieve some of his clothing left at the night halt.[22] The small detachment had discovered, and fired upon, two Indians[23] who were opening a box of hard bread that had been dropped during the night march of the 24th. The Indians had escaped and, not knowing that Medicine Bull and Red Cherries were members of Little Wolf's band of Cheyenne,[24] Tom Custer feared the village would be warned. In the best tradition of "shooting the messengers" Custer angrily ordered Calhoun and Tom back to the column. Custer might have convinced himself that the Indians were far enough in his rear to proceed with his original plan were it not for George Herendeen. Herendeen, who had also ridden back with Sergeant Curtiss' party, reported to Custer he had seen signs of a large war party in a ravine near the abandoned hard bread box.[25]

Herendeen's report was the last straw.[26] Custer could no longer deny that the command had been discovered. He had to move quickly now, lest the Indians escape as feared. Custer had his orderly of the day, Trumpeter John Martin (Giovanni Martini) of Company H, sound *"Officer's Call."* [27] Godfrey recalled Custer's instructions when the officers had assembled:

> *"He recounted Captain Keogh's report (Keogh had informed Tom Custer of Sergeant Curtiss' encounter at the hard bread box, DCE), and also said that the scouts had seen several Indians moving along the ridge overlooking the valley through which we had marched, as if observing our movements; he thought the Indians must have seen the dust made by the command. At all events our presence had been discovered and further concealment was unnecessary; that we would march at once to attack the village; that he had not intended to make the attack until the next morning, the 26th, but our discovery made it imperative to act at once, as delay would allow the village to scatter and escape. Troop commanders were ordered to make a detail of one non–commissioned officer and six men to accompany the packs; to inspect their troops and report as soon as they were ready to march; that the troops would take their places in the column of march in the order in which reports of readiness were received, and that the last one to report would escort the pack–train."[28]*

While the other officers went to check their companies, Benteen, knowing that his troop was in compliance, immediately claimed the post of honor.[29] Just prior to the officer's conference, Godfrey had ridden over to headquarters and observed Custer and Bloody Knife in conversation:

> *"Bloody Knife was talking to the Genl & said we would find enough Sioux to keep us fighting two or three days. Genl remarked laughingly that he thought we would get through in one day."[30]*

Dr. Lord had not recovered from his dysentery and Custer suggested he remain with the pack train while Dr. Porter would take his place. Lord, a first lieutenant, insisted upon accompanying the main column and Custer relented.[31] Burkman, tried to convince Custer's young nephew Reed to remain with the pack train:

"I went over to him whar he was settin' his horse close to Captain Tom Custer.

"'Autie,' I says, 'don't go with the General today. Pears like they's goin' to be considerable fightin'. You stay and guard camp.'

"The youngster threw back his head and laughed. He pulled his foot from the stirrup and give me a friendly kick. 'Me stay!' he says. 'When they's goin' to be a fight! Why, John, you're crazy! That's what I come out West fur, to see an Indian fight.'

"I kept on arguin' with him. Bud, I coaxed him with tears in my eyes. Seemed like I couldn't bear his goin' into battle that mornin'. But it want no use. He jist laughed. 'You're mad,' he said, "cause you can't go along.'

"When the battle was over he was found close to his uncle, Boss Custer, jist a leetle below whar General Custer was layin'.

"Custer called to me then and ordered me to saddle Vic. (Dandy was in the fight up on Reno Hill. I disremember who rid him. He was wounded in the neck but he got well and was arterwards sent back to the General's father.)

"Whilst I was holdin' Vic's bridle, him (Vic, short for Victory, was a mare, DCE) prancin' considerable, I said to Custer, ' 'Pears like I ought to be goin' along General.'

"He leaped into the saddle and then he leaned over and put his hand fur a minute on my shoulder. He smiled at me. His moustache was long, almost hidin' his mouth. He was wearin' one of his big, white hats, o'course, and a fringed, buckskin coat. (Custer had discarded the jacket before his trip to the Crow's Nest, DCE)

" 'No John,' he says to me. 'You've been doin' guard duty three nights in recession. You're tired out. Your place is with McDougall (sic) and the pack train. But if we should have to send fur more ammunition you can come in on the home stretch.'

"Them's the last words he ever spoke to me."[32]

Stabbed, who functioned as the Arikara medicine man, exhorted the young men to behave well and be brave. Knowing many of the young men were preparing for their first fight, he anointed their chests with clay as protection against the Lakota.[33] With Captain McDougall's report that Company B was ready,[34] the column moved out; crossing the divide between the Rosebud and Little Big Horn valleys at noon.[35]

Custer has been severely criticized for pressing his attack, without benefit of a proper reconnaissance, at mid–day; the usual charges being "recklessness," and "glory hunting."[36] We need to judge Custer's actions, however, in light of what he knew then, not what we 'Monday Morning Quarterbacks" know now. He knew his night movement of the 24th had been unsuccessful as the command had been rediscovered by at least three, and possibly more, scouting parties, thereby depriving him of the element of surprise. From his Washita campaign he knew the dangers attendant to an attack without proper reconnaissance; only abandoning his plan for reconnaissance when the weight of evidence the village would be alerted to his presence became too great. The trail signs, and the information from his scouts, all indicated a large, perhaps unprecedented, warrior force in his front. He did not know of the defeat of Crook on the Rosebud, nor the resolve of the force about to be encountered. He knew that Indians seldom offered battle to large bodies of troops, being more inclined to disperse when their village was threatened. As General Sherman stated, Custer had no option, given the circumstances, other than to press an immediate attack.[37] As we shall see in the next chapter, Custer would remember the lessons of the Washita and, displaying extreme caution, conduct a reconnaissance–in–force rather than the rash assault that is typically depicted. Perhaps Walter Camp best summed up this penchant for second guessing:

> *"Custer in his Indian fighting was a good deal like Admiral Farragut and the torpedoes (sic) in Mobile Harbor. If Farragut had run upon torpedoes and sunk most of his ships he would have been called reckless. He missed the torpedoes (sic) and became a hero."*[38]

---

[1] U. S. Naval Observatory data indicates sunrise on June 25, 1876 occurred at 5:22 AM. See Joe Sills, Jr. "Weir Point Perspectives" page 45.

[2] See John M. Carroll "Custer's Chief of Scouts" page 87.

[3] See John M. Carroll "Custer's Chief of Scouts" page 87. This, of course, was the famous "lone tepee" the location of which will be key to understanding the spatial relationships between Custer's various detachments during the battle.

[4] See O. G. Libby "The Arikara Narrative" page 83. The Arikara scout Red Star says that Charley Reynolds wrote the message, but this is unlikely. See O. G. Libby "The Arikara Narrative" page 88.

[5] See John M. Carroll "Custer's Chief of Scouts" page 87. There is no doubt that breakfast fires were lighted on June 25th, as we have the testimony of many of the officers, Benteen and Godfrey among them, as well as that of the Indian scouts. That the command was permitted to light fires after just completing a night march to mask their location from enemy scouting parties seems incredible.

[6] See O. G. Libby "The Arikara Narrative" page 90.

[7] As previously mentioned, had large herds of antelope not been sighted to the north, the Indians would have turned south and passed by Custer's left as Terry had feared. See Thomas B. Marquis "Wooden Leg: A Warrior Who Fought Custer" page 204.

[8] See Thomas Marquis "Custer on the Little Big Horn" page 20.

[9] See Thomas B. Marquis "Wooden Leg: A Warrior Who Fought Custer" page 208.

[10] See Thomas B. Marquis "Wooden Leg: A Warrior Who Fought Custer" page 209. Note that with the exception of the Uncpapa circle being furthest south, and the Cheyenne circle being furthest north, there is little agreement in Indian accounts regarding the location of the circles.

[11] See Thomas B. Marquis "Wooden Leg: A Warrior Who Fought Custer" page 205. Little Wolf, whose band was closely following Custer's command would enter the village shortly after the Custer portion of the fight ended.

[12] Due to the warm morning Custer had discarded his buckskin jacket. According to the diary of Sergeant James Wilson, the maximum temperature recorded on board the Far West on June 25 was 91 degrees. See Michael J. Koury "Diaries of the Little Big Horn" page 79.

[13] See O. G. Libby "The Arikara Narrative" page 90.

[14] See Glendolin Damon Wagner "Old Neutriment" page 149.

[15] Varnum recalled Tom Custer being sent back to the command, but did not comment on the reason for it. In his account, Girard has the General questioning Tom Custer about the forward movement of the troops upon the General's return from the Crow's Nest. See O. G. Libby "The Arikara Narrative" page 171. Custer may have authorized a movement of the regiment to a point within about 3 miles of the divide, and there are indications such a movement took place. This second movement, however, brought the regiment too close to the divide for adequate concealment causing Custer's consternation.

[16] See Dale T. Schoenberger "The End of Custer" page 48.

[17] See John M. Carroll "Custer's Chief of Scouts" page 88. Varnum was impressed by Custer's mild profanity as he had only heard him swear once previously, during one of the 1873 engagements with the Lakota along the Yellowstone (Custer had promised Libbie to stop swearing upon their marriage – see Karol Asay "Gray Head and Long Hair" page 7). Red Star's account has Custer initially disbelieving positive evidence of a village has been obtained, then agreeing after an examination of the valley through his field glasses. See O. G. Libby "The Arikara Narrative" page 91.

[18] This was the party of the Oglala Black Bear returning to Red Cloud Agency after tracking some stolen horses. Also in the group were Knife and his wife, Owl Bull, Medicine Bird, Blue Cloud, and Kills Enemy In Winter. Despite having seen the soldiers, they continued on toward the agency, making no attempt to warn the village. This party also encountered Little Wolf's Cheyenne and learned of the incident at the hard bread box from them. See Watler Camp "Custer in '76" page 203.

[19] See John M. Carroll "Custer's Chief of Scouts" pages 87 – 88.

[20] See O. G. Libby "The Arikara Narrative" pages 91 – 93. Some accounts claim Half Yellow Face told Custer that they would both die that day. To push for a major offensive action, while believing it would result in one's own death, is inconsistent with an Indian's nature. I am therefore unable to accept this account in the absence of further corroboration.

[21] The members of this detail were Company F privates William Brown, Patrick Bruce, Sebastian Omling and James Rooney. All except Rooney would die with Custer. See Richard G. Hardorff "Hokahey! A Good Day To Die!" page 28.

[22] See Colonel W. A. Graham "Abstract of the Official Record of Proceedings of The Reno Court of Inquiry" page 68.

23 Richard G. Hardorff believes there were 3 Cheyenne encountered at the hard bread box and names Big Crow, Black Horse, and Medicine Bull. See "Hokahey! A Good Day To Die" page 27.

24 See Peter John Powell "People of the Sacred Mountain" page 1032.

25 See David Humphreys Miller "Custer's Fall: The Indian Side of the Story" pages 18 – 19.

26 It is possible that Varnum and the scouts saw a small party that had camped the night of the 24th at the lone tepee site break camp and head for the main village. Varnum apparently concluded the village was breaking up and so informed Custer. These may have been the 40 to 50 Indians Lieutenant Hare testified he saw in the vicinity of the lone tepee. See Edgar I. Stewart "Custer's Luck" pages 323 – 324. Herendeen had a narrow escape when, riding in advance of the column, he had come within 150 yards of one of the Indians pursued by Varnum's party. See Richard G. Hardorff "Hokahey! A Good Day To Die!": page 24.

27 See Frank Perfetti "John Martin, An Italian With Custer" page 18. Captain Benteen had ordered Martin to report for duty as Custer's orderly around 8:00 AM while the column was halted for a rest and coffee stop. See Frank Perfetti "John Martin, An Italian With Custer" page 17.

28 See E. S. Godfrey "Custer's Last Battle 1876" page 21. Sergeant Windolph's account indicates he overheard the size of the village and the division into battalions being discussed at the conference, Captain Benteen being opposed to dividing the regiment. As no other officers recalled those topics of conversation, and they certainly should have been remembered as they would have been among the most important items discussed, I conclude that this conversation between Custer and Benteen, if it took place at all, occurred after crossing the divide. See Neil C. Mangum "Battle of the Little Big Horn: As Related by Charles Windolph, Company H, Seventh Cavalry, U.S.A." page 3.

29 See Colonel W. A. Graham "The Custer Myth" page 179.

30 See Edgar I. Stewart "The Field Diary of Lt. Edward Settle Godfrey" page 10. The reader is reminded that Custer was given the same council, too many Indians for the soldiers to whip, by his Osage scouts just prior to the Washita fight.

31 See John M. Carroll "They Rode With Custer."

32 See Glendolin Damon Wagner "Old Neutriment" pages 150 – 151.

33 See O. G. Libby "The Arikara Narrative" page 84. Ben Innis believes this ceremony took place at the Crow's Nest. See "Bloody Knife!" pages 132 - 133.

34 This tardiness may have saved the lives of McDougall and his men as they probably would have been assigned to Keogh's battalion as they had been throughout the march.

35 As noted previously, very few participants could agree on the time of day certain events took place. This time is from Lieutenant Wallace's official itinerary. See Captain Michael J. Koury "Diaries of the Little Big Horn" page 17.

36 Historians have been highly selective in their mention of actions conducted against Indian villages in daylight. Seldom, if ever, mentioned are Mackenzie's 4 PM attack on a Comanche village on the North Fork of the Red River in September of 1872 (see Bill O'Neal "Fighting Men of the

Indian Wars" page 160) or Eugene Carr's attack at Summit Springs which was conducted in broad daylight with a divided command against a numerically superior Indian force (see Michael J. Koury "The Myth of the Indian Warrior" page 58). As both Carr's and Mackenzie's actions preceded the Little Big Horn, it may be logical to assume Custer knew of these actions and, while not pleased by having to abandon his initial plan, was not overly concerned with pressing his attack in daylight.

37 See Edgar I. Stewart "Custer's Luck" page 280.

38 See Jim Schneider "The Humor of Walter M. Camp" page 13.

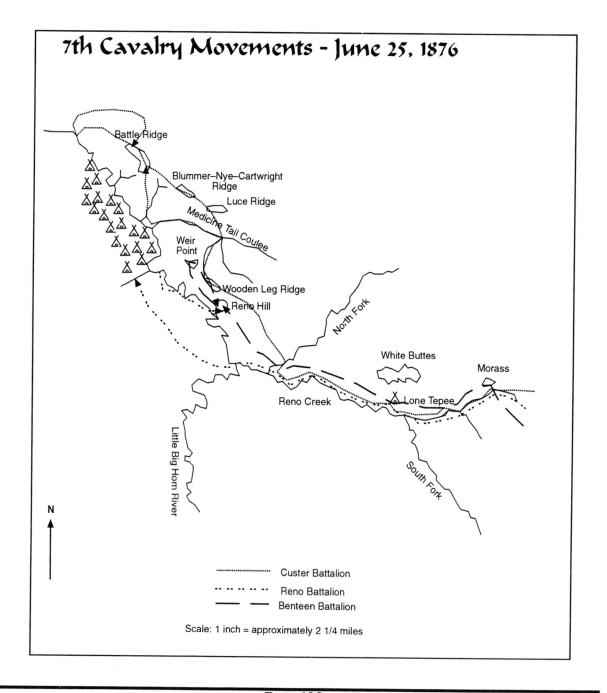

Chapter 12

The Approach To The Valley

About 15 minutes after crossing the divide,[1] Custer halted the column and went aside with his adjutant, Lieutenant Cooke. Cooke was seen to do some "figuring" in his notebook, which was undoubtedly calculating the relative strengths of the various battalions. Upon his return, Custer divided the regiment into battalions. Reno was to command companies A, G, and M; Benteen, companies D, H, and K; Keogh, companies C, I, and L; and Yates, companies E and F.[2] McDougall's Company B, by virtue of being the last company to report being ready, was detailed to escort the pack train which remained under the command of Lieutenant Mathey.[3] The assignment of Company B to escort the packs may have been fortuitous as B's troopers were the least experienced in the regiment.[4]

One of the scouts, William Jackson, a half–breed Pikuni Blackfoot, remembered that Mitch Boyer tried to dissuade Custer from attacking:

> "... Bruyer (Boyer, DCE) said to Custer: 'General, we have discovered the camp,
> down there on the Little Horn. It is a big one! Too big for you to tackle! Why, there
> are thousands and thousands of Sioux and Cheyennes down there.'

> "For a moment the general stared at him, angrily, I thought, and then sternly
> replied: 'I shall attack them! If you are afraid, Bruyer –'

> "'I guess I can go wherever you do,' Bruyer quickly answered; and at that, the
> general turned back to the command, we following him. He had the bugler sound
> the officers' call, and the command rested while they got together, and Custer gave
> his orders for the attack upon the camp."[5]

While Custer conferred with his officers, Boyer described the camp to the scouts. Jackson remembered that after Boyer finished, the scouts were quiet for a time, then:

> "Bloody Knife looked up and signed to the sun: 'I shall not see you go down behind
> the mountains to–night.' And at that I almost choked. I felt that he knew that his
> end was near, that there was no escaping it. I turned and looked the other way. I
> thought that my own end was near. I felt very sad."[6]

As a consequence of the Indian trail being comprised of alkali dust up to 4 inches deep, Custer wanted Mathey to keep the pack train off the trail in order to hold down the dust.[7] Reno was ordered to march parallel to the main column on the left of the creek that would one day bear his name, while Benteen was ordered to "... move with my command to the left, to send well–mounted officers with about six men who would ride rapidly to a line of bluffs about five miles (actually 2 miles, DCE) to our left and front, with instructions to report at once to me if anything of Indians could be seen from that point. I was to follow the movement of this detachment as rapidly as possible. Lieutenant Gibson was the officer selected. . ."[8].

Custer scholars have argued incessantly over Benteen's orders. Some believe that Benteen was sent to the left to keep him out of the fight all together; citing as rationale for their position

---

that Benteen's was the only command element not to be accompanied by a doctor.[9] Lieutenant Gibson, Benteen's second in command, wrote his wife on July 4: *"Benteen's battalion was sent to the left about five miles to see if the Indians were trying to escape up the valley of the Little Big Horn, after which* **we were to hurry and rejoin the command as quickly as possible.** *(emphasis the author's)"*[10] His daughter repeated that rationale in her book *"With Custer's Cavalry."*[11] Thomas B. Marquis believed that Custer, or his scouts, may have seen the trail made by the warriors when they went to attack Crook and Benteen was sent to investigate.[12] Edgerly told Walter Camp that he believed Benteen was ordered to the left to prevent the escape of any Indians up the valley.[13] Others have viewed Custer's action as a belated attempt to satisfy Terry's caution to not let the Indians escape around his left flank. I personally believe that Custer, unaware of the precise location of the village, but knowing it to be in the valley, and cognizant of the Washita where the villages were strung out for miles along the stream, was conducting a reconnaissance in force. As Benteen would not be expected to engage the Indians alone, not sending a doctor would be appropriate. Similarly, it would be appropriate for Benteen to have the smallest detachment, as was the case (see Table 12 – 2). Godfrey seems to confirm this hypothesis with his statement that Benteen was ordered to the left either to intercept Indians fleeing up the valley, and drive them back toward the supposed location of the village, below the mouth of Reno Creek, or perhaps because Custer was concerned *"the village might be strung out along the valley for several miles. . ."*[14]

Keogh, realizing that action was close at hand, exchanged Paddy, who he had ridden for most of the expedition, for his old "war horse" Comanche.[15] The division of the regiment being completed, the command moved forward once again. The assignment of personnel to the various commands is presented in Table 12 – 1[16] and the combat strength of the various battalions is presented in Table 12 – 2. The main command hadn't traveled very far when Custer noted that there was a second line of bluffs behind the line to which he had just ordered Benteen. He immediately dispatched Chief Trumpeter Henry Voss to tell Benteen to go on to the second line of bluffs if he didn't find anything prior. As the main command moved down Reno Creek the country opened up and Custer saw that he had still constrained Benteen too severely. He then dispatched Sergeant Major Sharrow with the message that, if Benteen didn't encounter any Indians, he was to push on and enter the valley.[17]

Benteen, mounted on his fast–walking horse Dick,[18] had set a furious pace over the uneven terrain; Godfrey, whose Company K was at the end of the column, having to *"quite often"* give the command to trot in order to keep closed up.[19] Realizing that it would be too fatiguing to the horses to continually climb the bluffs, the command began skirting around the base of them. This had the effect of bringing the line of march back toward Reno Creek. At the Reno court of inquiry, Benteen testified that, after receiving the message carried by Sharrow, he noticed the Gray Horse Troop moving at a gallop. His testimony, which did not elicit any questions from the recorder, indicates he believed it useless to continue on his mission and that he would be of more use if he struck out at once for Custer's trail.[20] Lieutenant Gibson, who led the detachment in advance of Benteen's column, had a different recollection of the reason Benteen turned back toward Custer's trail. In an 1898 letter to Godfrey, Gibson stated that, from his last observation point, he had *"looked far up the valley of the Little Big Horn without seeing any signs of Indians, and had so reported to Benteen who had then given the order to return to the trail."*[21] There is no reason to suspect Gibson's information is in error. Benteen's testimony may be explained by the supposition that it was more important for him to attempt to discredit Custer for giving superfluous orders, than to take credit for having completed his assigned mission. It is of interest to note that Benteen did not attempt to send a messenger to Custer informing him of the results of the reconnaissance. The failure to properly communicate much needed intelligence in a timely manner would plague the 7th Cavalry throughout the day. In any event, Benteen returned to the main trail just above a morass where he stopped to water his thirsty horses.

Given the broken nature of the country, Benteen's gait was necessarily irregular making it hard to estimate the distance traveled. While it is uncertain exactly how far, and how long, it took Benteen to complete his reconnaissance, some judgments may be made. A chronology of the major events of June 25 is presented in Appendix 12. Much controversy has arisen over the years because of the lack of agreement as to the time of day certain events transpired. Some authors attempt to deal with this controversy by the obtuse argument that, since there were no time zones in 1876,[22] some of the officers had their watches set to "Chicago Time" while others were, apparently on "local time." All of which, of course, implies the existence of time zones! It is difficult enough to try to understand what happened on June 25 without inventing such useless controversy. The rate and distance analysis used in establishing the times presented in Appendix 12 are therefore based upon relative time. That is, it is of no importance to know when Custer passed the lone tepee, but it is critical to know where Benteen was at the time Custer passed the lone tepee. To that end, all times presented in Appendix 12 are based upon relative times using the time Custer passed the lone tepee as the reference point.

From this analysis, I conclude that Benteen, moving at a walk pace,[23] must have left his watering place at the morass 35 minutes after Custer passed the lone tepee. If one accepts Godfrey's testimony that they watered and rested for 20 to 30 minutes, Benteen must have reached the morass within 5 to 15 minutes after Custer passed the lone tepee. That being the case, and the morass generally believed to have been about 4 miles from where the regiment was divided into battalions and the lone tepee about 3 1/2 miles beyond the morass, Benteen would have consumed between 2 hours 35 minutes and 2 hours 45 minutes on his scout.[24] We will leave Benteen watering at the morass for the moment and return to the movement toward the Little Big Horn by Custer and Reno.

The command moved down Reno Creek in column of fours, with Reno's battalion on the left (south) bank and Custer's command on the right; Lieutenant Varnum being to the left, while Lieutenant Hare and the remainder of the scouts were in front.[25] Scouts were constantly riding in and out, providing a steady stream of intelligence to Custer.[26] During the march down Reno Creek the two commands were sometimes almost abreast; at other times as much as 100 yards apart. Finding themselves almost abreast, Private Byron L. Tarbox, Company L, had some final advice for his half–brother, Private William Ephraim Morris of Company G:

> ". . . called to me and laughingly said: 'Look out, Bill, the Indians are h– – –for red–headed fellows.' I replied: 'You look out for number one hundred!' That was the last I ever saw of my half–brother. (Private Tarbox was killed with the Custer Column, DCE)"[27]

Shortly before reaching the site of the lone tepee,[28] Custer motioned to Reno with his hat to cross the stream and join the main command on the right bank.[29] The crossing was somewhat difficult to accomplish and left Reno's battalion in the rear of Custer's column. Lieutenant Cooke then rode up with an order from Custer for Reno to move his battalion to the front. Reno immediately complied reaching the head of the column at the lone tepee.

The lone tepee, located at the upper, or south, fork of Reno Creek lies under an unmistakable chalk white bluff.[30] This had been the campsite of the main village during the Battle of the Rosebud. All that remained was a solitary tepee, the burial lodge of the Sans Arc warrior Old She Bear who had died of wounds received in the fight with Crook.[31] The night of the 24th, some Lakota traveling to join the main village had camped on this site. Being warned, probably by Deeds and Brown Ass, of the soldier's approach, they had hurriedly broken camp, leaving cooking utensils on the fires.[32] Earlier, Lieutenant Hare and his contingent of scouts had seen 40 to 50 Indians as they approached the lone tepee.

Unit of Origin	Custer's Command	Reno's Command	Benteen's Command	Pack Train & Escort
Headquarters				
Officers (3)	2	1		
Non Comms (1)	1			
Enlisted (1)	1			
Medical (3)	1	2		
Civilians (2)	2			
Guides (3)	3			
Interpreters (2)	2			
Courier (1)	1			
Company A				
Officers (3)	1	2		
Non Comms (9)		8		1
Enlisted (40)		34		6
Company B				
Officers (2)		1		1
Non Comms (7)				7
Enlisted (41)		1		40
Company C				
Officers (2)	2			
Non Comms (8)	7			1
Enlisted (43)	37			6
Company D				
Officers (2)			2	
Non Comms (5)			4	1
Enlisted (45)			39	6
Company E				
Officers (2)	2			
Non Comms (8)	7			1
Enlisted (37)	30	2		5
Company F				
Officers (2)	2			
Non Comms (8)	7			1
Enlisted (41)	28	2		11
Company G				
Officers (2)	1	1		
Non Comms (8)		7		1
Enlisted (36)	1	29		6
Company H				
Officers (2)			2	
Non Comms (9)			8	1
Enlisted (36)	1		29	6
Company I				
Officers (2)	2			
Non Comms (6)	5			1
Enlisted (40)	30	3		7
Company K				
Officers (2)	1		1	
Non Comms (8)	1		6	1
Enlisted (34)		1	27	6
Company L				
Officers (2)	2			
Non Comms (7)	6			1
Enlisted (49)	38			11
Company M				
Officers (2)		1		1
Non Comms (8)		7		1
Enlisted (46)		39		7
Crow Scouts (6)	6			
Arikara Scouts(24) [33]	23			1
Lakota Scouts (5)	5			
Teamsters/Packers (12)				12
Total	**258**	**141**	**118**	**150**

Table 12 – 1 Assignments As Of Division Into Battalions– June 25, 1876

As Fred Girard rode to a small knoll just northwest of the tepee, a large dust cloud could be seen rising from the valley beyond.[34] Upon reaching the summit, Girard apparently saw the same fleeing Indians sighted earlier by Lieutenant Hare and his scouts. Waving his hat to attract Custer's attention, he called out: *"Here are your Indians, running like devils!"*[35] At those words, Custer's heart must have leapt into his mouth. Coupled with the huge dust clouds in the valley and the signs of this obviously hastily abandoned camp site, Girard's warning could mean only one thing – the village was breaking up and scattering! Immediate action was required – or all would be lost!

Command Element	Strength	Percent of Regiment
Custer's Command	**258**	**38.7**
Headquarters	9	
Scouts/Guides	42	
Civilians	2	
Keogh's Battalion	**129**	**19.3**
Company C	46	
Company I	37	
Company L	46	
Yates' Battalion	**76**	**11.4**
Company E	39	
Company F	37	
Reno's Battalion	**141**	**21.1**
Headquarters	13	
Company A	44	
Company G	37	
Company M	47	
Scouts	0	
Interpreters/Courier	0	
Benteen's Battalion	**118**	**17.7**
Company D	45	
Company H	39	
Company K	34	
Pack Train	**150**	**22.5**
Company B	48	
Mathey's Command	89	
Civilian Packers	12	
Scouts	1	
Total	**667**	**100**

Table 12 – 2 Battalion Combat Strength – June 25, 1876

Custer now turned to his Arikara scouts. Although ordered ahead earlier in the day to seek the enemy and drive off the pony herd, if possible, they had halted at the lone tepee.[36] Young Hawk had slit open the tepee to view the remains, and One Feather went inside and drank the soup left for the dead warrior and ate some of the meat; after which the scouts apparently set fire to the tepee.[37] Custer, through the interpreter Girard, now ordered them after the fleeing Lakota:

"I told you to dash on and stop for nothing. You have disobeyed me. Move to one side and let the soldiers pass you in the charge. If any man of you is not brave, I will take away his weapons and make a woman of him.

"One of the scouts cried out: 'Tell him if he does the same to all his white soldiers who are not so brave as we are, it will take him a very long time indeed.' The scouts all laughed at this and said by signs that they were hungry for the battle."[38]

As the scouts prepared to move forward again, Lieutenant Varnum rode up to Custer. Varnum, who had been on the left earlier in day, had been on the white bluffs and had seen at least a portion of the village as well as a sizable warrior force in the bottom.[39] After making his report, he inquired where Reno was going, Custer responding *"To begin the attack."*[40] Custer, informed by Varnum that the village was not fleeing, sent Lieutenant Cooke forward to order Reno to open the attack upon a fixed objective. Reno testified he had progressed only a short distance past the lone tepee when:

"Lieutenant Cooke came to me and said, 'General Custer directs you to take as rapid a gait as you think prudent and charge the village afterwards, and you will be supported by the whole outfit.'"[41]

Already moving at a trot, Reno pressed forward. Meanwhile, Varnum was attempting to secure Custer's permission to go in with the advance:

". . . he said to go on with them if you want to. Lt. Hare & I and my whole party (including Girard, DCE) started at the trot. Lieut. Geo. D. Wallace, a classmate of mine & dear friend & old roommate, was riding at the head of the column with the Genl. He was acting topographical officer. I called back to him, 'Come on Nick, with the fighting men. I don't stay back with the coffee coolers.' Custer laughed and waved his hat and told Wallace he could go & Wallace joined me."[42]

Seeing all this movement to the front must have confused Crow scouts White Swan and Half Yellow Face as they went with Reno's column instead of up on the bluffs as they had been ordered.[43] Varnum, Hare, Wallace, Girard and the Arikara scouts spurred forward, but one of Reno's companies would already be across the Little Big Horn before they caught up to the battalion.[44] After the departure of White Swan and Half Yellow Face with Reno's command, Mitch Boyer led the remaining Crow scouts up onto the bluffs while Custer's column continued to follow Reno's trail.

It was at this juncture that things began to go terribly wrong for Custer and the 7th Cavalry. Benteen had erred in not sending a courier through to Custer with the results of his reconnaissance of the upper valley. Custer compounded this "failure to communicate" by opening the attack without making any move to either consolidate the regiment, or inform the other command elements that combat was being initiated in the valley. Even if one accepts the hypothesis that Custer was still uncertain whether he was attacking a fixed or a mobile objective, he should have ordered Mathey, and McDougall to hurry along, following his trail, until they received further orders.

At the lone tepee, or shortly thereafter, Lieutenants Hare, Varnum, and Wallace, guide Charley Reynolds, interpreters Fred Girard and Isaiah Dorman, courier George Herendeen, 2 Crow, 5 Lakota, 1 Pikuni Blackfoot, and 22 Arikara scouts joined Reno's command. In addition to reducing the strength of the Custer command by the 37 men mentioned above, Boston Custer at some point prior to the lone tepee had returned to the pack train to obtain a new mount from the remuda. The assignment of personnel to the various commands at the time Reno received his attack order is presented in Table 12 – 3 and the corresponding combat strength of the various battalions is presented in Table 12 – 4.

The Indian camp was not unaware of Custer's presence. According to the Cheyenne American Horse, they had very detailed information regarding the command's movements:

"The next day some men were back on the Rosebud watching to see where the troops with whom they had fought, were going. These went the other way (Crook moved away from the village, DCE), but these scouts discovered Custer going up the Rosebud. A short time after the scout who made this discovery got into the camp, four or five lodges of Sioux, who had set out to go to Red Cloud Agency (probably the Oglala Bad Faces mentioned by David Humphreys Miller, DCE), discovered Custer's troops close to them. These lodges got frightened and turned back, and when they reached the main camp, their report caused great alarm. . .

"About this time the troops turned and went to the head of Reno Creek and on Reno Creek they separated. The next thing I heard an old man haranguing in the camp,

that the soldiers were about to charge the camp from both ends, the upper and the lower. I was in the Cheyenne camp at the lower end of the village."[45]

Unit of Origin	Custer's Command	Reno's Command	Benteen's Command	Pack Train & Escort
Headquarters				
Officers (3)	2	1		
Non Comms (1)	1			
Enlisted (1)	1			
Medical (3)	1	2		
Civilians (2)	2			
Guides (3)	1	1		1
Interpreters (2)	0	2		
Courier (1)	0	1		
Company A				
Officers (3)	0	3		
Non Comms (9)		8		1
Enlisted (40)		34		6
Company B				
Officers (2)		1		1
Non Comms (7)				7
Enlisted (41)		1		40
Company C				
Officers (2)	2			
Non Comms (8)	7			1
Enlisted (43)	37			6
Company D				
Officers (2)			2	
Non Comms (5)			4	1
Enlisted (45)			39	6
Company E				
Officers (2)	2			
Non Comms (8)	7			1
Enlisted (37)	30	2		5
Company F				
Officers (2)	2			
Non Comms (8)	7			1
Enlisted (41)	28	2		11
Company G				
Officers (2)	0	2		
Non Comms (8)		7		1
Enlisted (36)	1	29		6
Company H				
Officers (2)			2	
Non Comms (9)			8	1
Enlisted (36)	1		29	6
Company I				
Officers (2)	2			
Non Comms (6)	5			1
Enlisted (40)	30	3		7
Company K				
Officers (2)	0	1	1	
Non Comms (8)	1		6	1
Enlisted (34)		1	27	6
Company L				
Officers (2)	2			
Non Comms (7)	6			1
Enlisted (49)	38			11
Company M				
Officers (2)		1		1
Non Comms (8)		7		1
Enlisted (46)		39		7
Crow Scouts (6)	4	2		
Arikara Scouts (24) [46]	0	23		1
Lakota Scouts (5)	0	5		
Teamsters/Packers (12)				12
Total	**220**	**178**	**118**	**151**

Table 12 – 3 Assignments As Of Reno's Attack Order– June 25, 1876

Command Element	Strength	Percent of Regiment
Custer's Command	**220**	**33.0**
Headquarters	8	
Scouts/Guides	5	
Civilians	2	
Keogh's Battalion	**129**	**19.3**
Company C	46	
Company I	37	
Company L	46	
Yates' Battalion	**76**	**11.4**
Company E	39	
Company F	37	
Reno's Battalion	**178**	**26.7**
Headquarters	15	
Company A	44	
Company G	38	
Company M	47	
Scouts	30	
Interpreters/Courier	4	
Benteen's Battalion	**118**	**17.7**
Company D	45	
Company H	39	
Company K	34	
Pack Train	**151**	**22.6**
Company B	48	
Mathey's Command	89	
Civilian Packers	12	
Scouts	1	
Guides	1	
Total	**667**	**100**

Table 12 – 4 Battalion Combat Strength After Reno's Attack Order– June 25, 1876

Feather Earring also told of a warning to the village:

"Reno's men came down Reno Creek; they were seen by two Sans Arc young men, who went up Reno Creek to get a horse that had been wounded in the Rosebud fight. Two Bear was killed by Reno's scouts;[47] *Lone Dog, the other, went back and gave the alarm, riding from side to side. Feather Earring saw him signaling that soldiers were coming, calling, 'One of us got killed; they are right behind me.' He had no sooner arrived at the village than Reno's command began firing at the tepees."*[48]

The village had received ample warning of Custer's approach for several days, and were well aware of his proximity on the 25th. Given their response to Crook's presence a week earlier when that column was still 40 miles away, it is amazing that the Indians did not respond in a more aggressive manner to the approach of the 7th Cavalry. Although the 7th Cavalry had achieved tactical surprise, they would fail to capitalize on their advantage.

---

[1] Lieutenant Wallace thought the division into battalions occurred about 12:15 P.M., while McDougall thought Custer ordered him to escort duty with the pack train at 11:00 A.M. and Reno testified that Adjutant Cooke ordered him to take personal command of A, G, and M at about 10:00 A.M. As before, I have relied on the account of Wallace, who was charged with keeping the official itinerary. See Col. W. A. Graham "Abstract of the Official Record of Proceedings of The Reno Court of Inquiry" pages 13,193 and 211.

[2] While many authors believe that Custer retained personal command of the 5 companies comprising his detachment, Edgerly and Moylan testified at the Reno Court of Inquiry that the regiment was divided into 4 battalions. The court agreed, making the division into 4 battalions one of its findings. Lieutenant Gibson probably also believed this to be the case as his daughter mentions it in "With Custer's Cavalry."

[3] In addition to the 48 officers and men of Company B, Custer had detailed an additional 77 men from the other companies to Mathey. (Actually, 89 troopers joined Mathey's pack train. When the scouts and packers are added, the combined force was 150 men, roughly 22% of Custer's force). Custer has been criticized for leaving such a large escort with the pack train in the absence of a strong enemy force in his rear. The argument is, in my opinion, specious. Not only did Custer not know precisely where the Indians were, he had one report, Herendeen's, of a large war party in his rear. When we recall his near disaster with the reserve ammunition at the Washita, it appears this assignment was prudent on Custer's part. Indeed, McDougall would lose sight of the other elements of the command after only a short time and, as he marched in the rear of the train, he would not sight them again until he reached Reno Hill. See Col. W. A. Graham "Abstract of the Official Record of Proceedings of The Reno Court of Inquiry" page 193.

[4] See Salvatore A. Caniglia "Profile of the Seventh" page 16.

[5] See James Willard Schultz "William Jackson Indian Scout" page 133. Custer has been soundly criticized for failing to heed his scout's council regarding the size of the village. It should be noted that the Indian scouts were typically pessimistic in the extreme regarding their chances when going into a fight. For example, Frank Grouard told Mills that the village at Slim Buttes was too big to attack (see Jerome A. Greene "Battles and Skirmishes of the Great Sioux War 1876 - 77" page 112). Even the hyper-critical Benteen, in a letter to Theodore Goldin, didn't criticize Custer for attacking, stating the 7th Cavalry had no previous inclination they would meet the number of Indians they encountered. See John M. Carroll "The Benteen – Goldin Letters" page 214.

[6] See James Willard Schultz "William Jackson Indian Scout" page 134.

[7] See Ronald H. Nichols "The Reno Court of Inquiry" page 512, W. Kent King "Massacre: The Custer Cover–Up" page 187, and Walter Camp "Custer in '76" page 78.

[8] See Benteen's official report of July 4, 1876 in Appendix 6.

[9] See Walter Camp "Custer in '76" page 249.

[10] See John S. gray "Centennial Campaign" page 304.

[11] See Katherine Gibson Fougera "With Custer's Cavalry" page 268.

[12] See Thomas B. Marquis "Keep the Last Bullet for Yourself" page 96.

[13] See Walter Camp "Custer in '76" page 54.

[14] See Colonel W. A. Graham "The Custer Myth" apge 138.

[15] See Elizabeth Atwood Lawrence "His Very Silence Speaks" page 55. It is possible that Keogh exchanged Paddy for Comanche at the Crow's Nest at the same time Custer exchanged Dandy for Vic.

[16] While there has never been an adequate explanation for the high number of enlisted personnel from companies F and L accompanying the pack train, it may be presumed that some of these were stragglers who were unable to keep up with, or by some other means became separated from, the Custer column.

[17] See Ronald H. Nichols "Reno Court of Inquiry" page 403. Benteen testified that if he didn't find any Indians in the first valley, he was to continue on to the next valley and so forth. Of course by this date Benteen had changed his recollection of his orders so that instead of looking for Indians, he was to *"pitch into anything he found."* Interestingly, Benteen was not questioned about the discrepancies between his testimony and his official report. I believe the evidence is clear that Benteen's mission was one of reconnaissance and was to have terminated in the valley of the Little Big Horn.

[18] See Charles K. Mills "Harvest of Barren Regrets" page 251.

[19] See Godfrey's testimony in Ronald H. Nichols "Reno Court of Inquiry" page 479.

[20] See Ronald H. Nichols "Reno Court of Inquiry" page 404.

[21] See Charles Khulman "Legend Into History" apges 89 – 90.

[22] Time Zones were established in 1884. See Colonel W. A. Graham "Reno Court of Inquiry" page 37.

[23] We shall see subsequently that if one assumes Benteen left the morass at a trot, he would have to slow to a walk pace after meeting Custer's first messenger, Sergeant Kanipe, else he could not meet Custer's second messenger, Trumpeter Martin, at the location where he testified the meeting took place. Setting aside for a minute whether or not Benteen believed he should increase his battalion's rate of march to the front in response to Kanipe's message, there can be no valid rationale for slowing the pace of the march after meeting Kanipe, and there is no historical record that indicates this took place.

[24] This assumes Custer moved from the point of division to the lone tepee at a walk rate. Benteen's testimony about E Troop moving at a gallop notwithstanding, there is no testimony that Custer moved faster than a walk until after passing the lone tepee. If one assumes an average rate of march of 4.5 miles per hour (between a walk and trot for cavalry), Benteen would have covered between 11.6 and 12.4 miles, which is in good agreement with the 12 to 15 miles Godfrey estimated.

[25] See Charles Khulman "Legend Into History" page 85.

[26] See Edgar I. Stewart "Custer's Luck" page 322.

[27] See Neil C. Mangum "Reno's Battalion in the Battle of the Little Big Horn" page 4.

[28] Reno testified the tepee was in sight when Custer beckoned him to cross the creek.

[29] See Ronald H. Nichols "Reno Court of Inquiry" page 560.

[30] As with everything else connected with the Little Big Horn, there is controversy over whether the lone tepee was located at the North or South Fork of Reno Creek. While some of the officers, notably Varnum, place the site at the North Fork, the accounts of the Crow scouts, Wooden Leg and White Bull (Ice Bear) clearly mention the white bluffs which identifies the location as the South, or Upper Fork. See Walter Camp "Custer in '76" page 211, John M. Carroll "Custer's Chief of Scouts" page 155, and John S. Gray "Custer's Last Campaign" page 246.

[31] See Colonel W. A. Graham "The Custer Myth" page 98. J. W. Vaughn names the Uncpapa Little Wing as the dead warrior. See "With Crook at the Rosebud" pages 186 – 187. For the most complete discussion of the possible identity of the slain warrior, the reader is referred to Richard G. Hardorff's "Cheyenne Memories of the Custer Fight" page 153. While Captain Moylan remembered two tepees, most accounts agree that only a single tepee was standing.

[32] See Edgar I. Stewart "Custer's Luck" pages 323 – 324. David Humphreys Miller believes these to have been a band of "bad faces" Oglala heading for Red Cloud Agency. When they spotted the troops they returned to the village. For his interpretation, see "Custer's Fall: The Indian Side of the Story" pages 80 – 82.

[33] Note that although William Jackson was a half–breed Pikuni Blackfoot, I have included him in the count for the Arikara for brevity.

[34] See Colonel W. A. Graham "The Custer Myth" page 258.

[35] See Ronald H. Nichols "Reno Court of Inquiry" page 112.

[36] The Arikara One Feather said the reason they originally remained at the lone tepee site was they had become separated from Girard and, without their interpreter, they didn't know what was expected of them. See Bruce Liddic and Paul Harbaugh "Camp on Custer" page 128.

[37] See O. G. Libby "The Arikara Narrative" page 121. The Crow scouts would later insist that it was the soldiers who had fired the tepee. It is really of no consequence who set the tepee afire, what is important to developing the chronology of Appendix 12, is that the tepee was burning when Custer's command was at that location.

[38] See O. G. Libby "The Arikara Narrative" pages 121 – 122, and Tom O'Neil "Sagas of Greasy Grass" pages 13 - 14. Luther Hare told Walter Camp that when the Arikara stopped at the lone tepee, Varnum and his aide had continued on toward the Little Big Horn. See Kenneth Hammer "Custer in '76" page 65.

[39] See W. Boyes "Custer's Black White Man" page 27, and See W. Kent King "Massacre: The Custer Cover–Up" page 179. While Hare didn't state Varnum had actually seen the village, it seems probable that he had, else he would not have continued on to a meeting with Custer after passing his scouts moving toward the river.

[40] See John M. Carroll "Custer's Chief of Scouts" page 64.

[41] See Ronald H. Nichols "Reno Court of Inquiry" page 561. Captain Myles Keogh may have gone with Cooke to deliver the attack order as Sergeant Davern testified that both Keogh and Cooke accompanied Reno to the river (See W. A. Graham "Reno Court of Inquiry" page 121). Captain Moylan (W. A. Graham "Reno Court of Inquiry" page 69), Lieutenant Hare ("Custer in '76" page 64), Fred Girard (W. A. Graham "Reno Court of Inquiry" page 36), Dr. Porter (W. A. Graham

"Reno Court of Inquiry" page 62), and George Herendeen (W. A. Graham "Reno Court of Inquiry" page 80) all recalled having heard Custer personally give the attack order at the lone tepee, while Major Reno and Lieutenant Wallace recalled the order coming shortly after passing the tepee. It appears that Reno and Wallace are corrrect in their rememberance of where the attack order was given and the others have confused the order to move to the front, which was given at the lone tepee, with the attack order. Private Tom O'Neill, who also claimed to have heard Custer personally give Reno the attack order, although he didn't say where this occurred, is also possibly confused about the two orders given Reno (John M. Carroll "A Seventh Cavalry Scrapbook #3" page 26). John Martin, not only claimed to have heard Custer give the attack order, but also heard Custer say he would attack the village on the lower end and recall Benteen to strike the center. I personally find this highly questionable. I am positive Custer formulated such a plan, but the formulation occurred later in the day. Had he formed this plan at the lone tepee, there would be no reason for further delay and he would have immediately dispatched a courier to recall Benteen. See Colonel W. A.. Graham "The Custer Myth" page 289.

[42] See John M. Carroll "Custer's Chief of Scouts" page 65. Varnum's seeking his old friend's presence with the strike force undoubtedly saved his life. Wallace would survive the Little Big Horn only to die at the hands of these same Lakota at Wounded Knee 14 years later.

[43] See Edgar I. Stewart "Custer's Luck" page 329.

[44] See John M. Carroll "Custer's Chief of Scouts" page 107.

[45] See Grinell Interviews.

[46] As before, William Jackson has been included in the count of the Arikara.

[47] The boy Deeds was also killed on the east bank of the river, probably near the mouth of Reno Creek. He was most likely killed by the scouts. See Richard G. Hardorff "Lakota Recollections Of The Custer Fight" page 58.

[48] See John S. Gray "Custer's Last Campaign" page 271. Interestingly, none of the government scouts mentions the killing of Two Bear, Deeds, or of Gall's family. Given the reported locations of their deaths, it seems most likely that they were killed by the scouts rather than the troopers.

Chapter 13

The Valley Fight

The scouts had ridden hard to the crossing of the Little Goat River,[1] fourteen of them diverting to capture some Lakota ponies they spotted on the east bank:

> *"Six (14, DCE) of the scouts turned off to the right sharply, where the Dakota horses were by the timber. Boy Chief and Red Star were ahead, then followed Strikes Two, Black Fox, Little Sioux, and One Feather. The other party led by Bloody Knife went on toward the point of the Dakota camp. Bloody Knife was far ahead and he brought back three horses toward his party, calling out: 'Someone take these horses back to the hill. One of them is for me.' Red Bear did not see Bloody Knife because of the dust, but he heard afterwards who it was . In this party were Bloody Knife, Young Hawk, Goose, Forked Horn, Little Brave, Red Bear, Bob Tailed Bull, and the two Crow scouts (Half Yellow Face and White Swan, DCE). 'Now we all came to the point of the Sioux camp, the guns began to go off and we got off our horses and began to shoot.' The Dakotas were shooting at them from the bluffs or hills, lying down out of sight."*[2]

Upon reaching the river, Reno crossed in column of twos, as prescribed for crossing such streams, the order being M, A, then G;[3] pausing briefly to water his horses and reform his command.[4] This crossing was witnessed by the Minneconjou Standing Bear who was on Weir Point attempting to retrieve some horses. When Standing Bear saw Custer's column approaching, he forgot about the horses and recrossed the Little Big Horn to prepare for the fight.[5] Lieutenant Cooke, observing from the river bank, thought M was attempting to cross too rapidly as Private James Wilber recalled:

> *"We were galloping fast, and just as we got to the river Cooke called out: 'For God's sake men, don't run those horses like that; you will need them in a few minutes.'"*[6]

Cooke then wheeled and headed back for Custer's command. At this juncture Girard became aware he had given Custer some potentially damaging information:

> *"The scouts were to my left and called my attention to the fact that all the Indians were coming up the valley. I called Major Reno's attention to the fact that Indians were all coming up the valley.[7] I halted there a little time. I thought it was of importance enough that General Custer should know it, and I rode back towards Custer's command. At this knoll (a knoll near the Little Big Horn, not the small knoll near the lone tepee from which Girard had sighted the fleeing Indians, DCE) I met Colonel Cooke and he asked me where I was going. I told him I had come back to report to him that the Indians were coming up the valley to meet us, and he says, 'All right, I'll go back and report.'"*[8]

On his way back to rejoin Reno, Girard passed Reno's striker, Private Archibald McIlhargey of Company I. McIlhargey had been sent by Reno to inform Custer that *"the Indians were in front of me and in strong force."*[9] Reno then moved the command out onto the plain, formed in column of fours and ordered the trot. Lieutenant Varnum and the scouts were now slightly ahead, and to the left of the column. Sergeant John M. Ryan of Company M recalled:

"Lieutenant Varnum, a very brave officer in command of the scouts, rode ahead of . . . [the] battalion, he swung his hat around in the air and sung out to the men: 'Thirty days' furlough to the man who gets the first scalp.' We were very anxious for the furlough, but not so particular about the scalp."[10]

After proceeding a short distance, Reno ordered the command "left front into line," holding G in reserve. They proceeded down the river in this formation until the number of Indians began to increase, at this point Reno dispatched a second messenger, his cook, Private John E. Mitchell, also of Company I, with a similar message for Custer:[11]

"Receiving no instructions in response to that (McIlhargey had probably been sent no more than 15 minutes earlier, DCE), I sent a second time a man named Mitchell who was about me in the capacity of cook. They (McIlhargey and Mitchell, DCE) were the nearest men I could get hold of quick. That was some minutes after, and I was convinced that my opinions were correct (that the Indians were in overwhelming numbers, DCE). I still heard nothing to guide my movements, and I went on down the valley to carry out my orders."[12]

The foregoing testimony is a clear indication that Reno was becoming extremely anxious regarding the size of the enemy force, although all that could really be seen was the huge dust being kicked up by the warriors as they circled their ponies to give them their second wind. Prior to this time there was nothing in Reno's actions to warrant criticism. Lieutenant DeRudio, an outspoken critic who would say of Reno *"If we had not been commanded by a coward we would have been killed,"*[13] testified that Reno was constantly checking the formation, and keeping it in good order, during the advance down the valley.[14] The situation changed, however, after the second messenger was dispatched. Although he had brought the command into line via bugle call,[15] Reno now sent his adjutant, Lieutenant Hodgson, to bring G up on the line.[16] All companies now being in line, the gallop was taken, per the prescribed tactics of the day. It appears that Reno was beginning to lose control of the situation. He had moved in good order, using easily heard bugle calls to control his column. Although the order to charge was never given[17] he had moved at a rapid pace. As his concern for the size of the enemy force grew, he abandoned bugle calls and became very tense, ordering the men to stop the cheering that commenced as the gallop was taken.[18]

While the river bottom is flat and devoid of trees except along the stream, where the cottonwoods grew thickly, the bank and bluff line is very irregular with some of the northern promontories pushing so far westward as to obscure the view of the valley from points further south. As Reno approached the Uncpapa circle, located at the southern end of the village, his attention became fixed on one of these promontories that almost completely screened his view of the lower valley. While there were, perhaps, as many as 1,500 tepees in the village, sheltering approximately 2,500 warriors,[19] Reno would have been able to see very few of the lodges as they were nestled in the numerous bends on the river, close to the sheltering cottonwoods. Reno remarked at his court of inquiry how easily he had driven the 40 to 50 warriors[20] in his front all the way down the bottom, but, apparently, he now began to sense it was too easy. He thought he was being led into a trap.

Perhaps those woods reminded him of the spring day in 1865 when he had chased Confederate Colonel John Singleton Mosby, the Gray Ghost, only to be ambushed, from just such woods as these, suffering a loss of 21 men.[21] Although he had "no absolute contact" with the enemy and had fired very few shots, if any,[22] Reno ordered a halt and dismounted his command about 100 yards short of the point of timber in question. Unfortunately, four troopers of Company M, Privates John H. Meier , Roman Rutten, George E. Smith, and Henry Turley, were unable to unable to check their horses and they were carried into the village. While Meier and Rutten returned after a harrowing circuit, the former being wounded and the latter unscathed, Turley was killed and Smith was presumed killed as his body was never recovered.[23] Despite having lost 3 of his 47 troopers before he had even dismounted, Captain French, according to Sergeant White, was the only officer to get his company properly deployed, *"the other two companies. . . huddled into a bunch."*[24]

Immediately, Sergeant John Ryan and a detail of ten men from Company M were sent forward to skirmish the woods.[25] Finding no Indians in the woods, the horses, led by every fourth man,[26] were taken into a little glade in the woods, and the skirmish line, now manned by 92 non commissioned officers and enlisted men, advanced until the right of the line rested on the timber.[27] Fred Girard recalled the termination of the charge and the continuing melancholia of Charley Reynolds:

> *"I halted forty–five or fifty yards back from the edge of the timber and there were Charlie Reynolds, Dr. Porter, George Herendeen, and Bloody Knife and myself, and Charlie Reynolds asked me if I had any whisky. He said he had never felt so [worried] in all the days of his life and he felt depressed and discouraged, and he thought it would be well to have something to stimulate him, and I gave him some and I offered it to the balance and they refused it. I took a little myself, and told him not to take too much, that he needed a very cool head, that we had plenty of business on our hands for that day. We then dismounted and just as we dismounted here this skirmish line was being drawn up.*

> *"While the skirmish line was being drawn up, the Indians were coming up. They were distant, as well as I could judge from where I stood, about one thousand yards from the left flank of the skirmish line, and in front, not directly in a line with it. We fired a few shots at the first Indians that came up. The firing started with some of our scouts that had left the command and gone into a little valley to capture some ponies, and more Indians were coming up here and riding around the command."*[28]

Private Thomas Dean O'Neill, Company G, confirmed Girard's impression of the main body of Indians being about 1000 yards distant when the skirmish line was formed, but recalled there were great numbers of Indians at about 500 yards also.[29] From their positions on the skirmish line, both Lieutenants DeRudio and Varnum claimed to have seen Custer on the bluffs across the river, although neither officer reported this valuable information to Reno.[30]

The performance of the scouts in this action, primarily the Arikara, has been grossly misunderstood and misrepresented. Varnum, and others, indicate the scouts disappeared from their position on the left of the skirmish line at virtually the first shot. We know that Half Yellow Face, White Swan, Goose, Billy Jackson, Bloody Knife, Bob Tailed Bull, and Little Brave remained with the command throughout the valley fight, the latter three being killed in action. The other scouts, rather than fleeing as has been popularly reported, were merely following their orders from Custer to pursue their traditional way of fighting by capturing as many Lakota ponies as possible.[31] While the Lakota were successful in recapturing some of the ponies before they could be driven across the Little Big Horn, a contingent of scouts did manage to drive some captured ponies back to the Powder River Camp.[32]

We cannot be positive exactly when Cooke rejoined Custer, but it was probably prior to Custer's turn to the north; else there would have been trail signs of a retrograde movement to the North Fork of Reno Creek. Cooke's intelligence must have convinced Custer that he was attacking a fixed, rather than a mobile, objective point. Knowing the futility of massed charges against Indians, Custer elected to use the only other cavalry tactic in the manual, envelopment. He ordered a turn to the right (north), halting to water his horses in the North Fork of Reno Creek. While at this watering stop, Private McIlhargey probably reported to Custer. The tone of the message may have given Custer a sense of urgency and he proceeded up the slope to Wooden Leg Ridge at a trot. From the summit, Custer [33] could see that Reno was in for trouble. He saw that the charge had been halted and a skirmish line formed, its left hanging in the air. Custer knew it was only a matter of minutes before Reno was flanked and forced onto the defensive. Thus when Private Mitchell, Major Reno's second messenger, arrived, he provided Custer with no new tactical information. Having noted the horde of warriors confronting Reno, and recognizing that the clear upper valley, which is visible from this vantage point, meant Benteen could be immediately recalled to the main command, Custer ordered a consolidation of the regiment. Custer had made a serious error, however;. he had not sent a messenger to a subordinate who was obviously in need of reassurance. [34]

When Custer returned to the command from his observations of the valley, he called Lieutenant Cooke and Tom Custer aside and spoke with them briefly. Tom Custer selected Sergeant Daniel A. Kanipe, of his own Company C, to carry a message to the pack train. Captain McDougall was to hurry up and bring the train straight across country. If any packs came lose, they were to be cut and abandoned, unless they were ammunition. Tom added that if Kanipe saw Benteen, he was to tell him to come on quick as it was a big Indian camp. [35] As Kanipe turned, Custer started the column forward. Some of the horses became excited and broke into a gallop, passing Custer at the head of the column. Kanipe heard Custer shout: *"Boys, hold your horses, there are plenty of them down there for us all."* [36]

With the dispatching of Sergeant Kanipe, Reno's two messengers, McIlhargey and Mitchell, and the scout's pursuit of the pony herd, the assignment of personnel to the various commands is as presented in Table 13 – 1 and the corresponding combat strength of the various battalions as presented in Table 13 – 2.

Reno, despite the multiple sightings[37] of the 7th Cavalry by the Indians, had taken the village completely by surprise. Black Elk, a thirteen year old Oglala, and many of the other young boys were enjoying a midday swim. He recalled: *". . . we heard the crier shouting in the Hunkpapa camp, which was not very far from us 'The chargers are coming! They are charging! The chargers are coming!' Then the crier of the Ogalalas shouted the same words; and we could hear the cry going from camp to camp northward clear to the Santees and Yanktonais.'*[38] Crazy Horse was watching a game of ring–toss when the warning came.[39] Red Horse, a Minneconjou chief, was digging tipsina, wild turnips, with four women:

> *"Suddenly one of the women attracted my attention to a cloud of dust rising a short distance from camp. I soon saw that the soldiers were charging the camp. To the camp I and the women ran. When I arrived a person told me to hurry to the council lodge. The soldiers charged so quickly we could not talk (council). We came out of the council lodge and talked in all directions. The Sioux mount horses, take guns, and go fight the soldiers. Women and children mount horses and go, meaning to get out of the way."*[40]

So great was the shock associated with Reno's appearance, that Four Robes, Sitting Bull's wife, initially ran for safety leaving Crow Foot, one of her three week old twins, behind. Regaining her composure, she returned and carried Crow Foot to safety.[41]

It was no different in the Cheyenne circle, northernmost of the camp circles and furthest away from Reno's attack. After a night of dancing, Wooden Leg and his brother, Yellow Hair, were napping on the river bank; Brave Bear was asleep in his lodge.[42] Two Moon was watering his horses while White Shield, a hero of the Rosebud Fight, was fishing.[43] Wooden Leg remembered the panic among the women, children and old ones:

"We heard shooting. We hurried out from the trees so we might see as well as hear. The shooting was somewhere at the upper part of the camp circles. It looked as if all of the Indians there were running away toward the hills to the westward or down toward our end of the village. Women were screaming and men were letting out war cries. Through it all we could hear old men calling: 'Soldiers are here! Young men, go out and fight them.'"[44]

Low Dog, Oglala chief, could not believe what he was hearing:

"I was asleep in my lodge at the time. . . I heard the alarm, but I did not believe it. I thought it was a false alarm. I did not think it possible that any white men would attack us, so strong as we were. . . When I got my gun and came out of my lodge the attack had begun at the end of the camp where Sitting Bull and the Uncpapas were."[45]

The warriors reacted quickly, some not even pausing to put on their war cloths and charms. Grabbing their weapons, they mounted the first available pony and sped toward the Uncpapa circle. Some of the Cheyenne, including Brave Bear, Scabby, and Wooden Leg, moved quickly enough to arrive while Reno's troopers were still on their skirmish line out on the prairie. Crow King, Uncpapa chief, recalled the arrival of scouts immediately before the attack and the delaying tactics employed by the Uncpapa as the fight opened:

"One (a scout, DCE) came back and reported that an army of white soldiers was coming, and he had no more than reported when another runner came in with the same story, and also told us that the command had divided, and that one party was going round to attack us on the opposite side (this second messenger may have been Standing Bear, DCE).

"The first attack was at the camp of the Uncpapas tribe. The shots neither raised nor fell. (Here he indicated that the whites commenced firing at about four hundred yards distance). The Indians retreated – at first slowly, to give the women and children time to go to a place of safety. Other Indians got our horses. By that time we had warriors enough to turn upon the whites. . ."[46]

In this earliest phase of the fighting, the Indians suffered some casualties. The Minneconjou Three Bears was mortally wounded near the Uncpapa tepees and Gall's two wives and three children were slain in some woods.[47] Most authorities believe Gall's family to have been killed by the Arikara scouts, but the Cheyenne believed they were killed by fire from Reno's skirmish line.[48]

Unit of Origin	Custer's Command	Reno's Command	Benteen's Command	Pack Train & Escort
Headquarters				
Officers (3)	2	1		
Non Comms (1)	1			
Enlisted (1)	1			
Medical (3)	1	2		
Civilians (2)	2			
Guides (3)	1	1		1
Interpreters (2)	0	2		
Courier (1)	0	1		
Company A				
Officers (3)	0	3		
Non Comms (9)		8		1
Enlisted (40)		34		6
Company B				
Officers (2)		1		1
Non Comms (7)				7
Enlisted (41)		1		40
Company C				
Officers (2)	2			
Non Comms (8)	6			2
Enlisted (43)	37			6
Company D				
Officers (2)			2	
Non Comms (5)			4	1
Enlisted (45)			39	6
Company E				
Officers (2)	2			
Non Comms (8)	7			1
Enlisted (37)	30	2		5
Company F				
Officers (2)	2			
Non Comms (8)	7			1
Enlisted (41)	28	2		11
Company G				
Officers (2)	0	2		
Non Comms (8)		7		1
Enlisted (36)	1	29		6
Company H				
Officers (2)			2	
Non Comms (9)			8	1
Enlisted (36)	1		29	6
Company I				
Officers (2)	2			
Non Comms (6)	5			1
Enlisted (40)	32	1		7
Company K				
Officers (2)	0	1	1	
Non Comms (8)	1		6	1
Enlisted (34)		1	27	6
Company L				
Officers (2)	2			
Non Comms (7)	6			1
Enlisted (49)	38			11
Company M				
Officers (2)		1		1
Non Comms (8)		7		1
Enlisted (46)		39		7
Crow Scouts (6)	4	2		
Arikara Scouts (24) [49]	0	9		15
Lakota Scouts (5)	0	5		
Teamsters/Packers (12)				12
Total	**221**	**162**	**118**	**166**

Table 13 – 1 Assignments As Of Custer's First Message– June 25, 1876

Reno has been much maligned, and I believe the evidence will show rather unfairly, for terminating his charge short of the village. As was the case when he disobeyed Terry's orders on his reconnaissance, he did a poor job in explaining his actions. He offered only rather lame explanations in his report on the battle and subsequent testimony at the court of inquiry, stating his Indian–fighting experience, of which he had none to speak of, told him that he was being led into a trap and that he could see 400 to 500 Indians concealed in a coulee 800 – 900 yards from where he halted, although it was obvious to all concerned that no one could have seen any warriors in the coulee at that distance.[50] Captain Moylan thought there were 400 Indians within 200 – 400 yards when Reno dismounted and Lieutenants Hare and DeRudio confirmed about 400 – 500 Indians coming out of a coulee about 300 to 400 yards in their front shortly after dismounting.[51] In contrast, Fred Girard, and Doctor Porter thought there were only about 50 to 75 Indians in view when Reno dismounted, while George Herendeen *". . . did not see any Indians oppose the advance, and I was in front. They were sitting still on their horses, and seemed to be awaiting our approach and did not move till we dismounted."*[52]

Command Element	Strength	Percent of Regiment
Custer's Command	**221**	**33.1**
Headquarters	8	
Scouts/Guides	5	
Civilians	2	
Keogh's Battalion	**130**	**19.5**
Company C	45	
Company I	39	
Company L	46	
Yates' Battalion	**76**	**11.4**
Company E	39	
Company F	37	
Reno's Battalion	**162**	**24.3**
Headquarters	13	
Company A	44	
Company G	38	
Company M	47	
Scouts	16	
Interpreters/Courier	4	
Benteen's Battalion	**118**	**17.7**
Company D	45	
Company H	39	
Company K	34	
Pack Train	**166**	**24.9**
Company B	48	
Mathey's Command	90	
Civilian Packers	12	
Scouts	15	
Guides	1	
Total	**667**	**100**

Table 13 – 2 Battalion Combat Strength At Time of Custer's First Message– June 25, 1876

While Reno's abandoning of the charge marked the only occasion during 19 attacks on Indian villages between 1868 and 1876 where the troops failed to carry the village,[53] in my estimation, halting and forming the skirmish line was the proper course of action. At a general court–martial, Reno would have been judged on what happened to his own command as well as Custer's. While his orders gave him no discretion, other than his rate of advance, clearly Reno's small command would not have lasted long had they entered the village as ordered. In fact, halting his command actually provided better support for Custer's plan than continuing the charge. The 7th Cavalry was attacking a fixed objective point and Reno's halting did not, of itself, compromise his effectiveness either as a threat to the village or serving as a blocking, or holding, force for Custer's enveloping movement. On the skirmish line, Reno was better able to defend himself, thus preserving the blocking force to support Custer's thrust on the enemy flank, or rear. Had he continued into the village as ordered, it is doubtful any of his command would have remained by the time Custer got into action.

The warriors fought in their usual fashion. While the main body remained comfortably out of carbine range, small groups would dash at the soldiers, turning their ponies at the last minute to make a bravery run along the *wasichu* line. The Cheyenne are the only tribe to recall specific bravery runs in front of Reno's skirmish line. Brave Bear was prominent early in the fighting and is listed as making a run, although it may have occurred after the troops pivoted to the timber, while Scabby is credited with no less than 5 such runs. Unfortunately, Scabby's medicine would not hold throughout the day as he would succumb to wounds received on another part of the field. [54] Captain French, using his infantry "Long Tom," is credited with downing a warrior while on the skirmish line: *"The Captain told some of the men there to take notice of that Indian on the gray horse to see if he'd fall after he fired, he fired and shortly after the Indian reeled out of his saddle and was dragged off into the brush."* [55] While the Lakota recall 4 casualties in front of Reno's skirmish line, the warrior referred to cannot be positively identified. The warrior shot by French might have been either of the two fatalities, Dog With Horns of the Minneconjou or Hawk Man of the Uncpapa, or, perhaps he was the wounded Uncpapa Good Bear Boy who was rescued under fire by Lone (One) Bull. The wounded Oglala, Knife Chief, does not appear to be a candidate.

The skirmish line was short lived with little, if any, fire control being exercised. [56] There were too few troopers to anchor the line on the bluffs to the west, so the left of the line hung in the air. To make matters worse, Reno, in response to a report that Indians were infiltrating the woods in an effort to turn his right, was obliged to take a portion of G Troop off the line, reducing it by 12 to 15 men, and lead them into the woods as skirmishers. [57]

The skirmish line, now being manned by less than 80 men, stretched less than half way across the bottom. The Lakota quickly sped around Reno's left and threatened his rear. After no more than 15 minutes, [58] the skirmish line was forced to fall back to the edge of the timber. Apparently no one could agree on just how the line came to withdraw to the timber. Varnum testified that he was with Reno in the woods while the line was being withdrawn, while Moylan testified Reno ordered the movement after he called Reno's attention to the Indians flanking the line. Reno testified that after his adjutant, Lieutenant Hodgson, informed him the line had been flanked, he ordered Hodgson to have the line withdrawn. [59] Whoever ordered the movement, it was accomplished in an unsupervised manner. Sergeant Miles F. O'Hara, Company M, had been wounded and sought the assistance of Private Edward D. Pigford, also of Company M, to gain the shelter of the timber. Pigford ignored his pleas and ran for the woods. [60]

Although they had suffered only two casualties on the skirmish line, Sergeant O'Hara being killed, and Sergeant Charles White, also of M, being wounded, [61] the timber offered a much better defensive position. [62] The position was horseshoe shaped and lay in an old channel of the river. There was an eight foot bank thickly covered with underbrush which served as a breastwork, backed by 30 to 40 yards of woods and then the river. It was also possible to retrieve reserve ammunition under cover as Lieutenant Varnum recalled:

"The command was lying in the timber, and I could not see all of the men. I saw Captain Moylan the first when I got onto the edge of the line, and he called out – I don't know that he intended to speak to me – that the horses that we had dismounted from were beyond the left flank of our line, that the Indians were circling into the timber toward his left flank, and would cut off our horses, and that all our extra ammunition was there, and that something must be done. I told him that I would bring them up, and I went back. In order to go down the line, I had to go down into the woods to this opening, and I rode down to the left of the line, and calling out for 'A' Company men to follow me with their horses. I went up with my own company, and we came right in the rear of where Captain Moylan was. This was about at the rear of his own line. I dismounted then, and went up on the line,

and as I did so I heard Captain Moylan call that his men were out of ammunition; and he ordered that each alternate man should fall back from the line and get ammunition out of their saddlebags, and return to the line, so as to let the others go back and get ammunition from their saddlebags."[63]

Shortly after entering the timber, some of the officers began to consider the feasibility of sending a courier through to Custer. Captain Moylan recalled:

"While the command was in the timber I remember having a conversation with Lt. Wallace about the lodges in the village; not the hostile forces. He asked me if I could not send word back to Gen. Custer of the facts. There was a half-breed (sic) Indian by the name of Jackson (William Jackson, half-breed Pikuni Blackfoot, DCE) there and I asked him if he would take a message back.

"He looked around before he made reply, then sweeping his hand as in the manner of Indians, to the left and rear, said 'No one man could get through there alive.'"[64]

Jackson was right. After Reno's left had been turned, the country between the ford used earlier by the troops and their present position was swarming with Lakota and Cheyenne. It would have been impossible for any couriers to, or from,[65] Custer to get through in that direction. Jackson was probably also correct in his assessment that Custer couldn't be reached by crossing the river in the rear of their current position. It didn't matter. Reno was not thinking of couriers. He had reached a decision; one that was to have disastrous consequences for Custer. Reno had decided upon a retreat.[66] It had been about three quarters of an hour since he started down the valley and, despite having sent two couriers, he had received neither direct aid from Custer, nor received further orders. Reno would testify:

"The regiment had evidently got scattered or someone would have sent me an order or come to aid me. And in order to secure a union of the regiment, which I thought absolutely necessary, I moved to the hill to get where I could be seen and where I thought I could so dispose the men that they would hold their own till someone came to aid us."[67]

Although Reno had not been posted to the 7th Cavalry until August of 1869, he had undoubtedly heard the story of Battle of the Washita and the fate of Major Elliott. The first sentence of his testimony, which he had 3 years to perfect seems to me a clear statement that he felt Custer had abandoned him. Note that in the second sentence, Reno is concerned both that his command needs to be seen, a clear indication he believed himself abandoned, and that he personally would effect a concentration of the regiment although that was Custer's prerogative, not Reno's. I believe Reno's statement is crystal clear – he <u>knew</u> Custer had abandoned him to his fate. That Reno lacked confidence in Custer's promise of support is clearly demonstrated in his exchange with the Recorder at the court of inquiry:

"Q: Did you go into that fight with feelings of confidence or distrust in your commanding officer, General Custer?

"A: No, sir, our relations were friendly enough, and if my own brothers had been in that column, I could have not done any more than I did.

"Q: The question is, whether you went into that fight with feelings of confidence or distraught?

"A: My feelings towards General Custer were friendly.

"Q: I insist that the question shall be answered.

"A: Well, sir, I had known General Custer a long time and I had no confidence in his ability as a soldier. I had known him all through the war."[68]

Despite the fact he was encountering very little resistance while in the timber, Reno believed his only chance for survival lay in regaining the safety of the main command.[69] He had made up his mind to retreat. Appendix 2 lists 7th Cavalry casualties both by engagement and by organization. A study of the tables indicates that Reno would suffer 40 of his 45 casualties after he made the fateful decision to retreat from the timber.[70]

Reno has also been severely criticized for his decision to retreat from the timber. While I agree that Reno is deserving of censure for retreating from the valley, I disagree with the commonly accepted basis for that censure. Most who criticize Reno for the retreat cite that, as it freed the entire warrior force to concentrate on Custer, it was a major contributing factor in the annihilation of Custer's command. This, to my mind, is 'Monday morning quarterbacking." Reno's action in leaving the timber must be evaluated in the context of what he knew, or should have known, at the time, not in the light of subsequent events.[71] Reno had not been informed of any of the numerous sightings of Custer's command on the bluffs across the Little Big Horn, neither had either of his two messages to Custer been answered. He had only the vaguest notion of where Benteen might be. He very rightly believed himself to be on his own, and the fault for this lies solely with Custer for failing to inform his subordinate of his evolving tactical plan. Additionally, Reno's command was beginning to run low on ammunition. While it is true this latter situation was the result of poor fire control on the part of the cavalry, the fault for the needless expenditure of ammunition, against targets that were mostly out of range, lies with the company officers and sergeants, not the battalion commander. To put this lack of fire control into perspective, it should be noted that Major Forsyth and his fifty scouts expended an average of 60 rounds during the Beecher's Island Fight, which included repulsing 3 charges.[72]

While Reno could have probably remained safely in the timber for a rather protracted length of time, he believed he would ultimately have to abandon the position.[73] That being the case, he probably reasoned, there's no time like the present. Had Reno posessed the frontier, or Indian–fighting, experience he tried to effect at his court of inquiry, he'd have known that turning one's back in flight on mounted warriors was tantamount to suicide.[74] A seasoned veteran would only have ordered such a retreat as an absolte last resort, and the movement would have been properly covered. As Colonel Gibbon once remarked: *"When I once dismount my men to fight Indians, I never remount except to pursue them."*[75] Any other course would result in a horse race with the trooper's lives as the stakes.

Boldness was not only the trademark of the cavalryman, it was essential when fighting Indians. For this reason Major George Alexander Forsyth, hero of the Beecher's Island Fight in which 50 civilian scouts held off a force of 800 – 900 Cheyenne and Lakota for nine days, believed Reno should never have been in the timber in the first place: *"I never could understand why Reno did not charge desperately on the Indians in front of him. His dismounting his men was against all sound military judgment. 'Audacity always audacity,' is the motto for a cavalryman."*[76] As grave as his error in judgment was in determining to abandon the timber, it was compounded was compounded by the manner in which the movement was conducted. There can be no excuse for Reno's actions during the retreat and the lack of control of the movement serves as a monument to his everlasting shame and discredit.

Having decided to withdraw, Reno personally went to McIntosh and Moylan to inform them of the movement, sending Hodgson, his adjutant, to advise French. As none of the trumpeters was ordered to sound the retreat, it is not surprising that a good portion of the command, which strangely included Reno's orderly Private Edward Davern of Company F, were ignorant of the movement. Typical of the accounts is that of Lieutenant Varnum:

"(Varnum had left Moylan and was visiting with Girard and Reynolds when the following occurred, DCE). . . I heard from the woods cries of 'Charge! Charge! We are going to charge!' There was quite a confusion, – something about a charge down in the woods, and I jumped up and said: 'What's that?' and started down into the woods and grabbed my horse. Everybody was mounted. I didn't hear any orders. I just understood the men calling that they were going to charge, and I grabbed my horse and mounted him, and this being in the bushes and the men mounting just outside of the bushes kept me in and I couldn't get out until the men had passed."[77]

Private Morris recalled he had some difficulty in retrieving his mount:

"Private Summers (David "Sandy" Summers, Company M was killed during the retreat from the valley, DCE) was number 4 of the first set of 4's, and he had my horse. When I reached him, a man from another troop was endeavoring to secure my horse. Summers told him: 'Let go, or I will blow your head off!' I took in the situation and leveled my carbine at the fellow's head and told him to quit, it was my horse, and he did. I secured my horse, 'Stumbling Bear' and mounted. . ."[78]

Those who did hear the order, apparently turned and ran for their horses, no one covering the withdrawal. Private William C. Slaper, with 9 months service to his credit, summed up the feelings of the average soldier:

"I remember that I ducked my head and tried to dodge bullets which I could hear whizzing through the air. This was my first experience under fire. I know that for a time I was frightened, and far more so when I got my first glimpse of the Indians riding about in all directions and firing at us and yelling and whooping like incarnate fiends, all seemingly as naked as the day they were born, and painted from head to foot in the most hideous manner possible."[79]

In the absence of resistance from the firing line, a small party of warriors filtered into the timber.[80] George Herendeen testified as to the result:

"The Indians came around our left and into the timber. As there was no firing on the line they came closer and closer. I saw twenty or twenty five where I fired at them and more coming. They were not firing at the troops. They fired 3 or 4 shots at me. Ten men could have checked them from getting in the timber at that point. I was there 6 or 7 minutes and fired 7 or 8 shots.

"Maj. Reno was sitting on his horse in the park. The troops were in line, in close order, their left toward the river. I heard him order "Dismount,' and there was a

volley fired by the Indians; I judge the ones I had seen coming in and had fired at. There was an Indian named 'Bloody Knife' standing[81] in front of Maj. Reno, within eight feet from him and he and a soldier were hit.[82] The soldier halloed and then Maj. Reno gave the order to dismount, and the soldiers had just struck the ground when he gave the order 'Mount' and then everything left the timber on the run.

"Major Reno started out and the line broke to get out as far as I could see; they were getting out at any place they could find. There was dense underbrush and not more than one man could pass at a time, so they had to go single file on a trail that had been made by buffalo or some animals.

"That volley and the man hollering seemed to startle everybody and they ran."[83]

Private O'Neill echoed Herendeen's statement about the slackening of fire while the troops mounted:

"The order was thereupon given by Major Reno to 'get to your horses, men.' While this order was being given and executed, the fire from the troopers slackened very materially – in fact, it practically ceased. This gave the Indians greater confidence than ever, and they pressed in on us in greatly increasing numbers."[84]

Colonel Graham provides an excellent commentary on the "mount/dismount/mount" scenario, which he accepts, although Herendeen's is the only account to mention it[85]:

". . . Reno was 'startled and disconcerted;' and well he might be, for the sudden volley came as a complete surprise, and to be splattered with the blood and brains of his Indian scout leader was certainly disconcerting.

"In ordering his men instantly to dismount, however, he did, as it seems to me, precisely what the occasion required, for if the Indians who fired the volley were to be engaged or driven out, there was no practical way to go about it but on foot. A mounted charge into underbrush and timber was obviously not to be thought of, and it was equally clear that to remain in the clearing mounted would be to make of his men mere sitting ducks. The order to dismount was therefore proper in the circumstance, so long as the concealed Indians continued to be a menace.

"Evidently however, in characteristic Indian fashion, they 'hit and ran,' and for the time being, ceased to be a menace. Reno at once ordered his men to remount; and to obviate another such incident, immediately led them out. That he was startled and disconcerted does not necessarily imply that his action was cowardly. If there is any implication of want of courage in his conduct at this juncture, it is rather to be found in his hasty departure, which left a considerable number of his men behind to shift for themselves as best they could."[86]

Lakota accounts of the death of Bloody Knife, who was half Uncpapa, include the bizarre story that his body was unknowingly decapitated[87] by his nieces who showed the trophy to, among others, their mother, who instantly recognized her brother. Theodore Goldin, for one, did not believe the story, and I personally don't see how it may be credited. Burial accounts do not mention the corpse as being decapitated and, given the circumstances of his death, a shot to the rear of the head that, upon exit, took a portion of the skull and brain with the bullet, it seems implausible that his features would have been recognizable.[88]

In describing the British disaster at Isandhlwana, which has been likened to the Little Big Horn on more than one occasion, Donald R. Morris wrote: *"There came a point, however, when a cause was lost and gallantry could do no more, and a man who had discharged his responsibilities might then seek safety in flight. There was even a term to cover such an eventuality – sauve qui peut. . ."*[89] Despite the justification for Reno's actions presented above, this point had not been reached in the valley fight, and although the term *sauve qui peut* has often been used to describe Reno's retreat, it has been in the more popular context of *save himself who can.*

The testimony of the survivors, and the witnesses at Reno's court of inquiry makes for fascinating reading. Captain Moylan, virtually the sole proponent of the retreat being a properly conducted military movement, testified:

"The order was then given to mount up the companies.

"The companies were mounted up and being unable to form in any order in the timber, I gave my men orders to mount up as rapidly as possible individually and move up out of the timber in order that they might be formed out there. When about one half of my company was mounted up, I went out of the timber and formed the men in column–of–fours as they came up.

*"M Company came up very soon after and formed on my left at an interval of 15 or 20 yards. G Company, as I understood, did not mount quite so soon or did not get up quite so soon as the other two companies, but they were in column **before it reached the river.** (emphasis the author's) During the time the companies were being formed, Major Reno was there on his horse overlooking the formation of the companies. He asked me as to my opinion as to the point we had better retreat to as it became evident to him that our movement would be entirely on the defensive. It must necessarily be owing to the force of Indians then in sight and coming down.*

"I have almost forgotten what reply I made but at any rate he designated a point across the river at some high hills where we would go to establish ourselves there, if possible, and await further developments. I don't know what his intentions were. In a few minutes he gave the order to move forward and the command moved forward at a trot and then at a gallop. After the command was in motion at a gallop, the heads of the companies were almost on a line. The Indians closed in very close on the other flank and on the inner flank, toward the timber, very close also, as there were a number of Indians in the timber, in fact, I know there were a great many Indians in there.

"While the men were mounting up one of my men was wounded just after mounting his horse by a shot fired by an Indian who was between us and the river in the woods. About half the distance from where we started for the river, to the river, I dropped from the head of my company down to a point about the middle of the company and I found the rear of my company was very much broken up, as the shooting into it was very severe. A good many men had been wounded and some killed while the company was in motion. I rode in that position until the head of the company reached the river. When I reached the river myself I found the river full of

horses and men. There was no regular ford there where they attempted to cross. They simply moved on the trail and into the river and got onto the other side."[90]

Upon further questioning from the Recorder, an entirely different story, in consonance with the accounts of other survivors, would surface. Moylan would admit that two members of his company, one enlisted man, unnamed, and Lieutenant DeRudio, were left in the timber; that no bugle calls announcing the movement were sounded; that he did not know if the other companies had been formed prior to moving toward the bluffs; that he did not know if any officer had been assigned to look after the rear of the column; that the proper position for an officer during the movement, in his opinion, was at the rear of the column; that he did not know where Reno rode, but saw him twice at the column's head; and that the crossing of the Little Big Horn was not covered.[91]

Herendeen, in returning to the timber after his horse fell and ran away, recalled hearing an officer imploring Moylan's company: *"Company 'A' men, halt. Let us fight them. For God's sake, don't run."*[92] Hare was also heard to exhort the men of Company A, shouting: *"If we've got to die, let's die like men!"* Hare then directed the following at Captain Moylan: *"Don't run off like a pack of whipped curs!"*[93] Varnum gave a graphic, account of the retreat in his personal reminiscences:

> *"When I got on the plain the column was racing for the bluffs. A heavy column in front – about eight or ten feet – and from there back for two or three hundred yards the men were scattered in twos & single file & the Indians surrounding on the flank with their Winchesters laying across their saddles and pumping them into us. There was a long gap for me to ride to catch up and I had a thoroughbred horse under me. I soon made it & fortunately without being hit. I was soon at the head of the column and tried to check it saying we could not run away from Indians. We must get down & fight.*

> *"Maj. Reno was there, however, & informed me that he was in command. I subsided. We soon struck the river & nearly all the Indians left us."*[94]

In his testimony, Varnum, who had sufficient frontier Indian–fighting experience to know that attempting to flee from a mounted warrior force was tantamount to suicide, would omit mention of trying to check the column and his exchange with Reno during the retreat. Lieutenant Hare, however, testified: *"Before I got to the top of the hill I heard Lieutenant Varnum calling to the men to halt. . ."*[95]Doctor Henry Rinaldo Porter confirmed Hare's recollection with his testimony:

> *"I saw First Lieutenant Varnum, he had his hat off and he said, 'For God's sake men, don't run. There are a good many officers and men killed and wounded and we have got to go back and get them.' I went up to the Major (Reno, DCE) and said, 'Major, the men were pretty well demoralized, weren't they?' And he replied, 'No, that was a charge, sir.'"*[96]

First Lieutenant Jesse M. Lee, Recorder at the Reno court of inquiry, gave an excellent summation of the indisputable facts concerning the retreat:[97]

1. After the death of Bloody Knife, Major Reno, in rapid succession, gave the order to 'Dismount' then 'Mount'; immediately after which the portion of the command at hand departed the timber without further orders.

2.   There is no evidence to show that the retreat order was properly communicated to Company G.[98]

3.   One officer, Lieutenant DeRudio, at least 14 soldiers, and two citizens, Herendeen and Girard, were left in the timber, or ran back to it from the plain seeing they had no chance of escape. That only through the merest chance of having a faithful orderly,[99] was Lieutenant Hare not abandoned.

4.   No Indians barred, or met, the front of the column during the movement to the river.[100]

5.   All of the casualties, killed and wounded, were left to the enemy with no attempt made to carry them off.[101]

6.   No attempt was made to cover the crossing of the Little Big Horn.[102]

7.   The movement only ceased on the top of the hill when the Indians ceased to pursue.

Some authorities have characterized Reno as incompetent. While a strong case may be made that Reno lacked the ability to motivate and inspire, to question his knowledge of the military art is to ignore his Civil War record. The manner in which the valley fight was handled, especially the retreat, was uncharacteristic of the man who was personally mentioned for his coolness under fire in covering the retreat of the infantry at Gaines Mill in June of 1862.[103] The inescapable conclusion is that Reno lost his head,[104] and control of his command, when Bloody Knife was killed in the timber. The withdrawal then degenerated into a panic rout, or, as the Cheyenne American Horse characterized it, "*It was like chasing buffalo, a grand chase.*"[105] The Uncpapa Little Knife recalled Reno's men firing wildly over their shoulders, killing some of their own comrades in the process. Little Knife also remembered several of Reno's troopers, who had been unhorsed, raising their hands in an appeal for mercy; an appeal that was, of course, ignored.[106] Red Feather thought the soldiers leaving the timber was a remarkable stroke of luck for the Indians, telling General Hugh L. Scott some warriors called out to let the soldiers pass because "*we can't get at them in there.*"[107]

Wooden Leg gave a more graphic account of the rout:

"Suddenly the hidden soldiers came tearing out on horseback, from the woods. I was around on that side where they came out. I whirled my horse and lashed it into a dash to escape from them. All others of my companions did the same. But soon we discovered they were not following us. They were running away from us. They were going as fast as their tired horses could carry them across an open valley space and toward the river. We stopped, looked a moment, and then we whipped our ponies into swift pursuit. A great throng of Sioux also were coming after them. My distant position put me among the leaders in the chase. The soldier horses moved slowly, as if they were very tired. Ours were lively. We gained rapidly on them.

". . . Our war cries and war songs were mingled with many jeering calls, such as: 'You are only boys. You ought not to be fighting. We whipped you on the Rosebud. You should have brought more Crows or Shoshones with you to do your fighting.'

"Little Bird and I were after one certain soldier. Little Bird was wearing a trailing warbonnet. He was at the right and I was at the left of the fleeing man. We were lashing him and his horse with our pony whips. It seemed not brave to shoot him. Besides, I did not want to waste my bullets. He pointed back his revolver, though, and sent a bullet into Little Bird's thigh. Immediately I whacked the white man fighter on his head with the heavy elk-horn handle of my pony whip. The blow dazed him. I seized the rifle strapped on his back.[108] I wrenched it and dragged the looping strap over his head. As I was getting possession of this weapon he fell to the ground. I did not harm him further. I do not know what became of him."[109]

Characteristically, the warriors on the plain had fallen back from Reno's initial movement out of the timber. When they discovered that the troops were actually retreating, rather than charging, the warriors raised the buffalo killing cry: *Yi-hoo!* Whipping their ponies, the warriors soon overtook the column on their struggling horses. While most of the warriors remained on the column's right flank, pumping their Winchesters into the troops, several warriors rode among the soldiers, clubbing and pulling them from their saddles. Sergeant Ryan, riding near the rear of the column, personally dispatched two warriors by putting his revolver *"square against their breasts."*[110] This counterattack, estimated to comprise 200 to 300 warriors, forced the command to the left, toward the timber bordering the river,[111] so that Reno reached the river below his attack ford.

At this location, and for some distance down river, the banks of the Little Big Horn are both abrupt and soft, a condition posing a significant hindrance to a large body attempting to ford. While steepness of the bank is an important consideration on the west bank, conditions are even less favorable on the east bank. Fortunately for Reno, the spot they were driven to was opposite a small ravine used by buffalo and other animals seeking water. As the command became bunched up waiting to enter the water, men in the rear dispersed both up and down stream, leaping their horses from the high bank. As the troops crossed the river, they again became bunched up as they entered the narrow, slippery funnel that was the buffalo trail, or tried to force their tired mounts to jump the 8 foot barrier that was the east bank. The warriors kept up a continuing fire into the densely packed troops. Wooden Leg used his captured carbine to good advantage at this juncture, clubbing two troopers off their horses in the river.[112] Finally, the congestion cleared and the demoralized command struggled to the summit of the bluffs.

The retreat had been a costly one. Including scouts and civilians, Reno left 36 dead behind him in the valley, at least 31 of which were sustained during his retreat. Fortunately, nine of the wounded were able to remain mounted and escaped. His total casualty count of 45 amounted to about 28% of his command. In sharp contrast to this figure are the 28 Indians, including 10 women and children, killed in the valley fight.[113] A listing of Indian fatalities by engagement is provided in Appendix 2, while a listing of Indians known to have been in the village on June 25th is provided in Appendix 9. When the minimum number of 17 men abandoned in the valley is accounted for, Reno reached the hill with about 60% of the men he had led into combat less than an hour and a half earlier. Despite his heavy losses, Reno had been lucky, as Lieutenant Hare observed: *"If the Indians had followed us in force to the hill-top, they would have got us all, though not before Benteen came up."*[114] While American Horse said the Indians did not pursue Reno to the top of the bluff so they could plunder the dead and assess their own losses;[115] the real reason the warriors withdrew was to counter Captain Yates' demonstration at Minneconjou Ford at the mouth of Medicine Tail Coulee. Although we cannot be certain of how and where all of these men died, we know about many of them. Their stories follow.

Reno's skirmish line from Wooden Leg Ridge. The road running diagonally across the center of the photo marks the approximate location where Reno dismounted and formed his skirmish line. From this vantage point Custer had an excellent view of Reno's advance down the valley but would not be able to see the full extent of the village. Viewed from the valley, a group on this point would appear to be on the edge of the bluffs as was noted by several in Reno's command. *Photo by the author.*

Reno's timber position from Wooden Leg Ridge. Reno's skirmish line position is visible at the far left of the photo. After advancing about a hundred yards on foot, Reno was forced into the timber in the center of the picture approximately where the white trailer is located. Custer would have had a good view of the skirmish line pivoting into the timber from this vantage point. *Photo by author.*

Reno's retreat crossing of the Little Big Horn taken from a point midway between the Reno-Benteen Defense Site and Weir Point. The second ridge from the left is where Dr. DeWolf was killed. *Photo by author.*

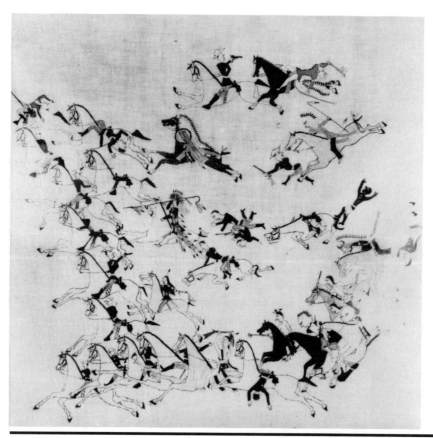

This painting by White Bird, 15-year-old Northern Cheyenne participant in the battle, depicts Reno's retreat from the valley. Note the body of Isaiah Dorman, the only black man in Custer's command, at right center. *Photo Courtesy Little Bighorn Battlefield National Monument.*

As had been the case during their charge toward the village, some of the men had a difficult time restraining their horses during the retreat. Private Goldin recalled:

"I saw the horse of Farrier Gideon Wells (Benjamin J. Wells, Company G, DCE) break from the lines and charge directly into the ranks of the pursuing Indians. I did not see him go down, but later we found his body, stripped, scalped and mutilated, some distance to the right, or south of the trail of the retreating column."[116]

There are two versions of the death of Charley Reynolds. Dr. Porter gave his version to Captain Grant Marsh when the wounded were brought aboard the *Far West*:

"He fell at my side. I was tending a dying soldier in a clump of bushes, just before the retreat to the bluffs, when it happened. The bullets were flying, and Reynolds noticed that the Indians were making a special target of me, though I didn't know it. He sprang up and cried: 'Doctor, the Indians are shooting at you!' I turned to look and in the same instant saw him throw up his hands and fall, shot through the heart."[117]

Sergeant Stanislaus Roy, Company A, may have confused Charley Reynolds with Isaiah Dorman when he informed Walter Camp: *"About 75 or 100 yds. from timber I saw Charlie Reynolds dismounted and wounded with pistol standing still and showing fight."[118]* George Herendeen, in a 1909 interview with Walter Camp, provided the following version of the death of Charley Reynolds:

"I saw Reynolds come out of timber, and said: 'Charley, don't try to ride out. We can't get away from this timber.' Reynolds was then trying to mount his horse. He finally mounted and got about 150 yds. when he was shot. . ."[119]

Herendeen continued, describing the death of Isaiah Dorman:

". . . and Isaiah fell near him (Reynolds, DCE), and while I was in the timber, I saw Indians shooting at Isaiah and squaws pounding him with stone hammers.[120] His legs below the knees were shot full of bullets only an inch or two apart."[121]

As Dorman was well known to the Lakota, being married to a Santee woman, they apparently reserved special treatment for him. In addition to peppering his legs with bullets, he was slit open and his coffee pot, filled with his blood, was left by the body.[122] A prime example of the fanciful stories told about the Little Big Horn, is the story of Sitting Bull succoring the mortally wounded Dorman, whom the Lakota called "teat." While the story cannot be credited, I have provided it as an example of the genre.

"As he (Sitting Bull, DCE) approached the end of the brush near the prairie-dog town, he came upon the Negro, 'Teat' Isaiah Dorman. Two Bull, Shoots Walking, and several others rode up at the same time. 'Teat' was badly wounded, but still able to talk. He spoke Sioux, and was well-liked by the Indians. He had joined the troops as interpreter because, he said, he wanted to see that western country once more before he died. And now, when he saw the Sioux all around him, he pleaded with them, 'My friends, you have already killed me; don't count coup on me.' He had been shot early in the fight.

"Sitting Bull arrived just then, recognized 'Teat' and said, 'Don't kill that man; he is a friend of mine.' The Negro asked for water, and Sitting Bull took his cup of polished black buffalo horn, got some water, and gave him to drink. Immediately after, Isaiah died. The warriors rode away. Afterward, some spiteful woman found the Negro's body and mutilated it with her butcher knife."[123]

The Two Kettle Lakota, Runs The Enemy, recalled seeing Dorman during the retreat:

"We passed a black man in a soldier's uniform and we had him. He turned on his horse and shot an Indian right through the heart.[124] Then the Indians fired at this one man and riddled his horse with bullets. His horse fell over on his back and the black man could not get up. I saw him as I rode by. I afterward saw him lying there dead."[125]

Lieutenant Donald McIntosh and several troopers of Company G did not hear the order to withdraw. While trying to rally his men in the timber, Private John Rapp, Company G, who was McIntosh's striker, was killed and the Lieutenant's horse stampeded. Seeing his Lieutenant without a mount, Private Samuel McCormick gave up his horse with the remark that as they were all dead men anyway, he might as well die on foot as horseback.[126] McIntosh was driven to the river bank shortly after leaving the timber and killed. Ironically, Private McCormick rejoined Reno's command with the Herendeen party and survived the battle.

Just as he was preparing to mount, Private Daniel Newell was shot in the left leg. Sergeant Patrick Carey told him: *"Mount your horse and stick to him as long as you can. You are fighting Indians, not white men."* Newell was able to mount his horse from the right side and started after his companions.[127] As Newell closed on the retreating command, he noticed Corporal Henry M. Scollin, Company M go down and heard him cry out: *"Good–bye, boys!"*[128] Private Morris recalled the event somewhat differently:

"David Summers (private, Company M, DCE) was killed just as he emerged from the timber. About half way to the river, Scollin's horse was shot and went down, and Scollin took his carbine and said: 'For God's sake boys, don't leave me here.' Thorpe (Private Rollins L. Thorpe, Company M, DCE) stopped and took him on behind his horse and just as he did so his horse was shot down. Thorpe then caught an Indian pony and escaped, and Scollin was left there and killed."[129]

Private Daniel J. Newell described his escape from the valley:

"Some of the men started to run. . . 1st Sgt Ryan of M said 'For God's sake, don't run! Fight as you retreat or not one of us will ever get out.' . . .We finally reached the horses. . .As I was about to mount was shot in left thigh. . . Called to paddy Ryan, Sgt. of M Troop: 'I am hit.' He said: 'Mount your horse my boy and stick to him. You are fighting Indians now.' I tried to, but could not mount. . . Then remembered Pete, my horse, was trained to let me mount on either side. . . After several efforts was able to get on him. . . My horse was hit as I came to the river, but he jumped in and took me across, but he was hit again and fell. . . I threw myself off and crawled about ten yards to where a corporal of my troop lay. . . He said: 'You are wounded. Come around here Dan and you will be under cover.' . . .We laid there for about a half hour and firing slackened. . . Corporal Ruder (Private Roman Rutten, DCE) helped me up the hill."[130]

As previously mentioned, Private Davern, Reno's orderly, did not hear the order to mount, only going for his horse when he saw the men of G Company run for their horses. Davern was somewhat delayed in leaving the timber as he stopped to turn over the G Company horse he found tied to his mount's bridle.[131] Godfrey relates what transpired as Davern spurred to catch the command: *". . . his horse was killed; he then shot the Indian, caught the Indian's pony, and rode to the command."*[132]

Captain French, had attempted to keep his men in good order during the retreat. His men remembered:

". . . French, a fat man with a falsetto voice, had called out: 'A – a – steady there men. Steady. Keep up a continual fire, you damned fools! Don't turn your back to the enemy. Steady, you damned fools!'

"The Captain waited until all his men got out of the timber then followed up in the rear. He drew his revolver and [was] firing at the Indians as they were riding alongside of him some twenty yards on either side of him. The Captain had barely chance to get to the ford and the Indians were so thick that you could hardly see what was going on until the Captain got on the other side of the river. He then dismounted from his horse, took his rifle and fired on the Indians while standing on the river bank."[133]

Black Elk, the young Oglala, also recalled the heroic soldier captain:

"The soldiers were running by this time up the stream – soldiers and Indians mixed up. Just then I could see a Sioux charge at one of the soldiers and try to get ahold of his horse and the soldier shot the Sioux off his horse with a revolver he had. Then I saw that this white man had shot two of the Indians at that time."[134]

French had become a sick, embittered man, literally drinking himself to death, as had Weir, when he wrote to Lieutenant Cooke's mother on June 16, 1880:

"What made Major R run away when he did I cannot positively know, and he did not tell me. What made him halt and dismount when he did is a matter in regard to which I am equally ignorant. It was not the kind of warfare to which I had been accustomed – and that was this – to be watchful, and prudent, and never to take less than an even chance, but when once in to do as is said to be the custom at Donnybrook Fair, – 'if you see a head, hit it' – I thought that we were to charge headlong through them all, – that was the only chance. To turn one's back on Indians, without being better mounted than they, is throwing away life. When he started to that hill he had told me, not one minute before, that he was going to fight – this was in reply to a question of mine.

*"And when all had gone for safety was when I sought death – and tried to fight the battle alone – and did so for nearly a mile – If one man could hold back seven or eight hundred what might not a hundred and twenty have done at the **right instant** .(emphasis in the original, DCE) Sometimes one minute is of far more value than years afterward, or before, – and military life consists simply, in waiting for opportunities. . .*

"I don't wonder that old Red Horse thought me a spirit from the bad place – for, and there is no mistake in this, for I saw them fall, eighteen of his men, who rode up to within a few yards of me – tumbled off as I fired and their ponies ran loose, – How many were dead I don't know, and [did] not stop to see. Just before I had killed one with my rifle, and, on crossing the creek, two more, and on the next day one – this is the evidence taken at Fort Lincoln in January, 1879, given by men who saw it. . .

"It is not nice, I know, to mention these things, but they do not rest on my own version. – What I mean to get at is this. – If I were able to do all this single–handed what might I not have done with the coveted opportunity, [135] – but a friendly bullet did not come to assist me – and although the idea flashed through my mine, yet I did not dare to resort to murder – the latter, I now believe would have been justifiable."[136]

As the command reached the river, Lieutenant Hodgson was one of those that jumped his horse into the stream. He and his horse were hit, apparently with the same shot. Dismounted, and wounded[137] in the river, Hodgson's story is continued by Private Slaper:

"As I glanced about me, the first thing that engaged my attention was Trumpeter Henry Fisher of M Troop, riding in the river some distance up, with Lieut. Benny Hodgson hanging to one stirrup. Hodgson had been wounded and was on foot in the stream, when Fisher came dashing into the water. Noting Hodgson's helpless condition, he thrust one of his stirrups toward him, which Hodgson grasped and was thus towed across to the opposite bank, under a galling fire from the Indians, who were now riding into the stream, shooting into the ranks of the stampeding troopers, and actually pulling many of them from their horses right there in the river. As Fisher gained the opposite bank, dragging Hodgson at the end of his stirrup, and the latter was trying to struggle up the incline, another shot rang out and Hodgson dropped. I did not see him move again, and suppose he was killed right there."[138]

Hodgson''s premonition of being carried out of immediate danger by the expedient of a trooper's stirrup had proven true; but the final outcome, withheld from his prophetic vision, rendered his rescue from the river a futile exercise.

Apparently, the young warrior Roman Nose rode too close to the troopers at this location and was killed on the river bank.[139]

Heroics during the retreat were not limited to French and Fisher, Sergeant Benjamin C. Criswell, Company B, *"rode back under a furious fire and brought off the body (Hodgson's, DCE), as well as all the ammunition in the saddle–bags on several dead horses."*[140] For his courage under fire, Sergeant Criswell was awarded the Medal of Honor.

During the retreat, Red Bear's horse stumbled and threw him. The Arikara quickly regained his feet and gave chase. He was able to secure his mount when the animal stopped in some thick underbrush. Before Red Bear could remount, he was charged by one of the pursuing warriors. Red Bear fired at the Indian, killing him instantly. He then remounted and crossed the river.[141] Little Brave was not so lucky. Being poorly mounted, he was easily overtaken and cut off near Reno's retreat crossing.[142] Before being overrun and killed by a party containing the Cheyenne Wooden Leg and the Oglala Kicking Bear,[143] Little Brave dispatched the Sans Arc warrior Elk Stands Above.[144] Crow King's brothers, White Bull and Swift Bear, as well as the Two Kettle Chased By Owl, were killed during Reno's retreat from the valley. It is probable that the two Uncpapas were killed by the Arikara Young Hawk.[145]

Bob Tailed Bull,[146] leader of the Arikara scouts, joined Bloody Knife and Little Brave on their journey to the spirit land during the retreat from the valley. Although several accounts list him as being killed on, or near, the skirmish line at the start of the fighting, the accounts of the Arikara are clear. Both Young Hawk and Strikes Two state that Bob Tail Bull was not only present during the retreat from the valley, but actually crossed to the east bank. At that point he was cut off and killed by the Oglala Running Eagle,[147] his blood stained horse joining the command on Reno Hill.[148] While Captain Keogh's horse, Comanche, is the most famous animal from the battle, his survival does not match the feat of Bob Tailed Bull's horse. The Arikara commemorate the event:

> "To this day, the Arikaras in North Dakota and the Pawnees in Oklahoma, sing a war dance song that has reference to a warrior and his horse. For it was sometime after the Battle of the Little Big Horn that an emaciated spotted horse walked into the Arikara village, alone. It was in the early morning when they found him. Scarred and showing signs of a hard journey, the horse carried an Army saddle intact. The reins were up as if he had just been ridden. He had returned home. (A journey of some 300 miles, DCE)"[149]

Despite a manner of dress and hair style in sharp contrast to the Cheyenne and Lakota, the government scouts were in danger of being fired upon by the troops. This may have happened to the Arikara scout Goose, severely wounded in the right hand during the retreat. Private Morris, himself wounded in the breast during the retreat recalled his encounter with Goose in Dr. Porter's hilltop field hospital on the morning of the 26th:

> "A Ree Indian, one of our scouts, about seventeen or eighteen years of age, was sitting at the foot of my blanket with a bandage on his arm (he had been shot in the right hand, DCE). I said to him, 'How cooler?' He held up his hand, pointing to me and pointed to his arm and smiled, accusing me in the sign language of shooting him in the wrist. I then recognized him as one of the two Indians that I was shooting at while crossing the bottom."[150]

The retreating soldiers and scouts soon discovered the east bank was no sanctuary. Upon reaching the flat just east of the retreat crossing, the Crow scout White Swan, who may have been wounded prior to crossing the river, noticed Whirlwind, sixteen year old Cheyenne warrior, bearing down on him. Wheeling his mount to the left, White Swan charged. The two warriors fired at the same instant. Whirlwind was killed, and White Swan wounded.[151]

Private Morris, who had jumped his horse off a ten foot bank into the Little Big Horn, told of his own narrow escape from death:

> "Upon reaching the level above the cut (buffalo trail, DCE) I dismounted and led my horse as fast as possible up the bluff, and overtook Tinker (unknown. no one serving with the 7th at the Little Big Horn had the surname of Tinker, DCE), Bill Meyer (Private William D. Meyer, Company M, DCE) and Gordon (Private Henry Gordon, Company M, DCE) about half way up the bluff. We stopped a moment to rest. (The bluffs, rising about 200 feet above the river are quite steep in this area, DCE). The bodies of the fallen soldiers were plainly visible. they marked the skirmish line and the line of the charge from the timber to the ford, and were in the river

and at the top of the cut. At this instant a shower of lead sent Meyer and Gordon to the happy hunting–ground, and a fifty caliber passed through the left breast of your humble servant. Our horses were also hit. I continued up the hill alone and joined the command; was then assisted to the improvised hospital." [152]

After Lieutenant Varnum crossed the river, he started up a ridge just to the left of Reno Hill and the route followed by the majority of the command. Fortunately he heard the men shouting to call him back and he returned and went up on the right with the column. Dr. DeWolf and his orderly, Private Elihu F. Clear, Company K, had been just ahead of Varnum and as DeWolf turned to see who was doing the shouting, he, and Clear [153] were shot and killed from ambush. [154] Although Lieutenant Wallace tried to protect DeWolf's body with long range carbine fire, he was scalped in full view of the command. Fortunately for history, Dr. Porter was able to recover De Wolf's diary from the body shortly after the Indians moved down stream to attack Custer.

Thirteen year old Black Elk recalled the aftermath of Reno's retreat:

"We followed [Maj. Marcus A.] Reno's retreat. Then when we got up the creek a little ways we went into the river – three of us boys about the same age together. I noticed a six–shooter so I got off and picked it up. Everyone was weaving in and out – that was really all I could see. I was very small and I had no chance to shoot anyone. There were a lot of Indians ahead of me. We stopped on a flat and everyone would get a soldier and strip him and put on his clothes for himself. We took everything they had – pistols, guns, ammunition, etc. We went to the river and turned back from there. As we turned from the river we saw a kicking soldier and a man came up and said: 'Boys, get off and scalp him.' So I got off and began to take my knife. Of course the soldier has short hair so I started to cut it off. Probably it hurt him because he began to grind his teeth. After I did this I took my pistol out and shot him in the forehead. This was down by the river where we jumped in." [155]

As the troops labored up the steep 200 foot rise of the bluffs, they represented easy prey for the jubilant warriors. Fortunately for Reno and his command, Custer's column had been sighted and, even before Yates fired his first volley into the village, the warriors were galloping to counter the new threat. Although Lieutenant Hare recalled, after a night's reflection, he heard Reno personally forming a skirmish line on the bluffs as he rode up, [156] and Private Davern testified about a calm, collected Reno giving him a drink of water, [157] it appears that it was some time before Reno regained his composure.

Godfrey, in his *Century Magazine* article, charged that Reno, after discharging the loads in his pistol during the retreat, threw his revolver away. [158] This account is apparently supported by the testimony of Private Davern, who recalled that after informing the major he had lost his carbine when thrown from his horse in the valley, Reno told him *". . . he had lost his carbine and pistol also. He did not say how or when."* [159] Arikara scout Red Bear claimed that Reno, his eyes wildly rolling, was foaming at the mouth when he reached the summit. [160] While I find Red Bear's account hard to accept, it cannot be denied that Reno and his command were thoroughly demoralized and had ceased to function as a fighting force. Only Custer's feint at Minneconjou Ford, and the timely arrival of Benteen, saved Reno's command from complete annihilation.

---

[1] Arikara name for the Little Big Horn. See Walter Camp "Custer in '76" page 181.

2 See O. G. Libby "The Arikara Narrative" pages 122 – 123.

3 See Edgar I. Stewart "Custer's Luck" page 331.

4 My analysis indicates no more than about 20 minutes were consumed in crossing, watering and reforming. See Appendix 12.

5 See John G. Neihardt "Black Elk Speaks" page 113 – 114.

6 See Walter Camp "Custer in '76" page 148.

7 Girard said Reno ordered his command 'Forward' after being informed the Indians were coming up the valley to meet him. See Colonel W. A. Graham "Reno Court of Inquiry" page 38. Reno denied that Girard had passed this intelligence to him, testifying: *"I received no communication from Girard at the Ford 'A'; he had no right to speak to me officially. I had had trouble with Girard, and discharged him because I thought he was stealing from the government."* See Colonel W. A. Graham "Reno Court of Inquiry" page 223.

8 See Ronald H. Nichols "Reno Court of Inquiry" page 87.

9 See Ronald H. Nichols "Reno Court of Inquiry" page 561.

10 See Don Rickey, JR. "Forty Miles a Day on Beans and Hay" page 286.

11 Although Reno testified Mitchell was dispatched while the command was moving down the valley, some authorities believe he was dispatched when Reno halted to form his skirmish line.

12 See Ronald H. Nichols "Reno Court of Inquiry" page 561.

13 Testimony of Lieutenant, then captain, Edward G. Mathey. See Ronald H. Nichols "Reno Court of Inquiry" pages 551 – 552. DeRudio, testifying prior to Mathey, said he had *"admired"* Reno's conduct on the skirmish line and, under cross examination, stated he had seen no signs of cowardice on Reno's part. It is interesting to note that DeRudio was not recalled by the court after Mathey's testimony. See Ronald H. Nichols "Reno Court of Inquiry" pages 323 and 328.

14 See Colonel W. A. Graham "Reno Court of Inquiry" page 105.

15 See Ronald H. Nichols "Reno Court of Inquiry" page 277.

16 See Ronald H. Nichols "Reno Court of Inquiry" page 561. This occurred about half way from the attack ford to where Reno formed his skirmish line and was about the point where Private O'Neill said he saw Custer's command on the bluffs east of the river. This sighting of Custer's command was not reported to Reno. See Walter Camp "Custer in '76" page 106. The order of the companies at this point seems to have been G on the left, M in the middle, and A on the right.

17 From the court of inquiry: "Q: *Then you consider that you charged the enemy there?* A: *I don't consider that I charged the enemy, but I went near enough to discover that it was impossible to do it.*" See Ronald H. Nichols "Reno Court of Inquiry" page 590.

18 See Edgar I. Stewart "Custer's Luck" page 345.

[19] John S. Gray has done the definitive research in this area and the reader is directed to his excellent "Centennial Campaign." Other than placing the Uncpapas at the extreme upper (southern) end, and the Cheyenne at the extreme lower (northern) end of the village, there is no agreement in Indian accounts as to the placement of the various camp circles.

[20] The names of the Oglalas Bad Heart Bull, Hard To Hit, and Kicking Bear have come down to us as the first Lakota to meet Reno's advance. See Helen H. Blish "A Pictographic History of the Oglala Sioux" page 217.

[21] See John Upton Terrell and Colonel George Walton "Faint The Trumpet Sounds" page 59.

[22] See John M. Carroll "Custer's Chief of Scouts" pages 121 – 122. Reno testified at the Court of Inquiry that the command had not fired any shots prior to dismounting.

[23] See Daniel O. Magnussen "Peter Thompson's Narrative" page 243. Although many authorities state Turley's body was never identified, Private William C. Slapper, in one of his accounts, mentioned the discovery of Turley's body with a knife thrust into one eye up to the hilt. See Tom O'Neil "Little Big Horn Memories" page 14. William E. Morris, however, was equally positive Turley was killed at the retreat ford. See E. Elden Davis and James W. Wengert MD "That Fatal Day" page 27.

[24] See Barry C. Johnson "A Captain of Chivalric Courage" page 13.

[25] See Fred Dustin "The Custer Tragedy" page 112.

[26] The frontier army never adopted the practice of their Indian scouts of tying their horses' bridles to their belts while fighting dismounted. See Dale T. Schoenberger "Custer's Scouts" page 44.

[27] Table 13 – 1 shows that, after dispatching his two messengers, Reno had 109 enlisted men and 22 sergeants to man his skirmish line. Including the 9 officers and 2 doctors, it would take 36 men just to hold the horses. Subtracting these 36 men and the 3 initial casualties left Reno only 92 men for the skirmish line. It is interesting to note that Reno maintained the traditional 4 horses per holder specified in the tactics of the day. Custer had used one holder for every eight horses during his August 4, 1873 skirmish on the Yellowstone, and there is evidence that Calhoun used a similar tactic on the hill that bears his name later that same day. The fact that Reno did not exercise another available option, picketing the horses in the security of the woods under a smaller guard, is either due to inexperience, or indicates Reno was beginning to fail to exercise proper judgment and control.

[28] See Ronald H. Nichols "Reno Court of Inquiry" page 88.

[29] See E.A. Brininstool "Troopers With Custer" page 130. Lieutenant Wallace said there were about 200 – 300 Indians in view when they formed the skirmish line (See Colonel W. A. Graham "Reno Court of Inquiry" page 18) while Lieutenant Varnum thought they faced 300 – 400 warriors while on the skirmish line, the heaviest concentration being 800 – 1000 yards away. See Colonel W. A. Graham "Reno Court of Inquiry" page 50.

[30] See Fred Dustin "The Custer Tragedy" page 114. Among others, Private Daniel Newell sighted Custer's command on the bluffs as Reno charged down the valley. See John M. Carroll "The Sunshine Magazine Articles" page 10. It is interesting to speculate as to Reno's actions had he been advised of these sightings. Reno undoubtedly would have surmised, as he stated in his report of

July 5th (See Appendix 7), that Custer was maneuvering to strike the village on its flank, or lower extremity. Armed with this knowledge, it is doubtful Reno would have abandoned the timber as readily as he did. Who can say what the results might have been had the Indians been forced to fight on two fronts simultaneously? In any event, when Reno abandoned the timber, all the warriors were freed to concentrate on Custer, making this, and the subsequent failures to report the sighting of Custer's command to Reno, a contributing factor in the defeat of Custer's immediate command.

[31] In addition to the ponies captured in the valley, the Arikara captured 27 ponies and 2 mules on the east bank of the Little Big Horn. See Richard G. Hardorff "Lakota Recollections of the Custer Fight" page 110. Had the scouts not been detailed to this important duty, Custer would have been forced to further divide his force as at least a company would have been assigned to this task.

[32] The best accounts of the scouts' participation in the valley fight are found in John S. Gray "Custer's Last Campaign" and Dale T. Schoenberger "Custer's Scouts." See also O. G. Libby "The Arikara Narrative" pages 131 – 134.

[33] Again, much useless controversy surrounds exactly who was seen on the bluffs at Wooden Leg Ridge and Weir Point. If Custer did not personally observe the valley from those locations, as would have been in character for him, he certainly ordered scouts to observe and report to him. Clearly what is important here is the intelligence obtained by Custer, rather than the identity of the person gathering that intelligence. I will use the name "Custer" to apply to that "intelligence gatherer" as I believe that it was indeed Armstrong Custer who was observed in both locations.

[34] Private Theodore Goldin claimed to have been dispatched with a written message from Custer to Reno. Inaccuracies and changes in his various accounts leave this subject to some question. See footnote 65. It is unnecessary to speculate whether or not a messenger could have gotten through to Reno. What is important is that, apparently, Custer made no attempt to communicate with Reno.

[35] See Walter Camp "Custer in '76" pages 92 – 93. It is interesting to note that although Lieutenant Mathey commanded the pack train the order was directed to McDougall, the commander of the escort. Perhaps this was because McDougall was the senior officer serving with that command element.

[36] See Robert M. Utley "Cavalier in Buckskin" page 186.

[37] The troops had been sighted many times on the morning of June 25. In addition to the sightings at the Crow's Nest, the Minneconjou Standing Bear had seen both Reno's and Custer's columns while looking for his horses in the vicinity of Weir Point. A hunter, perhaps Fast Horn, had killed a buffalo on Reno Creek but had to abandon it when the soldiers approached (See Richard G. Hardorff "Lakota Recollections of the Custer Fight" pages 21, 54, 57 - 58, and 82). Fat Bear brought the news of the encounter with Sergeant Curtiss' detail to Sitting Bull at the council lodge just as Reno attacked the Uncpapa circle (see Stanley Vestal "Sitting Bull" page 160). Gall maintained that Custer's column had been sighted by buffalo scouts on the 24th and word of the discovery had reached the village that same night (see Usher L. Burdick "David F. Barry's Indian Notes On The Custer Battle" page 23). When one considers the warrior's response to the sighting of Crook's column eight days earlier, this lack of concern with a column in the immediate vicinity of their village defies comprehension.

[38] See John G. Neihardt "Black Elk Speaks" page 109.

[39] See Charles A. Eastman "Indian Heroes & Great Chieftains" page 99.

[40] See Colonel W. A. Graham "The Custer Myth" page 61.

[41] See Richard G. Hardorff "Lakota Recollections of the Custer Fight" page 119. Afterwards, Crow Foot was know as Abandoned One, or Fled and Abandoned. See Gregory F. Michno "Lakota Noon" page 48.

[42] See Peter John Powell "People of the Sacred Mountain" page 1012.

[43] See Peter John Powell "People of the Sacred Mountain" pages 1010 and 1012.

[44] See Thomas B. Marquis "Wooden Leg" page 217.

[45] See Colonel W. A. Graham "The Custer Myth" page 75.

[46] See Colonel W. A. Graham "The Custer Myth" pages 76 – 77.

[47] Contemporary newspaper reports indicate the bodies of several women and children were found near where Reno attacked. See Richard G. Hardorff "Lakota Recollections of the Custer Fight" page 48. There is also a report that one of the women gathering roots and herbs along Reno Creek was killed as she and her companions fled from Reno's advancing troopers. See James Brust "Lt. Oscar Long's Early Map Details Terrain, Battle Positions" page 6.

[48] See Peter John Powell "People of the Sacred Mountain" page 1011.

[49] Note that although William Jackson was a half–breed Pikuni Blackfoot, I have included him in the count for the Arikara for brevity.

[50] In his direct testimony Reno stated the coulee was in the foothills. This description does not agree with the topography of the valley, any of the maps of the region, or the testimony of others including his own cross examination where Reno stated: *"It was afterward developed that if I had gone 2[00] or 300 yards further I should have thrown my command into a ditch 10 yards wide and 3 or 4 deep."* In response to a question about whether there were Indians in the coulee, now called a ditch by Reno, he responded: *"Yes, sir, I saw them coming out of it."* See Ronald H. Nichols "Reno Court of Inquiry" page 590.

[51] See Colonel W. A. Graham "Reno Court of Inquiry" pages 72 and 90.and Walter Camp "Custer In '76" page 88. While the existence of this coulee has been debated, there seems to be no question of its existence and that a substantial warrior force had entered it. It is highly improbable however, that Reno, or anyone else in the command, was aware of either the coulee or the warriors prior to the formation of the skirmish line. A good description of this coulee and its location on the west bank of the Little Big Horn, rather than the benchlands, is given in Charles Khulman "Legend Into History" page 55 and accompanying map on page 48.

[52] DeRudio also testified that at the time the charge was halted the Indians appeared to be standing still waiting for the troops. See Colonel W. A. Graham "Reno Court of Inquiry" pages 40, 65, 81, 90 and 106.

[53] See Jay Smith "A Hundred Years Later" page 105.

[54] John Stands In Timber lists Scabby as dying of wounds received in the fighting, but, as Peter John Powell says he survived the bravery runs in the valley without a scratch, his wounds were probably received during Reno's retreat from the valley. See Peter John Powell "People of the Sacred Mountain" page 1013.

[55] See Barry C. Johnson "A Captain of Chivalric Courage" page 13.

[56] Sergeant Ferdinand A. Culbertson, Company A, recalled that some of the men on the skirmish line were firing very fast. See Colonel W. A. Graham "Reno Court of Inquiry" page 122. Company A ran out of ammunition after only about 15 minutes indicating they were firing at just about half the maximum rate for the Springfield carbine. DeRudio testified that Reno was on the firing line at that time encouraging the men and directing the fire (See Colonel W. A. Graham "Reno Court of Inquiry" page 106) while Sergeant Ryan would make the same observation about Lieutenant Hodgson (See Don Rickey Jr. "Forty Miles a Day on Beans and Hay" page 288).

[57] See Colonel W. A. Graham "Reno Court of Inquiry" page 214.

[58] Estimates given at the Reno Court of Inquiry as to the length of time the command was on the skirmish line varied from 5 to 20 minutes. My analysis indicates 15 minutes is about right.

[59] See Colonel W. A. Graham "Reno Court of Inquiry" pages 47 and 70, and Ronald H. Nichols "Reno Court of Inquiry" pages 562 – 563.

[60] See Richard G. Hardorff "Lakota Recollections on the Custer Fight" page 83. Red Feather told General Hugh L. Scott, that a trooper took the guidon from Sergeant O'Hara before running to the timber. Although his body was never identified, both Pigford and Sergeant Ryan reported that O'Hara's charred head was found suspended by a wire from a tripod inside a tepee in the abandoned village. See Dale T. Schoenberger "End of Custer" pages 100 and 288.

[61] When Sergeant White was wounded, Lieutenant DeRudio borrowed his carbine to fire at the Indians. See Charles K. Mills "Charles C. DeRudio" page 26. Apparently DeRudio "freelanced" throughout the engagement. Although assigned to Company A, we find him on the firing line with Company M. Further evidence of his unwillingness to remain with his troop will be forthcoming. Sergeant White, who reached the bluffs as part of the Herendeen party, would help care for the wounded during the siege. See Kenneth Hammer "Little Big Horn Biographies" page 51. Private Daniel Newell recalled White "... *had a glassful of jelly in his bags and each wounded man got a small spoonful of that.*" See John M. Carroll "The Sunshine Magazine Articles" page 13.

[62] By a strange twist of fate, these same cottonwoods would be used in the construction of Fort Custer. See Cyrus Townsend Brady "Indian Fights and Fighters" page 391.

[63] See John M. Carroll "Custer's Chief of Scouts" page 113.

[64] See Colonel W. A. Graham "Reno Court of Inquiry" page 80.

[65] Private Theodore W. Goldin, Company G, claimed to have carried a written message from Custer to Reno. Goldin claimed he never knew the contents of the message and Reno put the message in his pocket after reading it. Over the years, Goldin's story changed many times as to when and where he joined Reno's command. It is possible that he began the day with the Custer column as Private Henry Petring, Company G, was adamant Goldin was not in the valley fight and Corporal John E. Hammon, Company G, was equally sure he wasn't with the pack train. If Goldin did

indeed begin the day with Custer, it is highly unlikely he joined Reno's command prior to their arrival on Reno Hill. In fact, it is possible that Goldin may have been the dismounted soldier encountered on the bluffs by the Crow scouts and the member of Company G that Sergeant Ferdinand A. Culbertson, Company A, found hiding in the brush on the side of bluffs. If such a message from Custer to Reno existed, it has been lost to history. See Larry Skenlar "Private Theodore W. Goldin: Too Soon Discredited?" pages 11 and 15.

[66] Although Captain French was the senior captain in the valley fight, apparently only Captain Moylan was consulted about the movement prior to its execution. See Barry C. Johnson "A Captain of Chivalric Courage" page 19.

[67] See Ronald H. Nichols "Reno Court of Inquiry" page 563.

[68] See Ronald H. Nichols "Reno Court of Inquiry" page 585. As is the case in a great portion of his understandably self–serving testimony, Reno exaggerates his relationship with Custer. While both served with the Army of the Potomac, it is doubtful that Reno knew *"him throughout the war."* What is most likely is that along about the summer of 1863 Reno became aware of Custer's reputation.

[69] Varnum testified that, at the time the command left the timber, they were taking a heavy fire in their rear from warriors on the east bank. While there no doubt were warriors firing into the rear of the command, it must be noted that, if the skirmish line were deployed behind the bank, the timber would serve to screen the command's rear. It should also be noted that no steps were taken to return this fire from the east bank. See Colonel W. A. Graham "The Reno Court of Inquiry" page 51.

[70] Although there may have been more, we know of only 3 casualties, all fatalities, in the timber. All of these were sustained while the command was mounting in preparation for the retreat and should therefore be tallied against the retreat.

[71] The officers were split in their opinion on the matter. Benteen and Weir, who were not in the valley fight, told Hare, while the dead were being buried on June 28, they believed Reno should have remained in the bottom. Hare, who had survived the valley fight, disagreed. See Tom O'Neil "Mysteries Solved, Mysteries Unsolved" page 22. The foregoing is typical of the officer accounts, those who were in the valley fight supported Reno's decision to withdraw, while those who were not in the valley criticized the decision.

[72] See Fred H. Werner "The Beecher Island Battle" pages 41 and 66.

[73] Indian accounts list only one casualty during this phase of the fighting, the Uncpapa Young Black Moon (aka Flying Charge). See Richard G. Hardorff "Hokahey! A Good Day To Die!" pages 42 and 135. Several authors have confused him with Chief Black Moon who was not killed in the fighting, surrendering his band at Standing Rock Agency in 1881. In any event, the minimal casualties on both sides prior to Reno's retreat indicates the position could have been held for an extended period.

[74] For a prime example, witness the Kidder Massacre. See E. A. Brininstool "Troopers With Custer" page 329. Reno was not totally without experience with Indians, having chased Indians on the Great Plains, rescued some survivors of an Indian attack and even captured some Indians in the northwest before the Civil War. According to his career list of battles and skirmishes, as compiled by the Adjutant General's office, however, Little Big Horn was his first time under fire against Indians. See Dale T. Schoenberger "End of Custer" page 79.

[75] See Colonel John Gibbon "Arms To Fight Indians" page 15.

[76] See Cyrus Townsend Brady "Indian Fights and Fighters" page 239. At the court of inquiry, Reno would invoke the action at Beecher's Island in an attempt to support his claim that the timber could not be held. It is probable some members of the court realized Reno's position in the timber was much stronger than was the scout's on Beecher's Island, but they failed to press the matter. Crook's aide, Lieutenant Bourke, was less tolerant of Reno's actions, writing: *"Reno saved, more by luck than good management, the remnant of the 7th Cavalry at the Custer Massacre. He saw enough at that fight to scare him for the rest of his life. He will never make a bold movement for ten years to come."* See Mark H. Brown "The Plainsmen of the Yellowstone" page 288.

[77] See John M. Carroll "Custer's Chief of Scouts" page 114.

[78] See Neil C. Mangum "Reno's Battalion in the Battle of the Little Big Horn" page 5.

[79] See Thomas B. Marquis "Keep the Last Bullet For Yourself" page 54.

[80] Indian accounts differ as to whether Crazy Horse or Gall is to be credited with encouraging the warriors to infiltrate the timber. It is believed that this group included Crooked Nose, Old Man, and Young Turkey Leg of the Cheyenne as well as the fourteen year old Uncpapa Iron Hawk. See Peter John Powell "People of the Sacred Mountain" page 1014 and Richard G. Hardorff "Lakota Recollections of the Custer Fight" pages 64 – 65.

[81] It is probable that Bloody Knife was mounted at the time of his death and that Herendeen's memory was faulty on that point. See Ben Innis "Bloody Knife!" page 139.

[82] Actually two troopers, Henry Klotzbucher and George Lorentz, both of Company M, were hit in addition to the Arikara scout Bloody Knife. Klotzbucher, clerk of Company M and Captain French's striker, yelled out as he was hit: *"Oh, my God! I have got it."* See Richard G. Hardorff "The Custer Battle Casualties" pages 137 – 139. At various times Private William E. Morris claimed that either Lorentz, or Klotzbucher, but never both, had been wounded as the retreat was starting and he had helped in getting the man under cover. Since he never mentions the ministrations of Dr. Porter to the wounded man, but does indicate that after the battle they found Klotzbucher's body unmolested where they had left him, it is probable that Morris and his comrades attended to Klotzbucher while Dr. Porter ministered to Lorentz.

[83] See Colonel W. A. Graham "Reno Court of Inquiry" pages 82 – 83. Many authorities believe it was the blood and brains of Bloody Knife spattering into Reno's face that precipitated the panic movement.

[84] See E.A. Brininstool "Troopers With Custer" page 131.

[85] Second Lieutenant Charles Francis Roe, Company F, 2nd Cavalry, maintained an officer of the 7th Cavalry confirmed Herendeen's account. Unfortunately, Roe did not divulge the officer's name. See Charles Francis Roe "Custer's Last Battle" page 9.

[86] See Colonel W. A. Graham "The Custer Myth" page 265.

[87] See George Bird Grinnell "The Fighting Cheyennes" page 355.

[88] For a complete treatment of the issue, See Richard G. Hardorff "The Custer Battle Casualties" pages 153 – 154 and Ben Innis "Bloody Knife!" pages 141 - 143.

[89] See Donald R. Morris "The Washing of the Spears" page 378.

[90] See Ronald H. Nichols "Reno Court of Inquiry" pages 217 – 218.

[91] See Ronald H. Nichols "Reno Court of Inquiry" pages 233 – 234.

[92] While most authorities credit this statement to Varnum, Charles Kuhlman believes the officer in question was Lieutenant Wallace. See "Legend Into History" page 69.

[93] See Charles K. Mills "Harvest of Barren Regrets" page 261.

[94] See John M. Carroll "Custer's Chief of Scouts" page 66 – 67.

[95] See Ronald H. Nichols "Reno Court of Inquiry" page 281.

[96] See Ronald H. Nichols "Reno Court of Inquiry" page 191.

[97] See Ronald H. Nichols "Reno Court of Inquiry" pages 619 – 620.

[98] A large, perhaps as many as one half, portion of G was initially left in the woods.

[99] Private Elihu F. Clear brought Hare his horse. This was the first intimation Hare had that the command was leaving. Assigned as orderly to Dr. DeWolf, Clear was killed along with the doctor while ascending the bluffs during the retreat.

[100] Per their usual practice when confronted by an aggressive movement, the Indians initially retreated when Reno broke from the timber. When they saw the soldiers were actually running away, it was the Indians who charged. See Thomas B. Marquis "Wooden Leg: A Warrior Who Fought Custer" page 220.

[101] In his court of inquiry testimony, Reno, after stating that it would have taken six or seven hundred men to hold the timber position, dismissed the subject of his wounded as follows:

"I suppose the Indians killed the wounded left in the timber. I could make no effort to take them out; and none was made. I do not know what became of the wounded left on the plain; the Indians would not permit me to take care of them." See Colonel W. A. Graham "Reno Court of Inquiry" page 226.

[102] An additional point could have been made here, that the command was forced to attempt a panic crossing of the river at an almost unfordable location. The east bank was so high, around 8 feet, that many horses and men fell back into the river, crashing into those crowding below them. Varnum himself almost slid off over his mount's rump. See Time Life Books "The Soldiers" page 214.

[103] See John Upton Terrell and Colonel George Walton "Faint the Trumpet Sounds" pages 36 – 37. Reno commented in a letter dated July 4, 1876: *". . . never saw during the whole war, such an awful fire."* See E. Elden Davis and James W. Wengert MD "That Fatal Day" page 14.

[104] I am not sure that Reno's actions may properly be labeled as "combat fatigue". As he, apparently, regained command function in a relatively short time, the condition seems to have been temporary in nature. The fact that his conduct in the hilltop fight was uninspiring and he abrogated his authority to a more capable subordinate, Benteen, is, in my opinion, more a question of personal style and interest than of continuing to experience the numbing melancholia effects of classic "combat fatigue" cases. Further, given his exceptional civil war record, I am unable to conclude the cause was cowardice.

[105] See George Bird Grinnell papers.

[106] See Richard G. Hardorff "Lakota Recollections of the Custer Fight" page 53.

[107] See Dale T. Schoenberger "End of Custer" pages 110 - 111.

[108] The carbine was attached to a sling–belt worn over the left shoulder, the barrel of the carbine being inserted into a 2 3/4 inch diameter, 2 1/2 inch length round leather socket suspended from the off side of the McClellan saddle. See Daniel O. Magnussen "Peter Thompson's Narrative of the Little Bighorn Campaign 1876" Page 37.

[109] See Thomas B. Marquis "Wooden Leg: A Warrior Who Fought Custer" pages 220 – 222.

[110] See E. Elden Davis and James W. Wengert MD "That Fatal Day" page 7.

[111] See Margot Liberty and John Stands in Timber "Cheyenne Memories" page 200. There are numerous accounts that indicate Reno's column, acting more like a mob than a military unit, actually retreated along two different routes. For an excellent synopsis of this evidence, the reader is referred to James Brust " Lt. Oscar Long's Early Map Details Terrain, Battle Positions" pages 11 -12.

[112] See Peter John Powell "People of the Sacred Mountain" page 1015.

[113] It is not possible to obtain precise figures on Indian casualties. Each individual had multiple names and would often be known by different names to different bands. In addition to the problems associated with an oral history tradition, the culture was not one to place any importance upon "rosters" and other such lists. As a result, in Appendix 9 I have only been able to document the presence of 389 different Indians at the battle. While the list undoubtedly contains some duplications, it represents only a small fraction of the Indians actually present. Despite these difficulties, it is highly improbable that the Indians suffered significantly more casualties than reported here.

[114] See Colonel W. A. Graham "Reno Court of Inquiry" page 91. Captain Walter Clifford, Company E, 7th Infantry, wrote in his diary of Reno's retreat: *"Had the pursuers been white men, hardly one of the fleeing party could have reached the summit unhurt."* See Michael J. Koury "Diaries of the Little Big Horn" page 47.

[115] See Grinnell Interviews.

[116] See John M. Carroll "The Benteen – Goldin Letters on Custer and His Last Battle" pages 47 – 48.

[117] See Joseph Mills Hanson "The Conquest of the Missouri" page 295.

[118] See Walter Camp "Custer in '76" page 112.

[119] See Walter Camp "Custer in '76" page 223.

[120] The Oglala Eagle Elk said that Dorman was killed by the Uncpapa Her Eagle Robe who succeeded in shooting Dorman after her gun initially misfired. See Richard G. Hardorff "Lakota Recollections of the Custer Fight" page 102.

[121] See Walter Camp "Custer in '76" pages 223 – 224.

[122] See Walter Camp "Custer in '76" page 224. A very complete discussion of the condition of Dorman's body and why the mutilation of his legs must have occurred while he still lived is presented in W. Boyes "Custer's Black White Man" pages 38 – 42 and Richard G. Hardorff "Lakota Recollections of the Custer Fight" page 102.

[123] See Stanley Vestal "Sitting Bull" page 165 – 166.

[124] The identity of this warrior has not been established, but the Two Kettle Chased By Owls, and Uncpapas Swift Bear, and White Buffalo Bull, brothers of Crow King, were killed between the timber and river during Reno's retreat.

[125] See Richard Upton "The Custer Adventure" page 115.

[126] See John M. Carroll "The Benteen – Golden Letters" page 44. David Humphreys Miller states McIntosh's horse was shot as he attempted to leave the timber, and he obtained McCormick's mount at that time. See "Custer's Fall" pages 105 – 106.

[127] See John M. Carroll "The Sunshine Magazine Articles" page 10.

[128] Scollin's real name was Henry Cody. See John M. Carroll "Troopers With Custer." For consistency among sources, I have retained the name carried on the muster rolls. On June 24th, Scollin had told his bunkmate Newell *"If anything happens to me, notify my sister Mary, who lives in Gardiner, Massachusetts. My name is Henry Cody."* After the fight, Newell recovered Scollin's prayer book, *The Key of Heaven*, from his saddlebag. Newell mailed the prayer book to the sister, lying about the mutilation of her brother's body when questioned by return mail, but did not recover the diary: *"I would have given most anything if I could have recovered his diary, but I suppose the squaws got that when they stripped his body. Poor boy."* See Evan S. Connell "Son of the Morning Star" page 6.

[129] See Walter Camp "Custer in '76" page 131.

[130] See John M. Carroll "A Seventh Cavalry Scrapbook" page 20.

[131] See Charles Kuhlman "Legend Into History" apge 68.

[132] See E. S. Godfrey "Custer's Last Battle 1876" page 25.

[133] See Charles K. Mills "Harvest of Barren Regrets" page 260. While there is no denying French's valor under fire, he did not completely discharge his responsibilities as an officer during the retreat. Once across the Little Big Horn, it was incumbent upon either Moylan or French to cover the

crossing of the trailing company, "G." There is no evidence that either officer attempted to form such a line.

[134] Dr. Charles E. McChesney, army surgeon and later an acting Indian agent, working from the description of Red Horse, was able to identify this man as Captain French. See John G. Neihardt "The Sixth Grandfather" page 182.

[135] As senior captain in the valley fight, French would have assumed command had Reno become incapacitated.

[136] See Barry C.Johnson "A Captain of Chivalric Courage" pages 17 – 18 and Colonel W. A. Graham "The Custer Myth" pages 341 – 342. Whether French really seriously considered shooting Reno at the time of the retreat is highly questionable. After the full story came out, including Reno's plan to abandon his wounded on the night of the 25th, many officers of the 7th became very bitter toward Reno. Moylan, who was such a staunch supporter of Reno at the court of inquiry, thought Reno was correct in leaving the timber but *"of his personal conduct in the bottom or subsequently on the hill the least said the better."* Speaking of the charge Reno had intended to abandon his wounded, Moylan would say that if the charge were true: *". . . then Reno ought to have been shot."* See Colonel W. A. Graham "The Custer Myth" page 335.

[137] Reno maintained that Hodgson was first wounded, in the waist, in the timber. There may be confirmation of this in the account of Private Thomas W. Coleman, Company B, who claimed that when he buried Hodgson on the 27th, he noticed three wounds, one by arrow and two by ball. See Jud Tuttle "Who Buried Lieutenant Hodgson?" page 15 and Thomas W. Coleman "Coleman Diary" pages 19 – 20.

[138] See E. A. Brininstool "Troopers With Custer" page 52. While private Morris also claimed to have been the one assisting Hodgson across the stream, and Cyrus Townsend Brady credits Sergeant Criswell with the feat, the preponderance of evidence favors "Bounce" Fisher.

[139] See Peter John Powell "People of the Sacred Mountain" page 1016.

[140] See Cyrus Townsend Brady "Indian Fights and Fighters" page 242. While Brady credits Criswell with assisting Hodgson across the river, there is no evidence that he had been detached from his company. It is probable that the acts, cited above, for which he was decorated, occurred after the pack train had joined Reno's command on the hill, and that Criswell braved sniper fire from across the river.

[141] See Dale T. Schoenberger "Custer's Scouts" page 47. This may have been the Cheyenne Old Man. Peter John Powell believed Old Man's killer to have been Bloody Knife, but, as the account shows Old Man was killed during a running fight with an Arikara scout, Bloody Knife could not have been the scout mentioned. See Peter John Powell "People of the Sacred Mountain" page 1014.

[142] See Dale T. Schoenberger "Custer's Scouts" page 47.

[143] See Richard G. Hardorff "Hokahey! A Good Day To Die!" page 126.

[144] See Richard G. Hardorff "Lakota Recollections of the Custer Fight" page 103.

[145] See Richard G. Hardorff "Lakota Recollections of the Custer Fight" page 110.

[146] Ironically, the brother of Bob Tailed Bull and Little Brave, had been captured some years previously by the Cheyenne. Known as Plenty Crows, he fought in the battle that claimed the lives of his two brothers.

[147] See Richard G. Hardorff "Lakota Recollections of the Custer Fight" page 103.

[148] See Richard G. Hardorff "The Custer Battle Casualties" pages 154 – 155 and John S. Gray "Custer's Last Campaign" pages 304 – 305. Note that Little Brave's horse also returned riderless to Reno Hill. There are indications that Bob Tailed Bull may have killed the Oglala White Eagle at the foot of Reno Hill. See Richard G. Hardorff "Lakota Recollections of the Custer Fight" page 110.

[149] See Elizabeth Atwood Lawrence "His Very Silence Speaks" page 210. Although Lawrence says the Arikara oral tradition names this pony as belonging to Little Brave, it was probably the mount of Bob Tailed Bull as his horse was spotted and carried a saddle resembling an army saddle.

[150] See Neil C. Mangum "Reno's Battalion in the Battle of the Little Big Horn" page 7.

[151] See Thomas B. Marquis "Wooden Leg: A Warrior Who Fought Custer " page 224. Note that when White Swan reached Reno Hill he had sustained wounds in both the right hand and leg. From the accounts, it does not seem possible for Whirlwind to have inflicted both wounds. While he might have successfully defended himself with an injured hand, it is most likely that White Swan suffered the leg wound prior to crossing the river and that Whirlwind's shot injured his hand. Note that Richard G. Hardorff names Bob Tailed Bull as the slayer of Whirlwind. See "Lakota Recollections of the Custer Fight" page 103.

[152] See Cyrus Townsend Brady "Indian Fights and Fighters" page 404.

[153] This soldier is listed as Clear on the monument and muster rolls, but other documents, and Godfrey's assertion that Clear was an assumed name, indicate his real name may have been Clair. Thomas Marquis claimed to have received the following account in a 1929 letter from Godfrey: *". . . Godfrey knew he was a gambler. On the night of June 21, at the mouth of the Rosebud River, Clair came to Godfrey's tent and asked Godfrey to accept $320 for safekeeping. After some hesitation and conversational exchange, Godfrey took the money. Four days later, Clair was killed in the Reno fight. Godfrey had some trouble in disposing of the money and finally turned it over to the army paymaster."* See Thomas B. Marquis "Keep the Last Bullet For Yourself" page 49.

[154] See John M. Carroll "Custer's Chief of Scouts" page 67. Although not mentioned by Varnum, Clear was killed along with DeWolf.

[155] See John G. Neihardt "The Sixth Grandfather" page 183.

[156] See Colonel W. A. Graham "Reno Court of Inquiry" page 104. William E. Morris shed further light on the situation when he recalled: *"Here I saw one of the bravest deeds of the day. Reno, like most of the rest of us, was stampeded, and with what head he had, was trying to hunt out the highest bluff on which to make a stand. Capt. Moylan had started to continue on his own hook, with what was left of his men from the retreat ordered by Reno. Lieut. Hare, who had passed me on his fast horse across the stream, yelled out with a voice that could be heard all over the field: 'If we've got to die, let's die like men. I'm a fighting – from Texas.' Then turning to Moylan he called out: 'Don't run off like a pack of whipped curs.'*

"That gave Reno the cue and recovering himself, he said, 'Captain Moylan, dismount those men.' Moylan didn't obey at once, and Reno repeated the order. So A Troop dismounted and deployed as skirmishers." See E. Elden Davis and James W. Wengert MD "That Fatal Day" page 27.

[157] See Colonel W. A. Graham "Reno Court of Inquiry" page 119.

[158] See E. S. Godfrey "Custer's Last Battle 1876" page 24.

[159] See Colonel W. A. Graham "Reno Court of Inquiry" page 133.

[160] See O. G. Libby "The Arikara Narrative" page 128 and Colonel W. A. Graham "The Custer Myth" page 41.

This painting was made by White Bird, 15-year-old Northern Cheyenne participant in the battle. All three actions: Custer Fight, Reno's Valley Fight, and the Hilltop Fight are depicted, as well as two of the major topographical features: Medicine Tail Coulee and Reno Creek. *Photo Courtesy Little Bighorn Battlefield National Monument.*

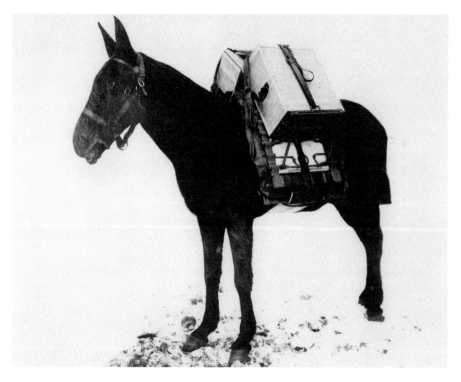

Army pack mule laden with ammunition boxes. Each box held 1,000 rounds of carbine ammunition. While pack trains, especially those comprised of specially selected and trained mules, made the army much more mobile in their pursuit of Indians, they were still no match for what Custer termed the finest light cavalry in the world. *Photo Courtesy Little Bighorn Battlefield National Monument.*

Chapter 14

Benteen Joins Reno

As noted in Chapter 12, Benteen concluded his scout and joined the trail followed by the Custer and Reno detachments a little above a large marshy area, or morass. Benteen took advantage of this opportunity to water his horses. Despite the fact he had clearly been ordered on a reconnaissance, Benteen did not dispatch a messenger to Custer with the results of the completed scout.[1] During this watering stop, Lieutenant Edgerly noticed Boston Custer passing the detachment on his way to rejoin his brother's command.[2] Godfrey described the watering stop in his *Century Magazine* article:

> *"While watering we heard some firing in advance,[3] and Weir became a little impatient at the delay of watering and started off with his troop, taking the advance,[4] whereas his place in column was second. The rest of the battalion moved out very soon afterward and soon caught up with him. Just as we were leaving the water-hole the pack-train was arriving, and the poor thirsty mules plunged into the morass in spite of the efforts of the packers to prevent them. . ."[5]*

Godfrey would testify at the Reno court of inquiry that the water stop took between 20 and 30 minutes. This timing, which is used in the timing analysis presented in Appendix 12, correlates quite well with future events using the standard rates of march for cavalry.

About an hour and a half after leaving the morass, Benteen's battalion passed the lone tepee.[6] Within the next mile, Sergeant Kanipe reported to Captain Benteen with Custer's first message. Although he was not called to testify at the Reno court of inquiry, the accounts Kanipe gave in later years are quite clear: his primary mission was to order the pack train forward to the protection of the main command; he was also to speed Benteen to the front should that detachment be encountered.[7] Benteen would not acknowledge disobeying that order, maintaining that Kanipe's message was solely for the pack train and he therefore directed the sergeant to that detachment. Since Custer had an unobstructed view of the upper valley of the Little Big Horn from Wooden Leg Ridge, he knew there was no village in that direction and therefore Benteen's reconnaissance could not discover a large enemy force. Armed with this knowledge, failure to recall Benteen at that juncture would make no sense. It is therefore almost certain that Kanipe was indeed ordered to hurry Benteen along as well as have the packs press forward. Benteen's statement may reflect either an honest misunderstanding of Kanipe's message, or the beginning of a sulking episode, or an attempt to divert attention from his disobedience. The argument in support of an honest misunderstanding of orders is found in Lieutenant Edgerly's court of inquiry testimony:

> *"A sergeant of C Company came back from General Custer's command and gave General Custer's compliments to Captain Benteen and he wanted him to bring up the packs. Captain Benteen said he thought he had made a mistake, that Captain McDougall was in charge of the pack train and showed him the place and he went."[8]*

On the other hand, Benteen may have been sulking because he felt Custer had left him out of the fight yet again.[9] As Godfrey related:

> *". . . as he (Kanipe, DCE) passed the column he said to the men, 'We've got 'em, boys.' From this and other remarks **we inferred that Custer had attacked and captured the village** . (emphasis the author's)"*

This may explain why Benteen did not comply with the order to increase his rate of march. Appendix 12 clearly shows that Benteen must have proceeded at the same walk pace initiated upon leaving the morass until the arrival of Custer's second messenger, Trumpeter John Martin. Private Morris recalled Benteen moved at a pace *". . . as slow as though he were going to a funeral. . ."*[10] Benteen would acknowledge he had not ordered a trot prior to the arrival of Trumpeter Martin, claiming there was no need as his horse walked at 5 miles per hour.[11] Interestingly, both Captain McDougall and Lieutenant Mathey, by that time a captain, would testify that they never received such a message[12] although Kanipe's presence with the pack train is well established. While the pack train was not brought *"across country"* as ordered, the analysis of Appendix 12 shows a dramatic increase in the rate of march of the pack train between the time it left the morass and the time it arrived on Reno Hill. This increased gait can only be attributed to the receipt of Kanipe's message. Discussion of Benteen's disobedience of orders will be deferred to Chapter 20.

From Wooden Leg Ridge Custer had an unobstructed view of the upper valley as well as Reno's skirmish line. He could not, however, see much of the village that lined the west bank of the river for perhaps another 2 or 3 miles. After dispatching Kanipe, Custer therefore continued northward toward the highest point in view on the east side of the river. Ascending this elevation, now known as Weir Point, Custer was able, for the first time, to comprehend the magnitude of the task at hand. Instead of a simple village, he beheld a mighty city laid out along the west bank of the Little Big Horn. Reno's small command could not possibly successfully contend with the horde of warriors contained in a village of such magnitude. Reno must be relieved in short order. The anticipated victory would require every available man in the regiment. Custer now became concerned over his first messenger dispatched only a few minutes previously. If Kanipe failed to come upon Benteen prior to reaching the pack–train, Benteen's 118 men might be out to the fight entirely. The recall of Benteen's battalion could not be left to chance. Trumpeter John Martin, of Benteen's own Company H, recalled:

> *". . . Then the General took me with him, and we rode to the top of the hill, where we could see the village in the valley on the other side of the river. It was a big village, but we couldn't see it all from there, though we didn't know it then;[13] but several hundred tepees were in plain sight.*

> *"There were no bucks to be seen; all we could see was some squaws and children playing and a few dogs and ponies. The General seemed both surprised and glad, and said the Indians must be in their tents, asleep.[14]*

> *"We did not see anything of Reno's column when we were up on the hill.[15] I am sure the General did not see them at all, because he looked all around with his glasses, and all he said was that we had 'got them this time.'*

> *"He turned in the saddle and took off his hat and waved it[16] so the men of the command, who were halted at the base of the hill, could see him, and he shouted to them, 'Hurrah, boys, we've got them! We'll finish them up and then go home to our station.'*

"Then the General and I rode back down to where the troops were, and he talked a minute with the Adjutant, telling him what he had seen. We rode on, pretty fast, until we came to a big ravine that led in the direction of the river, and the General pointed down there and then called me. This was about a mile down the river from where we went up on the hill, and we had been going at a trot and gallop all the way. It must have been about three miles from where we left Reno's trail.[17]

"The General said to me, 'Orderly, I want you to take a message to Colonel Benteen. Ride as fast as you can and tell him to hurry. Tell him it's a big village and I want him to be quick, and to bring the ammunition packs.' He didn't stop at all when he was telling me this, and I just said, 'Yes, sir,' and checked my horse, when the Adjutant said, 'Wait, orderly, I'll give you a message.' and he stopped and wrote it in a big hurry, in a little book, and then tore out the leaf and gave it to me.

"And then he told me, 'Now, orderly, ride as fast as you can to Colonel Benteen. Take the same trail we came down. If you have time, and there is no danger, come back; but otherwise stay with your company.'[18]

With Custer's famous last message, *"Benteen. Come on. Big village. Be quick, bring packs. W. W. Cooke. (P. S. Bring pac–s),"*[19] safely tucked in his pocket, Martin spurred to the rear as fast as his tired mount would carry him. With the dispatch of Martin, and accounting for Reno's casualties and missing in the valley fight, the assignments of personnel and battalion strengths were as depicted in Tables 14 – 1 and 14 – 2 (for Reno's battalion A means available, K Killed, W wounded, and M missing). When in the vicinity of Weir Point, Martin encountered the General's brother, Boston:

"Just before I got to the hill I met Boston Custer. He was riding at a run, but when he saw me he checked his horse and shouted 'Where's the General?' and I answered, pointing back of me, 'Right behind that next ridge you'll find him.' And he dashed on. That was the last time he was ever seen alive."[20]

Martin mentioned seeing Indians firing at Custer and waving buffalo robes. Although he was unaware of it at the time, Martin's horse was wounded by this firing. From Martin's various accounts it is unclear whether this took place shortly before, or immediately after, the meeting with Boston Custer. In any event, Boston was able to join his brother as his body was found on the Custer Battlefield. This meeting of Boston Custer and Martin also establishes that Benteen was only about a half hour behind Custer when he received Martin's message (see Appendix 12).[21]

Continuing on the back trail, Martin met Benteen, riding in advance of his battalion, about two miles west of the lone tepee. It must have come as a surprise to Benteen to encounter a second messenger from Custer within a mile of the first. Benteen scanned the message, then handed it to Captain Weir. Lieutenant Edgerly told Walter Camp that after reading Cooke's message Benteen was heard to remark: *"Well! If he wants me in a hurry, how does he expect that I can bring the packs? If I am going to be of service to him I think I had better not wait for the packs. . ."*[22] Lieutenant Edgerly, who said he had also been shown the message (probably by his commander, Captain Weir) supported Benteen's position in his court of inquiry testimony: *"The remark was made by someone, either by Captain Weir or myself, that he could not possibly want us to go for the packs as Captain McDougall was there and would bring them up."*[23]

Benteen's and Martin's recollection of the meeting differ markedly. Benteen testified at the court of inquiry that Martin told him *". . . the Indians were all skedaddling, therefore there was less necessity for me going back for the packs."*[24] Benteen, when questioned about his rate of march after meeting Martin, testified: *"I don't think the gait was increased as we were going as fast as we could without going at a gallop, but **I gave the command 'trot.'** (emphasis the author's) I don't think it increased the gait at all. Martin has testified that I sent him back to the pack train. I did no such thing, if he went back to the pack train he went there of his own accord."*[25] It is of interest to note that Mathey also apparently felt the gait of his command could not be increased, as he would testify at the court of inquiry that loose packs did not slow his rate of march as he would leave two troopers to repack the offending mule while the balance of the train continued forward.[26]

Martin's recollection of events was that he never told Benteen the Indians were skedaddling, rather that Custer was three miles away and under attack.[27] This is substantially the same story Martin told Colonel Graham, but it differs in marked respects from his testimony at the court of inquiry. Martin's testimony omitted all reference to Boston Custer, stating he did not stop from the time he was handed the message by Cooke until he reached Benteen. He also testified that, in response to a question from Benteen regarding Custer's whereabouts, he had told Benteen he supposed Custer had charged through the village by that time. He further testified Benteen had ordered him to go to McDougall, only about 150 yards in Benteen's rear, to hurry the packs along.[28]

In terms of what Martin told Benteen when he delivered Custer's message, it appears that Benteen's recollection is more valid than Martin's as Edgerly testified at the court of inquiry: *"I heard him (Martin, DCE) speak to the orderly behind Captain Benteen. He was laughing and seemed very much elated, said it was the biggest village he ever saw,[29] that they had found the Indians all asleep in their tepees, that Major Reno was charging it and killing everything, men, women and children."*[30] While it would have been necessary for Benteen to send a messenger to the pack train in order to comply with his written orders, it seems he did not do so as neither Lieutenant Mathey nor Captain McDougall mentioned receiving any such message. In any event, the analysis of Appendix 12 clearly shows that, regardless of the testimony, the rate of march of Benteen's column was increased after the arrival of Martin.

Shortly after increasing his rate of march, Benteen came to the point in the trail where Custer's command diverted toward the north while Reno's continued toward the river. Lieutenant Gibson recalled Benteen remarking: *"Here we have the two horns of a dilemma."*[31] Incredibly, rather than ask Trumpeter Martin which trail should be followed[32] to reach Custer, Weir and Company D started off on the left hand (Reno's) trail while the other two companies followed the right hand (Custer's) trail. Benteen, accompanied by his orderly, rode between the two diverging detachments.[33] Godfrey related:

> *"We now heard firing, first straggling shots, and as we advanced the engagement became more and more pronounced and appeared to be coming toward us. The column took the gallop with pistols drawn, expecting to meet the enemy which we thought Custer was driving before him in his effort to communicate with the pack–train, never suspecting that our force had been defeated. We were forming in line to meet our supposed enemy, when we came in full view of the valley of the Little Big Horn."*[34]

And what a sight they beheld! The smoke and dust choked valley was literally filled with mounted warriors; Benteen and his officers estimating the number of warriors at 700 to 900. While the major portion of Reno's demoralized force climbed the bluffs in a mad dash to escape their pursuers, a small detachment of about a dozen men deployed in skirmish order at the ford. Despite their officers' failure to attempt to cover the panic recrossing of the Little Big Horn, these doomed men courageously held their line on the west bank, buying the precious time necessary for their comrades to escape.[35] As Benteen recalled:

"There I saw an engagement going on and I supposed it was the whole regiment. There were twelve or thirteen men in skirmish line that appeared to have been beaten back. The line was then parallel with the river and the Indians were charging and recharging through those men. I thought the whole command was thrashed, and that was not a good place to cross."[36]

While we can never know with certainty, who commanded that valiant little detail, Sergeant Edward Botzer of Company G was killed at the retreat ford and may have been the non–commissioned officer responsible for organizing the heroic covering of the crossing.[37]

Turning aside from his embattled comrades without the slightest regret for failing to render them assistance, Benteen *". . . noticed 3 or 4 Indians, probably 4[00] or 500 yards from me. I thought they were hostiles and rode with my orderly towards them, and saw as I approached them that they were Crows.[38] They said there was a big 'pooh poohing' going on, which I had already seen. Then I saw the men who were up on the bluff and I immediately went there, and was met by Major Reno."[39]*

As Benteen neared Reno's position on the bluffs, his battalion was mistaken for Custer's column and the demoralized and beleaguered[40] troops raised a cheer for their perceived deliverance.[41] When Benteen reached the position, Reno rushed forward to meet him, exclaiming: *"For God's sake, Benteen, halt your command and help me. I've lost half my men."[42]* While Reno must have gone on to describe the action in the valley, Benteen would maintain: *"Reno did not explain to me why he had retreated from the river bottom to the hill."[43]*

In reality, Reno had lost much more than his casualties (lists of 7th Cavalry casualties by organization and by engagement are provided in Appendix 2). As we shall see, he had lost both the desire and ability to command, as noted by Dr. Porter: *"Reno was the ranking officer, but Benteen appeared to be the officer actually in command."[44]* Reno, who had lost his hat and firearms during the retreat, was not the only officer to have lost his composure. Varnum, who had tried unsuccessfully to steam the stampede to the bluffs, along with Reno, was "excitedly" firing at warriors well out of range.[45] Moylan, the only officer to claim his portion of the retreat was accomplished in a military manner, was reportedly in tears.[46] Private Windolph would note that *"Reno and all his officers and men were, excited, mad, and bewildered."[47]* Lieutenant Hare rushed up to his friend Godfrey and, clasping his hand *"heartily, said with a good deal of emphasis: 'We've had a big fight in the bottom, got whipped, and I am —— glad to see you.'"[48]*

The hilltop position was far from secure as the Lakota were still in force in the bottom opposing the bluff. While the warriors were momentarily content to strip and mutilate Reno's dead, they represented a serious threat.[49] Benteen ordered skirmishers forward to clear the bluffs of the various small parties of warriors and establish a defensive perimeter. That duty accomplished, Benteen showed Reno his message from Cooke and expressed the opinion that they should immediately move to junction with Custer;[50] heavy firing already being heard from downstream.[51] According to Trumpeter Martin, the excited Reno could only blurt out: *"Well I have lost about half of my men, and I could do no better than I have done."[52]* Reno, acknowledging at the court of inquiry that Benteen had shown him Custer's message, testified: *"It did not occur to me that Custer with 225 men needed anyone quickly . . ."[53]*

Unit of Origin	Custer's Command	Reno's Command (A/K/W/M)	Benteen's Command	Pack Train & Escort
Headquarters				
Officers (3)	2	1/0/0/0		
Non Comms (1)	1			
Enlisted (1)	1			
Medical (3)	1	1/1/0/0		
Civilians (2)	2			
Guides (3)	1	0/1/0/0		1
Interpreters (2)	0	0/1/0/1		
Courier (1)	0	0/0/0/1		
Company A				
Officers (3)	0	2/0/0/1		
Non Comms (9)		7/1/1/0		1
Enlisted (40)		27/6/1/0		6
Company B				
Officers (2)		0/1/0/0		1
Non Comms (7)				7
Enlisted (41)		1/0/0/0		40
Company C				
Officers (2)	2			
Non Comms (8)	6			2
Enlisted (43)	37			6
Company D				
Officers (2)			2	
Non Comms (5)			4	1
Enlisted (45)			39	6
Company E				
Officers (2)	2			
Non Comms (8)	7			1
Enlisted (37)	30	2/0/0/0		5
Company F				
Officers (2)	2			
Non Comms (8)	7			1
Enlisted (41)	28	2/0/0/0		11
Company G				
Officers (2)	0	1/1/0/0		
Non Comms (8)		4/3/0/0		1
Enlisted (36)	1	8/8/0/13		6
Company H				
Officers (2)			2	
Non Comms (9)			8	1
Enlisted (36)	0		30	6
Company I				
Officers (2)	2			
Non Comms (6)	5			1
Enlisted (40)	32	1/0/0/0		7
Company K				
Officers (2)	0	1/0/0/0	1	
Non Comms (8)	1		6	1
Enlisted (34)		0/1/0/0	27	6
Company L				
Officers (2)	2			
Non Comms (7)	6			1
Enlisted (49)	38			11
Company M				
Officers (2)		1/0/0/0		1
Non Comms (8)		3/3/1/0		1
Enlisted (46)		28/7/4/0		7
Crow Scouts (6)	4	1/0/1/0		
Arikara Scouts (24)[54]	0	4/3/1/1		15
Lakota Scouts (5)	0	0/0/0/5		
Teamsters/Packers (12)				12
Total	**220**	**95**	**119**	**166**

Table 14 – 1 Assignments At Conclusion of Valley Fight– June 25, 1876

The firing became so heavy as Yates withdrew from Minneconjou Ford and Keogh skirmished on Luce and Blummer–Nye–Cartwright Ridges that one of the officers expressed the conviction that *"our command ought to be doing something or Custer would be after Reno with a sharp stick."*[55] After hearing two distinct volleys, someone was heard to remark: *"Custer is giving it to them for all he's worth."*[56] Captain Moylan rather prophetically added: *"Gentlemen, in my opinion General Custer has made the biggest mistake of his life, by not taking the whole regiment*

regiment in at once in the first attack."[57] The warriors in the valley also heard the firing and in moments they had sped downstream leaving the soldiers on the hilltop unopposed and unthreatened.

Command Element	Strength	Percent of Regiment
Custer's Command	**220**	**36.7**
Headquarters	7	
Scouts/Guides	5	
Civilians	2	
Keogh's Battalion	**130**	**21.7**
Company C	45	
Company I	39	
Company L	46	
Yates' Battalion	**76**	**12.7**
Company E	39	
Company F	37	
Reno's Battalion	**95**	**15.8**
Headquarters	9	
Company A	36	
Company G	13	
Company M	32	
Scouts	5	
Interpreters/Courier	0	
Benteen's Battalion	**119**	**19.8**
Company D	45	
Company H	40	
Company K	34	
Pack Train	**166**	**27.7**
Company B	48	
Mathey's Command	90	
Civilian Packers	12	
Scouts	15	
Guides	1	
Total	**600**	**100**

Table 14 – 2 Battalion Combat Strength At Conclusion of Valley Fight– June 25, 1876

Despite this lack of opposition, Reno refused to move without first replenishing his ammunition.[58] Lieutenant Hare was therefore dispatched to hurry up some of the ammunition. As his own horse had been wounded, he borrowed Godfrey's mount and galloped toward the rear.[59] Benteen, despite the heavy and prolonged firing that everyone in the command knew could only be coming from Custer's column and his direct order to *"be quick"* about rejoining his commander, assumed de facto command of Reno's battalion and settled down to await the arrival of the packs. While Lieutenant Wallace would testify at the court of inquiry that the command was concerned about Custer, he admitted: "*. . . there was a great deal of swearing about Gen. Custer's running off and leaving us.*"[60] Benteen would attempt to cover his culpability by maintaining that he believed Custer had been annihilated before Martin reached him with Custer's message. Regarding a movement down river, Benteen would testify: *"A movement could have been made down the river in the direction Custer had gone immediately upon my arrival on the hill, but we would all have been there yet.*"[61]

Reno used the respite to personally attend to the burial of his adjutant, the popular Benny Hodgson. [62] Reno was so consumed with Hodgson's death that, when Captain McDougall reported to him that he had heard heavy firing from his right upon his approach to the bluffs, he could only remark: *"Captain, I lost your Lieutenant and he is lying down there.*"[63] As the few spades that were with the regiment were with the pack train, Hodgson's burial had to be deferred, the burial party contenting themselves with retrieving some of the Lieutenant's personal property.

Captain Weir, who had moved from the morass without orders when he felt the stop too lengthy, was becoming impatient again as the sound of Custer's firing increased in volume. He asked Edgerly if he would take the troop to Custer even if none of the other companies would go. Receiving an affirmative reply, Weir set out to confront Reno. Apparently rethinking his position, and wanting to get a better appreciation of the situation, Weir, without talking to either Reno or Benteen,[64] mounted and, accompanied by his orderly, set out toward the "sound of the guns." Interpreting Weir's departure as an indication that permission for a movement downstream had been obtained, Edgerly mounted D Troop and started downstream after his captain. About the time Edgerly and the troop reached Wooden Leg Ridge, Lieutenant Hare, followed closely by packers R. C.. Churchill and Frank C. Mann escorting two mules, each laden with two 1,000 round boxes of ammunition,[65] returned to Reno's position.[66]

Apparently having regained some of his composure, Reno sized up the situation and concluded he had better make a show of complying with Custer's written order to Benteen, dispatching Hare with an order to Weir to attempt to establish communication with Custer. When Captain McDougall arrived, he was met by Captain Moylan who mentioned he had just heard two faint volleys from down river; McDougall expressing the opinion it was Custer firing at the other end of the village.[67] McDougall also consulted with Godfrey concerning the firing heard from Custer's position: *"I think we ought to be down there with him."* Godfrey undoubtedly told McDougall he had heard two very distinct volleys shortly after Hare had returned with the two ammunition laden mules.[68] McDougall had then gone and expressed his opinion to Reno and Benteen.[69] During the twenty or so minutes it took for the rest of the pack train to arrive, Benteen also apparently concluded he would be on dangerous ground with Custer should Weir establish contact. Soon after the arrival of the packs[70] he mounted the rest of his battalion and started after Weir's troop.[71] Like a spring under tension that is finally released, the rest of the command followed suit and a general movement downstream began; French's Company M leading with Moylan's Company A, assisted by a platoon of McDougall's Company B in carrying the wounded, bringing up the rear.

As the trailing elements of Reno's command commenced their movement, a small party was seen scaling the bluffs. This proved to be George Herendeen and 13 men, mostly from Company G, who had been left behind in the timber.[72] Herendeen had left the timber with the van of Reno's command, but only traveled about 150 yards before his horse was shot forcing him to return to the timber on foot. Troopers were still leaving the timber when Herendeen returned, but he found a small party of about 15 soldiers with 5 or 6 horses and convinced them to remain with him in the timber: *"There were also some soldiers, and, seeing no chance to get away, I called on them to come into the timber and we would stand off the Indians. Three of the soldiers were wounded, and two of them so badly they could not use their arms. The soldiers wanted to go out, but I said no, we can't get to the ford, and, besides, we have wounded men and must stand by them. The soldiers still wanted to go, but I told them I was an old frontiersman, understood Indians, and, if they would do as I said, I would get them out the scrape, which was no worse than scrapes I had been in before."*[73] (See Table 14 – 3 for a list of the men left in the timber with Herendeen). After retrieving the spare ammunition from the saddle bags the horses were turned loose. Herendeen recalled: *"Most of the men with me in the timber were a badly scared lot of fellows, and they were already as good as whipped. They appeared to be without experience as soldiers."*[74]

Herendeen remembered that about a half hour after Reno left the timber, firing began down river. There were a great many volleys fired, especially in the early part of the firing. He thought the heavy firing lasted about an hour.[75] Continuing Herendeen's narrative after Custer's firing ceased to be heard:

"Once in awhile while in the timber, I would go to the edge and look, and finally seeing only a few Indians, I told the men we would go out and that we must walk and not run and go across the open flat. There was a wounded corporal or sergeant.[76] On the way out of the timber only one shot was exchanged with these Indians.[77] I told the men not to shoot unless necessary, that I did not wish to stir up a general engagement with them – not to run but to go in skirmish order, take it cool, and we would get out. I told them I had been in just such scrapes before and knew we could get out if we kept cool. I told them I could get out alone, and if they would do what I told them I could get them out also. The wounded sergeant then spoke up and said: 'They will do what you want, for I will compel them to obey. I will shoot the first man who starts to run or to disobey orders.' This wounded sergeant helped me out in good shape. When we got to the river, the water was rather deep where we forded. This sergeant and I remained on the west bank while the balance forded, and we told them when they would get over to protect us while we forded, and they did so.

"We forded the river some distance below where Reno did and went up the bluff farther north than where Reno retreated up. This was farther north than where DeWolf was killed. The Indians were now coming up the valley to attack Reno.

"When we got to the top of the bluff, we met Reno's advance toward Custer just as they stopped and fell back.[78] Had we been twenty minutes later, we never would have been able to join Reno. I found that my horse had jumped up after being shot in the bottom and had followed along in the retreat and was on top of the bluff when I got there. After we were corralled (sic) on Reno hill, my horse was killed, and he was one of the dead horses piled up on Moylan's line. I lay behind him on June 26, and he was bloated up with gas, and two or three times when the body was struck, I could hear the hiss of escaping gas."[79]

Name	Company
Sgt Patrick Carey	M
Sgt Charles White	M
Pvt John E. Armstrong[80]	A
Pvt Benjamin Johnson	G
Pvt John Lattmann	G
Pvt Samuel McCormick	G
Pvt John J. McGinnis[80]	G
Pvt Hugh McGonigle	G
Pvt Andrew J. Moore	G
Pvt Henry Petring	G
Pvt Eldorado J. Robb	G
Pvt John Sivertsen	M
Blacksmith Walter O. Taylor	G
Trumpeter Henry C. Weaver	M
Pvt Markus Weiss	G

Table 14 – 3 Men Left In The Timber With Herendeen

The members of Herendeen's party were not the only ones left in the timber that would survive to rejoin the command. Fred Girard, William Jackson, Lieutenant DeRudio and Private O'Neill would also rejoin their comrades on the hill, although after some narrow escapes.

As O'Neill was mounting, his horse was shot. Spotting a riderless horse, he mounted it. Informed that the horse belonged to trooper Martin, O'Neill was obliged to give him up. O'Neill reported that Martin was killed during the retreat.[81] Initially attempting to follow in the wake of the retreat on foot, O'Neill soon became convinced he would be cut off and killed by the Indians and returned to the relative safety of the timber position.[82] Private Henry Seafferman, of Company G, who was also dismounted, was killed near O'Neill as he tried to hide in some brush.[83] Girard testified at the court of inquiry that he had not left the woods with the main command as he thought they would return after charging the enemy.[84] William, or Billy, Jackson had started with the column on the retreat from the timber but had turned back when he became convinced there were too many Lakota between him and the river to have a chance of gaining the far bank.[85] The adventures of these men in the valley makes fascinating reading. They all speak of the heavy firing heard from downstream, including volley firing,[86] as well as being witnesses to the mutilation of Reno's dead. Excerpts from their various accounts are presented below.

The account of Lieutenant Charles DeRudio was first published in the July 30, 1876 edition of the *New York Herald*[87] and tells substantially the same story as given to Walter Camp by Thomas O'Neill:

"... *When we were half way over the creek, I, being in the rear, noticed a guidon planted on the side we had left and returned to take it. When coming through the wood, the guidon entangled itself in the branches and slipped out of my hand. I dismounted to pick it up and led my horse to the south bank of the creek. As I was about to mount, my horse was struck with a bullet, and becoming frightened, he ran into the Indians, leaving me dismounted in the company of about 300 Sioux not more than 50 yards distant.[88] They poured a whistling volley at me, but I was not wounded, and managed to escape to the thicket near by, where I would have an opportunity of defending myself and selling my life at a good high figure. In the thicket I found Mr. Girard, the interpreter; a half-breed Indian;[89] and private O'Neill, of Co. 'G', 7th Cav. The first two of the quartet had their, horses, while O'Neill like myself, was dismounted. I told the owners of the horses that the presence of the animals would betray us, suggesting at the same time that they be stampeded. They declined to act on the suggestion and I left them and crawled through the thick underwood into the deep dry bottom of the creek, where I could not easily be discovered, and from whence I hoped to be able under cover of darkness to steal out and rejoin the command. I had not been in this hiding place more than 10 minutes when I heard several pistol shots fired in my immediate vicinity, and shortly thereafter came the silvery, but to me diabolical voices of several squaws. I raised my head with great caution to see what the women were at and to discover their exact location. I found the women at the revolting work of scalping a soldier who was perhaps not yet dead. Two of the ladies were cutting away, while two others performed a sort of war dance around the body and its mutilators. I will not attempt to describe to you my feelings at witnessing the disgusting performance...*

"... *I crawled out of the creek bottom the same way I had approached, and as I was about to ascend the bank, I heard a voice calling 'Lieutenant, Lieutenant.' I could see no one, but the call was repeated, and advancing a few yards in the direction from which it proceeded, I found all three of the party I had left, a short time before, hidden in the bottom of the creek... Finally the time came when under the protection of night (it was very cloudy) we were able to come out of our hiding places and take the direction of the ford, which was two miles to the south, through an open plain. Mr. Girard and the scout mounted their horses and the soldier and myself took hold, each one, of a horse's tail, and followed them... Once we forded myself took hold, each one, of a horse's tail, and followed them. . . Once we forded the stream but found it was at a bend and that we would have to ford it again. When we recrossed the river, we ran full into a band of eight savages. The two mounted men ran for their lives, the soldier and myself jumped into the bushes near us. I cocked my revolver and in a kneeling position was ready to fire at the savages if they should approach me. They evidently thought, from the precipitate retreat of the two mounted men, that all of us had decamped; and began to talk among themselves. In a few minutes to my surprise they continued their course, and soon after went out of hearing. I raised up from my position, approached the bank of the river and called to the soldier, who immediately answered. We then saw that all the fords were well guarded by the savages, and it would be very dangerous to attempt to cross any part of the river. . . The night passed and in the dim dawn of day we heard an immense tramping, as of a large cavalry command, and the splashing of the water convinced us that some troops were crossing the river. I imagined it was our command, as I could distinctly hear the sound of the horses shoes striking the stones. I cautiously stepped to the edge of the bushes to look out (I was then no more than three yards from the bank of the river), and thought I recognized some gray horses mounted by men in military blouses, and some of them in white hats. They were, I thought, going out of the valley, and those that had already crossed the river were going up a very steep bluff, while others were crossing after them. I saw one man with a buckskin jacket, pants, top boots and white hat, and felt quite sure I recognized him as Capt. Tom Custer which convinced me that the cavalrymen were of our command.*

"With this conviction I stepped boldly out on the bank and called to Capt. Custer, 'Tom, don't leave us here.' The distance was only a few yards and my call was answered by an infernal yell and a discharge of 300 or 400 shots. I then discovered my mistake and found the savages were clad in clothes and mounted on horses which they had captured from our men. Myself and the soldier jumped into the bushes (the bullets mowing down the branches at every volley), and crawled off to get out of range of the fire. In doing so we moved the top branches of the undergrowth, and the Indians on the top of the bluff covered us with their rifles. We now decided to cross a clearing of about twenty yards and gain another wood; but before doing this, I took the precaution to look out. The prospect was terribly discouraging for on our immediate right, not more than fifty yards distant, I saw four or five Indians galloping toward us. Near by me there were two cottonwood stumps nearly touching each other, and behind this slender barricade myself and the soldier knelt down, he with his carbine and I with my revolver, ready to do for a few of the savages before they could kill us. . . They had not seen us and when the foremost man was just abreast of me and about ten yards distant, I fired. They came in Indian file, and at my fire they turned a right–about and were making off when Pvt. O'Neill fired his carbine at the second savage, who at that moment was reining his pony to turn him back. The private's eye was true, and his carbine trusty, for Mr. Indian dropped his rein, threw up his paws and laid down on the grass to sleep his long sleep. The gentleman I greeted rode a short distance and then did likewise. The rest of the party rode on, turned the corner of the wood and disappeared. . .

". . . By 6 o'clock everything around us was apparently quiet and no evidence or signs of any Indians were near us. We supposed the regiment had left the field, and all that remained for us to do was wait for the night and then pass the river and take the route for the Yellowstone River, and there construct a raft and descend to the mouth of the Powder River, our supply camp . . . After marching two miles, I

thought I would go up on a very high hill to look around and see if I could discover any sigh of our command; and on looking around I saw a fire on my left and in the direction where we supposed the command was fighting during the day, probably two miles from us. Of course we made two conjectures on this fire: it might be an Indian fire and it might be from our command. The only way to ascertain was to approach it cautiously and trust to chance. Accordingly we descended the hill, and took the direction of the fire. Climbing another and another hill, we listened a while and then proceeded on for a mile or more, when on the top of a hill we again stopped and listened. We could hear voices, but not distinctly enough to tell whether they were savages or our command. We proceeded a little farther and heard the bray of a mule, and soon after, the distinct voice of a sentry challenging with the familiar words 'Halt; Who goes there?' The challenge was not directed to us, as we were too far off to be seen by the picket, and it was too dark; but this gave us courage to continue our course and approach, though carefully, lest we should run into some Indians again. We were about 200 yards from the fire and . . . I cried out 'Picket,[90] *don't fire; it is Lt. DeRudio and Pvt. O'Neill,' and started to run. We received an answer in a loud cheer from all the members of the packet and Lt. Varnum. This officer, one of our bravest and most efficient, came at once to me and was very happy to see me again, after having counted me among the dead; . . ."*[91]

Billy Jackson described his and Girard's adventures after they became separated from DeRudio and O'Neill:

". . . We had not gone more than two hundred yards, when, from a clump of brush not far ahead, a deep voice demanded in Sioux: 'Who are you?'

"The sudden challenge almost stunned me. I saw DeRudio and O'Neill drop down into the waist–high grass, heard Girard reply, as he checked up his horse: 'Just us few.'

"'And where are you going.'

"'Out here a way,' Girard calmly answered as he turned and rode back past me, saying: 'Quick! We must draw them after us!'

"We rode swiftly down the island for several hundred yards, saw that we were not pursued, and stopped, then heard a few shots up where we had left DeRudio and O'Neill . . .

". . . We tied our horses in a dense growth of willows, left the island, and went on up the valley.

". . . On the other side we ran up into the brush, put on our clothes, and, with rifles cocked and ready, started on. Moving cautiously, we began climbing a steep brush and timber slope. We had reached a height from which, looking down the valley, we could see the many dancing fires of the enemy, when I stepped upon a dry stick that broke with a loud snap.

"Close above us, a Sioux said: 'Spotted Elk, did you hear that?'

'Yes. Maybe a deer,' came the reply, up off to our left.

'I am thirsty; let us go down to the river,' said another picket, above on our right, and at that, Girard and I turned and went leaping down the slope. I stumbled and fell over a log and crashed into a clump of rose–brush.

"Below me, still another picket cried out: 'What is the trouble up there?'

'Something running; sounds like a bear,' one off to my left replied.

"As I sat up, I could no longer hear Girard, and did not know whether he had stopped or gone back to the river. . ."[92]

Lying in his position all day, the Lakota sometimes passing within 15 feet of his hiding place, Billy Jackson escaped discovery. After nightfall, he went down to the river for a drink. His narrative continues:

". . . I was about to kneel and drink when, close on my left, I heard in Sioux: 'Who are you?' and though I flinched, I recognized the voice. 'Girard!' I cried. 'Don't shoot!'

"We ran to grip each other's hands. I told him my experiences, and he said that he had found a good hiding–place in an old driftwood pile overgrown with high rose–brush, and had run little risk of discovery, though many of the enemy had ridden near him.

". . . But just then we heard a strange noise, nudged one another, listened more intently, heard it again, knew what it was: the husky, coughing groan of a horse. 'Hi there!' cried Girard.

"And oh, how glad we were when we heard some one close above us, reply in good American: 'Who are you?'"[93]

Girard and Jackson returned to Reno's lines about 11 P. M. on June 26th, while DeRudio and O'Neill wouldn't arrive until nearly 2 A. M. the morning of June 27th.[94]

Encumbered as they were with Moylan's wounded, the last elements of Reno's command[95] had barely reached Wooden Leg Ridge before they were met by the earlier departing companies racing pell mell for the rear; the Cheyenne and Lakota hot on their heels. Hurriedly, they retired to a saucer–like depression and flattened themselves on the ground, seeking what meager protection the vegetation provided, in anticipation of the onslaught of the red wave. The siege of Reno Hill had begun.

[1] While the withholding of this piece of important intelligence probably had no direct impact on the final outcome, it is another example of how poor communication would plague the 7th Cavalry on this day. While no single "failure to communicate" caused the defeat of the 7th Cavalry, the totality of these failures was more than could be overcome.

[2] Boston Custer had returned to the pack train to obtain a fresh horse from the remuda. While there he had spoken to Captain McDougall. See Walter Camp "Custer in '76" page 69. This sighting of Boston Custer is important as it corroborates the subsequent sighting by Trumpeter John Martin which, in turn, establishes how quickly Benteen could have reached Custer had he obeyed his orders.

[3] While Godfrey may indeed have heard some scattering shots to his front, the analysis presented in Appendix 12 demonstrates that Benteen's battalion must have left the morass at least 45 minutes to an hour before either Custer's or Reno's commands became actively engaged. The only firing that might have occurred during Benteen's water stop would have been either the scouts killing Deeds or the woman gathering turnips.

[4] There is some indication that Weir attempted to enlist Godfrey's support in petitioning Benteen to initiate this movement, but was rebuffed. See Charles K. Mills "Harvest of Barren Regrets" page 255. Weir would repeat this action later in the day in the movement to the high point that bears his name. Interestingly, in neither instance when Weir insubordinately moved his troop forward without orders, is there any evidence that he requested authorization from the cognizant commander, Benteen or Reno. Since Weir died without leaving a record pertaining to these events, his rationale for the unauthorized movements must forever remain in the realm of speculation.

[5] See E. S. Godfrey "Custer's Last Battle 1876" page 22.

[6] Although Benteen described the tepee as "burning," his statement that he couldn't recall if he had gone inside indicates the lodge poles were smoldering at best. As a further indication the tepee had not been consumed, Benteen, in a letter to Theodore Goldin, described the tepee's colorful decorations. See John M. Carroll "The Benteen-Goldin Letters" page 184. See Appendix 12 for further discussion.

[7] See Walter Camp "Custer in '76" pages 92 – 93.

[8] See Ronald H. Nichols "Reno Court of Inquiry" page 441.

[9] Benteen had not been personally involved in the August 1873 skirmishes with the Lakota.

[10] See William Hedley "'PS Bring Pacs' The Order That Trapped the Custer Battalion" page 61.

[11] See Ronald H. Nichols "Reno Court of Inquiry" page 497.

[12] McDougall testified that while he never received such a message, Mathey did and had discussed it with him. McDougall's response had been to tell Mathey to hurry up the packs. See Ronald H. Nichols "The Reno Court of Inquiry" page 531. It is interesting to note that a certificate from McDougall, dated January 9, 1897, states he did indeed receive Kanipe's message. See J. E. Kanipe "Tarheel Survivor of Custer's Last Stand" page 30.

[13] This appears to refer to Wooden Leg Ridge rather than Weir Point.

[14] An Italian immigrant, whose real name was Giovanni Martini, Martin probably misunderstood Custer who may have said: we've caught them napping.

[15] At this juncture, the second sighting of Custer on the bluffs, Reno's command was in the timber.

[16] This confirms Lieutenant DeRudio's sighting from the timber position of Custer waving his hat on Weir Point.

[17] Martin, whose story changed somewhat from his court of inquiry testimony, may have been a little confused as to when he was dispatched. Knowing that Benteen needed to be immediately recalled, and given the number of warriors that were available to confront Reno, it makes no sense for Custer to have ridden another mile or so before dispatching Martin. It is possible that Martin was with Custer on Wooden Leg Ridge rather than Weir Point and afterwards confused the two locations.

[18] See Colonel W. A. Graham "The Custer Myth" pages 289 – 290. Note that when testifying before the Reno court of inquiry, Martin stated that Custer did not speak with him directly but dictated the order to Cooke who then wrote it down. See Ronald H. Nichols "Reno Court of Inquiry" page 390.

[19] See Colonel W. A. Graham "The Custer Myth" page 297.

[20] See Colonel W. A. Graham "The Custer Myth" page 290.

[21] Custer would move between 1 and 2 miles further away from the point where Martin was dispatched within the next hour, putting Benteen perhaps as much as 50 minutes behind the Custer column.

[22] See Walter Camp "Custer in '76" pages 54 – 55. Although I believe it is clear that Custer was only concerned about the potential loss of the ammunition packs, Benteen reached the only interpretation possible from the written order: Custer wanted all the packs.

[23] See Ronald H. Nichols "Reno Court of Inquiry" page 440.

[24] See Ronald H. Nichols "Reno Court of Inquiry" page 404.

[25] See Ronald H. Nichols "Reno Court of Inquiry" page 433.

[26] See Ronald H. Nichols "Reno Court of Inquiry" pages 512 – 513.

[27] See Walter Camp "Custer in '76" page 101.

[28] See Ronald H. Nichols "Reno Court of Inquiry" page 390 – 391. Martin would tell Walter Camp in 1908 that he had testified as he did because it was not desired that he tell all that he knew. See Walter Camp "Custer in '76" page 101. The statement that McDougall, who marched in rear of the packs, was only 150 yards in Benteen's rear at this juncture cannot be credited. Noted Custer historian Edgar I. Stewart felt that Martin not only had trouble with English, but that Benteen's sarcastic comment on Martin: *"thick-headed, dull-witted Italian, just as much cut out for a cavalryman as he was for a King"* was justified. See Edgar I. Stewart "Custer's Luck" page 386. Later in life, Martin would tell Colonel Graham he had been misunderstood at the court of inquiry and had only given Custer's message to Benteen. Given that Martin was struggling to learn English at

in life, Martin would tell Colonel Graham he had been misunderstood at the court of inquiry and had only given Custer's message to Benteen. Given that Martin was struggling to learn English at the time of the battle, this seems to be a plausible explanation. See Frank Perfetti "John Martin, An Italian With Custer" page 28.

29 Not a very impressive statement given Martin had only been in the states since 1873 and had enlisted in 1874.

30 See Ronald H. Nichols "Reno Court of Inquiry" page 441.

31 See Walter Camp "Custer in '76" page 80.

32 Benteen also never inquired of Martin which side of the river Custer was on, testifying he believed the information was unnecessary as he thought the troops had already captured the village. See Ronald H. Nichols "Reno Court of Inquiry" page 497.

33 See Walter Camp "Custer in '76" page 75.

34 See E. S. Godfrey "Custer's Last Battle 1876" page 25. It was apparently this firing that caused Benteen's two detachments to reunite on Reno's trail.

35 Even Captain French, who had performed heroically during the retreat from the bottom, apparently became caught up in the panic behavior characteristic of a mob. Stopped on the east bank by Company G's Private George Loyd, who implored him to order a covering fire for the wounded crossing the river, French excitedly replied *"I'll try! I'll try!"* French, however, did nothing and rode to the top of the bluff. See Dale T. Schoenberger "End of Custer" page 127.

36 See Ronald H. Nichols "Reno Court of Inquiry" page 405.

37 When Dull Knife's village was captured by Colonel Ranald Mackenzie on November 26, 1876, one of the items recovered was a Company G roster book that may have been carried by Sergeant Botzer. Subsequent to the Little Big Horn, the Cheyenne High Bear had used the book for his drawings. See George Bird Grinnell "The Fighting Cheyennes" page 367.

38 These were the Crow scouts Goes Ahead, White Man Runs Him, and Hairy Moccasin, all released by Custer from the vicinity of Weir Point, and the Arikara Black Fox. See John S. Gray "Custer's Last Campaign" page 283. These scouts continued on toward the rear and informed Lieutenant Mathey that Custer had been defeated.

39 See Ronald H. Nichols "Reno Court of Inquiry" page 405.

40 Dr. Porter would testify at the court of inquiry that *"The command was demoralized. They seemed to think they had been whipped."* See Colonel W. A. Graham "The Reno Court of Inquiry" page 63. Private John B. McGuire, Jr., of Company C, told Walter Camp that when he arrived on Reno Hill with the pack train, all 6 companies were in confusion. See "Custer in '76" page 124.

41 According to Dr. Porter, when Benteen was first sighted, some of the men shouted *"Here comes Custer!"* See John Upton Terrell and Colonel George Walton "Faint the Trumpet Sounds" page 242.

42 See Colonel W. A. Graham "The Custer Myth" page 291. While there are indications that command and control was being restored prior to Benteen's arrival (notably the story of Sergeant Charles Windolph, Company H, who related Reno, Varnum and French were trying to rally the

Charles Windolph, Company H, who related Reno, Varnum and French were trying to rally the men when Benteen's battalion arrived, and Lieutenant Hare's testimony that, shortly after Benteen's arrival, he heard Reno say: *"We have assistance now, and we will go and avenge the loss of our comrades."* See Neil C. Mangum "Battle of the Little Big Horn" page 4 and Colonel W. A. Graham "The Reno Court of Inquiry" page 98) it is more probable that Benteen encountered the beaten and demoralized mob described by Benteen , Dr. Porter, and Lieutenant Edgerly. For the statistically minded, Reno, at this point, had less than 60 percent of the force he had taken into the valley fight. See the casualty lists in Appendix 2.

[43] See E.A. Brininstool "Troopers With Custer: Historic Incidents of the Battle of the Little Big Horn" page 81.

[44] See Colonel W. A. Graham "The Reno Court of Inquiry" page 64.

[45] See the testimony of Lieutenant Edgerly in Colonel W. A. Graham "The Reno Court of Inquiry" page 160. Edgerly stressed in a March 1, 1924 letter to Colonel Graham that Varnum was not frightened, merely excited and angry. See Tom O'Neil "Marcus A. Reno: What Was Said Of Him At The Little Big Horn" pages 9 - 10.

[46] See John M. Carroll "The Benteen – Goldin Letters" page 243.

[47] See Neil C. Mangum "Battle of the Little Big Horn" page 4.

[48] See E. S. Godfrey "Custer's Last Battle 1876" page 25.

[49] Godfrey would remark in his Field Diary that he thought it strange the Indians did not demonstrate against them (see page 12).

[50] See Charles K. Mills "Harvest of Barren Regrets" page 259. In a display that would be astonishing in other men, but completely in character for Benteen, he would not tell the court of inquiry about urging Reno to junction with Custer. Instead, he testified he had not asked for permission (although permission to obey a superior officer's order was not required) to proceed down river in Custer's direction as he supposed Custer could take care of himself. See Ronald H. Nichols "Reno Court of Inquiry" page 462.

[51] At the court of inquiry only Reno, Benteen and Wallace would deny hearing firing from Custer's position. Sergeant Ferdinand A. Culbertson of Company A claimed to have been near Reno, while waiting to start down the slope to bury Lieutenant Hodgson, during the heavy portion of Custer's firing. See Colonel W. A. Graham "The Reno Court of Inquiry" page 125. Interestingly, Reno mentioned hearing the firing in his official report of July 5, See Appendix 7. Others on the bluffs recalled hearing the firing commence about the time Benteen arrived and continuing for upwards of 45 minutes. The analysis of Appendix 12 shows this firing could have only been the engagements in Medicine Tail Coulee (Yates at Minneconjou Ford and subsequent withdrawal to Calhoun Hill and Keogh on Luce and Blummer–Nye–Cartwright Ridges).

[52] See Walter Camp "Custer in '76" page 105.

[53] See Colonel W. A. Graham "The Reno Court of Inquiry" page 224. It is instructive to note this questioning of a superior's orders, although unheard of in the 19th century army, went unchallenged at the court of inquiry.

[54] Note that although William Jackson was a half–breed Pikuni Blackfoot, I have included him in the count for the Arikara for brevity.

[55] See E. S. Godfrey "Custer's Last Battle 1876" page 26.

[56] See E. S. Godfrey "Custer's Last Battle 1876" page 26.

[57] See E. S. Godfrey "Custer's Last Battle 1876" page 26. This quote was in the original *Century Magazine* article published in 1892 but was deleted from later reprints. See Colonel W. A. Graham "The Custer Myth" page 141.

[58] Although it was reputed that Reno's command was virtually unarmed due to their lack of ammunition, only 1,000 rounds of the reserve carbine ammunition would be taken by Reno's troops indicating that probably only Moylan's Company A had significantly depleted their store of ammunition.

[59] See Walter Camp "Custer in '76" page 66.

[60] See Colonel W. A. Graham "The Reno Court of Inquiry" page 21. This is an obvious reference to the fate of Major Elliott at the Washita and this opinion was undoubtedly held, if not expressed, by at least some of the officers.

[61] See Colonel W. A. Graham "The Reno Court of Inquiry" page 139.

[62] Lieutenant Varnum would later recall two expeditions to Hodgson's body (one led by Reno and accompanied by some troopers attempting to fill their canteens, and the other the "burial" party) and state that Lieutenant Hare was not dispatched until after the Hodgson "burial" party had returned to Reno Hill. While this scenario is definitely within the realm of possibility, the analysis of Appendix 12 indicates that Varnum was most probably in error on this score. See John S. Gray "Custer's Last Campaign" pages 310 – 311. If Varnum was correct in his recollection, then an additional half hour would have to be allocated to the delay before starting down river.

[63] See Colonel W. A. Graham "The Reno Court of Inquiry" page 194.

[64] There are indications that Weir had a heated exchange with Reno regarding the movement to Custer (see Neil Mangum "The Battle of the Little Big Horn" page 4). As Reno was preoccupied with the burial of Hodgson, and since Weir insisted he did not ask Reno's permission for his movement, it appears that this argument, if it took place, occurred only after Weir had made his personal observations from Weir Point.

[65] There were a total of 12 mules allocated to carry the reserve ammunition. See Jim Schneider "'Rations, Forage and Ammunition" page 29.

[66] See John S. Gray "Custer's Last Campaign" pages 285 – 286. While Sergeants Ryan and Windolph, and Lieutenants Godfrey and Wallace believed Reno's command to have been virtually out of ammunition, Lieutenant Hare, Fred Girard and packers Churchill and John McGuire believed that very little ammunition had been expended by Reno's troops as witnessed by drawing only 1,000 rounds of the reserve ammunition when the first two mules arrived (a fact confirmed by Wallace's testimony). See Colonel W. A. Graham "The Custer Myth" page 243, Colonel W. A. Graham "The Reno Court of Inquiry" pages 17, 171, and 201, Neil C. Mangum "The Battle of the Little Big Horn" page 4, E. S. Godfrey "The Field Diary of Edward Settle Godgrey" page 12, Walter

Camp "Custer in '76" page 124, and Ronald H. Nichols "Reno Court of Inquiry" page 104. There is no support from other sources for Godfrey's statement that Benteen's men were ordered to share their ammunition with Reno's men prior to the arrival of the ammunition mules. See Don Rickey Jr. "Forty Miles A Day on Beans and Hay" page 291.

[67] See Colonel W. A. Graham "The Reno Court of Inquiry" page 75. Private Jacob Adams, on duty with the pack train, also recalled hearing *"sharp firing"* from Custer's position when the pack train arrived on Reno Hill. See Horace Ellis "A Survivor's Story of the Custer Massacre" page 9.

[68] See Colonel W. A. Graham "The Reno Court of Inquiry" page 178. While it is impossible to pinpoint the exact nature of the volley fire heard at this juncture, the analysis of Appendix 12 indicates it was probably firing from the Calhoun Hill position that was heard after the arrival of the pack train.

[69] See Walter Camp "Custer in '76" page 70.

[70] Although McDougall recalled he was on the hill for between one and one-half to two hours prior to the movement down river, the analysis of Appendix 12 shows this recollection to have been erroneous.

[71] There are indications that Benteen was preparing to belatedly obey Custer's written order even before the pack train arrived. Captain McDougall told Walter Camp that, when he arrived on Reno Hill, no line had been formed so he sent out skirmishers. This indicates that Benteen had withdrawn the line he had established upon his arrival on Reno Hill. Being the experienced soldier that he was, Benteen would only have withdrawn his line in anticipation of a movement. See Walter Camp "Custer in '76" page 70.

[72] Varnum remembered the sequence of events somewhat differently than Herendeen, whose account is used here. Varnum recalled that after the arrival of the two ammunition laden mules, he obtained 2 spades from the packs and started down the hill to bury Hodgson. About 1/3 of the way down the bluff, he saw Herendeen and party. He went on to state that he was recalled before he could complete his burial task as the arrival of the remainder of the pack train was imminent. See John S. Gray "Custer's Last Campaign" page 312. As Varnum's accounts changed somewhat over time, and as Herendeen's did not, I have used Herendeen's recollection of events in preference to Varnum's.

[73] See John M. Carroll "A Seventh Cavalry Scrapbook #12" page 23.

[74] See Walter Camp "Custer in '76" pages 223 – 224.

[75] See Walter Camp "Custer in '76" page 224.

[76] This was Sergeant Charles White, Company M. He had been wounded in the right arm in the valley fight and his horse had been killed when the retreat began.

[77] The lack of resistance encountered by the Herendeen party proves that virtually all of the Indians had left Reno's vicinity to attack Custer.

[78] Actually this was the rear of Reno's command.

[79] See Walter Camp "Custer in '76" pages 224 – 225.

[80] The decapitated heads of Armstrong and McGinnis were found in the abandoned village indicating they were the two troopers who refused to leave the timber with Herendeen.

[81] There were four Martins serving with the 7th that day: Corporal James Martin, Company G, Trumpeter John Martin, Company H, First Sergeant Michael Martin, Company D, and Private William Martin, Company B. Trumpeter Martin, of course was serving as orderly to General Custer, there is no indication that either Sergeant Martin or Private Martin were on detached duty from their companies, leaving us with Corporal Martin. As Corporal Martin was killed in the Hilltop Fight on June 25th, while O'Neill was "lost" in the valley, it is likely that Corporal James Martin is the trooper mentioned by O'Neill.

[82] See Walter Camp "Custer in '76" page 107.

[83] See Dale T. Schoenberger "End of Custer" page 115.

[84] See Colonel W. A. Graham "Reno Court of Inquiry" page 45.

[85] Ironically, Jackson's enlistment was up on June 25. See James Willard Shultz "The Custer Massacre" page 14.

[86] The reports of Custer's firing are somewhat mixed, but everyone, except Reno, Benteen, and Wallace heard at least 2 volleys indicating the firing was directed rather than random. Fred Girard testified: *"Ten or fifteen minutes after Major Reno left the bottom I heard the firing on these hills. . . . To the left of where Major Reno was, it was to my right. . . . On the right hand side (east bank, DCE) and I could see Indians going up these ravines on the right hand side of the stream. I saw Indians going up there and I could hear the firing as though they were firing at troops going up there. I knew that there was some troops going by because I had seen them back of that. . . . I heard continuous firing clear on down as if there was a general engagement. . . . Down to where I afterward went and saw General Custer's battlefield and I heard firing to the left of the village, three or four volleys, as if there were fifty or one hundred guns at a volley. Lieutenant DeRudio was in the woods with me and when he heard this firing he said, 'By God, There's Custer coming, let's go and join him.' I told him to wait, that we had plenty of time, that when the firing got opposite to us we could go out and join him, that he was now too far away. . . . It was during the firing down there, after the heavy firing down there, indicating a general engagement at that point, where Custer was afterward found. . . . There was a continuous firing all the time the troops were marching down there, not regular volleys, but scattering shots, sometimes three or four and sometimes only one, and then it was kept up irregularly, and when it got down below there, where Custer's battlefield was, it became heavy. There was a skirmish fire all the way down from where I first heard it."* See Ronald H. Nichols "The Reno Court of Inquiry" pages 97 - 98. The Cheyenne Tall Bull also recalled two distinct volleys, the first being fired from Calhoun Ridge early in the fight. See Kenneth Hammer "Custer in '76" page 213.

[87] Colonel Graham adds the notation "Alleged to have been written by Major Brisbin though signed by DeRudio" to the title of the article in "The Custer Myth" page 253.

[88] Prior to the episode with the guidon, Private David McVeigh, a trumpeter in Company A, had brought DeRudio's horse to the Lieutenant, but DeRudio had refused to mount. While not necessarily indicative of cowardice, it is obvious DeRudio had no intention of leaving the timber with the rest of the command making the circumstances, as he reported them, of his remaining in the timber highly suspect. Benteen would write: *" DeRudio was supposed to have been lost, but the same night the Indians left their village he came sauntering in dismounted, accompanied by McIntosh's cook. They had hidden away in the woods. He has a thrilling romantic story made out*

*already – embellished you bet! The stories of O'Neill (the man who was with him) and DeRudio's of course, couldn't be expected to agree, but far more of the truth, I am inclined to think, will be found in the narrative of O'Neill; at any rate, it is not at all colored – as he is a cool, level-headed fellow – and tells it plainly **and the same way all the time** – which is a big thing towards convincing one of the truth of a story."* (emphasis from the original). See Charles K. Mills "Charles C. DeRudio" pages 26 and 34.

89 This was Billy Jackson the half–breed Pickuni Blackfoot.

90 The picket was Private George A. Bott of Company A. See Charles K. Mills "Charles C. DeRudio" apge 32.

91 See Colonel W. A. Graham "The Custer Myth" pages 253 – 256.

92 See James Willard Schultz "William Jackson Indian Scout" pages 143 – 146.

93 See James Willard Schultz "William Jackson Indian Scout" pages 151 – 153.

94 See John S. Gray "Custer's Last Campaign" page 305.

95 According to John Burkman, Private Thomas Blake of Company A was so paralyzed with fear he refused to accompany the command in its move down river. See Dale T. Schoenberger "End of Custer" page 219.

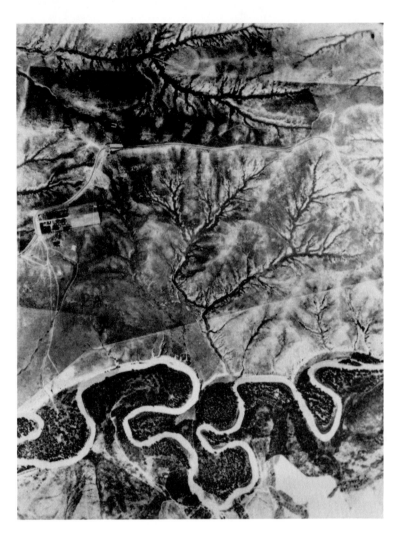

Aerial view looking straight down on the battlefield. Calhoun Hill is at the top right where the road forms a loop. Custer Hill lies along the ridge line at picture's left. Deep Ravine is shown in the center connecting to the river. *Photo Courtesy Little Bighorn Battlefield National Monument.*

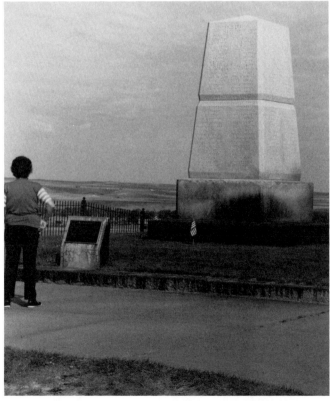

Last Stand, or Custer Hill. The stone marker, inscribed with the names of the slain troopers, is actually a marker for a mass grave rather than a monument to the 7th Cavalry. Prior to the road being put in, this area was a knoll approximately 30 feet in diameter and rising about 6 feet above the ridge. Custer's body was found approximately 6 feet to the right of the marker. *Photo by author.*

Chapter 15

A Reconstruction of The Custer Fight

The question of the precise movements of the Custer column, from the point Reno was given his attack order until the command was annihilated a few hours later, has plagued historians and devotees ever since that fateful June day. Fortunately, we have more than the marble markers commemorating the fallen cavalrymen to guide us in our reconstruction of the movements of that ill–fated column. The 1984 archaeological survey mapped 252 markers on the Custer Battlefield.[1] These markers, one for each of the soldier dead, were originally placed in April of 1890 by Captain Owen Sweet. The original markers, supplemented by minor additions over the years, were all placed on Custer's field.[2] This may have been due to two primary factors. First, the remainder of the battlefield was privately held, although markers for Dorman, Reynolds and McIntosh were subsequently placed in the valley. The second, and perhaps most relevant factor, is the positions of the soldier dead in the valley and hilltop fights were not marked as they were on Custer's field. Forty three of the markers appear to be paired, yielding what is referred to as a "double marker." If the 43 "double markers" truly represent a single soldier burial, as the 1984 and 1985 archaeological evidence indicates,[3] then only 209 bodies were found on the Custer Battlefield proper, the exact number of soldier deaths accounted for in Appendix 2. While there are obvious errors in specific marker locations,[4] as a whole the archaeological investigations have proven the markers to be reliable locations of soldier dead.[5] The empirical evidence generated by the archaeological investigations poses quite a dilemma for those theorists who espouse the opinion that the bodies of 28 soldiers, mostly from Company E, lie in Deep Ravine, where they were slaughtered like sheep in a pen as they crouched in a panic stricken bunch. If the 43 "double markers" are spurious, as the hard evidence indicates, and if the 209 "correctly placed" markers represent the locations where soldier bodies were discovered, also as the hard evidence indicates,[6] then there are no bodies unaccounted for and the reason the archaeological investigations of 1984 and 1985 failed to discover bodies in Deep Ravine is crystal clear; there simply are no bodies there to find! The reader is referred to Gregory Michno's excellent work on the location of the 28 "phantom" bodies, "The Mystery of E Troop."

In addition to several stragglers, who had something to hide in their narratives, Custer dispatched at least two messengers during his march, and, although often in conflict with other established facts, their narratives form an important part of our understanding of the command's movements prior to their departure.[7] In addition, Custer's column was sighted on the bluffs by various members of Reno's battalion during the valley fight. The last elements of the verbal evidence, and the most difficult to assess,[8] are the accounts of the surviving Crow scouts and the Arapaho, Cheyenne, and Lakota battle participants. The final pieces of data are the physical evidence and artifacts. This includes the trail made by the shod cavalry horses[9] as well as the bullets and shell casings discovered at various locations in the years following the conflict. The account that follows draws on all of the data sources mentioned above, tempering the conclusions drawn with an appreciation for both the tactics of the period and the personality of George Armstrong Custer.

After Reno was given his attack order near the lone tepee, Custer slowed the pace of his column to a walk to provide some separation between the two commands.[10] Custer had attempted to send Crow scouts Half Yellow Face and White Swan up to the ridge to view the village, but they had misinterpreted his intention and followed Reno's battalion.[11] Mitch Boyer then took the remaining Crow scouts, Curly, Goes Ahead, Hairy Moccasin, and White Man Runs Him, up on the ridge to observe the village.[12]

Unit of Origin	Custer's Command	Reno's Command (A/K/W/M)	Benteen's Command	Pack Train & Escort
Headquarters				
Officers (3)	2	1/0/0/0		
Non Comms (1)	1			
Enlisted (1)	1			
Medical (3)	1	1/1/0/0		
Civilians (2)	2			
Guides (3)	2	0/1/0/0		0
Interpreters (2)	0	0/1/0/1		
Courier (1)	0	1/0/0/0		
Company A				
Officers (3)	0	2/0/0/1		
Non Comms (9)		7/1/1/0		1
Enlisted (40)		27/6/1/0		6
Company B				
Officers (2)		0/1/0/0		1
Non Comms (7)				7
Enlisted (41)		1/0/0/0		40
Company C				
Officers (2)	2			
Non Comms (8)	6			2
Enlisted (43)	28			14
Company D				
Officers (2)			2	
Non Comms (5)			4	1
Enlisted (45)			39	6
Company E				
Officers (2)	2			
Non Comms (8)	7			1
Enlisted (37)	30	2/0/0/0		5
Company F				
Officers (2)	2			
Non Comms (8)	7			1
Enlisted (41)	28	2/0/0/0		11
Company G				
Officers (2)	0	1/1/0/0		
Non Comms (8)		4/3/0/0		1
Enlisted (36)	1	21/8/0/0		6
Company H				
Officers (2)			2	
Non Comms (9)			8	1
Enlisted (36)	0		30	6
Company I				
Officers (2)	2			
Non Comms (6)	5			1
Enlisted (40)	32	1/0/0/0		7
Company K				
Officers (2)	0	1/0/0/0	1	
Non Comms (8)	1		6	1
Enlisted (34)		0/1/0/0	27	6
Company L				
Officers (2)	2			
Non Comms (7)	6			1
Enlisted (49)	38			11
Company M				
Officers (2)		1/0/0/0		1
Non Comms (8)		3/3/1/0		1
Enlisted (46)		28/7/4/0		7
Crow Scouts (6)	0	1/0/1/0		
Arikara Scouts (24)[13]	0	4/3/1/1		15
Lakota Scouts (5)	0	0/0/0/5		
Teamsters/Packers (12)				12
Total	**208**	**109**	**119**	**173**

Table 15 – 1 Assignments At Start of Custer Fight– June 25, 1876

* Nathan Short dispatched as messenger and dismissal of 4 Crow scouts.

Command Element	Strength	Percent of Regiment
Custer's Command	**208**	**34.2**
Headquarters	7	
Scouts/Guides	2	
Civilians	2	
Keogh's Battalion	**121**	**19.9**
Company C	36	
Company I	39	
Company L	46	
Yates' Battalion	**76**	**12.5**
Company E	39	
Company F	37	
Reno's Battalion	**109**	**17.9**
Headquarters	9	
Company A	36	
Company G	26	
Company M	32	
Scouts	5	
Interpreters/Courier	1	
Benteen's Battalion	**119**	**19.5**
Company D	45	
Company H	40	
Company K	34	
Pack Train	**173**	**28.4**
Company B	48	
Mathey's Command	98	
Civilian Packers	12	
Scouts	15	
Guides	0	
Total	**609**	**100**

Table 15 – 2 Battalion Combat Strength At Start of Custer Fight– June 25, 1876

After trailing Reno for about 2 miles, Custer turned his column to the right. The speculation as to Custer's motivation for this change in direction is confined to two possible causes. Sergeant Kanipe , Custer's first messenger, told Walter Camp that Custer turned to pursue some Indians sighted on the bluff ahead.[14] The alternate view is that Custer turned in response to Lieutenant Cooke's intelligence that the Indians were coming up the valley to meet Reno.[15] The reasoning supporting this theory is as follows: as there are no accounts of sighting a trail indicating a retrograde movement on the part of the Custer column, Cooke must have rejoined the command prior to the change in direction. Given Cooke's information that the village was not fleeing as previously feared, the probability of a successful attack would be greatly enhanced by a flanking, or enveloping, movement on Custer's part. Therefore, the turn to the right was made in order to seize an unanticipated tactical opportunity. The choice in motivations typically involves the author's personal feelings about Armstrong Custer's capabilities as a combat officer. Those who feel Custer was reckless and rash favor the scenario where the turn to the right was prompted by the appearance of a small "target of opportunity." Those who believe Custer was a highly competent combat officer, as, in my opinion, the events of Chapter 10 clearly demonstrate, favor the latter scenario: that the change in direction was simply a response to an evolving tactical situation. Regardless of his motivation for changing his direction of march, Custer should have sent messengers to both Reno and Benteen informing them of his column's proposed future movements and alerting them to expect future changes in their own orders. His failure to do so made it difficult for his various units to properly cooperate in the upcoming action.

After the turn to the right, Custer's next action was to water his thirsty mounts. During this halt, I believe Reno's first messenger, Private McIlhargey, reported to Custer.[16] As Cooke had already reported the fact the Indians were coming up the valley to meet Reno, the only new information provided by McIlhargey was the emotional state of his commander, Major Reno. This cast a new light on the unfolding events and Custer moved at a rapid pace up the steep incline leading to Wooden Leg Ridge to observe events for himself.[17] About this time, privates Brennan and Fitzgerald turned their horses toward the rear.[18]

The command scaled the incline in column of twos; Company F, the Band Box Troop, in the lead.[19] The General and his Aide–de–camp, Tom Custer, watched the troops from a slight elevation. When they reached the hill, the command reformed in column of fours, the companies riding abreast; the order from the river being E, F, L, I, and C.[20] From his vantage point on Wooden Leg Ridge, Custer had an unobstructed view of the upper valley. He was thus able to determine that Benteen's battalion would not encounter any significant warrior force; rendering the continuance of Benteen's reconnaissance pointless. Custer was also able to observe Reno's initial actions in the valley fight. Eyewitnesses sighted Custer on the bluffs both during the charge down the valley[21] and from the skirmish line.[22] Although he was unable to see much of the village from this vantage point, Custer was aware that Reno had ceased offensive operations and was operating on the defensive. He also knew that the entire village was north of his command and that Benteen's 118 troopers were effectively out of the fight. An immediate consolidation of the regiment was required, and that's exactly what Custer ordered.

Custer called for a messenger. Because his horse was almost played out, Sergeant August Finckle had to relinquish the duty to his comrade in Company C, Sergeant Daniel A. Kanipe.[23] Kanipe was ordered to have the pack train and escort come straight across country so that they would rejoin the command in the minimum amount of time; Custer did not want a repeat of his Washita experience where the reserve ammunition was brought up under fire. If Kanipe happened upon Benteen's battalion, they were to be hurried to the front as well. It was probably at this point that Custer, or perhaps Mitch Boyer, waved his hat.[24]

Although he had obtained valuable information from his observations on Wooden Leg Ridge, one critical point was still very much in doubt: how far downstream did the village extend? In order to conceal his movements, Custer sent the command down Cedar Coulee[25] in column of fours;[26] a detail from F serving as the point.[27] Custer, accompanied by Mitch Boyer and the Crow scouts, marched down the line of bluffs until a clear view of the lower valley could be obtained.

The view, and tactical intelligence, Custer sought was obtained from Weir Point. This is the first position on the bluffs from which a clear view of the lower valley and the entire village could be obtained.[28] Custer was generally pleased by what he saw. Although Reno had been forced to pivot into the timber when his left was turned,[29] his battalion was in a strong defensive position. While the village was of unprecedented size, it was in a single location rather than spread out as had been the case at the Washita. The item that encouraged Custer most however, was his observation that the warrior force seemed to be concentrating solely on Reno. The opinion that his immediate command had not been detected was reinforced by the observation that the village appeared to be deserted. Custer therefore exulted to his troops with the remark misunderstood by Martin: *"We've caught them napping!"*

After completing his observations from Weir Point,[30] Custer had no further need of his Crow scouts. Goes Ahead remembered that Custer had told the scouts they had taken him to the enemy and need not go into the fight.[31] To this, Mitch Boyer added his personal admonition *". . . to leave the fighting to the soldiers, watch from the hills and if we are getting licked make your way back to Terry and tell him we are all killed."*[32] After dismissing his scouts, Custer returned to the main column which had halted in upper Medicine Tail Coulee. While Reno might be expected to hold the timber for some time, a consolidation of the regiment must be effected without delay. Custer could not take the risk that Kanipe would fail to encounter Benteen. He therefore dispatched Martin with a message specifically for Benteen to hurry to the front with the ammunition packs. Lieutenant Cooke, recognizing that Martin had some difficulty with English, called on him to wait, then handed him a hastily scribbled message. While the note was ambiguous regarding Custer's intentions (Benteen would quite properly interpret the order as calling for the entire pack train rather than just the reserve ammunition, thus causing some confusion on Benteen's part), it left no margin for interpretation, or freedom of action, by its recipient. The enemy was close at hand, and the pack train, escorted by Benteen's battalion, was to immediately effect a junction with the regiment's commander.

Shortly after Martin was dispatched with the order for Benteen, Boston Custer rejoined his brothers in upper Medicine Tail Coulee (see Appendix 12) and informed the general that Benteen was close behind. Custer then determined to strike the village in the center with Benteen's battalion, perhaps augmented by one of Keogh's companies, while he would continue north with the remaining troops to strike the village at its lower end. When there was still no sign of Benteen after a wait of about 10 minutes, Custer's hand was forced. He could wait no longer to relieve the pressure on Reno and therefore dispatched Yates' battalion,[33] Troops F and E, to demonstrate at the ford[34] while the remainder of the command assumed position on Luce Ridge,[35] which afforded Custer an unobstructed view of Yates' demonstration at the ford. While Custer was undoubtedly surprised, and disappointed, in Benteen's tardiness, his plan was still workable. When Benteen arrived, part of his battalion could be dispatched to reinforce Yates at the ford in a holding action. The remainder of the column would proceed down stream to strike the lower end of the village.

While Yates marched toward the ford,[36] Custer dispatched a messenger to the north, toward Terry's column.[37] The message was probably to inform Terry that a very large village had been found and that Custer was attacking. I believe there is compelling, although circumstantial, evidence that Private Nathan Short of Company C was that messenger. Curly recalled seeing a trooper, riding a sorrel–roan horse,[38] dispatched northward from Medicine Tail Coulee. On August 3rd, the body of a sorrel–roan 7th Cavalry horse, shot in the forehead, was found on the Yellowstone opposite the mouth of the Rosebud; an army–issue Springfield carbine lying ten feet from the horse's head.[39] On August 8th, somewhere between 2 and 9 miles up the Rosebud from the Yellowstone, Terry's flankers found the body of an enlisted man near the trail lying in heavy rosebrush. The hat had been marked "7 C" under the brass crossed saber insignia, indicating the owner was assigned to Company C. The cartridge belt had an informal serial number inked on it which Sergeants Kanipe and Richard P. Hanley of Company C identified as being assigned to Private Short.[40] While soldier accounts make no mention of the cause of death, the Minneconjou Lights recalled hearing *"one soldier was found some days afterwards and many miles away. Wounded, he had been subsisting on raw frogs and some were found in his pockets after he was killed."*[41]

Captain Freeman's journal contains the following provocative entry for August 11, 1876: *"Dead white man found today and the remains of another who is supposed to have been burned at the stake."*[42] The date of the entry being 3 days later than the initial report of the finding of a body may indicate the length of time it took Freeman to learn of the discovery, or, if he didn't keep up his journal daily, he may have been in error as to the date when he finally transcribed the entry. In any event, we have no other sources that indicate a body, or bodies, was discovered on two separate occasions, so Freeman apparently is referring to the discovery of the body of Nathan Short. The presence of a second body, showing evidence of being burned is a mystery – Freeman's terse comment being the only surviving soldier account. The Minneconjou Flying By, however, recalled hearing other Indians mentioning finding, and presumably killing, two nearly starved soldiers on the Rosebud, at least one of whom had been eating frogs.[43] This may explain the inscription on the manila envelope stolen from the Two Moon Monument on the Cheyenne Reservation in October of 1960: *". . . two soldiers got away from Custer Battle alive . . ."*[44] Tables 15 – 1 and 15 – 2 show the available combat strengths and assignments at the time the Custer

Fight began. For simplicity, the return of the Herendeen party is included in the portion of the table dealing with Reno's battalion.

Yates arrived at the ford[45] about the time the advance elements of Reno's retreat reached Reno Hill.[46] Yates dismounted Company F on the first bench and volley fired into the village[47] while E Troop continued to the crossing.[48] Although it was never Custer's intention to attempt a crossing at that point, the Cheyenne believe they stopped Custer's advance at that point, perhaps killing as many as three men:[49]

> "White Shield overtook a group of four Cheyennes, among whom were Roan Bear, Bobtail Horse, and Calf. (Note Peter John Powell in "People of the Sacred Mountain" omits mention of White Shield and names Dull Knife as the first warrior to fire on the soldiers from the ford. DCE) . . . As the Cheyennes rode out of the river toward the troops, who were still at a distance, they saw that the soldiers were following five Sioux who were running from them. They gradually circled away from in front of the soldiers, and the troops did not follow them, but kept on toward the river. The troops were headed straight for the ford – about half a mile above the battlefield – and White Shield and the other Cheyennes believed that Custer was about to cross the river and get into the camp. The troops were getting near them, but suddenly, before the troops reached the river, the gray–horse company halted and dismounted, and all who were following them, as far as could be seen, also stopped and dismounted.

> "White Shield rode off to the left and down the river, while Bobtail Horse, Calf, and the two or three who were with them stopped close to the river, and under cover of a low ridge began to shoot at the soldiers. The five Sioux whom the troops had at first seemed to be pursuing now joined Calf and Bobtail Horse, and the ten Indians were shooting at the soldiers as fast as they could. About the time the soldiers halted, one was killed."[50]

There is no agreement in the various Indian accounts as to how long the demonstration at Minneconjou Ford lasted,[51] but it probably consumed no more than about 20 minutes. When the Lakota began arriving in strength, the troops began to withdraw up Deep Coulee[52] in the direction of Calhoun Hill; Troop E covering the movement as dismounted skirmishers.[53] The Lakota, of course, attributed this withdrawal to their overwhelming numbers. The Cheyenne accounts, supported by physical evidence, paint an entirely different picture, as will be explained shortly.

While the feint at the ford had accomplished Custer's objective in relieving the pressure on Reno, it had been perhaps even more beneficial to the Lakota and Cheyenne. Their morale already high from the thrashing of Reno in valley, the exultant warriors could only interpret the lack of aggressiveness at the ford as timidity on the part of these new soldiers. The ease with which the Lakota perceived they drove Custer from the ford made strong hearts of all the warriors.

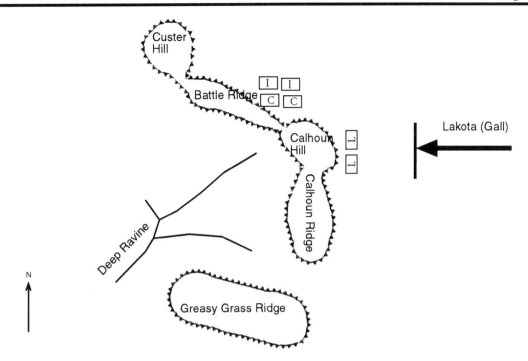

Figure 15 – 1 Initial Positions Of The Keogh Battalion

Recall that a party of about 50 Cheyenne, including Wolf Tooth and Big Foot, had slipped away from the village and crossed to the east, or right, bank of the Greasy Grass the night of June 24 – 25. This band was about 4 miles from the battlefield when they were informed of the presence of soldiers, not on the Rosebud as expected, but in close proximity to the village. Turning their ponies, they arrived in Medicine Tail Coulee while Keogh's battalion was on Luce Ridge and Yates was demonstrating at the ford.[54] The arrival of this warrior force presented a grave threat being in the rear of Yates' 76 man battalion. Dismounted volley fire[55] from Luce Ridge[56] failed to dislodge the warriors and Custer was forced to move toward the high ground (Calhoun Hill) to the north.[57] From this point on, Custer was forced to react to the evolving tactical situation rather than dictating it by aggressive action. There is evidence that Custer sent a detail to Yates at the ford to order his withdrawal.[58] This detail may have been commanded by First Sergeant James Butler, explaining the presence of his body near the ford.[59] In any event, Keogh's battalion, accompanied by Custer,[60] engaged in a running fight along Blummer–Nye–Cartwright Ridge[61] as they moved toward Calhoun Hill.[62]

Reconcentrating the two battalions in the vicinity of Calhoun Hill,[63] Custer realized that his feint had worked too well; Benteen, encumbered by the pack train, would never be able to fight his way through the ever increasing horde of warriors streaming toward Calhoun Hill. Quickly surveying the situation, Custer seized on the only remaining chance for the total victory he sought. The warriors were not pressing the command too closely; Keogh's battalion should be able to hold them from the advantageous terrain offered by Calhoun Hill. Custer had also noticed the non–combatants fleeing down stream from the village. If he could capture a major portion of the women and children with Yates' small battalion, he could use them as a shield as he had done when extricating his command at the Washita. Leaving Keogh's battalion engaged in some noisy, but ineffective in terms of inflicting casualties, long range firing.[64] Custer mounted E Troop and proceeded northward over Last Stand Hill.[65] As the 7th marched through the present national cemetery, Wolf Tooth's party appeared on Last Stand Hill and fired ineffectively on the rear of the column.[66]

Arriving at the northern ford, which I will refer to as Crazy Horse Ford, Custer attempted to force a crossing.[67] Receiving fire from a warrior force of indeterminate size, he was forced to halt his advance.[68] He withdrew to the flats near the present trading post[69] and remained there some little time before returning, via the present national cemetery,[70] to Last Stand Hill.[71] During this withdrawal, newspaper correspondent Mark Kellogg[72] and perhaps two troopers were killed. While the main portion of the command waited on the flats below the cemetery and present superintendent's house, E Troop, dismounted as skirmishers, cleared the ridge of warriors.[73]

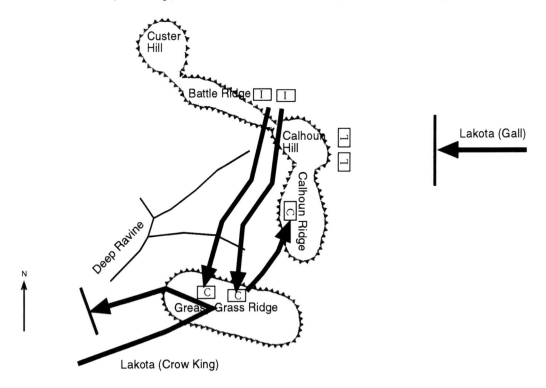

Figure 15 – 2 Deployment Of Company C
Keogh Battalion Second And Third Positions

Having failed in his attempt to capture the non–combatants, Custer was finally forced squarely on the defensive. Initially, Keogh had been able to keep the warriors at bay solely with Company L, holding the inexperienced C[74] and his own I in reserve.[75] After some little time, however, circumstances forced Keogh to deploy C Troop in two platoons. Custer had too few men to defend the entire ridge line[76] and undoubtedly knew that the warriors were already moving to outflank Keogh. Custer decided to consolidate the battalions in the most advantageous defensive position – Calhoun Hill. To accomplish the consolidation, and protect his flank and rear, one platoon of Company E was dispatched to the so–called South Skirmish Line,[77] while the remaining platoon, perhaps commanded by Lieutenant Smith, covered the "back door" to Last Stand Hill in the vicinity of the present stone house.[78] Company F, and the regimental staff began to move toward Calhoun Hill on the east side of Battle Ridge. Previously Keogh had dispatched platoons of Company C to Greasy Grass and Calhoun Ridges,[79] the former already occupied by a warrior force threatening Company L's right flank.[80] The position on Calhoun Ridge supported Company L while the position on Greasy Grass Ridge commanded the head of Deep Coulee and supported the platoon of E Troop on the South Skirmish Line.[81] It was at this crucial moment,[82] when the platoon from Company E was deploying along the South Skirmish Line, supported by a platoon of Company C on Greasy Grass Ridge,[83] that the Southern Cheyenne Old Man Chief, Lame White Man, seized the moment, and fulfilled his destiny.

Lame White Man, accompanied by his brother–in–law Tall Sioux, purifying himself via the sweat bath ritual when news of Reno's attack reached the Cheyenne circle:

"Lame White Man, Tall Sioux, and the others were still inside the sweat lodge when the first sounds of fighting were heard. During a sweat bath, the lodge cover is opened and closed the sacred four times, and water is sprinkled on the hot stones each time, to make the purifying steam. The sweat lodge cover had been closed for the second or third time when Twin Woman, Lame White Man's wife, heard the noise of shooting and excitement in the upper camp.

"When Lame White Man and the others heard the sounds they quickly crawled out of the sweat lodge. They ran up the riverbank, heading back to their families to help them catch horses and get away. When Lame White Man reached his tipi, he found his war horse still picketed there. Twin Woman had already caught a pony for herself, so Lame White Man swung Red Hat [Red Hood], their little son, up behind his mother. Crane Woman, their young daughter, waited alongside on another horse.

"Lame White Man was still stripped for the sweat bath, and there was no time now for him to dress in war clothing. He quickly wrapped a blanket about his waist and grabbed a belt, moccasins, and a gun. Then he jumped on his horse, and he and his family dashed off. They rode hard, heading for the hills west of the camp, toward which many of the People were now running.

"About halfway there, Lame White Man called to his wife, 'I must go across the river. I must follow my boys!' He rode away from his family, while Twin Woman continued on with the children to a nearby hill."[84]

Crossing at Crazy Horse Ford[85] along with the Cheyenne and Oglala warriors, Lame White Man had turned south, while Crazy Horse had continued east, to arrive in Deep Ravine. In Deep Ravine Lame White Man was joined by Crow King and his warriors who crossed at that point.[86] Noting the pitifully few soldiers on Greasy Grass Ridge and the South Skirmish Line,[87] Lame White Man rose up shouting his war cry: *"Come, we can kill all of them!"* Mounted on his war pony, he was eagerly supported by a horde of warriors, dissatisfied with the long range firing that precluded the winning of any war honors,[88] in the charge that overwhelmed the platoon of E,[89] who probably didn't have an opportunity to draw their pistols after expending the round in their carbines.[90] As Hump, the Minneconjou Chief, whipped his horse forward he received a wound in the leg above the knee, the ball exiting his hip. His horse also having been hit, Hump was thrown to the ground. Despite being in great pain, he encouraged his warriors, who forked around their fallen chief, shouting his war cry: *"Hi–yi–yi!"*[91] White Bull, who claimed 7 coups in the fighting, describes his involvement at this stage of the fighting:[92]

"Soldier aims [at] White Bull and does not fire; then, when White Bull gets close, he throws gun at White Bull, and White Bull wrestles with him. After [wrestling] so long, [White Bull] gets on top and hits him on head. Wrestling soldier tries to take White Bull's gun from White Bull's left hand, and soldier about gets it. So, White Bull hits him in face with whip, and soldier lets go. Then, [the soldier] comes back with fists and hits White Bull on jaw and shoulder, then grabs his hair and tries to bite White Bull's nose [who] yelled all the time to scare soldier. Then White Bull hits him

several times on the head and pushed him over, and takes his gun and cartridge belt and counted coup. [The] soldier did not make any noise, and as White Bull was afraid he could not get the best of the soldier, he yelled all the time to scare the soldier."[93]

The force of the charge carried almost to the top of Battle Ridge and forced Custer to execute a retrograde movement of Company F toward Last Stand Hill.[94] But the warriors were not interested in the troopers east of Battle Ridge for the moment, they had already turned their attention toward the platoon of C Troop occupying Greasy Grass Ridge.[95] Inexperienced as they were, their right flank now totally unprotected, the platoon broke and ran. Their path of retreat took them in a roughly semicircular path through the second platoon of Company C, perhaps commanded by First Sergeant Edwin Bobo,[96] defending Calhoun Ridge. These troopers also broke and ran; the combined force moving, in order, through the position on Calhoun Hill occupied by Company L, then through the reserve position held by Company I in the ravine east of Battle Ridge with, finally, a few survivors reaching Last Stand Hill.[97] During this rout, one of the soldiers broke away and was pursued for some little distance before he was killed.[98] One trooper[99] almost made good his escape at this point as the Oglala Flying Hawk related:

> *"The man supposed to have been Lt. Harrington was driven back along the ridge with the rest from Calhoun Hill to Custer Hill, and on arriving there he did not stop going but went right on, and so he knows this man left the field before Custer was killed, because Custer was not yet surrounded. This man fired two shots back and was seen to fall. He got about half a mile away."[100]*

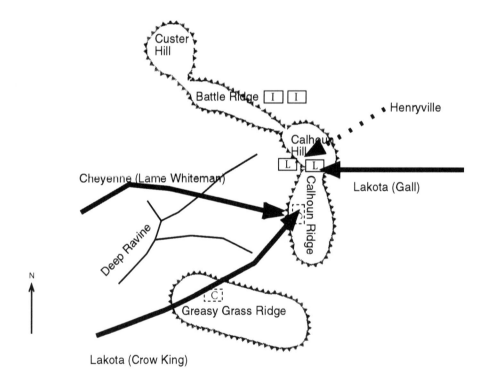

Figure 15 – 3 Keogh Battalion Final Positions

The warriors were in hot pursuit of the remnants of C Troop, inflicting the same heavy losses on these fleeing troopers as they had on Reno's column a short time before. The Two Kettle Lakota Runs The Enemy recalled: *"Another charge was made and they retreated along the line of the ridge; it looked like a stampede of buffalo. On this retreat along the ridge, the soldiers were met by my band of Indians as well as other Sioux. The soldiers now broke the line and divided, some of them going down the eastern slope of the hill, (toward Keogh's reserve company, DCE) and some of them going down to the river. The others came back to where the final stand was made on the hill, but they were few in numbers then."*[101] The Minneconjou White Bull also described the rout of Company C:

> *". . . now many bunches on south and west took charge at one company and drove them back to where Custer monument [now] is. There was much dust, and we rode among them and pulled them off their horses."*[102]

The Cheyenne Yellow Nose,[103] may have captured Company C's guidon[104] which he used to count coup on a trooper on Calhoun Hill:

> *"One trooper was carrying a flag. As he saw Yellow Nose coming, he jumped on his horse and started to run. Yellow Nose was too quick for him. Riding up to the ve?ho?e (Cheyenne for white soldier, DCE), he grabbed the flag out to the trooper's hand. The soldier was bleeding badly, and now, as Yellow Nose wrenched the flag from him, he dropped from his horse. Yellow Nose did not bother to touch him. Instead, he charged ahead, striking soldiers right and left with the flag, counting coup on them, touching the soldier horses as well, claiming them as his own."*[105]

Calhoun's L Company had been holding Gall and his Lakota south of Calhoun Hill at bay, apparently repulsing at least the charge that stampeded the led horses.[106] The failure of Company C to hold forced Company L to pivot to the west to counter the pursuing warriors. Volley fire checked this advance, but just at that moment a large force of warriors, armed with repeating rifles (Winchesters and Henrys),[107] rose up east of Calhoun Hill, in the region now referred to as Henryville,[108] and poured a murderous fire into Calhoun's rear. At virtually the same instant, Gall led a charge against Calhoun's exposed left flank. In less time than it takes to tell it, Company L virtually disintegrated, the men falling in perfect skirmish order,[109] before the three–pronged onslaught.[110] The Indian accounts and archaeological evidence are crystal clear in their agreement that Company L behaved in a highly skilled and professional manner throughout the fight.[111] The valiant Calhoun had been true to his word;[112] the time had come and, although he was unable to work the miracle his brother–in–law so desperately needed, he had not been found wanting.[113]

The exultant warriors pouring over and around Calhoun Hill fell next on Keogh's own Company I, which had been held in reserve,[114] before they had time to deploy.[115] In an instant the warriors were on the troopers and the fighting, described by the triumphant warriors as the fiercest on the field,[116] was hand to hand.[117] These descriptions are supported by the scarcity of soldier shell casings recovered from this area;[118] they simply didn't have an opportunity to reload. The fists and rifle butts of the soldiers were poor matches for the clubs, hatchets and lances of the warriors for close in fighting. Had the 7th retained their sabers, they would have inflicted greater damage, but the result would have been the same.[119]

Crazy Horse was prominent during this phase of the fighting, making a bravery run in front of Company I that drew a hail of bullets, emptying the soldier's single shot carbines. The Arapaho, Waterman, recalled the courage of Crazy Horse: *"Crazy Horse, the Sioux Chief, was the bravest man I ever saw. He rode closest to the soldiers, yelling to his warriors. All the soldiers were shooting at him, but he was never hit."*[120] Crazy Horse then led the charge that split and isolated I Company, leading to their extermination.[121] The Oglala Red Feather, a brother–in–law of Crazy

Horse, told General Scott in 1921: *"At this point Crazy Horse came up and rode between the two parties. The soldiers all fired at once, but missed him. The Indians got the idea the soldier guns were empty and charge immediately. They charged right over the hill. Red Feather, yelling, shot into the soldiers who tried to get away. That made it easier for the Indians who shot them from behind. He did not follow the soldiers very far because he was interested in taking the soldiers' saddle bags."*[122] The Cheyenne Brave Bear may have been the slayer of Captain Keogh as he related:

> *"Only one officer among them was still mounted.[123] He was a brave man, riding a sorrel horse (While Comanche was a bay, he had a mixture of red coloring and may have been mistaken for a sorrel, DCE[124]) and covering the rear of his retreating men (Keogh's body was found in the group of bodies closest to Calhoun Hill which would have put him in rear of his company as it withdrew toward Last Stand Hill, DCE). A Lakota scalp–shirt wearer charged the officer, who turned and shot the Lakota through the head with a pistol – the soldier chief's only weapon. Then a Cheyenne warrior charged the officer, who raised his pistol and shot him through the breast, killing him. Now the soldier chief had killed two fighting men. Brave Bear, watching all this, drew careful aim. He fired, and the soldier chief dropped from his sorrel horse, dead."*[125]

The archaeological evidence suggests a detailed scenario for the demise of one of Keogh's troopers. The marker in question, number 174, stands near the eastern boundary of the monument. Excavation in this area yielded 3 carbine casings (fired from the same weapon), a Colt cartridge, a Colt bullet, and a deformed .50/70 bullet. With this evidence we can correlate Indian accounts of a trooper fleeing from the Keogh area toward the east. As the man ran toward the east he drew fire from the warriors in his rear. He stopped and returned fire, perhaps expending the final 3 rounds for his Springfield. He then attempted to use his pistol as the warriors closed in. The spent Colt bullet indicates he may have pulled the trigger on his Colt for the last time just as he received his fatal wound. If the .50/70 was the fatal round, it is ironic to note it was probably an army surplus round obtained by the Indians.[126]

The remnants of Keogh's battalion, using their remaining horses as shields,[127] struggled toward Last Stand Hill under a murderous fire from the pursing warriors on their flank and rear. Those that reached Last Stand Hill owed the few additional precious minutes of their lives to the covering fire of the remnant of Company E as the Cheyenne recalled: *"They poured out such a heavy hail of bullets that, for a time, the pursuing warriors on horseback had to pull back over the top of a nearby hill."*[128]

In the space of a few minutes Custer's command was reduced to Company F, a platoon of E, and some stragglers from Keogh's decimated battalion. It was at this juncture that the so called "last stand" was made. Shooting their horses to form a breastwork against warriors attacking from the southwest, the survivors hunkered down in anticipation of a siege.

The Indians now halted their charge and employed a tactic on the remnants of the 7th huddled on Last Stand Hill that had proven successful a decade earlier against Fetterman. The fighting regressed to a somewhat long–range affair, with one deadly difference. The warriors now relied on the bow and arrow, sending high arching arrows to fall among the exposed troopers while not exposing the archer to return fire.[129] This phase of the fighting is described by Wooden Leg:

> *"We were lying down in gullies and behind sagebrush hillocks. The shooting at first was at a distance, but we kept creeping in closer all around the ridge. Bows and*

arrows were in use much more than guns. From the hiding places of the Indians, the arrows could be shot in a high and long curve, to fall upon the soldiers or their horses. An Indian using a gun had to jump up and expose himself long enough to shoot.[130] *The arrows falling upon the horses stuck in their backs and caused them to go plunging here and there, knocking down the soldiers."*[131]

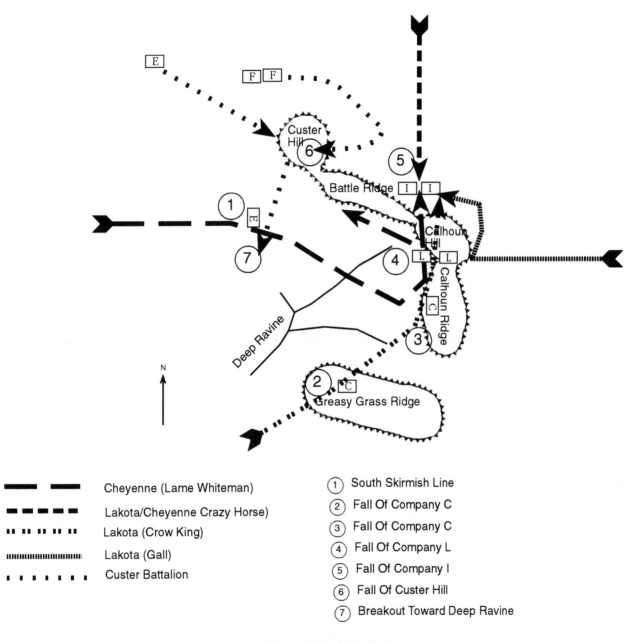

▬ ▬ ▬ ▬ Cheyenne (Lame Whiteman)	① South Skirmish Line
▬ ▬ ▬ ▬ Lakota/Cheyenne Crazy Horse)	② Fall Of Company C
■ ■ ■ ■ ■ Lakota (Crow King)	③ Fall Of Company C
▥▥▥▥▥▥ Lakota (Gall)	④ Fall Of Company L
▪ ▪ ▪ ▪ ▪ Custer Battalion	⑤ Fall Of Company I
	⑥ Fall Of Custer Hill
	⑦ Breakout Toward Deep Ravine

Figure 15 – 4 Battle Sequence

After some little time, the suicide boys charged through the remaining troopers. This attack, launched from the site of the present national cemetery, struck the survivors on their flank and rear. According to Stands In Timber: *"They galloped up to the level ground near where the museum now is. Some turned and stampeded the gray horses of the soldiers. By then they were mostly loose, the ones that had not been shot. The rest charged right in at the place where the soldiers were making their stand, and the others followed them as soon as they got the horses away.*

The group of markers on Last Stand Hill. Custer's marker, marking the location of his burial rather than kill site, is in the center with the black shield. The South Skirmish Line can be faintly seen in the upper left as can the mouth of Deep Ravine. A portion of the National Cemetery is visible at the upper left. *Photo by author.*

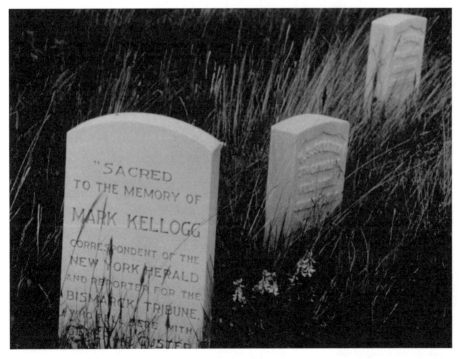

Kellogg marker on the east side of Battle Ridge. Burial accounts clearly establish Kellogg's body was found very near the river making this marker's location in error by perhaps as much as a mile. While several individual markers (the Kellogg marker, the Algernon Smith marker, and the markers for unidentified officers Henry Harrington, James Porter, George Lord and Jack Sturgis) are obviously improperly placed, the archaeological evidence clearly demonstrates the markers are valid representations of trooper burial locations. *Photo by author.*

Mouth of Deep Ravine from Last Stand Hill. Note the markers on the lower portion of Deep Ravine Trail are hidden from vantage points on Last Stand Hill as well as the upper portion of Deep Ravine Trail by the rise in the picture's center. In my opinion, this indicates the South Skirmish Line could not have extended beyond that rise. The far side of the rise could be effectively covered from extended positions based upon either Greasy Grass or Calhoun Ridge. *Photo by author.*

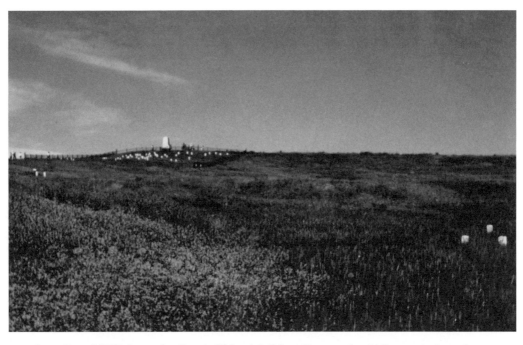

Last Stand Hill from the South Skirmish Line. Fore and middle ground markers represent isolated troopers. *Photo by author.*

Markers along the upper portion of Deep Ravine Trail taken from Last Stand Hill look-ing Southwest. The archaeological evidence indicates an organized resistance at this location and the spacing of the markers approximates dismounted skirmish intervals. I believe this portion of Deep Ravine Trail, clearly visible from Last Stand Hill, repre-sents the South Skirmish Line. *Photo by author.*

Markers along the lower portion of Deep Ravine Trail Looking Northwest. I believe these markers represent the group led by Mitch Boyer that attempted to breakout at the end of the Custer Fight rather than an extension of the South Skirmish Line. *Photo by author.*

The Custer clan was decimated at the Little Big Horn, Margaret Custer Calhoun, sister of the general, lost her husband, three brothers, and a nephew. Top to bottom, left to right: Lieutenant James Calhoun, Captain Tom Custer, Lieutenant Colonel George Armstrong Custer, Armstrong Reed (named for his uncle who once thought of adopting the boy), and Boston Custer. *Photo Courtesy Little Bighorn Battlefield National Monument.*

Captain Myles W. Keogh in full dress uniform. In his first major action against Indians with the 7th Cavalry, his battalion checked the advance of the warriors from Medicine Tail and Deep Coulees while Custer attempted to capture the non-combatants. *Photo Courtesy Little Bighorn Battlefield National Monument.*

Lieutenant William W. Cooke in full dress uniform, taken in 1875. As Custer's adjutant, he scribbled the famous "Be quick. Bring Packs" message to Benteen. His body, along with others of the regimental staff, being found in close proximity to Armstrong Custer's indicates Custer was exercising direct command until near the end of the fight. One of his distinctive side whiskers was taken as a trophy by the Cheyenne Wooden Leg. *Photo Courtesy Little Bighorn Battlefield National Monument.*

[At left] Lieutenant Colonel, Brevet Major General, George Armstrong Custer, taken in 1875. Note the close cropped hair, similar to how he wore it on his final campaign, and the receding hair line. *Photo Courtesy Little Bighorn Battlefield National Monument.*

[Below left] Lieutenant James Calhoun in full dress uniform, taken in 1875. His company, the most actively engaged on Custer's part of the field, held the warriors at bay until, attacked on three sides, it virtually disintegrated. *Photo Courtesy Little Bighorn Battlefield National Monument.*

[Below right] Captain, then Lieutenant, Thomas W. Custer in full dress uniform, taken in 1873. Note the two Medals of Honor won during the final days of the Civil War. *Photo Courtesy Little Bighorn Battlefield National Monument.*

Portrait of the Uncpapa Lakota Crow King, who lost two brothers in the fight and was involved in the pivotal fighting for Calhoun Hill. Like Low Dog, he believed the soldiers would have won had Reno held his position in the timber. *Photo Courtesy Little Bighorn Battlefield National Monument.*

Portrait of the Oglala Lakota Low Dog. Credited by Stands in Timber with killing a fleeing trooper on the second rise east of the battlefield. Like Crow King, he believed the soldiers would have won had Reno held his position in the timber. *Photo Courtesy Little Bighorn Battlefield National Monument.*

Portrait of the Uncpapa Lakota Gall, taken in 1881. After his two wives and three children were killed in the valley fight, he was a leader in the fighting culminating in the collapse of the Calhoun Hill position. *Photo Courtesy Little Bighorn Battlefield National Monument.*

Portrait of the Uncpapa Lakota Rain in the Face, taken in 1881, showing full war bonnet. Rain in the Face was believed by many to have cut out and eaten the heart of Tom Custer. *Photo Courtesy Little Bighorn Battlefield National Monument.*

The Cheyenne Wooden Leg, taken in 1927. Wooden Leg holds the "trapdoor" Springfield carbine he wrenched from one of Reno's fleeing troopers in the valley fight. Wooden Leg's account furnishes a wealth of information about Custer's movements and the fighting on that part of the field. *Photo Courtesy Little Bighorn Battlefield National Monument.*

Portrait of the Uncpapa Lakota Sitting Bull. Spiritual leader of his people, Sitting Bull counciled, and practiced, a policy of isolationism regarding the white man. He had prophetic visions of the victory on the Little Big Horn during the two sundances preceding the fight. *Photo Courtesy Little Bighorn Battlefield National Monument.*

Custer's striker John Burkman holds the general's mounts Dandy and Victory, or Vic, in 1869. One of the enduring myths of the Little Big Horn is that Custer, a man mounted on a blazed faced sorrel with four white stockings, was killed in the river at the mouth of Medicine Tail Coulee at the start of the fight. Although the right foreleg is obscured in this view, the mare Vic obviously did not have four white stockings. *Photo Courtesy Little Bighorn Battlefield National Monument.*

The suicide boys started the hand–to–hand fighting, and all of them were killed or mortally wounded." [132] Gall, the Uncpapa, apparently either participated in, or witnessed, this event: "*. . . went on down to where the last soldiers were. They were fighting good. The men were loading and firing, but they could not hit the warriors in the gully and the ravine. The dust and smoke was black as evening. Once in a while we could see the soldiers through the dust, and finally we charged through them with our ponies. When we had done this, right here on this ground and just a few rods south of us, the fight was over."* [133] This charge stampeded the remaining horses of E Company. The Uncpapa, Iron Hawk describes that portion of the action:

> *"We looked up and saw the cavalry horses stampeding. They were all gray horses. Little Bear began to get ready. He put on his pretty saddle blanket. He was riding a pinto gray horse. Little Bear said: 'Take courage, the earth is all that lasts.' Then Little Bear's horse reared up and started out. He began to charge at Custer (the troops on Last Stand Hill, DCE) and when he got right near him his horse was shot out from under him. Little Bear jumped off and decided to run back and got shot. He got up again after being shot in the leg and started back. His friend, Elk Nation, started out to save him. As he went up there the soldiers shot at him and Little Bear got on with Elk Nation. The soldiers kept pumping shots at them both."* [134]

The survivors of the suicide boys' charge knew they were doomed. All that remained was for Mitch Boyer, clad in his unmistakable calf–skin vest, to lead a small group of soldiers toward the tantalizing perceived safety of the river. They made it as far west, and a little to the south of the South Skirmish Line, [135] so that the bodies along this line appeared to all have been killed at the same time when they actually died about 30 minutes apart. Two Moon describes the final moments of the Custer Fight:

> *"At last about a hundred men and five horsemen stood on the hill all bunched together. All along the bugler kept blowing his commands. He was very brave too. Then a chief was killed. I hear it was Long Hair, I don't know; and then the five horsemen and the bunch of men, may be so forty, started toward the river. The man on the sorrel horse led them, shouting all the time. He wore a buckskin shirt, and had long black hair and mustache.[136] He fought hard with a big knife. His men were all covered with white dust."* [137]

Iron Hawk gave a more detailed account of his participation in the end of the Custer Fight:

> *"Just as the two (Little Bear and Elk Nation, DCE) got back everyone hollered: 'Now they have gone.' We looked up and the soldiers all were running toward the Hunkpapas on foot. I had nothing but bow and arrows. Someone on the right side began charging first – his name was Red Horn Buffalo. The Hunkpapas said: 'Hokahey!' and charged at them. The soldiers were running downhill and the Hunkpapas were charging (probably refers to the final breakout toward the South Skirmish Line, DCE). When they saw us, the soldiers swung down and Red Horn Buffalo rode right into the soldiers. This was the last we saw of this man. The Hunkpapas ran right up to the soldiers and encircled them from all sides. I noticed that Red Horn Buffalo's horse was going alone, empty saddled.*

> *"By this time I was up among the soldiers. Of course they came to fight us and we had to fight. I was there to fight. I went among them and met the soldiers, so I just took my bow and arrow and shot one of them straight through under the ribs and I heard him scream. Just about this time I looked over there and I saw two soldiers*

fleeing alone and Indians on top of them. Then I went after them. There was a little creek going up there and one of the soldiers got killed by Brings Plenty. There are headstones all over there (apparently refers to Keogh area, DCE) and the furthest headstone shows where the second man that I killed lies. These white men wanted it, they called for it and I let them have it. The first time I did not kill this man, as I hit him crosswise over the back of the shoulders. Then I let him have it with the bow over the head until I killed him. Because they wanted it and called for it, I was very mad because the women and children had run away scared and I was thinking about this when I did this killing. I said: 'Hownh!' (the sound of an angry grizzly bear sometimes used by the Lakota in battle, DCE) three times while hitting the man. After the man fell off the horse I got off and was still beating him because I was so mad. Probably this was the last of Custer's men to be killed and I killed him."[138]

The Arapaho Waterman witnessed the end on Custer Knoll:

"When I reached the top of the hill I saw Custer.[139] He was dressed in buckskin, coat and pants, and was on his hands and knees. He had been shot through the side and there was blood coming from his mouth. He seemed to be watching the Indians moving around him. Four soldiers were sitting up around him, but they were all badly wounded. All the other soldiers were down. Then the Indians closed in around him, and I did not see any more."[140]

All that remained now was for the victors to collect their spoils and vent their rage on the bodies of the wounded and the slain. According to the Oglala Lone Bear: *". . . there were numbers of soldiers wounded and alive after the fight. They were mostly killed by the squaws who followed the warriors in the fight."*[141] The Brule Two Eagles recalled one woman dispatching a wounded soldier: *"There was one squaw that he noticed particularly as she had her hair cut short. (She was mourning for a son killed a few days before at the fight on [the] Rosebud.) She was carrying an ax, [and] just before he (Two Eagles, DCE) reached the place where she was, a soldier got up, but was quickly caught by two warriors who held him while the squaw killed him with the ax. This was a private soldier. This squaw was a Cheyenne."*[142] Undoubtedly some of these soldiers attempted to escape by feigning death. Black Elk, an Oglala youth of 13 who took two scalps in the battle, described one such attempt:

"I saw something funny. Two fat old women were stripping a soldier, who was wounded and playing dead. When they had him naked, they began to cut something off that he had, and he jumped up and began fighting with the two fat women. He was swinging one of them around, while the other was trying to stab him with her knife. After awhile, another woman rushed up and shoved her knife into him and he died really dead. It was funny to see the naked Wasichu fighting with the fat women."[143]

Wooden Leg, who is named by Thomas Marquis as the source for his mass suicide theory of the battle, also is one of the main sources of the theory that the troopers were drunk.[144] He relates his observations at the conclusion of the fighting:

"I found a metal bottle, as I was walking among the dead men. It was about half full of some kind of liquid. I opened it and found that the liquid was not water. Soon afterward I got hold of another bottle of the same kind that had in it the same

kind of liquid. I showed these to some other Indians. Different ones of them smelled and sniffed. Finally a Sioux said: 'Whiskey.'

"Bottles of this kind (Wooden Leg is probably referring to the soldier's canteens, DCE) were found by several other Indians. Some of them drank the contents. Others tried to drink, but had to spit out their mouthfuls. Bobtail Horse got sick and vomited soon after he had taken a big swallow of it. It became the talk that this whisky explained why the soldiers became crazy and shot each other and themselves instead of shooting us. One old Indian said, though, that there was not enough whisky gone from any of the bottles to make a white man soldier go crazy. We all agreed then that the foolish actions of the soldiers must have been caused by the prayers of our medicine men. I believed this was the true explanation. My belief became change, though, in later years. I think now it was the whisky.

"I took a folded leather package from a soldier having three stripes on the left arm of his coat. It had in it lots of flat pieces of paper having pictures or writing I did not then understand (this was the pay the soldiers had received on the Heart River the evening of May 17, DCE). The paper was of green color. I tore it all up and gave the leather holder to a Cheyenne friend. Others got packages of the same kind from other dead white men. Some of it was kept by the finders. But most of it was thrown away or was given to boys, for them to look at the pictures."[145]

While there were undoubtedly some suicides among the troops,[146] Wooden Leg would later recant his testimony that virtually all of Custer's soldiers died as the result of suicide.[147] Similarly, there is no foundation in fact for a theory of mass drunkenness.[148] Custer, who had not taken a drink since 1862, would never have allowed the troops to reach such a condition. While there was no doubt some liquor in the command, primarily among the officers and civilians, to believe that a majority of the troopers had large quantities of whisky that they had left untouched for three days and finally drained the morning of the fight, is beyond the acceptance of even the most credulous. It is ironic to note that these theories,[149] typically espoused by so-called Native American proponents, merely serve to deny the demonstrated prowess of the warriors. Rather than continue to search for obtuse and convoluted explanations for the soldiers loosing, credit should be given where it is due. The warriors simply overpowered the soldiers on this occasion. The fact that the Indians themselves were dumbfounded with the magnitude of their achievement should not obscure the simple facts of the engagement. Lame White Man recognized and seized the decisive moment in the conflict; becoming the catalyst that, for a brief time, molded the warriors into an irresistible fighting force.

Among the carnage there was an officer whose description resembles Second Lieutenant William Van Wyck Reily of Company F. After all the soldiers had been killed, this officer, who apparently had only been stunned, raised himself on an elbow and gazed upon the field without comprehending what was happening. Initially the warriors fell back as they believed this soldier had returned from the dead. Finally a Lakota strode up to the officer, wrenched the revolver from his clutch, and dispatched him with a shot from his own weapon.[150] Gall, who had fought primarily on the south end of the ridge, had a different recollection of the last trooper to fall:

"There was one soldier on the hill southeast of us[151] still firing when the battle ended and we had a hard time to kill him. He killed several of our braves. Finally some of the braves crawled up the hill on all of the four sides. While he was killing some in front of him, those behind him finally killed him."[152]

Although Wooden Leg maintained there was no dancing or celebrating in the village that night due to the large number of Indian casualties, many on Reno Hill recalled hearing what they believed to be the wild revelry of the Indians as they tortured their helpless victims (see the report of Major Reno in Appendix 7). In 1879, the Uncpapa Little Knife admitted that a soldier with stripes on his arm had been taken prisoner and killed during a wild dance held late that night. [153] The Cheyenne Two Moon, while not admitting any prisoners were taken, said some of the soldiers killed at the ford were dragged into the village, dismembered and burned at a big dance that night. [154] The Cheyenne recall another incident of torture:

> *"As Antelope Woman watched this last fighting, she saw a lone soldier, still alive, back along the ridge. He was sitting on the earth in plain sight, out in the open, rubbing his head as if he were in a daze. Three Lakota warriors ran up and seized him. Slowly, deliberately, they stretched the soldier out on his back. Then, while two of them held his arms, the third man cut off his head with a sheath knife."* [155]

The Cheyenne Wooden Leg took what he considered to be a very unique scalp:

> *"I took one scalp. As I went walking and leading my horse among the dead I observed one face that interested me. The dead man had a long beard growing from both sides of his face and extending several inches below the chin (undoubtedly this was the body of Lieutenant Cooke with his unmistakable Dundreary side whiskers. The burial accounts mention that one of Cooke's side whiskers had been taken. DCE). He had also a full mustache. . . I skinned one side of the face and half of the chin, so as to keep the long beard yet on the part removed."* [156]

Despite the concerted effort to conceal the condition of the dead from their grieving families, we have eye–witness testimony to the ghastly scenes attendant to that butcher's yard after the women had finished their grisly work. [157] In addition to the numerous incidents of dismemberment, there were several decapitations, including the body of Lieutenant Jack Sturgis, son of the regiment's commander, whose head was discovered in the village. [158] The condition of the bodies was such that Corporal John E. Hammon, Company G, could not identify the remains of his own brother, Private George W. Hammon of Company F. [159] Perhaps the most mutilated body on the battlefield was that of Tom Custer. His entire scalp had been taken, leaving only a few tufts on the nape of his neck. His head had been crushed, the features, driven into the ground so as to be unrecognizable. His entire body and head literally bristled with arrows. The only way his body could be identified was via a tattoo on his arm bearing the initials TWC. The condition of the corpse, and the fact that his chest was slashed, gave rise to the legend that Rain In The Face had cut out his heart and eaten it. Longfellow immortalized the grisly deed in verse but chose Armstrong Custer as the victim. Major Reno summed up the sickening sight:

> *"Many of their skulls had been crushed in; eyes had been torn from their sockets; hands, feet, arms, legs and noses had been wrenched off; many had their flesh cut in strips the entire length of their bodies, and there were others whose limbs were closely perforated with bullet holes, showing that the torture had been inflicted while the wretched victims were yet alive."* [160].

One of the persistent legends associated with the Little Big Horn is that Armstrong Custer's body was not mutilated. This has been ascribed by various authors as due to his having committed suicide, which was supposedly somehow sacred to the Indians, or to his demonstrated courage as an adversary. Neither claim has even the slightest basis in fact. Recalling that the purpose of mutilation was to render harm to the victim in the next life, it would be contrary to all logic to spare an especially brave adversary. That was exactly the manner of man that the warriors would want incapacitated in the next life. Similarly, there was no need to spare the body of a suicide in the next life. While most Indian accounts state that they did not know who led the soldiers until long after the battle, the Cheyenne claim to have recognized Custer's body after the fight. I believe that rather than accepting the following account literally, it should be viewed in the context of a morality lesson as to the fate of those who break their word:

> *"Soon after the last of the troopers were dead, two of these Southern women, wandering around the battlefield, came upon a soldier they recognized. He was Long Hair, who lay there, dead. They stood gazing at him, and as they did so, some Lakota warriors came along and were about to cut up his body. The Southern women, thinking of Monahsetah,[161] (made signs, saying, 'He is a relative of ours.' However, they said nothing more about him. So the Lakotas cut off only one joint of a finger.*

> *"The women then pushed the point of a sewing awl into each of Long Hair's ears, on into his head. They did this to improve his hearing, for it seemed he had not heard Stone Forehead's warning eight springs before this, when Custer smoked with the Southern Chiefs in the presence of Maahotse, (the Everywhere Spirit, DCE) vowing that he came in peace. [162] Only truth can be spoken in the hearing of the Sacred Arrows, and Stone Forehead had warned the soldier chief that if he were lying, he and all his men would die."[163]*

None of the contemporary accounts verify this minor mutilation of Custer's body. While it is true that the actual conditions attendant to the discovery of Custer's body were concealed out of deference to his widow, none of the later accounts mention anything resembling the wounds described in the Cheyenne account. Lieutenant Bradley, who discovered the bodies of Custer's command, distorted the facts out of compassion for the families of the slain. In a letter to the editor of the Helena *Herald*, Bradley attempted to dispel the rumors beginning to circulate of the mass mutilations on the battlefield. In regard to Custer's body he wrote:

> *". . . Later in the day I was sent to guide Colonel Benton (Benteen, DCE) of the 7th Cavalry to the field, and was a witness to his recognition of the remains of Custer. Two other officers of that regiment were also present and they could not be mistaken, and the body so identified was wholly unmutilated. Even the wounds that caused his death were scarcely discoverable (though the body was entirely naked), so much so that when I afterwards asked the gentlemen whom I accompanied whether they had observed his wounds, they were forced to say that they had not.*

> *"Probably never did a hero who had fallen upon the field of battle appear so much to have died a natural death. His expression was rather that of a man who had fallen asleep and enjoyed peaceful dreams than that of one who had met his death amid such fearful scenes as that field had witnessed, the features being wholly without ghastliness or any impress of fear, horror, or despair."[164]*

In an account published after the death of Libbie Custer, former Private Jacob Adams, of Company H, confirmed the two wounds in Custer's temple and breast stating that the head wound, which had bled down Custer's face was probably the fatal one. Adams rejected out of hand any consideration that Custer had committed suicide. due to the absence of powder burns.[165] While allowing that Custer had not been scalped, a condition due more to his receding hairline than any mercy on the part of the Indians, Adams mentioned an 6 to 11 inch gash in the left thigh, exposing the bone. In addition to the gash in the thigh, Godfrey confided to his friend, Colonel Charles F. Bates, that Custer's genitals had been mutilated by an arrow which had been forced up his penis.[166] The mutilation of Custer's thigh was typical of that inflicted by the Lakota while the Cheyenne often used arrows in the manner described by Godfrey.

When the fighting was over on Custer's field, Little Wolf's band finally arrived in the village. Many of the Lakota wanted to kill Little Wolf and his party, believing them to have been scouts for the soldiers. After much discussion, during which Little Wolf described his band's sighting of Custer in camp on the Rosebud and the encounter with Sergeant Curtiss' detail over the hard bread box, the newcomers were allowed to join the Cheyenne circle unmolested. There was still some residual resentment that the band had remained so long on the reservation, missing the 3 major fights of the season.[167]

According to custom, the village was moved slightly that night as it was considered bad luck to remain in a camp where a death had occurred. Wooden Leg recalled that most of the tepees were not put up once they had been moved, the people retiring in brush wickiups. This movement of the village is one of the causes of the endless debate over the number of warriors present in the camp. While members of Colonel Gibbon's command counted between 1,500 and 1,800 lodge circles, it is impossible to know how many of these were "duplicates" representing two distinct locations of a single tepee.[168] Similarly, it cannot, at this stage, be determined how many, if any, unattached young men were permanently residing in wickiups. When all is said and done, it is of no consequence whether Custer was opposed by as few as 1,000 or as many as 4,000 warriors. What is important, is the Indians, in a pitched battle, defeated and annihilated, five companies of cavalry. It is also important that we have an historical record, comprised not only of eye–witness testimony, but supported by archaeological evidence, that describes the combat performance of both sides. The historical record is rich enough for our national heritage, it doesn't require "re–engineering" by revisionist historians.

After the village had been moved, Wooden Leg visited his friend, Noisy Walking, who had been mortally wounded in the charge of the suicide boys:

"After sundown I visited Noisy Walking. He was lying on a ground bed of buffalo robes under a willow dome shelter. His father White Bull was with him. His mother sat just outside the entrance. I asked my friend: 'How are you?' He replied: 'Good, only I want water.' I did not know what else to say, but I wanted him to know that I was his friend and willing to do whatever I could for him. After a while I said: 'You were very brave.' Nothing else was said for several minutes. He was weak. His hands trembled at every move he made. Finally he said to his father:

"I wish I could have some water – just a little of it.'

"No. Water will kill you.'

"White Bull almost choked as he said this to his son. But he was a good medicine man, and he knew what was best. As I sat there looking at Noisy Walking I knew he was going to die. My heart was heavy. But I could not do him any good, so I excused myself and went away."[169]

But what of the catalyst of the battle? The individual who turned what would probably have been a drawn contest into the grist of myth and legend? After charging through the platoon of E Troop, Lame White Man had turned, possibly to charge a C Company position. Mistaken for an Arikara, he was killed and scalped by his Lakota comrades:[170]

> *"Lame White Man [Mad Hearted Wolf] must have charged in right behind the suicide warriors, whom he called 'my boys'; for when some Lakota warriors found his body, he was lying in the very midst of the dead soldiers. When the Lakotas saw him there they mistook him for an Indian soldier scout. So one of them scalped Lame White Man, taking the side of his hair, including the long braid. Later, when the Lakotas learned of their mistake, they carried the scalp back and placed it back on his head.[171] So Lame White Man, the Elk Society chief who fought as bravely as a mad-hearted wolf, died in the midst of these enemies, killing the soldiers who had come to kill the Northern People, while the People themselves were keeping the peace with the whites."[172]*

Ironically, Lame White Man, who, more than any other individual, enshrined the Little Big Horn in our history and national heritage, is largely unknown today; while the men whose defeat he architected have attained immortality.

---

[1] See Douglas Scott "Archaeological Insights Into The Custer Battle" page 27. A total of 263 men were killed during the 3 engagements comprising the Battle of the Little Big Horn, and an additional 5 men died later, either aboard the *Far West* or in the hospital at Fort Lincoln. See Appendix 2.

[2] See Douglas D. Scott "Archaeological Insights into The Custer Battle" pages 17 – 18.

[3] Twenty-one percent of the paired markers were excavated and they all showed, at most, the remains of a single individual. See Douglas D. Scott "Archaeological Perspectives on The Battle of the Little Bighorn" pages 58 and 62.

[4] Prior to the construction of the road, a small knoll, on the site of the current monument, rose about 6 feet above the rest of the ridge. Upon this knoll, the bodies of Armstrong Custer, Tom Custer, Lieutenant Cook, and 7 others, 2 of whom were not identified, were found. The leveling of this knoll required the removal of the markers for these bodies to their present locations which are in error by about 40 feet. This displacement of markers from Custer Knoll was verified by the archaeological evidence when the bones excavated from the marker designated for Lieutenant Algernon Smith were shown to belong to another individual, although the burial accounts are clear than Smith's body was discovered in the group of 10 with Custer. See Jerome A. Greene "Evidence and the Custer Enigma" page 69, Douglas D. Scott "Archaeological Perspectives on The Battle of the Little Bighorn" page 61, and Douglas Scott "Archaeological Insights Into The Custer Battle" page 101. The burial accounts also indicate that the markers for Armstrong Reed and Boston Custer should have been located some hundreds of feet nearer the river. Similarly, Captain Sweet erected the marker for Doctor Lord on the South Skirmish Line when he found a "surgeon's button" there although some burial accounts indicate his body was indeed recognized and lay about 20 feet southwest of Custer (See John S. Gray "Custer's Last Campaign" page 393). While the following miss locations of markers do not inhibit our understanding of the progress of the battle, that is not the case with the marker for Mark Kellogg. The burial accounts are clear that his body was found near the river, approximately 3/4 mile from his marker's current location. The relatively undisturbed state of his body indicates he was killed early in the fight, probably during the withdrawal from Crazy Horse Ford. See Sandy Barnard "Mark Kellogg's Role During the 1876 Campaign" pages 8 – 9, and 11.

[5] See Douglas D. Scott "Archaeological Perspectives on The Battle of the Little Bighorn" page 88.

[6] Statistically speaking, each marker represents the location of a soldier body. We know that at least 6 of the 209 Custer dead died, and were presumably buried, outside the present boundaries of Custer's Battlefield. If all of the markers were excavated, we would expect to find no remains at six of the markers. This minor discrepancy, less than 3%, would not, from the viewpoint of mathematical probability, invalidate the assertion that the markers are true indicators of the locations of soldier dead.

[7] There is also evidence that a messenger, who did not survive, was dispatched to General Terry. Also Private Theodore Goldin claimed to have been a messenger from Custer to Reno. While this may be true, the details of Goldin's narrative defy belief.

[8] It is extremely difficult to assign place names to the events described in the Indian accounts. The first difficulty the researcher encounters is the differing cultural perspective. While we are interested in Custer's tactical movements as a means of ascertaining his driving motivations at various points, the Indian's accounts are given from their traditional viewpoint of individual combat waged for personal glory and aggrandizement, devoid of all tactical objectives. When this situation is compounded by the traditionally poor quality of interrogation and interpretation attendant to most of the accounts (this is especially true in the accounts of the Crow scout Curly and the Uncpapa Rain in the Face), it is difficult to assign either a definitive place or unit name in any but the most obvious of instances.

[9] While physical evidence is very important, it has the same potential for misinterpretation as the Indian accounts and must therefore be weighed just as carefully. While shod tracks definitely show the presence of a cavalry horse, they do not show who, if anyone, was riding the horse at the time, or when, in relation to known battle events, the tracks were made. Similarly, while a government Springfield shell casing definitely establishes that a particular weapon was used in a given location (assuming artifact "harvesting" over the years has neither displaced the chronicled finds nor materially altered the distribution of artifacts on the field), it does not, of itself, tell us who fired the weapon, or when it was fired.

[10] See John S. Gray "Custer's Last Campaign" page 278.

[11] See John S. Gray "Custer's Last Campaign" page 278.

[12] See John S. Gray "Custer's Last Campaign" page 279.

[13] Note that although William Jackson was a half–breed Pikuni Blackfoot, I have included him in the count of the Arikara for brevity.

[14] See Kenneth Hammer "Custer in '76" page 92.

[15] This hypothesis is supported by the presence of both Cooke and Keogh at Reno's attack ford. As regimental adjutant and battalion commander respectively, neither Cooke nor Keogh was at liberty to accompany Reno. It is therefore logical to assume they were ordered forward by Custer to obtain further intelligence on the size and disposition of the enemy force. The required information was supplied by Girard. For a comprehensive discussion of this too little noted incident, the reader is referred to Don Horn's excellent "Custer's Turn To The North At The Little Big Horn: The Reason" pages 17 - 19.

[16] See the time line analysis of Appendix 12.

17 See Kenneth Hammer "Custer in '76" page 94. It was about this time that Private Mitchell, Reno's second messenger, reached Custer. Mitchell provided no new information on the tactical situation over that obtained by personal observation from Wooden Leg Ridge.

18 The implication here is that Brennan and Fitzgerald had no stomach for the coming fight. Thompson, who was not at all reticent to criticize others for their actions at Little Big Horn, reported the incident without further comment. See Daniel O. Magnussen "Thompson's Narrative" page 117. Private John B. McGuire of Company C told Walter Camp that the members of C Troop always believed Brennan and Fitzgerald left the column due to cowardice. See Kenneth Hammer "Custer in '76" page 126. Privates John Welch Brennan and John Fitzgerald , both of Company C, would survive the battle. When Privates Peter Thompson and James Watson fell behind, due to their horses having played out, an entire set of fours from Company C had dropped out of the column. While the stories of Thompson and Watson are somewhat convoluted, and Thompson's personal account requires an extreme amount of credulity to be taken seriously, their performance, especially Thompson's, during the siege was thoroughly professional. Thompson, who would win a Medal of Honor as a water carrier, apparently joined the pack train about the time it reached Reno Hill. See Kenneth Hammer "Custer in '76" page 125. While these were the most celebrated, they were by no means the only stragglers from the Custer column that would eventually wind up with Reno. The account of how Frank Hunter came to be with Reno's command is an excellent example of a fertile imagination. The reader is referred to Kenneth Hammer "Custer in '76" page 139.

19 Peter Thompson speaks of a detail (a non–commissioned officer and four men) from Company F being detached to investigate the lone tepee and serve as the command's point. This indicates that Company F occupied the lead position in the column. See Daniel O. Magnussen "Thompson's Narrative" pages 119 and 120. Thompson is supported by Indian testimony that indicates a detail of 6 men was sighted in the vicinity of Luce Ridge by a woman on the east side of the river. See Richard G. Hardorff "Cheyenne Memories of the Custer Fight" page 43.

20 See Daniel O. Magnussen "Thompson's Narrative" pages 116 – 117 and Richard G. Hardorff "Markers, Artifacts, and Indian Testimony: Preliminary Findings on the Custer Battle" page 9.

21 See the accounts of Private O'Neill (Company G) and Sergeant Stanislaus Roy (Company A) in Kenneth Hammer "Custer in '76" pages 106 and 112 as well as the accounts of Private Daniel Newell (Company M) and Private Henry Petring (Company G) in John S. Gray "Custer's Last Campaign" page 292.

22 Varnum's account in John M. Carroll "Custer's Chief of Scouts" page 65 is confirmed by Crow scout Goes Ahead in Colonel W. A. Graham "The Custer Myth" page 20.

23 See Robert J. Ege "Settling the Dust" page 17. While much has been made by some authorities of the alleged poor condition of Custer's horses, only Sergeant Finckle and troopers Thompson and Watson are known to have dropped out of the column due to played out mounts. Noting that the heavy laden pack train was able to keep up on the march, frontiersman George Herendeen maintained that Custer neither marched to the Little Big Horn at too rapid a pace nor were his horses spent.

24 John Martin told Walter Camp that Custer did not wave his hat while Crow scout Curly told Walter Camp that it was Mitch Boyer who waved his hat. See "Custer in '76" pages 100 and 157. Crow scout White Man Runs Him was equally certain it was Custer , accompanied by his brother Tom, who waved his hat. See Colonel W. A. Graham "The Custer Myth" page 23.

[25] On two separate occasions the Crow scout Hairy Moccasin related that the troops passed down Cedar Coulee. See John S. Gray "Custer's Last Campaign" page 342.

[26] Custer may have sent each of the battalions (F and E under Captain Yates, and I, C, and L under Captain Keogh) along different routes. This would account for Godfrey's insistence that Custer's trail was further east of Reno Hill than would be the case had Cedar Coulee been used exclusively.

[27] See Daniel O. Magnussen "Thompson's Narrative" page 120.

[28] The western-most portion of Weir Point affords an unobstructed view of the entire valley. From this location Custer would have been able to observe the entire village with the exception of any lodges that might be concealed by the timber lining the stream.

[29] Fred Girard testified he saw the column on the bluffs while Reno's command was in the timber. This observation was supported by the testimony of Lieutenant DeRudio. See Colonel W. A. Graham "Reno Court of Inquiry" pages 42 and 115.

[30] Some authorities believe that Custer was never on Weir Point. Given that the village extended at least as far down stream as Minneconjou Ford, Weir Point would have to be ascended to obtain a view of the entire village. To make two observations of the village while ignoring the most advantageous vantage point seems incredible to me. I believe Custer, who personally went to the Crow's Nest, would have insisted on viewing the village from Weir Point.

[31] See Kenneth Hammer "Custer in '76" page 174. For a detailed account of the journey of the scout Curly from the battlefield to the steamer *Far West,* the reader is referred to John S. Gray's excellent "Custer's Last Campaign" pages 373 – 380.

[32] See Richard Upton "The Custer Adventure" page 66.

[33] The accounts of Captain Moylan, Lieutenant Edgerly, and Sergeant Kanipe all agree that Custer's immediate command was divided into two battalions. Only Kanipe, a member of Company C mentions that his troop was assigned to Keogh's battalion. As Keogh was senior to Yates, and Companies I, L, and a portion of C, died on Keogh's portion of the field, there is no reason to doubt that Keogh's battalion consisted of Companies I, L, and C. See John S. Gray "Custer's Last Campaign" page 360.

[34] On June 27 Lieutenants DeRudio and Edward McClernand (of Terry's Engineering Staff) followed a **regular cavalry trail** in lower Medicine Tail Coulee. DeRudio mentioned the troops were marching in column of fours, changing to column of twos where the coulee narrowed. McClernand, however, reported two distinct sets of fours. See Robert E. Doran "Battalion Formation and the Custer Trail" page 17.

[35] John Martin's last view of the troops was of the column ascending the rise of land north of the mouth of Cedar Coulee; the formation known as Luce Ridge. See Richard G. Hardorff "Markers, Artifacts and Indian Testimony" page 10.

[36]There is evidence that Yates' point, probably the same detail from F that had ridden in the advance previously, was spotted by Lakota women digging turnips on the east side of the river. They noted a squad of six troopers near Luce Ridge well in advance of Custer's column. See Richard G. Hardorff "Lakota Recollections" page 74. Gall also mentioned seeing troops mounted on

white horses (Company F) when Custer was first observed east of the village. See Usher L. Burdick "David F. Barry's Indian Notes On The Custer Battle" page 23.

[37] See John S. Gray "Custer"'s Last Campaign" page 358 and Colonel W. A. Graham "The Custer Myth" pages 18 and 19. The young Crow scout Curly has been ill treated by history; his accounts distorted by unscrupulous interviewers and interpreters. His first account was interpreted by Thomas Leforge for Lieutenant Bradley just a few days after the fight. As his descendant, Dan Old Elk, told the author, Curly never changed this first account when discussing the fight with family members. This first account is the only one I have used in reconstructing Custer's movements. See Fred Dustin 'The Custer Tragedy' page 164.

[38] While C Troop rode sorrels, a sorrel–roan was something of a rare occurrence. Curly recalled: *"Custer wrote a message and handed to a young man – on a sorrel roan horse – who galloped away. Boyer (sic) called me to him – he said – 'You ride back over the trail a ways and then go to one of the high points' – pointing eastward over to the high ridge east of the Custer hill – 'watch awhile, and see if the Sioux are besting us, and you make your way back to Terry and tell him we are all killed.'"* See Frank Perfetti "John Martin, An Italian With Custer" pages 53 - 54.

[39] See Robert E. Doran "The Man Who Got to the Rosebud" page 20.

[40] See Robert E. Doran "The Man Who Got to the Rosebud" page 21. Private Frank Sniffin believed the trooper to have been Private Oscar T. Warner of Company C and maintained the body was identified by means of the name being in the hat. See Bruce Liddic and Paul Harbaugh "Camp on Custer" pages 86 - 87. While Sniffin may have been correct in his assertion, both sergeants Kanipe and Hanly claimed to have examined the effects, including the hat, and concluded the remains to have been Short's. As both sergeants were members of C Troop, they should have been in a position to know and I am therefore inclined to accept their identification of the remains in preference to Sniffin's.

[41] See Richard G. Hardorff "Lakota Recollections" page 170.

[42] See George A. Schneider "The Freeman Journal" page 74.

[43] See Jerome A. Greene "Lakota and Cheyenne" page 61. If Flying By's account is accurate, then Short and Warner may have been the two soldiers mentioned.

[44] See Carl L. Pearson "Sadie and the Missing Custer Battle Papers" page 17.

[45] Many authorities persist in the belief that no element of the 7th Cavalry reached the river at the mouth of Medicine Tail Coulee. The Indian testimony is quite clear that at least two companies reached the river at this point and that some little firing took place there. At least 15 shell casings and slugs from army weapons, along with Indian slugs and casings, horseshoes and an iron tent pin, have been found at the mouth of both Medicine Tail and Deep Coulees; leaving no room for doubt that 7th Cavalry elements penetrated that far. See Jerome A. Greene "Evidence and the Custer Enigma" pages 22 – 24 and Douglas Scott "Archaeological Insights Into The Custer Battle" page 13. For a description of the action at Minneconjou Ford based upon the various accounts of the Crow scout Curly, See John S. Gray "Custer's Last Campaign" pages 364 - 365.

[46] White Man Runs Him recalled: *"The scouts (Crow scouts, DCE) believed that Reno's outfit was all killed. It was hard to tell because the dust was flying and they were retreating so fast. I know for sure that Custer went right to the river bank. I saw him go that far."* See Colonel W. A. Graham "The Custer Myth" page 15.

[47] See the account of Rain In The Face in "The Teepee Book" page 646 and Jim Holly "Indian Accounts Paint Last Stand Picture" page 67. Other than the Uncpapa and Cheyenne circles being located at the extreme southern and northern ends of the village respectively, there is no agreement in Indian accounts as to the layout of the village. While the layout of the village is really of no importance in understanding the battle, the location of the Cheyenne circle, in relation to landmarks on the east, or right, bank of the Little Big Horn is an aid in understanding Custer's movements. Unfortunately, there is no agreement as to the terminus of the northern end of the village; various authorities placing it from just north of Medicine Tail Coulee to opposite Last Stand Hill. See S. L. A. Marshall "Crimsoned Prairie" page 146, Charles Kuhlman "Legend Into History" page 14, Mari Sandoz "The Battle of the Little Bighorn" pages 108 – 109, Frazier and Robert Hunt "I Fought With Custer" page 100, and Custer Battlefield Chief Historian Doug McChristian to the author, April 2, 1991.

[48] Foolish Elk, an Oglala, recalled: *"These men sat on their horses and fired across the river into the village, without getting into it."* See Kenneth Hammer "Custer in '76" page 198. The Crow Scout Goes Ahead indicated at least a portion of the troops formed a dismounted skirmish line. See O. G. Libby "The Arikara Narrative" page 160. Rain In The Face also indicated the troopers dismounted before firing into the village: *"The soldiers had dismounted, and were firing into the camp from the top of the cliff."* See Dr. Charles A. Eastman "Rain In The Face: The Story of A Sioux Warrior," Bighorn Yellowstone Journal, Summer 1993, page 18. See also Jim Holly "Indian Accounts Paint Last Stand Picture" page 67.

[49] Joseph White Cow Bull, in a 1938 interview with David Humphreys Miller, claimed that a guidon bearer, a trooper, and an officer Miller claimed to be Custer, were killed as the 7th attempted to force a crossing. There are several problems with the assertion that Custer was killed at this juncture. First is that the man in question was clad in buckskin jacket and pants. While Custer indeed wore that outfit on the campaign, he had shed the jacket early in the morning. Although First Lieutenant James E. Porter was apparently wearing his buckskin jacket at the time of his death despite the near hundred degree heat, I doubt Custer would have put his jacket back on as the heat of the day increased. The second problem with the story is the unnamed Indian eyewitnesses just happen to recall that, although the river was at least 3 feet deep at that point, the buckskin clad officer rode a blaze faced sorrel with four white stockings. This horse is immediately recognized as Vic, the mount Custer rode that day. The problem with this is two fold. First I find it incredible the Indians, in the heat of battle, would recall a particular horse, especially one whose markings were not that unusual. Secondly, as anyone who has seen the photograph of Custer's striker, John Burkman, holding Dandy and Vic can readily ascertain – Vic did not have four white stockings! Next we have the testimony of Sergeant John Ryan that he had retrieved, and sent to Mrs. Custer, some spent shell casings from Custer's Remington sporting rifle that he found <u>under</u> the body (See Jud Tuttle "Remnants of A Regiment" page 38). Last, but the most telling argument for Custer dying late in the fight, is the evidence that either of his two wounds would have been almost instantly fatal coupled with the fact that the regimental staff, including Adjutant Cooke, died near the general. Had Custer died early in the fight, Keogh, as senior captain on the field, would have assumed command and Cooke should have died near Keogh. While a scenario might be concocted that Custer died early and Cooke and the rest of the regimental staff served with Keogh, only reaching Last Stand Hill after Keogh had been killed, it is standard practice to embrace the simplest scenario that satisfies the facts. That scenario is simply that Custer died late in the conflict surrounded, as was proper, by his staff. The Lakota and Cheyenne participants who guided Colonel Nelson Miles to the battlefield in 1878 claimed that one of Custer's officers (the man had a compass and field glasses) was killed in the position nearest the river. Although this account does not state the officer was killed in the river, it may refer to Minneconjou Ford, but, most probably refers to Greasy Grass Ridge, in which case the officer in question could only be Lieutenant Harrington. See James Brust "Lt. Oscar Long's Early Map Details Terrain, Battle Positions" page 8. Cheyenne Tribal Historian John Stands In Timber believes no soldiers were killed at the ford. He cites the warrior

Hanging Wolf as his authority: *". . . they hit one horse down there, and it bucked off a soldier, but the rest took him along when they retreated north."* See John Stands In Timber "Cheyenne Memories" page 199. Historian Brian C. Pohanka believes that Lieutenant Algernon E. Smith may have been the buckskinned officer shot in the river. See "Their Shots Quit Coming" page 24.

[50] See George Bird Grinnell "The Fighting Cheyennes" page 350.

[51] Brave Wolf, in speaking of the action at the ford, recalled: *"They began fighting, and for quite a long time fought near the river, neither party giving back."* See George Bird Grinnell "The Fighting Cheyennes" page 350. Soldier Wolf and Tall Bull also told Grinnell the fight at the ford lasted some time, Tall Bull recalling: *"For quite a long time the troops stood their ground right there; then they began to back off, fighting all the time, for quite a distance, working up the hill, until they got pretty close to where the monument now is. . ."* See George Bird Grinnell interviews, Southwest Museum. The Brule Two Eagles however stated it was a *"short fight only."* See Richard G. Hardorff "Lakota Recollections" page 145. Thomas Disputed, an Oglala known at the time as Shave Elk, said the soldiers stopped and fought *". . . just a little while, but not long . . ."* He also noted the soldiers were in two detachments. See Bruce Liddic and Paul Harbaugh "Camp on Custer" page 122.

[52] The artifactual evidence, and Lieutenant Charles Roe's observations indicate that one troop may have withdrawn directly from the Ford while the second company proceeded down river, turning east at the mouth of Deep Coulee. See Charles Francis Roe "Custer's Last Battle" page 10. Benteen also believed that the troops withdrew in two columns. See John M. Carroll "The Benteen – Goldin Letters" page 155.

[53] Sitting Bull's account, which is highly questionable in many areas, describes an orderly withdrawal from Minneconjou Ford: *"The bugle blew. It was an order to fall back. All the men fell back fighting and dropping."* See Colonel W. A. Graham "The Custer Myth" page 72. Two Moon supports Sitting Bull's account with his recollection: *"The [Custer's command] dismounted and slowly moved back up the ridge with their horses on the inside and the soldiers around them."* See Richard G. Hardorff "Lakota Recollections" page 137. See also Jim Holly "Indian Accounts Paint Last Stand Picture" page 68.

[54] See Peter John Powell "People of the Sacred Mountain" page 1018, and John Stands In Timber "Cheyenne Memories" pages 197 – 198.

[55] 152 Springfield shell casings have been found at regular skirmish intervals of 9 to 10 feet along Luce Ridge. See Richard G. Hardorff "Markers, Artifacts and Indian Testimony" page 38

[56] Cheyenne Tribal Historian John Stands In Timber is adamant that the Custer fight started in this location and that the soldier fire was directed against Wolf Tooth's party. See John Stands In Timber "Cheyenne Memories" page 198. Going over the ground with historian J. W. Vaughn and Battlefield Historian Don Rickey, Stands In Timber pointed out the ridge where the fighting started. According to Rickey's notes: *". . . as pointed out by Stands–in–Timber, this would be above and east of the Nye–Cartwright Ridge area (that is, Luce Ridge, DCE) – shells have subsequently been found there, but more field work is needed to prove or disprove this account of fighting in that location."* See Rickey interview with John Stands In Timber, August 8, 1956, Folder H – 14, Little Big Horn Battlefield National Monument. See also interviews with John Stands In Timber, Folder 15878, Little Bighorn Battlefield National Monument. Although the Crow scouts do not mention any action at this location, the artifactual evidence is too strong to ignore. John Gray has theorized that the Crow actually witnessed this action but ascribed it to Minneconjou Ford. See John S. Gray "Custer's Last Campaign" page 351. In fact, the portion of the account of Goes Ahead that deals with volley firing may refer to Luce Ridge. See O. G. Libby "The Arikara Narrative" page 160.

[57]Gall apparently entered the Custer Fight at this stage as his description seems to support the Cheyenne accounts of the action on the ridges bordering Medicine Tail Coulee. Gall's account was obtained on the field by a correspondent of the St. Paul Pioneer Press in 1886. *"Gen. Custer was attacked fully three–quarters of a mile back from the river, near the crest of the ridge lining the coulee he was descending, and was forced back step by step, at right angles to his former course, to the summit now crowned by the battle monument where all finally perished."* See Colonel W. A. Graham "The Custer Myth" page 90.

[58] Minneconjou Ford cannot be seen from Blummer–Nye–Cartwright Ridge and Custer may have sent a detail to alert Yates to the warrior presence in his rear.

[59] See Jerome A. Greene "Evidence and the Custer Enigma" pages 28 – 29. The bodies and horses of four troopers, including that of Henry C. Dose (Trumpeter of Company G who was serving as an orderly to Custer on June 25) were found on a line from Blummer–Nye–Cartwright Ridge to the Sergeant Butler Marker. While there is no way of determining when these men died, and there are Indians accounts of troopers attempting to escape from Custer's battlefield toward the south (See John P. Langellier "Myles Keogh: Irish Dragoon" page 147), it is possible that this was a detail, commanded by Sergeant Butler, sent by Custer to Yates. See Richard G. Hardorff "Markers, Artifacts and Indian Testimony" page 37. The most popular opinions for the location of Butler's body are that he was either a messenger from Custer (although it would have been highly irregular for a first sergeant to be selected for such duty, Godfrey believed it to have been the case – see Colonel W. A. Graham "The Custer Myth" page 96) or that he was cut off when Calhoun Hill was overrun and escaped as far as his marker before being killed. See Charles Kuhlman "Legend Into History" pages 230 – 231 and James Willert "Little Big Horn Diary" page 357.

[60] Brass 50 – 70 shell casings have been found in the soldier position on Blummer–Nye–Cartwright Ridge. As this was the same load used in Custer's personal Remington sporting rifle, it is a further indication (in addition to the tactical considerations previously presented), although certainly not proof positive as at least 14 different weapons of that caliber have been identified as used on the battlefield (See Douglas Scott "Archaeological Insights Into The Custer Battle" pages 51 – 52), that Custer was with Keogh's battalion. See Henry and Don Weibert "Sixty–six Years in Custer's Shadow" page 113.

[61] By 1971 some 200 casings, mostly in groups of three, had been found along this ridge. See Richard G. Hardorff "Markers, Artifacts and Indian Testimony" page 38. The firing line appears to face Medicine Tail and Deep Coulees with an Indian position having been identified about 300 yards from the army firing line. See Daniel O. Magnussen "Thompson's Narrative" page 170 and Henry and Don Weibert "Sixty Six Years In Custer's Shadow" page 53. The Indian accounts given at the battlefield to Lieutenant Oscar Long in 1878 describe a company, mounted on bay horses, being fired upon by other soldier companies. This reference to action in Medicine Tail Coulee can only refer to either Company I or L and probably represents the informant's lack of understanding the concept of covering fire. See James Brust "Lt. Oscar Long's Early Map Details Terrain, Battle Positions" pages 8 and 10.

[62] Artifactual evidence as well as Indian testimony indicate that volleys were fired both from Blummer–Nye–Cartwright Ridge and Calhoun Hill. See Richard G. Hardorff "Lakota Recollections" pages 43 – 44. While the remains of four troopers and three horses were found just north of Luce Ridge years after the battle, these may have been soldiers fleeing from the collapse of Calhoun Hill rather than casualties taken during the withdrawal from Luce and Blummer–Nye–Cartwright Ridges. See Richard G. Hardorff "Lakota Recollections" note 15, page 43.

[63] This junction of Custer's command was apparently witnessed by the Brule Two Eagles and the Minneconjou Lights. See Gregory Michno "The Mystery of E Troop" page 89.

[64] Kate Bighead recalled that the Cheyenne used mostly arrows during this phase of the fighting, not only due to a shortage of guns, but so that the warriors would not have to expose themselves to the soldier's fire. She recalled *"There was a long time – the old men now say they think it must have been about an hour and a half – of this fighting slowly, with not much harm to either side."* See Thomas B. Marquis "Custer on the Little Bighorn" page 87. The account of Wooden Leg agrees with that of Kate Bighead in all important details of this phase of the fighting. See Thomas B. Marquis "Wooden Leg" pages 230 – 231. Tall Bull and Nicholas Ruleau maintained that volleys were fired from Calhoun Hill during this phase of the fighting. See Kenneth Hammer "Custer in '76" page 213 and Richard G. Hardorff "Lakota Recollections" page 43. The Oglala Lone Bear thought that the entire Custer Fight took about 4 hours. See Richard G. Hardorff "Lakota Recollections" page 159.`

[65] Two Moon saw this battalion disappear over Last Stand Hill. See Michael Moore "Gibbon's Route to Custer Hill" page 30.

[66] See interviews with John Stands In Timber, Folder 15878, Little Bighorn Battlefield National Monument. Crazy Horse believed Custer was after the non-combatants. His account indicates the warriors were divided into two groups, one intercepting Custer before he could reach the women and children, while the other concentrated in Custer's rear. See "South Dakota Historical Collections" page 227. Two Moon also recalled he first heard of Custer's column from Lakota messengers who said the soldiers were going to kill the women. See Tom O'Neil "Indians At Greasy Grass" page 10.

[67] The map drawn by an Indian participant for Lieutenant Philo Clark shows very definitely that Custer attempted a crossing of the Little Big Horn well north of Deep Ravine. See Thomas R. Buecker "Lt. Philo Clark's Sioux War Report" page 12. Reno court of inquiry Recorder, Lieutenant Jesse Lee, in his summation, stated his belief that Custer did not attempt to cross at Minneconjou Ford but probably attempted a crossing lower down. See Colonel W. A. Graham "The Reno Court of Inquiry" page 259. The Blackfoot Kills Eagle may have described action at this ford when he reported : *"After the Indians hemmed in the troops about 60 yards north of the river they drove the soldiers up the hill (this would have to be either Custer or Calhoun Hill, DCE) where they were all killed."* See Edward A. Milligan "High Noon On The Greasy "Grass" page 8.

[68] Over the years, two Indian shell casings have been found at this ford and a bone was found north of this crossing in the direction of the old trading post. These finds are identified as #34 and #23 respectively on the aerial map maintained at the battlefield.

[69] Although Richard Fox attributes the position to Cemetery Ridge, Captain Freeman's sketch map of the battlefield clearly shows a cavalry position on the flats in this approximate location. See "Archaeology, History, and Custer's Last Battle" page 188.

[70] See interviews with John Stands In Timber, Folder 15878, Little Bighorn Battlefield National Monument.

[71] In "Cheyenne Memories" Stands In Timber devotes only one paragraph to the action north of the monument: *"The soldiers followed the ridge down to the present cemetery site. Then this bunch of forty or fifty Indians (Wolf Tooth Party, DCE) came out by the monument and started shooting down at them again. But they were moving on down toward the river, across from the Cheyenne camp.*

Some of the warriors there had come across, and they began firing at the soldiers from the brush in the river bottom. This made the soldiers turn north, but they went back in the direction they had come from, and stopped when they got to the cemetery site. And they waited there a long time – twenty minutes or more." See John Stands In Timber "Cheyenne Memories" page 199. During his 1956 survey of the field with Battlefield Historian Don Rickey, Stands In Timber gave a more detailed interpretation that changes some of the locations in the previous account: *"They all went along Custer Ridge, then turned east (actually northwest, DCE) to try and cross the river. Repulsed at the river, the soldiers then halted on the flats below the superintendent's house and below the cemetery."* Rickey's notes continue: *"Note: Battle proper began below and west of the cemetery, moved to Custer Ridge – the troops were moving in a generally southerly or southeasterly direction, as seen from a Cheyenne viewpoint."* See Don Rickey Interview with John Stands In Timber, August 8, 1956, Folder H – 14, Little Bighorn Battlefield National Monument.

[72] Despite the present location of Kellogg's marker to the east of Last Stand Hill, the soldier accounts, including that of Colonel Gibbon, are quite clear that Kellogg's body was found near the river in a small valley whose description uniquely identifies it as the terrain leading to the cemetery from Crazy Horse Ford. The fact that Kellogg's body was not stripped, and that, although he had been scalped and had an ear missing, he was not mutilated to a significant extent, indicates the warriors had other things on their minds when they reached his body. While not conclusive, this indicates Kellogg was not one of those who attempted to flee at the end of the fighting, but died while the fight was still being hotly contested.

[73] See John Stands In Timber "Cheyenne Memories" page 200. If Lieutenant Smith was either killed or mortally wounded during this action, it would account for the presence of his body on Last Stand Hill.

[74] With the exception of McDougall's Company B, Company C, commanded by a Second Lieutenant 4 years out of West Point, was the most inexperienced troop in the 7th Cavalry.

[75] In an interview with Hamlin Garland, Two Moon recalled the initial deployment on Calhoun Hill: *"They formed into three branches with a little ways between (companies C, I and L, DCE). Then a bugle sounded, and they all got off (their) horses, and some soldiers led the horses back over the hill."* Two Moon also recalled that bugle calls were used extensively throughout the Custer Fight indicating the officers exercised control throughout the fight. See Richard G. Hardorff "Cheyenne Memories of the Custer Fight" page 102. White Bull also noted the use of bugle calls on Custer's battlefield. See Tom O'Neil "Indians At Greasy Grass" page 4.

[76] It is approximately 1/2 mile, or 2640 feet, from Last Stand Hill to Calhoun Hill. Using the standard skirmish interval of 9 feet, it would require 293 troopers just to adequately man the firing line.

[77] Many authorities have come to doubt that a "South Skirmish Line" actually existed, concluding the markers in this area are either erroneously placed or correspond to troopers attempting to escape toward the river at the end of the fight. During the archaeological investigations conducted under the supervision of Douglas D. Scott in 1984 and 1985, the evidence gathered showed that the markers on the South Skirmish Line contained at least as high, and in many cases higher, correlation to body locations as any other area of the battlefield investigated; the report concluding: *"no spurious markers were excavated at either the South Skirmish Line or the Keogh area."* (See Douglas D. Scott "Archaeological Perspectives On The Battle of The Little Bighorn" page 87). Having thus established that the markers on the South Skirmish Line are as valid in marking the locations of soldier bodies as at any other location on the field, the question remains, at what point in the fight did those men die? While we cannot determine with certainty the timing of their demise, there are some relevant points, in addition to the Cheyenne accounts, to consider. If the

deaths had occurred near the end of the fighting, they would probably exhibit the "bunching" behavior associated with near panic under combat conditions. The spacing of the markers, as well as the accounts of Lieutenants Wallace and Hare (who described the dead in that location as being in skirmish order), and the map of Lieutenant Edward Maguire (which also indicates the bodies were in skirmish order) makes a compelling case for the existence of an organized defense in this area of the field (See Douglas D. Scott "Archaeological Perspectives On The Battle of The Little Bighorn" pages 47 – 48 and page 123). While it is becoming fashionable at this date to attribute the defeat to "combat fatigue", now popularly called "bunching", there is absolutely no support in soldier accounts or the archaeological data to support such a conclusion. Indian accounts that seem to indicate "bunching" of the troops in this location are, at best, subject to various interpretations. The simplest explanation, which I have accepted, is to believe the Cheyenne accounts, the archaeological evidence and the accounts, and map, left by Lieutenants Wallace, Hare and Maguire; the South Skirmish Line existed, and was overrun relatively early in the fight.

[78] White Bull's map of the troop locations shows Company E, or at least a platoon from that company, deployed considerably north of the present monument. See Wayne Wells "Little Big Horn Notes: Stanley Vestal's Indian Insights" page 15. Shell casings indicating a soldier skirmish line have been found about 400 to 500 yards north of the National Cemetery. See Robert E. Doarn "Battalion Formation and the Custer Trail" page 18.

[79] The account of the Brule Two Eagles is very clear regarding a deployment along Greasy Grass Ridge: *"Soldiers went from 'C' (Refers to letters on the map used by Walter Camp to interrogate Indian participants. In this case 'C' refers to the western terminus of Calhoun Ridge, DCE) to 'D' (Calhoun Hill, DCE). Some soldiers on reaching 'K' (area where the bodies of Company I were found, DCE) made a dash to the river, and went down on a line about half way between 'C' and 'H' (while Hardorff interprets this as a deployment from Deep Ravine eastward, the scale of the map is such that it could equally well refer to Greasy Grass Ridge. In any event, it is clear that these troopers came from east of the ridge, where the companies held in reserve would be placed, to deploy in skirmish order, DCE). They scattered some in going down. (Two Eagles was, of course, unfamiliar with skirmish intervals and viewed this as a 'scattering' of the troops, DCE). There were from 10 to 12 in this bunch. (Clearly the deployment of a platoon rather than a full company is being described, DCE)"* See Richard G. Hardorff "Lakota Recollections" page 146 Two Moon also indicates a deployment of three distinct units: *"They formed in three bunches . . . Then a bugle sounded, and they all got off their horses, and some soldiers led the horses back over the hill (the horses were positioned in the ravine east of Calhoun Hill, DCE)."* See Robert M. Utley "Custer and the Great Controversy" page 111. Some 20 members of C Troop died on Greasy Grass and Calhoun Ridges, including Sergeants August Finckle and Jeremiah Finley. While there are only 3 soldier markers on Greasy Grass Ridge, evidence gathered by Walter Camp indicates as many as 8 soldiers may have died there. As there are no markers in line with the South Skirmish Line lying east of Deep Ravine, I have concluded the deployment of the platoon of C Troop was to Greasy Grass Ridge rather than as a junction with the platoon of E Troop on the South Skirmish Line. See Richard G. Hardorff "Lakota Recollections" pages 31 and 180.

[80] The accounts of Colonel Miles' Lakota and Cheyenne scouts describe a charge to clear Greasy Grass Ridge of warriors. While Lieutenant Long interpreted the action to have been on the part of Company L, the markers and burial party evidence seem to clearly demonstrate that this deployment must have been accomplished by Company C. See James Brust "Lt. Oscar Long's Early Map Details Terrain, Battle Positions" page 9.

[81] For a discussion of the discovery of government shell casings at the western terminus of Calhoun Ridge as well as bodies found near the head of Deep Ravine and along Calhoun Ridge See Richard G. Hardorff "Markers, Artifacts and Indian Testimony" pages 41 – 42.

82 The accounts of both Kate Bighead and Wooden Leg indicate the deployment to the South Skirmish Line occurred about 1 1/2 hours after the opening of Custer's portion of the fight. See Gregory Michno "The Mystery of E Troop" pages 106 and 108.

83 Wooden Leg recalled: *"About 40 of the soldiers came galloping from the east part of the ridge down toward the river, toward where most of the Cheyennes and many Ogallalas were hidden. The Indians ran back to a deep gulch. The soldiers stopped and got off their horses when they arrived at a low ridge where the Indians had been."* This account also states that the Indians are uncertain as to the color of horses ridden by these soldiers. See Thomas B. Marquis "Wooden Leg" page 231. Marquis put the number of troops deployed at between 30 and 40 in "Keep the Last Bullet For Yourself" pages 158 – 159. Foolish Elk seems to coroborate these accounts when he recounted that Custer's men charged twice, perhaps referring to the deployment of platoons from E and C. Foolish Elk went on to say the charges were ineffectual and shortly after the charges the battle became furious. See Kenneth Hammer "Custer in '76" page 199.

84 See Peter John Powell "People of the Sacred Mountain" page 1019.

85 See Stand In Timber interview with Don Rickey folder H – 14 Little Bighorn Battlefield National Monument.

86 See Usher L. Burdick "David F. Barry's Indian Notes On The Custer Battle" page 25.

87 At most, there were 36 officers and men in C Troop and 39 officers and men in E Troop at this juncture; the two platoons being roughly equivalent in size. It is probable both E and C had taken some casualties prior to this portion of the action.

88 See Stanley Vestal "Sitting Bull" page 128. Thomas B. Marquis, relying on the accounts of Cheyenne participants, concluded the long range fighting with little chance to win honors lasted about one and one half hours. See "Custer On The Little Big Horn" pages 25 – 26.

89 Walter Camp and Stanley Vestal believed that Thomas Marquis was incorrect in his assertion that Lame White Man's charge came against E Troop on the South Skirmish Line. They felt that this charge came against either C Troop on Calhoun Ridge, or L Troop on Calhoun Hill. Young Little Wolf's account states the charge was against Calhoun Ridge. See Richard G. Hardorff "Cheyenne Memories of the Custer Fight" page 90. My analysis and reconstruction of the fight indicates all of the accounts are correct, the charge carrying successively from the South Skirmish Line to Greasy Grass and Calhoun Ridges, then to Calhoun Hill. At this point, Lame White Man apparently turned toward Custer Hill, rather than cross the ridge line to the Keogh Sector, as his body was found just below the crest on the west side of the ridge. While the account of White Bull clearly states that soldiers were fighting below Custer Hill and toward the river after Troops I and L were over run, the style of the narrative indicates heavy editing by Vestal and, for that reason, I have accepted the accounts of Kate Bighead and Wooden Leg in preference to that of White Bull.

90 The reconstruction of the progression of the battle relies heavily on the excellent research conducted by Bruce Trinque as documented in "The Cartridge – Case Evidence on Custer Field: An Analysis and Re–interpretation."

91 See Dale T. Schoenberger "The End of Custer" pages 190 – 191.

92 Stanley Vestal, in his zeal to honor his friend White Bull, undoubtedly over emphasized this warrior's importance in the fighting, magnifying White Bull's role above that of Crazy Horse. While

it is difficult to pinpoint locations and times associated with these coups, the map attendant to While Bulls' coups indicates this action took place near Deep Ravine, although it may have occurred at the end of the fighting rather than the initial encounter with the South Skirmish Line. See Richard G. Hardorff "Lakota Recollections" pages 116 – 126.

[93] See Richard G. Hardorff "Lakota Recollections" page 126.

[94] Turtle Rib who arrived on the field about the time Keogh was overrun, seems to have witnessed this retrograde movement as he talks of units moving toward both ends of the ridge at the same time. Obviously, Keogh's Company I would have to turn to face the Indians coming from the south and east. See Kenneth Hammer "Custer in '76" page 201.

[95] The location of Corporal Foley's body (near Minneconjou Ford), coupled with the Indian accounts of a fleeing noncommissioned officer in that location, indicates, but, of course cannot prove, that the attack against C Troop came from north of Calhoun Ridge, forcing the survivors to flee either toward the east, as the majority of the C Company survivors apparently did, or toward the south.

[96] We have no direct evidence as to which of the platoons was commanded by First Sergeant Edwin Bobo and Lieutenant Harrington since Harrington's body was never identified and Bobo's was found near that of Captain Keogh. See Richard G. Hardorff "Markers, Artifacts and Indian Testimony: Preliminary Findings on The Custer Battle" pages 32 – 33. The account given to Lieutenant Oscar Long in 1878 by Cheyenne and Lakota participants may indicate that Lieutenant Harrington commanded the platoon on Greasy Grass Ridge. See James Brust "Lt. Oscar Long's Early Map Details Terrain, Battle Positions" page 8.

[97] Historian Brian Pohanka believes that the C Troop bodies adjoining those of E Troop near Deep Ravine came from troopers fleeing the collapse of Calhoun Ridge. See "There Shots Quit Coming" page 13.

[98] While some Cheyenne accounts label this man as both an officer, usually presumed to have been Lieutenant Harrington as his remains were never identified, and a suicide, Brave Wolf insists that this soldier was killed by the Cheyenne Old Bear. See George Bird Grinnell "The Fighting Cheyennes" page 353. The Minneconjou Turtle Rib told Walter Camp of a soldier suicide after being pursued some distance by 3 warriors. This may, or may not, have been the same incident. See Kenneth Hammer "Custer in '76" page 202. The Uncpapa Spotted Horn Bull and his wife also tell of an officer suicide during an attempt to escape on horseback to the east. See Colonel W. A. Graham "The Custer Myth" page 85. Perhaps the Oglala He Dog solves the mystery with his statement: *". . . he was beating the horse with the revolver and was yelling away. He fired backward now and then. He (He Dog, DCE) thinks the revolver went off accidentally in the beating of the horse. . ."* See Richard G. Hardorff "Lakota Recollections" page 76. This individual is usually identified as either Lieutenant Harrington or Corporal John Foley, Company C. As He Dog was positive that Foley was a suicide, he could not have been this individual. See Kenneth Hammer "Custer in '76" page 207. While the original account of Wooden Leg attributes virtually all the soldier deaths to suicide, he later claimed to have been misinterpreted and stated there were very few soldier suicides. See John Stands In Timber "Cheyenne Memories" page 205. In addition to this story of an escaping mounted trooper, the Oglala Lone Bear thought one trooper committed suicide but did not give either a location or point in the conflict for the event. These are the only Lakota accounts of soldier suicides. See Richard G. Hardorff "Lakota Recollections" page 162.

[99] There is great confusion, and controversy, over the identify of this soldier. Apparently two men broke out at this point; one riding north along the ridge, the other, probably Corporal John Foley of Company C, attempting to escape to the south. He Dog, Turtle Ribs and Gall all mention a

soldier death at the southern location near the marker for Sergeant Butler. Gall's suicide account, coupled with the accounts of Fred Girard, and Lieutenants Wallace and DeRudio, seems to indicate the man in question was Foley. See Richard G. Hardorff "Markers, Artifacts and Indian Testimony" pages 29 – 30.

[100] See Richard G. Hardorff "Markers, Artifacts and Indian Testimony" page 52. Hardorff feels, as do I, that history has not dealt kindly with Harrington, labeling him either a suicide or coward, or both. Hardorff feels that the man mentioned may have been Sergeant Major Sharrow as his body, along with another trooper, was found furthest north. While this is possible, the place for Sharrow would have been with Custer and the headquarters staff. His presence on Calhoun Hill would not seem to be logical.

[101] See Richard G. Hardorff "Markers, Artifacts and Indian Testimony" pages 49 – 50.

[102] See Richard G. Hardorff "Lakota Recollections" page 112.

[103] Yellow Nose was actually a Ute who had been captured by the Cheyenne in 1858.

[104] Although some accounts credit Yellow Nose with capturing Custer's personal battle flag, a red over blue swallowtail with white crossed sabers, it is most probable that a company guidon was his prize. See Richard G. Hardorff "Lakota Recollections" page 140. John Stands In Timber clearly states that it was a company guidon *"an American flag"* Yellow Nose captured, however, Stands In Timber says Yellow Nose merely took the guidon from the ground rather than wresting it from a soldier. See "Cheyenne Memories" page 202. Hardorff believes that the Oglala Stands First may have captured Custer's personal battle flag. See Richard G. Hardorff "Lakota Recollections" page 104.

[105] See Peter John Powell "People of the Sacred Mountain" pages 1023 – 1024.

[106] The Two Kettle Lakota, Runs The Enemy, recalled the repulse of a charge on Calhoun Hill: *"While Custer was all surrounded, there had been no firing from either side. The Sioux then made a charge from the rear side, shooting into the men, and the shooting frightened the horses so that they rushed upon the ridge and many horses were shot. The return fire was so strong that the Sioux had to retreat back over the hill again."* See Richard G. Hardorff "markers, Artifacts and Indian Testimony: pages 46 – 47. See also Joe E. Milner "California Joe" pages 309 – 310. The Uncpapa Moving Robe Woman, who witnessed the stampeding of the horses east of Calhoun Hill, noticed: *"One soldier was holding the reins of eight or ten horses."* While it was standard military procedure for one trooper to be responsible for 4 horses, Custer had halved the normal number of horse holders during the 1873 Stanley expedition. Calhoun's apparent use of a similar tactic is witness to the increasing warrior pressure and demonstrates an attempt to maximize the troops' fire power. See Richard G. Hardorff "Lakota Recollections" page 95.

[107] The archaeological evidence disclosed that a minimum of 124 Indian guns were used on the Custer Battlefield, of which 55% were repeating, or magazine, weapons. Statistical projections yield a estimate of 354 to 414 guns used against Custer's immediate command, of which 198 to 232 would have been repeaters. See Douglass D. Scott "Archaeological Perspectives on The Battle of the Little Bighorn" page 118.

[108] The archaeological evidence shows that at least 7 distinct Indian weapons were used both on Greasy Grass Ridge and Henryville. Coupled with the Indian accounts, we have a strong case for inferring that the progress of the fight went as stated. See Wayne Wells "The Fight On Calhoun Hill" page 27. Scott, however, believes that the battle progression was Calhoun Hill, Keogh, South

Skirmish Line and Last Stand Hill. See "Archaeological Perspectives on The Battle of the Little Bighorn" page 129.

[109] Lieutenant Edgerly, remarked on the positions of the bodies on Calhoun Hill: *"The first dead soldiers we came to were Leuts. Calhoun, Crittenden and enlisted men of L troop (obviously D Troop's route to Custer's battlefield did not take them in the vicinity of Butler, Foley, or the four troopers at the end of Blummer–Nye–Cartwright Ridge, DEC). The bodies of these officers were lying a short distance in rear of their men, in the very place where they belonged, and the bodies of their men forming a very regular skirmish line."* See Jerry Cecil "Lt. Crittenden: Striving For The Soldier's Life" page 34. The entire company did not perish on the skirmish line as, for example, Private John Duggan's body was found in Deep Coulee. See Dale T. Schoenberger "The End of Custer" page 198.

[110] The archaeological evidence uncovered during the 1984 and 1985 excavations appears to verify Indian accounts that Company L was caught in a murderous cross fire. See Jerome A. Greene "Evidence and the Custer Enigma" page 67.

[111] The Oglala Red Feather was witness to the tenacity of the soldiers defending Calhoun Hill. Red Feather *"came to an officer (the Indians were confused about military rank and markings, especially during service in the field so the attribution to a particular rank must be viewed with some skepticism, DCE) who was shot through the stomach who was sitting on the ground, holding a gun in his hand. Red Feather tried to take the gun away, but the officer dropped the gun and grabbed Red Feather. Red Feather was scared to death until someone shot the officer."* See Richard G. Hardorff "Lakota Recollections" page 85.

[112] Upon his appointment to the 7th Cavalry, Calhoun had written Custer: *"I shall do my best to prove my gratitude. If the time comes you shall not find me wanting."* See Edgar I. Stewart "Custer's Luck," page 451.

[113] Burial parties attested to seeing piles of cartridges, some containing as many as 30 casings, between the bodies on Company L's skirmish line. Hardorff believes that 11 of the 17 Indian fatalities he has determined to have occurred on Custer's field were inflicted by Company L. See "Markers, Artifacts and Indian Testimony" page 46.

[114] Despite the construction of the road along Battle Ridge, had Company I been deployed along the ridge line and pushed off the crest into the hollow to the east, some artifactual evidence should have survived on at least one side of the ridge. As none was found, I conclude Keogh's company was never deployed along the crest of the ridge; being held in reserve, as would be proper since Keogh was the battalion commander. See Douglas Scott "Archaeological Insights Into The Custer Battle" page 115.

[115] This action was, according to He Dog, immediately preceded by a charge, led by Crazy Horse, that split the two platoons of Company I. See Gregory Michno "The Mystery of E Troop" page 87. The account of Foolish Elk indicates that a unit, mounted on bays, was headed for Last Stand Hill and did not stop and make a stand. Both Companies I and L were mounted on bays and both made a stand. Either Foolish Elk was mistaken, or what he witnessed was the movement of some stragglers rather than a full company. See Kenneth Hammer "Custer in '76" page 199. The archaeological investigation disclosed that several Springfield carbines were used both on Calhoun Hill and in the Keogh sector. This indicates that either some survivors of Company L joined Company I, or that the weapons were captured and used by the Indians. See Douglas Scott "Archaeological Insights Into The Custer Battle" page 117.

[116] See Lone Bear interview in Richard G. Hardorff "Lakota Recollections" pages 157 and 159. Red Horse described five separate stands by the troops on Custer's Field (South Skirmish Line, Greasy Grass Ridge/Calhoun Ridge, Calhoun Hill, Keogh, and Last Stand Hill). He may have been referring to the stand made in the Keogh Sector when he related that most of the Indian losses were inflicted by *"men in ravine."* See Colonel W. A. Graham "The Custer Myth" page 60.

[117] See John P. Langellier "Myles Keogh: Irish Dragoon" page 147.

[118] See Douglas Scott "Archaeological Insights Into The Custer Battle" page 122.

[119] On Calhoun Hill, all of the evidentiary sources: Indian accounts, burial party accounts, and archaeological evidence, are in complete agreement. This mutual corroboration allows us to construct a very detailed scenario for the action on that part of Custer's Field. While we are tempted to assign the same degree of confidence to the reconstruction of the action in the Keogh, Sector, we must recall that, in terms of proper application of the scientific method, the absence of data (in this case archaeological evidence) may not be used to "prove" a conclusion. While the absence of artifacts in the Keogh Sector supports the Indian testimony, it cannot be concluded that this lack of artifacts proves that testimony is accurate.

[120] See Colonel W. A. Graham "The Custer Myth" page 110.

[121] See Richard G. Hardorff "Lakota Recollections" pages 87 – 88 and the interview with He Dog in "Custer in '76" page 207. Stanley Vestal, a proponent of White Bull, indicates that warrior led the charge in question after Crazy Horse had refused his challenge. It seems unlikely that a warrior of the stature of Crazy Horse would refuse such a challenge and the story, having no impartial witness, is not to be credited. See Wayne Wells "The Fight on Calhoun Hill" pages 29 – 30.

[122] See Richard G. Hardorff "Markers, Artifacts and Indian Testimony" page 49.

[123] There is compelling circumstantial evidence that Keogh fought mounted as his left knee had been shattered by a ball that, apparently, had first penetrated Comanche's chest.

[124] See Ernest L. Reedstrom "Bugles, Banners and War Bonnets" page 229.

[125] See Peter John Powell "People of the Sacred Mountain" page 1024.

[126] See Douglas Scott "Archaeological Insights Into The Custer Battle" page 124. The Uncpapa Iron Hawk claimed to have killed this trooper.

[127] See Richard G. Hardorff "Lakota Recollections" page 157.

[128] See Peter John Powell "People of the Sacred Mountain" page 1025.

[129] See Peter John Powell "People of the Sacred Mountain" page 1025. The use of arrows against the troops on Custer Hill is confirmed by the archaeological evidence. See Richard Allan Fox, Jr. "Archaeology, History, and Custer's Last Battle" page 116.

[130] Wooden Leg described the dangers of this form of fighting: *"A Sioux wearing a warbonnet was lying down behind a clump of sagebrush on the hillside only a short distance north of where now is the big stone having the iron fence around it (the monument on Last Stand Hill, DCE). . . The Sioux*

was peeping up and firing a rifle from time to time. At one of these times a soldier bullet hit him exactly in the middle of the forehead. His arms and legs jumped in spasms for a few moments, then he died." See Thomas B. Marquis "Wooden Leg" page 236.

[131] See Thomas B. Marquis "Wooden Leg" page 230.

[132] See John Stands In Timber "Cheyenne Memories" page 201.

[133] See Richard G. Hardorff "Markers, Artifacts and Indian Testimony: page 53.

[134] See John G. Neihardt "The Sixth Grandfather" page 191.

[135] There are various accounts of a small number of men attempting to escape toward the river near the end of the fighting. See Peter John Powell "People of the Sacred Mountain" page 1028 for an account of a sergeant and six men attempting to escape. See also James Brust "Lt. Oscar Long's Early Map Details Terrain, Battle Positions," page 7, for the most popular description of 40 men attempting to break out. The archaeological investigation of the South Skirmish Line has positively placed Mitch Boyer's body at paired markers 33 and 34 on the South Skirmish Line (confirming the accounts of Sergeant Kanipe and Lieutenant John G. Bourke. See John S. Gray "Custer's Last Campaign" page 397), giving credence to the account that places Mitch Boyer, the man in the calfskin vest, at the head of this contingent. See Douglas D. Scott, et al "Archaeological Perspectives on the Battle of the Little Bighorn" pages 74 and 84. One of these men may have been Sergeant Robert M. Hughes of Company K. As the bearer of Custer's personal battle flag, the location of his body in Deep Ravine points to a breakout from the command position on Custer Knoll sometime near the conclusion of the fight. See Dale T. Schoenberger "The End of Custer" page 208. If Private William Brown of Company F was another of these men, he made it further than any of his comrades; his body being found on the west bank of the river opposite the mouth of Deep Ravine. See Dale T. Schoenberger "The End of Custer" page 208.

[136] Given the poor visibility, due to smoke dust and distance, it seems likely that Two Moon is referring to Lieutenant Cooke whose prodigious side whiskers could well have been mistaken for a mustache.

[137] See Richard G. Hardorff "Markers, Artifacts and Indian Testimony" page 53.

[138] See John G. Neihardt "The Sixth Grandfather" pages 191 – 192.

[139] Waterman believed he saw the general, but Wooden Leg states that this officer was the one with the tattoo on his arm, establishing his identity as Captain Tom Custer. See Thomas Marquis "Wooden Leg" page 264.

[140] See Colonel William A. Graham "The Custer Myth" page 110.

[141] See Richard G. Hardorff "Lakota Recollections" page 160.

[142] See Richard G. Hardorff "Lakota Recollections" page 150.

[143] See John G. Neihardt "Black Elk Speaks" page 124.

[144] Later Wooden Leg would later claim to have been misquoted on the mass suicides. See John Stands In Timber "Cheyenne Memories" page 205.

[145] See Thomas B. Marquis "Wooden Leg" page s 246 – 247. Other Indian accounts mention the boys using the greenbacks as saddle blankets for their clay horses.

[146] See "The Teepee Book" pages 193 – 194 for an account of troopers at the Wagon Box Fight tieing their bootlaces to the triggers of their muskets so that they could commit suicide should they be over run.

[147] See John Stands In Timber "Cheyenne Memories" page 205.

[148] See Thomas B. Marquis "Keep the Last Bullet For Yourself" page 128 for an accounting of the amount of whisky found by the Indians on the battlefield.

[149] The latest theory of this genre, espoused by Richard Fox, is that "mass combat fatigue" caused the defeat. This theory builds on the discredited mass suicide theory as well as the recorded instances of a small number of soldiers foolishly attempting to surrender (See "The Teepee Book" page 590 for Red Horse's account of attempted surrenders). While there were undoubtedly isolated instances of both suicides and "combat fatigue" there is no credible eyewitness testimony that this occurred on the large scale Fox proposes. The major deficiency I find with Fox's analysis is his misuse of the archaeological data. Fox's conclusions rest on the absence of artifactual data, although Fox should know that scientific methodology does not allow one to draw a positive conclusion from the absence of data. This error is especially obvious in the case of Keogh's Company I where Fox completely ignores the voluminous Indian testimony of fierce hand–to–hand fighting and cites the lack of government shell casings uncovered during the archaeological investigations as "proof" the soldiers offered little resistance.

[150] See Peter John Powell "People of the Sacred Mountain" page 1029.

[151] While this account is usually considered to describe the death of Sergeant Butler, it could apply equally well to anyone on Calhoun Hill.

[152] See Usher L. Burdick "David F. Barry's Indian Notes On The Custer Battle" pages 27 – 29.

[153] First Sergeant John M. Ryan, Company M, did not believe the Indian accounts that no prisoners were taken: *"I think the Indians took some of our men prisoners, and when the reinforcements joined us, we found what appeared to be human bones and parts of blue uniforms where the men had been tied to stakes and trees. . . We found three of our men's heads, suspended by wires through the back of the ears from a lodge pole, with the hair burned off."* See Richard G. Hardorff "Lakota Recollections" page 96.

[154] See Francis B. Taunton "Custer's Field" page 40.

[155] See Peter John Powell "People of the Sacred Mountain" page 1029.

[156] See Thomas B. Marquis "Wooden Leg" page 240.

[157] According to Marquis, the women and children were still about their ghoulish work on the morning of June 26. See "Wooden Leg" page 263.

[158] In order to spare the feelings of his mother, the details of Sturgis' mutilation were concealed for years. The official story was that the young lieutenant's body could not be identified. This situation backfired when his mother decided to visit the field in 1878. Hurriedly, a marker for young Sturgis

was erected on the South Skirmish Line so that the mother's grief could be brought to closure. Interestingly, that spurious marker, bearing the name of Lieutenant Sturgis, is replicated by one of today's marble markers.

[159] See Daniel O. Magnussen "Thompson's Narrative" page 251.

[160] See Richard G. Hardorff "Lakota Recollections" page 96.

[161] The Cheyenne maintain that Custer took this young maiden as a mistress after the Washita and that she bore him a son. As the only birth of a child to this young Cheyenne that we can verify occurred within a matter of weeks after the Washita, this story is highly suspect.

[162] This is a reference to Custer's negotiations for the release of two captive white women which culminated his successful campaign on the southern plains.

[163] See Peter John Powell "People of the Sacred Mountain" page 1030.

[164] See Lieutenant James H. Bradley "The March of the Montana Column" pages 172 – 173.

[165] In those days of black powder loads, it would have been impossible for a suicide not to have his face streaked with a quantity of black powder. No account of finding Custer's body indicates powder burns on the body. A fantastic explanation that the Cheyenne women actually washed Custer's body is given in D. A. Kinsley "Favor the Bold" page 229.

[166] See Richard G. Hardorff "The Custer Battle Casualties" pages 19 – 20 and 21.

[167] See Thomas B. Marquis "Wooden Leg" pages 248 – 251 and Peter John Powell "People of the Sacred Mountain" page 1031.

[168] For example Lieutenant McClernand thought Medicine Tail Coulee was about opposite the village's midpoint (see E. J. McClernand "The Fight On Custer Hill" page 38) while White Bird's pictograph indicates the village extended at least to opposite the mouth of Deep Ravine (see Lawrence A. Frost "Custer Legends page 175) and Lieutenant Philo Clark's map shows the village extended north of Custer Hill (see Thomas R. Buecker "Sioux War Report" page 12).

[169] See Thomas B. Marquis "Wooden Leg" pages 255 – 256. Noisy Walking died that night of his wounds.

[170] While the slaying of Lame White Man cannot be attributed with absolute certainty to any individual, or group, there is no question that he was mistakenly scalped by the Lakota. See John Stands In Timber "Cheyenne Memories" page 203. While the account in "Wooden Leg" states Lame White Man was recognized by his war cloths, Stands In Timber is adamant that his grandfather was dressed only in a blanket. According to John G. Neihardt in "The Sixth Grandfather," page 186, the Minneconjou Standing Bear scalped Lame White Man under the impression he was an Arikara scout for the soldiers; however, in "Black Elk Speaks," page 116, also by John G. Neihardt, Standing Bear claimed only to have witnessed the event. The Minneconjou White Bull maintained that another Minneconjou, Little Crow was responsible for mistakenly scalping Lame White Man. See Richard G. Hardorff "Lakota Recollections" page 121.

[171] The Lakota believed a scalped individual could not enter heaven so it was imperative to return their ally's scalp.

172 See Peter John Powell "People of the Sacred Mountain" page 1028.

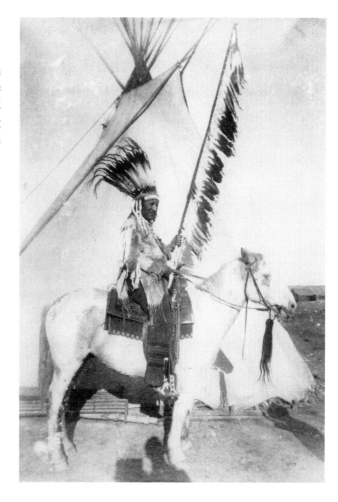

Crow scout White Swan, taken in 1898. Although severely wounded, he repeatedly tried to crawl from the field hospital to take his place on the firing line. *Photo Courtesy Little Bighorn Battlefield National Monument.*

Crow scout Curly, taken in 1877. Unscrupulous interpreters and journalists misrepresented his accounts of the battle causing his early account to be rejected by many early battle scholars. *Photo Courtesy Little Bighorn Battlefield National Monument.*

View from the west bank of the Little Big Horn. The bluffs in the background are where Reno's panic withdrawal from the valley terminated. *Photo Courtesy Little Bighorn Battlefield National Monument.*

Weir Point. This elevation actually consists of two saddles at roughly a right angle. The road from Last Stand Hill to the Reno-Benteen Defense Site passes through the saddle in the picture's center. The saddle that runs roughly north and south is bounded by the high points on the photo's left. While any of the elevations offers a good view of Calhoun Hill, it is only from the northern most of these peaks (left rear of photo) that a complete view of the village could be obtained. *Photo by author.*

Chapter 16

The Siege of Reno Hill

According to Lieutenant Edgerly, after Benteen's junction with Reno, Company D had been deployed as skirmishers to dislodge the few warriors who had taken position on Wooden Leg Ridge.[1] The high ground having been secured, Edgerly recalled:

> *"Then came a time of suspense. We could hear heavy firing down the river and knew it must be Custer. D Troop (Weir's) was for a long while standing to horse, every man apparently anxious to move down to the firing. I wondered what we were waiting for and said to Captain Weir; 'We ought to go down there.' Weir went away for a few minutes then came back again and asked me what I thought we ought to do. I replied: 'Go to Custer, of course.' He then asked if I would be willing to go with him and D Troop, even if the other troops did not go. I told him I would and he then left me saying he would ask permission of Reno and Benteen. Before reaching those officers, however, he changed his mind and concluded that before he asked permission to take the troop down he would go out to a high point that overlooked the valley and see what was going on there, so he came back toward the troop, called to an orderly to bring his horse, mounted and started towards the Custer battleground without saying a word to me. I, supposing from our conversation and his action, that he had received the desired permission, mounted the troop and started after him."[2]*

Weir's movement, coupled with the arrival of 4,000 rounds of reserve ammunition, overcame the command's inertia[3] and the companies, individually, and without orders, started down river, the order being M, K, then H.[4] Benteen's account of his movement to Weir Point, documented in a March 1, 1892 letter to Theodore Goldin, makes for fascinating reading:

> *"I followed, with the remaining two troops of my battalion, the trail that Weir had 'sallied on,' he having no orders to proceed – some ten minutes later perhaps; anyway, just as soon as I learned of his insubordinate and unauthorized movements. . . On arriving at elevation (Weir Point, DCE) I then had my first glimpse of the Indian village from the height. Still I saw enough to cause me to think that perhaps this time we had bitten off quite as much as we would be able to well chew. Then I got the guidon of my own troop and jammed it down in a pile of stones which were on the high point, thinking perhaps the fluttering of same might attract attention from Custer's command if any were in close proximity."[5]*

Reno, who had lost control of his command,[6] hastily dispatched Lieutenant Hare with an order for Weir to establish contact with Custer.[7] This much of the "Weir Point Episode" is clear, although still subject to some debate.[8]

The details of the movement, how far the troops advanced down river, how long did they remain on Weir Point, and, most importantly, what did they observe from that vantage point, are not nearly so clear. For example, despite Edgerly's statement that Weir told him he had started down river without consulting either Reno or Benteen,[9] there are indications, including the accounts of Fox, Martin and Windolph, that Weir had a heated argument with Reno prior to starting down stream. [10] Martin told Colonel Graham:

> *"It sounded like a big fight was going on, and the men thought it was General Custer, and that he was whipping the Indians, and we all wanted to hurry on and join him, but they wouldn't let us go. Captain Weir had some words with Colonel Reno, and I could tell by the way he was acting that he was excited and angry. He waved his arms and gestured and pointed down the river. Then we heard some volleys, and Captain Weir jumped on his horse and started down the river all alone. But his troop followed him right away."* [11]

Private John Fox, Company D, claimed the following exchange between Weir and Reno was witnessed by Moylan and Benteen:

> *"Weir remarked, 'Custer must be around here somewhere and we ought to go to him.' Reno said 'We are surrounded by Indians and we ought to remain here.' Weir said, 'Well, if no one else goes to Custer, I will go.' Reno replied, 'No you can not go. For if you try to do it you will get killed and your company with you.'"* [12]

Edgerly's description of the movement continues:

> *"He (Weir, DCE) rode along the crest of the bluffs where Custer was last seen alive by any of our command, and I took the troop a little to the right following a shallow ravine. The Indians from the Custer battlefield saw us cross the highest point of the bluff and a large number of them started for us. Weir, from his high point, saw them start and signalled for me to move to the right, continuing his signals until he had swung the troop completely around and brought it to where he was."* [13]

While this account seems to indicate that Edgerly had encountered the full force of the warriors after they had dispatched Custer, that could not have been the case as Edgerly goes on to state: *"We stayed out there about two hours according to my recollection, doing considerable shooting but I imagine very little hitting."* [14] Varnum's account is clear that, at most, Company D was engaged in long range sniping: *"I went to where his (Edgerly's, DCE) company was dismounted and firing at the Indians, who seemed to be coming from out on the prairie and turning back. It was quite long range, but there was a good many shots being fired at him, and he was firing away– a slow fire– a shot now and then at quite a little distance."* [15] Varnum, who was probably the last man to reach Weir Point, would testify about one and one half hours were consumed from the time he reached Weir's company on the point until they returned to the defensive position on Reno Hill. [16] These two accounts make it abundantly clear that the troops remained on Weir Point for an extended period of time being engaged, although not pressed, a good portion of that time.

Regarding what the troops observed from Weir Point, Corporal George Washington Wylie, Company D, maintained that they could see mounted men with guidons. Believing this to be Custer's command, Weir was about to start forward when stopped by Sergeant James Flanagan: *"Here Captain, you had better take a look through the glasses, I think those are Indians."* After looking, Weir agreed and went no further down river. [17] While this statement seems fairly innocuous today, it has tremendous impact when viewed against the background of officers, such as Weir, who had served with distinction in the Civil War. These officers would maintain they had no inkling Custer had met with disaster prior to General Terry's arrival on June 27th. This statement immediately arouses suspicion when one recalls the importance placed upon the colors by the military. Great honor and glory accrued for capturing an enemy's colors during combat; witness Tom Custer's two Medals of Honor during the Civil War. Similarly, a unit losing their colors in combat could only regain their honor and prestige by recapturing them. Note further that the plural, guidon**s**, is used in the narrative. Given this background, how could one possibly view a minimum of two captured guidons, out of a total of 5, from a commander who never lost a color during the Civil War,[18] and not know that an unprecedented disaster had taken place?

There are other indications of a "cover up" on the part of the officers. Both Captains French and Weir, began drinking very heavily after the battle, a situation that resulted in the untimely death of Weir 6 months later, and French being court–martialed and dismissed from the service in 1879. Both men appear to have been suffering from extreme melancholia, as witnessed by Weir's letters to Libbie Custer. In October he wrote:

> *"You know I can't tell you now but will sometime tell it to you . . . I have so much to tell you that I will tell you nothing now. . . ."*

and again in November:

> *"It is my life business to vindicate my friends of that day. . . . I know if we were all of us alone in the parlor, at night, the curtains all down and everybody else asleep, one or the other of you would make me tell you everything I know"*

French, in writing to Lieutenant Cooke's mother, as quoted in Chapter 13, may have referred to more than the valley fight when he wrote *". . . when I sought death. . . If one man could hold back seven or eight hundred, what might not a hundred and twenty have done at the right instant. Sometimes one minute is of far more value than years afterward. . . I want revenge for my friends."*[19]

But why hide the fact that a disaster was known to have occurred prior to the troops' arrival on Weir Point? The reasoning will become clear once the entire Weir Point Episode is understood.

While most witnesses at the court of inquiry were firm in their belief that Custer had already been defeated prior to the arrival of troops on Weir Point, a few dissenting voices were heard. Godfrey spoke of a few scattering shots beyond the ridge that they thought was Custer's rear guard retreating toward Terry.[20] Sergeant Ryan, upon observing the Indians firing into the ground, correctly deduced they were killing Custer's wounded.[21] Edgerly provided another key piece of information when he admitted they could see the bodies of Custer's men and slain horses from Weir Point.[22] But it was Private Edward A. Pigford, Company M, who first hinted at the whole truth. Pigford stated: *". . . looked over toward Custer ridge the Indians were firing from a big circle, but it gradually closed until they seemed to converge into a large black mass on the side hill toward the river and all along the ridge."*[23] Lieutenant Hare apparently confirmed this when he told Walter Camp that both he and Weir thought Custer was actively engaged while the troops were on Weir Point.[24] The formal accusation was made public in the December 28, 1878 edition of the *New York Herald*. This account, claiming to quote Captain Weir who had died two years previously, maintained the troops on Weir Point witnessed the end of the Custer fight and were prevented from going to their comrades" aid by Major Reno.[25] The statement in the *Herald* had been obtained from Frederick Whittaker, as biased in his support of Custer as others have been in their denunciation of the general, who was never able to produce an original of Weir's alleged statement.[26]

Whittaker's lack of credibility has caused most authorities to dismiss the possibility the troops on Weir Point witnessed a portion of the Custer Fight. Despite my personal belief that the Weir statement was a fabrication on the part of Captain Whittaker, I believe his hypothesis to have been essentially correct; the troops on Weir Point witnessed the Custer Fight, probably from the point of Lame White Man's charge until it ended some 30 minutes later.[27]

The first piece of circumstantial evidence supporting this theory is the Cheyenne accounts of the action north of Last Stand Hill. The timing analysis contained in Appendix 12 is based upon time and distance formulations, that is, standard rates for given gaits of cavalry are used to calculate the time required to transverse the known distances involved. The times are adjusted, if necessary, at those points where multiple detachments were in visual contact, such as the sightings of Custer's column on the bluffs by members of Reno's battalion in the valley. As such, the analysis is conservative in nature, ignoring the possibility of enroute delays. That analysis indicates, it was not possible for Custer to have withdrawn from Medicine Tail Coulee, gone to the northern ford, returned, and been annihilated prior to Weir's movement down river, unless Weir waited well over an hour after the junction with Reno before proceeding down stream. While there is less than unanimous agreement among the survivor's accounts as to when Weir proceeded down river, the majority of witnesses indicate the movement occurred fairly soon after the junction with Reno.[28]

Pigford's account, if it is credited at all, is assumed by most authorities to refer to Last Stand Hill. The key term in Pigford's account, and the term that locates the position described, is "big circle." Pigford's account clearly states the position on Custer's field under observation from Weir Point was seen to be encircled by the Cheyenne and Lakota warriors. All that is required to identify the position being described is a short climb to the northernmost peak of the surviving saddle[29] formed by Weir Point. From that vantage point it is obvious that the only hill <u>encircled</u> by warriors that can be viewed from Weir Point is Calhoun Hill – the north, or back, side of Last Stand Hill being totally obscured from view from any position on Weir Point. No *"side hill toward the river"* exists in the vicinity of Last Stand Hill, but this description very aptly fits Greasy Grass Ridge, while *"all along the ridge"* could easily refer to Calhoun Ridge rather than Battle Ridge as is usually assumed despite the fact no Indian accounts tell of a general engagement along the entire length of the ridge. What Pigford's account describes, therefore, is the action precipitated by the charge of Lame White Man against the South Skirmish Line, resulting in the successive collapse of the positions on Greasy Grass Ridge, Calhoun Ridge, and Calhoun Hill.

Another piece of circumstantial evidence is contained in Stanley Vestal's notes in the Western History Collections at the University of Oklahoma. Vestal quotes Two Moon as stating: *"Middle-aged and young in fight (Custer fight, DCE). Many Indians not in fight, so remainder charged Reno while Custer battle [was going] on."*[30] There are no accounts that indicate Reno was actively engaged on Reno Hill during the time the Custer Fight was in progress. In fact, Indian accounts indicate Reno was totally unopposed at that time; a contention supported by the ease with which the Herendeen party rejoined the command. The foregoing considerations leave us but a single option for the location of the "charge" on Reno – Weir Point. The final piece of evidence is contained in a letter to Libbie Custer from Lieutenant John Garland on December 4, 1877. The letter contains the following interesting passage:

"Capt. Nowlan[31] told me last winter that he heard Mr. Edgerly (Lt W. S. Edgerly, 7th Cavalry, DCE) tell Gen. Sturgis (Colonel Samuel D. Sturgis, Commanding Officer, 7th Cavalry, DCE) at the camp fire last fall at Standing Rock that he saw and heard the General's devoted band from where he and Weir stood."[32]

As to why the troops did not proceed to Custer's aid one can only speculate. My personal belief is the close fighting phase of the battle happened too quickly for the officers to comprehend what was happening and then react to it. Most probably only troops D and M were on Weir Point when Calhoun Hill fell. By the time Companies K and H arrived (A and B, along with Major Reno, apparently never got further down river than Wooden Leg Ridge),[33] Custer's entire command had been wiped out. I find no evidence what–so–ever that Major Reno, who had ceased to exercise command, was informed that Custer had been observed hotly engaged, much less that he refused to allow the companies to go to the aid of their commander.[34] Given the insubordinate actions of Weir, French and Benteen prior to this time, had such an order been given, it is doubtful it would have been obeyed.

Once the warriors had dispatched Custer's immediate command, they turned their attention to the troops now highly visible on Weir Point where Benteen had planted the guidon to identify their position to Custer. The warriors hastened toward the high point, becoming engaged by companies D and M as they came within range:

> *"At this point there were a few Indians who commenced firing at us from behind some rocks.*
>
> *"I dismounted the troop, and also from behind rocks, we had an interesting duel, until Capt. French called up to me that Reno had sent orders for us to return to his position."*[35]

Godfrey, who like French and Edgerly[36] had deployed his company to defend around Weir Point, was startled by the verbal order brought to him by Reno's acting adjutant, Lieutenant Hare,[37] as he related in his *Century Magazine* article:

> *"Weir's and French's troops were posted on the high bluffs and to the front of them; my own troop along the crest of the bluffs next to the river; the rest of the command moved to the rear, as I supposed to occupy other points in the vicinity, to make this our defensive position. Busying myself with posting my men, giving direction about the use of ammunition, etc., I was a little startled by the remark that the command was out of sight. At this time Weir's and French's troops were being attacked. Orders were soon brought to me by Lieutenant Hare, Acting–Adjutant, to join the main command. I had gone some distance in the execution of this order when, looking back, I saw French's troop come tearing over the bluffs, and soon after Weir's troop followed in hot haste. Edgerly was near the top of the bluff trying to mount his frantic horse, and it did seem that he would not succeed, but he vaulted into his saddle and then joined the troop."*[38]

Edgerly indeed had some difficulty in withdrawing from Weir Point. He had given the command to mount and was just approaching his own horse when *"I saw one Indian who looked so inviting that I couldn't resist the temptation to take a shot at him. . . Meanwhile the Indians who had seen our preparations for leaving, had closed in on us and were on a knoll less than twenty paces from us shooting as rapidly as they could."*[39] His horse, terrified by the firing, proved impossible to mount encumbered by the carbine, so Edgerly handed his weapon to his orderly, Private Charles Sanders:

> *"When I handed my carbine to Private Saunders, (the muster rolls list him as Sanders, DCE) I noticed that he had a broad grin on his face, altho' he was sitting in a perfect shower of bullets. I didn't have time to question him then, but the next day after the firing ceased I asked him what he was laughing at at such a time. He replied, 'I was laughing to see what poor shots those Indians were; they were shooting too low and their bullets were spattering dust like drops of rain.' I never saw a cooler man under fire than Saunders."*[40]

The troops had progressed only a few hundred yards when the farrier of D Troop, Private Charlie Vincent,[41] fell from his horse; shot through the hips.[42] Unable to mount, the unfortunate wretch implored Lieutenant Edgerly not to abandon him. Edgerly testified as to the result during the Reno Court of Inquiry:

> *"On going back I passed a man of D Company wounded. He looked at me and I told him to get into a hole and I would form a line, come back and save him. As soon as I got by K Company I met Captain Weir and told him about the wounded soldier and that I had promised to save him and asked him to throw out a skirmish line for that purpose. He said he was sorry but the orders were to go back on the hill. I said that I had promised to save the man. He said he could not help it, the orders were positive to go back and we must go back."[43]*

There being no convenient hole for Vincent to hide in, he was last seen crawling after his departing comrades.[44] The Minneconjou Standing Bear was present at the conclusion of the episode:

> *"And we started for the soldiers (the troops on Weir Point, DCE). They ran back to where they came from. One got killed, and many of us got off and couped him."[45]*

As a maximum of 4 coups were allowed to be struck on an enemy, Standing Bear's reference to "many" warriors couping the unfortunate Vincent may be an indication that he was tortured to death. A further indication of torture is that Vincent's body[46] was discovered with a stick rammed down the throat.[47] As the Lakota believed that a person's spirit exited the body via the mouth, this indicates the stick was forced into position while Vincent was still alive. Fortunately, this was the final time during the '76 campaign a wounded trooper would be left to the clemency of an enemy that did not subscribe to the concept of showing mercy to wounded adversaries.

Sergeant Thomas W. Harrison, who was with Edgerly on Weir Point, gave an entirely different view of the Charlie Vincent episode to Walter Camp. Harrison maintained that as he and Edgerly left the point *"They had to throw their bridles over their heads and draw revolvers and ride through the Indians as they came by Charley. He (Charley) cried out that he was wounded and needed assistance. Edgerly stopped and told him to get into a ravine and he would try and come back and save him as soon as they could get reinforcements. After going a piece they looked back and saw the Indians finishing up Charley. At the moment they were talking with Charley, perhaps 200 Indians were in the immediate neighborhood, all advancing."[48]*

If this account is true, it casts an entirely new light on Edgerly's court of inquiry testimony. Weir had died in 1876 and Harrison had been discharged the same year. There were, therefore, no witnesses to Edgerly's abandoning Vincent and he could easily shift the responsibility to the deceased Weir. With so many having so much to hide about the Weir Point episode, it is little wonder a reconstruction of the true events is so difficult.

The troops were in a potentially disastrous position. Troop M, for the second time in the space of a couple of hours, had turned its back to these warriors and was rushing to the rear, closely pursued by D Troop galloping to the rear unaccompanied by either of their officers. As in Reno's panic withdrawal from the valley, the soldier's rear was totally unprotected. While the warriors were preparing for another "buffalo hunt" of the fleeing bluecoats, a humorous incident occurred which was related by Lieutenant Edgerly:

> *"We had in our troop a corpulent old tailor, known throughout the regiment as 'Jimmy' Wynn (Private James Wynn, Company D, DCE), who was riding an old*

horse, blind in one eye, and ordinarily very quiet. The instant he mounted, his
horse started for the rear at full speed and one of the most laughable sights I ever
saw was 'Jimmy' pulling at the reins with both hands, his carbine dangling at his
side, a veritable fat John Gilpin. He wasn't able to stop until he reached the horses of
the rest of the command."[49]

While Edgerly, despite the danger, saw the humor in trooper Wynn's rapid departure for the rear, Godfrey was anything but amused by the rapid pace of the movement; recalling troops D and M[50] passing him in *"hot haste."*[51] The reason behind this rapid withdrawal has never been adequately explained, there being no indication that the warriors either pushed the troops off the high ground or that the troops were closely pressed. Professor William James makes an interesting observation in his book "Principle of Psychology" that may be relevant. The professor states that, contrary to popular belief, we don't run because we are frightened, rather we become frightened because we have run. Charles Kuhlman extended this argument to conclude that troops D and M started at too rapid a pace, resulting in the officers being unable to check their troops. A repeat of Reno's panic withdrawal from the valley was avoided when Company K was dismounted to cover the retreat in skirmish order.[52] Godfrey's company was fairly green *"many had not been under fire before,"* [53]necessitating the reformation of the skirmish line on two occasions to prevent bunching by the troopers.

As they neared the position on Reno Hill chosen for defense, Godfrey noted the tactical importance of the high ground afforded by Wooden Leg Ridge which commanded the soldier's position. Exercising sound military judgment, Godfrey ordered Lieutenant Hare, who had elected to remain with Company K after delivering the recall order,[54] to take ten men and secure the high ground. Before the order could be executed, further orders came from Reno to fall back as quickly as possible, and this tactical objective was abandoned to the oncoming warriors.[55]

The site selected for defense was a rather poor one, but probably the best available on "short notice." The position, about 100 feet above the river, is variously described as a saucer with part of the rim broken away, or the arc of a circle. It probably is best compared to a horseshoe with one elongated prong; the lower central portion being a swale. The position was not entirely devoid of advantage as the natural depression in the center of the position allowed the animals to be picketed so that all of the troopers could be deployed on the firing line.

The problem of being "under the guns" of Wooden Leg Ridge was compounded by improper placement of the troops. The proper position to take on a slope is forward of, rather than behind, the rise. While this results in a somewhat exposed position, it affords the maximum field of fire for the troops which, of course, is the main purpose. An examination of the reconstructed rifle pits at the Reno–Benteen Defense Site reveals that, with the exception of companies A and H,[56] all of the troops were positioned on the reverse side of the crest. In some cases the field of fire, from a prone position, was less than 30 feet. This positioning of the firing lines seems to indicate that, with the exception of Benteen, the officers had ceased to exercise proper military judgment and control of the troops, allowing the men to indulge their instincts of self preservation. Captain Moylan, for example, lost his original nickname of "Hardy" and became known throughout the regiment as "Aparoho Michie" because he spent virtually the entire siege laying behind the relative safety of one of the mule aparohos.[57] Similarly, Corporal Daniel Nealon of Company H, became known as "Cracker Box Dan" for taking refuge behind a barricade of hardtack boxes during the hottest of the fighting. [58] There are recorded instances of the warriors being able to advance, without exposing themselves to the fire of the troops, close enough to the lines to be able to throw arrows and rocks among the troopers. Clearly a determined and aggressive attack by the Indians would have resulted in the complete annihilation of the 7th Cavalry. Fortunately for those corralled on Reno Hill, the warrior's blood lust had been satiated and Benteen would effectively extinguish any further sparks of warrior aggressiveness before they could be fanned into a conflagration similar to that which overwhelmed Custer.

It would be incorrect to assume that all of the troopers forgot their military training and obligations. As mentioned previously, what little proper positioning of troops was accomplished was largely due to the efforts of Benteen whose performance of duty in defense of Reno Hill was as magnificent as it had been derelict in his earlier failing to comply with Custer's written orders.[59]

As the troops arrived at the defensive position, the mule Barnum broke from his position in line and hurried toward the on–rushing warriors with his cargo of 2,000 rounds of carbine ammunition. Sergeant Richard P. Hanley of Company C, realizing the criticality of the situation, sped in pursuit. Withstanding a hail of lead, Hanley, after a wild circuit consuming twenty minutes, was able to capture Barnum and secure him safely within the lines.[60] For this heroic action, Hanley would receive the Medal of Honor.

Barnum's irreplaceable ammunition secured, the troops braced for the impending onslaught that continued unabated until dark.[61] Sergeant John Ryan, Company M, recalled the start of the siege:

> *"We had been in this position but a short time when they advanced in great numbers from the direction in which we came.*
>
> *"They made several charges upon us and we repulsed them every time. Finally they surrounded us. Soon the firing became general all along the line, very rapid and at close range. The company on the right of my company had a number of men killed in a few minutes. There was a high ridge on the right and an opening on the right of our lines, and one Indian in particular I must give credit for being a good shot.*
>
> *"While we were lying in this line he fired a shot and killed the fourth man on my right. Soon afterward he fired again and shot the third man. His third shot wounded the man on my right,[62] who jumped back from the line, and down among the rest of the wounded. I thought my turn was coming next. I jumped up, with Captain French, and some half a dozen members of my company; instead of firing straight to the front, as we had been doing up to the time of this incident, we wheeled to our right and put in a deadly volley, and I think we put an end to that Indian, as there were no more men killed at that particular spot."*[63]

The warriors would fire heavily on the troops for 20 to 30 minutes and then follow up with a charge.[64] Notable among the casualties[65] were Sergeant Benjamin C. Criswell,[66] and Private Charles Cunningham,[67] both of Company B, civilian packer Frank C. Mann,[68] and Private Frank Braun of Company M, the last fatality of the Little Big Horn.[69] Private Andrew J. Moore, of Company G, initially left behind in the timber, had rejoined the command with the Herendeen party. Although cautioned by Private Hugh McGonigle, another of the G Company men initially left in the timber, not to expose himself, Moore complained he could not properly aim unless standing. Taking a bullet through the kidneys, he died in the field hospital begging for the opiates Dr. Porter didn't have.[70] At dusk, Company K's First Sergeant, Dewitt Winney raised his head above his barricade. He was instantly struck by a bullet in the forehead. Winney screamed: *"I am hit!"* Godfrey, being nearby attempted to reassure the wounded man, but Winney expired before Godfrey could finish speaking.[71] While there should have been ample opportunity during the charges for the warriors to win war honors, the oral history of the Lakota and Cheyenne is quite meager for this phase of the fighting. A notable exception is the story of the Minneconjou Breech Cloth, killed near dusk during a bravery run on the east side of Reno Hill. The Minneconjou Dog Backbone was positioned to the northeast some distance from Reno Hill. Despite the distance separating them from the troops, Dog Backbone kept warning the young warriors: *"Look out, now, boys. Those soldiers are a good way off, but their bullets are coming over mighty fierce."* Just as he finished his admonition, he was killed by a ball in the forehead.[72]

During this period of the fighting, some of the Springfield carbines began to jam. Daniel Newell describes French's coolness under fire while removing the jammed cartridges: *"During all this fighting I was near Captain French helping get the guns loaded whenever an empty shell would stick, and this happened to most[73] of the guns as soon as they got hot. Captain French was a crack shot and always carried a 'Long Tom' infantry rifle. This gun had a ramrod carried under the barrel and I think it was the only ramrod in the outfit. Whenever a shell would stick he would recover the gun and either pick it out with his knife or I would push it out with the ramrod. We would then load the gun and return it to its owner. In doing this Captain French was exposed most of the time, but was perfectly cool and for some reason or other escaped unhurt."[74]*

With the cessation of firing, the troops were put into regular positions[75] and ordered to entrench as best they could. Entrenching proved an ordeal. The troopers had gone nearly 24 hours with little or no sleep and food and they had emptied their canteens during the heat of the day. To make matters worse, there were only a handful of axes and spades in the entire command.[76] The exhausted troopers were forced to scratch out what protection they could from the arid soil using tin cups and knives.[77] Benteen, alone of all the officers, did not order his men to entrench as he explained at the Reno court of inquiry: *"I was pretty tired and did not think there was much necessity for building them (breastworks, DCE) as I had an idea the Indians would leave us, but I sent for spades to carry out his (Reno's, DCE) instruction, but could get none."[78]* His exposed company would pay for this error in judgment, sustaining nearly one third of the command's total casualties on the 26th.

Unable to choke down their dry biscuits due to the lack of water, the exhausted troopers tried to gain what little respite was available in slumber. Even this was denied them, as the incessant beating of the drums in the village below filled their imaginations with the most terrifying of visions. While the soldier's accounts indicate wild revelry and celebration in the Indian village, the Lakota custom of observing a 4 day mourning period precluded a victory dance being held the night of the 25th.[79] The state of mind of the beleaguered troops is aptly described by Godfrey:

> *"Men imagined they could see a column of troops over on the hills or ridges, that they could hear the tramp of the horses, the command of officers, or even the trumpet-calls. Stable-call was sounded by one of our trumpeters; shots were fired by some of our men, and familiar trumpet-calls were sounded by our trumpeter immediately after, to let the supposed marching column know that we were friends. Every favorable expression or opinion was received with credulity, and then ratified with a cheer. Somebody suggested that General Crook might be coming, so some one, a civilian packer, I think, mounted a horse, and galloping along the line yelled: 'Don't be discouraged, boys, Crook is coming.' But they gradually realized that the much-wished-for reinforcements were but the phantasma of their imaginations, and settled down to their work of digging rifle-pits."[80]*

Godfrey went on to describe the activity in the Indian village:

"Their camp was a veritable pandemonium. All night long they continued their frantic revels; beating tom-toms, dancing, whooping, yelling with demoniacal screams, and discharging firearms. We knew they were having a scalp-dance. In this connection the question has often been asked 'if they did not have prisoners at the torture?' The Indians deny that they took any prisoners. We did not discover any evidence of torture in their camps. It is true that we did find human heads, severed from their bodies, but these probably had been paraded in their orgies during that terrible night." [81]

There are first hand accounts of that harrowing night purporting to have observed prisoners being burned at the stake in the village. Private Jacob Adams recalled: *"On the night of the 25th of June I saw the Indians burn two of our men at the stake. They just put a stake into the ground and rawhided the man fast to the stake and built a fire all around him. They don't put this fire close enough to kill him at once, they torture him to death. After they ran around it whooping and hollering. I do not know if they got those men out of General Custer's command or Major Reno's command. There was a woods between us and the Indians and they took them back far enough from the woods so we could see plainly from the hills where we were at. They wanted to show us how brave they were and to show what would become of us if we were captured."* [82] The officers were not immune to this form of hysteria, Major Reno stating: *"I am strongly of the opinion that . . . he (Lieutenant Harrington, DCE) was burned at the stake, for while the great battle was going on I and some other officers looking through field glasses saw the Indians miles away, engaged in a war dance about three captives. They were tied to a stake and my impression was that Lieutenant Harrington was one of them."* [83] While Little Knife admitted that a soldier had been tortured to death in the village that night, the troopers couldn't possibly have witnessed the event from their great distance. Peter Thompson recalled a classic case of "combat fatigue":

"After the firing of the Indians had ceased, I went where I had left my horse in charge of a man named McGuire (Private John B. McGuire Jr. of Company C, DCE). Here I saw something that under other conditions would have been laughable. McGuire had been given charge of five horses. When I left mine with him he was sitting on the ground, his head shrunk down between his shoulders, and his eyes bulged out to their fullest extent; and when I returned, he was in exactly the same position, still holding the reins of five horses in his hand, but three were lying dead. I asked him if he knew that three of the horses were dead; he mournfully shook his head. . ." [84]

Although the immediate threat had passed, the besieged troopers were in dire straits, and they knew it. Speculation ran rampant, and, at the core of this speculation, was the specter of Major Elliott at the Washita. Benteen testified at Reno's court of inquiry: *"It was the belief of the officers on the hill during the night of the 25th that General Custer had gone to General Terry and that we were abandoned to our fate."* [85] Wallace supported Benteen in his testimony: *"I heard a great deal of swearing about General Custer running off and leaving us."* [86] Godfrey agreed the enlisted men held this opinion when he testified: *"I think everybody thought he had been repulsed and the Indians had driven him away. There was such a feeling and I heard the men say during the night that they thought General Custer had abandoned them as he did not come back."* In response to the question: *"Was there in your mind or in the minds of others as far as you know, any impression that General Custer would abandon any part of his command if it were a possible thing for him to get to it?"* Godfrey testified: *" I don't think there was any such impression."* [87] Varnum, and Sergeant Culbertson, agreed in their testimony, stating: *"I certainly had an idea myself that he had been driven off in his attack on the other end of the village and that he was either corralled, as we were, in the hills, or had got away towards General Terry's command."* [88] and *"It was the general belief among the men that General Custer had been wounded*[89] *and could not come to us just as we could not go to him."*[90]

Captain McDougall also did not feel Custer had abandoned them, testifying:

> *"During the night of the 25th I think the conclusion was that Custer had met the same crowd and they were either following him or else he had gone to General Terry. . . We had heard firing down there, and all the Indians had come back after us, and I thought perhaps he had retreated to General Terry, and they had come back to finish our command . . . We had no idea they (Custer's command , DCE) were destroyed (in this opinion, all the Reno court of inquiry testimony was unanimous, DCE)."*[91]

What else were the corralled troopers to think? The frontier army usually considered a force of 3 companies more than adequate to handle any contingency against Indians, and Custer had 5 companies in his immediate command. Except for the Fetterman ambush of the previous decade, there were no instances in the frontier army of such a large body of troops being annihilated by Indians. Benteen, however, could not resist a last dig at his fallen commander for the Washita when he testified: *"Except for the battle of the Washita there was no historical example, as far as I know, of the destruction of a command equipped as his (Custer's, DCE) was."*[92] Since Custer couldn't have been annihilated, and he certainly had not come to Reno's aid, he must have withdrawn in the direction of the Terry–Gibbon Column. Hadn't Custer, when confronted by a large warrior force, marched away from the Washita 8 years before without ascertaining the fate of Elliott and his small force? The few officers who knew, or suspected, the truth, undoubtedly remained silent.

Godfrey believed that the command, although hampered by their casualties, should attempt to effect a junction with Custer: *"We (Captain Weir and Godfrey, DCE) thought he had been repulsed and was unable to make a junction with us. We thought that the command ought to move that night and effect a junction with him, as we had fewer casualties there to take care of than we would have in the future."*[93] Others were thinking along similar lines as Walter O. Taylor, blacksmith of Company G, related in a 1909 letter to Walter Camp:

> *"After twilight had come on the evening of the 25th and the fire of the Indians had slackened or ceased altogether, the men moved about quite freely, and were naturally rather anxious to know what our next move would be, the First Sergeant of my company had been wounded (there is no record of Sergeant Alexander Brown being wounded at the Little Big Horn, DCE) and his duties fell upon Sergeant Fehler (Sergeant Henry Fehler of Company A, DCE), an elderly German, of a rather placid nature, our company was considerably scattered and when I saw the Sergeant (Fehler, DCE) near the lower end of the herded horses and pack mules, I approached and asked him 'What are we going to do, stay here all night, or try to move away?' Major Reno was then standing quite near and heard my question, he turned at once with the remark, 'I would like to know how the Hell we are going to move away.'"*[94]

But a movement was discussed quite seriously among the officers. Godfrey, who knew the full story by the time *Century Magazine* published his 1892 article, feeling compelled to protect the honor of the regiment at all costs, would cryptically write: *"The question of moving was discussed, but the conditions coupled to the proposition caused it to be indignantly rejected."*[95]

And just what were those conditions that required indignant rejection? Much to his everlasting shame, Major Reno had determined upon another retreat, abandoning his wounded to the enemy![96] Perhaps Lieutenant Mathey was aware of Reno's decision[97] when he testified at the court of inquiry regarding the fate of Custer: *"My impression was that General Custer was surrounded as we were and **had wounded men and would not abandon them** (emphasis the author's, DCE). That probably he was in the same fix we were."*[98] It is also possible that Mathey knew nothing of Reno's plan and merely selected some interesting phraseology during his testimony. Godfrey would learn of the plan in 1881 but, his devotion to the honor of the regiment, would preclude his making a public statement for almost half a century. Godfrey relates how he learned of the contemplated action:

> *"On June 28, as we were marching to Custer field to bury the dead, Benteen and I were riding together, apart from the rest of the command, and I said to him, 'Benteen, it's pretty damned bad.'*

> *"Benteen asked, 'What do you mean' I replied, 'Reno's conduct.' Benteen then faced me and said, with great earnestness, 'God (my nickname among my fellows), I could tell things that would make your hair stand on end.' I responded, 'What is it? Tell me.' Just then some one rode up near us, and Benteen jerked his head in the direction of the intruder and said, 'I can't tell you now.' I asked, 'Will you tell me some time?' and he replied, 'Yes.' Time after time I besought him to tell me, but always there appeared some excuse for putting off the narration.*

> *"In 1881 we were on a fishing trip at Point Pleasant, N. J., and one evening all the other members of the party had gone to the beach for a swim. I recalled his statement to me on June 28, and said, 'Benteen, now we are absolutely alone, and no one can hear. You promised to tell me what you had in mind, and I want you to tell me now.' He hesitated a moment, and then asked, 'Don't you think it is just as well to let bygones be bygones?" I replied, 'No, I insist on your promise.' A moment of silence followed, when he said:*

> *"Well, on the night of the 25th Reno came to me after all firing had ceased and proposed that we mount every man who could ride, destroy such property as could not be carried, abandon our position and make a forced march back to our supply camp. (The supply camp was on the Yellowstone River, at the mouth of the Powder, distant about 120 miles, map measurement.) I asked him what he proposed to do with the wounded, and he replied, 'Oh, we'll have to abandon those that can not ride.' I said, 'I won't do it.'"*[99]

From our twentieth century perspective, it is difficult to comprehend how Godfrey could confuse the honor of the regiment with the personal honor of Major Reno. It seems logical that, even in the nineteenth century, the honor of the Seventh Cavalry would have been able to withstand the dishonoring of its junior major. As Captain Moylan, a staunch defender of Reno at the court of inquiry, wrote to Godfrey in 1892:

> *"I desire to be understood that my defense of Reno is entirely confined **to his act of taking his three troops out of the bottom** (emphasis by Moylan, DCE). Of his personal conduct in the bottom or subsequently on the hill the least said the better. If what Col. Benteen told me at Meade in 1883 (Reno's plan to abandon the wounded, DCE) was true, and I know of no reason to doubt it, then Reno ought to have been shot."*[100]

In describing the removal of Reno's wounded from the field, Colonel John Gibbon could only hint at their anguish as they had lain helplessly amid decaying flesh, without water, at the mercy of swarms of flies, tirelessly attended by the regiments sole surviving physician:

> *"Poor fellows! an impression had, in some way, gained a footing amongst them during the long weary hours of the fight on the 26th that, to save the balance of the command, they were to be abandoned."[101]*

Abandoning the wounded was not the only reason to conceal the entire story of the events of June 25th. Godfrey's second reason, if ever made public, would stain the honor of the regiment beyond repair. While Godfrey would never used the term in public, his various accounts, when coupled with the knowledge of the plan to abandon the wounded, makes it indisputably clear that had Reno insisted on abandoning the wounded, the officers would have mutinied. A mutiny, while always a serious offense, is doubly so when executed during a active engagement. What evidence is there that such a action was contemplated? First we have a statement provided by McDougall to Walter Camp on the condition that, if used, it would not be attributed:

> *"Finally when the column started to fall back (from Weir Point, DCE) he (being on very good terms with Benteen) quietly remarked to him that if not careful there would be a second Ft. Phil Kearney affair. He then said quietly to Benteen that Reno was doing nothing to put the command on the defensive and that he (Benteen) being the senior capt., had better take charge and run the thing. . . Benteen grinned and did as was suggested."[102]*

In later years Godfrey would expand on his *Century Magazine* article. While still trying to be obscure, the meaning of the following passage concerning Reno's conduct becomes clear within the context of a contemplated revolt among the officers:

> *"His faltering advances down the valley, his halting, his falling back to the defensive position in the woods in the old river bed before his command had suffered a single casualty in the ranks; his disorganized, panic retreat to the bluffs with practically no resistance, his conduct up to and during the siege, and until the arrival of General Terry was not such as to inspire confidence or even respect, except for his authority; and **there was a time during the night of the 25th, when his authority, under certain conditions, was to be ignored** (emphasis the author's, DCE)."*

Weir apparently was consulted by Benteen regarding the situation for Godfrey mentions that on the night of June 25th Weir, who was greatly agitated and distressed, came to him with the question if a difference of opinion arose between Benteen and Reno, whom would Godfrey follow; Godfrey affirming he would follow Benteen.[103] As Godfrey stated in his field diary: *"We (Weir and himself, DCE) both thought that to Col Benteen we must look for the wisdom to deliver us from our situation or defend us as it was evident that Col Reno carried no vigor nor decision, and his personal behavior gave no confidence in him."[104]*

Fortunately, Reno apparently never insisted on implementing his plan and the contemplated revolt never materialized. There was much to do to shore up the defense. As previously mentioned, the companies were placed in line by unit, and meager breastworks were constructed. Captain Moylan placed a four man picket, commanded by Sergeant Stanislaus Roy, outside his barricade to give early warning should the Indians attempt to steal upon them in the dark.[105] Lieutenant Mathey assisted Dr. Henry Renaldo Porter in selecting the site for the field hospital, which lay in the depression, or swale, in the center of the position.[106] Upon their arrival on the hill, Mathey had sent all of his men up to the firing line, leaving the horses and mules loose, a potentially dangerous situation, as Benteen related:

> *"Mathey paid no attention to his pack-train on the hill until I gave him a square heel-and-toe 'cussing out' in broad Saxon, which was when I returned to him two mules, loaded with ammunition (4 boxes, or 4,000 rounds, DCE), which mules I had personally caught while they were hell-bent on getting to the blue water which was so plainly in sight."*[107]

Lieutenant Mathey then had picket lines run to tether the horses and mules, although this apparently wasn't accomplished until near daylight. The picket lines were so arranged as to afford some protection to the wounded.[108] Benteen also had to contend with the near exhaustion of the troops. Despite having been detailed to command Company G[109] after the death of Lieutenant McIntosh, Lieutenant Gibson was ordered to assist Benteen with the Company H sentries:

> *"I judged of the condition of the men of my troop somewhat by my own condition; though that is one of almost physical never tire; but not having had sleep for the two nights previous to this one, was getting just a trifle weary myself; so, up and down the line of 'H' Troop 1st Lieut. Gibson and myself tramped, the night of June 25th & 26th, doing our very best to keep the sentinels awake, but we just could not do it. Kicking them; well, they didn't care anything about that."*[110]

Sleepy sentries were not the only personnel problem faced by the command that night. A major problem for the command was "skulkers" leaving the firing line to seek the relative safety of the packs. Custer's striker, Private John Burkman recalled the fate of one skulker: *"Billy Blake,*[111] *a private, made believe he was hurt and lay with the wounded at Reno Hill. Fact was he was not hurt. He was very much ashamed of it afterward and could not stand the scorn of his comrades and joined another company."*[112] A high percentage of these skulkers were from Company G, where Lieutenant Wallace, left without assistance when Benteen had Gibson accompany him on his continuous round of the sentries, was apparently unable to keep order. Benteen went to the packs on multiple occasions during the siege to return the troopers to the firing line. Lying wounded in the field hospital on June 26th, Private Peter Thompson recalled one such incident: *"I saw Capt. Benteen dash into the midst of our horses and drive out several men who were hiding and skulking about them. 'Get out of here,' he cried, 'And do your duty!'"*[113]

Reno, very active the night of June 25 according to private Slapper, was also plagued by the skulkers. *"I then went round the line and came into the pack train, and I found a good many men and packers who were skulking, and I drove them out. I did this several times. I thought the mules and the horses were safe and that those men had no business there."*[114] Reno's problem with the skulkers cut two ways as packer B. F. Churchill[115] testified:

> *"We had been without anything the whole day. We went out to find our own mess (the command had been plagued by stealing of supplies, DCE). We thought we could not find it from everything being piled up together. The officer's mess kits and company kits were piled in together without any regard to whose they were. We went to the line and saw Major Reno standing there. We did not notice him till he spoke to Frett (Packer John Frett who testified to substantially the same story as Churchill, DCE), at least, I did not. I don't know whether he did or not. He spoke to Frett and asked him what he wanted. Frett said he was after something to eat. Major Reno then asked him if the mules were 'tight,' it sounded like 'tight' but Frett thought he meant 'tied' and said 'yes.' Major Reno again asked the question if the mules were 'tight' and Frett asked him what he meant by 'tight.' Then some more*

words passed between them. I don't know what they were but it seemed that Major Reno made a pass to strike Frett and some whiskey flew over myself and Frett and that Major Reno stepped back and picked up a carbine, but whether he intended to strike Frett with it, I don't know. I took Frett by the shoulders and pulled him away. That was the last I saw of Major Reno that night."[116]

Reno admitted to striking Frett, but denied being drunk[117]: *"The last time I went there the packs had been taken off. That was the time I saw those men. I had been there several times to drive out men and I felt annoyed, and so I asked one of the men what he was doing there. I cannot recall the words of his reply, but I know they angered me more, and as I thought that was not exactly the time for moral suasion, I hit him, and I may have told him that if I found him there again I would shoot him."*[118]

About 9 PM, Edgerly noticed gaps in the line between troops M and B as well as between troops G and A. Receiving permission from Reno to plug the gaps, Edgerly redeployed Company D.[119] Lieutenant Varnum, despite having virtually no sleep for 48 hours, volunteered to try to get a message through the lines:[120]

> *". . . went to Capt. Moylan's line & with other officers talked over our situation. I suggested I would try and get away during the night if I could get a good man to go with me & carry the news & try to get relief. I talked to Herendine (Herendeen, DCE), but he thought it too risky. Sergt. Geo. McDermott (George Michael McDermott, also known as Michael Burke, DCE), of A Troop agreed to go with me & I went to see Major Reno about it. He was with Capt. Weir. I made my proposition to him. He did not reply for some time & then said he could not afford to lose two good shots & that we would get killed anyway. I said we might as well get killed trying to get relief as to get killed where we were. He said, 'Varnum, you are a very uncomfortable companion.' I left him.*

> *"Weir came to me afterwards & said Reno would let me send scouts if they would go. I had only four left with me,[121] White Swan, who was badly wounded, & Half Yellow Face, of the Crows, and Goose (also wounded) and Forked Horn of the Rees. After long talks they finally agreed to try to get out that night & Reno gave me notes to give them. They did not go, however, & I doubt if they tried."*[122]

Too little notice has been taken of the heroism displayed by White Swan during the siege. White Swan had been grievously wounded in the right hand and leg as a result of his duel with the Cheyenne Whirlwind, and was unable to walk. Private Dennis Lynch of Company F recalled seeing White Swan dragging himself to the firing line by grabbing the grass with his hands and pulling himself and his gun along to get a shot at the Lakota. The men would then return him to the field hospital only to discover him a little while later again trying to drag himself up to the skirmish line.[123] Being an Indian scout, he was ineligible for a decoration, but no member of the government forces was more deserving of a Medal of Honor than White Swan. Another hero who has received too little attention, was Dr. Porter, the command's only surviving surgeon.[124] Without relief, he toiled for over 36 hours to bring what comfort and succor he could to the wounded. As if that weren't enough, he even attempted to take an active part in the defense, as recalled by Peter Thompson:

> *"While the hottest of the fight was going on and the tide of battle seemed to be against us, our doctor dropped his bandages, and grasping a gun started toward the skirmish line.[125] Some of the men, seeing his action, begged him to stay telling*

*him that it would go hard with the command if anything should go wrong with him
and to enforce their arguments a wounded man was brought in who needed his
immediate attention. This, for a time, seemed to deter him for he laid down his gun
and commenced work at his former occupation. He was kept very busy for some
time."*[126]

Having failed to convince Reno to let him attempt to penetrate the lines, Varnum fell into a deep sleep. *"I was awakened by being carried & found myself in the arms of Pvt. 'Tony' Siebelder (Anton Siebelder, DCE), Troop A, who, when firing opened in the morning about 3 o'clock, found me in a very exposed position. He laid me down & I slept for a while & felt better."*[127]

With the resumption of hostilities, Private Richard B. Dorn went to wake Captain McDougall. Kneeling beside his commanding officer, Dorn was shot and died instantly.[128] Benteen, like Varnum and McDougall, had anything but a peaceful slumber; recalling that one round hit him in the heel of his boot, while another impacted the dust under an arm pit.[129] Private Julian D. Jones of Company H had helped scoop out a rifle pit that he shared with Private Windolph. Early in the morning Jones told Windolph he was going to remove his overcoat and rolled onto one side. As he did so, a bullet ripped through some nearby boxes of hardtack and drilled the unlucky Jones in the heart.[130]

The animals also suffered considerably, both of Benteen's horses being wounded in the fighting.[131] When Captain French's prized gray horse was wounded in the head the morning of June 26, a compassionate Private Henry C. Voight of Company M immediately went to the poor beast's aid. While leading him away from the other horses, Voight was shot through the head and killed.[132]

Although the survivors of the siege would continue to deny they had any thought that Custer had met with disaster prior to their relief by Terry's column, McDougall told Walter Camp that on June 26 many of the warriors were wearing soldier's uniforms. He cited one warrior in particular who paraded back and forth in front of Reno's lines brandishing a guidon.[133] Finally, a trooper tumbled this unknown warrior from his horse.[134]

The warriors were present in great numbers. McDougall mentioned there were too many to occupy the firing line at the same time; the hills to their rear being black with warriors waiting to take their turn. While Godfrey had written in his field diary for June 25: *"I thought we were a little too niggardly of our ammunition. . .,"*[135] by the 26th the command had been ordered to fire only with the permission of the officers. This extreme measure was taken not only to conserve ammunition, but in recognition of the poor marksmanship of many of the troopers.[136] Godfrey commented on one trooper preparing to fire: *". . . he pulled the trigger. There was a very perceptible dropping of the muzzle, and a flinch, but no report. He had forgotten to cock his piece."*[137] The warrior's firing was especially heavy on the 26th, any movement on the part of the troopers eliciting a hail of bullets. Despite this galling fire, Private Henry Holden of Company D repeatedly went for the precious ammunition necessary to keep the warriors at bay.[138] For his heroic action he was awarded the Medal of Honor. During this period of heavy firing occurred one of those strange and unexplainable incidents so common to combat situations. A spent bullet ricocheted off the head of chief packer John C. Wagoner. Wagoner kicked convulsively for several seconds and then sat up rubbing his head. He survived with no more than a bad headache.[139]

There were unsung heroes throughout the hilltop fight. Private Windolph recalled the death of Corporal George Lell of Company H:

"I will never forget Sgt. Lell (Lell was a corporal, DCE). He was fatally wounded and dragged to the hospital. He was dying and knew it. 'Lift me up, boys,' he said to some of the men. 'I want to see the boys again before I go.' So they held him up to a sitting position where he could see his comrades in action. A smile came to his face as he saw the beautiful fight the Seventh was making. Then they laid him down and he died soon after."[140]

The warriors were becoming bolder and more aggressive, Varnum noting they would assume positions varying from 100 to 500 yards from the soldier's line.[141] In addition to their failure to erect breastworks and entrench, Company H's position was dominated by Wooden Leg Ridge in their rear. The troop suffered heavy casualties and Benteen had some difficulty in keeping his troopers on the firing line. The situation became critical when Private Thomas E. Meador of Company H was killed at about 9 AM.[142] Immediately Long Road,[143] a young Sans Arc, sprang forward to count the first coup.[144] He joined his brother, killed at the Battle of the Rosebud,[145] when he was shot by Private Edward D. Pigford;[146] his body falling so near the soldier line that the Lakota were unable to recover it.

Benteen knew he must quickly defuse this act of bravado and determined to drive the Indians from the ravine in his front that posed such a threat to his position. As Benteen recalled:

"I gathered up all the skulkers who were hiding away among the pack mules, some 16 or 18, compelled them to carry pack-saddles, sacks of bacon, boxes of hardbread, &c, to the left flank of my Troop, and with the miscellaneous collection of "Stuff," built a small breastwork; I then turned the men I had so gathered over to my 1st Lieut., telling that I intended taking the Troop and drive those Indians out of the ravine that he must hold that position, no matter what became of my party, and to shoot the 1st man that showed the slightest disposition to "flunk;" then the men were notified what I expected of them, and away we started."[147]

Private Patrick Corcoran, lying wounded in the field hospital, recalled, as did Sergeant Kanipe, that about half of Benteen's men had run over toward the hospital.[148] This mass departure from the firing line is undoubtedly what encouraged Long Road to attempt to count coup on Private Meador's body. This also explains why a private in Company M dispatched the warrior rather than a member of Benteen's own company. Corcoran recalled Benteen admonishing his men: *"Where are you running to, men? Come on back and we will drive them off. You might as well be killed out there as in here."[149]*

Captain Benteen described the charge in an unpublished manuscript:

"Then I walked along the front of my troop and told them that I was getting mad, and I wanted them to charge down the ravines with me when I gave the yell: then, each to yell as if provided with a thousand throats. The Chinese act was sufficiently good enough for me if it would work; but I hadn't so much real trust in its efficacy. However, when the throttles of the 'H sters' were given full play, and we dashed into the unsuspecting savages who were amusing themselves by throwing clods of dirt, arrows by hand, and otherwise, for simply pure cussedness among us, to say that 'twas a surprise to them, is mild form, for they somersaulted and vaulted as so many trained acrobats, having no order in getting down those ravines, but quickly getting; de'il take the hindmost!

"Then, then, I had the key to the beautiful blue water that had been flowing so rippling at our very feet for two days – and which wounded and well longed so much for, – there it was, ours, for the getting."[150]

As was the case on every occasion when the troopers acted with audacity and aggressiveness, the Lakota fell back almost to the river, dragging their casualties with them;[151] abandoning the ravine and clearing a path to the precious water the command so desperately needed. Private Edwin F. Pickard of Company F recalled the torture of being without water: *"Our throats were parched, the smoke stung our nostrils, and it seemed as if our tongues had swollen so we couldn't close our mouths, and the heat of the sun seemed fairly to cook the blood in our veins."*[152] Jacob Adams agreed stating his mouth was so swollen, swallowing became impossible.[153] Perhaps most tormented of the non-wounded was Private Cornelius Cowley of Company A who went berserk from his maddening thirst and had to be tied down. Benteen, acting on his own initiative,[154] had successfully countered the apparent boost to warrior morale and routed the enemy[155] in his immediate front at the cost of only three wounded.[156] Lieutenant Varnum described his participation in the action:

"We were opened on by the whole circle. I felt a pain in both legs at once, and thought for a second I had lost both legs. I got a bullet through the calf of one leg, and as my foot was up, while I was running, the other went down my leg cutting the yellow stripes off my trousers and denting the leather of my boot over the ankle bone. It did not touch my person, but acted like a blow on my ankle bone and the foot swelled up, turned black & blue and was really the worst wound of the two.[157]

"We had no trouble after that from that quarter. I dropped into a shallow trench when I got back and tried to examine the hole in my leg to see how bad it was, but every time I did so, a bullet cut the dirt very near it.

"A young private of B Troop[158] got to laughing at my endeavors, and while doing so a bullet went from the top of his head down through his body. He probably never knew what happened to him."[159]

After Benteen's successful charge, the fire of the warriors slackened; Benteen using the respite to build breastworks and dig rifle pits. About 2 PM,[160] the warriors opened a heavy fire. Godfrey describes Benteen's response:

"The firing almost ceased for a while, and then it recommenced with greater fury. From this fact, and their more active movements, it became evident that they contemplated something more serious than a mere fusillade. Benteen came back to where Reno was,[161] and said if something was not done pretty soon the Indians would run into our lines. Waiting a short time, and no action being taken on his suggestion, he said rather impatiently: 'You've got to do something here pretty quick; this won't do, you must drive them back.' Reno then directed us to get ready for a charge, and told Benteen to give the word. Benteen called out 'All ready now, men. Now's your time. Give them hell. Hip, hip, here we go!' and away we went with a hurrah, every man, but one who lay in his pit crying like a child. The Indians fired more rapidly than before from their whole line. Our men left the pits with their carbines loaded, and they began firing without orders soon after we started. A large body of Indians had assembled at the foot of one of the hills, intending probably to make a charge, as Benteen had divined, but they broke as soon as our line started. When we had advanced 75 or 100 yards, Reno called out 'Get back, men, get back,

[Above left] Captain Frederick W. Benteen, taken in 1874. Disobeying a direct order to aid his commander, he was nevertheless instrumental in saving the command during the Hilltop Fight. His irrational hatred for his commander is the source of most of the derogatory comments directed at Custer's performance. *Photo Courtesy Little Bighorn Battlefield National Monument.*

[Above right] Doctor Henry R. Porter, taken in 1886. Porter's tireless tending of the wounded during the Hilltop Fight and subsequent transportation to Fort Lincoln undoubtedly saved many lives. *Photo Courtesy Little Bighorn Battlefield National Monument.*

[Right] Major Marcus A. Reno, taken in 1875. His conduct during the valley fight, especially the retreat, is deserving of the most severe criticism. Unlike Benteen, there is no evidence that Reno harbored any active dislike toward Custer prior to the battle. *Photo Courtesy Little Bighorn Battlefield National Monument.*

Lakota camp on Tongue River, 1879. Spotted Eagle's camp is typical of the period.
Photo Courtesy Little Bighorn Battlefield National Monument.

and back the whole line came. A most singular fact of this sortie was that not a man who advanced with the lines was hit; but directly after every one had gotten into the pits again, the one man who did not go out was shot in the head and killed instantly. The poor fellow had a premonition that he would be killed, and had so told one of his comrades."[162]

While Godfrey was upset believing the charge had been terminated too early, his diary entry indicates his understanding that the charge had achieved the desired result: *"Col Benteen ordered us to charge although Col Reno was then on the line – Col Reno went with us*[163] *and ordered us back to the trenches before we had gone twenty yards **as the firing became very warm & there were no breast work to hide behind** (emphasis the author's. Note Godfrey's private feelings about Reno's bravery were not voiced in his court of inquiry testimony or his Century Magazine Article,. DCE). But still it had its effect."*[164]

Lieutenant Edgerly apparently recalled the same tragic affair Godfrey reported regarding Benteen's charge:

"Pvt. Golden (Patrick M. Golden, DCE), a handsome Irishman of D troop, behaved very well during the first day's fighting but, after the firing ceased, he went to a veteran sergeant, in whom he had great confidence, and asked him if he tho't the Indians would come back. The Sergt. said they would probably come back at about daylight, when Golden commenced to cry. The Sergt. asked what the matter was and he replied, 'Tom! If they come back they will kill me.'[165] *The Sergt. tried to comfort or encourage him but without success. I didn't observe him until next morning, until we were ordered to our pits by Reno. . . as soon as the charge was completed we were ordered to get in the pits again. Private Stivers (Thomas W. Stivers, Company D, DCE) who had been in the pit with me saw Golden. . . and asked him whose (pit, DCE) it was. He said he didn't know and as there was room enough for three men there Stivers and I got into it. We hadn't been there a minute before a shot came throwing dirt all over us and striking Golden in the head. He never knew what hit him but died instantly."*[166]

Once again, Benteen's timely and decisive action had averted a potential tragedy. As Godfrey would testify: *"It was my opinion then that Captain Benteen was exercising the functions principally of commanding officer."*[167] Godfrey was also critical of Reno's conduct during a tour of the lines on the 26th. When Reno and Godfrey came under fire, Reno remarked: *"Damned if I want to be killed by an Indian. I've gone through too many fights for that."* Godfrey then went on to state: *"I don't think Reno's conduct was such as tended to inspire the command with confidence in resisting the enemy."*[168]

Godfrey was not the only one who recognized Benteen's indispensable contributions to the defense. Private William Morris of Company M noted: *"Benteen was unquestionably the bravest man I ever met."* First Sergeant John M. Ryan, also of Company M, a man who had many reasons to dislike Benteen, summed up Benteen's contributions best: *"Too much cannot be said in favor of Captain Benteen. His prompt movements saved Reno from utter annihilation, and his gallantry cleared the ravines of Indians."* His views were echoed by Lieutenant Varnum: *"Benteen was really the only officer looking out for the whole command and he handled things well and fought very gallantly."*[169]

After the first charge, an avenue was opened to the precious water so desperately needed by the command in general, and the wounded in particular. Almost immediately, volunteers stepped forward to run the gauntlet to the river. While the Indian's fire slackened during this period, several warriors noted what the troopers were up to and worked there way to positions commanding the route the troopers must follow. The troopers took anything that could hold water: canteens, cooking pots and camp kettles. The troopers seeking the water would be exposed to enemy fire on two occasions; first they had to transverse a shot distance to reach the ravine from their lines. While they would be exposed at this juncture, it would only be to relatively long range firing. Once inside the ravine, the steep banks effectively shielded them until they reached its mouth, about 30 feet from the river. Here they would have to cross the open space completely vulnerable to fire from warriors posted in the bushes along the west bank of the river.

Medal of Honor for Non-water Carrier Action	Medal of Honor for Carrying Water	Water Carrier No Medal of Honor
Sgt Benjamin C. Criswell, Co B	Sgt Rufus D. Hutchinson, Co B	Sgt John Rafter, Co K
Sgt George H. Geiger, Co H	Cpl Stanislaus Roy, Co A	Sgt Louis Rott, Co K
Sgt Richard P. Hanley, Co C	Pvt Neil Bancroft, Co A	Cpl John E. Hammon, Co G
Sgt Thomas Murray, Co B	Pvt Abraham B. Brant, Co D	Cpl George H. King, Co A
Pvt Charles Cunningham, Co B	Pvt Thomas J. Callan, Co B	Pvt Jacob Adams, Co H
Pvt Henry Holden, Co D	Blacksmith Frederick Deitline, Co D	Pvt Ansgarius Boren, Co B
Blacksmith Henry W. B. Mecklin, Co H	Pvt Theodore W. Goldin,[170] Co G	Pvt Charles Campbell, Co G
Saddler Otto Voit, Co H	Pvt David W. Harris, Co A	Pvt Thomas W. Coleman, Co B
Pvt Charles Windolph, Co H	Pvt William M. Harris, Co D	Pvt Augustus L. DeVoto, Co B
	Pvt James Pym, Co B	Pvt Edmond Dwyer, Co G
	Pvt George D. Scott, Co D	Pvt John Foley, Co K
	Pvt Thomas W. Stivers, Co D	Pvt John M. Gilbert, Co A
	Pvt Peter Thompson, Co C	Pvt Frank Hunter, Co F
	Pvt Frank Tolan, Co D	Pvt John Kanavagh, Co D
	Pvt Charles H. Welch, Co D	Pvt William D. Nugent, Co A
		Pvt Edwin F. Pickard, Co F
		Pvt James M. Rooney, Co F
		Pvt William C. Slaper, Co M
		Pvt James Weeks, Co M
		Pvt James Wilber, Co M
		Saddler Michael P. Madden, Co K

Table 16 – 1 Medal of Honor Winners And Water Carrriers

After the first party had made the round trip without benefit of protection, Benteen detailed four of the best marksmen from Company H: Sergeant George H. Geiger, Blacksmith Henry W. B. Mecklin, Saddler Otto Voit, and Private Charles Windolph,[171] to provide cover fire for the water carriers.[172] Despite the best efforts of the sharpshooters, the water carriers suffered several casualties. Wooden Leg described the death of one of the water carriers:[173]

> *"Some soldiers came to get water from the river, just as our old men had said they likely would do. The white men crept down a deep gulch and then ran across an open space to the water. Each one had a bucket, and each would dip his bucket for water and run back into the gulch. I put myself, with others, where we could watch for these men. I shot at one of them just as he straightened up after having dipped his bucket into the water. He pitched forward into the edge of the river. He went wallowing along the stream, trying to swim, but having a hard time at it. I jumped out from my hiding place and ran toward him. Two Sioux warriors got ahead of me. One of them waded after the man and struck him with a rifle barrel. Finally he grabbed the man, hit him again, and then dragged him dead to the shore, quite a distance down the river."[174]*

The most celebrated casualty among the water carriers was Saddler Michael P. Madden of Company K. Wounded in the ankle as part of the first water party, Dr. Porter was forced to amputate his leg in the field hospital the next day.[175] According to William Slaper, Madden was given a stiff drink of brandy prior to the operation which he bore without a whimper. Given another drink after the ordeal was over, Madden smacked his lips and replied: *"Docthor, cut off me other leg!"*[176]

Fifteen men would be awarded the Medal of Honor, the only military decoration available at the time,[177] for obtaining water for the wounded; while twenty-one additional water carriers, Madden and Slaper among them, would go unrecognized.[178] Table 16 – 1 lists Medal of Honor winners as well as the water carriers that did not earn the Medal of Honor. Madden would be promoted to sergeant on the field by Godfrey, but it was a hollow honor as his disability ended his military career. There was another unfortunate incident attendant to the quest for water. Upon returning with the second group of water carriers, Private James Weeks of Company M was hailed by Captain Moylan. Responding to Moylan's request for a drink, Weeks blurted out: *"You go to hell and get your own water; this is for the wounded."* As Private Slaper recalled: *"Nothing more was said but I know that must have been a hard pill for Moylan to swallow."*[179]

About an hour after the second charge, the firing ceased almost completely as the warriors turned their attention to the Terry–Gibbon Column approaching up the valley. Unwilling to pay the price necessary to defeat this third column of troops within the span of 10 days, the Indians struck camp, fired the prairie, and moved off unmolested except for the few shots fired in frustration by Sergeant Ryan and Captain French. Benteen, a qualified judge of such matters, remarked on the size of the Indian column *"It started about sunset and was in sight till darkness came. It was in a straight line about three miles long, and I think half a mile wide, as densely packed as animals could be. They had an advance guard and platoons formed, and were in as regular military order as a corps or division."*[180] The column slowly wound its way up the valley exiting in the direction of the Big Horn Mountains. The Battle of the Little Big Horn was over.

---

[1] See Francis B. Taunton "No Pride In The Little Big Horn" page 19.

[2] See John M. Carroll "The Gibson And Edgerly Narratives" page 10.

[3] See Colonel W. A. Graham "The Reno Court of Inquiry" page 33.

[4] See Francis B. Taunton "No Pride in the Little Big Horn" page 30.

[5] See John M. Carroll "The Benteen – Goldin Letters" page 215. It is instructive to note that the only rationale for moving down river cited by Benteen was to follow the *"insubordinate"* Weir. Benteen would recognize in later letters to Goldin that he was not required to obey Reno's orders in preference to Custer's written order, claiming he had satisfied that order by moving down river. See John M. Carroll "The Benteen – Goldin Letters" page 246.

[6] Benteen claimed to have moved down river despite Reno *"having his trumpeter sound the halt continuously and assiduously"* (See John M. Carroll "The Benteen Goldin Letters" page 186 and Francis B. Taunton "No Pride in the Little Big Horn" page 29) acknowledging, under oath, to having moved without orders from Reno (See Ronald H. Nichols "The Reno Court of Inquiry" page 463). Herendeen told the court of inquiry that, when he talked to Reno after leading his party from the valley, all of the companies except A had already moved down stream. See Francis B. Taunton "No Pride in the Little Big Horn" page 29.

[7] See Colonel W. A. Graham "The Reno Court of Inquiry" page 278. Reno's July 5, 1876 report states he sent Weir to open communications with Custer only after personally reaching Weir Point. Of course, Reno personally never reached Weir Point. See Appendix 7.

[8] Sergeant Ryan's account of the movement, as well as the stories given to the *New York Herald* by Reno and Benteen in August of 1876, indicate Weir may have made two movements down river. The statements given to the *Herald* by Benteen and Reno were apparently made in conjunction with one another rather than separately. Benteen told the *Herald*: *"While the command was awaiting the arrival of the pack mules a company was sent forward in the direction supposed to have been taken by Custer. After proceeding about a mile **they were attacked and driven back** . . The rest of the story you must get from Colonel Reno. . ."* (emphasis the author's). Reno's statement then completed the narrative: *"On **the return of the company** (emphasis the author's) and the closing up of the pack mules, which occurred about the same time, the whole command moved forward, proceeding about a mile and a half. . . So numerous were the masses of Indians encountered that the command was obliged to dismount and fight on foot, retiring to the point which had first been selected."* See Colonel W. A. Graham "The Custer Myth" page 228. For Sergeant Ryan's account see Richard Upton "The Custer Adventure" page 51.

[9] See Kenneth Hammer "Custer in '76" page 55 and E. S. Godfrey "Custer's Last Battle 1876" page 26.

[10] See Bruce Liddic and Paul Harbaugh "Camp on Custer" pages 94 - 96, Francis B. Taunton "No Pride in the Little Big Horn" pages 21 – 23, Glendolin Damon Wagner "Old Neutriment" page 198, Earle R. Forrest "Witnesses at the Battle of the Little Big Horn" page 5, and John S. Gray "Custer's Last Campaign" page 317.

[11] See Colonel W. A. Graham "The Custer Myth" page 291.

[12] See Bruce Liddic and Paul Harbaugh "Camp on Custer" pages 94 - 95.

[13] See John M. Carroll "The Gibson And Edgerly Narratives" page 10.

[14] See John M. Carroll "The Gibson And Edgerly Narratives" page 11.

[15] See John M. Carroll "Custer's Chief of Scouts" page 117.

[16] See John M. Carroll "Custer's Chief of Scouts" page 144.

[17] See Walter Camp "Custer in '76" page 129 and Wayne Wells "The Fight on Calhoun Hill" page 23.

[18] When surrounded at Trevilian Station, Custer tore his colors from their staff and secured them inside his blouse. See Jay Monaghan "Custer: The Life of General George Armstrong Custer" page 200 and D. A. Kinsley "Custer: Favor The Bold" page 217.

[19] See Colonel W. A. Graham "The Custer Myth" page 341.

[20] See Colonel W. A. Graham "The Custer Myth" page 142.

[21] See Richard Upton "The Custer Adventure" page 51.

[22] Although his account indicates he is discussing Last Stand Hill, Edgerly is clearly referring to Calhoun Hill as will become clear in the discussion of Pigford's account. See George M. Clark "Scalp Dance" page 20.

[23] See Walter Camp "Custer in '76" page 143.

[24] See Charles Kuhlman "Legend Into History" pages 225 – 226.

[25] See John M. Carroll "A Seventh Cavalry Scrapbook #11" pages 21 – 22.

[26] See John M. Carroll "A Seventh Cavalry Scrapbook #11" page 22.

[27] According to noted historian Robert M. Utley, Gall maintained that Custer's men were over run before any troops appeared on Weir Point. See "Custer and the Great Controversy" page 108. It is instructive to note however, that Standing Bear is quoted on page 187 of Raymond J. DeMallie's "The Sixth Grandfather" as stating the warriors didn't **notice** the troops on Weir Point until after Custer was annhilated. This crucial distinction perhaps puts Gall's statement in an entirely new light, for, if the troops remained on Weir Point for at least one, and perhaps as long as two, hours, what could have been occupying the attention of the warriors during that interval if they were not actively engaged with Custer's command?

[28] Weir, unfortunately, left no personal account, or at least no account of the battle attributable to him has surfaced. Benteen, who had much to gain personally from a tardy movement on Weir's part, thought that Weir had gone down river very soon after the junction with Reno was effected (See John M. Carroll "The Benteen – Goldin Letters" page 171). This viewpoint is echoed by Lieutenant Edgerly, who was in immediate command of Company D during the movement, when he testified the movement occurred within a half hour of the junction (See Colonel W. A. Graham "The Reno Court Of Inquiry" page 161). Sergeants Davern and Culbertson believed the movement to have commenced about one hour after the junction, but while the sounds of Custer's firing could still be heard (See George M. Clark "Scalp Dance" pages 66 – 67). Godfrey, who became admittedly confused in later years as to what time the junction with Reno occurred, is the lone dissenter, believing Weir's movement came almost two and one half hours after the junction (See E. S. Godfrey "Custer's Last Battle 1876" page 27).

[29] At the time of the battle a second saddle existed at right angles to the present one which parallels the river. This second saddle was destroyed when the present road was constructed.

[30] See Wayne Wells "Little Big Horn Notes: Stanley Vestal's Indian Insights" page 11.

[31] Henry James Nowlan was assigned to Department Headquarters in the field during the campaign and ultimately replaced Keogh as commander of Company I.

[32] See Tom O'Neil "John Garland to Libbie" Newsletter of the Little Big Horn Associates, page 8. A Copy of the letter is in the Historical Society of North Dakota Archives in Bismarck, North Dakota.

[33] See John S. Gray "Custer's Last Campaign" page 327. Upon his arrival with the pack train, Captain McDougall had gone to where Benteen and Reno were engaged in conversation and expressed to them his opinion that they should move toward the sound of the guns. McDougall, who had heard Custer's heavy firing for about the last 15 minutes of the pack train's approach to Reno Hill, later remarked: *"Reno did not appear to regard the seriousness of the situation."* See Charles K. Mills "Harvest of Barren Regrets" pages 262 – 263.

[34] The following dispatch, from the December 30, 1878 edition of the *St. Paul Pioneer Press* stirred the controversy: *"The Washington correspondent of a New York paper, telegraphed yesterday that Col. Thomas B. Weir (Captain Thomas Bell Weir, DCE), one of the officers commanding a company under Major Reno on the day of the disaster to Custer, had declared before his death, last December, that he was in full view of the fight when he was sent out to reconnoiter during the action, and that he reported to Reno and urged that help be given their comrades. The dying officer is said also to have asserted that Reno refused to make the movement as argued, and was openly accused, at the time, of cowardice, by his own officers. Col . Weir's statement alleges that when he moved out with his company the sound of the firing from Custer's column was distinctly heard by the whole command, and that the point from which he obtained a view of the battle was not more than a mile and a half from where Reno's command lay."* See E. Eldon Davis "The Reno Court of Inquiry: The Pioneer Press" page 17.

[35] See Edward C. Bailly "Echoes From Custer's Last Fight" page 179.

[36] One of the mysteries of the Weir Point episode is the whereabouts of Captain Weir and his reason for not remaining with his company. Clearly he was not present when the troops began their withdrawal as the order was given to Edgerly (Edgerly would write *"My captain left me about an hour before we started back and went to Reno."* See John M. Carroll "The Gibson And Edgerly Narratives" page 11). As will become clear shortly, Weir would reappear with his company before the final position on Reno Hill was reached. This question of Weir's whereabouts has fueled speculation he was in the rear arguing for a movement in force toward Custer who, as the speculation goes, was known to be hotly engaged. While Weir was clearly some little distance in the rear of his troop when the withdrawal was initiated, and I believe Weir did know that Custer was still actively engaged, there is no direct evidence or testimony of a confrontation between Reno and Weir at that time.

[37] Benteen, supported by his Lieutenant, Francis Gibson, would maintain that he, not Reno, ordered the retreat to Reno Hill. See John M. Carroll "The Benteen–Goldin Letters" pages 215 – 216 and Kenneth Hammer "Custer In '76" page 81.

[38] See E. S. Godfrey "Custer's Last Battle 1876" pages 27 – 28.

[39] See Francis B. Taunton "No Pride In The Little Big Horn" page 25.

[40] See Don Rickey, Jr. "Forty Miles a Day on Beans and Hay" page299 – 300 and Kenneth Hammer "Little Big Horn Biographies" page 43.

[41] While his battlefield marker, and many authorities, list this man as Vincent Charlie, the regimental muster role for June 1876 clearly shows his name to have been Charlie Vincent. As there was only one casualty during the movement from Weir Point, there is no confusion as to whom is referred to.

[42] See Kenneth Hammer "Custer In '76" page 57.

[43] See Ronald H. Nichols "The Reno Court of Inquiry" page 446.

[44] See Dale T. Schoenberger "The End of Custer" page 222. The performance of the army regarding removing their wounded from the field was nothing short of disgraceful during the entire campaign. While Godfrey would verbalize the cavalryman's credo: *"We of the cavalry had been imbued with the principle to take any risk to attempt the rescue of a comrade in peril."* (see Elmo Scott Watson and Don Russell "The Battle of the Washita, or Custer's Massacre?" page 8) the evidence of the 1876 campaign indicates this to have been barracks rhetoric that was seldom practiced in the field.

[45] See John G. Neihardt "Black Elk Speaks" page 117.

[46] While Vincent's remains were transferred to the national cemetery in 1903, they had not been positively identified. Government red tape prevented the installation of a headstone bearing his name. In 1995, after 92 years, the situation was finally rectified when scientists at Chico University in California furnished positive proof of his identity. A headstone reading "Vincent Charley" has since been installed in place of the one labeled "unknown soldier."

[47] See Kenneth Hammer "Custer In '76" page 57.

[48] See Bruce Liddic and Paul Harbaugh "Camp on Custer" pages 97 - 98.

[49] See Kenneth Hammer "Little Big Horn Biographies" pages 52 – 53.

[50] Captain French presents one of the fascinating enigmas of the Little Big Horn. While he displayed uncommon individual bravery, he apparently totally abrogated his responsibilities as an officer in failing to cover Reno's retreat crossing of the Little Big Horn despite the entreaties of the non-commissioned officers, improperly placed his men on the reverse slope in the defensive position on Reno Hill, and disobeyed an order to cover the withdrawal from Weir Point (while Benteen didn't name the company he had ordered to cover the withdrawal from Weir Point during his testimony at the Reno court of inquiry, he could only have been referring to Company M. See Ronald H. Nichols "The Reno Court of Inquiry" page 410).

[51] See E. S. Godfrey "Custer's Last Battle 1876" page 28.

[52] Benteen would testify that he ordered Godfrey to cover the retreat (See Colonel W. A. Graham "The Reno Court of Inquiry" page 140) while Godfrey indicates he covered the movement on his own initiative. See E. S. Godfrey "Custer's Last Battle 1876" page 28. While Luther Hare told Walter Camp that Company K didn't dismount as skirmishers until they were within about 500 yards of Reno Hill (See Kenneth Hammer "Custer In '76" page 66), Godfrey's account of forcing the Indians back over Weir Point indicates the covering action commenced almost immediately. Godfrey's

recollection is supported by Edgerly's court of inquiry testimony that Godfrey had dismounted his troop within 60 yards of the point formerly occupied by Company D. See Ronald H. Nichols "The Reno Court of Inquiry" page 446. See Charles Kuhlman "Legend Into History" page 116 for his fine analysis of this action.

53 See Edgar I. Stewart "The Field Diary of Edward Settle Godfrey" page 13.

54 According to Godfrey: *"Lieutenant Hare expressed his intention of staying with me, 'Adjutant or no Adjutant.'"* See E. S. Godfrey "Custer's Last Battle, 1876" page 28.

55 See E. S. Godfrey "Custer's Last Battle 1876" page 28.

56 See William G. Rector "Fields of Fire" page 66. Rector gives an excellent treatment of this subject in his article.

57 See Don Rickey, Jr. "40 Miles A Day On Beans And Hay" page 291.

58 See Robert J. Ege "Curse Not His Curls" page 49.

59 Benteen would admit in a letter to Theodore Goldin that he was not obligated to obey Reno's orders upon their junction and go on to state that he had satisfied Custer's written order when he moved down river. See John M. Carroll "The Benteen – Goldin Letters" page 246.

60 See Kenneth Hammer "Custer in '76" page 127, Cyrus Townsend Brady "Indian Fights and Fighters" pages 249 – 250, and Daniel O. Magnussen "Thompson's Narrative" page 179. Daniel Newell maintained that Private James W. Severs of Company M also recovered an ammunition laden mule but was not recognized for his action. See John M. Carroll "The Sunshine Magazine Articles" page 12.

61 According to U. S. Naval Observatory data, sunset on June 25, 1876 was at 9:04 PM. See Joe Sills, Jr. "Weir Point Perspectives" page 45.

62 As Ryan does not name these troopers, it is likely that they were not from Company M. This fits with Godfrey's testimony that the companies were intermingled on June 25 and with the casualty lists which show only one casualty, Frank Braun, from Company M on June 25.

63 See Richard Upton "The Custer Adventure" page 53. During the battle Ryan used a non government issue sharps sporting rifle chambered for the government .45/55 round. Interestingly, the archaeological investigations uncovered a government bullet on Wooden Leg Ridge whose land and groove impressions indicated it had been fired from a Sharps sporting rifle. See Douglas D. Scott "Archaeological Perspectives on the Battle of the Little Bighorn" page 116. While we are unable to ascertain the identity, and subsequent fate, of the warrior in question, the Minneconjou Big Ankles, along with Cheyennes Big Foot, Sandstone, Sleeping Rabbit, Spotted Elk, and Wolf Tooth were known to have joined Wooden Leg, as sharpshooters. See Don Rickey interview with John Stands In Timber, August 8, 1956 and Appendix 9.

64 See John M. Carroll "Custer's Chief of Scouts" page 93.

65 For a complete listing of casualties, see Appendices 1 and 9.

66 Prior to being wounded in the neck, Criswell would recover precious ammunition from the saddlebags of fallen 7th Cavalry horses on the east bank of the Little Big Horn despite a galling fire

from the warriors. For this action, he would be awarded the Medal of Honor. His citation also states he recovered the body of Lieutenant Hodgson and bore it to the hilltop position (See W. F. Beyer and O. F. Keydel "Acts of Bravery" page 216). While it is not clear who actually buried Hodgson, it is clear that he was buried on the east bank near the site of his marker. It is extremely unlikely that Hodgson would have been interred at the base of the bluff had his body been carried to the top by Criswell. While Criswell may have been a member of Hodgson's burial party, it appears highly unlikely that he secured the body and carried it to the top of the bluff as his citation states.

[67] Also wounded through the neck, Cunningham refused to leave the firing line. For his heroic action he was awarded the Medal of Honor. See W. F. Beyer and O. F. Keydel "Acts of Bravery" page 220. Note this source improperly lists Cunningham's rank as corporal.

[68] Sergeant Stanislas Roy, Company A, told Walter Camp of Mann's death: *"He was behind breastwork with carbine on A Co.'s line. He was aiming a carbine over a breastwork about 3 ft. high, and after he had been observed in this position about 20 min., some one made remark that 'something must be wrong with the packer.' Upon going up he was found stone dead, having been hit in the temple and killed so quick that he did not move from position sighting his gun."* See Kenneth Hammer "Custer In '76" page 114. Although Sergeant Roy recalled that Mann had been shot on the 26th, he actually was killed on the 25th, see John M. Carroll "Roll Call On The Little Big Horn" page 167.

[69] Wounded in the face and left thigh, when Braun died in the hospital at Fort Lincoln on October 4, 1876, the Little Big Horn had claimed its last victim.

[70] See Dale T. Schoenberger "The End of Custer" page 238.

[71] See Dale T. Schoenberger "The End of Custer" page 228.

[72] See Stanley Vestal "Sitting Bull" pages 173 - 174.

[73]Newell exaggerates. See Chapter 20 for a discussion of extractor failure in the Springfield carbine.

[74] See John M. Carroll "The Sunshine Magazine Articles" page 12.

[75] Godfrey testified at the Reno court of inquiry that no officer supervised the forming of the initial line on Reno Hill, the companies all being *"interpolated"* together. After the cessation of hostilities for the day, the companies were assigned to regular positions in the line but Godfrey could not recall who gave that order. See Ronald H. Nichols "The Reno Court of Inquiry" page 489 - 490. Benteen, perhaps in an effort to sustain the honor of the regiment, as well as bolster his own cause should his failure to comply with Custer's written order be questioned, had testified: *"The first I knew of the formation of that line was my telling Lieutenant Wallace to place his company there, pointing out the spot. He said, 'I have no company, I have only 3 men.' I said, 'Put yourself and your three men there, I will see that you are supported.' He did so, and from that the line was formed."* See Ronald H. Nichols "The Reno Court of Inquiry" page 410.

[76] Benteen testified he thought there were 5 spades in the command and that *"no doubt there were some"* axes. See Ronald H. Nichols "The Reno Court of Inquiry" pages 415 – 416. Wallace, who believed there were 3 spades in the command, said the troopers used their tin cups and knives and axes to entrench. See Ronald H. Nichols "The Reno Court of Inquiry" page 63.

[77] Varnum testified that the command used tin cups and sabers to entrench. Since, with the possible exception of Mathey and DeRudio, there were no sabers in the command, Varnum is in error. See John M. Carroll "Custer's Chief of Scouts" page 118.

[78] See Ronald H. Nichols "The Reno Court of Inquiry" page 412.

[79] See Stanley Vestal "Sitting Bull" page 174. Apparently the Cheyenne had no such social prohibition and, while the distance from Reno Hill to the Cheyenne circle (which was moved even further away after Custer's annihilation) seems to preclude it, it is possible the troopers may have witnessed a dance conducted by the Cheyenne.

[80] See E. S. Godfrey "Custer's Last Battle 1876" page 30.

[81] See E. S. Godfrey "Custer's Last Battle 1876" page 30.

[82] See Jacob Adams "A Story of the Custer Massacre" page 30.

[83] See Dale T. Schoenberger "The End of Custer" page 188.

[84] See Daniel O. Mangnssen "Thompson's Narrative" page 192. Note that McGuire was wounded in the right arm on June 26th.

[85] See Colonel W. A. Graham "The Reno Court of Inquiry" page 149.

[86] See Ronald H. Nichols "The Reno Court of Inquiry" page 37.

[87] See Ronald H. Nichols "The Reno Court of Inquiry" page 501.

[88] See Ronald H. Nichols "The Reno Court of Inquiry" page 182.

[89] Culbertson's statement obviously refers to the fact that Custer's command must have sustained significant casualties rather than to the physical condition of his commander.

[90] See Ronald H. Nichols "The Reno Court of Inquiry" page 379.

[91] See Ronald H. Nichols "The Reno Court of Inquiry" page 536.

[92] See Colonel W. A. Graham "The Reno Court of Inquiry" page 148. It is of interest to note that no one questioned Benteen on his testimony equating the loss the of 19 men at the Washita to the loss of the 208 men killed in Custer's immediate command. Obviously the incidents were linked in Benteen's mind more by animosity than logic.

[93] See Ronald H. Nichols "The Reno Court of Inquiry" page 491.

[94] See Kenneth Hammer "Custer In '76" page 142.

[95] See E. S. Godfrey "Custer's Last Battle 1876" page 30. In a letter dated January 3, 1886, Benteen requested that Godfrey not include Reno's planned movement in his forthcoming article. See Tom O'Neil "Marcus A. Reno: What Was Said Of Him at the Little Big Horn" page 3.

[96] While Reno, perhaps in an attempt to defuse damaging testimony he feared would be introduced, would repeatedly volunteer he had no thought of moving from the hill or leaving the wounded, he was forced to admit, under oath , that he had indeed abandoned his wounded in the valley fight without making any effort to save them. See Ronald H. Nichols "The Reno Court of Inquiry' pages 569, 576, 586, and 587.

[97] Among 7th Cavalry officers, Benteen told Varnum and Moylan, in addition to Godfrey, of Reno's plan. It will become obvious that Weir also knew of the plan, but how Mathey learned of it, if he did, has not been explained.

[98] See Ronald H. Nichols "The Reno Court of Inquiry" page 520.

[99] See Colonel W. A. Graham "The Custer Myth" page 333.

[100] See Colonel W. A. Graham "The Custer Myth" page 335.

[101] See Colonel John Gibbon "Hunting Sitting Bull" page 667.

[102] See Kenneth Hammer "Custer In '76" pages 70 – 71. Francis B. Taunton notes that Hammer inadvertently omitted the non attribution request from his manuscript. See "No Pride In The Little Big Horn" page 33.

[103] See Frazier and Robert Hunt "I Fought With Custer" pages 204 and 206, and Colonel W. A. Graham "The Custer Myth" pages 333 – 334. Godfrey, in a March 2, 1926 letter to J. A. Shoemaker, stated he was convinced Benteen had asked Weir to sound him out in case a contest over abandoning the wounded (i.e. a mutiny) became necessary. See Tom O'Neil "Marcus A. Reno: What Was Said of Him at the Little Big Horn" page 2.

[104] See Edgar I. Stewart "The Field Diary of Lt. Edward Settle Godfrey" page 15.

[105] See Charles K. Mills "Harvest of Barren Regrets" page 270.

[106] See Ronald H. Nichols "The Reno Court of Inquiry" pages 516 – 517.

[107] See John M. Carroll "The Benteen–Goldin Letters" page 210.

[108] See Ronald H. Nichols "The Reno Court of Inquiry" page 517.

[109] See Kenneth Hammer "Little Big Horn Biographies" page 21.

[110] See John M. Carroll "The Benteen–Goldin Letters" pages 172 – 173.

[111] Only one Blake was serving with the 7th Cavalry, Private Thomas Blake of Company A. Burkman may have been confused about the trooper's first name, or Billy may have been a nickname.

[112] See Don Rickey "Forty Miles A Day On Beans And Hay" page 303.

[113] See Daniel O. Magnussen "Peter Thompson's Narrative" page 201.

[114] See Ronald H. Nichols "The Reno Court of Inquiry" page 576.

[115] Per Army Quartermaster records he is listed as R. C. Churchill in Appendix 1, but the court records list him as B. F. Churchill, so those initials have been retained in this section of the narrative.

[116] See Ronald H. Nichols "The Reno Court of Inquiry" page 470.

[117] Reno did admit to having between a pint and a quart of whiskey, stating he took a drink about midnight. Much has been made by some authors of the statements of DeRudio, Girard, Frett and Churchill (who all had reason to dislike Reno) that Reno had been drinking throughout the day and was drunk the night of the 25th. While Reno was probably "feeling his liquor" due to the tension of the situation as well as his empty stomach, I find it difficult to believe he was incapacitated by alcohol on the 25th and therefore accept the testimony of the officers that he was sober. (For example, see Colonel W. A. Graham "The Reno Court of Inquiry" page 192). It is true that Reno purchased, on credit, a total of 7 gallons and 2 demijohns of whiskey from traders operating on the steam boats between August 1 and August 22. The fact that credit purchases for all other 7th Cavalry officers combined during this same period totaled 10 gallons, demonstrates only that Reno was a heavy drinker; a fact that is hardly in dispute. In no way, however, does this prove Reno had either the opportunity or capacity to be drunk on June 25th. See Ben Innis "Bloody Knife!" pages 150 - 151.

[118] See Ronald H. Nichols "The Reno Court of Inquiry" page 576.

[119] See Colonel W. A. Graham "The Reno Court of Inquiry" page 163.

[120] While Varnum recalled the following conversation with Reno as occurring on June 26th, it appears that Sergeant Culbertson, who overheard Varnum's discussion with Sergeant McDermott, was correct in his recollection that the incident actually transpired on the 25th. See Ronald H. Nichols "The Reno Court of Inquiry" page 379.

[121] The other Crow scouts had left Reno Hill at sundown. The account of Goes Ahead indicates they had met Company A, the black horse troop, and obtained permission to leave, but doesn't mention who granted them permission to leave. See "The Teepee Book" pages 601 and 604.

[122] See John M. Carroll "Custer's Chief of Scouts" page 94. Young Hawk claimed that the attempt was indeed made by four Arikara: himself, Forked Horn, Red Foolish Bear, and the wounded Goose, as well as an unnamed sergeant. When fired upon by the Lakota, they returned to the defensive position. See O. G. Libby "The Arikara Narrative" page 105.

[123] See Kenneth Hammer "Custer In '76" page 140.

[124] Porter had a narrow escape from the bottom as described in the *St. Paul Pioneer Press*: *"Porter was by the side of a dying soldier (this was either private Klotzbucher or Lorentz, DCE). His orderly and supplies were gone, and the command was off several hundred yards. He was alone. Bullets were piercing the trees and a terrific yell was sounding the alarm of universal death. Porter left his lost patient and led his horse to the embankment that protected the woods. He was startled by Indians dashing by him within ten feet. They were rushing along the foot of the little bluff. Their aim was so directed in the line of the flying battalion that Porter's presence was unnoticed. He was unarmed, and his powerful black horse reared and plunged as if he was mad. Porter saw the fate that was in the immediate future if that horse escaped before he was on his back. He held on with*

superhuman strength. He could hold him, but that was all. To gain the saddle seemed a forlorn hope. Leap after leap with the horse quicker than he. It was a brief ordeal, but in the face of death it was a terrible one. One supreme effort and, half in his saddle, the dusky charger bore away his master like the wind. He gained the full seat, and lying close upon his savior's neck, was running a gauntlet where the chances of death were a thousand to one. The Indians were quick to see the lone rider and as storm of leaden hail fell around him. He had no control of his horse. It was only a half-mile dash, but it was a wild one. The horse was frenzied. He reached the river in a minute and rushed up the bluff, where Reno had gone, and was then recovering himself. The horse and rider were safe." See Joseph Mills Hanson "Conquest of the Missouri" pages 293 - 294.

[125] Daniel Newell confirms Thompson's account of Porter attempting to join the firing line. See John M. Carroll "The Sunshine Magazine Articles" page 12.

[126] See Daniel o. Magnussen "Thompson's Narrative" pages 202 – 203.

[127] See John M. Carroll "Custer's Chief of Scouts" pages 71 – 72.

[128] See Kenneth Hammer "Custer In '76" page 71.

[129] See John M. Carroll "The Benteen – Goldin Letters" page 173.

[130] See Dale T. Schoenberger "The End of Custer" page 236.

[131] See John M. Carroll "The Benteen–Goldin Letters" page 156.

[132] See Dale T. Schoenberger "The End of Custer" page 236.

[133] McDougall did not comment as to how the troopers thought the warriors had come by their war trophies.

[134] See Kenneth Hammer "Custer In '76" page 71.

[135] See Edgar I. Stewart "The Field Diary of Edward Settle Godfrey" page 16.

[136] See Don Rickey "Forty Miles A Day On Beans And Hay" page 101.

[137] See Don Rickey "Forty Miles A Day On Beans And Hay" page 101.

[138] See W. F. Beyer and O. F. Keydel "Acts of Bravery" page 220.

[139] See Dale T. Schoenberger "The End of Custer" page 227.

[140] See Kenneth Hammer "Little Big Horn Biographies" page 31.

[141] See Edgar I. Stewart "Custer's Luck" page 421.

[142] See Kenneth Hammer "Custer In '76" page 81.

[143] Also often referred to as Long Robe. He is known to the Cheyenne as Thunder Shield.

144 See Edgar I. Stewart "Custer's Luck" page 425, "The Battlefield Dispatch" Summer 1991, page 7, Stanley Vestal "Sitting Bull" page 176, Daniel O. Magnussen "Thompson's Narrative" page 209, and Paul I. Wellman "Death on Horseback" page 149.

145 See John Stands In Timber "Cheyenne Memories" page 207.

146 See Kenneth Hammer "Custer In '76" page 144. Company H's Private Jacob Adams also claimed to have killed Long Road. See Horace Ellis "A Survivor's Story of the Custer Massacre" page 10.

147 See John M. Carroll "A Seventh Cavalry Scrapbook" pages 6 – 7.

148 See Kenneth Hammer "Custer In '76" page 150.

149 See Kenneth Hammer "Custer In '76" page 150.

150 See John M. Carroll "The Benteen – Goldin Letters" pages 173 – 174.

151 See E. S. Godfrey "Custer's Last Battle 1876" page 30. Included among the casualties was the Sans Arc Eagle Hat. See Dale T. Schoenberger "The End of Custer" page 239.

152 See Dale T. Schoenberger "The End of Custer" page 242.

153 See Dale T. Schoenberger "The End of Custer" page 242.

154 See John M. Carroll "A Seventh Cavalry Scrapbook" pages 6 – 7 and Ronald H. Nichols "The Reno Court of Inquiry" page 412.

155 Unfortunately, as was all too often the case with Benteen, his brilliant achievement was accompanied by an act of pettiness. Miffed by what he thought was tardiness on the part of Company M to support this charge, Benteen would refuse to endorse Captain French's recommendation for a Medal of Honor for Sergeant Ryan who performed with distinction during the siege. See Edgar I. Stewart "Custer's Luck" page 424. A corollary to this story is that several months before the Little Big Horn, Benteen had presided over Sergeant Ryan's court martial for harsh punishment of a soldier. Found guilty and reduced to the ranks, Ryan was reinstated by Custer in time for the '76 campaign. See Don Rickey "Forty Miles A Day On Beans And Hay" pages 139 – 140, and 311.

156 Although the Medal of Honor citation for Private Peter Thompson lists him as *"wounded through the head"* while attempting to secure water for the wounded, Thompson always maintained he was shot through the right hand while moving to join Benteen's charge. Given the debilitating nature of a "wound through the head" it seems unlikely Thompson could have rendered further service to his comrades after being hit. As it also seems that Thompson would be the best source as to the time and location of his wound I have therefore accepted his account. See Daniel O. Magnussen "Thompson's Narrative" page 197. In addition to Thompson and Lieutenant Varnum, Private James J. Tanner, Company M, was wounded, dying in the field hospital on June 27. Kenneth Hammer "Little Big Horn Biographies" pages 46 – 47.

157 Charles Kuhlman believed Varnum was wounded in the second charge. See "Legend Into History" page 137.

[158] Almost certainly Private George B. Mask as only two privates from Company B were killed in the hilltop fight and Private Dorn was known to have been killed while attempting to awaken Captain McDougall.

[159] See John M. Carroll "Custer's Chief of Scouts" page 72.

[160] See Edgar I. Stewart "Custer's Luck" pages 426 – 427.

[161] The troops were under a very heavy fire and Benteen's sojourn to Reno's position was not undertaken without some personal risk. Godfrey testified as to Benteen's exposed position during the conversation with Reno: *"It was so exposed that I told him he had better come away from the place he was, that he would get hit. He said something about the bullet not having been moulded yet to shoot him, that he had been through too many dangerous places to care anything about their shooting."* See Ronald H. Nichols "The Reno Court of Inquiry" page 500.

[162] See E. S. Godfrey "Custer's Last Battle 1876" pages 30 – 31.

[163] As with most events associated with the battle, there is controversy regarding whether or not Reno participated in this charge. Benteen testified at the court of inquiry that he believed Reno did not accompany the troops (See Ronald H. Nichols "The Reno Court of Inquiry" page 413). While Reno was not questioned about the incident at the court of inquiry, his official report indicates he accompanied the troops. Given Godfrey's displeasure with Reno's entire performance, it seems reasonable to conclude he would not have credited Reno with joining the charge had he remained in the rear. I therefore conclude Reno did accompany the second charge.

[164] See Edgar I. Stewart "The Field Diary of Edward Settle Godfrey" page 17.

[165] There were two sergeants in Company D at the Little Big Horn whose first names were Tom. As Thomas Russell had enlisted in August of 1872 and had been promoted sergeant while in the field on June 6, 1876, it appears that Edgerly was referring to Sergeant Thomas W. Harrison who had enlisted for his second hitch in 1871.

[166] See Kenneth Hammer "Little Big Horn Biographies" page 22, Edgar I. Stewart "The Field Diary of Edward Settle Godfrey" page 15, Colonel W. A. Graham "The Custer Myth" page 145, and Richard G. Hardorff "The Custer Battle Casualties" page 163.

[167] See Ronald H. Nichols "The Reno Court of Inquiry" page 493. Benteen had hinted he had assumed command when testifying about the withdrawal from Weir Point: *"Mind you, I was looking after things probably more than it was my business or duty to do."* See Ronald H. Nichols "The Reno Court of Inquiry" page 410.

[168] See Colonel W. A. Graham "The Reno Court of Inquiry" page 182. While Reno's statement seems rather innocuous today, in the nineteenth century any concern for one's personal safety was looked on as tantamount to cowardice.

[169] See Charles K. Mills "Harvest of Barren Regrets" page 273.

[170] While some authorities doubt that Goldin was a member of either of the two water parties, Lieutenant Wallace recalled Goldin had been a water carrier. See Larry Skenlar "Private Theodore W. Goldin: Too Soon Discredited?"

[171] See Edgar I. Stewart "Custer's Luck" page 425. Note Stewart incorrectly names the Blacksmith as Meckling.

[172] While it is not clear exactly how many trips for water were made, the Medal of Honor citation for Peter Thompson credits him with a total of three circuits.

[173] Edgar I. Stewart believed this unfortunate trooper to have been Private James J. Tanner, of Company M. As both Sergeant Ryan and Private Newell name Tanner as being wounded in Benteen's charge to clear Water Carrier's Ravine, I believe Stewart to be in error in this instance and therefore list this trooper as unknown.

[174] See Thomas B. Marquis "Wooden Leg" pages 259 – 260.

[175] Private John Sivertsen, Company M, recalled that when they went to bring Madden into the lines, the warriors shooting from the opposite bank would call out in perfect English: *"Come on over on this side, you Sons of . . . and we will give it to you! Come over! "* See Bruce Liddic and Paul Harbaugh "Camp on Custer" page 110.

[176] See E. A. Brininstool "Troopers With Custer" pages 57 – 58. Although he was not close enough to observe the entire operation, Private William H. White, Company F, Second Cavalry, saw Madden immediately afterwards, helping to carry him aside to relieve himself. White doubts that Madden made the statement attributed, or that there was any liquor in the command. See Thomas B. Marquis "Custer on the Little Big Horn" page 40.

[177] See Daniel O. Magnussen "Thompson's Narrative" page 210. When added to the 9 Medals of Honor awarded to non-water carriers, the resulting total of 24 represents the most Medals of Honor awarded for a single engagement in U. S. history. See Richard G. Hardorff "Lakota Recollections of the Custer Fight" page 47. Ironically, prior to the Little Big Horn, no member of the 7th Cavalry had won a Medal of Honor.

[178] John Henley, who was not present, said that Private Thomas W. Coleman was the first man to go for water. See Bruce Liddic and Paul Harbaugh "Camp on Custer" page 109.

[179] See Kenneth Hammer "Little Big Horn Biographies" page 50.

[180] See Edgar I. Stewart "Custer's Luck" page 428.

Chapter 17

The Relief Of The Seventh

Captain Freeman's column, consisting of Companies E, H and K of the Seventh Infantry,[1] had marched from the camp at the mouth of the Rosebud at 6:00 AM on June 21, bound for the mouth of the Big Horn River; the cavalry, commanded by Captain Ball, following at 1:30 PM. General Terry, Colonel Gibbon, and Major Brisbin had remained behind for the officer's conference held on board the *Far West* and to see the Seventh Cavalry off on the 22nd. Lieutenants William H. Low and Frank Kenzie were vocally indignant their battery of gatling guns had not been allowed to accompany Custer's column, sharing the belief of most of the Montana Column that they would be out of the fight entirely.[2] Gibbon would echo those sentiments on the 23rd when he remarked: *"I am satisfied that if Custer can prevent it, we will not get into the fight."*[3] This, of course, is the most heated controversy associated with the Battle of the Little Big Horn; did Custer violate his orders and attack too soon? The facts will be presented, in their proper sequence, and the reader will judge accordingly.

A curious event transpired on June 22nd. The gatling gun battery, which had left the camp on the Rosebud after midnight on the 21st, had brought Captain Ball an order from Gibbon to separate from the infantry and, along with the artillery, hasten to Fort Pease.[4] The purpose of this division of Gibbon's small command, deep in enemy territory, seems to defy explanation. This event was followed by one even more difficult to understand. For some unexplained reason, Captain Ball rescinded Gibbon's standing order against bugle calls, which had been instituted a month previously. Bradley recalled:

> *"Our cavalry comrades have been particularly restless under this [bugle call] prohibition, and it was observed today that no sooner did they cut loose from us than they began to sound their bugles with hearty good will. So much did the buglers glory in their new found freedom and the bellow notes they poured forth that they exerted themselves fit to crack their throats, and repeated the calls far more freely than was necessary for the mere information of the command."*[5]

History offers no explanation for this breech of security which seemed to invite detection and attack. The next day, an Indian hunting party was seen on the south bank. This turned out to be fortuitous for the troops as the buffalo the hunters were pursuing swam the Yellowstone and became easy pickings for the cavalry. The cavalry unselfishly left several carcasses hanging in trees for the infantry. Inexplicably Lieutenant Joshua Jacobs, the Montana Column's quartermaster, refused to allow the wagons to halt long enough to take on this load of badly needed fresh meat. Captain Freeman, although present, refused to overrule his subordinate so, as one disgusted soldier put it, they *". . . supped on bacon, instead of the excellent buffalo steaks we might have had."*[6]

That same night, Gibbon was taken violently ill with hepatic-colic of the stomach and bowels. By morning he was unable to move and remained in his cabin on the *Far West* until rejoining his command on June 26. His two day absence would be keenly felt with the inexperienced Terry in command of the column. The cavalry and infantry reunited about two miles below Fort Pease at 7:30 AM on the 24th.[7] Captain Thaddeus Sanford Kirtland, commanding Company B of the Seventh Infantry, was ordered to remain behind and guard the wagons.[8] The remaining companies, about 385 officers and men all told, accompanied by a pack train containing supplies for 8 days, were to be ferried across the Yellowstone and commence the march up the Tullock. The decision to carry rations for eight days was not an arbitrary one. The selection ensured that the Montana and Custer Columns were rationed for the same period of time,[9] upon expiration of which, according to Terry's orders to Custer, they were to reunite.

While the difficulties the command had encountered previously were not serious in terms of consequences, they undoubtedly had an adverse effect on the morale of the troops which was already at low ebb from the belief Custer's force would be the only one to strike the enemy. Now, however, these minor difficulties would be magnified as their true significance would be revealed; the Montana Column was being ineptly commanded. It would take from 6 AM until nearly noon for the movement of the troops to the south bank of the Yellowstone to commence. The *Far West* accomplished the task of ferrying the troops across in five trips, completing the movement shortly after 4 PM.[10] About 11 AM, Terry, who had assumed personal command of the column upon Gibbon's incapacity, ordered twelve Crow scouts to cross the Yellowstone and proceed up the Tullock *". . . until they found a Sioux village on a recent trail."*[11]

Unconcerned about fragmenting his command in hostile territory, Terry ordered the cavalry, along with a portion of the infantry, forward about 5 PM. Bradley was to seek a campsite in the vicinity of the mouth of Tullock's Fork. The remainder of the infantry remained in the staging area to receive a crash course in mule packing.[12] The command was reunited about 7:30 PM in the cavalry camp established by Bradley a mile above the mouth of Tullock's Fork. This camp was located approximately 47 miles from the junction of the Little Big Horn and Big Horn rivers; a two day march for the infantry. In light of subsequent assertions of a plan for a combined attack on June 26, it is well to note that Terry did not order a night march on the 24th; thereby resigning himself to an arrival time in the valley of the Little Big Horn late on the 26th.

That night, an enthusiastic Bradley would write prophetically in his journal:

*"We are now fairly en route to the Indian village, which is supposed to be on the Little Big Horn. It is undoubtedly a large one, and **should** (emphasis the author's) Custer's command and ours unite,[13] we, too, will have a large force numbering all told about one thousand men, armed with the splendid breech-loading Springfield rifles and carbines, caliber forty-five, and strengthened by the presence of Low's battery of three Gatling guns. Should we come to blows **it will be one of the biggest Indian battles ever fought on this continent**, (emphasis the author's) and the most decisive in its results, for such a force as we shall have if united will be invincible, and the utter destruction of the Indian village, and overthrow of Sioux power will be the certain result. There is not much glory in Indian wars, but **it will be worth while to have been present at such an affair as this** (emphasis the author's)."*[14]

The command started up the Tullock at 5:45 AM on June 25th.[15] Almost immediately, Terry made an ill advised command decision as explained by the column's engineering officer, Second Lieutenant Edward J. McClernand:

"The General (Terry, DCE) used me as a staff officer and as I had recently passed over the ground directed me to select the trail.

"It was my intention to follow along the little stream to a point three or four miles short of where Captain Ball struck it on April 29th, during his scout, previously mentioned, then turn to the right and cross the divide between Tullock's Fork and the Little Big Horn River so as to reach the latter stream about five miles above its junction with the Big Horn. Along that route the distance from our camp of the

*night of the 24th – 25th, to the Little Big Horn would have been about 47 or 48
miles, and to the top of the divide between it and Tullock's Fork considerably less;
probably about forty miles, or less. I am dwelling somewhat upon details here in
view of the tragedy we are now approaching. . .*

*"The trail we were following along Tullock's Fork crossed that small stream
frequently, but was nevertheless quite a good one, although the battery of Gatling
guns found some trouble now and then at the crossings; nothing though that
caused serious difficulty, or delay. However, after passing up the creek for 3.3 miles
[16] General Terry sent word to me that he intended to ascend the divide between the
Fork and the Big Horn River, and follow it to the mouth of the Little Big Horn. In
adopting this course the General accepted the advice of a civilian scout, 'Muggins'
Taylor, in Gibbon's employ. Taylor was not familiar with the trail along the Fork, or
the country between it and the Big Horn. He was, in general terms a good and
brave man, who had long lived near the Indian frontier, but mostly in small towns,
and was in no sense an experienced 'plainsman.' It is only fair to say that usually a
good trail can be found along the top of a divide between two streams, but this rule
does not apply where 'bad lands' intervene, as was the case in the country selected
by Taylor."[17]*

Terry never explained his reasons for moving to the divide. Many authors have speculated
that the movement was conducted in an attempt to shorten the march, but this does not seem
plausible. In addition to his Crow scouts, who were intimately familiar with the country, the
members of Captain Ball's April scout had been over the route McClernand intended to follow. It
seems incredible, given the resources at his disposal who were known to be familiar with the
country, that Terry would apparently consult only Muggins Taylor as to the line of march to be
followed.

The movement to the divide was accomplished in a most precipitous manner. Bradley, in
command of the scouts, found himself 9 miles in advance blazing a trail the command was not
following. Finding himself alone, Bradley ordered a halt. Finally, he was informed by a squad of
cavalry of the change in line of march and recalled to the main column.[18] Only the most dire of
circumstances could justify putting the command at such risk by moving, in what was considered
to be close proximity to the enemy, without benefit of an advance scouting party. No
circumstances of the sort existed, of course, and the command was indeed fortunate they did not
encounter a sizable warrior force. While, a few miles to the north, Custer's fabled luck was
deserting him, Terry would have much more than his allotted portion of luck this day. Despite
the lack of rationale for this movement, one fact is clear; the recall of Bradley's scouting
detachment, leaving the valley devoid of any troops or scouts, demonstrated that Terry had
abandoned his plan to thoroughly scout the lower regions of the Tullock.

Along the new route the column began to experience the types of problems Custer had
foreseen when the pole of one of the gun carriages was broken in mid morning, requiring a half
hour delay to repair.[19] The march along the divide would prove arduous in the extreme, as
summarized by Lieutenant McClernand:

*"Once having reached the summit of the divide it became absolutely necessary to
follow it, although it was very narrow and tortuous. Rough ravines, hundreds of
feet deep, and filled with scrubby pines, ran back almost to the summit from both
sides. The day was excessively warm, and the infantry, toiling along over the rough
ground, suffered greatly for water, which was not found at any place on the divide.*

After marching 21.35 miles, and after descending a long and precipitous hill, where it was necessary to fasten many lariats together, tie them to the Gatling gun carriages and then lower the latter by hand, the cavalry reached the Big Horn where the troopers and their mounts first quenched their own intense thirst, after which many canteens were filled and sent back to the weary and even more thirsty foot troops."[20]

Incredibly, Captain R. P. Hughes, Terry's brother-in-law, places the entire blame for the unnecessary suffering this change of direction inflicted on the troops solely on the shoulders of George Armstrong Custer! Hughes reasoned that had Custer sent Herendeen through to Terry as ordered, a change in the line of march would not have been necessary, hence the suffering inflicted on the troops by Terry's ill-advised change in route was Custer's fault. Neither Hughes or any other proponent of this theory has ever attempted to explain how Terry knew that Herendeen was to reach him within 3.3 miles of leaving his camp on June 25, or how the planned meeting with Herendeen, who was supposed to be coming down the Tullock, would be facilitated by abandoning the valley in favor of the divide. Bradley echoed the sentiments of his brother officer, but placed the blame for the ill-chosen route on the assignment of guide Mitch Boyer to the Seventh Cavalry, rather than the judgment of his commanding officer:

"I soon rejoined, taking a short cut across the hills, and found the command involved in a labyrinth of bald hills and deep, precipitous ravines completely destitute of water. The men had emptied their canteens of the wretched alkali water they started with and were parched with thirst as well as greatly fatigued with clambering over such ground. A worse route could not have been chosen, but destitute of a guide as we are,[21] it is not to be wondered that we entangled ourselves in such a mesh of physical obstacles."[22]

Upon rejoining the command, Bradley and his party were ordered to Tullock's Peak in the command's left front as Terry believed a view of the valley of the Little Big Horn might be obtained from that height. Again the order was given without consultation with the Crow scouts who could have told Terry that an unobstructed view of the valley could not be obtained from that point. Even had an unobstructed view been obtained, the valley, being some 22 miles from Tullock's Peak, was too distant to be able to discern any village that might be present. In any event, while the command began their descent to the Big Horn River, Bradley was forced to complete a worthless 16 mile circuit; reporting all that could be seen from Tullock's Peak was a higher ridge that completely obscured the view. As his orders prevented him from proceeding beyond Tullock's Peak, Bradley was obligated to return to the command with this worthless information.

As the exhausted troopers stumbled to a rest halt on the banks of the Big Horn, Terry was preparing for yet another movement. Although the troops had already covered an exhausting 23.65 miles and a heavy rain began falling at 4:30, the General was contemplating a night march to position the command at the junction of the Little Big Horn and Big Horn early on the 26th. Lieutenant Roe recalled Terry stating: *"I have agreed with Custer to be at or near the mouth of the Little Big Horn on the morning of the 26th."[23]* Terry then continued, perhaps thinking out loud: *"I will take the cavalry and push on to-night. If Major Freeman is able to march his men, I will also take the infantry on to-night."[24]*

Roe also recalled Terry's subsequent conversations regarding the movement:

"Terry asked him (Freeman, DCE). 'Major, is it possible to take your infantry on to-night?' He replied, 'It is not – the men are worn out,' which was true, as they had

marched fully twenty-five difficult miles that day. He added, however, 'If you will allow me to remain here to-night, I will agree to start at four o'clock in the morning.'

"The General turned to me with the question, 'What do you think of the cavalry?' My answer as a troop commander was that the horses were not used up, and we could go on practically any distance the circumstances required, say from twenty-five to fifty miles.[25] He replied, 'That being the case, the cavalry will push on to-night.'"[26]

Some of the Crow scouts who had gone up the Tullock early in the morning had reported seeing smoke in the valley of the Little Big Horn. While Terry may have correctly discerned the smoke indicated the presence of the village they sought, and he may have feared the failure to rendezvous with Herendeen indicated Custer was not in the vicinity, splitting his command was a tactical error which could have had the most dire of consequences. The movement split the command into two segments numbering respectively about 200 and 185 men; either force woefully inadequate to deal with the Lakota should they be encountered.

McClernand vastly understated the difficulties encountered during the night march when he wrote:

"At 5:15 PM, we were again in the saddle. Our course took us over rough hills and across deep ravines. Night came on very dark and the rain continued to fall dismally until 10:30 PM. It was difficult for those parts of the column in the rear to see those in their front. The battery, especially, had great difficulty in keeping up.[27] Several times it was lost [28] and only brought back by repeated trumpet calls. It was impossible, due to the darkness, to follow a straight course even when the nature of the country would have permitted it, and the General decided we were taxing the strength of the command to small gain. At midnight he halted where some water was standing in holes, and near which the grass was fortunately tolerably good, for our animals were in sore need of food. There was also a little wood nearby, but to prevent all danger of signaling our approach no fires were permitted, and we passed what remained of the night sitting, or tramping about in the mud, chilled to the bone in our wet clothing. We had marched 12.10 miles (a rate of 1.8 mph [29] which demonstrates the nature of the terrain, DCE) after parting from the infantry and 35.75 during the day."[30]

The order against fires, of course, was the proper precaution to take regardless of the condition and discomfort of the troops. It seems the concern was somewhat belated, however, when viewed within the context of having bugle calls sounded to recall the lost battery. Had any enemy scouts been in the vicinity, Terry's small command would have long since been discovered.

Bradley provides a more detailed, and graphic account of the march:

"The cavalry officers who scouted up the Big Horn last April were acting as guides,[31] for want of better, and, as their knowledge of the country was far from profound, we were continually encountering serious obstacles to our march – now a precipitous hillside, now a deep ravine. . .

". . . and once the cry did go up: 'The battery is missing!' A halt was made, and after some racing and hallooing (this may refer to the trumpet calls mentioned by McClernand, DCE) the missing guns were set right again, having lost the human thread and so wandered a mile or so out of the way. At another time some of the cavalry went astray and lost half an hour getting back to us.

"At length, after hours of such toil, getting out of one difficulty only to plunge at once into another,[32] the head of the column came plump on the brink of a precipice at whose foot swept the roaring waters of the Big Horn. The water gleamed in front 150 feet below, and to the right hand to the left the ground broke off into a steep declivity, down which nothing could be seen but forbidding gloom. Our cavalry guides were wholly bewildered, and everybody was tired out, and dripping with wet, and impatient to get somewhere and rest. When General Terry saw the walls of Fort Fisher before him (a reference to Terry's brilliant conquest of the 'Confederate Gibraltar' and the highlight of his military career, DCE), he knew what to do. He threw his battalions against them, and carried them by storm, and gained a glorious victory and won a star; but when he saw to what a pass we had now come and reflected that every step we took seemed only to render our situation more perplexing, he appeared uncertain and irresolute. For several minutes we sat our horses, looking by turn at the water and into the black ravines, when I ventured to suggest to the General that we trust ourselves to the guidance of Little Face, one of my Crow scouts who had roamed this country as a boy fifty years ago and had previously assured me that he knew every foot of it. Little Face was called up, said he could guide us to a good camping-ground, was accepted as a guide, and led off in the dark with as much confidence as though he was in the full light of day. The aimless, profitless scrambling was over; he conducted us by an easy route a mile or two to the left, where we found ourselves in a commodious valley with water enough in its little channel to suffice for drinking purposes."[33]

After a night's reflection, Terry apparently decided his top priority was to close up his widely scattered command and ordered the cavalry to remain in camp until 9:15 AM, the magnitude of the delay negating the progress made during the night march. McClernand discovered that the previous day's misadventures had neither bolstered Terry's confidence in his Crow scouts, nor shaken it in regard to Muggins Taylor. In describing the events of June 26, McClernand wrote:

"The column soon reached quite a broad valley, destitute of trees, and in which there was doubtless a considerable stream in the early spring, fed by the melting snows, but at the time of our visit the water course was dry except for such moisture as might be expected from the rain of the night before. Nevertheless, Scout Taylor told General Terry the ravine in our front was the Little Big Horn River, the water of which sank near its mouth, or as he expressed it, 'which ran dry at its mouth.' To this statement I strongly protested, and said to the General that while I had not actually gone to the mouth of the river on the scout under Captain Ball some two months earlier, we were within ten or twelve miles of its junction with the Big Horn, and that from the divide to the east I had, with the aid of my field glasses, followed its course to the junction of the two rivers and that beyond question it was a fine flowing stream, and well timbered. My statements were so positive that the General was convinced, and we again moved forward, and from the top of the next ridge, two or three miles in advance, we looked down upon the beautiful little valley and clear running stream we had been seeking, with the junction of the two rivers but a

short distance to our right and front. General Terry seemed much pleased, saying in substance, 'Well; I have kept faith with Custer – I promised to be here today.'"[34]

While the reunited command, including a recovered Colonel Gibbon,[35] was halted atop this ridge, Lieutenant Bradley reported to General Terry some important intelligence the morning's scout had uncovered:

"Major Brisbin, who in General Gibbon's absence commands the column, roused me up this morning at daylight and ordered me out on a scout at once, not allowing my men to get breakfast. As I had traveled some twenty miles farther yesterday than anybody else, so that my horses were tired and my men hungry, it struck me as rather rough treatment. I was too much vexed to hurry much, and did not get off till 4 AM, having sent six Crows ahead half an hour earlier. My orders were to scout to the Little Big Horn, looking out for Sioux sign and sending back word of any important discoveries. Having advanced about three miles, we entered a valley cut by a dry creek, and here came upon the fresh tracks of four ponies. As we entered the ravine, we had seen a heavy smoke rising in our front, apparently fifteen or twenty miles away, and I at once concluded we were approaching the Sioux village and that the trail had been made by a party of scouts therefrom.

"Sending back a written report of the discovery, I took the trail of the four supposed Sioux in the hope of catching them in the Big Horn valley, toward which the trail led and where we thought they might have camped, as there was no convenient way of leaving the valley into which they had gone except that by which they had entered it.

"At the distance of less than two miles the trail struck the river, and we found that they had there crossed, leaving behind a horse and several articles of personal equipment, indicating that they had fled in great haste. An examination of the articles disclosed to our great surprise that they belonged to some of the Crows whom I had furnished to General Custer at the mouth of the Rosebud, which rendered it probable that the supposed Sioux were some of our own scouts who had for some reason left Custer's command and were returning to the Crow agency. While speculating upon the circumstance, three men[36] were discovered on the opposite side of the Big Horn about two miles away, apparently watching our movements. We at once signaled to them with blankets that we were friends, for a long time to no purpose, but when we were about to give up and seek some other method of communicating with them, they responded by kindling a fire that sent up a small column of smoke, indicating that they had seen signals and trusted our assurances. We gathered wet sage-brush and assured them with a similar smoke, and soon afterwards they came down to the river and talked across the stream with Little Face and one or two more of the scouts who went down to meet them. While the interview went on, I kept the remainder of the detachment on the bluffs. Presently our Indians turned back and, as they came, shouted out at the top of their voices a doleful series of cries and wails that the interpreter, Bravo, explained was a song of mourning for the dead. That it boded some misfortune there was no doubt; and when they came up, shedding copious tears and appearing pictures of misery, it was evident that the occasion was of no common sort. Little Face in particular wept with a bitterness of anguish such as I have rarely seen. For awhile he could not speak, but at last composed himself and told his story in a choking voice, broken with frequent sobs. As he proceeded, the Crows one by one broke off from the group of listeners and going aside a little distance sat down alone, weeping and chanting

that dreadful mourning song, and rocking their bodies to and fro. They were the first listeners to the horrid story of the Custer massacre,[37] and, outside of the relatives and personal friends of the fallen, there were none in this whole horrified nation of forty millions of people to whom the tidings brought greater grief . . ."

". . . It was a terrible, terrible story,[38] so different from the outcome we had hoped for this campaign, and I no longer wondered at the demonstrative sorrow of the Crows. My men listened to it with eager interest, betrayed none of the emotion of the Crows, but looking at each other with white faces in pained silence, too full of the dreadful recital to utter a word. Did we doubt the tale? I could not; there was an undefined vague something about it, unlooked for though it was, that commanded assent, and the most I could do was to hope that in the terror of the three fugitives from the fatal field their account of the disaster was somewhat overdrawn. But that there had been a disaster – a terrible disaster – I felt assured."[39]

Bradley's acceptance of the story was not shared by Terry's staff officers:

". . . narrated to the General the ghastly details as I had received them from Little Face. He was surrounded by his staff and accompanied by General Gibbon, who had that morning joined [them], and for a moment there were blank faces and silent tongues and no doubt heavy hearts in that group, just as there had been among the auditors of Little Face at its rehearsal by him. But presently the voice of doubt and scorning was raised, the story was sneered at, such a catastrophe it was asserted was wholly improbable, nay, impossible; if a battle had been fought, which was condescendingly admitted might have happened, then Custer was victorious, and these three Crows were dastards who had fled without awaiting the result and told this story to excuse their cowardice. General Terry took no part in these criticisms, but sat on his horse silent and thoughtful, biting his lower lip and looking to me as though he by no means shared in the wholesale skepticism of the flippant members of his staff."[40]

Lieutenant McClernand supplied the rationale for the officer's disbelief in his recounting of the event:

"At this time a big smoke was seen up the valley of the Little Big Horn, but the report of the Crows was not generally believed, and many thought the smoke arose from the Indian village, and that Custer was burning it. The Crows said the Sioux had fired the grass.

"As said, the statement of the two Crows (actually there were three, DCE) was not generally accepted. Many in our column were willing to admit that Custer's advance guard might have been driven back, but scoffed at the idea of his entire regiment being beaten. In fact Custer commanded the admiration, and excited the enthusiasm of most of the young men in the army. His well known reputation for courage and dash was contagious and caught the fancy even of those among us who had never met him. It is recalled that one young officer attached to General Terry's Headquarters, Lieutenant Thompson of the 6th Infantry if I remember correctly, announced loudly that of course Custer had beaten the Indians and was now fifty miles away in pursuit. Many undoubtedly thought likewise. My captain, James N. Whelan, fell into general disfavor because he insisted the Crows were

reliable, and that their report should be accepted. I do not know what General Terry thought; so far as I know he kept his opinion to himself."[41]

Lieutenant Roe is the only diarist who credits Terry with voicing an opinion at the time:

"I find it impossible to believe that so fine a regiment as the Seventh Cavalry should have met with such a catastrophe."[42]

Gibbon echoed the opinion of his commander:

"I do not suppose there was a man in the column who entertained for a moment the idea that there were Indians enough in the country to defeat, much less annihilate, the fine regiment of cavalry which Custer had under his command."[43]

The column was halted for a rest and food stop from 1 PM to about 5 PM. Becoming more apprehensive with each passing minute, Terry offered an inducement of $200 for anyone able to get a message through to Custer.[44] Terry, who had previously turned down two officers who attempted to volunteer, accepted the offers of Muggins Taylor and Henry Bostwick to attempt to reach Custer, dispatching them up the west and east bank of the Little Big Horn respectively about 3 PM. Unconvinced that the Seventh Cavalry had met with disaster, yet with nagging unvoiced doubts gnawing at the roots of consciousness, the command would push forward up the valley of the Little Big Horn without their Crow scouts who, upon the advice of Barney Bravo, had deserted enmass to return to Crow Agency.[45] This was not Bravo's first "French Leave" taking in a tight situation; having deserted from Fort Phil Kearny on May 9, 1867.[46]

Exercising extreme caution, Bradley and his scouts were sent on ahead and the column was formed in a defensive posture as recorded by Roe: *". . . we were formed in two parallel columns, the infantry on the left toward the river and the cavalry on the right, with orders to march at exactly the same pace as the infantry. The Gatling guns were in the rear, and the general officers (Terry and Gibbon, DCE) and their staffs in front, between the two lines."[47]* They had not gone far when a rider, who proved to be Bostwick, was sighted. Roe described the meeting:

"Galloping up to within hearing distance, he said excitedly, 'You have been looking for Indians all summer; you'll find all you want there'– pointing to a section of bench land which ran out into the valley and about six miles up. General Terry sent word to the leading cavalry (which happened to be my Troop) to go up onto the bench land and act as advance guard and right flank."[48]

Roe had not gone far before he noted two mounted men on a ridge perhaps 4 or 5 miles distant. As he studied the men through his field glasses, 14 warriors came out of a ravine about a mile in Roe's front and proceeded toward the men on the ridge. After observing many Indians on his right flank, Roe sent a written message describing the situation to Terry. At the halt to send this message, Roe was joined by Muggins Taylor who reported: *"The country is alive with Indians – I haven't been able to get anywhere near that smoke."[49]* Taylor then remained with Roe's detachment. Roe gives a very detailed and vivid description of what transpired next:

"We moved along up onto this bench land when suddenly, as if it had come out of the ground, appeared in our front a perfect skirmish line of mounted Indians reaching from the edge of the bench land all the way across and up to where the two men had been seen on horseback. Knowing that General Custer had some

Arikaras from the Missouri River, it occurred to me that perhaps a portion of the Seventh Cavalry had been successful; and being naturally anxious to know who we were, had put them out in an effort to locate us.

"At once I decided to try to communicate with them. Turning to the first sergeant, a man named Anderson (Alexander Anderson, Company F, Second Cavalry, DCE) – twenty years in the regiment and one of the best soldiers I have ever known – I said, 'Sergeant, take any two men in the Troop you wish and go ahead about fifteen or twenty yards. Leave an interval between yourselves, approach within a reasonable distance of those Indians, put a handkerchief on a gun, wave it, and see what the effect will be.'

"We observed some distance in the rear of that skirmish line a large body (undoubtedly three or four hundred) mounted men. While we were looking what was from all appearances a troop of cavalry – at least sixty or seventy men – dressed in dark clothes, marching by twos and with a guidon flying, started out from among them. They continued to the ridge where the original two had been seen, and halted; then one man went forward and joined those two.

"What appeared to be a second troop of cavalry now left the main body and merged with the others on the ridge; then two men – as though it might be the Captain and Lieutenant – joined the group, which would ordinarily be taken for officers. It soon developed that these apparent troops were Indians dressed in the clothing of General Custer's men whom they had killed.

"I immediately ordered the sergeant to move forward, saying that we would support him; he did so and soon disappeared, while I sighted him going down a slope into the very wide ravine of a creek (dry at that season), some seventy-five yards wide at the bottom, with a few cottonwood trees. He took to a trot and gallop; I did the same with the Troop, and just as we went up the slope on the far side came pop, pop, pop, pop, from the hostile skirmish line.

"As we appeared on the plateau, however, their ranks were breaking, and the Indians were circling their horses, which means 'Come on!' We could distinctly hear their war-whoops. The whole force on the ridge and the original two men were running helter-skelter to join the main body, which stood fast. Apparently all the plateau was alive with Indians.

"Anderson came over to me and said, 'As soon as I was within about seven hundred yards of the line I got off my horse and told Sullivan (Private John O'Sullivan, Company F, Second Cavalry, DCE) to wave his handkerchief. They at once opened fire.' The sergeant was a dead shot – could hit an antelope running. To show his good sense and judgment he said to me, 'I could have killed one or two Indians, but I didn't know whether the Lieutenant wanted to bring on an engagement or not.'

"In this wholly unexpected situation, with a prospect that our single Troop might soon be in a fight against overwhelming odds, our first thought was naturally, 'Where are Terry, Gibbon and Custer?' We instinctively turned and marched directly back to the edge of the bench land, having gone a quarter or a half mile

from it, expecting to find the main command near us; but it was back some two miles in the valley. I sent an orderly down with a message, and received word to stay where we were until dark and then come into camp, the orderly saying that they had bivouacked for the night. I remained on the ridge until about eight o'clock in the evening."[50]

Roe's observations were echoed by Private William H. White, a member of Roe's Company F:

"We saw hundreds of Indians on horseback as we were going into camp for that night. They were on the benches at the southwestward, and occasionally some of them raced their ponies past us, between us and the river. No shots were fired by them nor toward them, but my Troop F, led by Lieut. Charles F. Roe, exchanged a few long distance harmless shots with the Sioux warriors on the benchland. But darkness soon came, and we all settled for the night, with plenty of sentinels on guard."[51]

One aspect of the campaign which has not received enough scrutiny is the Montana Column going into camp in the face of an enemy at least their equal in strength. The purpose of the expedition was to find, and bring to battle, these very warriors. The Montana Column, particularly Colonel Gibbon, had been shamed early in the campaign by not striking the village when the opportunity presented itself on two separate occasions. This time the fault for the failure to act aggressively rested solely upon General Terry, the expedition's commander who was present on the field. Clearly Terry and Gibbon had no stomach for a fight and would only engage if forced by the Indians. Consequently, Roe was told to remain in his position to report on future developments in case the Lakota determined to carry the fight to the soldiers.

While Terry's writings are entirely devoid of reference to the situation faced by the command of June 26, Gibbon would explain the situation away in his own writings by indicating by the time the commander learned of the presence of large numbers of the enemy it was too dark to take action: *". . . the scouting parties were called in, who reported seeing quite a large number of Indians on the distant hills, but in the gathering darkness nothing could be plainly made out"[52]* and pleading inability to fathom the demeanor of the Indians. *"If he (Custer, DCE) had defeated the Indians and destroyed their camp, as the fires seemed to indicate, it was difficult to account for the presence of these Indians in our front, who were evidently watching us; whereas, if the report of the Crows was correct, and the Indians had defeated Custer, their bearing was equally inexplicable."[53]* This is a truly incredible argument, the premise being that no warrior force could have logically remained on the field after a battle regardless of the outcome. That being the case, it was apparently acceptable to simply ignore the presence of the enemy! The explanation offered by Lieutenant McClernand, while also weak, was much to be preferred to Gibbon's:

"It was rapidly growing dark when 'Muggins' Taylor returned and said what we saw in the distance was Custer and his cavalry. He was angry and excited, saying some of Custer's Indian scouts had ridden out from the column and fired on him, and he swore he would kill them when we joined forces. Captain Hughes of General Terry's staff said to his chief – 'for God's sake, General, let us push on.' The General replied, 'No, Hughes, if that supposed column be Custer's and he is in the same doubt that we are, we may fire into each other in the night."[54]

While this all sounds plausible on the surface, there are two major flaws with this story. First we are asked to believe that the General Terry, who had been almost frantic with apprehension over the location of Custer the previous day, has been informed that the same Custer has met with an unprecedented disaster – the same Terry who endangered his entire command in an attempt to contact Custer, went peacefully and unconcernedly into camp without establishing whether or not the force in his front was indeed the Seventh Cavalry. Secondly, as neither Gibbon nor McClernand is able to deal with the contents of the messages exchanged between Roe and the command element, they are simply dismissed as vague reports lacking substance and verification.

Fortunately for the faint-hearted Terry and Gibbon, the warriors were only attempting to screen the withdrawal of the village; an event witnessed by Roe before rejoining the command:

> *"In the rear of the main body of Indians, I could see a large extent of country almost literally covered with horses and people apparently going in the direction of the Big Horn Mountains further south [in what is now northern Wyoming]; and subsequently learned that this was the large Indian village moving away. We also noticed, across the river, the bench lands and the stream coming together to make a valley on the other side. On a hill beyond this valley a number of dark objects could be dimly seen; looking at them for some time, we concluded that they were dead buffalo.*

> *"They were in fact Custer, his five Troops of the Seventh Cavalry and their horses – all dead."*[55]

Roe was not the only officer to nearly march into a situation from which it would be extremely difficult to extricate himself. Bradley, with his detachment of 11 men, formed the advance party on the left flank of the command. As he proceeded down the valley, he too noticed large numbers of Indians beginning to gather in his front. At about the same time Roe was being fired upon, *"a few shots were exchanged by the Indians and a few of our eager men who pushed to the front."*[56] What concerned Bradley most, however, was observing *"squad after squad of mounted savages"*[57] filtering into some woods in his front through which his small detachment must pass. Fortunately, just before reaching the woods, he received orders to halt and hold his position until the cavalry had finished watering their horses. After the cavalry had finished watering, Bradley's detachment was to return to camp, a task accomplished soon after dark.

Despite the nonchalant tone of Gibbon's writings, the command was obviously concerned they would be attacked as the organization of their camp revealed: *"No fires were allowed, and* **we lay upon our arms** *,(emphasis the author's) arranged in a square, but with a very weak face indeed down the river, that side (the command's rear, DCE), I believe, being occupied by only a guard of twenty-odd men. The animals were secured within the square."*[58] Although omitted by Bradley, McClernand mentions the Gatling guns being *"placed to the best advantage to repel a possible attack"* and that the troopers were sent, by company, to the river to fill all possible vessels with water.[59]

All being secure in the camp: *". . . the officers assembled in groups and talked over the events of the day. I found that a majority of the infantry officers placed confidence in the report brought by the Crows of Custer's overthrow, and were prepared for unpleasant disclosures upon the morrow. Some of the cavalry officers also shared in this conviction, but the majority of them and about all of the staff were wholly skeptical and still had faith that Custer had been victorious if he had fought at all."*[60] It seems incredible that the command could have had no apprehension about Custer after exchanging fire with Indians wearing uniforms and carrying guidons. Bradley's comment on the inability of some of his fellow officers to comprehend the events of the day is insightful: *"So obstinate is human nature in some of its manifestations that there were actually men in the command who lay down to sleep that night in the firm conviction, notwithstanding all the disclosures of the day, that there was not an Indian in our front and that the men seen were members of Custer's command."*[61]

Morning dawned without an Indian in sight. The command pushed forward with flanking parties on the high ground on both sides of the river. McClernand described the command's arrival at the abandoned village site:

"... we had gone but a short distance when two tepees were seen through the trees, and ascending the low sandstone bluff at the extreme western sweep of the Little Big Horn, we saw in our immediate front a large bottom where an immense Indian village had stood but a few hours before. A few tepees were still standing, in which several dead Indians were found. The enemy had evidently left in haste; numerous buffalo-robes, blankets, tepee-poles, and camp utensils were scattered over the ground, together with great quantities of dried meat. Fifty or sixty ponies had also been left behind."[62]

McClernand was obviously unfamiliar with the plains Indian custom of abandoning the property of the dead. The debris from the village were erroneously interpreted as signs the Indians had departed in great haste, probably due to the advance of the Terry-Gibbon Column, when the Indians had, in actuality, made a very orderly and methodical withdrawal. It was also the custom to move the camp whenever a death occurred. Accordingly, the village was moved the night of the 25th slightly to the north and away from the river. Unwilling to re-erect their tepees, many families constructed brush wickiups.[63] The presence of these wickiups, reported by military observers as shelters for unattached warriors from the agencies,[64] has made the attempt to determine the size of the warrior force almost impossible. Any elation felt by the command over these discoveries was only temporary. McClernand's account continues:

"A buckskin shirt, a garment much affected on the plains in those days by some officers, was found with the name Sturgis on it. It was discolored by blood stains, and had been pierced in two places by a bullet. It was assumed to have been the property of Lieutenant Sturgis of the 7th Cavalry."[65]

The mood of apprehension slowly changed to one of horror as each new discovery was made and reported: Dr. Paulding found a bloodstained buckskin jacket marked *"Lieut Porter, 7th Cavalry"*[66] with a bullet entry hole in the right breast and the exit hole under the right shoulder;[67] a pair of cavalry officer pants;[68] the scalp of Bloody Knife;[69] Dr. Lord's pocketcase;[70] gloves marked *"Yates, 7th Cav."*;[71] several items belonging to Lieutenant Sturgis: spurs;[72] bloody drawers marked *"Sturgis – Seventh Cavalry"*;[73] and his shirt, with *"collar button still in the neck"*;[74] and a man's heart with a lariat tied to it.[75] Unfortunately these grisly discoveries was just the beginning. Private Homer Coon, Company I, 7th Infantry, reported: *"In passing through their camp we came across a dead cavalry horse which had been cut open and a dead naked soldier was forced head foremost into the horse's belly."*[76] An indeterminate number of decapitated remains were also found. John Burkman reported: *".3 heads were tied to a lodge pole in the village, with wire strung behind the ears, and burned."*[77]; while Herendeen reported that the heads of four soldiers were found.[78] Gibbon's advance had discovered three heads under an overturned kettle, identifying two of them as Private John E. Armstrong, of Company A, and John J. McGinnis, of Company G.[79] Private John Foley reportedly identified a head found under an overturned kettle, which may have been the kettle containing the remains of Armstrong and McGinnis, as belonging to a red-haired corporal of Company G.[80] Although brown-haired, Otto Hagemann was the only corporal of Company G killed in the valley fight.[81] With Varnum's revelation that Sturgis' head was also found in the village, the minimum number of heads discovered was four, three of which came from troopers in Reno's battalion.

Although suffering far fewer casualties than the soldiers (see Appendix 2 for the known Indian fatalities), many dead warriors were discovered by the troops. Lieutenant Roe described the discovery of the dead warriors left in the village:

> *". . . we found that they were funeral tepees, in one of which were five dead Indians and in the other three;[82] around the outside were dead ponies, indicating that the slain warriors were chiefs. These tepees were hung with black blankets, the bodies raised a foot from the ground, with all their war bonnets, heavily beaded shirts, leggings and moccasins on them."[83]*

Private William H. White, a member of Lieutenant Gustavus C. Doane's party collecting bedding material for the wounded on June 27 described what became of these bodies:

> *"We roughly tumbled the corpses around on the ground in the tepees, to get from them the buffalo robes and blankets wrapped about them. These were to be used for making beds and litter hammocks for the wounded men with Reno. Incidentally, we looked with great interest upon the fine costumes and the Indian implements and trinkets wrapped in with the dead warriors. With one of them we found a 50-caliber single-shot Sharps rifle, and with one or two others we found cap-and-ball revolvers. Of course, I believe that all of the warrior bodies that could be found were robbed of their wrappings as well as their buffalo-skin shelters, and it is likely that not many of their personal belongings were left with them."[84]*

Ordered on a scout up the valley, Captain Ball subsequently discovered some 30 bodies on scaffolds [85] and many more in a coulee. [86] According to General Terry's June 28th dispatch, Ball discovered a heavy trail leading into the valley that was no more than 5 days old *". . . and would seem to show that at least two large bands united here just before the battle."[87]*

While the soldiers contemplated the meaning of their horrifying discoveries in the village, they received word of Bradley's discovery of the bodies of Custer's command on the hills to the east. Indicative of the shock experienced by the command over this intelligence is the disparity in the officer's accounts. McClernand related: *"All were horrified by a message received about this time from Lieutenant Bradley, our chief of scouts, saying he had counted 196 dead cavalrymen on the hills across the river. The objects seen the day before looking like buffaloes lying down were probably dead comrades and their horses."[88]* Roe agreed with McClernand that Bradley had sent an orderly with the report, but recalled the message to have been: *"Up to this time I have counted two hundred dead officers and soldiers. I have never met Custer, but from photographs which I have seen of him I think one of the bodies is the General's."[89]* Gibbon, in addition to remembering a different number of bodies, recalled that Bradley reported in person: *". . . the officer in charge of the mounted infantry party, in the hills to the north (Gibbon means east, DCE) of us, rode up to where General Terry and I sat upon our horses, and his voice trembled as he said, 'I have a very sad report to make. I have counted one hundred and ninety-seven dead bodies lying in the hills!' 'White men?' was the first question asked. 'Yes, white men.'"[90]* Bradley was killed in 1877 at the Battle of the Big Hole before he could complete his journal beyond the events of June 26th. His July 25, 1876 letter to the *Helena Herald* concerning the mutilation of Custer's dead briefly mentions the discovery of the bodies: *"I was scouting the hills some two or three miles to the left of the column upon the opposite bank of the river from that traversed by the column itself, when the body of a horse attracted our attention to the field of Custer's fight, and hastening in that direction the appalling sight was revealed to us of his entire command in the embrace of death. This was the first discovery of the field, and the first hasty count made of the slain, resulting in the finding of the 197 bodies reported by General Terry."*[91]

The evening of the 26th Reno had buried his dead and shifted his position slightly to get away from the stench of the decaying animals. On the morning of the 27th Godfrey was frustrated by Reno's apparent lack of resolve as to how to proceed: *"Our commanding officer seemed to think the Indians had some 'trap' set for us, and required our men to hold themselves in readiness to occupy the pits at a moment's notice. Nothing seemed determined except to stay where we were. Not an Indian was in sight, but a few ponies were seen grazing down in the valley."*[92] About 9:30 AM a dust cloud was observed and Reno ordered Arikara scouts Young Hawk and Forked Horn to determine if the approaching column were soldiers or the Lakota returning.[93] The scouts, after observing the dust was raised by troops, returned to report this fact to Reno without making their presence known to Terry. Lieutenants Wallace and Hare were then dispatched by Reno to contact the troops, leaving in such haste they didn't bother to saddle their horses. Wallace and Hare related the details of Reno's engagements and were then asked if they knew Custer's whereabouts. McClernand recalled:

> *"'Where is Custer,' they were asked. Wallace replied, 'The last we saw of him he was going along that high bluff' (pointing in a general direction to the bluffs down stream from the position where he had located Reno), 'toward the lower end of the village. He took off his hat and waved to us. We do not know where he is now.' We have found him,' said General Terry, his eyes filling with tears, for all now felt the truth of the statement shouted to us by our Crow scouts from across the Big Horn, and fully expected to find Custer's remains on the stricken field discovered by Bradley.*
>
> *"Reno's messengers sat their horses aghast at the information given them, and seemed slow to grasp the fact that their detachment had not played the major role in the drama that had been enacted."*[94]

Apparently, about this same time Muggins Taylor made contact with Reno's detachment on the bluffs as Godfrey reported: *"A white man, Harris, I think, soon came up with a note from General Terry, addressed to General Custer, dated June 26, stating that two of our Crow scouts had given information that our column had been whipped and nearly all had been killed; that he did not believe their story, but was coming with medical assistance. The scout said that he could not get to our lines the night before,*[95] *as the Indians were on the alert."*[96] Taylor, according to Godfrey's account, was followed in turn by Bradley and Terry with his staff:

> *". . . Lieutenant Bradley, 7th Infantry, came into our lines, and asked where I was. Greeting most cordially my old friend, I immediately asked, 'Where is Custer?' He replied, 'I don't know, but I suppose he was killed, as we counted 197 dead bodies. I don't suppose any escaped.' We were simply dumfounded. This was the first intimation we had of his fate. It was hard to realize; it did not seem possible.*
>
> *General Terry and staff, and officers of General Gibbon's column soon after approached, and their coming was greeted with prolonged, hearty cheers. The grave countenance of the General awed the men to silence. The officers assembled to meet their guests. There was scarcely a dry eye; hardly a word was spoken, but quivering lips and hearty grasping of hands gave token of thankfulness for the relief and grief for the misfortune."*[97]

According to Godfrey, the remainder of the day was occupied in conveying the wounded to Gibbon's camp and some visiting among the officers. Apparently some uncomplimentary remarks regarding Reno's conduct were made to officers of the Montana Column. Mathey testified: *"Captain Newlan [98] on the 27th asked me about Major Reno's conduct. Someone seemed to have said something about it. I declined saying anything to him, though he seemed to have information from someone . . . the most they seemed to question was his conduct in the charge, and I know nothing about that."* [99]

Godfrey was not the only one who could not believe what had happened. Benteen questioned Terry about Custer's whereabouts and was informed: *"To the best of my knowledge and belief he lies on this ridge about four miles below here with all of his command killed."* Benteen replied: *"I can hardly believe it. I think he is somewhere down the Bighorn grazing his horses. At the battle of the Washita he went off and left part of his command, and I think he would do it again."* [100] This reply, linking an illogical act of grazing horses in the midst of a combat situation while the remainder of the command is abandoned to its fate, represents an almost textbook case of psychological defense mechanism. Terry then told Benteen to go and look for himself. Consistent with the behavior associated with massive feelings of guilt, Benteen apparently could not stay away; needing to verify the disaster for himself. Arriving on the knoll where Custer's body lay, Benteen was heard to remark: *"There he is God damn him, he will never fight anymore."* [101] According to Walter Camp's interview with Charles F. Roe, a pale and troubled looking Benteen remarked upon his return to Reno Hill: *"We found them, but I did not expect that we would."* [102]

While Terry had gone with Wallace and Hare to Reno's hilltop position, Gibbon had continued up the valley to select a campsite. He described the scene in his 1877 article:

> *"Nearly the whole valley was black and smoking with the fire which had swept over it (the Indians had fired the grass to screen their withdrawal, DCE), and it was with some difficulty I could find grass sufficient for our animals, as it existed only in spots close to the stream where too green to burn. Except the fire, the ground presented but few evidences of the conflict which had taken place. Now and then a dead horse was seen; but as I approached a bend of the creek (for it is little more than a creek), just below the hill occupied by the troops, I came upon the body of a soldier lying on his face near a dead horse. He was stripped, his scalp gone, his head beaten in, and his body filled with bullet-holes and arrows. Close by was another body, also close to a dead horse, lying, like the other, on its face, but partially clothed, and this was recognized by one of our officers as the body of Captain McIntosh (The body was recognized by Lieutenant Gibson, Lieutenant McIntosh's brother-in-law, there is no record of a brevet to captain for McIntosh, DCE). More bodies of both men and horses were found close by, and it was noted that the bodies of men and horses laid almost always **in pairs** (emphasis by Colonel Gibbon, DCE), and as this was the ground over which Colonel Reno's command retired towards the hills after its charge down the valley, the inference was drawn, that in the run the horses must have been killed first, and the riders after they fell."* [103]

First Lieutenant William Lewis English, Company I, 7th Infantry, entered the following in his diary for June 27: *"Stench of dead bodies and horses, fearful around us. I shall write the account of the disaster in another place (as far as is known he never wrote an account of the fight, DCE)."* [104] The vivid description of the camp to which Reno's wounded were conveyed contained in the diary of Captain Walter Clifford, Company E, 7th Infantry, reveals him to have been a man of great compassion and an artist in describing his feelings. While an artist is able to express what most of us cannot, he too is unable to express the totality of his feeling. The haunting images portrayed makes one wonder about the much deeper feelings Clifford could not describe.

"Our camp is surrounded with ghastly remains of the recent butchery. The days are scorching hot and still, and the air is thick with the stench of the festering bodies. We miss the laughing gaiety that usually attends a body of soldiery even on the battlefield. A brooding sorrow hangs like a pall over our every thought. It seems too horrible for belief – that we must wake and find it only a shuddering dream. Every sound comes to us in a muffled monotone, and a dull, dogged feeling of revenge seems to be the prevailing sentiment. The repulsive looking green flies that have been feasting on the swollen bodies of the dead, are attracted to the camp fires by the smell of cooking meat. They come in such swarms that a persevering swing of a tree branch is necessary to keep them from settling on the food . . . They crawl over the neck and face, into eyes and ears, under the sleeves with a greedy eagerness and such clammy, sticky feet as to drive taste and inclination for food away . .

"Let us bury our dead and flee from this rotting atmosphere.

"A hush has fallen over the sleeping camp. The silence is death-like. Half fearfully I hasten to the river bank and listen to the sobbing gurgle of its waters as they hasten towards the busy east with their heart-breaking story . . . the polluted air is here also, and one is forced to lie with face close to the water to be rid of the deadly poison that is permeating the clothing and filling the lungs with every respiration. A little delay on this death-stricken ground and we will remain forever."[105]

---

[1] See Lieutenant James H. Bradley "The March of the Montana Column" pages 142 – 143.

[2] See Edgar I. Stewart "Custer's Luck" page 284.

[3] See Barbara Zimmerman "Gibbon's Montana Column" page 7.

[4] See Roger Darling "A Sad And Terrible Blunder" page 126.

[5] See Roger Darling "A Sad And Terrible Blunder" page 128.

[6] See Roger Darling "A Sad And Terrible Blunder" page 128.

[7] See Roger Darling "A Sad And Terrible Blunder" page 140.

[8] See Edgar I. Stewart "Custer's Luck" page 286. Stewart lists Kirtland as a lieutenant, but he had been promoted captain on July 28 , 1866 when the number of regiments in the peacetime army was increased. See John M. Carroll "Roll Call on the Little Big Horn" page 139.

[9] As rationed, the Montana Column would exhaust their supplies by July 3, while Custer would exhaust his full rations (he carried an extra three days supply of hard bread) by July 4.

[10] See Roger Darling "A Sad And Terrible Blunder" page 142.

[11] See Lieutenant James H. Bradley "The March of the Montana Column" page 147.

[12] See Roger Darling "A Sad And Terrible Blunder" page 144. The Montana Column suffered from their unfamiliarity with pack mules as had the Seventh Cavalry before them. It is difficult to reconcile the post battle image of a Terry anxious to junction with Custer and carry out his plan of cooperative action, with the plodding events and indecisive actions that indicated a total lack of planning. In fairness to Terry, it is difficult to determine how much blame for the lack of preparation to ascribe to Gibbon who, until his illness, was in complete charge of the column.

[13] Note that Bradley is unaware of any contemplated joint action with the Seventh Cavalry. It would seem logical, although by no means necessary, that the chief of scouts would have been aware of such a contemplated junction as, under those circumstances, it would be a priority to locate Custer's command.

[14] See Lieutenant James H. Bradley "The March of the Montana Column" page 148.

[15] See Edward J. McClernand "On Time For Disaster" page 47.

[16] Distances marched were determined by two odometers fastened to either wheel of a light cart under the charge of Sergeant Becker. See Edward J. McClernand "On Time For Disaster" page 55.

[17] See Edward J. McClernand "On Time For Disaster" pages 47 – 49.

[18] See Lieutenant James H. Bradley "The March of the Montana Column" page 149.

[19] See Roger Darling "A Sad And Terrible Blunder" page 168.

[20] See Edward J. McClernand "On Time For Disaster" page 49.

[21] Bradley apparently suffered from the same false impression as Terry. His Crow scouts, who undoubtedly showed him his "short cut" to the command, were well acquainted with the country, as were the officers and men who had participated in Captain Ball's April 29 scout. The problem here was not lack of a guide, but failure to use the competent guides available. While Terry would not learn from his error in judgment, Bradley would finally come to his senses and extricate the command from a tight spot.

[22] See Lieutenant James H. Bradley "The March of the Montana Column" page 149.

[23] See Charles Francis Roe "Custer's Last Battle" page 4. Of all the statements made after the fact concerning a plan for mutual cooperation, Roe's seems to fit best with the actual events. Custer planned a dawn attack on June 26 and Terry's *"at or near"* remark clearly indicates the intention to serve as a blocking force to seal a potential escape route, rather than as an actively participating cooperating force. The Montana Column's serving as blocking force would also be consistent with the offer to Custer of the Gatling guns and the entire cavalry force.

[24] See Charles Francis Roe "Custer's Last Battle" page 4.

[25] Here the young and inexperienced Roe obviously overestimated the capabilities of the troops in an attempt to please his commander. Fortunately, he was not called upon to make good on his estimate.

[26] See Charles Francis Roe "Custer's Last Battle" page 4.

[27] Lieutenant Roe reported: *"About 11 o'clock word has passed along the column from the rear that the two Gatling guns were lost; so the command halted and the General told Captain Hughes to see if he could locate those guns, order them abandoned if necessary, and tell the men to come on with the horses."* See Charles Francis Roe "Custer's Last Battle" page 5.

[28] There is only one documented instance of the battery becoming separated; that occurring about 11 PM.

[29] Contrasting this rate with the 2.7 mph, almost equal to the 3 mph walk rate for cavalry, Custer averaged on his night march of June 24 gives an indication of the rigors of the march. It should also be noted that while Custer's march was undertaken in an attempt to conceal his presence from the enemy, Terry's march had no such tactical imperative.

[30] See Edward J. McClernand "On Time For Disaster" page 50.

[31] Captain Ball's troop had the lead during this phase of the march. Why Ball, who had not been on the divide in April, should be chosen as the pathfinder in preference to the Crow scouts, remains a mystery.

[32] Lieutenant Roe was fortunate to escape injury when his horse made a misstep, plunging them in a 15 foot drop into a side ravine. See Roger Darling "A Sad And Terrible Blunder" page 178.

[33] See Lieutenant James H. Bradley "The March of the Montana Column" pages 150 – 151.

[34] See Edward J. McClernand "On Time For Disaster" pages 50 – 51. John Gray feels Terry had been hurrying to reach a blocking position at the junction of the Little Big Horn and Big Horn Rivers. Terry's statement, especially in the absence of any definite plan of mutual cooperation in the written orders to Custer, may very well indicate that the overall strategy determined on the *Far West* on June 21 was for the Terry–Gibbon Column to function as a blocking force while Custer's force struck the blow. See "Centennial Campaign" pages 186 – 187.

[35] See George A. Schneider "The Freeman Journal" page 57. Brisbin, in an 1892 letter to Godfrey would recall that Gibbon was anything but well when he rejoined the column: *"Gibbon, although still sick . . . took command. . . . I remember he rode with his pants open and his belly was much swelled. He must have suffered greatly, but did not complain."* See Roger Darling "A Sad and Terrible Blunder" page 238.

[36] These were Goes Ahead, White Man Runs Him and Hairy Moccasin.

[37] Dr. Paulding noted in his diary entry of June 26: *". . . Custer had attacked a village of 1900 lodges yesterday a few miles up the Little Horn, had got corralled with a large portion of his command in a ravine down which he was going and that his men had all been shot down like buffalo, none or very few at any rate escaping except themselves. We did not believe this story, but our scouts did and were afraid to go any further. Said the smoke was from the timber set fire to by the Sioux to burn out some of Custer's men."* See W. Boyes "Surgeon's Diary With The Custer Relief Column" page 21.

[38] Goes Ahead revealed to Walter Camp the reason the Crow scouts told Bradley Custer's command had been annihilated although they had not personally witnessed the event; they had seen Reno's panic retreat and assumed all of the soldiers would suffer the same fate. See Kenneth Hammer "Custer in '76" page 174.

[39] See Lieutenant James H. Bradley 'The March of the Montana Column" pages 152 – 154

[40] See Lieutenant James H. Bradley "The March of the Montana Column" page 155.

[41] See Edward J. McClernand "On Time For Disaster" page 52.

[42] See Charles Francis Roe "Custer's Last Battle" page 5.

[43] See Colonel John Gibbon "Last Summer's Expedition Against the Sioux" page 295.

[44] See Captain Michael J. Koury "Diaries of the Little Big Horn" page 5. While McClernand set the fee at $500, $200 was paid for similar service during the campaign and, as Terry was the authorizing entity, his figure has been accepted.

[45] See Lieutenant James H. Bradley "The March of the Montana Column" pages 156 – 157.

[46] See John S. Gray "Custer's Last Campaign" page 100.

[47] See Charles Francis Roe "Custer's Last Battle" page 7.

[48] See Charles Francis Roe "Custer's Last Battle" page 7.

[49] See Charles Francis Roe "Custer's Last Battle" page 7.

[50] See Charles Francis Roe "Custer's Last Battle" page 7.

[51] See Thomas B. Marquis "Custer On The Little Bighorn" page 34.

[52] See Colonel John Gibbon "Last Summer's Expedition Against the Sioux and Its Great Catastrophe" page 297.

[53] See "Gibbon on the Sioux Campaign of 1876" page 27.

[54] See Edward J. McClernand "On Time For Disaster" pages 57 – 58.

[55] See Charles Francis Roe "Custer's Last Battle" pages 7 – 8. There was at least one live observer on the battlefield as the Oglala Fears Nothing observed the approach of Terry's column from the battlefield aided by captured field glasses. See Dale T. Schoenberger "End of Custer" page 248.

[56] See Lieutenant James H. Bradley "The March of the Montana Column" page 158.

[57] See Lieutenant James H. Bradley "The March of the Montana Column" page 158.

[58] See Lieutenant James H. Bradley "The March of the Montana Column" page 160.

[59] See Edward J. McClernand "On Time For Disaster" page 58.

[60] See Lieutenant James H. Bradley "The March of the Montana Column" pages 160 – 161.

[61] See Lieutenant James H. Bradley "The March of the Montana Column" page 161. While Bradley names no officers, McClernand's account indicates he was one of those in question.

[62] See Edward J. McClernand "On Time For Disaster" page 59.

[63] See Thomas B. Marquis "Custer On The Little Big Horn" page 91.

[64] For example see Charles Francis Roe "Custer's Last Battle" page 10.

[65] See Edward J. McClernand "On Time For Disaster" page 59. McClernand's is the only account to mention finding a buckskin jacket belonging to Sturgis. There are many accounts of recovering the bloodstained buckskin jacket of Lieutenant Porter and McClernand may have confused Porter's jacket with the discovery of Lieutenant Sturgis' bloody drawers.

[66] See Michael J. Koury "Diaries of the Little Big Horn" page 47.

[67] See Francis B. Taunton "Custer's Field" page 23. On February 8, 1876, with a second child on the way, and the hardship of separation from his family weighing heavily on his mind, Porter wrote to the Adjutant General of the Army to request a transfer to the General Staff. Although his application was endorsed by senior officers and the Maine delegation in the House of Representatives, no immediate action was taken by the army and James Porter marched to his death with the Custer column. See Lenora Snedeker "The Tragedy of the James Porter Family" page 4.

[68] See Francis B. Taunton "Custer's Field" page 23.

[69] O. G. Libby "The Arikara Narrative" page 111.

[70] See Edgar I. Stewart "Custer's Luck" page 465.

[71] See Francis B. Taunton "Custer's Field" page 23.

[72] See Francis B. Taunton "Custer's Field" page 23.

[73] See Colonel John Gibbon "Last Summer's Expedition Against the Sioux" page 298.

[74] See Francis B. Taunton "Custer's Field" page 23. This is an indication that Sturgis was decapitated, an event disclosed by Varnum at the 50th reunion.

[75] See Charles Francis Roe "Custer's Last Battle" page 10. Roe, who apparently believed Longfellow's tale of the revenge of Rain In The Face, felt the heart may have been Tom Custer's. Most probably it belonged to one of Reno's troopers killed in the valley.

[76] See Francis B. Taunton "Custer's Field" page 23. Captain Walter Clifford, Company E, 7th Infantry, and Private James M. Rooney, Company F, 7th Cavalry, both mention finding the body of a trooper and horse in the village although the locations are unclear and they do not mention the body as being thrust into the horse. If Kanipe was mistaken in identifying Sergeant Bustard's body as being found in the village (Edgerly reported that Bustard's body was found in the group around Keogh) these reports may all refer to a single individual.. Hardorff believes this individual to have

been Private William Brown of Company F, 7th Cavalry. See Richard G. Hardorff "The Custer Battle Casualties" pages 108 - 109.

[77] See Francis B. Taunton "Custer's Field" page 24.

[78] See Francis B. Taunton "Custer's Field" page 23.

[79] See Richard G. Hardorff "The Custer Battle Casualties" page 16. Private William D. Nugent of Company A, 7th Cavalry, claimed, however, that Armstrong's head was found on a pole. See John M. Carroll "They Rode With Custer" page 20.

[80] See Kenneth Hammer "Custer In '76" page 147.

[81] Corporal James Martin of Company G, also brown-haired, was killed in the hilltop fight. See John M. Carroll "They Rode With Custer" page 170.

[82] The Arikara Young Hawk identified one of the bodies as *Chat-ka*, a Lakota who had been a scout at Fort Lincoln. See O. G. Libby "The Arikara Narrative" page 109. This same warrior has been identified as Left Hand, who scouted for the army from June 9 until December 9, 1875. See Kenneth Hammer "Custer In '76" page 284. Richard G. Hardorff believes these burial lodges were located opposite the mouth of Deep Ravine. See "Lakota Recollections of the Custer Fight" page 28.

[83] See Charles Francis Roe "Custer's Last Battle" page 10.

[84] See Richard G. Hardorff "Hokahey! A Good Day To Die!" pages 109 - 110.

[85] See George M. Clark "Scalp Dance" page 23.

[86] Members of Ball's scouting party told Private Dennis Lynch, Company F, 7th Cavalry, they had found many dead warriors in a coulee but the stench was so overpowering they had been unable to count them. See Kenneth Hammer "Custer In '76" page 139.

[87] See Fred Dustin "The Custer Tragedy" page 190.

[88] See Edward J. McClernand "On Time For Disaster" page 60.

[89] See Charles Francis Roe "Custer's Last Battle" page 11. Godfrey, who was personally informed of the disaster by Bradley would report that Bradley was unsure whether Custer's body was among those discovered.

[90] See Colonel John Gibbon "Last Summer's Expedition Against the Sioux" page 299.

[91] See Lieutenant James H. Bradley "The March of the Montana Column" page 172.

[92] See E. S. Godfrey "Custer's Last Battle 1876" page 35.

[93] See O. G. Libby "The Arikara Narrative" page 107.

[94] See Edward J. McClernand "On Time For Disaster" page 61.

[95] As only Taylor and Bostwick had attempted to contact Custer's command on the 26th, Godfrey was obviously mistaken as to the name. John Gray names Taylor as this messenger. See "Centennial Campaign" page 193.

[96] See E. S. Godfrey "Custer's Last Battle 1876" pages 35 – 36.

[97] See E. S. Godfrey "Custer's Last Battle 1876" page 36.

[98] First Lieutenant Henry James Nolan, Quartermaster of the 7th Cavalry, had been serving as Acting Assistant Quartermaster on Terry's staff. He was promoted captain effective June 25, 1876.

[99] See Ronald H. Nichols "The Reno Court of Inquiry" page 522.

[100] See Evan S. Connell "Son of the Morning Star" page 78.

[101] See Evan S. Connell "Son of the Morning Star" page 78. There has been some controversy over whether Benteen actually made this statement. In a letter to Theodore Goldin, dated February 17, 1896, Benteen comments on the events of the 27th: *"At my own request, Gen. Terry permitted me to mount what was left of my troop and go to Custer's field, soon after he joined us on the 27th. When I returned, I said to Lieut. Maguire of Engineers, 'By the Lord Harry, old man, 'twas a ghastly sight; but what a big winner the U. S. Govt. would have been if only Custer and his gang could have been taken!' The Lord, in His own good time had at last rounded the scoundrels up, taking, however, many good and innocent men with them!"* See John M. Carroll "The Benteen–Goldin Letters" page 271.

[102] See Kenneth Hammer "Custer in '76" page 250.

[103] See Michael J. Koury "Gibbon on the Sioux Campaign of 1876" page 30.

[104] See Francis B. Taunton "Custer's Field" page 22.

[105] See Francis B. Taunton "Custer's Field" pages 22 – 23.

Fort Abraham Lincoln with the Missouri River on the extreme left. Note the tents near the river. *Photo Courtesy Little Bighorn Battlefield National Monument.*

Crazy Horse Ford. The northern ford, variously referred to as Ford D and Crazy Horse Ford, from the west bank. Note the narrow opening between the trees which screen the high banks behind. This is the only place on the river that corresponds with Colonel Gibbon's description of the crossing used when he visited the battlefield. Gibbon's account indicates that the body of Mark Kellogg was found within a short distance of this crossing. The relatively unmolested nature of the corpse indicates, in my opinion, that Kellogg died early in the fight, when the warriors were still preoccupied with fighting the soldiers rather than plundering and mutilating the bodies. Kellogg was probably killed during the withdrawal from this ford when Custer abandoned his attempt to capture the noncombatants. *Photo by author.*

Chapter 18

Requiem

On the morning of the 28th, the Seventh Cavalry gathered together the pitifully few tools in the combined commands[1] and headed down river to bury their dead. Godfrey described their first view of the field:

"The morning was bright, and from the high bluffs we had a clear view of Custer's battle-field. We saw a large number of objects that looked like white boulders scattered over the field. Glasses were brought into requisition, and it was announced that these objects were the dead bodies. Captain Weir exclaimed, 'Oh, how white they look!'"[2]

Corporal John E. Hammon, Company G, 7th Cavalry, recalled his sojourn to Custer's field:

"Upon arriving at the Custer battle ground each troop was marched in column of fours, dismounting, and each troop burying dead to a certain point, covering the whole battle ground. The men's bodies were found all stripped, scalped, heads knocked in, and bodies mutilated. Many times in taking hold of a body to lift it into the grave the skin would slip from the wrists, or the shoulders became dislocated, etc. Custer's body was found at the western end of the field on a little knoll, a little to the south of its crest; lying on his back, head uphill, his left foot lying natural, his right heel lying upon a dead horse. His left hand was lying natural, his right lay out at right angles from the body at full length, the hand twisted as if something had been wrenched out of it. There was a dead soldier lying under the calf of his right leg alongside of the dead horse. Three bullet holes were found on his person; one in the left side under the heart in the ribs; one in the left side of the head in the ear; the other in the right forearm.[3] He was not scalped or mutilated a particle.[4] Tom Custer, his brother, was found dead a little north of where Custer lay, and on top of the knoll. I did not see where he was hit, but he was scalped clear down around the ears, his skull mashed, and his abdomen slashed crosswise and longitudinally; and but for his initials on his left arm I would not have recognized him. Four men in G Troop buried Custer where it lay; and I signed the proofs of his death for the life insurance company, which was done on Powder River before Capt. Smith of Gen. Terry's staff, some six weeks or thereabouts afterwards."[5]

As the location of the bodies provides a major clue in any reconstruction of the Custer fight, significant emphasis must be placed on the condition of the field as observed on June 28. For a more complete account than the following, refer to Francis B. Taunton *"Custer's Field: A Scene of Sickening Ghastly Horror,"* Douglas D. Scott, et al *"Archaeological Perspectives on the Battle of the Little Bighorn,"* Douglas D. Scott and Richard A. For, Jr. *"Archaeological Insights into The Custer Battle,"* and two works by Richard G. Hardorff *"Markers, Artifacts and Indian Testimony: Preliminary Findings on The Custer Battle,"* and *"The Custer Battle Casualties: Burials, Exhumations, and Reinterments."*

One or more bodies were located in 8 distinct regions of the field: the region comprising Minneconjou Ford at the mouth of Medicine Tail and Deep Coulees; Calhoun and Greasy Grass Ridges; Calhoun Hill; the Keogh position in the coulee east of Calhoun Hill; the region between the Keogh position and Custer Hill; Last Stand, or Custer Hill; the basin west of the present monument comprising the often referred to South Skirmish Line and Deep Ravine; and the area from Crazy Horse Ford to the National Cemetery which is northwest of the monument. Each of these regions will be described below.

The body furthest upstream was that of Corporal John Foley of Company C[6] which lay on a rise between Medicine Tail and Deep Coulees. [7] The body of First Sergeant James Butler of Company L was found in Deep Coulee along with the bodies of 4 other troopers[8] including trumpeter Henry C. Dose of Company G,[9] detailed as an orderly to General Custer. As there are no markers in Deep Coulee, it is impossible at this date to determine whether the deaths of Butler and the four other troopers were connected. [10] As has been shown in Chapter 17, at least one body[11] was found on the west bank of the river, opposite the mouth of Deep Ravine. Coupled with the discovery of the body of Nathan Short on the Rosebud, this means at least eight bodies were discovered outside of the present boundaries of Custer's field.

Benteen, in an obvious attempt to justify his failure to comply with his commander's orders to quickly come to his aid, needed the battle to have been of short duration, certainly less than an hour.[12] He would therefore testify that he believed Custer's command had already been annihilated when Martin reached him with Cooke's written order. [13] In reviewing the position of the bodies on Custer's field, he would be forced to assert there were no signs of an active resistance (*". . . it was a rout, a panic, till the last man was killed, that there was no line formed. There was no line on the battlefield; you can take a handful of corn and scatter it over the floor and make just such lines."*[14]), else the battle could not have been the short one necessary to make his inactivity somewhat defensible. McClernand's account would have been extremely galling to Benteen: *"The line he (Custer, DCE) established on the ridge mentioned, running from this position toward the river, showed more care taken in deploying and placing the men than, in my opinion, was shown on any other part of the entire field, including, of course, Reno's several positions."*[15] Even Benteen was unwilling to adhere to his fabrication without exception, stating: *"Only where General Custer was found were there any evidences of a stand."*[16] Fortunately for history, others, who had less to hide than Benteen, described, in detail, evidence of lines of resistance. The first such position encountered was the one occupied by Company L on what is now known as Calhoun Hill.

Edgerly, [17] Wallace [18] and Moylan[19] agreed that Company L was found in skirmish order, with Calhoun and Crittenden [20] in rear of the two platoons;[21] exactly the position prescribed for officers directing the fire of the troops. That Company L had been engaged for some time was evidenced by piles of shell casings found by the bodies. [22]

As Custer had "colored the companies" the officers attempted to use dead horses to determine the position of the various troops. In general this was a difficult task as most of the dead horses were found on, or near, Custer Hill. [23] Specifically, in the case of Company C, this proved extremely difficult as few of their horses were found. In an uncharacteristic display of empathy, Benteen stated that the bodies were *"as recognizable as if they were in life."*[24] Perhaps some of the members of C Troop were not as badly mutilated as others on the field. That may have been the reason men from Company C were identified on Greasy Grass and Calhoun Ridges. At the latter location were found the bodies of Company C Sergeants Jeremiah Finley[25] and August Finckle. [26]

In terms of the Keogh Sector, Edgerly thought the bodies showed signs that the company was in the process of falling back on Custer's position. [27] Keogh's company died in two distinct groups, indicating they fought by platoons. In the group surrounding Keogh were recognized the bodies of First Sergeant Frank E. Varden, [28] Sergeant James Bustard,[29] Corporal John Wild,[30] and Trumpeter John W. Patton. [31] Keogh's unmutilated body was discovered with the *Agnus Dei* around his neck, but his *Medaglia di Pro Petri Sede* which had been in a pocket was missing.[32] According to Captain Edward S. Luce, former member of the 7th Cavalry and also a former superintendent of the battlefield: *"Keogh's left leg and knee were badly shattered by a gunshot wound, and Comanche had suffered a severe bone-hit, the bullet entering the right shoulder and emerging from the left – exactly where Keogh's knee would have been."*[33]

Between the Keogh and Custer, or Last Stand Hill positions, all is confusion. Private Jacob Adams, of Company H recalled:

> *"I went with Benteen over to Custer battlefield on p.m. of June 27. Down near the river and before we came to any dead men we found three or four dead horses. Custer lay within a circle of dead horses on a flat place at the end of the ridge. Tom Custer lay back of him and not near the horses. Quite a distance east of Custer (down near Keogh and between Keogh and Custer) the dead bodies lay thick, and among these were identified dead men from all of the five companies. We came to the conclusion then and there that the fight had been a rout, a running fight."*[34]

McClernand stated that Custer's mare Vic, short for Victory, was found about 100 to 150 feet from Custer Hill in the direction of Keogh with her head pointed toward Custer Knoll.[35] Proving that virtually nothing associated with the battle is without controversy, Lieutenant Roe believed that Vic was one of the horses forming the breast works atop Custer Knoll.[36]

Undoubtedly, the most attention was paid to the group surrounding Custer. Prior to the erection of the present monument, a small knoll rising about six feet above the surrounding ridge occupied the location of the present monument. It was atop this knoll that the bodies of Armstrong and Tom Custer, Algernon Smith,[37] and William Cooke were found.[38] Godfrey recalled that a total of 42 bodies and 39 horses were found on Custer Hill.[39] Private Thomas W. Coleman of Company B also recalled 42 bodies surrounding Custer,[40] but Lieutenant Roe's count was 34.[41] Private Dennis Lynch said that 14 of his comrades from Company F lay in the group around Custer.[42] Edgerly remembered that Yates and Van Wyck Reily were found at the base of the knoll along with a *"great many"* enlisted men, presumably of Company F.[43] The current location of the Custer family markers within the fence on Custer Hill is incorrect. Armstrong and Tom Custer were found on the top of the knoll within 6 feet of where the current monument stands and about 40 feet from where their markers are placed.[44] Boston Custer and Armstrong Reed were found at the base of the ridge leading to the present museum, about 100 yards from where Armstrong and Tom met their end.[45] In the case of Armstrong and Tom Custer, the discrepancy is probably due to the markers being placed near their burial site. Why the markers for Boston Custer and Armstrong Reed are improperly placed is subject to speculation.[46]

One of the most controversial elements of the Custer Fight is the location of the dead troopers of the Gray Horse Troop, Company E. While only two members of Company E have been positively identified as dying within the confines of Deep Ravine,[47] many authorities believe that the majority of the company perished in an unorganized mass within the ravine while attempting a mad dash for freedom at the end of the battle. Captain Walter Clifford of the 7th Infantry however, stated there was a definite skirmish line, followed by the circle of 40 men near Custer.[48] Lieutenant Wallace appeared to confirm Clifford's statement with his court of inquiry testimony as to the presence of a line in Deep Ravine: *"I afterward saw in the ravine some men lying in skirmish order but they were at the bottom of a deep ravine and I don't know how it was."*[49] Lieutenant Hare's testimony is most revealing in this matter:

> *"Q: State whether you found any men in skirmish line except those about Captain Calhoun.*

"A: I did not see his company. Lieutenant Smith's was the only one I saw and 28 of his men were in a coulee.

"Q: Did the position of those men indicate a prolonged resistance?

"A: It indicated a skirmish order. They were about at skirmish intervals."[50]

Captain McDougall's 1909 letter to Godfrey provides some interesting points to ponder concerning E Troop and Deep Ravine:

"Reno . . . ordered me to bury Troop 'E' which I had commanded so many years. In the ravine I found most of the troop, who had used the upper sides of the ravine for a kind of breastwork, falling to the bottom as they were shot down. In burying the men the stench was so great that the men (my men) began to vomit, so we had to pile large chunks of earth upon them, broken off from the sides of the ravine. . . Only a few of the men could be recognized. I knew Sergeant Hohmeyer[51] *(sic) at once; he had one sock left on his foot with his name on it."*[52]

McDougall, who said he found the body of Company K's Sergeant Robert H. Hughes, responsible for carrying Custer's personal battle flag, among the dead in the ravine,[53] went on to testify: *"That (referring to Deep Ravine on the Maguire map, DCE) is where the most of Company E were found to the best of my recollection, about half were in the ravine and the other half on a line outside."*[54] Hughes was not the only man from a unit other than E Troop found in that location as the bodies of Corporals John Briody and William Teeman[55], and Privates Gustave Klein[56] and Timothy Donnelly[57], all of Company F were also recognized. Lieutenant Thompson and Captain McDougall recalled that only about a dozen bodies were found between this position and Custer Hill.[58]

The four accounts stated above agree that the bodies were in skirmish order, indicating an organized resistance, and were found in a ravine, although not necessarily Deep Ravine. Even the most cursory examination of the battlefield terrain reveals that a tactical deployment into Deep Ravine would be an absurdity as the steepness of the walls does not offer an effective firing position and the ravine is commanded by higher points only a few yards distant. In other words, Deep Ravine is obviously a death trap. Any body of troops found in such a location could only be due to the popularly held "last ditch" escape theory. It seems, to my mind, impossible to reconcile the panic break for freedom scenario with the discovery of bodies in orderly intervals; especially when that line was perpendicular to the line of retreat. The account of Two Moon, given to J. M. Thralls on the battlefield in 1901, would appear to substantiate this position. Two Moon said that 19 men (down from his earlier estimate of 40) broke away at the end of the fight and that their kill sites are marked with haeadstones. If their kill sites were properly marked in 1901, they couldn't have died in Deep Ravine.[59] This account is confirmed by the Uncpapa Iron Hawk who claimed he killed one the last of Custer's troopers at the site marked by the last headstone on the South Skirmish Line. If Iron Hawk was correct, very few of Custer's troopers could have made it to Deep Ravine.[60]

Although all of the affected burial accounts mention approximately 28 bodies being found in, or near, Deep Ravine, if the placement of the markers is correct, as the archaeological evidence clearly indicates, where did the 28 bodies come from? Regimental muster roles do not allow for an additional 28 men, making a total of 236 on Custer's field, to have ridden with Custer. If the bodies were removed from the ravine prior to burial, why wasn't that fact recorded? According to Lieutenant Roe, who restaked the graves in 1881: *"There never was 28 dead men in the ravine. . .*[61] Perhaps Roe was correct and the reason no bodies have ever been recovered from Deep Ravine is that there simply were not bodies there to find.

One of the most important accounts of the discovery of bodies, in terms of understanding the movements of Custer's command, is that given by Colonel John Gibbon who visited the battlefield on June 29th. Due to its importance, I will quote the passage at length:

> *"Close by us are two such fords as I have described, and crossing one of these we move up the right bank of the stream which here runs nearly due south. On our right is the wooded bank of the river, the intervening space between the cottonwood trees being filled up with brushwood. On our left the valley opens out into a grass-covered prairie, fringed on its southern side, and again on its western side, where the stream curves to the north again, with timber and brushwood. Riding along up the stream we come to the point where, after cutting the bluffs skirting it on the north, it turns sharply to the south. Here the ground commences to rise before us in gently sloping hills separated by little valleys, one of which seems to lead in about the direction we want to take. Just before this valley joins the valley of the river, the bottom has been cut into a gulch some eight or ten feet deep, and this is filled with brushwood nourished by the moisture of the rain-water, which doubtless cut out the gulch. Struck with the fact that this little valley seemed to be a natural outlet from the scene of the fight, and the possibility that individuals might have sought shelter in the gulch on their way to the timber below, we closely examined the place up to the point where the gulch headed , but found no 'signs.' As we proceeded up the valley, now an open grassy slope, we suddenly came upon a body lying in the grass. It was lying upon its back, and was in an advanced state of decomposition. It was not stripped, but had evidently been scalped and one ear cut off. The clothing was not that of a soldier, and, with the idea of identifying the remains, I caused one of the boots to be cut off and the stocking and drawers examined for a name, but none could be found. On looking at the boot, however, a curious construction was observed. The heel of the boot was reinforced by a piece of leather which in front terminated in two straps, one of which was furnished with a buckle, evidently for the purpose of tightening the instep of the boot. This led to the identification of the remains,[62] for on being carried to camp the boot was recognized as one belonging to Mr. Kellogg,[63] a newspaper correspondent who accompanied General Custer's column. Beyond this point the ground commenced to rise more rapidly, and the valley was broken up into several smaller ones which lead up towards the higher ground beyond. Following up one of these we reach a rolling but not very broken space, the ground rising higher and higher until it reaches a culminating knoll dominating all the ground in the immediate vicinity. This knoll, by common consent now called Custer's Hill, is the spot where his body was found. . ."*[64]

The conclusions I have reached from the forgoing accounts, which form the basis for the reconstruction presented in Chapter 15, are that C Troop was deployed along both Greasy Grass and Calhoun Ridges; that Company L offered significant resistance before being overwhelmed; that Company I was overrun while still in the reserve position; that a platoon[65] of Company E was deployed on the so called South Skirmish Line early in the fight; that Company F was deployed around Custer Hill; that Kellogg's body verifies that Custer went to the northern (Crazy Horse) ford; and that the remnants of the regiment, comprised of representatives of probably all of the companies, met their end during a final dash for freedom at the end of the battle in the vicinity of, but not in, Deep Ravine. The fact that only two dead Indian ponies were found on Custer's field[66] indicates that the warriors fought mostly dismounted, charging only when in close proximity to the troops; a further indication of a prolonged engagement.

On the 28th, the 7th Cavalry, formed in skirmish order by company, had gone over the field identifying the horribly mutilated bodies[67] as best they could and giving meager burial to the remains. The ground was hard and extremely arid making digging difficult even if the proper tools had been on hand. Due to the shortage of tools and the sickening stench of the decaying flesh, many bodies were only given a covering of sage brush and left where they had fallen. Private John Fox, Company D, recalled the burial squad he was in had only one shovel. *"They dug up the ground with knives and chopped it with an axe. They threw dirt and sage brush on the bodies. They covered only the faces of some of the bodies."*[68] The best of the graves, with the exception of the common grave for Armstrong and Tom Custer, were only 12 to 14 inches deep.[69] These graves were dug adjacent to the body which was then rolled in and covered. Fortunately for history, the locations of the bodies were marked with wooden stakes so that their locations have been, in general, preserved. In the case of the officers, the names were inscribed on paper, folded into a shell casing, and driven into the head of the stake.[70] Although, officially, the bodies of Lieutenants Porter, Sturgis, Harrington and Lord were never identified[71]; Lieutenant Roe recalled that, upon his return from the battlefield on the 7th, Benteen said he had identified all of the officers except Harrington and Lord.[72] Richard Edward Thompson, a Second Lieutenant in Company K of the 6th Infantry at the time of the battle, told Walter Camp the body of Dr. Lord had been identified as lying about 20 feet southeast of Custer on the side of the hill.[73]

Of course, there is controversy associated with who actually buried Custer. Sergeant Ryan claimed to have superintended the burial of Armstrong and Tom Custer and went on to describe the burial process:

> *"We dug a shallow grave 15 to 18 inches deep. We laid the General in as tenderly as a soldier could with his brother Captain along side of him, covering the bodies with pieces of blankets and tents and spreading earth on top, spreading it as well as we could, making it look as near a mound as possible. We then took a basket off an Indian 'travois' placing it upside down over the grave and pinning it to the ground with stakes, placing large stones around it to keep the wolves from digging it up, and this simple and sad mode of burial was the best of all those heroes on that terrible field of Little Big Horn, and I helped bury 45 enlisted men and commissioned officers. . . . The company commanders went in a body over the field, to find the bodies of the commissioned officers. The first sergeants of each troop had orders to advance with their companies over a certain space of the field, burying what men were found, and keeping an account of the number and who they were. . . . The burials did not amount to much, as we had only a few tools, so we simply dug up a little earth beside the bodies and threw it over them. In a great many instances their arms and legs protruded. . . . Some of the companies burying those men had no shovels. They had a few axes and chopped down some sage brush and put it over the bodies."*[74]

Private O'Neill, however, claimed that Company G, not Ryan's M, buried Custer:

> *"I was a member of that party that buried General Custer and about from thirty to thirty-five officers and men who fell within fifty yards of him. I do not suppose Custer was in exactly the position where he fell when we found him, for he had been stripped naked, not even a stocking on. The last stand was made on what we call a 'hogback hill.' It appeared to me that the general had been placed by the warriors in a comfortable position, his head higher than his feet, lying on his back, arms by his side, features calm, without any contortion. One bullet wound on the body and one through the temples were visible. The wound on the body seemed to enter on the left side, a little behind and below the left breast, the bullet traveling*

between the back and breastbone and coming out on the right side near the lower ribs. This wound was apparently made by an Indian on horseback, while the general was on foot. The other wound was squarely through the temples, and from the absence of powder marks, left no doubt in my mind that it was inflicted by an Indian on foot, and on the same level as the general. There was not any in the burial party who thought the general shot himself. Nearly all other officers and soldiers were scalped; also the bodies were slashed with knives. Tom Custer was the worst mutilated; his whole scalp was taken off, supposed to have been done by Rain In The Face. When we arrived at the place where the last stand was made, the company to which I belonged, about thirty men with several officers from other companies, held a consultation about the burying of the dead. It was decided not to remove the bodies from the spot where they fell, but to dig up the earth and throw it over the bodies. Some of the bodies were lying on the top of other bodies; one case in particular, the body of the chief trumpeter (Henry Voss, DCE), was lying downward over the face of a very dear friend of mine, named Jack Vickory (Sergeant John Vickory of Company F who was the regimental color bearer, DCE). All the bodies were naked, except that of Vickory, which had one white sock on, with his name on it. I rolled the body of the trumpeter off Vickory and began to cover up Vickory's body. I made considerable of a mound over him, and in doing so I made quite an excavation in the ground. Captain Wallace, who was afterwards killed at Wounded Knee by the Indians in 1901 (1890, DCE), and who was in charge of my company at the time, said:

"'O'Neill, that will be a good place to bury the general.'

"So, with the assistance of another soldier[75], we squared the hole, and lifted the general's body a few yards away, and placed it in the grave. Captain Wallace wrote the general's name on a piece of paper, put it in an empty shell, and placed it at his head; the doctor (Dr. Porter, DCE) cut a lock of the general's hair for Mrs. Custer. Later the body was taken up and was removed to West Point, where it now lies."[76]

Reno's dead in the valley were also buried on the 28th. Private Adams recalled the burial of Lieutenant McIntosh: *"Lieut. Gibson and I went to McIntosh's body. The fire had run through the grass and scorched it. Gibson wanted me to get a pack mule and take it up on Reno hill, but I disliked the job and told him I knew of no way to pack it, so he decided to have it buried where it lay, and I buried it there."[77]* In addition to the effects of the fire, McIntosh's body had been horribly mutilated, being scalped from the forehead to the back of his neck.[78] Gibson was only able to identify the remains of his brother-in-law by means of a gutta-percha button lying near the body which was identical to the type given McIntosh by his wife prior to the departure from Fort Lincoln.[79]

The body of the popular Hodgson was attended to by his company commander, Captain McDougall:

"On the night of the 26th of June 1876, I took Privates Ryan and Moore (Stephen L. Ryan and Farrier James E. Moore, DCE) of my company, and we went and got Lieutenant Hodgson's body, and carried it to my breastworks, and kept it there until the next morning on the 27th. After sewing him up in a blanket and a poncho, I proceeded with those two men to bury him."[80]

Name	Reburial Location
George Armstrong Custer	Post Cemetery, U. S. Military Academy, West Point, New York on October 10, 1877.
Thomas Ward Custer	Grave number 1488, Section "A", National Cemetery, Fort Leavenworth, Kansas on August 3, 1877.
George Walter Yates	Grave number 1487, Section "A", National Cemetery, Fort Leavenworth, Kansas on August 3, 1877.
James Calhoun	Grave number 1489, Section "A", National Cemetery, Fort Leavenworth, Kansas on August 3, 1877.
Algernon Emory Smith	Grave number 1486, Section "A", National Cemetery, Fort Leavenworth, Kansas on August 3, 1877.
Donald McIntosh	Grave number 1490, National Cemetery, Fort Leavenworth, Kansas on August 3, 1877. Exhumed October 28, 1909 and reinterred October 31, 1909 in Lot No. 107–D, Officers' Section, Western Division, Arlington National Cemetery.
Myles Wyles Keogh	Throop Martin Lot, Fort Hill Cemetery, Auburn, N. Y. on October 25, 1877.[81]
William Winer Cooke	Hamilton, Ontario, Canada.
William Van Wyck Reily	Washington, D. C.
George Edwin Lord	Common grave at the site of the Monument on the battlefield.
James Madison DeWolfe	Norwalk, Ohio.
John Jordan Crittenden	Originally reinterred where he had fallen on the battlefield in July 1877. Exhumed on September 11, 1931 and reinterred in the Custer Battlefield National Cemetery on September 15, 1931.
Benjamin Hubert Hodgson	Chestnut Hill Cemetery, Philadelphia, Pa. in October 1877.

Table 18 – 1 Reburial Sites of Seventh Cavalry Officers[82]

These interments were burials in name only. The shallow coverings, or graves, were unable to withstand the ravages of either the elements, or the scavenging by wolves, coyotes and human ghouls.[83] Visitors to the field were appalled by the conditions they beheld; the ground being strewn with bones. Although these bones were almost exclusively those of 7th Cavalry horses, the resulting outcry forced the army to take action. In 1877, the first of two reburial parties, this one commanded by Captain Michael Sheridan, brother of General Sheridan, arrived at the battlefield. Sheridan reported he had buried all exposed human remains, remounded all the graves he could find, and marked each grave with a cedar stake. His detail had the additional duty of recovering the bodies of the officers (see Table 18–1 for a list of reburial sites for the officers). In compliance with the wishes of his family, Lieutenant Crittenden was reinterred where he had fallen, being removed to the National Cemetery in 1931.[84]

Of course, there is the apparently requisite controversy over whether the actual remains of Armstrong Custer were recovered. Sergeant Michael C. Caddle, who was on detached duty at the time of the battle but accompanied the 1877 reburial party that exhumed the bodies of the officers, is the source of this controversy. Caddle maintained that when the grave indicated by the numbered stake as being Custer's was opened, the body was found lying on a corporal's blouse. Caddle went on to state that he believed they recovered the correct body on their second attempt.[85] Captain Michael Sheridan felt compelled to write Libbie Custer in response to a *New York Herald* statement about the deplorable conditions on the battlefield:

> "*Thinking perhaps this may have come to your eyes (the New York Herald statement, DCE) I desire now to say that **no** person connected with that paper was with me, and that any statement it may have made was manufactured in the Herald office and was untrue. Nowlan and myself properly identified by the stakes driven into the ground at the head of each grave the body of **every** officer I brought*

in without the slightest difficulty (emphasis from the original). In addition to this Nowlan had superintended the burial and easily went to each grave in the presence of myself and Lt. Scott and found the stakes and was fully sustained in his identification by a number of men who assisted in the burial, and whom I purposely took out with me to make assurance doubly sure. Although I know you have the good sense not to believe such stuff as was published in the face of what you know I would have written you, I still pledge you my honor as an officer and a gentleman that the remains of each officer was fully identified, and I regret exceedingly that a newspaper that has pretended to be so friendly to Genl. Custer – and whose editor claims to have been his personal friend – should for the mere purpose of being called enterprising, have manufactured this outrageous story, with the possibility of increasing the doubts and uncertainties that must have filled your heart for the past year."[86]

The matter of whether or not Custer's body was recovered and subsequently buried at West Point should be resolved by the following letter from Major Joseph G. Tilford to Libbie Custer, which contained physical evidence the correct body had been recovered:

"On yesterday I shipped by U. S. Express via Chicago, the remains of your heroic husband Genl.. Custer to West Point, N. Y., care of the Commanding Officer of the Post. Those were my instructions from Genl. Sheridan. I presume an officer will accompany the remains from Chicago on.

"It may be some consolation for you to know that I personally superintended the transfer of the remains from the box in which they came from the battlefield to the casket which conveys them to West Point.

"I enclose you a lock of hair from the remains which are so precious to you. I also kept a few hairs for myself as having been worn by a man who was my beau ideal of a soldier and honorable Gentleman."[87]

In 1879 the army sent a second burial detail, this one commanded by Captain George K. Sanderson.[88] Sanderson erected an eleven foot high cordwood memorial on Custer Knoll. Parts of four or five bodies, all that Sanderson could find, were buried in a common grave beneath the memorial. In addition, the horse bones were collected and placed inside of the cordwood structure. The field was finally in acceptable shape as it was noted in 1881 that the graves were thickly covered with grass and there were no exposed remains.

Finally, in 1881, Lieutenant Roe returned to the field tasked with erecting a permanent monument, inscribed with the names of the slain, which still stands today. Acting upon Sanderson's earlier recommendation, the graves were opened and the remains reinterred in a common grave beneath the monument. Fortunately, Roe marked each opened grave with a stake.

In April of 1890, Captain Owen J. Sweet placed the marble markers[89] where he could locate stakes. As the rest of the battlefield was privately owned at that time, Sweet placed all of his markers on the Custer battlefield proper. Over the years several other markers were rather indiscriminately placed. Despite this haphazard treatment, the archaeological investigations recently conducted at the battlefield indicate the markers, when obviously paired markers are viewed as a single marker, are a good indication of where 7th Cavalry troopers were interred.

Another of the myths of the Little Big Horn is that Captain Keogh's mount, Comanche, was the only living thing found on the battlefield. In addition to Comanche, a gray horse named Nap and the mascot of Company I, a black and white bulldog named Joe Bush, survived the battle.[90] The troopers also found a number of wounded horses which they put out of their misery. As with everything else associated with the battle, who found Comanche, and where he was found, is unclear. The various accounts have Comanche being found in the abandoned village, near his fallen master, or on either bank of the Little Big Horn. At least six men, including Lieutenant Nowlan and Private Francis Johnson Kennedy,[91] of Company I, claimed to have found and cared for Comanche. If Nowlan didn't find Comanche, he certainly took charge of him shortly after his discovery.

In addition to the controversy surrounding his discovery, no one could agree on the number of wounds Comanche had sustained which are variously reported as 2, 3, 4, 6, 7 (the most popular number), 10, 12, or 20.[92] Private Dennis Lynch, who dressed Comanche's wounds aboard the *Far West*, demonstrated that the wound in Comanche's breast and left side were made by the same bullet when he noted that blowing in the breast wound through a quill caused a discharge from the side wound.[93]

After his return to Fort Lincoln in a specially constructed stall on the *Far West*, Comanche became an object of veneration for the regiment. Colonel Samuel D. Sturgis, who had lost his youngest son at the Little Big Horn, issued the following order:

Headquarters Seventh U.S. Cavalry,
Fort A. Lincoln, D. T.,
April 10, 1878

GENERAL ORDERS NO. 7:

(1) – The horse known as "Comanche," being the only living representative of the bloody tragedy of the Little Big Horn, June 25, 1876, his kind treatment and comfort shall be a matter of special pride and solicitude on the part of every member of the Seventh Cavalry, to the end that his life shall be preserved to the utmost limit. Wounded and scarred as he is, his very existence speaks in terms more eloquent than words, of the desperate struggle against overwhelming numbers of the hopeless conflict, and the heroic manner in which all went down on that fatal day.

(2) – The commanding officer of Company I will see that a special and comfortable stall is fitted up for him, and he will not again be ridden by any person whatsoever, under any circumstances, nor will he ever be put to any kind of work.

(3) – Hereafter, upon all occasions of ceremony of mounted regimental formation, Comanche, saddled, bridled and draped in mourning, and led by a mounted trooper of Company I, will be paraded by the regiment.

By command of Colonel Sturgis.

E. A. GARLINGTON,
First Lieutenant and adjt. Seventh Cavalry[94]

As the new blacksmith of Company I, replacing Henry Bailey who was killed with the Custer column, Private Gustave Korn, a survivor of Reno's valley fight, was detailed to look after Comanche. A special bond was forged between man and horse, Comanche being known to follow Korn around like a puppy – even accompanying the blacksmith on visits to the home of his female acquaintances,[95] which was only broken upon the death of Korn at Wounded Knee in December of 1890. Without his long time attendant, Comanche grew increasingly morose and finally died on November 7, 1891. Regimental blacksmith Samuel Winchester, who was tending to Comanche when he died, spoke for the entire regiment when he wrote the following note to himself:

"Fort Riley, Kansas, Nov. 7th, 1891 – in memory of the old veteran horse who died at 1:30 o'clock with the colic in his stall while I had my hand on his pulse and looking him in the eye – this night long to be remembered."[96]

Wishing to preserve Comanche, the officers of the 7th contacted Professor Dyche, a naturalist associated with the University of Kansas in Lawrence. Dyche offered to have Comanche mounted for $400 or to donate his services if the officers would donate Comanche to the State University. The officers accepted Dyche's proposal and Comanche may be seen today in the museum bearing Dyche's name at the university in Lawrence.

The dead having been attended to, the command prepared to transport the wounded to the steamer *Far West*. While 12 of the wounded were able to ride,[97] hand litters had to be constructed for the other 40 troopers.[98] Eight men were assigned to each litter to work in relays. The command started in the late afternoon of the 27th to spare the wounded and litter bearers the midday heat. Progress was slow and tortuous for the wounded who were jostled by the rough terrain. By midnight, although they had only progressed four and one half miles, the litter bearers and wounded were exhausted and the column went into camp.

During the night it was mercifully decided that another means of transportation for the wounded must be adopted. While Gibbon wanted to construct rafts and float the wounded down river to the steamer, it was eventually decided to have First Lieutenant Gustavus Cheeny Doane, Company G, 2nd Cavalry, supervise construction of mule litters. The greater portion of the 28th was spent in selecting lodge poles for use in the construction. The litters were made of two poles about 20 feet long with two 3 foot cross pieces spaced about six and one half feet apart. The dead horses and mules were skinned and the hides cut into strips to form a lattice work between the cross pieces. On top of the lattice work, blankets and buffalo robes were spread and the wounded man rode with his head under the muzzle of the trailing horse or mule to preclude the possibility of being kicked in the head.

In another example of the failure of the typical frontier commander to learn from his adversaries, the wounded scouts White Swan and Goose[99] were transported via the far superior travois made by their fellow scouts. While mule litters were adequate, Crook had recognized the travois to be a superior form of transport for wounded[100] and, although he would use some mule litters to transport his wounded after Slim Buttes, he had used the travois to remove his wounded from the Rosebud.[101]

It was decided to make a short trial march and the command moved out at 6 PM on the 28th. Everything had gone so nicely that when Terry's two couriers, Henry Bostwick and Private James E. Goodwin, Company A, 7th Infantry, returned with the news that the steamer was at the mouth of the Little Big Horn, Terry, in another of his ill advised actions, decided to continue the march until the *Far West* was reached. The moon went down about midnight and the column grouped forward in the dark despite the fact that it had begun to rain. The wounded suffered greatly from the jostling and stumbling of the mules; unlucky amputee Mike Madden being thrown from his litter into a bed of cactus.[102] Finally a road to the steamer was discovered and the nearly exhausted command struggled down the last ravine, guided by the fires ordered by Captain Freeman to illuminate the path; reaching the steamer shortly after 2 AM on June 30th.

Shortly before dawn, the wounded were secured aboard their floating hospital still under the supervision of the tireless Dr. Porter.

Shortly before casting off, General Terry summoned Captain Grant Marsh, master of the *Far West*, to his cabin. Marsh related Terry spoke with a great deal of emphasis and emotion which was considered unusual:

> *"Captain, you are about to start on a trip with fifty-two wounded men on your boat. This is a bad river to navigate and accidents are liable to happen. I wish to ask of you that you use all the skill you possess, all the caution you can command, to make the journey safely. Captain, you have on board the most precious cargo a boat ever carried. Every soldier here who is suffering with wounds is the victim of a terrible blunder; a sad and terrible blunder."[103]*

The *Far West* steamed to the base camp on the Yellowstone where it awaited the arrival of the command to ferry them to the north bank; that duty being completed on the 2nd of July. When he arrived at Pease Bottom aboard the steamer on June 30th, Terry found a dispatch from Sheridan informing him that the latest intelligence revealed the village to contain about 1800 lodges and as many as 3000 warriors.[104] Fourteen of the wounded had sufficiently recovered to be returned to duty and Captain Spephen Baker's Company B of the 6th Infantry was replaced as boat guard by seventeen dismounted 7th Cavalry troopers. [105] When the *Far West* set out for Fort Lincoln at five o'clock in the afternoon of July 3rd, [106] there were only 37 wounded aboard; Corporal George H. King having died of his wounds the previous day. [107] The journey began on an ominous note as Private William Montell George died of his wounds shortly after the departure and was buried at the Powder River camp.[108]

The *Far West* was only to make two more stops on its record setting journey; at Fort Buford to land the wounded scout Goose [109] and briefly at Fort Stevenson on the afternoon of the July 5th. Here, in accordance with the custom of the day, and Terry's direct orders, Captain Marsh had the derrick and jack staff draped in black and the flag lowered to half staff. At eleven PM, [110] just fifty-four hours after leaving the mouth of the Big Horn, the *Far West* completed its historic 710 mile journey and landed at Bismarck. Unfortunately the steamer arrived too late for Private James C. Bennett who died of his wounds about 3 PM. [111]

Dr. Porter told the story of the voyage of the *Far West* to Clement A. Lounsberry, editor of the *Bismarck Tribune*. The story was published in the February and March 1897 issues of *The Record*:

> *"The steamer Far West was moored at the mouth of the Little Big Horn. She was the supply boat of the expedition and had made her way up the Big Horn farther than any other boat. She had performed one exploit unprecedented in western river navigation in reaching the mouth of the Little Big Horn, and was ready to perform another unequaled in steamboating in the west. The wounded were carried on board the steamer and Dr. Porter was detailed to go down with them. Terry's adjutant general, Colonel Ed. Smith (Captain Edward Worthington Smith, Company G, 18th Infantry, DCE), was sent along with the official dispatches and a hundred other messages. He had a traveling bag full of telegrams for the Bismarck office. Captain Grant Marsh was in command of the Far West. He put everything in the completest order and took on a large amount of fuel. He received orders to reach Bismarck as soon as possible. He understood his instructions literally, and never did a river man obey them more conscientiously. On the evening of the third of July the steamer weighed anchor. In a few minutes the Far West, so fittingly*

named, was under full head of steam. It was a strange land, and an unknown river. What a cargo on that steamer! What news for the country! What a story to carry to the government, to Fort Lincoln, to the widows!

"It was running from a field of havoc to a station of mourners. The steamer Far West never received the credit due her. Neither has the gallant Marsh. Nor the pilots David Campbell and John Johnson. Marsh, too, acted as pilot. It required all their endurance and skill. They proved the men of emergency. The engineer, whose name is not known to me (George Foulk, DCE), did his duty. Every one of the crew is entitled to the same acknowledgment. [112] They felt no sacrifice was too great upon that journey, and in behalf of the wounded heroes. A very moderate imagination can picture the scene upon that floating hospital.

"There were wounds of every character, and men more dead than alive. The suffering was not terminated with the removal from the field to the boiler deck. It continued and ended in death more than once before Fort Lincoln was hailed. Porter watched for fifty-four hours. He stood the test. The Big Horn is full of islands, and a successful passage, even on the bosom of a 'June rise' is not an easy feat. The Far West would take a shoot on this or that side of an island, as the quick judgment of the pilot would dictate . . . A steamboat moving as fast as a railway train in a narrow, winding stream is not a pleasure. It was no pleasant sensation to be dashing straight at a headland, and the pilot the only power to save. Occasionally the bank would be touched and the men would topple over like ten-pins. It was a reminder of what the result would be if a snag was struck. Down the big Horn the heroine went, missing islands, snags and shore. It was a thrilling voyage. The rate of speed was unrivaled in the annals of boating. Into the Yellowstone the staunch craft shot, and down that sealed river . . . she made over twenty miles an hour (the Far West would average 13.15 miles per hour on this voyage, a record unequaled on the Yellowstone, DCE). The bold captain was taking chances, but he scarcely thought of them. He was under flying orders. Lives were at stake. His engineer was instructed to keep up steam at the highest pitch. Once the steam gauge marked a pressure that turned his cool head and made every nerve in his powerful frame quiver. The crisis passed and the Far West escaped a fate more terrible than Custer's. . . . Down the swift Yellowstone, . . . into the broad Missouri, and then there was clear sailing. There was a deeper channel and more confidence. A few minutes were lost at Fort Buford. Everybody at the fort was beside himself. The boat was crowded with inquirers, and their inquiries were not half answered when the steamer was away. At [Buford] a wounded scout (Goose, DCE) was put off, and at Fort Stevenson a brief stop to tell in a word what had happened. There was no difference in the speed from Stevenson to Bismarck. The same desperate rate was kept up to the end. They were approaching home with something of that feeling which always moves the human heart. At 11 o'clock on the night of the 5th of July they reached Bismarck, and Fort Abraham Lincoln. One thousand miles (actually 710 miles, DCE) in fifty-four hours was the proud record. You have Captain Marsh's challenge to produce a duplicate.

"Dr. Porter and Colonel Smith hurried from the landing up town, calling up the editor of the [Bismarck] Tribune and the telegraph operator. The latter, J. M. Carnahan, took his seat at the key the next morning and scarce raised himself from his chair for twenty-two hours. He, too, was plucky, and what he sent vibrating around the world is history.

"What a night! Colonel Lounsberry was editor of the Tribune then . . . Porter, Smith, Fred Girard, Grant Marsh, and nearly a score of others were interviewed that night. A brief bulletin to the New York Herald. 'Custer and his whole command massacred. Not one left to tell the tale.' Terry gathered up the notes written by Mark Kellogg's hand, of the progress of the march up to the beginning of the battle. General James S. Brisbin sent notes of the battlefield as he found it and saw it. These were filed. There was a column or two of Mark's work and two or more of Brisbin's. 'Take this,' said Lounsberry, as he handed Carnahan a copy of the New Testament. 'Fire that in when you run out of copy. Hold the wires. Tell 'em it's coming and to hold the key!' With almost the speed of lightning flew the editor's hand . . . Porter, Girard, Marsh and others told their stories and they were put on the wires. The list of the dead, of those wounded, and the incidents in relation to each, were poured into his ears or brought the editor by willing hands. To sleep, or even tire under such circumstances was not likely. The story grew. Fifteen thousand words had gone and still there was more, and the story grew in interest. The wee small hours had gone and daylight came and still the keys were busy. What Custer said. What Custer did. The story of Curley, of Reynolds, what the wounded said . . . A hundred messengers working all bent on giving the story to the world, one newspaper writer and two telegraph operators. That story cost the New York Herald $3,000. It was worth the money. It was the greatest scoop ever known in newspaper circles. It was the finest job of reporting ever done on the American continent. Porter, the hero of Little Big Horn, was one of the most interesting features in it . . ."113

The arrival of the *Far West* at Bismarck marked the first "official" confirmation of the tragedy.114 Earlier in the day, three Lakota had brought news of the disaster into Fort Rice, some 25 miles south of Fort Lincoln, and the message was brought by courier to Bismarck for transmission by telegraph to the Adjutant General's office in St. Paul. Similarly, the *Bismarck Tribune*, was not the first newspaper to print the tragic news. On July 1st, Muggins Taylor had been dispatched to Fort Ellis with news of the defeat. The *Bozeman Times* put out an "Extra" at 7 PM the evening of July 3rd. While the *Times* reported the story was brought by Taylor, it is possible that a settler from the Stillwater River named Horace Countryman may have carried the news into Fort Ellis in Bozeman, when Taylor arrived at his ranch too exhausted to continue. In any event, the telegraph wires out of Bozeman were down and Countryman was convinced by W. H. Norton, special correspondent of the *Helena Herald*, to carry the news to Helena. The *Helena Herald* published an "Extra" on July 4, the day of the centennial. Andrew Fisk, editor of the *Herald*, wired the story to the Associated Press at Salt Lake City; from which point it was flashed to the east coast, making headlines on the 5th, a full day prior to receipt of the *Tribune's* detailed story. The official message from Captain D. W. Benham, commanding the garrison at Fort Ellis, was forwarded by mail without notifying the captain of the change in media. General Terry's official dispatches did not reach Sheridan's Chicago headquarters until July 6.

After only a short stay in Bismarck, the *Far West* dropped the short distance down the river to Fort Lincoln on the opposite bank. Lieutenant Charles Lawrence Gurley of the 6th Infantry told of the receipt of the sad tidings in the same article from the *Record* quoted previously:

"The news came to us about 2 A.M. Captain William S. McCaskey, Twentieth Infantry, summoned all the officers to his quarters at once, and there read to them the communication he had just received – per steamer Far West, from Captain Smith, General Terry's adjutant general. After we had recovered from the shock, Captain McCaskey requested us to assist him in breaking the news to the widows. It fell to my lot to accompany Captain McCaskey and Dr. J. V. D. Middleton, our post surgeon, to the quarters of Mrs. Custer – immediately east of those occupied by

myself. We started on our sad errand a little before 7 o'clock on that 6th of July morning. I went to the rear of the Custer house, woke up Maria, Mrs. Custer's housemaid, and requested her to rap on Mrs. Custer's door, and say to her that she and Mrs. [Margaret] Calhoun and Miss [Emma] Reed (sister of Armstrong Reed and a niece of the general, DCE) were wanted in the parlor. On my way through the hall to open the front door, I heard the opening of the door of Mrs. Custer's room. She had been awakened by the footsteps in the hall. She called me by name and asked me the cause of my early visit. I made no reply, but followed Captain McCaskey and Dr. Middleton into the parlor. There we were almost immediately followed by the ladies of the Custer household, and there we told to them their first intimation of the awful result of the battle of the Little Big Horn.

"Imagine the grief of those stricken women, their sobs, their flood of tears. The grief that knew no consolation. The fearful depression that had hung over the fort for the past two days had its explanation then. It was almost stifling."[115]

In her writings, Libbie Custer was unable to bring herself to write of the campaign in any detail; leaving only the following brief account:

"A picture of one day of our life in those disconsolate times is fixed indelibly in my memory.

"On Sunday afternoon, the 25th of June, our little group of saddened women, borne down with one common weight of anxiety, sought solace in gathering together in our house. We tried to find some slight surcease from trouble in the old hymns; some of them dated back to our childhood's days, when our mothers rocked us to sleep to their soothing strains. I remember the grief with which one fair young wife threw herself on the carpet and pillowed her head in the lap of a tender friend. Another sat dejected at the piano, and struck soft chords that melted into the notes of the voices. All were absorbed in the same thoughts, and their eyes were filled with far-away visions and longings. Indescribable yearning for the absent, and untold terror for their safety, engrossed each heart. The words of the hymn,

> *'E'en though a cross it be,*
> *Nearer, my God, to Thee,'*

came forth with almost a sob from every throat.

"At that very hour the fears that our tortured minds had portrayed in imagination were realities, and the souls of those we thought upon were ascending to meet their Maker.

"On the 5th of July – for it took that time for the news to come – the sun rose on a beautiful world, but with its earliest beams came the first knell of disaster. A steamer came down the river bearing the wounded from the battle of the Little Big Horn, of Sunday, June 25th. This battle wrecked the lives of twenty-six women at Fort Lincoln, and orphaned children of officers and soldiers joined their cry to that of their bereaved mothers.

"From that time the life went out of the hearts of the 'women who weep,' and God asked them to walk on alone and in the shadow."[116]

Libbie Custer felt her life had ended. Yet her sister-in-law had suffered the greater loss. *"Captain McCaskey did his painful duty. He would never forget the flood of tears, the sobs, the grief. Nor would he forget Maggie Calhoun – who had lost her brothers Autie, Tom, Boston, her nephew Autie Reed, and her husband Jim – running after him as he left and crying out: 'Is there no message for me?'"*[117] The widows, no longer being attached to the army, soon departed for the east. Their over night stop in Fargo is described in *The Record* for August of 1895:

"Mrs. Custer came first with drooping head, her slender figure bowed, her face perfectly colorless, and so little strength left she could scarcely reach the top of the stairway.

"Hackneyed as is the smile of a broken lily, it could not but suggest itself as we looked upon her, and none other seemed so exactly fitting. With her walked Mrs. Calhoun, (the 'Sister Margaret' she had written of so lovingly), and on Mrs. Calhoun's face, fixed in its marble pallor, was an expression which long haunted those who saw it. Her large eyes gazed straight ahead, yet seemed to see nothing that was near. Away, away, a strained, far-off gaze, her whole face expressed horror of one who sees visions too frightful for speech. Burned upon her brain was the terrible picture of that battlefield, and to her had been denied the blessed relief of tears. All that night did the kind-hearted physician watch over one and another of the stricken women, and for her he feared the loss of reason. Her husband – cut down in his bright, brave, young manhood – her three brothers, the Custers – her darling nephew, loving little Autie Reed – a mere child, whose unconquerable desire to see something of wild life with his uncles, had at last induced his reluctant mother to intrust him to Custer's care. 'Gone! Are they all Gone? All?' had been her first wild cry, when the tidings were brought to the fort, and her face assumed that marble pallor, her eyes that expression of frozen horror, and not yet had the terrible tension been relaxed; not yet the overburdened brain and heart been relieved by tears."[118]

Maggie Calhoun was not the only widow to be haunted by memory and tormented by imagination. Benteen's 1879 court of inquiry testimony that Dr. Lord's body had not been identified rekindled hope in the heart of his widow residing in Maine. She *"has an intuitive belief that he is still alive and she will yet see him. She reproaches herself for some little things she did, thinking it sent him off with Custer, and that he was indifferent as to the consequences."*[119] Mrs. Grace Harrington, perhaps haunted by her husband's fears of being burned alive, had a very difficult time dealing with her grief; spending some time in an institution due, no doubt, to a nervous breakdown.[120] Maggie Calhoun did not suffer a nervous breakdown and had apparently come to grips with her grief by the time her husband and brother Tom were reinterred at Fort Leavenworth in August of 1877. After the ceremony, she accepted the five cartridge casings fired from her husband's revolver and found by his side on the battlefield.[121] It is hoped Mrs. Lord also achieved closure for her grief.

While the grief and suffering of the army widows was duly noted by history, they were not the only ones to acutely feel the sting of their personal loss. Many women in the Indian village mourned for loved ones who had passed into *wanagi-yata*, the gathering place of the souls: *". . . on this particular scaffold had been place the body of a certain young Sioux killed during the fighting. The mother was grief-stricken, of course. As the people moved away from the camp scene on Monday afternoon she lingered behind, as Indian mourners customarily did. Her friends in the main body kept watch for her, but after a while she disappeared from their view. Some of them went back to find her. They found her pony grazing near the burial scaffold of her son, but she was not anywhere in sight. Then it was observed that the original wrapped body on the scaffold appeared to be double its proper bulk. Investigation cleared up the strange condition. The mourning mother had climbed up there, had wrapped herself in the buffalo robe shroud with her son, and had made a fatal plunge of her sheath-knife into her own heart.*"[122]

---

[1] Captain McDougall testified that he had searched the abandoned village for any implements that could be of use in the burials. See Ronald H. Nichols "The Reno Court of Inquiry" page 535.

[2] See E. S. Godfrey "Custer's Last Battle 1876" page 38.

[3] This is the only account to mention a third wound, in the right forearm, on Custer's body. Several accounts mention that Tom Custer's arm was broken by a bullet and Hammon may have mistakenly ascribed that wound to the General.

[4] A discussion of the mutilation of Custer's body and the attempt to spare the feelings of the families of the slain is presented in Chapter 15.

[5] See John M. Carroll "A Seventh Cavalry Scrapbook" pages 15 – 16.

[6] See Francis B. Taunton "Custer's Field" page 30.

[7] See Kenneth Hammer "Custer In '76" page 116.

[8] See Francis B. Taunton "Custer's Field" page 6.

[9] See Francis B. Taunton "Custer's Field" page 27.

[10] Richard G. Hardorff on page 33 of "Markers, Artifacts and Indian Testimony" provides a map showing that the bodies of Butler and the four troopers were separated by approximately one half mile. Additionally, there is Indian testimony indicating that the soldier death occurring at the Butler marker was very near the end of fighting and not connected with the early action in Medicine Tail Coulee.

[11] This may have been Private William Brown of Company F. See Francis B. Taunton "Custer's Field" page 19.

[12] Benteen stated on several occasions that the fight took less than an hour. See E. A. Brininstool "Troopers With Custer" page 88.

[13] See E. A. Brininstool "Troopers With Custer" page 89. There was an additional reason, grounded in military law, for Benteen's assertion that Custer was already dead when Martin reached Benteen. That reason will be explored in Chapter 20.

[14] See Colonel W. A. Graham "The Reno Court of Inquiry" pages 145 – 146.

[15] See Edward J. McClernand "On Time For Disaster" page 92.

[16] See Colonel W. A. Graham "The Reno Court of Inquiry" page 146.

[17] See Colonel W. A. Graham "The Custer Myth" page 220.

[18] See Colonel W. A. Graham "The Reno Court of Inquiry" pages 31 – 32.

[19] See Colonel W. A. Graham "The Reno Court of Inquiry" page 76.

[20] Second Lieutenant John Jordan Crittenden III, on temporary duty from Company G, 20th Infantry, as a replacement for Lieutenant Edwin Eckerson. Commissioned on October 15, 1875. The unlucky son of Colonel Thomas L. Crittenden, had lost an eye just ten days after his commissioning due to the explosion of a cartridge at Fort Abercrombie, Dakota Territory. See John M. Carroll "They Rode With Custer" page 63 and "Roll Call on the Little Big Horn" page 124. Another account lists the cause of the eye injury as the result of a shotgun shell exploding in his face during a hunting trip. See Jerry Cecil "Lt. Crittenden" page 32. According to Lieutenant Hugh L. Scott, not present at the battle but a member of the first reburial party the following year, Crittenden's body was recognized because an arrow, shot into his glass eye, had broken it. See Richard G. Hardorff "The Custer Battle Casualties" page 104. Young Crittenden, apparently already aware of a soldier's duty, had once reproached his father for a Civil War retreat: *"Father, John J (the father's horse, DCE) never would have retreated if you hadn't turned him around."* The burial parties could testify that Lieutenant Crittenden had heeded his father's final advice: *"My boy, do your duty! Never retreat! Die, if need be, with your face to the foe!"* See Jerry Cecil "Lt Crittenden" page 32.

[21] Testimony of Edgerly. See Colonel W. A. Graham "The Reno Court of Inquiry" page 166.

[22] Wallace testified to seeing 25 to 30 cartridge shells in "little piles" on Calhoun Hill. See Colonel W. A. Graham "The Reno Court of Inquiry" page 32.

[23] See Colonel W. A. Graham "The Custer Myth" page 346.

[24] See Colonel W. A. Graham "The Custer Myth" page 298.

[25] Finley, apparently an accomplished tailor who had made Custer's buckskin jacket, was found with 12 arrows in his body. See John P. Langellier "Myles Keogh: Irish Dragoon" page 42. He had reportedly been scalped and decapitated. See E. Elden Davis and James W. Wengert MD "That Fatal Day" page 18.

[26] See Francis B. Taunton "Custer's Field" page 21.

[27] See Colonel W. A. Graham "The Custer Myth" page 220.

[28] See Kenneth Hammer "Custer In '76" page 58.

[29] See Kenneth Hammer "Custer In '76" page 58. Trumpeter William G. Hardy of Company A maintained that Sergeant Bustard was riding the mount of Sergeant Milton J. De Lacy, also of Company I, on June 25. This horse was found dead on the west bank of the river near Minneconjou Ford. As Hardy also felt that Keogh's long time mount Comanche actually belonged to Private John McGuinnes of Company I, sick in hospital at Fort Lincoln, his account is somewhat suspect. See Ray Meketa "A Survivor of the Little Big Horn" page 65.

[30] Private Francis Johnson Kennedy said Wild was identified *". . . because the corporal was the biggest. . ."* member of Company I, a highly suspect method of identification under the circumstances. Kennedy went on to state: *"The corporal was uninjured (not mutilated, DCE) because he had been kind to Rain In The Face when he was in the Guard House, giving him tobacco, etc. I understood that Rain In The Face said if he (Wild, DCE) had not been killed outright,*

he would have left him near us where we could have taken care of him." See Bruce Liddic and Paul Harbaugh "Camp on Custer" page 160. This fantastic tale, which has no corroboration, tends to cast doubt on Kennedy's credibility.

[31] See Richard G. Hardorff "The Custer Battle Casualties" page 115.

[32] See Robert J. Ege "Legend Was A Man Named Keogh" pages 38 – 39.

[33] See "Keogh, Comanche And Custer" page 76.

[34] See Kenneth Hammer "Custer In '76" page 121.

[35] See Edward J. McClernand "On Time For Disaster" page 92.

[36] See Charles Francis Roe "Custer's Last Battle" page 10.

[37] Some authors cite the presence of Algernon Smith and Tom Custer as proof the battle was a running rout as they did not die with their companies. As Tom Custer was serving as aid-de-camp to his brother, only Smith was out of place on Custer Knoll. As there are indications that Dr. Lord actually died on the knoll, rather than the south skirmish line, it is possible that Smith had been wounded and was in the field hospital at the time of his death.

[38] The erection of the monument necessitated the relocation of some of the markers. It is assumed that the present marker for Armstrong Custer marks his burial spot, which was at the base of the knoll, rather than the spot where he fell which was within about six feet of the monument. See Richard G. Hardorff "Markers, Artifacts and Indian Testimony" page 5.

[39] See Richard G. Hardorff "The Custer Battle Casualties" page 24. This total obviously includes the bodies found at the base of the small knoll.

[40] See Evan S. Connell "Son of the Morning Star" page 412.

[41] See Charles Francis Roe "Custer's Last Battle" page 10.

[42] See Kenneth Hammer "Custer In '76" page 139.

[43] See Richard G. Hardorff "The Custer Battle Casualties" page 100.

[44] See Richard G. Hardorff "Markers, Artifacts and Indian Testimony" page 7.

[45] See Chris Summitt "Beyond the Markers" page 17.

[46] In addition to the markers already mentioned, an error has been made in the location of the marker for Lieutenant Harrington, which resides within the fence on Custer Hill. As Harrington's body was never identified, it is obviously impossible to mark the site of his death.

[47] See Richard G. Hardorff "Markers, Artifacts and Indian Testimony" pages 57 – 58.

[48] See Michael J. Koury ""Diaries of the Little Big Horn" page 47.

[49] See Ronald H. Nichols "The Reno Court of Inquiry" page 67.

[50] See Ronald H. Nichols "The Reno Court of Inquiry" page 304.

[51] First Sergeant Frederick Hohmeyer.

[52] See Colonel W. A. Graham "The Custer Myth" page 377.

[53] See Richard G. Hardorff "The Custer Battle Casualties" page 115.

[54] See Ronald H. Nichols "The Reno Court of Inquiry" page 53.5

[55] See Chris Summitt "Beyond the Markers" page 17.

[56] See Chris Summitt "Beyond the Markers" page 17.

[57] See Richard G. Hardorff "The Custer Battle Casualties" page 111. Neil Mangum noted that the body of Corporal Briody was one of those found on the South Skirmish Line. See "Little Bighorn Faces" page 11.

[58] See Richard G. Hardorff "Markers, Artifacts and Indian Testimony" page 57 and Kenneth Hammer "Custer In '76" page 248.

[59] See Richard G. Hardorff "Cheyenne Memories of the Custer Fight" page 111. Note that no headstones, used to mark kill sites, have ever been placed in Deep Ravine.

[60] See Gregory Michno "The Mystery of E Troop" pages 93 - 94.

[61] See Michael Donahue "Redefining Deep Ravine" page 49.

[62] The remains must have been discovered previously as Kellogg's notes were recovered (see Kenneth Hammer "Custer In '76" page 252) and, had Gibbon recovered them, he would surely have mentioned it. Gibbon mistakenly believed that the body had been overlooked by the burial party due to its almost complete lack of covering. Unfortunately, the exposure of Kellogg's body to the elements was probably the rule rather than an exception for this first burial of the Custer dead.

[63] Although this account clearly establishes the fact that Kellogg's remains were found to the west of Custer Hill, his marker is located to the east among the group of markers between the Keogh Sector and Custer Hill positions. This is due to the fact that the party erecting the markers in 1890 found a stake with Kellogg's name on it at the site of the present marker. See Kenneth Hammer "Custer In '76" page 252. Second Lieutenant Richard E. Thompson, Company K, 6th Infantry, confirmed Kellogg's body was discovered about 100 yards from the river. See Gregory Michno "The Mystery of E. Troop" page 164.

[64] See John Gibbon "Gibbon on the Sioux Campaign of 1876" page 39. Many authorities believe Gibbon refers to crossing the Little Big Horn near the mouth of Deep Ravine and that Kellogg's body was found near the head of that ravine. There are two keys to understanding the location described, the fact that Gibbon moved *"up the right bank"* after crossing and his description of *"sloping hills separated by little valleys, one of which seems to lead in about the direction we want to take"* and that *"just before this valley joins the valley of the river, the bottom has been cut into a gulch."* While Deep Ravine is definitely a gulch *"some eight or ten feet deep"* it most certainly is headed by what could be described as a basin, or valley, but certainly not by *"an open grassy*

slope" that is *"broken up into several smaller ones (valleys, DCE)."* In fact, this description exactly matches the terrain in the vicinity of Crazy Horse Ford where the river takes a turn to the southwest. We know that Gibbon's terrain description cannot possibly be Deep Ravine, but what can this account tell us about the death of Kellogg? The state of mutilation of the body is key here. As the body was not stripped, and only partially mutilated, it indicates he may have been killed early in the fight while the warriors were still preoccupied with resisting the soldiers (had the women and children found his body, it almost certainly would have been stripped and suffered more mutilation). It is therefore possible that Kellogg was a casualty sustained during Custer's withdrawal from Crazy Horse Ford.

[65] The basis for assuming a platoon action is based upon Indian accounts and tactical considerations rather than the location of bodies.

[66] See Brian C. Pohanka "Their Shots Quit Coming" page 24.

[67] After viewing the desecrated bodies of their comrades, several 7th Cavalry troopers vented their rage on the Indian dead. Private Homer Coon, Company I, 7th Infantry, saw Indian bodies dismembered and thrown on a brush fire by the infuriated cavalrymen. See Don Riuckey, Jr. "Forty Miles a Day on Beans and Hay" page 315.

[68] See Bruce Liddic and Paul Harbaugh "Camp on Custer" page 96.

[69] See Douglas Scott "Archaeological Insights Into The Custer Battle" page 15.

[70] Sergeant George Gaffney, Company I, who had been aboard the *Far West* as part of the Quartermaster Department, claimed to have cut the lodge poles used to mark the officer's graves. Gaffney said a heated ramrod was used to burn a Roman numeral into the stake thus identifying the bodies. See Bruce Liddic and Paul Harbaugh "Camp on Custer" page 93

[71] See the June 28 entry in the Godfrey's field diary.

[72] See Richard G. Hardorff "The Custer Battle Casualties" pages 105 – 106.

[73] See Kenneth Hammer "Custer in '76" page 248. It should be noted that Dr. Lord's marker is on the South Skirmish Line. Placed there because of the discovery of a button that was recognized as belonging to the doctor.

[74] See Colonel W. A. Graham "The Custer Myth" page 364.

[75] O'Neill told Walter Camp that this was Corporal John E. Hammon of Company G. Se Kenneth Hammer "Custer In '76" page 110.

[76] See John M. Carroll "A Seventh Cavalry Scrapbook #5" pages 20 – 21.

[77] See Kenneth Hammer "Custer In '76" page 122.

[78] See E. Elden Davis and James W. Wengert MD "That Fatal Day" page 11.

[79] See Evan S. Connell "Son of the Morning Star" page 21. Private John Lattman, Company G, told Walter Camp the body was clothed in a calico shirt which allowed identification. See Bruce Liddic and Paul Harbaugh "Camp on Custer" page 80.

[80] See Ronald H. Nichols "The Reno Court of Inquiry" page 554.

[81] Keogh's monument carries the following inscription:

"Sleep soldier still in honored rest

Your truth and valor wearing.

The bravest are the tenderest

The loving are the daring."

See Lenora A. Snedeker "Attention! An Article of Historical Opinion" Newsletter of the Little Big Horn Associates, May 1995, page 6.

[82] The bodies of First Lieutenant James Ezekiel Porter and Second Lieutenants Henry Moore Harrington and James Garland Sturgis were never officially identified. Varnum confirmed on the 50th anniversary of the fight that Sturgis' head had been found in the village. As there were also some reports that Porter's body had been recognized, the bodies of these two officers may lay with that of Doctor Lord under the present monument. It is of interest to note that all of these officers have markers bearing their names on the battlefield.

[83] Authorities at Fort Custer ordered a man to return a skull he had "collected" on the battlefield. See Douglas D. Scott "Archaeological Insights Into The Custer Battle" page 15.

[84] Contrary to popular belief, Crittenden's remains were not removed to make way for the road along Battle Ridge, but because the superintendent of the cemetery had received a letter of complaint that *"the custodian of the Custer Battlefield was not taking proper care of Lt. John Jordan Crittenden's grave."* See Jerry Cecil "Lt. Crittenden" page 35.

[85] See Joseph Mills Hanson "Conquest of the Missouri" pages 378 - 379.

[86] See John S. Manion, Jr., Blaine L. Beal, W. Donald Horn, and Dr. Lawrence Frost "Addressing the Custer Story" pages 50 - 51.

[87] See John S. Manion, Jr., Blaine L. Beal, W. Donald Horn, and Dr. Lawrence Frost "Addressing the Custer Story" pages 61 - 62.

[88] See James Brust "Learning About the Battle of The Little Big Horn From Photos Old and New" page 51.

[89] See James brust "Learning About the Battle of The Little Big Horn From Photos Old and New" page 52.

[90] Wounded, Nap was abandoned but followed the troops to the Yellowstone and he eventually wound up at Fort Lincoln. Joe Bush was recovered from the Lakota some years after the battle. See Richard G. Hardorff "Markers, Artifacts and Indian Testimony" page 66. John Burkman, Custer's striker, recalled that two of Custer's dogs, Bleuch and Tuck, tried to follow Custer into the fight but Burkman restrained them. See Glendolin Damon Wagner "Old Neutriment" page 152.

[91] See John M. Carroll "A Seventh Cavalry Scrapbook" pages 26 – 27. In addition to finding Comanche, Kennedy claimed there was no room on the *Far West* for the horse. His account doesn't state how Comanche got to Fort Lincoln. See Bruce Liddic and Paul Harbaugh "Camp on Custer" pages 159 and 162.

[92] See Elizabeth Atwood Lawrence "His Very Silence Speaks" page 96.

[93] See Kenneth Hammer "Custer In '76" page 140.

[94] See E. A. Brininstool "Troopers With Custer" pages 271 – 272.

[95] See Lawrence A. Frost "Custer Legends" page 216.

[96] See Evan S. Connell "Son of the Morning Star" page 297.

[97] See Edgar I. Stewart "Custer's Luck" page 476.

[98] Gibbon's concern for the conduct of the mules is what made hand litters initially attractive. See Colonel John Gibbon "Hunting Sitting Bull" pages 665 – 666.

[99] See O. G. Libby "The Arikara Narrative" page 114. While the horse Comanche was tenderly cared for on the voyage, the wounds of Arikara scout Goose were not attended to by Dr. Porter.

[100] Gibbon would write that the army should take lessons from the Indians in removing wounded from the field. See Colonel John Gibbon "Hunting Sitting Bull" page 694. It should be noted that Dr. Paulding's diary states 6 travois were used to transport Reno's wounded. See W. Boyes "Surgeon's Diary With the Custer Relief Column" page 26.

[101] See John M. Carroll "A Seventh Cavalry Scrapbook #8" page 19.

[102] See Kenneth Hammer "Custer In '76" page 73 and Colonel John Gibbon "Hunting Sitting Bull" page 674.

[103] See Joseph Mills Hanson "Conquest of the Missouri" page 298. It should be noted that when Walter Camp interviewed Captain Marsh, Marsh made no mention of Terry's alleged *"sad and terrible blunder"* comment.

[104] See John S. Gray "Centennial Campaign" page 196.

[105] See Daniel O. Magnussen "Thompson's Narrative" page 287.

[106] See John S. Gray "Centennial Campaign" page 197.

[107] See Kenneth Hammer "Custer In '76" page 241.

[108] See Kenneth Hammer "Custer In '76" page 241.

[109] See Fred Dustin "The Custer Tragedy" page 200.

[110] See John S. Gray "Centennial Campaign" page 197.

[111] See Daniel O. Magnussen "Thompson's Narrative" page 296.

[112] Members of the ship's company were: Grant Marsh, captain and pilot; Dave Campbell, pilot; Ben Thompson, mate; George Foulk and John Hardy, engineers; and Walter Burleigh, clerk. See Joseph Mills Hanson "Conquest of the Missouri page 239.

[113] See Richard Upton "The Custer Adventure" pages 101 – 104.

[114] Godfrey provided the following insight from his wife in a letter to Joseph Mills Hanson: *"I have heard the women, wives of officers, tell of their intense excitement when they heard the whistle blast of the Far West as she approached Bismarck on that July evening; how they waited and waited for tidings, each afraid to tell her thoughts and anxieties, till near midnight, when, with heavy hearts, almost with sobs, they separated and went to their homes. My wife told me how she tossed with restlessness till dawn, when she was startled from a doze by a tap on her window and instantly, suppressing a scream, exclaimed:*

"'Is my husband killed?'

"She was answered by a voice choked with emotion:

"'No, dear, your husband is safe and Mrs. Moylan's is safe, but all the rest are killed.'

"Then came the heart-breaking task of telling the news to the widows." See "Conquest of the Missouri" page 312.

[115] See Richard Upton 'The Custer Adventure" pages 104 – 105.

[116] See Elizabeth B. Custer "Boots and Saddles" pages 267 – 269.

[117] See Lawrence A. Frost "General Custer's Libbie" page 227.

[118] See John M. Carroll "A Seventh Cavalry Scrapbook #8" pages 6 – 7.

[119] See John M. Carroll "A Seventh Cavalry Scrapbook #10" page 17.

[120] See Thomas E. O'Neil "Custer Chronicles II" page 27.

[121] See Charles M. Cook "Little Big Horn Survivors"

[122] See Thomas Marquis "Custer, Cavalry and Crows" page 73.

Chapter 19

Epilogue

The Battle of the Little Big Horn had ended, but the campaign of 1876, frustrated by a continued lack of success was still in progress. Terry, the morale of his force at low ebb due to the mauling by the Lakota and Cheyenne as well as inept leadership, would make no attempt to follow the village until after being reinforced by Colonel Nelson A. Miles and Companies B, E, F, G, H, and K of the Fifth Infantry on August 1st.[1] On August 8th, Terry's 1,700 man force reentered the campaign as it commenced its march up the Rosebud to effect a junction with Crook's Bighorn and Yellowstone Expedition.[2] Conspicuous by their absence were the gatling guns left behind at the supply depot. In their place, Lieutenant Low commanded a battery comprised of two ten-pound and one welve-pound, rifles.[3]

While awaiting his reinforcements, Terry had continued to send out scouting parties and knew that the village had divided into at least two groups, one continuing toward the Big Horn Mountains and the other moving south and east. Terry, unwilling to face the Lakota and Cheyenne alone despite Sheridan's tender of the 5th Infantry, believed the final hope for a successful campaign rested in uniting his command with that of General Crook. Recognizing the danger inherent in attempting to reach Crook, Terry posted a notice calling for volunteers on a cottonwood tree on July 8.[4] Privates William Evans, Benjamin F. Stewart, and James Bell, all of Company E, 7th Infantry,[5] responded and were sent out on July 9th with three copies of dispatches detailing Custer's defeat and urging a junction of the commands sewn in the lining of their blouses.[6] Ignoring the caution to travel only at night, the small detail almost met with disaster on July 10th. Stopping on a small tributary of the Rosebud, they had counted 30 burial scaffolds of warriors they surmised had died from wounds received in the battle of the Little Big Horn when suddenly *"around the bend of the stream came the head of a herd of ponies, driven by about sixty hostile Indians."*[7] Being in the bottom of a small ravine, the couriers were not immediately detected, but they knew it was only a matter of time before they were discovered and flight across the open prairie was tantamount to suicide. After a hurried consultation, they settled on a daring scheme that saved their lives. When the head of the herd came opposite the ravine, they led their own horses into the herd and meandered along with the ponies, concealed by the dust. Evans recalled that when darkness fell: *"it did not take us long to get out of that vicinity."*[8] The couriers rode into Crook's camp on Goose Creek the morning of July 12th after witnessing the usual morning harassing raid on the pickets by a small party of Lakota and Cheyenne.[9] For their heroic exploit, Evans, Stewart and Bell were awarded the Medal of Honor.[10]

Crook was unable to receive the couriers in person until the next morning as he was away hunting in the mountains and had to be recalled by Captain Mills. Crook attempted to send a courier through with a reply to Terry's dispatches, but the scout turned back after two attempts, believing himself to have been spotted by the Lakota. Finally Crook asked Evans, Stewart and Bell if they would be willing to attempt the return trip. Evans and Stewart immediately volunteered, but Bell, whose horse had died the day they reached Crook's camp, was forced to decline. Accompanied by three of Crook's Crow scouts, Evans and Stewart departed at dark on July 23rd; reaching Terry's camp on the Yellowstone on July 25th.[11]

Crook has been soundly criticized, and deservedly so, for his inactivity after the defeat at the Rosebud. Already the largest force in the field, he had reported suffering only minimal casualties at the Rosebud. Crook, despite being reinforced by Major Alexander Chambers and 7 companies of the 4th Infantry on July 13th, had been ordered by Sheridan not to resume the campaign until the arrival of Colonel Wesley Merritt and his 10 companies of the 5th Cavalry; but to immediately resume operations upon their arrival.[12] Colonel Merritt was somewhat delayed in reaching Crook as he first had to intercept a party of Cheyenne who had left Red Cloud Agency for the unceded territory. Marching his command 85 miles in 31 hours, Merritt reached Warbonnet Creek ahead of the Cheyenne.[13] In an small engagement, noted in history for the slaying of the warrior Yellow Hair[14] by William F. "Buffalo Bill" Cody, Merritt turned the Cheyenne back to their reservation. After taking this "first scalp for Custer," Merritt effected his junction with Crook on August 3rd, bringing, in addition to his 10 companies of the 5th Cavalry, 76 recruits for the 2nd and 3rd Cavalry as well as over 60 "surplus" horses.[15]

While Crook was justified in awaiting the arrival of Merritt before moving, his lack of discipline and unwillingness to continue military operations in the meantime cannot be excused. The camp resembled a summer resort more than a military installation. There were constant recreational hunting and fishing parties and, despite the almost daily raids on the camp, the infantry and cavalry even managed to get in a game of baseball.[16] Crook would finally march toward his junction with Terry on August 5th; after a 49 day hiatus from the campaign.

While he waited for reinforcements, Crook did little to prepare for a resumption of active operations. He had reluctantly sent out a 25 man scouting party under Second Lieutenant Frederick William Sibley, Company E, 2nd Cavalry, on July 6th.[17] While Lieutenant Bourke would record the purpose of the scout as being to *". . . ascertain with some definiteness the whereabouts of the Sioux. . .,"* it is obvious from subsequent events Crook had no intention of acting on any intelligence the scout might provide. Crook's worst fears were realized when the small force accomplished their objective, encountering a large portion of the village on July 7th. Barely escaping with their lives, Sibley had to abandon his horses to effect a 50 mile withdrawal over the mountains. Exhausted and nearly starving, the scouting party stumbled into camp on July 9th to learn that Crook, apparently unable to deal with the suspense of waiting for their intelligence, had departed on yet another of his mountain outings the morning after their departure. Fortunately for his reputation, Crook was able to delay taking action on Sibley's intelligence until he received his written orders from Sheridan on July 13 to await the arrival of Merritt and the 5th Cavalry before resuming the campaign. With Sheridan's telegram in hand, Crook was able to send an extraordinary return wire on the 15th: *". . . The best information I can get from my front is that the Sioux have three fighting men to my one. Although* **I have no doubt of my ability to whip them with my present force, the victory would be one barren of results** *(emphasis the author's), and so I have thought it better to defer the attack until I get the Fifth here, and then end the campaign with one crushing blow. . . ."*[18]

The commands united on August 11 in a comical scene in which Terry's force deployed for battle, after mistaking Crook's advancing column for Indians. Instead of deciding to form a single strike force comprised of the 36 companies of cavalry in the combined commands, Terry and Crook decided to pursue the highly mobile enemy encumbered by the infantry. As Lieutenant McClernand would wryly remark:

> *"In my humble opinion the Cavalry of both commands – 36 troops – should have been united and sent rapidly forward to attack the enemy. A good cavalryman, General Merritt, was there to command. The defeat of the 7th Cavalry had, however, shaken the confidence of many in the ability of cavalry alone to contend successfully with Indians. I am not aware, however, that any such conclusions should have been drawn. The disaster of the Little Big Horn was the legitimate result not only of the greatly superior strength of the enemy, but of a badly planned battle, badly fought, perhaps, in many places.*

"The experience of the next two years showed that cavalry could charge and beat Indians. Besides, we could have fought on foot and have put probably 1500 men in line – exclusive of the horse holders. The Indians were retreating from their favorite hunting grounds, and it is fair to presume they were not equal to presenting as bold a front as formerly.

"Both on the Rosebud under Crook, and at the Little Big Horn, the troops were put in in piecemeal and beaten in detail. Fought in that way, either cavalry or infantry, at any time and under any circumstances, will probably be beaten."[19]

A disgusted Nelson Miles escorted the wagon train back to the Yellowstone with orders to keep the Indians on the south bank.[20] Freed of the direct participation of the department commanders, Miles and Mackenzie would achieve great success in winter campaigns. After plodding along together for two weeks, accomplishing nothing but wearing out themselves and their animals, Terry and Crook parted company; Terry disbanding his expedition shortly thereafter with the Montana Column being sent home on September 6th.[21]

Crook, left alone in the field, emulated Terry's predilection for marching hither and yon, accompanied by great ceremony and sense of urgency in responding to every fresh rumor, without achieving any concrete results. As Private Alfred McMackin sardonically remarked: *"The general supposition is that in order to draw the veil of obscurity over his (Crook, DCE) being outgeneralled by Sitting Bull, and his signal failure to accomplish anything towards the defeat of the Indians, he conceived the brilliant idea of marching hither and thither. . ."[22]*

The failure to close the distance on the enemy was not the saddest part of this phase of the campaign however. Crook had left himself totally cut off from any base of supply. While he had a fortunate experience in discovering a corn field to feed his famished horses along the Little Missouri River grown from the seed dropped by Terry's wagons in May;[23] overall this march was one of extreme privation. While the starvation march Crook's troops endured during the winter campaign might be attributed to a mistake made in the heat of combat, this second starvation march was coldly calculated. With his supplies almost exhausted, he turned his column away from Fort Lincoln toward the Black Hills. Crook would boast in his annual report he had accomplished a ten days march on *"a little over two day's rations."[24]* Citing his concern for the safety of the civilian population as the rationale for the privation he inflicted upon his command rings hollow when his 49 day period of inactivity following the Rosebud fight is recalled.

On September 5th[25] Crook ordered that 3 of the weakest horses from each battalion be shot each night for food.[26] By the time the starvation march ended, Crook had slaughtered over 400 horses,[27] leading to a standing joke by the infantry that if they only marched far enough, they would eat all the cavalry horses.[28] Second Lieutenant Walter Scribner Schuyler, Company B, 5th Cavalry, Aide–de–Camp to General Crook described the suffering of the troops to his father:

"I have told you of what I experienced on this march, but you can gather from that no realization of the suffering of the men, particularly the infantry. I have seen men become so exhausted they were actually insane . . . . I saw men who were very plucky sit down and cry like children because they could not hold out."[29]

While Crook would blame the hardships of the march on the small size of his pack train, citing that he could carry only enough provisions to march between supply points with no time to search the country for the enemy,[30] even this consummate "buck passer" was unable to find an individual to blame for the fiasco other than himself. By the 7th of September the command was on the verge of starvation. To meet the enemy now in a pitched battle was to invite total annihilation. Crook therefore detached Captain Mills and a 150 man escort,[31] mounted on the command's fittest horses, to ride ahead to Deadwood and obtain supplies. To lighten the load on the worn mounts, Mills allowed each trooper to carry only 50 rounds of carbine ammunition.[32]

The next evening, September 8, Mills stumbled across a small Lakota village comprised of Oglalas, Brules and Minneconjous, under the leadership of the Oglala American Horse, near Slim Buttes, Dakota Territory. Enroute to Spotted Tail Agency,[33] some of the inhabitants that had taken part in the Custer fight may have felt they had achieved a degree of safety by camping in that location. The fact that the tepees were pitched well inside the boundary of the Sioux Reservation was of no importance to Mills or his troopers. Immediately deciding to attack in three detachments at dawn the next morning, Mills inexplicably did not send word to Crook of his discovery or intentions, and he allowed his troopers to build fires.[34] Mills' luck held and he was not discovered until he launched his attack.

Mills carried the village on his initial assault achieving such surprise that many of the warriors cut their way out of the tepees.[35] Securing the village was another matter, however, as the warriors rallied and counterattacked with great ferocity. Mills was able to hold on for 3 hours until Crook arrived with the main force, despite the small amount of ammunition he had allowed the troopers to carry. Recovered from the village, in addition to the much needed dried meat that fed the command for a week,[36] were three 7th Cavalry horses and the gauntlets of Captain Keogh found wrapped in Company I's guidon.[37]

Having again been sent ahead to Deadwood on the 11th, Mills' arrival on the 13th with the supply wagons and a beef herd signaled the end of the starvation march.[38] Crook formally disbanded his expedition at Camp Robinson on October 24th.[39] While the victories of Mackenzie in the Dull Knife Fight and Miles at Wolf Mountain in the following winter demonstrated to the tribes the determination of the troops to bring the conflict to a final conclusion, two other events sealed the ultimate fate of these plains Indians. First, the military assumed control of the agencies. The troops enforced Sheridan's directive that any Indian returning to the reservation had to surrender his pony and all guns and ammunition. This policy, coupled with the disarming of the Indians already on the reservation, eliminated the agencies as a source of supply for warriors in the unceded territory. Finally, the establishment of Forts Keogh and Custer along the Yellowstone and Big Horn Rivers ensured that no sizable party of warriors could remain in the Powder River country in security. When the reservation Lakota were coerced into signing the Black Hills agreement on September 26, 1876, the government had finally achieved its campaign objective.

Hounded by Miles and his "Walk a Heaps",[40] Sitting Bull led his followers to Canada where he remained until surrendering on July 19, 1881.[41] A victim of the despair manifest in the ghost dance craze of 1890, Sitting Bull was killed by Indian policemen Lieutenant Bull Head and Sergeant Red Tomahawk while being placed under arrest on December 15, 1890.[42] Ironically, General Terry died in New Haven Connecticut the next day.

While the death of Sitting Bull deprived the Lakota of their spiritual leader, the symbol of their resistance, Crazy Horse, had died even earlier. Surrendering in May of 1877, Crazy Horse fell prey to petty tribal jealousies. Unused to politics, he tried to remain aloof, but the whispers of unscrupulous Lakota finally wrought his downfall. The army attempted to enlist Crazy Horse for the Nez Perce campaign. Tired of war, Crazy Horse initially refused, but finally consented to fight. Frank Grouard, however, misinterpreted the words of Crazy Horse and translated them not as *"we will fight until not a Nez Perce is left"* but as *"we will fight until not a white man is left."* [43] Arrested while journeying from Spotted Tail Agency to Fort Robinson, he was ordered to be confined in the guard house. When Crazy Horse realized what was happening, he broke free of his captors and pulled a knife. He was bayoneted in the kidney by a trooper while Little Big Man held his arms, just as his vision had foretold. Attended by his father and Minneconjou friend Touch The Clouds, Crazy Horse died painfully that night. The death of Crazy Horse was witnessed by Shave Elk, one of the scouts who escorted Crazy Horse from Spotted Tail Agency to Fort Robinson:

> *"When we got over there (Fort Robinson, DCE) an officer (Captain James Kennington, Company B, 14th Infantry, the officer of the day, DCE) took Crazy Horse by one hand and Little Big Man (Wicharta Taukala) by the other and led him off. I had turned to look the other way when I heard Crazy Horse say, 'So you intend to put me in the guard house, do you' and he turned to run back. A soldier (Private William Gentles, Company F, 14th Infantry, DCE) stabbed him with a bayonet in the right side, the bayonet going nearly through him (Crazy Horse was stabbed through the kidneys, DCE). About this time and while he was struggling to get away from Little Big Man, he drew a knife and cut Little Big Man on the wrist and also in the side under his left arm. This struggle was the end of Crazy Horse."[44]*

With the passing of Crazy Horse and Sitting Bull, the hoop of the nation had been smashed into a thousand fragments. Forced to live in the white man's rectangular houses, the sacred hoop could never hope to be reconstructed without the guidance of another leader in the mold of Crazy Horse and Sitting Bull. The Lakota still await such a leader.

A petition, dated July 4, 1876 and purportedly signed by 236 survivors of the 7th Cavalry, requesting Major Reno be promoted Lieutenant Colonel to fill the vacancy caused by Custer's death and that Captain Benteen be promoted major to fill the vacancy created by Reno's requested promotion, was forwarded to General Sherman, who politely replied that vacancies in grades above captain must be filled by the rule of seniority. An FBI analysis of the document conducted in 1954 revealed some startling facts. The petition contained signatures of 3 men who were known to have been in the Powder River camp on July 4,[45] as well as the signatures of 17 men who habitually signed for their pay with an "X."[46] The FBI concluded that as many as 79 signatures may have been forgeries[47] and were probably written by a single individual. The candidate most mentioned as the suspected forger is First Sergeant Joseph McCurry of Benteen's Company H. Regardless of the identity of the forger, a cover-up, designed to protect the honor of the regiment, was in full swing.[48]

General Terry, although apparently requiring some heavy convincing, also entered into the plot to cast the sole blame for the defeat on Custer.[49] Although he would never publicly fault Custer, it is instructive to view his official reports presented in Appendix 5. Terry's initial report, written on June 27th makes no mention of a cooperative plan of action between the columns of Gibbon and Custer, merely stating he had told Custer he planned to be at the mouth of the Little Big Horn on the 26th, the day Custer had wanted to attack. Terry sent telegrams on June 28 and July 2 detailing the burials and removal of the wounded, again without mentioning a plan of cooperative action.[50]

Finally, on July 2 he sent Sheridan a dispatch marked confidential.[51] It is instructive to quote the opening passage: *"I think **I owe it to myself** (emphasis the author's) to put you more fully in possession of the facts of the late operations."* The report details Custer's deviation from Terry's letter of instruction by immediately following the trail and not sending Herendeen down the Tullock. The report then goes on to state that a cooperative plan of action involving the two columns was planned for the 26th. The report, of necessity, omits any reference as to how the precise timing of such a movement would be determined and communicated once the location of the enemy was finally established. The report also doesn't explain why, if there was indeed such a plan, only inconsequential elements were included in the written instructions to Custer while the plan's critical element was left out! Terry, trapped perhaps by his own inherent honesty, then goes on to state he offered to accompany Custer and take the detachment of the 2nd Cavalry with him. While Terry clearly offered Custer the 2nd Cavalry, it is absurd to think that a general officer would seek a subordinate's approval to accompany the strike force. While Major Brisbin clearly suggested the offer of his cavalry be contingent upon Terry going in command, had Terry thought the idea of merit he would have simply ordered Custer to accept the 2nd Cavalry. Terry proves the lie in his own words when he attempts to argue both sides of the issue. Terry's point is that if you don't believe Custer disobeyed orders for a cooperative attack, then Custer is still to blame because he refused to accept the offer of the 2nd Cavalry and serve under the command of the expedition commander. This illogical subterfuge, which only serves to demonstrate Terry's ineptness as a field commander, could not have fooled Sheridan or Sherman even momentarily, but a scapegoat was needed and dead men tell no tales. Or so they thought.

What the army hadn't counted on was Custer's popularity and the devotion of Elizabeth Bacon Custer as well as some former subordinates, especially Frederick Whittaker. Libbie Custer spent the remaining 57 years of her widowhood in glorifying her husband's name and memory. Whittaker rushed a highly romanticized biography of Custer into print and then hammered on the War Department and congress to order an investigation of the Little Big Horn, if not a court–martial for Reno. Such a hue and cry was raised, primarily against Reno, that the embattled major was forced to seek a court of inquiry in an attempt to preserve his reputation. It is instructive to note that Reno requested the court of inquiry, which had no power to order punishment, 3 days prior to the expiration of the statute of limitations on potential courts martial for conduct at the Little Big Horn.[52]

The court of inquiry, which convened in Chicago's Palmer House on January 13, 1879 and adjourned 23 witnesses later on February 11, 1879, was a travesty. There was almost a total lack of pointed cross examination with discrepancies and contradictions in the testimony going unchallenged. Proving that it's a small world, the court recorder was Lieutenant Jesse Matlock Lee of the 9th Infantry,[53] who had been the military agent in charge of Spotted Tail Agency in 1877 and had witnessed the death of Crazy Horse.[54] The fact that Lee was inexperienced in questioning witnesses was of no concern to an army that had decided two years previously that Reno's conduct did not require investigation. Given his inexperience, the lack of pointed cross examination is perhaps understandable.

It was clear from the beginning there was much to cover up. A nervous Reno set up a hospitality suite in his room where 7th Cavalry officers were treated to whiskey and cigars prior to testifying. Although Benteen had urged his attendance, apparently only Godfrey refused to attend.[55] Benteen would brag in later years that, although the court knew he was withholding information, they weren't able to get him to divulge it.[56] Benteen, who had no fondness for Reno, was probably the architect of the officers closing ranks behind Reno to preserve the honor of the regiment. As Lieutenant McClernand wrote:

> *"It was in leadership that Custer's lieutenant (Reno, DCE) seems to have failed, and that he had so failed and that Benteen was the man who stood between utter destruction and such safety as was found, was heard on all sides from his subordinates when Terry arrived. Many of the criticisms heard were severe. Later, before the Court of Inquiry that followed, many were toned down."[57]*

Toned down indeed! When DeRudio testified, he was not asked about his comment that they'd have all been killed had they not been commanded by a coward. Instead, only Lieutenant Mathey was asked if he had heard DeRudio make the statement. The only really damaging piece of testimony to come from an officer during the testimony was Godfrey's comment that he believed Reno to have exhibited *"nervous timidity."*[58] While seasoned plainsmen Herendeen and Girard were extremely critical of Reno's conduct, they were not military men and their testimony carried little weight.[59]

Captain Robert G. Carter wrote the following two memoranda concerning what he had heard regarding a cover up:

"July 6, 1923

"General D. S. Brainard told me this date that he often heard Capt. (later General) Whelan (Captain James Nichols Wheelan, Company G, DCE) and Lieut. (later General) C. F. Roe, both of the Second U. S. Cavalry and of Terry's command, say that when they reached Reno's defensive line on the bluff all of Reno's officers talked wildly and excitedly about the fight, and of Reno's cowardice, etc. A little later they shut their mouths like clams and would not talk. It seemed to them (Brainard was later in Whelan's troop) that there suddenly sprang up among the Seventh Cavalry officers a understanding and resolve among themselves that they would say nothing further about that affair which would reflect in any way upon the honor of their regiment or regimental esprit, even if they had to sacrifice their own individual opinions concerning the plan of campaign or the conduct of the battle, either by Reno or Custer. This was later shown by their testimony before the Reno Court of Inquiry, where all but Godfrey refused to charge Reno with cowardice.

"It is also shown by my interview with Col. (John) Merrill (son of Major Lewis Merrill, 7th Cavalry) who as a boy heard the battle discussed in the post trader's store at Fort Abraham Lincoln for months and was astounded to learn that three years later (1879) nearly every officer went before the Reno Court and testified to absolutely nothing, which, in 1876, they had uttered as a positive conviction."[60]

*"I have frequently heard Major-General Eben Swift, who for a period was Adjutant of the Fifth U. S. Cavalry when General Wesley Merritt commended it – declare that General Merritt who was a member of the Reno Court of Inquiry held in Chicago in 1879 told him that the Court in its finding – **'damned Reno with faint praise'** – because they were compelled to base the finding according to the evidence – and most of the witnesses seemed reluctant **'to tell the truth, the whole truth and nothing but the truth'** but testified only to such facts as would sustain the honor and uphold the reputation of the Seventh U. S. Cavalry (emphasis from the original, DCE).*

"R. G. Carter

Capt. U. S. Army, Ret'd

July 11, 1932"[61]

While the name of the correspondent for the *St. Paul Pioneer Press* appears to have been lost to history, his dispatch of February 3, 1879, signed "Winearls," supports Carter's memoranda: *"It is hoped the Reno inquiry will close by the end of next week. There is no probability of his being found guilty of cowardice. I cannot refrain from remarking that the manner some of the officers have talked in private and to their friends in regard to the events of that day has been strangely at variance with their sworn testimony. It shows conclusively that they are either cowardly talking behind Reno's back, or else that they have not courage enough to face his resentment by speaking the truth on the witness stand."*[62]

Despite the fact the officers covered up for Reno and some very obvious questions were not asked in relation to the failure to obey Custer's written order, much of interest did come out of the testimony. Reno defended his actions in withdrawing from the timber by comparing his defensive position to the one on Beecher's Island that was repeatedly charged by the Cheyenne. Although Beecher's Island was covered with brush as opposed to Reno's heavily timbered positon, Reno's assertion that the Lakota would have certainly charged his position, which was too extensive to defend with the number of troopers available, went unchallenged. His reputation being dependent on Custer's command having been annihilated in a very short time, Reno would testify that he believed Custer's command had been annihilated before he left the timber; while Benteen, who had disobeyed a direct order in the presence of the enemy, supported Reno's testimony with his belief that Custer was already dead by the time trumpeter Martin reached him with Custer's message. Neither was asked the basis for his belief and, in concert with their positions, Reno and Benteen were the only ones to offer testimony that they could not hear Custer's firing from Reno's temporary position on the bluffs. Benteen even went so far as to testify that Custer's field could not even be seen from Weir Point, an obvious falsehood that could have been easily refuted had the recorder been interested in pursuing the matter.

Reno admitted under oath, he had not charged the village as ordered. He also admitted he had abandoned his wounded in the valley. Reno was not questioned as to why he didn't attempt to cover his retreat crossing of the Little Big Horn, nor did he offer any explanation other than stating he was at the head of the column as he thought proper in a "charge." Reno was not the only one to be damaged by the testimony, Captain Myles Moylan admitting under oath that it was better to be a live coward on the hill than a dead hero in the timber.[63]

In his summation, which was far stronger than either his direct or cross examination of witnesses, Lieutenant Lee damned Reno for failing to charge the village, failing to remain in the timber, and for the character of his retreat from the valley. Nothing of importance was said regarding his conduct during the hilltop fight. The findings of the court, presented in Appendix 8, was akin to the old Scottish verdict of "not proven" whereby the sentence is remitted but the stigma remains. Wesley Merritt, a member of the court, summed it up with the following remark: *"Well, the officers wouldn't tell us anything, and we could do nothing more than damn Reno with faint praise."*[64] The army was well satisfied with the verdict, but it apparently haunted Lieutenant Lee as his 1897 letter to Libbie Custer testifies:

> *"I want to say to you in all frankness, that at one time I was in some degree influenced by the prejudicial opinions of those whose motives I did not understand, and whose sources of information I then had no means of testing. But soon after I was brought into close contact with thousands of Indians, the Sioux, Cheyennes and others; and In January 1879, I was Recorder of the Reno Court of Inquiry; a year later I visited the field of battle.*

> *"Now, I tried to be honest and fair minded and allow nothing but **facts** to make an impression on my mind. So it came about in the light of long and confidential talks with Indians under my charge, in the light of what was said to me by witnesses **before** they went on the stand, and in the light of much testimony **on the stand**, and finally in the light of my visit to the field, my judgment could no more escape the conclusion of **facts** than to deny that I am penning these lines. That conclusion I referred to in my letter to General Miles and I am glad you consider it 'generous and fair.' **It is true!** I do not believe an unprejudiced mind – any one whose heart is free from the contact of jealousy could with a knowledge of all the facts come to*

*any other conclusion. When I got all the facts it was easy to understand how **self interest** influenced opinions; how jealousy being unopposed could unmask its horrid power and loosen its tongue of calumny – with none to answer; how the living could extol themselves for **prudence** and **delay** – and condemn the dead as **rash** and **impetuous**, how Authority through inexperience, sought to evade the responsibility through a loophole of escape. Had some one blundered? Then how easy to censure those who could not answer. It was both cruel and unjust for **anyone** to send that dispatch: 'Orders were disobeyed but the penalty paid.'(emphasis from the original)*

"This dispatch reveals both weakness and incompetency. The sender, as I believe, knew but little if anything about Indians, but he did know General Custer, and it verges on imbecility to suppose that any one would expect Indians to be held in position several days by one column waiting and making it convenient for another column to attack them.

*"I was glad to see that General Miles had gotten at all the material facts, and of course there could be but one conclusion. I think Capt. Philo Clark in his life time – got the fact, and the conclusion was the same. Major Godfrey when Captain of the 7th Cavy – wrote a very fair article on this subject. There has been so much misrepresentation – so much from personal and interested motives, that it would seem that the truth is hard to separate from the chaff, but I believe that the **impartial historian** will do justice to your distinguished husband.(emphasis from the original)*

*"My opinion, as such, is of but little account one way or the other, but I believe as an unprejudiced person I have had better opportunities to get at the **facts** than almost any other person. These facts show beyond successful contradiction: (emphasis from the original)*

*"1st: That General Custer was **not** disobeying General Terry's orders in attacking the Indians. Any other course under the circumstances would have been ridiculous and absurd. (emphasis from the original)*

*"2nd: Major Reno, according to General Gibbon's testimony – left, **abandoned**, a splendid position where he threatened the entire village and thus enabled the entire force of Indians to concentrate on general Custer, who was thus compelled to meet them with **less** than 2/5 of the effective force of his regiment. (emphasis from the original)*

*"3rd: Major Reno's disastrous retreat in **keeping out of the battle at a critical period fully 3/5 of the effective force**, and in doing this all chance for victory over the Indians was lost. (emphasis from the original)*

"I had not the honor of a personal acquaintance with General Custer. I saw him but once in my life; but I feel that I would be remiss to Truth were I to fail to say and write on appropriate occasions that which I know is in accord with his great reputation."[65]

Reno did not fare well after the Little Big Horn. On the very evening the 7th Cavalry returned to Fort Lincoln, September 26, Reno became involved in a drunken brawl. Sent to Fort Abercrombie, he almost immediately became involved in a scandal with Emiline Bell, the rather notorious wife of a brother 7th Cavalry officer. As a result, he was court–martialed and sentenced to be dismissed from the service; President Hayes reducing the sentence to suspension without pay for two years. Reno was serving out this suspension during the tenure of the court of inquiry. Re-instated, Reno immediately got into trouble again. Already under arrest for another drunken brawl, this time involving Lieutenant Nicholson, Reno became embroiled in a controversy involving his commanding officer's daughter. Colonel Sturgis preferred charges against Reno when he was caught peeping through the parlor window at young Ella Sturgis. Reno was found guilty of *"disorders and neglects . . . to the prejudice of good order and military discipline"*, known as the "Devil's Article," and sentenced to be dismissed from the service; this time, despite the protests of Generals Terry and Sherman that the punishment was excessive, the sentence was not commuted. Although there was more than a little truth in Reno's lament: *"it has been my misfortune to have attained a widespread notoriety through the country by means of the press, open to any enemy who know not why they are so, but like the village cur, bark when their fellows do, and a greater attention will be called to what I do than other officers not so widely advertised"*,[66] and some justification for comparing Reno with World War II's Eddie Slovick, Reno's drunkenness and overbearing behavior were the root cause of his problems.

In 1967 Reno's biographers, John Upton Terrell and Colonel George Walton, received a hearing before the Board for the Correction of Military Records at the Pentagon, Washington, D. C., which resulted in the reversal of the two court martial decisions.[67] All this came much too late for Reno, of course who died of cancer on April 1, 1889, the ninth anniversary of his dismissal from the service. He was buried in a pauper's grave in Washington D. C.; being exhumed and reinterred in the Custer Battlefield National Cemetery after his court–martials had been overturned.

Benteen fared somewhat better than Reno. Ironically, he wound up his military service as a major in a black regiment, the Ninth Cavalry; after having turned down a commission as major in the black Tenth Cavalry 17 years previously. Benteen was court–martialed and found guilty on 3 of 6 counts of drunkenness and of conduct unbecoming an officer, a charge related to an alleged incident of relieving himself upon a tent in which women were seated.[68] Sentenced to be dismissed from the service, President Grover Cleveland mitigated the sentence to suspension at half pay for one year *"in view of his long and honorable service and the reputation he has earned for bravery and soldierly qualities."*[69] Within three months of returning to active duty, Benteen was retired for medical reasons: *"incapacitated for active service because of defective vision, frequent micturition caused by either spinal lesion and inflammation of the prostate gland and neuralgia; all of which are incident to the service."*[70] During his retirement he engaged in a lengthy correspondence with Theodore Goldin, a former private in the Seventh Cavalry. This correspondence reveals Benteen to have been an embittered man whose obsessive hatred for Custer increased with the passing years. A year and a half into retirement, he was breveted a brigadier general for his actions at the Little Big Horn and at Canyon Creek during the Nez Perce campaign. Stricken with malarial fever, he suffered a stroke and died June 22, 1898. He is buried in Arlington National Cemetery.

---

[1] See Norm Davis "A Tale of Two Privates" page 71.

[2] See Edward J. McClernand "On Time For Disaster" page 96.

[3] See C. Lee Noyes "The Guns 'Long Hair' Left Behind" page 96.

4 See Paul L. Hedren "Three Cool, Determined Men" page 20.

5 See Paul L. Hedren "Three Cool, Determined Men" page 15.

6 See Paul L. Hedren "Three Cool, Determined Men" page 21.

7 See Paul L. Hedren "Three Cool, Determined Men" page 22.

8 See Paul L. Hedren "Three Cool, Determined Men" page 22.

9 See Paul L. Hedren "Three Cool, Determined Men" page 23.

10 See Paul L. Hedren "Three Cool, Determined Men" page 15.

11 See Paul L. Hedren "Three Cool, Determined Men" page 26.

12 See John G. Bourke "On the Border With Crook" page 336.

13 See Paul Andrew Hutton "Soldiers West" page 247.

14 This warrior is referred to as Yellow Hand by some authors.

15 See John G. Bourke "On The Border With Crook" page 344.

16 See John G. Bourke "On The Border With Crook" page 343.

17 See "On The Border With Crook" page 331.

18 See John M. Carroll "A Seventh Cavalry Scrapbook # 12" page 28. After his near debacle on the Rosebud there was no need for Crook to explain how a "victory" could be *"barren of results."*

19 See Edward J. McClernand "On Time For Disaster" pages 97 – 98. McClernand's opinion was echoed by Lieutenant Frank D. Baldwin whose diary records: *". . . it is the general opinion (of surviving 7th Cavalry officers, DCE) that if Genl. Terry had at once put his fresh forces in pursuit he could have used the Indians up at one stroke. . ."* See James S. Brust "Baldwin Talks With Reno, Writes About Custer's Final Battle" page 20.

20 See Colonel John Gibbon "Hunting Sitting Bull" pages 682 – 683.

21 See Edward J. McClernand "On Time For Disaster" pages 98 – 99.

22 See Evan S. Connell "Son of the Morning Start" page 336.

23 See Martin F. Schmitt "General George Crook: His Autobiography" page 212.

24 See John M. Carroll "General Custer and the Battle of the Little Big Horn: The Federalist View" page 124.

25 See Jerome A. Greene "Slim Buttes, 1876" page 42.

[26] See John M. Carroll "Papers of The Order of Indian Wars" page 41.

[27] See John M. Carroll "Papers of The Order of Indian Wars" page 31.

[28] See Martin F. Schmitt "General George Crook: His Autobiography" page 209.

[29] See Don Rickey, Jr. "Forty Miles A Day on Beans and Hay" pages 262 – 263.

[30] See Martin F. Schmitt "General George Crook: His Autobiography" page 213.

[31] See Cyrus Townsend Brady "Indian Fights and Fighters" page 306.

[32] See Jerome A. Greene "Slim Buttes, 1876" page 48.

[33] See Jerome A. Greene "Slim Buttes, 1876" page 50.

[34] See Jerome A. Greene "Slim Buttes, 1876" page 56.

[35] See John F. Finerty "War Path and Bivouac" page 282.

[36] See Martin F. Schmitt "General George Crook: His Autobiography" page 206.

[37] See John M. Carroll "General Custer and the Battle of the Little Big Horn: The Federalist View" page 126 and John P. Langellier, et al "Myles Keogh: Irish Dragoon" page 154.

[38] See Paul Andrew Hutton "Soldiers West" page 248.

[39] See Jerome A. Greene "Slim Buttes, 1876" page 111.

[40] Crazy Horse's name for infantry.

[41] See Robert M. Utley "Frontier Regulars" page 288.

[42] See E. A. Brininstool "Fighting Indian Warriors" page 183.

[43] See Mari Sandoz "Crazy Horse" page 392. Louis Bordeaux claimed Grouard feared Crazy Horse and sought to get him in trouble with the authorities. The implication being Grouard intentionally misinterpreted Crazy Horse's remarks. See Bruce Liddic and Paul Harbaugh "Camp on Custer" page 140. Grouard, apparently omitting all mention of translating Crazy Horse's remarks, told his biographer that he had discovered a plot by Crazy Horse to kill not only himself and Lieutenant Clarke, but also all of the whites at Red Cloud Agency. See Joe De Barthe "The Life and Adventures of Frank Grouard" page 338. Insight into Grouard's attitude toward Crazy Horse may be gained from his description of the Reynolds Fight, which Grouard assumed to have taken place against the village of Crazy Horse:

> ". . . I yelled to Crazy Horse. I recalled what he had told me during my endeavors to secure the Black Hills Treaty – that he would rather fight than make a treaty – and told him that now was the time to come out and get all the fighting he wanted, as the troops were all around his camp."

See Joe De Barthe "The Life and Adventures of Frank Grouard" page 192.

[44] See Bruce Liddic and Paul Harbaugh "Camp on Custer" pages 126 - 127 and Richard G. Hardorff "The Oglala Lakota Crazy Horse" page 15.

[45] See Charles G. du Bois "Kick the Dead Lion" page 55.

[46] See Charles G. du Bois "Kick the Dead Lion" page 53.

[47] See Charles G. du Bois "Kick the Dead Lion" page 55.

[48] A detailed account of the forgeries may be found in Robert J. Ege "Curse Not His Curls" page 116.

[49] Terry's letter of August 1st to his sisters indicates a growing concern for salvaging his reputation and expresses the hope that the presidential election will refocus the nation's attention away from the campaign: *"I have not a very lively expectation of meeting the Indians in a large body. I don't (sic) see how they can keep together such a force as they have had and subsist. I am inclined to think that both Crook's & my future operations will be fruitless, & then wont there be a howl? Perhaps the excitement over the presidential (sic) election will wax so warm by that time affairs in this quarter will seem to be of very slight importance."* See James Willert "The Terry Letters" page 35.

[50] According to Terry's brother-in-law, Captain R. P. Hughes, Terry read his dispatch of June 27 to his staff officers prior to sending it. Hughes said the officers protested vigorously about omitting Custer's disobedience of orders, which was rectified in Terry's confidential dispatch of July 2. See pages 19 and 20 of the appendix to Colonel W. A. Graham's "The Story of the Little Big Horn."

[51] Upon receiving the report, General Sherman, who was in Philadelphia attending the Centennial Exposition with Sheridan, determined it should be forwarded to the Secretary of War. Sherman gave the report to a reporter he had mistaken for a messenger, who then made the report public. See pages 19 and 20 of the appendix to Colonel W. A. Graham's "The Story of the Little Big Horn."

[52] See Colonel W. A. Graham "The Reno Court of Inquiry" page iv.

[53] See Francis B. Taunton "No Pride in the Little Big Horn" page 24.

[54] See Robert M. Utley "Custer and the Great Controversy" page 92.

[55] See Colonel W. A. Graham "The Custer Myth" plage 319. Godfrey noted in a 1925 letter to retired Captain Robert G. Carter: *"I never heard that there was a compact by officers as to testimony. I only know that I was importuned many times by Benteen, and by others, to call on Reno and visit him in his room, drink his whiskey and smoke his cigars, etc. I did know by circumstances that there was a lot of drinking going on in his room. I refrained from reading the proceedings of the court, when I overheard someone express surprise at the testimony given by one witness, which was summarized by 'he believes in Reno.' So, I did not visit Reno nor read the testimony given during the trial."* See Steven Wright "Edward Settle Godfrey and the Custer Myth" page 12.

[56] While Benteen withheld testimony on Reno's plan to abandon the wounded, he had discussed it with Reno's attorney should the subject surface. See Colonel W. A. Graham "The Custer Myth" page 192.

[57] See Edward J. McClernand "On Time For Disaster" page 88.

[58] See Colonel W. A. Graham "The Reno Court of Inquiry" page 184.

[59] Robert Utley notes that the marked difference in testimony between the civilians, most of whom had a personal ax to grand with Reno, and the officers gave rise to the supposition that the army had closed ranks behind Reno. See "Custer and the Great Controversy" page 61.

[60] See Tom O'Neal "Marcus A. Reno: What Was Said Of Him At The Little Big Horn" page 11.

[61] See Tom O'Neal "Marcus A. Reno: What Was Said Of Him At The Little Big Horn" page 11.

[62] See E. Eldon Davis "The Reno Court of Inquiry: The Pioneer Press" page 17.

[63] See Colonel W. A. Graham "The Reno Court of Inquiry" page 79.

[64] See Francis B. Taunton "No Pride in the Little Big Horn" page 42.

[65] See Lawrence A. Frost "Custer Legends" pages 99 - 100.

[66] See Charles K. Mills "Harvest of Barren Regrets" page 324.

[67] See Robert M. Utley "Frontier Regulars" page 84 and Ronald H. Nichols "Marcus Albert Reno" page 14.

[68] See Charles K. Mills "Harvest of Barren Regrets" page 364.

[69] See Charles K. Mills "Harvest of Barren Regrets" page 364.

[70] See Charles K. Mills "Harvest of Barren Regrets" page 367.

Chapter 20

A Campaign Gone Awry

The campaign of 1876 was a catastrophic military failure by any measure. In addition to the Little Big Horn disaster, the United States Army had been dealt a humiliating defeat at the Rosebud and the national press was not at all reticent in reciting the army's timid approach to the anticipated conquest of the plains tribes as well as the campaign's military failures. Even the minor victories at Powder River in March and Slim Buttes in September were tainted by the failure to follow up on the initial success, and, in the case of the Reynolds Fight, actually had the adverse effect of strengthening warrior morale and resolve. The campaign also pointed out a lack of capability for waging this style of warfare that was far too common among the high command elements.

Terry, Gibbon and Crook proved themselves incapable of dealing with the extant situation and relied on the expedients of "no comment" or placing the blame for the campaign's failures on the shoulders of others. These three officers, while major contributors not only to the Little Big Horn disaster, but the failure of the overall campaign, must be judged against the standard of their times, just as Armstrong Custer's performance must be judged against that of his peers in the campaign. As an aid in understanding the performance of Terry, Gibbon and Crook, it must be pointed out that the United States Army has never been able to deal effectively with irregular or guerrilla forces. To believe otherwise is to deny the experience of the Philippine and Pancho Villa Campaigns as well as the entire Vietnam experience. It is instructive to note that military objectives for the 1876 campaign were finally realized when active campaigning was removed from the personal control of the department commanders and senior staff, and vested in the capable hands of prominent younger officers, Nelson Miles and Ranald Mackenzie. The fact that an officer of this ilk, Armstrong Custer, had been in command at the Little Big Horn only increased the disbelief associated with the disaster. A mighty industrial giant, poised on the threshold of a technological revolution unparalleled in the history of mankind, had picked a fight with a stone age culture of nomadic hunters and been soundly whipped!

Institutions and political power structures cannot survive this class of debacle. Accordingly, the situation could not be simply ignored. A scapegoat had to be found. To preclude some embarrassing, and unanswerable, questions, those most intimately involved did not take an active part in the burgeoning controversy, relying upon others to cast the necessary aspersions.

The controversies associated with the battle of the Little Big Horn commenced almost before the sound of the final shot had faded away and continues unabated to the present day. There have been almost as many theories advanced as to the causes of the disaster as there have been writers on the subject. The earliest theories revolved around the central theme that Custer must have been ambushed. This theme was modified somewhat by one author in the recent past who believed that Mitch Boyer intentionally led the 7th Cavalry into a trap. The next set of theories to emerge dealt with variations on the theme of Custer as the vain egotistical glory hunter who, against his better judgment, rushed pell mell to the slaughter. Equally popular over the years with the glory hunter theme has been the hue and cry that the defeat was directly attributable to a combination of the cowardice of Reno and the indifference of Benteen. A variation on the theme of the incompetent subordinates lays the cause of the defeat on a movement from Custer Hill to Calhoun Hill to open a corridor for Benteen when Custer sighted the troops on Weir Point. The final category of themes revolves around the theory that Custer's immediate command gave a poor account of themselves. The first manifestations of this theme were in the theories that the troops had committed mass suicide, or were too exhausted to fight, or were drunk. The latest variant on this theme is that Custer's immediate command suffered from mass hysteria, or, if you prefer, combat fatigue.

Despite the apparent diversity of the foregoing opinions, they have a common central thesis; rather than having been beaten by the Indians, the army lost this fight! This attitude is prevalent in the American psyche and culture and is especially manifest in sports where the home team is never outmatched and beaten, but, through some fatal error, or foul play, manages to lose the contest. The proponents of the above theories will continue to insist their theory is the only logical explanation as to how the army lost the battle. I do not intend to enter into the never ending debate regarding the relative merit of the arguments and counter-arguments associated with each of the theories mentioned above. Suffice it to say, I believe that all of the above theories suffer from the same defect; they are based on a common false assumption – the inherent infallibility of the frontier army. While there is much to criticize in the army's performance during the campaign in general, and the battle of the Little Big Horn in particular, the Indian testimony and the archaeological evidence are clear – this was a fight won by the Indians, not one lost by the soldiers. The fact that a victory of this magnitude was unprecedented and, given the plains Indian's method of fighting, impossible to predict absent detailed knowledge of the Battle of the Rosebud, cannot be allowed to shape our interpretation of the historical record as revealed by eyewitness testimony, an examination of the terrain, a study of the tactics of the period, an appreciation for the personalities involved, and the archaeological evidence. It is ironic that Frederick Benteen, one of the men most responsible for the vast amount of misinformation surrounding this fight, should have said it most succinctly. Benteen's explanation for the defeat was simply: *"Too many Indians, good shots, good riders and the best fighters the sun ever shone on."*[1]

I believe the historical record is both clear and straight forward. The fight began as one of those typically ineffectual long range sniping affairs that did little damage and allowed both sides to boast of their prowess. The fight continued in this manner for perhaps as long as an hour and a half and seemed destined to result in another drawn battle, where both sides could claim victory, for which the 1876 campaign is notorious. In this case destiny, in the person of the Southern Cheyenne Old Man Chief Lame White Man, would decree otherwise. Noticing the weakness in a tactical deployment by Custer, probably undertaken to screen a reunification of his command at Calhoun Hill, Lame White Man led a charge setting off a chain of events culminating in the virtual annihilation of three and one half of Custer's five companies in the time required for *"a hungry man to eat his dinner."* Reduced to one full company and the shattered, demoralized remnants of the other four, it was not long before the men on Custer Hill joined their comrades in "Fiddler's Green."

In the following pages I will briefly discuss the major controversies associated with the Battle of the Little Big Horn, including an analysis of the performance of the principal participants in the campaign: George Crook, Alfred Terry, John Gibbon, Marcus Reno, Frederick Benteen, and Armstrong Custer. While there is much to criticize in the performance of the officers mentioned, their conduct must be evaluated against the standard of their times, not against twentieth century military science, social mores or "political correctness." Whatever the shortcomings of these officers, at most their errors were contributing factors, similar in scope to those mentioned throughout the narrative, rather than the principal causes of the defeat. Had the military performed flawlessly, the result would have been the same, given that Custer would attack the village on June 25. The outcome of this fight hinged on Lame White Man seizing the decisive moment, nothing more. To postulate a chain of events that would not have Lame White Man in the right place at the right time would be only the wildest conjecture incapable of proof. The essential elements of the fight on Custer's field were five:

1. Custer's attempt to seize victory by capturing the non-combatants.

2. The division of his immediate command to attempt the capture required a reunification and associated screening deployment, carried out in this instance by E Troop.

3. Lame White Man seizing the initiative and overwhelming the platoon of E Troop posted on the South Skirmish Line.

4. C Troop, the second most inexperienced in the regiment, was the next to fall. Commanded by a relatively inexperienced second lieutenant and a first sergeant, they did not give a good account of themselves breaking under the pressure of the warrior's charge.[2]

5. Company L disintegrated under extreme pressure from simultaneous attacks on three sides.

If one accepts the foregoing as the principal elements causing the defeat, then a faultless performance by Custer, Reno and Benteen, while causing more warrior casualties, would have yielded the same result. Concocting a scenario in which either items 1 or 3 above do not occur is akin to postulating a scenario where the battle takes place on entirely different terrain with different numbers, and strengths, of army units involved. Of course, any such scenario can neither be proven nor disproven and, as such, must be relegated to the realm of fiction, not historical narrative. Why then discuss the controversies at all? As I stated in the foreword, I agonized for a long time before including this chapter. Two reasons finally compelled me to write it. First, there have been so many preposterous theories advanced that I felt obligated to attempt to "set the record straight." Secondly, a criticism of the principals involved is a valuable exercise not only in understanding what the "standard of performance" was like in the late 19th century army, but in humanizing the personalities involved. Before assessing the performance of the six principal officers, there are three additional elements of controversy: the number of warriors involved, Indian armament, and the performance of the 1873 Model Springfield Carbine, that must be discussed.

The first element of controversy is associated with the number of warriors present at the Little Big Horn. The root cause of this controversy is the same as for the earlier theories about the defeat – the invincibility of the frontier army. In the mind set of the late nineteenth century military establishment, it was an incontrovertible fact that a force of 3 companies was able to handle any contingency when dealing with plains Indians. As Custer had 5 companies under his direct command, it therefore follows that a primary cause of the defeat must have been the Indians were massed in overwhelming numbers. To that end, early estimates ranged as high as 7,000 warriors.[3] From that ridiculously high figure, the number of warriors believed to have been engaged has steadily decreased over the years until an equally ridiculous figure of a maximum of 700 - 800 warriors was proposed. While I personally believe that the number of warriors present in the village was around 2,500, the actual number of warriors engaged is really not of prime importance.

Going into the '76 campaign, the military was not concerned with numbers of warriors; that only became an issue in the final reports of the commanders as they attempted to justify an universally poor performance. The concern of the military had always been that they would be unable to force the warriors to battle. Strength and terrain were unimportant as witnessed by Gibbon's, Terry's and Crook's willingness to make detailed plans and dispositions of troops without firm intelligence[4] relating to the enemy's strength and location. Those details were not overlooked by these professional military men, they were deemed unnecessary impediments to the sole problem at hand – bringing the enemy to battle. In the final analysis, the number of warriors present was not nearly so important to the battle's outcome as was the manner in which they fought. *"Never before or after were the northern Plains tribes better prepared for war. They were numerous, united, confident, superbly led, emotionally charged to defend their homeland and freedom, and able, through design or good fortune, to catch their adversary in unfavorable tactical situations. Even flawless generalship might not have prevailed over Sitting Bull's mighty coalition that summer. In large part the generals lost the war because the Indians won it."[5]*

The second element of controversy, and corollary to the first, is the question of the warrior's armament. Archaeological investigations at the battlefield have uncovered evidence that the warriors were better armed than previously supposed and supports Varnum's recollection that all the warriors he observed were armed with guns.[6] Statistical analysis of the recovered shell casings indicates that as many as 414 warriors had firearms, of which perhaps 232 were magazine guns (Winchester and Henry repeating rifles).[7] These repeating rifles apparently played a decisive role in the action on Calhoun Hill. The archaeological evidence also indicates that at least 29 warriors,[8] armed with Winchesters or Henrys, concentrated in the area known as Henryville, southeast of Calhoun Hill.

The archaeological evidence is also clear that Company L's skirmish line pivoted until being re-established at about a right angle to their previous position. The Indian accounts are clear that the company initially faced southward to check the warriors streaming up Deep Coulee. The archaeological evidence, which confirms the skirmish line faced southward at one time, indicates that the line was pivoted to face in a westward direction. I have postulated this movement was in response to the charge of Lame White Man and the subsequent collapse of Company C. Facing Greasy Grass Ridge, Company L's left flank was exposed to the charge of Gall's warriors, while the marksmen located in Henryville poured what must have been a galling fire into the company's rear. Pressured on three sides, Company L must have disintegrated in short order.

While the armaments of these warriors was undoubtedly used to good advantage on Calhoun Hill, there are no indications this was universally true on the other portions of Custer's field. To the contrary, the Indian accounts, borne out by the archaeological evidence, indicates the fighting in the Keogh sector was mostly hand to hand, while the bow and arrow were used to good advantage against the troops on Custer Hill. In any event, prior knowledge by the army of these weapons would not have changed the planning of the campaign one iota. The fear of the military was focused and constant; would the Indians escape before they could be brought to battle?

The final item of controversy that must be dealt with prior to discussing the campaign's major personalities, is related to the second. While many warriors were armed with magazine guns, the army relied on the single shot Model 1873 Springfield Carbine. This controversy revolves around two issues, firepower and the Springfield's extractor. While there is no question that either a Henry or a Winchester could deliver more rounds per minute, the single shot Springfield, when handled by an experienced marksman, was capable of delivering up to 17 rounds per minute. As a practical matter, the only time such rapid fire was necessary was to counter a massed charge when the enemy was relatively close in; an event that, although rare in Indian warfare, occurred at least three times (the South Skirmish Line, Calhoun Hill and the Keogh Sector) during the Custer Fight. For all other battle scenarios, including the usual long range sniping attendant to most actions with plains Indians, the superior range (highly accurate at 250 yards, the cavalry load of 55 grains of black powder could propel the 405 grain slug over 1,000 yards[9]) and stopping power of the Springfield would make it the weapon of choice.[10] While it is undoubtedly true that equipping the soldiers with either Henrys or Winchesters would have resulted in more Indian casualties, the outcome would, in my estimation, have been unaltered.

The second factor associated with the Springfield deals with the extractor mechanism. A single pin is used to push the shell from the breech and the concurrent opening of the "trapdoor" mechanism then expels the spent cartridge. The carbine, and the infantry 'Long Tom," both in .45 caliber, fired a 405 grain bullet with a black powder load; 70 grains for the infantry musket and 55 grains for the carbine, although the carbine was capable of firing the 70 grain load as well. A common casing was used with the addition of a wad for the carbine load.

The copper casings were slow to cool, and the Springfield was consequently prone to jamming. What happened was the hot casing expanded to fill the breech. The extractor pin then often tore through the lip of the soft casing leaving the spent shell jammed in the breech. Prior to issuing a ramrod for the carbine (issued via a modification in 1884 in direct response to jamming concerns expressed after the Little Big Horn), the usual method for freeing the breech was to pry the expended cartridge from the breech with a knife. Major Reno, in his report on the performance of the Springfield during the battle, noted that 6 of the 380 carbines in his command were rendered unserviceable due to such failures of the extractor system. While Reno did not mention how many carbines experienced the problem and continued to be serviceable, the archaeological investigations at the battlefield noted a potential for 1.8% of the carbines at the Reno-Benteen defense site and 3.3% of the carbines on Custer's field[11] to have exhibited such failures. This projects to approximately 7 of the 199 carbines used by Custer's troops having experienced the problem; a number far too small to have had an appreciable effect on the outcome of the fight.

Having disposed of the controversies associated with numbers and armaments of the warriors and the performance of the Springfield carbine, we are ready to discuss the performance of the principal military leaders: Reno, Benteen, Terry, Gibbon, Crook and Custer.

Major Marcus A. Reno was a casualty of the Little Big Horn just as certainly as if he'd met his death on that field. In addition to having his every action scrutinized[12] and criticized, he is frequently branded a coward; a term only slightly less onerous to a military man than that of traitor. This branding of Reno as coward apparently occurred almost immediately following the fight. Apparently Colonel Gibbon joined the debate, twitting Reno, until restrained by Terry with his observations: *"I have seen many dead soldiers and dead soldier horses in this vicinity, but I have not seen many dead Indians nor dead ponies."*[13] Richard A. Roberts noted that on his journey to Fort Lincoln aboard the *Far West* with the 7th Cavalry's wounded: *"From the officers on the steamer I learned very minute details of the battle and appearance of the field and even at that early date they branded Reno and others, cowards."*[14]

Captain Robert G. Carter of the 4th Cavalry, an accomplished Indian Wars campaigner in his own right was even more outspoken on the subject:

> *"Reno showed the white feather from the start, and his entire conduct was that of a white-livered, yellow-streaked coward. He was terrorized and panic stricken. . . . He should have been tried and cashiered for the part he took in 'Custer's Last Fight.' If ever there was a pusillanimous poltroon in the army whose name should be handed down to future generations as an arrant coward, Marcus A. Reno is the man."*[15]

Varnum had a difficult time dealing with the question of Reno's cowardice. Initially declining to answer the question posed by the court of inquiry recorder, when pressed, he testified: *"Certainly there was no sigh of cowardice or anything of that sort in his conduct and nothing specially the other way. I didn't see anything special to say on either side."*[16]

Godfrey developed an abiding hatred for Reno in the years after he learned of Reno's plan to abandon the wounded the night of June 25th; going so far as to block the inscribing of names on the monument on Reno Hill because, of necessity, Reno's name would have appeared thereon.[17]

Captain McDougall, however, defended Reno's honor at the court of inquiry, testifying: *"He had no enthusiasm as far as I could observe, but he was as brave as any man there; they were all brave; I saw no officer or man show the white feather."*[18] Charges of cowardice on Reno's part were not confined to the military. Lakota and Cheyenne participants told Lieutenant Oscar Long in 1878: *"All the Indians thought **Custer** a brave man – he did not run, but **Reno** ran – he was not a brave man – he was not a man at all but a squaw; else he would have come down to the aid of **Custer** ."*[19] (emphasis from the original)

While there is much deserving of criticism in Reno's performance at the Little Big Horn, it is difficult to label a man who had withstood the hail of lead at Mechanicsville and Antietam, coward. While it cannot be denied it was a much younger Reno that faced down the horrors of the Civil War, the passage of time tends to make military men less willing to take the chances necessary for success in desperate situations. It doesn't tend to make them cowards.

It is clear that Reno "lost his head" and, for a prolonged period, either forgot, or ignored, his military training and experience. This was recognized by Private William O. Taylor, Company A, who wrote to Godfrey in 1910: *"Reno proved incompetent and Benteen showed his indifference . . . When an enlisted man sees his commanding officer lose his head entirely and several other officers showing greater regard for their personal safety than anything else, it would be apt to demoralize anyone . . ."*[20] Lieutenant Mathey would testify at the court of inquiry that Reno was *"somewhat excited"* when the pack train arrived. While Mathey said he considered Reno's behavior to have been normal under the circumstances, the pack train arrived on Reno Hill about one and a quarter hours after Reno, which should have been ample time for Reno to have completely regained his composure.[21] While Reno had some previous experience in Indian campaigning in the Pacific Northwest, it was limited in scope and his situation in the valley was totally alien to his experience. His conduct, commencing with his movement down the valley to the attack, is an almost textbook case of panic behavior. Reno's failings at Little Big Horn are summarized below:

1. Failure to charge the village as ordered. Reno testified at his court of inquiry that he did not actually charge the village, fearing an ambush. When one recalls that the coulee purported to contain hundreds of warriors could not be seen prior to Reno's halting, it becomes clear there was no physical evidence supporting Reno's decision to halt his battalion. Reno's action would be justified in terms of late twentieth century military science, but was considered inexcusable by many of his fellow officers. The only method to firmly establish whether Reno's action was justified in terms of nineteenth century military practices would have been a court martial. While some may argue that failure to file charges against Reno was defacto evidence of the army's acceptance of his conduct, other actions cannot be so easily explained away. We will see that several of Reno's actions demanded a court martial. The fact no charges were filed is attributable to the army's desire to "save face" and "cut its losses" rather than an affirmation of Reno's conduct.

2. Failure to communicate his intended withdrawal from the valley to his entire command.[22] At the court of inquiry, Reno explained his decision to leave the timber was based upon three factors: a desire to effect a junction with Custer, insufficient personnel to adequately defend the position, and a shortage of ammunition. Reno, who was not asked any probing questions by Lieutenant Lee, likened his valley

position to Beecher's Island. While the besieged scouts on Beecher's Island were repeatedly charged by mounted warriors, their position was brush covered rather than being heavily timbered[23] with a natural breastwork afforded by the cut bank as was Reno's valley position. While Reno's decision to abandon the timber was supported by all the participating officers who testified at the court of inquiry, the civilian plainsmen universally condemned it. It is of interest to note that the highly pessimistic Arikara believed Reno could have held out indefinitely in the timber.[24] The Cheyenne concurred, noting: *"We could never understand why the soldiers left the timber, for if they had stayed there the Indians could not have killed them."*[25]

In any event, once the decision was reached, Reno did not properly communicate his intention to the command with the result that virtually all of Company G was initially left behind. Reno claimed that either himself or his adjutant verbally passed the word to the company commanders. While this may have been the case, given the uproar that must have been in progress with the firing, whooping of the warriors, and screaming of the horses, it appears to me that choosing this method of passing the command, rather than by bugle call, indicates, at least to my mind, Reno was exhibiting panic behavior. While there is some justification for Reno's determining to leave the timber, the manner in which his withdrawal was carried out can only be described as a panic rout.[26]

3. Abandoning his wounded in the timber. There is no indication what-so-ever that any attempt was made to evacuate wounded privates Lorenz and Klotzbucher from the timber or to attempt to rescue any troopers that fell wounded during the retreat. Reno testified at the court of inquiry: *"I suppose the Indians killed the wounded left in the timber. I could make no effort to take them out; and none was made. I do not know what became of the wounded left on the plain; the Indians would not permit me to take care of them."*[27]

4. Failure to cover his line of retreat or his crossing of the Little Big Horn. No attempt was made to keep the Indians at a distance from the column with the result the warriors rode among the troopers, pulling them from their horses. As the command had to move in the direction of the warriors to reach their objective, there is some justification for describing the intended movement as a charge. When describing this movement, there are several points to be recalled:

   a. Reno led the advance elements of the command out of the timber before the entire command was mounted, in fact before the order to mount had been communicated to the entire command.

   b. Upon reaching the plain, Reno immediately set out for the bluffs without properly forming the command, designating a rallying point, or assigning an element to protect the flanks and rear. While Reno would argue he was charging, the command was not formed in a mounted skirmish line, nor was the enemy solely in their front, a circumstance that required establishing a screening element before commencing the movement. The line of Reno's dead clearly shows he merely skirted the timber, rather than making the aggressive movement a charge would indicate.[28]

   c. The retreating command was forced to their left and arrived on the river bank at a location where the bank was both high and steep. Reno and the advance jumped their horses into the stream and raced for the bluff making no attempt to establish a dismounted skirmish line on the west bank to hold the warriors at a distance from the rear of the column which must become subject to bunching given the terrain. Once across the river, Reno sped to the top of the bluff, again without establishing a skirmish line on the east bank to cover the column's crossing.

Given the above, it is obvious Reno's withdrawal from the timber was anything but the standard military maneuver he described – it was a panic rout. The Indian testimony clearly demonstrates they knew the movement to be the rout it was. The army couldn't have been fooled either. The unprofessional conduct of this movement resulted in loss of life for about one-third of Reno's command. The fact that no charges were filed over this unnecessary sacrifice of troops may be attributed to the army being solely interested in quelling the controversy.

5. Failure to move to Custer's aid upon the junction with Benteen. Nelson Miles would prove the severest critic on this point stating: *"No commanding officer can win victories with seven-twelfths of his command remaining out of the engagement when within sound of his rifle shots."*[29] Reno would argue that he moved as rapidly as possible, but was inhibited by his wounded and the need to replenish his ammunition. Neither claim is supported by the evidence. Reno had several wounded troopers upon his arrival on top of the bluff, primarily in Moylan's Company A. The officers testified it took all of Moylan's able-bodied men as well as a platoon of B Troop to carry the wounded toward Custer.[30] Two aspects of this testimony went unchallenged. First there is the question of how the litters used to carry the wounded were constructed. If such litters were indeed constructed, then why did litters have to be constructed for all of the wounded when they were subsequently transported to the *Far West?*

The second factor that was ignored at the court of inquiry was that each of these wounded men had to make the steep ascent to the top of the bluff without assistance. Company A's William O. Taylor summarized: *"A few of our men had been wounded, but none so seriously that they could not ride with the pack train."*[31] Given the above two considerations, it appears the professed difficulty in moving the wounded downstream has been greatly exaggerated. As for the question of being low on ammunition, the testimony at the court of inquiry was clear and concise: fewer than 1000 rounds, or about 10 rounds per trooper, were drawn from the reserve by Reno's men after Lieutenant Hare rushed 4000 rounds to the hilltop. While Moylan's men may have nearly exhausted their supply, Reno's command clearly had enough ammunition in aggregate to conduct the movement without waiting for the reserve ammunition. While it might have been argued that Reno needed to wait for the pack train to afford it adequate protection from the Indians, such a claim was never made and, therefore, clearly was not an item of concern to Reno.

As a final argument, Reno would fall back on Benteen's self-serving expedient, testifying *"I believe that when I came out of the timber Custer's command was all dead."*[32] Continuing this deception required both Reno and Benteen to be unable to hear the firing of Custer's command that was so obvious to everyone else on the hilltop. Fortunately for Reno and Benteen, neither was questioned regarding McDougall's testimony that he brought the sound of Custer's firing to their attention. It is of interest to note that Reno's report on the battle states *'We heard firing in that direction and knew that it could only be Custer . . .(emphasis the author's, DCE)'*[33] Gibson, in a 1915 letter to George L. Yates, son of the late captain, described Benteen's junction with Reno charging: *"Benteen asked Reno where Custer was, and when told said: 'Well, let us make a junction with him as soon as possible.' This I know, for I heard it.*[34] Finally, Benteen would confide to Theodore Goldin Reno had informed him that he had heard firing down river that he presumed to have been Custer's.[35]

6. Decision to abandon the wounded the night of June 25. To even contemplate such an action, which would result in a horrible death by torture for the abandoned men, is proof positive of extended panic behavior on Reno's part. The only circumstances under which such an eventuality could be rationally discussed would be in the certain knowledge that, without resorting to that odious expedient, the entire command faced <u>certain</u> annihilation. While Reno may have harbored such an opinion, it clearly was not shared by his officers. As we have seen, abandonment of the wounded was all too common during the 1876 campaign. While it may have been a common occurrence, the practice was not, and, for obvious reasons, could not, be condoned by the army.

7. Abrogation of command. Reno clearly relinquished command to Benteen on June 25. While there are indications he assumed command again on June 26, the active defense, on both days, was conducted solely by Benteen. The record is also clear that Reno had not delegated a portion of his command function to Benteen, rather Benteen had moved expeditiously to fill the void created by Reno's incapacity. As Lieutenant Gibson would write to his wife after swearing her to secrecy *"Reno did not know which end he was standing on, and Benteen just took the management of affairs in his own hands, and it was very fortunate for us that he did."*[36]

By any standard, be it nineteenth or twentieth century, in any army in the world, items 4 and 7, and perhaps others, of the foregoing actions demanded questioning within the context of a court martial. The fact that no charges were pressed is further indication that the army was uninterested in either information or justice, they just wanted the controversy, and attendant bad publicity, to cease.

The controversy involving Benteen typically revolves around the issue of malingering, but should focus on disobedience of orders. The testimony taken at the court of inquiry, and the insubordinate actions of Captain Weir, makes it clear that Benteen did not rush to rejoin the regiment after his return to the main trail, as Private William E. Morris recalled:

> *"Benteen, arriving about an hour later, came up as slow as though he were going to a funeral. By this statement I do not desire to reflect in any way upon him; he was simply in no hurry; and Muller (probably Private Jan Moller, DCE), of his troop, who occupied an adjoining cot to mine in the hospital at Fort Abraham Lincoln, told me that they walked all the way, and that they heard the heavy firing while they were watering their horses."*[37]

It is equally clear, from the analysis presented in Appendix 12, that Benteen moved rapidly from the receipt of Custer's written message until his junction with Reno. Once he reached Reno's position, Benteen was faced with a moral, but not a military, dilemma. Benteen must have instantly recognized Reno's command was shattered and incapable of conducting military operations. To ride off in such a situation was to assure annihilation of Reno's battalion should they be attacked in force prior to regaining their senses and reorganizing themselves. While this presented Benteen a moral quandary, his duty as a military man was clear – he had to obey Custer's written order. Benteen admitted as much in a letter to Theodore Goldin stating Custer's order could not be countermanded by Reno after their junction.[38]

In an attempt to defend his failure to comply with his written orders, and, no doubt, to assuage his conscience, Benteen adopted the expedient of "knowing" that Custer's command had been annihilated prior to his receipt of the message carried by Martin: *"I wish to say before that order reached me that I believe that General Custer and his whole command were dead."*[39] Benteen's position, which has its foundation in military law, of course was that if Custer was dead at the time Benteen received his orders, how could those orders be disobeyed? In terms of the army wanting to ignore the incident entirely, it is instructive to note that no one on the court asked Benteen any questions relating to how he could possibly know when Custer's command was wiped out; especially in view of the weight of evidence that heavy firing from Custer's position was heard for a prolonged period after the junction of Reno's and Benteen's commands. The answer must have been as clear to the members of the court as it is to us.

Benteen's defenders typically argue from a twentieth-century perspective on the issue of disobedience. While the U. S. Army has always been subject to "political realities," if such an oxymoron may be applied, the tenant that a positive result precludes malfeasance in execution, and the corollary statement that a disastrous result precludes proper execution, are twentieth-century concepts that continue to evolve, or descend, if you prefer, to new levels as the ideal of "political correctness' is further refined.

The question of Benteen's disobedience is really very simple to understand and the circumstances are crystal clear. The operative portion of the Articles of War for 1874, which remained in effect until revised in 1895, is Section 21, which states:

*"Any officer or soldier who, **on any pretense whatsoever**, strikes his superior officer, or draws or lifts up any weapon, or offers any violence against him, **being in the execution of his office**, or **disobeys any lawful command** of his superior officer, **shall suffer death**, or **such other punishment** as a court-martial may direct.[40] (emphasis the author's)"*

There can be no valid debate over whether or not Reno countermanded Custer's order. As Colonel William Winthrop, the leading American commentator on military law points out:

". . . the only exceptions recognized to the rule of obedience being cases of orders so manifestly beyond the legal power or discretion of the commander as to admit of no rational doubt of their unlawfulness."[41]

Benteen was undoubtedly aware of this and never attempted to argue the point, admitting in a letter to Theodore Goldin that Reno had no authority to countermand Custer's order. Instead, Benteen seized upon the only loophole in the article: *"being in execution of his office."* If Custer were dead at the time Benteen received his written order, by law, Benteen was not obligated to obey. It is not surprising then that Benteen became convinced that Custer had been annihilated prior to his receiving Cooke's written order.[42] It was unnecessary to add that Custer's death voided the order. Fortunately for Benteen, the army was solely interested in putting an end to the bad publicity. A court-martial, and subsequent conviction of Benteen, would only prolong the pain and controversy. Besides, how could the man who almost single handedly saved the regiment from complete destruction be prosecuted for a capital offense? The honor of the army was obviously best served by ignoring the question of Benteen's disobedience entirely. That, of course, is exactly what happened and explains why Benteen's conduct was not investigated and why no probing questions were asked of him at Reno's court of inquiry. It may also explain why Benteen never attacked Custer publicly after the Reno court of inquiry and why he never went on the lecture circuit although he would have done well financially had he chosen to participate.

The arguments presented above, in my opinion, make an unassailable case. The American judicial system, military law included, however is not based solely upon the law and justice, but rather on precedent. In addition to the judicial theoretical arguments already presented, there was a single precedent prior to the Little Big Horn. At Second Manassas, or Bull Run if you prefer, General John Pope ordered Major General Fitz John Porter to attack "Stonewall" Jackson's right. Believing himself outnumbered at least 3 to 1, Porter refused.[43] His conviction was automatic.

While Second Manassas was another humiliating defeat for the Army of the Potomac, it was not a disaster of the magnitude of Little Big Horn. Perhaps that was the reason the army was content to order Fitz John Porter's dismissal from the service[44] rather than order a firing squad.

Had Benteen obeyed his orders, the battle of the Little Big Horn would have been fought in an entirely different manner. With what result, who can say? As Custer scholar Edgar I. Stewart noted, it is difficult enough to determine what did happen, let alone what might have happened given a different set of circumstances.

Another, and often overlooked failing of Benteen on this occasion, and typical of others, including Custer, was his failure to communicate badly needed intelligence. Benteen, as the record left by Lieutenant Gibson makes abundantly clear, knew he had been sent to the left on a reconnaissance mission. Upon completing that mission, he was obligated to send a messenger to his commander with the results of that reconnaissance. There is no evidence that any such messenger was dispatched. Similarly, Benteen was obligated to, at the very least, send a messenger to the pack train after his receipt of Custer's written order. Although Trumpeter Martin would testify he was such a messenger, Benteen, under oath, would deny he had sent any messenger, leaving the troops assigned to the pack train to figure out the tactical situation for themselves. Finally, when he halted with Reno for a protracted period, he was obliged to send Custer a messenger indicating he couldn't *"be quick."* Not only did Benteen not do so, but he failed to recognize, as Reno did, the attendant danger to himself in Weir's unilateral movement to Custer. Reno, therefore dispatched Hare to belatedly "order" Weir to attempt a junction with Custer while Benteen remained silent.

Benteen, to a much greater extent than Reno, was fortunate the army wanted to bury the controversy of the Little Big Horn with the dead. A court martial for Benteen would, at best, have ended in his dismissal from the service, and, although unlikely, could have resulted in a firing squad.

Terry's performance during the 1876 campaign branded him as unfit to command an expedition against plains Indians. When his military record is examined, this poor performance is not that surprising. A lawyer by profession, the only bright spot on his record was the capture of Fort Fisher, the largest coastal fortification in the confederacy and guardian of its last open seaport. While other officers had failed to take the "Confederate Gibraltar," Terry, using very basic tactics, had succeeded. A combined naval and army operation, Terry had demonstrated the ability of a competent staff officer to effect compromise. Compromise is fine for a staff officer in a combined operations war room, but it is disastrous for a commander in the field. Terry's failings in the campaign are attributable to his deficiencies both as a commander and as a strategist.

Terry was constantly aggravated by his inability to control his subordinates. Reno had violated the chain of command and gone over Terry's head to Sheridan in an attempt to obtain command of the 7th Cavalry during the summer campaign. Since Terry had ignored this insubordinate action, one wonders how he could have been surprised by Reno's further disobedience of orders on his scout of the Tongue.[45] Similarly, there is no indication of a reprimand for Brisbin in going over Gibbon's head to inform Terry of the campaign's failures prior to the junction of the Dakota and Montana columns. This failure to exercise firm command prevented the well liked Terry from earning the respect of his men and inhibited the restoration of confidence and morale after the disaster at Little Big Horn. Godfrey would confine his disrespectful statements to his diary,[46] while Miles would confide a scathing remark on morale to his wife, Mary: *"I never saw a command so completely stampeded as this."*[47]

Miles amplified in an August letter to his wife: *"The more I see of movements here the more admiration I have for Custer and I am satisfied that his likes will not be found very soon again."*[48] Miles' comments were echoed by Lieutenant Charles King who remarked the combined Terry-Crook force *"would never catch or scare 40 Indians. . . . The caution of Headquarters surpasses everything."*[49] "Buffalo Bill" Cody was even more critical as quoted in the *Chicago Tribune* for September 22, 1876:

> *"He (Cody, DCE) said plainly that the soldiers did not want or intend to fight; that he had worn himself out finding Indians; and, when he did discover their whereabouts, there was no one ready to 'go for them.' To use his own language, it was evident to him that no one connected with the army had lost any Indians, and consequently they were not going to hunt any. He said he had pointed out fresh trails, and they had been pooh-poohed as old; and, when he reported bodies of the enemy, no troops could be got ready until all hope of successful pursuit had faded away. This, and much more to the same effect, fell from the lips of the noted scout, who seemed untiring and outspoken in his denunciation of the entire business."*[50]

Terry's tactics during the 1876 campaign were, at best, highly suspect. In fact, his performance was so poor one wonders if his alleged *"sad and terrible blunder"* comment to Captain Grant Marsh wasn't more suited to his own performance than to Custer's. As Major Alfred L. Hough observed: *"I was impressed with the opinion that both of them (Sheridan and Terry, DCE) felt that the campaign against the Sioux . . . was a failure for which they would be held responsible by the people. Especially was this the case with General Terry who was nervous, excited, and depressed in spirits; he had changed much since I had last seen him in 1869."*[51] In ordering Custer after the Indians, Terry was guilty of the offense so often attributed to Custer; splitting his force in the presence of superior enemy strength without benefit of proper reconnaissance. While Custer, believing his command to have been discovered, had some justification in splitting his forces in response to an evolving tactical situation, there is no such justification for Terry's actions. Reno's scout had furnished some valuable information on where the village had been 3 weeks previously, a fact already known to, but not admitted by, Gibbon. Mitch Boyer could certainly have told Reno and Terry that the trail was about 3 weeks old, as Charley Reynolds was subsequently able to inform Custer. Similarly, the size of the village represented stale intelligence as it was known that the young warriors continued to leave the reservations in large numbers bound for the unceded territory. Prudence would seem to have dictated that Terry keep his entire command together until the enemy's strength and location were positively determined. Instead, Terry's actions, as demonstrated by Reno's orders for his scout, were more concerned with determining where the enemy wasn't, the Tongue, than with determining where they in fact were; west of the Rosebud.

Proving this tactical blunder was no oversight, Terry would reduce an already small force to ineffectual proportions (based upon the assertion in his final report that removing the Second Cavalry made the remainder of the Montana Column too weak to be effective) when he split the cavalry and infantry on his night march of June 25. He wound up with his command widely dispersed and the artillery missing. That there was no purpose to such a movement was demonstrated on the morning of the 26th when Terry delayed the march of his cavalry to allow his exhausted infantry to close up.

Terry's other major failing was as a strategic planner. Although he would allow himself to be convinced by his staff that he had crafted an infallible plan for mutual cooperation of the

Terry's other major failing was as a strategic planner. Although he would allow himself to be convinced by his staff that he had crafted an infallible plan for mutual cooperation of the Custer and Gibbon columns, such was far from the case.[52] Sheridan knew the virtual impossibility of coordinating movements against even a fixed objective in such country,[53] as the following excerpt from a letter to General Sherman demonstrates. *"As no very correct information can be obtained as to the location of the hostile Indians, and as there would be no telling how long they would stay at any one place if it were known, I have given no instructions to Genls. Crook or Terry, preferring that they should do the best they can under the circumstances, . . . as I think it would be unwise to make any combinations in such a country as they will have to operate in, as hostile Indians, in any great numbers, can not keep the field as a body, or at most ten days. I therefore consider, and so do Terry and Crook, that each column will be able to take care of itself, and of chastising the Indians should it have the opportunity. . . ."*[54] Nelson Miles would put it most bluntly: *"It is folly to suppose that either a small or large band of Indians would remain stationary, and allow one body of troops to come up on one side of it while another body came up on the other side and engaged it in battle."*[55] Despite overwhelming evidence to the contrary, Terry came to believe he had established a definite time table for cooperative action between Custer's and Gibbon's columns in the valley of the Little Big Horn. Apparently, Terry had forgotten to communicate the one vital piece of information critical to the success of his plan in Custer's written orders as those orders contain no mention of cooperative action between the columns on the 26th, or any other date. It is instructive to note that Terry required an examination of the Tullock in these same orders, although the Indians could not possibly be found there if they were to be caught in a combined operation in the valley of the Little Big Horn. While Terry was reasonably sure the village was on the Little Big Horn, he had no way of knowing whether it would be located on the upper, or lower, reaches of that stream. In fact, the best information available indicated they would be found on the upper reaches of the Little Big Horn. Had the village been located at either the source or mouth of the stream, either Gibbon or Custer, respectively, would have required an extra day to come within supporting distance of that location.

The shallowness of the planning effort, which included sealing only one of the potential escape routes for the Indians, was not the only problem associated with the planning element. Terry's indecisiveness was a major hurdle. Clearly without a clue regarding how to proceed, Terry vacillated over the composition of his strike force, finally delegating the decision, and attendant strategy, to Custer. As Terry freely admitted in his annual report, had Custer accepted his offer of the Second Cavalry and the gatling gun battery, Gibbon's remaining force would have been too weak to actively participate. How a command that was too weak to participate was to have cooperated in attacking the village is, for obvious reasons, not discussed by Terry's supporters.

Even forgetting the foregoing inconsistencies, Terry's plan to use Gibbon's column as a blocking force was basically flawed. While General Harney had used the tactic with great success against Little Thunder's Brule village on Blue Water Creek in September of 1855, Terry did not understand the essence of the strategy. Harney had attacked the village with his infantry, utilizing the cavalry as the blocking force where their mobility could be used to greatest advantage for the inevitable pursuit. Terry, had such a plan for cooperative action actually existed, was going to try it backwards, using his infantry, supported by an inadequate cavalry force, as the pursuit force. Even green Second Lieutenant Hugh L. Scott knew better: *"How it was expected of foot soldiers to catch Indian was always a puzzle to me."*[56] When all is said and done, however, Terry's bungling, including his personal direction of the march of the Montana Column which has been detailed in Chapter 17, and its deleterious effect on morale, had no direct bearing on Custer's defeat, but did preclude any possible chance for a successful conclusion of the campaign. Fortunately for Terry, and George Crook, the army's high command, while aware of their failings, preferred, for the good of the service, to let the blame rest upon the fallen Custer. As Sheridan confided to Sherman: *"The fact of the case is the operations of Generals Terry and Crook will not bear criticism, bear criticism, and my only thought has been to let them sleep. I approved what was done, for the sake of the troops, but in doing so, I was not approving much, as you know."*[57] Major Eugene Carr would have heartily concurred: *"It has reached beyond a joke that we should be kept out and exposed because two fools (Terry and Crook, DCE) do not know their business. I would leave the expedition today, if I could."*[58]

Unlike General Terry, Colonel John Oliver Gibbon had a long and distinguished Civil War record, with one success following another.[59] As the commander of the famed "Iron Brigade," Gibbon's high water mark coincided with that of the confederacy at Gettysburg's angle. Gibbon had also cooperated effectively with the other expedition commanders, Crook and Custer, during the Appomattox Campaign.

Given his successful Civil War record, Gibbon's subsequent performance during the Indian Wars is difficult to reconcile. He was involved in two major Indian campaigns, the 1876 campaign and the 1877 campaign against the Nez Perce. Gibbon's performance during the 1876 campaign was spotty and uninspired while his Nez Perce campaign performance was almost disastrous. At the Battle of the Big Hole, Gibbon's surprise attack on the Nez Perce village was quickly converted to the Indian's advantage. The action ended with a wounded Gibbon completely corralled by the Nez Perce in a siege reminiscent of the Little Big Horn.[60] Gibbon suffered the additional indignity of losing the only piece of artillery captured by the enemy during the Indian Wars. Gibbon was fortunate the Nez Perce were intent upon escape, else historians would be writing of the "Gibbon Massacre."

In chapter 6 we described Gibbon's timid response to Lakota provocative acts and his ineffectual attempt to ford the Yellowstone. This performance is summarized in a letter from Dr. Paulding to his mother, dated June 14, 1876:

> *". . . A large camp was found up the Rosebud about 18 miles off, but our genial C. O. did not deem it advisable to attack it, a chance any other commander would give any price for, and after laying there for 10 days with the Indians showing themselves everyday in plain sight, as though they knew what a harmless concern they were dealing with, he at last began to do something.* **not** *to cross the command in boats & attack – but to* **go away** *(emphasis Paulding's, DCE). and this he did, keeping on down the river till we met Terry & were turned back as soon as he heard of it.*

> *"Our C. O.'s excuse was that he had rec'd orders from St. Paul to guard* **this** *side of the Yellowstone (emphasis Paulding's, DCE).*[61] *There's literal obedience for you. The whole trip has been a miserable farce and everything has been as disagreeable as idiotic, pig headed stupidity could make it.*

> *". . . having missed our golden opportunity to catch Indians (a hard thing to do in summer) they won't be able to do much & we may either go home very soon or else spend the rest of the summer chasing a few scattered bands around & through the mountains."*[62]

While a steamer to convey the strike force to the south bank was not available for his use on May 17, the *Josephine* could have been available on the 19th or 20th had Gibbon been desirous of striking a blow. If Gibbon had any question about his ability to launch a successful operation against the village, his orders from General Terry required him to remain on the north bank and deny the enemy passage from the south bank. Had Gibbon made this decision, and

[Above left] General George Crook. Brilliant in planning and logistics, his performance during the 1876 campaign was, at best, highly questionable. His failure to provide key intelligence to Terry and Custer was a contributing factor in the defeat of the 7th Cavalry. *Photo Courtesy Little Bighorn Battlefield National Monument.*

[Above right] Colonel John Gibbon. History has dealt too kindly toward his performance in the 1876 campaign. He, more than any other commander, was in a position to ensure a successful campaign. His failure to keep the village under continuing surveillance was a major factor in the defeat of the 7th Cavalry. *Photo Courtesy Little Bighorn Battlefield National Monument.*

[Right} General Alfred H. Terry in later life. His experience in Indian warfare and his tactical limitations were all too apparent during the 1876 campaign. His staff attempted to divert adverse publicity from him by casting aspersions on the dead Custer. *Photo Courtesy Little Bighorn Battlefield National Monument.*

there is no indication he did – at least we have no record that he ever communicated such a decision to his staff, he was still obligated to maintain surveillance over the village.

Gibbon's failure to maintain a continuing surveillance of the village, once sighted on May 16, is difficult to understand, and impossible to condone. In addition to Bradley's mounted infantry, Gibbon had the services of the Crow scouts at his disposal. To fail to even attempt to conduct this critical reconnaissance, and then hide the fact in official dispatches behind the expedient of denying the village had been sighted, can be construed as nothing short of dereliction of duty. Had Gibbon attempted a continuing surveillance and failed due to activity of the Lakota, it would have furnished valuable information regarding enemy activity and possible strength. Had such a reconnaissance been successful, the strength and location of the enemy would have been determined by the time the Dakota Column arrived, allowing a plan of action to be formulated based upon fact rather than supposition. Gibbon's failure to conduct this reconnaissance, and subsequent attempt to cover up this failure, caused Terry to plan and Custer to march in ignorance against the enemy. As such, Gibbon's inaction was a major factor in the defeat of the Seventh Cavalry. History has been far too kind to Gibbon. As he was in a perfect position to ensure the successful outcome of the campaign, he, to a much greater extent than Reno or Benteen, was responsible for the defeat.

What we have here, is basically a failure to communicate. This cliché from the 1970's is a perfect description of Crook's major failing during the 1876 campaign. While Gibbon failed to collect much needed intelligence on the enemy's strength and location, this information, including unanticipated information about enemy resolve and determination, literally fell into Crook's lap while he was engaged in a card game. Crazy Horse's assault on the Rosebud provided three valuable pieces of intelligence to Crook. First the enemy was concentrated in unanticipated strength. Second, the village could not be too distant from the Big Bend of the Rosebud as such a large war party would be difficult to sustain and keep together over a great distance. Third, and perhaps most important, the warriors fought with unusual determination and cohesiveness. This crucial information, along with the fact that Crook's command would be leaving the theater of operations for a protracted period, was denied Terry and Custer, although Crook would complain bitterly to his staff about not receiving any information from Terry's command.

By 1876 the Indian fighting army had learned three truths about fighting plains Indians. First, Indians did not attack large bodies of troops. A troop armed with breech-loading rifles should be able to adequately defend itself as Indians would not charge into organized fire and were not psychologically prepared to sustain casualties. Second, it was practically impossible to surprise a village in the summer. Finally, if a village were attacked, Indians would fight only to expedite their escape. Commencing with the Battle of the Rosebud, it would take the Lakota and Cheyenne only 8 days to teach the army an entirely new set of lessons.

Crook, like Gibbon, would not even attempt to send a courier, whether military, civilian, or Indian scout, all of whom were available, through to Terry; preferring instead to content himself and his command with prospecting, hunting, fishing, and even a game of baseball. What makes this failure to attempt to provide critical information even more damning, is the dispatch written by *Chicago Inter-Ocean* correspondent Thomas C. MacMillan on June 15. This dispatch, citing Crook's Crow scouts, states that Sitting Bull had a force of 3,000 warriors and correctly located Gibbon's various camp sites.[63] Crook's inactivity made him the target of the resident bards:

"I'd like to be a packer

And pack With George F. Crook (Crook had no middle name, DCE)

And dressed up in my canvas suit

To be for him mistook,

I'd braid my beard in two long tails,

And idle all the day

In whittling sticks and wondering

What the New York papers say."[64]

The following item from the *Army and Navy Journal* of July 6, 1878 undoubtedly expressed the view of more than one of Crook's officers:

"The N. Y. Herald says: An officer who was with Crook in the battle of the Rosebud, June 17, 1876, writes (on the anniversary of that day) as follows: 'I shall always believe that all subsequent trouble with the Sioux – the Custer massacre and all – can be traced to one or two pivotal points: Leaving our pack trains on Goose Creek and making it impossible or inadvisable to follow up such a little fracas as that of the Rosebud; or our failure to seek the enemy again immediately after our return to Goose Creek, on the 19th. In either event we would have met Custer's army. The two commands would have been united. The whole Sioux Nation was there and keen for a fight. There would have been one great battle and our troubles with the Sioux would have been forever ended."[65]

What makes Crook's inactivity even more incredible was his failure to request the re-enforcements he felt he must have before re-entering the campaign.[66] As *New York Herald* reporter James J. O'Kelly commented: *"The conduct of this officer through the campaign has been, to say the least, peculiar."*[67] The much sought intelligence almost reached Custer in any event. Libbie Custer's last letter to her husband, which arrived shortly after his departure up the Rosebud, very succinctly described the warrior determination and aggressiveness that had dealt Crook his stunning defeat on the Rosebud. That civilian correspondence could reach Terry's command almost in time to influence the planning, speaks volumes about Crook's failure. As with Gibbon's failure to obtain intelligence, Crook's failure to communicate this crucial information led to Terry planning, and Custer attempting to execute, in ignorance. Crook's failure was almost as crucial as Gibbon's in sealing the fate of the Seventh Cavalry and its long-haired leader.[68] Had Benteen been court martialed for his disobedience of orders, he should have had the company of fellow defendants Gibbon and Crook.

Although Crook's failure to send a courier to Terry was his major error in terms of the defeat of Custer and the Seventh Cavalry, it was far from being his only significant blunder of the campaign. Crook had anticipated Terry's blunder by dividing his force for Reynolds' attack on Old Bear's village without definite knowledge of the enemy's location or strength. Any criticism that might have accrued to Crook was effectively deflected when he brought charges against Colonel Reynolds. Like Terry, Crook would prove his blunder was no fluke when he repeated it at the Rosebud. Crook's decision to detach half of his cavalry to go "village hunting" while hotly engaged could have resulted in a disaster of epic proportions. While Crook's audacity in ordering such a movement must be accorded a certain degree of admiration for its inherent aggressiveness, his timing demonstrated a total lack of appreciation for the current tactical situation. Fortunately, Mills' timely recall averted the disaster Crook had labored so assiduously to architect. A brief catalog of Crook's failings at the Rosebud follows:

1. Failed to follow basic military procedures. Although he had been warned by his scouts that the enemy was near, he allowed his men to unsaddle without posting adequate pickets.

2. Overconfidence. In a failing he shared with many of the officers on the expedition, Crook was not concerned with fighting Indians, only with catching them. As George E. Hyde has observed: *"Crook was of the opinion at this time that the Sioux would not put up much of a fight. Unlike the Apaches, who had nothing but their lives to lose and therefore fought desperately, the Sioux, he told his officers, were rich in ponies and other property and when they lost this wealth they would lose heart and give up."*[69]

3. Failure to exercise proper command. The command became widely scattered after the initial attack. While Crook continued to observe the situation for a protracted period of time, his subalterns deployed the troops piece meal and they wound up out of effective supporting distance of each other. Crook would complain, with some validity, in later years that this scattering was the sole responsibility of his subordinates. In reality, if all of his subordinates, most especially his Crow and Shoshoni scouts, had waited for Crook's personal order to deploy, the command would have been destroyed by the surging Lakota and Cheyenne while Crook was still struggling with his decision on how to respond.

4. Failure to grasp the tactical situation. Crook's decision to attack a phantom village opened the way for the Indians to press their attacks. When Crook finally grasped the seriousness of his situation, the timely return of Mills' column was all that averted disaster.

Colonel Nelson A. Miles, in a letter to General Sherman, was uncomplimentary to Crook in the extreme. He described Crook as *"A man who was a failure during the war and has been ever since."* Continuing, Miles felt that Crook's performance during the 1876 campaign *"accomplished nothing but give the Indians renewed confidence."*[70] There is more than a little truth in Miles' statement. In terms of his Civil War record, the most vivid images of Crook are of his failures; marching to and fro in front of the confederate position at Antietam in a vain attempt to locate the bridge while his ranks were being decimated,[71] and his rout at Cedar Creek. Similarly, his handling of the Rosebud Fight is an almost classic case of total ineptitude. Had Crook believed his subordinates, Royall and Nickerson, were really at fault for his humiliating defeat at the Rosebud, as he claimed in later years, he would have had no compunction what-so-ever in having them court-martialed. General of the Army William T. Sherman wasn't fooled. He believed Crook had been guilty of mismanagement both at Powder River and the Rosebud.[72] It is instructive to note that Crook's single shining example in the Indian Wars was the Tonto Basin Campaign; being nothing short of brilliant in planning and execution. It was also one other thing – an operation planned by Crook but solely conducted by subordinates as active command was delegated to the commanders in the field. Lieutenant Bourke described Crook's orders to his subordinate commanders: *"The trail must be struck and never lost. No excuse was to be accepted for leaving a trail; if horses played out, the enemy must be followed on foot, and no sacrifice should be left untried to make the campaign short, sharp, and decisive."*[73] This strategy capitalized on Crook's brilliance in planning, logistics and understanding of the enemy while neutralizing his inherent weaknesses that seemed to come to the fore whenever he took an active part in the details of an action. How differently might the '76 campaign have gone if the Crook of the Tonto Basin Campaign had been present.

Finally we come to Lieutenant Colonel, Brevet Major General, George Armstrong Custer. In some quarters, Custer was blamed for the defeat almost immediately. In their editorial of July 7, 1876, the *Chicago Tribune* set the tone for the attacks on Custer that have continued to this day:

> *"Custer . . . was a brave, brilliant soldier, handsome and dashing, but he was reckless, hasty and impulsive, preferring to make a dare-devil rush and take risks rather than to move slower and with more certainty, and it was his own mad-cap haste, rashness and love of fame that cost him his own life, and cost the service the loss of many brave officers and gallant men. No account seems to have been taken of the numbers or leadership of the Sioux, . . . no account was even taken of the fact that General Gibbon was coming to the Little Big Horn with reinforcements, only a day's march behind, **although General Custer was aware of it** (emphasis in the editorial, DCE). He preferred to make a reckless dash and take the consequences, in the hope of making a personal victory and adding to the glory of another charge, rather than wait for the sufficiently-powerful force to make the fight successful and share the glory with others. **He took the risk, and he lost** (emphasis in the editorial, DCE)."[74]*

For good measure, the same *Chicago Tribune* critiqued its own editorial on June 5, 1932, stating: *"Printed at a time when it could not be popular, the Tribune utterance was a masterpiece of editorial judgment and courage."*[75]

I believe this narrative has demonstrated that the usual controversies associated with Armstrong Custer are the result of his having been "wrong for all the right reasons." As Edgerly summarized in a April 16, 1925 letter to Colonel Graham concerning his *"Story of the Little Big Horn"*: *"I wish you could see your way to state that Custer found the trail of the village told of by Bradley, that it was approximately about the size estimated by him, that we had no means of knowing or reason for suspecting that it had been reinforced by thousands and finally upon nearing the village he had every reason to believe the Indians were running away."*[76] Until the very end, Custer was attempting to control an evolving tactical situation and turn it to his advantage. For the first time in his career, his impeccable sense of timing deserted him. With our 20:20 hindsight, we know Custer waited too long for Benteen to join him, allowing the warriors to mass in his front and preclude any entry into the village. We also know, as Custer could not, that he should have pressed an attack at Minneconjou Ford rather than feinting to relieve the pressure on Reno. It is most ironic that one of the major failings of the man held up as the very symbol of rashness,[77] on the fatal day, was a super abundance of conservatism.[78] Noted historian Robert M. Utley has put it most succinctly:

> *"George Armstrong Custer does not deserve the indictment that history has imposed on him for his actions at the Little Bighorn. Given what he knew at each decision point and what he had every reason to expect of his subordinates, one is hard pressed to say what he ought to have done differently.*[79] *In truth, at the Little Bighorn 'Custer's Luck' simply ran out. Although the failures of subordinates may have contributed and the strength and prowess of the foe certainly contributed, Custer died the victim less of bad judgment than of bad luck."*[80]

This is not to say Custer made no errors at the Little Big Horn. He made several major errors, some of them years before the battle was joined. The post Civil War Custer had mellowed as a disciplinarian. He made a fatal error in not eradicating Benteen's insubordination when it first surfaced in 1868. Instead, Custer chose not to be confrontational, banishing the "anti–Custer" faction of the regiment to remote posts where they were "out of sight and out of mind." Custer should have known this was only a cosmetic fix that obscured, rather than resolved, the root problem. Perhaps he would have handled the situation better had his rise in rank not been so meteoric, allowing him the seasoning in dealing with personalities at the unit level he so badly needed. While he could not recognize this failing in himself, Custer ascribed the downfall of his idolized former commander, George Mc Clellan, to this very cause. Custer noted in his incomplete Civil War memoirs: *". . . he alone, of all the commanders of the Army of the Potomac, was thrust into high and almost supreme command of an army without having first had an opportunity to prepare himself by apprenticeship, as his successors had, by working their way up, step by step, through intermediate grades, from colonels or captains to that of general commanding–in–chief, and thus acquiring a self confidence and resolution which sudden elevation to high and supreme command was not calculated to give."*[81]

Another major failing of Custer was his propensity to withhold information from his subordinates.[82] Sergeant Culbertson commented on this failing during his court of inquiry testimony: *"I heard Captain Weir ask Captain Moylan if, when he was Adjutant, General Custer gave him any particular orders about doing anything. Captain Moylan said 'No,' that when he was Adjutant, General Custer never told him what he was going to do; he would order him to tell the company commanders to go to such and such places and that was all."*[83] Reno's actions in the valley might have been entirely different had Custer recognized the need for taking a few minutes to explain the tactical situation, as he understood it, and his objectives. How long would it have taken to inform Reno that his job was to attempt to initiate an engagement while Custer sought an avenue to deliver a decisive blow? In any event, it was an opportunity missed, and one, I believe, that cost Custer dearly.

Custer was guilty of another "communications failure." While he may, or may not, have attempted to send a messenger to Reno in the valley,[84] Custer clearly waited too long to recall Benteen from his scout. The only possible explanation is that Custer was not convinced there were no villages up the Little Big Horn from the mouth of Reno Creek. There is circumstantial evidence this was the case as Kanipe was dispatched almost immediately after Custer reached a vantage point from which he could ascertain the upper valley was clear of villages. While the lack of this piece of intelligence may have kept Custer from recalling Benteen at the time Reno was ordered into action, Custer still should have apprised Benteen of the evolving tactical situation and ordered McDougall and Mathey to close up with the pack train.

The final, and from an American cultural viewpoint, the most serious failure of Armstrong Custer at the Little Big Horn was he failed to deliver a victory. George C. Scott, in his role as George S. Patton, said it best – *"Americans love to win, they play to win all the time, and they will not tolerate a loser as the very thought of losing is hateful to Americans."* From our cultural perspective as "Monday morning quarterbacks," it's easy to understand how the disaster must have been Custer's sole fault. If Custer was correct and had acted in a thoroughly professional military manner, why was he lying dead on that knoll surrounded by slaughtered cavalrymen?[85] Apparently, in the final analysis of historians, it matters not that Custer's performance was superior to every other commander in the summer campaign. One incontestable fact remains. Custer failed to win – and paid the ultimate price.

It is my hope this narrative has shed some light, not only on what happened to Lieutenant Colonel, Brevet Major General, George Armstrong Custer and five companies of the Seventh Regiment of United States Cavalry on a ridge overlooking the Little Big Horn River on June 25, 1876, but on the men, red and white, who participated in that campaign. I believe the record shows Custer has been unfairly criticized as the result of a cover up initiated by his old nemesis Benteen and Terry's brother-in-law, Robert Hughes. Custer's performance, while resulting in disaster for his immediate command, was superior to that of every other commander in the summer campaign.[86] Perhaps the foregoing will best be understood by those in the medical profession who see neither irony nor contradiction in the adage *"well, the operation was a success, however, the patient died."*

In the final analysis, perhaps Armstrong Custer hasn't done too badly. While he has undeservedly become a symbol for failure, and a stereotype of all that was onerous in our

dealings with the Indians,[87] he did achieve something denied all of the other commanders –
immortality. In that respect, perhaps Custer won his last fight after all!

---

[1] See "The Teepee Book" page 613.

[2] 37% of Company C's men had less than a year's service to their credit, versus 39% for Company B. See Salvatore A. Caniglia "Profile of the Seventh" page 16.

[3] See Roger Darling "A Sad And Terrible Blunder" page 246. Initially estimating the village's fighting strength at 1,800, the surviving 7th Cavalry officers revised their estimate upward to 3,000 after visiting the abandoned village site. See Colonel W. A. Graham "The Reno Court of Inquiry" page 29. In 1877 Captain Philo Clark went over the battlefield with two of the warrior participants. They informed him that at the time of the Rosebud Fight (prior to the arrival of the bands led by Gall and Crow King) the village was comprised of about 1200 lodges and 400 wickiups housing about 3500 warriors. See Colonel W. A. Graham "The Custer Myth" page 116.

[4] From our twentieth century perspective, this is clearly unacceptable performance. When one recalls the failure of Reynolds to gather intelligence prior to attacking Old Bear's village, and the similar action by Anson Mills at Slim Buttes in addition to the actions of Terry, Gibbon, Crook and Custer, it is seen that this was a frequent occurrence in fighting Indians. While the pitfalls of such a course of action are obvious to us, the historical record is clear that, in terms of 19th century military values, failure to adequately reconnoiter was common practice and only deserving of censure if the result of the fight proved unfavorable. It is therefore somewhat ironic to note that Armstrong Custer, the only commander in the campaign who apparently realized the importance of a thorough reconnaissance, being forced by circumstances as he knew them to abandon that plan, is the officer most criticized for failing to conduct a proper reconnaissance.

[5] See Robert M. Utley "Frontier Regulars" page 262.

[6] See Colonel T. M. Coughlan "Varnum – The Last of Custer's Lieutenants" page 32.

[7] See Douglas D. Scott "Archaeological Perspectives on the Battle of the Little Bighorn" page 118. This evidence supports Grinnell's statement that about half of the Indians (Grinnell was probably referring only to the Cheyenne) at the Little Big Horn had guns. See George Bird Grinnell "The Fighting Cheyennes" page 352. In this fight, the army was clearly "out gunned" in terms of number of firearms employed.

[8] See Douglas D. Scott "Archaeological Perspectives on the Battle of the Little Bighorn" page 126. While 29 guns doesn't seem like a great number, it must be recalled that Company L entered the Custer Fight with 46 men. Allowing only 6 horseholders leaves a maximum of 40 combat effectives, assuming none were incapacitated in the actions on Luce and Blummer-Nye-Cartwright ridges. Twenty nine rapid firing weapons, used against 40 troopers, represents a considerable amount of firepower.

[9] The Springfield out ranged the Winchester by 100 yards and had twice the penetrating power. See Robert M. Utley "Frontier Regulars" page 72.

[10] The Springfield, a common arm to be used by both cavalry and infantry, was selected by a five member board of officers, chaired by General Terry, of which the cavalry representative was Major Reno. See Ron Nichols "The Springfield Carbine at the Little Big Horn" page 56. It should be noted that the officer corps was not unanimously supportive of the Springfield. Colonel Gibbon, for example, favored retention of the Springfield musket for the infantry, but preferred the Winchester, or similar arm, for the cavalry. See Colonel John Givvon "Arms To Fight Indians" page 15.

11 See Douglas D. Scott "Archaeological Perspectives on the Battle of the Little Bighorn" page 114.

12 Such an account, written by Captain Robert G. Carter in response to Colonel W. A. Graham's "The Story of the Little Big Horn" is presented in "The Custer Myth" pages 303 - 304.

13 See Thomas B. Marquis "Keep The Last Bullet For Yourself" page 169.

14 See Richard A. Roberts "Custer's Last Battle" page 25.

15 See Evan S. Connell "Son of the Morning Star" page 48.

16 See Ronald H. Nichols "The Reno Court of Inquiry" page 169.

17 See Colonel W. A. Graham "The Custer Myth" page 335. For a detailed treatment of the subject see John M. Carroll "A Seventh Cavalry Scrapbook #3" page 25. The complete text of Godfrey's January 18,. 1929 letter to Crow Agent C. H. Asbury follows: *"My dear Major Asbury:*

"Your letter of January 2nd has been before me as a matter of great interest. Several times when in Washington I have been tempted to see the Interior officials in reference to the appropriation for grounds and marker at the upper battlefield, but thought better to await progress of purchases, etc.

"I have always felt that no individual names should be placed on the marker (the one at the Reno-Benteen Defense Site, DCE).

"1st – Because I always felt that Major Reno utterly failed in his part in the valley attack in the disposition of his command when he fell back in the old stream bed; that he failed to exercise any fire control; that he **could** *and* **should** *have held that position (emphasis from the original, DCE).*

"2nd – Having made the decision to retreat, he made no disposition to cover the retreat or to properly inform the command of such decision; that he in person led a panic, straggling retreat, hereby sacrificing many lives and the morale of his command. The shock from the killing of Bloody Knife at his side or near him seems to have bereft him of the sense of official responsibility and to impel him to seek safety in flight.

"3rd – After the command had taken the position, when we were besieged he seemed resigned to inactivity except when urged by Captain Benteen. After all firing had ceased the night of June 25th he planned to abandon the position, destroy property that could not be transported, mount all men who could ride and retreat to the supply camp at the mouth of Powder River. When asked what he proposed to do with the wounded who could not ride, he said they would have to be **abandoned** *and Benteen told him he would not do it (emphasis from the original, DCE). This I had from Captain Benteen himself.*

"I protest the name of Major Reno on the marker, and as the commander's name should not be engraved thereon, therefore no individual names of survivors should appear and I suggest the following inscription:

"This area was occupied by Companies A, B, D, G, H, K, and M, 7th U. S. Cavalry, and the pack train where they were besieged June 25th and 26th, 1876. (The marker at the Reno-Benteen Defense Site bears this inscription today, DCE).

"With best wishes for you and yours,

"Cordially,

"E. S. Godfrey" See Tom O'Neil "Marcus A. Reno: What Was Said Of Him At The Little Big Horn" pages 5 - 6.

[18] See Colonel W. A. Graham "The Reno Court of Inquiry" page 196.

[19] See James Brust "Lt. Oscar Long's Early Map Details Terrain, battle Positions" page 9.

[20] See Colonel W. A. Graham "The Custer Myth" page 344.

[21] See John Upton Terrell and Colonel George Walton "Faint the Trumpet Sounds" page 257.

[22] Similarly, Reno's order to withdraw from Weir Point was also not communicated to the entire command.

[23] See Fred H. Werner "The Beecher Island Battle" pages 35 and 84.

[24] See O. G. Libby "The Arikara Narrative" page 12.

[25] See George Bird Grinnell "The Fighting Cheyennes" page 349. The Lakota Spotted Horn Bull was also surprised by Reno's withdrawal from the bottom, recalling the warriors hadn't done much firing prior to Reno's retreat. See Colonel W. A. Graham "The Custer Myth" page 84.

[26] After interviewing 7th Cavalry officers, including Major Reno, the night of August 6, 1876, Lieutenant Frank D. Baldwin of the 5th Infantry confided to his diary that Reno's withdrawal from the valley was *". . . done with more rapidity than discipline or the good of the service would admit of."* See James S. Brust "Baldwin Talks With Reno, Writes About Custer's Final Battle" page 20.

[27] See Colonel William A. Graham "The Reno Court of Inquiry" page 226.

[28] See Edward J. McClernand "On Time For Disaster" page 73.

[29] See Robert J. Ege "Settling the Dust" page iii. Kanipe would echo these sentiments: *"Speaking now as a private citizen I do not hesitate to express it as my opinion that if Reno and Benteen had carried out their orders Custer and the five troops would not have met their sad fate."* See Glendolin Damon Wagner "Old Neutriment" page 193.

[30] William Morris' account indicates that although he had been wounded in the left breast, he made the movement toward Custer without being offered any assistance. See Tom O'Neil "Mysteries Solved, Mysteries Unsolved" page 27.

[31] See William O. Taylor "With Custer On The Little Bighorn" page 48.

[32] See Colonel W. A. Graham "The Reno Court of Inquiry" pagse 226 - 227.

[33] Reno's report is reproduced in full in Appendix 7.

[34] See Charles Kuhlman "Legend Into History" page 222.

[35] See John M. Carroll "The Benteen-Goldin Letters" page 185.

[36] See Katherine Gibson Fougera "With Custer's Cavalry" page 272.

[37] See Cyrus Townshend Brady "Indian Fights and Fighters" page 404. It doesn't seem possible that heavy firing from Custer''s position could be heard from the morass.

[38] See John M. Carroll "The Benteen-Goldin Letters" page 246. The countermanding of a superior's order is purely a twentieth century concept.

[39] See Ronald H. Nichols "Reno Court of Inquiry" page 430.

[40] See William Winthrop "Military Law and Precedents" pages 987 - 988.

[41] See Edward M. Byrne "Military Law, Third Edition" page 165.

[42] The Articles are equally clear that an adjutant's orders are presumed to come from the commander and therefore carry the full weight of the commander's prerogatives. Again, Benteen never attempted to argue the point.

[43] See Shelby Foote "The Civil War: A Narrative, Fort Sumter to Perryville" pages 634 - 635.

[44] See Shelby Foote "The Civil War: A Narrative, Fort Sumter to Perryville" page758.

[45] Although Custer preferred to avoid conflict with his officers, he never shied away from a confrontation. His direct confrontation with Reno over the scout contrasts markedly with Terry's approach in sending Hughes to find out why Reno had gone to the Rosebud. See Edgar I. Stewart "Custer's Luck" page 237.

[46] Godfrey's entry for August 14 reads in part: "... *very much to our disgust we are under Genl Gibbon again. Something must be wrong about Genl Terry that he cannot hold control of cavalry & Infty without having merely nominal command.*" See Edward S. Godfrey "The Filed Diary of Edward Settle Godfrey" pages 35 - 36.

[47] See Paul Andrew Hutton "Soldiers West" page 216.

[48] See Charles G. DuBois "Kick The Dead Lion" page xviii.

[49] See Jerome A. Greene "Slim Buttes" page 30.

[50] See Jerome A. Greene "Slim Buttes" page 30.

[51] See Robert M. Utley "Frontier Regulars" page 292.

[52] For a concise dissertation on the plot to shield Terry from blame, see John S. Gray "Centennial Campaign" page 196. A very thorough examination of the question of Custer's disobedience may be found in Charles Kuhlman's "Did Custer Disobey Orders at the Battle of the Little Big Horn?"

[53] See Robert M. Utley "Cavalier in Buckskin" page 170.

[54] See Lt Col Melbourne C. Chandler "Of Garryowen In Glory" page 46.

[55] See Charles G. du Bois "Kick the Dead Lion" page 101.

[56] See Colonel William A. Graham "The Custer Myth" page 114.

[57] See Robert M. Utley "Frontier Regulars" page 271.

[58] See Wayne Michael Sarf "The Little Bighorn Campaign" page 283.

[59] Gibbon served with distinction at Second Manassas, Antietam, South Mountain, Fredericksburg, Gettysburg, the Wilderness, and Petersburg, being severely wounded both at Fredericksburg and Gettysburg. His performance and fidelity to duty was rewarded when he was accorded one of the honorary positions in the room where Grant accepted Lee's surrender at Appomattox. See Roger Darling "A Sad And Terrible Blunder" page 107.

[60] Gibbon's loss of 60 men at the Battle of the Big Hole is exceeded only by the Fetterman and Custer Fights in plains Indian warfare. Reno, by contrast, suffered 45 casualties in the valley fight and an additional 59 casualties in the two day hilltop fight. See John M. Carroll "A Seventh Cavalry Scrapbook #7" pages 24 - 25 and Appendix 2.

[61] As stated previously, Gibbon had been ordered to remain on the north bank unless he was assured of making a successful attack. This passage, and the entire tone of Paulding's letter, appears to indicate that Gibbon, at one point, felt compelled to justify his inaction to his officers.

[62] See Paul L. Hedren "The Great Sioux War 1876-77" pages 130 -131.

[63] See Thomas C. MacMillan "Crook's Expedition" page 10.

[64] See Robert M. Utley "Frontier Regulars" pages 270 - 271.

[65] See John M. Carroll "A Seventh Cavalry Scrapbook #10" page 12.

[66] See Daniel O. Magnussen "Thompson's Narrative" page 284. Having supreme faith that Sheridan would rush all available replacements to the front without being asked, Crook must have been shocked by Sheridan's dispatch, which he received June 19, urging him to attack again. See Martin F. Schmitt "General George Crook: His Autobiography" page 197.

[67] See John Upton Terrell and Colonel George Walton "Faint The Trumpet Sounds" page 204.

[68] Charles A. Eastman, a full blooded Lakota, related that the Lakota generally believed that Crook, not Reno, was the real coward of the Little Big Horn. See "Indian Heroes and Great Chieftains" page 97.

[69] See George E. Hyde "Red Cloud's Folk" page 260.

[70] See Paul Andrew Hutton "Soldiers West" page 219.

[71] See Martin F. Schmitt "General George Crook: His Autobiography" pages 97-98.

[72] See Robert M. Utley "Frontier Regulars" page 262.

[73] See Robert M. Utley "Frontier Regulars" page 196.

[74] See E. A. Brininstool "Troopers With Custer" page 34.

[75] See E. A. Brininstool "Troopers With Custer" page 34.

[76] See Tom O'Neil "Marcus A. Reno: What Was Said Of Him At the Little Big Horn" page 10.

[77] Sheridan did not believe his principal lieutenant guilty of rashness, stating: *"I do not attribute Col. Custer's action to either recklessness or want of judgment, but to a misapprehension of the situation and to a superabundance of courage."* See Colonel William A. Graham "The Custer Myth" page 117.

[78] Custer had once remarked on what others thought to be impetuousity: *"I am not impetuous or impulsive, I resent that. Everything that I have ever done has been the result of the study I have made of imaginary military situations that might arise. When I became engaged in campaign or battle and a great emergency arose, everything that I had ever read or studied focused in my mind as if the situation were under a magnifying glass and my decision was the instantaneous result. My mind worked instantaneously, but alway as the result of everything I had ever studied; being brought to bear on the situation."* See Evan S. Connell "Son of the Morning Star" page 351.

[79] One of Custer's sharpest critics, Captain Hughes, observed *"Everything indicates that he was convinced that the Indians were in full flight, and, if this were true, his tactics are not to be criticized."* See Francis B. Taunton "Sufficient Reason?" page 68.

[80] See Robert M. Utley "Cavalier in Buckskin" page 202.

[81] See John M. Carroll "Custer In The Civil War" page 112.

[82] Custer was far from unique in this regard. Crook, for example, *". . . incessantly pumped his subordinates for information but never revealed his plans to them. He did not bother his officers with detailed instructions, expecting them to exercise initiative."* See Bill O'Neal "Fighting Men of The Indian Wars" page 97.

[83] See Colonel William A. Graham "The Reno Court of Inquiry" page 127.

[84] It would have been appropriate for Custer to have dispatched a messenger to Reno in response to the message delivered by McIlhargey. This messenger could have reassured Reno by explaining the regiment had turned north in an attempt to flank the enemy.

[85] Luther Hare summed up this pragmatic position in a December 1893 letter to R. P. Hughes: *'**With the results of that fight before him** how any one can seek to defend the tactics used is an enigma to me. (emphasis the author's)"* See Ray Meketa "A Letter From Luther Hare" pages 209 - 210.

[86] It would be exceeded by both Mackenzie and Miles in the coming winter campaign

[87] Custer's sentiments on the "Indian problem" were well known, although infrequently quoted: *"If I were an Indian, I often think I would greatly prefer to cast my lot among those of my people adhered to the free open plains rather than submit to the confined limits of a reservation, there to be the recipient of the blessed benefits of civilization, with its vices thrown in without stint or measure."* See Sherry L. Smith "The View From Officer's Row" page 38.

Appendix 1

Seventh Cavalry Roster by Company

(Includes all personnel accompanying the expedition)
(Where conflicts in spelling occur, the spelling on the June 1876 Regimental Muster Roll has been used)

Headquarters

Officers(5)

Lieutenant Colonel George Armstrong Custer — Commanding regiment. Killed June 25th. One of 10 bodies found on Custer Knoll.

Major Marcus A. Reno — Commander in valley and hilltop fights.

First Lieutenant William W. Cooke — Regimental Adjutant. Killed with the Custer Column June 25th. One of 10 bodies found on Custer Knoll.

First Lieutenant Henry J. Nowlan — Detached Service on General Terry's Staff as Acting Assistant Quartermaster

Veterinary Surgeon C. A. Stein — At Powder River Camp

Non-commissioned Officers(3)

Sergeant Major William H. Sharrow — Killed with the Custer Column June 25th
Quartermaster Sergeant Thomas Causby — At Powder River Camp
Saddler Sergeant John G. Tritten — At Powder River Camp

Enlisted(1)

Chief Trumpeter Henry Voss — Killed with the Custer Column June 25th. One of 10 bodies found on Custer Knoll.

Effective strength on June 25th: 3 Officers, 1 non-commissioned officer, and 1 enlisted man.

Medical(3)

James Madison DeWolf — Killed during the retreat from the valley, June 25th

First Lieutenant George Edwin Lord — Killed with the Custer Column June 25th. While at the Powder River Camp, he was detailed to replace Dr. John Winfield as chief medical officer.

Henry Rinaldo Porter

Civilians(2)

Mark Kellogg — Newspaper correspondent. Killed with the Custer Column June 25th

Harry Armstrong Reed — Custer's nephew. Killed with the Custer Column June 25th

Guides(3)

Mitch Bouyer — Killed with the Custer Column June 25th
Boston Custer — Killed with the Custer Column June 25th
Charles Alexander Reynolds — Killed during the retreat from the valley, June 25th

Interpreters(2)

Isaiah Dorman — Killed during the retreat from the valley, June 25th

Frederick F. Girard

Couriers(1)

George Herendeen

Band – White Horses

Non-commissioned Officers(1)
Chief Musician Felix Villiet Vinatieri   At Powder River Camp

Enlisted(13)
Private Otto Arndt (aka Max Cernow)   At Powder River Camp
Private Conrad Baumbach   At Powder River Camp
Private Benjamin Beck   At Powder River Camp
Private Edmond Burli   At Powder River Camp
Private Joseph Carroll   At Powder River Camp
Private Andrew Carter   At Powder River Camp
Private Peter Eisenberger   At Powder River Camp
Private Julius Griesner   At Powder River Camp
Private Jacob Huff (aka Jacob Emerich)   At Powder River Camp
Private Julius Jungsbluth   At Powder River Camp
Private Bernard O'Neill   At Powder River Camp
Private George Rudolph   At Powder River Camp
Private Thomas Charles Sherborne   At Powder River Camp

Company A – Coal Black Horses

Officers(3)
Captain Myles Moylan   Company Commander
First Lieutenant Charles C. DeRudio   Temporary Duty from Company E. Abandoned in the timber.

Second Lieutenant Charles A. Varnum   Temporary Duty Commanding Indian Scouts, wounded in the leg during Benteen's charge on June 26th

Non-commissioned Officers(10)
First Sergeant William Heyn   Wounded in the left knee during the valley fight, June 25th
Sergeant Samuel Alcott   At Powder River Camp
Sergeant Ferdinand A. Culbertson
Sergeant John Thomas Easley
Sergeant Henry Fehler
Sergeant George Michael McDermott (aka Michael Burke)
Corporal James Dalious   Killed in action. Probably in the valley fight, June 25th
Corporal John Thomas Easley   Promoted Sergeant June 1, 1876
Corporal George H. King   Promoted Corporal June 1, 1876. Water carrier on June 26. Wounded in hilltop fight June 26th. Died on steamer *Far West* July 2nd
Corporal Stanislaus Roy   Awarded the Medal of Honor for bringing water to the wounded.

Enlisted(43)
Trumpeter William G. Hardy (aka Charles Laurse)
Trumpeter David McVeigh
Blacksmith Andrew Hamilton
Farrier John Bringes
Saddler John Muering
Private Charles Aller
Private John E. Armstrong   Killed in action. Abandoned in the timber.
Private Neil Bancroft   Awarded the Medal of Honor for bringing water to the wounded.
Private Louis Baumgartner

Private August Bockerman	At Powder River Camp
Private Wilbur F. Blair	
Private Thomas Blake	
Private George A. Bott	
Private Benjamin F. Burdick	At Powder River Camp
Private Andrew Conner	
Private Michael Coveney	Deserted May 17, 1876
Private Cornelius Cowley (aka John Sullivan)	
Private Jacob Deihle	Wounded in the face during hilltop fight June 26th
Private James Drinan	Killed in action. Probably in the valley fight, June 25th
Private Otto Durselen	
Private Samuel James Foster	Wounded in the right arm , probably during the hilltop fight, June 25th
Private John W. Franklin	
Private John M. Gilbert	Water carrier on June 26th.
Private David W. Harris	Awarded the Medal of Honor for bringing water to the wounded.
Private Frederick Holmstead	Wounded in the left wrist, probably during the hilltop fight, June 25th
Private Stanton Hook	
Private Samuel Johnson	
Private Emil O. Jonson	
Private William McClurg (aka William Irvine)	
Private James McDonald	Killed in action. Probably in the valley fight, June 25th
Private William Moodie	Killed in the hilltop fight June 25th
Private William D. Nugent	Water carrier on June 26th.
Private George W. Proctor	
Private John S. Ragsdale	At Powder River Camp
Private Francis M. Reeves	Wounded in the left side and body, probably during the hilltop fight, June 25th
Private Richard Rollins	Killed in action. Probably in the valley fight, June 25th
Private Thomas Seayers	
Private Anton Siebelder	
Private Elijah T. Strode	Wounded in the right ankle during the valley fight on June 25th
Private John Sullivan	Killed in action. Probably in the valley fight, June 25th
Private Thomas P. Sweetser	Killed in action. Probably in the valley fight, June 25th
Private William O. Taylor	
Private Howard H. Weaver	

Effective strength on June 25th: 3 Officers, 9 non-commissioned officers, and 39 enlisted men.

Company B – Bay Horses

Officers(2)

Captain Thomas M. McDougall	Company Commander
Second Lieutenant Benjamin H. Hodgson	Temporary duty as Adjutant to the Reno Battalion. Killed during the retreat from the valley June 25th

Non-commissioned Officers(8)
First Sergeant James Hill

Sergeant Benjamin C. Criswell	Promoted Sergeant June 4, 1876. Wounded in the neck during the hilltop fight on June 25th. Awarded Medal of Honor for recovery of Hodgson's body and bringing ammunition under heavy fire.
Sergeant Peter Gannon	At Powder River Camp
Sergeant Rufus D. Hutchinson	Awarded the Medal of Honor for bringing water to the wounded.
Sergeant Thomas Murray	Wounded during the hilltop fight June 26th. Awarded Medal of Honor for bringing up pack train and bringing rations under heavy fire.
Corporal James Dougherty	
Corporal William M. Smith	Promoted Corporal May 15, 1876. Wounded in the hilltop fight June 26th
Corporal Adam Wetzel	Promoted Corporal June 4, 1876

Enlisted(58)

Trumpeter John Connell	At Powder River Camp
Trumpeter James Kelly	
Blacksmith John Crump	Appointed Blacksmith May 15, 1876
Farrier James E. Moore	
Saddler John E. Bailey	
Private Peter Orlanda Barry	Temporary duty with Department Headquarters in the field.
Private James F. Barsantee (aka William Evans)	
Private William Boam	
Private Hugh Boner	
Private Ansgarius Boren	Water carrier on June 26th.
Private George Brainard	
Private James Brown (aka Richard J. Nolan)	
Private Charles Burns	At Powder River Camp
Private William M. Caldwell	At Powder River Camp
Private James Callan	At Powder River Camp
Private Thomas J. Callan	Awarded the Medal of Honor for bringing water to the wounded.
Private Charles A. Campbell	Reduced from Sergeant June 4, 1876
Private Thomas Carmody	
Private John J. Cary	
Private Frank Clark	
Private Thomas W. Coleman	Water carrier on June 26th.
Private Harry Criswell	
Private Michael Crowe	
Private Patrick Crowley	
Private Charles Cunningham	Wounded in the neck during the hilltop fight June 25th, he remained on the firing line. Awarded the Medal of Honor for this action.
Private William H. Davenport	
Private Louis DeTourriel	At Powder River Camp
Private Augustus L. DeVoto	Water carrier on June 26th.
Private Jacob W. Doll	At Powder River Camp
Private Richard B. Dorn	Killed in the hilltop fight, June 26h
Private William Frank	
Private Frederick Henry Gehrmann	At Powder River Camp
Private John R. Gray	At Powder River Camp
Private John J. Keefe	At Powder River Camp
Private John L. Littlefield	At Powder River Camp
Private John McCabe	
Private Bernard McGurn	At Powder River Camp

Private Terrence McLaughlin
Private William McMasters
Private George B. Mack   Killed in the hilltop fight June 26th
(Mask is shown as an alternative name on June Regimental Muster Roll)
Private William Martin
Private William E. Morrow   At Powder River Camp
Private Thomas O'Brien   At Powder River Camp
Private John O'Neill
Private James Pym   Awarded the Medal of Honor for bringing water
                                                 to the wounded.

Private George F. Randall
Private Stephen L. Ryan
Private Hiram Wallace Sager
Private Daniel Shea
Private Patrick Simons   At Powder River Camp
Private Philipp Spinner
Private Edward Stout
Private Thomas James Stowers (aka James Thomas)
Private Henry L. Tinkham   At Powder River Camp
Private William Trumble   Hodgson's orderly. In the valley fight.
Private Richard A. Wallace
Private Edwin B. Wight   At Powder River Camp
Private Aaron Woods

Effective strength on June 25th: 2 Officers, 7 non-commissioned officers, and 41 enlisted men.

Company C – Light Sorrel Horses

Officers(2)
Captain Thomas W. Custer   Temporary duty as Aide-de-camp to Lieutenant
                                                 Colonel Custer. Killed with the Custer Column
                                                 June 25th. One of 10 bodies found on Custer
                                                 Knoll.
Second Lieutenant Henry M. Harrington   Missing in action, presumed killed with the
                                                 Custer Column June 25th

Non-commissioned Officers(9)
First Sergeant Edwin Bobo   Killed with the Custer Column June 25th
Sergeant August Finckle   Killed with the Custer Column June 25th
Sergeant Jeremiah Finley   Killed with the Custer Column June 25th
Sergeant Richard P. Hanley   With the pack train. Awarded Medal of Honor for
                                                 recovery of mule laden with ammunition from
                                                 between the lines
Sergeant Daniel Alexander Kanipe   Courier to the pack train
Corporal Charles A. Crandall   At Powder River Camp
Corporal John Foley   Killed with the Custer Column June 25th
Corporal Henry Eldon French   Killed with the Custer Column June 25th
Corporal Daniel Ryan   Killed with the Custer Column June 25th

Enlisted(52)
Trumpeter Thomas J. Bucknell   Killed with the Custer Column June 25th
Trumpeter William Kramer   Killed with the Custer Column June 25th
Blacksmith John Fitzgerald   At Powder River Camp
Farrier John King   Killed with the Custer Column June 25th
(Listed as blacksmith on June Regimental Muster Roll)
Saddler George Howell   Killed with the Custer Column June 25th
Wagoner Frank Stark   At Powder River Camp
Private Fred E. Allan   Killed with the Custer Column June 25th

Private Charles L. Anderson (aka Levi Henry Anderson)	Deserted June 20, 1876
Private James C. Bennett	Wounded in the body during the hilltop fight June 26th. Died on steamer *Far West* July 5th.
Private Charles H. Bischoff	At Powder River Camp
Private William Brandle	At Powder River Camp
Private John Welch Brennan	Straggler, joined Reno's Battalion
Private John Brightfield	Killed with the Custer Column June 25th
Private Christopher Criddle	Killed with the Custer Column June 25th
Private George Eiseman	Killed with the Custer Column June 25th
Private Gustave Engle	Killed with the Custer Column June 25th
Private James Farrand	Killed with the Custer Column June 25th
Private Morris Farrar	Unknown. Possible straggler.
Private John Fitzgerald	Straggler, joined Reno's Battalion.
Private Isaac Fowler	With pack train
Private Patrick Griffin	Killed with the Custer Column June 25th
Private James Hathersall	Killed with the Custer Column June 25th
Private John Jordan	With pack train
Private William Kane	At Powder River Camp
Private John Lewis	Killed with the Custer Column June 25th
Private John B. McGuire, Jr.	Wounded in the right arm during the hilltop fight on June 26th
Private John Mahoney	With the pack train
Private Frederick Meyer	Killed with the Custer Column June 25th
(Meier is shown as alternative name on June Regimental Muster Roll)	
Private August Meyer	Killed with the Custer Column June 25th
Private Martin Mullin	With the pack train
Private Ottocar Nitsche	With pack train
Private Charles M. Orr	At Powder River Camp
Private Edgar Phillips	Killed with the Custer Column June 25th
Private John Rauter	Killed with the Custer Column June 25th
Private Edward Rix	Killed with the Custer Column June 25th
Private James Henry Russell	Killed with the Custer Column June 25th
Private Samuel S. Shade	Killed with the Custer Column June 25th
Private Jeremiah Shea	Killed with the Custer Column June 25th
Private Nathan Short	Died near the Yellowstone River, date unknown
(June Regimental Muster Roll lists him as killed in action on June 25th)	
Private Ludwick St. John	Killed with the Custer Column June 25th[1]
Private Alpheus Stuart	Killed with the Custer Column June 25th
Private Ygnatz Stungwitz	Killed with the Custer Column June 25th
Private John Thadus	Killed with the Custer Column June 25th
Private Peter Thompson	Straggler, joined Reno's Battalion. Wounded in the right hand on June 26th. Awarded Medal of Honor for bringing water to the wounded
Private Garrett Van Allen (aka Garrett H. Niver)	Killed with the Custer Column June 25th
Private Julius Von Arnim	At Powder River Camp
Private Robert Walker	At Powder River Camp
Private Oscar T. Warner	Killed with the Custer Column June 25th
Private James Watson	Straggler, joined Reno's Battalion
Private Alfred Whittaker	With pack train. Wounded in the right elbow during the hilltop fight on June 26th
Private Willis B. Wright	Killed with the Custer Column June 25th
Private Henry Wyman	Killed with the Custer Column June 25th

Effective strength on June 25th: 2 Officers, 8 non-commissioned officers, and 43 enlisted men.

Company D – Bay Horses

Officers(2)

Captain Thomas B. Weir   Company Commander
Second Lieutenant Winfield Scott Edgerly

Non-commissioned Officers(6)

First Sergeant Michael Martin
Sergeant James Flanagan
Sergeant Thomas W. Harrison
Sergeant Thomas Russell   Promoted Sergeant June 6, 1876
Corporal Albert J. Cunningham   At Powder River Camp
Corporal George Washington Wylie

Enlisted(55)

Trumpeter Aloys Bohner (aka Louis Braun)
Blacksmith Frederick Deitline   Awarded the Medal of Honor for bringing water
                                                to the wounded.
Farrier Charley Vincent   Wounded and abandoned to the Indians during
                                                retreat from Weir Point June 25th. Commonly
                                                known as Vincent Charley, the June Regimental
                                                Muster Roll contains a notation by Captain
                                                Wallace indicating the surname to be Vincent.

Saddler John Myers
Private James H. Alberts
Private John B. Ascough
Private Abraham B. Brant   Awarded the Medal of Honor for bringing water
                                                to the wounded.
Private Thomas Conlan   At Powder River Camp
Private Stephen Cowley   At Powder River Camp
Private Thomas Cox
Private George Dann
Private David E. Dawsey
Private John J. Fay
Private Harvey A. Fox   At Powder River Camp
Private John Fox
Private Patrick M. Golden   Killed in the hilltop fight June 25th
Private John Green (aka Henry Gross)   At Powder River Camp
Private Joseph H. Green
Private John Hager
Private Curtis Hall
Private William Hardden
Private Gustav Harlfinger   At Powder River Camp
Private James Harris
Private William M. Harris   Awarded the Medal of Honor for bringing water
                                                to the wounded.
Private Jacob Hetler   Wounded in the left leg on June 25th and in the
                                                back on June 26th
Private Henry Holden   Awarded Medal of Honor for bringing
                                                ammunition under heavy fire.
Private Charles Horn
Private Charles H. Houghtaling
Private Edward Housen (aka Edward Dellienhousen) Killed in action, June 25th
Private George Hunt
Private James Hurd (aka James Hood)
Private John Kanavagh   Water carrier on June 26th.
Private John J. Keller
Private Fremont Kipp

Private John Kretchmer
Private Jesse Kuehl   At Powder River Camp
Private Uriah S. Lewis   At Powder River Camp
Private Patrick McDonnel   Wounded in the left leg during the hilltop fight
                                                       June 25th

Private David Manning
Private William A. Marshall
Private John Meadwell (aka J. R. Meadville)
Private William O'Mann
Private John Quinn   At Powder River Camp
Private William J. Randall
Private Elwyn S. Reid
Private William Sadler   At Powder River Camp
Private Charles Sanders
Private George D. Scott   Awarded Medal of Honor for bringing water to
                                                       the wounded.
Private John J. Sims   At Powder River Camp
Private Henry G. Smith
Private William E. Smith
Private Thomas W. Stivers   Awarded Medal of Honor for bringing water to
                                                       the wounded

Private Frank Tolan   Awarded Medal of Honor for bringing water to
                                                       the wounded

Private Charles H. Welch   Awarded Medal of Honor for bringing water to
                                                       the wounded

Private James Wynn

Effective strength on June 25th: 2 Officers, 5 non-commissioned officers, and 45 enlisted men.

Company E – Gray Horses

Officers(2)
First Lieutenant Algernon E. Smith   Temporary duty from Company A, Company
                                                       Commander. Killed with the Custer Column June
                                                       25th. One of 10 bodies found on Custer Knoll.

Second Lieutenant James G. Sturgis   Temporary duty from Company M, Missing in
                                                       action, presumed killed with the Custer Column
                                                       June 25th

Non-commissioned Officers(9)
First Sergeant Frederick Hohmeyer   Killed with the Custer Column June 25th
Sergeant William B. James   Killed with the Custer Column June 25th
Sergeant Lawrence Murphy   Probably at Powder River Camp
Sergeant John S. Ogden   Killed with the Custer Column June 25th
Sergeant James F. Riley   With pack train. Wounded in the back and left
                                                       leg during the hilltop fight on June 26th

Corporal George C. Brown   Killed with the Custer Column June 25th
Corporal Thomas P. Eagan (aka Thomas Hagan)   Killed with the Custer Column June 25th
Corporal Henry S. Mason   Killed with the Custer Column June 25th
Corporal Albert H. Meyer   Killed with the Custer Column June 25th

Enlisted(44)
Trumpeter Thomas McElroy   Killed with the Custer Column June 25th
Trumpeter George A. Moonie   Killed with the Custer Column June 25th
Blacksmith Henry Miller   Probably at Powder River Camp
Farrier Abel B. Spencer   Probably at Powder River Camp
Saddler William Shields   Probably at Powder River Camp

Private Harry Abbots	Extra duty as hospital attendant, with the Reno Battalion
Private David Ackinson	On steamer Far West, sick
Private William H. Baker	Killed with the Custer Column June 25th
Private Robert Barth	Killed with the Custer Column June 25th
Private Frank Berwald	Probably at Powder River Camp
Private Owen Boyle	Killed with the Custer Column June 25th
Private James Brogan	Killed with the Custer Column June 25th
Private Latrobe Bromwell	With pack train
Private William H. Chapman (aka Smith, Dutton)	Transferred from Company B on June 1, he was probably at Powder River Camp
Private Edward Conner	Killed with the Custer Column June 25th
Private John Darris	Killed with the Custer Column June 25th
Private William Davis	Killed with the Custer Column June 25th
Private Richard Farrell	Killed with the Custer Column June 25th
Private John Heim	Killed with the Custer Column June 25th
Private John Henderson	Killed with the Custer Column June 25th
Private Sykes Henderson	Killed with the Custer Column June 25th
Private John S. Hiley	Killed with the Custer Column June 25th[2]
Private William Huber	Killed with the Custer Column June 25th
Private John James (aka John Casella)	With pack train
Private John G. Kimm	With pack train
Private Andy Knecht	Killed with the Custer Column June 25th
Private Henry Lang	With pack train
Private Herod T. Liddiard	Killed with the Custer Column June 25th
Private Patrick O'Conner	Killed with the Custer Column June 25th
Private Francis O'Toole	With pack train
Private Christopher Pandtle	Extra duty as hospital attendant, with the Reno Battalion
Private William H. Rees	Killed with the Custer Column June 25th
Private William H. Reese	Probably at Powder River Camp
Private Edward Rood	Killed with the Custer Column June 25th
Private Henry Schele	Killed with the Custer Column June 25th
Private William Smallwood	Killed with the Custer Column June 25th
Private Albert A. Smith	Killed with the Custer Column June 25th
Private James Smith (first)	Killed with the Custer Column June 25th
Private James Smith (second)	Killed with the Custer Column June 25th
Private Benjamin F. Stafford	Killed with the Custer Column June 25th
Private Alexander Stella	Killed with the Custer Column June 25th
Private William A. Torrey	Killed with the Custer Column June 25th
Private Cornelius Van Sant	Killed with the Custer Column June 25th
Private George Walker (aka George P. Weldon)	Killed with the Custer Column June 25th

Effective strength on June 25th: 2 Officers, 8 non-commissioned officers, and 37 enlisted men.

Company F – White Horses

Officers(2)

Captain George W. Yates	Company Commander. Killed with the Custer Column June 25th
Second Lieutenant William Van Wyck Reily	Killed with the Custer Column June 25th

Non-commissioned Officers(9)

First Sergeant Michael Kenney	Killed with the Custer Column June 25th
Sergeant William A. Curtiss	With pack train
Sergeant Frederick Nursey	Killed with the Custer Column June 25th

Sergeant John Vickory	Regimental color bearer. Killed with the Custer Column June 25th. One of 10 bodies found on Custer Knoll.
Sergeant John K. Wilkinson	Killed with the Custer Column June 25th
Corporal John Briody	Killed with the Custer Column June 25th
Corporal Edward Clyde	Probably at Powder River Camp
Corporal Charles Coleman	Killed with the Custer Column June 25th
Corporal William Teeman (aka William A. Adams)	Killed with the Custer Column June 25th

Enlisted(51)

Trumpeter Thomas N. Way (Listed as a private on the June Regimental Muster Roll)	Killed with the Custer Column June 25th
Blacksmith James R. Manning	Killed with the Custer Column June 25th
Farrier Benjamin Brandon	Killed with the Custer Column June 25th
Saddler Claus Schleiper	With pack train
Private Thomas Atcheson	Killed with the Custer Column June 25th
Private William Brady	Killed with the Custer Column June 25th
Private Benjamin Franklin Brown	Killed with the Custer Column June 25th
Private Hiram E. Brown	Probably at Powder River Camp
Private William Brown	Wounded under Yates at the Washita, he was killed with the Custer Column June 25th[3]
Private Patrick Bruce	Killed with the Custer Column June 25th
Private Lucien Burnham	Killed with the Custer Column June 25th
Private James W. Butler	Extra duty as hospital attendant, with Reno's battalion
Private James Carney	Killed with the Custer Column June 25th
Private Armantheus D. Cather	Killed with the Custer Column June 25th
Private Edward Davern	Temporary duty as Reno's orderly
Private Anton Dohman	Killed with the Custer Column June 25th
Private Timothy Donnelly	Killed with the Custer Column June 25th
Private William Eades	Probably at Powder River Camp
Private Thomas J. Finnegan	With pack train
Private William J. Gardiner (Some sources show him as John William Gardiner)	Killed with the Custer Column June 25th
Private William J. Gregg	Probably at Powder River Camp
Private George W. Hammon	Killed with the Custer Column June 25th
Private Francis Hegner	Probably at Powder River Camp
Private Frank Howard (aka Morris H. Thompson)	With pack train
Private Frank Hunter	Straggler. Water carrier on June 26th.
Private John P. Kelly	Killed with the Custer Column June 25th
Private Gustave Klein (aka Henry or Heinrich Klein)	Killed with the Custer Column June 25th
Private Herman Knauth	Killed with the Custer Column June 25th
Private Meig Lefler	Probably at Powder River Camp
Private William H. Lerock	Killed with the Custer Column June 25th
Private Werner L. Liemann	Killed with the Custer Column June 25th
Private William A. Lossee	Killed with the Custer Column June 25th
Private Dennis Lynch	With pack train
Private Bernard Lyons	With pack train
Private Christian Madson	Killed with the Custer Column June 25th
Private Francis E. Milton	Killed with the Custer Column June 25th
Private Joseph Milton	At Powder River Camp
Private Joseph Monroe	Killed with the Custer Column June 25th
Private Frank Myers	Probably at Powder River Camp
Private Sebastian Omling	Killed with the Custer Column June 25th
Private Edwin F. Pickard	With pack train. Water carrier on June 26th.
Private Michael Reiley	Probably at Powder River Camp
Private James M. Rooney	With pack train. Water carrier on June 26th.
Private Patrick Rudden	Killed with the Custer Column June 25th

Private Richard D. Saunders	Killed with the Custer Column June 25th
Private Paul Schleiffarth	Probably at Powder River Camp
Private Frederick Shulte (aka Charles Miller)	With pack train
Private Francis W. Sicfous	Killed with the Custer Column June 25th
Private John W. Sweeney	With pack train
Private Thomas Walsh	With pack train
Private George A. Warren	Killed with the Custer Column June 25th

Effective strength on June 25th: 2 Officers, 8 non-commissioned officers, and 42 enlisted men.

Company G – Sorrel Horses

Officers(2)

First Lieutenant Donald McIntosh	Company Commander. Killed during the retreat from the valley, June 25th
Second Lieutenant George D. Wallace	

Non-commissioned Officers(8)

Sergeant Edward Botzer	Acting First Sergeant.[4] Killed at the ford during the retreat from the valley June 25th
Sergeant Alexander Brown	Recovered Charley Reynolds' diary.
Sergeant Martin Considine	Killed in action. Probably in the valley fight, June 25th
Sergeant Olans H. Northeg	
Corporal James Akers	Promoted Sergeant June 25th
Corporal Otto Hagemann	Killed in action. Probably in the valley fight, June 25th
Corporal John E. Hammon	Promoted Sergeant June 25th. Water carrier on June 26th.
Corporal James Martin	Killed in the hilltop fight June 25th

Enlisted(52)

Trumpeter Henry C. Dose	Assigned as an headquarters orderly. Killed with 3 others near the head of Blummer–Nye–Cartwright Ridge on June 25th.
Blacksmith Walter O. Taylor	Abandoned in the timber. Rejoined Reno's command as a member of the Herendeen party.
Farrier Benjamin J. Wells	Killed during the retreat from the valley June 25th
Saddler Crawford Selby	Killed in action. Probably in the valley fight, June 25th
Private Charles Clinton Barnett	At Powder River Camp
Private James P. Boyle	Wounded, probably during the hilltop fight, date unknown
Private Henry M. Brinkerhoff	Promoted Corporal June 25th
Private Charles Campbell	Wounded in the right shoulder as part of the first water party June 26th
Private Michael Cornwall	
Private Melancthon H. Crussy	At Powder River Camp. Promoted Corporal June 25th
Private Edmond Dwyer	Member of the first water party June 26th
Private Frank J. Geist	At Powder River Camp
Private Theodore W. Goldin (John Stillwell)	Awarded Medal of Honor for bringing water to the wounded
Private Thomas E. Graham	
Private William S. Gray	At Powder River Camp
Private Edward Grayson	
Private John Hackett	
Private George W. Henderson	At Powder River Camp

Private Benjamin Johnson	Abandoned in the timber. Rejoined Reno's command as a member of the Herendeen party.
Private Jacob Katzenmaier	At Powder River Camp
Private Martin Kilfoyle	At Powder River Camp
Private John Lattmann	Abandoned in the timber. Rejoined Reno's command as a member of the Herendeen party.
Private Frank Lauper	At Powder River Camp
Private George Loyd	Promoted Corporal June 25th
Private Samuel McCormick	Ready to leave the timber, he gave his horse to dismounted Lieutenant McIntosh. Rejoined Reno's command as part of the Herendeen party
Private John McDonnell	
Private John McEagan	
Private John J. McGinniss	Abandoned in the timber. Killed in action June 25th
Private Hugh McGonigle	Abandoned in the timber. Rejoined Reno's command as a member of the Herendeen party.
Private Edward J. McKay	At Powder River Camp
Private John McKee	At Powder River Camp
Private John McVay	Wounded in the hips, June 25th
Private Andrew J. Moore	Abandoned in the timber, he rejoined Reno's command only to be killed in the hilltop fight June 25th
Private John Morrison	Wounded, probably during the hilltop fight, date unknown
Private Thomas Dean O'Neill	Originally abandoned in the timber. Rejoined Reno's command the night of June 26th
Private Henry Petring	Abandoned in the timber. Rejoined Reno's command as a member of the Herendeen party.
Private John Rapp	Killed in the valley fight June 25th while holding Lieutenant McIntosh's horse
Private John A. Reed	
Private Eldorado J. Robb	Abandoned in the timber. Rejoined Reno's command as a member of the Herendeen party.
Private Benjamin F. Rogers	Killed in action. Probably in the valley fight, June 25th
Private Robert Rowland	At Powder River Camp
Private Henry Seafferman	Killed during the retreat from the valley, June 25th
Private John Shanahan	At Powder River Camp
Private John R. Small	
Private Edward Stanley	Killed in action. Probably in the valley fight, June 25th
Private George W. Stephens	At Powder River Camp
Private Thomas W. Stevenson	
Private Daniel Sullivan	At Powder River Camp
Private Joseph Tulo	At Powder River Camp
Private John W. Wallace	Promoted Corporal June 25th
Private Markus Weiss	Abandoned in the timber. Rejoined Reno's command as a member of the Herendeen party.
Private Pasavan Williamson	At Powder River Camp

Effective strength on June 25th: 2 Officers, 8 non-commissioned officers, and 36 enlisted men.

Company H – Blood Bay Horses

Officers(2)

Captain Frederick W. Benteen — Company Commander. Slightly wounded in the thumb during the hilltop fight.

First Lieutenant Francis M. Gibson

Non-commissioned Officers(9)

First Sergeant Joseph McCurry — Wounded in action June 26.

Sergeant Patrcik Conelly — Wounded in action June 26.

Sergeant George H. Geiger — Awarded Medal of Honor as sharpshooter covering water party.

Sergeant Thomas F. McLaughlin — Wounded in action June 26.

Sergeant Mathew Maroney

Sergeant John Pahl — Wounded in the back (right shoulder) June 25th

Corporal Alexander B. Bishop — Wounded in the right arm June 25th

Corporal George Lell — Killed in the hilltop fight June 26th

Corporal Daniel Nealon

Enlisted(38)

Trumpeter John Martin (aka Giovanni Martini) — Carried Custer's last message to Benteen

Trumpeter William Ramell — Wounded in action June 26.

Blacksmith Henry W. B. Mecklin — Awarded Medal of Honor as sharpshooter covering water party.

Saddler Otto Voit — Wounded in action June 26. Awarded Medal of Honor as sharpshooter covering water party.

Private Jacob Adams — With the pack train. Water carrier on June 26.

Private Henry P. Bishley — Wounded in action June 26.

Private Charles H. Bishop — Wounded in the right arm June 25th

Private Henry Black — Wounded in the right arm June 25th

Private William Channell

Private John Cooper — Wounded in the right elbow June 25th

Private John H. Day

Private George W. Dewey

Private Edward Diamond

Private William Farley — Wounded in action June 26.

Private William Montell George — Wounded in the left side June 25th. Died on steamer *Far West* July 3rd.

Private George W. Glease (aka George W. Glenn)

Private Henry Haack

Private Timothy Haley

Private Thomas Hughes (aka Charles Hughes) — Wounded in action June 26.

Private John Hunt

Private Julien D. Jones — Killed in the hilltop fight June 26th

Private George Kelly

Private James Kelly

Private Thomas Lawhorn

Private Thomas McDermott

Private James McNamara

Private David McWilliams — At Powder River Camp. Wounded in right leg while mounting his horse on June 6th.

Private Thomas E. Meador — Killed in the hilltop fight June 26th

Private Jan Moller — Wounded in right thigh during hilltop fight June 25th

Private Edler Nees

Private Joshua S. Nicholas

Private William O'Ryan

Private John J. Phillips — Wounded in the face and both hands June 25th

Private John S. Pinkston	
Private Samuel Severs	Wounded in both thighs June 25th
Private Aloyse L. Walter	At Powder River Camp
Private William C. Williams	
Private Charles Windolph (aka Charles Wrangel)	Wounded in the buttock June 25th. Awarded Medal of Honor as sharpshooter covering the water party.

Effective strength on June 25th: 2 Officers, 9 non-commissioned officers, and 36 enlisted men.

Company I – Bay Horses

Officers(2)

Captain Myles W. Keogh	Company Commander. Killed with the Custer Column June 25th
First Lieutenant James E. Porter	Killed with the Custer Column June 25th

Non-commissioned Officers(9)

First Sergeant Frank E. Varden	Killed with the Custer Column June 25th
Sergeant James Bustard	Killed with the Custer Column June 25th
Sergeant Michael C. Caddle	At Powder River Camp
Sergeant Milton J. De Lacy	Probably with pack train
Sergeant George Gaffney	Temporary duty with Department Headquarters in the field.
Sergeant Robert L. Murphy	Temporary duty with Department Headquarters in the field.
Corporal George C. Morris	Killed with the Custer Column June 25th
Corporal Samuel Frederick Staples	Killed with the Custer Column June 25th
Corporal John Wild	Killed with the Custer Column June 25th

Enlisted(45)

Trumpeter John McGucker	Killed with the Custer Column June 25th
Trumpeter John W. Patton	Killed with the Custer Column June 25th
Blacksmith Henry A. Bailey	Killed with the Custer Column June 25th
Farrier John Rivers	At Powder River Camp
Private John Barry	Killed with the Custer Column June 25th
Private Franz C. Braun	Temporary duty with Reno's battalion.
Private Joseph H. Broadhurst	Killed with the Custer Column June 25th
Private Thomas Conners	Killed with the Custer Column June 25th
Private David Cooney	With pack train. Wounded in the right hip during the hilltop fight June 26th. Died of wounds at Fort Lincoln July 20
Private Thomas Patrick Downing	Killed with the Custer Column June 25th
Private Edward C. Driscoll	Killed with the Custer Column June 25th. One of 10 bodies found on Custer Knoll.
Private Gabriel Geesbacher	At Powder River Camp
Private David C. Gillette	Killed with the Custer Column June 25th
Private George H. Gross	Killed with the Custer Column June 25th
Private Adam Hetismer	Killed with the Custer Column June 25th
Private Edward P. Holcomb	Killed with the Custer Column June 25th
Private Marion E. Horn	Killed with the Custer Column June 25th
Private Henry P. Jones	Probably with pack train
Private Patrick Kelley (aka Edward H. Kelly)	Killed with the Custer Column June 25th
Private Francis Johnson Kennedy (aka Francis Johnson)	With pack train
Private Gustave Korn	Initially missing in the valley fight. Rejoined the Reno Battalion the night of June 25th
Private Mark E. Lee	On steamer Far West, sick.
Private Frederick Lehman	Killed with the Custer Column June 25th

Private Henry Lehmann	Killed with the Custer Column June 25th
Private Edward W. Lloyd	Killed with the Custer Column June 25th
Private Patrick Lynch	Temporary duty with Department Headquarters in the field.
Private Archibald McIlhargey	Carried the first message from Reno to Custer. Killed with the Custer Column June 25th
Private James P. McNally	With pack train
Private John McShane	With pack train
Private John E. Mitchell	Carried the second message from Reno to Custer. Killed with the Custer Column June 25th
Private Fred Myers	At Powder River Camp
Private Jacob Noshang	Killed with the Custer Column June 25th
Private John O'Bryan	Killed with the Custer Column June 25th
Private Eugene Owens	With pack train
Private John Parker	Killed with the Custer Column June 25th. One of 10 bodies found on Custer Knoll.
Private Felix James Pitter	Killed with the Custer Column June 25th
Private George Post	Killed with the Custer Column June 25th
Private James Quinn	Killed with the Custer Column June 25th
Private Charles Ramsey	With pack train
Private William Reed	Killed with the Custer Column June 25th
Private John W. Rossbury	Killed with the Custer Column June 25th
Private Darwin L. Symms	Killed with the Custer Column June 25th
Private James E. Troy	Killed with the Custer Column June 25th
Private Charles Von Bramer	Killed with the Custer Column June 25th
Private William B. Whaley	Killed with the Custer Column June 25th

Effective strength on June 25th: 2 Officers, 6 non-commissioned officers, and 40 enlisted men.

Company K – Sorrel Horses

Officers(2)

First Lieutenant Edward S. Godfrey	Company Commander
Second Lieutenant Luther R. Hare	Temporary duty with Indian Scouts

Non-commissioned Officers(10)

First Sergeant DeWitt Winney	Killed in the hilltop fight June 25th
Sergeant Jeremiah Campbell	
Sergeant Andrew Frederick	
Sergeant Robert M. Hughes	Carried Custer's personal battle flag. Killed with the Custer Column June 25th
Sergeant John Rafter	Water carrier on June 26.
Sergeant Louis Rott	Water carrier on June 26.
Corporal John J. Callahan	Killed in the hilltop fight June 25th
Corporal George Hose	
Corporal Henry Murray	At Powder River Camp
Corporal John Nolan	At Powder River Camp

Enlisted(53)

Trumpeter George B. Penwell	
Trumpeter Christian Schlafer	
Blacksmith Edmund H. Burke	
Farrier John R. Steintker	
Saddler Michael P. Madden	Wounded in the right leg as part of first water party on June 26th. Leg amputated on the field by Dr. Porter
Wagoner Albert Whytefield	At Powder River Camp

Private Charles Ackerman   At Powder River Camp
Private George Blunt
Private Christian Boissen
Private Cornelius Bresnahan
Private Joseph Brown
Private Charles J. Burgdorf   At Powder River Camp
Private Charles Burkhardt
Private Elihu F. Clear   Temporary duty as orderly to Dr. DeWolf. Killed
                                                   during the retreat from the valley June 25th

Private Patrick Coakley (aka Patrick Redican)
Private Patrick Corcoran   Wounded in the right shoulder during the hilltop
                                                   fight on June 25th

Private William L. Crawford   At Powder River Camp
Private John C. Creighton (aka Charles Chesterwood)
Private Michael Delaney   At Powder River Camp
Private John F. Donahue
Private Charles Fisher   At Powder River Camp
Private John Foley   Water carrier on June 26.
Private William Gibbs
Private Thomas Albin Gordon
Private Thomas Green   At Powder River Camp
Private Walter Hayt   At Powder River Camp
Private Julius Helmer   Killed in the hilltop fight on June 25th
Private Andrew Holahan   At Powder River Camp
Private Jacob Horner   At Powder River Camp
Private Alonzo Jennys (aka John Folsom)
Private William W. Lasley
Private Daniel Lyons   At Powder River Camp
Private Wilson McConnell
Private Martin McCue
Private Max Mielke   Wounded in the left foot during the hilltop fight
                                                   on June 26th

Private Michael Murphy
Private Thomas Murphy (aka Thomas Anderson)
Private Michael Ragan   At Powder River Camp
Private Henry W. Raichel
Private Michael Reilly   At Powder River Camp
Private Jonathan Robers
Private Francis Roth   At Powder River Camp
Private John Schauer
Private Christian Schlafer
Private John Schwerer
Private August Seifert
Private Frederick Smith   At Powder River Camp
Private Emil Taube   At Powder River Camp
Private William E. Van Pelt   At Powder River Camp
Private Ernest Wasmus
Private William Whitlow
Private George A. Wilson   At Powder River Camp
Private Henry Witt   At Powder River Camp

Effective strength on June 25th: 2 Officers, 8 non-commissioned officers, and 34 enlisted men.

Company L – Bay Horses

Officers(2)

| First Lieutenant James Calhoun | Company Commander. Temporary duty from Company C. Killed with the Custer Column June 25th |
| Second Lieutenant John J. Crittenden | Temporary duty from Company G, 20th Infantry. Killed with the Custer Column June 25th |

Non-commissioned Officers(9)

First Sergeant James Butler	Killed with the Custer Column June 25th
Sergeant Henry Bender	At Powder River Camp
Sergeant William Cashan	Killed with the Custer Column June 25th
(Casman is shown as alternative name on June Regimental Muster Roll)	
Sergeant John Mullen (aka James Hughes)	With pack train
Sergeant Amos B. Warren	Killed with the Custer Column June 25th
Corporal William H. Gilbert	Killed with the Custer Column June 25th
Corporal William H. Harrison	Killed with the Custer Column June 25th
Corporal John Nunan (aka Noonan)	At Powder River Camp
Corporal John Seiler	Killed with the Custer Column June 25th

Enlisted(55)

Trumpeter Frederick Walsh	Killed with the Custer Column June 25th
Blacksmith Charles Siemon	Killed with the Custer Column June 25th
Farrier William H. Heath	Killed with the Custer Column June 25th
Saddler Charles Perkins	Killed with the Custer Column June 25th
Private William G. Abrams	With pack train
Private George E. Adams	Killed with the Custer Column June 25th
Private William Andrews	Killed with the Custer Column June 25th
Private Anthony Assadily	Killed with the Custer Column June 25th
Private Elmer Babcock	Killed with the Custer Column June 25th
Private Charles Banks	With pack train
Private Nathan T. Brown	Probably at Powder River Camp
Private John Burke	Killed with the Custer Column June 25th
Private John Burkman	Custer's striker. With pack train
Private Ami Cheever	Killed with the Custer Column June 25th
(Andrew Hester is shown as alternative name on June Regimental Muster Roll)	
Private Michael Conlon	At Powder River Camp
Private William B. Crisfield	Killed with the Custer Column June 25th
Private John Duggan	Killed with the Custer Column June 25th
Private William Dye	Killed with the Custer Column June 25th
Private William Etzler	With pack train
Private James J. Galvan (aka Michael J. Miller)	Killed with the Custer Column June 25th
Private Charles Graham	Killed with the Custer Column June 25th
Private Henry Hamilton	Killed with the Custer Column June 25th
Private Weston Harrington	Killed with the Custer Column June 25th
Private Louis Hangge	Killed with the Custer Column June 25th
Private Max Hoehn	At Powder River Camp
Private Francis Thomas Hughes	Dr. Lord's orderly. Killed with the Custer Column June 25th
Private Thomas G. Kavanagh	Killed with the Custer Column June 25th
Private Michael Keegan	At Powder River Camp
Private Ferdinand Lepper	At Powder River Camp, sick.
Private Louis Lobering	Killed with the Custer Column June 25th
Private William J. Logue	Probably with pack train
Private Charles McCarthy	Killed with the Custer Column June 25th
Private Peter McGue	Killed with the Custer Column June 25th
Private Bartholomew Mahoney	Killed with the Custer Column June 25th

Private Philip McHugh	With pack train
Private Alexander McPeake	At Powder River Camp
Private Jasper Marshall	With the pack train. Wounded in the left foot during the hilltop fight on June 26th.
Private Thomas E. Maxwell	Killed with the Custer Column June 25th
Private John Miller	Killed with the Custer Column June 25th

(James Miller is shown as alternative name on June Regimental Muster Roll)

Private Lansing Moore	With the pack train
Private David J. O'Connell	Killed with the Custer Column June 25th
Private Christian Reibold	Killed with the Custer Column June 25th
Private Henry Roberts	Killed with the Custer Column June 25th
Private Walter B. Rogers	Killed with the Custer Column June 25th
Private Peter E. Rose	With pack train
Private Charles Schmidt	Killed with the Custer Column June 25th
Private Charles Scott	Killed with the Custer Column June 25th
Private Bent Siemonson	Killed with the Custer Column June 25th
Private Andrew Snow	Killed with the Custer Column June 25th
Private Henry Stoffel	With pack train
Private Timothy Sullivan	With pack train
Private Byron L. Tarbox	Killed with the Custer Column June 25th
Private Edward D. Tessier	Killed with the Custer Column June 25th
Private Thomas L. Tweed	Lt. Cooke's orderly. Killed with the Custer Column June 25th
Private Michael Vetter	Killed with the Custer Column June 25th

Effective strength on June 25th: 2 Officers, 7 non-commissioned officers, and 49 enlisted men.

Company M – Mixed Colors for Horses

Officers(2)

Captain Thomas H. French	Company Commander
First Lieutenant Edward G. Mathey	Temporary duty commanding the pack train.

Non-commissioned Officers(9)

First Sergeant John M. Ryan	
Sergeant William Capes	At Powder River Camp
Sergeant Patrick Carey	Abandoned in the timber, rejoined Reno to be wounded in the right hip during the hilltop fight on June 26th
Sergeant John McGlone	Probably with pack train. Promoted sergeant June 17th
Sergeant Miles F. O'Hara	Killed on the skirmish line during the valley fight on June 25th
Sergeant Charles White (Henry Charles Weihe)	Wounded in the right arm during the valley fight on June 25th, he was abandoned in the timber, rejoining Reno's command as a member of the Herendeen party.
Corporal Henry M. Scollin	Killed during the retreat from the valley, June 25th
Corporal William Lalor	Promoted corporal June 17th
Corporal Frederick Streing	Killed in action. Probably in the valley fight, June 25th

Enlisted(51)

Trumpeter Charles Fisher	
Trumpeter Henry C. Weaver	Abandoned in the timber, rejoined Reno's command as a member of the Herendeen party.
Saddler John Donahue	

Wagoner Joseph K. Rickets	At Powder River Camp
Private Joseph Bates (aka Joseph C. Murphy)	
Private Frank Braun	Wounded in the face and left thigh, probably during the hilltop fight, on June 25th. Died of wounds at Fort Lincoln on October 4th
Private Morris Cain	
Private Harrison Davis (aka Henry Harrison Davis)	
Private John Dolan	At Powder River Camp
Private Bernard Golden	
Private Henry Gordon	Killed during the retreat from the valley on June 25th
Private George Heid	
Private Charles Kavanaugh	
Private Henry Klotzbucher	Captain French's striker. Killed in the timber during the valley fight on June 25th
Private George Lorentz	Killed in the timber during the valley fight on June 25th
Private James McCormick	At Powder River Camp
Private Daniel Mahoney	
Private John H. Meier	Wounded in the back of the neck during the valley fight on June 25th
Private William D. Meyer	Killed during the retreat from the valley on June 25th
Private Hugh N. Moore	
Private William Ephraim Morris	Wounded in the left breast during the retreat from the valley on June 25th.
Private Frank Neely	
Private Daniel J. Newell	Wounded in the left leg during the retreat from the valley on June 25th
Private Edward A. Pigford	Wounded in the right hip during the retreat from the valley on June 25th
Private William E. Robinson	
Private Roman Rutten	Wounded in the right shoulder during the hilltop fight on June 26th
Private Hobart Ryder	With pack train.
Private William W. Rye	
Private John Seamans	
Private Robert Senn	
Private James W. Severs	
Private John Sivertsen (Silvertsen)	Originally abandoned in the timber. Rejoined Reno's command night of June 25th
Private William C. Slaper	Water carrier on June 26.
Private George E. Smith	His horse bolted into the Indian village while Reno was halting to form the skirmish line in the valley. Presumed dead, his body was never recovered
Private Frank Sniffin	Carried company guidon.
Private Walter S. Sterland	At Powder River Camp
Private Frank Stratton	
Private David Summers	Killed during the retreat from the valley on June 25th
Private James J. Tanner	Wounded during Benteen's charge on June 26th, died in the field hospital June 27th
Private Levi Thornberry	
Private Rollins L. Thorpe	

Private Henry Turley	His horse bolted into the Indian village while Reno was halting to form the skirmish line in the valley. Presumed dead, his body was never recovered
Private Thomas B. Varner	Wounded in the right ear during the hilltop fight on June 26th
Private Henry C. Voight	Killed during the hilltop fight on June 26th
Private George Weaver	
Private James Weeks	Water carrier on June 26.
Private John Whisten	
Private Ferdinand Widmayer	At Powder River Camp
Private Charles Theodore Wiedman	Wounded during the hilltop fight on June 26th
Private James Wilber	Water carrier on June 26. Wounded in the left leg during the hilltop fight on June 26th
Private Charles Williams	

Effective strength on June 25th: 2 Officers, 8 non-commissioned officers, and 46 enlisted men.

Indian Scouts(43)

Bear Comes Out (aka Bear Waiting)	Lakota
Bear Running in the Timber (aka Buffalo Ancestor)	Lakota
Black Fox	Arikara. Initially with Reno, did not cross the river
Black Porcupine	Arikara. At Powder River Camp.
Bloody Knife	Arikara. Killed while preparing to retreat from the valley, June 25th. Served as scout during 1874 Black Hills Expedition.
Bob Tailed Bull	Leader of the Arikaras. Killed during the valley fight June 25th.
Boy Chief (aka Black Calf)	Arikara. Participant in the valley fight. Captured ponies.
Bull	Arikara. Initially with Reno, did not cross the river
Bull Stands in Water (aka Bull in the Water)	Arikara. Initially with Reno, did not cross the river but participated in driving captured ponies to the pack train
Chara ta (aka William Baker)	Half–breed Arikara. At Powder River Camp.
William "Billy" Cross	Half-breed Lakota
Curly	Crow
Curly Head	Arikara. At Powder River Camp.
Forked Horn	Arikara. Participant in the valley fight.
Goes Ahead	Crow
Goose	Arikara. Severely wounded in the right hand during the retreat from the valley, June 25th. Served as scout during 1874 Black Hills Expedition.
Hairy Moccasin	Crow
Half Yellow Face	Crow
Horns in Front	Arikara. At Powder River Camp.
Howling Wolf (aka Wolf)	Arikara. At Powder River Camp.
William Jackson	Half-breed Pikuni Blackfoot. Abandoned with Girard in the timber during Reno's retreat.
Little Brave	Arikara. Killed during the valley fight, June 25th
Little Sioux	Arikara. Participant in the valley fight. Captured ponies. Served as scout during 1874 Black Hills Expedition.
One Feather	Arikara. Participant in the valley fight. Captured ponies.
Pretty Face (aka Good Face)	Arikara. With the pack train.

Red Bear (aka Good Elk, Handsome Elk)	Arikara. Participant in the valley fight.
Red Foolish Bear (aka Foolish Bear)	Arikara. Participant in the valley fight.
Red Star (aka Strikes the Bear)	Arikara. Participant in the valley fight. Captured ponies.
Red Wolf (aka Bush, Red Brush)	Arikara. Initially with Reno, did not cross the river
Round Wooden Cloud (aka Ca–roo)	Lakota
Running Wolf (aka Wolf Runs)	Arikara. At Powder River Camp.
Rushing Bull (aka Charging Bull)	Arikara. Initially with Reno, did not cross the river
Scabby Wolf (aka Laying Down)	Arikara. At Powder River Camp.
Soldier	Arikara. Initially with Reno, did not cross the river
Stabbed (aka Stab)	Arikara. Initially with Reno, did not cross the river
Strikes the Lodge	Arikara. Initially with Reno, did not cross the river
Strikes Two	Arikara. Participant in the valley fight. Captured ponies. Served as scout during 1874 Black Hills Expedition.
Tall Bear (aka High Bear)	Arikara. At Powder River Camp.
White Cloud	Lakota
White Eagle	Arikara. Initially with Reno, did not cross the river
White Man Runs Him	Crow
White Swan	Crow. Severely wounded in the right hand and leg during a duel with the Cheyenne warrior Whirlwind after recrossing the Little Big Horn during the retreat from the valley, June 25th
Young Hawk	Arikara. Participant in the valley fight. Served as scout during 1874 Black Hills Expedition.

Totals

31 Arikara
6 Crow
5 Lakota
1 Pikuni Blackfoot

Teamsters/Packers(12)

John C. Wagoner	Chief Packer. Wounded in the head during the hilltop fight on June 26th
William Alexander	
R. C.. Churchill	While the Reno court of inquiry records list him as Benjamin F. Churchill, U. S. Army Quartermaster records of the Seventh Cavalry list him as R. C. Churchill.
George Edwards	
Moses E. Flint	
John Frett	
John Lainplough	
William Lawless	
Chris Loeser	
Harry McBratney	
Frank C. Mann	Killed during the hilltop fight on June 25th
E. L. Moore	

[1] Ironically, St. John, who had deserted from Fort Rice on May 8, 1875, surrendered to the authorities on June 25, 1875; exactly one year before he was to die with Custer. He obtained an early release from his

sentence in order to march with the regiment. See John M. Carroll "A Bit of Seventh Cavalry History With All Its Warts" page 13.

[2] Of noble birth, Hiley, whose real name was John Stuart Forbes, had enlisted under his brother-in-law's name. A letter from his mother was found in his trunk stating: *"You can return home now, as the trouble causing your departure has been settled."* See John M. Carroll "They Rode With Custer" page 119.

[3] See Brian Pohanka "George Yates: Captain of the Band Box Troop" page 15.

[4] Botzer ranked Brown by 17 days.

Appendix 2

Battle Casualties

7th Cavalry Casualties By Organization

ORG	OFFICERS TOT	KIA	WIA	NON COMMS TOT	KIA	WIA	ENLISTED TOT	KIA	WIA	OTHER[1] TOT	KIA	WIA
Headquarters	3	2	0	1	1	0	1	1	0	3	2	0
Company A	3	0	1	9	1	2[2]	39	7	5	0	0	0
Company B	2	1	0	7	0	3	41	2	1	0	0	0
Company C	2	2	0	8	6	0	43	30	4[3]	0	0	0
Company D	2	0	0	5	0	0	45	3	2	0	0	0
Company E	2	2	0	8	7	1	37	30	0	0	0	0
Company F	2	2	0	8	7	0	42	29	0	0	0	0
Company G	2	1	0	8	4	0	36	9	4	0	0	0
Company H	2	0	1	9	1	5	36	2	13[4]	0	0	0
Company I	2	2	0	6	5	0	40	31	1[5]	0	0	0
Company K	2	0	0	8	3	0	34	2	3	0	0	0
Company L	2	2	0	7	6	0	49	38	1	0	0	0
Company M	2	0	0	8	3	2	46	9	9[6]	0	0	0
Civilians	0	0	0	0	0	0	0	0	0	20	7	1
Scouts	0	0	0	0	0	0	0	0	0	35	3	2
TOTALS	28	14	2	92	44	13	489	193	43	58	12	3

1. Scouts, Civilians, and Medical Staff
2. Corporal George H. King died of wounds on board the Far West on July 2, 1876
3. Private James C. Bennett died of wounds on board the Far West on July 5, 1876
4. Private William Montell George died of wounds on board the Far West on July 3, 1876
5. Private David Cooney died of wounds at Fort Lincoln on July 20, 1876
6. Private Frank Braun died of wounds at Fort Lincoln on October 4, 1876
Note: Nathan Short, Company C, died near the Yellowstone River, date unknown, and is not listed here among the killed in action

7th Cavalry Casualties By Engagement

Valley Fight – June 25th

ORG	OFFICERS			NON COMMS			ENLISTED			OTHER[1]		
	TOT	KIA	WIA	TOT	KIA	WIA	TOT	KIA	WIA	TOT	KIA	WIA
Headquarters	1	0	0	0	0	0	0	0	0	2	1	0
Company A	3	0	0	8	1	1	34	6	1	0	0	0
Company B	1	1	0	0	0	0	0	0	0	0	0	0
Company E	0	0	0	0	0	0	2	0	0	0	0	0
Company F	0	0	0	0	0	0	2	0	0	0	0	0
Company G	2	1	0	7	3	0	29	7	0	0	0	0
Company I	0	0	0	0	0	0	3[2]	0	0	0	0	0
Company K	1	0	0	0	0	0	1	1	0	0	0	0
Company M	1	0	0	7	3	1	40	7	4	0	0	0
Civilians	0	0	0	0	0	0	0	0	0	4	2	0
Scouts	0	0	0	0	0	0	0	0	0	30	3	2
TOTALS	9	2	0	22	7	2	111[3]	21	5	36	6	2

1. Scouts, Civilians, and Medical Staff
2. Privates Archibald McIlhargey and John E. Mitchell were sent as messengers to Custer. Their bodies were found with those of their
comrades of Company I.
3. Only 109 were in the valley fight.

7th Cavalry Casualties By Engagement

Custer Fight – June 25th

ORG	OFFICERS			NON COMMS			ENLISTED			OTHER[1]		
	TOT	KIA	WIA	TOT	KIA	WIA	TOT	KIA	WIA	TOT	KIA	WIA
Headquarters	2	2	0	1	1	0	1	1	0	1	1	0
Company C	2[2]	2	0	6	6	0	30	29[3]	0	0	0	0
Company E	2	2	0	7	7	0	30	30	0	0	0	0
Company F	2	2	0	7	7	0	29	29	0	0	0	0
Company G	0	0	0	0	0	0	1	1	0	0	0	0
Company I	2	2	0	5	5	0	31	31	0	0	0	0
Company K	0	0	0	1	1	0	0	0	0	0	0	0
Company L	2	2	0	6	6	0	38	38	0	0	0	0
Civilians	0	0	0	0	0	0	0	0	0	4	4	0
Scouts	0	0	0	0	0	0	0	0	0	0	0	0
TOTALS	12	12	0	33	33	0	160	159	0	5	5	0

1. Scouts, Civilians, and Medical Staff
2. Tom Custer was serving as Aid–de–Camp to his brother
3. Nathan Short died near the Yellowstone River, date unknown

7th Cavalry Casualties By Engagement

Hilltop Fight – June 25th & 26th

(First number is casualties on June 25, second is casualties on June 26)

ORG	OFFICERS			NON COMMS			ENLISTED			OTHER[1]		
	TOT	KIA	WIA	TOT	KIA	WIA	TOT	KIA	WIA	TOT	KIA	WIA
Headquarters	1	0	0	0	0	0	0	0	0	1	0	0
Company A	2[2]	0	0/	8	0	0/1[3]	33	1/0	3/1	0	0	0
Company B	1	0	0	7	0	1/2	40	0/2	1/0	0	0	0
Company C	0	0	0	2	0	0	12	0	0/4[4]	0	0	0
Company D	2	0	0	5	0	0	45	3/0[9]	2/0	0	0	0
Company E	0	0	0	1	0	0/1	7	0	0	0	0	0
Company F	0	0	0	1	0	0	13	0	0	0	0	0
Company G	1	0	0	5	1/0	0	28	1/0	3/1[10]	0	0	0
Company H	2	0	0/	9	0/1	2/3	36	0/2	8/5[5]	0	0	0
Company I	0	0	0	1	0	0	9	0	0/1[6]	0	0	0
Company K	2	0	0	7	2/0	0	33	1/0	1/2[7]	0	0	0
Company L	0	0	0	1	0	0	11	0	0/1	0	0	0
Company M	2	0	0	5	0	0/1	39	0/2[11]	1/4	0	0	0
Civilians	0	0	0	0	0	0	0	0	0	12[8]	1/0	0/1
Scouts	0	0	0	0	0	0	0	0	0	10	0	0
TOTALS	13	0/0	0/2	52	3/1	3/8	306	6/6	19/19	23	1/0	0/1

Total by Day 31/38

1. Scouts, Civilians, and Medical Staff
2. Charles DeRudio rejoined the regiment after the hilltop fight
3. Corporal George H. King died of wounds on board the Far West on July 2, 1876
4. Private James C. Bennett died of wounds on board the Far West on July 5, 1876
5. Private William Montell George died of wounds on board the Far West on July 3, 1876
6. Private David Cooney died of wounds at Fort Lincoln on July 20, 1876
7. Private Frank Braun died of wounds at Fort Lincoln on October 4, 1876
8. Fred Gerard rejoined the regiment after the hilltop fight
9. Charles Vincent killed during withdrawal from Weir Point
10. The dates that James Boyle and John Morrison were wounded is unknown but have been arbitrarily assigned to June 25.
11. James Tanner, wounded on the 26th, died in the field hospital on June 27.

Indian Fatalities

	Valley Fight	Custer Fight	Hilltop Fight	Other	Description
Blackfeet (1)	**(1)**	**(0)**	**(0)**	**(0)**	
Flying Charge	X				Location unknown.
Cheyenne (14)	**(4)**	**(10)**	**(0)**	**(0)**	
Old Man	X				Killed during Reno's retreat to the bluffs.
Roman Nose	X				Killed on West bank of the river during Reno's retreat.
Scabby	X				Died of wounds received in valley fight.
(Little) Whirlwind	X				Killed on the East bank near Reno's retreat crossing.
Black Bear		X			Killed on the North slope of Custer Hill.
Black Cloud		X			Location unknown.
Black Coyote		X			Location unknown.
Lame White Man		X			Killed halfway down Custer Ridge.
Limber Bones (Flying By)		X			Killed on the North slope of Custer Hill.
Noisy Walking		X			Died of wounds received near big bend of Deep Ravine.
Open Belly		X			Died of wounds received near present museum.
Owns Red Horse		X			Location unknown.
Red Horn Buffalo		X			Killed in Deep Ravine/Last Stand Hill area.
Swift Cloud		X			Location unknown.
Minneconjou (5)	**(2)**	**(1)**	**(2)**	**(0)**	
Dog With Horns	X				Killed in front of Reno's first skirmish line.
Three Bears	X				Died of wounds received near Uncpapa tepees.
High Horse		X			Location unknown.
Breech Cloth			X		Killed on East side of Reno Hill 6/25.
Dog's Backbone			X		Killed Northeast of Reno Hill 6/26.
Oglala (6)	**(2)**	**(4)**	**(0)**	**(0)**	
Big Design	X				Location unknown.
White Eagle	X				On slope near Reno Hill.
Bad Light Hair		X			Location unknown.
Black White Man		X			Died of wounds received on West slope of Custer Hill.
Many Lice		X			Location unknown.
Young Skunk		X			Location unknown.
Two Kettle (1)	**(1)**	**(0)**	**(0)**	**(0)**	
Chased by Owls	X				Killed between timber and the river during Reno's retreat.
Unidentified (12)	**(10)**	**(0)**	**(0)**	**(2)**	
Black Fox				X	Location and circumstances unknown.
Standing Rabbit				X	Identified as killed by kicking bear.
Unnamed Women	6				Killed South of village just prior to valley fight.
Unnamed Children	4				Killed South of village just prior to valley fight.

Indian Fatalities
(Continued)

	Valley Fight	Custer Fight	Hilltop Fight	Other	Description
Sans Arc (10)	**(3)**	**(6)**	**(1)**	**(0)**	
Elk Stands Above	X				Killed on hillock North of Reno Hill.
High Elk	X				Location unknown.
Two Bear	X				Killed on the East side of the river prior to the valley fight.
Bear With Horns		X			Location unknown.
Cloud Man		X			Location unknown.
Elk Bear		X			Location unknown.
Hump Nose		X			Location unknown.
Kills Him		X			Location unknown.
Lone Dog		X			Location unknown.
Long Road (Robe)			X		Killed on South side of Reno Hill 6/26.
Uncpapa (9)	**(5)**	**(3)**	**(0)**	**(1)**	
Deeds	X				Killed on East bank of the river prior to the valley fight.
Hawk Man	X				Killed in front of Reno's 1st skirmish line.
Swift Bear	X				Killed between timber and the river during Reno's retreat.
White Buffalo Bull	X				Killed between timber and the river during Reno's retreat.
Young Black Moon	X				Killed in front of Reno's second skirmish line.
Bear With Horns		X			Killed along Custer Ridge.
Guts		X			Location unknown.
Red Face		X			Location unknown.
Chatka				X	Found dead in burial tepee after the fight.
Totals	**28**	**24**	**3**	**3**	**58 Total Dead**

Appendix 3

Terry's Order For Reno's Scout

Headquarters Department of Dakota
(In the Field)

Camp on Powder River, June 10, 1876

Special Field Orders
No. 11

    1. The Quartermaster of the expedition is hereby ordered to purchase, for public use, two Mackinac boats, at a price not to exceed twenty–five dollars apiece.

    2. Major M. A. Reno, 7th Cavalry, with six companies (the right wing) of his regiment, and one gun from the Gatling battery, will proceed, at the earliest practicable moment, to make a reconnaissance of the Powder River from the present camp to the mouth of the Little Powder. From the last–named point he will cross to the head waters of Mizpah Creek, and descend that creek to its junction with Powder River; thence he will cross the Pumpkin Creek and Tongue River, and descend the Tongue to its junction with the Yellowstone – where he may expect to meet the remaining companies of the 7th Cavalry and supplies of subsistence and forage.

    Major Reno's command will be supplied with subsistence for twelve days, and with forage for the same period, at the rate of two pounds of grain per day for each animal.

    The guide, Mitch Bouyer, and eight Indian Scouts, to be detailed by Lieutenant Colonel Custer, will report to Major Reno for duty with his column.

    Acting Assistant Surgeon J. E. Porter* is detailed for duty with Major Reno.

    By Command of Brigadier General Terry:

Ed. W. Smith,
Captain 18th Infantry, A.D.C.,
Acting Assistant Adjutant General

* An obvious error on the part of Captain Smith, or a clerk who copied the letter, as J. E. Porter was a first lieutenant in Company I, 7th Cavalry. The surgeon was Henry R. Porter.

Appendix 4

Terry's Order to Custer

Headquarters Department of Dakota
(In the Field)

Camp at Mouth of Rosebud River,
Montana, June 22nd, 1876.

Lieut. Col. G. A. Custer, 7th Cavalry.

Colonel:

The Brigadier–General Commanding directs that, as soon as your regiment can be made ready for the march, you will proceed up the Rosebud in pursuit of the Indians whose trail was discovered by Major Reno a few days since. It is, of course, impossible to give you any definite instructions in regard to this movement, and were it not impossible to do so, the Department Commander places too much confidence in your zeal, energy, and ability to wish to impose upon you precise orders which might hamper your action when nearly in contact with the enemy. He will however, indicate to you his own views of what your action should be, and he desires that you should conform to them unless you shall see sufficient reason for departing from them. He thinks that you should proceed up the Rosebud until you ascertain definitely the direction in which the trail above spoken of leads. Should it be found (as it appears almost certain that it will be found) to turn towards the Little Horn, he thinks that you should still proceed southward, perhaps as far as the headwaters of the Tongue, and then turn towards the Little Horn, feeling constantly, however, to your left, so as to preclude the possibility of the escape of the Indians to the south or southeast by passing around your left flank.

The column of Colonel Gibbon is now in motion for the mouth of the Big Horn. As soon as it reaches that point it will cross the Yellowstone and move up at least as far as the forks of the Big and Little Horns. Of course its further movements must be controlled by circumstances as they arise, but it is hoped that the Indians, if upon the Little Horn, may be so nearly inclosed by the two columns that their escape will be impossible. The Department Commander desires that on your way up the Rosebud you should thoroughly examine the upper part of Tullock's Creek, and that you should endeavor to send a scout through to Colonel Gibbon's Column, with information on the results of your examination. The lower part of the creek will be examined by a detachment from Colonel Gibbon's command.

The supply steamer will be pushed up the Big Horn as far as the forks if the river is found to be navigable for that distance, and the Department Commander, who will accompany the Column of Colonel Gibbon, desires you to report to him there not later than the expiration of the time for which your troops are rationed, unless in the meantime you receive further orders.

Very Respectfully,
Your Obedient Servant,
Ed. W. Smith, Captain, 18th Infantry
Acting Assistant Adjutant General

Appendix 5

General Terry's Reports

(Telegram)

Headquarters Department of Dakota
Camp on Little Big Horn River, Montana
June 27, 1876

To the Adjutant General of
the Military Division of the Missouri,
Chicago, Ill., via Fort Ellis:

It is my painful duty to report that day before yesterday, the 25th instant, a great disaster overtook General Custer and the troops under his command. At 12 o'clock of the 22d he started with his whole regiment and a strong detachment of scouts and guides from the mouth of the Rosebud. Proceeding up that river about twenty miles, he struck a very heavy Indian trail which had previously been discovered, and, pursuing it, found that it led, as it was supposed it would lead, to the Little Big Horn River. Here he found a village of almost unexampled extent, and at once attacked it with that portion of his force which was immediately at hand. Major Reno, with three companies, A, G, and M, of the regiment, was sent into the valley of the stream, at the point where the trail struck it. General Custer, with five companies, C, E, F, I, and L, attempted to enter it about 3 miles lower down. Reno forded the river, charged down its left bank, dismounted, and fought on foot until finally, completely overwhelmed by numbers, he was compelled to mount, recross the river, and seek a refuge on the high bluffs which overlook its right bank. Just as he recrossed, Captain Benteen, who, with three companies, D, H, and K, was some two miles to the left of Reno when the action commenced, but who had been ordered by General Custer to return, came to the river, and, rightly concluding that it was useless for his force to attempt to renew the fight in the valley, he joined Reno on the bluffs. Captain McDougall, with his company, B, was at first some distance in the rear, with the train of pack–mules; he also came up to Reno. Soon this united force was nearly surrounded by Indians, many of whom, armed with rifles of long range, occupied positions which commanded the ground held by the cavalry – ground from which there was no escape. Rifle–pits were dug, and the fight was maintained, though with heavy loss, from about half past two o'clock of the 25th till 6 o'clock of the 26th, when the Indians withdrew from the valley, taking with them their village. Of the movements of General Custer and the five companies under his immediate command scarcely anything is known from those who witnessed them, for no officer or soldier who accompanied him has yet been found alive. His trail, from the point where Reno crossed the stream, passes along and in the rear of the crest of the bluffs on the right bank for nearly or quite three miles. Then it comes down to the bank of the river, but at once diverges from it as if he had unsuccessfully attempted to cross; then turns upon itself, almost completes a circle, and ceases. It is marked by the remains of his officers and men and the bodies of his horses, some of them dotted along the path, others heaped in ravines and upon knolls, where halts appear to have been made. There is abundant evidence that a gallant resistance was offered by the troops, but that they were beset on all sides by overpowering numbers. The officers known to be killed are: General Custer, Captains Keogh, Yates, and Custer, Lieutenants Cook, Smith, McIntosh, Calhoun, Porter, Hodgson, Sturgis, and Reily, of the cavalry; Lieutenant Crittenden, of the Twentieth Infantry, and Acting Assistant Surgeon DeWolf; Lieutenant Harrington, of the cavalry, and Assistant Surgeon Lord are missing; Captain Benteen and Lieutenant Varnum, of the cavalry are slightly wounded. Mr. Boston Custer, a brother, and Mr. Reed, a nephew, of General Custer, were with him and were killed. No other officers than those whom I have named are among the killed, wounded, and missing.

It is impossible as yet to obtain a nominal list of the enlisted men who were killed and wounded; but the number of killed, including officers, must reach 250; the number of wounded is 51. At the mouth of the Rosebud, I informed General Custer that I would take the supply–steamer *Far West* up the Yellowstone to ferry General Gibbon's column over the river; that I should personally accompany that column; and that it would, in all probability reach the mouth of the Little Big Horn on the 26th instant. The steamer reached General Gibbon's troops, near the mouth of the Big Horn, early in the morning of the 24th, and at 4 o'clock in the afternoon all his men and animals were across the Yellowstone. At 5 o'clock, the column, consisting of five companies of the Seventh Infantry, four companies of the Second Cavalry, and a battery of three Gatling guns, marched out to and across Tullock's Creek. Starting soon after 5 o'clock in the morning of the

25th, the infantry made a march of twenty–two miles over the most difficult country I have ever seen. In order that scouts might be sent into the valley of the Little Big Horn, the cavalry, with the battery, was then pushed on thirteen or fourteen miles further, reaching camp at midnight. The scouts were sent out a half past 4 in the morning of the 26th. They soon discovered three Indians, who were at first supposed to be Sioux but, when overtaken, they proved to be Crows, who had been with General Custer. They brought the first intelligence of the battle. Their story was not credited. It was supposed that some fighting, perhaps severe fighting, had taken place; but it was not believed that disaster could have overtaken so large a force as twelve companies of cavalry. The infantry, which had broken camp very early, soon came up, and the whole column entered and moved up the valley of the Little Big Horn. During the afternoon efforts were made to send scouts through to what was supposed to be General Custer's position, to obtain information of the condition of affairs; but those who were sent out were driven back by parties of Indians, who, in increasing numbers, were seen hovering in General Gibbon's front. At twenty minutes before 9 o'clock in the evening, the infantry had marched between twenty nine and thirty miles. The men were very weary and daylight was fading. The column was therefore halted for the night, at a point about eleven miles in a straight line above the mouth of the stream. This morning the movement was resumed, and after a march of nine miles, Major Reno's entrenched position was reached. The withdrawal of the Indians from around Reno's command and from the valley was undoubtedly caused by the approach of General Gibbon's troops. Major Reno and Captain Benteen, both of whom are officers of great experience, accustomed to see large masses of mounted men, estimate the number of Indians engaged at not less than twenty–five hundred. Other officers think that the number was greater than this. The village in the valley was about three miles in length and about a mile in width. Besides the lodges proper, a great number of temporary brush–wood shelters was found in it, indicating that many men besides its proper inhabitants had gathered together there. Major Reno is very confident that there were a number of white men fighting with the Indians. I have as yet received no official reports in regard to the battle; but what is stated herein is gathered from the officers who were on the ground then and from those who have been over it since.

Alfred H. Terry
Brigadier General

(Telegram)

Headquarters Department of Dakota
Camp on Little Horn, June 28, 1876

Assistant Adjutant General
Military Division of the Missouri, Chicago, Ill.:

The wounded were brought down from the bluffs last night and made as comfortable as our means would permit. To–day horse and hand litters have been constructed, and this evening we shall commence moving the wounded toward the mouth of the Little Big Horn, to which point I hope that the steamer has been able to come. The removal will occupy three or four days, as the marches must be short. A reconnaissance was made to–day by Captain Ball, of the Second Cavalry, along the trail made by the Indians when they left the valley. He reports that they divided into two parties, one of which kept the valley of Long Fork, making, he thinks, for the Big Horn Mountains; the other turned more to the eastward. He also discovered a very heavy trail leading into the valley that is not more than five days old. This trail is entirely distinct from the one which Custer followed, and would seem to show that at least two large bands united here just before the battle. The dead were all buried to–day.

Alfred H. Terry
Brigadier General

(Telegram)

Headquarters Department of Dakota
Camp on Yellowstone,
near Big Horn River, Montana,
July 2, 1876

Lieut. Gen. P. H. Sheridan, Chicago, Ill.,
The Adjutant General, Military Division
of the Missouri, Chicago, Ill.

In the evening of the 28th we commenced moving down the wounded, but were able to get on but four miles, as our hand–litters did not answer the purpose. The mule–litters did exceedingly well, but they were insufficient in number. The 29th, therefore, was spent in making a full supply of them. In the evening of the 29th we started again, and at 2 A.M. of the 30th the wounded were placed on a steamer at the mouth of the Little Big Horn. The afternoon of the 30th they were brought to the depot on the Yellowstone. I now send them by steamer to Fort Lincoln, and with them one of my aids, Capt. E. W. Smith, who will be able to answer any questions which you may desire to ask. I have brought down the troops to this point. They arrived to–night. They need refitting, particularly in the matter of transportation, before starting again. Although I had on the steamer a good supply of subsistence and forage, there are other things which we need, and I should hesitate to trust the boat again in the Big Horn.

Colonel Sheridan's dispatch informing me of the reported gathering of Indians on the Rosebud, reached me after I came down here. I hear nothing of General Crook's movements.

At least a hundred horses are needed to mount the cavalrymen now here.

Alfred H. Terry
Brigadier General

(Telegram)
CONFIDENTIAL [to Gen. Sheridan]

Headquarters Department of Dakota
Camp on Yellowstone,
near Big Horn River, Montana,
July 2, 1876

I think I owe it to myself to put you more fully in possession of the facts of the late operations. While at the mouth of the Rosebud I submitted my plan to Genl. Gibbon and General Custer. They approved it heartily. It was that Custer with his whole regiment should move up the Rosebud till he should meet a trail which Reno had discovered a few days before but that he should send scouts over it and keep his main force further to the south so as to prevent the Indians from slipping in between himself and the mountains. He was also to examine the headwaters of Tullock's Creek as he passed it and send me word of what he found there. A scout was furnished him for the purpose of crossing the country to me. We calculated it would take Gibbon's column until the twenty–sixth to reach the mouth of the Little Big Horn and that the wide sweep which I had proposed Custer should make would require so much time that Gibbon would be able to cooperate with him in attacking any Indians that might be found on that stream. I asked Custer how long his marches would be. He said they would be at first about thirty miles a day. Measurements were made and calculation based on that rate of progress. I talked with him about his strength and at one time suggested that perhaps it would be well for me to take Gibbon's cavalry and go with him. To this suggestion he replied that without reference to the command he would prefer his own regiment alone. As a homogeneous body, as much could be done with it as with the two combined and he expressed the utmost confidence that he had all the force that he could need, and I shared his confidence. The plan adopted was the only one that promised to bring the Infantry into action and I desired to make sure of things by getting up every available man. I offered Custer the battery of Gatling guns but he declined it saying that it might embarrass him: that he was strong enough without it. The movements proposed for Genl. Gibbon's column were carried out to the letter and had the attack been deferred until it was up I cannot doubt that we should have been successful. The Indians had evidently nerved themselves for a stand, but as I learn from Capt. Benteen, on the twenty–second, the cavalry marched twelve miles; on the twenty–third, thirty–five miles; from five A.M. till eight P.M. on the twenty–fourth, forty–five miles and then after night ten miles further; then after resting but without unsaddling, twenty–three miles to the battlefield. The proposed route was not taken but as soon as the trail was struck it was followed. I cannot learn that any examination of Tullock' Creek was made. I do not tell you this to cast any reflection upon Custer. For whatever errors he may have committed he has paid the penalty and you cannot regret his loss more than I do, but I feel that our plan must have been successful had it been carried out, and I desire you to know the facts. In the action itself, so far as I can make out, Custer acted under a misapprehension. He thought, I am confident, that the Indians were running. For fear that they might get away he attacked without getting all his men up and divided his command so that they were beaten in detail. I do not at all propose to give the thing up here but I think that my troops require a little time and in view of the strength which the Indians have developed I propose to bring up what little reinforcement I can get. I should be glad of any that you can send me. I can take two companies of Infantry from Powder River and there are a few recruits and detached men whom I can get for the cavalry. I ought to have a larger mounted force than I now have but I fear cannot be obtained. I hear nothing from General Crook's operations. If I could hear I should be able to form plans for the future much more intelligently.

I should very much like instructions from you, or if not instructions, your views of the situation based as might be on what has taken place elsewhere as well as here.

I shall refit as rapidly as possible and if at any time I should get information showing that I can act in conjunction with General Crook, or independently, with good results, I shall leave at once.

I send in another dispatch a copy of my written orders to Custer, but these were supplemented by the distinct understanding that Gibbon could not get to the Little Big Horn before the evening of the 26th.

Alfred H. Terry
Brigadier General

Appendix 6

Benteen's Report

Sir:

In obedience to verbal instructions received from you, I have the honor to report the operations of my battalion, consisting of Companies D, H, and K, on the 25th ultimo.

The directions I received from Lieutenant–Colonel Custer were, to move with my command to the left, to send well–mounted officers with about six men who would ride rapidly to a line of bluffs about five miles to our left and front, with instructions to report at once to me if anything of Indians could be seen from that point. I was to follow the movement of this detachment as rapidly as possible. Lieutenant Gibson was the officer selected, and I followed closely with the battalion, at times getting in advance of the detachment. The bluffs designated were gained, but nothing seen but other bluffs quite as large and precipitous as were before me. I kept on to these and the country was the same, there being no valley of any kind that I could see on any side. I had then gone about fully ten miles; the ground was terribly hard on horses, so I determined to carry out the other instructions, which were, that if in my judgment there was nothing to be seen of Indians, Valleys, etc., in the direction I was going, to return with the battalion to the trail the command was following. I accordingly did so, reaching the trail just in advance of the pack–train. I pushed rapidly on, soon getting out of sight of the advance of the train, until reaching a morass, I halted to water the animals, who had been without water since about 8 P.M. of the day before. This watering did not occasion the loss of fifteen minutes, and when I was moving out the advance of the train commenced watering from that morass. I went at a slow trot until I came to a burning lodge with the dead body of an Indian in it on a scaffold. We did not halt. About a mile further on I met a sergeant of the regiment with orders from Lieutenant–Colonel Custer to the officer in charge of the rear–guard and train to bring it to the front with as great rapidity as was possible. Another mile on I met Trumpeter Morton (Martin, DCE), of my own company, with a written order from First Lieut. W. W. Cook to me, which read:

"Benteen, come on. Big village. Be quick. Bring packs. W. W. Cook"
"P. Bring Pac's"

I could then see no movement of any kind in any direction; a horse on the hill, riderless, being the only living thing I could see in my front. I inquired of the trumpeter what had been done, and he informed me that the Indians had "skedaddled," abandoning the village. Another mile and a half brought me in sight of the stream and plain in which were some of our dismounted men fighting, and Indians charging and recharging them in great numbers. The plain seemed to be alive with them. I then noticed our men in large numbers running for the bluffs on the right bank of the stream. I concluded at once that those had been repulsed, and was of the opinion that if I crossed the ford with my battalion, that I should have had it treated in like manner; for from long experience with cavalry, I judged there were 900 veteran Indians right there at that time, against which the large element of recruits in my battalion would stand no earthly chance as mounted men. I then moved up to the bluffs and reported my command to Maj. M. A. Reno. I did not return for the pack–train because I deemed it perfectly safe where it was, and we could defend it, had it been threatened, from our position on the bluffs; and another thing, it savored too much of coffee–cooling to return when I was sure a fight was progressing in the front, and deeming the train as safe without me.

Very respectfully,

F. W. Benteen
Captain Seventh Cavalry

Lieut. Geo. D. Wallace
Adjutant Seventh Cavalry

Appendix 7

Reno's Report

Headquarters 7th U.S. Cavalry,
Camp on Yellowstone River,
July 5th 1876

Captain E. W. Smith
A.D.C. and A.A.A.G.

The command of the regiment having devolved upon me as the senior surviving officer from the battle of the 25th and 26th of June between the 7th Cavalry and Sitting Bull's band of hostile Sioux on the Little Big Horn River, I have the honor to submit the following report of its operations from the time of leaving the main column until the command was united in the vicinity of the Indian village.

The regiment left the camp at the mouth of the Rosebud River after passing in review before the Department Commander under command of Brevet Major General G. A. Custer, Lieutenant Colonel, on the afternoon of the 22nd of June and marched up the Rosebud twelve miles and encamped; – 23d marched up the Rosebud passing many old Indian camps and following a very large lodge–pole trail, but not fresh making thirty–three (33) miles; 24th the march was continued up the Rosebud, the trail and signs freshening with every mile until we had made twenty–eight (28) miles, and we then encamped and waited for information from the scouts; at 9–25 p.m. Custer called the officers together and informed us that beyond a doubt the village was in the valley of the Little Big Horn, and in order to reach it, it was necessary to cross the divide between the Rosebud and the Little Big Horn, and it would be impossible to do so in the day time without discovering our march to the Indians; that we would prepare to march at 11 p.m.; this was done, the line of march turning from the Rosebud to the right up one of its branches which headed near the summit of the divide. About 2 a.m. of the 25th the scouts told him that he could not cross the divide before daylight. We then made coffee and rested for three hours, at the expiration of which time the march was resumed, the divide crossed and about 8 a.m. the command was in the valley of one of the branches of the Little Big Horn; by this time Indians had been seen and it was certain that we could not surprise them and it was determined to move at once to the attack. Previous to this no division of the regiment had been made since the order had been issued on the Yellowstone annulling wing and battalion organization, but Custer informed me that he would assign commands on the march.

I was ordered by Lieutenant W. W. Cook Adjutant, to assume command of companies M, A, and G; Captain Benteen of companies H, D, and K, Custer retained C, E, F, I, and L under his immediate command and company B, Captain McDougall, in rear of the pack train.

I assumed command of the companies assigned to me and without any definite orders moved forward with the rest of the column and well to its left. I saw Benteen moving further to the left and as they passed he told me he had orders to move well to the left and sweep everything before him. I did not see him again until about 2–30 p.m. The command moved down the creek towards the Little Big Horn valley, Custer with five companies on the right bank, myself and three companies on the left bank and Benteen farther to the left and out of sight. As we approached a deserted village, and in which was standing one tepee, about 11 a.m. Custer motioned me to cross to him, which I did, and moved nearer to his column until about 12–30 a.m. [p.m.] when Lieutenant Cook, Adjutant, came to me and said the village was only two miles ahead and running away; to move forward at as rapid a gait as prudent and to charge afterwards, and that the whole outfit would support me. I think those were his exact words. I at once took a fast trot and moved down about two miles where I came to a ford of the river. I crossed immediately and halted about ten minutes or less to gather the battalion, sending word to Custer that I had everything in front of me and that they were strong. I deployed and with the Ree scouts on my left charged down the valley driving the Indians with great ease for about 2 1/2 miles. I however soon saw that I was being drawn into some trap as they would certainly fight harder and especially as we were nearing their village, which was still standing, besides I could not see Custer or any other support and at the same time the very earth seemed to grow Indians and they were running towards me in swarms and from all directions. I saw I must defend myself and give up the attack mounted. This I did, taking possession of a point of woods, and which furnished (near its edge) a shelter for the horses, dismounted and fought on foot. Making headway through the woods I soon found myself in the near vicinity of the village, saw that I was fighting odds of at least five to one and that my only hope was to get out of the woods where I would soon have been surrounded, and gain some ground. I accomplished this by mounting and charging the Indians between me and the bluffs on the opposite side of the river. In this charge 1st Lieutenant Donald McIntosh, 2nd Lieutenant Benj. H. Hodgson, 7th Cavalry and A.A. Surgeon J. M. DeWolf were killed. I succeeded in reaching the top of the bluff with a loss of three officers and twenty–nine enlisted men killed, and seven men wounded. Almost at the same time I reached the top, mounted men were seen to be coming towards us and it proved to be Colonel Benteen's battalion, companies H, D, and K. We joined forces and in a short time the pack train came up. As senior my command was then A, B, D, and G, H, K, M, and 380 men and the following officers, Captains Benteen, Weir, French, and McDougall, 1st Lieutenants Edgerly, Wallace, Varnum, and Hare and A.A. Surgeon Porter. 1st Lieutenant DeRudio was in the dismounted fight in the woods but having some trouble with his horse, did not join the command in the charge out, and hiding himself in the woods joined the command after night–fall on the 26th. Still hearing nothing of Custer and with this reinforcement, I moved down the river in the direction of the village, keeping on the bluffs. We heard firing in that direction and knew it could only be Custer. I moved to the summit of the highest bluff but seeing and hearing nothing, sent Capt. Weir with his company to open communications with him. He soon sent back word by Lieut. Hare that he could go no further and that the Indians were getting around him. At this time he was keeping up a heavy fire from his skirmish line. I at once turned everything back to the first position I had taken on the bluff and which seemed to me the best. I dismounted the men and had the horses and mules of the pack train driven together in a depression, put the men on the crests of the hills making the depression and had hardly done so when I was furiously attacked, – this was about six p.m. We held our ground with a loss of eighteen enlisted men killed and forty–six wounded until the attack ceased about 9 p.m. As I knew by this time their overwhelming numbers and had given up any hope of support from that portion of the regiment with Custer, I had the men dig rifle pits; barricaded with dead horses and mules and boxes of hard bread the opening of the depression towards the Indians in which the animals were herded, and made every exertion to be ready for what I saw would be a terrific assault the next day. All this night the men were busy, and the Indians holding a scalp dance underneath us in the bottom and in our hearing. On the morning of the 26th I felt confident that I could hold my own and was ready as far as I could be when at daylight about 2–30 a.m. I heard the crack of two rifles. This was the signal for the beginning of a fire that I have never seen equaled. Every rifle was handled by an expert and skilled marksman and with a range that exceeded our carbine, and it was simply impossible to show any part of the body before it was struck. We could see as the day brightened, countless hordes of them pouring up the valley from out the village, and scampering over the high points towards the places designated for them by their chiefs and which entirely surrounded our position. They had sufficient numbers to completely encircle us, and men were struck from opposite sides of the lines and where the shots were fired. I think we were fighting all the Sioux nation, and also all the desperadoes, renegades, half–breeds and squawmen between the Missouri and the Arkansas and east of the Rocky mountains, and they must have numbered at least twenty–five hundred warriors. The fire did not slacken until about 9–30 a.m. and then we found they were making a last desperate effort and which was directed against the lines held by companies H, and M. In this charge they came close enough to use their bows and arrows, and one man lying dead within our lines was touched with the coup stick of one of the foremost Indians. When I say the stick was only ten or twelve feet long, some idea of the desperate and reckless fighting of these people may be understood. This charge of theirs was gallantly repulsed by the men on that line led by Colonel Benteen. They also came close enough to send their arrows into the line held by Co's. D, and K, but were driven away by a like charge of the line which I accompanied. We now had many wounded and the question of water was vital, as from 6 p.m. of the previous evening until near 10 a.m., about 16 hours, we had been without.

A skirmish line was formed under Colonel Benteen to protect the descent of volunteers down the hill in front of his position to reach the water. We succeeded in getting some canteens although many of the men were hit in doing so. The fury of the attack was now over, and to our astonishment the Indians were seen going in parties toward the village. But two solutions occurred to us for this movement, that they were going for something to eat, more ammunition (as they had been throwing arrows) or that Custer was coming. We took advantage of this lull to fill all vessels with water, and soon had it by camp kettles full. But they continued to withdraw and all firing ceased soon; [except] occasional shots from sharp–shooters sent to annoy us about the water. About 2 p.m. the grass in the bottom was set on fire and followed up by Indians who encouraged its burning, and it was evident to me it was done for a purpose, and which purpose I discovered later on, to be the creation of a dense cloud of smoke behind which they were packing and preparing to move their village. It was between six and seven p.m. that the village came out from behind the dense clouds of smoke and dust. We had a close and good view of them as they filed away in the direction of Big Horn Mountains, moving in almost perfect military order. The length of the column was fully equal to that of a large division of the Cavalry Corps of the Army of the Potomac as I have seen it in its march.

We now thought of Custer, of whom nothing had been seen and nothing heard since the firing in his direction about six p.m. on the eve of the 25th, and we concluded that the Indians had gotten between him and us, and driven him towards the boat at the mouth of the Little Big Horn River. The awful fate that did befall him never occurred to any of us as within the limits of possibility.

During the night I changed my position in order to secure an unlimited supply of water and was prepared for their return, feeling sure they would do so, as they were in such numbers; but early in the morning of the 27th and while we were on the *qui vive* for Indians, I saw with my glass a dust some distance down the valley. There was no certainty for some time what they were, but finally I satisfied myself they were cavalry, and if so could only be Custer, as it was ahead of the time that I understood that General Terry could be expected. Before this time however, I had written a communication to General Terry and three volunteers were to try and reach him. I had no confidence in the Indians with me and could not get them to do anything. If this dust were Indians, it was possible they would not expect anyone to leave. The men started and were told to go as near as it was safe to determine whether the approaching column was white men, and to return at once in case they found it so; but if they were Indians to push on to General Terry. In a short time we saw them returning over the high bluffs already alluded to. They were accompanied by a scout who had a note from Terry to Custer, saying Crow scouts had come to camp saying he had been whipped but that it was not believed. I think it was about 10–30 a.m. that General Terry rode into my lines; and the fate of Custer and his brave men was soon determined by Captain Benteen proceeding with his company to his battle ground, and where was recognized the following officers who were surrounded by the dead bodies of many of their men: General G. A. Custer; Col. W. W. Cook, Adjutant; Captains M. W. Keogh, G. W. Yates, and T. W. Custer; 1st Lieuts. A. E. Smith, James Calhoun; 2nd Lieutenants W. V. Reily of the 7th Cavalry, and J. J. Crittenden of the 20th Infantry, temporarily attached to this regiment. The bodies of Lieutenant J. E. Porter and 2nd Lieutenants H. M. Harrington and J. G. Sturgis, 7th Cavalry and Assistant Surgeon G. W. Lord, U.S.A., were not recognized, but there is every reasonable probability they were killed. It was now certain that the column of five companies with Custer had been killed.

The wounded in my lines were during the afternoon and eve of the 27th, moved to the camp of Gen'l Terry, and at 5 a.m. of the 28th I proceeded with the regiment to the battle ground of Custer and buried 204 bodies, including the following named citizens: Mr. Boston Custer, Mr. Reed (a young nephew of General Custer) and Mr. Kellogg, a correspondent for the *New York Herald.* The following named citizens and Indians who were with my command were also killed: Charles Reynolds (guide and hunter); Isaiah Dorman (colored) interpreter; Bloody Knife who fell from immediately by my side; Bobtail Bull and Stab of the Indian scouts.

After traveling over his trail, it is evident to me that Custer intended to support me by moving further down the stream and attacking the village in flank, that he found the distance greater to the ford than he anticipated; that he did charge, but his march had taken so long, although his trail shows he had moved rapidly, that they were ready for him. That Co's. C, and I, and perhaps part of E, crossed to the village or attempted it, at the charge; were met by a staggering fire, and that they fell back to find a position from which to defend themselves, but they were followed too closely by the Indians to permit time to form any kind of line. I think had the regiment gone in as a body, and from the woods from which I fought advanced upon the village, its destruction was certain. But he was fully confident they were running away or he would not have turned from me. I think (after the great number of Indians there were in the village) that the following reasons obtain for the misfortune. His rapid marching for two days and one night before the fight; attacking in the daytime at 12 M and when they were on the *qui vive* instead of early in the morning, and lastly his unfortunate division of the regiment into three commands.

During my fight with the Indians I had the heartiest support from officers and men, but the conspicuous service of Bvt. Col. F. W. Benteen, I desire to call attention to especially; for if ever a soldier deserved recognition by his government for distinguished service, he certainly does. I enclose herewith his report of the operations of his battalion from the time of leaving the regiment until we joined commands on the hill. I also enclose an accurate list of casualties as far as it can be made at the present time, separating them into two lists: "A", those killed in General Custer's command; "B", those killed and wounded in the command I had. The number of Indians killed can only be approximated until we hear through the Agencies. I saw the bodies of 18 and Captain Ball, 2d Cavalry, who made a scout of thirteen miles over their trail says that their graves were many along their line of march. It is simply impossible that numbers of them should not be hit in the several charges they made so close to my lines. They made their approaches through the deep gulches that led from the hill top to the river, and when the jealous care with which the Indian guards the bodies of killed and wounded is considered, it is not astonishing that their bodies were not found. It is probable that the stores left by them, and destroyed the next two days, was to make room for many of them on their travois. The harrowing sight of the dead bodies crowning the height on which Custer fell, and which will remain vividly in my memory until death, is too recent for me not to ask the good people of this country whether a policy that sets opposing parties in the field armed, clothed and equipped by one and the same government should not be abolished.

All of which is respectfully submitted.

M. A. Reno,
Major 7th Cavalry,
Com'd'g Regiment.

Appendix 8

Findings of The Reno Court of Inquiry

The following may be found in Ronald H. Nichols "Reno Court of Inquiry Proceedings Of A Court Of Inquiry In The Case Of Major Marcus A. Reno Concerning His Conduct At The Battle Of The Little Big Horn River On June 25 – 26, 1876", pages 627 – 629.

FINDINGS

The Court of Inquiry assembled by Special Orders No. 255, dated Headquarters of the Army, A.G.O., Washington, November 25, 1878, reports in obedience to that order the following facts involving the conduct of Major Marcus A. Reno, 7th Cavalry, in regard to the Battle of the Little Big Horn fought June 25 and 26, 1876.

First: On the morning of the 25th of June 1876, the 7th Cavalry, Lieutenant Colonel G. A. Custer commanding, operating against the hostile Indians in Montana Territory, near the Little Big Horn River, was divided into four battalions, two of which were commanded by Colonel Custer in person with the exception of one company in charge of the pack train, one by Major Reno and one by Captain F. W. Benteen.

This division took place from about 12 to 15 miles from the scene of the battle or battles afterwards fought.

The column under Captain Benteen received orders to move to the left for an indefinite distance (to the first and second valleys) hunting Indians with orders to charge any it might meet with.

The battalion under Major Reno received orders to draw out of the column, and doing so, marched parallel and only a short distance from the column commanded by Colonel Custer.

Second: About three or four miles from what afterwards was found to be the Little Big Horn River where the fighting took place, Major Reno received orders to move forward as rapidly as he thought prudent until coming up with the Indians who were reported fleeing, he would charge them and drive everything before him, and would receive the support of the column under Colonel Custer.

Third: In obedience to the orders (given by Colonel Custer) Captain Benteen marched to the left (south) at an angle of about 45 degrees, but meeting an impracticable country, was forced by it to march more to his right than the angle above indicated, and nearer approaching a parallel route to that trail followed by the rest of the command.

Fourth: Major Reno, in obedience to the orders given him moved on at a fast trot, on the main Indian trail until reaching the Little Big Horn River, which he forded, and halted for a few minutes to reform his battalion.

After reforming, he marched the battalion forward towards the Indian village, downstream or in a northerly direction, two companies in a line of battle and one in support, until about half–way to the point where he finally halted, when he brought the company in reserve forward to the line of battle, continuing the movement at a fast trot or gallop until after passing over a distance of about two miles, when he halted and dismounted to fight on foot, at a point of timber upon which the right flank of his battalion rested.

After fighting in this formation for less than half an hour, the Indians passing to his left rear, and appearing in his front, the skirmish line was withdrawn to the timber and the fight continued for a short time, half an hour or 45 minutes in all, when the command, or nearly all of it, was mounted, formed, and at a rapid gait was withdrawn to a hill on the opposite side of the river.

In this movement one officer and about 16 soldiers and citizens were left in the woods, besides one wounded man or more; two citizens and 13 soldiers rejoining the command afterwards.

In this retreat Major Reno's battalion lost some 29 men in killed and wounded, and three officers, including Dr. DeWolf, killed.

Fifth: In the meantime, Captain Benteen having carried out as far as was practicable the spirit of his orders, turned in the direction of the route taken by the remainder of the regiment and reaching the trail followed it to near the crossing of the Little Big Horn, reaching there about the time Reno's command was crossing the river in retreat lower down, and finally joined his battalion with that of Reno on the hill.

Forty minutes or an hour later the pack train, which had been left behind on the trail by the rapid movement of the command, and the delays incident to its march, joined the united command, which then consisted of seven companies, together with about 30 or 35 men belonging to the companies under Colonel Custer.

Sixth: After detaching Benteen's and Reno's columns, Colonel Custer moved with his immediate command on the trail followed by Reno to a point within about one mile of the river, where he diverged to the right (or northward) following the general direction of the river to a point about four miles below that afterwards taken by Major Reno, where he and his command were destroyed by the hostiles. The last living witness of this march, Trumpeter Martin, left Colonel Custer's command when it was about two miles distant from the field where it afterward met its fate. There is nothing more in evidence as to this command, save that firing was heard proceeding from its direction, from about the time Reno retreated from the bottom up to the time the pack train was approaching the position on the hill.

All firing which indicated fighting was concluded before the final preparations in Major Reno's command for the movement which was afterwards attempted.

Seventh: After the distribution of ammunition and a proper provision for the wounded men, Major Reno's entire command moved down the river in the direction it was thought Custer's column had taken and in which it was known General Terry's command was to be found.

This movement was carried sufficiently far to discover that its continuance would imperil the entire command, upon which it returned to the position formerly occupied, and made a successful resistance, till succor reached it. The defense of the position on the hill was a heroic one against fearful odds.

The conduct of the officers throughout was excellent, and while subordinates in some instances did more for the safety of the command by brilliant displays of courage than did Major Reno, there was nothing in his conduct which requires the animadversion from this Court.

OPINION

It is the conclusion of this Court in view of all the facts in evidence, that no further proceedings are necessary in this case, and it expresses this opinion in compliance with the concluding clause of the order convening the Court.

John H. King
Colonel 9th Infantry
President

J. M. Lee
First Lieutenant & Adjutant, 9th Infantry
Recorder

Appendix 9

Indians Present At The Battle Of The Little Big Horn

The following Indians are known to have participated in the Battle of the Little Big Horn, or to have been in the village during its prosecution. It is a difficult task to assemble such a list as many Indians were known by several names within their own band or tribe in addition to the name by which they were known to other tribes. Although great care has been exercised in compiling this list, there may be multiple listings of the same individual due to the difficulties mentioned above.

Arapaho (5)

Left Hand	One of a party of 5 Arapaho, mistaken for army scouts, they reluctantly joined the fight to prove their innocence.[1] Killed a wounded Lakota he had mistaken for an army scout. Claimed one of Custer's soldiers gave him his gun in surrender; Lakota then killed the unarmed soldier.[2]
Waterman	One of a party of 5 Arapaho, mistaken for army scouts, they reluctantly joined the fight to prove their innocence.[3] Told of a bravery run by Crazy Horse in front of Custer's position. Claimed to have shot and killed one of Custer's soldiers during the charge on Last Stand Hill.[4]
Well Knowing One (Green Grass)	One of a party of 5 Arapaho, mistaken for army scouts, they reluctantly joined the fight to prove their innocence.[5]
Yellow Eagle	One of a party of 5 Arapaho, mistaken for army scouts, they reluctantly joined the fight to prove their innocence.[6]
Yellow Fly	One of a party of 5 Arapaho, mistaken for army scouts, they reluctantly joined the fight to prove their innocence.[7]

Cheyenne (159)

A Crow Cut His Nose[8]	
American Horse	Fought Reno in the valley and participated in the action at Medicine Tail Ford (Ford B).[9] He described Reno's withdrawal from the valley as "It was like chasing buffalo, a grand chase."[10]
Antelope Woman[11] (Kate Bighead)	Described the mutilation of Custer's wounded by the Cheyenne women, and dwitnessed the torture of one of Custer's troopers.[12] Her account furnishes the basis for the flow of action on Custer's field.
Bald Eagle[13]	
Bear Walks On A Ridge[14]	
Beaver Claws[15]	
Beaver Heart	Fought in the valley fight.[16]
Big Beaver	Captured gun from soldier killed at eastern-most marker (#174 Keogh Sector)[17]

Big Crow	Leader of Crooked Lance Society. [18] Member of Little Wolf's band. One of three scouts seen by Sergeant Curtiss at the box of hardtack. This report would convince Custer the command had been discovered, requiring an immediate attack to prevent the escape of the Indians. [19]
Big Foot	Member of the party that engaged Custer's command while on Luce Ridge. [20] Identified by John Stands In Timber as a Cheyenne sharpshooter stationed on Wooden Leg Hill during the hilltop fight. [21]
Big Nose [22]	
Black Bear (Closed Hand, Fist)	One of the suicide boys, killed during their charge on the North slope of Custer Hill. [23]
Black Bird [24]	
Black Cloud	Identified as killed in the Custer Fight by the Minneconjou white Bull. [25]
Black Coyote	Husband of Buffalo Calf Road Woman. Identified as killed in the Custer fight by the Minneconjou White Bull. [26]
Black Horse	Member of Little Wolf's band. One of three scouts seen by Sergeant Curtiss at the box of hardtack. This report would convince Custer the command had been discovered, requiring an immediate attack to prevent the escape of the Indians. [27]
Black Knife [28]	
Black Moccasin	The Blackfoot Kill Eagle claimed this warrior beat him with the arms of a dismembered soldier after the Custer fight. [29]
Black Shield [30]	
Black Stone [31]	
Black White Man	Member of Little Wolf's band. Arrived after the Custer Fight. [32]
Black Wolf [33]	
Bobtail Horse	Member of Elk Warrior Society. One of the four Cheyenne who engaged Custer's troops at Medicine Tail Ford. [34]
Box Elder [35]	Prophet. Predicted both the attacks by Custer at the Little Big Horn and by Mackenzie on Dull Knife's village in November of 1876. [36]
Braided (Locks) Hair (Wrapped Braids)	Wounded in the Custer Fight. [37] Identified by Wooden Leg as wearing a war bonnet in the fighting. [38]
Brave Bear	Made a bravery run in front of Reno's skirmish line. [39]
Brave Wolf	A contrary, he fought in the valley and Custer fights. [40] His account of the Custer fight indicates an attack on the Cheyenne circle by Custer's troops. [41] Gave an account of the Custer Fight to Lt. Oscar Long in 1878. [42]
Broken Jaw [43]	
Buffalo Calf (Calf)	One of the four Cheyenne who engaged Custer's troops at Medicine Tail Ford. [44]
Buffalo Calf Road Woman	Wife of Black Coyote and sister of Comes in Sight. Participated in Custer fight, as she had at the Rosebud, armed with a revolver. [45]
Bull Bear	Fought against both Reno's and Custer's commands. Participated in Gall's charge on Company L. [46]
Bull Hump [47]	
Bullet Proof [48]	
Charcoal Bear [49]	

Chief Coming Up	Identified by Wooden Leg as wearing a war bonnet in the fighting.[50]
Coal Bear	Holy man and keeper of the sacred buffalo hat (*esevone*).[51]
Comes in Sight	Made a bravery run, probably in front of C Troop on Greasy Grass Ridge.[52]
Contrary Belly	Made a bravery run, probably in front of C Troop on Greasy Grass Ridge.[53]
Crane Woman	Young daughter of Lame White Man.[54]
Crazy Head[55]	Identified by Wooden Leg as wearing a war bonnet in the fighting.[56]
Crazy Mule[57]	
Crazy Wolf[58]	
Crooked Nose	One of the party that infiltrated the timber and killed the scout Bloody Knife and privates Henry Klotzbucher and George Lorentz.[59]
Crooked Nose	Sister of Wooden Leg.[60]
Crow Necklace[61]	Identified by Wooden Leg as wearing a war bonnet in the fighting.[62]
Cut Belly (Open Belly, Owns Red Horse)	One of the Suicide Boys. Died of wounds received near the site of the present museum.[63]
Dirty Moccasins[64]	
Dives Backward[65]	
Dog Friend[66]	
Dull Knife	The first Cheyenne to fire on Custer's troops at Medicine Tail Ford.[67]
Eagle Feather On The Forehead	Mother of Wooden Leg.[68]
Eagle Tail Feather	One of the party that chased and killed two of Reno's troopers that attempted to escape south down the valley.[69]
Fast Walker[70]	
Fingers Woman	Sister of Wooden Leg.[71]
Flat Iron[72]	
Goes After Other Buffalo[73]	
Hanging Wolf	Crossed the river and fired at Custer's column as they approached Medicine Tail Ford.[74]
High Bear	Captured the roster of Troop G in the valley fight. Later drew battle scenes in the roster.[75]
High Walking[76]	Given a government compass by Long Shield.[77]
Hollow Wood[78]	
Horse Road[79]	
Howling Wolf[80]	Identified by Wooden Leg as wearing a war bonnet in the fighting.[81]
Iron Shirt	Started to strip a wounded officer of his buckskin jacket, but stopped when he noticed a blood stain that ruined the jacket.[82]
Issues	Captured a carbine in the fighting.[83]
Kills in the Night	Along with Old Bear, chased one of Custer's troopers who attempted to escape south along the ridge near the end of the fight.[84] Hardorff notes a Lakota by this name.
Lame White Bull	Participated in the Custer Fight.[85]

Lame White Man[86] (Bearded Man, Mustache)	Killed in the Custer fight about half way down Custer Ridge leading the charge that elevated the battle into the realm of legend. Mistakenly thought to be an Arikara scout, he was probably scalped by the Minneconjou Little Crow. Head soldier of the Elk Warriors. [87]
Last Bull[88]	
Left Handed Shooter[89]	
Limber Bones (Flying By)	Killed on the North slope of Custer Hill. [90]
Limpy[91]	
Little Bird	Wounded in the thigh during Reno's retreat from the valley. [92]
Little Coyote[93]	
Little Creek[94]	
Little Hawk	Fought Reno in the valley. [95]
Little Horse	Accounts indicate he may have stripped the buckskins from Tom Custer's body. [96] Identified by Wooden Leg as wearing a war bonnet in the fighting.[97] A famous Cheyenne warrior, he led the assault at the Fetterman Fight. [98]
Little Robe[99]	
Little Shield[100]	Identified by Wooden Leg as wearing a war bonnet in the fighting. [101]
Little Sun	One of the party that chased and killed two of Reno's troopers that attempted to escape south down the valley. [102]
Little Wolf	Arrived with his band after the Custer Fight. His band had trailed Custer from the night stop on 6/24. [103]
Lone Bear[104]	
Long Shield	Took a compass as a war trophy. [105]
Mad Wolf (Rabid Wolf, Mad Hearted Wolf)[106]	Member of the Dog Soldiers.[107] Participated in the Custer Fight. [108] Identified by Wooden Leg as wearing a war bonnet in the fighting. [109]
Magpie Eagle[110]	
Medicine Bear	Claimed Custer was killed early in the fight. [111]
Medicine Bull	Member of Little Wolf's band. One of three scouts seen by Sergeant Curtiss at the box of hardtack. This report would convince Custer the command had been discovered, requiring an immediate attack to prevent the escape of the Indians. [112] Participated in the hilltop fight on June 26. [113]
Mosquito[114]	
Noisy Walking (Left Handed Ice)	One of the Suicide Boys. Died of wounds received in the big bend of Deep Ravine.[115]
Old Bear[116]	Old Man Chief. Leader of the village destroyed by Reynolds on the Powder River.
Old Bear	Not the Old Man Chief from the Powder River fight. Along with Kills in the Night chased one of Custer's troopers who attempted to escape south along the ridge near the end of the fight. Old Bear is credited with killing the trooper. [117]
Old Man (Old Man Coyote)	One of the party that infiltrated the timber and killed the scout Bloody Knife and privates Henry Klotzbucher and George Lorentz. Killed during Reno's retreat to the bluffs.[118]

Owns Red Horse

Identified as killed in the Custer Fight by the Minneconjou White Bull.[119]

Pawnee[120]
Pig[121]
Pine

Fought against both Reno's and Custer's commands.[122]

Plenty Bears[123]
Plenty Crows

An Arikara captive, his two brothers, Bobtail Bull and Little Brave, fought with Reno in the valley fight.[124]

Plenty Of Buffalo Meat[125]
Rattlesnake Nose[126]
Red Bird (Young Little Wolf)[127]
Red Cherries[128]

Named by Peter John Powell as one of the two scouts (Medicine Bull being the other) encountered by Sergean t Curtiss' detail at the hard bread box.

Red Cloud

Named as a leading warrior in the fighting by John Stands In Timber.[129]

Red Hat (Red Hood)

Young son of Lame White Man.[130]

Red Horn Buffalo

Killed in the Custer Fight.[131]

Red Owl[132]
Red Robe[133]
Red Tomahawk

Identified by John Stands In Timber as sighting Custer's column in their second camp on the march up the Rosebud.[134]

Rising Fire[135]
Rising Sun

Took a watch as a war trophy.[136]

Roan Bear

Member of the Fox Warrior Society.[137] One of the four Cheyenne who engaged Custer's troops at Medicine Tail Ford.[138]

Roman (Hump) Nose

Killed on the West bank of the river near the ford during Reno's retreat from the valley.[139]

Sandstone

Identified by John Stands In Timber as a Cheyenne sharpshooter stationed on Wooden Leg Hill during the hilltop fight.[140]

Scabby

Made five bravery runs in front of Reno's first skirmish line.[141] Identified as dying of wounds received in the fighting by John Stands In Timber.[142]

Sits Beside His Medicine[143]
Sleeping Rabbit

Identified by John Stands In Timber as a Cheyenne sharpshooter stationed on Wooden Leg Hill during the hilltop fight.[144]

Snow Bird[145]
Soldier Wolf

At the age of 17 he fought in the valley and Custer fights. His account of the Custer fight indicates that after the withdrawal from Medicine Tail Ford, some of Custer's troops went over the hill north of the present monument.[146] Credited with killing a soldier.[147]

Spotted Blackbird[148]
Spotted Elk

Identified by John Stands In Timber as a Cheyenne sharpshooter stationed on Wooden Leg Hill during the hilltop fight.[149]

Strong Left (Arm) Hand[150]

Sun Bear — One of the party that chased and killed two of Reno's troopers that attempted to escape south down the valley. [151] Wounded in the Custer Fight. [152] Identified by Stands In Timber as, along with Low Dog, pursuing a soldier that attempted to escape beyond the east boundary of the monument. [153] Identified by Wooden Leg as wearing a war bonnet in the fighting. [154]

Swift Cloud — Identified as killed in the Custer fight by the Minneconjou White Bull. [155]

Tall Bear (White Antelope) — Participated in the Custer fight. Killed during the Sibley scout July 7, 1876. [156]

(Jacob) Tall Bull — Fought in the valley and Custer fights. His account indicates soldier action at Cheyenne, or Crazy Horse, Ford. [157] Had his pony killed in the charge against Custer Hill. [158]

Tall Sioux — Was taking a sweat bath with Lame White Man when Reno attacked. [159]

Tall White Man [160]

Tangled Horn Elk — Captured a carbine in the Custer Fight. [161]

Turkey Legs [162]

Twin — Brother of Wooden Leg. [163]

Twin Woman — Wife of Lame White Man. [164]

Two Birds [165]

Two Feathers [166]

Two Moon(s) — Participated in valley and Custer fights. Claimed that some of Custer's troopers were killed at Medicine Tail Ford (Ford B) and later dragged into the village, dismembered and burned at a big dance the night of June 25. [167]

Walks Last — Had his pony killed during a bravery run in the Custer Fight. [168]

Weasel Bear [169]

(Little) Whirlwind — Sixteen years old at the time of the battle, he was killed on the East bank of the river near Reno's retreat crossing, possibly by the Arikara Bobtail Bull. [170]

White Bird [171] — Wounded in the leg during the Custer Fight. [172]

White Body [173] — Identified by Wooden Leg as wearing a war bonnet in the fighting. [174]

White Buffalo Shaking Off The Dust — Father of Wooden Leg. [175]

White Bull (Ice Bear, Ice) [176] — Father of Noisy Walking. Participated in the valley and Custer fights. [177] Gave an account of the Custer Fight to Lt. Oscar Long in 1878. [178]

White Elk — Captured a carbine and cavalry horse in the fighting. [179] Identified by Wooden Leg as wearing a war bonnet in the fighting. [180]

White Frog — Participated in the Custer Fight. [181]

White Hawk — Participated in the Custer Fight. [182]

White Horse — Participated inthe Custer Fight. [183]

White Shield — Name was changed from Young Blackbird after Rosebud fight. [184] Witnessed Little Horse stripping the body of Tom Custer. [185]

White Wolf (Shot In The Head) — Used a repeating rifle in the fighting. [186]

Wild Hog — Elk Warrior. [187]

Wolf Medicine [188] — Identified by Wooden Leg as wearing a war bonnet in the fighting. [189]

Wolf Tooth	Member of the party that engaged Custer's command while on Luce Ridge.[190] Identified by John Stands In Timber as a Cheyenne sharpshooter stationed on Wooden Leg Hill during the hilltop fight.[191]
Wooden Leg	One of the warriors stationed on the ridge North of Reno's hilltop position. The ridge should properly be called Wooden Leg Ridge rather than Sharpshooter Ridge for consistency with other battlefield names. Claims the Custer fight began with an hour and a half of long range firing. Quoted, although he later claimed never to have made the statment, as stating most of Custer's men committed suicide.[192] Probably one of the party that killed the Arikara scout Little Brave.[193] Captured a carbine in the retreat from the valley.[194]
Wooden Thigh[195]	
Wool Woman	Mother of Noisy Walking.[196]
Yellow Hair	Older brother of Wooden Leg.[197]
Yellow Horse[198]	
Yellow Nose	Ute captive and a Dog Soldier.[199] Usually credited with taking Custer's personal flag, he probably captured the guidon of Company C on Greasy Grass Ridge.[200] Wounded in the heels during the Custer fight.[201]
Yellow Weasel[202]	Took a bugle as a war trophy.[203]
Young Little Wolf[204]	
Young Turkey Leg	One of the party that infiltrated the timber and killed the scout Bloody Knife and privates Henry Klotzbucher and George Lorentz.[205]
Young Two Moon[206]	

Lakota (259)

Tribal Affiliation Unknown (48)

Bear's Cap	Participated in the Custer Fight.[207]
Bear King	Member of Medicine Man's band. Left Standing Rock Agency with Kill Eagle's band of Blackfeet.[208]
Big Leggins[209]	
Big Nose[210]	
Black Fox	Killed. Location unknown.[211]
Blind Water[212]	
Brave Crow	Counted coup in the Custer Fight.[213]
Brave Hawk	Member of Belly Fat's band. Left Standing Rock Agency with Kill Eagle's band of Blackfeet.[214]
Brings Plenty	Reported to have killed a soldier with a war club.[215]
Burst Thunder	Observed the scalping of Lame White Man by Little Crow.[216]
Dog	Member of Running Antelope's band. Left Standing Rock Agency with Kill Eagle's Blackfoot band.[217]
Eagle Chase[218]	
Eagle Man	Member of Wounded Head's band. Left Standing Rock Agency with Kill Eagle's band of Blackfeet.[219]
Fat Bear	Credited with bringing the story of Deeds to the council lodge[220] after a run of 15 miles.[221]
Fool Bull[222]	
Four Horns[223]	

Gray Whirlwind (Sunken Ass)   Reported Sitting Bull's horse was wounded at start of the valley fight inducing Sitting Bull to fight.[224]

Hairy Chin   Lakota Medicine Man[225]
Has Horn   Participated in the Custer Fight.[226]
Iron Bull[227]
Iron Lightning   Participated inthe Custer Fight.[228]
Kills Alive[229]
Limping Black Elk[230]
Little Eagle   Member of Plenty Crow's band. Left Standing Rock Agency with Kill Eagle's band of Blackfeet.[231]

Little Horse[232]
Makes Enemy[233]
Owns Horn   Participated in the Custer Fight.[234]
Paints Brown[235]
Pemmican[236]
Red Fish[237]
Scarlet Bear   Member of Two Heart's band. Left Standing Rock Agency with Kill Eagle's band of Blackfeet.[238]

Scarlet Eagle   Member of Sitting Crow's band. Left Standing Rock Agency with Kill Eagle's band of Blackfeet.[239]

Scarlet Thunder   Member of Horn's band. Left Standing Rock Agency with Kill Eagle's band of Blackfeet.[240]

Shoots Bear As He Runs   Participated in the Custer Fight.[241]
Shot in the Face[242]
Sitting Hawk[243]
Spotted Rabbit[244]   Participated in the Custer Fight.[245]
Standing Black Bear   Claimed to have accompanied Deeds the morning of June 25.[246]

Standing Rabbit   Identified as killed by Kicking Bear.[247]
Strong   Member of Two Heart's band. Left Standing Rock Agency with Kill Eagle's band of Blackfeet.[248]

The Man Who Walks With His Dogs   Member of Belly Fat's band. Left Standing Rock Agency with Kill Eagle's band of Blackfeet.[249]

Thin Elk[250]
Whirling[251]
White Beard[252]
White Buffalo[253]
With Horns   Participated in the Custer Fight. Removed the wounded Lazy White Bull from the battlefield.[254]

Wounded Lice   Scouting with Lazy White Bull on June 26, he encountered the Montana Cloumn.[255]

Worm[256]

Blackfeet (3)

Flying Charge   Killed in the valley fight.[257]
Kill Eagle *Wambli Kte*   Claimed that he and his followers were held as virtual prisoners by the Uncpapa . Witnessed, but claims not to have participated in the battle.[258]

Scabby Head[259] *Pa Hayuhpu*

Brule (9)

Buffalo Horse[260]
Charging Hawk   Eight years old at the time of the battle.[261]

Crow Dog	Remembered for his murder of Spotted Tail rather than any part he took in the fighting.[262]
Flying Chaser[263] *Wakuya Kinyan*	
Hollow Horn Bear[264]	
Short Bull	Participated in the valley fight.[265]
Thunder Hawk	Wounded in the left hip at the Battle of the Rosebud, he was in the village but not an active participant at the Little Big Horn.[266]
Two Eagles	His account describes Custer's movement in two battalions down Medicine Tail Coulee and from Nye–Cartwright Ridge to Calhoun Hill. Said the Cheyenne circle was North of Deep Ravine.[267]
Two Strikes	Credited with killing two soldiers riding double.[268]

Minneconjou (47)

Bear Lice *Mato Heya*	Along with Crow Boy assisted the Minneconjou Lazy White Bull engaged in hand to hand combat with one of Custer's troopers.[269]
Beard[270]	
Big Ankles	Identified by John Stands In Timber as a Lakota sharpshooter, and nephew of Lame Deer, stationed on Wooden Leg Hill during the hilltop fight.[271]
Black Shield[272] *Wahacanka Sapa*	
Breech Cloth *Miyapahe*	Killed on East side of Reno Hill during a bravery run near dusk on June 25.[273]
Buffalo Bull[274]	
Bull *Ptebloka*	Member of Bad Hand's band. Left Standing Rock Agency with Kill Eagle's band of Blackfeet.[275]
Charging Hawk[276]	
Comes Flying[277]	
Crazy Heart	Shirt Wearer, son of Lame Deer.[278]
Dog Backbone *Sunka Cankahu*	Killed Northeast of Reno Hill on June 25.[279]
Dog With Horns *Sunka Yuha*	Brother of Feather Earring.[280] Killed in the valley fight in front of Reno's first skirmish line.[281]
Fast Bull[282] *Ptebloka Iuzahan*	
Feather Earring *Owinpi Aopazan*	Brother of Dog With Horns.[283] Said the Indians would have surrendered if Custer had parlayed instead of attacking.[284]
Flying By[285] *Kinyan*	Son of Lame Deer, his horse was shot during Reno's retreat and securing another mount made him late in arriving for the Custer Fight.[286] He was armed with a winchester during the fight and claimed that the Lakota later found 2 soldiers on the Rosebud nearly starved to death.[287]
Foolish Heart	Brother of Flying By.[288]
Four Times Woman	Sister of Lazy White Bull.[289]
Good Fox[290]	
High Back (High Backbone)[291]	
High Horse *Wankal Sunka Wakan*	Killed in the Custer fight, location unknown.[292]
Hump *Canhahake*	Wounded above the knee in the Custer fight.[293] Brother of Little Crow.[294] Gave an account of the fight to Lt. Oscar Long in 1878.[295]
Humped Little Crow[296]	
Iron Hail[297]	

Iron Thunder *Hoton Mazasapa*

Brother of Hump. Arriving too late to fight Reno in the valley, his horse became lame and he missed the Custer fight as well. Speaks of Custer attempting to capture the women and children.[298]

Kills Standing

Brother of Lazy White Bull.[299]

Lame Deer[300] *Tahca Huste*

Lazy White Bull *Pte San Hunka*[301]

Counted 7 coups, captured two guns and 12 horses, and survived a vicious hand to hand encounter with one of Custer's troopers. Had his horse shot from under him and was wounded in the ankle by a spent bullet.[302] Although a Uncpapa by birth, he is listed with the Minneconjou because he had gone to live with his wife's people.

Lights[303] (Runs After the Clouds)

Little Crow *Kangi Cicala*

Probably the Lakota who mistakenly scalped the Cheyenne Lame White Man.[304] Brother of Hump.[305]

Lone Horn[306]

Long Elk

Wounded in the fighting near Calhoun Hill.[307]

Looking Elk *Hehaca Wakita*[308]

Makes Room[309] *Kipana*

Father of Lazy White Bull. Did not take an active part in the fighting.[310]

One Bull[311]

One Horn[312]

Red Horse *Hinsa*

Drew a large number of pictographs of the battle. Claimed many of Custer's soldiers tried to surrender and that they used little of their ammunition. Said that while fighting Reno, they received word that the women and children had been captured by Custer.[313]

Roman Nose[314]

Shell Woman

Sister of Lazy White Bull.[315]

Spotted Elk (Big Foot)[316] *Hehank Gleska*

Killed at Wounded Knee.[317]

Standing Bear *Mato Najin*

Saw Custer's approach from Weir Point.[318] Did not participate in Reno's valley fight, but fought against Custer[319] capturing a buckskin coat and counting coup.[320]

Takes the Horses[321]

Brother of Dog Backbone.

Three Bears *Mato Yamni*

Died near the foot of the Big Horn Mountains of wounds received near Uncpapa tepees during Reno's valley fight.[322]

Touch The Clouds [323] *Mahpihpiya Putaka*

Turtle Rib[324]

May have killed one of the Arikara scouts.[325] Claims that soldiers were moving toward Custer and Calhoun Hills at the same time.[326] Claimed to have witnessed several soldier suicides.[327]

Uses Her Own Words

Sister of Lazy White Bull.[328]

White Hollow Horn[329]

Wounded Hand[330]

Oglala (65)

American Horse[331]

Bad Heart Bull *Tatanka Cante Sica*

One of the first 3 Lakota to meet Reno's advance in the valley.[332]

Bad Light Hair *Sica Zi Pehin*

Killed in the Custer fight, location unknown.[333]

Bear Lying Down His account indicates some wild firing, perhaps induced by panic, on the part of Custer's troops.[334]

Big Design Named as killed in the valley fight by He Dog.[335]
Big Elk[336]

Big Man Named by the Blackfoot Kill Eagle as a leader at the Custer fight.[337]

Big Road *Canku Tanka* Principal chief in the Oglala camp.[338]
Black Bear *Mato Sapa* Member of small party starting back to Red Cloud Agency the morning of June 25, he saw Custer's column on the divide.[339]

Black Elk[340] *Hehaka Sapa* Although only 13 years of age, he took two scalps in the valley fight.[341]

Black Fox[342] *Sungila Sapa*
Black White Man *Wasichu Sapa* Died near foot of Big Horn Mountains of wounds received on West slope of Custer Hill.[343]

Blue Cloud One of 7 Lakota members of Black Bear's party who heard the hard bread box story from the 3 Cheyenne while watching Custer from the divide.[344]

Comes Again[345]
Crazy Horse[346] *Suska Witko* His arrival during the valley fight encouraged the warriors to infiltrate Reno's timber position.[347] Always where the fighting was thickest, led a charge that split Company I into two platoons[348] and made a bravery run in front of Custer's position. Acknowledged by Lakota and Cheyenne alike as the bravest warrior in the fight.[349]

Crow Dog[350] *Kangli Sunka*
Eagle Bear[351]
Eagle Elk *Wambli Hehaka* Witnessed the killing of Isaiah Dorman, by the woman Her Eagle Robe, in the valley.[352] Used a winchester in the fighting.[353] Participated in the charge on Greasy Grass Ridge.[354] Claimed to have captured a bay and sorrel bridled together indicating Company C shared horse holders with either Company I or, most probably, Company L.[355]

Fast Horn May have killed the buffalo Custer found partially skinned on Reno Creek.[356]

Fast Thunder[357]
Flying By *Kinyan* An old man at the time, he was in the forefront of the Custer fight exhorting the young men.[358]

Flying Hawk *Cetan Kinyan* Brother of Kicking Bear of Ghost Dance fame and nephew of Sitting Bull.[359] Fought in the valley and Custer fights. Says many Indians were between Custer's two detachments in Medicine Tail Coulee forcing the move from Luce Ridge.[360] He said that Custer Hill is directly opposite where the women were congregated during the fighting.[361]

Foolish Elk[362] *Hehaka Witko* Said that Custer made two charges; one on Calhoun Hill and the other from the monument toward the river.[363]

Hard To Hit *Oosicela* One of the first 3 Lakota to meet Reno's advance in the valley.[364]

He Dog *Sunka Bloka* A Shirt Wearer and leader of the military lodge of Crow Owners. Did not fight against Reno in the valley. Engaged Custer's troops at Medicine Tail Ford and, apparently on Nye–Cartwright Ridge.[365] Named Corporal John Foley, Company C, as a suicide.[366]

High Eagle[367]

Horn Chips[368] (Encouraging Bear)

Horned Horse *Sunka Wakan He Yuha* — Father of White Eagle. [369]

Hunts The Enemy[370]

Jack Red Cloud[371] — Son of Red Cloud. Humiliated at Rosebud Fight.

Julia Face — Wife of the Brule, Thunder Hawk. [372]

Kicking Bear *Mato Anablaga* — May have killed the Arikara scout Little Brave. [373] One of the first 3 Lakota to meet Reno's advance in the valley. [374]

Kills Enemy In Winter — One of 7 Lakota members of Black Bear's party who heard the hard bread box story from the 3 Cheyenne while watching Custer from the divide.[375]

Kills In The Night[376]

Knife — One of 7 Lakota members of Black Bear's party who heard the hard bread box story from the 3 Cheyenne while watching Custer from the divide.[377]

Knife Chief *Itancan Mila* — Wounded through both arms and in the body in front of Reno's first skirmish line. [378] (Note that Hardorff lists him as a Uncpapa in "Hokahey! A Good Day to Die!" page 39).

Little Hawk[379]

Lone Bear — Thought the Custer fight lasted about 4 hours.[380]

Lone Man[381]

Lone Elk — Witnessed the last group of troopers leaving Custer Hill heading for the river.[382]

Long Dung[383]

Low Dog *Sunka Kuciyela* — Asleep in his lodge when Reno attacked, he fought in the valley and Custer fights. Tells of a charge against a dismounted skirmish line that held its own horses. Felt the soldiers would have won if Reno had remained in the timber and fought as Custer's command did. [384] Identified by John Stands In Timber as sighting Custer's column in their second camp on the march up the Rosebud. Stands In Timber credits him with killing a fleeing soldier on the second rise beyond the east boundary. [385]

Magpie[386]

Many (Plenty) Lice *Heya Ota* — Wounded in the Battle of the Rosebud, he was killed in the Custer fight, location unknown.[387]

Medicine Bird — One of 7 Lakota members of Black Bear's party who heard the hard bread box story from the 3 Cheyenne while watching Custer from the divide.[388]

No Neck[389]

One Who Walks With The Stars — Credited with killing a wounded soldier. [390]

Owl Bull — One of 7 Lakota members of Black Bear's party who heard the hard bread box story from the 3 Cheyenne while watching Custer from the divide.[391]

Red Feather — Just getting up when Reno attacked. Says Reno pulled back into the timber just as they charged his exposed left flank. May have counted first coup on Sergeant Myles F. O'Hara, M Company, who was abandoned on Reno's skirmish line by Private Edward D. Pigford. Had his horse killed under him in charge on Calhoun Hill. Claimed to have found some whiskey in one of the Company I saddlebags. [392]

Red Hawk[393] *Cetan Luta*

Red Horn Buffalo — Wounded in the jaw during Reno's retreat from the valley. [394]

Red Horn Buffalo	Wounded in the jaw during Reno's retreat from the valley.[394]
Respects (Fears) Nothing	Joined the fight after Reno withdrew into the timber. His account indicates the action on Custer's field began against Company C on Greasy Grass Ridge. Thought the Custer fight took 3 hours.[395]
Running Eagle	Probable killer of the Arikara Bobtail Bull.[396]
Runs Fearless	May have counted the second coup on the Arikara scout Bobtail Bull.[397]
Shave Elk[398] (Thomas Disputed) *Eccoca Taskla*	
Short Bull[399]	
Soldier Hawk	Participated in the valley fight.[400]
Stands First	May have captured Custer's personal flag.[401]
Walking Blanket Woman	Took the place of her brother, killed at the Rosebud, in fighting the soldiers.[402]
Walking White Cow[403]	Brother of White Eagle.
White (Cow) Bull[404] *Tatanka Pte Ska*	Indian sharpshooter. Fired at Reno Hill, killing or wounding several soldiers.[405]
White Cow Robe	Wife of Respects Nothing.[406]
White Eagle *Wambli Ska*	Killed during Reno's retreat on the slope near Reno Hill, possibly by the Arikara Bobtail Bull.[407]
Yellow Horse[408]	
Young Skunk *Maka Cincala*	Killed in the Custer fight, location unknown.[409] May have counted first coup on the Arikara scout Bobtail Bull.[410]

Sans Arc (23)

Bear With Horns	Identified as killed in the Custer fight by the Minneconjou White Bull.[411]
Black Eagle[412]	
Blue Coat[413]	
Cloud Man *Mahpihpiya Wicasa*	Killed in the Custer fight, location unknown.[414]
Crow Boy *Kangli Hoksila*	May have been a Crow captive raised among the Sans Arcs. Along with Bear Lice assisted the Minneconjou Lazy White Bull engaged in hand to hand combat with one of Custer's troopers.[415]
Did not Go Home *Ignigla Sni*	Along with the Cheyene Old Bear and Kills in the Night, chased two of Reno's retreating troopers. He reported one soldier was killed by the Lakota, the other was a suicide.[416] Counted coup in the Custer Fight.[417]
Eagle Hat	Killed in Benteen's charge to clear Water Carrier's Ravine.[418]
Elk Bear *Mato Hehaka*	Killed in the Custer fight, location unknown.[419]
Elk Stands Above[420] *Hehaka Haneya*	Killed on hillock near the river, probably by the Arikara Little Brave.[421]
Fast Bear[422]	
High Bear[423]	
High Elk[424] *Hehaka Waskal*	Killed in the valley fight.
High Horse[425]	
Holy Lodge	Wife of the Minneconjou White Bull.[426]
Hump Nose[427]	
Iron White Man	Father of Holy Lodge.[428]
Kills Him *Kte Iya*	Killed in the Custer fight, location unknown.[429]
Lone (Long) Dog *Sunka Wan*	Warned the village of Reno's advance.[430] Killed in the Custer fight, location unknown.[431]

Lone (Long) Dog *Sunka Wan*

Warned the village of Reno's advance.[430] Killed in the Custer fight, location unknown.[431]

Long Road (Long Robe) *Sina Hanska*

Killed almost within the soldier's lines on the South side of Reno Hill on June 26.[432]

Red Bear[433] *Mato Luta*
Spotted Eagle[434] (Two Eagles)
Two Bear *Mato Nunpa*

Killed by Reno's scouts on the East side of the river prior to the valley fight.[435]

Yellow Cloud[436]

Santee (4)

Gray Earth Track Oye Makasan   Reputed to have Custer's mount, Vic, after the battle.[437]
Red Point (Inkpaduta, Red Top)[438] *Inkpa Luta*
Plenty Of Meat   Discovered Custer's column at the divide.[439]
Walks Under The Ground[440]

Two Kettle (2)

Chased by Owls *Wawok uwa Hinhan*

Killed between the timber and the river during Reno's retreat from the valley.[441]

Runs the Enemy

One of the Lakota to pressure Reno's left flank forcing the movement to the timber.[442]

Uncpapa (58)

Afraid of Eagles *Nihan Wambli*

Member of Bare Ribs' band. Left Standing Rock Agency with Kill Eagle's band of Blackfeet.[443]

Bad Soup (Bad Juice) *Ohanpi Sica*

Reported to have pointed out Custer's body to the Minneconjou White Bull.[444]

Bear Ears

Member of Bare Ribs' band. Left Standing Rock Agency with Kill Eagle's band of Blackfeet.[445]

Bear With Horns *Mato Heton*   Killed along Custer Ridge.[446]
Beautiful White Cow

Watched the battle from the west bank of the Little Big (Pretty White Buffalo, Mrs. Spotted Horn Bull) *Pte San Waste Win*   Horn, probably opposite Deep Ravine.[447]

Black Moon *Hokeluta Sapa Cincala*

Mistakenly named as killed in the valley fight, he survived to surrender his band at Standing Rock Agency in 1881.[448]

Blue Cloud

Left Standing Rock Agency with the Blackfoot band of Kill Eagle.[449]

Blue Mountain   Step son of Sitting Bull.[450]
Brown Ass[451] *Ozogila*

Probable father of Deeds.[452] There is great confusion over his true band affiliation and relationship, but he was most likely an Uncpapa.

Buffalo Calf Pipe[453]
Chatka

Had been a scout at Fort Linclon. His body was found in one of the tepees in the abandoned village.[454]

Crow Foot[455]

One of Sitting Bull's twin daughers. Initially left behind by Four Robes during Reno's attack.[456]

Crow King *Kangli Yatapi*	Claimed to have received reports of both Reno's and Custer's movement on the village shortly before Reno attacked. Participated in valley, hilltop and Custer fights. Agreed with Low Dog that the soldiers would have won if Reno had remained in the timber and fought as Custer fought. Had two brothers, Swift Bear and White Buffalo Bull, killed in the fighting.[457]
Deeds [458]	Killed on the East bank of the river near the mouth of Reno Creek, probably by Reno's scouts. There is great confusion over his true band affiliation, but he was most likely an Uncpapa.[459]
Elk Heart	Slightly wounded in the valley fight.[460]
Elk Nation	Rescued his wounded friend, Little Bear, under fire near Custer Hill.[461]
Flat Hip[462]	
Four Robes	Wife of Sitting Bull.[463]
Gall *Pizi*	Lost his two wives and three children in the valley fight, probably killed by Reno's Arikara scouts. Led the warriors who stampeded the led horses of Keogh's battalion. Led the charge that overwhelmed Company L.[464]
Good Bear Boy	Wounded in front of Reno's first skirmish line, he was rescued, under fire, by Lone (One) Bull.[465]
Good Voiced Elk	Witnessed the movement of about 30 men from Custer Hill toward the river at the end of the fight.[466]
Gray Eagle	Brother-in-law of Sitting Bull.[467]
Guts (Rectum) *Tezi Ikpi*	Killed in the valley fight.[468]
Hawk Man *Cetan Wicasa*	Killed in front of Reno's first skirmish line.[469]
Hawk Stays Up	Counted coup in the Custer Fight.[470]
Her Eagle Robe *Tashina Wamnbli*	Reported to have killed Dorman.[471]
Iron Cedar *Hante Mazasapa*	According to Gall, he brought word of Custer's advance on the village while the warriors were fighting Reno.[472]
Iron Elk[473]	
Iron Hawk *Cetan Mazasapa*	May have been with the party that infiltrated Reno's timber position and killed the scout Bloody Knife and privates Henry Klotzbucher and George Lorentz.[474] Wounded in the Custer fight,[475] this 14 year old warrior is credited with killing a soldier in the Custer Fight.[476]
Jumping Bull	Asiniboine captive adopted by Sitting Bull.[477]
Knife King	Wounded while recalling the warriors from the firing line on June 26.[478]
Little Bear	Wounded in the leg and his pony killed under him charging Custer Hill, he was rescued under fire by Elk Nation.[479]
Little Knife *Mila Cicala*	In 1879 he admitted one of Custer's noncommissioned officers had been taken prisoner and tortured to death in the village the night of June 25.[480]
Little Soldier	Step son of Sitting Bull.[481]
Little Voice *Hola (Hona)*	Brother of Deeds.[482]
Little Warrior[483]	
Lone (One) Bull *Ptebloka Okinihan*	Brother of Lazy White Bull.[484] Rescued Good Bear Boy under fire in front of Reno's skirmish line.
Lone Man[485]	
Long Elk	Wounded slightly in the valley fight.[486]
Looking Elk	Refused to take Good Bear Boy off the field while under fire.[487]

Moving Robe Woman [488]	Took an active part in the valley and Custer fights after her younger brother, Deeds, was killed. [489] Her account indicates Calhoun assigned 8 – 10 horses to each horse holder to increase his fire power. Reported to have killed two of Custer's wounded troopers. [490]
Old Bull[491]	
Pretty Bear *Mato Washte*	Wounded slightly in the valley fight. [492]
Rain In The Face [493] *Ite Magaju*	
Red Face *Aposina Luta*	Killed in the Custer fight, location unknown. [494]
Red Horn Buffalo	Wounded charging the party that tried to escape from Custer Hill toward the river at the end of the fight. [495]
Red Whirlwind Woman (Scarlet Woman)[496]	
Seen By The Nation	Wife of Sitting Bull.[497]
Shoots Walking	His account indicates he witnessed some cases of "combat fatigue" in the Custer fight. [498]
Sitting Bull[499] *Tatanka Iyotaka*	Spiritual leader of the Lakota. Did not take an active part in the fighting.
Spotted Eagle [500] *Wambli Gleska*	
Spotted Horn Bull[501] *Tatanka He Gleska*	
Swift Bear *Luzahan Matoi*	One of Crow King's brothers. [502] Killed between the timber and the river during Reno's retreat from the valley possibly by the Arikara Young Hawk. [503]
Two Bulls[504]	
White Buffalo Bull *Hehutela Ska*	One of Crow King's brothers. [505] Killed between the timber and the river during Reno's retreat from the valley possibly by the Arikara Young Hawk. [506]
White Eyebrows	Brother of Beautiful White Cow.[507]
White Hair On Face[508]	
Young Black Moon[509] *Kuwa Kiyapi*	Killed in front of Reno's second skirmish line.[510]

Yanktonai (2)

Two Bulls	Said Custer's troopers fought like boys, not men. [511]
White Eagle[512]	

---

[1] See Colonel W. A. Graham "The Custer Myth" page 109.

[2] See Colonel W. A. Graham "The Custer Myth" page 111.

[3] See Colonel W. A. Graham "The Custer Myth" page 109.

[4] See Colonel W. A. Graham "The Custer Myth" page 110.

[5] See Colonel W. A. Graham "The Custer Myth" page 109.

[6] See Colonel W. A. Graham "The Custer Myth" page 109.

[7] See Colonel W. A. Graham "The Custer Myth" page 109.

[8] See Steven W. Myers "Roster of Known Hostile Indians at the Battle of the Little Big Horn" page 10.

[9] See Grinnell interviews, Southwest Museum, Highland Park, Ca.

[10] See Peter John Powell "People of the Sacred Mountain"page 1014.

[11] See Peter John Powell "People of the Sacred Mountain"page, 1009.

[12] See Peter John Powell "People of the Sacred Mountain"page 1029.

[13] See Steven W. Myers "Roster of Known Hostile Indians at the Battle of the Little Big Horn" page 10.

[14] See Steven W. Myers "Roster of Known Hostile Indians at the Battle of the Little Big Horn" page 10.

[15] See Steven W. Myers "Roster of Known Hostile Indians at the Battle of the Little Big Horn" page 10.

[16] See Peter John Powell "People of the Sacred Mountain"page 1013.

[17] See Richard G. Hardorff "Cheyenne Memories of the Custer Fight" pages 111 and 149.

[18] See Richard G. Hardorff "Cheyenne Memories of the Custer Fight" page 144.
[19] See Richard G. Hardorff "Hokahey! A Good Day to Die!" page 27.
[20] See Peter John Powell "People of the Sacred Mountain" page 1018.
[21] See Don Rickey interview with John Stands In Timber, August 18, 1956, Packet H – 14, Little Bighorn Battlefield National Monument.
[22] See Steven W. Myers "Roster of Known Hostile Indians at the Battle of the Little Big Horn" page 10.
[23] See Peter John Powell "People of the Sacred Mountain" page 1028.
[24] See Gregory F. Michno "Lakota Noon" page 309.
[25] See Steven W. Myers "Roster of Known Hostile Indians at the Battle of the Little Big Horn" page 5.
[26] See Richard G. Hardorff "Lakota Recollections of the Custer Fight" page 121.
[27] See Richard G. Hardorff "Hokahey! A Good Day to Die!" page 27.
[28] See Steven W. Myers "Roster of Known Hostile Indians at the Battle of the Little Big Horn" page 10.
[29] See Colonel W. A. Graham "The Custer Myth" page 52.
[30] See Steven W. Myers "Roster of Known Hostile Indians at the Battle of the Little Big Horn" page 10.
[31] See Richard G. Hardorff "Cheyenne Memories of the Custer Fight" page 50.
[32] See Richard G. Hardorff "Cheyenne Memories of the Custer Fight" page 144.
[33] See Steven W. Myers "Roster of Known Hostile Indians at the Battle of the Little Big Horn" page 10.
[34] See Peter John Powell "People of the Sacred Mountain" page 1020.
[35] Also known as Dog Stands On Ridge, Horn, and Old Brave Wolf.
[36] See Richard G. Hardorff "Lakota Recollections of the Custer Fight" page 135.
[37] See Steven W. Myers "Roster of Known Hostile Indians at the Battle of the Little Big Horn" page 10.
[38] See Thomas B. Marquis "Wooden Leg: A Warrior Who Fought Custer" page 244.
[39] See Peter John Powell "People of the Sacred Mountain" page 1013.
[40] See Peter John Powell "People of the Sacred Mountain" page 1013.
[41] See Grinnell interviews, Southwest Museum, Highland Park, Ca.
[42] See James Brust "Lt. Oscar Long's Early Map Details Terrain, Battle Positions" page 9.
[43] See Steven W. Myers "Roster of Known Hostile Indians at the Battle of the Little Big Horn" page 10.
[44] See Peter John Powell "People of the Sacred Mountain" page 1020.
[45] See Peter John Powell "People of the Sacred Mountain" page 1025.
[46] See Steven W. Myers "Roster of Known Hostile Indians at the Battle of the Little Big Horn" page 10.
[47] See Richard G. Hardorff "Cheyenne Memories of the Custer Fight" page 84.
[48] See Steven W. Myers "Roster of Known Hostile Indians at the Battle of the Little Big Horn" page 10.
[49] See Steven W. Myers "Roster of Known Hostile Indians at the Battle of the Little Big Horn" page 10.
[50] See Thomas B. Marquis "Wooden Leg: A Warrior Who Fought Custer" page 244.
[51] See Gregory F. Michno "Lakota Noon" page 132.
[52] See Peter John Powell "People of the Sacred Mountain" page 1023.
[53] See Peter John Powell "People of the Sacred Mountain" page 1023.
[54] Peter John Powell "People of the Sacred Mountain" page 1019.
[55] See Steven W. Myers "Roster of Known Hostile Indians at the Battle of the Little Big Horn" page 10.
[56] See Thomas B. Marquis "Wooden Leg: A Warrior Who Fought Custer" page 244.
[57] See Thomas B. Marquis "Wooden Leg: A Warrior Who Fought Custer" page 212.
[58] See Steven W. Myers "Roster of Known Hostile Indians at the Battle of the Little Big Horn" page 10.
[59] See Peter John Powell "People of the Sacred Mountain" page 1014.
[60] See Charles Hamilton "Cry of the Thunderbird" page 201.
[61] See Steven W. Myers "Roster of Known Hostile Indians at the Battle of the Little Big Horn" page 10.
[62] See Thomas B. Marquis "Wooden Leg: A Warrior Who Fought Custer" page 244.
[63] See Richard G. Hardorff "Hokahey! A Good Day to Die!" page 82.
[64] See Steven W. Myers "Roster of Known Hostile Indians at the Battle of the Little Big Horn" page 10.
[65] See Gregory F. Michno "Lakota Noon" page 104.
[66] See Steven W. Myers "Roster of Known Hostile Indians at the Battle of the Little Big Horn" page 10.

[67] See Peter John Powell "People of the Sacred Mountain" page 1020.

[68] See Gregory F. Michno "Lakota Noon" page 35.

[69] See Peter John Powell "People of the Sacred Mountain" page 1015.

[70] See Steven W. Myers "Roster of Known Hostile Indians at the Battle of the Little Big Horn" page 12.

[71] See Gregory F. Michno "Lakota Noon" page 35.

[72] See Steven W. Myers "Roster of Known Hostile Indians at the Battle of the Little Big Horn" page 12.

[73] See Steven W. Myers "Roster of Known Hostile Indians at the Battle of the Little Big Horn" page 12.

[74] See Margot Liberty and John Stands In Timber "Cheyenne Memories" page 199.

[75] See Steven W. Myers "Roster of Known Hostile Indians at the Battle of the Little Big Horn" page 12.

[76] See Steven W. Myers "Roster of Known Hostile Indians at the Battle of the Little Big Horn" page 12.

[77] See Charles Hamilton "Cry of the Thunderbird" page 204.

[78] See Thomas B. Marquis "The Cheyennes of Montana" page 263.

[79] See Steven W. Myers "Roster of Known Hostile Indians at the Battle of the Little Big Horn" page 12.

[80] See Steven W. Myers "Roster of Known Hostile Indians at the Battle of the Little Big Horn" page 12.

[81] See Thomas B. Marquis "Wooden Leg: A Warrior Who Fought Custer" page 244.

[82] See Peter John Powell "People of the Sacred Mountain" page 1028.

[83] See Thomas B. Marquis "The Cheyennes of Montana" page 256.

[84] See Peter John Powell "People of the Sacred Mountain" page 1027.

[85] See Steven W. Myers "Roster of Known Hostile Indians at the Battle of the Little Big Horn" page 12.

[86] See Richard G. Hardorff "Lakota Recollections of the Custer Fight" page 121.

[87] See Richard G. Hardorff "Cheyenne Memories of the Custer Fight" page 87.

[88] See Steven W. Myers "Roster of Known Hostile Indians at the Battle of the Little Big Horn" page 12.

[89] See Steven W. Myers "Roster of Known Hostile Indians at the Battle of the Little Big Horn" page 12.

[90] See Richard G. Hardorff "Hokahey! A Good Day to Die!" page 82.

[91] See Thomas B. Marquis "The Cheyennes of Montana" page 263.

[92] See Peter John Powell "People of the Sacred Mountain" page 1015.

[93] See Richard G. Hardorff "Lakota Recollections of the Custer Fight" page 38.

[94] See Steven W. Myers "Roster of Known Hostile Indians at the Battle of the Little Big Horn" page 12.

[95] See Peter John Powell "People of the Sacred Mountain" page 1013.

[96] See Peter John Powell "People of the Sacred Mountain" pages 1028 – 1029.

[97] See Thomas B. Marquis "Wooden Leg: A Warrior Who Fought Custer" page 244.

[98] See Richard G. Hardorff "Cheyenne Memories of the Custer Fight" pages 58 - 59.

[99] See Steven W. Myers "Roster of Known Hostile Indians at the Battle of the Little Big Horn" page 12.

[100] See Steven W. Myers "Roster of Known Hostile Indians at the Battle of the Little Big Horn" page 12.

[101] See Thomas B. Marquis "Wooden Leg: A Warrior Who Fought Custer" page 244.

[102] See Peter John Powell "People of the Sacred Mountain" page 1015.

[103] See Steven W. Myers "Roster of Known Hostile Indians at the Battle of the Little Big Horn" page 12.

[104] See Richard G. Hardorff "Hokahey! A Good Day to Die!" page 148.

[105] See Charles Hamilton "Cry of the Thunderbird" page 204.

[106] See George Bird Grinnell "The Fighting Cheyennes" page 350. Although Lame White Man is often referred to as Mad Hearted Wolf, a check of the reference will demonstrate that this is a different warrior.

[107] See Richard G. Hardorff "Cheyenne Memories of the Custer Fight" page 52.

[108] See Steven W. Myers "Roster of Known Hostile Indians at the Battle of the Little Big Horn" page 12.

[109] See Thomas B. Marquis "Wooden Leg: A Warrior Who Fought Custer" page 244.

[110] See Peter John Powell "People of the Sacred Mountain" page 1009.

[111] See Steven W. Myers "Roster of Known Hostile Indians at the Battle of the Little Big Horn" page 12.

[112] See Richard G. Hardorff "Hokahey! A Good Day to Die!" page 27.

[113] See Steven W. Myers "Roster of Known Hostile Indians at the Battle of the Little Big Horn" page 12.

[114] See Steven W. Myers "Roster of Known Hostile Indians at the Battle of the Little Big Horn" page 12.

[115] See Richard G. Hardorff "Lakota Recollections of the Custer Fight" pages 32 – 33.

116 See Thomas B. Marquis "Wooden Leg: A Warrior Who Fought Custer" page 211.

117 See Peter John Powell "People of the Sacred Mountain"page 1027.

118 See Peter John Powell "People of the Sacred Mountain"page 1014.

119 See Steven W. Myers "Roster of Known Hostile Indians at the Battle of the Little Big Horn" page 6.

120 See Steven W. Myers "Roster of Known Hostile Indians at the Battle of the Little Big Horn" page 12.

121 See Steven W. Myers "Roster of Known Hostile Indians at the Battle of the Little Big Horn" page 12.

122 See Steven W. Myers "Roster of Known Hostile Indians at the Battle of the Little Big Horn" page 12.

123 See Steven W. Myers "Roster of Known Hostile Indians at the Battle of the Little Big Horn" page 12.

124 See Margot Liberty and John Stands In Timber "Cheyenne Memories" page 210.

125 See Steven W. Myers "Roster of Known Hostile Indians at the Battle of the Little Big Horn" page 12.

126 See Steven W. Myers "Roster of Known Hostile Indians at the Battle of the Little Big Horn" page 12.

127 See Gregory F. Michno "Lakota Noon" page 159.

128 See Peter John Powell "People of the Sacred Mountain" page 1032.

129 See Don Rickey interview with John Stands In Timber, August 18, 1956, Packet H – 14, Little Bighorn Battlefield National Monument.

130 See Peter John Powell "People of the Sacred Mountain" page 1019.

131 See Gregory F. Michno "Lakota Noon" page 211.

132 See Steven W. Myers "Roster of Known Hostile Indians at the Battle of the Little Big Horn" page 12.

133 See Richard G. Hardorff "Cheyenne Memories of the Custer Fight" page 157

134 See Don Rickey interview with John Stands In Timber, August 18, 1956, Packet H – 14, Little Bighorn Battlefield National Monument.

135 See Richard G. Hardorff "Cheyenne Memories of the Custer Fight" page 142.

136 See Steven W. Myers "Roster of Known Hostile Indians at the Battle of the Little Big Horn" page 12.

137 See Richard G. Hardorff "Cheyenne Memories of the Custer Fight" page 51.

138 See Peter John Powell "People of the Sacred Mountain"page 1020.

139 See Richard G. Hardorff "Lakota Recollections of the Custer Fight" page 110.

140 See Don Rickey interview with John Stands In Timber, August 18, 1956, Packet H – 14, Little Bighorn Battlefield National Monument.

141 See Peter John Powell "People of the Sacred Mountain"page 1011.

142 See Don Rickey interview with John Stands In Timber, August 18, 1956, Packet H – 14, Little Bighorn Battlefield National Monument.

143 See Steven W. Myers "Roster of Known Hostile Indians at the Battle of the Little Big Horn" pages 12 – 13.

144 See Don Rickey interview with John Stands In Timber, August 18, 1956, Packet H – 14, Little Bighorn Battlefield National Monument.

145 See Steven W. Myers "Roster of Known Hostile Indians at the Battle of the Little Big Horn" page 13.

146 See Grinnell interviews, Southwest Museum, Highland Park, Ca.

147 See Steven W. Myers "Roster of Known Hostile Indians at the Battle of the Little Big Horn" page 13.

148 See Bruce Liddic and Paul Harbaugh "Camp on Custer" page 62.

149 See Don Rickey interview with John Stands In Timber, August 18, 1956, Packet H – 14, Little Bighorn Battlefield National Monument.

150 See Steven W. Myers "Roster of Known Hostile Indians at the Battle of the Little Big Horn" page 13.

151 See Peter John Powell "People of the Sacred Mountain"page 1015.

152 See Steven W. Myers "Roster of Known Hostile Indians at the Battle of the Little Big Horn" page 13.

153 See Don Rickey interview with John Stands In Timber, August 18, 1956, Packet H – 14, Little Bighorn Battlefield National Monument.

154 See Thomas B. Marquis "Wooden Leg: A Warrior Who Fought Custer" page 244.

155 See Richard G. Hardorff "Lakota Recollections of the Custer Fight" page 121.

156 Identified as being in the Battle of the Little Big Horn by the Blackfoot Kill Eagle. See Colonel W. A. Graham "The Custer Myth" page 54.

[157] See Grinnell interviews, Southwest Museum, Highland Park, Ca.

[158] See Peter John Powell "People of the Sacred Mountain" page 1028.

[159] See Peter John Powell "People of the Sacred Mountain" page 1011.

[160] See Steven W. Myers "Roster of Known Hostile Indians at the Battle of the Little Big Horn" page 13.

[161] See Steven W. Myers "Roster of Known Hostile Indians at the Battle of the Little Big Horn" page 13.

[162] See Steven W. Myers "Roster of Known Hostile Indians at the Battle of the Little Big Horn" page 13.

[163] See Gregory F. Michno "Lakota Noon" page 35.

[164] See Peter John Powell "People of the Sacred Mountain" page 1019.

[165] See Steven W. Myers "Roster of Known Hostile Indians at the Battle of the Little Big Horn" page 13.

[166] See Steven W. Myers "Roster of Known Hostile Indians at the Battle of the Little Big Horn" page 13.

[167] See Richard G. Hardorff "Lakota Recollections of the Custer Fight" pages 129 – 140.

[168] See Steven W. Myers "Roster of Known Hostile Indians at the Battle of the Little Big Horn" page 13.

[169] See Richard G. Hardorff "Hokahey! A Good Day to Die!" page 129.

[170] See Richard G. Hardorff "Lakota Recollections of the Custer Fight" page 103.

[171] See Steven W. Myers "Roster of Known Hostile Indians at the Battle of the Little Big Horn" page 13.

[172] See Richard G. Hardorff "Cheyenne Memories of the Custer Fight" page 84.

[173] See Steven W. Myers "Roster of Known Hostile Indians at the Battle of the Little Big Horn" page 13.

[174] See Thomas B. Marquis "Wooden Leg: A Warrior Who Fought Custer" page 244.

[175] See Gregory F. Michno "Lakota Noon" page 35.

[176] See Kenneth Hammer "Custer in 76" page 211.

[177] See Grinnell interviews, Southwest Museum, Highland Park, Ca.

[178] See James Brust "Lt. Oscar Long's Early Map Details Terrain, Battle Positions" page 9.

[179] See Steven W. Myers "Roster of Known Hostile Indians at the Battle of the Little Big Horn" page 13 and See Richard G. Hardorff "Cheyenne Memories of the Custer Fight" pages 37 - 38.

[180] See Thomas B. Marquis "Wooden Leg: A Warrior Who Fought Custer" page 244.

[181] See Steven W. Myers "Roster of Known Hostile Indians at the Battle of the Little Big Horn" page 13.

[182] See Steven W. Myers "Roster of Known Hostile Indians at the Battle of the Little Big Horn" page 13.

[183] See Steven W. Myers "Roster of Known Hostile Indians at the Battle of the Little Big Horn" page 13.

[184] See Jerome A. Greene "Lakota and Cheyenne: Indian Views of the Great Sioux War, 1876 – 1877" page 30

[185] See Peter John Powell "People of the Sacred Mountain" page 1028.

[186] See Steven W. Myers "Roster of Known Hostile Indians at the Battle of the Little Big Horn" page 13.

[187] See Richard G. Hardorff "Cheyenne Memories of the Custer Fight" page 84.

[188] See Steven W. Myers "Roster of Known Hostile Indians at the Battle of the Little Big Horn" pages 13 – 14.

[189] See Thomas B. Marquis "Wooden Leg: A Warrior Who Fought Custer" page 244.

[190] See Richard G. Hardorff "Lakota Recollections of the Custer Fight" page 165.

[191] See Don Rickey interview with John Stands In Timber, August 18, 1956, Packet H – 14, Little Bighorn Battlefield National Monument.

[192] See Colonel W. A. Graham "The Custer Myth" page 105.

[193] See Richard G. Hardorff "Lakota Recollections of the Custer Fight" page 103.

[194] See Steven W. Myers "Roster of Known Hostile Indians at the Battle of the Little Big Horn" page 14.

[195] See Steven W. Myers "Roster of Known Hostile Indians at the Battle of the Little Big Horn" page 14.

[196] See Gregory F. Michno "Lakota Noon" page 145.

[197] See Peter John Powell "People of the Sacred Mountain" page 1012.

[198] See Steven W. Myers "Roster of Known Hostile Indians at the Battle of the Little Big Horn" page 14.

[199] See Richard G. Hardorff "Cheyenne Memories of the Custer Fight" page 53.

[200] See Richard G. Hardorff "Lakota Recollections of the Custer Fight" pages 104 and 140. A pictograph in the Spotted Wolf – Yellow Nose Ledger clearly shows him counting coup with a guidon. See Peter John Powell "People of the Sacred Mountain" pages 972 – 973.

[201] See Richard G. Hardorff "Lakota Recollections of the Custer Fight" page 104.

[202] See Steven W. Myers "Roster of Known Hostile Indians at the Battle of the Little Big Horn" page 14.

[203] See Charles Hamilton "Cry of the Thunderbird" page 204.

[204] See Steven W. Myers "Roster of Known Hostile Indians at the Battle of the Little Big Horn" page 14.

[205] See Peter John Powell "People of the Sacred Mountain" page 1014.

[206] See Jerome A. Greene "Lakota and Cheyenne: Indian Views of the Great Sioux War, 1876 – 1877" page 65.

[207] See Steven W. Myers "Roster of Known Hostile Indians at the Battle of the Little Big Horn" page 14.

[208] See Colonel W. A. Graham "The Custer Myth" page 48.

[209] See Steven W. Myers "Roster of Known Hostile Indians at the Battle of the Little Big Horn" page 14.

[210] See Steven W. Myers "Roster of Known Hostile Indians at the Battle of the Little Big Horn" page 14.

[211] See Steven W. Myers "Roster of Known Hostile Indians at the Battle of the Little Big Horn" pages 14 – 15.

[212] See Richard G. Hardorff "Hokahey! A Good Day to Die!" page 92.

[213] See Steven W. Myers "Roster of Known Hostile Indians at the Battle of the Little Big Horn" page 15.

[214] See Colonel W. A. Graham "The Custer Myth" page 48.

[215] See Steven W. Myers "Roster of Known Hostile Indians at the Battle of the Little Big Horn" page 15.

[216] See Raymond J. DeMallie "The Sixth Grandfather" page 186.

[217] See Colonel W. A. Graham "The Custer Myth" page 48.

[218] See Richard G. Hardorff "Hokahey! A Good Day to Die!" page 92.

[219] See Colonel W. A. Graham "The Custer Myth" page 48.

[220] See Richard G. Hardorff "Hokahey! A Good Day to Die!" page 22.

[221] See Steven W. Myers "Roster of Known Hostile Indians at the Battle of the Little Big Horn" page 15.

[222] See Steven W. Myers "Roster of Known Hostile Indians at the Battle of the Little Big Horn" page 16.

[223] See Steven W. Myers "Roster of Known Hostile Indians at the Battle of the Little Big Horn" page 16.

[224] See Gregory F. Michno "Lakota Noon" pages 40 - 41.

[225] See Charles M. Robinson III "A Good Year To Die" page 153.

[226] See Steven W. Myers "Roster of Known Hostile Indians at the Battle of the Little Big Horn" page 16.

[227] See Richard G. Hardorff "Lakota Recollections of the Custer Fight" page 39.

[228] See Steven W. Myers "Roster of Known Hostile Indians at the Battle of the Little Big Horn" page 16.

[229] See Richard G. Hardorff "Hokahey! A Good Day to Die!" page 144.

[230] See Steven W. Myers "Roster of Known Hostile Indians at the Battle of the Little Big Horn" page 16.

[231] See Colonel W. A. Graham "The Custer Myth" page 48.

[232] See Richard G. Hardorff "Hokahey! A Good Day to Die!" page 92.

[233] See Richard G. Hardorff "Hokahey! A Good Day to Die!" page 92.

[234] See Steven W. Myers "Roster of Known Hostile Indians at the Battle of the Little Big Horn" page 17.

[235] See Bruce Nelson "Land of the Dacotahs" page 178.

[236] See Richard G. Hardorff "Hokahey! A Good Day to Die!" page 120.

[237] See Steven W. Myers "Roster of Known Hostile Indians at the Battle of the Little Big Horn" page 18.

[238] See Colonel W. A. Graham "The Custer Myth" page 48.

[239] See Colonel W. A. Graham "The Custer Myth" page 48.

[240] See Colonel W. A. Graham "The Custer Myth" page 48.

[241] See Steven W. Myers "Roster of Known Hostile Indians at the Battle of the Little Big Horn" page 18.

[242] See Richard G. Hardorff "Lakota Recollections of the Custer Fight" page 39.

[243] See Richard G. Hardorff "Hokahey! A Good Day to Die!" page 92.

[244] See Richard G. Hardorff "Hokahey! A Good Day to Die!" page 140.

[245] See Steven W. Myers "Roster of Known Hostile Indians at the Battle of the Little Big Horn" page 18.

[246] See Richard G. Hardorff "Hokahey! A Good Day to Die!" page 23.

[247] See Richard G. Hardorff "Hokahey! A Good Day to Die!" page 132.

[248] See Colonel W. A. Graham "The Custer Myth" page 48.

[249] See Colonel W. A. Graham "The Custer Myth" page 48.

[250] See Steven W. Myers "Roster of Known Hostile Indians at the Battle of the Little Big Horn" page 18.

[251] See Richard G. Hardorff "Lakota Recollections of the Custer Fight" page 73.

[252] See Steven W. Myers "Roster of Known Hostile Indians at the Battle of the Little Big Horn" page 18.

[253] See Steven W. Myers "Roster of Known Hostile Indians at the Battle of the Little Big Horn" page 19.

[254] See Steven W. Myers "Roster of Known Hostile Indians at the Battle of the Little Big Horn" page 19

[255] See Richard G. Hardorff "Lakota Recollections of the Custer Fight" page 123.

[256] See Steven W. Myers "Roster of Known Hostile Indians at the Battle of the Little Big Horn" page 19.

[257] See Richard G. Hardorff "Hokahey! A Good Day to Die!" page 134.

[258] See Colonel W. A. Graham "The Custer Myth" pages 46 – 47.

[259] See Colonel W. A. Graham "The Custer Myth" page 63.

[260] See Richard G. Hardorff "Lakota Recollections of the Custer Fight" page 178.

[261] ee Richard G. Hardorff "Camp, Custer, and the Little Bighorn" page 93.

[262] See David Humphreys Miller "Custer's Fall" page 48.

[263] See Richard G. Hardorff "Lakota Recollections of the Custer Fight" page 38.

[264] See Richard G. Hardorff "Lakota Recollections of the Custer Fight" page 177.

[265] See Steven W. Myers "Roster of Known Hostile Indians at the Battle of the Little Big Horn" page 18.

[266] See Richard G. Hardorff "Lakota Recollections of the Custer Fight" page 188.

[267] See Richard G. Hardorff "Lakota Recollections of the Custer Fight" page 141 – 151.

[268] See Steven W. Myers "Roster of Known Hostile Indians at the Battle of the Little Big Horn" page 18.

[269] See Richard G. Hardorff "Lakota Recollections of the Custer Fight" page 116.

[270] See Gregory F. Michno "Lakota Noon" page 315.

[271] See Don Rickey interview with John Stands In Timber, August 18, 1956, Packet H – 14, Little Bighorn Battlefield National Monument.

[272] See Richard G. Hardorff "Lakota Recollections of the Custer Fight" page 39.

[273] See Richard G. Hardorff "Hokahey! A Good Day to Die!" page 86.

[274] See Richard G. Hardorff "Lakota Recollections of the Custer Fight" page 38.

[275] See Colonel W. A. Graham "The Custer Myth" page 48.

[276] See Gregory F. Michno "Lakota Noon" page 315.

[277] See Steven W. Myers "Roster of Known Hostile Indians at the Battle of the Little Big Horn" page 15.

[278] See Steven W. Myers "Roster of Known Hostile Indians at the Battle of the Little Big Horn" page 15.

[279] See Richard G. Hardorff "Lakota Recollections of the Custer Fight" page 123.

[280] See Richard G. Hardorff "Hokahey! A Good Day to Die!" page 42.

[281] See Richard G. Hardorff "Lakota Recollections of the Custer Fight" pages 109 – 110.

[282] See Colonel W. A. Graham "The Custer Myth" page 63.

[283] See Richard G. Hardorff "Hokahey! A Good Day to Die!" page 42.

[284] See Colonel W. A. Graham "The Custer Myth" page 98.

[285] See Richard G. Hardorff "Lakota Recollections of the Custer Fight" page 87.

[286] See Kenneth Hammer "Custer in 76" page 209.

[287] See Kenneth Hammer "Custer in 76" page 210.

[288] See Gregory F. Michno "Lakota Noon" page 81.

[289] See Gregory F. Michno "Lakota Noon" page 25.

[290] See Steven W. Myers "Roster of Known Hostile Indians at the Battle of the Little Big Horn" page 16.

[291] See Steven W. Myers "Roster of Known Hostile Indians at the Battle of the Little Big Horn" page 16.

[292] See Richard G. Hardorff "Hokahey! A Good Day to Die!" page 144

[293] See Colonel W. A. Graham "The Custer Myth" page 78.

[294] See Steven W. Myers "Roster of Known Hostile Indians at the Battle of the Little Big Horn" page 16.

[295] See James Brust "Lt. Oscar Long's Early Map Details Terrain, Battle Positions" page 9.

[296] See Richard G. Hardorff "Hokahey! A Good Day to Die!" page 29.

[297] See Richard G. Hardorff "Hokahey! A Good Day to Die!" page 120.

[298] See Colonel W. A. Graham "The Custer Myth" page 79.

[299] See Gregory F. Michno "Lakota Noon" page 25.

[300] See Richard G. Hardorff "Lakota Recollections of the Custer Fight" page 39.

[301] See Richard G. Hardorff "Lakota Recollections of the Custer Fight" page 109.

[302] See Richard G. Hardorff "Lakota Recollections of the Custer Fight" pages 107 – 126.

[303] See Richard G. Hardorff "Lakota Recollections of the Custer Fight" page 163.

[304] See Richard G. Hardorff "Lakota Recollections of the Custer Fight" page 33.

[305] See Steven W. Myers "Roster of Known Hostile Indians at the Battle of the Little Big Horn" page 16.

[306] See Steven W. Myers "Roster of Known Hostile Indians at the Battle of the Little Big Horn" page 16.

[307] See Richard G. Hardorff "Hokahey! A Good Day to Die!" pages 62 – 63.

[308] See Richard G. Hardorff "Camp, Custer, and the Little Bighorn" page 85

[309] See Richard G. Hardorff "Lakota Recollections of the Custer Fight" page 39.

[310] See Richard G. Hardorff "Lakota Recollections of the Custer Fight" page 119.

[311] See Gregory F. Michno "Lakota Noon" page 315.

[312] See Steven W. Myers "Roster of Known Hostile Indians at the Battle of the Little Big Horn" page 17.

[313] See Colonel W. A. Graham "The Custer Myth" pages 56 – 62.

[314] See Steven W. Myers "Roster of Known Hostile Indians at the Battle of the Little Big Horn" page 17.

[315] See Gregory F. Michno "Lakota Noon" page 25.

[316] See Richard G. Hardorff "Lakota Recollections of the Custer Fight" page 164.

[317] See Richard G. Hardorff "Camp, Custer, and the Little Bighorn" page 91.

[318] See Richard G. Hardorff "Lakota Recollections of the Custer Fight" page 145.

[319] See Richard G. Hardorff "Lakota Recollections of the Custer Fight" pages 57 – 60.

[320] See Steven W. Myers "Roster of Known Hostile Indians at the Battle of the Little Big Horn" page 18.

[321] See Richard G. Hardorff "Hokahey! A Good Day to Die!" page 91.

[322] See Richard G. Hardorff "Lakota Recollections of the Custer Fight" page 109.

[323] See Richard G. Hardorff "Lakota Recollections of the Custer Fight" page 39.

[324] See Richard G. Hardorff "Hokahey! A Good Day to Die!" page 79.

[325] See Steven W. Myers "Roster of Known Hostile Indians at the Battle of the Little Big Horn" page 18.

[326] See Kenneth Hammer "Custer in 76" page 201.

[327] See Kenneth Hammer "Custer in 76" page 202.

[328] See Gregory F. Michno "Lakota Noon" page 25.

[329] See Steven W. Myers "Roster of Known Hostile Indians at the Battle of the Little Big Horn" page 19.

[330] See Stanley Vestal "Sitting Bull" page 159.

[331] See Steven W. Myers "Roster of Known Hostile Indians at the Battle of the Little Big Horn" page 14.

[332] See Helen H. Blish "A Pictographic History of the Oglala Sioux" page 217.

[333] See Richard G. Hardorff "Lakota Recollections of the Custer Fight" page 121.

[334] See Richard G. Hardorff "Lakota Recollections of the Custer Fight" page 87.

[335] See Richard G. Hardorff "Hokahey! A Good Day to Die!" page 142.

[336] See Steven W. Myers "Roster of Known Hostile Indians at the Battle of the Little Big Horn" page 14.

[337] See Colonel W. A. Graham "The Custer Myth" page 54.

[338] See James McLaughlin "My Friend The Indian" page 134.

[339] See Kenneth Hammer "Custer in 76" page 203

[340] See Richard G. Hardorff "Lakota Recollections of the Custer Fight" page 64.

[341] See Steven W. Myers "Roster of Known Hostile Indians at the Battle of the Little Big Horn" page 15.

[342] See Richard G. Hardorff "Lakota Recollections of the Custer Fight" page 49.

[343] See Richard G. Hardorff "Lakota Recollections of the Custer Fight" page 123.

[344] See Kenneth Hammer "Custer in 76" page 203

[345] See Richard G. Hardorff "Hokahey! A Good Day to Die!" page 120.

[346] See Colonel W. A. Graham "The Custer Myth" pages 62 – 65.

[347] See Richard G. Hardorff "Lakota Recollections of the Custer Fight" page 65.

[348] See Richard G. Hardorff "Lakota Recollections of the Custer Fight" page 75.

[349] See Richard G. Hardorff "Lakota Recollections of the Custer Fight" pages 87 – 88.

[350] See Richard G. Hardorff "Lakota Recollections of the Custer Fight" page 46.

[351] See Richard G. Hardorff "Hokahey! A Good Day to Die!" page 20.

[352] See Richard G. Hardorff "Lakota Recollections of the Custer Fight" pages 101 – 102.

[353] See Steven W. Myers "Roster of Known Hostile Indians at the Battle of the Little Big Horn" page 15.

[354] See Richard G. Hardorff "Lakota Recollections of the Custer Fight" page 104.

[355] See Richard G. Hardorff "Lakota Recollections of the Custer Fight" page 105.

[356] See Richard G. Hardorff "Hokahey! A Good Day to Die!" page 20.

[357] See Edward Kadlecek and Mabell Kadlecek "To Kill An Eagle" pages 124 and 130.

[358] See Richard G. Hardorff "Lakota Recollections of the Custer Fight" page 87.

[359] See Richard G. Hardorff "Lakota Recollections of the Custer Fight" page 49.

[360] See Richard G. Hardorff "Lakota Recollections of the Custer Fight" page 52.

[361] See Richard G. Hardorff "Lakota Recollections of the Custer Fight" page 54.

[362] See Richard G. Hardorff "Lakota Recollections of the Custer Fight" page 69.

[363] See Kenneth Hammer "Custer in 76" page 199.

[364] See Helen H. Blish "A Pictographic History of the Oglala Sioux" page 217

[365] See Richard G. Hardorff "Lakota Recollections of the Custer Fight" pages 73 – 77.

[366] See Kenneth Hammer "Custer in 76" page 207.

[367] See Richard G. Hardorff "Hokahey! A Good Day to Die!" page 120.

[368] See Richard G. Hardorff "Hokahey! A Good Day to Die!" page 126.

[369] See Richard G. Hardorff "Hokahey! A Good Day to Die!" page 51.

[370] See Richard G. Hardorff "Lakota Recollections of the Custer Fight" page 69

[371] See Gregory F. Michno "Lakota Noon" page 278.

[372] See Richard G. Hardorff "Lakota Recollections of the Custer Fight" page 187.

[373] See Richard G. Hardorff "Lakota Recollections of the Custer Fight" page 84.

[374] See Helen H. Blish "A Pictographic History of the Oglala Sioux" page 217.

[375] See Kenneth Hammer "Custer in 76" page 203

[376] See Richard G. Hardorff "Cheyenne Memories of the Custer Fight" page 56.

[377] See Kenneth Hammer "Custer in 76" page 203

[378] See Richard G. Hardorff "Lakota Recollections of the Custer Fight" page 48.

[379] See Steven W. Myers "Roster of Known Hostile Indians at the Battle of the Little Big Horn" page 16.

[380] See Richard G. Hardorff "Lakota Recollections of the Custer Fight" page 159.

[381] See Richard G. Hardorff "Camp, Custer, and the Little Bighorn" page 88.

[382] See Richard G. Hardorff "Lakota Recollections of the Custer Fight" page 114.

[383] See Steven W. Myers "Roster of Known Hostile Indians at the Battle of the Little Big Horn" page 16.

[384] See Colonel W. A. Graham "The Custer Myth" page 75.

[385] See Don Rickey interview with John Stands In Timber, August 18, 1956, Packet H – 14, Little Bighorn Battlefield National Monument.

[386] See Richard G. Hardorff "Lakota Recollections of the Custer Fight" page 81.

[387] See Richard G. Hardorff "Lakota Recollections of the Custer Fight" page 192.

[388] See Kenneth Hammer "Custer in 76" page 203

[389] See Steven W. Myers "Roster of Known Hostile Indians at the Battle of the Little Big Horn" page 17.

[390] See Steven W. Myers "Roster of Known Hostile Indians at the Battle of the Little Big Horn" page 17.

[391] See Kenneth Hammer "Custer in 76" page 203

[392] See Richard G. Hardorff "Lakota Recollections of the Custer Fight" pages 81 – 88.

[393] See Richard G. Hardorff "Lakota Recollections of the Custer Fight" page 39.

[394] See Richard G. Hardorff "Hokahey! A Good Day to Die!" page 74.

[395] See Richard G. Hardorff "Lakota Recollections of the Custer Fight" pages 25 – 34.

[396] See Richard G. Hardorff "Lakota Recollections of the Custer Fight" page 103.

[397] See Helen H. Blish "A Pictographic History of the Oglala Sioux" page 246.

[398] See Bruce Liddic and Paul Harbaugh "Camp on Custer" page 125

[399] See Gregory F. Michno "Lakota Noon" page 315.

[400] See Helen H. Blish "A Pictographic History of the Oglala Sioux" page 250.

[401] See Richard G. Hardorff "Lakota Recollections of the Custer Fight" page 104.

[402] See Steven W. Myers "Roster of Known Hostile Indians at the Battle of the Little Big Horn" page 18.

[403] See Richard G. Hardorff "Hokahey! A Good Day to Die!" page 52.

[404] See Colonel W. A. Graham "The Custer Myth" pages 96 – 97.

[405] See Steven W. Myers "Roster of Known Hostile Indians at the Battle of the Little Big Horn" page 19.

[406] See Gregory F. Michno "Lakota Noon" page 27.

[407] See Richard G. Hardorff "Lakota Recollections of the Custer Fight" page 110.

[408] See Richard G. Hardorff "Hokahey! A Good Day to Die!" page 125.

[409] See Richard G. Hardorff "Lakota Recollections of the Custer Fight" page 121.

[410] See Helen H. Blish "A Pictographic History of the Oglala Sioux" page 246.

[411] See Richard G. Hardorff "Lakota Recollections of the Custer Fight" page 121.

[412] See Richard G. Hardorff "Lakota Recollections of the Custer Fight" page 151.

[413] See Richard G. Hardorff "Lakota Recollections of the Custer Fight" page 151.

[414] See Richard G. Hardorff "Lakota Recollections of the Custer Fight" page 121.

[415] See Richard G. Hardorff "Lakota Recollections of the Custer Fight" page 116.

[416] See Richard G. Hardorff "Lakota Recollections of the Custer Fight" page 114.

[417] See Steven W. Myers "Roster of Known Hostile Indians at the Battle of the Little Big Horn" page 15.

[418] See Dale T. Schoenberger "End of Custer" page 239.

[419] See Richard G. Hardorff "Lakota Recollections of the Custer Fight" page 121.

[420] Also known as Standing High.

[421] See Richard G. Hardorff "Lakota Recollections of the Custer Fight" page 103.

[422] See David Humphreys Miller "Custer's Fall" page 48.

[423] See Steven W. Myers "Roster of Known Hostile Indians at the Battle of the Little Big Horn" page 16.

[424] See Colonel W. A. Graham "The Custer Myth" page 54.

[425] See Richard G. Hardorff "Lakota Recollections of the Custer Fight" page 151.

[426] See Richard G. Hardorff "Lakota Recollections of the Custer Fight" page 108.

[427] See Steven W. Myers "Roster of Known Hostile Indians at the Battle of the Little Big Horn" page 16.

[428] See Gregory F. Michno "Lakota Noon" page 25.

[429] See Richard G. Hardorff "Lakota Recollections of the Custer Fight" page 121.

[430] See Colonel W. A. Graham "The Custer Myth" page 97.

[431] See Richard G. Hardorff "Lakota Recollections of the Custer Fight" page 121.

[432] See Richard G. Hardorff "Lakota Recollections of the Custer Fight" page 122.

[433] See Colonel W. A. Graham "The Custer Myth" page 63.

[434] See Richard G. Hardorff "Lakota Recollections of the Custer Fight" pages 38 and 151.

[435] See Colonel W. A. Graham "The Custer Myth" page 97.

[436] See Richard G. Hardorff "Lakota Recollections of the Custer Fight" page 151.

[437] See Richard G. Hardorff "Camp, Custer, and the Little Bighorn" page 88.

[438] See Richard G. Hardorff "Lakota Recollections of the Custer Fight" page 38.

[439] See Steven W. Myers "Roster of Known Hostile Indians at the Battle of the Little Big Horn" page 17.

[440] See David Humphreys Miller "Custer's Fall" page 267.

[441] See Richard G. Hardorff "Lakota Recollections of the Custer Fight" page 110.

[442] See Richard G. Hardorff "Lakota Recollections of the Custer Fight" page 26.

[443] See Colonel W. A. Graham "The Custer Myth" pages 48 and 56.

[444] See Richard G. Hardorff "Lakota Recollections of the Custer Fight" page 120.

[445] See Colonel W. A. Graham "The Custer Myth" page 48.

[446] See Richard G. Hardorff "Hokahey! A Good Day to Die!" pages 132 and 142.

[447] See James McLaughlin "My Friend The Indian" page 173.
[448] See Richard G. Hardorff "Hokahey! A Good Day to Die!" page 42.
[449] See Colonel W. A. Graham "The Custer Myth" page 48.
[450] See Gregory F. Michno "Lakota Noon" page 48.
[451] See Richard G. Hardorff "Lakota Recollections of the Custer Fight" page 58. Also known as Brown Back or Eagle, Crawler, and Pants.
[452] See Richard G. Hardorff "Lakota Recollections of the Custer Fight" page 109.
[453] See Steven W. Myers "Roster of Known Hostile Indians at the Battle of the Little Big Horn" page 15.
[454] See Richard G. Hardorff "Hokahey! A Good Day to Die!" page 105.
[455] Also known as Abandoned One, and Fled and Abandoned.
[456] See Gregory F. Michno "Lakota Noon" page 48.
[457] See Colonel W. A. Graham "The Custer Myth" pages 76 – 77.
[458] Also known as Trouble, Plenty of Trouble, Business, and One Hawk.
[459] See Richard G. Hardorff "Lakota Recollections of the Custer Fight" page 58.
[460] See Richard G. Hardorff "Hokahey! A Good Day to Die!" page 39.
[461] See Richard G. Hardorff "Hokahey! A Good Day to Die!" page 73.
[462] See Steven W. Myers "Roster of Known Hostile Indians at the Battle of the Little Big Horn" page 15.
[463] See Gregory F. Michno "Lakota Noon" page 48.
[464] See Colonel W. A. Graham "The Custer Myth" pages 89 – 95.
[465] See Richard G. Hardorff "Hokahey! A Good Day to Die!" pages 37 – 38.
[466] See Richard G. Hardorff "Hokahey! A Good Day to Die!" page 75.
[467] See Gregory F. Michno "Lakota Noon" page 48.
[468] See Helen H. Blish "A Pictographic History of the Oglala Sioux" page 215.
[469] See Richard G. Hardorff "Lakota Recollections of the Custer Fight" page 93.
[470] See Steven W. Myers "Roster of Known Hostile Indians at the Battle of the Little Big Horn" page 16.
[471] See Richard G. Hardorff "Lakota Recollections of the Custer Fight" page 102.
[472] See Colonel W. A. Graham "The Custer Myth" page 94.
[473] See Gregory F. Michno "Lakota Noon" page 39.
[474] See Richard G. Hardorff "Lakota Recollections of the Custer Fight" page 64.
[475] See Richard G. Hardorff "Lakota Recollections of the Custer Fight" page 67.
[476] See Steven W. Myers "Roster of Known Hostile Indians at the Battle of the Little Big Horn" page 16.
[477] See Richard G. Hardorff "Lakota Recollections of the Custer Fight" page 120.
[478] See Stanley Vestal "Sitting Bull: Champion of the Sioux" page 176.
[479] See Richard G. Hardorff "Hokahey! A Good Day to Die!" page 73.
[480] See Richard G. Hardorff "Lakota Recollections of the Custer Fight" page 96.
[481] See Gregory F. Michno "Lakota Noon" page 48.
[482] See Richard G. Hardorff "Hokahey! A Good Day to Die!" page 20.
[483] See Richard G. Hardorff "Hokahey! A Good Day to Die!" page 92
[484] See Richard G. Hardorff "Lakota Recollections of the Custer Fight" page 119.
[485] See Richard G. Hardorff "Hokahey! A Good Day to Die!" page 78.
[486] See Richard G. Hardorff "Hokahey! A Good Day to Die!" pages 39 – 40.
[487] See Richard G. Hardorff "Hokahey! A Good Day to Die!" page 37.
[488] Also known as She Walks With Her Shawl.
[489] See Richard G. Hardorff "Lakota Recollections of the Custer Fight" page 46.
[490] See Richard G. Hardorff "Lakota Recollections of the Custer Fight" pages 94 – 95.
[491] See Richard G. Hardorff "Hokahey! A Good Day to Die!" page 86.
[492] See Richard G. Hardorff "Hokahey! A Good Day to Die!" pages 39 – 40
[493] See Colonel W. A. Graham "The Custer Myth" page 96.
[494] See Richard G. Hardorff "Lakota Recollections of the Custer Fight" page 121.
[495] See Richard G. Hardorff "Hokahey! A Good Day to Die!" page 74.

[496] See Gregory F. Michno "Lakota Noon" page 27.

[497] See Gregory F. Michno "Lakota Noon" page 48.

[498] See Richard G. Hardorff "Lakota Recollections of the Custer Fight" page 86.

[499] See Colonel W. A. Graham "The Custer Myth" pages 65 – 73.

[500] See Colonel W. A. Graham "The Custer Myth" page 96.

[501] See Colonel W. A. Graham "The Custer Myth" page 82.

[502] See Richard G. Hardorff "Hokahey! A Good Day to Die!" page 43.

[503] See Richard G. Hardorff "Lakota Recollections of the Custer Fight" page 110.

[504] See Richard G. Hardorff "Hokahey! A Good Day to Die!" page 81.

[505] See Richard G. Hardorff "Hokahey! A Good Day to Die!" page 43

[506] See Richard G. Hardorff "Lakota Recollections of the Custer Fight" page 110.

[507] See James McLaughlin "My Friend The Indian" page 165.

[508] See Gregory F. Michno "Lakota Noon" page 148.

[509] Also known as Flying Charge.

[510] See Richard G. Hardorff "Hokahey! A Good Day to Die!" pages 42 and 135.

[511] See Richard G. Hardorff "Lakota Recollections of the Custer Fight" page 87.

[512] See Richard G. Hardorff "Lakota Recollections of the Custer Fight" page 38.

Appendix 10

Indians Who May Have Been Present At The Battle Of The Little Big Horn

The following Indians are suspected to have participated in the Battle of the Little Big Horn, or to have been in the village during its prosecution, although no direct evidence establishes their presence. It is a difficult task to assemble such a list as many Indians were known by several names within their own band or tribe in addition to the name by which they were known to other tribes. This is further complicated by some officer's propensity to assign derogatory names to certain individuals after their surrender (this will be obvious, I believe, when reviewing the names of some of the warriors surrendering with Crazy Horse). Although great care has been exercised in compiling this list, there may be multiple listings of the same individual due to the difficulties mentioned above.

Cheyenne(6)

Black Eagle[1]	Present at the Powder River fight on March 17, 1876. Presumed to have joined the camp of Crazy Horse after the fight.
Puffed Cheek[2]	Present at the Powder River fight on March 17, 1876. Presumed to have joined the camp of Crazy Horse after the fight.
Star[3]	A cousin of Wooden Leg. Present at the Powder River fight on March 17, 1876. Presumed to have joined the camp of Crazy Horse after the fight.
White Bull	Brother of Antelope Woman.[4]
White Moon	Brother of Antelope Woman.[5]
Yellow Eagle[6]	Participated in Rosebud fight.

Lakota(3)

Bad Lake[7]	Brother in law of the Minneconjou Lazy White Bull. He was in the village at the time of the Rosebud fight.
Rattling Hawk	Wounded in the Rosebud Fight.[8]
Yells at Daybreak[9]	Participated in Rosebud fight.

Oglala (205)[10]

Around The Quiver
Ass Hole
At The End
Bad Hand
Bad Horse
Bad Minneconjues
Bad Partisan
Bad Sucker
Bad Warrior
Bear Jaw
Bear Star
Belly
Belly Full
Belly Inside
Big Belly Mule
Big Bend
Big Eater
Big Lodge Chimney
Big Owl
Black Eye Lid

Blackbird
Blind Woman
Blind Woman #2
Bloody Knife
Blue Horse
Bluff
Brave Wolf
The Bud
The Buggar
The Bull'
Bull Man
Bull Proof
Butt Horn
Charging Hawk
The Chief
Chief Man
Circled Lodge
Clown
Clown #2
Cockeyed Woman
Comes From War
Comes In Day
Contrary
Crawler
Crazy Bear
Crazy Head
Crazy Heart
Crooked Mouth
Cross Prick
Crossways
Dancing Arrow
Dog Ear
Dog Nothing
Don't Amount To Anything
Don't Get Out Of The Way
Dried Prick
Dry Lake
Duck Belly
Ear Ring Prick
Enemy
Face Turner
Fat Rump
Feather Moon
Fills The Pipe
Fills Up
Four Bullets
Four Crows
Gets Married
Gets Together
Gives Out
Good Boy
Gopher
Grandfather
Greases His Arm
Green Blanket
Grey Head
Hairy
The Hand

Hangs His Head
Heap Bear Lays Down
The Hill
Hoarse
Hole In Face
Hollow Sunflower
Horse Bear
Iron Magpie
Iron White Man
Iroquois Limitation
Kills The Married
The Last
Laugher
Lays Laughing
Leggings
Lightning Killer
The Lights
Likes To Fight
Little Back
Little Big Man
Little Boy
Little Bull
Little Prick
Living Bear
Loafer
Long Handle
Long Name
Long Visitor
Looks Like A Dog
Looks White
Looks Yellow
Makes Widows Cry
Man On Top
Melter
Moccasin HIde
Mountain
Neck Prick
None In Sight
Old
One Brings Shit Far Away
One Grass
One Kills At Eight Steps
One Teat
One That Searches
One That Steals
Owns Arrow
Pisses In The Horn
Plenty Dogs
Plenty Shells
Poor Bear
Poor Dog
Pretty Legs
Pulls Out
Pumpkin Hill
Red Rock
Red Shirt
Red Tail
Ree

Rider
The Rump
Runner
Runs Close To Camp
Runs In Sight
Runs On Top
Saddle
Scabby Face
Scaring Bear
Sees The Cow
The Shield
Shits On His Hand
Shits On The Eagle
Short Short Brule
Side Rib
Singing Bear
Singing Prick
Sits Up Above
Sitting Bear
Sitting Horse
Skunk Guts
Skunk Head
Sleeps There
Slow White Cow
Snake Creek
Snatch Loser
Snatch Steale
Soft Prick
Soldier
Spotted Hand
Spread Pine
Spunker
Stinking Tie
Strong Fox
Tall Bull
Tanned Nuts
Thick Face
Three Hawks
Thunder Hawk
Thunder Tail
Tobacco'
Top Lodge
Torn Belly
Tripe Fold
Undone
Walks In Mud
War Shanty'
Warms His Blanket
Water Snake
Whistler
White Bear
White Cloud
White Face
White Hair
White Rabbit
White Twin
The Whore
Widow

Widow #2
Woman Bone
Wood Boat
Wood Root
Wound In Back
Wrinkled Face
Wrinkler
Yellow Left
Yellow Robe

Uncpapa (5)

Bear Bonnet[11]

He was with Sitting Bull on the Milk River when interviewed by Stanley Huntley for The Chicago Tribune.

Broad Trail[12]

A chief and one of the leading Uncpapa warriors. He was with Sitting Bull on the Milk River when interviewed by Stanley Huntley for The Chicago Tribune.

Long Dog[13]

Reputed to have been one of the leading Uncpapa warriors, his direct participation in the battle is not recorded. He was with Sitting Bull on the Milk River when interviewed by Stanley Huntley for The Chicago Tribune.

Stone Dog[14]

He was with Sitting Bull on the Milk River when interviewed by Stanley Huntley for The Chicago Tribune.

White Gut[15]

He was with Sitting Bull on the Milk River when interviewed by Stanley Huntley for The Chicago Tribune.

[1] See Jerome A. Greene "Lakota and Cheyenne: Indian Views of the Great Sioux War, 1876 – 1877" page 8.
[2] See Jerome A. Greene "Lakota and Cheyenne: Indian Views of the Great Sioux War, 1876 – 1877" page 6.
[3] See Jerome A. Greene "Lakota and Cheyenne: Indian Views of the Great Sioux War, 1876 – 1877" page 6.
[4] See Gregory F. Michno "Lakota Noon" page 22.
[5] See Gregory F. Michno "Lakota Noon" page 22.
[6] See Jerome A. Greene "Lakota and Cheyenne: Indian Views of the Great Sioux War, 1876 – 1877" page 24.
[7] See Jerome A. Greene "Lakota and Cheyenne: Indian Views of the Great Sioux War, 1876 – 1877" page 17.
[8] See Charles M. Robinson III "A Good Year To Die" page 153.
[9] See Jerome A. Greene "Lakota and Cheyenne: Indian Views of the Great Sioux War, 1876 – 1877" page 20. Also known as Rooster, and His Voice is Loudest at Daybreak.
[10] The following surrendered at Red Cloud Agency with Crazy Horse in May of 1877. The animosity of the army is evident in some of the names recorded. See Thomas R. Buecker and R. Eli Paul "The Crazy Horse Surrender Ledger" pages 157 - 164.
[11] See The Chicago Tribune July 5, 1879.
[12] See The Chicago Tribune July 5, 1879.
[13] See The Chicago Tribune July 5, 1879.
[14] See The Chicago Tribune July 5, 1879.
[15] See The Chicago Tribune July 5, 1879.

Appendix 11

Experience of Seventh Cavalry Officers With the Regiment

Name	Prior to 1867	Washita	Stanley	Black Hills	LBH
L/C G. A. Custer	+	+	+	+	kia
1 Lt W. W. Cooke	+	+			kia
Maj M. A. Reno					+
1 Lt E. G. Mathey		+	+	+	+
Capt M. Moylan	+	+	+	+	+
1 Lt C. C. DeRudio			+		+
2 Lt C. A. Varnum			+	+	wia
Capt T. M. McDougall			+	+	+
2 Lt B. H. Hodgson			+	+	kia
Capt T. W. Custer	+	+	+	+	kia
2 Lt H. M. Harrington			+	+	kia
Capt T. B. Weir	+	+			+
2 Lt W. S. Edgerly					+
1 Lt A. E. Smith		+	+	+	kia
2 Lt J. G. Sturgis					kia
Capt G. W. Yates		+	+	+	kia
2 Lt W. V. W. Reily					kia
1 Lt D. McIntosh			+	+	+
2 Lt G. D. Wallace			+	+	+
Capt F. W. Benteen	+	+	+	+	wia
1 Lt F. M. Gibson		+	+	+	+
Capt M. W. Keogh	+				kia
1 Lt J. E. Porter					kia
1 Lt E. S. Godfrey		+	+	+	+
2 Lt L. R. Hare					+
1 Lt J. Calhoun			+	+	kia
2 Lt J. J. Crittenden					kia
Capt T. H. French			+	+	+

Appendix 12

Chronology

The following table presents what I believe to be the times associated with the movements of the various elements of the 7th Cavalry on June 25, 1876. The time of day that certain events took place has been a consistent source of meaningless controversy, serving only to obscure the real issues of where each of the elements were in relation to specific events. I have therefore not provided any "clock times" for the various events; rather, I have assigned relative times to the events using for a reference the time the Custer column passed the lone tepee. My rationale for the times assigned follows the table.

Event	Relative Time (Minutes)	Distance (Miles)	Rate of March (mph)
The Custer column passes the lone tepee.	T	N/A	N/A
Reno receives attack order from Cooke	T + 5	0.5	6.0
Boston Custer passes Benteen's battalion	T + 25[1]	N/A	6.0
Benteen leaves morass. Lead mules from pack train arrive	T + 35[2]	N/A	3.0
Reno reaches the river	T + 45	4.0	6.0
Cooke rejoins Custer with message from Girard	T + 57[3]	1.5	7.0
Custer reaches North Fork of Reno Creek	T + 60	3.0	3.0
Custer waters his horses in North Fork	T + 60 – T + 75[4]	N/A	N/A
Private McIlhargey delivers Reno's first message to Custer	T + 65[5]	1.75	7.0
Reno forms skirmish line in the valley. First Custer sighting.	T + 85[6]	2.0	6.0 & 9.0
Custer reaches first lookout. Observes Reno's skirmish line	T + 90[7]	1.5	6.0
Sergeant Kanipe dispatched with first message	T + 95	N/A	7.0
Private Mitchell delivers Reno's second message to Custer	T + 97[8]	3.75	7.0
Reno pivots into the timber	T + 100[9]	N/A	N/A
Custer reaches Weir Point. Observes Reno's command engaged in the timber	T + 105[10]	1.0	6.0
Second Custer sighting	T + 105[10]	N/A	N/A
Trumpeter Martin dispatched with second message	T + 115	.25	6.0

Event	Relative Time (Minutes)	Distance (Miles)	Rate of March (mph)
Martin passes Boston Custer	T + 119[11]	0.5	7.0
Reno begins retreat from the timber	T + 120[12]	N/A	N/A
Benteen passes lone tepee	T + 120[13]	3.5	3.0
Boston Custer joins the Custer column	T + 123[14]	9.5	6.0
Kanipe reports to Benteen	T + 125[15]	3.5	7.0
Kanipe reports to McDougall and Mathey	T + 140[16]	1.2	6.0
Martin delivers Custer's order to Benteen	T + 145[17]	3.5	7.0
Yates' battalion arrives at Minneconjou Ford	T + 150[18]	1.5	6.0
Reno's advance reaches Reno Hill	T + 150[19]	3.0	6.0
Benteen witnesses the annihilation of the rear of Reno's column	T + 160[20]	1.5	6.0
Yates withdraws from Minneconjou Ford.	T + 170[21]	N/A	N/A
Benteen reaches Reno Hill. Heavy firing is heard from Custer's position	T + 170[22]	1.0	6.0
Custer's battalions reunite at Calhoun Hill	T + 190[23]	N/A	N/A
Weir starts downstream	T + 190[24]	N/A	6.0
Hare and two ammunition mules reach Reno	T + 200[25]	2.0	6.0
Weir reaches Weir Point	T + 210[26]	2.0	6.0
Pack train reaches Reno Hill	T + 222[27]	5.5	4.0
Custer completes sortie to Crazy Horse Ford	T + 230[28]	2.0	6.0
Charge of Lame White Man	T+230 – T+245[29]	N/A	N/A
Benteen reaches Weir Point	T+242 – T+262[30]	2.0	3.0 or 6.0
Custer's command destroyed	T+260 – T+275[31]	N/A	N/A
Retreat begins from Weir point	T+272 – T+292[32]	N/A	N/A

1. There is no solid basis for establishing this time, but we can tie this event to Benteen's watering stop at the morass. We know that Edgerly mentioned Boston Custer passing the battalion while watering. Since Weir moved out from the morass in advance of the remainder of the column, but after Boston Custer passed, I have assumed that Boston Custer passed the morass 10 minutes prior to Benteen's departure.

2. Assuming Benteen proceeded at a walk (the same rate he must have traveled between the meetings with Kanipe and Martin) after leaving the morass, he would have to depart by T + 35 in order to meet Kanipe at T + 125 and Martin at T + 145.

3. Cooke had to rejoin the Custer column prior to their arrival at the North Fork of Reno Creek as there is no evidence to suggest a retrograde movement by the Custer column that would have been necessary had Custer passed the fork prior to Cooke's arrival. If Custer continued at a walk pace, he would arrive at the fork about 1 hour after passing the lone tepee. Reno, who either received his attack order at, or shortly after passing, the lone tepee, would, at a fast trot, arrive at the Little Big Horn within 40 minutes. This allows 5 minutes for Cooke to receive Girard's message and rejoin Custer prior to arrival at the forks assuming Cooke returned to Custer at a fast trot.

4. I have allowed Custer 15 minutes to water his horses in the North Fork of Reno Creek due to the wide frontage on the bank.

5. McIlhargey was dispatched while Reno was still forming in the timber after crossing the Little Big Horn, or shortly thereafter. He was probably dispatched as a result of the intelligence passed on by Girard and should have departed within about 5 minutes of Cooke. The timing indicates that McIlhargey probably joined Custer during the watering stop and his message indicating Reno's concern over the enemy's strength, in conjunction with Cooke's, was probably the reason Custer ascended the bluffs at a rapid gait.

6. I have allocated 20 minutes for Reno to cross the river and reform his command, 10 minutes to trot one mile down the valley then 7 minutes to travel the second mile at a gallop, and 3 minutes to dismount and form the skirmish line.

7. I have allowed Custer 15 minutes to trot the 1.5 miles to Wooden Leg Ridge.

8. Private Mitchell must have been dispatched within about 15 minutes of private McIlhargey, else the command would have already been at the gallop. Mitchell probably joined Custer near Wooden Leg Ridge.

9. All testimony indicates that Reno was on the skirmish line only a short time. This is verified by the "Custer sighting" on Weir Point after Reno's command entered the timber. I have estimated Reno's command remained on the skirmish line for 15 minutes.

10. This timing is derived by estimating Custer observed Reno's action on the skirmish line for 5 minutes prior to trotting the one mile to Weir Point. I have assumed the command was in the timber for 5 minutes before Custer was observed on Weir Point.

11. Martin said he met Boston at about Weir Point. Boston could easily have been in the vicinity of Weir Point at this time if he rode from the morass at a trot, which seems reasonable given he was anxious to join his brothers.

12. All testimony indicates Reno was only in the timber a very short time. I have estimated 20 minutes.

13. Note that surviving members of the 7th Cavalry passing the lone tepee both with Custer's and Benteen's detachments mentioned the tepee was burning. I feel that it is improper to take them strictly at their word, that is, that the tepee was blazing while each command passed. I have therefore assumed the tepee was just "igniting" as Custer passed and just "smoldering" prior to burning itself out when Benteen passed. In any event, we don't really know how long the hides and lodge poles would take to burn, but an hour and 45 minutes doesn't seem excessive for wood to continue to smolder.

14. Assuming Boston Custer continued at a trot after leaving Martin, he would have reached Custer in Medicine Tail Coulee at T + 123.

15. This allows 30 minutes for Kanipe to cover the approximately 3.5 miles required to reach Benteen who testified at the Reno Court of Inquiry that he was a mile west of the lone tepee when he met Kanipe.

16. This estimate assumes that the pack train left the morass 20 minutes after the departure of Benteen's battalion, T + 55, and marched at a walk rate of 3 mph, placing them about .9 mile east of the lone tepee when Kanipe met Benteen. The effective rate of closure would be 9 mph since Kanipe was traveling at 6 mph (I believe his horse was probably tiring by this time so have reduced the rate of travel from 7 mph to 6 mph) toward the pack train which was moving at 3 mph. This analysis places the meeting location as about 1/4 mile east of the lone tepee.

17. My analysis indicates Martin was dispatched about 20 minutes after Kanipe. I have assumed the same rate of travel for both messengers, 7 mph, and they both traversed the same distance: Martin was dispatched from about one mile further than Kanipe and he met Benteen, according to Benteen's testimony, about one mile west of where Benteen met Kanipe. Note that if the one mile separation between meeting Kanipe and Martin is correct, it demonstrates Benteen could have been moving no faster than at a walk rate.

18. Herendeen testified that the men left in the timber heard firing from down river about 1/2 hour after Reno's retreat. Since this is the first firing heard from the Custer command, I believe it to have been the volleys fired into the village by Yates' battalion. This timing would allow Custer 8 minutes to confer with Boston and Yates, 15 minutes for Yates to trot to Minneconjou Ford, and 4 minutes to deploy and demonstrate at the ford. It therefore seems reasonable that the volleys Herendeen heard were fired by Yates' battalion.

19. Given the worn condition of the horses, and Indian testimony that they had no trouble overtaking the troops ("it was like hunting buffalo") a gallop rate appears totally unrealistic. I have therefore estimated a trot, 6 mph, which yields a transit time from timber to bluff of approximately 30 minutes.

20. This timing is derived from the estimate of Martin reaching Benteen. After receiving Custer's order from Martin, Benteen had to cover approximately 1.5 miles, which he could have comfortably accomplished in the 15 minutes allocated if he moved at a trot.

21. It would have taken approximately 20 minutes for the warriors chasing Reno to arrive in the large numbers mentioned in various accounts as being present during the withdrawal of Yates' battalion from Minneconjou Ford. Since those warriors could not have left Reno prior to T + 143, I have estimated Yates' withdrawal to have occurred no earlier than T + 163.

22. I have allocated 10 minutes for Benteen to witness the annihilation of the rear of Reno's column, the encounter with the Crow scouts, and the transit up the bluffs.

23. I estimate Yates took 20 minutes to reach Calhoun Hill after withdrawing from the ford.

24. Hare could see Weir's troop as he returned from the pack train indicating that Company D had traveled no more than a mile which would indicate a departure about 10 minutes before Hare's return.

25. Hare testified that as soon as Benteen joined Reno he was ordered back to hurry up the ammunition. He testified that he was gone a total of 20 minutes. I have assumed that there was a relatively short delay of 10 minutes prior to Hare being ordered after the packs (includes the time to obtain Godfrey's horse). Note that the timelines presented indicate the ammunition mules must have been moving at a gait of about 5.5 mph for them to have been only about 1 mile away, while the remainder of the train was progressing at about 4.0 mph. I believe this demonstrates that Kanipe delivered his message to the pack train and the ammunition was being hurried to the front, although following the trail rather than moving straight across country as ordered.

26. The exact route Weir took is not known, but we know he went some distance north of Weir Point, so distances must be estimated. To be conservative I have assumed a distance of 2 miles to be covered at a trot due to the urgency Weir obviously felt.

27. This is the time for the arrival of the final elements of the pack train whose gait was undoubtedly increased, after the arrival of Kanipe, for the final 5.5 miles of the march.

28. This estimate includes the 20 minute delay on the flats near the trading post mentioned by Stands in Timber.

29. Lame White Man couldn't have charged prior to Custer's return from Crazy Horse Ford and the deployment of troopers from Company E. Since Custer was now definitely on the defensive and anxious to reunite the command for an integrated defense based at Calhoun Hill, the deployment of E Troop probably occurred very soon after Custer reached Last Stand Hill at T + 230. I have assumed the maximum time for this deployment was 15 minutes.

30. Benteen and French started for Weir Point after the entire pack train was up. If they moved at a walk rate of 3 mph, they would arrive at T + 262; at a trot, the arrival time could be as early as T + 242.

31. The Indian accounts indicate that from the time Lame White Man charged until Custer's command was destroyed was no more than 30 minutes, or between T + 260 and T + 275. Working backwards, if you assume a 20 minute time for the Indians to recognize the troops on Weir Point and arrive at that location, forcing the troops to withdraw, you obtain a time for the destruction of Custer's command between T + 252 and T + 272 which is in good agreement with the time generated by basing the analysis upon Custer's return from Crazy Horse Ford. The total elapsed time from Yates' demonstration at Minneconjou Ford (T + 150) until Custer's annihilation at T + 260 or T + 275 is in good agreement with the two hour estimate of Sitting Bull for the duration of the Custer Fight.

32. Kanipe remembered being on Weir Point for about a half hour. While he doesn't state which troop he accompanied, given that he had gone to join the pack train, he probably arrived with the second contingent to reach Weir Point (either at T + 242 or T + 262).

Appendix 13

Annual Report of Lieutenant General P. H. Sheridan for 1876[1]

No. 1.

HEADQUARTERS MILITARY DIVISION OF THE MISSOURI,
New Orleans, La., November 25, 1876

GENERAL: I have the honor to submit, for the information of the General of the Army, a brief report of the events occurring in the Military Division of the Missouri since my last annual report.

The division covers a large extent of territory, reaching from the eastern line of Illinois to Nevada, and from the line of the British possessions to the Gulf of Mexico, embracing within these limits three–fourths of all our Indian population.

For the convenience of administration, it is divided into five military departments, named as follows:

Department of Dakota, embracing the State of Minnesota and Territories of Montana and Dakota;

Department of the Platte, embracing the States of Iowa and Nebraska, the Territories of Wyoming and Utah, and so much of the Territory of Idaho as lies east of a line formed by the extension of the western boundary of Utah to the northeastern boundary of Idaho;

Department of the Missouri, embracing the States of Illinois, Missouri, Kansas, Colorado, the Indian Territory, and the Territory of New Mexico;

Department of Texas, embracing the State of Texas; and the

Department of the Gulf, embracing the States of Louisiana, Arkansas, Mississippi, Alabama, and those portions of Tennessee and Kentucky lying west of the Tennessee River;

Commanded respectively, by Brig. Gens. Alfred H. Terry, George Crook, John Pope, Edward O. C. Ord, and Christopher Augur.

These departments are units of administration, each department commander being alone responsible for the administration and executive working of his department, and for economy in expenditure of public money and the discipline of the troops.

The duties of the division commander are supervisory and corrective. He adjusts the wants of each department, and transfers the troops from one department to another to meet any new condition which may arise and to correct any abuses of administration and executive management.

The troops in the Department of Texas have been constantly on the alert to meet the depredations of Indians from Mexico and from Mexican cattle–thieves along the Rio Grande, but I am happy to state that both these causes of complaint have greatly diminished, and, with the increase of our cavalry regiments authorized by Congress last session, we hope to remove all anxiety by giving full protection. For the operation of the troops, I respectfully refer you to the report of Brig. Gen. E. O. C. Ord, commanding the department.

The Department of the Missouri has been entirely quiet since the campaign of 1874–'75, when the hostile Indians were dismounted and disarmed and the worst leaders sent to Florida. For a detailed account of the affairs of the department, I refer to the report of Brig. Gen. John Pope, accompanying.

In the Department of the Gulf no events have occurred other than those incident to the disturbed condition of affairs arising from the political contest of this year. The department has been somewhat changed, by taking from it the Gulf posts of Florida and adding to it Alabama and those portions of Kentucky and Tennessee which lie west of the Tennessee River.

In the Departments of Dakota and the Platte serious Indian troubles have existed, which have been attended by some disasters, much labor, and considerable expense, but there is a fair prospect of a complete settlement by the defeat and surrender of all the hostile Indians, with their arms, ponies, men, women, and children, before the winter is over.

On the 9th of November, 1875, United States Indian Inspector E. C. Watkins reported to the Commissioner of Indian Affairs the attitude of certain wild and hostile Indians in Dakota, Montana, and Wyoming, composed of a small band of thirty or forty lodges, under Sitting Bull, who had been an out–and–out anti–agency Indian, and the bands of other chiefs and headmen under Crazy Horse, an Ogallalla Sioux, belonging formerly to the Red Cloud agency, numbering about one hundred and twenty lodges. Mr. Watkins stated that these hostile bands had never accepted the reservation policy of the Government, were continually making war on the Arickarees, Mandans, Gros Ventres, Assinaboines, Blackfeet, Piegans, Crows, and other friendly tribes, as well as upon frontier settlers and emigrants, and recommended that the Government send troops to operate against them and reduce them to subjection. The report of Inspector Watkins, with the views of the Commissioner of Indian Affairs and the recommendation of the honorable Secretary of the Interior, that these Indians be informed that they must remove to a reservation before the 31st of January, 1876, and that, in the event of their refusal to come in by the time specified, they would be turned over to the War Department for punishment, were referred to me by the General of the Army, December 13, 1875.

As Generals Terry and Crook command the departments in which these Indians were located, I submitted the subject to them, and General Terry was of the opinion that Sitting Bull's band was encamped near the mouth of the Little Missouri; that it could be reached by a quick movement, which might be decisive at that season of the year, and that he had sufficient troops to make such a movement. General Crook was of the opinion that operations could be undertaken in his department against the hostiles whenever, in the judgment of the Indian Bureau, such action became necessary.

As the commands of these two officers embraced all the Indians against whom military action was contemplated, and as they felt competent and able to move, I requested that, should operations be determined upon, directions to that effect be communicated as speedily as possible, so that the enemy might be taken at the greatest disadvantage; in other words, in midwinter, when they could not well get out of the way of the troops.

On February 4, 1876, I again stated, by endorsement on a letter of the Commissioner of Indian Affairs, that if it was intended to operate against these Indians, I could safely say that every possibility of success would vanish unless directions were immediately given; saying further that I fully comprehended the difficulties of the country, and that unless they were caught before early spring they could not be caught at all.

On February 7, 1876, authority was received, by endorsement of the General of the Army on letter of the honorable Secretary of the Interior, to commence operations against the hostile Sioux. They were, at that time, Sitting Bull's band, of 30 or 40 lodges, and not exceeding 70 warriors, and Crazy Horse's band, not exceeding 120 lodges, and numbering probably 200 warriors. Meantime General Terry had learned that Sitting Bull's band was on the Dry Fork of the Missouri, some 200 miles farther west, instead of the Little Missouri.

On the 8th of February, the letter of the honorable Secretary of the Interior was referred to General Terry, with directions to take such steps with the forces under his command as would carry out the wishes of the Interior Department and the orders of the General of the Army. No specific directions could be given, as no one knew exactly, and no one could have known where these Indians were, as they might be here to–day and somewhere else to–morrow.

General Terry was also informed that General Crook would operate from the south in the direction of the headwaters of Powder River, Pumpkin Buttes, Tongue River, Rosebud and Big Horn Rivers, where Crazy

Horse and his allies frequented, and that departmental lines would be disregarded by the troops until the object requested by the Secretary of the Interior was attained. General Terry was further informed that the operations of himself and General Crook would be made without concert, as the Indian villages are movable and no objective point could be fixed upon, but that, if they should come to any understanding about concerted movements, there would be no objection at division headquarters.

On the same date, February 8, 1876, a copy of the same paper was referred to General Crook, with similar general instructions, informing him also that the operations conducted by General Terry would be communicated to him for his information whenever received at division headquarters.

During the time this correspondence was taking place, from December 12, 1875, to February 4, 1876, efforts were being made by the Interior Department to have these hostile Indians come in and settle down on reservations. Communications had been sent them from various agencies, informing them of the wishes and intentions of the Government, and every inducement held out to them to become peaceable and obedient. The only end gained, however, by all these communications was that of informing the hostiles that troops were to be sent out to compel them to come in.

Immediately on receipt of his instructions, General Crook commenced concentrating the available cavalry of his command at Fort Fetterman, consisting of ten companies, numbering about 50 or 60 men to a company, and this force, with the addition of two companies of infantry, formed an expedition, which moved out from Fort Fetterman on March 1 against the hostiles, who were believed to be located on the headwaters of Powder River, Tongue River, or the Rosebud. On the 17th of March the main portion of the expedition, under the immediate command of Col. J. J. Reynolds, struck an Indian village under Crazy Horse on Powder River, destroying all the lodges, 105 in number, and the ammunition and stores it contained, and killing some of the Indians as well as capturing a large herd of horses.

The success of this attack was to some extent compromised, however, by afterward allowing the Indians to recover their horses by a surprise, on the morning after the engagement. The command had suffered so much from the severity of the weather (the mercury having congealed in the thermometer on several occasions) that it had to return to Fort Fetterman without inflicting any further blow than the burning of one hundred and five lodges or tepees.

The failure to retain the captured horses greatly modified the success of the expedition, and the troops had to be redistributed to their various winter–stations to protect them from the extreme cold.

About the same time that General Crook was making his preparations to move, as just described, General Terry also projected an expedition against Sitting Bull's band, which was then believed, from information he had received, was located on the Little Missouri River, but afterward found to be on the Dry Fork of the Missouri, some two hundred miles farther west. Before, however, the Seventh Cavalry could be concentrated at Fort Abraham Lincoln the season became so inclement – a great number of men being badly frost–bitten in reaching the fort – and the snow so deep that it was thought advisable to abandon the expedition until later in the season. The impracticability of operations against these Indians from Fort Lincoln, on the Missouri River, during the existence of the wild storms of Dakota in the early spring, became pretty well settled by the result already experienced, and satisfied me that the recommendation for the establishment of the two military posts in what is known as the Yellowstone country, made in my last annual report and in my report of 1874, in anticipation of hostilities with the Sioux, was the only view to take of this subject which promised undoubted success, and I again renewed my solicitations for the establishment of the posts at the mouth of Tongue River and the Big Horn. This advice, if adopted, would have given us abundant supplies at convenient points, to operate in the very heart of the country from whence all our troubles came.

For some years it had been apparent to me that the marauding bands who lived in this country, and who formed a nucleus for all the dissatisfied and unmanageable Indians at the Missouri River, Red Cloud and Spotted Tail agencies, would have to be subjugated and made to feel the power of the Government; and as a means to this end I recommended the occupation of the country in which these hostiles roamed by two permanent and large military posts. Had my advice been taken, there would have been no war. These posts, would not only have been the means of preventing the assembling of Indians in large bodies in that great buffalo region, but they would have given us depots of supplies and shelter for troops that could, on account of the short distances from these supplies, operate at any season of the year. In addition to these advantages, the troops would have become familiar with the haunts of the Indians, learned the country thoroughly, and would not have been obliged, as they afterward were, to operate blindly in an almost totally unknown region, comprising an area of almost ninety thousand square miles.

Early in the spring, as no change had then been made in the orders, Generals Terry and Crook made preparations to resume the operations, General Crook concentrating at Fort Fetterman fifteen companies of cavalry and five companies of infantry; and on May 29 he marched from that point for Goose Creek, and established his supply camp there on the 8th of June.

From this camp he moved out toward the headwaters of the Rosebud, on the morning of the 13th of June, and on the 17th his scouts discovered the Indians in large numbers about forty miles north of Goose Creek. A few minutes after this information was received, the command was attacked with considerable desperation. The Indians displayed strong force at all points, and contested the ground with tenacity which proved they were fighting for time to get their village away. The command finally drove them off, with a loss of 13 Indians killed, left on the field; and on our side, of 9 men killed, one officer and 23 men wounded. The victory was barren of results, however, as, on account of his wounded and a lack of rations for his troops, General Crook was unable to pursue the enemy. The next day he returned to his supply camp on Goose Creek and awaited re–enforcements and supplies, considering himself too weak to make any movement until additional troops reached him.

It now became apparent that he had not only Crazy Horse and his small band to contend against, but that the hostile force had been augmented by large numbers of the young warriors from the agencies along the Missouri River and the Red Cloud and Spotted Tail agencies in Nebraska, and that the Indian agents at these agencies had concealed the fact of the departure of these warriors; and that, in most cases, they continued to issue rations as though they were present. I had feared such a movement from the agencies, and early in May had asked that power should be given to the military to exercise supervisory control over the agencies and keep in all who were then there and all out who were then out and hostile, but no attention was paid to this representation.

General Terry concentrated at Fort Lincoln the Seventh Cavalry, three Gatling guns, and six companies of infantry, and on the 17th of May marched from that post for the mouth of the Powder River, where he arrived and established his supply camp on the 7th of June. From this point, Major Marcus A. Reno, Seventh Cavalry, with six companies of that regiment, scouted up the Powder River to its forks, across the country to the Rosebud, and down the Rosebud to its mouth. In the mean time, General Terry moved with his main forces up the south bank of the Yellowstone and formed a junction with Col. John Gibbon's command, consisting of four companies Second Cavalry and six companies of the Seventh Infantry, that had marched from Fort Ellis, in Montana, to the mouth of the Rosebud.

During Major Reno's scout a large Indian trail was discovered leading up the Rosebud, but as his orders did not contemplate an attack with his small force, it was only followed a sufficient distance to enable him to definitely locate the Indians in the vicinity of the Little Big Horn River. He then returned to the mouth of the Rosebud.

General Terry, now pretty well informed of the locality of the Indians, directed Lieut. Col. George A. Custer to move with the Seventh Cavalry up the Rosebud until he struck the trail discovered by Major Reno, with instructions that he should not follow it directly to the Little Big Horn, but that he should send scouts over it and keep his main force farther south, to prevent the Indians from slipping in between himself and the mountains. He was also to examine the headwaters of Tullock's Creek as he passed it, and send word to General Terry of what he found there.

Custer moved on the 22d of June, following the trail as soon as he struck it, and after marching about 125 miles from the place of starting, attacked the Indians in their village on the west bank of the Little Big Horn, and about 30 miles above its mouth, between 10 and 12 o'clock on the morning of the 25th of June. In the mean time General Terry moved up the Yellowstone River with Colonel Gibbon's column, arriving at the mouth of the Little Big Horn on June 26.

The attack of General Custer proved disastrous, resulting in the destruction of himself, twelve officers, and five companies of the Seventh Cavalry, and in a heavy loss in killed and wounded to the detachment commanded by Major Reno, whose command of three companies was saved from annihilation by the timely arrival of Major Benteen with four companies, and by entrenching its position on an eminence on the east bank of the river. His position at this point was soon completely enveloped by the Indians, who kept up a constant fire until the approach of General Terry with Gibbon's column, on the evening of June 26.

As much has been said in regard to the misfortune that occurred to General Custer and the portion of his regiment under his immediate command in this action, I wish to express the conviction I have arrived at concerning it. From all the information that has reached me, I am led to believe that the Indians were not aware of the proximity of Custer until he had arrived within about eight or nine miles of their village, and that then their scouts who carried the intelligence back to the valley were so closely followed up by Custer that he arrived on the summit of the divide overlooking the upper portion of the village almost as soon as the scouts reached it. As soon as the news was given, the Indians began to strike their lodges and get their women and children out of the way, a movement they always make under such circumstances. Custer, seeing this, believed the village would escape him if he awaited the arrival of the four companies of his regiment still some miles in his rear. Only about 75 or 100 lodges or tepees could be seen from the summit or divide, and this probably deceived him as to the extent of the village. He therefore directed Major Reno with three companies to cross the river and charge the village, while he with the remaining five companies would gallop down the east bank of the river, behind the bluff, and cut off the retreat of the Indians. Reno crossed and attacked gallantly with his three companies, about 110 men, but the warriors, leaving the women to strike the lodges, fell on Reno's handful of men and drove them back to and over the river with severe loss. About this time Custer reached a point about 3 1/2 or 4 miles down the river, but instead of finding a village of 75 or 100 lodges, he found one of perhaps from 1,500 to 2,000, and swarming with warriors, who brought him to a halt. This, I think, was the first intimation the Indians had of Custer's approach to cut them off, for they at once left Reno and concentrated to meet the new danger. The point where Custer reached the river, on the opposite side of which was the village, was broken into choppy ravines, and the Indians crossing from Reno got between the two commands, and as Custer could not return, he fell back over the broken ground with his tired men and tired horses, (they had ridden about seventy miles with but few halts,) and became, I am afraid, an easy prey to the enemy. Their wild savage yells, overwhelming numbers, and frightening war paraphernalia made it as much as each trooper could do to take care of his horse, thus endangering his own safety and efficiency. If Custer could have reached any position susceptible of defense, he could have defended himself, but none offered itself in the choppy and broken ravines over which he had to pass, and he and his command were lost without leaving any one to tell the tale. As soon as Custer and his gallant officers and men were exterminated, and the scenes of mutilation by the squaws commenced, the warriors returned to renew the attack upon Reno, but he had been joined by Captain Benteen and the four companies of the regiment that were behind when the original attack took place, and the best use had been made of the respite given by the attack on Custer to entrench their position. Reno's command was thus enabled to repulse every attack made by the Indians, until relieved by General Terry on the morning of the 27th, as before mentioned.

Had the Seventh Cavalry been kept together, it is my belief it would have been able to handle the Indians on the Little Big Horn, and under any circumstances it could have at least defended itself; but, separated as it was into three distinct detachments, the Indians had largely the advantage, in addition to their overwhelming numbers. If Custer had not come upon the village so suddenly, the warriors would have gone to meet him, in order to give time to the women and children to get out of the way, as they did with Crook only a few days before, and there would have been, as with Crook, what might be designated a rear–guard fight, a fight to get their valuables out of the way, or, in other words, to cover the escape of their women, children, and lodges.

After the disaster to poor Custer, General Terry withdrew his command to the mouth of the Big Horn, there to refit and await re–enforcements. Additional troops were at once put in motion for General Terry's command, as had already been done for General Crook's, but, as these additional troops had to be collected from all the various stations on the frontier, some of them very remote from railroads, considerable time was consumed before their arrival. During this period the bands which had broken off from the main body of hostiles and the young men at the agencies continued their old and well–known methods of warfare – stealing horses on the frontier and killing small parties of citizens; while the constant communications by the hostiles with Indians at the agencies made it evident that supplies of food and ammunition were being received. To prevent this, I had deemed it necessary that the military should control the agencies, and, as before mentioned, on the 29th of May requested that the Interior Department would so co–operate with the military as to enable us to carry out the policy of arresting, disarming, and dismounting such of the hostiles as made their appearance at the agencies. On July 18 I renewed this request, and on the 22d the honorable Secretary of the Interior authorized the military to assume control of all the agencies in the Sioux country, but it was too late.

I at once directed the commanding officers at Camps Robinson and Sheridan to take possession at Red Cloud and Spotted Tail agencies, and sent Colonel Mackenzie to Red Cloud with a sufficient force to arrest any hostiles who might come in, and to count and enroll the Indians. A careful count was made by September 1, and it was found that those at Red Cloud numbered 4,760, nearly one–half less than had been reported by the agent. The count at Spotted Tail's agency was less than 5,000, whereas nearly double that number was alleged to be present at their agency, and were issued to.

Troops were also sent to occupy the Missouri River agencies to accomplish the same purposes, and the number of Indians found present was less from one–half to one–third than was reported present and issued to by the agents. It was then easy to see where the small bands, originally out and on whom war was made, got their strength from, as well as their supplies.

Congress having at last passed the bill, late in the session, July 22, authorizing the construction of two posts in the Yellowstone country, preparations were made to build them at once and all the material was prepared as rapidly as possible, but the season had now become so far advanced that it was found impracticable to get this material up the Yellowstone River on account of low water, and the building of them was consequently deferred until next spring, when the work will be speedily done, as the material is now at the mouth of the Yellowstone ready for shipment; but as soon as I found the post could not be built this year, I directed a cantonment to be formed at the mouth of the Tongue River, the place selected for one of the two posts, and a strong garrison to be detailed under the command of Colonel Miles, Fifth Infantry, to occupy it.

On August 3 General Crook had received all the re–enforcements that could be sent him, and all that he wanted, and having received information that the hostiles had moved eastwardly from the Big Horn Mountains, and crossed the Fort C. F. Smith road on the 26th of July, his column moved out on the 5th of August down Tongue River in pursuit. He followed the trail across Powder River and some distance to the east of it, when it separated and became indistinct. He then marched his command southward in the direction of the Black Hills, the command of Captain Mills, Third Cavalry, capturing a village of 35 lodges on the morning of September 17, killing a number of Indians and capturing a few women and children. For the details of this action I respectfully refer to the report of General Crook.

As soon as I learned from General Crook of his contemplated movement to the Black Hills, and the great need of food and clothing for his command, supplies were pushed out from the Red Cloud agency and Fort Laramie to meet him and to reach Custer City before his arrival there.

General Terry, finding that most of his troops would be engaged in the protecting and forwarding of supplies, and in hutting for the winter, and that would be consuming the supplies sent out, broke up his command, sending Colonel Gibbon back to Montana before the extreme cold weather began, and returned to Fort Lincoln with the Seventh Cavalry. From Fort Lincoln he proceeded down the Missouri River with the Seventh to the Standing Rock and Cheyenne River agencies, dismounting and disarming the Indians at these two points – a policy that had been resolved upon as offering unquestionably a final settlement of all further difficulties with the Sioux.

While this was going on, the hostiles attacked the trains carrying supplies to the Tongue River cantonment, and Col. Nelson A. Miles, Fifth Infantry, marched out his command, and, after an engagement on the 21st of October and a successful pursuit, over 400 lodges of the Missouri River Indians surrendered to him, giving hostages for the delivery of men, women, children, ponies, arms, and ammunition at the Cheyenne River agency on the 2d of December; Sitting Bull, with his band of about 30 lodges, escaping to the north, and, no doubt, to the British possessions.

General Crook, after refitting at Custer City, detailed Colonel Merritt, Fifth Cavalry, to make a scout down to the forks of Cheyenne River, and thence in to the Red Cloud agency, where it had been resolved to disarm and dismount the Indians; but before Colonel Merritt's arrival, it was found necessary to direct Colonel Mackenzie, Fourth Cavalry, to perform this duty, and it was successfully accomplished without firing a shot.

With the view of continuing operations during the winter, I had directed the establishment of a cantonment at old Fort Reno, and had ordered that a considerable amount of supplies of forage and rations be sent there, and as soon as the Indians at the Red Cloud agency were dismounted and disarmed, General Crook re–organized a new column to operate from Reno. This column is now in the field, under Colonel Mackenzie, and accompanied by General Crook, and I anticipate the very best results from it.

The surrender of the Indians from the Missouri River agencies to Colonel Miles on the 27th of October, numbering, in men, women, and children at least 2,000, and the escape of Sitting Bull with his small band to the north, leaves now out and hostile only the Northern Cheyenne and the band of Crazy Horse and his allies from the Red Cloud agency, and it is against these Indians that General Crook is now operating, and when these are killed, captured, or surrendered, the Sioux war will be at an end, and I think all future trouble with them, as it is intended to put most of them on foot, and a Sioux on foot is a Sioux warrior no longer.

If the posts on the Yellowstone had been established according to my recommendation, there would have been no war. If the Indian Bureau had turned over to the military the control of the agencies before the troops took the field, as I had represented, it would not have assumed the magnitude that it did. But it seems to have required some disaster like that which happened to Custer before good judgment or common sense could be exercised on this subject.

The operations against these Indians during the summer were the same as summer campaigns against them generally are, and not much success can attend them other than preventing the Indians from accumulating winter supplies and the demoralizing effects that result to the men, women, and children from being constantly harassed, and when winter comes they are but ill–prepared to pass over it safely.

The undersigned has no good evidence to show that Sitting Bull was the leader of the hostile Indians during the summer; on the contrary, it is more than probable he was in that respect quite insignificant, as he has never had but a few followers, and is old, and very much crippled by disease. His reputation was accidental, and I am inclined to believe he is totally unconscious of it, as he never did anything to acquire it. Sitting Bull, as I have said further back in this report, had only 30 or 40 lodges of the Uncpapa band of Sioux, not exceeding 70 warriors. He was an anti–agency Indian – that is, he never came in to any of the agencies, or to any of the councils of his tribe whose agency is at Standing Rock, on the Missouri River; and some of his followers, strange to say, were so wild as to have never seen a white man's face until the past summer. They were hostile out and out, and always had been. When the Interior Department requested the military to commence operations against the hostiles, (which embraced Crazy Horse and his allies and Sitting Bull and his small band,) the request was to "make war on Sitting Bull and other hostile Indians." And the name of Sitting Bull and the word "hostile" became synonymous, and whenever the name "Sitting Bull" was read it was understood by me to mean hostile Indians; and by this confusion, and by the aid of newspaper correspondents, Sitting Bull in person became a great leader, when it is known he has never been more than an insignificant warrior, with a few thieving followers. I believe Crazy Horse's band and the Northern Cheyenne have done nearly all the fighting, especially the Northern Cheyenne and I doubt if there was any special or distinguished leader.

The troops did as well as could be done during the summer, and certainly as well as I expected; for long experience has taught me how difficult it is to catch an Indian in the summer season. They were, however, harassed, and prevented from accumulating supplies for the winter, and no doubt the balance will be caught when the cold weather comes on.

I recommend that the whole Sioux Nation be established on the Missouri River, between Standing Rock and Fort Randall. They can be cheaply fed there, and can be sufficiently isolated to be controlled. To take so many wild Indians to the Indian Territory would be a difficult undertaking at this time, and would, in my opinion, be attended with the worst results to those now there, as well as to the Sioux. They should go gradually, form time to time, and when the Indians there are ready to receive them.

I have been obliged to delay this report to await the report of General Terry, which is not yet in, until I could delay no longer on account of the near approach of the day when Congress meets; and now, when I do submit it, I am obliged to write it here, and have not been able to make it as full as it should be on account of the absence of data now in my office at Chicago.

Very respectfully, your obedient servant,

P. H. SHERIDAN.
Lieutenant–General Commanding

Brig. Gen. E. D. TOWNSEND
Adjutant–General of the Army, Washington, D. C.

---

[1] See John M. Carroll "General Custer and the Battle of the Little Big Horn: The Federal View"

pages 71 – 80. I have corrected spelling as necessary.

Appendix 14

Report of Colonel John Gibbon[1]

HEADQUARTERS DISTRICT OF MONTANA,
Fort Shaw, Montana, October 17, 1876

SIR: I have the honor to submit the following report of the military operations of the troops under my command during the past spring and summer:

In accordance with telegraphic instruction from the brigadier–general commanding the department, five companies of the Seventh Infantry left Fort Shaw on the 17th of March, and proceeded toward Fort Ellis.

The ground was covered with a heavy snow and the roads a mass of mud and slush, but the command made good time and reached Fort Ellis on the 28th, a distance of 183 miles. In the mean time, one company of the Seventh (Clifford's) had been ordered to march from Camp Baker, and the snow being too deep on the direct road to Fort Ellis, Captain Clifford dug his way through snow–drifts to the Missouri River and reached Fort Ellis on the 22d of March. From that point he was instructed by telegraph to proceed as an escort to our supply train as far as the new Crow agency.

The battalion of the Seventh Infantry from Fort Shaw, under command of Captain Freeman, left Fort Ellis on the 30th of March, and on the 1st of April the four companies of the Second Cavalry left the post under command of Captain Thompson. Major Brisbin, although on crutches from rheumatism, and unable to mount a horse, insisted so strongly upon accompanying the expedition that I consented to his going, although he was obliged to travel in an ambulance.

The road over the divide, between Fort Ellis and the Yellowstone River, was in an almost impassable condition, and to add to our difficulties a furious snow–storm set in on the 3d of April, and it was midnight on the 4th before our train succeeded in getting across and reaching Shields River, a distance of thirty miles. From there the cavalry and wagon train was pushed down the river after the infantry, fording the Yellowstone twice, and overtook Captain Freeman's command in camp on the river opposite the new agency on the 7th. On the 8th I proceeded to the agency, 18 miles, held a council with the Crows the next day, and the day after (10th) enlisted 25 of them as scouts. Lieutenant Jacobs having arrived with wagons, our supplies were loaded up to transfer them to the north bank of the Yellowstone.

Clifford's company having left the agency the day before, (9th) on the 11th the train was started in a furious snow–storm which had raged all night, and, pulling for a part of the way through snow two feet deep, reached the point selected for our depot; the command in the mean time having marched there.

Having established the supply camp, and left "A" Company (Logan's) in charge of it, the command resumed the march down the river on the 13th. The ground, however, was very soft, and our heavily–loaded wagons made but slow progress, but after fording the Yellowstone four times we reached the vicinity of Fort Pease on the 20th. The next day I received a dispatch from the department commander to proceed no farther than the mouth of the Big Horn for the present, and placed the command alongside of Fort Pease. On the 23d, Captain Freeman's company was sent back with the wagon train to bring up the supplies; and on the 24th Captain Ball with two companies of the Second Cavalry, was started on a scout to old Fort C. F. Smith. He returned by the way of the Little Big Horn and Tullock's Fork on the 1st of May without having seen any signs of Indians. Captain Freeman, with Logan's company and our train got back on the 8th of May, and on the 10th the march down the river was resumed with the consolidated command, and all our supplies in the train.

Up to the 3d of May we had seen no sign of Indians, but on the morning of that day the ponies of the Crow scouts, which had been carelessly permitted to roam at large, were found to be missing, together with two animals belonging to one of our guides, and the signs demonstrated the fact that a war party had been in our vicinity.

Page 519

On the 14th we went into camp near the Little Porcupine, (Table Creek of Lewis and Clarke,) where we were visited by a terrific storm of hail and rain which rendered the prairies impassable for our wagons and detained us till the 20th. Scouts had been sent out constantly, not only on the north side toward the mouth of Tongue River, but on the south side of the Yellowstone. These reported seeing various war parties of Sioux, and finally the smoke of a camp on the Rosebud about thirty–five miles from us. With the design of striking this camp and surprising it by a night march, I attempted to cross the Yellowstone on the 17th, but that river had become a rapid torrent, and after drowning four of our horses in attempting to get them across, the effort was abandoned. On the 20th, our scouts having reported a large body of Indians moving toward the mouth of the Rosebud with an evident design of crossing the Yellowstone, I moved with the whole of the command, except Kirtland's company, hastily down the river and camped for the night below the mouth of the Rosebud, but saw no Indians, and the next day brought Captain Kirtland's company and the train down to the new position.

On the 23d Lieutenant English, with I Company, Seventh Infantry, and Lieutenant Roe's Company F, Second Cavalry, to accompany it a part of the way, was started back to meet and escort in a contract train, bringing us supplies from Fort Ellis. The morning the escort left (23d) two soldiers and a citizen teamster, while hunting in the hills a few miles from camp, were murdered by Indians, who, however, rapidly disappeared before a scouting party of two companies, under Captain Ball, sent after them. On the 27th I started a dispatch for the department commander down the river in a small boat in charge of Privates Evans and Stewart, Company E, Seventh Infantry, and Scout Williamson, the two soldiers having volunteered for the service; and the next day I received the department commander's dispatch of the 15th instant, directing me to march at once for the stockade above Glendive Creek, cross the Yellowstone, and move out eastward to meet him. Captain Sanno, Seventh Infantry, with two companies – his own and Lieutenant Roe's, Second Cavalry – was at once started, with all our wagons under charge of Lieutenant Jacobs, regimental quartermaster Seventh Infantry, back to lighten the contract train and hurry it forward; and on the 4th of June it reached camp after a rapid march in spite of a furious storm of snow and sleet, which raged all day on the 1st. The next day (5th) the march was resumed down the river, but we were delayed by steep hills and rugged country, and in four days made only 57 miles, which brought us about 17 miles below the mouth of Tongue River. That night (8th) I received by scouts the department commander's dispatch of that day from Powder River, and the next morning met him on the steamboat *Far West* a few miles below our camp. In accordance with his instructions the command was at once prepared to move up the rive again, but a furious rain–storm that afternoon delayed the movement by converting the alkali flats surrounding us into impassable ground. The cavalry, however, got off on the afternoon of the 10th and the infantry the next day, and after a march of 50 miles was again concentrated in camp below the mouth of the Rosebud on the 14th. On the 18th Major Reno, with a force of cavalry, arrived opposite our camp after a scout on Powder, Tongue, and Rosebud Rivers, during which he reported he had seen no Indians, and the next day he proceeded down the river.

A cavalry scout up the river having reported the side streams almost impassable, by reason of floods from recent rains, I started Captain Freeman with three companies of infantry on the 21st, up the road to build bridges. General Terry reaching the camp by steamer shortly afterward, the whole command was started up the river. I, at his request, accompanied him on the *Far West*, for the purpose of conferring with Lieutenant–Colonel Custer, who reached a point on the opposite side of the river with the whole of the Seventh Cavalry that afternoon.

That evening the plan of operations was agreed upon. Lieutenant–Colonel Custer, with the Seventh Cavalry, was to proceed up the Rosebud till he struck an Indian trail, discovered during Major Reno's scout. As my scouts had recently reported smoke on the Little Big Horn, the presence of an Indian camp some distance up that stream was inferred.

Lieutenant–Colonel Custer was instructed to keep constantly feeling toward his left, well up toward the mountains, so as to prevent the Indians escaping in that direction, and to strike the Little Big Horn, if possible, above (south of) the supposed location of the camp, while my command was to march up the Yellowstone to the mouth of the Big Horn, there to be ferried across by the steamer, then to move up the Big Horn to the mouth of the Little Big Horn, and up that stream, with the hope of getting the camp between the two forces. As it would take my command three days to reach the mouth of the Big Horn, and probably a day to cross it over the Yellowstone, besides two more to reach the mouth of the Little Big Horn, and Lieutenant–Colonel Custer had the shorter line over which to operate, the department commander strongly impressed upon him the propriety of not pressing his march too rapidly. He got off with his regiment at 12 o'clock the next day, (22d,) three Gatling guns, under Lieutenant Low, Twentieth Infantry, being detached from his regiment and sent to join my command. The steamer got away at 4 o'clock that day, and reached Fort Pease early on the morning of the 24th. My command, except the train and Captain Kirtland's company, (B, Seventh Infantry,) being at once ferried across, was, that evening, moved out to the crossing of Tullock's Fork. I did not accompany it, and General Terry took command of the troops in person. The next day the steamer entered the mouth of the Big Horn and proceeded up that stream.

The next morning early, (26th,) I left the *Far West* and overtook the infantry portion of the command, General Terry having made a night march with the cavalry and Gatling guns, and later in the day that portion of the command was overtaken on a high ridge overlooking the valley of the Little Big Horn near its mouth, where, by direction of General Terry, I resumed command of my troops. Shortly afterward our scouts brought in news that they had encountered some Indians, and, giving chase, had run them across the Big Horn. They had dropped articles in their flight which proved them to be Crows, assigned to duty with Lieutenant–Colonel Custer's command. They, having discovered that their pursuers belonged to their own tribe, refused to come back, and called across the river that Custer's command had been entirely destroyed by the Sioux, who were chasing the soldiers all over the country and killing them. We now pushed up the valley of the Little Big Horn as rapidly as the men could march, large fires being seen in the distance. Efforts were made to communicate with Lieutenant–Colonel Custer by scouts, but our Crow interpreter deserted and took the Crows with him, and two attempts made by white men to precede the command with dispatches failed, the scouts in both cases running into Indians. As we proceeded up the valley the fires increased in number and volume, giving rise to the impression that Custer had captured the camp and destroyed it. The Indians, who late in the afternoon remained in sight on the hills in front of us, rather militated against the supposition, however, and after marching until dark we halted and bivouacked on the prairie.

The next morning the march was resumed and after proceeding about 3 miles we came in sight of a large deserted Indian camp, in which two tepees were still standing, and these were found to contain the dead bodies of Indians. Many lodge poles were still standing, and the quantity of property scattered about testified to the hasty departure of the Indians. Our scouts reported only a few scattering horsemen in sight on the distant hills. We continued to move rapidly forward, still uncertain as to the fate of Custer's command, Captain Ball's company about a mile in advance. While passing through the Indian camp a report reached me from our scouts in the hills to the north of the river that a large number of bodies of white men had been discovered, and shortly afterward Lieutenant Bradley came in with the information that he had counted 194 bodies of dead soldiers. All doubt that a serious disaster had happened to Lieutenant–Colonel Custer's command now vanished, and the march was continued under the uncertainty as to whether we were going to rescue the survivors or to battle with the enemy who had annihilated him. At length we caught sight of a number of animals congregated upon the slope of a distant hill, and on a point nearer to us three horsemen were evidently watching us. After Captain Ball's company had passed them these cautiously approached us, our troops being in pain sight and marching in two columns abreast of each other. At length, being convinced we were friends, they came forward more rapidly and announced that the Seventh Cavalry had been cut to pieces and the remnant, under Major Reno, were entrenched in the bluffs close by. Communication was now soon opened with Major Reno. His command was found entrenched upon the tops of several small ridges, their dead and living horses lying about them, with some fifty wounded men lying on the hot, dusty hill–tops, where, until about 6 o'clock on the evening before, they had been unable to obtain any water except at the imminent risk of life. We were informed that in this spot they had been surrounded by overwhelming numbers of Indians from the close of Major Reno's charge on the 25th (about 2 1/2 p. m.) until about 6 p. m. the next day, the Indians pouring upon them all that time a very close and almost continuous fire from the neighboring ridges, some of which commanded the position in reverse. The first inquiry made was if General Custer was with us, and the command appeared to know nothing of the fate of himself and that portion of his command immediately with him until we informed them of it. As described to us, the whole movement of the Indians when they abandoned their camp was visible from Major Reno's position, and the last portion disappeared in the hills to the south just at dusk on the 26th, when my command was 8 3/4 miles from Major Reno's position.

My command was at once placed in camp, and arrangements made to bring down and properly care for the suffering wounded. This was effected by night–fall. The next day, 28th, Captain Ball, Second Cavalry, was sent out with his company, and followed the main trail some ten or twelve miles. He found that it led directly south toward the Big Horn Mountains, and in returning to camp he discovered a large fresh trail leading down the Little Big Horn toward the scene of the battle. The day was occupied in burying the dead and in constructing litters for the wounded. In the performance of this latter duty Lieut. G. C. Doane, Second Cavalry, was detailed to devise mule litters, and with the very crudest material, (cottonwood poles, raw–hide, and ropes,) made some six or eight. But the mules, when attached to them, proved so intractable that the attempt was abandoned, and hand litters of lodge poles and canvas constructed, with these, and the men to carry them, the command left camp at sunset on that day. The movement, however, was exceedingly slow and tedious. The whole command, afterward assisted by two companies of the Seventh Cavalry, was used by relays, and it was long past midnight when camp was reached, at a distance of four and one–half miles.

The next day (29th) was occupied in destroying the large quantity of property abandoned by the Indians in their hasty flight. An immense number of lodge poles, robes, and dressed skins, pots, kettles, cups, pans, axes, and shovels, were found scattered through the camp and along the trail followed by the Indians. Our progress with the hand litters having proved so exceedingly slow and tedious Lieutenant Doane was called upon to continue the construction of the mule litters, and by selecting from all the pack mules in the command he succeeded in obtaining fifty gentle enough for the service, and in constructing a sufficient number of litters to carry all the wounded. With these a second start was made at 6 p. m., with the expectation of making a short march. But the litters worked so admirably as to call forth the most unbounded commendation in praise of the skill and energy displayed by Lieutenant Doane, and after proceeding a few miles information was received by courier that the *Far West* was waiting for us at the mouth of the Little Big Horn. The department commander therefore decided to continue the march with the view of placing the wounded in comfort and rest as soon as possible. The march was then resumed, but the night proved dark and stormy and the road down from the plateau to the steamer rough and obscure, so that it was two o'clock on the morning of the 30th before the wounded were safely housed on board the boat. This was done without a single accident of any moment, and I desire to invite special attention to the invaluable services of Lieutenant Doane in the construction of the requisite litters in so short a time out of the rude material of clumsy poles, horse raw–hide, and refractory mules. But for his energy, skill, and confidence our suffering wounded would probably have been several days longer on the road.

The *Far West* left that day for the mouth of the Big Horn, which point I reached with the command, after a two days' march, on the 2d of July. The whole command was then ferried across the Yellowstone River and placed in camp. Here it remained until the 27th, when, in obedience to the orders of General Terry, it was transferred down the river to the new depot at the mouth of the Rosebud, and on the 3d of August my portion of it was ferried across the Yellowstone, preparatory to the movement up the Rosebud.

The troops in the field were now re–organized, and I was assigned to the command of the four battalions of infantry belonging to the Fifth, Sixth, Seventh, and twenty–second Infantry. On the 8th the command started up the Rosebud, but the road was difficult, required a great deal of work, and our progress was slow.

On the 10th we encountered General Crook's command coming down, and the next day the united commands started with pack mules on the Indian trail which General Crook was following, the battalion of the Fifth Infantry being sent back to escort our supply train and scout the river to prevent the Indians crossing to the north of it. In the midst of very heavy rain the command moved across to Tongue River, down that and across to Powder River, and down that to its mouth, which it reached on the 17th. On the 25th my command, further reduced by the detachment of the Sixth Infantry, started up Powder River again, but the following day, on information that the Indians were below us, on the Yellowstone, we retraced our steps, and marched across the country to a point on the river near O'Fallon's Creek, and the day following, 27th, were ferried across the Yellowstone by steamer. That night the whole command made a night march to the north, entering upon an almost entirely unknown country without guides, where, for the next four days, our movements were hampered by the necessity for marching toward the water pools, which had to be first sought for. Our general course, however, was northward, and scouting parties sent across the main divide and down the Yellowstone having demonstrated that no large bodies of Indians had made their way north, toward the Fort Peck agency, the command came in again to the Yellowstone, near Glendive Creek, on the 31st.

On the 5th of September I received orders for my command to return to its station in Montana.

Starting on the 6th, we reached our wagon train a few miles above the mouth of powder River, 81 miles, on the 9th, and placing our pack mules in harness, resumed the march the next day. On the 12th we reached the mouth of Tongue River, and on the 17th passed Fort Pease. On our arrival at the mouth of Big Timber, on the 26th, the command was divided, the cavalry companies under Captain Ball marching to Fort Ellis, and the infantry to Camp Baker, via the forks of the Muscleshell. The cavalry reached Fort Ellis on the 29th of September, and the five companies of the Seventh Infantry arrived at Fort Shaw on the 6th instant, having left Company E (Clifford's) at Camp Baker on the 2d. I preceded the cavalry into Fort Ellis, and, having arranged for the muster out and payment of the Crow scouts, returned to this post on the 4th instant.

It gives me great pleasure to testify to the cheerful manner in which the whole command performed the long marches and arduous duties of the campaign. Starting out in the depths of winter, with the expectation of an absence of two or three months, they submitted to the tedious delays, long marches, and exposures of an unprecedentedly wet and cold season during six months with a soldierly cheerfulness worthy of the highest praise

In concluding this report I beg leave to submit the following suggestions:

It became evident during the campaign that we were attempting to carry on operations in an extensive region of something like four or five hundred miles square with inadequate means. Had we been called upon to operate against only the Indians known to be hostile, any one of the three columns sent against them would have been amply sufficient to cope with any force likely to be brought against it; but when the hostile body was largely re–enforced by accessions from the various agencies where the malcontents were doubtless in many cases driven to desperation by starvation and the heartless frauds perpetrated upon them, the problem became less simple, and when these various bands succeeded in finding a leader who possessed the tact, courage, and ability to concentrate and keep together so large a force, it was only a question of time as to when one or other of the exterior columns would meet with a check from the overwhelming numbers of the interior body. The first information we had of the force and strategy opposed to us was the check given to Custer's column, resulting in a disaster which might have been worse but for the timely arrival of General Terry's other column.

The inadequate means at the disposal of the troops became painfully apparent at an early day. Operating on one bank of a deep and rapid stream for a distance of several hundred miles, my column was entirely without the means of crossing to the other bank to strike exposed camps of the hostile bands.

Encumbered with heavily loaded wagon trains, our movements were necessarily slow, and when we did cut loose from these our only means of transporting supplies were the mules taken from the teams, and unbroken to packs, unsuitable pack saddles, and inexperienced soldiers as packers. These latter soon learned to do their part tolerably well, but at the expense of the poor animals, whose festering sores after a few days' marching appealed not only to feelings of humanity, but demonstrated the false economy of the course pursued.

At the end of one scout with pack mules most of our animals had to be replaced by others from the train, and at the end of the campaign many of them were in anything but a serviceable condition for either pack or draught purposes. The contrast between the mobility of our force and that of General Crook's was very marked, especially for rapid movements. General Crook's well organized pack train, with trained mules and its corps of competent packers, moved almost independently of the column of troops, and as fast as they could move. His ranks were not depleted by drafts to take charge of the packs and animals, for each mule faithfully followed the sound of the leader's bell and needed no other guide, and his pack mules were neither worn out nor torn to pieces by bad saddles and worse packing.

In addition to our other wants, we were entirely devoid of any proper means for the transportation of sick or wounded. This, with a well organized pack train, was comparatively easy. As it was, a few wounded men were all-sufficient to cripple, for offensive operations, a large body of troops; for in savage warfare to leave one's wounded behind is out of the question.

Maps of the route passed over by the command will be forwarded as soon as they can be completed. The country visited by the troops is by no means the desert it has been frequently represented. There is, of course, a great deal of barren, worthless land, but there is also much land in the valleys susceptible of cultivation, and an immense region of good grazing country which will in time be available for stock raising. Even where from the valleys the appearance of the so-called "bad lands" was most forbidding, we found on the plateau above excellent grass in the greatest abundance covering the country for great distance. This was particularly noticeable in the region north of Powder River, between the Yellowstone and Missouri Rivers, and along the Tongue and Rosebud and the country between the two. The country along the Little Big Horn is also a fine grass country, and along the Big Horn itself immense valleys of fine grass extend.

During the summer's operations the cavalry marched nearly 1,500 miles, and the infantry nearly 1,700, besides some 900 miles by portions of the cavalry and 500 miles by portions of the infantry in scouting and escort duty.

I am, sir, very respectfully, your obedient servant,

JOHN GIBBON,
Colonel Seventh Infantry, Commanding District.

Maj. GEO D. RUGGLES,
Assistant Adjutant–General, Department of Dakota.

---

[1] See John M. Carroll "General Custer and the Battle of the Little Big Horn: The Federal View"

pages 97 – 102. I have corrected spelling as necessary.

Appendix 15

Annual Report of General Crook for 1876[1]

HEADQUARTERS DISTRICT OF THE PLATTE,
Omaha, Nebr., September 25, 1876

SIR: At the date for my annual report for 1875, September 15, the settlers along the line of the Pacific Railroad and in Wyoming, Nebraska, and Colorado, were very much excited and exasperated by the repeated incursions made upon them by Indians coming from the north, and although many of the trails of stolen stock ran directly upon the Sioux reservation, the agency Indians always asserted that the depredations were committed by certain hostile bands under Crazy Horse, Sitting Bull, and other outlaw chiefs.

These bands roamed over a vast extent of country, making the agencies their base of supplies, their recruiting and ordnance depots, and were so closely connected by intermarriage, interest, and common cause with the agency Indians that it was difficult to determine where the line of the peaceably disposed ceased and the hostile commenced.

In fact it was well known that the treaty of 1868 had been regarded by the Indians as an instrument binding on us but not binding on them.

On the part of the Government, notwithstanding the utter disregard by the Sioux of the terms of the treaty, stringent orders, enforced by military power, had been issued prohibiting settlers from trespassing upon the country known as the Black Hills.

The people of the country, against whom the provisions of the treaty were so rigidly enforced, naturally complained that if they were required to observe this treaty some effort should be made to compel the Indians to observe it likewise.

Although in the treaty of 1868, the Indians expressly agree –

> *"3d. That they will not attack any persons at home, or traveling, nor molest or disturb any wagon trains, coaches, mules, or cattle belonging to the people of the United States, or to persons friendly therewith.*

> *"4th. That they will never capture or carry off from the settlements white women or children.*

> *"5th. That they will never kill or scalp white men, nor attempt to do them harm."*

It is notorious that, from the date of the treaty to the present, there has been no time that the settlers were free from the very offenses laid down in the sentences quoted.

Indians have, without interruption, attacked persons at home, murdered and scalped them, stolen their stock; in fact, violated every leading feature in the treaty.

Indeed, so great were their depredations on the stock belonging to the settlers that at certain times they have not had sufficient horses to do their ordinary farming work, all the horses being concentrated on the Sioux reservation, or among the bands which owe allegiance to what is called the Sioux Nation.

In the winter months these renegade bands dwindle down to a comparatively small number, while in summer they are recruited by restless spirits from the different reservations, attracted by the opportunity to plunder the frontiersmen, so that by midsummer they become augmented from small bands of one hundred to thousands.

Sitting Bull's band has been regarded by the white people and Indians as renegades, and when it was decided by the Interior Department that they should no longer be permitted to roam at large, but be required to come in and settle down upon the reservation set apart for them, messengers were dispatched to them setting forth these facts, and that from and after a certain time, unless they came in upon the reservation, they would be regarded and treated as hostile.

The time having expired, and the Indians failing to embrace the terms offered by the Government, by direction of the Lieutenant–General commanding I commenced preparations for a campaign against these bands.

I believe that the most successful campaign, though of course involving the most hardship, would be that prosecuted in winter, or, at least, in the early spring months. So, in the latter end of February, 1876, I took the field, with Fort Fetterman as the base.

Of the movements which transpired during this campaign, the surprise and destruction of the village of Crazy Horse on Powder River, and the subsequent failure of the command to fully profit by the success thus far obtained, reference may be had to my report of May 7, 1876, copy herewith, marked "A."

My second expedition was organized in May, and marched from Fort Fetterman on May 29.

Of the movements which transpired during this campaign, up to and including the fight on the Rosebud, reference may be had to my report of June 20, herewith enclosed, marked "B."

Knowing as I do, from personal knowledge, the large numbers of Indians in other localities who require the restraining influence of troops, I have carefully refrained from embarrassing the division commander by calls for re–enforcements. I have rather left that matter entirely to him, satisfied that he understood the necessities of the case, and would send me troops as fast and as early as he could get them. I mention this simply from the fact that there has been much of an unpleasant nature said in regard to the matter. I repeat that I did not ask for re–enforcements because I felt that we were abundantly able to take care of ourselves until they came, and that when they could be sent they would be; and they were.

The troops assigned to my command having reached me, the second movement of this expedition commenced on the morning of August 5, from our camp on Tongue River, Wyoming Territory.

For the details of this movement, reference may be had to my expedition report, copy enclosed, and marked "C."

The expedition reached the mining camp of Deadwood, Dakota, on the 16th instant, where our temporary necessities were supplied by purchase.

The march from the head of Heart River to this point was one of unusual hardship, and tested the endurance of the command to its fullest extent.

During the campaign, from May 29 to this date, our losses, embracing those in the engagements on Tongue River, Rosebud, and Slim buttes, have been but twelve killed, thirty–two wounded, (most of whom have since been returned to duty,) one death by accident, and one by disease.

Of the difficulties with which we have had to contend, it may be well to remark that when the Sioux Indian was armed with a bow and arrow he was more formidable, fighting as he does most of the time on horseback, than when he got the old fashioned muzzle loading rifle. But when he came into possession of the breech loader and metallic cartridge, which allows him to load and fire from his horse with perfect ease, he became at once ten thousand times more formidable.

With the improved arms, I have seen our friendly Indians, riding at full speed, shoot and kill a wolf, also on the run, while it is a rare thing that our troops can hit an Indian on horseback, though the soldier may be on his feet at the time. The Sioux is a cavalry soldier from the time he has intelligence enough to ride a horse or fire a gun. If he wishes to dismount, his hardy pony, educated by long usage, will graze around near where he has been left, ready when his master wants to mount either to move forward or escape.

Even with their lodges and families, they can move at the rate of fifty miles per day. They are perfectly familiar with the country; have their spies and hunting parties out all the time at distances of from twenty to fifty miles each way from their villages; know the number and movements of all the troops that may be operating against them, just about what they can probably do, and hence can choose their own times and places of conflict, or avoid it altogether.

At the fight on the Rosebud, June 17, the number of our troops was less than one thousand, and within eight days after that the same Indians we there fought met and defeated a column of troops of nearly the same size as ours, killing and wounding over three hundred, including the gallant commander, General Custer himself.

I invite attention to the fact that in this engagement my troops beat these Indians on a field of their own choosing, and drove them in utter rout from it, as far as the proper care of my wounded and prudence would justify. Subsequent events proved beyond dispute what would have been the fate of the command had the pursuit been continued beyond what judgment dictated.

The occupation by settlers of the Black Hills country had nothing to do with the hostilities which have been in progress. In fact, by the continuous violations by these Indians of the treaty referred to, the settlers were furnished with at least a reasonable excuse for such occupation, in that a treaty so long and persistently violated by the Indians themselves should not be quoted as a valid instrument for the preventing of such occupation. Since the occupation of the Black Hills there has not been any greater number of depredations committed by the Indians than previous to such occupation; in truth, the people who have gone to the Hills have not suffered any more and probably not as much from Indians as they would had they remained at their homes along the border.

The Sioux Nation numbers many thousands of warriors, and they have been encouraged in their insolent, overbearing conduct by the fact that those who participated in the wholesale massacre of the innocent people in Minnesota during the brief period that preceded their removal to their present location, never received adequate punishment therefor.

Following hard upon and as the apparent result of that horrible affair, the massacre of over eighty officers and men of the Army at Fort Phil Kearney, the Government abandoned three of its military posts and made a treaty of unparalleled liberality with the perpetrators of these crimes, against whom any other nation would have prosecuted a vigorous war. Since that time the reservations, instead of being the abode of loyal Indians, holding the terms of their agreement sacred, have been nothing but nests of disloyalty to their treaties and the Government, and scourges to the people whose misfortune it has been to be within the reach of the endurance of their ponies.

And in this connection, I regret to say, they have been materially aided by subagents who have disgraced a bureau established for the propagation of peace and good–will to man.

What is the loyal condition of mind of a lot of savages who will not allow the folds of the flag of the country to float over the very sugar, coffee, and beef they are kind enough to accept at the hands of the nation to which they have thus far dictated their own terms?

Such has been the condition of things at the Red Cloud agency.

The agents have informed us that the hoisting of a flag over the agency or a persistence in the determination to find by actual count the number ŏf warriors out on the war–path would result in their massacring all the people there. When, therefore, the present campaign was inaugurated against the hostile bands it was impossible to find out what force we should probably meet. It has transpired that they could and did re–enforce the hostiles by thousands of warriors. If, therefore, by the placing of these agencies under control of the military, and insisting upon the points not heretofore required, any portion of those ostensibly peaceable Indians go out, I submit that it will be better than a doubtful loyalty, as we shall know something about what we have to encounter.

The nature of the duties of the department commander have required me to be absent from headquarters much of the time, and the duties of Col. R. Williams, assistant adjutant general, Maj. J. P. Hawkins, chief commissary of subsistence, and Maj. M. I. Ludington, chief quartermaster, have been complicated not only by this absence but by the changing phases of the campaign from time to time.

It gives me pleasure to be able to say that they have discharged their duties in the most able and satisfactory manner, and I am under obligations to them therefor.

Capt. J. V. Furey, assistant quartermaster, who has been field quartermaster for me this summer and fall, has had a multitude of duties not properly belonging to him devolving upon him, while at the same time he has been performing the onerous duties pertaining to his department. He has at times been thrown upon his own responsibility in situations not only involving the safety of his trains and our supplies, but the future of the entire command itself. He has performed all these duties with ability and a zeal that merits the highest commendation.

I am also under obligations to the other staff officers on duty at department headquarters, to the officers of my personal staff, and the officers on duty with my headquarters in the field. For details of the affairs of the several staff departments, I refer to copies of their several reports, enclosed, and marked, respectively, D, E, F, G, H, I, and K.

I have the honor to be, very respectfully, your obedient servant,

GEORGE CROOK,
Brigadier–General, U. S. A., Commanding .

ASSISTANT ADJUTANT GENERAL,
Military Division of the Missouri, Chicago, Ill.

A. – Subreport of General Crook[2]

HEADQUARTERS DEPARTMENT OF THE PLATTE,
Omaha, Nebr., May 7, 1876.

SIR: For a long time it has been the opinion of well–informed men that the principal source of all the depredations committed by Indians along the line of the Union Pacific Railroad has been in the camps of certain hostile bands of renegade Sioux, Cheyenne, and other tribes, who have roamed over the section known as the Powder, Big Horn, and Yellowstone country.

Having the run and many of the privileges of all the reservations, were those of these tribes who are supposed to be at peace are located, and enjoying immunity from any restraint upon their movements, they have been able to procure arms and ammunition, and when any important raid was contemplated, re–enforcements from the restless young warriors on these reservations, thus inflicting incalculable damage to the settlements upon which their raids have fallen.

To correct this and remove the principal cause, the Interior Department caused these hostile bands to be notified that they must come in upon the reservations set apart for them by a certain date, January 31, current year, or, thereafter be considered and treated as hostile.

The date up to which they were allowed to accomplish this movement having arrived, and the bands notified having treated the summons with the utmost contempt, acting under the instructions of the Lieutenant–General commanding, I commenced operations against them in March with a detachment of troops known as the Big Horn expedition.

The object of this expedition was to move, during the inclement season, by forced marches, carrying by pack animals the most meager supplies, secretly and expeditiously surprise the hostile bands, and, if possible, chastise them before spring fairly opened, and they could receive, as they always do in summer, re–enforcements from the reservations; the number of hostiles being largely augmented in summer, while in winter the number is comparatively small.

The campaign was, up to the moment our troops entered the large camp on the Powder River, on the 17th of March, a perfect success; the Indians were surprised, the troops had their camp and about 800 ponies before the Indians were aware of their presence, or even proximity.

Of the mismanagement, if not worse, that characterized the actions of portions of the command during the skirmish that followed, and its movements for the following twenty–four hours, it is unnecessary to speak, as they have been made the subject of serious charges against several officers, notably the immediate commander of the troops, Col. J. J. Reynolds, Third Cavalry.

The failures, however, may be summed up thus:

1st. A failure on the part of portions of the command to properly support the first attack.

2d. A failure to make a vigorous and persistent attack with the whole command.

3d. A failure to secure the provisions that were captured for the use of the troops, instead of destroying them.

4th. And most disastrous of all, a failure to properly secure and take care of the horses and ponies captured, nearly all of which again fell into the hands of the Indians the following morning.

The successes many be summed up thus:

1st. A complete surprise of the Indians.

2d. The entire destruction of their village, with their camp equipage, and large quantities of ammunition.

The undersigned accompanied the expedition, not as its immediate commander, but in his capacity of department commander, for several reasons, chief of which may be mentioned that it had been impressed upon him, and he had almost come to believe, that operations against these Indians were impossible in the rigors of the climate during the winter and early spring, and he wished to demonstrate by personal experience whether this was so or not.

When the attacking column was sent to surprise the village, the department commander, having given the immediate commander ample instructions as to his wishes, did not accompany it, but remained with the train–guard, to the end that the command might not be embarrassed by any division or appearance of such on the field, and the commander himself might feel free from all embarrassment that he might otherwise feel if the department commander were present; my intention being to take the horses and ponies, which I was certain we should capture, and from them remount my command, and with the supplies we captured push on and find whatever other force there might be.

The failure, therefore, to properly secure the captured horses rendered a further prosecution of the campaign, at this time abortive, and the expedition returned, reaching Fort Fetterman on the 26th of March.

Attention is respectfully invited to copies of the report of Colonel Reynolds, commanding the expedition, with subreports and accompanying papers, delays in receipt of which have caused my delay in forwarding this.

I am, sir, very respectfully, your obedient servant,

GEORGE CROOK,
Brigadier–General, Commanding.

The ASSISTANT ADJUTANT–GENERAL, U. S. A.,
Headquarters Military Division of the Missouri, Chicago, Ill.

HEADQUARTERS DEPARTMENT OF THE PLATTE,
ASSISTANT ADJUTANT–GENERAL'S OFFICE,
Omaha, Nebr., September 28, 1876

Official copy.

R. WILLIAMS,
Assistant Adjutant–General

B. – Subreport of General Crook[3]

HEADQUARTERS BIG HORN AND YELLOWSTONE EXPEDITION, CAMP CLOUD PEAK,
Base Big Horn Mountains, W. T., June 20, 1876.

SIR: I have the honor to report that the detachments of Crow and Shoshone Indian scouts I had been negotiating for, reached me on the night of the 14th Instant. I immediately parked my trains, pack animals, &c., in a secure place, so arranged that the civilian employees left with them could, if necessary, defend them till our return, and marched on the morning of the 16th with every available fighting man and four days' rations, carried by each officer and man on his person or saddle.

I allowed no led horses, each officer and man being equipped alike, with one blanket only, and every man who went, whether citizen, servant, or soldier, armed and with some organization for fighting purposes only.

The Crow Indians were under the impression that the hostile village was located on Tongue River or some of its smaller tributaries, and were quite positive that we would be able to surprise it. While I hardly believed this to be possible, as the Indians had hunting parties out, who must necessarily become aware of the presence of the command, I considered it would be worth while to make the attempt. The Indians, (ours,) of course, being experts in this matter, I regulated my movements entirely by their efforts to secure this end.

Marching from our camp on the South Fork of Tongue River, or Goose Creek, as sometimes called, towards the Yellowstone, on the evening of the first day's march we came to a small stream near the divide that separates the waters of the Tongue and Rosebud. We discovered that a small party of hunters had seen us. We crossed the divide that evening and camped on the headwaters of a small stream, laid down on the maps as Rosebud Creek, and about 35 or 40 miles from our camp on Tongue River.

Pushing on next morning down the Rosebud, with my Indian scouts in front, when about 5 miles down the stream, near the mouth of a deep canon, the scouts came in, reported that they had seen something and wished me to go into camp where we were, lying close till they could investigate, and very soon after others came in, reporting the Sioux in the vicinity, and within a very few minutes we were attacked by them in force.

The country was very rough and broken; the attack made in greater or less force on all sides, and, in advancing to meet it, the command necessarily soon became much separated. Under the circumstances I did not believe that any fight we could have would be decisive in its results unless we secured their village, supposed to be in close proximity. I therefore made every effort to close the command and march on their village. I had great difficulty in getting the battalions together, each command being pressed by the Indians, as the effort to concentrate them was made; the roughness of the ground facilitating this, the Indians apparently being aware of the reason for the movement, and assembling on the bluffs overlooking the canon through which the command would have to pass.

While the engagement was in progress I succeeded, however, in throwing a portion of the command into and down the canon for several miles, but was obliged to use it elsewhere, and, before the entire command was concentrated, it was believed that the canon was well covered, and our Indians refusing to go into it, saying it would be certain death. The bluffs on the side of the canon being covered with timber, they could fire upon the command at short range, while a return fire would be of no effect.

The troops having repulsed the attacks, and, in connection with the Indian scouts, driven the Sioux several miles, and our Indians refusing to go down the canon to the supposed location of the village, it remained to follow the retreating Sioux, without rations, dragging our wounded with us on rough mule litters or return to our train, where they could be cared for. The latter being the course adopted, we camped that night on the field, and marched next morning, reaching camp yesterday evening, having been absent, as intended when we started, four days.

Our casualties during the action were ten killed, including one Indian scout, and twenty–one wounded, including Capt. Guy V. Henry, Third Cavalry, severely wounded in the face. It is impossible to correctly estimate the loss of the enemy, as the field extended over several miles of rough country, including rocks and ravines not examined by us after the fight; thirteen of their dead bodies being left in close proximity to our lines.

I respectfully call attention to the enclosed reports of Lieutenant–Colonel Royall, Third Cavalry, and Major Chambers, Fourth Infantry, commanding the cavalry and infantry battalions respectively, and commend the gallantry and efficiency of the officers and men of the expedition as worthy of every praise.

Lieutenant–Colonel Royall and Major Chambers have given me great strength by the able manner in which they have commanded their respective columns. I am particularly grateful to them for their efficiency during the trip and engagement.

I am, sir, very respectfully, your obedient servant,

GEORGE CROOK,
Brigadier–General, Commanding.

The ASSISTANT ADJUTANT–GENERAL, U. S. A.,
Headquarters Military Division of the Missouri, Chicago, Ill.

Ba. – Telegram From General Crook[4]

BIG HORN AND YELLOWSTONE EXPEDITION,
Camp at head of Heart River, Dak. Ty., September 5, 1876.

Lieutenant–General SHERIDAN, Chicago, Ill.:

On 26th August I left Powder River on the trail of the Indians that we had followed down from the Rosebud, General Terry going north of the Yellowstone to intercept the trail of any Indians taking that direction. My column followed this trail down Beaver Creek to a point opposite Sentinel Buttes, where the Indians scattered, and the deluging rains to which we have been exposed during the past week have so obliterated their trails as to make it very difficult and laborious to work up the case, but undoubtedly a very large majority of the trails led over toward the Little Missouri, going in the direction of the Black Hills, the separation taking place apparently about twelve days ago.

I have every reason to believe that all the hostile Indians left the Big Horn, Tongue, and Powder River country in the village the trail of which we followed.

This village was very compact, and arranged in regular order of seven circles of lodges, covering an area of at least two thousand acres. With the exception of a few lodges that had stolen off toward the agencies, there was no change in the size or arrangement of the village until it disintegrated. All indications show the hostile Indians were much straitened for food, and that they are now traveling in small bands, scouting the country for small game.

I feel satisfied that if they can be prevented from getting ammunition or supplies from the agencies, a large majority of them will surrender soon.

I have with me only about two days' provisions, but I shall push out for the Black Hills, to try to reach there in advance of the hostiles or as soon as they do, scouting the country on the march as thoroughly as the circumstances will admit. We have traveled over four hundred miles since leaving our wagon train; our animals are now much jaded, and many of them have given out, while our men begin to manifest symptoms of scorbutic affections. As things look now, Custer City will probably be the base to operate from. I would like to have 200,000 pounds of grain sent there at once, together with twenty days' full rations of vegetables for the men. I would also like to have two companies of cavalry sent across the country from Red Cloud, via Pumpkin Buttes, by forced marches, to escort my wagon train from the Dry Fork of Powder River, by the miner's road, to Deadwood City in the Black Hills, so as to get it there with all possible dispatch.

I make these requests of you, as I have not heard anything reliable from the outside world since your telegram of July 26, and do not know what changes may have transpired to modify the disposition of troops in my department.

GEORGE CROOK,
Brigadier–General

Bb. – Telegram From General Crook[5]

HEADQUARTERS DEPARTMENT OF THE PLATTE,
BIG HORN AND YELLOWSTONE EXPEDITION,
Camp on Owl River, Dakota, September 10, 1876.

GENERAL SHERIDAN, Chicago:

Marched from Heart River, passing a great many trails of Indians going down all the different streams we crossed between Heart River and this point, apparently working their way in toward the different agencies.

Although some to the trails seemed fresh, our animals were not in condition to pursue them.

From the North Fork of Grand River, I sent Captain Mills, of the Third Cavalry, with 150 men, mounted on our strongest horses, to go in advance to Deadwood and procure supplies of provisions.

On the evening of the 8th, he discovered, near the Slim Buttes, a village of thirty–odd lodges, and lay by there that night and attacked them by surprise yesterday morning, capturing the village, some prisoners, and a number of ponies, and killing some of the Indians. Among the Indians was the chief American Horse, who died from his wounds, after surrendering to us. Our own casualties were slight, but among them was Lieutenant Von Leuttwitz, of the Third Cavalry, wounded seriously in knee, and leg since amputated.

In the village were found, besides great quantities of dried meat and ammunition, an army guidon, portions of officers' and non–commissioned officers' uniforms, and other indications that the Indians of this village had participated in the Custer massacre.

Our main column got up about noon that day, and was shortly after attacked by a considerable body of Indians, who, the prisoners said, belonged to the village of Crazy Horse, who was camped somewhere between their own village and the Little Missouri River. This attack was undoubtedly made under the supposition that Captain Mills' command had received no re–enforcements.

The prisoners further stated that most of the hostile Indians were now going into the agencies, with the exception of Crazy Horse and Sitting Bull with their immediate followers. Crazy Horse intended to remain near the headwaters of the Little Missouri; and about one–half of Sitting Bull['s band, numbering from sixty to one hundred lodges, had gone north of the Yellowstone, while the remainder of that band, with some Sans–Arcs, Minneconjous, and Uncpapas, had gone in the vicinity of Antelope Buttes, there to fatten their ponies and to trade with the Rees and others.

I place great reliance in these statements, from other corroboratory evidence which I have.

Those Indians with Sitting Bull will amount probably to three hundred or four hundred lodges, and in my judgment can very easily be struck by General Terry's column, provided it go in light marching order and keep under cover.

Our prisoners in their conversation also fully confirmed in every particular my opinions as already telegraphed you.

We had a very severe march here from Heart River eighty four consecutive miles. We did not have a particle of wood; nothing but a little dry grass, which was insufficient even to cook coffee for the men. During the greater portion of the time we were drenched by cold rains, which made traveling very heavy. A great many of the animals gave out and had to be abandoned. The others are now in such weak condition that the greater number of them will not be able to resume the campaign until after a reasonable rest.

I should like to have about five hundred horses, preferably the half–breed horses raised on the Laramie plains or in the vicinity of Denver and already acclimated to this country.

I intend to carry out the program mentioned in my last dispatch via Fort Lincoln, and shall remain in the vicinity of Deadwood until the arrival of my wagon train.

GEORGE CROOK,
Brigadier–General

C. – Subreport of General Crook[6]

HEADQUARTERS BIG HORN AND YELLOWSTONE EXPEDITION,
Fort Laramie, Wyo., September 25, 1876.

SIR: Having been advised by the Lieutenant–General that ten companies of the Fifth Cavalry would re–enforce me, I waited with my command in the vicinity of the Big Horn Mountains till they arrived August 3d, and the expedition moved out on the morning of the 5th of August.

In view of the fact that I had been somewhat embarrassed by the care of our wounded, in the movement we made on the Rosebud in June, our organization was made with a view to the possible contingencies that constantly arise in conflict with a savage foe. In war with a civilized foe it has been considered that the wounding of the enemy was better than to kill him, inasmuch as the force is not only deprived of the services of the wounded man but of those required to take care of him.

Hence it sometimes happens that a hospital falling into the hands of an enemy is a decided advantage to the army losing it. In such case the wounded would be tenderly cared for.

But in this war the case is different. The falling into the hands of our savage foe of our wounded would be a calamity not necessary to expatiate upon to be appreciated.

In starting on this second movement I first stripped the command of everything in excess of the absolute necessities of the officers and men, and after selecting the best position available for it, left my wagon train in charge of Captain Furey, assistant quartermaster, with only the men belonging to it to guard it, with the sick and hospital attendants.

My pack trains were in five detachments, each led by a bell–animal and so well drilled that the train would go wherever the troops were required to, leaving absolutely nothing to guard or embarrass us, and in case of an engagement it was impossible to separate the mules from the bell animals.

Material for travaux for our wounded was transported on the pack train and the entire command was in the most perfect fighting condition, ready to move in any direction and over any country with celerity, and to attack with power.

The wounded needed no guard as they, with the pack animals, were kept up with the troops all the time. Three days' march from our camp, and on Rosebud Creek, we found the trail of the hostile force going down that stream toward the Yellowstone.

Their camps were made in seven distinct circles, and were compact encampments covering an area of at least two thousand acres.

These camps and the trail showed that there was no material scattering or diminution of their force until they separated on Beaver Creek.

We followed this trail down the Rosebud to within thirty miles of where it empties into the Yellowstone, when we met General Terry's column, in conjunction with which we followed it across to Powder River, and down that stream to within twenty miles of its mouth. Here the trail left Powder River and ran in an easterly direction, while our command marched down to the Yellowstone River to replenish our rations. Here we were detained seven days by the difficulties the steamer carrying supplies experienced in navigating that stream.

Both columns then marched back up Powder River to renew pursuit on the trail, when we received information that the Indians had attacked the entrenched camp at the mouth of Glendive Creek, and fired on the steamer on the Yellowstone.

This was evidently for the purpose of covering some movement embracing a possible breaking into smaller bands and a crossing of the Yellowstone by some portion of them.

General Terry then returned to and crossed the Yellowstone to the north side to intercept any movement in that direction, while I moved with my column south on the trail to a point on Beaver Creek opposite Sentinel Buttes, where it broke up into small parties, the majority going toward the agencies and the Black Hills.

As the whole frontier of my department was thus exposed, and the people in the Black Hills in imminent danger, I marched via the head of Heart River toward their camps in the hills.

This march of ten days was made on a little over two days' rations, eighty–odd miles being over a country that had no wood, shrubbery, or even weeds with which to make fires for cooking coffee; ten days being in a deluging rain, the men not having during that time a dry blanket; the deep sticky mud making a toilsome march, which for severity and hardship has but few parallels in the history of our Army.

Notwithstanding this, when we reached "Belle Fourche," there was but two and one–tenth percent of the command sick, and this included fifteen wounded in the engagement near Slim Buttes.

On the march down, our advance, under Capt. Anson Mills, Third Cavalry, attacked and destroyed a village of thirty–seven lodges containing a large quantity of robes and property of value to the hostiles.

A report of this engagement is enclosed and marked C.

The trains of supplies sent to meet us are now with the command, which is comfortably camped in the vicinity of Custer City, waiting future movements.

I cannot close my report without expressing my deep sense of gratitude for the courtesy with which I was treated by Brigadier–General Terry during the time our expeditions acted in conjunction. He not only did not assume command of my column, as he might have done, but shared everything he had with us.

I have the honor to be, very respectfully, your obedient servant,

GEORGE CROOK,
Brigadier–General U. S. Army, Commanding,

ASSISTANT ADJUTANT–GENERAL
Military Division of the Missouri, Chicago, Ill.

[1] See John M. Carroll "General Custer and the Battle of the Little Big Horn: The Federal View" pages 114 – 118. I have corrected spelling as necessary.

[2] See John M. Carroll "General Custer and the Battle of the Little Big Horn: The Federal View" pages 118 – 119. I have corrected spelling as necessary.

[3] See John M. Carroll "General Custer and the Battle of the Little Big Horn: The Federal View" pages 120 – 121. I have corrected spelling as necessary.

[4] See John M. Carroll "General Custer and the Battle of the Little Big Horn: The Federal View" pages 121 – 122. I have corrected spelling as necessary.

[5] See John M. Carroll "General Custer and the Battle of the Little Big Horn: The Federal View" pages 122 – 123 I have corrected spelling as necessary.

[6] See John M. Carroll "General Custer and the Battle of the Little Big Horn: The Federal View" pages 123 – 125. I have corrected spelling as necessary.

Appendix 16

Text Of The Treaty of 1868

And

Text Of The Agreement To Purchase The Black Hills

The following texts are taken from "Custer's Gold" by Donald Jackson, pages 127 – 141.

Treaty of April 29, 1868

Articles of a treaty made and concluded by and between Lieutenant–General William T. Sherman, General William S. Harney, General Alfred H. Terry, General C. C. Augur, J. B. Henderson, Nathaniel G. Taylor, John B. Sanborn, and Samuel F. Tappan, duly appointed commissioners on the part of the United States, and the different bands of the Sioux Nation of Indians, by their chiefs and headmen, whose names are hereto subscribed, they being duly authorized to act in the premises.

ARTICLE I. From this day forward all war between the parties to this agreement shall forever cease. The government of the United States desires peace, and its honor is hereby pledged to keep it. The Indians desire peace, and they now pledge their honor to maintain it.

If bad men among the whites, or among other people subject to the authority of the United States, shall commit any wrong upon the person or property of the Indians, the United States will, upon proof made to the agent and forwarded to the Commissioner of Indian Affairs at Washington city, proceed at once to cause the offender to be arrested and punished according to the laws of the United States, and also reimburse the injured person for the loss sustained.

If bad men among the Indians shall commit a wrong or depredation upon the person or property of any one, white, black, or Indian, subject to the authority of the United States, and at peace therewith, the Indians herein named solemnly agree that they will, upon proof made to their agent and notice by him, deliver up the wrong–doer to the United States, to be tried and punished according to its laws; and in case they willfully refuse so to do, the person injured shall be reimbursed for his loss from the annuities or other moneys due or to become due to them under this or other treaties made with the United States. And the President, on advising with the Commissioner of Indian Affairs, shall prescribe such rules and regulations for ascertaining damages under the provisions of this article as in his judgment may be proper. But no one sustaining loss while violating the provisions of this treaty or the laws of the United States shall be reimbursed therefor.

ARTICLE II. The United States agrees that the following district of country, to wit, viz: commencing on the east bank of the Missouri river where the forty–sixth parallel of north latitude crosses the same, thence along low–water mark down said east bank to a point opposite where the northern line of the State of Nebraska strikes the river, thence west across said river, and along the northern line of Nebraska to the one hundred and fourth degree on longitude west from Greenwich, thence north on said meridian to a point where the forty–sixth parallel of north latitude intercepts the same, thence due east along said parallel to the place of beginning; and in addition thereto, all existing reservations on the east bank of said river shall be, and the same is, set apart for the absolute and undisturbed use and occupation of the Indians herein named, and for such other friendly tribes or individual Indians as from time to time they may be willing, with the consent of the United States, to admit amongst them; and the United States now solemnly agrees that no persons except those herein designated and authorized so to do, and except such officers, agents, and employees of the government as may be authorized to enter upon Indian reservations in discharge of duties enjoined by law, shall ever be permitted to pass over, settle upon, or reside in the territory described in this article, or in such territory as may be added to this reservation for the use of said Indians, and henceforth they will and do hereby relinquish all claims or right in and to any portion of the United States or Territories, except such as is embraced within the limits aforesaid, and except as hereinafter provided.

ARTICLE III. If it should appear from actual survey or other satisfactory examination of said tract of land that it contains less than one hundred and sixty acres of tillable land for each person who, at the time, may be authorized to reside on it under the provisions of this treaty, and a very considerable number of such persons shall be disposed to commence cultivating the soil as farmers, the United States agrees to set apart, for the use of said Indians, as herein provided, such additional quantity of arable land, adjoining to said reservation, or as near to the same as it can be obtained, as may be required to provide the necessary amount.

ARTICLE IV. The United States agrees, at its own proper expense, to construct at some place on the Missouri river, near the centre of said reservation, where timber and water may be convenient, the following buildings, to wit: a warehouse, a storeroom for the use of the agent in storing goods belonging to the Indians, to cost not less than twenty–five hundred dollars; an agency building for the residence of the agent, to cost not exceeding three thousand dollars, a residence for the physician, to cost not more than three thousand dollars; and five other buildings, for a carpenter, farmer, blacksmith, miller, and engineer, each to cost not exceeding two thousand dollars; also a school–house or mission building, so soon as a sufficient number of children can be induced by the agent to attend school, which shall not cost exceeding five thousand dollars.

The United States agrees further to cause to be erected on said reservation, near the other buildings herein authorized, a good steam circular saw–mill, with a grist–mill and shingle machine attached to the same, to cost not exceeding eight thousand dollars.

ARTICLE V. The United States agrees that the agent or said Indians shall in the future make his home at the agency building; that he shall reside among them, and keep an office open at all times for the purpose of prompt and diligent inquiry into such matters of complaint by and against the Indians as may be presented for investigation under the provisions of their treaty stipulations, as also for the faithful discharge of other duties enjoined on him by law. In all cases of depredation on person or property he shall cause the evidence to be taken in writing and forwarded, together with his findings, to the Commissioner of Indian Affairs, whose decision, subject to the revision of the Secretary of the Interior, shall be binding on the parties to this treaty.

ARTICLE VI. If any individual belonging to said tribes of Indians, or legally incorporating with them, being the head of a family, shall desire to commence farming, he shall have the privilege to select, in the presence and with the assistance of the agent then in charge, a tract of land within said reservation, not exceeding three hundred and twenty acres in extent, which tract when so selected, certified, and recorded in the "land book," as herein directed, shall cease to be held in common, but the same may be occupied and held in the exclusive possession of the person selecting it, and of his family, so long as he or they may continue to cultivate it.

Any person over eighteen years of age, not being the head of a family, may in like manner select and cause to be certified to him or her, for purposes of cultivation, a quantity of land not exceeding eighty acres in extent, and thereupon be entitled to the exclusive possession of the same as above directed.

For each tract of land so selected a certificate, containing a description thereof and the name of the person selecting it, with a certificate endorsed thereon that the same has been recorded shall be delivered to the party entitled to it, by the agent, after the same shall have been recorded by him in a book to be kept in his office, subject to inspection, which said book shall be known as the "Sioux Land Book."

The President may, at any time, order a survey of the reservation, and, when so surveyed, Congress shall provide for protecting the rights of said settlers in their improvements, and may fix the character of the title held by each. The United States may pass such laws on the subject of alienation and descent of property between the Indians and their descendants as may be thought proper. And it is further stipulated that any male Indians over eighteen years of age, of any band or tribe that is or shall hereafter become a party to this treaty, who now is or who shall hereafter become a resident or occupant of any reservation or territory not included in the tract of country designated and described in this treaty for the permanent home of the Indians, which is not mineral land, nor reserved by the United States for special purposes other than Indian occupation, and who shall have made improvements thereon of the value of two hundred dollars or more, and continuously occupied the same as a homestead for the term of three years, shall be entitled to receive from the United States a patent for one hundred and sixty acres of land including his said improvements, the same to be in the form of the legal subdivisions of the surveys of the public lands. Upon application in writing, sustained by the proof of two disinterested witnesses, made to the register of the local land office when the land sought to be entered is within a land district, and when the tract sought to be entered is not in any land district, then upon said application and proof being made to the commissioner of the general land office, and the right of such Indian or Indians to enter such tract or tracts of land shall accrue and be perfect from the date of his first improvements thereon, and shall continue as long as he continues his residence and improvements, and no longer. And any Indian or Indians receiving a patent for land under the foregoing provisions, shall thereby and from thenceforth become and be citizen of the Unites States, and be entitled to all the privileges and immunities of such citizens, and shall, at the same time, retain all his rights to benefits accruing to Indians under this treaty.

ARTICLE VII. In order to insure the civilization of the Indians entering into this treaty, the necessity of education is admitted, especially of such of them as are or may be settled on said agricultural reservations, and they therefore pledge themselves to compel their children, male and female, between the ages of six and sixteen years, to attend school; and it is hereby made the duty of the agent for said Indians to see that this stipulation is strictly complied with; and the United States agrees that for every thirty children between said ages who can be induced or compelled to attend school, a house shall be provided and a teacher competent to teach the elementary branches of an English education shall be furnished, who will reside among said Indians, and faithfully discharge his or her duties as a teacher. The provisions of this article to continue for not less than twenty years.

ARTICLE VIII. When the head of a family or lodge shall have selected lands and received his certificate as above directed, and the agent shall be satisfied that he intends in good faith to commence cultivating the soil for a living, he shall be entitled to receive seeds and agricultural implements for the first year, not exceeding in value one hundred dollars, and for each succeeding year he shall continue to farm, for a period of three years more, he shall be entitled to receive seeds and implements as aforesaid, not exceeding in value twenty–five dollars.

And it is further stipulated that such persons as commence farming shall receive instruction from the farmer herein provided for, and whenever more than one hundred persons shall enter upon the cultivation of the soil, a second blacksmith shall be provided, with such iron, steel, and other material as may be needed.

ARTICLE IX. At any time after ten years from the making of this treaty, the United States shall have the privilege of withdrawing the physician, farmer, blacksmith, carpenter, engineer, and miller herein provided for, but in case of such withdrawal, an additional sum thereafter of ten thousand dollars per annum shall be devoted to the education of said Indians, and the Commissioner of Indian Affairs shall, upon careful inquiry into their condition, make such rules and regulations for the expenditure of said sum as will best promote the educational and moral improvement of said tribes.

ARTICLE X. In lieu of all sums of money or other annuities provided to be paid to the Indians herein named, under any treaty or treaties heretofore made, the United States agrees to deliver at the agency house on the reservation herein named, on or before the first day of August of each year, for thirty years, the following articles, to wit:

For each male person over fourteen years of age, a suit of good substantial woolen clothing, consisting of coat, pantaloons, flannel shirt, hat, and a pair of home–made socks.

For each female over twelve years of age, a flannel skirt, or the goods necessary to make it, a pair of woolen hose, twelve yards of calico, and twelve yards of cotton domestics.

For the boys and girls under the ages named, such flannel and cotton goods as may be needed to make each a suit as aforesaid, together with a pair of woolen hose for each.

And in order that the Commissioner of Indian Affairs may be able to estimate properly for the articles herein named, it shall be the duty of the agent each year to forward to him a full and exact census of the Indians, on which the estimate from year to year can be based.

And in addition to the clothing herein named, the sum of ten dollars for each person entitled to the beneficial effects of this treaty shall be annually appropriated for a period of thirty years, while such persons roam and hunt, and twenty dollars for each person who engages in farming, to be used by the Secretary of the Interior in the purchase of such articles as from time to time the condition and necessities of the Indians may indicate to be proper. And if within the thirty years, at any time, it shall appear that the amount of money needed for clothing under this article can be appropriated to better uses for the Indians named herein, Congress may, by law, change the appropriation to other purposes; but in no event shall the amount of this appropriation be withdrawn or discontinued for the period named. And the President shall annually detail an officer of the army to be present and attest the delivery of all the goods herein named to the Indians, and he shall inspect and report on the quantity and quality of the goods and the manner of their delivery. And it is hereby expressly stipulated that each Indian over the age of four years, who shall have removed to and settled permanently upon said reservation and complied with the stipulations of this treaty, shall be entitled to receive from the United States, for the period of four years after he shall have settled upon said reservation, one pound of meat and one pound of flour per day, provided the Indians cannot furnish their own subsistence at an earlier date. And it is further stipulated that the United States will furnish and deliver to each lodge of Indians or family of persons legally incorporated with them, who shall remove to the reservation herein described and commence farming, one good American cow, and one good well-broken pair of American oxen within sixty days after such lodge or family shall have so settled upon said reservation.

ARTICLE XI. In consideration of the advantages and benefits conferred by this treaty and the many pledges of friendship by the United States, the tribes who are parties to this agreement hereby stipulate that they will relinquish all right to occupy permanently the territory outside their reservation as herein defined, but yet reserve the right to hunt on any lands north of North Platte, and on the Republican Fork of the Smoky Hill river, so long as the buffalo may range thereon in such numbers as to justify the chase. And they, the said Indians, further expressly agree:

Ist. That they will withdraw all opposition to the construction of the railroads now being built on the plains.

2d. That they will permit the peaceful construction of any railroad not passing over their reservation as herein defined.

3d. That they will not attack any persons at home, or traveling, not molest or disturb any wagon trains, coaches, mules, or cattle belonging to the people of the United States, or to persons friendly therewith.

4th. They will never capture, or carry off from the settlements, white women and children.

5th. They will never kill or scalp white men, nor attempt to do them harm.

6th. They withdraw all pretense of opposition to the construction of the railroad now being built along the Platte river and westward to the Pacific ocean, and they will not in future object to the construction of railroads, wagon roads, mail stations, or other works of utility or necessity, which may be ordered or permitted by the laws of the United States. But should such roads or other works be constructed on the lands of their reservation, the government will pay the tribe whatever amount of damages may be assessed by three disinterested commissioners to be appointed by the President for that purpose, one of said commissioners to be a chief or headman of the tribe.

7th. They agree to withdraw all opposition to the military posts or roads now established south of the North Platte river, or that may be established, not in violation of treaties heretofore made or hereafter to be made with any of the Indian tribes.

ARTICLE XII. No treaty for the cession of any portion or part of the reservation herein described which may be held in common shall be of any validity or force as against the said Indians, unless executed and signed by at least three fourths of all the adult male Indians, occupying or interested in the same; and no cession by the tribe shall be understood or construed in such manner as to deprive, without his consent, any individual member of the tribe of his rights to any tract of land selected by him, as provided in Article VI. of this treaty.

ARTICLE XIII. The United States hereby agrees to furnish annually to the Indians the physician, teachers, carpenter, miller, engineer, farmer, and blacksmiths, as herein contemplated, and that such appropriations shall be made from time to time, on the estimates of the Secretary of the Interior, as will be sufficient to employ such persons.

ARTICLE XIV. It is agreed that the sum of five hundred dollars annually, for three years from date, shall be expended in presents to the ten persons of said tribe who in the judgment of the agent may grow the most valuable crops for the respective year.

ARTICLE XV. The Indians herein named agree that when the agency house and other buildings shall be constructed on the reservation named, they will regard said reservation their permanent home, and they will make no permanent settlement elsewhere; but they shall have the right, subject to the conditions and modifications of this treaty, to hunt, as stipulated in Article XI. hereof.

ARTICLE XVI. The United States hereby agrees and stipulates that the country north of the North Platte river and east of the summits of the Big Horn mountains shall be held and considered to be unceded Indian territory, and also stipulates and agrees that no white person or persons shall be permitted to settle upon or occupy any portion of the same; or without the consent of the Indians, first had and obtained, to pass through the same; and it is further agreed by the United States, that within ninety days after the conclusion of peace with all the bands of the Sioux nation, the military posts now established in the territory in this article named shall be abandoned, and that the road leading to them and by them to the settlements in the Territory of Montana shall be closed.

ARTICLE XVII. It is hereby expressly understood and agreed by and between the respective parties to this treaty that the execution of this treaty and its ratification by the United States Senate shall have the effect, and shall be construed as abrogating and annulling all treaties and agreements heretofore entered into between the respective parties hereto, so far as such treaties and agreements obligate the United States to furnish and provide money, clothing, or other articles of property to such Indians and bands of Indians as become parties to this treaty, but no further.

Agreement of August 15, 1876

Articles of agreement made pursuant to the provisions of an act of Congress entitled "An act making appropriations for the current and contingent expenses of the Indian Department, and for fulfilling treaty stipulations with various Indian tribes, for the year ending June thirtieth, eighteen hundred and seventy seven, and for other purposes," approved August 15, 1876, by and between George W. Manypenny, Henry B. Whipple, Jared W. Daniels, Albert G. Boone, Henry C. Bulis, Newton Edmunds, and Augustine S. Gaylord, commissioners on the part of the United States, and the different bands of the Sioux Nation of Indians, and also the Northern Arapahoes and Cheyennes, by their chiefs and headmen, whose names are hereto subscribed, they being duly authorized to act in the premises.

ARTICLE 1. The said parties hereby agree that the northern and western boundaries of the reservation defined by article 2 of the treaty between the United States and different tribes of Sioux Indians, concluded April 29, 1868, and proclaimed February 24, 1869, shall be as follows: The western boundaries shall commence at the intersection of the one hundred and third meridian of longitude with the northern boundary of the State of Nebraska; thence north along said meridian to its intersection with the South Fork of the Cheyenne River; thence down said stream to its junction with the North Fork; thence up the North Fork of said Cheyenne River to the said one hundred and third meridian; thence north along said meridian to the South Branch of Cannon Ball River or Cedar Creek; and the northern boundary of their said reservation shall follow the said South branch to its intersection with the main Cannon Ball River, and thence down the said main Cannon Ball River to the Missouri River; and the said Indians do hereby relinquish and cede to the Untied States all the territory lying outside the said reservation, as herein modified and described, including all privileges of hunting; and article 16 of said treaty is hereby abrogated.

ARTICLE 2. The said Indians also agree and consent that wagon and other roads, not exceeding three in number, may be constructed and maintained, from convenient and accessible points on the Missouri River, through said reservation, to the country lying immediately west thereof, upon such routes as shall be designated by the President of the United States; and they also consent and agree to the free navigation of the Missouri River.

ARTICLE 3. The said Indians also agree that they will hereafter receive all annuities provided by the said treaty of 1868, and all subsistence and supplies which may be provided for them under the present or any future act of Congress, at such points and places on the said reservation, and in the vicinity of the Missouri River, as the President of the United States shall designate.

ARTICLE 4. The Government of the United States and the said Indians, being mutually desirous that the latter shall be located in a country where they may eventually become self–supporting and acquire the arts of civilized life, it is therefore agreed that the said Indians shall select a delegation of five or more chiefs and principal men from each band, who shall, without delay, visit the Indian Territory under the guidance and protection of suitable persons, to be appointed for that purpose by the Department of the Interior, with a view to selecting therein a permanent home for the said Indians. If such delegation shall make a selection which shall be satisfactory to themselves, the people whom they represent, and to the United States, then the said Indians agree that they will remove to the country so selected within one year from this date. And the said Indians do further agree in all things to submit themselves to such beneficent plans as the Government may provide for them in the selection of a country suitable for a permanent home, where they may live like white men.

ARTICLE 5. In consideration of the foregoing cession of territory and rights, and upon full compliance with each and every obligation assumed by the said Indians, the United States does agree to provide all necessary aid to assist the said Indians in the work of civilization; to furnish to them schools and instruction in mechanical and agricultural arts, as provided for by the treaty of 1868. Also to provide the said Indians with subsistence consisting of a ration for each individual of a pound and a half of beef (or in lieu thereof, one half pound of bacon,) one–half pound of flour, and one–half pound of corn; and for every one hundred rations, four pounds of coffee, eight pounds of sugar, and three pounds of beans, or in lieu of said articles the equivalent thereof, in the discretion of the Commissioner of Indian Affairs. Such rations, or so much thereof as may be necessary, shall be continued until the Indians are able to support themselves. Rations shall, in all cases, be issued to the head of each separate family; and whenever schools shall have been provided by the Government for said Indians, no rations shall be issued for children between the ages of six and fourteen years (the sick and infirm excepted) unless such children shall regularly attend school. Whenever the said Indians shall be located upon lands which are suitable for cultivation, rations shall be issued only to the persons and families of those persons who labor, (the aged, sick, and infirm excepted;) and as an incentive to industrious habits the Commissioner of Indian Affairs may provide that such persons be furnished in payment for their labor such other necessary articles as are requisite for civilized life. The Government will aid said Indians as far as possible in finding a market for their surplus productions, and in finding employment; and will purchase such surplus, as far as may be required, for supplying food to those Indians, parties to this agreement, who are unable to sustain themselves; and will also employ Indians, so far as practicable, in the performance of Government work upon their reservation.

ARTICLE 6. Whenever the head of a family shall, in good faith, select an allotment of land upon such reservation and engage in the cultivation thereof, the Government shall, with his aid, erect a comfortable house on such allotment; and if said Indians shall remove to said Indian Territory as herein before provided, the Government shall erect for each of the principal chiefs a good and comfortable dwelling–house.

ARTICLE 7. To improve the morals and industrious habits of said Indians, it is agreed that the agent, trader, farmer, carpenter, blacksmith, and other artisans employed or permitted to reside within the reservation belonging to the Indians, parties to this agreement, shall be lawfully married and living with their respective families on the reservation; and no person other than an Indian of full blood, whose fitness, morally or otherwise, is not, in the opinion of the Commissioner of Indian Affairs, conducive to the welfare of said Indians, shall receive any benefit from this agreement or former treaties, and may be expelled from the reservation.

ARTICLE 8. The provisions of said treaty of 1868, except as herein modified, shall continue in full force, and, with the provisions of this agreement, shall apply to any country which may hereafter be occupied by the said Indians as a home; and Congress shall, by appropriate legislation, secure to them an orderly government; they shall be subject to the laws of the United States, and each individual shall be protected in his rights of property, person, and life.

ARTICLE 9. The Indians, parties to this agreement, do hereby solemnly pledge themselves, individually and collectively, to observe each and all of the stipulations herein contained, to select allotments of land as soon as possible after their removal to their permanent home, and to use their best efforts to learn to cultivate the same. And they do solemnly pledge themselves that they will at all times maintain peace with the citizens and Government of the United States; that they will observe the laws thereof and loyally endeavor to fulfill all the obligations assumed by them under the treaty of 1868 and the present agreement, and to this end will, whenever requested by the President of the United States, select so many suitable men from each band to co–operate with him in maintaining order and peace on the reservation as the President may deem necessary, who shall receive such compensation for their services as Congress may provide.

ARTICLE 10. In order that the Government may faithfully fulfill the stipulations contained in this agreement, it is mutually agreed that a census of all Indians affected hereby shall be taken in the month of December of each year, and the names of each head of family and adult person registered; said census to be taken in such manner as the Commissioner of Indian Affairs may provide.

ARTICLE 11. It is understood that the term reservation herein contained shall be held to apply to any country which shall be selected under the authority of the United States as the future home of said Indians.

This agreement shall not be binding upon either party until it shall have received the approval of the President and Congress of the United States.

Appendix 17

List of Seventh Cavalry Actions against Indians

Date	Location	KIA OF	KIA EN	WIA OF	WIA EN
4/15/67	Near Ft. Lyon, Colo (Lt. Matthew Berry)	0	0	0	1
4/19/67	Cimarron Crossing, Kansas (Lt Matthew Berry)	0	0	0	1
5/27/67	Pond Creek Station, Kansas (Capt M. W. Keogh) (no Indian casualties)	0	0	0	0
6/8/67	Chalk Bluffs, Kansas (Lt H. J. Nowlan) (no Indian casualties)	0	0	0	0
6/11/67	Near Big Timbers, Kansas (Lt J. M. Bell)	0	1	0	0
6/12/67	Near Ft. Dodge, Kansas	0	0	0	1
6/21/67	Near Ft. Wallace, Kansas (Lt J. M. Bell)	0	2	0	2
6/22/67	Near Ft. Wallace, Kansas (Lt H. J. Nowlan) (no Indian casualties)	0	0	0	0
6/24/67	North Fork Republican River, Kansas (Lc G. A. Custer)	0	0	0	1
6/24/67	North Fork Republican River, Kansas (Capt L. M. Hamilton)	0	0	0	0
6/26/67	Republican River (south fork), Kansas (Lt S. M. Robbins)	0	0	0	2
6/26/67	Near Ft. Wallace, Kansas (Capt Albert Barnitz)	0	6	0	6
6/27/67	Near Ft. Wallace, Kansas (Lt H. J. Nowlan) (no Indian casualties)	0	0	0	0
8/2/68	Cimarron River, Kansas (Capt R. M. West) (no Indian casualties)	0	0	0	0
8/12/68	Saline River, Kansas (Capt F. W. Benteen) (no Indian casualties)	0	0	0	0
8/13/68	Saline River, Kansas (Capt F. W. Benteen)	0	0	0	0
9/10/68	Rule Creek, Colo (Co L)	0	2	0	1
9/11-15/68	Sand Hills, Indian Territory (Sully Expedition Maj J. H. Elliott)	0	3	0	5
9/17/68	Saline River, Kansas (Detachment)	0	0	0	3
10/12/68	Big Bend of Arkansas River, Kansas (Maj J. H. Elliott)	0	0	0	0
11/3/68	Big Coon Creek, Kansas (Capt F. W. Benteen) (no Indian casualties)	0	0	0	0
11/27/68	Washita River, Indian Territory (Black Kettle – Lc G. A. Custer)	2	19	3	13
1/28/69	Solomon River, Kansas	0	0	0	2
6/1/69	Solomon River, Kansas	0	0	0	1
6/19/69	Near Sheridan, Kansas	0	0	0	2
6/1/70	Solomon River, Kansas	0	0	0	0
8/4/73	Tongue River, Montana (Capt Myles Moylan)	0	0	0	1
8/11/73	Yellowstone River near Big Horn, Montana (Lc G. A. Custer)	0	3	1	3
4/23/74	Near Ft. Lincoln, Dakota (Lc G. A. Custer)	0	0	0	0
6/25/76	Little Big Horn River, Montana (Lc G. A. Custer)	13	189	0	0
6/25/76	Little Big Horn River, Montana (Maj M. A. Reno)	2	46	2	44
9/13/77	Canyon Creek, Montana (Col S. D. Sturgis)	0	3	1	10
9/30/77	Bear Paw Mountains, Montana (total army casualties)	2	22	4	38
8/17/80	Little Missouri River, Montana (Sgt E. Davern)	0	0	0	0
1/2/81	Popular River, Monatan	0	0	0	0

Date	Location	KIA		WIA	
		OF	EN	OF	EN
11/5/86	Crow Agency, Montana	0	1	0	2
	(total army casualties)				
12/28/90	Near Porcupine Creek, South Dakota	0	0	0	0
12/29/90	Wounded Knee Creek, South Dakota (Col J. W. Forsyth)	1	24	3	32
12/30/90	White Clay Creek, South Dakota (Col J. W. Forsyth)	0	1	1	6

Engagements With More Than Twenty Casualties 1850 – 1891

Date	Location	KIA		WIA	
		OF	EN	OF	EN
6/25/76	Little Big Horn River, Montana (Custer's command) (Sioux and Cheyenne)	13	189	0	0
6/25-26/76	Little Big Horn River, Montana (Reno's command) (Sioux and Cheyenne)	2	46	2	44
12/21/66	Fetterman Fight Near Ft. Kearny, Dakota (Sioux and Cheyenne)	3	76	0	0
9/30/77	Bear Paw Mountains, Montana (Nez Perce)	2	22	4	38
12/29/92	Wounded Knee Creek (Sioux)	1	24	3	32
8/9-10/77	Big Hole Basin, Montana (Nez Perce)	2	21	5	31
9/29-10/1/79	Milk River, Colorado (Ute)	1	9	2	43
8/21-22/67	Prairie Dog Creek, Kansas	0	8	0	35
7/11-12/77	South Fork of Clearwater, Idaho (Nez Perce)	0	13	2	25
1/17/73	Modoc Caves near Tule Lake, Cal (Modoc)	0	9	1	20
4/26/73	Lava Beds, Cal (Modoc)	4	18	1	16
11/27/68	Black Kettle's Village, Washita River, Indian Territory (Cheyenne)	2	19	3	13
6/17/77	White Bird Canyon, Idaho (Nez Perce)	1	33	0	2
11/25-26/76	North Fork Powder River, Montana Territory (Cheyenne)	1	5	0	25
8/19/54	Grattan Fight near Ft. Laramie, Nebraska (Brule Sioux)	1	28	0	1
6/17/76	Rosebud River, Montana (Sioux and Cheyenne)	0	9	1	20
3/30/54	Cianeguilla, New Mexico (Apache)	0	22	0	2
4/11-20/73	Lava Beds, Cal (Modoc)	1	6	2	13
1/9-22/79	Fort Robinson, Nebraska (Cheyenne revolt)	0	7	1	13

Total Army Casualties on Plains vs Indians

KIA		WIA	
OF	**EN**	**OF**	**EN**
40	642	38	555

Total Engagements by Cavalry Regiment vs Indians

1st Dragoons	39
2nd Dragoons	14
1st Cavalry	111
2nd Cavalry	73
3rd Cavalry	63
4th Cavalry	47
5th Cavalry	68
6th Cavalry	56
7th Cavalry	39
8th Cavalry	95
9th Cavalry	68
10th Cavalry	49

Engagements by Cavalry Regiment vs Indians From July 1866 to June 1876

1st Dragoons	0
2nd Dragoons	0
1st Cavalry	83
2nd Cavalry	37
3rd Cavalry	51
4th Cavalry	34
5th Cavalry	60
6th Cavalry	26
7th Cavalry	32
8th Cavalry	95
9th Cavalry	26
10th Cavalry	28

Field Grade Officers Killed in Action Against Indians 1835 - 1891

General E. R. S. Canby 4/11/73 by Modocs, Lava Beds, California

Lieutenant Colonel A. R. Thompson, 6th Infantry 12/25/37 by Seminoles at Lake Okeechobee, Florida

Lieutenant Colonel C. VanCamp, 2nd Cavalry 10/1/58 by Comanches near Wichita Village, Choctaw Nation, Indian Territory

Lieutenant Colonel G. A. Custer, 7th Cavalry 6/25/76 by Lakota Cheyenne and Arapahoe at the Little Big Horn River, Montana Territory

Major F. L. Dade, 4th Infantry 12/28/35 by Seminoles near Fort King, Florida

Major J. H. Elliott, 7th Cavalry 11/27/68 by Cheyenne and Arapahoe during attack on Black Kettle's Village, Washita River, Indian Territory

Major T. T. Thornburgh, 4th Infantry 10/1/79 by Utes at Milk River, Colorado

Appendix 18

Selected Biographies

Myths and legends are composed of more than epic events. They flourish and remain in our cultural heritage only in proportion to the fame and charisma of the participants. It is no different with the Battle of the Little Big Horn. It is therefore appropriate to provide the following brief biographical sketches of key participants.

Frederick William Benteen. Born August 24, 1834 in Petersburg, Virginia. Died June 22, 1898.[1] He remained loyal to the Union during the Civil War entering military service as a First Lieutenant on September 1, 1861. This act so enraged his father, who with the rest of the family remained loyal to their native state, that he was disinherited and his father was heard to pray aloud for the death of this disloyal son at the hands of a relative. Benteen gained a measure of "revenge" when his company participated in the capture of his father, who was running supplies to the confederates.[2] Like Custer, Benteen turned down a higher commission in a black regiment to serve in the 7th.[3] An officer of unquestioned ability and courage, he received two brevets for Civil War actions, attaining the rank of colonel, and two for the Indian Wars, including Little Big Horn.

Appointed Captain, 7th Cavalry, to rank from July 28, 1866, the date the regiment was organized. Commanded Company H in the attack on Black Kettle's Cheyenne village on the Washita River in 1868. Suspended at half pay for one year for drunkenness, he retired from the army April 7, 1888, three days after returning to active duty.[4] He was appointed Brigadier General February 27, 1890, for his service at the Little Big Horn and against the Nez Perce at Canyon Creek.[5]

His belief that he was continually commanded by inferiors led to friction wherever he served and deprived him of attaining the brilliant military record of which he was capable. Benteen was the most vocal of the anti Custer group of 7th Cavalry officers. He was insolent and bordered on insubordination with his superiors on numerous occasions.[6] *"In fact, Benteen's dominant characteristic seems to have been jealousy of, and hostility toward, almost everyone and everything."*[7] In later years he was fond of recounting his confrontations with Custer and his success in withholding information at the Reno court of inquiry. This abiding hatred for Custer, which grew in intensity rather than diminishing with the passage of years, and, perhaps, remorse for his inaction during Custer's death struggle, led to false statements concerning conditions found on the battlefield. This in turn has caused much confusion among students of the battle and propagated many myths concerning the battle and Armstrong Custer. General Hugh L. Scott referred to Benteen as *"my model . . . and the idol of the 7th Cavalry."*[8] Lieutenant Charles A. Varnum, giving a more balanced assessment, said *"Benteen drank & played poker, and when under the influence of liquor could utter sneering remarks. He was a law unto himself, and a soldier of undoubted courage."*[9]

As the captain of H Troop at the Little Big Horn, Benteen was the recipient of the famous *"Be quick. Bring Packs"* message written by regimental adjutant Lieutenant William W. Cooke. He has deservedly been both criticized and praised for his conduct at the Little Big Horn. His sulking and dawdling on the trail made him late in reaching the river. While he was instrumental in the defense of the position on the bluffs, his refusal to entrench on the night of June 25th contributed to extremely heavy casualties for his company on the 26th. His bravery was without question. Although suffering from malarious dysentery, and wounded in the right thumb during the hilltop fight, he refused confinement after treatment in the field hospital. While many authors place a large portion of the blame for the defeat squarely upon his shoulders, it is incontestable that he, virtually single-handedly, saved the remainder of the regiment. Thus the enigmatic Benteen deserved both a court martial for disobeying Custer's written order to hurry to him with the ammunition packs and a Medal of Honor for saving the 7th during the hilltop fight.

Crazy Horse (Suska Witko). Oglala Lakota born in 1839.[10] Killed while resisting arrest at Fort Robinson, Nebraska Territory on September 5, 1877 by Private William Gentles, Company F, 14th United States Infantry.[11] The most famous Lakota War Chief, he had an appreciation for tactics and strategy that was unique among the plains Indians. He led the decoy party resulting in the annihilation of Fetterman's command in 1866.[12] He reportedly had a major role in the Wagon Box Fight as well. He was a decoy in the attack on the Platte River Bridge Station.[13] He organized and led the attack on Crook's force on the Rosebud River on June 17th. During this battle, rather than meeting Crook's cavalry charges head on, the Indians enveloped the flanks and struck at weak points.

Crazy Horse, like all plains Indians war chiefs, led by example, inspiring his warriors to feats of bravery. He Dog described Crazy Horse's personal style of fighting: *"All the times I was in fights with Crazy Horse, in critical moments of the fight Crazy Horse would always jump off his horse to fire. He is the only Indian I ever knew who did that often. He wanted to be sure he hit what he aimed at. That is the kind of fighter he was. He didn't like to start a battle unless he had it all planned out in his head and knew he was going to win. He always used judgment and played it safe."*[14]

At the Little Big Horn, Crazy Horse may have thwarted Custer's attempt to capture the non–combatants north of the Cheyenne circle. Dr. V. T. McGillycuddy, assistant post surgeon at Fort Robinson where Crazy Horse was killed, summed up the great leader quite well:

> *"In him everything was made a second to patriotism and love of his people. Modest, fearless, a mystic, a believer in destiny, and much of a recluse, he was held in veneration and admiration by the younger warriors who would follow him anywhere . . . I could not but regard him as the greatest leader of his people in modern times."* [15]

George Crook. Born near Dayton, Ohio September 23, 1829; died of heart failure at his Chicago residence on March 21, 1890. The 1573rd graduate of West Point, Crook stood 38th in a class of 43.[16] A Brigadier General at the age of 32 and a Major General at 35, Crook received 5 Civil War Brevets for gallantry and meritorious service.[17]

Crook, famous for his winter campaigns and innovative use of pack trains and Indian scouts to track their own people, began honing his Indian fighting techniques against the Paiutes and Klamaths during the period 1866 – 1868.[18] Crook believed *"that a pack train can only be efficient when composed of mules expressly selected and used solely for that purpose."*[19] Crook organized his first pack train in 1867 under the civilian packer, Thomas Moore who would continue in that capacity for the next two decades.[20] Crook knew that Indians were far superior trackers to white scouts and their presence on campaign contributed to the psychological disintegration of the bands being pursued. Crook therefore always endeavored to use members of the tribe being pursued.[21] Crook's brilliant strategy of using small, mobile forces supported by Indian scouts and pack trains during the Tonto Basin Campaign in Arizona brought peace to the region and a promotion from Lieutenant Colonel to Brigadier General.

At the time of the 1876 Campaign Crook was the commander of the Department of the Platte. Action by his forces both opened (Cheyenne village on the Powder River, March 17th) and closed (Slim Buttes, September 9th) the campaign of 1876. His winter campaign was patterned after his Tonto Basin success in that he accompanied the column only as an observer, leaving the operational command to Colonel J. J. Reynolds. When the campaign ended in failure, Crook was quick to press charges against three of the officers involved. At the Battle of the Rosebud, Crook, although he would later attempt to deny it, exercised personal command and was decisively defeated by the combined force of Lakota and Cheyenne led by Crazy Horse. The defeat on the Rosebud, and Crook's subsequent lack of effort in communicating with Terry, was a major factor in the defeat of Custer 8 days later.

In late August he ran out of supplies and his command was forced to subsist on horse meat. The second "starvation march" Crook's troops were forced to endure during the '76 campaign culminated in Captain Anson Mills being dispatched to Deadwood to obtain supplies. Before reaching his destination, Mills discovered and attacked the Lakota village at Slim Buttes, thus ending the campaign, as it had begun, with a minor victory. As with most of the participants of the 1876 Campaign, Crook's is not an easy character to comprehend. He was undeniably innovative. He was equally inflexible and stubborn.[22]

Neil Mangum, former chief historian of the Custer Battlefield, offered an invaluable insight when he concluded Crook was just as ambitious as Nelson A. Miles or Armstrong Custer but he concealed it from view.[23] Upon being informed of Crook's death, General William T. Sherman remarked that he had been the greatest Indian fighter and manager the army ever had.[24] The late John M. Carroll, noted Custer historian, however, believed *"him to be the most over–rated officer in the U. S. Army, and one who deserved censure for his retreat (from the Rosebud, DCE) in 1876."*[25] Whatever your opinion as to Crook's character and culpability, it is clear his withdrawal from the Rosebud with only minor casualties allowed the opening for the escape of the Indians so dreaded by the military. It is also an unassailable fact that, of all the commanders in the 1876 Campaign, Crook knew that the Indians were concentrated in large numbers and were fighting with uncharacteristic skill and determination. He never attempted to communicate this intelligence to either Colonel Gibbon or General Terry although his Crow scouts informed him of Gibbon's location and he complained constantly of the lack of word from their columns.

Curly (Shes–his). Probably born about 1858. Died of pneumonia at his log cabin near Crow Agency, Montana on May 21, 1923. He enlisted with the 7th Infantry on April 10, 1876. With Custer's column on June 25th until dismissed from further service by Mitch Boyer acting under Custer's orders. He brought the first word of the disaster to the men on the steamer *Far West*; although, without an interpreter, they had great difficulty in discerning his message. Curly has become a center of controversy and the protagonist in many outlandish stories about the fight; my personal favorite being the one where Curly hides inside the carcass of a dead horse until the victorious warriors leave the field. This has led many authors to totally disregard any account attributed to this source.[26] Undoubtedly the victim of interpreters of questionable skill and unscrupulous authors, it is instructive to note that in his first interview about the battle Curly flatly denied any actual participation in the fighting.[27]

George Armstrong Custer. Born December 5, 1839 in New Rumley, Ohio. Killed in action June 25, 1876. The 1966th graduate of West Point, he stood last in a class of 34.[28] While much has been made of the number of demerits Custer received at West Point, other cadets, including Marcus A. Reno, received significantly more demerits.[29]

A Brigadier General at the age of 23 and a Major General at 25, Custer received 6 brevets for gallant and meritorious service during the Civil War[30] while having 11 horses shot from under him.[31] Known as "the Murat of the American Army,"[32] He played a key role in the union victory at Gettysburg when his division thwarted J. E. B. Stuart's attempt to gain the federal's rear. Captured Robert E. Lee's supply train outside Appomatox Court House and received Lee's messenger under flag of truce requesting surrender terms on April 9, 1865. Custer captured more armaments, more prisoners and more battle standards than any other commander in the Civil War.[33] A man of unquestioned courage and almost super–human stamina, he was one of the brilliant young Federal generals that wrested the mantle of invincibility from the shoulders of Stuart's cavalry corps. During the Civil War, Custer displayed *"rare combat talents and instincts and built his success on swift perception and almost instant reaction."*[34] These characteristics explain why Custer was such a favorite of Sheridan's who, himself, *"didn't care how many men he lost if he carried his objective and once he had identified his objective he went for it by the most direct means with little respect for the conventions of 'civilized' warfare."*[35] Much of the man and his Civil War record may be learned from his order to the Third Cavalry Division after the capitulation at Appomatox:

> *"During the past six months, though in most instances confronted by superior numbers, you have captured from the enemy in open battle 111 pieces of field artillery, 65 battle–flags, and upwards of 10,000 prisoners of war, including several general officers. Within the past ten days, and included in the above, you have captured 46 field–pieces of artillery, and 37 battle–flags. You have never lost a gun, never lost a color, and never been defeated; and, notwithstanding the numerous engagements in which you have borne a prominent part, including those memorable battles of the Shenandoah, you have captured every piece of artillery which the enemy has dared to open upon you."*[36]

In 1866 Custer accepted the lieutenant colonelcy of the 7th U. S. Cavalry, becoming one of four officers that served with the regiment from its inception to Little Big Horn.[37] Shortly after joining the 7th Cavalry, Custer turned down the colonelcy of the 9th Cavalry, a black regiment.[38] Court martialed and suspended from pay and rank for one year in 1867. Although technically second in command, through the patronage of Sheridan,[39] Custer commanded the 7th from its inception until his death, excepting only the period of his

his suspension. During the 1867 Hancock expedition Custer learned that you couldn't successfully chase Indians on the plains; they must be attacked in their villages.[40] This lesson was applied with great success at the Washita the following year; giving the post Civil War army its first major success against plains Indians. The prowess of the Lakota was probably overestimated by Custer and his military contemporaries during the 1873 Stanley expedition and equally underestimated during the 1876 campaign. In January of 1876 he had prophetically written his brother Tom from New York:

> *". . . I have no idea of obtaining my promotion this spring or summer.[41] On the contrary, I expect to be in the field, in the summer, with the 7th, and think there will be lively work before us. I think the 7th Cavalry may have its greatest campaign ahead."[42]*

Custer *"was by nature an irrepressible romantic who saw himself and the service in cavalier terms."[43]* He was extremely fond of animals, usually being accompanied in the field by his dogs and various specimens he'd collect along the way including a "tamed" antelope and a pelican.

Successful tactics employed at the Battle of the Washita in November of 1868 proved disastrous at the Little Big Horn when the elements of his divided command wound up out of supporting distance of each other and were easily defeated individually. According to the accounts of burial parties, his marker is too far down the slope. This is probably due to the construction of the monument and the access road. His body was actually found about 6 feet south of the present monument.

At the time of his death Custer was the senior lieutenant colonel of cavalry in the army and would have been promoted in 1877.[44] The controversies dealing with Custer's actions leading up to and at the Little Big Horn are dealt with in depth in the narrative. There are, however, probably two points about this complex individual upon which all can agree. First, it is just as difficult today to be ambivalent about the man as it was during his lifetime. One either admires or loathes him; there are no half measures. Second, while victory at Little Big Horn might have won him fleeting fame, death at that place secured him immortality.

Thomas Ward Custer. Younger brother of George Armstrong Custer, Tom was born March 15, 1845, in New Rumley, Ohio. Killed in action with the Custer Column June 25, 1876.[45] Entered military service as a private September 2, 1861. During the Civil War he rose from the ranks to second lieutenant. One of only nineteen men in U. S. history to be awarded two Medals of Honor, Tom Custer was the first recipient of the dual award and the only man honored for two Civil War actions.[46] He received four brevets for Civil War service, attaining the rank of lieutenant colonel for his exploits at Saylor's Creek.[47] One of four officers to serve with the 7th Cavalry from its inception to Little Big Horn[48], he was promoted Captain in December 1875.[49]

An accomplished practical joker, Tom once told Lieutenant Gibson's daughter that he wore his hat tilted almost over his eyes as a disguise because he was wanted for killing a chinaman. During the Washita Campaign, he managed to run afoul of a skunk and was liberally dosed. Rather than immediately attend to rectifying the situation, Tom set out on making the rounds of the other officers, staying in a tent only long enough for the occupants to notice the change in the atmosphere and begin to accuse one another.[50]

Although the captain of Company C, he apparently served as Aide–de–Camp to his brother throughout the campaign as he neither accompanied his company on Reno's scout nor died on the same part of the field on June 25th. One of the most mutilated bodies found on the battlefield, he was identified by a tattoo containing his initials. The condition of his body fostered the myth that the Uncpapa warrior Rain In The Face had killed both Custers and cut out and eaten Tom's heart; a pure fabrication that was believed by many, including Libbie Custer.[51] Finding his body, and the body of Lieutenant Algernon E. Smith , so near his brother, and so far from his company, has led many authors to speculate that most 7th Cavalry officers with Custer did not die with their units. According to accounts of burial parties, his marker is too far down the slope. This is probably due to the construction of the monument and the access road. His body was actually found about 6 feet further up the slope than General Custer's. Tom's buckskin jacket was recovered after the attack on Dull Knife's Cheyenne village on November 25, 1876.[52]

Charles Camilus DeRudio. Born Carlo Camillo di Rudio[53] in Belluno, Italy on August 26, 1832.[54] Died November 1, 1910.[55] He took the name Charles Camilius DeRudio when he enlisted in the Union Army in 1864.[56] He was educated at the Austrian Military Academy and served on the staff of General Garabaldi. An extremely interesting and controversial individual, he escaped from a life sentence on Devil's Island where he was confined for his role in the attempt to assassinate Emperor Louis Napoleon in 1858. [57] Entered U. S. Military service as a private on August 25, 1864. Second Lieutenant DeRudio was assigned to the 7th Cavalry on July 14, 1869. He was promoted first lieutenant of Troop E on December 10, 1875, to fill the vacancy created by the promotion of Thomas M. McDougall to Captain of Troop B.[58]

DeRudio was neither liked nor respected by his fellow officers and was "exchanged" with Lieutenant Algernon Smith of Troop A, preventing him from commanding Company E. Hence DeRudio, serving under Reno in the valley, survived while Smith rode to his death in command of Company E, the Gray Horse Troop.[59] While in the valley, he saw Custer wave his hat from a high point on the bluffs across the Little Big Horn River. He was left in the timber during Reno's retreat from the valley on June 25th. After many narrow escapes, he and Private Thomas Dean O'Neill rejoined the command the night of June 26th. DeRudio was an outspoken critic of Reno, actually accusing him of cowardice. Referred to as "Count No Account" by members of the 7th cavalry due to his sometimes conflicting stories about the Little Big Horn Battle, his reputation for unreliability has caused many authorities to ignore his accounts of the battle.

Gall (Pizi). Probably born along the Moreau River in South Dakota about 1840. Died December 5, 1893 (some authorities give the year as 1894). Gall, although an orphan, rose to prominence among Uncpapa Lakota fighting men. Gall once led a war party that killed many Arikara warriors including Bloody Knife's two brothers.[60] This act, coupled with the personal abuse Gall heaped upon Bloody Knife when the Arikara lived with the Uncpapa, led to a long–standing feud. In November of 1865 Bloody Knife led a platoon of soldiers to Gall's tepee south of Fort Berthold. According to Joseph H. Taylor, who got the story from Bloody Knife in 1875, the soldiers believed they were going to the camp of Long Dog and his renegades. During the subsequent melee, Gall was shot and stabbed through the breast three times with a bayonet. The officer in charge prevented Bloody Knife from blowing Gall's head off. Miraculously Gall survived. He recounted substantially the same story to Father Pierre DeSmet in 1868 but did not name Bloody Knife or any other Indian as a principal in the affair.[61] His band probably did not join the village until after the Rosebud fight.

At Little Big Horn, Gall was one of the principal Uncpapa war chiefs, rallying the warriors to repulse Reno in the valley. His two wives and three children were killed during Reno's attack on the village:

". . . it made my heart bad. After that I killed my enemies with the hatchet."[62]

Taking his cue from Lame White Man's successful assault on platoons of C and E Companies near Deep Ravine, Gall led the charge that overwhelmed L and I Companies.

After the Little Big Horn, Gall retreated into Canada along with Sitting Bull. Following a dispute with Sitting Bull, Gall returned to the United States with part of the Uncpapa band in early 1881. He surrendered to General Nelson A. Miles and, after a short confinement at Fort Buford, sent to the Standing Rock Indian Reservation in South Dakota, where he cultivated land and attempted to live up to treaty agreements. He converted to Christianity and is said to have attended the mission church service carrying his weapons and painted, as if for a war council. Lieutenant Godfrey *"perceived Gall as a man of tremendous character, natural ability, and great common sense, a chief whose massive physiognomy reminded him of Daniel Webster."*

John Oliver Gibbon. Born April 20, 1827 in Holmesburg, Pennsylvania. Died February 6, 1896. The 1350th graduate of West Point, Gibbon stood 20th in a class of 38.[63] Fought against the Seminole Indians in 1848 - 49. A Brigadier General at age 34 and a Major General at 37, Gibbon's Civil War record is nothing short of brilliant. He received 5 Civil War brevets for gallant and meritorious service and was wounded during the battles of Fredericksburg and Gettysburg.[64] The capstone of his brilliant Civil War career was the breaking of Pickett's charge at Gettysburg.[65] Retired as a Brigadier General, U. S. Army, on April 30, 1891.

In contrast to his daring Civil War exploits, his Indian War service record is replete with indecision and inaction. At the Battle of the Big Hole he narrowly avoided a disaster tantamount to Little Big Horn when Chief Joseph continued his flight rather than storm Gibbon's fragile defensive position.[66]

During the 1876 campaign Gibbon commanded the Montana Column. For over a month, his was the only force in the field. His chief of scouts, Lieutenant James H. Bradley, secured just the information needed for a successful campaign, but Gibbon, at various times, either ignored it or misrepresented it. After the first sighting of the village on May 16th, Gibbon attempted a movement that was abandoned virtually before it was begun when he was unable to get the cavalry's horses across the swollen Yellowstone. The second sighting, eleven days later on the Rosebud, the sight that Reno was to "discover" on his June scout, was totally ignored. Both Lieutenant Bradley and Doctor Paulding speak derisively of Gibbon's inaction in their respective journal and diary. It is clear from Gibbon's own reports that his inaction while "guarding the Yellowstone" increased the confidence and belligerence of the Indians. Gibbon's failure to maintain surveillance over the village, and his withholding of vital intelligence, was a major factor in Custer's subsequent defeat.

Edward Settle Godfrey. . Born October 9, 1843, in Kalida, Putnam County, Ohio. Died April 1, 1932. Entered military service as a private in Company D, 21st Ohio Volunteer Infantry, on April 26, 1861. Honorably discharged on August 12, 1861. Entered the U. S. Military Academy July 1, 1863, graduating 53rd in a class of 63 (the 2208th graduate) on June 17, 1867, and was appointed a Second Lieutenant in Company G, 7th Cavalry effective that date. In addition to the Little Big Horn, Godfrey served with the 7th Cavalry at the Washita, Bear Paw Mountains, and Wounded Knee. Promoted First Lieutenant on February 1, 1868, Godfrey was in charge of burning the village at the Battle of the Washita, November 27, 1868. Participated in Colonel David Stanley's expedition protecting the Northern Pacific Railroad Survey along the Yellowstone in 1873, and was engaged in the action against the Lakota at the mouth of the Big Horn River on August 11th. Assistant Engineering Officer with Custer in the Black Hills expedition of 1874. Wounded in action against the Nez Perce at the Bear Paw Mountains September 30, 1877, he subsequently received the Medal of Honor and a brevet of Major for this action.[67] He retired from active service with the rank of Brigadier General on April 30, 1891.

In the absence of Captain Owen Hale, on detached duty in St. Louis, commanded Company K, the "Dude Troop," at the Little Big Horn and was responsible for averting disaster when he dismounted his company to cover the retreat from Weir Point. He then courted disaster by entrenching in a position that had virtually no field of fire. His diary and article for *Century Magazine* in January of 1892 comprise a large portion of our knowledge of the Little Big Horn Campaign. Never an admirer of Reno, he grew to believe that Reno was both *"cowardly and craven"* at Little Big Horn. While his loyalty to the regiment precluded his making a public statement until 1924, he developed a loathing for Major Reno when informed by Benteen that Reno had proposed abandoning the wounded the night of June 25th. This hatred of Reno reached such an extent that Godfrey felt compelled to block placing Reno's name, and of necessity all others, on the monument at the Reno–Benteen Defense Site. He maintained that on the night of the 25th, Captain Thomas B. Weir had come to him, greatly agitated and distressed, soliciting his support for Benteen should a conflict arise between Reno and the 7th's senior captain. We are indebted to Godfrey as one of the primary chroniclers of the 1876 campaign.

Miles Walter Keogh. Born March 25, 1840, at Orchard House, Leighlinbridge, County Carlow, Ireland. Killed in action with the Custer Column June 25, 1876.[68] A professional soldier, Keogh fought briefly in Algeria before serving in the Pope's army, being commissioned a lieutenant in the Papal Guards on November 9, 1860. Twice wounded during the Civil War, he was awarded three brevets for gallant and meritorious service, including one for his actions at Gettysburg. Appointed Captain of U. S. Volunteers effective April 9, 1862. Captured with General Stoneman at Sunshine Church, Georgia on July 31, 1864, he was exchanged September 30, 1864. Commissioned Captain in the 7th Cavalry to rank from July 28, 1866, the date the regiment was organized. Assigned to command of Company I, 7th U. S. Cavalry on November 16, 1866, Keogh served in that capacity until his death. Interestingly, Keogh was absent from all of the 7th's major campaigns (Washita Battle, Yellowstone and Black Hills Expeditions) with the single exception of the Little Big Horn. Keogh is generally credited with introducing *"Garry Owen"* to the regiment.[69]

Keogh's horse, Comanche, was reputed to be the only living thing found on the battlefield. Keogh's body, his leg shattered by a bullet that had passed through Comanche's chest, was found surrounded by his noncommissioned officers. Keogh's body was not mutilated, probably due to the *Agnus Dei* found still around his neck, [70] but the *Medaglia di Pro Petri Sede*, awarded by Pope Pius IX, which he habitually carried was missing. Keogh's fame and popularity have grown over the years until they rival that of Custer himself. The position of Keogh's Company seems to verify that he was serving as a battalion commander at the Little Big Horn. The location of the bodies from Company I, when coupled with Indian accounts and the accounts of the troops on Weir Point, gives valuable insight as to the progress of the fight as it reached its crescendo. Keogh's company guidon, his watch, gauntlets, and a blood stained photo of Captain McDougall's sister that he had carried into the fight were recovered after the Battle of Slim Buttes. [71]

Lame White Man. Born about 1838. [72] Killed near Deep Ravine June 25, 1876. An "Old Man Chief" of the Southern Cheyenne, he had lived for many years among the Northern Cheyenne and had been accepted as a chief by them. He led his people off the White River Reservation to join the non reservation Indians in early April. [73] Participated in the Rosebud fight against General Crook on June 17th. Principal Cheyenne war chief in the Custer fight.

Lame White Man was the catalyst of the Little Big Horn. Without his direct intervention, Little Big Horn might have been relegated the status of just another "drawn" fight during the 1876 campaign. His bold stroke at the crucial moment elevated the conflict to the plateau of saga and legend. Shouting his war cry, *"Come! We can kill all of them!"*, he was killed leading the charge that over–ran the "South Skirmish Line" near Deep Ravine preventing the junction of the two battalions of Custer's immediate command that was already in progress and precipitating the subsequent rout. Probably mistaken in the heat of battle for an Arikara scout, he may have been mistakenly killed by the Lakota. [74]

Rain In The Face (Ite Magaju). Uncpapa Lakota warrior born near the forks of the Cheyenne River in North Dakota in 1835. [75] Died in September 1905. Received his name after an all day battle in the rain that smeared and streaked his war paint. Participated in the Fetterman fight. Arrested in 1875 by Lieutenant Tom Custer and Captain George W. Yates for the murder of the sutler Balliran and veterinary surgeon Honsinger during the Yellowstone Expedition of 1873. Years after the Little Big Horn, he was tried for, and acquitted of, the murders.

Captured a guidon at Little Big Horn and had two horses shot from under him during the fight. Severely wounded in the right leg, he cut the bullet out himself, severing several tendons in the process so that thereafter he walked with a limp. [76] He is best known for his alleged threat to cut out and eat the heart of Tom Custer. [77]

Marcus Albert Reno. Born on November 15, 1834, in Carrollton, Greene County, Illinois. [78] Died following a cancer operation on April 1, 1889 (some sources list the date as either March 30th or 31st). [79] The 1779th graduate of West Point, Reno stood 20th in a class of 38. [80] Reno, once wounded during the Civil War, was breveted 4 times for gallant and meritorious service, attaining the rank of Brigadier General of Volunteers. His August 1869 posting to the 7th Cavalry was his first permanent attachment to a regiment. [81] Cavalry representative on the five officer board, chaired by General Terry, that selected the Springfield Model 1873 rifle as the weapon to be used by the combined U. S. Army forces. When it appeared that Custer would not be allowed to accompany the 1876 expedition, he implored Terry to place him in command of the cavalry. Incurred General Terry's displeasure for violating orders on his scout of June 10th to the 19th. He was court martialed and suspended from rank and pay for two years in 1877. Shortly after his return to active duty, he was court martialed and dismissed from the service for *"disorders and neglects. . . to the prejudice of good order and military discipline.*'[82]

Commanded companies A, G, and M in the valley fight and A, B, D, G, H, K, M, and the pack train during the hilltop fight. Probably the most maligned officer in the United States Army since Benedict Arnold, he has been accused of cowardice for his conduct in the valley following the death of Bloody Knife. He was also accused, although not publicly, of suggesting abandoning the wounded the night of June 25th. He has been further accused of being drunk on the 25th and 26th of June. At Little Big Horn, Reno's first Indian fight, [83] he was ordered by Custer to take three troops and charge the village; a movement that would be supported by the entire command. Instead of charging into the village, Reno dismounted his command and formed a skirmish line. After a short time, he retired to a defensive position in the timber along the river bottom. He almost immediately led a panic retreat to the heights across the river attendant with great loss of life.[84] For this, and his subsequent inaction during the siege on the hilltop, he has been accused of cowardice.

On the other side of the coin, Private William C. Slaper, Company M, 7th Cavalry, had high praise for the coolness displayed by Reno both in the valley and on the hilltop. His July 4, 1876 letter not withstanding, it is very difficult, and I believe unjustified, to label a veteran officer, who was in the thick of the fighting at Antietam and Mechanicsville, coward.[85] Historically, Reno has been cast as the villain of the piece. While he may properly be heavily censured for the timid manner in which his "charge" down the valley was conducted, that the order to withdraw from the timber was not communicated to all elements of the command, the failure to cover the retreat crossing of the Little Big Horn, and abrogating his command to Captain Benteen during the siege on the hill, others were far more responsible for the disaster that befell the 7th Cavalry. He demanded a court of inquiry into his actions at the Little Big Horn to clear his name. The court gave a lukewarm endorsement of his actions; finding no case for misconduct.

Sitting Bull (Tatanka Iyotaka). Uncpapa Lakota born on the Grand River near the present town of Bullhead, South Dakota in March of 1831.[86] Murdered by Indian policemen Bull Head and Red Tomahawk at Pine Ridge Reservation on December 15, 1891.[87] A more proper translation of his name is "A Buffalo Bull Lives Permanently Among Us." A powerful warrior and war leader in his youth,[88] by 1876 Sitting Bull had become the spiritual advisor of the entire Lakota Nation. Contrary to popular belief, Sitting Bull was not spoiling for a fight in 1876; rather he was following his policy of isolation from the white man. His sundance torture induced dream of *"many soldiers falling into camp"* did much to bolster the confidence of Lakota warriors.

Much controversy has arisen about him and especially his role at the Little Big Horn. Much of this controversy is due to Indian Agent James McLaughlin's frustration over his failed attempt at "civilizing" Sitting Bull. Sitting Bull maintained that if Custer would have parlayed before attacking, the Indians would have surrendered and gone on the reservation. He did not lead his people to Slim Buttes after the Little Big Horn, camping instead on Grand River to mourn the loss of his young son who had died after being kicked in the head by a mule. After the battle Sitting Bull led his people to Canada. Returning in 1881, he was held a virtual prisoner for a year at Fort Randall before being sent to Standing Rock Reservation. Some authorities believe the reason he was allowed to travel with Buffalo Bill and his Wild West Show, organized in 1883, was to keep Sitting Bull away from the reservation.

W. H. H. Murray, in a New York World article, provided a suitable eulogy:

> *"I knew this man; knew him in his relation to his high office among his people and in his elements as a man. This man Sitting Bull was a prophet, not war chief, to his people. What was a misnomer, to us in our ignorance of facts and things, to the Red Man . . . was a rank above all ranks won or bestowed by the tribe, an office . . . connected with, and symbolic of the highest truths and deepest mysteries of their religion. Hence by virtue of his office he was the counselor of chiefs, . . . the oracle of mysteries and of knowledge hidden from the mass; even from the chiefs, . . . Such was Sitting Bull as to his office, as interpreted from a standpoint of knowledge of the religion, the traditions and superstitions of his people. That he was faithful to his high office all knew, . . . that leaf of laurel none can deny to his fame, . . . I met him often; I studied him closely . . . and I knew him well, and this I say of him, he was A Sioux of the Sioux, . . . in him his race, in physique, in manners, in virtues, in faults stood incarnate, . . . His word once given was a true bond. . . . He was a born diplomat, . . . there was no surface to him, he was the embodiment of depths, . . ."[89]*

Alfred Howe Terry. Born November 10, 1827 in Hartford Connecticut. Died December 16, 1890.[90] A lawyer in civilian life, he entered military service as Colonel, 2nd Connecticut Volunteers May 7, 1861. Twice breveted for gallant and meritorious service, he attained the rank of Major General of Volunteers and Brigadier General U. S. Army, during the Civil War. He fought at First Bull Run, his regiment being last off the field.[91] Achieved his greatest military success with the capture of Fort Fisher, the "Gibraltar of the South" in January 1865. A member of the peace commission of 1868 that granted the Lakota their hunting grounds in perpetuity, unless 3/4 of the adult males agreed to a sale, (the same lands that the 1876 expedition was attempting to take by force) Terry had favored the distribution of guns and ammunition to the Indians. President of the board of officers that selected the Springfield Model 1873 rifle as the weapon to be used by the combined U. S. Army forces. Terry had no prior experience fighting Indians and, in fact, did not gain any first hand experience during the campaign. His appointment as brigadier in the regular army was the highest rank any non–West Point graduate earned in the postwar army.[92]

Sent in overall command of the expedition when Custer fell into disfavor with the Grant administration due to his testimony regarding the Belknap impeachment hearings. He has been criticized for going into camp the night of June 26th with a strong Indian force in view. While charges of Custer's disobedience of orders became prominent after his death, Terry's two reports of the Little Big Horn, written six days apart, hint at a cover-up designed to make Custer the scapegoat for the disaster.

White Bull. Sitting Bull's nephew. Participated in both the Fetterman and Wagon Box Fights. Head Chief of the Fox Soldier Warrior Society.

Fought against both Reno and Custer. Reached the Custer portion of the battlefield before the soldiers took their final positions on Battle Ridge. His account of the battle seems to confirm recent archaeological findings indicating some soldier positions north of the present monument. Participated in the charge that split Calhoun's and Keogh's companies ending the fighting on the east end of Battle Ridge. At the Little Big Horn he counted 7 coups (6 firsts), killed two men, captured 2 guns and 12 horses, had his horse killed under him, and was wounded in the ankle.

Became a scalp Shirt Man (one of 6 head chiefs) in 1881. In later life he became an Indian Policeman and joined the Congressional Church. He was honored at the 50th anniversary of the Battle of the Little Big Horn.

Wooden Leg (Kum–mok–quiv–vi–ok–ta). Probably born in 1858. Member of the Elk Warrior Society. This Cheyenne warrior received his name because of his ability to walk long distances without tiring. Was in the Cheyenne–Ogalala village attacked by Colonel J. J. Reynolds on March 17th. He lost all of his personal possessions in that fight but gained some measure of revenge by participating in the recapture of the pony herd. Participated in the Rosebud fight against General Crook.

Fought in both the Custer and Reno fights. He claimed to have "scalped" one of Lieutenant W. W. Cooke's sideburns as a trophy.[93] As he is the best known of the warriors identified as taking position on Sharpshooter Ridge, that landmark should, I believe, carry his name to be in concert with other landmarks on the battlefield that have been named for participants.
Served as a scout for the army during the Ghost Dance troubles in 1890. Although not an active participant, he was present at the Battle of Wounded Knee. Went to Washington as a Cheyenne delegate just as his grandfather, No Braids, had many years before. Served two terms as a judge at the Cheyenne agency. His detailed account of the Custer fight has been largely ignored, perhaps due to the claim of mass suicide among the troopers of Custer's immediate command.

---

[1] See John M. Carroll "Roll Call on the Little Big Horn."

[2] See pages 39–45 of "Harvest of Barren Regrets" by Charles K. Mills for a complete description of the *Fair Play* affair. It is interesting to note that Theodore C. ("Charley") Benteen was the only non–military prisoner in that action not to be released, remaining in custody for the duration of the war. The reader will have to judge whether this was the act of a loving son concerned for his father's welfare, or one of spiteful vengeance. It should also be noted that Karol Asay, in "Gray Head and Long Hair" pp 3 – 4, doubts Benteen had any direct involvement in the incident.

[3] In 1866 Benteen was offered a major's commission in the 10th Cavalry, but chose the captaincy of H Troop in the 7th instead. See Colonel W. A. Graham "The Custer Myth," pages 159 – 160.

[4] See Evan S. Connell "Son of the Morning Star," page 39.

[5] See John M. Carroll "Roll Call on the Little Big Horn."

[6] See "The Benteen – Golden Letters" edited by John M. Carroll pages 201 – 202 and Charles K. Mills "Harvest of Barren Regrets" pages 303 - 304 for Benteen's difficulties with Colonel Samuel Sturgis during the 1877 Nez Perce Campaign and page 221 of Carroll for Benteen's gloating over his perceived thwarting of Colonel Nelson Miles' plans for an 1877–78 winter campaign.

[7] See Edgar I. Stewart "Custer's Luck," page 169.

[8] See John Upton Terrell and Colonel George Walton, "Faint the Trumpet Sounds," page 73.

[9] See D. A., Kinsley "Favor the Bold: Custer the Indian Fighter," page 124.

[10] See Evans S. Connell "Son of the Morning Star," page 71.

[11] See Richard G. Hardorff "The Oglala Lakota Crazy Horse" page 9. This excellent work provides genealogical information about Crazy Horse as well as biographical information on Gentles.

[12] See Jason. Hook "American Indian Warrior Chiefs," page 76.

[13] See Jason. Hook "American Indian Warrior Chiefs," page 73.

[14] See Jim Holly "Crazy Horse on the Greasy Grass" pages 107 - 108.

[15] See Jason Hook "American Indian Warrior Chiefs," page 53.

[16] When Crook was appointed a Major General, USA in 1888 to fill the vacancy created by the retirement of Alfred H. Terry, he became the lowest ranking cadet to rise to that rank. See Martin F. Schmitt, "General George Crook: His Autobiography,: page xvii. and Neil Mangum "Battle of the Rosebud: Prelude to the Little Bighorn," page 11.

[17] See John M. Carroll "Roll Call on The Little Big Horn," page 48.

[18] See Paul Andrew Hutton "Soldiers West," pages 117 – 118.

[19] See Paul Andrew Hutton "Soldiers West," page 120. Crook could not have been surprised by the trouble Terry had with his pack train which was comprised of mules that had pulled the freight wagons from Fort Lincoln.

[20] See Paul Andrew Hutton "Soldiers West," page 120.

[21] See Paul Andrew Hutton "Soldiers West," page 121.

[22] See Paul Andrew Hutton "Soldiers West," page 118.

[23] See Neil Mangum "Battle of the Rosebud: Prelude to the Little Bighorn," page 17.

[24] See John G. Bourke "On the Border With Crook," page vi.

[25] See John M. Carroll "Custer's Chief of Scouts: The Reminiscences of Charles A. Varnum," page 63.

[26] Many authors probably feel as Russell White Bear felt when he told Curly shortly before Curly's death that he had interpreted for him many times but still didn't have his story straight. See Joe Sills Jr. "The Crow Scouts: Their Contribution in Understanding the Little Big Horn Battle," page 15.

[27] This interview, conducted by Lieutenant James H. Bradley with Thomas H. Leforge acting as interpreter, occurred about one week after the battle. See Thomas Marquis "Custer on the Little Big Horn," pp 116 – 117. Dan Old Elk, Curly's great grandson, told this author that it has been handed down through the family that Curly did not participate in the fight.

[28] See John M. Carroll "They Rode With Custer."

[29] In fact, Custer's 726 demerits pale in comparison to Reno's academy record of 1031; a total that caused Reno to spend an extra year in order to graduate. See Evan S. Connell "Son of the Morning Star," pages 40 and 107. Custer, in fact, had only the third highest demerit total in his own regiment. He was exceeded not only by Reno, but also Lieutenant Benjamin Hodgson who accumulated a total of 747. See Tom O'Neil, "Cadet George Armstrong Custer: Demerits and Academics" page 1 and Brian Pohanka "Schooled for Conflict: 7th Cavalry Officers at West Point 1863 – 1875" page 28. It should be noted that there is currently a school of thought that Reno should only be charged with 657 demerits; the demerits for his two suspended years (1854 – 1855, and 1855 – 1856) having been crossed out in the Delinquency Register. To my mind this is much like the argument over Roger Maris' 61st home run coming in a 162 game season versus Babe Ruth hitting 60 homers in 154 games. See "The Battlefield Dispatch: A Quarterly Newsletter of the Custer Battlefield Historical & Museum Association, Inc." Summer 1994, Volume 13, No. 3, page 7.

[30] See John M. Carroll "They Rode With Custer."

[31] See Robert Paul. Jordan "Ghosts on the Little Big Horn," page 789.

[32] See Frederic F. Van de Water "Glory Hunter: A Life of General Custer," page 358.

[33] See D. Mark Katz "Custer in Photographs," page xiii.

[34] See Robert M. Utley "Life in Custer's Cavalry," page 256.

[35] See Robert M. Utley "Frontier Regulars." page 142.

[36] See Frederic F. Van de Water "Glory Hunter: A Life of General Custer," pages 116 – 117.

[37] See Fred Dustin "The Custer Tragedy," page 8.

[38] Like many officers of the period, Benteen among them, Custer preferred service in a lower grade with a white regiment to service with a black regiment. In Custer's case this was probably due more to a fear of being left out of the mainstream than to racial prejudice. See Fred Dustin, "The Custer Tragedy," page15 and Frederic Van de Water, "Glory Hunter: A Life of General Custer," pg 142.

[39] Sheridan and Custer both would have subscribed to Theodore Roosevelt's credo: *"Far better it is to dare mighty things, to win glorious triumphs, even though checkered by failure, than to take rank with those poor spirits who neither enjoy much nor suffer much, because they live in the gray twilight that knows not victory nor defeat."* See Robert J. Ege "Curse Not His Curls" page 22.

[40] See Stan Hoig "The Battle of the Washita," page 20. At the battle of Williamsburg, Custer had learned from the same General Hancock that disobedience of orders could sometimes bring victory. See Jay Monaghan, "Custer," page 372.

[41] Custer was the senior lieutenant colonel of cavalry. His promotion to full colonel would have necessitated a transfer to another regiment.

[42] See Marguerite Merington "The Custer Story," page 277.

[43] See Stan Hoig "The Battle of the Washita," page 2.

[44] See Francis B. Taunton "Sufficient Reason?," page 91.

[45] See John M. Carroll "Roll Call on the Little Big Horn."

[46] See John M. Carroll "They Rode With Custer." During an attack on a confederate cavalry unit near Namozine Church on April 3rd, 1865, he shot the rebel color bearer and captured the colors as well as 14 prisoners, including 3 officers. For this action he was awarded his first Medal of Honor . See Raymond J. Tassin "Double Winners of the Medal of Honor," page 17. Three days later Tom won his second Medal of Honor for capturing a flag in the action at Saylor's Creek. Although shot in the right cheek, the bullet exiting behind the right ear, he had to be ordered from the field by his brother before he would seek medical attention. See "Double Winners of the Medal of Honor, pages 21 – 22. While some authorities list as many as 5 civil war double Medal of Honor winners, the data is ambiguous and Tom Custer is generally accepted as the only double award winner from that conflict.

[47] See John M. Carroll "Roll Call on the Little Big Horn."

[48] See Fred Dustin "The Custer Tragedy," page 8.

[49] See John M. Carroll "They Rode With Custer."

[50] See Carl Day "If You Want To Know" page 7.

[51] The "Revenge of Rain in the Face" theory was popularized by Longfellow's poem. See Elizabeth B. Custer, "Boots and Saddles," page 178.

[52] See James S. Hutchins "Boots and Saddles At the Little Big Horn," page 15 and Jud Tuttle "Remnants of a Regiment, pg 39, 2nd Symposium.

[53] See Kenneth Hammer "Little Big Horn Biographies," page 15. and Charles K. Mills "Charles C. DeRudio," page 10.

[54] See Charles K. Mills "Charles C. DeRudio," page 3.

[55] See John M. Carroll "Roll Call on the Little Big Horn."

[56] See Charles K. Mills "Charles C. DeRudio," page 10.

[57] See Charles K. Mills "Charles C. DeRudio," pages 5 – 8.

[58] See John M. Carroll "They Rode With Custer."

[59] While Custer denied responsibility for the "swap" it seems improbable that any other officer with the authority to order such an exchange would have done so. Benteen felt that the exchange was made at least partly upon the request of General Terry. See Charles K. Mills "Charles C. DeRudio," page 22. When his personal appeal to General Terry failed, DeRudio petitioned the Adjutant General of the Army to place him in command of Troop E. Custer wrote a scathing "endorsement" of the request which reads in part:

". . . Lieut. DeRudio possesses neither the experience nor the ability which can be claimed for Lieut.

Smith nor is he a fit person in my opinion to exercise not only the command of, but to be the only

officer present with a cavalry company, liable to be called upon at any moment to engage in

important service against hostile Indians. . . The transfer of Lieut. DeRudio to A Company was made

partially at his request and to give two officers to each company. No better commentary could

probably be made upon the value of Lieut. DeRudio's services as a company officer than to state that

the Captain of the company to which Lieut. DeRudio has been assigned protested in respectful terms

against having Lieut. DeRudio in the company, preferring to perform the entire duty alone. . . "

See Robert M. Utley "Gossip and Scandal," pages 18 – 19.

[60] See Neil Mangum "Gall: Sioux Gladiator or White Man's Pawn?," page 29 and Evan S. Connell "Son of the Morning Star," page 17.

[61] See Ernest Lisle Reedstrom "Bloody Knife: Custer's Favorite Scout" page 21.

[62] See Colonel W. A. Graham "The Custer Myth," page 90.

[63] See John M. Carroll "Roll Call on the Little Big Horn"

[64] See John M. Carroll "Roll Call on the Little Big Horn"

[65] See Jack McLaughlin "Gettysburg: The Long Encampment," page 153.

[66] See Robert M. Utley, "Frontier Regulars," page 16 and Merrill D. Beal, "I Will Fight No More Forever," pages 115 – 126.

[67] See John M. Carroll "Roll Call on the Little Big Horn."

[68] See G. A. Hayes–McCoy "Captain Myles Walter Keogh: United States Army 1840 – 1876" page 1. Note that John M. Carroll in "Roll Call on the Little Big Horn" cites Keogh's birth year as 1842. It is probable that the 1840 date is correct as that would have made Keogh 20 at the time he received his commission in the papal guard rather than the apparently too youthful 18 the 1842 date requires.

[69] See "The Field Diary of Edward Settle Godfrey," page 61.

[70] See Robert J. Ege "Legend Was a Man Named Keogh," pages 38 – 39 and Evan S. Connell "Son of the Morning Star," pages 290 – 291.

[71] See John M. Carroll Papers of The Order of Indian Wars page 43 and James S. Hutchins "Boots and Saddles At the Little Big Horn: page 18.

[72] See Thomas B. Marquis "Wooden Leg: A Warrior Who Fought Custer," page 268.

[73] See Thomas B. Marquis "Wooden Leg: A Warrior Who Fought Custer," page 183.

[74] Lame White Man had been participating in the sweat bath ritual when Reno attacked and had time only to wrap a blanket around himself before entering the fight. His loose flowing hair may have caused the Lakota to confuse him for an army scout. In any event, his body was mistakenly scalped by the Lakota. See Thomas B. Marquis "Wooden Leg: A Warrior Who Fought Custer," pages 241 – 242.

[75] See Bruce. Grant "Concise Encyclopedia of the American Indian," page 261.

[76] See Cyrus Townsend. Brady "Indian Fights and Fighters," page 289.

[77] Rain in the Face had been arrested by Tom Custer in December of 1875 and vowed revenge. The horribly mutilated condition of Tom's body gave rise to the legend that Rain had made good his threat. Despite the difficulty of identifying anyone covered with grime and gunpowder amidst the dust and turmoil of a battlefield, and despite the lack of reliable information to confirm the story, many people, including Libbie Custer, believed it. See Bruce Grant "Concise Encyclopedia of the American Indian," page 261 and Evan S. Connell "Son of the Morning Star," pages 386 – 392, for an account of the arrest of Rain in the Face. See also Elizabeth Custer "Boots and Saddle," page 178.

[78] There has been some debate over Reno's true birthdate. The date used here has been confirmed by Reno's grand–nephew, Charlie Reno (Reno himself had "calculated" his birth as occurring in 1832).

[79] See John M. Carroll "Roll Call on the Little Big Horn."

[80] Reno was a 6 year cadet having twice been suspended, once for excessive demerits. While many authors have made much of Custer's demerits while at the academy, Reno still holds the rather dubious academy record for demerits with 1031. Before too much is made of this statement, which is only intended to set the record straight and not to prolong a meaningless controversy, it must be noted that Philip Sheridan also took 6 years to complete the West Point course. In Sheridan's case he was suspended for one year for assaulting his drill instructor. Further, Sheridan was only 11 demerits from expulsion at graduation. It should also be noted that Robert E. Lee is the only graduate of the military academy to have completed the course without a single demerit. See Paul Andrew Huton "General Philip Sheridan: Civil War Memoirs," page ix and Evan S. Connell, "Son of the Morning Star," page 40, Tom O'Neil, "Cadet Marcus Albert Reno: Record of Demerits and Academics." page 24 and John Upton Terrell and Colonel George Walton "Faint the Trumpet Sounds," pages 24 and 27.

[81] See John Upton Terrell and Colonel George Walton "Faint the Trumpet Sounds," page 4.

[82] The offense for which Reno was dismissed was peering at the daughter of his commanding officer, Colonel Samuel D. Sturgis, through the parlor window. The article under which he was dismissed was appropriately known as the "Devil's Article." In 1967 his biographers, John Upton Terrell and Colonel

George Walton, received a hearing before the Board for the Correction of Military Records at the Pentagon, Washington, D. C., which resulted in the reversal of the two court martial decisions. See Robert M. Utley, "Frontier Regulars," page 84 and Ronald H. Nichols, "Marcus Albert Reno," page 14.

[83] See Robert M. Utley "Custer and the Great Controversy," page 17.

[84] At Gaines Mill, June 27, 1862, Reno demonstrated very effectually the manner in which a retreat is covered by cavalry. Apparently this lesson deserted him 14 years later. See John Upton Terrell and Colonel George Walton "Faint the Trumpet Sounds," pages 36 – 37.

[85] Although Reno had written to a friend in Harrisburg, PA : *"I never saw, during the whole war, such an awful fire"* as he encountered at the Little Big Horn, it is doubtful that he was speaking literally. It denies credibility to suggest that the firepower and carnage attendant at either Mechanicsville or Antietam was duplicated on any part of the field at the Little Big Horn. See Wengert, James W., MD, and E. Elden Davis, "That Fatal Day: Eight More With Custer."

[86] See Stanley Vestal "Sitting Bull," page 3.

[87] See Stanley Vestal "Sitting Bull," pages 293 – 302, Virginia Driving Hawk Sneve "They Led A Nation," page 28, and Evan S. Connell "Son of the Morning Star," page 392.

[88] At age 25 he killed a Crow chief in hand to hand combat receiving a wound that caused him to limp for the remainder of his life. Sitting Bull became leader of the Midnight Strong Hearts, an elite splinter group of the Brave Hearts. See John Menta "Sitting Bull: The Life of a Sioux Patriot," page 68 and Stanley Vestal "Sitting Bull," page 27.

[89] See William O. Taylor "With Custer On The Little Bighorn" pages 128 – 129.

[90] See John W. Bailey "Pacifying the Plains: General Alfred Terry and the Decline of the Sioux, 1866 – 1890," page 4 and Roger Darling "A Sad and Terrible Blunder," page 278.

[91] See Roger Darling "A Sad and Terrible Blunder," page 81.

[92] See John W. Bailey "Pacifying the Plains: General Alfred Terry and the Decline of the Sioux, 1866 – 1890," page 8.

[93] Cooke's unique side whiskers, were known as Dundrearies, after the character Lord Dundreary in the play "Our American Cousin." See Evan S. Connell "Son of the Morning Star" page 289.

Bibliography

Unpublished Documents and Manuscripts

Church, Bob. "Did Custer Believe His Scouts?" 5th Annual Symposium, Custer Battlefield Historical and Museum Association, Inc., held at Hardin, Montana on June 21, 1991.

Custer, Elizabeth B. "General Custer at The Battle of The Little Big Horn June 25, 1876". Printed, not published in New York. 1897

Grinnell, George Bird. "Notes on the Custer Fight." MS 5 #497, Braun Research Library, Southwest Museum, Highland Park, California.

Kanitz, Jay. "Varnum: The Later Years of Custer's Last Lieutenant." 5th Annual Symposium, Custer Battlefield Historical and Museum Association, Inc., held at Hardin, Montana on June 21, 1991.

Karselis, Terry. "Disaster in Duplicate: An Examination of the Similarities Between the Battle of Isandhlawana and the Little Big Horn." 5th Annual Symposium, Custer Battlefield Historical and Museum Association, Inc., held at Hardin, Montana on June 21, 1991.

Mangum, Neil. "Gall: Sioux Gladiator or White Man's Pawn?" 5th Annual Symposium, Custer Battlefield Historical and Museum Association, Inc., held at Hardin, Montana on June 21, 1991.

McWilliams, Mary Ellen. "A Self-Guided Tour: Fort Phil Kearny, Fetterman Battle, Wagon Box Fight". Fort Phil Kearny/Bozeman Trail Association. 1988.

Rickey, Donald. "Interviews with John Stands–in–Timber." Folder #15878. Custer Battlefield National Monument. August 18, 1956.

Scott, Douglas. "So As to Render Unserviceable to the Enemy: Archaeology at the Reno – Benteen Equipment Disposal Site." 5th Annual Symposium, Custer Battlefield Historical and Museum Association, Inc., held at Hardin, Montana on June 21, 1991.

Sills, Joe Jr. "The Crow Scouts: Their Contribution in Understanding the Little Big Horn Battle." 5th Annual Symposium, Custer Battlefield Historical and Museum Association, Inc., held at Hardin, Montana on June 21, 1991.

Trinque, Bruce. "The Cartridge Case Evidence on Custer Field: An Analysis and Re–interpretation." 5th Annual Symposium, Custer Battlefield Historical and Museum Association, Inc., held at Hardin, Montana on June 21, 1991.

Zimmerman, Barbara. "Gibbon's Montana Column." 5th Annual Symposium, Custer Battlefield Historical and Museum Association, Inc., held at Hardin, Montana on June 21, 1991.

Symposiums

Barnard, Sandy. "Clement A. Lounsberry: Claim for Glory". 2nd Annual Symposium, Custer Battlefield Historical and Museum Association, Inc., held at Hardin, Montana on June 24, 1988.

Barnard, Sandy. "Mark Kellogg's Role during the 1876 Campaign". 1st Annual Symposium, Custer Battlefield Historical and Museum Association, Inc., held at Hardin, Montana on June 26, 1987.

Barnard, Sandy. "Newspaper Coverage of the Little Big Horn: Summer 1876". 3rd Annual Symposium, Custer Battlefield Historical and Museum Association, Inc., held at Hardin, Montana on June 23, 1989.

Batten, Derel. "An Englishman's View of the Little Big Horn Affair". 1st Annual Symposium, Custer Battlefield Historical and Museum Association, Inc., held at Hardin, Montana on June 26, 1987.

Blackburn, Theodore. "Tragedy on the Little Big Horn: The Story of Sergeant Butler". 2nd Annual Symposium, Custer Battlefield Historical and Museum Association, Inc., held at Hardin, Montana on June 24, 1988.

Brust, James. "Learning About the Battle of the Little Big Horn From Photos Old and New." 8th Annual Symposium, Custer Battlefield Historical and Museum Association, Inc., held at Hardin, Montana on June 24, 1994.

Clark, Lt Col Dennis K. "Reno's Charge Out of the Timber." 8th Annual Symposium, Custer Battlefield Historical and Museum Association, Inc., held at Hardin, Montana on June 24, 1994.

Clark, Lt Col Dennis. "7th U. S. Cavalry Command and Control System 25 June 1876." 7th Annual Symposium, Custer Battlefield Historical and Museum Association, Inc., held at Hardin, Montana on June 25, 1993.

Davis, Norm. "A Tale of Two Privates." 8th Annual Symposium, Custer Battlefield Historical and Museum Association, Inc., held at Hardin, Montana on June 24, 1994.

Donahue, Michael. "Redefining Deep Ravine." 8th Annual Symposium, Custer Battlefield Historical and Museum Association, Inc., held at Hardin, Montana on June 24, 1994.

Doran, Bob. "Battalion Formation and the Custer Trail". 3rd Annual Symposium, Custer Battlefield Historical and Museum Association, Inc., held at Hardin, Montana on June 23, 1989.

Doran, Robert E. "The Man Who Got to the Rosebud". 1st Annual Symposium, Custer Battlefield Historical and Museum Association, Inc., held at Hardin, Montana on June 26, 1987.

Hedley, William. "'We've Caught Them Napping!' - The Little Big Horn Time Warp". 3rd Annual Symposium, Custer Battlefield Historical and Museum Association, Inc., held at Hardin, Montana on June 23, 1989.

Hedley, William. "'Ps Bring Pacs: The Order That Trapped the Custer Battalion." 4th Annual Symposium, Custer Battlefield Historical and Museum Association, Inc., held at Hardin, Montana on June 22, 1990.

Heier, Vince. "Fiction Stranger Than Truth: A 'Novel' Approach to Custer in Literature". 3rd Annual Symposium, Custer Battlefield Historical and Museum Association, Inc., held at Hardin, Montana on June 23, 1989.

Holly, Jim. "Crazy Horse on the Greasy Grass." 8th Annual Symposium, Custer Battlefield Historical and Museum Association, Inc., held at Hardin, Montana on June 24, 1994.

Holly, Jim. "Indian Accounts Paint Last Stand Picture." 7th Annual Symposium, Custer Battlefield Historical and Museum Association, Inc., held at Hardin, Montana on June 25, 1993.

Keenan, Jerry. "Rosebud, Oh Rosebud." 6th Annual Symposium, Custer Battlefield Historical and Museum Association, Inc., held at Hardin, Montana on June 26, 1992.

Keller, Doug. "Myths of the Little Big Horn". 2nd Annual Symposium, Custer Battlefield Historical and Museum Association, Inc., held at Hardin, Montana on June 24, 1988.

Koury, Michael J. "The Myth of the Indian Warrior." 6th Annual Symposium, Custer Battlefield Historical and Museum Association, Inc., held at Hardin, Montana on June 26, 1992.

Krause, Wesley. "The Guns of '76." 6th Annual Symposium, Custer Battlefield Historical and Museum Association, Inc., held at Hardin, Montana on June 26, 1992.

Kush, George F. "In the Great Mother's Land: The Mounted Police and the Sioux." 6th Annual Symposium, Custer Battlefield Historical and Museum Association, Inc., held at Hardin, Montana on June 26, 1992.

Mangum, Neil C. "Popular Reaction to Custer - The Public's Perception". 1st Annual Symposium, Custer Battlefield Historical and Museum Association, Inc., held at Hardin, Montana on June 26, 1987.

McChristian, Doug. "'Hurrah, Boys! We've Got Them!': An Analysis of Custer's Observation Point". 3rd Annual Symposium, Custer Battlefield Historical and Museum Association, Inc., held at Hardin, Montana on June 23, 1989.

Meketa, Ray. "A Survivor of the Little Big Horn". 1st Annual Symposium, Custer Battlefield Historical and Museum Association, Inc., held at Hardin, Montana on June 26, 1987.

Menta, John. "Sitting Bull: The Life of a Sioux Patriot". 1st Annual Symposium, Custer Battlefield Historical and Museum Association, Inc., held at Hardin, Montana on June 26, 1987.

Miller, David Humphreys. "Personal Recollections by the Author of Custer's Fall". 3rd Annual Symposium, Custer Battlefield Historical and Museum Association, Inc., held at Hardin, Montana on June 23, 1989.

Nichols, Ron. "A Brief Analytical Study of Reno's Fight in the Valley". 3rd Annual Symposium, Custer Battlefield Historical and Museum Association, Inc., held at Hardin, Montana on June 23, 1989.

Nichols, Ron. "The Springfield Carbine at the Little Big Horn". 2nd Annual Symposium, Custer Battlefield Historical and Museum Association, Inc., held at Hardin, Montana on June 24, 1988.

Noyes, C. Lee. "The Guns 'Long Hair' Left Behind: The Gatling Gun Detachment and the Little Big Horn." 8th Annual Symposium, Custer Battlefield Historical and Museum Association, Inc., held at Hardin, Montana on June 24, 1994.

Pohanka, Brian. "Schooled for Conflict: 7th Cavalry Officers at West Point 1863 – 1875." 6th Annual Symposium, Custer Battlefield Historical and Museum Association, Inc., held at Hardin, Montana on June 26, 1992.

Sills, Joe Jr. "Messages and Messengers." 4th Annual Symposium, Custer Battlefield Historical and Museum Association, Inc., held at Hardin, Montana on June 22, 1990.

Sills, Joe, Jr. "Weir Point Perspectives." 7th Annual Symposium, Custer Battlefield Historical and Museum Association, Inc., held at Hardin, Montana on June 25, 1993.

Sills, Joe Jr. "Were There Two Last Stands?". 2nd Annual Symposium, Custer Battlefield Historical and Museum Association, Inc., held at Hardin, Montana on June 24, 1988.

Treece, James William, Jr. "The Glory That Was Custer's." 4th Annual Symposium, Custer Battlefield Historical and Museum Association, Inc., held at Hardin, Montana on June 22, 1990.

Tuttle, Judd. "Remnants of a Regiment". 2nd Annual Symposium, Custer Battlefield Historical and Museum Association, Inc., held at Hardin, Montana on June 24, 1988.

Tuttle, Judd. "Who Buried Lieutenant Hodgson?" 4th Annual Symposium, Custer Battlefield Historical and Museum Association, Inc., held at Hardin, Montana on June 22, 1990.

Urwin, Dr. Gregory. "Was the Past Prologue? Meditations on Custer's Tactics at the Little Big Horn." 7th Annual Symposium, Custer Battlefield Historical and Museum Association, Inc., held at Hardin, Montana on June 25, 1993.

Wells, Wayne. "Custer's Arrival Time at the River". 1st Annual Symposium, Custer Battlefield Historical and Museum Association, Inc., held at Hardin, Montana on June 26, 1987.

Wells, Wayne. "The Fight on Calhoun Hill". 2nd Annual Symposium, Custer Battlefield Historical and Museum Association, Inc., held at Hardin, Montana on June 24, 1988.

Wright, Steven. "Edward Settle Godfrey and the Custer Myth." 6th Annual Symposium, Custer Battlefield Historical and Museum Association, Inc., held at Hardin, Montana on June 26, 1992.

Zimowski, Francis. "Military Awards for Bravery Given to Participants of the Little Big Horn Battle". 3rd Annual Symposium, Custer Battlefield Historical and Museum Association, Inc., held at Hardin, Montana on June 23, 1989.

Articles

Brockway, Michael D. "Custer's Winter in Austin." Volume 39, No. 6 of True West Magazine, June 1992, Stillwater, OK, Western Publications.

Brown, Lisle G. "Like a Feather Borne by the Wind." Vol. XII Research Review 1978 – 6. El Paso, Texas.

Brust, James. "Lt. Oscar Long's Early Map Details Terrain, Battle Positions." Volume 11 of Greasy Grass, May 1995, Billings, Montana, Fenske Printing Inc.

Buecker, Tom. "Frederic S. Calhoun: A Little–Known Member of the 'Custer Clique'" Volume 10 of Greasy Grass, May 1994, Billings, Montana, Fenske Printing Inc.

Burst, James. "Baldwin Talks With Reno, Writes About Custer's Final Battle." Volume 9 of Greasy Grass, May 1993, Billings, Montana, Fenske Printing, Inc.

Brust, James. "Fouch Photo May Be the First." Volume 7 of Greasy Grass, May 1991, Billings, Montana, Fenske Printing Inc.

Buecker, Thomas R. "Lt. William Philo Clark's Sioux War Report." Volume 7 of Greasy Grass, May 1991, Billings, Montana, Fenske Printing Inc.

Calhoun, Samuel W., "Did Custer Disobey?", Volume 6 of Greasy Grass, May 1990, Billings Montana, Fenske Printing Inc.

Caniglia, Salvatore A. "Profile of the Seventh", vol. XI of Research Review, 1977–6,El Paso, Texas, June 1977.

Cecil, Jerry. "Lt. Crittenden: Striving For The Soldier's Life" Volume 11 of Greasy Grass, May 1995, Billings, Montana, Fenske Printing Inc.

Cecil, Jerry. "Researching The Tale of Lt. Crittenden's Pocket Watch" Volume 11 of Greasy Grass, May 1995, Billings, Montana, Fenske Printing Inc.

Davis, E. Elden "A Look At The Reno Court of Inquiry and The Defense: A Correspondent's View." "Newsletter: Little Big Horn Associates." Vol. XXVIII, November 1994–9, Four Star Printing and Office Supply, Inc., Boaz, Alabama. 1994.

Davis, E. Elden and Karen L. Daniels. "Big Horn – Yellowstone Journal." Vol. I., No. I., Winter, 1992. Powder River Press, Howell, Michigan.

Davis, E. Elden and Karen L. Daniels. "Big Horn – Yellowstone Journal." Vol. I., No. 2., Spring, 1992. Powder River Press, Howell, Michigan.

Davis, E. Elden and Karen L. Daniels. "Big Horn – Yellowstone Journal." Vol. I., No. 3., Summer, 1992. Powder River Press, Howell, Michigan.

Davis, E. Elden and Karen L. Daniels. "Big Horn – Yellowstone Journal." Vol. I., No. 4., Autumn, 1992. Powder River Press, Howell, Michigan.

Davis, E. Elden and Karen L. Daniels. "Big Horn – Yellowstone Journal." Vol. 2., No. I., Winter, 1993. Powder River Press, Howell, Michigan.

Davis, E. Elden and Karen L. Daniels. "Big Horn – Yellowstone Journal." Vol. 2., No. 2., Spring, 1993. Powder River Press, Howell, Michigan.

Davis, E. Elden and Karen L. Daniels. "Big Horn – Yellowstone Journal." Vol. 2., No. 3., Summer, 1993. Powder River Press, Howell, Michigan.

Davis, E. Elden and Karen L. Daniels. "Big Horn – Yellowstone Journal." Vol. 2., No. 4., Autumn, 1993. Powder River Press, Howell, Michigan.

Davis, E. Elden and Karen L. Daniels. "Big Horn – Yellowstone Journal." Vol. 3., No. 1., Winter, 1994. Powder River Press, Howell, Michigan.

Davis, E. Elden and Karen L. Daniels. "Big Horn – Yellowstone Journal." Vol. 3., No. 2., Spring, 1994. Powder River Press, Howell, Michigan.

Day, Carl. "If You Want to Know." Volume 9 of Greasy Grass, May 1993, Billings, Montana, Fenske Printing, Inc.

Duncan, Charles and Jay Smith. "The Captives." Research Review. McNaughton & Gunn, Inc., El Paso, Texas, Vol. 7, No. 2, June 1993.

Duncan, David Ewing. "The Object at Hand." Volume 22, Number 6 of Smithsonian, September 1991, Washington D. C.

Ege, Robert J. "The Bravest Man the Sioux Ever Fought." Real West Magazine. September 1967. Volume X, Number 55.

Ege, Robert J. "Legend Was A Man Named Keogh". Helena, Montana. Montana Magazine. Spring 1966.

Faeder, Gustav S.. "Superb Was The Day." Leesburg, VA, America's Civil War Magazine, March 1991, Empire Press.

Fox, Arthur B. "Stinging Defeat Suffered." Leesburg, VA, Military History Magazine, February 1993, Empire Press.

Gibbon, Colonel John. "Last Summer's Expedition Against the Sioux" (continued as "Hunting Sitting Bull"). American Catholic Quarterly Review, Vol. II, April and October 1877.

Godfrey, E. S. "Some Reminiscences, Including the Washita Battle, November 27, 1868." The Cavalry Journal, October, 1928. Baltimore. The United States Cavalry Association. 1928.

Gray, John S. "Arikara Scouts With Custer." North Dakota History, volume 35, No. 2. Bismarck, North Dakota. State Historical Society of North Dakota. Spring 1968.

Grover, David H. "Custer's Navy: The Steamboat 'Far West'" America's Combat History Magazine. Challenge Publications, Canoga Park, California. Spring 1993.

Hardorff, R. "Dutch" "Captain Keogh's Insurance Policy" Vol. XI of Research Review, 1977–9, El Paso, Texas. September 1977

Hedren, Paul L. "'Three Cool, Determined Men: The Sioux War Heroism of Privates Evans, Stewart, and Bell.'" Helena, Montana. Montana Magazine. Winter 1991.

Heidenreich, C. Adrian. "The Native Americans' Yellowstone." Montana: The Magazine of Western History. Helena, Montana. Montana Historical Society. Volume 35, No. 4, Autumn, 1985.

Hutton, Paul A. "Phil Sheridan's Pyrrhic Victory: The Piegan Massacre, Army Politics and the Transfer Debate." Montana: The Magazine of Western History. Helena, Montana. Montana Historical Society. Volume 32, Number Two, Spring, 1982.

Jordan, Robert Paul. "Ghosts on the Little Bighorn". Washington, D. C. National Geographic Magazine, Volume 170, Number 6, December 1986 .

Kanipe, J. E. "Tarheel Survivor fo Custer's Last Stand." Research Review. McNaughton & Gunn, Inc., El Paso, Texas, Vol. 7, No. 2, June 1993.

Lalire, Gregory. "Ghost Dancers' Last Stand." Wild West Magazine. Empire Press Inc., Leesburg, Virginia. June 1993.

Lane, Harrison. "Custer's Massacre." Helena, Montana. Montana Historical Society Press. 1955.

Langley, Harold D. "The Custer Battle and the Critique of an Adventurer." Montana: The Magazine of Western History. Helena, Montana. Montana Historical Society. Volume XXII, No. 2, April, 1972.

Lass, William E. "Steamboats on the Yellowstone." Montana: The Magazine of Western History. Helena, Montana. Montana Historical Society. Volume 35, No. 4, Autumn, 1985.

Luce, Edward S. "North Dakora History: The Diary and Letters of Dr. James M. DeWolf." Bismarck, North Dakota. The State Historical Society. April – July 1958.

Mangum, Neil C. "Battle of the Little Big Horn." Volume 1 of Greasy Grass, May 1985.

Mangum, Neil C. "Reno's Battalion in the Battle of the Little Big Horn." Volume 2 of Greasy Grass, May 1986.

Michno, Greg. "Little Big Horn Mystery Solved." El Paso, Texas. Research Review Magazine. January 1992.

Morre, Michael and Michael Donahue. "Gibbon's Route to Custer Hill." Volume 7 of Greasy Grass, May 1991, Billings, Montana, Fenske Printing Inc.

Morris, Roy Jr. "It Was Just Madness: An Interview With Shelby Foote." Leesburg, VA, America's Civil War Magazine, March 1991, Empire Press.

Munn, Fred. "Memoirs of a Cavalry Veteran". Helena, Montana. Montana Magazine. Spring 1966.

Myers, Steven W. "Roster of Known Hostile Indians at the Battle of the Little Big Horn" Research Review Magazine, Vol. 5, No. 2, June 1991.

Nichols, Ronald H., "Marcus Albert Reno." Volume 2 of Greasy Grass, May 1986.

O'Donnell, J. P. "Battle of Ash Hollow." Volume 39, No. 6 of True West Magazine, June 1992, Stillwater, OK, Western Publications.

O'Neil, Alice. "Custe and Politics." Newsletter, Little Big Horn Associates. May 1994. Vol XXVIII.

O'Neil, Tom and Hoyt S. Vandenberg. "A Modern Look at Custer's Orders." Research Review. Printers Inc., El Paso, Texas, Vol. 8, No. 2, June 1994.

Pearson, Carl L. "Sadie and the Missing Custer Battle Papers." Montana: The Magazine of Western History. Helena, Montana. Montana Historical Society. Volume XXVI, No. 4, October, 1976.

Pennington, Jack. "The Reno Court – The Second Cover–Up," Research Review. Printers Inc., El Paso, Texas, Vol. 9, No. 1, January 1995.

Pohanka, Brian C.,"Profile: Lieutenant William Van Wyck Reily 7th U. S. Cavalry." Volume 2 of Greasy Grass, May 1986.

Pohanka, Brian C.,"Their Shots Quit Coming", Military History Magazine's Great Battles, Volume 1 Number 1, Leesburg Va., Empire Press. 1986.

Rector, William G. "The Reno-Benteen Defense Perimeter". Helena, Montana. Montana Magazine. Spring 1966.

Reedstrom, Ernest Lisle. "Bloody Knife: Custer's Favorite Scout." True West, February 1989. Vol 36, No 2.

Reedstrom, Ernest Lisle. "Tom Custer: In The Shadow Of His Brother." True West, November 1994. Vol 41, No 11.

Saum, Lewis O. "Stanley Huntley Interviews Sitting Bull: Event, Pseudo–event or Fabrication?" Montana: The Magazine of Western History. Helena, Montana. Montana Historical Society. Volume 32, Number Two, Spring, 1982.

Schneider, Jim. "The Humor of Walter M. Camp." Vol. XII Research Review 1978 – 9. El Paso, Texas.

Schneider, Jim "Rations, Forage, & Ammunition: Logistical Problems Facing the Dakota Column in the Summer of 1876." Research Review. McNaughton & Gunn, Inc., El Paso, Texas, Vol. 5, No. 2, June 1991.

Schoenberger, Dale T. "Custer's Scouts". Helena, Montana. Montana Magazine. Spring 1966.

Scott, Douglas and Douglas Owsley. "Oh, What Tales Bones Could Tell – And Often Do!" Volume 7 of Greasy Grass, May 1991, Billings, Montana, Fenske Printing Inc.

Sills, Joe Jr.. "The Recruits Controversy: Another Look". Volume 5 of Greasy Grass, May 1989, Billings Montana, Fenske Printing Inc.

Skenlar, Larry. "Private Theodore W. Goldin: Too Soon Discredited?" Research Review. Printers Inc., El Paso, Texas, Vol. 9, No. 1, January 1995.

Smith, Cornelius C. Jr. "Crook and Crazy Horse". Helena, Montana. Montana Magazine. Spring 1966.

Smith, Jay. "The Indian Fighting Army." El Paso, Texas. Research Review Magazine. June, 1989.

Smith, Jay "What Did Not Happen At The Battle of the Little Big Horn." El Paso, Texas. Research Review Magazine. June 1992.

Snedeker, Lenora A. "Attention! An Article of Historical Opinion," Newsletter of the Little Big Horn Associates, May 1995 – 4, Vol. XXIV.

Snedeker, Lenora A. "The Tragedy of the James Porter Family." Newsletter of the Little Big Horn Associates, August 1996 – 6. Vol. XXV.

Stewart, Edgar I. "I Rode With Custer." Helena, Montana. Montana Historical Society Press. 1955.

Stewart, Edgar I. "The Custer Battle and Widow's Weeds." Montana: The Magazine of Western History. Helena, Montana. Montana Historical Society. Volume XXII, No. 1, January, 1972.

Stewart, Edgar I. "The Little Big Horn: 90 Years Later". Helena, Montana. Montana Magazine. Spring 1966.

Summitt, Christopher M. "Apologia Pro "Custer's Last Stand'". Volume 5 of Greasy Grass, May 1989, Billings Montana, Fenske Printing Inc.

Summitt, Chris. "Beyond the Markers." Volume 1 of Greasy Grass, May 1985.

Trinque, Bruce A. "The Defense of Custer Hill." Research Review. Printers Inc., El Paso, Texas, Vol. 8, No. 2, June 1994.

Trinque, Bruce A. "Elusive Ridge." Research Review. Printers Inc., El Paso, Texas, Vol. 9, No. 1, January 1995.

Utley, Robert M. "Gossip and Scandal." El Paso. Texas. Research Review Magazine. June 1989.

Utley, Robert M. "War Houses in the Sioux Country: The Military Occupation of the Lower Yellowstone." Montana: The Magazine of Western History. Helena, Montana. Montana Historical Society. Volume 35, No. 4, Autumn, 1985.

Wells, Wayne. "Little Big Horn Notes: Stanley Vestal's Indian Insights". Volume 5 of Greasy Grass, May 1989, Billings Montana, Fenske Printing Inc.

Wengert, James W., MD. and E. Elden Davis, "That Fatal Day: Eight More With Custer." Powder River Press. Howell, Michigan. 1992.

Newspapers

New York Times, July 6, 1876.

New York Times, July 7, 1876.

New York Times, July 8, 1876.

Books

Adams, Alexander B. "Sitting Bull. An Epic of the Plains" New York. Barnes and Noble Books. 1992.

Adams, Jacob. "A Story of the Custer Massacre." Privately printed. 1965.

Adjutant General's Office, "Chronological List of Actions, Etc., With Indians from January 15, 1837 to January, 1891." Fort Collins, Colorado. Old Army Press. 1979.

Ambrose, Stephen E. "Crazy Horse and Custer: The Parallel Lives of Two American Warriors". New York. Meridian. 1986.

Anders, Major Frank L. "Critical Notes On The Line Of March." Brooklyn, New York. Arrow and Trooper. 1995.

Anderson, Harry H. "Cheyennes at the Little Big Horn – A Study of Statistics." Reprinted from North Dakota Historical Society Quarterly, Vol. 27, No. 2, Spring 1960.

Andrist, Ralph K. "The Long Death: The Last Days of the Plains Indian." New York, Toronto, Oxford, Singapore, and Sydney. Collier Books, MacMillan Publishing Company. 1993.

Anglo, Michael. "Custer: Man and Myth." London. Jupiter Books. 1976.

Arnold, Steve and Tim French. "Custer's Forgotten Friend: The Life of W. W. Cooke." Howell, Michigan. Powder River Press. 1993.

Asay, Karol. "Gray Head and Long Hair: The Benteen – Custer Relationship." New York. The Mad Printers of Mattituck. 1983.

Axelrod, Alan. "Chronicle of the Indian Wars." New York, London, Toronto, Sydney, Tokyo and Singapore. Prentice Hall General Reference. 1993.

Bailey, John W. "Pacifying the Plains: General Alfred Terry and the Decline of the Sioux, 1866 – 1890." Westport, Connecticut and London, England. Greenwood Press. 1979.

Barnard, Sandy. "Custer's First Sergeant John Ryan." Terre Haute, Indiana. AST Press. 1996.

Barnett, Louise. "Touched By Fire: The Life, Death, and Mythic Afterlife of George Armstrong Custer." New York. Henry Holt And Company. 1996.

Bates, Charles Francis. "Custer's Indian Battles." Fort Collins, Colorado. Old Army Press.

Beal, Merrill D. "I Will Fight No More Forever." Seattle. University of Washington Press. 1963.

Beyer, W. F. and O. F. Keydel. "Acts of Bravery: Deeds of Extraordinary American Heroism." Stamford, CT and Woodbury, NY. Longmeadow Press. 1993.

Billington, Ray Allen. "Soldier & Brave." New York, Evanston, and London. Harper & Row, Publishers. 1963.

Blish, Helen H. "A Pictographic History of the Oglala Sioux." Lincoln, University of Nebraska Press. 1967.

Blumenson, Martin. "Patton: The Man Behind the Legend: 1885 – 1945." New York. Berkley Books. 1987.

Bourke, John G. "On the Border With Crook". New York. Charles Scribner's Sons. 1891.

Boyes, W. "Custer's Black White Man." Washington, D. C. South Capitol Press. 1972.

Boyes, W. "Surgeon's Diary with the Custer Relief Column." Washington, D. C., South Capitol Press. 1974.

Bradley, James H., "The March of the Montana Column: A Prelude to the Custer Disaster". Norman. University of Oklahoma Press. 1961.

Brady, Cyrus Townsend. "The Sioux Indian Wars." (Originally Published as Indian Fights and Fighters) New York. Indian Head Books. 1992.

Brininstool, E. A. "Fighting Indian Warriors". New York. Bonanza Books. 1953.

Brininstool, E. A. "The Custer Fight: Captain Benteen's Story." Brooklyn, New York. Arrow and Trooper. 1994.

Brininstool, E. A. "Troopers With Custer: Historic Incidents of the Battle of the Little Big Horn". Lincoln and London. University of Nebraska Press. 1989.

Brown, Dee. "Bury My Heart at Wounded Knee". New York, Chicago and San Francisco. Holt, Rinehart and Winston. 1971.

Brown, Dee. "Fort Phil Kearny – An American Saga." New York. G. P. Putnam's Sons. 1962.

Brown, Mark H. "The Flight of the Nez Perce." New York. G. P. Putnam's Sons. 1967.

Brown, Mark H. "The Plainsmen of the Yellowstone." New York. G. P. Putnam's Sons. 1961.

Buecker, Thomas R. and R. Eli Paul. "The Crazy Horse Surrender Ledger" Lincoln. Nebraska State Historical Society. 1994.

Burdick, Usher L. "David F. Barry's Indian Notes on The Custer Battle." Baltimore. Wirth Brothers. 1949.

Byrne, Edward M. "Military Law, Third Edition." Annapolis, Maryland. Naval Institute Press. 1981.

Byrne, P. E. "Soldiers of the Plains." New York, Minton, Balch & Company. 1926.

Carroll, John M. "A Bit of Seventh Cavalry History With All Its Warts." Bryan, Texas. Privately printed. 1987.

Carroll, John M. "The Benteen – Goldin Letters on Custer and His Last Battle." Lincoln and London. University of Nebraska Press. 1991.

Carroll, John M. "Cavalry Bits: The Yellowstone Expedition of 1873." Mattituck, New York and Bryan, Texas. J. M. Carroll and Company. 1986.

Carroll, John M. "Custer in Texas." New York. Sol Lewis and Liveright. 1975.

Carroll, John M. "Custer in the Civil War: His Unfinished Memoirs." San Rafael, California. Presidio Press. 1977.

Carroll, John M. "Custer's Chief of Scouts: The Reminiscences of Charles A. Varnum". Lincoln and London. University of Nebraska Press. 1987.

Carroll, John M. "General Custer and the Battle of the Little Big Horn: The Federalist View." New Brunswick, New Jersey. Garry Owen Press. 1976.

Carroll, John M. "General Custer and the Battle of the Washita: The Federal View." Bryan, Texas. Guidon Press. 1978.

Carroll, John M. "The Gibson and Edgerly Narratives." Bryan, Texas. Privately printed, no date.

Carroll, John M. "I Varnum." Glendale, California. The Arthur H. Clark Company. 1982.

Carroll, John M. "The Papers of the Order of Indian Wars". Fort Collins, Colorade. Old Army Press. 1975.

Carroll, John M. and Price, Byron. "Roll Call On The Little Big Horn, 28 June 1876". Fort Collins, Colorado. Old Army Press. 1974.

Carroll, John M. "A Seventh Cavalry Scrapbook." Bryan, Texas. Privately printed. 1978.

Carroll, John M. "A Seventh Cavalry Scrapbook #2." Bryan, Texas. Privately printed. 1978.

Carroll, John M. "A Seventh Cavalry Scrapbook #3." Bryan, Texas. Privately printed. 1978.

Carroll, John M. "A Seventh Cavalry Scrapbook #4." Bryan, Texas. Privately printed. 1978.

Carroll, John M. "A Seventh Cavalry Scrapbook #5." Bryan, Texas. Privately printed. 1979.

Carroll, John M. "A Seventh Cavalry Scrapbook #7." Bryan, Texas. Privately printed. 1979.

Carroll, John M. "A Seventh Cavalry Scrapbook #8." Bryan, Texas. Privately printed. 1979.

Carroll, John M. "A Seventh Cavalry Scrapbook #9." Bryan, Texas. Privately printed. 1979.

Carroll, John M. "A Seventh Cavalry Scrapbook #10." Bryan, Texas. Privately printed. 1979.

Carroll, John M. "A Seventh Cavalry Scrapbook #11." Bryan, Texas. Privately printed. 1979.

Carroll, John M. "A Seventh Cavalry Scrapbook #12." Bryan, Texas. Privately printed. 1979.

Carroll, John M. "The Sunshine Magazine Articles" Bryan, Texas. 1979.

Carroll, John M. "The Teepee Book" New York. Sol Lewis. 1974.

Carroll, John M. "They Rode With Custer:A Biographical Directory of the Men That Rode With General George A. Custer". Mattituck, New York. J. M. Carroll and Company. 1987.

Chalfant, William Y. "Without Quarter." Norman and London. University of Oklahoma Press. 1991.

Champagne, Duane. "Native America: Portrait of the Peoples." Detroit, Michigan, Visible Ink Press. 1994.

Chandler, Lt Col Melbourne C. "Of Garryowen in Glory." Annandale, Virginia. The Turnpike Press. 1960.

Clark, George M., "Scalp Dance: The Edgerly Papers on the Battle of the Little Big Horn". Oswego, New York, Heritage Press. 1985.

Clark, Robert A. "The Killing of Chief Crazy Horse." Lincoln and London. University of Nebraska Press. 1988.

Connell, Evan S. "Son of the Morning Star: Custer and the Little Bighorn". New York. Promontory Press. 1993.

Cook, Charles M. "The Little Big Horn Survivors." Champaign, Illinois. The Grinding Stone Press. 1988.

Convis, Charles L. "The Honor of Arms: A Biography of Myles W. Keogh." Tucson, Arizona. Westernlore Press. 1990.

Coughlan, Colonel T. M. "Varnum – The Last of Custer's Lieutenants." Privately printed. 1980.

Criqui, Orvel A. "Fifty Fearless Men." Marceline, Missouri. Walsworth Publishing Company. 1993.

Custer, Elizabeth B. "Boots and Saddles". Norman and London. University of Oklahoma Press. 1987.

Custer, Elizabeth B. "Following the Guidon." New York. Harper & Brothers, Franklin Square. 1890.

Custer, Elizabeth B. "Tenting on the Plains." Norman. University of Oklahoma Press. 1971.

Custer, George A. "The Civil War Memoirs of General George Armstrong Custer." Brooklyn New York. Arrow and Trooper Publishing Company. 1991.

Custer, George A. "My Life on the Plains". Lincoln and London. University of Nebraska Press. 1966.

Darling, Roger. "A Sad and Terrible Blunder." Vienna, Virginia. Potomac–Western Press. 1990.

Davis, E. Elden and Karen I. "Reno Court of Inquiry: St. Paul Pioneer Press." Howell, Michigan. Powder River Press. 1993.

DeMallie, Raymond J., "The Sixth Grandfather." Lincoln and London. University of Nebraska Press. 1985.

Diessner, Don. "There Are No Indians Left But Me! Sitting Bull's Story." El Segundo, California. Upton and Sons. 1993.

Dillon, Richard H. "North American Indian Wars." Secaucus, New Jersey. Chartwell Books, Inc. 1983.

Dippie, Brian W. "Custer's Last Stand: The Anatomy of an American Myth." Missoula, Montana. University of Montana Publications in History. 1976.

Donnelle, A. J., "Cyclorama of General Custer's Last Battle." New York. Promontory Press. 1966.

Downey, Fairfax. "Indian–Fighting Army." Fort Collins, Colorado. Old Army Press. 1971.

Downey, Fairfax. "Indian Wars of the U. S. Army (1776 – 1865)." Garden City, New York. Doubleday & Company, Inc. 1963.

Drimmer, Frederick. "Captured By The Indians" New York. Dover Publications, Inc. 1985.

du Bois, Charles G., "The Custer Mystery." El Segundo. Upton and Sons.1986.

du Bois, Charles G., "Kick the Dead Lion: A Casebook of the Custer Battle". El Segundo. Upton and Sons.1987.

duMont, John S. "Custer Battle Guns." Canaan, New Hampshire. Phoenix Publishing. 1988.

Dunn, J. P. "Massacres of the Mountains: A History of the Indian Wars of the Far West 1815 - 1875". New York. Archer House Inc. 1886.

Dustin, Fred "Reno's Positions in the Valley." Brooklyn, New York. Arrow and Trooper Publishing. 1995.

Dustin, Fred. "The Custer Tragedy: Events Leading Up to and Following the Little Big Horn Campaign of 1876.". Ann Arbor, Michigan. Edwards Brothers, Inc. 1939.

Eastman, Charles A. "Indian Heroes and Great Chieftains." Lincoln and London. University of Nebraska Press. 1991.

Ediger, Theodore A. and Vinnie Hoffman. "Some Reminiscences of The Battle of the Washita." Reprinted from The Chronicles of Oklahoma. Summer, 1955, Volume XXXIII, No. 2.

Ege, Robert J. "Curse Not His Curls." Fort Collins, Colorado, The Old Army Press. 1974.

Ege, Robert J. "Settling the Dust: The Story of the Custer Battle". Greeley, Colorado. Werner Publications. 1981.

Faulk, Odie B. "Crimson Desert." New York. Oxford University Press. 1974.

Finerty, John F. "War-Path and Bivouac". Chicago. The Lakeside Press. 1955.

Foote, Shelby. "The Civil War: A Narrative. Fort Sumter to Perryville." New York. Random House. 1958.

Forrest, Earle R. "Witnesses at the Battle of the Little Big Horn." Monroe, Michigan. Monroe County Library System. 1986.

Fougera, Katherine Gibson. "With Custer's Cavalry". Lincoln and London. University of Nebraska Press. 1986.

Frost, Lawrence A. "The Court–Martial of General George Armstrong Custer." Norman and London. University of Oklahoma Press. 1987.

Frost, Lawrence A. "The Custer Album". Norman and London. University of Oklahoma Press. 1990.

Frost, Lawrence A. "Custer Legends." Bowling Green, Ohio. Bowling Green University Popular Press. 1981.

Frost, Lawrence A. "First Last Stand of the 7th Cavalry: The Kidder Massacre." Brooklyn, New York. Arrow and Trooper. 1995.

Frost, Lawrence A. "General Custer's Libbie." Seattle, Washington. Superior Publishing Company. 1976.

Frost, Lawrence A. "With Custer in '74: James Calhoun's Diary of the Black Hills Expedition." Provo, Utah. Brigham Young University Press. 1979.

Gaff, Alan and Maureen, Editors. "Adventures on the Western Frontier by Major General John Gibbon." Bloomington and Indianapolis. Indiana University Press. 1994.

Gibson, Captain Frank M. "Our Washita Battle." Brooklyn, New York. Arrow and Trooper Publishing. Not dated.

Goble, Paul. "Brave Eagle's Account of The Fetterman Fight." Lincoln and London. University of Nebraska Press. 1972.

Goble, Paul. "Red Hawk's Account of Custer's Last Battle." Lincoln and London. University of Nebraska Press. 1969.

Godfrey, E. S. "The Field Diary of Lt. Edward Settle Godfrey". Portland, Oregon. The Champoeg Press. 1957.

Godfrey, E. S. "Custer's Last Battle 1876". Golden, Colorado. Outbooks, Inc. 1986.

Goldin, Theodore W. "With the Seventh Cavalry in 1876." Privately printed. 1980.

Graham, W. A. "Abstract of the Official Record of Proceedings of The Reno Court of Inquiry". Harrisburg, Pennsylvania. The Stackpole Company. 1954

Graham, W. A. "Custer's Battle Flags". Los Angeles. Brand Book. 1950.

Graham, W. A. "The Custer Myth: A Source Book of Custeriana". New York. Bonanza Books. 1953.

Graham, W. A. "The Story of the Little Big Horn". New York. Bonanza Books. 1959.

Gragg, Rod. "Confederate Goliath: The Battle of Fort Fisher" New York. Harper Perennial. 1992.

Grant, Bruce. "Concise Encyclopedia of the American Indian". New York. Bonanza Books. 1989.

Gray, John S. "Centennial Campaign: The Sioux War of 1876". Norman and London. University of Oklahoma Press. 1988.

Gray, John S. "Custer's Last Campaign." Lincoln and London. University of Nebraska Press. 1991.

Greene, Jerome A. "Battles and Skirmishes of the Great Sioux War, 1876 – 1877: The Military View." Norman and London. University of Oklahoma Press. 1993.

Greene, Jerome A. "Evidence and the Custer Enigma". Golden, Colorado. Outbooks, Inc. 1986.

Greene, Jerome A. "Lakota and Cheyenne: Indian Views of the Great Sioux War, 1876 – 1877." Norman and London. University of Oklahoma Press. 1994.

Greene, Jerome A. "Slim Buttes, 1876: An Episode of the Great Sioux War." Norman and London. University of Oklahoma Press. 1982.

Greene, Jerome A. "Yellowstone Command." Lincoln and London. University of Nebraska Press. 1991.

Grinnell, George Bird. "By Cheyenne Campfires" Lincoln and London. University of Nebraska Press. 1971.

Grinnell, George Bird. "The Cheyenne Indians, Volume I", Lincoln and London. University of Nebraska Press. 1972.

Grinnell, George Bird. "The Cheyenne Indians, Volume II", Lincoln and London. University of Nebraska Press. 1972.

Grinnell, George Bird. "The Fighting Cheyennes." Norman, Oklahoma. University of Oklahoma Press. 1989.

Gump, James O. "The Dust Rose Like Smoke: The Subjugation of the Zulu and the Sioux." Lincoln and London. University of Nebraska Press. 1994.

Hamilton, Charles. "Cry of the Thunderbird: The American Indian's Won Story." New York, The MacMillan Company. 1951.

Hammer, Kenneth. "Custer in 76: Walter Camp's Notes on the Custer Fight". Provo. Brigham Young University Press. 1981.

Hammer, Kenneth. "Little Big Horn Biographies." Printed in South Dakota, 1965.

Hammer, Kenneth. "Men With Custer: Biographies of the 7th Cavalry." Huntington Beach, CA., Ventana Graphics. 1995.

Hammer, Kenneth M. "The Springfield Carbine on the Western Frontier." Bellevue, Nebraska. Old Army Press. 1970.

Hans, Fred M. "The Great Sioux Nation." Chicago. M. A. Donohue and Company. 1907.

Hanson, Joseph Mills. "The Conquest of the Missouri." New York and Toronto. Murray Hill Books, Inc. 1946.

Hardorff, Richard G. "Camp, Custer, and the Little Bighorn" El Segundo, California. Upton and Sons, Publishers 1997.

Hardorff, Richard G. "Cheyenne Memories of the Custer Fight: A Source Book" Spokane, Washington. The Arthur H. Clark Company. 1995.

Hardorff, Richard G. "Hokahey! A Good Day to Die!" Spokane, Washington. The Arthur H. Clark Company. 1993.

Hardorff, Richard G. "Lakota Recollections of the Custer Fight." Spokane, Washington. The Arthur H. Clark Company. 1991.

Hardorff, Richard G. "Markers, Artifacts and Indian Testimony: Preliminary Findings on the Custer Battle". Short Hills, New Jersey. Don Horn Publications. 1985.

Hardorff, Richard G. "The Oglala Lakota Crazy Horse" Mattituck, N. Y. and Bryan, Tx. J. M. Carroll & Company. 1985.

Hassrick, Royal. "The Sioux". Norman and London. University of Oklahoma Press. 1989.

Hedren, Paul L. "The Great Sioux War 1876 – 77". Helena, Montana. Montana Historical Society Press. 1991.

Herr, John K. and Edward S. Wallace. "The Story of the U. S. Cavalry 1775 – 1942." New York. Bonanza Books. 1953.

Hixon, John C. "Custer's 'Mysterious Mr. Kellogg.'" Bismarck, North Dakota. State Historical Society of North Dakota. 1950.

Hofling, Charles K., "Custer and the Little Big Horn: A Psychobiographical Inquiry". Detroit. Wayne State University Press. 1981.

Hoig, Stan. "The Battle of the Washita". Garden City, New York. Doubleday and Company, Inc. 1976.

Hook, Jason. "American Indian Warrior Chiefs." New York. Sterling Publishing Co. Inc. 1990.

Horn, W. Donald. "Witnesses For The Defense of General George Armstrong Custer." West Orange, New Jersey. Midland Press. 1981.

Hunt, Frazier and Robert. "I Fought With Custer: The Story of Sergeant Windolph, Last Survivor of the Battle of the Little Big Horn". Lincoln and London. University of Nebraska Press. 1987.

Hunt, Frazier "The Romantic Soldier" Brooklyn, New York. Arrow and Trooper. 1994.

Hutchins, James S. "Boots and Saddles At The Little Bighorn". Fort Collins, Colorado. Old Army Press. 1976.

Hutton, Paul A. "Custer and His Times." El Paso, Texas. Little Big Horn Associates. 1981.

Hutton, Paul Andrew. "The Custer Reader." Lincoln and London. University of Nebraska Press. 1992.

Hutton, Paul Andrew. "General Philip Sheridan: Civil War Memoirs." New York, Toronto, London, Sydney, Auckland. Bantam Books. 1991.

Hutton, Paul Andrew. "Soldiers West: Biographies from the Military Frontier". Lincoln and London, University of Nebraska of Press. 1987.

Hyde, George E. "Red Cloud's Folk". Norman. University of Oklahoma Press. 1937.

Hyde, George E. "Spotted Tail's Folk". Norman. University of Oklahoma Press. 1974.

Innis, Ben "Bloody Knife: Custer's Favorite Scout." Fort Collins, Colorado. Old Army Press. 1973.

Izzard, Bob. "Adobe Walls Wars." Amarillo, Texas. Amarillo Speed Print, Inc. 1993.

Jackson, Donald. "Custer's Gold: The United States Cavalry Expedition of 1874." New Haven and London, Yale University Press. 1966.

Jensen, Rivhard E., R. Eli Paul and John E. Carter. "Eyewitness at Wounded Knee." Lincoln and London. University of Nebraska Press. 1991.

Johnson, Barry C. "A Captain of 'Chivalric Courage': Thomas H. French, 7th Cavalry". London. The English Westerners' Society. 1989.

Johnson, Barry C. "Case of Marcus A. Reno." London, England. The English Westerner's Scoiety. 1969.

Johnson, Barry C. "Custer, Reno, Merrill and the Lauffer Case." London. English Westerners' Society. 1970.

Johnson, Dorothy M. "The Bloody Bozeman". Missoula. Mountain Press Publishing Company. 1987.

Josephy, Alvin M. Jr. "The Patriot Chiefs." New York. The Viking Press. 1961.

Kadlecek, Edward and Mabell. "To Kill An Eagle: Indian Views on the Last Days of Crazy Horse." Boulder, Colorado. Johnson Books. 1993.

Kain, Robert C. "In the Valley of the Little Big Horn." Newfane, Vermont. Privately published. 1969.

Kansas Corral of the Westerners. "Custer's Last Stand." Abilene, Kansas. The Kansas Corral of the Westerners. 1972.

Katz, D. Mark, "Custer in Photographs". New York. Bonanza Books. 1985.

Keenan, Jerry, "The Wagon Box Fight." Sheridan, Wyoming. The Fort Phil Kearny/Bozman Trail Association. 1990.

Kelly, Fanny. "My Captivity Among the Sioux Indians.' New York. Citadel Press. 1993.

Kidd, J. H. "A Cavalryman With Custer." New York, Toronto, London, Sydney, and Auckland. Bantam Books, 1991.

King, Captain Charles. "Campaigning With Crook and Stories of Army Life," New York. Harper & Brothers, Franklin Square. 1890.

King, Captain Charles. "Custer's Last Battle." Grand Rapids, Michigan. Custer Ephemera Publications. 1975.

King, W. Kent. "Massacre: The Custer Cover-Up". El Segundo. Upton and Sons. 1989.

Kinsley, D. A., "Custer: Favor the Bold: A Soldier's Story." New York. Promontory Press. 1992.

Koury, Michael J., "The Field Diary of General Alfred H. Terry." Bellevue, Nebraska. Old Army Press. 1970.

Koury, Michael J., "Diaries of the Little Big Horn", Bellevue, Nebraska. Old Army Press. 1970.

Kraft, Louis. "Custer and the Cheyenne." El Segundo, CA. Upton and Sons. 1995.

Kuhlman, Charles. "Custer and the Gall Saga." Bellevue, Nebraska. Old Army Press. 1969.

Kuhlman, Charles. "Legend into History". Ft. Collins, Colorado. Old Army Press. 1977.

Kuhlman, Charles. "Massacre Survivor! The Story of Frank Finkel A Trooper With Custer at the Little Big Horn." Fort Collins, Colorado. Old Army Press. 1972.

Langellier, John P., Kurt Hamilton Cox and Brian C. Pohanka. "Myles Keogh: The Life and Legend of an 'Irish Dragoon' in the Seventh Cavalry." El Segundo, California. Upton and Sons. 1991

Lawrence, Elizabeth Atwood. "His Very Silence Speaks." Detroit. Wayne State University Press. 1989.

Leckie, Shirley A. "Elizabeth Bacon Custer and the Making of a Myth." Norman and London. University of Oklahoma Press. 1993.

Leckie, William H. "The Buffalo Soldiers." Norman and London. University of Oklahoma Press. 1987.

Leighton, Margaret. "Bride of Glory". New York. Ariel Books. 1962.

Leighton, Margaret. "The Story of General Custer." New York. Grosset & Dumlap. 1954.

Libby, O. G. "The Arikara Narrative of the Campaign Against the Hostile Dakotas June, 1876". Bismark . J. M. Carroll and Company. 1920.

Liddic, Bruce R. and Paul Harbaugh "Camp On Custer: Transcribing the Custer Myth" Spokane, Washington. The Arthur H. Clark Company. 1995.

Liddic, Bruce R. "I Buried Custer: The Diary of Pvt. Thomas W. Coleman, 7th U. S. Cavalry." College Station, Texas. Creative Publishing Company. 1979.

Longstreet, Stephen. "War Cries on Horseback." Garden City, New York. Doubleday and Company, Inc. 1970.

Luce, Edward Smith. "Keogh, Comanche and Custer." John S. Swift Co., Inc. 1939.

Lummis, Charles R. "General Crook and the Apache Wars." Flagstaff, Arizona. Northland Press. 1985.

Lydic, F. A. "The Far West's Race With Death." Joliet, Illinois. Privately printed, 1980.

Magnussen, Daniel O. "Peter Thompson's Narrative of the Little Bighorn Campaign 1876". Glendale, California. The Arthur H. Clark Company. 1974.

Mails, Thomas E. "The Mystic Warriors of the Plains." New York. Mallard Press. 1991.

Mangum, Neil C. "Battle of the Rosebud:Prelude to the Little Bighorn". El Segundo, California. Upton & Sons. 1987.

Manion, John S. Jr., Blaine L. Beal, W. Donald Horn, and Dr. Lawrence A. Frost. "Addressing the Custer Story" Monroe, Michigan. Garry Owen Publishers. 1980.

Marquis, Thomas B. "The Cheyennes of Montana." Algonac, Michigan. Reference Publications, Inc. 1978.

Marquis, Thomas B. "Custer, Cavalry & Crows." Fort Collins, Colorado. Old Army Press. 1975.

Marquis, Thomas B. "Custer on the Little Bighorn". Algonac, Michigan. Reference Publications, Inc. 1987.

Marquis, Thomas B. "Keep The Last Bullet For Yourself: The True Story of Custer's Last Stand". Algonac, Michigan. Reference Publications, Inc. 1985.

Marquis, Thomas B. "Memoirs of a White Crow Indian". Lincoln and London. University of Nebraska Press. 1974.

Marquis, Thomas B. "Rain-in-the-Face; Curly, the Crow" Scottsdale, Arizona. Cactus Pony. 1934.

Marquis, Thomas B. "Sitting Bull and Gall, the Warrior" Scottsdale, Arizona. Cactus Pony. 1934.

Marquis, Thomas B. "Wooden Leg: A Warrior Who Fought Custer". Lincoln and London. University of Nebraska Press. 1931.

Marshall, S.L.A. "Crimsoned Prairie: The Indian Wars". New York. Da Capo Press, Inc. 1972.

McCann, Lloyd E., "The Grattan Massacre." Reprinted from Nebraska History, Vol. XXXVII, Number 1, March 1956.

McClernand, Edward J. "On Time for Disaster: The Rescue of Custer's Command". Lincoln and London. University of Nebraska Press. 1989.

McLaughlin, James. "My Friend The Indian". Lincoln and London. University of Nebraska Press. 1989.

Merington, Marguerite. "The Custer Story: The Life and Intimate Letters of General George A. Custer and His Wife Elizabeth". Lincoln and London. University of Nebraska Press. 1987.

Michno, Gregory. "Lakota Noon" Missoula, Montana. Mountain Press Publishing Company. 1997.

Michno, Gregory. "The Mystery of E Troop" Missoula, Montana. Mountain Press Publishing Company. 1994.

Miles, Nelson A. "Personal Recollections & Observations of General Nelson A. Miles Vols 1 & 2." Lincoln and London. University of Nebraska Press. 1992.

Miller, David Humphreys. "Custer's Fall: The Indian Side of the Story". Lincoln and London. University of Nebraska Press. 1985.

Miller, David Humphreys. "Ghost Dance." Lincoln and London. University of Nebraska Press. 1985.

Milligan, Edward A. "High Noon on the Greasy Grass." Bottineau, North Dakota. Bottineau Courant Print. 1972.

Mills, Anson. "My Story." Washington, D. C., Press of Bryon S. Adams. 1921.

Mills, Charles K. "Charles C. DeRudio." Mattituck, New York. J. M. Carroll and Company. 1983.

Mills, Charles K. "Rosters From 7th U. S. Cavalry Campaigns 1866 – 1896." Mattituck, New York. J. M. Carroll and Company. 1983.

Mills, Charles K. "Harvest of Barren Regrets: The Army Career of Frederick William Benteen 1834 – 1898." Glendale, California. The Arthur H. Clark Company. 1985.

Milner, Joe E. "California Joe." Caldwell, Idaho, The Caxton Printers, Ltd. 1935.

Monaghan, Jay. "Custer: The Life of General George Armstrong Custer." Lincoln and London. University of Nebraska Press. 1971.

Monnett, John H. "The Battle of Beecher Island and the Indian War of 1867 – 1869." Niwot, Colorado. University Press of Colorado. 1992.

Morris, Donald R., "The Washing of the Spears." New York, Simon & Schuster, Inc. 1965.

Nadeau, Remi. "Fort Laramie and the Sioux". Lincoln and London, University of Nebraska Press, 1982.

Neihardt, John G. "Black Elk Speaks: Being the Life Story of a Holy Man of the Oglala Sioux". Lincoln and London. University of Nebraska Press. 1988.

Nelson, Bruce. "Land of the Dacotahs." Minneapolis. University of Minnesota Press. 1946.

Nichols, Ronald H. "Custer Approaches the Little Big Horn." Crow Agency, Montana. Custer Battlefield Historical & Museum Association, Inc. 1992.

Nichols, Ronald H. "Reno Court of Inquiry." Costa Mesa, California. Privately Printed. 1983.

Olson, James C. "Red Cloud and the Sioux Problem". Lincoln and London. University of Nebraska Press. 1965.

O'Neal, Bill. "Fighting Men of the Indian Wars." Stillwater, Oklahoma. Barbed Wire Press. 1991.

O'Neil, Alice Tomlinson "Custer Recollections." Brooklyn, New York. Arrow and Trooper. 1995.

O'Neil, Alice Tomlinson "My Dear Sister." Brooklyn, New York. Arrow and Trooper. 1994.

O'Neil, Tom. "And So It Goes: Arguments on the Little Big Horn." Brooklyn New York. Arrow and Trooper Publishing Company. 1993.

O'Neil, Tom. "Cadet George Armstrong Custer: Demerits & Academics." Brooklyn, New York. Arrow and Trooper Publishing Company. 1992.

O'Neil, Tom. "Cadet Marcus Albert Reno: Record of Demerits & Academics." Brooklyn, New York. Arrow and Trooper Publishing Company. 1992.

O'Neil, Tom "Captain Myles Walter Keogh, United States Army 1840 – 1876: O'Donnell's National University of Ireland Lecture." Brooklyn, New York. Arrow and Trooper. 1994.

O'Neil, Tom "The Cavalry Campaign Outfit At The Little Big Horn." Brooklyn, New York. Arrow and Trooper. 1994.

O'Neil, Tom "Custer Chronicles. Volume 1." Brooklyn, New York. Arrow and Trooper. 1994.

O'Neil, Tom "Custer Chronicles. Volume II." Brooklyn, New York. Arrow and Trooper. 1994.

O'Neil, Tom "Custer Chronicles. Volume III." Brooklyn, New York. Arrow and Trooper. 1995.

O'Neil, Thomas E. "Custer to the Little Big Horn: A Study in Command." Brooklyn, New York, Arrow and Trooper Publishing Company. 1991.

O'Neil, Tom. "Decision at Little Big Horn: A Custer Retrospective." Brooklyn, New York. Arrow and Trooper Publishing Company. 1993.

O'Neil, Tom "E. A. Brininstool Exposed!" Brooklyn, New York. Arrow and Trooper. 1994.

O'Neil, Tom. "50th Anniversary Celebration." Brooklyn New York. Arrow and Trooper Publishing Company. 1991.

O'Neil, Tom. "Garry Owen Tid Bits III." Brooklyn, New York. Arrow and Trooper Publishing Company. 1991.

O'Neil, Tom. "Garry Owen Tid Bits V." Brooklyn, New York. Arrow and Trooper Publishing Company. 1992.

O'Neil, Tom. "Garry Owen Tid Bits VI." Brooklyn, New York. Arrow and Trooper Publishing Company. 1992.

O'Neil, Tom. "Garry Owen Tid Bits VII." Brooklyn, New York. Arrow and Trooper Publishing Company. 1993.

O'Neil, Tom. "Garry Owen Tid Bits IX." Brooklyn, New York. Arrow and Trooper Publishing Company. 1993.

O'Neil, Tom. "Garry Owen Tid Bits X." Brooklyn, New York. Arrow and Trooper Publishing Company. 1994.

O'Neil, Tom. "George Armstrong Custer: A Historical Overview." Brooklyn, New York. Arrow and Trooper Publishing Company. 1995.

O'Neil, Tom. "The Gibson – Edgerly Narratives of the Little Big Horn." Brooklyn New York. Arrow and Trooper Publishing Company. 1993.

O'Neil, Tom "In Reply to Van de Water." Brooklyn, New York. Arrow and Trooper. 1994.

O'Neil, Tom "Indians at Greasy Grass." Brooklyn, New York. Arrow and Trooper. 1994.

O'Neil, Tom. "Letters From Boston Custer." Brooklyn New York. Arrow and Trooper Publishing Company. 1993.

O'Neil, Tom. "Lonesome Charley Reynolds." Brooklyn New York. Arrow and Trooper Publishing Company. 1995.

O'Neil, Tom "Marcus A. Reno: What Was Said of Him at the Little Big Horn." Brooklyn, New York. Arrow and Trooper Publishing. 1995.

O'Neil, Tom "Memories. William C. Slapper, company M, Rev. John E. Cox." Brooklyn, New York. Arrow and Trooper. 1994.

O'Neil, Tom "Mrs. Custer On The Plains." Brooklyn, New York. Arrow and Trooper. 1994.

O'Neil, Tom "Mysteries Solved. Mysteries Unsolved." Brooklyn, New York. Arrow and Trooper. 1994.

O'Neil, Tom and William G. Rector. "The Official Reports of Major Reno and Captain Benteen: Little Big Horn. 25 June 1876 and Fields of Fire: The Reno Benteen Defense Perimeter." Brooklyn, New York. Arrow and Trooper Publishing Company. 1992.

O'Neil, Thomas E. "Passing Into Legend: The Death of Custer." Brooklyn, New York. Arrow and Trooper Publishing Company. 1991.

O'Neil, Tom "Politics and 1876." Brooklyn, New York. Arrow and Trooper. 1994.

O'Neil, Tom. "Sagas of Greasy Grass." Brooklyn, New York. Arrow and Trooper Publishing Company. 1992.

O'Neil, Tom. "Testimony: Custer on the Sale of Post Traderships – The Clymer Committee." Brooklyn, New York. Arrow and Trooper Publishing Company. 1993.

O'Neil, Tom. "U. S. Army Weapons at the Little Big Horn." Brooklyn New York. Arrow and Trooper Publishing Company. 1993.

Overfield II, Loyd J., "The Little Big Horn, 1876: The Official Communications, Documents and Reports with Rosters of the Officers and Troops of the Campaign". Lincoln and London. University of Nebraska Press. 1971.

Palmer, Robert G. "The Death of Custer." Brooklyn New York. Arrow and Trooper Publishing Company.

Perfetti, Frank. "John Martin, an Italian With Custr at the Little Big Horn, 1876 – 1976." New York. Carlton Press, Inc. 1976.

Perrett, Bryan. "Last Stand! Famous Battles Against the Odds." London. Arms and Armour Press. 1993.

Perry, James M. "Arrogant Armies: Great Military Disasters and the Generals Behind Them." New York, Chichester, Brisbane, Toronto, and Singapore. John Wiley & Sons Inc. 1996.

Members of the Potomac Corral of the Westerners. "Great Western Indian Fights". Lincoln and London, University of Nebraska Press. 1966.

Powell, Father Peter John. "People of the Sacred Mountain." San Francisco, California. Harper and Row Publishers. 1981.

Reedstrom, E. Lesle. "Apache Wars: An Illustrated Battle History." New York, Sterling Publishing Co., Inc. 1990.

Reedstrom, Ernest L., "Bugles, Banners and War Bonnets". New York. Bonanza Books. 1977.

Reedstrom, Ernest L., "Custer's 7th Cavalry: From Fort Riley to the Little Big Horn." New York. Sterling Publishing Co., Inc. 1992.

Regan, Geoffrey. "Snafu: Great American Military Disasters." New York. Avon Books. 1993.

Remsburg, John E. and George J. " Charley Reynolds: Soldier, Hunter, Scout and Guide." Mattituck, New York. J. M. Carroll Company. 1978.

Reusswig, William. "A Picture Report of The Custer Fight." New York. Hastings House, Publishers. 1967.

Reynolds, Arlene. "The Civil War Memories of Elizabeth Bacon Custer." Austin, Texas. University f Texas Press. 1994.

Rickey, Don Jr. "Forty Miles a Day on Beans and Hay". Norman and London. University of Oklahoma Press. 1989.

Riggs, David F. "East of Gettysburg, Custer vs Stuart." Fort Collins, Colorado. Old Army Press. 1985.

Rister, Carl Coke. "Border Command: General Phil Sheridan in the West." Norman. University of Oklahoma Press. 1944.

Roberts, Richard A. "Custer's Last Battle: Reminiscences of General Custer". Monroe, Michigan. Monroe County Library System. 1978.

Robinson, Charles M. III. "A Good Year To Die: The Story of the Great Sioux War." New York. Random House. 1995.

Roe, Charles Francis. "Custer's Last Battle." New York City. Privately Printed. 1927.

Sandoz, Mari. "Crazy Horse: The Strange Man of the Oglalas". Lincoln and London. University of Nebraska Press. 1961.

Sandoz, Mari. "The Battle of the Little Bighorn". Lincoln and London, University of Nebraska Press. 1978.

Sandoz, Mari. "These Were the Sioux". Lincoln and London. University of Nebraska Press. 1985.

Sarf, Wayne Michael. "The Little Bighorn Campaign: March – September 1876." Cornshohocken, PA. Combined Books, Inc. 1993.

Schmidt, Joseph C. "General George Crook: His Autobiography." Norman and London. University of Oklahoma Press. 1986.

Schneider, George A. "The Freeman Journal: The Infantry in the Sioux Campaign of 1876." San Rafael, California. Presidio Press. 1977.

Schneider, James V. and Richard Campbell. "Behind Custer at the Little Big Horn." Ft. Wayne, Indiana. Privately printed, no date.

Schoenberger, Dale T. "The End of Custer: The Death of an American Military Legend" Surrey, British Columbia and Blaine, Washington. Hancock House. 1995.

Schultz, James Willard. "William Jackson, Indian Scout." Springfield, Illinois. William K. Cavanagh. 1976.

Scott, Douglas D., and Richard A. Fox Jr., "Archaeological Insights into The Custer Battle." Norman, and London, University of Oklahoma Press, 1987.

Scott, Douglas D., Richard A. Fox Jr., Melissa A. Connor, and Dick Harmon. "Archaeological Perspectives on the Battle of the Little Bighorn". Norman, and London, University of Oklahoma Press, 1989.

Scudder, Ralph E. "Custer Country" Portland, Oregon. Binfords & Mort, Publishers. 1963.

Shanor, Charles A. and Timothy P. Terrell. "Military Law In A Nutshell," St. Paul, Minnesota. West Publishing Co., 1980.

Smith, Sherry L. "Sagebrush Soldier: Private William Earl Smith's View of the Sioux War of 1876." Norman and London. University of Oklahoma Press. 1989.

Smith, Sherry L. "The View From Officers' Row." Tucson, AZ. University of Arizona Press. 1990.

Sneve, Virginia Driving Hawk. "They Led a Nation: The Sioux Chiefs." Sioux Falls, South Dakota. Brevet Press, Inc. 1975.

South Dakota State Historical Society Collections, Volume VI. 1912.

Spence, Lewis. "North American Indians." London. Senate. 1994.

Spotts, David L. "Campaigning With Custer 1868 – 69." Lincoln and London. University of Nebraska Press. 1988.

Chief Standing Bear "My People, The Sioux" Boston and New York. Houghton Mifflin Company. 1928.

Steinbach, Robert H. " A Long March: The Lives of Frank and Alice Baldwin." Austin. University of Texas Press. 1989.

Stewart, Edgar I. "Custer's Luck". Norman and London. University of Oklahoma Press. 1988.

Tassin, Dr. Raymond J. "Double Winners of The Medal of Honor." Canton, Ohio. Daring Books. 1986.

Taunton, Francis B. "Brand Book 1971-72." London. The English Westerners' Society. 1972.

Taunton, Francis B. "Custer's Field: 'A Scene of Sickening Ghastly Horror'". London. The Johnson-Taunton Military Press. 1989.

Taunton, Francis B. "No Pride in the Little Big Horn". London. The English Westerners' Society. 1987.

Taunton, Francis B. "Sufficient Reason?" London. The English Westerners' Society. 1977.

Taylor, William O. "With Custer On The Little Bighorn." New York and London. Viking Penguin. 1996.

Tebbel, John, and Keith Jennison. "The American Indian Wars." New York. Harper & Brothers Publishers. 1960.

Terrell, John Upton. "Apache Chronicle." New York. The World Publishing Company. 1972.

Terrell, John Upton and Colonel George Walton. "Faint the Trumpet Sounds: The Story of Major Marcus A. Reno and His Controversial Role in the Campaign Culminating in the Battle of the Little Big Horn and the Custer Massacre". New York. David McKay Company, Inc. 1966.

Thompson, Neil Baird. "Crazy Horse Called Them Walk–A–Heaps." Saint Cloud, Minnesota. 1979.

Thompson, Richard A., "Crossing The Border With The 4th Cavalry." Waco, Texas. Texian Press. 1986.

Thrapp, Dan L. "The Conquest of Apacheria." Norman. University of Oklahoma Press. 1967.

Thrapp, Dan L. "Victorio and the Mimbres Apaches." Norman and London. University of Oklahoma Press. 1980.

Timber, John Stands In and Margot Liberty. "Cheyenne Memories". Lincoln and London. University of Nebraska Press. 1972.

Time–Life Books. "The Great Chiefs." New York. Time–Life Books. 1975.

Time–Life Books. "The Indians." New York. Time–Life Books. 1973.

Time–Life Books. "The Scouts." New York. Time–Life Books. 1978.

Time–Life Books. "The Soldiers." New York. Time–Life Books. 1974.

Upton, Richard. "The Custer Adventure". El Segundo. Upton and Sons. 1990.

Urwin, Gregory J. W. and Roberta E. Fagan. "Custer and His Times, Book Three." Little Big Horn Associates, Inc. 1987.

Urwin, Gregory J. W. "Custer Victorious". Lincoln and London. University of Nebraska Press. 1990.

Utley, Robert M., and Wilcomb E. Washburn. "The American Heritage History of the Indian Wars". New York, American Heritage Publishing Co. Inc., 1977.

Utley, Robert M. "Cavalier in Buckskin: George Armstrong Custer and the Western Military Frontier". Norman and London. University of Oklahoma Press. 1988.

Utley, Robert M. "Custer and the Great Controversy". Pasadena, Ca. Westernlore Press. 1980.

Utley, Robert M. "Frontier Regulars: The United States Army and the Indian, 1866 - 1891". Lincoln and London. University of Nebraska Press. 1984.

Utley, Robert M. "The Indian Frontier of the American West 1846 – 1890." Albuquerque, New Mexico. University of New Mexico Press. 1989.

Utley, Robert M. "The Lance and The Shield: The Life and Times of Sitting Bull." New York. Henry Holt and Company. 1993.

Utley, Robert M. "Life in Custer's Cavalry: Diaries and Letters of Albert and Jennie Barnitz 1867 - 1868". Lincoln and London. University of Nebraska Press. 1987.

Utley, Robert M. "The Last Days of the Sioux Nation." New Haven and London. Yale University Press. 1963.

Utley, Robert M. "The Reno Court of Inquiry: The Chicago Times Account." Fort Collins, Colorado. Old Army Press. 1983.

Van de Water, Frederic F. "Glory-Hunter: A Life of General Custer". Lincoln and London. University of Nebraska Press. 1988.

Vaughn, J. W. "Indian Fights: New Facts on Seven Encounters." Norman. University of Oklahoma Press. 1966.

Vaughn, J. W. "The Reynolds Campaign on Powder River." Norman, Oklahoma. University of Oklahoma Press. 1961.

Vaughn, J. W. "With Crook at the Rosebud." Lincoln and London. University of Nebraska Press. 1988.

Vestal, Stanly. "Sitting Bull: Champion of the Sioux". Norman and London. University of Oklahoma Press. 1989.

Vestal, Stanly. "Warpath and Council Fire." New York. Random House. 1948.

Vestal, Stanly. "Warpath: The True Story of the Fighting Sioux Told in a Biography of Chief White Bull". Lincoln and London. University of Nebraska Press. 1984.

Wagner, Glendolin Damon. "Old Neutriment". Lincoln and London. University of Nebraska Press. 1989.

Walker, James R. "Lakota Belief and Ritual." Lincoln and London. University of Nebraska Press. 1991.

Walker, Judson Elliott, "Campaigns of General Custer." New York. Arno Press. 1966.

Watson, Elmo Scott and Don Russell. "The Battle of the Washita, or Custer's Massacre?" London, England. The English Westerner's Society. Brand Book 1972 – 73.

Weems, John Edward. "Death Song." New York. Indian Head Books. 1991.

Weibert, Don L. "The 1874 Invasion of Montana: A Prelude to the Custer Disaster." Billings, Montana. Don L. Weibert. 1993.

Weibert, Henry and Don. "Sixty-six Years in Custer's Shadow." Billings, Montana. Falcon Press Publishing Company, Inc. 1985.

Welch, James with Paul Stekler. "Killing Custer." New York and London. W. W. Norton and Company. 1994.

Wellman, Paul I. "Death on Horseback: Seventy Years of War for the American West". Philadelphia and New York. J. B. Lippincott Company. 1947.

Werner, Fred H. "The Beecher Island Battle." Greeley, Colorado. Werner Publications. 1989.

Werner, Fred H. "Before The Little Big Horn: Battle of the Rosebud, Montana Territory, June 17, 1876". Greeley, Colorado. Werner Publications. 1983.

Werner, Fred H. "The Slim Buttes Battle: September 9 - 10, 1876." Privately printed. 1981.

Werner, Fred H. "The Soldiers Are Coming!: The Story of the Reynolds Battle March 17, 1876". Greeley, Colorado. Werner Publications. 1982.

Wert, Jeffry D. "Custer: The Controversial Life of George Armstrong Custer." New York. Simon & Schuster. 1996.

Wheeler, Colonel Homer W. "Buffalo Days: The Personal Narrative of a Cattleman, Indian Fighter and Army Officer". Lincoln and London, University of Nebraska Press. 1990.

Whittaker, Frederick. "A Complete Life of General George A. Custer." Lincoln and London. University of Nebraska Press. 1993.

Willert, James. "Little Big Horn Diary." La Mirada, California. Privately Published. 1982.

Willert, James. "March of the Columns" El Segundo, California. Upton & Sons Publishers. 1994.

Willert, James. "The Terry Letters." La Mirada, California. Raul Brondarbit Printing Co. 1980.

Winthrop, William. "Military Law and Precedents." New York. Arno Press. 1979.

Woodyard, Darrel. "Dakota Indian Lore." San Antonio, Texas. The Naylor Company. 1968.

Wooster, Robert. "Nelson A. Miles and The Twilight of the Frontier Army." Lincoln and London. University of Nebraska Press. 1993.

Worchester, Donald E. "The Apaches: Eagles of the Southwest." Norman and London, University of Oklahoma Press. 1992.

Wormser, Richard. "The Yellowlags: The Story of the United States Cavalry." Garden City, New York. Doubleday & Company, Inc. 1966.

Zitkala-Sa. "Old Indian Legends". Lincoln and London, University of Nebraska Press. 1985.

Index

Reno 126, 403, responsibility for defeat of 7th cav 413, reviews 7th cav 158, transportation of wounded 371, upset with Brisbin 122, wounded at Big Hole 412
Gibson, Katherine
premonition of 147, Smith's watch fob 169
Gibson, Lt F. M. 5, 6, 149, 161
Benteen's scout 193, 194, 244, 409, burial of McIntosh 367, hilltop fight 316, neutrality of 113, offered positionon 147, officer's conference of 6/22 161, on Benteen assuming command 407, on Reno's delay in moving to Custer 406, Smith's watch fob 169, witnesses Cooke's will 167
Girard, Frederick F. 119, 165, 374
abandoned in timber 219, 249, 250, 252-253, Crow's Nest 185, estimate of warrior strength 171, High Bear-Reno confrontation 123, lone tepee 196, 197, relations with Reno 113, Reynolds' premonition 149, secures liquor for Bloody Knife 156, Terry's orders to Custer 158, valley fight 198, 205, 207, 211, witnesses mutilation of Reno's dead 250
Glendive Creek 26
Godfrey, Lt E. S. 390
Benteen's performance 321, Benteen's scout 194, 195, 241, 244, Davern's escape from valley 223, death of Winney 310, describes 6/21 officer's conference 153, 154, describes 6/22 officer's conference 159, 160, describes Custer/Bloody Knife confrontation 187, describes departure from Ft Lincoln 115, describes desecration of Indian burials 128, describes order of march 117, disbelief of disaster 352, hilltop fight 309, 311, 313, 318, 320, 321, 323, junction with Reno 245, 248, junction with Terry 351, 352, Kanipe 241, march up Rosebud 153, 154, 161, 164, 166, 167, Medicine Lodge Creek 22, mutiny 315, neutrality of 113, night

march of 6/24 167, 170, 171, on abandonment by Custer 312, on conditions on Custer Hill 361, 363, on death of Golden 321, on mutilation of Armstrong Custer 281, on Terry as commander 409, plan to abandon wounded 313, 314, poker game on Far West 154, premonition of disaster 143, 149, relations with Reno 114, 351, Reno's conduct 226, 314, 391, Reno's scout 123, role of recruits in defeat 113, Taylor correspondence 404, Washita 3, 6, 10, 11, Weir Point 305, 307, 309
Goes Ahead
observes village 263, on dismissal by Custer 266
Golden, Pvt P. M.
death of 321, premonition of death 321
Goldin, Pvt T.
Benteen correspondence 303, 394, 407, decapitation of Bloody Knife 216, retreat from valley 221
Good Bear boy 212
Good Heart 91
Goodwin, Pvt J. E. 371
Goose
Black Hills Expedition 30, hilltop fight 317, method of transportation to Far West 371, return to Fort Buford 372, 373, supplements pay by hunting 118, valley fight 205, 207, wounding of 225
Gordon, Pvt H.
death of 225
Grand River Agency 29
Grant, Fred 24
Grant, Orvil 45, 46, 47
Grant, Pres U. S. 46, 48, 49, 153
allows Custer on expedition 50, Black Hills strategy 39, Custer's request for reinstatement 49, denies Custer's request for Major Merrill 111, orders Taft to replace Custer as expedition commander 48, reaction to' New York World editorial 49, refuses to see Custer 48
Greasy Grass Ridge 361, 402
attack on C Troop 272, collapse of soldier position on 306, Company C bodies on 362, deployment of C Troop 270, 271, 365,

Pigford's observations of action along 306, weakness of soldier position on 271
Great Sioux Reservation 46
Grinnel, George Bird 29
Grouard, Frank 56, 88, 89, 91, 92
Reynolds' fight 57
Gurley, Lt C. L. 374

H
Hagemann, Cpl O. 350
Hairy Moccasin 263
Hale, Lt W. 9
Half Yellow Face
hilltop fight 317, valley fight 198, 205, 207, 263, joins Reno's battalion 263, on march up Rosebud 161, 171, scouts for Gibbon 74, urges Custer To attack 186
Hamilton, Capt L. M. 5, 6, 9
Hamilton, Lt S. T. 74
Hammon, Cpl J. E.
burial of Custer's dead 361, mutilations 279
Hammon, Pvt G. W. 279
Hancock Campaign 169
Hancock, Gen W. S. 22
Hanley, Sgt R. P.
awarded Medal of Honor 310, identifies effects of Nathan Short 267, recovers the mule Barnum 310
Hardy, Pvt W. G. 171
Hare, Lt L. R.
Harrington's morbid sketches 149, junction with Benteen 245, 247, 248, junction with Terry 351, 352, march up Rosebud 164, 195, night march of 6/24 170, on location of Company E 363, sights Indians near lone tepee 195, valley fight 198, 211, 218, 219, 220, 226, Weir Point 248, 303, 305, 307, 309, 409
Harney, Gen 411
Harney, Gen William S. 21
Harrington, Lt H. M.
body not identified 366, commands C Troop on Reno scout 125, marksmanship of 155, possible death of 272, premonition of torture 113, 149, torture of 312
Hartsuff, Capt A. 89
Hastings, James S. 40, 87
Hawk Man
death of 212
Hayes, President R. B. 394
Hayfield Fight 2